DIGEST OF INTERNATIONAL LAW

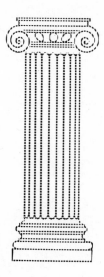

prepared by and under the direction of

Marjorie M. Whiteman, B.A., LL.B., M.P.L., J.S.D., LL.D. (HON.)

Assistant Legal Adviser, the Department of State

VOLUME

DEPARTMENT OF STATE PUBLICATION 7403

Released June 1963

For sale by the Superintendent of Documents, U.S. Government Printing Office
Washington 25, D.C. - Price $4.25

PREFACE

This *Digest of International Law* treats of public international law and related matters, particularly during the last two decades. It is the successor digest to Hackworth's *Digest of International Law.*[1]

To reflect the status of international law in this our time is to reveal a considerable evolution in both its range and content. The volumes reflect a moving scene. At times, in fact, during the preparation of manuscript for this *Digest*, it has seemed that international law would not jell long enough for accurate reflection of its current status.

While international law is comparatively clear and definite in many of its aspects, in others it is unclear and uncertain. It may be that a particular norm or principle, far from being at its zenith, may be either in its ascendency or in its descendency as international law. Further, the degree of acceptance of a particular practice may vary within a particular period.

The author has not attempted to adopt the role of prophetess. She has endeavored to treat of materials in an objective fashion, leaving it, in the main, for other determination whether a particular practice

---

[1] An early *Digest of the Published Opinions of the Attorneys-General, and of the Leading Decisions of the Federal Courts, with Reference to International Law, Treaties and Kindred Subjects*, published in 1877, prepared by John L. Cadwalader, Assistant Secretary of State, was the forerunner of the official digests of international law printed by the United States Government Printing Office. That early digest was comprised of a single volume of less than 300 pages, with subjects arranged in alphabetical order rather than under chapter headings. In 1886 there was published a second digest of international law prepared by Dr. Francis Wharton, then Chief Examiner of Claims of the Department of State. Wharton's *International Law Digest*, in three volumes, set the pattern for succeeding digests at least so far as table of contents and general format were concerned. The third digest, John Bassett Moore's *International Law Digest*, comprised of eight volumes, was published in 1906. Moore's volumes incorporated much of Wharton's Digest. The fourth digest, the first volume of which was published in 1940, is Hackworth's *Digest of International Law*, also in eight volumes. Judge Hackworth, then Legal Adviser of the Department of State, did not include in these volumes materials contained in either Wharton's or Moore's digests. The present *Digest* does not incorporate the Hackworth volumes.

or principle of international jurisprudence is in process of development or jettison.

The practice of States is not like a book. It does not occur under well-known headings. Correspondingly, international law does not arise in, or fall into, separate and clear-cut chapters. Thus, any arrangement of materials reflecting the practice of States is arbitrary, although some arrangements in the past have become almost time-honored. While the table of contents and the format of this *Digest* resemble those of the three immediately preceding digests, it was found necessary in the preparation of the manuscript for this *Digest* to depart, in considerable measure, from the tables of contents of those earlier digests because of new subject matter in the period dealt with and the changing emphasis on numerous concepts of international law. A system of cross-references to such corresponding chapters or sections as exist in predecessor digests is employed at the outset of each chapter.

In order to avoid undue repetition, a choice was necessarily made as to where the bulk of the materials treating of a particular matter should be printed. Materials dealing with certain incidents are, in some cases, dealt with in part in more than one chapter and under a number of different headings. A comprehensive index, to be found in the final volume, is intended to direct the user of the volumes to materials relating to similar subject matter.

The inclusion in this work of a particular quotation from or other reference to material—or its omission—is not to be construed as necessarily indicating approval—or disapproval—of a certain viewpoint or statement. In numerous instances a selection of differing opinions (including those of publicists) is set forth in order that a broader understanding of the matter may be had. In the light of events and a developing international law, presentation of various viewpoints may conceivably be of assistance to the user.

To the extent that documents are quoted in whole or in part in this *Digest*, the portions published may, of course, be quoted by others. In some instances portions quoted have been extracted from larger documents not yet declassified in whole or made available for publication. Every effort has been made so that portions quoted are quoted in context but publication of a portion of a document in this *Digest* does not constitute permission to consult or publish other portions of documents not included or merely cited.

The preparation of a digest of international law is a prodigious undertaking. Necessarily, a selection of documents was made if only because of their voluminous nature. It is hoped, however, that this *Digest of International Law* will constitute a compilation of materials, some official and others not, which by their presentation may serve to indicate in some measure the direction of prevailing currents in the development of international law, or at least supply a certain amount of background on particular subjects.

As new situations and problems arise, new solutions will evolve in many fields. International law thus grows. After all, international law reflects the distillation of man's experience through the ages in the conduct of relations between politically organized peoples.

MARJORIE M. WHITEMAN
Assistant Legal Adviser
The Department of State

WASHINGTON, D.C.
March 1963

Acknowledgments

The preparation of this *Digest of International Law* has been, in numerous ways, a joint enterprise. I desire to thank all those people who have assisted in making it possible.

The work has been done under two Presidents of the United States. While the task is being completed under President John F. Kennedy, a considerable amount of the manuscript was prepared under President Dwight D. Eisenhower. I am hopeful that in some measure at least the high standards set by Secretary of State Dean Rusk, for himself, are reflected in these volumes. His scholarly work has been an inspiration. Credit is also due the late Secretary of State John Foster Dulles whose interest in international law was well known, and Secretary of State Christian A. Herter under whose auspices the printing program for the *Digest* was begun.

Among those who gave early encouragement to the preparation of a new digest of international law were Vice President Lyndon B. Johnson, as a member of the Committee on Appropriations of the United States Senate, Senator Estes Kefauver who stressed the need for such a digest, and Representative John J. Rooney as a member of the House Appropriations Committee.

Without the cooperation of the former Deputy Under Secretary of State for Administration, Loy W. Henderson, and the continued cooperation of Deputy Under Secretaries of State for Administration Roger W. Jones and William H. Orrick, Jr., and their staffs, these volumes would not have been published.

To Herman Phleger, Legal Adviser of the Department of State, who selected the author for this task, and to Legal Advisers Adrian Fisher, Loftus Becker, Eric Hager, and Abram Chayes, who have lent their full support to the project, I express thanks. Also I express appreciation to Deputy Legal Advisers Jack B. Tate, John M. Raymond, Leonard C. Meeker, and Richard D. Kearney. The Executive Assistant, Office of the Legal Adviser, Jac. H. Bushong, has at all times been extremely helpful.

It should be recorded that a considerable amount of research on the chapters of the present *Digest* was done over a period of some years by the author working alone. In later years the author has had the invaluable assistance of a number of scholarly research assistants, members of the Office of the Legal Adviser, devoting full time to the project. The work of the following members of this staff is gratefully acknowledged: Harold S. Burman, Abigail J. Cooley, Edison W. Dick, Marcia M. Fleming, Mona H. Gagnon, Alice M. McDiarmid, Peter H. Pfund, Stephen C. Schott, Jerome H. Silber, and Julia W. Willis.

Other members of the Office of the Legal Adviser who have given generously of their time in preparing particular materials, are Charles I. Bevans, Eliezer Ereli, Thomas T. F. Huang, Katherine Fite Lincoln, John Maktos, Eleanor C. McDowell, Virginia V. Meekison, William E. Murnighan, Alan F. Neidle, Sylvia E. Nilsen, Herbert K. Reis, Frederick Smith, Jr., Marten H. A. Van Heuven, and William V. Whittington. Miss Marian Nash, Foreign Service Officer and Attorney, Robert D. Johnson, Chief Counsel, Passport Office, and John W. Perry, Office of the General Counsel, Department of the Air Force, have contributed valuable research in their respective fields of competence.

To the above-named persons, and others throughout the Department of State and other Departments and Agencies of the Government, who have supplied specific materials or have read manuscript or proofs, I express thanks.

Appreciation is also expressed to those of my staff who assisted in checking the manuscript and galley proofs. To date, those who have assisted in this meticulous work are Fred E. Arnold, Robert P. Bannerman, Lawrence Baskir, Russell S. Berman, Abigail J. Cooley, Joseph L. Liberati, Earle McCaskill, Scott R. Schoenfeld, and John Kirkwood White.

To the Librarian of the Department of State, Fred W. Shipman, and members of the Library staff, including Myra J. DeBerry, and to Rosine Pilliod, Law Librarian, I am indebted. Appreciation is expressed to the office of Records and Reference Branch of the Department of State, particularly to Eugene J. Hennigan, former Chief of the Reference Section, and Wilmer P. Sparrow, now Chief of the Reference Section, and their staff, charged with the Department's files. Additionally, thanks is given Paul T. Ayscue for his assistance in connection with making records available for publication. John O. Hemard, Chief, and Constance G. Gaynor, Alace M. Harvey, Dorothy B. Thomas, and Mae Hahlen of the Reference and Documents Section of the Bureau of International Organization Affairs have been extremely helpful in providing United Nations documentation. To the Staff of the Division of Reproduction and Distribution Services, thanks is expressed for their many services.

I am indebted to the Division of Publishing Services of the Department of State for the fine cooperation of the former Chief of the Division, Norris E. Drew, and for that of the present Chief of the Division, Jerome H. Perlmutter. I am extremely grateful to Joseph J. Moriarty, Acting Chief of the Law and Treaties Section of that Division, and those who have from time to time worked with him in editing the manuscript, including Ruth L. McKinnon, Blanche H. Mullan, Lorna K. Newby, Grace C. Reynolds, and Donald W. Ricketts. For painstaking proofreading, I am grateful to Otis E. Camp, Isla V. Davies, Bertha J. Hartman, Ruth McKinnon, Rozelle Parra, Mary Jane Yakshevich, and John J. Lee, who is also preparing a comprehensive index for the entire *Digest*.

To all those skilled people in the Government Printing Office who have been engaged on this project, I express thanks.

Additionally, I desire to thank those who were my secretaries throughout the period of the preparation of this *Digest of International Law*, particularly Lillie B. Dowrick for her long 'and devoted assistance.

M. M. W.

CONTENTS

CHAPTER I

CHAPTER II

Chapter I

INTERNATIONAL LAW[1]

GENERAL NATURE

§ 1

International law is the standard of conduct, at a given time, for Definition states and other entities subject thereto. It comprises the rights, privileges, powers, and immunities of states and entities invoking its provisions, as well as the correlative fundamental duties, absence of rights, liabilities, and disabilities. International law is, more or less, in a continual state of change and development. In certain of its aspects the evolution is gradual; in others it is avulsive. International law is based largely on custom, e.g., on practice, and whereas certain customs are recognized as obligatory, others are in retrogression and are recognized as nonobligatory, depending upon the subject matter and its status at a particular time.

Over varying periods of time certain international practices have been found to be reasonable and wise in the conduct of foreign relations, in considerable measure the result of a balancing of interests. Such practices have attained the stature of accepted principles or norms and are recognized as international law or practice. Accordingly, there are in the field of international law, public and private, certain well-recognized principles or norms.

The recognized customs prevailing between states and other subjects of international law are reflected not only in international practice *per se* but also in international treaties and agreements, in the general principles of law recognized by states, in judicial and arbitral decisions, and in the works of qualified scholars. Based largely on custom, thus reflected and recognized, international law is, to a considerable extent, unwritten in form and uncodified.

International law is evidenced by international agreement, by international custom or practice, and by the general norms of civilization. As evidence of such agreements, custom or practice, and norms, resort may appropriately be had to treaties and agreements and, secondarily, to their subsequent interpretation and application; to the practice

---

[1] In this connection, see prior U.S. digests of international law, particularly: I, Wharton, *International Law Digest* (2d ed., 1887), ch. I § 8; I Moore, *International Law Digest* (1906), ch. I, pp. 1 ff.; and I Hackworth, *Digest of International Law* (1940), ch. I, pp. 1 ff.

and custom of states and other entities subjects of international law, as set forth in primary sources and, secondarily, as reported elsewhere; and to accepted standards as revealed in agreements or in practice or in authoritative pronouncements. Decisions of international judicial tribunals and international arbitral bodies, depending upon their competence, constitute an important evidentiary source of international law. Decisions of local courts and tribunals bearing upon aspects of international law or international custom or practice may, according to their competence, also be resorted to for evidence of international law. The teachings of universities and the writings of publicists may constitute a secondary source of evidence as to the standard of conduct properly denominated international law, depending upon their merit.

Herman Phleger, as Legal Adviser of the Department of State, stated:

"International law has been defined as those rules for international conduct which have met general acceptance among the community of nations. It reflects and records those accommodations which, over centuries, states have found it in their interest to make. It rests upon the common consent of civilized communities. It is not to be found in any code. It is made up of precedent, judicial decisions, treaties, arbitrations, international conventions, the opinions of learned writers in the field, and a myriad of other acts and things, which represent in the aggregate those rules which enlightened nations and their people accept as being appropriate to govern international conduct. It is constantly changing, and expanding, as modern science shrinks the world and brings its peoples into ever closer contact.

"Skeptics define international law as the rules which countries obey if they feel like it. Some go even further—they say there is no such thing as international law.

"But there is such a thing as international law. It has had a long and honorable, though chequered, career. I predict that it will play an even more important part in world affairs in the future than it has in the past. Indeed, in this rapidly shrinking world, it becomes increasingly evident that our survival may depend upon our success in substituting the rule of law for the rule of force.

"When we speak of international law, we realize of course that it is made up of two distinct, though related, subjects: Public international law and private international law. The first is usually referred to as the law of nations, with sovereign states as its subjects.

"The latter, private international law, is commonly called the conflict of laws. It is an aspect of private law which involves such juridical relations between individuals as transcend the sphere of national law and, therefore, is not international law in the true sense."

Herman Phleger, Legal Adviser, Department of State, "Some Recent Developments in International Law of Interest to the United States", address before the Pennsylvania Bar Association, Harrisburg, Pa., Jan. 22, 1954, XXX *Bulletin*, Department of State, No. 763, Feb. 8, 1954, p. 196.

"1. International law can no longer be adequately or reasonably defined or described as the law governing the mutual relations of States, even if such a basic definition is accompanied by qualifications or exceptions designed to allow for modern developments; it represents the common law of mankind in an early stage of development, of which the law governing the relations between States is one, but only one, major division.

"2. By the common law of mankind is meant the law of an organised world community, constituted on the basis of States but discharging its community functions increasingly through a complex of international and regional institutions, guaranteeing rights to, and placing obligations upon, the individual citizen, and confronted with a wide range of economic, social and technological problems calling for uniform regulation on an international basis which represent a growing proportion of the subject-matter of the law. The imperfect development and precarious nature of the organised world community is reflected in the early stage of development of the law, but does not invalidate the basic conception."

Jenks, *The Common Law of Mankind* (1958) 58.

Article 5 of the Charter of the Organization of American States provides:

"The American States reaffirm the following principles:

"a) International law is the standard of conduct of States in their reciprocal relations;

"b) International order consists essentially of respect for the personality, sovereignty and independence of States, and the faithful fulfillment of obligations derived from treaties and other sources of international law".

Article 7 further provides:

"Every American State has the duty to respect the rights enjoyed by every other State in accordance with international law."

U.S. TIAS 2361 ; 2 UST 2394, 2418, 2419.

"It is particularly the Montevideo Convention of 1933 which Counsel for the Colombian Government has also relied on in this connexion. It is contended that this Convention has merely codified principles which were already recognised by Latin-American custom, and that it is valid against Peru as a proof of customary law. The limited number of States which have ratified this Convention reveals the weakness of this argument . . . ."

Asylum Case, Colombia/Peru, International Court of Justice, Judgment, Nov. 20, 1950, I.C.J. Reports (1950) 266, 277.

"International law differs in important respects from national law. [Usually designated by international lawyers as "municipal law".] It is not the result of enactment by any single legislature. Its rules are to be sought in law-making treaties, in international custom, in the principles of law recognized by all civilized peoples, in the decisions of international tribunals, and in the cautious use of the writings of jurists of recognized general authority. In the absence of an international legislative body international law tends to be more immutable than national law. It is important to avoid the resulting danger; the effort to achieve a collective system should be something different from an attempt to confine a dynamic world in the strait-jacket of the *status quo.*"

Report by a Group of Members of the Royal Institute of International Affairs, *International Sanctions* (Oxford, 1938) 6.

Private International Law, relationship

"Although public international law is usually defined as the body of norms binding upon civilized States in their relations with one another, a more accurate definition would include all norms having their source in the international community of States rather than in individual States. While at first blush a consideration of the relationship of private international law to this body of norms may seem of purely theoretical and abstract interest, it is in actuality the starting point in determining the framework within which individual States can develop rules of private international law responsive to the needs of the international community. . . ."

Stevenson, "The Relationship of Private International Law to Public International Law", 52 Colum. L. Rev. (1952) 561. For a discussion of the "Scope of Private International Law", see *ibid.* 561–564.

But see Backett, "What is Private International Law?", VII Brit. Yb. Int'l L. (1926) 73; Nussbaum, *Principles of Private International Law* (1943) § 23.

Comity

"Comity", defined as "the recognition which one nation allows within its territory to the legislative, executive, or judicial acts of another nation, having due regard both to international duty and convenience, and to the rights of its own citizens, or of other persons who are under the protection of its laws", "binds the courts as well as the diplomatic channels".

The Hanko (The Norsktank), 54 F. Supp. (E.D.N.Y. 1944) 241, 244, citing *Hilton v. Guyot,* 159 U.S. 113, 164 (1895). As to the "Comity of Nations", see further H. Lauterpacht, "Allegiance, Diplomatic Protection and Criminal Jurisdiction over Aliens", 9 Camb. L.J. (1947) 330–332.

Origin and Theory

"There is no precise time at which it may be said that the body of rules which now regulate, under the title of International Law, the intercourse of nations, came into being. As a science it assumed a definite form in the sixteenth and seventeenth centuries, in the works of the great philosophical jurists, of whom Grotius is the most eminent example. Their works are distinguished by the blending of moral and political principles as discovered by reason and revelation, with positive law and custom as found in the jurisprudence of nations and their practices. The first constituted what was called the law of nature (*jus naturae*); the second, the law of nations (*jus gentium*). Hence the title of some of the treatises—the Law of Nature and of Nations.

"Of the positive element of the new science the Roman Civil Law was the chief source, since it was the foundation of the jurisprudence of the countries of Continental Europe whose laws and practices were chiefly consulted. It is thus apparent that from the beginning the science in question embraced something more than the positive legislation of independent States; and the term 'international law', which has in recent times so generally superseded the earlier titles, serves to emphasize this fact. It denotes a body of obligations which is in a sense independent of and superior to such legislation. . . .

"... the Government of the United States has on various occasions announced the principle that international law as a system is binding upon nations not merely as something to which they may be tacitly assumed to have agreed, but as a fundamental condition of their admission to full participation in the intercourse of civilized States."

John Bassett Moore, "International Law", II *Collected Papers of John Bassett Moore* (1944) 277–278, 280.

–"... The *Law of Nations is the science of the rights which exist between Nations or States, and of the obligations corresponding to these rights.*

"Since Nations are composed of men who are by nature free and independent, and who before the establishment of civil society lived together in the state of nature, such Nations or sovereign States must be regarded as so many free persons living together in the State of nature.

"We must therefore apply to nations the rules of the natural **Natural Law** law to discover what are their obligations and their rights; hence the *Law of Nations* is in its origin merely the *Law of Nature applied to Nations*. Now the just and reasonable application of a rule requires that the application be made in a manner suited to the nature of the subject; but we must not conclude that the Law of Nations is everywhere and at all points the same as the natural law, except for a difference of subjects, so that no other change need be made than to substitute Nations for individuals. A civil society, or a State, is a very different subject from an individual person, and therefore, by virtue of the natural law, very different obligations and rights belong to it in most cases. The same general rule, when applied to two different subjects, can not result in similar principles, nor can a particular rule, however just for one subject, be applicable to a second of a totally different nature. Hence there are many cases in which the natural law does not regulate the relations of States as it would those of individuals. We must know how to apply it conformably to its subjects; and the art of so applying it, with a precision founded upon right reason, constitutes of the Law of Nations a distinct science.

"We use the term *necessary Law of Nations* for that law which results from applying the natural law to Nations. It is *necessary*, because Nations are absolutely bound to observe it. It contains those precepts which the natural law dictates to States, and it is no less binding upon them than it is upon individuals. For States are composed of men, their policies are determined by men, and these men are subject to the natural law under whatever capacity they act. This same law is called by Grotius and his followers the *internal Law of Nations*, inasmuch as it is binding upon the conscience of Nations. Several writers call it the *natural Law of Nations.*"

Vattel, *Le Droit des Gens* (1758), translated by Charles Fenwick, Carnegie Institution reprint (1916), vol. 3, bk. I, pp. 3, 4.

"About the beginning of the seventeenth century it is possible to detect a new direction in the study of law. Natural law had always been part of the philosopher's stock-in-trade. For many reasons, which have been amply discussed by Sir Henry Maine and Sir Frederick Pollock, it had to be brought again into the foreground, mainly in order to bridle the sovereign states, newly conscious of their status and power, especially in their relations to each other. At that time international law could not be built up without recourse to what were conceived to be first principles: international custom was far too rudimentary and barbarous to make a nineteenth century positivism even conceivable. Internal changes within the sovereign states spread the philosophical study of politics from international law to public law as a whole. There might have been no extension of the process to Civil Law had there been a distinct class of public lawyers; but the rise and development of such a profession, far from being anterior to these more general developments, was a phase of them, long-drawn out and strange in character. For long public lawyer meant international lawyer: to this day the Regius Chair of Public Law in the University of Edinburgh is a chair of international law, though the fact that its holder also teaches jurisprudence shows how much international law in its origins owed to legal theory. . . .

"If then some stuffing had to be put into international law, only the Civil lawyers could do it; and they almost inevitably found it by extracting the most rational and universal elements from the Roman Law with which they were most familiar. . . ."

Lawson, "A Common Lawyer Looks at the Civil Law" (University of Michigan Law School, Thomas M. Cooley Lectures, Fifth Series, 1953, published 1955) 31–32.

"For the Scholastic philosopher, . . . International Law is truly a law, and is as firmly grounded in fundamental principles as is the civil law of any individual state. He admits that the frequent violation of such a law is a disheartening thing, but he recognizes that these violations cannot destroy its real existence and fundamental nature.

.   .   .   .

". . . In its widest sense, therefore, a law is nothing more than a manner of acting in a way which will lead the agent to the end proportionate to its nature, the particular law followed by each agent likewise being determined by that agent's particular nature. In short, every agent, lacking from the outset the full perfection of its nature, seeks to overcome this initial deficiency by a series of acts which will lead it to the desired end wherein it will achieve the perfection due its nature. These acts, therefore, are the means to that end; and law, in its widest sense, is that which puts order into these acts whereby they will be duly proportionate to the end for which they are intended. 'It is an ordination of things to an end, by reason of which each creature by pursuing its own particular end, helps to attain the end of the whole universe.'

". . . Scholastics call this general law of the universe, this fundamental plan of action for all creatures, the Eternal Law. They reason that the Creator of the universe, Who is supremely intelligent, must have created for a purpose, and in order that that purpose will be accomplished, He must have instituted a plan of action for the universe, a law. Thus, in the words of St. Thomas, the Eternal Law is 'the Divine Wisdom in so far as it is directive of all actions and movements.' Every particular law of the universe, therefore, is but a manifestation of the Divine Plan by which the whole universe is directed to its end.

.   .   .   .

"Because . . . man has a natural inclination expressive of his need and aptitude for group living, society is natural to him and to that extent the state is a natural institution. . . . He requires the aids given by civil society in order to develop completely the virtues of his rational and moral nature. Hence the state owes its existence to the Natural Law. Further, since the state must have a ruler and laws by which the actions of its members are directed to the common good, it is evident that these necessary political elements are likewise justified by the Natural Law. Civil laws, therefore, owe their ultimate 'legality' to the Natural Law, in as much as they are the necessary means by which men can live together in society. . . .

"It is evident from this relationship between the civil law and the natural law that the justice of a civil law is determined by its conformity with the natural law and the obligation to obey it arises from this same relationship. . . .

"Man's natural bond to his fellow-man, however, does not disappear at the boundaries of each man's particular state, but rather it is co-extensive with all human society. The fundamental precepts of justice and charity, of mutual aid and respect for the rights of others, obtain just as truly among men of different states as among men of the same state. Consequently, the same intimate relationship which exists between the domestic civil law and the natural law also exists between International Law and the natural law.

"We may define the law of nations as 'the sum total of the duties and rights, customs and usages, by which states are bound together in their dealings with one another. Like the domestic laws of nations, it contains two elements: Natural and Positive. The former comprises those principles and rules governing international relations which are immediately drawn from the moral law of nature written there by its Creator. The positive element consists mainly of treaties, customs and usages which the states have formally accepted or sanctioned. In so far as accepted international law does not include pertinent precepts of the natural law, . . . it falls short of completeness; in so far as it contains articles contrary to the precepts of the natural law, it loses all binding force and frustrates its own purpose.'

". . . we maintain that all positive law, both domestic and international, that coincides with the fundamental principles of the natural law, is absolutely binding in conscience with a moral obligation,—regardless of whether or not there happens to be on hand a physical force capable of enforcing its observation.

.   .   .   .

"Not only is it evident that the moral law furnishes the natural element in international law, but a little consideration will make it clear that even the positive element (treaties, pacts, covenants, etc.) would have no binding force unless the various states recognized that there was a moral obligation under the natural law to keep faith with one another."

Baker, "The Scholastic Concept of International Law", 16 Notre Dame Law.   (1940) 1, 3, 4, 8, 9, 10, 11.

Positive Law

"Law between Nations is the law which is recognized in the community of different princes or peoples who hold sovereign power—that is to say, the law which has been accepted among most nations by customs in harmony with reason, and that upon which single nations agree with one another, and which is observed by nations at peace and by those at war."

Zouche, *Juris et Judicii Fecialis sive Juris inter Gentes* (1650), translated by J. L. Brierly, Carnegie Institution reprint (1911), vol. II, p. 1.

Consent

"Assuming for the moment the basic premise . . . that consent is the foundation of the international order of rights and duties, it does not follow by ineluctable logic that one state cannot be an object of international law without the consent of other states. It is sufficient to the argument (and nearer to the reality) that consent is given to international law as a system rather than to each and every relationship contained in it; and, in the final analysis, the position of an unrecognized state would be determined by whatever rules are given by international law with respect to the capacity of states."

Jaffe, *Judicial Aspects of Foreign Relations* (1933) 90.

"While recognized members of the community of nations are bound by the established rules of international law without any explicit act of acceptance, they cannot become bound by new rules without express or implied consent. [H. A. Smith, Great Britain and the Law of Nations, Vol. 1, pp. 12–13.] . . .

. . . .

"In principle it seems clear that a group of states cannot legislate for the world. The Declarations of Paris (1856) and of London (1909), while professing in the main to state accepted rules of international law, were asserted to bind only the parties *inter se.* In both cases the parties expressed the intention to gain accession by other states of the world, but it was recognized that these other states would not be bound until they had so acceded. [A. Pearce Higgins, The Hague Peace Conferences and other International Conferences concerning the Laws and Usages of War (Cambridge, 1909), pp. 2, 541, 565.] It would appear that the American Republics can, under international law, do no more, and this position has been asserted by belligerents in refusing to accept the Declaration of Panama. [Res. XIV, Res. XV, *Report on the Meeting of the Ministers of Foreign Affairs of the American Republics, Panamá, Sept. 23–Oct. 3, 1939* (P.A.U. 1939) 19, 22. See British, French, and German notes of Jan. 14, 23, and Feb. 16, 1940, in reply to protest of the American Republics of Dec. 23, 1939, on the *Graf Spee* incident, II *Bulletin*, Department of State, No. 35, Feb. 24, 1940, pp. 199–205.] In practice the accepted rules of neutrality have been applied by the American Republics in the case of the *Graf Spee* and other instances in which hostilities have occurred within the barred zone. [The zone described in the Declaration of Panamá. Uruguay based its action on Hague Convention XIII.] If the American Republics should go beyond the offer of voluntary accession to these resolutions, and attempt to apply the new principles against unwilling states, they will have to rely on policy and not on law, and in such an effort they might find themselves acting in violation of international law."

Quincy Wright, "Rights and Duties under International Law", 34 Am. J. Int'l L. (1940) 238, 247.

"International law—to use Bentham's innovation of 1789, which has found favor with the public, instead of the older, more expressive term, law of nations—has been variously denounced and praised as international morality or ethics; international courtesy or convention in the social sense of the word; comity as distinguished from rule of law; or merely and finally as the foreign policy, such as the Monroe Doctrine, which at a particular time happens to catch the fancy of nations. If admitted as law in general or as possessing some of the elements of ordinary municipal law, the principle that pinches is declared not to be law and to have no binding force whatever, because there is no supreme court of nations in which the dispute may be litigated and no

20th Century Positivists

sheriff to execute the decree, supposing that one had actually been delivered. But the judgment of a municipal court is not self-executing, as, for instance, when President Jackson stamped his foot, saying: 'John Marshall has made the decision; now let him execute it!' . . . It is submitted that the mere form of the sanction is immaterial, and that the nature of law cannot well depend upon the whim or ability of a sheriff, or the mere success or failure of an army in the field. If the principle is binding at all—that is, if nations admit that a principle binds them—it is of no great moment whether the force is moral, ethical, or physical. . . .

. . . .

"Admitting for a moment Austin's strictures, it is evident that a great deal of the body of international law would be law in the strict sense of the term; for a nation may and does bind itself by treaty, a positive agreement, and a violation of rights under the treaty would lead to a 'command' from the injured state to the state guilty of the infraction. It would likewise seem to follow that if nations should recognize a custom or the body of customs which make up the law of nations, and give full effect to this custom, when rights depending upon the custom arise and enforce through municipal courts the so-called law, the principle of decision might claim in such a case the epithet of law. The law administered in the various prize courts in civilized states is universal, practically identical, and is enforced by process of court. Each specific instance would make this law, at least for the purposes of the case, municipal law and the sanction required by Austin's definition would clearly be present. Austin would indeed allow the quality of positive law to these various instances, but he maintains that the law so applied becomes municipal or national law and loses the character of international law.

. . . .

". . . the presence of a sanction is not essential to the quality of law, for the law as such is simply a rule of conduct, and is neither self-applying nor self-executing. The rule of conduct exists, and in a perfect state, whether it be enforced or not.

. . . .

"If, then, the recognition of the body of usages and customs forming the bulk of international law involves their adoption both by the state so recognizing, subjects and citizens thereof, it follows, as said, that the usages and customs of international law become, for the purpose of state and citizen, municipal law of such state and citizen, and that such usages and customs become the common law of each and every state so recognizing and adopting. There then presents itself a body of fixed and binding law—the common law of nations—just as clearly and surely as the common customs and usages of England became the common law of that realm."

James Brown Scott, "The Legal Nature of International Law", 1 Am. J. Int'l L., pt. II (1907) 831, 837, 839, 851.

"... International law, like all other kinds of law, originated in the necessities of intercourse between human beings. Just as rules developed for the regulation of life within individual groups, so, as groups became permanent and were transformed into states, rules developed for the regulation of their intercourse with one another. The system thus gradually formed was not artificial in any sense other than that in which all legal systems are artificial. Regulation is just as essential to the relations between groups of men as it is to the relations between individual men.

.   .   .   .

"But, so far as obligation is concerned, it matters not whether the system was tacitly accepted or expressly adopted. In both cases, the obligation is the same.

.   .   .   .

"... Since the great conflict in Europe began, the days have perhaps been rare on which the teacher or student of international law has not been greeted with the profound remark that there is no such thing as international law, or that international law has come to an end. . . . The rules of international law are by no means so indefinite or uncertain as they are often supposed to be, or as interested persons often seek to make them appear to be; nor is their observance by any means so casual as is sometimes imagined. It would be difficult to find in international law an example of uncertainty greater than that which attended the interpretation and the enforcement of the so-called Sherman Anti-Trust Law, which, after twenty years of strenuous controversy, was left to be interpreted according to the 'rule of reason.' Nor is international law in ordinary times badly observed. It is, in fact, usually well enforced; and any differences in regard to its interpretation and enforcement are, except in matters of a political nature, commonly left to international tribunals for determination, in connection with individual claims."

John Bassett Moore, "Symposium on International Law: Its Origin, Obligation, and Future", IV *Collected Papers of John Bassett Moore* (1944) 131, 132–133.

"... The theorists, in their attempt to produce the new order by coercion, are driving out of existence international law, the only law that is able to survive among a congeries of states, none of whom is entitled to pass judgment on others, and none of whom is able to enforce its judgment without inviting war. The theorists thus propose to 'enforce' peace by war at a time when international relations are more irreconcilable than ever; yet they expect the promotion of law to accompany this essentially anarchistic process. This is the state of mind that the 20th century has attained. Perhaps two world wars, with their destruction of human values, were too great a shock to permit the survival of reason.

.   .   .   .

"... the law that can prevail among sovereign states is not a law dictated by superior to inferior, as is the case inside a state,

or in municipal law, as we call it, but only a system to which
states agree, whether created by custom or by treaty among
equals. . . .

.   .   .   .

"The assumption of numerous theorists that the weakness of
international law is due to the lack of force behind it is responsible for much of the sorry thinking of the present day. International law is a primitive system, not because it lacks the support of force but because it deals with sovereign states who cannot be coerced by other states without entailing war. There must
be a certain agreement on the law, at least among the majority.
But the law gains its strength through practice, invocation by
foreign offices and application by tribunals."

Borchard, "The Impracticability of 'Enforcing' Peace", 55 Yale L. J.
(1946) 966, 967–969.

"The law of nations which has developed during the course of
the past three centuries has rested chiefly on the custom and practise of the states which are members of the society of nations.
The jurisprudence of international and national tribunals has
become significant as one of its sources, only during the past century; though such tribunals have developed many of the customary standards and principles, their jurisprudence has generally been based on foundations for which there was historical
justification. The conception of a law of nations consciously
constructed by a community of states found little place in the
writings of the seventeenth and eighteenth centuries, and it has
been but slowly evolved out of the experience of the nineteenth
century. The needs of the international society of earlier times
had not been thought to call for effort to develop new law; but
the revolutionary changes of the nineteenth century created a
new international society, with which came the need for a different kind of international law. Such changes are still in progress; the industrial revolution of the nineteenth century is being
paralleled, in its effect on international relations, by the technical revolution of the twentieth century; and as new conditions
are produced, or old conditions are changed, need arises for
new law. The customary guidance does not fully serve this
need; nor are courts able to fill it. Law-making, legislation,
has come to be a process quite as important in the development
of the law of nations as administration, or arbitration, or adjudication. Whether expressly or otherwise, no study of international law in the twentieth century can ignore legislation as
one of its principal sources."

I Hudson, *International Legislation, 1919–21* (1931), sec. 1, p. xiii.

"What law does the Court [Permanent Court of International
Justice] apply in the disposition of controversies? It applies
international law. What is international law? It is the body
and principles and rules which civilized States consider as binding
upon them in their mutual relations. It rests upon the consent of

sovereign States. There are many questions which are discussed by international jurists with respect to principles which are not yet embodied in international law, as there is no satisfactory evidence of the consent of States to be bound by them. There are also particular principles and rules that are binding upon particular States, because they are established by treaties between such States. These rules are not, properly speaking, international law, but they govern the States that have agreed to them.

"If there is a dispute as to international law and the court finds that there is no international law on the subject, it says so. It is not its function to create rules of international law. It explores, hears arguments, and determines whether there is a rule of international law applicable to a given case. Its decisions on such questions expound and clarify international law. The law thus develops in a normal way by the unfolding of its accepted principles in their application to particular disputes. But the court does not assume the function of a legislature. The court is naturally very cautious in this part of its work; an international court would not long survive that took to itself the legislative function or the making of law for States."

Charles Evans Hughes, "Organization and Methods of the Permanent Court of International Justice", address before the Association of the Bar of the City of New York, 72 *Cong. Rec.*, Jan. 21, 1930, 71st Cong., 2d sess., pp. 2016, 2017.

"When the Court, in the *Asylum* case, was confronted with a contention relating to an alleged right of a unilateral and definitive qualification of the offence committed by the refugee, it based itself on the principle of State sovereignty and held that a party which relies on a custom derogating from that principle must prove that the rule invoked is in accordance with a constant and uniform State practice accepted as law. The same method would seem to be applicable in the present case. Having to base oneself on the ground that questions of naturalization are in principle within the exclusive competence of States, one should, as in the *Asylum* case, enquire whether a rule derogating from that principle is established in such a manner that it has become binding on Liechtenstein. The Government of Guatemala would have to prove that such a custom is in accordance with a constant and uniform State practice 'accepted as law' (Article 38, para. I(b) of the Court's Statute). But no evidence is produced by that Government purporting to establish the existence of such a custom."

Judge Klaestad, *Nottebohm Case* (Liechtenstein *v.* Guatemala), Judgment (Second Phase), Apr. 6, 1955, I.C.J. Reports (1955) 30, dissenting opinion.

". . . Observation proves that there is, in fact, a system regulating the Society of States which fulfills a function analogous to the system regulating individual conduct. This system is derived primarily from two elements: guiding forces, such as

public opinion, which center at times in actual institutions of
public enlightenment, education, *etc.*; norms of conduct, which
determine the limits and forms within which the conduct of
States one toward another must develop.

"A special category of these norms, certainly the most important, consists of those which are established by means of
agreements, tacit or express, between the States themselves;
agreements by which these States reciprocally undertake to act
in a given manner, so that, if certain hypotheses result, they are
bound to do or not to do such or such a thing and may advance
corresponding claims.

". . . The obligatory force of these norms is derived from the
principle that States must respect the agreements concluded between them: *pacta sunt servanda.* . . .

"Every legal order consists of a complex of norms which derive
their obligatory character from a fundamental norm to which they
all relate, directly or indirectly. The fundamental norm determines, in this way, which norms compose a given legal order and
gives unity to the whole. The international legal order is distinguished by the fact that, in this order, the principle *pacta
sunt servanda* does not depend, as in internal law, upon a superior norm; it is itself the supreme norm. . . . all norms, and
only the norms, which depend upon this principle as the necessary and exclusive source of their obligatory character, belong
to the category of those with which we are concerned here. These
norms constitute international law, that is to say, the legal order
of the Community of States."

Anzilotti, *Corso Di Diritto Internazionale*, vol. I (3d ed., 1928) 41–43,
translated in Hudson's *Cases on International Law* (2d ed., 1936) 6–7.

"Neo-
Kantian"

Neo-Kantian philosophy assumes that "international law can be
regarded as law in the same sense as national law. Its rules, in short,
are conceivable as hypothetical judgments 'making a coercive act,
forcible interference in the sphere of interests of a subject, the
consequence of a certain act of the same or another subject' ".

Stone, *Legal Controls of International Conflict* (1954), p. xlvi.

"Since national law has the reason of its validity, and hence
its 'source' in this sense, in international law, the ultimate source
of the former must be the same as that of the latter. Then the
pluralistic view cannot be defended by the assumption that national and international law have different and mutually independent 'sources'. It is the 'source' of national law by which that
law is united with international law, whatever may be the 'source'
of this legal order. Which is the source, then, that is, the basic
norm of international law?

"To find the source of the international legal order, we have to
follow a course similar to that which led us to the basic norm of
the national legal order. We have to start from the lowest norm
within international law, that is, from the decision of an inter-

national court. If we ask why the norm created by such a decision is valid, the answer is furnished by the international treaty in accordance with which the court was instituted. If, again, we ask why this treaty is valid, we are led back to the general norm which obligates the States to behave in conformity with the treaties they have concluded, a norm commonly expressed by the phrase *pacta sunt servanda*. This is a norm of general international law, and general international law is created by custom constituted by acts of States. The basic norm of international law, therefore, must be a norm which countenances custom as a norm-creating fact, and might be formulated as follows: 'The States ought to behave as they have customarily behaved'. Customary international law, developed on the basis of this norm, is the first stage within the international legal order. The next stage is formed by the norms created by international treaties. The validity of these norms is dependent upon the norm *pacta sunt servanda*, which itself is a norm belonging to the first stage of general international law, which is law created by custom constituted by acts of States. The third stage is formed by norms created by organs which are themselves created by international treaties, as for instance decisions of the Council of the League of Nations, or of the Permanent Court of International Justice."

Kelsen, *General Theory of Law and State* (1945) 369–370. For a dualist criticism of Kelsen's analytical monist approach to international law, see Borchard, "International Jurisprudence—Analytical and Functional", 38 Am. J. Int'l L. (1944) 95–98.

Contemporaneously there exists a school interested primarily in constructing a "scientific" juristic theory of international law. In order to do so, they seek to strip international law of all *a priori* existence or validity and set about to examine it as observable phenomena in time and space or as "fact". The law that actually exists by reason of consent (positive law), in this view, can only be founded on empirically verifiable facts which may themselves have causal relations.

"Empiricist-Positivists"

"No fact as such is regarded as having a legal character. It is qualified as legal through its relation to some other fact, which in turn derives its legal quality from some further fact, and so on, until we come to the final basis of the law. . . . Somewhere it is supposed to stop. A sort of fountain is to be discovered from which the legal character of the whole series of acts is to be derived. . . .

". . . the 'ultimate basis' must be placed outside the actual succession of events. No link in the chain of cause and effect fulfills the requirements of an ultimate basis because it always follows previous facts as their effect. No stop is therefore possible in the actual world of facts. The fixed and stable basis of the law, if there is any such basis, must be of an absolute nature, i.e. raised above the succession of cause and effect.

"However cherished the idea of such an ultimate and absolute basis of the law may be, it nevertheless makes no sense. The idea is contradictory in itself. Either the absolute character of the basis is really maintained—then it can have no connection with the succession of cause and effect—or it is conceived as a cause of some effects. In that case its absolute character is abandoned.

"Empirically, too, we arrive at the conclusion that there is no ultimate basis of the law. . . . Nowhere do we find an ultimate basis of the law, but only human actions as links in the chain of cause and effect.

". . . No more can the *end* of law be an object of scientific research. . . .

"In a discussion of the basis or the end of the law, some supposition is always made as to what the law *is*. Two elements are common to most theories on this matter: (1) Law consists of a system of *rules*, and (2) these rules are *obligatory* or endowed with 'binding force', i.e. they create *duties* for those subjected to them.

"From the second element originates the search for an ultimate basis of the law outside the world of mere facts. A duty can never be based on a fact as such. If the fact is a command, the authority by whom the command is given must have a *right* to command, or, in other words, there must already exist a duty to obey the command. If this duty is based on a command from a superior authority, this authority in its turn must have a right to command, and so on. Sooner or later it is necessary to come to an absolute basis of the right to command, if the whole theory is to be maintained.

"The quest for an ultimate basis of the law is therefore made necessary by the original assumption concerning the nature of the law. On the other hand, the quest is necessarily futile. . . .

"Very often an escape from the dilemma is sought by gliding over from the idea of the absolute foundation required to some fact. It is said, for example, that the obligatory force of the law is based on its being *recognized* as obligatory (Jellinek). In other words, the duty to follow the law is engendered by recognition of the existence of the duty. This makes no sense. Nothing can be called into existence by being recognized as existing. . . .

"There is only one way which promises some hope of solving the dilemma. We have to turn back on that concept of law which was the starting-point of the discussion. The question should be put whether the law really must be considered to have obligatory force, to create duties and corresponding rights. If this element can be dropped, the difficulties will be disposed of. Then law will be simply a set of social facts. It will not be particularly difficult to bring them in relation to other social facts with the usual scientific methods. No need for a basis outside the natural world will arise.

. . . .

". . . the judge never determines the existence of a right. On the basis of the facts presented to him he issues the command, for example, that B shall pay a sum to A. This activity can be accurately described only by speaking of facts, not of rights.

It is true that sometimes the judgment contains the concept of a right, e.g. when it acknowledges A as the owner of a thing. In that case the judgment itself has been transcribed into a pattern of conduct.

"When the ideas of an obligatory force of the law, of rights and duties, are dissolved into their component parts, the chief problems of traditional legal philosophy vanish into thin air. They are replaced by real problems which can be treated in a wholly scientific way. Instead of rights and duties, we have only the *ideas* of rights and duties; instead of the binding force of the law, men's *opinions* on the reasons why law is 'binding'. The only scientific task in this field is to investigate the ideas as such. With the fundamental legal concepts the idea of jurisprudence as a 'normative' science is dissolved too. The belief in the possibility of such a science is called forth by the doctrine that the 'shall' of the rules denotes something real instead of being merely an imperative word, psychologically associated to a pattern of conduct. In so far as jurisprudence expounds patterns of conduct set up in statutes or by precedent, it is concerned with the content of ideas and with past actions, i.e. with facts."

Olivecrona, "Law as Fact", in Sayre, *Interpretations of Modern Legal Philosophies* (Oxford, 1947) 542–544, 554. See also Velhelm Lundstedt, "Law and Justice: A Criticism of the Method of Justice", also published in the work cited, pp. 450–453, 474–476.

". . . the fundamental source of error in a number of apparently unconquerable contradictions in the modern theory of law is a dualism in the implied prescientific concept of law which more or less consciously forms the basis of the theories developed. It is a dualism of *reality* and *validity* in law, which again works itself out in a series of antinomies in legal theory. . . .

. . . .

". . . Altogether, 'validity' is nothing objective or conceivable, but merely a word used as a common term for such expressions by which certain subjective experiences of impulse are rationalised. There do not exist any conceptions of validity whatever, but merely conceptually rationalised experiences of validity, that is to say, certain experiences furnished with peculiar illusions of objectivity. . . .

"The hypothesis presented is to the effect that the common concept of law has come into existence by an intimate fusion of notions of validity in the sense indicated above, with notions of reality, a fusion which, when the former are accepted according to their rationalised logical claim, shows itself in the above-mentioned dualism with its immanent antinomies, but which, when the process of rationalising is reduced, and the expressions of validity are merely taken according to their symbolical value, expresses an interaction between actual elements of the legal reality. . . ."

Alf Ross, *Towards A Realistic Jurisprudence* (Copenhagen, Einar Munksgaard, 1946, translated from Danish by Fausbøll) 11–13.

Functional
theorists

The Functional School objects to the Positivists' narrow and unrealistic view of law—their legalism by which legal matters are dealt with as exclusively apart from ethics, mores, psychology, and sociology; their *etatist* monism by which valid law is restricted to rules enacted by the state or to decisions of the tribunals. Functional theorists purport to bring law closer to reality by giving it a basis in touch with all the social factors thereby making law at once both a directive and a resultant of these social forces.

"The fundamental weakness of the positivist doctrine of international law lies in its inadequacy to international law as it really is. Unfaithful to its own assumptions, it contains at the same time more and less than the actual rules of international law, which it furthermore submits to subjective evaluation in the light of ethical and political principles of assumedly universal, yet doubtful, validity. . . . realism has become a collective designation for several tendencies in modern jurisprudence, all aiming at replacing, by different means, the fictitious legalism of traditional jurisprudence with a conception nearer to the realities of the law. All these tendencies have this in common : They do not regard the legal rules as definitely determined by their legislative or judicial formulation, but search for the psychological, social, political and economic forces which determine the actual content and working of legal rules and which, in turn, are determined by them. In other words, their scientific goal is to formulate uniform functional relationships between those forces and the legal rules. Hence, 'realist' jurisprudence is, in truth, 'functional' jurisprudence.

". . . On the one hand, international law is the function of the civilization in which it originates, that is, of the regulative ideas laid down in the ethics and *mores* of this civilization, of the political, economic and general social forces prevailing in it, and finally, of the specific psychological factors manifesting themselves in the individuals determining it. On the other hand, international law is a social mechanism working towards certain ends within this same civilization which, in turn, as far as determined by it, becomes a function of this same international law. By systematizing the rules of a given international law under the viewpoint of this dual functional relationship between rules and social forces, the functional theory will arrive at a real scientific understanding of the material element of the legal rules which positivism even at its best was able to describe and systematize only according to superficial legalistic viewpoints. [Citing certain legal authorities.]

.   .   .   .

". . . It follows from this analysis that there exist two obviously different types of international law, one founded upon the permanent and stable interests, the other based upon the temporary and fluctuating interests of states. . . .

"The main bulk of the concepts and principles of international

law has been derived from municipal civil law. These concepts
and principles have been developed within a legal system characterized by the extraordinary stability of the interests underlying it. Hence its application is, of necessity, restricted to legal
systems based upon equally stable interests. In the international
field such stable interests exist, for instance, with respect to
diplomatic privileges, territorial jurisdiction, extradition, wide
fields of maritime law, arbitral procedure, and so forth. This
is the classical field of traditional international law as it has
gradually developed in the practice of states since the sixteenth
century. We propose to call these rules non-political international law, originating in the permanent interests of states
to put their normal relations upon a stable basis by providing
for predictable and enforceable conduct with respect to these
relations.

"But there is another type of international law which expresses,
in terms of rights and duties, temporary interests ever given to
change. In this category belong political agreements, especially
treaties of alliance and their modern substitutes, which, under
the legalistic disguise of treaties of general arbitration, consultation, or friendship, frequently pursue aims at least preparatory
to close political ties. The traditional science of international
law treats both types of international law alike, applying to both
the concepts and methods developed in municipal civil law. By
doing so, it cannot but draw a completely distorted picture of
those rules which belong in the category of political international
law. Under such treatment, their validity appears to be firmly
established, whereas it is actually always precarious; the interests
which they are supposed to serve appear to be permanent and
definite, whereas they are actually exposed to continuous change
and are more or less uncertain; and consequently, the rights and
duties established by them appear to be clearly determined,
whereas they are subject actually to the most contradictory
interpretations."

Morgenthau, "Positivism, Functionalism, and International Law", 34
Am. J. Int'l L. (1940) 260, 273, 274, 278, 279.

The phenomenological approach to international law constitutes a
reaction against the logical formalism of Kelsen, for it is interested
in the content rather than the form of knowledge. It also constitutes
a reaction against empiricism and positivism for it is interested more
in the meaning of concrete phenomena as objects of interpretation
through psychic acts and insists that reality lies in the psychological
experience of phenomena rather than in its supposed independent existence. Thus, a real international legal order or world community
exists, according to this school of thought, only in so far as it is an
"actual process of human actions".

Phenomeno-
logical
approach

". . . It is a commonplace that human society, in the sense of
the true social whole, is not to be found exclusively in the sphere

of factual acts of men as they occur.   If Verdross, in regard to
the problem of juridical positivity, has shown a deep insight into
the really *ideal sphere of existence* of 'objective values', including
the construct [*sic*] which is the law, and then, in sharp contradistinction to this ideal sphere of existence has recognized the *factual
sphere* of the 'concrete statutory acts' as the basis of the 'positivity' of the juridical order, it follows that he should also have
reached the conclusion, in regard to social existence, that social
association cannot possibly be identical with the totality of the
merely factual social acts, for that is *only* the 'ground' for the
reality of the association as an ideal mental construct.   The social
association or the juridical community is an ideal mental construct
which—if we may borrow the lofty words with which Verdross
has so aptly described the essential character of positive law—
points with its head beyond itself out into the world of values,
while with its feet it stands on the solid ground of the actual
process of human actions.   The problem of the objective existence
of the 'international juridical community' has in our view not been
solved by proposing the formulation of the 'totality of the factual
juridical acts regulated by international law.' "

Tomoo Otaka, *Grundlegung der Lehre vom sozialen Verband* (Vienna,
Springer, 1932), sec. 26, "The Idea of the World Association and Positive
International Law", pp. 109–110 (translation).   For Verdross, see Verdross,
Volkerrecht (Berlin, Springer, 1937).

"We need this contact with the experience for support, since the
egological theory is fundamentally at variance with traditional
juridical thought, which, by using rationalism, dispenses with such
a contact, and which, with empiricism and historicism, falsifies it
with two inauthentic contacts.

"The egological theory considers that the Dogmatic Science of
Law is a science of reality, consequently a factual science; but
only of cultural or human experience, and not of natural or causal
experience.   In this respect, the egological theory is profoundly
different from both the rationalism and empiricism dominant in
juridical trial. . . .

"In opposition to juridical rationalism, the egological theory
considers that the thing to be judged by the jurist is not the
standard, but human conduct as viewed from a certain particular
angle.   Just as the stars are the objects of the astronomer's perception, and not the laws of Kepler and Newton, since the latter
are only concepts with which the stars are perceived, so also
the objects of the jurist's perception in Dogmatic Science are not
standards, but rather human conduct in its inter-subjective interference, because juridical standards are only concepts with
which that conduct is judged as conduct.   Standards are simply
the concepts with which we consider that conduct.   In themselves, being concepts, they are ideal objects of a logical nature,
like all concepts; which explains why the study of norms in their
normative nature is the business of formal juridical logic, upon
which matter the investigations of Kelsen which are known as
pure theory of law, contain the general features and bases.   But

Dogmatic Science, as a science of reality, contains an extra feature with regard to juridical logic, which comes directly and immediately from human experience, as natural experience places in physics something which does not come from the mere logical structure of the perception of Nature . . .

"In its turn, and in opposition to juridical empiricism, the egological theory considers that human conduct is an object of experimentation that differs radically from natural objects, since, while the latter constitutes an experience of necessity governed by the identity of causes with effects, human conduct constitutes a free experience in which the creation of something original emerges at every instant. It is for this reason that conduct as such, that is to say, free conduct, cannot be thought of as being, according to the claim of empiricism, but as an existential 'must be'. And only through the possession of concepts which mention or represent conduct in its reality as the egological theory maintains. Therefore the egological theory accepts the normative logic of the pure theory of law which has shown us that norms are exactly such concepts. But it adds the specific intuition of the law, which is an intuition of liberty— and therefore an axiological intuition—as an extra feature of the judgment which is added to the logico-juridical structure on the basis of (*por cuenta de*) human experience."

Cossio, "Phenomenology of the Judgment, An Introduction to the Ego-logical Theory of Law"*, in Sayre, *Interpretations of Modern Legal Philosophies* (1947) 85, 86–87 (translated by Richard Tyler). ["*I have had to resort to the neologism 'egology' and the words derived from it (from ego 'I'), in order to avoid all the directions taken by the word 'subjective' when it lost its original connotation as a mere adjective denoting a subject. In this manner, I may clearly establish Law in a definite regional ontology without falling prey to misinterpretations that are verbal in origin."]

Certain sociological theories of our day may tend toward a revival of natural law because inherent in these sociological aspirations is an inborn sense of justice. This may constitute rather a "revision" of natural law since it admits a strain of natural law through sociological jurisprudence. Such sociological jurisprudence usually assumes without question the validity of positive law. Not all the writers quoted immediately *infra* necessarily fall completely within the generalizations just set forth. Thus, Judge de Visscher would give natural law, as such, a recognized place in a fuller concept of international law. (*Post*, p. 25.)

Revival of Natural Law

"This law [new international law] is the result and outcome of the great transformations in the life of nations which have taken place since the first world war, and mostly after the 1939 cataclysm.

"The *community* of States, which had hitherto remained *anarchical*, has become in fact an *organized international society*.

This transformation is a fact which does not require the consecration of an international agreement. . . .

"All these transformations have had a great influence on international law: a new international law has emerged. It is new for three reasons: it includes new questions in addition to traditional questions in a new form; it rests on the basic reconstruction of fundamental principles of classical international law, and brings them into harmony with the new conditions of the life of peoples; finally, it is based on the new social régime which has appeared, *the régime of interdependence*, which is taking the place of the individualistic régime which has, up to now, provided the basis of both national and international life. This new régime has given rise to what may be called *social interdependence* which is taking the place of traditional *individualism*. . . .

"The purposes of the new international law, based on social interdependence, differ from those of classical international law: they are to harmonize the rights of States, to promote co-operation between them and to give ample room to common interests; its purpose is also to favour cultural and social progress. In short, its purpose is to bring about what may be called *international social justice*.

"To achieve these purposes, this law must lay stress on the notion of *obligation* of States, not only between themselves, but also toward the international community. It must limit absolute international sovereignty of States according to the new requirements of the life of peoples, and must yield to the changing necessities of that life.

"Because of these characteristics the new international law is not of an exclusively juridical character. It has also political, economic, social, and psychological characteristics.

". . . In reality it takes root in the new conditions and the new requirements of the life of peoples in numerous recent social institutions of several countries, in the international judicial conscience which has been awakened mainly since the upheaval of 1914. . . ."

Judge Alvarez, *International Status of South-West Africa*, International Court of Justice, Advisory Opinion, July 11, 1950, I.C.J. Reports (1950) 128, dissenting opinion, pp. 175–176. In his proposals of "new law" based on the new social facts of interdependence and the requirements of the life of people, a natural-law strain can be identified in his reference to the notion of obligations of States quite independent of specific laws by which a State's sovereign will has consented to be bound.

". . . The 'law' that is being studied is still too often regarded as a body of doctrine or rules, divorced from power and social processes. . . . The conception of law as a decision-making process, and a process in which the decision-makers are influenced by many variables, has had as yet but few effects. . . .

.   .   .   .

". . . The process of decision-making is, indeed, one of continual redefinition of doctrine in the formation and application of policy to ever-changing facts in ever-changing contexts. The variables to which decision-makers respond, the factors which affect decision, are both environmental and predispositional. Environmental variables include the facts of a particular controversy, the competing claims of the parties, and the standards invoked (comprising both technical legal doctrines in terms of rights, duties, powers, property, title, contract, tort, sovereignty, due process, and so on, and policy propositions in terms of basic community values), as well as the whole community context. Predispositional variables include the attitudes (demands for values, identifications, and expectations), skills, class positions, and character structures of decision-makers. . . ."

McDougal, "The Comparative Study of Law for Policy Purposes: Value Clarification as an Instrument of Democratic World Order", 61 Yale L.J. (1952) 915, 919, 920, 921–922.

". . . Thus, the critics of 'law' who use the word to refer merely to authoritative rules or formal doctrine, policy crystallizations of the past, and who focus too sharply upon naked force as sanction may conceal from both themselves and others the true nature of the decision-making process. It is not suggested that past authoritative formulations of policy do not greatly influence decision-makers. Such formulations play varying rôles in the perspectives of different decision-makers and it is only rational for present decision-makers to seek guidance from the experience of their predecessors. Decision-making is also forward-looking, however, and decision-makers respond in fact not alone to prior prescriptions but to a great many environmental and predispositional variables, including doctrines which formulate the effects of alternative decisions upon the groups which they represent or with which they identify and which state objectives and policies for the future. The process of decision-making is indeed, as every lawyer knows, one of continual redefinition of doctrine in its application to ever-changing facts and claims. A conception of law which focuses upon doctrine to the exclusion of the pattern of practices by which it is given meaning and made effective is, therefore, not the most conducive to understanding. It may be emphasized, further, that official decision-makers, the people who have formal authority and are expected to make important decisions, may or may not make the decisions in fact. Effective control over decisions may be located in governmental institutions, but it may also be located in political parties or pressure groups or private associations and the people exercising control may rely for their power not upon formal authority but upon wealth, enlightenment, respect or other values. . . . A realistic conception of law must, accordingly, conjoin formal authority and effective control and include not only doctrine but also the pattern of practices of both formal and effective decision-makers. A democratic conception of law may also include, to add brief detail, a commitment to change by peaceful procedures and to policies which prescribe a wide sharing of power and other values, provision of procedures for the continual review and reformulation of policies and representation in those procedures of all people who are affected, provision of procedures for the interpretation and application of policies, and the balancing of effective power necessary to make procedures secure and to put policies into practice. . . .

"Law is neither a frozen cake of doctrine designed only to protect interests in *statu quo*, nor an artificial judicial proceeding, isolated from power processes . . .; when understood with all its commitments and procedures, law offers, as we have seen, a continuous formulation and reformulation of policies and constitutes an integral part of the world power process."

McDougal, "Law and Power", 46 Am. J. Int'l L. (1952) 102, 109–111.

Professor McDougal is included with the sociological school of theory because, according to his view, law must respond to environmental factors, changing social facts.

F. S. C. Northrop uses this approach of sociological jurisprudence with its concept of "living law pluralism" which fits positive law into a broader context linking it not only to the contents of the various "living laws" but also to their philosophies—thus embodying a strain of natural law. See Northrop, "Contemporary Jurisprudence and International Law", 61 Yale L.J. (1952) 623. See also Gidynski, "Duguit's Sociological Approach to the Bases of International Law", published in "Juristic Bases for International Law, a Symposium", 31 Iowa L. Rev. (1946) 493, 599.

"The positivist school had cherished the hope of reducing international law as a whole to the logical forms of a rigorous system. Its confidence in criteria which is regarded as established bore the marks of a stability and of a tranquil assurance in the value of experimental methods that were characteristic of the 19th Century. The school had the merit of substituting for the vague suggestions of a deformed natural law an attentive examination of inter-State relations. But its doctrine, voluntarist in its most widely received version, misrepresented reality by reducing law to nothing more than the rules evolving from agreements between states by a method of elaboration believed characteristic of international relations. Remaining in this sense essentially formal, it exaggerated the specificity of international law, separating it off from the moral, social, and political data which form its sphere of application and condition its effectiveness. Though this school's avowed aim was to exclude all political elements from the statement of legal norms, it adopted as the decisive criterion of the validity of such norms the manifestations of will proceeding from political authority. This attitude paralyzed the critical spirit and too often froze the law in positions ill-adapted to the profound changes demanded by the times.

"Law has its legitimate and necessary autonomy over against realities, when realities attain that degree of juristic integration and that formal 'setting apart' which protect them, at least temporarily, against social and political oscillations. But it is the weakness of neopositivism and the mark of its antihistorical spirit that it approaches the problem exclusively from this point of view; that it sees in the process by which norms are formed only the special procedure that constitutes its last phase and marks its full achievement; that, to satisfy purely logical requirements, it states as a principle a completeness of law that immediately brings all social facts within the legal order.

". . . The stake in the sphere of international organization, the great question posed by the minimum demands of international security, is nothing less than the social solidity of the present distribution of power among States. The central problem of the normative order is henceforth much less the legal validity of the formal process of elaborating international law than the obstacles confronting its extension. We must know why and how far certain aspects of the external activity of States, and those certainly the most fundamental, continue to be refractory to law, even at times immune from any common value-judgment, resistant to reasoned analysis and the test of general criteria. We must determine—since object or matter here provides no usable indication—the influence in this state of affairs of the present forms of political power and, still more, of the spirit animating those forms. We must understand in all its profound reality, that is to say at the national level and in the internal order first, what it is in the State that determines that other 'setting apart,' this time purely political, which in international relations bars the way to more complete legal integration and inspires discretionary decision."

De Visscher, *Theory and Reality in Public International Law* (Princeton, 1957, translated from French by P. E. Corbett), pp. xi, xii–xiii. Positive law is thus reduced by this author as a classification to but one of the component parts of international law the other part of which is natural law.

See also Ago, "Positive Law and International Law", 51 Am. J. Int'l L. (1957) 691, 696, 729. After tracing the historical development of the concept "positive law", Ago concludes, "traditional thought, in spite of its different attitudes, never gives up the basic idea that the adjective 'positive' joined to the noun 'law' stands to indicate the particular way in which the existence of the law so qualified came about historically. And this thought always sees positive law as being necessarily limited to only one part of that law which it considers as being endowed with obligatory force: a part which can even annul itself altogether, as in international law according to Pufendorf and his followers, but which can never extend to include the whole of the law in force in a given legal system." Having thus restricted the use of the term "positive law" to that law which is "posited" or enacted, he constructs his theory of "spontaneous law" meaning that law which "seems to be the product of spontaneous germination, and not of will or a 'laying down' ".

"It may be that in the present case we are not concerned with the 'positive law of nations', which is the law strictly laid down in treaties or conventions. There is no treaty which mentions, in a detailed manner, every one of the 'principles of international law' which States are bound to observe. The 'principles of ordinary international law' precede, inspire and govern treaties; they flow from treaties, from doctrine and from the general legal system. In present-day law, there is no finer or more fruitful principle than that providing for the distribution of burdens and of damage suffered. Where damage has been suffered by a member of the community in the interests of the latter it would be unjust that that member alone should bear the full burden of the sacrifice."

Judge Levi Carneiro, *Anglo-Iranian Oil Co.* (United Kingdom *v.* Iran), Judgment, July 22, 1952, I.C.J. Reports (1952) 92, dissenting opinion, p. 162.

"Modern" International Law

". . . In the international sphere there is little but the abstract rule. Only slowly, and with immense difficulties arising out of the value which governments and peoples continue to attach to the sovereignty of their States, are we beginning to construct some prototypes of the organization usually associated with the term 'law'. The preliminary condition of such organization, which is a sense of community, of shared values, is present in the international sphere only in a highly rarified form.

. . . .

". . . Centuries of fine moral and juristic reasoning have left us with an imposing web of norms. . . . What is needed—and what is difficult to achieve—is a tougher sort of institutions based upon interests so clearly defined and so broadly and firmly apprehended that they will prevail over particular and temporary defections. A jurisprudence which can render substantial aid in establishing such institutions must reinforce itself with the best in political science, sociology and social psychology.

. . . .

". . . whereas in the Renaissance recourse to metaphysics for the fundamental principles of any legal system was normal and open, today it is usually unconscious. Relatively rare in our time is the secular jurist who flouts the prevalently empirical style of thought and confesses openly, as Anzilotti does, that the fundamental norm upon which his system rests is a metaphysical hypothesis.

. . . .

"There is, however, an important truth hidden under the exaggerations of the historical school and the biological metaphor. They remind us that attempts to speed law far beyond the living and thinking habits of the entities that it is designed to govern are doomed to failure."

Corbett, *Law and Society in the Relations of States* (1951) 10, 12, 17, 288.

". . . the term 'international' is misleading since it suggests that one is concerned only with the relations of one nation (or state) to other nations (or states).

"Part of the difficulty in analyzing the problems of the world community and the law of regulating them is the lack of an appropriate word or term for the rules we are discussing. Just as the word 'international' is inadequate to describe the problem, so the term 'international law' will not do. Georges Scelle seeks to meet the difficulty by using the term *droit des gens*, 'not taken exclusively in its Latin etymology, which still implies the notion of a collectivity, but in its common and current meaning of *individuals*, considered simply as such and collectively as members of political societies.' [Georges Scelle, *Précis de droit des gens* (Paris, Recueil Sirey, 1932), pt. I, p. vii.] I find no satisfactory English equivalent along these lines. Professor Alf Ross of the University of Copenhagen, speaking of the term 'private international law,' has wisely said: 'Normally it is both hopeless and inadvisable to try to alter a generally accepted terminology, but in this case linguistic usage is so misleading that it seems to me right to make the attempt.' [Alf Ross, *A Textbook of International Law* (London, Longmans, Green, 1947), p. 73.] Ross's own experiment in word-coining—'interlegal law' for 'private international law'—is not encouraging to me. My choice of terminology will no doubt be equally unsatisfactory to others. Nevertheless I shall use, instead of 'international law,' the term 'transnational law' to include all law which regulates actions or events that transcend national frontiers. Both public and private international law are included, as are other rules which do not wholly fit into such standard categories.

.   .   .   .

"Transnational situations, then, may involve individuals, corporations, states, organizations of states, or other groups. . . ." Jessup, *Transnational Law* (1956) 1–2, 3. Professor Jessup stated in a footnote: "3. Myres McDougal has familiarized us with the use of the adjective 'transnational' to describe groups whose composition or activities transcend national frontiers, but he does not apply the term to law in the sense in which it is used here. Joseph E. Johnson suggested more broadly the utility of the word 'transnational' in place of 'international' in his address of June 15, 1955, at the annual meeting of the Harvard Foundation and Law School Alumni. Occasional use of the word has also been made by Percy Elwood Corbett, *The Study of International Law* (Garden City, N.Y., Doubleday, 1955), p. 50, and by Arthur Nussbaum, *A Concise History of the Law of Nations* (rev. ed., New York, Macmillan, 1954)." (*Ibid.* 2.)

"Yet there is a unity of law. It is a unity which overrides divergencies of substance and procedure. The doctrine of consideration is not a universal nor is our concept of a trust. Yet there are great legal maxims which express general legal truths. We recognize their universality by naturalizing them without anglicizing their labels. So it is that the fundamental writ of habeas corpus itself retains its Latin name as do the equitable rule *sic utere tuo* and the *de minimis* doctrine. So it is that article 38 of the Statute of the International Court of Justice—which forms an integral part of the Charter—can refer to 'the general principles of law recognized by civilized nations.'

"It is the opportunity of this and succeeding generations of lawyers to extend the range and volume of these general principles of law to the end envisaged by Cicero when:

> " 'There will not be one law for Rome and another law for Athens, nor one law today and another tomorrow, but among all peoples and for all time one and the same law will apply.'

"If we had already attained a Ciceronian unity of law and a spiritual unity in our philosophical concept of the place of the individual in human society, it could be argued that respect for human rights is not a matter for international concern. The ordinary processes of law enforcement are indeed matters within the domestic jurisdiction. Yet even here international law has long recognized and our government and international tribunals have long asserted that there is a standard of civilized justice. Failure to live up to that standard resulting in injury to an alien individual has long been acknowledged to engage a state's international responsibility to pay damages.

"The international society has come more slowly to recognize that what is involved is really a concern for the individual who has been the victim of barbarous treatment. In our traditional international system of interstate relationships we were impelled to confine ourselves largely to the legal fiction that the state was injured through the injury inflicted upon its citizen. But this was a procedural, not a substantive problem. The rule developed in the era of essentially bilateral relations between states and is still law. International law has not yet been fully modernized but it has progressed. We have progressed into a multilateral era. We have learned that international organization and international cooperation need not be confined to postage and statistics and weights and measures. The United States not only accepts this concept of international cooperation, it glories in it. We affirm and take pride in our leadership. I repeat it is not the leadership of monopoly or of domination but a participating and shared leadership.

"I repeat also that in ratifying the Charter of the United Nations we have pledged ourselves to cooperate in promoting 'universal respect for and observance of human rights and fundamental freedoms.' In 1945 we were free to choose. We could have chosen to go on down the isolationist path. Thank God we chose instead the upward path of cooperation.

"That choice has in a new sense set us free. We are now free to act internationally upon our deep convictions that the welfare of the individual is something we care about not just when that individual is an American citizen but because he is a human being.

"The law of the international society is catching up with the conscience of mankind. Four and five decades ago when American hearts were wrung and American sympathies went out to persecuted minorities in other lands, our government was hampered by the restrictive rules of the era. Jurists strove to grapple with the human problem and sought to develop the doctrine of humanitarian intervention. That doctrine failed to prosper not because it was humanitarian but because it was unilateral and unilateralism contained the germs of its own fatal malady.

"It is not a new thing in American history that we care and care deeply what happens to human beings throughout the world. What is new is our acceptance, along with that of the great majority of other members of the family of nations, of the principles which give us a legal as well as a moral interest in human happiness.

"There is not one shred of juridical support for the argument that we have no legal interest in human rights. There is no factual evidence that we have no concern about them. We as people here do care what happens to other people elsewhere."

Philip C. Jessup, Ambassador at Large, "The Conquering March of an Idea", address delivered before the 72d Annual Meeting of the American Bar Association, St. Louis, Mo., Sept. 6, 1949, XXI *Bulletin*, Department of State, No. 533, Sept. 19, 1949, pp. 432, 433–434.

"The topic that you have chosen for discussion at this meeting of the society—'International Law and the Political Process'—has a very real meaning for those of us who are charged with legal responsibilities in the Department. One of the first things that we learn is that abstract conceptions of international law, as it should be, must, of necessity, be qualified in application by the realities of the political process.

"I know that there are those who assert that international law, in order to be worth its salt, must be based solely upon logic and principle. But international law, notwithstanding the reasoned theses of the commentators, consists, in the last analysis, of those principles upon which sovereign nations can agree. Such agreement is seldom, if ever, reached without regard to the political process.

"Please do not imply from my remarks that I would throw logic and principle overboard in favor of pure political pragmatism. There is, however, a mean, a balancing between legal theory and political capabilities, that must be taken into account both in the formulation and in the application of the principles of international law."

Loftus Becker, Legal Adviser, Department of State, "Some Political Problems of the Legal Adviser", address before the American Society of International Law, Washington, D. C., Apr. 26, 1958, XXXVIII *Bulletin*, Department of State, No. 986, May 19, 1958, p. 832.

"Law, according to the Marxist doctrine, is one of the superstructures erected on the economic base. It appears with the formation of the State and after the division of society into classes. It is law which, through the State, governs social relationships, since it expresses the will of the dominant class in a given State.

U.S.S.R. concept

"In the various branches of municipal law, individuals and associations of individuals, considered to be juridical persons, appear as 'subjects.'

"International law, in short, regulates political and economic relations between States; the States themselves are its immediate subjects. This is the peculiarity of this branch of law; international law could be called inter-State, and, in fact, the term would be more correct. That is why very special attention will be given here to the problem of the State as a subject of international law.

. . . .

"International law is a collection of precepts that govern the relations between States in the course of their rivalry, struggle, and cooperation, which express the will of the ruling classes in those States, and are guaranteed by the coercion exercised by States separately or collectively.

. . . .

"This definition agrees with the general definition of law given by A. I. Vishinsky [See *Les Tâches principales de la science du droit soviétique socialiste*, 1938, p. 183. See also the publication *L'Etat soviétique* (*Sovietskoie gossoudarstvo*), 1939, No. 3.], a member of the Academy, which is the prevailing concept at the present time in the Soviet theory of law."

Krylov, "Les Notions Principales du Droit des Gens", ch. 1, "La Notion de Droit International", 70 *Recueil Des Cours* (1947, vol. I) 415, 420 (translation). See also Chakste, "Soviet Concepts of the State, International Law and Sovereignty", 43 Am. J. Int'l L. (1949) 21; Hazard, "The Soviet Union and International Law", 43 Ill. L. Rev. (1948) 591.

"International life and the precepts of international law that have crystallized in international life lead to the conclusion that in many cases one cannot speak of the universality of international law.

Nonuniversality

"Under certain historic conditions, in given relations between States, various classes of international law, with more or less democratic tendencies, can be distinguished.

"It is easy to confirm this statement with examples.

"Thus, the rules of international law established by England, France, and other States of Western Europe in the first half of the nineteenth century were more democratic than the rules of international law that governed relations between the absolutist States of Eastern Europe, such as Austria, Prussia, etc.

"The international law of the era of 'industrial capitalism' assumed a more democratic character than the bourgeois international law of the imperialist era. To demonstrate this, we have only to refer to the new forms of dependency of colonial and semicolonial countries in the twentieth century.

"The differences can also be noted from another standpoint.

"If one studies American international law, on the one hand, that is to say, the rules established in inter-American relations, and European international law, on the other hand, one cannot but observe certain differences and due note should be taken of them. In particular, Professor Alvarez brought out, in his work on American international law (1910), the modifications of European international law in the relations between the American States. The American States have not adopted the entire heritage and all the vestiges of feudalism that exist in European international law.

"One more example. The interests of the great maritime powers, England and the United States of America, lead them to formulate certain rules of international maritime law different from those of the powers of the European continent. The latter settle points of maritime law on other bases, defending, first of all, the law of the coastal State against the law of the flag State affirmed by the Anglo-Saxon countries. Thus, it is possible to speak of an Anglo-Saxon international maritime law and a European international maritime law.

"The same observation can be made in the field of private international law, based, in the Anglo-Saxon countries, on the concept of domicile, while the European countries defend the concept of nationality.

"We therefore have authority for concluding that, with respect to many questions, international law is not universal, but particular, that is to say, that it is expressed in a variety of international juridical principles. It is nonetheless true that in many fields there is a common, or general, international law."

Krylov, "Les Notions Principales du Droit des Gens", ch. 1, "La Notion de Droit International", 70 *Recueil Des Cours* (1947, vol. I) 415, 420–422 (translation).

"In the history of international relations the real and only sources of law have been treaties and international custom. Let us now examine what this fact has really meant. There is no question that if a State has expressly agreed to be bound by a treaty, it has made its own law, and it should be governed by it; but can we say the same thing of custom? Of course not. So far, custom, as a generative power of law, has been in the hands of a few, always the great Powers. They are the ones that have made the laws of war because they are the ones that have made important wars; they have made the laws of neutrality because, in their practices, they have accepted the restrictions upon their power to conduct belligerent operations; the maritime Powers have made the law of the sea because they are the only ones who have fleets that encompass the waters of the world. Those that have fishing industries have regulated international fishing rights. They have done it both by custom and convention, but always regardless of the idea or consent of those other countries which were not engaged in the particular activity that was to be legally regulated.

"This discriminating situation is rapidly becoming obsolete and unpopular and even the great Powers have come to realize that the imposition as international law of their own agreements and customs upon the whole world has become a practical impossibility; thus they now seek, through international organizations, to count upon the consent of the majority of States to uphold their interests, economic and political. International life, international relations and international law are in this way becoming more democratic, in keeping with the general trend of the times. Humanity has also come to realize that the Community of Nations has a very clear interest even in the most special and particular situation for even in the disarmament of the great nations, as in the destruction by the fishing industry of living resources of the sea, the interest of all nations is at stake. War is not any more a conflict between a few States, but a universal calamity which should be averted by universal means and the wealth of the world should not be at the disposal only of those who can take it simply because they have the practical means to do so, but it should be exploited to the benefit of all mankind."

Córdova, "The Development and Codification of International Law", published in *The United Nations—Ten Years' Legal Progress, Collection of Essays* (The Hague, 1956) 43, 53–54.

Change

". . . the unfortunate situation of the law of nations is due to certain great changes in habits of life which have been developing over a century or more of time. . . .

"First of these, and productive of the others, is the interdependence which has been developing since the Industrial Revolution. . . .

"His [the individual's] dependence is not confined to those who are within the confines of his own nation. His prosperity, his very livelihood, depends directly or indirectly upon persons and agencies beyond his own frontiers and beyond the control of his own government. He can not solve this problem by asking for more national law and administration. The system into which he has been caught up, intricate and world-wide, reaches far beyond his national government. The state which he has organized and maintained for the protection and advancement of his own welfare, and which he has for so long regarded as the ultimate in human organization and as his sufficient protection, is no longer able in an interdependent world to serve these purposes. . . .

"Obviously, the above change has significant consequences for international law. Since the state is no longer competent, can no longer perform its function properly, it can not set itself above the law of nations; on the contrary, it must rely upon that law. The theory that a state can not be bound save by its own consent— if such a theory ever had validity—can not be maintained in a situation in which a state has become actually dependent upon others. The factual situation is that the doctrine of sovereignty can no longer dominate, and that each state will have to give up some of its sovereign rights in order to get the protection and assistance which it must have. It is clear, too, that the complexities and dependences of today necessitate international organization and administrative agencies; and this implies the issuance of law by a common authority, and its application by a community judge.

"Development in this direction has been going on, of course, for many years, grudgingly and insufficiently. International public unions and administrative agencies of various kinds have been created; tribunals of justice have been established; a more comprehensive system has recently appeared in the League of Nations. But all of this growth has been checked—has indeed been wrecked—by another change, another pressure which must be taken into serious consideration in the rebuilding of law and order. This is modern war, itself changed by the industrialization and interdependence which have wrought so much change in our life. . . .

"It is obvious that international law can not stand against this sort of war. Of course, law and war have always been contradictory—a senseless antithesis within a legal system; but in the past, the strength of customary law has enabled it to exercise some degree of control over war itself, and to carry on outside of the areas involved in war. This is no longer true. . . .

". . . The desire of the individual for security has become a driving force which must be taken into the calculations for the future. . . . Since the state is unable to give him the security which he covets, he must look beyond domestic government to international government, beyond domestic law to international law. . . . Hitherto, international law has been a law for sovereign states only, and it has given little recognition to the individual who is, after all, the unity of human society. It must now recognize that its function is, directly or indirectly, to aid the individual. . . ."

Eagleton, "Forces Which Will Shape the Rebuilding of International Law", 36 Am. J. Int'l L. (1942) 640–643.

"The changing character of international law is, first, a consequence of a transformation of general conditions, a transformation the impact of which is equally felt in the municipal legal orders. The 'classic' international law presupposed the doctrines of democracy, capitalism, economic liberalism, 'laissez faire,' the principles of the sanctity of private property, the strict distinction between private enterprise and economic activities by states, the strict distinction between armed forces and the civilian population. All that has fundamentally changed. The coming of total war, of ever expanding economic activities by states, the control by states of the economic life of the nation even in times of peace, and more so in times of war, the appearance of totalitarian regimes, have profoundly influenced old and well-established rules of international law and brought about far-reaching uncertainty. These transformations, while particularly prominent in totalitarian states, are nevertheless more or less universal, to be seen also in the democracies of the free world. They have shaken the basis of many rules of the laws of war and of

the law of neutrality. They have changed and made insecure
the rules concerning immunity from jurisdiction of states in
their economic activities, of state instrumentalities, of govern-
ment-owned merchant vessels, government corporations; also
with regard to rules concerning state responsibility (political
parties, subversive and terrorist activities, hostile propaganda),
and finally with regard to rules concerning nationalization, expropriation, confiscation. [These transformations are dealt with
in the article of W. Friedmann, "Some Impacts of Social Organization on International Law," 50 A.J.I.L. 474–514 (1956).]

"There are tendencies to weaken or to question old and well-
established rules of international law: there is a tendency against
conquest as a title of acquisition of sovereignty; there is uncertainty as to the so-called 'doctrine of contiguity'; there is much
confusion as to the recognition of states and governments; there
are very doubtful areas as far as the law of international treaties
is concerned; a weakening of the requirement of effectivity where
sovereignty is acquired by occupation of a *terra nullius;* there
is a complete lack of agreement as to the acquisition of sovereignty in the Arctic and the Antarctic.

"Technological developments have led to uncertainties in the
laws of war, such as aerial war, chemical and bacteriological
warfare, magnetic mines and so on; or have led to completely
new norms in fields which before had not been of practical importance. The coming of aviation has led in a short time to the
new norm of general customary international law according to
which the legal status of the airspace is the same as the status
of the subjacent space. We are at the threshold of a completely
new 'international space law.' The new interest in making use
of the water of streams for purposes of irrigation, hydro-electric
power and so on, is transforming the law of international rivers,
hitherto dominated by the interests of navigation.

"Other changes stem from technological (geological and
engineering) advances combined with economic considerations,
neo-Malthusian fears of overpopulation and an upsurge of sovereignty: the new norms *in fieri,* concerning the continental shelf,
the disquieting developments with regard to the limits of territorial waters, contiguous zones, the law of high-seas fishing,
developments which, in extreme cases, threaten the survival of
the fundamental principle *juris cogentis* of the freedom of the
high seas.

"There is, further, the advent and enormous expansion of international organizations, quasi-universal and regional, general
and specialized. They have brought many new developments:
international organizations as subjects of international law, in
the field of international treaties, privileges and immunities,
responsibility, capacity to claim indemnities. There is no doubt
that the scope of international law, formerly restricted to relations between sovereign states, has expanded: stateless persons,
refugees, indigenous populations of trusteeship territories, solution of economic, financial, social, health, cultural, educational
problems on a worldwide scale, development of, and technical aid

and assistance to, underdeveloped countries. There is no doubt that the law of international organizations, although based on particular international law, has also deeply influenced general international law.

"The new quasi-universal general international organizations have not restricted themselves to international co-operation in the so-called non-political fields. They have attempted to regulate activities which the states hitherto have regarded as their exclusive domain. Hence new ideas and experiments have appeared which would have been unthinkable prior to 1914: the attempt to restrict or even abolish the use of force in international relations, the idea of 'international concern,' as expressed in Article XI of the League of Nations Covenant, the ideas of collective security, of international sanctions, the attempts at an international criminal law, at international protection of human rights. True, many of these attempts have hitherto been ineffective and have made whole departments of the law, like the laws of war and the law of neutrality, extremely insecure. These attempts have led scholars to question the whole philosophy on which the current concept of international organization is based. Scholars have insisted that it is impossible to make revolutionary changes without changing the sociological foundations on which present-day international law is based. Charles De Visscher has written that any advance in this direction must start with a change in the distribution of power which, at this time, is in the hands of the sovereign states. Yet, on the other hand, it is unlikely that these new ideas, inspired by a deep concern with the consequences of modern war, will, despite their ineffectiveness so far, disappear completely."

Kunz, "The Changing Law of Nations", 51 Am. J. Int'l L. (1957) 77, 80–82.

SUBJECTS

§ 2

". . . Sovereign and independent States are the principal— States though not exclusive—subjects of international law."

Survey of International Law in Relation to the Work of Codification of the International Law Commission, Memorandum submitted by the Secretary-General of the United Nations, A/CN.4/1/Rev. 1, Feb. 10, 1949, p. 24.

"Only states may be parties in cases before the Court".

Statute of the International Court of Justice, art. 34(1) ; 59 Stat. 1059.

In a claim espoused by the Greek Government resulting from injuries caused by the alleged failure of the British Government to recognize certain concessionary rights of M. Mavrommatis, a Greek national, the Permanent Court of International Justice in confirming its jurisdiction in the case declared:

". . . It is an elementary principle of international law that a State is entitled to protect its subjects, when injured by acts contrary to international law committed by another State, from whom they have been unable to obtain satisfaction through the ordinary channels. By taking up the case of one of its subjects and by resorting to diplomatic action or international judicial proceedings on his behalf, a State is in reality asserting its own rights—its right to ensure, in the person of its subjects, respect for the rules of international law.

". . . Once a State has taken up a case on behalf of one of its subjects before an international tribunal, in the eyes of the latter the State is sole claimant. . . ."

The Mavrommatis Palestine Concessions, (Judgment) Series A, No. 2, Aug. 30, 1924, pp. 6, 12; I Hudson, *World Court Reports* (1934) 297, 302.

In the case United States of America on behalf of *Dickson Car Wheel Company, Claimant*, v. *United Mexican States*, the United States-Mexican Claims Commission stated, "The relation of rights and obligations created between two States upon the commission by one of them of an act in violation of International Law, arises only among those States subject to the international juridical system. There does not exist, in that system, any relation of responsibility between the transgressing State and the injured individual for the reason that the latter is not subject to international law. The injury inflicted upon an individual, a national of the claimant State, which implies a violation of the obligations imposed by International Law upon each member of the Community of Nations, constitutes an act internationally unlawful, because it signifies an offense against the State to which the individual is united by the bond of nationality. The only juridical relation, therefore, which authorizes a State to exact from another the performance of conduct prescribed by International Law with respect to individuals is the bond of nationality. This is the link existing between that law and individuals and through it alone are individuals enabled to invoke the protection of a State and the latter empowered to intervene on their behalf."

Opinions of Commissioners under the Convention of Sept. 8, 1923, between United States and Mexico (1931), Docket No. 1074, July 1931, pp. 175, 187, 188.

"Her Majesty's Government take the view that States are the proper subject of international law; and that if individuals are given rights under international treaties, effect should be given to these rights through the national law of the States parties. The matter was discussed in 1949 and 1950, when hon. Members on both sides of the House took that view."

Joint Under-Secretary of State for Foreign Affairs Richard Hugh Turton, speaking in the House of Commons in answer to questions concerning right of individual petition in the Council of Europe's Convention on Human Rights and Fundamental Freedoms. 536 H.C. Deb. (5th ser.) cols. 1532–1533 (Feb. 7, 1955).

In reply to a question about the European Convention on Human Rights, the British Foreign Secretary (Selwyn Lloyd) stated that Her Majesty's Government have ratified the Convention but "have not made the optional declaration accepting the competence of the European Commission of Human Rights to receive petitions from individuals, nor that recognising the compulsory jurisdiction of the proposed European Court of Human Rights."

The Foreign Secretary also said:

"The position which Her Majesty's Government have continuously taken up is that they do not recognise the right of individual petition, because they take the view that States are the proper subject of international law and if individuals are given rights under international treaties effect should be given to those rights through the national law of the States concerned. The reason why we do not accept the idea of the compulsory jurisdiction of a European Court is that it would mean that British codes of common and statute law would be subject to review by an international Court. For many years it has been the position of successive British Governments that we should not accept that status."

574 H.C. Deb. (5th ser.) cols. 867–868 (July 29, 1957).

"Since the Law of Nations is based on the common consent of individual States, States are the principal subjects of International Law. This means that the Law of Nations is primarily a law for the international conduct of States, and not of their citizens. As a rule, the subjects of the rights and duties arising from the Law of Nations are States solely and exclusively. An individual human being, such as an alien or an ambassador, for example, is not directly a subject of International Law. Therefore, all rights which might necessarily have to be granted to an individual human being according to the Law of Nations are not, as a rule, international rights, but rights granted by Municipal Law in accordance with a duty imposed upon the State concerned by International Law. Likewise, all duties which might necessarily have to be imposed upon individual human beings according to the Law of Nations are, on the traditional view, not international duties, but duties imposed by Municipal Law in accordance with a right granted to, or a duty imposed upon, the State concerned by International Law".

I Lauterpacht, *Oppenheim's International Law* (8th ed., 1955) 19.

". . . The basic concept for Kelsen is the unity of national and international law, and 'an aspect of this unity is the fact that the States as acting persons are organs of international law, or of the community constituted by it. The creation and execution of an order are the functions of its organs, and the international legal order is created and executed by States. It is especially the creation of international law by treaty that clearly reveals the States as organs of the international community.' By virtue of international law, 'when two States conclude a treaty, they function as organs of international law. The representatives of the two contracting parties together form the composite organ that creates the contractual norm. . . . Of this composite order, the representatives of the contracting States are part organs. It is the international legal order which leaves it to each national order to determine the individual who, as a representative of the State, is competent to conclude treaties with the representative of another State. Hence, the representative of a contracting State is primarily a (partial) organ of the international community, and only secondarily an organ of his own State'."

Gross, "States as Organs of International Law and the Problem of Auto-interpretation", in *Law and Politics in the World Community*, Essays on Hans Kelsen's Pure Theory and Related Problems in International Law, compiled and edited by George Lipsky (1953), pp. 59, 70.

Juridical persons

"32. All these developments may be considered as rendering necessary, within the orbit of the codification of the general part of international law, the clarification and revision of some of the traditional notions. Such clarification and revision would do no more than give expression both to actual changes in the law and to the changing conditions of international society which no longer permit the maintenance of what, in the view of many, is becoming a fiction obstructive of progress. Previous efforts at codification have touched only the fringe of the question. Thus the League of Nations Committee of Experts for the Progressive Codification of International Law discussed in some detail draft rules for formulating, by way of an international convention, international provisions concerning the nationality of commercial corporations and for the recognition of the legal personality of foreign commercial corporations. [*Minutes of the Third Session*, 1927, pp. 57–63, 64–67.] At its fourth session in 1928 the Committee had before it a report on the legal position of private non-profit-making international associations and of private international foundations. [*Minutes of the Fourth Session*, 1928, p. 49.]"

Survey of International Law in Relation to the Work of Codification of the International Law Commission, Memorandum submitted by the Secretary-General of the United Nations, A/CN.4/1/Rev. 1, Feb. 10, 1949, p. 21.

"In addition to those matters which heretofore have come within the domain of international law, there belong other new matters arising out of the exigencies of modern social life, as well as the international rights of individuals, namely, the rights which natural or juridical persons can invoke in each nation in the cases expressly provided for in the convention on this subject."

"Fundamental Bases of International Law", art. 2, prepared by the American Institute of International Law (1925), 20 Am. J. Int'l L. Spec. Supp. (1926) 304.

"1. A claimant is entitled to present his claim directly to the State alleged to be responsible.

"2. A claimant is entitled to present his claim directly to a competent international tribunal if the State alleged to be responsible has conferred on that tribunal jurisdiction over such claim."

Art. 22, draft Convention on the International Responsibility of States for Injuries to Aliens, Harvard Law School (May 1, 1960), p. 11.

Section VI of part X of the Treaty of Versailles (article 304) contained provision for the establishment of Mixed Arbitral Tribunals. Paragraph (b) of that article provided:

"(b) The Mixed Arbitral Tribunals established pursuant to paragraph (a), shall decide all questions within their competence under Sections III, IV, V and VII.

"In addition, all questions, whatsoever their nature, relating to contracts concluded before the coming into force of the present Treaty between nationals of the Allied and Associated Powers and German nationals shall be decided by the Mixed Arbitral Tribunal, always excepting questions which, under the laws of the Allied, Associated or Neutral Powers, are within the jurisdiction of the National Courts of those Powers. Such questions shall be decided by the National Courts in question, to the exclusion of the Mixed Arbitral Tribunal. The party who is a national of an Allied or Associated Power may nevertheless bring the case before the Mixed Arbitral Tribunal if this is not prohibited by the laws of his country." (Underscoring added) (III Redmond, Treaties, Conventions, etc. (1923) 3477.)

Article 305 provided in part as follows, with respect to the case of a party who was not satisfied with a decision rendered by a German court:

"Whenever a competent court has given or gives a decision in a case covered by Sections III, IV, V or VII, and such decision is inconsistent with the provisions of such Sections, the party who is prejudiced by the decision shall be entitled to obtain redress which shall be fixed by the Mixed Arbitral Tribunal. At the request of the national of an Allied or Associated Power, the redress may, whenever possible, be effected by the Mixed Arbitral Tribunal directing the replacement of the parties in the position occupied by them before the judgment was given by the German court." (Underscoring added) (Ibid. 3479.)

Section III (article 296) related inter alia to debts due by a "national" of one of the Contracting Powers to a "national" of the Opposing Power, which became due before, or during, the war. Section IV (article 297) provided inter alia that property damage claims by "nationals" of Allied and Associated Powers should be determined by the Mixed Arbitral Tribunals.

It is important to note section 18 of the annex to article 296 provided as follows:

"Each of the Governments concerned shall appoint an agent who will be responsible for the presentation to the Mixed Arbitral Tribunal of the cases conducted on behalf of its Clearing Office. This agent will exercise a general control over the representatives or counsel employed by its nationals.

"Decisions will be arrived at on documentary evidence, but it will
be open to the Tribunal to hear the parties in person, or according to
their preference by their representatives approved by the two Governments, or by the agent referred to above, who shall be competent to
intervene along with the party or to re-open and maintain a claim
abandoned by the same." (Underscoring added) (*Ibid.* 3460.)

The Treaty thus contemplated that private individuals could present cases
to the Mixed Arbitral Tribunals. It may be noted that Arthur Burchard,
a member of the Bar of Berlin, stated:

". . . The proceedings before the Mixed Arbitral Tribunal are sometimes proceedings between governments, e.g., between Clearing Offices
(§ 16 Annex to Article 296) and sometimes between private parties,
e.g., in cases for determining the conditions of licenses (Article 310),
and sometimes between governments and private parties, e.g., in all
cases arising under Article 297 (e)." (21 Am. J. Int'l L. (1927)
472, 476–477.)

In the course of a debate on the nationalization of the Suez Canal
Company, August 2, 1956, the British Prime Minister, Sir Anthony
Eden, said:

"The Company, although it is registered in Egypt, is, of course,
an international organisation of the highest importance and
standing, and it has ensured that the Canal was administered both
with regard to the interests of international shipping and to those
of Egypt herself. . . ."

During the same debate, the Secretary of State for Foreign Affairs,
Selwyn Lloyd, said:

". . . this Canal Company . . . is not an ordinary domestic
concern which can properly be nationalised, however much we
may or may not agree with the principle of nationalisation, but
is a company of an international character. It has had an international character throughout the whole of its existence, and if
one looks at the Convention of 1888, it is recited in the Preamble
that the countries concerned wished

" 'to establish, by a Conventional Act, a definite system
destined to guarantee at all times, and for all Powers, the
free use of the Suez Maritime Canal . . .'

It was designed to establish an international system, and therefore I agree with the right hon. Gentleman that the principle
of nationalisation does not apply."

557 H.C. Deb. (5th ser.) cols. 1608, 1661–1662 (Aug. 2, 1956).

". . . Where the state . . . sets up a government corporation to
manage a fleet of merchant vessels or to operate a government
monopoly in matches or tobacco, international law has tended
toward the acceptance of a rule which would distinguish the corporation from the state. The development has taken place especially in connection with the law of sovereign immunity before
the courts of another state; such immunity is denied to govern-

ment corporations in the jurisprudence of many countries. Even where no governmental corporation is interposed, the sovereign character of the state has not been recognized by some courts when the state acts as a private trader. [Harvard Research in International Law, Draft Convention on Competence of Courts in Regard to Foreign States, Article 12 and Comment, Article 11 and Comment, 26 Am. J.I.L. Supp., 1932, pp. 597–641; cf. the changing view of the Supreme Court of the United States as reflected in *Republic of Mexico* v. *Hoffman*, 324 U.S. 30, 65 S. Ct. 530 (1945).]"

Jessup, "The Subjects of a Modern Law of Nations", 45 Mich. L. Rev. (1947) 383, 388.

". . . These [Insurgents]—although not States—are, in law, entitled to exercise belligerent rights in relation to the recognising States and their nationals. They are bound by the obligation to conduct hostilities in accordance with the rules of international law. This, indeed, is an acknowledged condition of recognition of belligerency. Moreover, substantial practice supports what is probably the accurate view on the subject, namely, that insurgents are entitled as a matter of law to recognition of belligerency provided that the requisite conditions of fact are present. . . . Moreover, it is also clear that unrecognised insurgents, without having acquired a specific status of belligerency, may be admitted to various forms of intercourse with outside States. Such intercourse, which involves the application of international law by and in relation to the insurgents, may include the conclusion of agreements, diplomatic and consular relations, and recognition of the insurgent authority as a government. . . ." _{Other entities}

Lauterpacht, "The Subjects of the Law of Nations", 63 L.Q. Rev. (1947) 438, 444, 445.

In upholding the international personality of the Sovereign Order of Malta, the Court of Cassation of Italy stated:

". . . the solution arrived at by the court below can be justified on other grounds. These grounds are based on the essential juridical character of the Sovereign Order of Jerusalem and Malta and on the position which is, in our judgment, held by it as an international person existing apart from the national sovereignty of the State. It is, accordingly, by virtue of a customary norm of international law, received by our own internal law, exempt from the necessity of obtaining the permission of the government for the acquisition of immovable property for its own institutional purposes.

"In order to dispose of the argument of the appellants it is necessary to trace the historical development of the international personality of the Sovereign Order of Jerusalem and Malta. Sovereignty is a complex notion, which international law, from the external point of view, contemplates, so to speak, negatively, having only in view independence vis-à-vis other States. For this reason it is sufficient to require merely proof of the autonomy of the Order in its relation to the Italian State. Historically, the essential element of such autonomy can be found in the political nature of the mission which the Order has been destined to fulfil, namely, by the aid of its arms to resist the Saracen and Mohammedan menace and to establish its hospitallers in the Levant. In the course of centuries it has aided in the establishment of Christianity and of European civilisation. The noble nature and military necessity of such a high and dangerous service brought about its transformation into an Order of Chivalry. . . ." (At cols. 1489–1490.)

The Court at this point recited in some detail the history of the Order and continued:

"With the recognition of the Church and of the Byzantine Empire, the Order established, after the conquest of territory of its own, its independence and sovereignty. . . . The Grand Master was recognised as Sovereign Head of Rhodes with all the attributes of such a position, which included, for instance, among other rights, the right to create and confer titles of Knight Commanders, the right to be accompanied on ceremonial occasions by three Knights of the Order . . . and finally, the right of active and passive legation together with the right of negotiating directly with other States and of making conventions and treaties. . . . Such attributes of sovereignty and independence have not ceased, in the case of the Order, at the present day—at least not from the formal point of view in its relations with the Italian State. Nor has its personality in international law come to an end, notwithstanding the fact that as a result of the British occupation of Malta such personality cannot be identified with the possession of territory. . . . With regard to this second aspect of the matter it is enough to point out that the modern theory of the subjects of international law recognises a number of collective units whose composition is independent of the nationality of their constituent members and whose scope transcends by virtue of their universal character the territorial confines of any single State. It must be admitted that only States can contribute to the formation of international law as an objective body of rules—States as international entities which are territorially identifiable. This is so because the fulfilment of this latter requirement makes them the principal objects and creators of such rules. But it is impossible to deny to other international collective units a limited capacity of acting internationally within the ambit and the actual exercise of their own functions, with the resulting international juridical personality and capacity which is its necessary and natural corollary. In accordance with these doctrines, such personality was never denied to the Holy See even before the Lateran Treaty of February 11, 1929, and it is unanimously conceded to the League of Nations, although it is neither a State, nor a Super-State, nor a Confederation of States. It is equally conceded to certain international administrative unions (see judgment of the

Court of Cassation of May 13, 1931, in the *International Institute of Agriculture* v. *Profili, Foro Italiano*, 1931, I, 1424) [*Annual Digest*, 1929–1930, Case No. 254] which aim at the protection and furtherance of collective economic interests. It would therefore be wrong to deny that the Sovereign Order of Jerusalem has preserved its original plurinational composition with its various languages. The definitely European and universal character of its aims and ideals must be admitted. These aims are charity, Christian piety, and spiritual enlightenment.

.   .   .   .

"We must therefore conclude that, given the position which is, according to our legal system, enjoyed by the Order as an international person, there was no necessity, for the valid acquisition of this property, to obtain the permission of the government." (At cols. 1490–1492.)

Nanni and Others v. *Pace and The Sovereign Order of Malta*, Court of Cassation, Italy, Decision affirming an order for restitution of certain property to the Order, Mar. 13, 1935, [1935–1937] Ann. Dig. 2, 4–6 (No. 2).

In another case the Italian Court of Cassation held that while the Italian Courts were not competent to review the decision of the Sovereign Order of Malta as to the existence of qualifications for succession to the Recanati-Giustiniani benefice (which was under the jurisdiction of the Order and which had fallen vacant on the death of the incumbent), the Order having decided that certain candidates lacked the prescribed requisites of nobility, morality and religious faith, the Italian Courts had jurisdiction, in conformity with the Charter of Incorporation, as a private-law matter, to ascertain who were qualified to stand as candidates for the benefice. The Court of Cassation said: "The reliance placed by the appellant Order on the recognition of its character as a juridical person in international public law, which character was conferred on the Sovereign Order of Malta by the decisions of June 17, 1913, and February 18, 1916, does not seem sufficient to exclude the competence of the Italian Courts. This character may indeed confer special powers on the Order, corresponding to the needs of its autonomy; but it is necessary to examine what are the limits of those powers and how far they may be exercised exclusively. The examination of claims of eligibility for the benefice is the exclusive right of the Order, not so much because the property the use of which constitutes a perquisite of the incumbent, belongs to the Order, as because the qualifications of fitness expressly laid down by its constitution have been inserted by the Order itself." The Court held that "the question of qualification for the benefice arises, in the first place, in a private law relationship, such as is laid down in the Charter of Incorporation, and therefore constitutes for the interested person a subjective right the vesting of which, however, is subject to the judgment of the Order with regard to other requirements like those of nobility and morality." *Sovereign Order of Malta* v. *Brunelli, Tacali and Others*, Court of Cassation, Italy, Decision, Dec. 17, 1931, [1931–1932] Ann. Dig. 88–89 (No. 46).

"31. Finally, account must be taken of the developments in modern international law amounting to a recognition of the international personality of public bodies other than States. The [International organizations]

international legal personality of the United Nations, of the
specialized agencies established under its ægis, and of other international organizations, call for a re-definition of the traditional
rule of international law in the matter of its subjects. That legal
personality is no longer a postulate of scientific doctrine. It is
accompanied by a recognized contractual capacity in the international sphere and, as with regard to the right to request an
advisory opinion of the International Court of Justice, by a
distinct measure of international procedural capacity."

*Survey of International Law in Relation to the Work of Codification of
the International Law Commission*, Memorandum submitted by the Secretary-General of the United Nations, A/CN.4/1/Rev. 1, Feb. 10, 1949, p. 21.

". . . it has been contended that the request for an opinion
would constitute an inadmissible interference by the General
Assembly and by States hitherto strangers to the Convention in
the interpretation of that Convention, as only States which are
parties to the Convention are entitled to interpret it or to seek
an interpretation of it. It must be pointed out in this connection
that, not only did the General Assembly take the initiative in
respect of the Genocide Convention, draw up its terms and open
it for signature and accession by States, but that express provisions of the Convention (Articles XI and XVI) associate the
General Assembly with the life of the Convention; and finally,
that the General Assembly actually associated itself with it by
endeavouring to secure the adoption of the Convention by as
great a number of States as possible. In these circumstances,
there can be no doubt that the precise determination of the conditions for participation in the Convention constitutes a permanent interest of direct concern to the United Nations which has
not disappeared with the entry into force of the Convention."

*Reservations to the Convention on the Prevention and Punishment of
the Crime of Genocide*, Advisory Opinion, May 28, 1951, I.C.J. Reports
(1951) 15, 19–20.

"The subjects of law in any legal system are not necessarily
identical in their nature or in the extent of their rights, and their
nature depends upon the needs of the community. Throughout
its history, the development of international law has been influenced by the requirements of international life, and the progressive increase in the collective activities of States has already
given rise to instances of action upon the international plane by
certain entities which are not States. This development culminated in the establishment in June 1945 of an international
organization whose purposes and principles are specified in the
Charter of the United Nations. But to achieve these ends the
attribution of international personality is indispensable.

　.　　　.　　　.　　　.　　　.　　　.　　　.

"In the opinion of the Court, the Organization was intended
to exercise and enjoy, and is in fact exercising and enjoying,
functions and rights which can only be explained on the basis

of the possession of a large measure of international personality and the capacity to operate upon an international plane. It is at present the supreme type of international organization, and it could not carry out the intentions of its founders if it was devoid of international personality. It must be acknowledged that its Members, by entrusting certain functions to it, with the attendant duties and responsibilities, have clothed it with the competence required to enable those functions to be effectively discharged.

"Accordingly, the Court has come to the conclusion that the Organization is an international person. That is not the same thing as saying that it is a State, which it certainly is not, or that its legal personality and rights and duties are the same as those of a State. Still less is it the same thing as saying that it is 'a super-State', whatever that expression may mean. It does not even imply that all its rights and duties must be upon the international plane, any more than all the rights and duties of a State must be upon that plane. What it does mean is that it is a subject of international law and capable of possessing international rights and duties, and that it has capacity to maintain its rights by bringing international claims."

Reparation for Injuries Suffered in the Service of the United Nations, Advisory Opinion, Apr. 11, 1949, I.C.J. Reports (1949) 174, 178, 179. The Court advised that the Organization has the capacity to bring an international claim against one of its Members which has caused injury to it by a breach of its international obligations towards it. *Ibid.* 184.

In answer to the question whether the General Assembly had the right to refuse effect to an award of compensation made by the Administrative Tribunal of the United Nations, in favor of a staff member of the United Nations whose contract of service had been terminated without his assent, the International Court of Justice in its Advisory Opinion on the *Effect of Awards of Compensation Made by the United Nations Administrative Tribunal* declared: ". . . If he [Secretary-General] terminates the contract of service without the assent of the staff member and this action results in a dispute which is referred to the Administrative Tribunal, the parties to this dispute before the Tribunal are the staff member concerned and the United Nations Organization, represented by the Secretary-General . . . . As this final judgment has binding force on the United Nations Organization as the juridical person responsible for the proper observance of the contract of service, that Organization becomes legally bound to carry out the judgment and to pay the compensation awarded to the staff member. It follows that the General Assembly, as an organ of the United Nations, must likewise be bound by the judgment."

Advisory Opinion, July 13, 1954, I.C.J. Reports (1954) 47, 53.

The head cashier of the International Institute of Agriculture sued the Institute for payment of compensation for his dismissal. The Court of Appeal in Rome in dismissing the appeal declared: "The International Institute of Agriculture was not a subject of international law seeing that it did not exercise sovereignty over a fixed territory and a population. It therefore had not the character of a State. . . ."

The Court of Cassation in sustaining a further appeal said: "The International Institute of Agriculture, which owes its origin to the common will of a number of States, expressed in the Pact of Union, for the protection and satisfaction of collective and common economic interests and needs, is an international entity, an International Administrative Union. . . . International practice knows of two kinds of international administrative unions: in some, the organisation is entrusted to one of the States by whose agreement it has been constituted; in others, the organisation remains autonomous and removed from the interference of any one State of the Union. . . . The International Institute of Agriculture, by the instrument creating it (Convention of 7 June, 1905) . . . belongs to the second category. . . . This is therefore a case of an autonomous union free, as regards its internal affairs, from interference by the sovereign power of the States composing the Union, except when it consents thereto. Following the better and more widely held doctrine, this Supreme Court holds that the International Institute of Agriculture is such an international legal person. . . ."

> *International Institute of Agriculture* v. *Profili*, [1929–1930] Ann. Dig. 413–415 (No. 254).

> The Constitution of the Food and Agriculture Organization of the United Nations provides "The Organization shall have the capacity of a legal person to perform any legal act appropriate to its purpose which is not beyond the powers granted to it by this Constitution." Art. XV(1). U.S. TIAS 1554; 60 Stat. 1886, 1891.

> The Constitution of the International Refugee Organization, approved by the First General Assembly in December 1946, Resolution 62(I), laid down that "The Organization shall enjoy in the territory of each of its members such legal capacity as may be necessary for the exercise of its functions and the fulfilment of its objectives." Art. 13. 18 UNTS 3, 14; U.S. TIAS 1846; 62 Stat., pt. 3, pp. 3037, 3046.

> Substantially identical wording is contained in art. 66 of the Constitution of the World Health Organization, July 22, 1946. 14 UNTS 185, 200; U.S. TIAS 1808; 62 Stat., pt. 3, pp. 2679, 2692.

Article 320 of the Treaty of St. Germain of 1919 provided that "any differences [between the private owning railroad companies and the States territorially concerned] on which agreement is not reached, including questions relating to the interpretation of contracts concerning the expropriation of the lines, shall be submitted to arbitrators designated by the Council of the League of Nations". The Sopron-Köszeg Local Railway Company, a concession-holder of a railway formerly situated entirely within Hungary but which, as a result of the territorial changes effected by the treaty, subsequently passed to Austria, brought its dispute over Austria's share of the receipts before the Council of the League which after recognizing the company's standing appointed arbitrators.

The Sopron-Köszeg Local Railway Company Case, [1929–1930] Ann. Dig. 57–59 (No. 34).

"What was the Reparation Commission? Was it a mere name for a temporary partnership of the Powers creditors of Germany on reparation account, or was it a *persona*, a right and duty-bearing entity of international and also in certain relations of municipal law?

"A study of the relevant articles of the Treaty of Versailles and observation of the actual proceedings of the Reparation Commission can hardly leave doubt that the Commission possessed international personality. The Treaty distinguishes the Commission from the Governments 'represented' upon it. The Commission possesses certain powers and has certain duties conferred upon it by a treaty to which the governments represented are not the only parties, and which therefore they could not revoke at their own arbitrary discretion. The Commission could not, for example, validly be ordered by the Allied Governments not to give Germany 'a just opportunity to be heard', nor could its discretion to extend the date and modify the form of payments have been withdrawn by unilateral action to which Germany was not a party. The Commission had judicial functions and its decisions, duly given in exercise of those functions, bound all parties to the treaties. A Delegate was not a diplomatic representative taking decisions *ad referendum*. A decision of the Commission was a final act; if a government was dissatisfied with its Delegate, it could recall him, but the governments possessed nothing in the nature of a general power of ratification, and therefore also disallowance, of what the Commission did. A Delegate was not in law the agent of his national government nor would it be accurate even to call him a plenipotentiary. He drew no salary from his government. Whether a Delegate acted always under instructions from his government or not, was the private affair of his government and himself. A Delegate had not to produce 'full powers' to be examined and found to be in 'good and due form'. And in most matters, and this is a strong confirmation of the independent character of the Commission, the Delegate was bound by the decision of the majority of his fellows. The Commission is thus clearly distinguished from a diplomatic congress. It had no resemblance to the Ambassadors' Conference. The fact that the Commission was the 'exclusive agency' of the Creditor Governments 'for receiving, selling, holding and distributing' reparation payments did not impair its personality or make it in law in other matters a mere agent of those Governments. And, indeed, an agent is a person distinct from his principal. Further, the Commission was itself recognized in the Treaty of Versailles as a principal in the international world; it had 'agents' of its own, who were not the agents of the Creditor Powers. These agents were to be accorded by Germany 'the same rights and immunities' as those of 'diplomatic agents of friendly Powers'. [Article 240(3) Treaty of Versailles.]

"This distinct personality of the Commission was implicit in its activities and its methods of business. The Commission conducted, as we have seen, arbitrations with the German and with the American Governments. The Commission took leases of property in Paris in its own name. The Commission never, so far as my recollection goes, treated itself as being a mere name for the general body of the Creditor Governments or as a collection of individuals with personal liability for ordinary contractual engagements, such as leases or contracts of service. The whole conduct of the Commission was in line with the theory of a distinct personality in the international world, carrying with itself that same status into the world of municipal law, so far as in the municipal sphere it had necessary activities. And that the Commission had what was thought to be a limited duration marked out for its existence is no evidence of lack of personality. Most, if not all, continental systems of law allow commercial companies to fix by their statutes, should they be so minded, what is to be the term of their legal lives. But the personality of these companies is not a matter of doubt.

"In these conditions, it would seem that some further qualification, beyond that resulting from the establishment of the League of Nations, is needed to the old rule that 'States solely and exclusively are the subjects of International Law'."

Williams, "A Legal Footnote to the Story of German Reparations", XIII Brit. Yb. Int'l L. (1932) 9, 33–35.

"With what, if any, rights and duties under international law are the various international organizations endowed? Theory and practice both suggest that any 'personality' which they may have in international law must be conferred upon them by states (or other international organizations already recognized as 'persons'), either expressly or through customary development. In practice it would seem that only international organizations created by states are treated as having international law rights and duties, although there is no inherent reason why international legal personality may not be conferred upon 'private' organizations. (Indeed, certain functions of the International Committee of the Red Cross, a privately created organization of Swiss individuals, in connection with prisoners of war come close to implying the international legal personality of that body.)

"Although the state itself is a fabrication of man as much as these international organizations, it is a fabrication of such long standing that it is regarded as the 'natural' person of the international legal system. Through centuries of custom and usage certain rights and duties have been attributed to states so consistently that they are regarded as flowing from the definition of statehood. International organizations, however, have not been so long known to the law, and for most purposes each is treated as a separate case. The extent of their capacity for rights and duties under international law depends upon the 'charter' (i.e., constitutional documents, usually in the form of a multilateral treaty) under which they are created, and the practice which has grown up around each organization. In general, it would appear that if a given right or duty is conferred neither by the charter, nor by customary international law, the international organization does not have it. The question to ask in each case is how far the organization acts as an entity in carrying on international relations, separate and distinct from the states which or private persons who are its members.

"The constitutional documents of many international organizations indicate that they have some degree of legal personality. It is not always clear, however, whether this refers to legal personality under the laws of the several member states, or to capacity for rights and duties under international law. For example, Article 104 of the United Nations Charter provides that 'The Organization shall enjoy in the territory of each of its Members such legal capacity as may be necessary for the exercise of its functions and the fulfillment of its purposes.' With respect to this, the Report of the Secretary of State to the President on the San Francisco Conference, June 26, 1945 says of this Article 104:

" 'This Article does not deal with what is called the "international personality" of the Organization. The Committee which discussed the matter was anxious to avoid any implication that the United Nations will be in any sense a "super-state". So far as the power to enter into agreements with states is concerned, the answer is given by Article 43 which provides that the Security Council is to be a party to the agreements concerning the availability of armed forces. International practice, while limited, supports the idea of such a body being a party to such agreements. No other issue of "international personality" requires mention in the Charter. Practice will bring about the evolution of appropriate rules so far as necessary.' Dept. of State, Conference, Ser. 71, pp. 157–158.

"Although no agreements have yet been concluded under Article 43, an example of an agreement between the United Nations and a state is afforded by its Headquarters Agreement with the United States. [61 Stat. 3416; T.I.A.S. 1676; 43 *Am. J. Int'l L. Supp.* 8 (1949). See also C. Parry, "The Treaty-Making Power of the United Nations," 1949 *Br. Y.B. Int'l L.* 108.] Furthermore, pursuant to Article 63 of the Charter, the United Nations, through its Economic and Social Council, has entered into agreements with various international organizations which are its 'specialized agencies.'

"It likewise seems clear that an international organization may be given the capacity to sue or be sued before an international court. International organizations have been parties to international arbitrations with states in various cases. [See *e.g.*, Germany v. Reparation Commission (1924), 1 *U.N. Rept. of Int. Arb. Awards* 429, *Ann. Dig.*, 1923–24, cases 194, 199, 200; Germany v. Reparation Commission, 1925, 2 *U.N. Rept. of Int. Arb. Awards* 745; *Interpretation of London Agreement of Aug. 9, 1924* (Germ. and Rep. Comm.), 2 *ibid.* 873, 20 *Am. J. Int'l L.* 556 (1926), *Ann. Dig.* 1925–1926, case 264; Germany v. Commissaire aux revenus gagés [Dawes Plan interpretation] 2 *U.N. Rept. of Int. Arb. Awards* 755, 21 *Am. J. Int'l L.* 326 (1927), *Ann. Dig.* 1925–26, case 151; The Standard Oil Tankers (Reparation Comm. and U.S.), 2 *U.N. Repts. of Int. Arb. Awards* 777, 22 *Am. J. Int'l L.* 404 (1928).; *Ann. Dig.* 1925–26, cases 169 and 353.

Regarding suits by international organizations in national courts, see Balfour, Guthrie & Co. v. United States, 90 F. Supp. 831 (N.D. Calif., 1950), holding that the United Nations, as a shipper of powdered milk sent by the United Nations' International Children's Emergency Fund to European ports, had capacity to sue a private charterer and also the United States as owner of the vessel on which the shipment was made (under the Suits in Admirality Act, . . .). See also International Refugee Organization v. Republic S.S. Co., 189 F. 2d 858 (4th Cir. 1951), holding that an international organization might bring suit in a federal court even though diversity jurisdiction was absent. Cf., United Nations Korean Reconstruction Agency *v.* Glass Production Methods, 143 F. Supp. 248 (S.D.N.Y. 1956), holding that the statute giving international organizations the right to sue did not affect usual venue provisions.]"

Bishop, *International Law, Cases and Materials* (1962, permission Little, Brown and Company) 257–259.

"A very large part of international affairs and thus of the process of international accommodation, concerns the relations between legal persons known as states. This is necessarily so. But it is no longer novel for the particular interest of the individual human being to break through the mass of interstate relationships. Jefferson could see the struggle between the colonies and the mother country in terms of individuals as well as of their political groupings. Wilson appealed to the Italian people over the heads of their government. Franklin Roosevelt is a symbol in many countries today because he felt and conveyed an interest in the living man and woman. The Communists pervert the process by seeking to subvert governments, alleging an

Individuals

interest in the common man whom they blatantly ignore when they succeed in imposing the power of their small elite governing class.

"When the representatives of 51 states met at San Francisco in 1945 to frame a world constitution, they too had a declaration of independence from tyranny as the background for their work. This was the Atlantic Charter incorporated in the United Nations declaration of January 1, 1942. They could not have ignored, if they had wished to do so, the need to provide for a decent respect for the welfare of mankind. Thus the Charter begins with its declaration that 'We, the Peoples of the United Nations,' (have) 'determined to reaffirm faith in fundamental human rights, in the dignity and worth of the human person, in the equal rights of men and women . . .' It recites that the peoples have drawn the Charter through the agency of their representatives. These representatives selected the promotion and encouragement of respect for human rights and fundamental freedoms as one of the purposes of the United Nations. They charged the General Assembly with the duty of assisting in the realization of these rights and freedoms. They devoted a chapter to international economic and social cooperation and therein made it mandatory that 'the United Nations shall promote: . . . universal respect for, and observance of human rights and fundamental freedoms . . .' For the achievement of this specific purpose as well as others, all members pledged themselves 'to take joint and separate action in cooperation with the Organization . . .' They directed the Economic and Social Council to set up a commission on human rights. Thus, as John Foster Dulles has said, the United Nations was created 'not merely to protect State against State, but to protect individuals.' "

Philip C. Jessup, Ambassador at Large, "The Conquering March of an Idea", address delivered before the 72d Annual Meeting of the American Bar Association, St. Louis, Mo., Sept. 6, 1949, XXI *Bulletin*, Department of State, No. 533, Sept. 19, 1949, pp. 432–433.

"Positive international law is moving towards wider recognition of the interests of the individual, even in so definitely inter-State an institution as diplomatic protection. . . . It may be thought that this trend will find its logical complement and sanction one day in easier access for the individual to international procedures. But though no doctrinal (dualistic) prejudice should close our eyes to these new developments, the grave objections to them from the point of view of the internal and external political order of States must be noticed."

De Visscher, *Theory and Reality in Public International Law* (Princeton, 1957, translated from French by P. E. Corbett) 125, n. 8.

"27. The question of the subjects of international law has, in particular in the last twenty-five years, ceased to be one of purely theoretical importance, and it is now probable that in some respects it requires authoritative international regulation. Practice has abandoned the doctrine that States are the exclusive subjects of international rights and duties. Although the Statute of the International Court of Justice adheres to the traditional view that only States can be parties to international proceedings, a number of other international instruments have recognized the procedural capacity of the individual. This was the case not only in the provisions of the Treaty of Versailles relating to the jurisdiction of the Mixed Arbitral Tribunals, but also in other treaties such as the Polish-German Convention of 1922 relating to Upper Silesia in which—as was subsequently held by the Upper Silesian Mixed Tribunal—the independent procedural status of individuals as claimants before an international agency was recognized even as against the State of which they were nationals.

"28. In the sphere of substantive law, the Permanent Court of International Justice recognized, in the advisory opinion relating to the postal service in Danzig, that there is nothing in international law to prevent individuals from acquiring directly rights under a treaty provided that this is the intention of the contracting parties. A considerable number of decisions of municipal courts rendered subsequently to the advisory opinion of the Permanent Court expressly affirmed that possibility.

"29. In the field of customary international law the enjoyment of benefits of international law by individuals as a matter of right followed from the doctrine, accepted by a growing number of countries, that generally recognized rules of the law of nations form part of the law of the land. In the sphere of duties imposed by international law the principle that the obligations of international law bind individuals directly regardless of the law of their State and of any contrary order received from their superiors was proclaimed in the Charter annexed to the Agreement of 8 August 1945, providing for the setting up of the International Military Tribunal at Nürnberg, as well as in the Charter of the International Military Tribunal at Tokyo of 19 January 1946. That principle was fully affirmed in the judgment of the Nürnberg Tribunal as flowing from the imperative necessity of making international law effective. The Tribunal said: 'Crimes against international law are committed by men, not by abstract entities, and only by punishing individuals who commit such crimes can the provisions of international law be enforced.' It was reaffirmed in the resolution of the General Assembly of 11 December 1946, expressing adherence to the principles of the Nürnberg Charter and judgment. It has loomed large in the discussions and statements bearing upon the resolution of the General Assembly in the matter of the codification of the law applied in the judgment of the International Military Tribunal. The General Assembly directed the Committee on Codification of International Law 'to treat as a matter of primary importance plans for the formulation, in the context of a general codification of offences against the peace and security of mankind, or of an International

Criminal Code, of the principles recognized in the Charter of the Nürnberg Tribunal and in the judgment of the Tribunal'. In a memorandum submitted by the representative of France to the Codification Committee in 1947 it was proposed that the general principle enunciated by the Tribunal and cited above should be confirmed as part of the codification of this aspect of the law: 'The individual is subject to international penal law. Without thereby excluding the penal responsibility of the criminal State, international penal law can inflict penalties on the authors of international offences and their accomplices.' [A/AC.10/34.]

"30. On a different plane the Charter of the Nürnberg Tribunal—and the judgment which followed it—proclaimed the criminality of offences against humanity, i.e., of such offences against the fundamental rights of man to life and liberty, even if committed in obedience to the law of the State. To that extent, in a different sphere, positive law has recognized the individual as endowed, under international law, with rights the violation of which is a criminal act. The repeated provisions of the Charter of the United Nations in the matter of human rights and fundamental freedoms are directly relevant in this connexion."

Survey of International Law in Relation to the Work of Codification of the International Law Commission, Memorandum submitted by the Secretary-General of the United Nations, A/CN.4/1/Rev. 1, Feb. 10, 1949, pp. 19–21.

The General Assembly "proclaims this Universal Declaration of Human Rights as a common standard of achievement for all peoples and all nations, to the end that every individual and every organ of society, keeping this Declaration constantly in mind, shall strive by teaching and education to promote respect for these rights and freedoms and by progressive measures, national and international, to secure their universal and effective recognition and observance, both among the peoples of Member States themselves and among the peoples of territories under their jurisdiction."

Universal Declaration of Human Rights, Dec. 6, 1948, U.N. General Assembly, 2d Sess., Doc. A/811.

As the Third Session of the General Assembly of the United Nations neared its final vote on the Declaration of Human Rights, Mrs. Franklin D. Roosevelt, Chairman of the Commission on Human Rights and member of the U.S. delegation, stated:

"In giving our approval to the declaration today, it is of primary importance that we keep clearly in mind the basic character of the document. It is not a treaty; it is not an international agreement. It is not and does not purport to be a statement of law or of legal obligation. It is a declaration of basic principles of human rights and freedoms, to be stamped with the approval of the General Assembly by formal vote of its members, and to serve as a common standard of achievement for all peoples of all nations." XIX *Bulletin*, Department of State, No. 494, Dec. 19, 1948, p. 751; see U.N. Gen. Ass. Off. Rec. 3d Sess., 1st pt., Summary Record, Dec. 9, 1948, 180th meeting, p. 862.

". . . Within several months of the adoption of the Charter of the United Nations, a Canadian court set aside a restrictive covenant in a private contract on the ground that it discriminated, on racial grounds, against one section of the community. In the view of the court, to uphold the contract would run counter to the obligations undertaken by Canada under Articles 1 and 55 of the Charter to promote universal respect for, and observance of, human rights and fundamental freedoms for all without distinction as to race, sex, language or religion. (*Re Drummond Wren*, (1945) O. R. 778).

"It would therefore appear that, to the extent to which the Charter incorporates obligations to respect the fundamental human rights and freedoms, it amounts to recognition of individuals as subjects of international law. . . ."

Lauterpacht, "Subjects of the Law of Nations", 64 L.Q. Rev. (1948) 97, 102–103.

Holding that the Charter, particularly that provision concerning the general obligation to promote human rights in cooperation with the Organization, was a non-self-executing treaty, the California Supreme Court in *Sei Fujii* v. *The State of California* (242 P. 2d 617 (1952)) reversed the District Court of Appeal's decision that the Alien Land Law, forbidding aliens from acquiring land in California, was contrary to both the letter and spirit of the Charter "which, as a treaty, is paramount to every law of every state in conflict with it." (217 P. 2d 481, 488 (Dist. Ct., 2d Dist., Div. 2, 1950)). Addressing its interpretation of the Charter to this issue, the California Supreme Court said, "The provisions in the charter pledging cooperation in promoting observance of fundamental freedoms lack the mandatory quality and definiteness which would indicate an intent to create justiciable rights in private persons immediately upon ratification. Instead, they are framed as a promise of future action by the member nations. . . ." It continued: "We are satisfied . . . that the charter provisions relied on by plaintiff were not intended to supersede existing domestic legislation, and we cannot hold that they operate to invalidate the alien land law." (242 P. 2d 621–622).

While, in a later case, the United States Supreme Court held the Alien Land Law unconstitutional solely on the ground that it contravened the Fourteenth Amendment, Justices Black and Douglas, in a concurring opinion, independently of the Court, observed: "There are additional reasons now why that law stands as an obstacle to the free accomplishment of our policy in the international field. One of these reasons is that we have recently pledged ourselves to cooperate with the United Nations to 'promote . . . universal respect for, and observance of, human rights and fundamental freedoms for all without distinction as to race, sex, language, or religion.' . . ." Justice Murphy, in a separate concurring opinion, mentioned the same provisions of the United Nations Charter and concluded: "The Alien Land Law stands as a barrier to the fulfillment of that national pledge. Its inconsistency with the Charter, which has been duly ratified and adopted by the United States, is but one more reason why the statute must be condemned." *Oyama et al.* v. *California*, 332 U.S. 633, 649–650, 673 (1948).

Article IV of the Convention on the Prevention and Punishment of the Crime of Genocide reads, "Persons committing genocide or any of the other acts enumerated in article III shall be punished, whether they are constitutionally responsible rulers, public officials or private individuals."

General Assembly Resolution 260(III) A, B, and C with text of Convention annexed, Dec. 9, 1948; 78 UNTS 277; S. Exec. O, 81st Cong., 1st sess.

The Charter of the Organization of American States, signed at Bogotá in 1948, affirms that—

"Each state has the right to develop its cultural, political and economic life freely and naturally. In this free development, the State shall respect the rights of the individual and the principles of universal morality."

Art. 13, U.S. TIAS 2361; 2 UST 2394, 2419.

"It was submitted that international law is concerned with the actions of sovereign States, and provides no punishment for individuals . . . Crimes against international law are committed by men, not by abstract entities, and only by punishing individuals who commit such crimes can the provisions of international law be enforced."

Judgment, Sept. 30, 1946, I *Trial of the Major War Criminals before the International Military Tribunal* (1947) 171, 222–223.

"We must lend our full support to the development and application of international law, particularly the laws against war which have been for the first time enforced against individuals by the Nürnberg and Far Eastern Tribunals."

Warren R. Austin, U.S. Representative to the United Nations, "The Goal of Collective Security", address, New York, N.Y., Mar. 4, 1947, XVI *Bulletin*, Department of State, No. 402, Mar. 16, 1947, pp. 474, 475.

"The point in dispute amounts therefore to this: Does the *Beamtenabkommen*, as it stands, form part of the series of provisions governing the legal relationship between the Polish Railways Administration and the Danzig officials who have passed into its service (contract of service)? The answer to this question depends upon the intention of the contracting Parties. It may be readily admitted that, according to a well established principle of international law, the *Beamtenabkommen*, being an international agreement, cannot, as such, create direct rights and obligations for private individuals. But it cannot be disputed that the very object of an international agreement, according to the intention of the contracting Parties, may be the adoption by the Parties of some definite rules creating individual rights and obligations and enforceable by the national courts. That there is such an intention in the present case can be established by reference to the terms of the *Beamtenabkommen.* . . ."

Jurisdiction of the Courts of Danzig (Pecuniary Claims of Danzig Railway Officials Transferred to the Polish Service), Advisory Opinion, Series B, No. 15, Mar. 3, 1928, pp. 4, 17–18; II Hudson, *World Court Reports* (1935) 237, 246–247.

The International Court of Justice, after referring to the "right of the population to have the Territory administered in accordance with these rules [mandate rules]", quoted in confirmation of this view "Article 80, paragraph 1, of the Charter, which maintains the rights of States and peoples and the terms of existing international instruments until the territories in question are placed under the Trusteeship System" and stated:

"These general considerations are confirmed by Article 80, paragraph 1, of the Charter, as this clause has been interpreted above. It purports to safeguard, not only the rights of States, but also the rights of the peoples of mandated territories until Trusteeship Agreements are concluded".

International Status of South–West Africa, Advisory Opinion, July 11, 1950, I.C.J. Reports (1950) 128, 133, 136.

". . . international law or the law of nations, must be defined as law applicable to states in their mutual relations and to individuals in their relations with states. International law may also, under this hypothesis, be applicable to certain interrelationships of individuals themselves, where such interrelationships involve matters of international concern. So long, however, as the international community is composed of states, it is only through an exercise of their will, as expressed through treaty or agreement, or as laid down by an international authority deriving its power from states, that a rule of law becomes binding upon an individual. When there is created some kind of international constituent assembly or world parliament, representative of the people of the world, and having authority to legislate, it will then be possible to assert that international law derives authority from a source external to the states. . . .

"There is no novelty in the suggestion that states may delegate the exercise of some of their customary attributes. The classic case is that of the European Commission of the Danube established under the Treaty of Paris of March 30, 1856. The commission was given legislative, administrative and judicial powers. The Central Commission for the Navigation of the Rhine established under Article 109 of the Final Act of Vienna of 1815 had comparable powers. The regulations of these commissions were directly applicable to individuals and individual infractions of the rules were directly cognizable by the commissions. Thus the international bodies dealt directly with individuals in the same manner in which national bodies customarily deal with them.

The same remark may be made in regard to those exceptional cases in which individuals have been given by treaty the right to appear before international tribunals. The notable cases are those of the Central American Court of Justice established in 1907, the Mixed Arbitral Tribunals established by the peace treaties at the end of World War I, and the Arbitral Tribunal for dealing with the rights of minorities in Upper Silesia under the Geneva Convention of 1922 between Poland and Germany. In such cases the international tribunal acted directly upon the claim of an individual and the judgment ran in favor of the individual. . . ."

Jessup, "The Subjects of a Modern Law of Nations", 45 Mich. L. Rev. (1947) 383, 385, 386. See also Korowicz, "The Problem of the International Personality of Individuals", 50 Am. J. Int'l L. (1956) 533; Eagleton, "Some Questions as to the Place of the Individual in the International Law of the Future", 37 Am. J. Int'l L. (1943) 642.

"Thus, the present Court [the International Court of Justice] deals with litigation between States. (I am not forgetting the very important right of the Security Council or the Assembly of the United Nations, or of any other organ of the United Nations or specialized agency [Charter, Article 96; Statute, Article 65] which may at any time be so authorized by the General Assembly, to request the Court to give an Advisory Opinion on a legal question.) Nevertheless, as you all know, it frequently happens that, when an individual makes a claim against a foreign State and cannot obtain satisfaction, that individual's Government may feel justified in espousing his claim and putting it forward against the defendant State upon an international level. The claim is thus transformed from a claim dependent on some system of national law into a claim involving a question of international law. It is in this way that you will often find the Permanent Court or the International Court dealing with a claim which began as a private claim by an individual against a foreign Government. I need merely mention the *Mavrommatis Palestine Concessions* case and the *Oscar Chinn* case.

"Many people consider that this is not enough and that there ought to be some machinery enabling an individual to bring a claim against a foreign Government before an international tribunal *as of right* and without the intervention of his own Government. It would take a long time for us to thresh out this question, and I shall not attempt to do so. I would however make the following observations:

"However attractive from the point of view of human rights the proposal may be, it must be remembered that the litigation of a claim between a private individual and a foreign Government before an international tribunal is capable of exciting national feelings between two States, and I submit that an individual uncontrolled by his Government ought not to be allowed to make that possible. I think that is the main reason in favor of the view that, if any machinery is to be created for enabling individuals to bring their claims against foreign Governments before international tribunals, their own Government ought to be in a position to give or withhold its imprimatur, for one of the main preoccupations of Governments must always be to avoid international friction.

"Sometimes the claims of individual persons may, though legal in form, raise or touch political issues."

Sir Arnold Duncan McNair, President of the International Court of Justice, *The Development of International Justice* (1954) 8–10 (from the first of two lectures delivered by Judge McNair at the Law Center of New York University in Dec. 1953).

SANCTION

§ 3

In setting forth *ante* reflections of the "positive" influence, fairly prevalent in the 20th century, it was observed at the same time that certain authorities addressed themselves, in their writings quoted, to a secondary but related issue: whether international law must be binding or enforceable in order to have the real character of law. James Brown Scott, finding that the binding force of international law is both moral and physical, stated more directly than certain others that international law is a rule of conduct even without the presence of a sanction. Professor Edwin M. Borchard seemed also to say that international law to be law is not dependent upon the element of enforceability. John Bassett Moore, while generally maintaining that international law is enforceable or regarded as binding, appeared also to agree with the view that the element of enforceability is not an essential element of the nature of law. Additionally, Anzilotti of Italy, a positivist who assumes the binding force of law, looked to an extra-legal norm in his answer to why international law is binding.

These authorities are quoted in § 1, *ante*, pp. 9–14.

". . . Violations of the law are extremely rare in any customary system, and they are so in international law. The common impression to the contrary arises from the unfortunate concentration of popular interest on the laws of war, and a consequent failure to observe that the less sensational but far more important part of the system, the laws of peace, is constantly and unobtrusively observed in the daily intercourse of states." Brierly, *The Law of Nations* (Oxford, 1928) 51.

". . . There are first those who, unable to discover any sanction meeting the requirements of their definition, deny to international law the status of positive law. [1 Austin, Lectures on Jurisprudence (3rd ed. 1869) 182; Patterson, Introduction of Jurisprudence (2nd, Mimeo, ed. 1946) 126, 131, 132; See also Kunz:

"The arguments of laymen and lawyers against the legal character of international law consist mostly in the lack of organization and of sanctions". Kunz, The Problem of the Progressive
Development of International Law (1946) 31 Iowa L. Rev. 544,
546.] A second group claims to find international sanctions of
equal, or nearly equal standing, with municipal sanctions. [Root,
The Sanctions of International Law (1908) 2 Am. J. Int. L.
451; Scott, The Modern Law of Nations and Its Municipal Law
Sanctions (1934) 22 Georgetown L. J. 139; Kelsen, Sanctions of
International Law under the Charter of the United Nations
(1946) 31 Iowa L. Rev. 498; Brierly, Sanctions (1931) 17 Grotius
Soc. Trans. 67, 68.] Finally there is an impressive number of
leading writers who, either conceding that no positive sanctions
exist or professing no opinion as to their existence, consider the
question of little significance. [2 Hyde, Int. Law (2nd Rev. ed.
1945) 1370; 1 Hackworth, Dig. Int. L. (1940) 12; Sir Frederick
Pollock, Introduction to 5th Eng. ed. of Wheaton, p. xli; Charles
Evans Hughes, quoted by Brierly, (1931) 17 Grotius Soc. Trans.
75]"

Sloan, "Comparative International and Municipal Law Sanctions", 27
Neb. L. Rev. (1947) 1.

"The observance of international law rests principally upon the **Honor**
honor of the American Republics, under the sanction of public
opinion.

.   .   .   .

"They may also have recourse to moral sanctions, such as an
appeal to public opinion, the publication of the official correspondence showing wherein the nation was at fault, a request for
arbitration, the severance of diplomatic relations."

"Fundamental Bases of International Law", arts. 20 and 22, prepared
by the American Institute of International Law (1925), 20 Am. J. Int'l L.
Supp. (1926) 304, 307–308.

"It may be thought that legislation can exist only where the
will declared is supported by some power that can enforce the
declaration. Certainly no such test can be applied to national
legislation, and it would seem to be no more applicable to international legislation. When the will of two or more states is
properly declared, the declaration seems to be binding on the
states concerned, in their relations to which it applies, because
of a general principle of international law that states must keep **Good faith**
faith with each other. The juristic force of the declaration is
not lost because one of the states concerned may fail to observe
it, no more than national legislation would lose its force because
of a violation. Penalties may or may not be laid down for a
violation of a national statute; they are seldom provided for in
international enactments. An 'intention to observe its international obligations' would seem to be as much a condition of

membership in the society of nations as a condition of eligibility
for membership in the League of Nations."

I Hudson, *International Legislation, 1919–21* (1931), p. xvii.

Trials

"Law in our national societies performs a number of functions.
One is restraint upon antisocial conduct—a negative function,
criminal law, for example. This requires courts and sheriffs,
police and prosecutors. Except for the trial of war criminals,
our international legal system is here in a rudimentary stage."

Secretary of State Acheson, "Law and the Growth of the International
Community", address, Apr. 24, 1952, before the American Society of Inter-
national Law, Washington, D.C., XXVI *Bulletin*, Department of State,
No. 671, May 5, 1952, p. 694.

"World opinion"

"International law has been described as law without a constitution. In the absence of effective juridical sanctions, world
opinion—aptly described in the Declaration of Independence as 'a
decent respect to the opinions of mankind'—remains·the most
effective means of preventing aggressive war. In the formation
of this opinion, we as lawyers, dedicated to the rule of law, bear a
heavy responsibility."

Herman Phleger, Legal Adviser, Department of State, "Progress in the
Rule of Law", address before the Philadelphia Bar Association, Oct. 10,
1955, XXXIII *Bulletin*, Department of State, No. 852, Oct. 24, 1955, pp.
647, 650–651.

"There is also a body of world opinion which, when it is
crystallized and brought to bear on particular situations, plays
a role equivalent to our 'common law.' There has been gratifying progress in developing this kind of community judgment,
and the gatherings of the nations at the General Assembly of
the United Nations greatly promote this result. There international conduct is judged, sometimes formally but more often
informally; and even the most powerful nations feel it expedient
to be able to represent their conduct as conforming to this body
of world opinion."

Secretary of State Dulles, "The Institutionalizing of Peace", address
before the American Society of International Law, Washington, D.C., Apr.
25, 1956, XXXIV *Bulletin*, Department of State, No. 880, May 7, 1956, pp.
739, 741.

By article 94 of the Charter of the United Nations, it is provided:

U.N. Charter: Decisions of ICJ

"1. Each Member of the United Nations undertakes to comply
with the decision of the International Court of Justice in any
case to which it is a party.

"2. If any party to a case fails to perform the obligations incumbent upon it under a judgment rendered by the Court, the
other party may have recourse to the Security Council, which
may, if it deems necessary, make recommendations or decide upon
measures to be taken to give effect to the judgment."

U.S. TS 993; 59 Stat. 1031, 1051.

"Let us turn now to the problem of the administration and enforcement of law. We have in the United Nations Security Council a body which, by the charter, is given primary responsibility for the maintenance of international peace and security. The charter contemplates (article 43) that the Security Council shall have at its disposal armed forces necessary for maintaining peace. *Other provisions*

"Unfortunately, the charter scheme for a Security Council action backed by an international police force has, up to now, not been realized because of the so-called veto power. Thereby confidence in the Security Council has been badly shaken and its usefulness impaired.

"In an effort to meet that situation the General Assembly adopted in 1950 a resolution known as 'Uniting for Peace.' It asked the members voluntarily to hold in readiness armed contingents available for United Nations use in maintaining international peace and security. Also the Assembly set up a procedure for meeting on 24 hours' notice in the event of a threat to the peace and a paralysis of the Security Council through exercise of the veto power.

"This partially compensates for the undependability of the Security Council as a law enforcement body. However, the General Assembly is primarily a deliberative body and includes so many members that it cannot serve effectively as an executive or enforcement agency.

"As further moves to reinforce the processes for peace, 45 nations have joined in collective security arrangements under article 51 of the charter, which acknowledges the inherent right of collective self-defense against armed attack. Most of these collective security arrangements are backed by the mobile striking power of the United States. These arrangements go far to deny aggressors the opportunity to follow the typical pattern of aggression which consists of picking up weaker nations one by one."

Secretary of State Dulles, "The Institutionalizing of Peace", address before the American Society of International Law, Washington, D.C., Apr. 25, 1956, XXXIV *Bulletin*, Department of State, No. 880, May 7, 1956, pp. 739, 742.

On the legal status of the United Nations Emergency Force (UNEF), see Chapman, "The United Nations Emergency Force—Legal Status", 57 Mich. L. Rev. (1958) 56.

"The process of negotiating a Suez Canal settlement was interrupted by the outbreak of hostilities in the Near East late last October.

.   .   .   .

"The steps in obtaining a cease-fire resulted in significant developments in the United Nations as an international institution. The steps in obtaining the withdrawal of the British and French, and ultimately Israeli, forces were a promising example of the actual operation of international law.

"In the General Assembly debate a preponderance of opinion was marshaled in support of the law of the charter and given expression in the Assembly's resolutions calling for cease-fire and withdrawal. Behind these resolutions was implicit the possibility of United Nations sanctions, which are open to the Assembly under articles 10 and 11 of the charter and are contemplated by the uniting-for-peace resolution. France and Britain to some degree and more especially Israel were subjected by other countries to strong pressures to comply with the Assembly's call—various and divergent as might have been the aims of those other countries.

"Thus in a situation of great peril, because of the possibility of a spreading of the conflict, the nations in effect agreed to apply the law of the charter. This, as I am sure you understand, did not result from the direct application of definitive rules by an international agency endowed with governmental power as we know it in domestic law. Much painstaking negotiation was involved both inside and outside the United Nations as to the means of applying the basic proposition that military forces should be withdrawn behind the armistice lines. This was done in order to take account of legitimate concerns and interests on both sides regarding security and legal rights. In the end, common ground was reached and the law had pragmatic effect."

Christian A. Herter, Under Secretary of State, address delivered at annual dinner of the American Bar Association, New York, N.Y., July 15, 1957, XXXVII *Bulletin*, Department of State, No. 945, Aug. 5, 1957, pp. 223, 225, 226.

Peaceful means

In February 1957, at a time when efforts were being made both by the United Nations and the United States and other Member States to secure the voluntary withdrawal of Israeli forces from Egyptian territory, President Eisenhower addressed the American people on "The Situation in the Middle East", in the course of which he said:

"Of course, we and all the members of the United Nations ought to support justice and conformity with international law. The first article of the charter states the purpose of the United Nations to be 'the suppression of acts of aggression or other breaches of the peace, and to bring about by peaceful means, and in conformity with . . . justice and international law, adjustment or settlement of international disputes.' But it is to be observed that conformity with justice and international law are to be brought about 'by peaceful means.' "

Address to the American people, Feb. 20, 1957, White House press release, Feb. 21, 1957; XXXVI *Bulletin*, Department of State, No. 924, Mar. 11, 1957, pp. 387, 389.

Enforcement by sanctions

"The strength of law depends essentially upon the consent—or at least the passive assent—of the more powerful elements among those who live under it. If the consent were conscious and universal there would hardly be need to buttress the law with sanctions, since no occasion for enforcing it would ever arise.

Such a condition may obtain in the millennium, but the human race has not experienced it yet.

.   .   .   .

"Sanctions are measures taken in support of law. It is of the essence of law that sanctions are applied with and by the general authority, not by any individual. With the substitution of the word 'state' for the word 'individual', this is true in principle, and ought to be true in fact, of the sanctions of international, as well as of national law. In so far as sanctions are punitive, they are applied only after due inquiry and judgement by a competent authority. Physical force enters into them but rarely and only in clearly defined circumstances; it must be remembered, however, that force is always present in the background.

"Not all sanctions are punitive; some are preventive. . . .

.   .   .   .   .   .

"There is no *corpus juris* of international law corresponding to national codes. When we write of 'the reign of law' in the international sphere we mean the observance of international engagements (whether they be multilateral treaties, such as the Geneva Convention, the Hague Conventions, or the Briand-Kellogg Pact, or whether they be ordinary bilateral treaties) and of the body of rules, usually termed 'international law', which, though not necessarily embodied in written instruments, command practically universal assent amongst civilized nations. It is therefore necessary to emphasize at this point the danger of stressing unduly the analogy with the internal development of nations—the 'policeman-burglar' analogy which has been responsible for so much loose thinking and slovenly argument. Edmund Burke has warned us against the attempt to indict a whole nation. Nations do not behave as individuals, nor can they be treated as individuals are treated."

Report by a Group of Members of the Royal Institute of International Affairs, *International Sanctions* (Oxford, 1938) 4–6.

"Law is, by its very nature, a coercive order. A coercive order is a system of rules prescribing certain patterns of behavior by providing coercive measures as sanctions to be taken in case of contrary behavior, or, what amounts to the same, in case of violation of the law. 'Violation' is a figurative and sometimes misleading expression. The term 'delict' (wrong, illegal act) more correctly designates any kind of behavior which is made the condition of a sanction because it is considered to be undesirable.

"Sanctions have the character of forcible deprivation of certain possessions, such as life, freedom, economic or other values. They are coercive in so far as they are to be taken even against the will of the subject to whom they are applied, if necessary by the employment of force. This is the way in which the law protects life, freedom, economic and other interests against delicts. Hence, sanctions are forcible interference in the sphere of interests normally protected by the law. They are legal sanctions if they shall be applied only on the condition that a delict has been com-

mitted or, what amounts to the same, that an obligation established by the law has been disregarded, and only against the
delinquent or individuals who are in a legally determined relation
to the delinquent, that is to the one who by his own behavior has
committed the delict. Sanctions are the specific reactions of the
community, constituted by the legal order, against delicts.

.   .   .   .

"International law is law in the true sense of the term, for its
rules, regulating the mutual behavior of states, provide sanctions
to be directed against the state which has committed an international delict, or, what amounts to the same, has disregarded its
obligations towards another state and thus violated the right of
the other state. The specific sanctions provided by general international law are: reprisals and war. Both are coercive acts,
the former a limited, the latter an unlimited interference in the
sphere of interests of a state. The distinction between reprisals
and war rests upon the degree of interference: whether the enforcement action undertaken against the state is aimed solely at
the violation of certain interests of this state, or is directed towards its complete submission or total annihilation and consequently performed by the armed forces of the opponent.
"It is a generally accepted principle of international law that
reprisals, i.e. limited interference in the sphere of interests of
one state by another are allowed only as a reaction against a
delict, that is to say, as a sanction. But, is this principle applicable also to an unlimited interference in the sphere of interests of another state, to war? As far as the answer to this question is concerned, two opposite views exist. According to one
opinion, war is neither a delict nor a sanction; any state that is
not bound by special treaty to refrain from warring upon another
state or to resort to war only under certain definite conditions,
may wage war against any other state on any ground, without
violating general international law. The opposite opinion, however, holds that according to general international law war is in
principle forbidden; it is permitted only as a reaction against an
international delict and only when directed against the state responsible for this delict. Like reprisals, war has to be a sanction
if it is not to be considered as a delict. This is the doctrine of
bellum justum, just war.
". . . Only if it is possible to interpret so-called international
law in this way can that order be considered as law in the true
sense of the term.

.   .   .   .

"The Charter of the United Nations goes much further than
its predecessors. It obligates the Members of the United Nations not only not to resort to war against each other but to
refrain from the threat or use of force and to settle their disputes
by peaceful means (Art. 2, par. 3 and 4). The use of force—
so-called enforcement action—is allowed by the Charter (except
in case of self-defense) only as a reaction of the Organization
against a threat to the peace or a breach of the peace (Art. 39).

If the enforcement actions provided for by the Charter are true sanctions, the Charter is a perfect realization of the *bellum-justum* principle."

Kelsen, "Sanctions in International Law Under the Charter of the United Nations," 31 Iowa L. Rev. (1946) 499–502.

"(cc) *Non-military sanctions.*

"As far as so-called diplomatic sanctions are concerned, it may appear that an international organization may apply these measures directly, that is to say, not through the governments of the member states, without losing its international character. The diplomatic means which may be employed are: a protest against an illegal conduct of a state, the withdrawal of the head of the embassy, the severing of all diplomatic relations, and also of all consular relations; the non-recognition of a situation established by an illegal action. . . .

"Financial sanctions consist of denying all financial assistance to a state guilty of aggression and its nationals, cutting off long-term loans, suspending short-term banking credits, and the like. Only an authority which is competent to impose legal obligations upon public and private banking institutions, which therefore can exercise legislative and executive power directly over individuals, can apply such measures. . . . Financial sanctions are less effective than other economic sanctions and consequently should be combined with them. These sanctions also presuppose legislative and executive powers which are characteristic of a state government.

"Economic sanctions may be applied in different degrees. The most important economic sanction consists of prohibiting the commerce in arms, ammunition and the raw materials essential to the production of arms and ammunition and to the prosecution of hostilities between the member states of the security organization and the aggressor. Among these prohibitions an oil embargo is of particular importance. The refusal to accept exports from a state is an economic sanction which may have a remarkable effect on the state against which it is applied. The highest possible degree of an economic sanction is achieved by prohibiting all commerce, which includes prohibiting the nationals of the member states from entering the territory of the aggressor, prohibiting the nationals of the aggressor state from entering the territory of the member states, controlling all transport and international exchanges of goods, and interrupting the diplomatic and consular relations between the member states and the aggressor. This is a complete international boycott of the aggressor. It stands to reason that the economic measures taken against the aggressor should be accompanied by economic measures, especially those of a financial nature, taken in favor of the victim, and that in this respect every possible assistance should be given to the state which is the victim of the aggression.

"(dd) *Military sanctions.*

"(A) The Opposition to Military Sanctions

"Any use of armed force as a reaction against a violation of international law is a military sanction, and if armed force is used for this purpose to an extent characteristic of war, a military sanction has the character of war. The fact that armed force is used as a sanction does not deprive this use of armed force of its legal character of war. Hence the rules of international law regulating the conduct of war apply to it.

.   .   .   .

"(B) The Organization of Military Sanctions

.   .   .   .

"(C) The International Police Force Organized as a Permanent and Separate Armed Force at the Direct Disposal of the Security Organization

"Most of the difficulties and insufficiencies involved in the organization of military sanctions discussed in the previous sections could be avoided by placing at the direct disposal of the security organization an international armed force which is not established on an *ad hoc* basis, as under the quota system. In other words, the international armed force would not be available only in case of a particular military action of the organization, but would be permanent and completely separate from and independent of the national armed forces of the member states, a separate armed force belonging exclusively to the security organization and not an armed force composed of parts of the armed forces of the member states."

Hans Kelsen, "Collective Security Under International Law", in XLIX *International Law Studies, 1954*, Naval War College (1957) 106–107, 110, 111, 113–114.

See further Sir Hartley Shawcross, "The Rules of Law—Their Enforcement in International Affairs", 51 *Law Society's Gazette* (Dec. 1954) 505.

SOURCE

Introductory

§ 4

Statute
of ICJ

Article 38 of the Statute of the International Court of Justice reads:

"1. The Court . . . shall apply:

"(*a*) international conventions, whether general or particular, establishing rules expressly recognized by the contesting States;
"(*b*) international custom, as evidence of a general practice accepted as law;

"(c) the general principles of law recognized by civilized nations;

"(d) subject to the provisions of Article 59, judicial decisions and the teachings of the most highly qualified publicists of the various nations, as subsidiary means for the determination of rules of law.

"2. This provision shall not prejudice the power of the Court to decide a case *ex aequo et bono,* if the parties agree thereto."

Art. 38, Charter of the United Nations, Statute and Rules of Court, Series D, Acts and Documents Concerning the Organization of the Court, No. 1, 1946, p. 47. The Statute of the International Court of Justice is "annexed" to and forms "an integral part of" the Charter of the United Nations (art. 92). U.S. TS 993; 59 Stat. 1031, 1051.

"Article 38 of the Statute sets out four categories of sources or materials which the Court is directed to apply: (1) international conventions; (2) international custom; (3) general principles of law; (4) judicial decisions and the teachings of publicists. As the text was proposed by the 1920 Committee of Jurists, the application of these categories was to be *in a successive order;* the deletion of this phrase would seem to have had little effect on the meaning of the direction. If an applicable rule has been laid down by the parties in a convention, it will be controlling and the Court may not need to look further; if that is not the case, a sufficient guide may be found in the customary law; if resort to general principles of law is necessary, however, the Court would naturally want to know at the same time how these principles have been applied by courts and how they have been evaluated in juristic writings. Yet Article 38 did not establish a rigid hierarchy. In applying a provision in a convention, the Court may have to take into account the customary law prevailing when the convention was entered into, or general principles of law, as well as judicial precedents. A distinction may also have to be drawn between the categories listed, for they are not on an equal footing; while it is possible to *apply* a conventional or a customary rule of law, it seems more proper to say that general principles of law, judicial precedents, and juristic writings have only the nature of sources from which an applicable rule may be deduced.

Order of importance

"Prior to 1920, agreements relating to the arbitration of particular disputes frequently set out in general terms the sources of the law to be applied. 'Justice and equity,' 'justice, equity and the law of nations,' and 'treaties and general principles of international law,' were favored formulations; and a series of nineteenth-century treaties referred to 'principles of international law, and the practice and jurisprudence established by analogous modern tribunals of highest authority and prestige.' General treaties, and those concluded under the inspiration of the Hague Peace Conferences, were often silent on this point, however. If the text of Article 38 did not represent a great departure, except perhaps in the reference to general principles of law, it supplied a ready enumeration which seemed to serve a need, and it has been adopted in whole or in part by several international tribunals and in a number of subsequent treaties. It is also incorporated by reference in Articles 18 and 28 of the Geneva General Act, and in a number of bipartite conventions inspired by the General Act."

Hudson, *The Permanent Court of International Justice, 1920–1942* (1943) 606–607.

In determining the international criteria for resolving the conflict between dual nationality, or for establishing a standard by which the nationality accorded must be recognized by other States, the International Court of Justice examined the principles applied by courts of other States, international arbitrators, writings of publicists, and the practice of certain States.

Nottebohm Case (Liechtenstein v. Guatemala), Judgment (Second Phase), Apr. 6, 1955, I.C.J. Reports (1955) 4, 22.

In 1949 the International Law Commission submitted its Draft Declaration on the Rights and Duties of States to the General Assembly. In connection with its consideration of the appropriate disposition of the Draft Declaration, the Sixth Committee considered the powers of the General Assembly. Professor Roling of the Netherlands commented that "The General Assembly had no legislative power", and that "Adoption, even unanimous adoption, of the draft declaration would not give it the authority of a law". The Summary Record states:

General
Assembly
adoption

"In that connexion, Mr. Roling remarked that there had been in the League of Nations a tendency to adopt resolutions whenever there was a setback in international relations, although every one knew very well that those resolutions would have no legal effect. Thus, following the failure of the Treaty of Mutual Assistance in 1923 and of the Geneva Protocol of 1924, the League of Nations had adopted a resolution proclaiming that aggressive war was an international crime. Similarly, after the failure of the three-Power conference on disarmament in 1927, and the failure of the unfortunate attempt to conclude an Eastern Locarno, another resolution had covered up the meagre results of international discussions by providing that international disputes should be settled by peaceful means, and once again describing a war of aggression as an international crime. It should be recalled that it had been expressly specified at the time that the resolution had no 'concrete legal significance'. Twenty years after its adoption, that resolution had been cited at the Nürnberg and Tokyo trials as proof of the fact that, pursuant to international law existing in 1927 and the years following, the war of aggression was an international crime for which individuals could be held responsible. Aggressive war should, of course, always be considered an international crime. But there was no justification for considering principles of international law, as set forth in a declaration with no binding force whatever, to be part of existing international law, as in the case referred to above."

U.N. Gen. Ass. Off. Rec. 4th Sess., 6th Comm., Summary Records, Sept. 20–Nov. 29, 1949, 173d meeting, pp. 205–206.

In discussing the Draft Declaration on Rights and Duties of States prepared by the International Law Commission in 1949, in the Sixth Committee of the General Assembly of the United Nations, Omar Loutfi of Egypt expressed the view that "Surely, the work of a body of jurists as eminent as those on the International Law Commission should be regarded as a subsidiary means for the determination of rules of law, on a par with the teachings of the most highly qualified publicists of the various nations." U.N. Gen. Ass. Off. Rec. 4th Sess., 6th Comm., Summary Records, Sept. 20–Nov. 29, 1949, 176th meeting, p. 223.

The representative of the Dominican Republic in the Sixth Committee (Miguel Ricardo Román) stated: "In international public law more than in any other field, the opinion of jurists played an important role as a source of law. It was important to remember that, under Article 38, paragraph 1, d, of the Statute of the International Court of Justice, judicial decisions and the teachings of the most highly qualified publicists of the various nations could be applied as subsidiary means for the determination of rules of law. It was therefore advisable to recognize the value of the work accomplished by the eminent jurists of the International Law Commission. . . ." U.N. Gen. Ass. Off. Rec. 4th Sess., 6th Comm., Summary Records, Sept. 20–Nov. 29, 1949, 173d meeting, p. 207.

With reference to the matter of considering the Draft Declaration on Rights and Duties of States prepared by the International Law Commission as a source of law, i.e., as the work of eminent jurists apart from whatever legal standing the Declaration might have or come to have, Professor Chaumont of France commented:

> "Owing to the currents of conflicting doctrines represented in the Commission, the declaration could not be the reflection of positive law, or of the teachings of the publicists composing the Commission who had had to sacrifice, at least in part, their personal opinions. Therefore, it could not reasonably be said that the declaration should constitute a source of law in the sense of Article 38, paragraph 1 d, of the Statute of the International Court of Justice." Statement, Oct. 25, 1949. U.N. Gen. Ass. Off. Rec. 4th Sess., 6th Comm., Summary Records, Sept. 20–Nov. 29, 1949, 172d meeting, pp. 196–197.

The Australian representative (Mr. Glasheen) on the Sixth Committee of the General Assembly stated with reference to the same matter that "while some articles represented the codification of the principles of positive law, others such as articles 4, 6, 8, 9, and 10 could be described as representing the progressive development of international law"; that the teachings of publicists referred to in Article 38, paragraph 1(d) of the Statute of the International Court of Justice "could concern only existing international law, not that of the future", and that "Consequently, he shared the doubts expressed by the French delegation that the draft declaration could be considered as a source of law within the meaning of Article 38 of the aforesaid Statute since it was not covered by any part of paragraph 1 of that Article." U.N. Gen. Ass. Off. Rec. 4th Sess.,

6th Comm., Summary Records, Sept. 20–Nov. 29, 1949, 176th meeting, p. 226.

At the same meeting—the 176th—the representative of Poland (Mr. Krajewski) observed that "The representative of France had rightly observed that Article 38 of the Statute of the International Court of Justice could not embrace the draft under consideration and that, in view of the contradictory opinions expressed in the International Law Commission during the drafting of the declaration, the draft could not be regarded as a reflection of positive law. Mr. Chaumont had nevertheless proposed (A/C.6/L.48) that the draft be used as a guide to international law and its progressive development. It was reasonable to wonder how an incomplete combination of elements of positive law and simple desires could serve as a guide in determining international law. . . ." *Ibid.*, p. 228.

International Agreements

§ 5

". . . There is no doubt that, when all or most of the Great Powers have deliberately agreed to certain rules of general application, the rules approved by them have very great weight in practice even among States which have never expressly consented to them. . . . As among men, so among nations, the opinions and usage of the leading members in a community tend to form an authoritative example for the whole. A striking proof of this tendency was given in the war of 1898 between Spain and the United States. Neither belligerent was a party to the article of the Declaration of Paris of 1856 against privateering; the United States had in fact refused to join in it. . . . Nevertheless, when the war of 1898 broke out, the United States proclaimed its intention of adhering to the Declaration of Paris, and the rules thereby laid down were in fact observed by both belligerents. . . .

"On the whole then the law of nations rests on a general consent which, though it may be supplemented, influenced, and to some extent defined, by express convention, can never be completely formulated under existing conditions. This is as much as to say that the law of nations must be classed with customary law."

Pollock, "Sources of International Law", 18 L.Q. Rev. (1902) 418–419.

"The nineteenth century is, however, specially distinguished for the modification and improvement of international law by what may be called acts of international legislation. Among the sources of international law the publicists commonly enumerate the stipulations of treaties. Where a certain rule of action is uniformly embodied in a succession of treaties between the leading Powers of the world, it assumes in course of time the character of a principle of international law. . . ."

John Bassett Moore, "Progress of International Law in the Century", II *Collected Papers of John Bassett Moore* (1944) 439, 445; reprinted from *The Nineteenth Century* (New York, 1901) 18–31.

Professor Krylov of the Union of Soviet Socialist Republics, speaking at the 1956 session of the International Law Association, discussing sources of international law, stated:

"I should like to say a few words concerning Lord Justice Hodson's remarks. He quoted a statement made by Mr. Bartoš to the effect that the Soviet doctrine with respect to international law does not recognize all the rules of international law but only a few, on the basis of political considerations. The same thought has been expressed by many Soviet writers. I do not share this way of thinking. I believe that all the rules of international law are binding on all States, if such rules correspond to the real needs of a peace policy. The Soviets, as I made it clear in my lecture at the Academy of The Hague, prefer to base their doctrine on bilateral and multilateral treaties of an equalitarian character. Practice is not a source of the same significance as the treaty. In recent years, there have been new sources of international law, such as, for instance, the decisions and resolutions unanimously adopted by the General Assembly of the United Nations. It goes without saying that the rules of international law are binding only on those who are parties to the treaty and that a number of rules, such as those of British colonial constitutional law are, as far as the Soviet Union is concerned, *res inter alios acta*.

"In conclusion, I should like to state once more that the active participation of Soviet jurists in the work of our Association may lead to mutual understanding."

International Law Association, *Report of the Forty-Seventh Conference, 1956* (1957) 42, 43 (translation).

"It is a common lay error to draw a sharp distinction between treaties and international law in general. Many who are not aware of the operation of the international legal process are wont to assert that 'there isn't any international law,' but that treaties are something different. . . . This reasoning overlooks the fact that no agreement has legal significance except against the background of a system of law which attaches legal consequences to the contractual act. . . . The confusion in the lay mind has not been dissipated by the common practice in the United States of referring to international law as embracing only customary law, which, to be sure, includes the law of treaties but not the treaties themselves. Thus it is frequently said that international conduct is regulated by international law and treaties. The European practice of distinguishing between customary and contractual international law and including both types when the term 'international law' is used alone is more helpful."

Jessup, *A Modern Law of Nations* (1948) 124, 125.

"It has often been pointed out that, in one sense, any binding agreement, even a bilateral one, 'makes' law (the so-called 'particular international law') for the subjects to it . . . aside from the preexisting law against the background of which the treaty is made."

Wilson, *The International Law Standard in Treaties of the United States* (1953) 2. At another point, Professor Wilson states:

". . . Seen from the point of view of preëxisting [international] rules, treaties afford means of affirming these rules, or of adapting, varying, suspending, or supplementing them in the relations of the parties *inter se.*" *Ibid.* 1.

"International law embodies the rules and principles established by international legislation . . .

"International legislation, often referred to as conventional law, includes the rules and principles contained in multipartite treaties and conventions, the number of which has greatly increased during the past fifty years. Rules and principles of international law may even become established as a consequence of their embodiment in a great number of bipartite treaties; thus, recent American and British treaties with China refer to 'the principles of international law and practice as reflected in the modern international procedure and in the modern treaties' concluded by the parties with other States. International legislation may also include some of the acts promulgated by organs of the Community of States, to the extent that such organs have been empowered to make dispositions which are binding on States; thus, in the *Mavrommatis Case*, Judge John Bassett Moore referred to the Palestine mandate as being 'in a sense a legislative act of the Council' of the League of Nations."

The International Law of the Future: Postulates, Principles and Proposals (Carnegie Endowment for International Peace, 1944) 25–26.

The International Law Commission of the United Nations included the following text in its Draft Declaration on Rights and Duties of States:

"Every State has the duty to carry out in good faith its obligations arising from treaties and other sources of international law, and it may not invoke provisions in its constitution or its laws as an excuse for failure to perform this duty." (Article 13.)

In the course of the Commission's consideration of an appropriate text for this article, the Chairman (Professor Hudson) stated that he "thought it was difficult to regard a treaty as a source of international law".

Report of the International Law Commission, 1st sess., 1949 (A/925), pp. 8–9; International Law Commission, 1st sess., 13th meeting, May 2, 1949, *Yearbook of the International Law Commission 1949*, pp. 103, 288. The expression "treaties and other sources of international law" is employed in the third paragraph of the Preamble to the Charter of the United Nations, and for that reason the Commission decided to employ that language in its draft of article 13.

"Article 38 of the Statute provides that the Court shall apply 'international conventions, whether general or particular, establishing rules expressly recognized by the contesting States.' The term *conventions* is used here, as in Article 63, in a general and inclusive sense. It would seem to apply to any treaty, convention, protocol, or agreement, regardless of its title or form. A convention may be *general* either because of the number of parties to it, or because of the character of its contents; it may be *particular* because of the limited number of parties, or because of the limited character of its subject-matter. A special agreement (*compromis*) or a stipulation between contesting parties may be in this sense a *particular convention.* The phrase *general or particular* seems to add little to the meaning in this connection.

"The phrase *establishing rules expressly recognized by the contesting States* seems to place two limitations upon the conventions which the Court is to apply: a limitation based upon the subject-matter of the instrument, and a limitation based upon the identity of the parties to the instrument. Yet it may be doubted whether the phrase creates either of these limitations. No precise distinction can be drawn between rule-establishing and other conventions. Any instrument which creates obligations for the States which are parties to it, which regulates the conduct of those States in any way, may be said to establish rules (Fr., *règles*) in a broad sense of the term. The rule-form may not be given to the obligation; it may be stated as a principle rather than as a rule, yet no reason exists for a limitation on the Court's application of the instrument for this reason. It was certainly not the purpose to restrict the Court to the application of what are sometimes called law-making treaties or conventions, like the Declaration of Paris of 1856 concerning maritime law. Moreover, a State may have recognized a rule established by a convention though it is not a party to the convention. It has frequently occurred that States have admitted formulations made by other States to be proper statements of the law and as such binding for themselves. In the course of years the classification of diplomatic agents embodied in the Protocol of Vienna of March 9, 1815 was accepted by most States without any formal accession, and the rules thus established may now be said to have been recognized by many States not parties to the Protocol. This result may be reached without saying that the rules have been incorporated into customary law, and it seems to be covered by the phrase in Article 38(1). To the extent that the rules laid down in an instrument must have been recognized by the contesting States before the Court, that phrase is limitative, but not otherwise."

Hudson, *The Permanent Court of International Justice, 1920–1942* (1943) 608–609. Hudson points out that "In the *Austrian-German Customs Régime Case*, the Court said that obligatory international engagements 'may be taken in the form of treaties, conventions, declarations, agreements, protocols, or exchange of notes.' Series A/B, No. 41, p. 47." He also points out that "In the *Eastern Greenland Case*, it recognized an oral statement as a binding undertaking.   Series A'/B, No. 53, p. 73."   In this connection, Hudson also comments: "The repeated formulation of a principle over a number of years in numerous international instruments may lead to a conclusion that the principle forms a part of the common international law."   Hudson, *ibid.*, notes 37, 38.

In addressing itself to the capacity of an international organization to bring an international claim against responsible governments for reparations when the defendant state is not a member of the organization, the International Court of Justice indicated in its advisory opinion on "Reparation for Injuries Suffered in the Service of the United Nations", the significance of an international agreement as a source of law when it declared: "fifty States, representing the vast majority of the members of the international community, had the power in conformity with international law, to bring into being an entity possessing objective international personality, and not merely personality recognized by them alone, together with capacity to bring international claims".

Reparation for Injuries Suffered in the Service of the United Nations, Advisory Opinion, Apr. 11, 1949, I.C.J. Reports (1949) 174, 185.

". . . It is useful to draw attention to the view according to which the incorporation in a treaty of certain rules and principles suggests that these rules and principles have not hitherto formed part of the law.   The court [the I.C.J.] relied on that reasoning in the *Asylum* Case when it stated that 'the fact that it was considered necessary to incorporate in that [the Montevideo] Convention an article accepting the right of unilateral qualification, seems to indicate that this solution was regarded as a new rule not recognised by the Havana Convention. . . .' "

Lauterpacht, *The Development of International Law by the International Court* (1958) 377.

"We seek honestly to try to follow policies that will sustain the basic principles of world law which we believe to be the indispensable foundation for peace.   Thus, we acted in 1956 in relation to Suez for precisely the same reasons that led us to act as we did in 1958 in relation to Lebanon, namely, to support, as we saw it, the principles of the United Nations Charter.

"To paraphrase George Washington's words, our conduct may be novel, but sound policy enjoins it.

"Unless the nations of the world will accept and abide by certain principles which are written into the charter as world law, then peace is in constant jeopardy."

Secretary of State Dulles, address before the Veterans of Foreign Wars, New York, N.Y., Aug. 18, 1958, XXXIX *Bulletin*, Department of State, No. 1002, Sept. 8, 1958, pp. 373, 377.

Custom

§6

"Art. 38 of the Statute also directs the Court to apply 'international custom, as evidence of a general practice accepted as law.' This might have been cast more clearly as a provision for the Court's applying customary international law. It seems to emphasize the general law, as opposed to the special law embodied in conventions accepted by the parties. It is not possible for the Court to apply a custom; instead, it can observe the general practice of States, and if it finds that such practice is due to a conception that the law requires it, it may declare that a rule of law exists and proceed to apply it. The elements necessary are the concordant and recurring action of numerous States in the domain of international relations, the conception in each case that such action was enjoined by law, and the failure of other States to challenge that conception at the time."

Hudson, *The Permanent Court of International Justice, 1920–42* (1943) 609. Mr. Hudson states in a footnote:

"Series A, No. 10, pp. 18, 21, 23, 28, 31. Judge Nyholm, dissenting, said: 'The ascertainment of a rule of international law implies consequently an investigation of the way in which customs acquire consistency and thus come to be considered as constituting rules governing international relations. . . . There must have been acts of State accomplished in the domain of international relations, whilst mere municipal laws are insufficient; moreover, the foundation of a custom must be the united *will* of several and even of many States constituting a *union of wills*, or a general *consensus of opinion* among the countries which have adopted the European system of civilization, or a manifestation of *international legal ethics* which takes place through the continual recurrence of events with an *innate consciousness of their being necessary.*' (Pp. 59–60.) Judge Altamira, also dissenting, said that in the process of the development of a customary rule there are often 'moments in time in which the rule, implicitly discernible, has not as yet taken shape in the eyes of the world, but is so forcibly suggested by precedents that it would be rendering good service to the cause of justice and law to assist its appearance in a form in which it will have all the force rightly belonging to rules of positive law appertaining to that category.' (Pp. 106–7.)
"*Cf.*, Judge Negulesco's dissent in the *Danube Commission Case*, in which he spoke of 'the necessity of immemorial usage consisting both of an uninterrupted recurrence of accomplished facts in the sphere of international relations and of ideas of justice common to the participating States and based upon the mutual convictions that the recurrence of these facts is the result of a compulsory rule.' Series B, No. 14, p. 105. See also *ibid.*, p. 114." Footnote 41, *ibid.* 610.

". . . The rules thereof [private international law or the doctrine of the conflict of laws] may be common to several States and may even be established by international conventions or customs, and in the latter case may possess the character of true international law governing the relations between States. . . ."

Payment of Various Serbian Loans Issued in France (France and the Serb-Croat-Slovene State), Permanent Court of International Justice,

Judgment, July 12, 1929, Series A, Nos. 20/21, pp. 5, 41; II Hudson, *World Court Reports* (1935) 340, 371.

The Court, although holding in the case concerning *Conditions of Admission to Membership in the United Nations* that political considerations could not constitute conditions in addition to those enumerated in article 4, nevertheless stated in an indirect reference to the principle prohibiting the abuse of rights, "Article 4 does not forbid the taking into account of any factor which it is possible reasonably and in good faith to connect with the conditions laid down in that Article. . . ."

Judge Azevedo in his individual opinion referred directly to this principle of good faith as applied to the exercise of rights when he said:

"Any legal system involves limitations and is founded on definite rules which are always ready to reappear as the constant element of the construction, whenever the field of action of discretionary principles, adopted in exceptional circumstances, is overstepped.

"This is a long-established principle, and has served, during centuries, to limit the scope of the principle *qui suo jure utitur neminem laedit.*

"The concept of the misuse of rights has now been freed from the classical notions of *dolus* and *culpa;* in the last stage of the problem an enquiry into intention may be discarded, and attention may be given solely to the objective aspect; i.e., it may be presumed that the right in question must be exercised in accordance with standards of what is normal, having in view the social purpose of the law."

Conditions of Admission of a State to Membership in the United Nations (Article 4 of the Charter), Advisory Opinion, May 28, 1948, I.C.J. Reports (1947–1948) 56, 63, 80.

"It is, in the opinion of the Court, generally recognized and in accordance with international custom that States in time of peace have a right to send their warships through straits used for international navigation between two parts of the high seas without the previous authorization of a coastal State, provided that the passage is *innocent.* . . ."

The Corfu Channel Case (United Kingdom *v.* Albania), Judgment (Merits), Apr. 9, 1949, I.C.J. Reports (1949) 4, 28.

". . . it is quite true that no international court is bound by precedents. But there is something which this Court is bound to take into account, namely the principles of international law. If a precedent is firmly based on such a principle, the Court cannot decide an analogous case in a contrary sense, so long as the principle retains its value."

Judge Zoričić, *Interpretation of Peace Treaties with Bulgaria, Hungary and Romania*, Advisory Opinion, Mar. 30, 1950, I.C.J. Reports (1950) 65, 104, dissenting opinion.

". . . In order properly to apply the rule [base lines drawn so as to respect the general direction of the coast], regard must be had for the relation between the deviation complained of and what, according to the terms of the rule, must be regarded as the *general* direction of the coast. Therefore, one can not confine oneself to examining one sector of the coast alone, except in a case of manifest abuse . . .

. . . .

". . . Such rights [rights reserved to the inhabitants of the Kingdom in the 1935 delimitation], founded on the vital needs of the population and attested by very ancient and peaceful usage, may legitimately be taken into account in drawing a line which, moreover, appears to the Court to have been kept within the bounds of what is moderate and reasonable."

Fisheries Case (United Kingdom *v.* Norway), Judgment, Dec. 18, 1951, I.C.J. Reports (1951) 116, 142.

"What are the principles of international law which the Court must have recourse to and, if necessary, adapt? And what are the principles which it must in reality create?

. . . .

"In the first place, many of the principles, particularly the great principles, have their origin in the legal conscience of peoples (the psychological factor). This conscience results from social and international life; the requirements of this social and international life naturally give rise to certain norms considered necessary to govern the conduct of States *inter se*.

"As a result of the present dynamic character of the life of peoples, the principles of the law of nations are continually being created, and they undergo more or less rapid modification as a result of the great changes occurring in that life.

"For the principles of law resulting from the juridical conscience of peoples to have any value, they must have a tangible manifestation, that is to say, they must be expressed by authorized bodies.

"Up to the present, this juridical conscience of peoples has been reflected in conventions, customs and the opinions of qualified jurists.

"But profound changes have occurred in this connection. *Conventions* continue to be a very important form for the expression of the juridical conscience of peoples, but they generally lay down only new principles, as was the case with the Convention on genocide. On the other hand, *customs* tend to disappear as the result of the rapid changes of modern international life; and a new case strongly stated may be sufficient to render obsolete an ancient custom. Customary law, to which such frequent reference is made in the course of the arguments, should therefore be accepted only with prudence.

"The further means by which the juridical conscience of peoples may be expressed at the present time are the resolutions of diplomatic assemblies, particularly those of the United Nations and especially the decisions of the International Court of Justice. Reference must also be made to the recent legislation of certain countries, the resolutions of the great associations devoted to the study of the law of nations, the works of the Codification Commission set up by the United Nations, and finally, the opinions of qualified jurists." Judge Alvarez, *Fisheries Case* (United Kingdom *v.* Norway), Judgment, Dec. 18, 1951, I.C.J. Reports (1951) 116, 148, 149, individual opinion.

In answer to the contention made in the case concerning Reservations to the Genocide Convention, that a general rule of international law required unanimous consent of all signatories of a treaty to a reservation appended by a state desiring to become a party thereto, the Court declared:

"It does not appear, moreover, that the conception of the absolute integrity of a convention has been transformed into a rule of international law. The considerable part which tacit assent has always played in estimating the effect which is to be given to reservations scarcely permits one to state that such a rule exists, determining with sufficient precision the effect of objections made to reservations. In fact, the examples of objections made to reservations appear to be too rare in international practice to have given rise to such a rule".

Reservations to the Convention on the Prevention and Punishment of the Crime of Genocide, Advisory Opinion, May 28, 1951, I.C.J. Reports (1951) 15, 24, 25.

"An international obligation may arise through local custom. If for a considerable period of time Portugal has been exercising this right, then the right may be upheld by international law. But in order that local custom should be established, it is not sufficient for Portugal merely to state that for a long period she maintained communications between Daman and the enclaves. She must go further and establish that the transit facilities that she had were enjoyed by her as a matter of right and not as a matter of grace or concession on the part of the Indian Government. . . . Therefore, India is right when she says that a right of passage subject to be revoked in whole or in part by somebody else is not a right at all. I think that Portugal realizes the weakness of her case under this head and therefore what has been really urged before us by Portugal is that this right which she claims is warranted by general principles of international law. General principles of international law would be applicable if Portugal establishes a general custom in contradistinction to a local custom by which a State has the right to have access to enclaves by transit facilities being given to her in order to maintain communications between herself and her enclaves. Now the only general custom which is comparable to the question we have to consider which international law recognizes is the right of innocent passage in territorial seas and in maritime parts of international rivers, and also immunity given to diplomatic representatives when they are in transit between one State and another. No general custom has ever been established permitting a State to have access to her enclaves as of right. Portugal has relied on a learned study made by Professor Bauer of other enclaves, but this study only shows that the right of passage either arises out of treaty or out of local custom which is not applicable to the present case.

"A principle of international law may also be imported from municipal law where the principle in municipal law is universally recognized and when that principle is not in conflict with any rule of international law itself; and the strongest reliance is placed by Portugal on the principle of municipal law which may be described as an easement of necessity. . . . In my opinion, it would be extremely unsafe to draw an analogy between the rights of an owner and the obligations of other owners under municipal law and the rights and obligations of States under international law. There can be no comparison between private property and territorial sovereignty nor can there be any comparison between a citizen and a sovereign State. A sovereign State can pass any legislation affecting private property. It can compel the owner of land to cede any right to neighboring owners. But that surely cannot be true of territorial sovereigns. Portugal cannot compel India to cede any right to her nor can India be placed under any obligation because Portugal is under a necessity to have access to her enclaves. Further, such a rule would obviously be in contradiction with the one undisputed well-established principle of international law, namely, territorial sovereignty, and therefore there is no scope for importing this principle of municipal law into the domain of international law.

". . . In this case, the relations between Portugal and the territorial sovereign of India clearly demonstrate that the conditions of Portugal's passage or transit over Indian territory were clearly settled and those conditions were that Portugal had no right to a passage or transit but she could only be afforded such facilities as the Indian government, in its absolute discretion, thought fit to concede. Therefore, Portugal has failed to make out any case, let alone an arguable case, that India's discretion with regard to this particular subject-matter, which clearly falls within her own domestic jurisdiction, is controlled by any international obligation or that there is any rule of international law which takes this matter out of the reserved domain. . . ."

Judge Chagla, *Case Concerning Right of Passage Over Indian Territory* (Portugal *v.* India), Judgment (Preliminary Objection), Nov. 26, 1957, I.C.J. Reports (1957) 125, 176–178, dissenting opinion.

"Article 24 of the Statute of the International Law Commission provides:

" 'The commission shall consider ways and means for making the evidence of customary international law more readily available, such as the collection and publication of documents concerning State practice and of the decisions of national and international courts on questions of international law. . . .'

. . . .

"Perhaps the differentiation between conventional international law and customary international law ought not to be too rigidly insisted upon, however. A principle or rule of customary international law may be embodied in a bipartite or multipartite agreement so as to have, within the stated limits, conventional force for the States parties to the agreement so long as the agreement is in force; yet it would continue to be binding as a principle or rule of customary international law for other States. Indeed, not infrequently conventional formulation by certain States of a practice also followed by other States is relied upon in efforts to establish the existence of a rule of customary international law. Even multipartite conventions signed but not brought into force are frequently regarded as having value as evidence of customary international law. For present purposes, therefore, the Commission deems it proper to take some account of the availability of the materials of conventional international law in connexion with its consideration of ways and means for making the evidence of customary international law more readily available.

"Article 24 of the Statute of the Commission seems to depart from the classification in Art. 38 of the Statute of the Court, by including judicial decisions on questions of international law among the evidences of customary international law. The departure may be defended logically, however, for such decisions, particularly those by international courts, may formulate and apply principles and rules of customary international law. Moreover, the practice of a State may be indicated by the decisions of its national courts."

Report of I.L.C. to the General Assembly on Work of Second Session, II *Yearbook of International Law Commission 1950*, pp. 367, 368.

"International practice is affected by the tensions which exist today as seriously as is the conclusion of international agreements. Untroubled times are conducive to the kind of generally accepted and lasting practice which turns into law. But at the present time practice is not contributing as much as it should to the law. We can all remember instances over the past few years when the practice of nations, large and small, has changed from case to case, so that courses of conduct have seemed to be decided upon a basis of temporary expediency rather than of principle.

"The existence of international organizations, and in particular the United Nations, means that there is an important new source of customary international law. The decisions of such organizations, if taken with due consideration and consistently adhered to, can afford abundant and easily accessible evidence of the growth of international custom. . . ."

Dr. Ivan S. Kerno, Assistant Secretary-General in Charge of the Legal Department of the United Nations, "International Law and International

Organization: Prospects for the Future", *Proceedings of the American Society of International Law* (1952) 12, 13.

". . . International custom is recognized and applied in diplomatic relations."

Krylov, "Les Notions Principales du Droit des Gens", ch. 1, "La Notion de Droit International", 70 *Recueil Des Cours* (1947, vol. I) 415–416 (translation).

"The practice of States, evidenced by the pronouncements of executive, diplomatic, and at times judicial agencies, is the basis of the customary international law. Before it can be said to establish a rule or principle of international law, a practice must be concordant and general, and it must be to some extent continuous. The practice of one State or the practice of several States, even though continuous, may not result in establishing rules and principles of international law."

The International Law of the Future: Postulates, Principles and Proposals (Carnegie Endowment for International Peace, 1944) 26.

In the *Asylum Case* between Colombia and Peru, the International Court of Justice stated:

"The Colombian Government has finally invoked 'American international law in general'. In addition to the rules arising from agreements which have already been considered, it has relied on an alleged regional or local custom peculiar to Latin-American States.

"The party which relies on a custom of this kind must prove that this custom is established in such a manner that it has become binding on the other Party. The Colombian Government must prove that the rule invoked by it is in accordance with a constant and uniform usage practised by the States in question, and that this usage is the expression of a right appertaining to the State granting asylum and a duty incumbent on the territorial State. This follows from Article 38 of the Statute of the Court, which refers to international custom 'as evidence of a general practice accepted as law'.

"In support of its contention concerning the existence of such a custom, the Colombian Government has referred to a large number of extradition treaties which, as already explained, can have no bearing on the question now under consideration. It has cited conventions and agreements which do not contain any provision concerning the alleged rule of unilateral and definitive qualification such as the Montevideo Convention of 1889 on international penal law, the Bolivarian Agreement of 1911 and the Havana Convention of 1928. It has invoked conventions which have not been ratified by Peru, such as the Montevideo Conventions of 1933 and 1939. The Convention of 1933 has, in fact, been ratified by not more than eleven States and the Convention of 1939 by two States only.

"It is particularly the Montevideo Convention of 1933 which Counsel for the Colombian Government has also relied on in this connexion. It is contended that this Convention has merely codified principles which were already recognized by Latin-American custom, and that it is valid against Peru as a proof of customary law. The limited number of States which have ratified this Convention reveals the weakness of this argument, and furthermore, it is invalidated by the preamble which states that this Convention modifies the Havana Convention.

"Finally, the Colombian Government has referred to a large number of particular cases in which diplomatic asylum was in fact granted and respected. But it has not shown that the alleged rule of unilateral and definitive qualification was invoked or—if in some cases it was in fact invoked—that it was, apart from conventional stipulations, exercised by the States granting asylum as a right appertaining to them and respected by the territorial States as a duty incumbent on them and not merely for reasons of political expediency. The facts brought to the knowledge of the Court disclose so much uncertainty and contradiction, so much fluctuation and discrepancy in the exercise of diplomatic asylum and in the official views expressed on various occasions, there has been so much inconsistency in the rapid succession of conventions on asylum, ratified by some States and rejected by others, and the practice has been so much influenced by considerations of political expediency in the various cases, that it is not possible to discern in all this any constant and uniform usage, accepted as law, with regard to the alleged rule of unilateral and definitive qualification of the offence.

"The Court cannot therefore find that the Colombian Government has proved the existence of such a custom. But even if it could be supposed that such a custom existed between certain Latin-American States only, it could not be invoked against Peru which, far from having by its attitude adhered to it, has, on the contrary, repudiated it by refraining from ratifying the Montevideo Conventions of 1933 and 1939, which were the first to include a rule concerning the qualification of the offence in matters of diplomatic asylum."

Asylum Case (Colombia/Peru), Judgment, Nov. 20, 1950, I.C.J. Reports (1950) 265, 276–278.

See also Briggs, "The Colombian-Peruvian Asylum Case and Proof of Customary International Law", 45 Am. J. Int'l L. (1951) 728–731.

"The sixth contention of the United States is that its consular jurisdiction and other capitulatory rights in Morocco are founded upon 'custom and usage'.

· · · · · · ·

"In the present case there has not been sufficient evidence to enable the Court to reach a conclusion that a right to exercise consular jurisdiction founded upon custom or usage has been established in such a manner that it has become binding on Morocco."

Case Concerning Rights of Nationals of the United States of America in Morocco (France v. United States of America), Judgment, Aug. 27, 1952, I.C.J. Reports (1952) 176, 199–200.

"The Court is thus led to conclude that the method of straight [base] lines, established in the Norwegian system, was imposed by the peculiar geography of the Norwegian coast; that even before the dispute arose, this method had been consolidated by a constant and sufficiently long practice, in the face of which the attitude of governments bears witness to the fact that they did not consider it to be contrary to international law."

Fisheries Case (United Kingdom v. Norway), Judgment, Dec. 18, 1951, I.C.J. Reports (1951) 116, 139. In his dissenting opinion Judge Read said:

"Customary international law is the generalization of the practice of States. This cannot be established by citing cases where coastal States have made extensive claims, but have not maintained their claims by the actual assertion of sovereignty over trespassing foreign ships. Such claims may be important as starting points, which, if not challenged, may ripen into historic title in the course of time." *Ibid.* 191.

Commenting upon this opinion, Sir Gerald Fitzmaurice states:

". . . While this point of view must probably not be pressed so far as to rule out the probative value, and the contribution to the formation of usage and custom, of State professions in their various forms (legislation, declarations, diplomatic statements, *etc.*), it is believed to be a sound principle that, in the long run, it is only the actions of States that build up practice, just as it is only practice ('constant and uniform', as the Court has said [in the *Asylum* case, I.C.J., 1950 Reports, p. 277]) that constitutes a usage or custom, and builds up eventually a rule of customary international law." Fitzmaurice, "The Law and Procedure of the International Court of Justice, 1951–54: General Principles and Sources of Law", XXX Brit. Yb. Int'l L. (1953) 1, 68.

". . . As flexible as it is, the growth of custom demands a minimum of stability. It cannot develop when state activities, because of their equivocal character and contradictory manifestations, cease to become crystallized in 'a general practice accepted as law' (Article 38 of the Statute of the International Court of Justice). The margin allowed for abstention, tolerance, the slow consolidation by the action of time, recedes when the abrupt development of new needs impels governments to take unilateral positions which are often reckless and inspired by an individualistic conception of sovereign rights. It cannot be denied that the traditional development of custom is ill suited to the present pace of international relations.

"We should be careful not to confuse this small productivity of custom with the tendency to particularize or individualize in the application of customary rules, which is already noticeable in certain recent judicial decisions. Certain authors have indicated uneasiness on this subject, and have expressed criticisms of the jurisprudence of the International Court of Justice which appear hardly justified to us.

"Some have reproved the Court for having followed too narrow a conception of custom so as to limit its field of application, and particularly for having avoided the exposition of firm and general criteria permitting the conclusion with certainty and, in some respects, *a priori*, of the existence of a customary rule. Still less than any other custom, international custom does not lend itself to the establishment of such criteria. The selection of the factual elements which, viewed as a whole, lead in a given case to the admission of the existence of a customary rule is subject to extremely variable considerations; it hardly permits efforts toward systematization.

"Other authors have devoted themselves with more justification to examining the logical process of the individualization of customary rules such as appears in certain decisions of the International Court of Justice, and more particularly in the *Fisheries Case* (United Kingdom-Norway, Judgment of December 18, 1951). We do not believe that any contribution is made to the clarification of the question by reasoning in abstract terms on the general relations between rules and exceptions. There is too much risk of being confined to a '*petitio principii.*' What is really important in order to comprehend the exact significance of what the Court in the *Fisheries Case* envisaged, not as an exception but as an 'application of general international law to a specific case,' is to remember the function of custom and its necessarily evolutionary character. The customary rule is a source of living law only insofar as, by adhering to the flexibility of its own process, it is capable of providing courts 'with an adequate basis for their decisions, which can be adapted to the diverse facts in question.' [I.C.J. 1951 Reports, p. 133.] Far from denoting a disintegration of the law, these adaptations, as long as they are inspired by the realities of international practice and become operative under the control of the judge, are proofs of the progress of the law. By being individualized in its applications, the rule of law becomes more refined; it is enriched by new additions which permit it to be adapted to situations which are not yet envisaged and to meet the necessities resulting therefrom."

De Visscher, "Reflections on the Present Prospects of International Adjudication", 50 Am. J. Int'l L. (1956) 467, 472–473.

"International Law is more than a scholarly collection of abstract and immutable principles. It is an outgrowth of treaties or agreements between nations and of accepted customs. But every custom has its origin in some single act, and every agreement has to be initiated by the action of some state. Unless we are prepared to abandon every principle of growth for International Law, we cannot deny that our own day has its right to institute customs and to conclude agreements that will themselves become sources of a newer and strengthened International Law. International Law is not capable of development by legislation, for there is no continuously sitting international legislature. Innovations and revisions in International Law are brought about by the action of governments designed to meet a change in circumstances. It grows, as did the Common-law, through decisions reached from time to time in adapting settled principles to new situations. Hence I am not disturbed by the lack of precedent for the inquiry we propose to conduct. . . ."

Report of Robert H. Jackson, United States Representative, *International Conference on Military Trials, London, 1945,* Department of State publication 3080 (1949), pp. 42, 51–52; XII *Bulletin,* Department of State, No. 311, June 10, 1945, pp. 1071, 1076.

"Custom in its legal sense means something more than mere habit or usage; it is a usage felt by those who follow it to be an obligatory one. There must be present a feeling that if the usage is departed from some sort of evil consequence will probably, or at any rate ought to, fall on the transgressor; in technical language there must be a 'sanction', though the exact nature of this need not be very distinctly envisaged. Evidence that a custom in this sense exists in the international sphere can be found only by examining the practice of states; that is to say, we must look at what states do in their relations with one another and attempt to understand why they do it, and in particular whether they recognize an obligation to adopt a certain course, or, in the words of Article 38, we must examine whether the alleged custom shows 'a general practice accepted as law'. Such evidence will obviously be very voluminous and also very diverse. There are multifarious occasions on which persons who act or speak in the name of a state do acts or make declarations which either express or imply some view on a matter of international law. Any such act or declaration may, so far as it goes, be some evidence that a custom, and therefore that a rule of international law, does or does not exist; but, of course, its value as evidence will be altogether determined by the occasion and the circumstances. States, like individuals, often put forward contentions for the purpose of supporting a particular case which do not necessarily represent their settled or impartial opinion; and it is that opinion which has to be ascertained with as much certainty as the nature of the case allows. Particularly important as sources of evidence are diplomatic correspondence; official instructions to diplomatists, consuls, naval and military commanders; acts of state legislation and decisions of state courts, which, we may presume, will not deliberately contravene any rule regarded as a rule of international law by the state; and opinions of law officers, especially when these are published, as they are in the United States.

"In applying the forms of evidence which have been enumerated above in order to establish the existence of an international custom what is sought for is a general recognition among states of a certain practice as obligatory. It would hardly ever be practicable, and all but the strictest of positivists admit that it is not necessary, to show that every state has recognized a certain practice, just as in English law the existence of a valid local custom or custom of trade can be established without proof that every individual in the locality, or engaged in the trade, has practised the custom. This test of *general* recognition is necessarily a vague one; but it is of the nature of customary law, whether national or international, not to be susceptible of exact or final formulation. . . .

"The growth of a new custom is always a slow process, and the character of international society makes it particularly slow in the international sphere. The progress of the law therefore has come to be more and more bound up with that of the law-making treaty. But it is possible even today for new customs to develop and to win acceptance as law when the need is sufficiently clear and urgent. A striking recent illustration of this is the rapid development of the principle of sovereignty over the air."

Brierly, *The Law of Nations* (5th ed., 1955) 60–63.

"Perhaps the most important distinction to be drawn for purposes of analysis is one between customary rules expressed as rights and customary rules expressed as obligations. As well as for those two types of customary rules, different considerations are appropriate for general, regional and exceptional customs respectively. The closer the approximation of a customary right or obligation to an historic or prescriptive right or obligation, the more relevant the doctrine of acquiescence becomes. The *opinio juris* is properly applicable to a practice only when that practice consists of submission to the exercise of a right, that is, when the practice is expressive of an obligation; and even then it is little more than the consequence of previous consent or acquiescence. It is this previous consent or acquiescence which is creative of the obligation: the consequent *opinio juris* may then accurately be said to be expressive of the rule in question, or evidence of it. Thus one difficulty which has perplexed a number of writers may be obviated: namely, how a rule can be created when the States creating it are considered as acting in the conviction that they are applying a pre-existing rule of identical content.

"A consideration of some of the relevant cases, even one as summary as the foregoing, appears to dictate the conclusion that, in practice, courts have tested the validity of rules of customary international law by reference to standards which are less artificial than those suggested by the more orthodox theories of custom. Where the material elements of custom, the constancy and generality of the practice in question, have not of themselves sufficed to satisfy the tribunal, the criterion on which reliance has been consistently placed has been that of general recognition or acceptance of the practice as lawful on the part of other States. Professor Briggs, in his comment on the *Asylum* case, put the matter clearly when he observed that 'the proper way to express the process by which customary international law is created is to say that a particular pattern of state conduct, hitherto legally discretionary, has acquired obligatory force through its general acceptance by states as a legal obligation.' ["The Colombian-Peruvian Asylum Case and Proof of Customary International

Law", in *American Journal of International Law*, 45 (1951), pp.
728–31, at p. 730.]   That general acceptance, or recognition, has
frequently assumed the form of acquiescence, which . . . miti-
gates the rigours of the positivist view and imparts a welcome
measure of controlled flexibility to the process of formation of
rules of customary international law."

Macgibbon, "Customary International Law and Acquiescence", XXXIII
Brit. Yb. Int'l L. (1957) 115, 144–145.   In the course of this article, the
writer discusses "Acquiescence as an element in the development of customary rights and obligations"; "General customary rights and obligations"; "Features common to the development of customary, historic and
prescriptive rights"; "The enhanced value of acquiescence as a result of
the historic or prescriptive character of special or exceptional customary
rights"; "The *opinio juris sive necessitatis*"; "The basis of the binding
force or rules of customary international law"; "Objections to the con-
sensual theory of custom"; and "The test applied by writers and tribunals
to determine the validity of customary rules".

"Custom is the older and the original source of International
Law in particular as well as of law in general [citing numerous
authorities]. . . . Custom must not be confused with usage.   In
everyday life and language both terms are used synonymously,
but in the language of the international jurist they have two distinctly different meanings.   International jurists speak of a *custom* when a clear and continuous habit of doing certain actions
has grown up under the aegis of the conviction that these actions
are, according to International Law, obligatory or right. . . .
Some conduct of States concerning their international relations
may therefore be usual without being the outcome of customary
International Law. . . .
"As usages have a tendency to become custom, the question
presents itself: at what stage does a usage turn into a custom?
This question is one of fact, not of theory.   All that theory can
say is this: Wherever and as soon as a line of international conduct frequently adopted by States is considered legally obligatory or legally right, the rule which may be abstracted from such
conduct is a rule of customary International Law."

I Lauterpacht, *Oppenheim's International Law* (8th ed., 1955) 25–27.

"It is necessary to distinguish between internal laws as evidence of the coming into existence of a customary rule of general
international law [*The Scotia* (U.S. Supreme Court, 1871), 14
Wallace 170] and a mere parallelism of municipal statutes.   [See
Giesler *v.* Giesler's Heirs, Swiss Federal Court, July 11, 1935,
Annual Digest and Reports of Public International Law Cases
1935–1937, pp. 1–2.]"

Kunz, "The Nature of Customary International Law", 47 Am. J. Int'l L.
(1953) 662, 668.

"The fact that a State has adopted a certain practice in matters affecting other States does not in itself prove that it admits

a legal obligation to this effect. To establish a legal duty, it is necessary that States act or refrain from acting on the conviction that they are bound by international law to do so."

I Schwarzenberger, *International Law* (1945) 13.

"It seems necessary to distinguish three cases:

"i. Where a *general* rule of customary international law is built up by the common practice of States, although it may be a little unnecessary to have recourse to the notion of agreement (and a little difficult to detect it in what is often the uncoordinated, independent, if similar, action of States), it is probably true to say that consent is latent in the mutual tolerations that allow the practice to be built up at all; and actually patent in the eventual acceptance (even if tacit) of the practice, as constituting a binding rule of law. It makes no substantial difference whether the new rule emerges in regard to (in effect) a new topic on which international law has hitherto been silent, or as a change in existing law. . . .

"ii. Where a special right different from, and in principle contrary to, the ordinary rule of law applicable, is built up by a particular State or States through a process of prescription—leading to the emergence of a usage or customary or historic right in favour of such State or States—it has already been seen . . . that the element of consent, that is to say, acquiescence with full knowledge, on the part of other States is not only present, but necessary to the formation of the right.

"iii. Special rights, i.e. such as would not exist under ordinary law, may, however, be acquired by one State, not as against the world in general (as under ii), but against another particular State, e.g. in its territory or waters or with reference to its vessels or nationals. This is the case to which the jointly dissenting Judges in the *Morocco* case were referring. [I.C.J. 1952 Reports, p. 220.] While the element of consent may be more difficult to detect here, and may have been lacking at the origin of the matter, it is believed that if the right has developed into a legal right, this is because consent, in the form of acquiescence, was given or can be presumed."

Fitzmaurice, "The Law and Procedure of the International Court of Justice, 1951–54; General Principles and Sources of Law", XXX Brit. Yb. Int'l L. (1953) 1, 68–69.

". . . The analysis of positive law allows us to conclude that all the subjects of law which are in close or even distant touch with international relations contribute to the formation of international custom. We have demonstrated that as a general rule the formation of custom does not depend on the presence in the minds of the parties of an *opinio juris*, but that on the contrary the content of the customary rule often plays the principal part. Sometimes it is merely the satisfactory and reasonable character of the custom which allows a decision whether a particular rule has or has not the character of a legal rule.

"This is where the strength and the weakness of the formation by custom of international law lie: its strength, because this is why custom is more closely adapted to life than legislative rule and consequently offers a better prospect for a satisfactory regulation of human relationships; its weakness, because more often the extra-legal elements which fix the needs of any given society cannot easily be distinguished, whence comes an element of uncertainty as to the existence of a customary rule; we have even seen that this uncertainty subsists when the custom is formed by the judge.

"A remedy might be found in the codification of custom. In view of what has been said above this would seem highly desirable. We are not afraid of the danger of stopping the evolution of custom or of making it lose contact with life. It is not very difficult to prove that the evolution of custom itself tends to a certain traditionalism which would not be in conflict with an attempt to define positive customary law."

Kopelmanas, "Custom as a Means of the Creation of International Law", XVIII Brit. Yb. Int'l L. (1937) 127, 151.

"From the perspective of realistic description, the international law of the sea is not a mere static body of rules but is rather a whole decision-making process, a public order which includes a structure of authorized decision-makers as well as a body of highly flexible, inherited prescriptions. It is, in other words, a process of continuous interaction, of continuous demand and response, in which the decision-makers of particular nation states unilaterally put forward claims of the most diverse and conflicting character to the use of the world's seas, and in which other decision-makers, external to the demanding state and including both national and international officials, weigh and appraise these competing claims in terms of the interests of the world community and of the rival claimants, and ultimately accept or reject them. As such a process, it is a living, growing law, grounded in the practices and sanctioning expectations of nation-state officials, and changing as their demands and expectations are changed by the exigencies of new interests and technology and by other continually evolving conditions in the world arena.

.   .   .   .

"The authoritative decision-makers put forward by the public order of the high seas to resolve all these competing claims include, of course, not merely judges of international courts and other international officials, but also those same nation-state officials who on other occasions are themselves claimants. This duality in function ('*dédoublement fonctionnel*'), or fact that the same nation-state officials are alternately, in a process of reciprocal interaction, both claimants and external decision-makers passing upon the claims of others, need not, however, cause confusion: it merely reflects the present lack of specialization and centralization of policy functions in international law generally. Similarly, it may be further observed, without deprecating the authority of international law, that these authoritative decision-

makers projected by nation states for creating and applying a
common public order, honor each other's unilateral claims to the
use of the world's seas not merely by explicit agreements but also
by mutual tolerances—expressed in countless decisions in foreign
offices, national courts, and national legislatures—which create
expectations that effective power will be restrained and exercised
in certain uniformities of pattern. This process of reciprocal
tolerance of unilateral claim is, too, but that by which in the
present state of world organization most decisions about jurisdiction in public and private international law are, and must be,
taken. [It is not of course the unilateral claims but rather the
reciprocal tolerances of the external decision-makers which create
the expectations of pattern and uniformity in decision, of practice
in accord with rule, commonly regarded as law.]"

McDougal, "The Hydrogen Bomb Tests and the International Law of the
Sea", 49 Am. J. Int'l L. (1955) 356–358.

In connection with this section generally, see also Kelsen, *Théorie du
droit international coutumier, Revue internationale de la théorie du droit*
(1939) ; Scelle, *Droit international public* (1944) 397 ; Sørensen, *Les sources
du droit international* (1946) ; Mateesco, *La coutume dans les cycles
juridiques internationaux* (1947) ; Rousseau, *Principes Généraux du Droit
International Public* (Paris, 1944) 815–862.

General Principles of Law

§7

". . . there has also been a significant widening of the circle
in which are included the states that acknowledge the obligations
and enjoy the advantages of international law. As the law of
nations was originally the product of the Christian states of
Europe, nations were classified, with reference to its acceptance
and rejection, as Christian and non-Christian. With the admission of Turkey, by the Treaty of Paris of 1856, 'to participate in
the advantages of the public law and concert of Europe,' this
classification ceased to be accurate. Lately we have witnessed a
further enlargement of the circle by the admission of Japan.
The admission of those states to the concert of nations does not
signify that the standards of international law have been altered
or abandoned. On the contrary, it denotes a more general acceptance of those standards as the test of advancement in law, in
morals, and in civilization."

John Bassett Moore, "Progress of International Law in the Century",
II *Collected Papers of John Bassett Moore* (1944) 439, 448–449; reprinted
from *The Nineteenth Century* (New York, 1901), pp. 18–31.

"Article 38 of the Statute also directs the Court to apply 'the
general principles of law recognized by civilized nations.' As all
nations are civilized, as 'law implies civilization,' the reference

to 'civilized nations' can serve only to exclude from consideration primitive systems of law. Members of the 1920 Committee of Jurists expressed varying views as to the meaning of this provision when it was drafted, and the confusion was not dissipated by the Committee's report. One of its purposes may have been, under the inspiration of the national legislation of some States, to prevent the Court's abstaining from a decision because 'no positive applicable rule exists.' The provision serves a useful purpose in that it emphasizes the creative role to be played by the Court. It confers such a wide freedom of choice that no fixed and definite content can be assigned to the terms employed. It has been widely hailed as a refutation of the extreme positive conception of international law, and even as revolutionary; on the other hand, it has been deprecated as adding to existing' confusion.

"Taken out of its context, the phrase 'general principles of law recognized by civilized nations' would refer primarily to the general principles of international law; following the provisions in Article 38 relating to international conventions and international custom, however, it must be given a different, perhaps one may say a larger, content. It empowers the Court to go outside the field in which States have expressed their will to accept certain principles of law as governing their relations *inter se*, and to draw upon principles common to various systems of municipal law or generally agreed upon among interpreters of municipal law. It authorizes use to be made of analogies found in the national law of the various States. It makes possible the expansion of international law along lines forged by legal thought and legal philosophy in different parts of the world. It enjoins the Court to consult a *jus gentium* before fixing the limits of the *droit des gens*.

"In the jurisprudence of the Court, this provision looms less large than in the literature which it has inspired. Whether from a sense of caution or because of the nature of the cases which have come before it, the Court has never professed to draw upon 'the general principles of law recognized by civilized nations' in its search for the applicable law. This does not mean that the provision has not influenced the thought and action of the Court, however; in dissenting or separate opinions, individual judges have frequently referred to it. On many occasions the Court has proceeded upon 'principles of international law,' or the 'generally accepted principles of international law,' or 'principles taken from general international law' (Fr., *droit international commun*), but usually without specification of the sources from which they are taken. It has assumed a broad competence to apply international law, and it has not felt itself confined within the limits of a law to be derived from conventions and custom. It has endeavored to give effect to what has been called the *common law* applicable to international affairs, but it has drawn no distinction between common law and customary law, nor between either and general principles of law. So far as the record goes, it fails to justify the view that the provision relating to general principles of law is 'revolutionary.' "

Hudson, *The Permanent Court of International Justice, 1920–1942* (1943) 610–612. Hudson cites generally on the topic: Kopelmanas in 43 *Revue générale de droit international public* (1936) 285–308; Scerni, I *Principi generali di diritto riconosciuti dalle nazioni civili* (1932); and Verdross, in 52 *Recueil Des Cours* (1935) 191–251. On the point of absence of a positive applicable rule of law, he states: "In some States, courts are required to decide cases before them and cannot evade this responsibility because of the non-existence of applicable law. The French Civil Code (Article 4) forbids a judge to refuse to decide under pretext of the silence, obscurity, or insufficiency of the law. The Swiss Civil Code of 1907 (Article 1) requires a judge, in default of applicable code provisions and customary law, to apply the rules which he would establish if he were acting as a legislator. Article 3 of the preliminary part of the Italian Civil Code of 1865 provided for resort to general principles of law when a precise disposition is lacking and analogy fails; this appears in somewhat different form in the Civil Code of 1938. *Cf.*, Article 1 of the Chinese Civil Code of 1929." *Ibid.* n.46.

Hudson further explains: "A suggestion made by Judge Kosters in 1931 led a *rapporteur* of the *Institut de Droit International* to formulate the proposition that in the absence of rules of conventional or customary law and of general principles of law, a tribunal may apply the principles of law common to the contesting States. *Annuaire de l'Institut*, 1932, pp. 303–5, 324–5. Such a principle was applied by the Supreme Court of the United States in *Wyoming* v. *Colorado* (1922) 259 U.S. 419." *Ibid.* 611, n.50.

Hudson also points out that the *Société Commerciale Case* is a clear case in which the Court applied a general principle of *res judicata*. Series A/B. No. 78; Hudson, *op. cit.* 612, n.51.

". . . Any measure affecting the property, rights and interests of German subjects covered by Head III of the Convention, which is not justified on special grounds taking precedence over the Convention, and which oversteps the limits set by the generally accepted principles of international law, is therefore incompatible with the régime established under the Convention. . . ."

German Interests in Polish Upper Silesia and the Factory at Chorzów, Permanent Court of International Justice, Judgment (Merits), May 25, 1926, Series A, No. 7, pp. 4, 22; I Hudson, *World Court Reports* (1934) 510, 523–524.

"The obligations incumbent upon the Albanian authorities consisted in notifying, for the benefit of shipping in general, the existence of a minefield in Albanian territorial waters and in warning the approaching British warships of the imminent danger to which the mine field exposed them. Such obligations are based, not on the Hague Convention of 1907, No. VIII, which is applicable in time of war, but on certain general and well-recognized principles, namely: elementary considerations of humanity, even more exacting in peace than in war; the principle of the freedom of maritime communication; and every State's obligation not to allow knowingly its territory to be used for acts contrary to the rights of other States."

The Corfu Channel Case (United Kingdom *v.* Albania), Judgment (Merits), **Apr. 9, 1949,** I.C.J. Reports (1949) 4, 22.

While the Colombian Government invoked the wording of the Bolivarian Agreement (29 Am. J. Int'l L. Supp. (1935) 282) in connection with its reference to principles of international law regarding asylum, the International Court of Justice said:

"In recognizing 'the institution of asylum', this article merely refers to the principles of international law. But the principles of international law do not recognize any rule of unilateral and definitive qualification by the State granting diplomatic asylum."

Asylum Case (Colombia/Peru), Judgment, Nov. 20, 1950, I.C.J. Reports (1950) 266, 274.

"It may be asked: What are these 'general principles of law recognized by civilized nations'? Where are they to be found? It is not possible to point to any code or book containing them. Much of the content of public international law proper has been developed by tribunals and by writers out of these general principles, and my view is that the same source will prove equally fruitful in the application and interpretation of those contracts which, though not interstate contracts and therefore not governed by public international law *stricto sensu*, can more effectively be regulated by general principles of law than by the special rules of any single territorial system. They will be developed both by contracting parties who realize the suitability of general principles of law and by tribunals which are called upon to adjudicate upon contracts of this type. I do not propose to prepare a list of the rules of law likely to be recognized as 'general principles'. 'Unjust enrichment' has been referred to above in the *Lena Goldfields* Award [Annual Digest, 1929–1930, Case No. 1 at 258; London *Times*, 3 September 1930.], and I shall mention only one other likely candidate, among many, for recognition [Respect for Acquired Rights]."

Lord McNair, "The General Principles of Law Recognized by Civilized Nations", XXXIII Brit. Yb. Int'l L. (1957) 1, 15–16. See Lauterpacht, *Private Law Sources and Analogies of International Law* (1927), which is, in effect, a commentary upon article 38, paragraph I(c) of the Statute of the Court, in particular pp. 67–71; see also Bin Cheng, *General Principles of Law* (1953).

See further the late Professor Gutteridge's discussion of general or universal principles common to civilized nations, in his article on "Comparative Law and the Law of Nations", in XXI Brit. Yb. Int'l L. (1944) 1 ff.

Contending that the status of occupied Germany was that of a state even though—he stated—occupation was neither by subjugation nor through belligerent occupation, Professor Kunz cited the principle of effectivity, "a norm of positive general international law", as a possible basis for establishing the fact of the German state. He argued:

> ". . . As an ultimate construction of the status of occupied Germany it could be said that even if the present status of Germany had been brought about illegally, yet this illegality would have been healed by the norm of effectivity. And this norm is not valid, as is sometimes asserted, only against the aggressor. Italy's conquest of Ethiopia was certainly illegal, but it was effective, and Italy's sovereignty was recognized *de jure* by Great Britain and by many other states."

Kunz, "The Status of Occupied Germany Under International Law: A Legal Dilemma", 3 *Western Political Quarterly* (1950) 538, 562.

Decisions of Tribunals

§ 8

" 'As subsidiary means [Fr., *moyen auxiliaire*] for the determination of rules of law,' the Court is also directed to apply 'judicial decisions and the teachings of the most highly qualified publicists of the various nations'; but this direction is expressly made 'subject to the provisions of Article 59' that 'the decision of the Court has no binding force except between the parties and in respect of that particular case.' Judicial decisions and the teachings of publicists are not rules to be applied, but sources to be resorted to for finding applicable rules. What is meant by *subsidiary* is not clear. It may be thought to mean that these sources are to be subordinated to others mentioned in the article, *i.e.*, to be regarded only when sufficient guidance cannot be found in international conventions, international custom and general principles of law; the French term *auxiliaire* seems, however, to indicate that confirmation of rules found to exist may be sought by referring to jurisprudence and doctrine. In view of the reference to Article 59, the term *judicial decisions* must include decisions of the Court itself; it includes also decisions of other international tribunals and of national courts. As to the decisions of national courts, a useful caution was given by Judge Moore in the *Lotus Case* that international tribunals 'are not to treat the judgments of the courts of one State on questions of international law as binding on other States, but, while giving to such judgments the weight due to judicial expressions of the view taken in the particular country, are to follow them as authority only so far as they may be found to be in harmony with international law.' No standards exist for saying who are 'the most highly qualified publicists of the various nations.' Judge Weiss said in the *Lotus Case* that 'international law is not created by an accumulation of opinions and systems; neither is its source a sum total of judgments, even if they agree with each other.' In the *Brazilian Loans Case*, Judge Bustamante emphasized the importance of the time in which a publicist writes, and observed that 'writers of legal treatises just as much as any one else, without wanting to and without knowing it, come under the irresistible influence of their surroundings, and the requirements of the national situation are reflected in their thoughts and have a great influence on their teachings.'

"In its judgments and opinions, the Court has frequently referred to what it had held and what it had said in earlier judgments and opinions, and within limits it has shown itself disposed to build a consistent body of case-law in its jurisprudence. On several occasions, it has referred to the decisions of other international tribunals: in the *Jaworzina Case*, the *Meerauge Case* decided by an arbitral tribunal in 1902, was cited to sustain a view taken by the Court. In the *Lotus Case*, reference having been made by a party to the *Costa Rica Packet Case* decided by an arbitral tribunal in 1897, it was cited by the Court but found to be distinguishable from the case in hand. In the *Chorzów Case*, it was said that 'in accordance with the jurisprudence of arbitral tribunals' contingent and indeterminate damage could not be taken into account, but no cases were cited. In the *Polish Postal Service Case*, the award of a tribunal of the Permanent Court of Arbitration in the *Pious Fund Case* was cited with approval; and in the *Eastern Greenland Case*, the award of a similar tribunal in the *Palmas Island Case* was cited.

"On the other hand, the Court has shown little disposition to concern itself with the decisions of national courts, even when they have been cited by parties. In the *Chorzów Case*, a bare reference was made to the jurisprudence of municipal courts. In the *Lotus Case*, in which national decisions concerning the jurisdiction of flag-States were cited by both parties, the Court cited some of the cases, but 'without pausing to consider the value to be attributed to the judgments of municipal courts in connection with the establishment of the existence of a rule of international law,' it concluded that the municipal jurisprudence was too divided to give any 'indication of the existence of a restrictive rule of international law'; the judgment of an English court in the *Franconia Case* was examined, but it was said that the conception of international law upon which a majority of the judges may have proceeded was 'peculiar to English jurisprudence,' not 'generally accepted even in common-law countries,' and 'abandoned in more recent English decisions' which were cited. In the *Personal Work of Employers Case*, a reference was made to municipal jurisprudence on the constitutionality of legislation, but no cases were cited. In its application of the rule as to exhaustion of local remedies in the *Panevezys Case*, the Court made an extended examination of the *Jeglinas Case* decided by Lithuanian Courts, but held that no 'course of decisions' of the Lithuanian Courts existed to relieve against the application of the rule. If it is called upon to apply the municipal law of a State, the Court may have to examine the decisions of courts of that State: in the *Serbian* and *Brazilian Loans Cases*, it referred to the 'doctrine' and 'jurisprudence' of French courts, but without citations. In dissenting and separate opinions, decisions of national courts are cited more freely and more frequently."

Hudson, *The Permanent Court of International Justice, 1920–1942* (1943) 612–615. Hudson's citations for cases referred to: *Lotus Case*, Series A, No. 10, pp. 74, 43; *Brazilian Loans Case*, Series A, No. 21, p. 133; *Jaworzina Case*, Series B, No. 8, pp. 42–3; *Meerauge Case*, 3 Martens, *Nouveau recueil général* (3d ser.) 71; *Costa Rica Packet Case*, 5 Moore, Internat. Arbs., p. 4948, 23 Martens, *Nouveau recueil général* (2d ser.) 808; *Chorzów Case*, Series A, No. 17, p. 57, *ibid.*, pp. 31, 47, *idem*, No. 9, p. 31; *Polish Postal Service Case*, Series B, No. 11, p. 30; *Pious Fund Case*, Scott, *Hague Court Reports* (1916) 3; *Eastern Greenland Case*, Series A/B, No. 53, p. 45; *Palmas Island Case*, Scott, *Hague Court Reports* (1932) 84; *Franconia Case*, *Regina* v. *Keyn* (1877) L.R. 2 Ex. Div. 63; *Personal Work of Employers Case*, Series B, No. 13, p. 20; *Panevezys Case*, Series A/B, No. 76, pp. 19–21; *Serbian* and *Brazilian Loans Cases*, Series A, No. 20, p. 47, *idem*, No. 21, pp. 124–125.

"International law embodies the rules and principles established by . . . international judicial decisions, and by the practice of States.

.   .   .   .

"The judicial decisions of international tribunals may also, in some cases, establish rules and principles of international law. All international tribunals are not on the same plane in this regard, however, the decisions of mixed bipartite commissions being obviously of less weight than those of tribunals of a more general character. In the past, few tribunals have had the support of a large number of States, and few have been permitted to function sufficiently continuously to develop a system of case-law; a great advance came with the establishment of the Permanent Court of International Justice. The decisions of national courts too have had influence on the development of international law, but as such courts function subject to national authority their decisions play a secondary rôle and cannot be said to establish rules and principles of law binding upon all States."

The International Law of the Future: Postulates, Principles and Proposals (Carnegie Endowment for International Peace, 1944) 25, 26.

In its Advisory Opinion on Awards of the United Nations Administrative Tribunal, the International Court of Justice referred to its opinion on *Reparation for Injuries Suffered in the Service of the United Nations* (I.C.J. Reports (1949) 182) concerning whether, having regard to its objects, the United Nations must be considered to possess an implied power to establish a judicial tribunal to adjudicate upon contracts of service between the United Nations and its employees. The Court stated:

"According to a well-established and generally recognized principle of law, a judgment rendered by such a judicial body [as the U.N. Administrative Tribunal] is *res judicata* and has binding force between the parties to the dispute."

Effect of Awards of Compensation Made by the United Nations Administrative Tribunal, Advisory Opinion, July 13, 1954, I.C.J. Reports (1954) 47, 53, 56.

A review of the opinions of the International Court of Justice, and also of individual concurring opinions and of dissenting opinions, reveals that, increasingly, previous opinions of the Court and of other international tribunals have been relied on in support of such opinions.

Works of Writers

§ 9

"The teachings of publicists are treated less favorably [than decisions of national courts] at the hands of the Court. No treatise or doctrinal writing has been cited by the Court. In connection with its conclusion in the *Lotus Case* that the existence of a restrictive rule of international law had not been conclusively proved, it referred to 'teachings of publicists' without attempting to assess their value, but it failed to find in them any useful indication. Individual judges have not been so restrained in their references to the teachings of publicists; they have not hesitated to cite living authors, and even the published works of members of the Court itself."

Hudson, *The Permanent Court of International Justice, 1920–1942* (1943) 615. For the *Lotus Case*, Hudson cites Permanent Court of International Justice, Judgment, Sept. 7, 1927, Series A, No. 10, pp. 27, 31. As to references by individual judges, the author cites: *idem*, No. 22, p. 44.

"The Court, having arrived at the conclusion that the arguments advanced by the French Government either are irrelevant to the issue or do not establish the existence of a principle of international law precluding Turkey from instituting the prosecution which was in fact brought against Lieutenant Demons, observes that in fulfilment of its task of itself ascertaining what the international law is, it has not confined itself to a consideration of the arguments put forward, but has included in its researches all precedents, teachings and facts to which it had access and which might possibly have revealed the existence of one of the principles of international law contemplated in the special agreement."

The S. S. Lotus (France and Turkey), Permanent Court of International Justice, Judgment, Sept. 7, 1927, Series A, No. 10, pp. 4, 31; II Hudson, *World Court Reports* (1935) 23, 45.

The International Court of Justice referred to the "opinions of writers" in its opinion in the *Nottebohm Case*. The reference was, however, not to the opinion of an individual writer or writers. In that case the Court referred to the need for genuine connection between a person and the state the nationality of which is claimed, and to the support given to this requirement by international and domestic tribunals. The Court stated:

> "According to the practice of States, to arbitral and judicial decisions and to the opinions of writers, nationality is a legal bond having as its basis a social fact of attachment, a genuine connection of existence, interests and sentiments, together with the existence of reciprocal rights and duties."

Nottebohm Case (Liechtenstein *v.* Guatamala), Judgment, Apr. 6, 1955, I.C.J. Reports (1955) 4, 23.

However, in individual concurring and in individual dissenting opinions with respect to opinions of the International Court of Justice, opinions of publicists have been cited.

Equity; Ex Aequo et Bono

§ 10

"As the Statute fails to provide expressly for the application of international law, so it fails to provide expressly for the Court's application of equity. In 1920, M. de Lapradelle proposed that the Court should 'judge in accordance with law, justice and equity,' and M. Ricci-Busatti would have included 'principles of equity' in what became Article 38 of the Statute; the rejection of these proposals at that time was partly due to the extent of the jurisdiction envisaged for the Court. Prior to 1920, numerous special and general arbitration treaties referred to the application of equity, the term *equity* being almost invariably coupled with *justice* or with *law*. Such references go back for many years, as indicated by a British-Netherlands *règlement* of 1654, and Article 25 of the Netherlands-Portugal treaty of 1661. Several outstanding multipartite instruments refer to equity: *e.g.*, Article 28 of a *règlement* adopted at the Congress of Vienna in 1815 provided for decisions by an arbitral commission *en toute justice, et avec la plus grand equité;* Article 7 of the 1907 Prize Court Convention provided for that Court's applying rules of international law, and where generally recognized rules do not exist *les principes généraux de la justice et de l'equité;* the Treaty of Versailles of 1919 provided that the Reparations Commission should 'not be bound by any particular code or rules of law,' but should be 'guided by justice, equity and good faith'; an annex to the Spitzbergen Treaty of 1920, to which many States were parties, envisaged a tribunal applying rules of international law and the general principles of justice and equity. References to equity have more frequently been made in bipartite treaties: an

American-British treaty of 1794 authorized a claims commission to decide according to 'justice, equity and the law of nations'; in claims conventions of 1853, 1854, 1863 and 1871, the United States and Great Britain required commissioners to take oath to decide 'to the best of their judgment, and according to justice and equity,' and in 1910, they agreed that a tribunal should decide 'in accordance with treaty rights and with principles of international law and of equity.' Both the United States and Great Britain concluded treaties of similar import with other States. Such provision was included, also, in treaties between various American States, and in some treaties between European States. Since 1920, the United States has concluded a series of arbitration treaties applying to disputes 'justiciable in their nature by reason of being susceptible of decision by the application of the principles of law or [and] equity'; and a series of treaties among Scandinavian States has provided for the arbitration of disputes not falling under Article 36 of the Statute of the Court, in accordance with the principles of law and equity. In some cases, also, recent special agreements have continued to refer to equity.

"While the jurisprudence of international tribunals has also associated *equity* with *law*, the tribunals which have been authorized to apply principles of equity have not gone far in determining what these principles are. Clearly, they are not to be derived from the municipal law of any particular State; an American-Norwegian tribunal stated in 1922 that 'the majority of international lawyers seem to agree that these words [law and equity] are to be understood to mean general principles of justice as distinguished from any particular system of jurisprudence or the municipal law of any State.' In 1923 an American-British tribunal held that 'no ground of equity' required the United States to pay compensation for cutting a cable; but in 1926 the same tribunal held that the Cayuga Indians had a 'just' claim against the United States. In 1933, the American-Panamanian Commission found 'no reason to scrutinize' whether the terms international law, justice and equity 'embody an indivisible rule or mean that international law, justice, and equity have to be con sidered in the order in which they are mentioned, because eithei of these constructions leads to the conclusion that the Commission shall be guided rather by broad conceptions than by narrow interpretations.'

"This long and continuous association of equity with the law which is applicable by international tribunals would seem to warrant a conclusion that equity is an element of international law itself. The conceptions introduced into the law as principles of equity cannot be listed with definiteness; but they are not to be discarded because they are vague, for that is a quality attaching to international law itself. They do not permit an individual judge to pursue merely personal predilections, and they must not be taken to undermine the established principles of the law. Their office is to liberalize and to temper the application of law, to prevent extreme injustice in particular cases, to lead into new directions for which received materials point the way. In this view, it may be possible to say that equity is a part of international law in the same way that it has been absorbed by various systems of municipal law, without drawing upon general principles of municipal law; yet it is easier for a tribunal to include equity in the law which it applies if it has been expressly authorized to apply 'the general principles of law recognized by civilized nations.'

"The Court may be said to have applied a principle of equity in the *Meuse Case* in 1937; it compared the Belgian lock against which the Netherlands complained to a lock previously built by the Netherlands, and declared that 'in these circumstances, the Court finds it difficult to admit that the Netherlands are now warranted in complaining of the construction and operation of a lock of which they themselves set an example in the past.' This was a clear application of a principle of equity requiring equality between the parties, as one of the judges stated more explicitly in a separate opinion."

Hudson, *The Permanent Court of International Justice, 1920–1942* (1943) 615–618. For the treaties and agreements referred to, see *ibid.* Hudson's citations to cases referred to: *American-Norwegian Case* (1922), Scott, *Hague Court Reports* (1932) 39; *Eastern Extension Telegraph Company Case*, 1923 American-British Tribunal, Nielsen's *Report*, p. 73; *Cayuga Indians Case, ibid.*, p. 307; *Perry Case*, American-Panamanian Commission, Hunt's *Report*, p. 71; *Meuse Case*, Series A/B, No. 70, p. 4.

Judge Hudson, concurring with the decision of the Court in the case of the *Diversion of Water from the River Meuse*, stated in his individual opinion:

"What are widely known as principles of equity have long been considered to constitute a part of international law, and as such they have often been applied by international tribunals. . . . A sharp division between law and equity, such as prevails in the administration of justice in some States, should find no place in international jurisprudence; even in some national legal systems, there has been a strong tendency towards the fusion of law and equity. Some international tribunals are expressly directed by the *compromis* which control them to apply 'law and equity'. See the Cayuga Indians Case, Nielsen's Report of the United States-British Claims Arbitration (1926), p. 307. Of such a provision, a special tribunal of the Permanent Court of Arbitration said in 1922 that 'the majority of international lawyers seem to agree that these words are to be understood to mean general principles of justice as distinguished from any particular systems of jurisprudence'. Proceedings of the United States-Norwegian Tribunal (1922), p. 141. Numerous arbitration treaties have been concluded in recent years which apply to differences 'which are justiciable in their nature by reason of being susceptible of decision by the application of the principles of law or equity'. Whether the reference in an arbitration treaty is to the application of 'law and equity' or to justiciability dependent on the possibility of applying 'law or equity', it would seem to envisage equity as a part of law.

"The Court has not been expressly authorized by its Statute to apply equity as distinguished from law. Nor, indeed, does the Statute expressly direct its application of international law, though as has been said on several occasions the Court is 'a tribunal of international law'. Series A, No. 7, p. 19; Series A, Nos. 20/21, p. 124. Article 38 of the Statute expressly directs the application of 'general principles of law recognized by civilized nations', and in more than one nation

principles of equity have an established place in the legal system.
The Court's recognition of equity as a part of international law is
in no way restricted by the special power conferred upon it 'to decide
a case *ex aequo et bono*, if the parties agree thereto.' . . . It must
be concluded, therefore, that under Article 38 of the Statute, if not
independently of that Article, the Court has some freedom to consider
principles of equity as part of the international law which it must
apply." Permanent Court of International Justice, Judgment, June
28, 1937, Series A/B, No. 70, pp. 4, 76–77; IV Hudson, *World Court
Reports* (1943) 178, 231–232.

The Special Arbitral Tribunal between Germany and Portugal in
the *Maziua* and *Naulilaa* cases, decided in 1928, recalled the sources
of law enumerated in article 38 of the Statute of the Permanent Court
of International Justice, and added: "Finally, in the absence of rules
of international law which are applicable to the facts in dispute, the
arbitrators are of opinion that it is their duty to fill the gap by applying principles of equity, fully taking into account the spirit of international law, which is applied by way of analogy, and its evolution."

8 M.A.T. (1929) 409, 413 (translation).
See also Berlia, *Essai sur la portée de la clause de jugement en équité
en droit des gens* (1937).

"It is, moreover, a principle generally accepted in the jurisprudence of international arbitration, as well as by municipal
courts, that one Party cannot avail himself of the fact that the
other has not fulfilled some obligation or has not had recourse
to some means of redress, if the former Party has, by some illegal
act, prevented the latter from fulfilling the obligation in question,
or from having recourse to the tribunal which would have been
open, to him."

German Interests in Polish Upper Silesia and the Factory at Chorzów,
Permanent Court of International Justice, Judgment, July 26, 1927, Series
A, No. 9, pp. 4, 31; I Hudson, *World Court Reports* (1934) 589, 610.

On "Decisions *ex aequo et bono*", Judge Hudson has the following
to say in his standard treatise on the Permanent Court of International Justice:

"Article 38 of the Statute also provides that the previous
enumeration in the Article 'shall not prejudice the power of the
Court to decide a case *ex aequo et bono*, if the parties agree
thereto.' The phrase *ex aequo et bono*, incorporated in the Statute
without much explanation, has its roots in Roman law. Modern
usage has invested the phrase with only a general meaning, without making it a term of art. In the last century Chile entered
into special arbitration agreements with several States providing
for decisions *ex aequo et bono*, and the example was later followed
by Brazil. The provision in Article 38 of the Court's Statute
inspired many general agreements after 1920. In a series of
German treaties, provision was made that if the parties agree,
an arbitral tribunal might decide in accordance with considera-

tions of equity instead of basing its decision on legal principles
(*anstatt sie auf Rechtsgrundsätze zu stützen, nach billigen
Ermessen treffen*). In 1924, an Italian-Swiss treaty provided
that if the Court should find a dispute to be of a non-juridical
nature, it should deal with the dispute *ex aequo et bono;* and this
provision was repeated in other treaties. A Belgian-Swedish
treaty of 1926 provided for the submission of disputes other than
those in which the parties are in conflict as to their respective
rights to arbitral tribunals for decision *ex aequo et bono;* this
provision, too, was employed in many treaties. The Belgian-
Turkish treaty of 1931 provided for decisions *ex aequo et bono*
in the absence of applicable rules of international law. The
Geneva General Act of 1928 has an especial importance in this
line of treaty-development; having provided that disputes in
which the parties were in conflict as to their respective rights
should be referred to the Court, it required other disputes to be
referred to arbitral tribunals which (Article 28) were to apply
the substantive rules enumerated in Article 38 of the Statute
of the Court, and which were to decide *ex aequo et bono* in so far
as there existed no such rule applicable to the dispute. This
provision was copied in numerous treaties.

"Though it was partly due to a tendency to imitate, this development of treaty law since 1920 indicates the views of many
States as to the office to be served by decisions *ex aequo et bono*,
and it must be taken into account in any effort to determine the
nature of such decisions. The jurisprudence is very meager.
In the *Pugh Case* in 1933, the arbitrator did not refer to the
direction given in the *compromis* to decide *ex aequo et bono.*

"Decisions applying the international law which includes equity,
as in the *Meuse Case*, are not to be confused with decisions *ex
aequo et bono* which may be given by the Court. For the latter,
the agreement of the parties is required; for the former it is
unnecessary. In a case where the parties are agreed that it may
decide *ex aequo et bono*, the provision in the Statute would seem
to enable the Court to go outside the realm of law for reaching
its decision. It relieves the Court from the necessity of deciding
according to law. It makes possible a decision based upon considerations of fair dealing and good faith, which may be independent of or even contrary to the law. Acting *ex aequo et bono*,
the Court is not compelled to depart from applicable law, but
it is permitted to do so, and it may even call upon a party to
give up legal rights. Yet it does not have a complete freedom
of action. It cannot act capriciously and arbitrarily. To the
extent that it goes outside the applicable law, or acts where no
law is applicable, it must proceed upon objective considerations
of what is fair and just. Such considerations depend, in large
measure, upon the judges' personal appreciation, and yet the
Court would not be justified in reaching a result which could not
be explained on rational grounds.

"No case has arisen to date in which the Court has been called
upon to decide *ex aequo et bono*. In the *Free Zones Case*, the

Court said that if it could be given power to prescribe a settlement disregarding recognized rights and taking into account considerations of pure expediency only, such power 'could only be derived from a clear and explicit provision to that effect.' Judge Kellogg said in that case that 'the authority given to the Court to decide a case *ex aequo et bono* merely empowers it to apply the principles of equity and justice in the broader signification of this latter word'; but Judge *ad hoc* Dreyfus thought it meant power 'to play the part of an arbitrator in order to reach the solution which, in the light of present conditions, appeared to be the best, even if that solution required the abolition of the zones.' "

Hudson, *The Permanent Court of International Justice, 1920–1942* (1943) 618–621. For the *Meuse Case*, see Series A/B, No. 70; for the *Free Zones Case*, see Series A, No. 24, Series A/B, No. 46.

Article 28 of the General Act of Geneva of 1928, as revised on April 28, 1949, by the General Assembly of the United Nations, reads:

"If nothing is laid down in the special agreement or no special agreement has been made, the Tribunal shall apply the rules in regard to the substance of the dispute enumerated in Article 38 of the Statute of the International Court of Justice. In so far as there exists no such rule applicable to the dispute, the Tribunal shall decide *ex aequo et bono.*"

93 LNTS 343, 355; 71 UNTS 101, 116. For a discussion of disputes to be settled *ex aequo et bono* under article 28 of the General Act, see Habicht, *The Power of the International Judge to Give a Decision "Ex Aequo et Bono"* (1935) 55–59. On article 28 generally, see Muûls, "L'article 28 de l'Acte général d'arbitrage", 11 *Revue de droit international et de législation comparée*, 3d Series (1930) 687–697; Brierly, "The General Act of Geneva, 1928", XI Brit. Yb. Int'l L. (1930) 119–133.

RELATION TO MUNICIPAL LAW

§11

". . . International law is a part of our law and as such is the law of all States of the Union (*The Paquete Habana*, 175 U.S. 677, 700), but it is a part of our law for the application of its own principles, and these are concerned with international rights and duties and not with domestic rights and duties."

Chief Justice Charles Evans Hughes, delivering the opinion of the Supreme Court, in *Skiriotes* v. *Florida*, 313 U.S. 69, 72–73 (1941).

"Although it is correct to say that international law governs only the relations between States, and that it has nothing to do directly with disputes between private individuals, the principle has been clearly adopted in the United States that it is part of the law of the land, because either we have signed international agreements, or have otherwise written it into our municipal law. . . ."

Aboitiz & Co. v. Price, 99 F. Supp. 602, 609 (D. Utah, Cent. Div., 1951).

". . . the words 'municipal law' often are used to refer to the laws of a country dealing with intra-mural matters as distinguished from 'international laws' dealing with its extra-mural affairs." *United States* v. *Forness et al.* (*Salamanica Trust Co. et al., Interveners*), 125 F.2d 928, 932 (2d Cir. 1942).

". . . the decisions of the United States courts bear witness to the fact that United States courts are competent to apply international law in their decisions when necessary. . . ."

Interhandel Case (Switzerland v. United States) (Preliminary Objections), Judgment, Mar. 21, 1959, I.C.J. Reports (1959) 6, 28.

". . . When it is said that international law cannot '*per se* create or invalidate municipal law nor can municipal law *per se* create or invalidate international law,' the fallacy lies in the inference that municipal law can disregard international law and that a country incurs no responsibility under international law when its municipal law violates international law to the injury of a foreign nation or its nationals. As we shall see, international law exerts a definite check upon municipal law and holds the State responsible to the State whose nationals are injured by excesses in conflict with international law. . . .

.   .   .   .

"What the dualists overlook is the fact that while departures from international law are occasionally successful in fact, this merely indicates that lawlessness, in the particular instance, has prevailed. . . . We have innumerable precedents which have held States liable for their failure to perform international obligations, whether the delinquency arises out of statute or administrative act. . . .

.   .   .   .

"In the United States the courts are by the Constitution bound to give effect to treaties which even an aggrieved individual may invoke. In England, the rule is different, for there treaties must be adopted or converted into legislation before they become invokable in the courts. But in both cases the treaty is binding on the nation and will be enforced, notwithstanding a conflicting municipal statute, by such instrumentalities as international law possesses. The American courts, like the English, are said to consider international law a part of the law of the land. And this is true, for international law will in principle be enforced directly in the municipal courts provided there is no statute *contra.* Where a reconciliation between international law and municipal law is possible, the courts will make it. Where there is a statute which conflicts with international law, instances of which will presently be noted, the courts must perforce give effect to the statute even as against the treaty, provided the treaty is earlier in time. . . .

"So in *United States v. La Jeune Eugenie*, the United States felt obliged to pay damages to France for the illegal seizure of a private vessel, although sustained by the Supreme Court. After the Civil War the United States submitted to arbitration twelve prize decisions of the United States Supreme Court during the Civil War. In six of those cases, the arbitral tribunal found the Supreme Court to have been wrong and awarded damages to Great Britain, a phenomenon very common in prize cases, especially where the prize court is bound by municipal order in council or regulation and not necessarily by international law. In the nineties, the United States had extended its jurisdiction in the Behring Sea by law beyond the three-mile limit, in order to police the manner of taking seals. The Behring Sea Arbitration held this to have been a legal error and the seizures made under the statute illegal, so that heavy damages had to be paid. Whenever a country by municipal statute or decree authorizes unlawful seizures from or arbitrarily discriminates against foreigners, under the criterion of international law and not merely municipal law, it incurs international responsibility and must repair the wrong in the most practicable manner possible. And when the President disregards the statute or pays damages through congressional appropriation for the municipal delinquency, he is not exercising the pardoning power but acts according to a supervening rule of law. Should he dispute the rule of international law with a foreign government the issue is generally submitted to arbitration or diplomatic negotiation, but in no case would it be consciously asserted that the Foreign Office—except for commanding political reasons which entail responsibility—has knowingly declined to give effect to an admitted or established rule of international law. Even an assertion that the issue involves a domestic question is internationally justiciable, for international law does determine the matters that are within the *domaine reservée*.

.   .   .   .

"But when the President or Secretary of State on the demand of foreign nations, invoking a rule of international law, releases an alien from the military service or releases a rumrunner seized outside the three-mile limit and thereby in effect overrules a statute of Congress and a supporting decision of a municipal court, he is acting as a societal agent of the American people and State and is recognizing the binding character of international law as law in the United States and everywhere else. When foreign nations refused to permit Russia and Japan to make foodstuffs contraband or in other respects to violate the rights of neutrals; when foreign nations deny to the countries of Latin-America the privilege of unilaterally defining the term 'denial of justice' or by contract with their citizens of exacting a waiver of the privilege of invoking diplomatic protection, they are invoking international law as a rule of law superior to any contrary rule of municipal law. . . ."

Borchard, "The Relation Between International Law and Municipal Law", 27 Va. L. Rev. (1940) 137, 140, 141, 144–147.

"In looking at the function and place of the law of nations in the national government, we are bound to begin asking how, and in what ways, the United States becomes concerned with the body of international law. First, I suppose, through the relationship of the law of nations to municipal law in the United States. The Constitutional provision is familiar which gives Congress the power 'To define and punish . . . Offenses against the Law of Nations;'. (Art. I., sec. 8, cl. 10.)
"Before the Constitution, it is interesting to note, the Chief Justice of Pennsylvania stated, in *Respublica* v. *de Longchamps*, that that case was 'one of the first impression in the United States. It must be determined on the principles of the laws of nations, which form a part of the municipal law of Pennsylvania;'. 1 Dall. 120, 123 (Pa. Oyer and Terminer, 1784). Interestingly enough, the case was a criminal prosecution for a non-statutory and uncodified offense against international law: assault upon the representative of a foreign country, France. The defendant was convicted, and sentenced to a fine, two years' imprisonment, and the posting of heavy bond for seven years to secure good behavior. The Chief Justice repeated his statement on international law, saying:

" 'The first crime in the indictment is an infraction of the law of nations. This law, in its full extent, is a part of the law of this state, and is to be collected from the practice of different nations, and the authority of writers.'

"The Constitutional provision mentioned earlier may have brought to an end the common law of crimes against the law of nations in this country, but for purposes of civil suit the rules of international law continued applicable. The United States Supreme Court in 1815 decided in favor of private claims in a prize case by reason of the law of nations. *The Nereide*, 9 Cr. 388 (U.S. 1815). In the Court's opinion, Chief Justice Marshall said that in the absence of an act of Congress 'the Court is bound by the law of nations which is a part of the law of the land.' "

Leonard C. Meeker, Assistant Legal Adviser, Department of State, "The Law of Nations in the National Government", address, Seattle, Wash., Apr. 20, 1956, Proceedings of the Pacific Northwest Regional Meeting, American Society of International Law, Bulletin No. 12, pt. 3, June 1956, p. 1.

"34. It must be a matter for consideration to what extent and in what detail the obligation of States to give effect, through their national law, to their duties arising out of international law should find a place in any general scheme of codification.

The problem is one which is closely related to the authority and the effectiveness of international law. To a large extent it is a question of the reaffirmation of what has now become a prominent feature of the law and of the practice of many States. The doctrine of incorporation, according to which the rules of international law form part of the municipal law of States, originated in England and in the United States. However, this is not now a doctrine confined to those countries. It has been adopted by other States, for instance in the German Constitution of 1919 and in the Constitutions of Argentina and Venezuela. The preamble to the French Constitution of 1946 contains a general declaration to the effect that France conforms to the principles of public international law. The courts of many other countries, the constitution of which does not expressly include the principle of incorporation, have acted upon it. The time would therefore appear ripe for the incorporation of the principle, suitably elaborated and defined, that treaties validly concluded by the State and generally recognized rules of customary international law form part of the domestic law of the State; that courts and other national agencies are obliged to give effect to them; that they cannot be unilaterally abrogated by purely national action; and that a State cannot invoke the absence of the requisite national laws and organs as a reason for the nonfulfilment of its international obligations.

"35. Admittedly a codification, on these lines, of this fundamental aspect of international law will raise difficult questions of constitutional law in various States, and the question will arise whether this is a suitable subject within the general scheme of codification. Thus in England treaties ratified by the Crown but affecting private rights are not enforced by the courts unless they are followed by an enabling Act of Parliament (though this difficulty has tended to disappear in view of the recent practice of submitting treaties for parliamentary approval, coupled with an enabling Act, prior to the ratification of the treaty). Similarly, in the United States though treaties ratified with the consent and advice of the Senate constitute the supreme law of the land, abrogating any law inconsistent with the terms of the treaties, a subsequent Act of Congress will be acted upon by the courts though its provisions may be inconsistent with the terms of a treaty binding upon the United States. These and similar problems bring to mind the difficulties of this aspect of codification. However, it is significant that it has formed the subject-matter of some previous efforts in this direction. Thus, for instance, article 3 of Project No. 4 adopted in 1925 by the American Institute of International Law—one of the series of 'projects of conventions for the preparation of a code of public international law'—on Fundamental Bases of International Law provides that 'international law forms a part of the national law of every country' and that 'in matters which pertain to it, it should therefore be applied by the national authorities as the law of the land'. Article 4 laid down that 'national laws should not contain provisions contrary to international law'. Similar provisions were

incorporated in articles 2 and 3 of Project No. 1 (Fundamental
Bases of International Law) submitted in 1927 by the International Commission of Jurists for the consideration of the Sixth
International Conference of American States. In the jurisprudence of international tribunals the principle of the supremacy
of international obligations over national law has found repeated
expression—as, for instance, in Advisory Opinion No. 17 (Greece
and Bulgaria, 'Communities' case) where the Permanent Court
of International Justice laid down that 'it is a generally accepted
principle of international law that in the relations between
Powers who are contracting Parties to a treaty, the provisions
of municipal law cannot prevail over those of the treaty' (Series
B, No. 17, at p. 32)."

*Survey of International Law in Relation to the Work of Codification of
the International Law Commission,* Memorandum submitted by the Secretary-General of the United Nations, A/CN.4/1/Rev. 1, Feb. 10, 1949, pp.
22–24.

For a survey of post World War II constitutional provisions concerning
international peace, and the relationship of international law to municipal
law, see Deener, "International Law Provisions in Post-World War II
Constitutions", 36 Cornell L.Q. (1951) 505.

"Several governments in their comments and proposed amendments in relation to the Dumbarton Oaks Proposals had displayed
interest in a provision for the Charter designed expressly to subordinate national internal law to international law and the obligations of the Charter. The text offered by the Belgian Delegation came under discussion first. It read: 'No state can evade
the authority of international law or the obligations of the present
Charter by invoking the provisions of its internal law.' [Docu-
mentation for Meetings of Committee IV/2, Relation of International Law and the Charter to Internal Law, UNCIO WD 12,
IV/2/24, May 22, 1945.] The summary report for the ninth
meeting of Committee IV/2 accurately sums up the debate on
the proposal: 'There was no disagreement with the principle underlying the proposal before the Committee. It was stated, however, that such a proposal did not need to be inserted in the
Charter, but more properly belonged in a codification of international law, if that were later to be undertaken by the General
Assembly.' [May 22, 1945, UNCIO Doc. 527, IV/2/27, May 23,
1945.] On the question of inclusion or exclusion of such a clause,
the vote of the committee was 21 in favor of insertion and 15
against. The motion was lost, however, for lack of a two-thirds
majority. The principal motion having failed of adoption, a
subordinate motion to commit the subject for study to the subcommittee, favored by various delegates who had objected to
insertion, was lost too. Nevertheless, the chairman, interpreting
the 'good will' of the committee and in the absence of objection,
referred the defeated proposal amidst general laughter to the
subcommittee. The subcommittee, IV/2/A, did not, however,

resume discussion of the subject. [Report of Committee IV/2, UNCIO Doc. 933, IV/2/42/(2), June 12, 1945.]"

Reiff, "Work of the United Nations 'Legal Committees'", XV *Bulletin*, Department of State, No. 366, July 7, 1946, pp. 3, 7–8.

The International Law Commission included the following article in its Draft Declaration on Rights and Duties of States:

"Every State has the duty to conduct its relations with other States in accordance with international law and with the principle that the sovereignty of each State is subject to the supremacy of international law." (Article 14.)

In urging the inclusion of the provision, Dr. Alfaro, whose own draft was worded somewhat differently (A/285), stated that "That was the principle of the pre-eminence of international over national law, . . . which should be stated formally in a declaration on the rights and duties of States, if only for its psychological effect on world opinion." Professor Scelle endorsed Dr. Alfaro's opinion, stating that "It was always useful to say that sovereignty was subject to the limitations of international law."

International Law Commission, 1st Sess., 14th meeting, May 3, 1949, *Yearbook of the International Law Commission 1949*, pp. 106, 288.

"Generally, within the realm of its internal affairs, each State may exercise its powers without restraint by international law. Nor can it be said that international law applies to all matters which arise in States' external affairs, that is in relations between States; just as municipal law does not cover the entire gamut of relations between individuals, so international law may not be complete enough at any given time to cover the entire range of inter-State relations.

"It was recognized in the Covenant of the League of Nations that some disputes between States may relate to matters which lie 'solely within the domestic jurisdiction' of a State, or as it is put in the French version, which are left by international law to the exclusive jurisdiction of a State; but in the case relating to *Nationality Decrees in Tunis and Morocco*, the Permanent Court of International Justice declared that 'the question whether a certain matter is or is not solely within the jurisdiction of a State is an essentially relative question,' depending upon 'the development of international relations.'

"The conception of a Community of States involves the supremacy of international law in inter-State relations. All conduct of States in their relations with other States is subject to being regulated by international law, hence subject to the applicable law."

The International Law of the Future: Postulates, Principles and Proposals (Carnegie Endowment for International Peace, 1944) 29. For the

Nationality Decrees in Tunis and Morocco Case referred to, see Permanent Court of International Justice, Advisory Opinion, Feb. 7, 1923, Series B, No. 4, p. 27.

"But the issue which the Court must decide is not one which pertains to the legal system of Liechtenstein. It does not depend on the law or on the decision of Liechtenstein whether that State is entitled to exercise its protection, in the case under consideration. To exercise protection, to apply to the Court, is to place oneself on the plane of international law. It is international law which determines whether a State is entitled to exercise protection and to seise the Court.

. . . .

". . . It has been considered that the best way of making such rules (international rules relating to nationality) accord with the varying demographic conditions in different countries is to leave the fixing of such rules to the competence of each State. On the other hand, a State cannot claim that the rules it has thus laid down are entitled to recognition by another State unless it has acted in conformity with this general aim of making the legal bond of nationality accord with the individual's genuine connection with the State which assumes the defence of its citizens by means of protection as against other States.

. . . .

"These facts clearly establish, on the one hand, the absence of any bond of attachment between Nottebohm and Liechtenstein and, on the other hand, the existence of a long-standing and close connection between him and Guatemala, a link which his naturalization in no way weakened. That naturalization was not based on any real prior connection with Liechtenstein, nor did it in any way alter the manner of life of the person upon whom it was conferred in exceptional circumstances of speed and accommodation. In both respects, it was lacking in the genuineness requisite to an act of such importance, if it is to be entitled to be respected by a State in the position of Guatemala. It was granted without regard to the concept of nationality adopted in international relations."

Nottebohm Case (Liechtenstein *v.* Guatemala), Judgment (Second Phase), Apr. 6, 1955, I.C.J. Reports (1955) 4, 20–21, 23, 26.

"There are times when an Arbitration Tribunal or this Court have to deal with municipal law, or any other kind of law and even with private contracts, when they have to take judicial notice of its existence, and perhaps even of its correct interpretation. Such a case was, for instance, the Nottebohm case, and there are many others, especially those involving the wrongful acts of Governments against foreigners, denial of justice, direct or indirect responsibility and the like; but even then, neither this Court nor the Arbitration Tribunals apply municipal law; they only have to judge such cases according to inter-State law. Municipal law, administrative laws and private contracts only concern them incidentally, in the same way as they have to concern themselves with the facts of the case submitted to them."

Judge Córdova, *Judgments of the Administrative Tribunal of the International Labour Organisation Upon Complaints Made Against the United Nations Educational, Scientific and Cultural Organization*, Advisory Opinion, Oct. 23, 1956, I.C.J. Reports (1956) 77, 165, dissenting opinion.

In the case of *Shri Krishna Sharma* v. *State of West Bengal*, the Calcutta High Court concluded that if the Indian statutes

". . . be in conflict with any principle of international law . . . municipal courts of India have got to obey the laws passed by the Legislature of the country to which they owe their allegiance. In interpreting and applying municipal law, these Courts will try to adopt such a construction as will not bring it into conflict with rights and obligations deducible from rules of international law. If such rules, or rights and obligations are inconsistent with the positive regulations of municipal law, municipal Courts cannot override the latter. It is futile in such circumstances to seek to reconcile, by strained construction, what are really irreconcilable."

55 Crim. L.J. (1954) 1722; 49 Am. J. Int'l L. (1955) 412, 413. See also III *The Indian Yearbook of International Affairs 1954* (1954) 393.

"(1) As regards Great Britain, the following points must be noted: (a) all such rules of customary International Law as are either universally recognised or have at any rate received the assent of this country are *per se* part of the law of the land. To that extent there is still valid in England the common law doctrine, to which Blackstone gave expression in a striking passage, that the Law of Nations is part of the law of the land. It has been repeatedly acted upon by courts. Apart from isolated *obiter dicta* it has never been denied by judges. The unshaken continuity of its observance suffered a reverse as the result of the *dicta* of some judges in *The Franconia* case in 1876 [R. v. Keyn (1876), 2 Ex. D. 63], but *West Rand Central Gold Mining Co.* v. *The King* [(1905), 2 K.B. 391], decided in 1905, must be regarded as a reaffirmation of the classical doctrine.

"(b) Such treaties as affect private rights and, generally, as require for their enforcement by English courts a modification of common law or of a statute must receive parliamentary assent through an enabling Act of Parliament. To that extent binding treaties which are part of International Law do not form part of the law of the land unless expressly made so by the legislature. That departure from the traditional common law rule is largely due to the fact that, according to British constitutional law, the conclusion and ratification of treaties are within the prerogative of the Crown, which would otherwise be in a position to legislate for the subject without obtaining parliamentary assent. The possible inconvenience of the rule rendering inoperative treaties which have not been transformed into Municipal Law is to a large extent one of theory rather than practice. This is so mainly for the reason that in practice opportunity is given, as a rule, to Parliament to approve treaties prior to their ratification and that enabling legislation is passed before the treaty is ratified. . . .

"(c) English statutory law is absolutely binding upon English courts, even if in conflict with International Law, although in doubtful cases there is a presumption that an Act of Parliament did not intend to overrule International Law. The fact that International Law is part of the law of the land and is binding directly on courts and individuals does not mean that English law recognises in all circumstances the supremacy of International Law. [It is of importance not to confuse, as many do, the question of the supremacy of International Law and of the direct operation of its rules within the municipal sphere. It is possible to deny the former while fully affirming the latter.]"

I Lauterpacht, *Oppenheim's International Law* (8th ed., 1955) 39–41. See also Holdsworth, "Relation of English Law to International Law", 26 Minn. L. Rev. (1942) 141–152.

"The principle that international law is a part of the law of the land does not find application in Italy. The opposite principle of absolute separation between international and national law prevails. Italian law alone governs legal relations within the national jurisdiction and is the only law applied by the courts and enforced by state agencies in Italy.

"International law, however, has a dual influence on Italian legislation. In the first place, reference to rules and concepts of international law is sometimes made by provisions of the domestic law. Article 553 of the Code of Commerce, which provides that naval blockade justifies the interruption of a ship's voyage, refers to international law for the concept of a naval blockade. The Code for Merchant Marine refers to international law for the definition of piracy. In this case there is no reception of international law as such in the Italian legal system, but the existence of the former is presupposed by the latter. In the second place, rules of international law creating obligations which the Italian state must fulfill within its domestic jurisdiction (for example, concession of certain rights to foreigners and the reduction of customs duties) result necessarily in the enactment of domestic legislation. This is the consequence of the separation between international and domestic law. Since the former does not apply within the state, Italy must enact domestic legislation in order to secure the fulfillment of her international duties within her domestic order. Concession of rights to foreigners and reduction of customs duties can only be provided for by legislative acts."

Sereni, *The Italian Conception of International Law* (1943) 321. For a discussion of the relation between municipal law and international law in Hungarian jurisprudence in the absence of a general incorporation of international law into municipal law, see Arató, "Hungarian Jurisprudence Relating to the Application of International Law by National Courts" 43 Am. J. Int'l L. (1949) 536.

"A clause which says that international law . . . is part of the municipal law of that country . . . has its difficulties for us. It is part of the theory of our municipal law that customary international law is part of the law of the land, but we have never extended this theory to treaty law. That extension has been made by the United States of America and at least some South American States. With us, therefore, most treaties only become the law of the land by Act of Parliament. It is more in keeping with our parliamentary practice that this should be so.

"There is little point in formally making international law part of municipal law. It is sufficient that, whatever the divergence between international and municipal law, the State should be liable at international law for any infraction by it of international law."

Paper by Professor R. O. McGehan, Victoria University College, Wellington, New Zealand, transmitted by the Government of New Zealand July 25, 1947, to the Secretary-General of the United Nations as an unofficial commentary on the Draft Declaration on Rights and Duties of States. *Preparatory Study Concerning a Draft Declaration on the Rights and Duties of States*, Memorandum submitted by the Secretary-General of the United Nations, A/CN.4/2, Dec. 15, 1948, pp. 175, 178–179.

". . . Danish courts of law and other public authorities are obliged to apply the principles and rules of international law generally acknowledged when their application is at issue. But, on the other hand, according to the Danish conception of law, Danish authorities cannot apply more specific rules of international law warranted by international treaties or other agreements till they have been publicly announced in Denmark, by way of acts of law or in other official ways, as legally binding."

Comment by the Government of Denmark on article 14 of the Draft Declaration of Rights and Duties of States submitted in 1947 to the General Assembly of the United Nations and later used as a basis of discussion by the International Law Commission. *Preparatory Study Concerning a Draft Declaration on the Rights and Duties of States*, Memorandum submitted by the Secretary-General of the United Nations, A/CN.4/2, Dec. 15, 1948, p. 90.

In the case of *Anglo-Iranian Oil Co. Ltd.* v. *Società S.U.P.O.R.*, decided by an Italian Court in 1954, the plaintiff had sued to recover oil extracted from the area of its 1933 concession in Iran and imported into Italy by defendant, contending that the Iranian legislation of 1951, whereby the oil industry in Iran was nationalized, was inapplicable in Italy as being repugnant to the Iranian Constitution, to Italian public order, and to generally accepted norms of international law, and as being political, discriminatory and confiscatory in character, since it provided for expropriation without compensation. The Court concluded that Italian courts may pass on the repugnance of a foreign law to the constitution of a foreign country, international public order, or generally recognized international law, and that they must deny effect in Italy to a foreign law providing for expropriation not for motives of public interest but for motives of political character, persecution, discrimination, race or confiscation, or without compensation. The Court held, however, that even if Iranian law was not applicable because of failure to provide compensation, the claim must be rejected because the Anglo-Iranian Oil Company did not sustain the burden of proof of ownership, the 1933 concession and the Iranian law then in force being interpreted to mean that the concessionaire became the owner only of oil extracted by it.

> *Anglo-Iranian Oil Co. Ltd.* v. *Società S.U.P.O.R.*, No. 3906/53, Civil Tribunal of Rome, Sec. I, July 14, 1954; see 49 Am. J. Int'l L. (1955) 259–261.

International law and private international law

"Finally, it is to be noted that some treaties refer in a general way to *international law* as controlling. The Provisional Agreement with Iran (1928, 47 Stat. 2644) for example, provides that the treatment of nationals shall be governed by the 'requirements and practices of generally recognized international law' (Art. 1, 3). The same rule appears, moreover, in some recent treaties, *e.g.*, with Thailand (1937, Art. I, 6), Yemen (1946, TIAS 1535), Nepal (1947, TIAS 1585), China (1946, Art. VI), Ireland (1950, Art. II), etc., as to the protection of persons and property. There can be no doubt that international law so referred to as controlling includes also conflict law applicable in private, especially jurisdictional and status matters. This seems to be indicated by the Judicial Agreement between Great Britain and Iraq (1922) recognized by the United States (47 Stat. 1844) where, in connection with a general reference to international law as applicable, the Agreement contains the following provision: 'In matters relating to personal status of foreigners or other matters of civil and commercial nature in which it is customary by international usage to apply the law of another country, such law shall be applied in a manner to be prescribed by law. . . .' (Art. 4)."

> Professor S. A. Bayitch, *Conflict of Law in United States Treaties—A Survey*, University of Chicago, International Legal Studies, No. 1, 1955, 17. For a survey of references in U.S. statutes, and treaties, to an international law standard, see Wilson, "International Law Standard in Statutes of the United States", 45 Am. J. Int'l L. (1951) 732.

". . . we are free under international law to choose our own theories of conflict of laws, and, that is particularly true, where the acts to which we refuse recognition are the acts of an enemy. Even neutral sovereign states enjoy considerable latitude in the solution of their own conflict-in-law problems according to their own choice of theories. *A fortiori*, that is true of a sovereign which is an ally of the occupied state, and which had as close a relationship to the Philippines as we had in 1942, in a war against the common enemy. It must be remembered that in this decision we are required to go back into war time relationships."

Aboitiz & Co. v. *Price*, 99 F. Supp. 602, 623 (D. Utah, Cent. Div., 1951).

In his treatise on the Permanent Court of International Justice, Judge Hudson comments as follows with reference to the Court and "Private International Law":

"In the application of the international law which governs the relations of States *inter se*, the Court may be called upon to deal with the principles governing the choice of the national law which regulates the creation or exercise of the rights or duties of States and individuals. It is not precluded from doing so by Article 38 of the Statute, and perhaps it may be said that the 'general principles of law recognized by civilized nations' include some principles of private international law. To some extent the latter have been embodied in international conventions, such as the six Hague Conventions of 1902 and 1905 [Kosters and Bellemans, *Les Conventions de la Haye sur le Droit International Privé* (1921) . . .], and the interpretation and application of these conventions may call into play the public international law which the Court is competent to apply; a protocol opened to signature at The Hague on March 27, 1931, confers on the Court jurisdiction to deal with disputes relating to them. [Series D, No. 6, p. 529; 167 League of Nations Treaty Series, p. 341; 5 Hudson, International Legislation, p. 933. . . .] Moreover, a dispute between two States may concern or may depend upon the application of a non-conventional principle of private international law. Referring to that branch of law 'usually described as private international law or the doctrine of conflict of laws,' the Court has said that its rules 'may be common to several States and may even be established by international conventions or customs, and in the latter case may possess the character of true international law governing the relations between States.' [Series A, No. 20, p. 41.]

"In numerous cases concerning questions of nationality and the status of aliens, the Court may be said to have applied private international law. In the *Serbian* and *Brazilian Loans Cases*, it was called upon to deal with questions of conflicts of laws: both cases related to disputes 'involving the question as to the law which governs the contractual obligations at issue,' and the Court said it could 'determine what this law is only by reference to the actual nature of these obligations and to the circumstances attendant upon their creation'; it admitted, however, that 'the same law may not govern all aspects of the obligations'; it held that the Serbian law and Brazilian law, respectively, governed the creation of the obligations in the two cases, but that 'the currency in which payment must or may be made in France' were 'governed by French law.' [Series A, No. 20, pp. 41, 44; *idem*, No. 21, pp.

121–122.]   The problem of choice of law may also have been involved in the *Société Commerciale Case*, but it was not dealt with by the Court.   [See, however, Series A/B, No. 78, p. 184.]"

Hudson, *The Permanent Court of International Justice, 1920–1942* (1943) 621–622.

Cited generally are Å. Hammarskjöld, 29 *Revue critique de droit international* (1934) 315–344; and Niboyet, 40 *Recueil Des Cours* (1932) 157–233.

DEVELOPMENT

§ 12

". . . In most of them [Judgments and Advisory Opinions of the Court], behind the formal complexion of interpretation, there reveals itself the entire legal background—in fact, we may say without fear of exaggeration the 'sociological background'— of the issue in a manner which makes international law and the study of the hidden springs of its development a reality in comparison with which doctrinal disquisitions as to whether international law is law or not appear to be academic.   The Advisory Opinion on *Reparation for Injuries Suffered in the Service of the United Nations*—an Opinion which is concerned with the interpretation of the Charter but which is of a quasi-legislative character on the question of subjects of international law—provides at the same time the most significant contribution made by the Court to the question of the nature, growth and functions of international law."

Lauterpacht, *The Development of International Law by the International Court* (1958) 29.

"This new law is in formation.   It is for the International Court of Justice to develop it by its judgments or its advisory opinions, and in laying down valuable precedents.   The theories of jurists must also share in the development of this law.

.   .   .   .

"The Court must, therefore, declare what is the new international law which is based upon the present requirements and conditions of the life of peoples: otherwise, it would be applying a law which is obsolete in many respects, and would disregard those requirements and conditions as well as the spirit of the Charter which is the principal source of the new international law.

"In so doing, it may be said that the Court *creates* the law; it creates it by modifying classical law; in fact it merely *declares* what is the law to-day. . . .

"The Court, moreover, already exercised this faculty of creating the law in its Advisory Opinion concerning Reparation for injuries suffered in the service of the United Nations; it declared on that occasion that the United Nations was entitled to present

an international claim; until that time only States had been recognized as possessing this right."

Judge Alvarez, *International Status of South-West Africa*, Advisory
Opinion, July 11, 1950, I.C.J. Reports (1950) 128, 176–177, dissenting
opinion.

". . . it is clear from the written proceedings and the oral arguments
that the Parties have attributed excessive importance to historic titles and
that they have not sufficiently taken into account the state of international
law or its present tendencies, in regard to territorial sovereignty.

". . . the task of the Court is to resolve international disputes by applying, not the traditional or classical international law, but that which exists
at the present day and which is in conformity with the new conditions of
international life, and to develop this law in a progressive spirit." Judge
Alvarez, *The Minquiers and Ecrehos Case* (France/United Kingdom), Judgment, Nov. 17, 1953, I.C.J. Reports (1953) 47, 73, individual opinion.

"We have already expressed the view that not all treaties are
concluded in strict compliance with international law, at least as
that law is now conceived by the leading minds of the world.
It is believed that practice and custom, the other great sources of
international law, in many instances are also far removed from
the principles of international law as generally conceived at present. The world has witnessed a great ideological revolution in
the past fifty years which has completely shaken the old foundations and principles of international law. One has merely to
think of the evolution which the juridical mind has traversed
within this period, with regard to the use of force, individual
responsibility for its use in connection with the use of the wealth
of the world and in so many other fields in which the old and
time-honoured postulates of international law have been superseded by new, more modern and more generous guiding principles. National sovereignty is fading before the ideas of international cooperation and of international responsibility. It is
no longer true that right is equal to might, and all efforts of the
human mind and all endeavours of statesmen, writers and jurists,
tend to replace—as the pattern for what is and what is not lawful—the absolute concept of selfish national sovereignty by the
new ideal of international solidarity. There is no question that
the old principles of international law, as derived from treaties
and custom, need to be revised in the light of these new ideals,
and adapted to the new standards of justice. The outlawry of
war and the use of individual force, its replacement by collective
security, the creation of international armies, the responsibility
of individuals before international law, the change in the basic
concepts for the distribution of wealth among nations, have rendered obsolete many of the traditional principles which used to
obtain not very long ago, just before the last world war. For
these reasons, codification, in the strict sense of the word would
not only be useless, but could even be detrimental.

May 82

"What is really necessary,—indeed indispensable—, is to bring the old principles up to date, to introduce the inevitable changes in the old rules, to reformulate them in accordance with the new basic legal ideas. International life is not static; international relations are dynamic and international law should be dynamic."

Córdova, "The Development and Codification of International Law", published in *The United Nations—Ten Years' Legal Progress, Collection of Essays* (The Hague, 1956) 43, 49–50.

"In order to endow law with the maximum of effectiveness it is necessary to provide means for the change of law. Such means, falling short of an international legislature, but grounded in the practice of States and in existing international law, have been discussed. . . . It has been shown here that in a large number of cases it is through law that the change of law will be most conveniently effected. Recent conventional law, by forbidding changes by force, has created the necessary basis for developing these means of peaceful change. The existing tendencies in the direction of the political integration of the community of States will in the future bring about the consummation of the machinery of change through the working of an effective international legislature. This will relieve obligatory judicial settlement of the strain—some real and some imaginary—imposed upon it as a result of the present imperfections of the legislative process. For this and other reasons it is a consummation devoutly to be wished. But it is improvident to reject a working minimum because the maximum cannot as yet be obtained, especially if the desired maximum cannot by the very nature of things constitute a final solution of all difficulties. The conflict between stability and change and between security and justice can never be finally obliterated. It is inherent in the life of a developing society. It can be removed only at the cost of eliminating either security or social change."

Lauterpacht, *The Function of Law in the International Community* (1933) 346–347.

"In considering the body of law to be applied by the Court one comes inevitably to the question of what methods exist for the clarification and development of international law. The question is especially timely at this moment in view of the provision in article 13 of the Charter of the United Nations that 'The General Assembly shall initiate studies and make recommendations for the purpose of . . . encouraging the progressive development of international law and its codification'.

"Continuing development of the law to make it more clear and certain and to adapt it to changing conditions of life is necessary in any judicial system. The accomplishment of this task is contributed to in various ways, including legislation, judicial decisions, rulings of administrative agencies, growth of commercial practices, writings of experts, and group-study projects, official and unofficial. The process called 'codification'

embodies several of these activities and may draw upon all of
them.

.   .   .   .

"Every judge, whatever the court, is faced with the problem of
applying the law understandingly. Judges interpret the law,
written or unwritten, as new situations arise. Whether they will
it or not, they mold the law. The international field is no
exception.

"Nor will codes of international law on all the major phases
solve the difficulty entirely. There will still be gaps in the law.
Agreements cannot possibly embody provisions with the minutiae
which one might desire. There will yet arise the great multitude
of new situations to be passed upon which were not envisioned
in the codes. Wisdom in the interpretation and application
of any law is always needed. Practice and custom, agreements
and writings, have not covered all aspects of the law of nations
with an equal degree of certainty. We must anticipate a growing and ever-developing international law. The nations have
an opportunity to frame codes which can be wisely developed
to fit the needs as they unfold."

Green H. Hackworth, Legal Adviser, Department of State, "The International Court of Justice and the Codification of International Law",
address, Cincinnati, Ohio, Dec. 19, 1945, XIII *Bulletin*, Department of
State, No. 339, Dec. 23, 1945, pp. 1000, 1002, 1006.

"But there are legal principles which do change, and the last
50 years have witnessed a fundamental change in one principle
of international law that affects us all.

"Fifty years ago war was accepted as a legitimate instrument
of national policy. Learned writers asserted its legality. Collective efforts were largely devoted to ameliorating the harsh
conditions of war—agreeing on the rules of the game, so to speak.
The Hague Conventions and the later Geneva Conventions regulating the treatment of prisoners of war represented efforts to
make war endurable, since its abolition seemed impossible.

"But two world wars and the harnessing of nuclear energy
have progressively convinced the world of the necessity for providing an effective means of preventing aggressive war. The
attempt to reach this objective has resulted in the establishing of
a new principle of international law and the taking of steps to
implement that principle."

Herman Phleger, Legal Adviser, Department of State, "Fifty Years of
Progress in International Law", address before the Association of the Bar
of the City of New York, Apr. 9, 1956, XXXIV *Bulletin*, Department of
State, No. 878, Apr. 23, 1956, pp. 663–664.

In advocating adherence by the United States to the Protocol of
Signature of the Statute of the Permanent Court of International
Justice, Secretary of State Stimson, in a letter to President Hoover
dated November 18, 1929, recognized the importance of the role which

the Court must play in the development and implementation of international law. He stated:

". . . it is . . . to the judicial action of a World Court, passing upon the individual controversies which arise between nations, that we must look not only for the application and interpretation of these compacts and codes but for the flexible and intelligent development in this way of all the subsidiary principles and detailed rules which will surely be found necessary in such application.

"No people are more familiar with this need than the American people, or have greater reason for confidence in this judicial method of developing the law of conduct between separate states. They have seen their own Supreme Court wisely and flexibly work out the myriad difficult and changing problems which in the course of one hundred and forty years have grown out of the compact in which thirteen sovereign states in 1787 agreed to settle their relations by pacific means. . . .

". . . The standards set up by international conferences will hardly be able safely to go beyond the statement of broad general principles; the development of details will necessarily grow out of the application of such principles by the Court. Here again to the American brought up under the common law, patiently and intelligently evolved by six hundred years of judicial decisions, this will be familiar as the method by which a system of law can be most safely, flexibly and intelligently produced."

Secretary of State Stimson to President Hoover, Nov. 18, 1929, 1929 For. Rel., vol. I, pp. 39–40.

"All of us who, as students or practitioners, are interested in this particular branch of jurisprudence, are profoundly conscious of the fact that today the subject of international law has an extraordinary significance. It is no exaggeration to say that never before, in the entire history of the human race, has the problem of the preservation and development of order under law presented itself with such urgent acuteness. Never before has it been so fraught with import for the future of mankind.

"The concept and the structure of a law of nations rose and evolved out of a spirit of protest against the ravages of international anarchy. In the ancient world and during the Dark Ages of the modern world, there widely prevailed a concept that each nation was a law unto itself, the sole arbiter of its international conduct, fully entitled—if it possessed sufficient strength—to engage in aggression and aggrandizement, to destroy by armed force the independence of other nations, and to subjugate other peoples. Force reigned supreme. Human liberty, national independence, confidence in safety and security on the part of nations and individuals, were in constant jeopardy.

"Over long centuries, voices raised in protest against the nightmare of international lawlessness grew in strength and influence, and ideas of how to achieve a law-governed world emerged more and more. Three hundred years ago the genius of Hugo Grotius gathered these scattered voices and ideas into a sharp focus and gave a powerful impetus to a new spirit, to a more and more insistent demand that relations among nations be based upon acceptance and application of well-defined rules of international conduct—upon a body of international law.

"Since then, enormous advances have been made in the character of relations among nations. There has been an ever-deepening and ever more widespread recognition of the inescapable fact that an attitude of unbridled license on the part of nations—in the same way that such an attitude on the part of individuals or groups within nations—is bound, sooner or later, to impair their own well-being and, in the end, lead them to destruction. There has been a wider and wider acceptance and application of the all-important fact that true social progress is possible only when nations in their relations with each other, as well as individuals and groups within nations, are willing to practice self-restraint and to cooperate for the greater good of all. Only thus can orderly processes exist and provide that social stability, security, and confidence without which individual liberty and a free play of creative forces must necessarily be precarious and the onward march of man must be halting if not altogether impossible.

"Institutions have been built up to give effect and reality to order under law within and among nations. They have been largely responsible for the flowering of our modern civilization in the spheres of political security, social justice, scientific progress, and economic betterment.

"This progress has not been achieved without stupendous effort. There have been interruptions and set-backs. Frequently, forces have arisen which have challenged the very concept of order under law, especially in the sphere of international relations, and have plunged nations into war, the greatest of all deterrents to human progress.

"That these challenges and the conditions of international lawlessness which they created have not been permanent set-backs is proof of the inherent vitality and virility of the great principles underlying the whole concept of world order under international law. These facts attest the indomitable strength of the spirit which has been the great driving force behind the determination of the human race to rise from the darkness of lawlessness to the light of law.

"Today, mankind is the unhappy victim of another challenge of this sort—a powerful challenge which threatens to wipe out the achievements of centuries in the development of international law and to destroy the very foundations of orderly international relationships. In the face of this challenge, it is of the utmost importance that every citizen visualize clearly the cardinal features of international law and of order based on law, as well as the conditions which would prevail if they were destroyed."

Address by Secretary of State Hull, before the American Society of International Law, as President of the Society, May 13, 1940, II *Bulletin*, Department of State, No. 47, May 18, 1940, pp. 532–533.

"I have received your letter of April 1, 1946 in which you refer to our previous correspondence concerning the Annual Meeting of the American Society of International Law and request that, in view of my inability to be present, I send you a written statement of my views in regard to 'the desirability of our maintaining and developing international law at the present time, and the policy of the United States in that regard'. I am glad to have an opportunity of doing so.

"The two devastating World Wars within our lifetime have shown the necessity of doing everything possible to prevent a third. In my opinion the only way to preserve our civilization is for peace-loving nations to give unstinted support to measures for insuring the observance of international law, and to do everything possible to see that it develops in such a way as to meet the needs of a rapidly changing world. Most of the inventions of recent years have enormous potentialities for good to the peoples of our own and other lands if they are directed along the right channels. On the other hand, inventions which are designed for, or may be turned to, purposes of destruction have been multiplied and made more and more deadly. The question then is: Which are to triumph, measures of peace or the machinery of destruction?

"It is the determination of our own Government and the Governments of other countries with which we are joined in the Organization of the United Nations that measures for the maintenance of peace under international law shall prevail.

"The development of international law has been a long and sometimes painful process, interrupted, as it has been over and over again, by bloody and destructive wars, the most devastating of which has just ended. But this is not a reason why those who have been hoping and working for the maintenance of peace should give up. On the contrary, it should strengthen their determination to have peace on earth firmly established.

"The observance and enforcement of the rules of international law have always been a matter of deep concern to the Department of State. It is an interesting fact that John Marshall, before he began his long and distinguished service as Chief Justice of the United States, served for a time as Secretary of State. As Chief Justice he rendered the opinion of the court in a number of cases which have ever since been recognized as landmarks in the development of international law. I refer especially to his opinions in *Murray* v. *The Schooner Charming Betsy*, 2 Cranch 64, and *The Schooner Exchange* v. *McFaddon*, 7 Cranch 116. In the former he expressed the opinion that 'An Act of Congress ought never to be construed to violate the law of nations if any other possible construction remains.' In the latter he laid stress upon the equality and sovereignty of states and the respect due from one state to another, and the 'common interest impelling them to mutual intercourse'.

"If the common interest of states pronounced by the great Chief Justice was of such importance in the year 1812, surely it is a matter of the greatest concern in our own time, when contacts between states, even those most widely separated, have multiplied and become so close. . . ."

Secretary of State Byrnes to Frederic R. Coudert, President of the American Society of International Law, Apr. 20, 1946, XIV *Bulletin*, Department of State, No. 357, May 5, 1946, p. 758.

". . . we are naturally inclined to view the future international order as merely a projection of the one we have evolved in this country.   Our institutions do contain a core of fundamental principles which we should never compromise.   Yet, to establish a workable system of international law, we must not confine our thinking to a mere extension of Anglo-Saxon law.   If it is to be international law with the support by all peoples, it must necessarily be a blend of many concepts and systems.   A genuine spirit of tolerance and understanding is the first ingredient in making the kind of world we want. . . ."

Secretary of State Marshall, "The United Nations Charter: A Standard for Conduct Among Nations", XIX *Bulletin*, Department of State, No. 482, Sept. 26, 1948, pp. 400, 401.

"While the restraining and accommodating functions of law are addressed to the task of defining and protecting existing rights, the legislative function is addressed to bringing about progress and change.   Adjustments are made in society so that we can go ahead, so that things happen.

"It is not easy to isolate and analyze this legislative function as it operates on the international scene.   There is no exact international equivalent of the national legislative bodies with which we are familiar.   And international adjudication provides little scope for the legislative role played by our national courts in, for example, the definition of unreasonable restraints on trade or of unfair labor practices.

"Nevertheless, as Judge Hudson's volumes on *International Legislation* so abundantly prove, members of the international community do utilize the legislative function which I have described.   Nations do consult together about international problems and adopt rules of action which subsequently guide and govern their conduct.   A glance at the index of documents collected in Judge Hudson's last volume shows such diverse matters as fisheries, patents, sugar, tin, banking, highway traffic, insurance, and health.

"The importance of the traditional judicial and administrative processes is clear beyond doubt.   But the dominant task which has to be performed in the international, as in the national community, is essentially legislative: that task is to pull the community together through dynamic, propulsive, and creative measures which will change unsatisfactory situations and create new ones responsive to human needs.

"What I have said suggests that this legislative task, on the national or the international level, is not simply a series of haphazard and disassociated actions. It is a cohesive whole, guided by certain operative principles leading toward the goals which the community is seeking.

"If you were to take from the shelves all the volumes which contain the statutes enacted by the British Parliament in the nineteenth and early twentieth centuries, you might well shrink from the effort of distilling any guiding principles from them. You would surely find the books full of unrelated minutiae, but I think you would also find yourselves drawn by a defined current.

"The other evening when I was thinking about this problem, I remembered a book which I had not read for over a quarter of a century, and took it from the shelf to see if my memory was right and whether some of its thought and analysis was as apposite as I remembered. The book was written before World War I. It attempted to isolate the basic principles lending cohesion and strength to the British Nation. Many of you are familiar with this book, *The Underlying Principles of Modern Legislation,* by an eminent and scholarly British constitutional lawyer, the late W. Jethro Brown.

"This study of nineteenth and early twentieth century British legislation may seem a far cry from the complex issues of international life with which we are grappling today. But as I turned over the pages, it seemed to me that this was not so.

"The task the author had set himself, in a world so different from ours, was to discover some philosophic consistency underlying the vast body of legislation with which the British people were attempting to meet the economic and political pressures of the time. He was writing in an era of golden placidity—on the surface, at least. But he was gravely concerned whether his countrymen would be able to solve their problems within the orderly pattern of legal processes. If British legislative ingenuity were unequal to the task, he foresaw the dangers of violent revolution which had overwhelmed less flexible societies.

"In the record of legislation before him, the British lawyer saw the unfolding of Acton's principle of liberty. Liberty, Jethro Brown pointed out, has two aspects—the citizen as an end in himself, and the citizen as a member of the community contributing to the general well-being. From these two aspects of liberty there are derived, in his own words, 'two fundamental principles—the Worth of Man and the Unity of Society.'

"These two principles underlay the broad range of legislation which he scrutinized. The principles seemed to work together, not in a conscious or deliberate way, to form a balanced and integrated national attitude. Making themselves felt in the concrete responses of the British Parliament, these two principles were, in a deeply practical sense, the major premises of the British community.

"We Americans see at once that these principles are also the touchstones of our American community.

.   .   .   .

"But these two principles—the worth of man and the unity of society—are not merely English principles or American principles. They are aspects of the ideal of liberty. And the ideal of liberty is going out across the world, as Jefferson said it would, 'to some parts sooner, to some later, and finally to all.'

"And so, when nations, seized of the ideal of liberty, group themselves together in a free international community, we should expect that larger community—if it is to be a valid and going concern—to build upon these two fundamental principles.

"I suggest to you this evening, that if we examine the recent growth of the international community, viewing that growth as a manifestation of international legislation at work, we will find Jethro Brown's thesis borne out on the international scene.

"We have no complete reference list of contemporaneous international legislation. But I would like to illustrate how international legislation has worked and is working; and at the same time, suggest what principles seem to me to underlie this body of legislation.

"In doing this it is unimportant to argue the traditional philosophic question whether a rule has the force of law if it lacks organized sanctions of power. The important question is whether the actors on the international scene, faced by complex problems, agree among themselves upon practical solutions, and thereafter govern their conduct accordingly."

Secretary of State Acheson, "Law and the Growth of the International Community", address, Apr. 24, 1952, before the American Society of International Law, Washington, D.C., XXVI *Bulletin*, Department of State, No. 671, May 5, 1952, pp. 694, 695.

"First of all, there is the problem of law. The charter [of the United Nations] itself establishes some basic international law, notably by article 2, which deals with sovereign equality, the settlement of international disputes by peaceful means, and the renunciation of the threat or use of force. Chapter XI, dealing with non-self-governing territories, also contains an important enunciation of legal principle.

"Article 13, as we have noted, calls for 'development of international law and its codification.' Under this provision the General Assembly has established the International Law Commission, which has since 1949 met annually to carry out this provision of the charter. Much useful work has been accomplished by the Commission. But progress in incorporating its proposals into the body of international law has so far been minimal.

"There is . . . a considerable body of so-called treaty law, represented by treaties as between the nations. But not all treaties represent 'law' in the sense we here use the term. Some treaties are multilateral and prescribe agreed rules of conduct in relation to such matters as the treatment of aliens and international trade.

Other treaties, usually bilateral, represent merely bargains and are not law in the sense of being a rule of conduct formulated in response to a community sentiment. They are somewhat the counterpart of private contracts within a national society. There has occurred a healthy growth in the multilateral, lawmaking type of treaty.

"There is also a body of world opinion which, when it is crystallized and brought to bear on particular situations, plays a role equivalent to our 'common law.' There has been gratifying progress in developing this kind of community judgment, and the gatherings of the nations at the General Assembly of the United Nations greatly promote this result. There international conduct is judged, sometimes formally but more often informally; and even the most powerful nations feel it expedient to be able to represent their conduct as conforming to this body of world opinion.

"While there is good progress, it must be admitted that the total of international law still falls far short of what is needed to institutionalize peace.

.   .   .   .

"If one were to summarize the present state of affairs, it could permissibly be concluded that considerable progress, even unprecedented progress, has been made in some of the essentials of an international order. There is more international law than ever before. There are greater enforcement possibilities than ever before, particularly in terms of deterrence to open armed aggression. There is more peaceful change than ever before.

"But even if we recognize, as we gladly do, that international society is moving in a sound direction, we must, I think, seriously ask ourselves whether we have adequately learned, and are with sufficient rapidity applying, the lessons of history. Humanity survived through World War II, despite the failure after World War I. But we cannot be sure that we shall be given a second reprieve. The new nature of warfare, as exemplified by the atomic bomb which burst upon a startled world just after the United Nations Charter was signed, gave notice that there may not be an amplitude of time with which to seek progress by the timid route of pragmatic trial and error.

"The foregoing analysis suggests that there are certain areas which particularly require development at the present time.

"One such area is the field of international law. There needs to be a greater and more significant body of such law. Popular attention tends to focus upon the police functions of an international order. These are more spectacular than law itself. But law is absolutely essential to prevent despotism. A policeman must know whom he is to apprehend and why, and a citizen must know when he can count upon the policeman to protect him and when he must fear arrest. Without law a policeman, whatever uniform he wears, is a despot or a tool of despotism.

"This necessity for law creates a perplexing problem because so much of the world is ruled by those who do not believe in law in our sense of the word. 'Law,' within the Communist bloc, is considered the means whereby those in power maintain their power and destroy their enemies. Since communism is materialistic and atheistic, its leaders cannot accept the view that law represents man's efforts to apply to human affairs principles of justice which derive from a higher being. For them there is no natural or moral law. Neither can they understand the concept of rulers being themselves subject to law since, by their creed, the rulers are themselves the source of law.

"Nevertheless, there is some glimmering of hope in this respect. Recent developments within the Soviet Union indicate an effort to provide greater personal security than existed when everyone was subject to liquidation through the secret police at the will of an enemy who possessed the greater power. Vyshinsky's code of 'trial by confession' rather than by evidence is being repudiated. So, despite the Communist doctrinal rejection of our concept of law, there may be emerging a de facto acceptance of law as a protection of the individual against the capricious will of those in authority.

"It is also a fact that on the international plane the Soviet rulers, if only grudgingly and as a matter of expediency, take some account of the opinions of mankind. And these, as we have observed, can form a body of common or unwritten international law.

"Therefore, it is not hopeless to seek to develop a greater body of law even on a universal basis.

"In view, however, of the great difficulty of gaining multilateral acceptance of formal codifications of international law, we shall have to place much reliance upon unwritten law. . . .

"There can also be a useful development of law among the free-world nations as a whole and also among those groups of free nations as naturally draw together. . . .

"When we consider the question of law, we must always consider it jointly with the problem of peaceful change. Law does not conduce to peace if it merely perpetuates the status quo after that status has ceased to serve the needs of a vital and changing community. So far, force or the threat of force has been by far the most effective means of bringing about change. If force is to be eradicated, adequate means for peaceful change must exist. While, as we have seen, peaceful change has already occurred to an unprecedented degree in the evolution of subject peoples to independence, there still remains danger of war from efforts to perpetuate situations which by any standard of equity ought to be changed.

"This makes it of the utmost importance that nations be responsive to informed world opinion and that the 'peaceful adjustment' article of the United Nations Charter (article 14) should be put to better use."

Secretary of State Dulles, "The Institutionalizing of Peace", address before the American Society of International Law, Washington, D.C., Apr. 25, 1956, XXXIV *Bulletin*, Department of State, No. 880, May 7, 1956, pp. 739, 741, 743–744.

In February 1957 Secretary of State Dulles commented as follows
with reference to the need for substituting an order under international law for armed force:

". . . I think that since the events of the last few months there
has come about on the part of all of the nations and members of
the United Nations a more lively realization of the interconnec-
tion of peace and justice and conformity with international law.
I have been constantly emphasizing this myself over the last 6
months, and while I believe that the avoidance of the use of armed
force is, you might say, a primary requirement, the exercise of
self-restraint in that regard calls for the exercise of great vigilance
and greater exertion than has been the case heretofore in trying to
assure that other aspects of international law are complied with.
I think we are going through what may prove to be a very significant stage in the development of an international order.   And
if the world can get through this present stage by liquidating the
armed attack, and then following that with a more vigilant effort
by the United Nations and its members to preserve and secure the
satisfaction of other rights under international law, I think we
will have made one of the great forward steps in history in the
development of an international order."

Secretary Dulles' news conference, Department of State press release
No. 76, Feb. 19, 1957, XXXVI *Bulletin*, Department of State, No. 924, Mar.
11, 1957, pp. 400, 402–403.

"It seems to me quite evident that one of the basic facts of this
age of thermonuclear weapons is that law itself must occupy a
higher place in it than in previous ages.   Until fairly recently
war was both a legal and a pragmatic means of settling international disputes.   The Kellogg-Briand Pact, however, some 30
years ago outlawed war as an instrument of policy; and then came
the charter of the United Nations, which forbids resort to armed
force unless authorized by the United Nations or undertaken in
defense against armed aggression.   And now that thermonuclear
weapons dominate the scene, war has also become so annihilating,
even for the victor, that it is unthinkable that it should be used
except as a defensive weapon.

"The rule of law must therefore in great measure supplant the
rule of war as the final arbiter of international intercourse, if this
intercourse is to continue at all.

"The fabric of social order is woven from a number of strands.
In the first place law and custom, written or unwritten, reflect the
consensus of the community as to what action is right and reasonable.   Second, there is some established and accepted means of
changing these rules of action, so that they may continue to meet
evolving needs and circumstances.   In the third place, there is
some person or agency empowered by the community to administer its law.   Fourth, there are organs of judgment which resolve
disputes under the law.   Fifth, there should be physical force suf-

ficient to deter violence by its capacity to punish breaches of the law. Finally, there must be sufficient material and spiritual health to cause people to act in reasonable and peaceful ways rather than to be driven by need, or fear, to acts of violence.

"There already exist the strands for weaving a world social order, but they are incomplete or imperfect, or have not yet been fully woven into the fabric of international life. A considerable body of international law exists—in the United Nations Charter, in so-called treaty law, and in that body of custom and practice which has attained the status of rules of international law. But the total still falls far short of what is needed to establish the rule of law among nations.

· · · · · · ·

". . . if we are to hope that the rule of law can supplant the rule of force in the world, our work is clear. We must continue to develop the body of law, the institutions of social order, the habit of public acceptance and resort to law, and the social, economic, and political health which are the essential bases of a law-abiding community. As the Greek philosopher Heraclitus said: 'The people must fight for their law as for their wall.' I would add that the people must create their law before they can defend it.

"It is often in time of gravest crisis, when law and order are most challenged and tested, that new techniques in law are invented or applied and the rule of law is thereby strengthened. It is strengthened, that is, if the challenges are met and the tests passed. Where law is flouted or ignored, then the fabric of order can be damaged or destroyed.

· · · · · · ·

"I have dealt with law today largely in its negative or preventive sense—the outlawing of war, the limiting of armaments. Let me say in closing, however, that the positive, permissive aspects of law will be at least as important as the negative ones in their contribution to the future of the world.

"The nations of Europe have under consideration at this moment treaties for a common market and for joint peaceful development of the atom. These developments hold promise of increased strength and independence for these nations and for the area as a whole. Such developments must inevitably break important new ground in international law. The skill with which the law is formulated can determine in substantial measure the success of these developments.

"History records both splendid successes and tragic failures in man's efforts to bring about the rule of law at the various levels of his social relationships. I believe that the further development of the rule of law among nations must come through a slow evolutionary process. It will depend in the first instance on the growth of mutual comprehension among all nations of the *need* for the peaceful machinery of law and of the horrors of the alternative machinery of war. Thereafter it will depend on the spread of confidence born of experience slowly accumulated in practical application of the machinery and techniques of law.

"In the final analysis, though, this development cannot go forward unless men everywhere are willing to make sacrifices of their personal and parochial prerogatives to the common welfare of the world community. . . ."

Under Secretary of State Herter, "The Rule of Law Among Nations", address before the American Bar Association, New York, N.Y., July 15, 1957, XXXVII *Bulletin*, Department of State, No. 945, Aug. 5, 1957, pp. 223–224, 227–228.

"Another direction in which the rule of law is moving is that of displacing force in relations among sovereign countries. We have an International Court of Justice. We have seen the exercise of an international police function, both in the United Nations force in Korea and in the United Nations force assigned to the Gaza Strip. We have agreements in article 2 of the United Nations Charter to the most fundamental concepts of international conduct.

"We have elaborate rules of international law—far more complete and detailed than most people realize. More than once nations have solemnly outlawed war as an instrument of national policy, most recently in the charter of the United Nations. We have, in short, at least the structure and machinery of an international rule of law which could displace the use of force. What we need now is the universal will to accept peaceful settlement of disputes in a framework of law.

"As for our own country, we have shown by our actions that we will neither initiate the use of force or tolerate its use by others in violation of the solemn agreement of the United Nations Charter. Indeed, as we contemplate the destructive potentialities of any future large-scale resort to force, any thoughtful man or nation is driven to a sober conclusion.

"In a very real sense the world no longer has a choice between force and law. If civilization is to survive, it must choose the rule of law. On this Law Day, then, we honor not only the principle of the rule of law but also those judges, legislators, lawyers, and law-abiding citizens who actively work to preserve our liberties under law.

"Let history record that on Law Day free man's faith in the rule of law and justice is greater than ever before. And let us trust that this faith will be vindicated for the benefit of all mankind."

President Eisenhower, "Freedom Under Law", White House press release, Apr. 30, 1958, XXXVIII *Bulletin*, Department of State, No. 986, May 19, 1958, p. 831. This statement by President Eisenhower was issued in connection with the observance of "Law Day", May 1, 1958, which by Presidential Proclamation No. 3221, Feb. 3, 1958, had been so designated. *Ibid.*, No. 974, Feb. 24, 1958, p. 293; 23 *Fed. Reg.* 821.

". . . The trend from anarchy to international order is quite clear, and we have today, in addition to the United Nations, a dozen specialized agencies, the Organization of American States, the North Atlantic Treaty Organization, the Council of Europe, the Arab League and so on. These organizations, and in particular the United Nations, represent an enormously important advance, and are the hope for the future. . . .

Effect of international organizations

"As the world becomes more and more completely organized, what will be the future of the law? International organization necessarily implies the development of law. In the first place, each organization must be constructed on a legal framework; in this field, as elsewhere, the law must serve its function as a means whereby men co-operate smoothly and effectively to gain their social ends. Once in existence, international organizations may promote their ends through the preparation of multilateral conventions. . . .

"International organizations, once operating, can be used to generate customary law. Indeed, this inevitably occurs to some extent as a body of precedent is built up and habitual courses of action come to have legal significance. The charters of these organizations are evolving constitutional instruments, and the legal frameworks established by the drafters must be filled out and completed by the accumulated experience of operation. But since an operating organization generates law, every decision and action which it takes must be carefully considered so that insofar as possible it will fit into a consistent body of precedent which will result in a sound development of international law. . . .

". . . It is clear that the use of force is illegal in international relations except in self-defense or in execution of a decision of a competent organ of the United Nations. But if force is ruled out as a means of settling disputes, it must be made certain that they are settled by peaceful means; and more than that, they must be settled in accordance with justice. . . . Legal techniques are the best means which mankind has yet devised for arriving at justice, and decisions must be taken on a basis of general principle rather than expediency. . . . The law should be a well-fitting jacket, but not a strait-jacket. . . ."

Ivan S. Kerno, Assistant Secretary-General in Charge of the Legal Department of the United Nations, "International Law and International Organization: Prospects for the Future", address before the American Society of International Law, Washington, D. C., Apr. 24, 1952, *Proceedings of the American Society of International Law* (1952) 12, 15–17.

CODIFICATION

§13

"From time to time since the middle of the nineteenth century various efforts have been made to codify international law. Most of these have dealt with administrative and international private law (the conflict of laws) and more particularly with the laws

Efforts in modern times

of war and neutrality. Some of these efforts, especially those of jurists of the Western Hemisphere, have included in their scope the whole field of public and private international law.

"In 1863 Professor Lieber of the Columbia University, at the request of President Lincoln, prepared a code of the laws and usages of war. Other writers on international law have at different times endeavored to bring together into code form the laws on different phases of international relations. The first international conference in relation to codification was that held in 1864 by representatives of twelve countries who met at Geneva and undertook the drafting of a convention embodying rules concerning land warfare. The convention drafted at that time was adopted by thirty-two Governments, including the United States. The 1864 conference was followed by another at Geneva in 1868 which drafted a convention pertaining to naval warfare. This convention, however, failed of ratification.

"In 1874 the representatives of the leading Powers, not including the United States, met at Brussels and drew up a code pertaining to rules of war. It failed of subsequent ratification.

"The next official step in this direction was that taken at the First Hague Peace Conference in 1899, at which were adopted three international conventions, namely, one concerning the Pacific Settlement of International Disputes, another respecting the Laws and Customs of War on Land, and the third applying to maritime warfare the principles of the Geneva Convention of 1868.

"The Second Peace Conference at The Hague in 1907, at which forty-four Nations were represented, made further progress in this direction by adopting fourteen conventions on different subjects pertaining to International Law.

"The Second Hague Conference recognized the need for a further conference to ascertain 'what subjects are ripe for embodiment in an international regulation.' This conference was to have met in 1914, but was not held because of the war.

"Article 14 of the Covenant of the League of Nations directed the Council of the League to prepare and submit to the League a plan for a Permanent Court of International Justice. The Council did not undertake this task itself, but invited eminent jurists to devise a plan. A Committee of Jurists, one of whom was Mr. Elihu Root, met at The Hague in the spring of 1920 and drafted a statute for a Permanent Court of International Justice. Mr. Root also took advantage of this meeting to suggest a succession of conferences at The Hague in order that the Nations in conference, with subsequent ratification of their work, should agree upon the law to be interpreted and applied by the Permanent Court. The Committee of Jurists adopted a resolution proposed by Mr. Root calling for such a conference.

"The Assembly and Council of the League in 1924 established a committee of experts for 'the Progressive Codification of International Law.' The committee, through the Secretariat of the League, addressed questionnaires to the various Governments, both member and non-member States, as to the subjects that might be ripe for codification. As a result of the replies of the various Governments, this committee in 1927 reported to the Assembly of the League which voted to hold the first Codification Conference at The Hague to consider the following subjects: (a) Nationality; (b) Territorial Waters; (c) Responsibility of States for damages done in their territory to the person or property of foreigners. Lengthy questionnaires covering these subjects were forwarded to the various Governments. Following the receipt of the replies of the Governments a Preparatory Committee of the League met at Geneva in January 1929 and again in May of that year and drew up bases of discussion. These bases were discussed at an international conference held at The Hague from March 13 to April 12, 1930, at which forty-eight States were represented. A limited convention and three protocols on nationality were approved by the conference, one of which, namely, the protocol relating to Military Service in Certain Cases of Dual Nationality, was later signed by the United States. No convention was agreed upon in either of the other two subjects.

"The codification of international law has been under active consideration in this hemisphere over a period of more than twenty-five years.

"In 1906 a convention ratified by fifteen American States, including the United States, established a Commission of Jurists charged with the duty of drafting a code of Private International Law and one of Public International Law to govern the relations between the American Republics.

"In 1927 this Commission met at Rio de Janeiro and prepared draft codes on twelve projects of Public International Law which were recommended for submission to and consideration by the Sixth Pan American Conference which convened in Habana in January 1928. Some of the projects, namely, those pertaining to the Status of Aliens, Treaties, Diplomatic Agents, Consuls, Maritime Neutrality, Asylum, Commercial Aviation, and Obligations of States in the Event of Civil Strife, were adopted at the Habana Conference, with modifications.

"Five of these conventions, namely, those pertaining to Civil Strife, Status of Aliens, Commercial Aviation, Consular Agents, and Maritime Neutrality have been ratified by the United States."

Acting Secretary of State W. R. Castle, Jr., to Senator Thomas J. Walsh, Apr. 15, 1932, MS. Department of State, file 500.C 111. Senator Walsh had, during an executive session of the Senate on the World Court, requested such a statement of the various efforts at codification of international law.

"The codification of law involves three basic processes: (1) the grouping together of the rules dealing with a given subject of law in an orderly and logical manner; (2) an attempt to correct defects in those rules, that is, the filling of omissions, the elimination of archaisms, and, in general, the modification of the rules to take into account changes in conditions and policies; and (3) the enactment of the new set of rules into binding law by some agency having the power to do this act. It is true, however, that 'codification' is sometimes used in a more limited sense to refer merely to the systematization of rules, or the systematization and modification of rules, without regard to the essential element of their being put into effect.

"I am certain that most of us in this meeting have had some personal experience with the process of codification in either the domestic or the international field and that we appreciate the difficulties in the way of achieving a useful code as well as the advantages that result from such an achievement.

"The sense in which we are here thinking of codification and some of the difficulties which inhere in the undertaking were aptly stated by Charles Evans Hughes, in an address as President of the American Society of International Law in 1925 in which, in speaking of the codification of public international law, he stated:

'. . . We are thinking both of the restatement of the existing law and of the process of international legislation; that is, of reinvigorating the old law by fresh declaration and of obtaining the formulation of principles and rules which will settle old juristic controversies and also meet the demands of new conditions. . . .

" 'We can be under no misapprehension as to the conditions in which this task is to be accomplished. The consent of nations must be had and this must be obtained from governments faced with political exigencies . . . the development of international law through codification cannot be had without the favorable action of foreign offices and national legislatures, and our problem is how to stimulate effective cooperative endeavor, how to assure both deliberation and purpose. And it must always be borne in mind by our lay friends, who are intent upon the immediate perfecting and declaring of international law, even in the most extreme applications which their paper programs demand, that it is agreement we are seeking on the part of states which according to our fundamental postulate we must recognize as independent and equal before the law; the general accord, if not absolute unanimity, which must characterize the recognition or assumption of international obligations.' (*Proceedings*, Amer. Soc. of Int. Law, 1925, pp. 1, 6–7.)

"In the past there has been a tendency to underestimate the difficulties of codification and to exaggerate the advantages that may result from it. There has been a rather general disregard of the fact that in some instances the most sincere efforts to codify international law may do more harm than good, although this possibility has been touched upon by several scholars, including John Bassett Moore, Noel-Baker, and J. L. Brierly.

"All the facets of the task of codifying international law are demonstrated in the history of the Hague Conference of 1930: the selection of a subject or subjects, the extent of the preparation in the international sphere and by national groups, the organization of the conference, the conflicts of interest between different participating states, the harmonizing of conflicting concepts in the international field carried over from differences in the several systems of domestic jurisprudence and varying political interests, and barriers of one kind or another.

"The preparatory work for this Conference extended over a period of approximately 6 years. It was begun in September 1924 when the Assembly of the League of Nations requested the Council to create a committee on codification. The Committee of Experts for the Progressive Codification of International Law, created by the Council, selected 11 subjects for investigation, of which 7 were reported to the Council as 'ripe for codification'. The Council transmitted this report to the Assembly, which in 1927 decided to submit three subjects, namely, 'Nationality', 'Territorial Waters', and the 'Responsibility of States for Damage Done in Their Territory to the Person or Property of Foreigners', to a first conference on codification. The Council created a Preparatory Committee for the Codification Conference and questionnaires on the three subjects were circulated among the governments. From the replies by 30 governments to the points stated in the questionnaires, bases of discussion were prepared. These bases were submitted to the Conference assembled in March 1930 at The Hague as a starting point for its deliberations. In addition to the painstaking preparation there was on hand at the Conference an excellent staff of more than 80 people from the secretariat of the League, well trained in the mechanics of international conferences. The three subjects were submitted to three separate committees, which in turn had their subcommittees and drafting committees, so that in effect three conferences were going on simultaneously.

"Meanwhile, the Harvard Research in International Law, functioning under the auspices of the Harvard Law School and composed of people from various parts of the country interested in international law, had prepared draft conventions on these same three subjects with copious comment. These were made available to the Conference at The Hague.

"Despite the groundwork thus laid through these preparatory efforts, and the facilities that were available, the Conference was attended with but little success. Its fruits consisted of a Convention on Certain Questions Relating to the Conflict of Nationality Laws and three protocols relating to the subject of nationality. . . .

.   .   .   .

"But one should not be too greatly discouraged by the modest results of the 1930 Hague Conference. I believe that we have learned some valuable lessons from that Conference that will make likely a greater degree of success in future undertakings of the sort.

530309 O–63—10

"Other efforts, official and unofficial, with varying degrees of success, have been made over a long period of years. Although the steps have been referred to repeatedly and in some detail, perhaps a brief reference to some of them may be useful at this time.

"During the first two years of our Civil War conflicting decisions and rulings on questions of the laws of warfare were of common occurrence in different armies and at times in the same theater of operations. The Secretary of War, seeing the need for remedying the situation, called upon Dr. Francis Lieber, an eminent jurist, to prepare a code of instructions for the government of armies of the United States in the field. Such a code was prepared by Dr. Lieber, and, as revised by a Board of Army Officers and approved by President Lincoln, was published in 1863 by the War Department as General Orders, No. 100. It covered such subjects as martial law, military necessity, retaliation, public and private property of the enemy, wanton violence, deserters, prisoners of war, hostages, booty, spies, exchange of prisoners, flags of truce, armistice, capitulation, et cetera.

"This code attracted wide-spread interest in Europe and was greatly relied upon by the Committee on Codification at the Conference held at Brussels in 1874 to consider the general question of the conduct of war. While the Declaration of Brussels was never ratified, it formed the basis of the regulations annexed to the Convention on Laws and Customs of War on Land concluded at the first Hague Peace Conference in 1899 and revised at the second Hague Conference in 1907.

"There was also signed at The Hague in 1899 a Convention for the Pacific Settlement of International Disputes, which comprised a code on good offices, mediation, and arbitration. This Convention, also revised at the second Hague Peace Conference in 1907, contained provision for a Permanent Court of Arbitration and marked an advanced step in the settlement of international disputes by peaceful means.

"Other conventions and declarations were signed at The Hague in 1899 and 1907, as, for example, those relative to the Opening of Hostilities, the Status of Enemy Merchant-Ships at the Outbreak of Hostilities, the Conversion of Merchant-Ships into War-Ships, the Laying of Automatic Submarine Contact Mines, the Bombardment by Naval Forces in Time of War, the Adaptation to Naval War of the Principles of the Geneva Convention of 1906, the Right of Capture in Naval War, the Rights and Duties of Neutral Powers and Persons in War on Land, the Rights and Duties of Neutral Powers in Naval War, and the Establishment of an International Prize Court.

.   .   .   .

"There emerged from the Conference, held in the latter part of 1908 and the early part of 1909, a declaration concerning the laws of naval war, known as the Declaration of London. It dealt with such questions as Blockade, Contraband, Unneutral Service, Destruction of Neutral Prizes, Transfer of Vessels to Neutral

Flags, Enemy Character, Convoy, and Resistance to Search. The Declaration did not reflect *in toto* the views of all or any of the nations participating in the Conference. In many respects it represented compromises on varying points, but by and large it was a commendable effort to codify the law in this important field. The Senate of the United States gave its advice and consent to ratification, but the Declaration was never ratified by any state. Efforts were made during the first World War to apply its provisions by common understanding but with little success.

"The American republics have been very active in the endeavor to codify international law. For example, at the Sixth International Conference of American States held at Habana in 1928, an effort was made to codify a number of subjects. Preliminary work had been done by a Commission of Jurists meeting in Rio de Janeiro, which presented 12 draft projects. The Conference agreed upon drafts relating to the Status of Aliens, Asylum, the Rights and Duties of States in the Event of Civil Strife, Commercial Aviation, Consular Agents, Diplomatic Officers, Copyright, Maritime Neutrality, Private International Law, and Treaties.

"A highly encouraging factor in the development of international law, and particularly in its codification, has been the work done on a voluntary basis by individuals and private organizations. Today's meeting is a token of the interest displayed in this subject by the American practicing lawyer. The Institute of International Law, the International Law Association, the American Society of International Law, the Carnegie Endowment for International Peace, the Harvard Research Group, as well as the Section on International and Comparative Law—and there are others—are private associations that have made a significant contribution to the codification of international law.

"The various efforts that have been made looking to the statement of international law in conventional form constitute a beginning. Conventions heretofore agreed upon will need to be reexamined and subjects not heretofore covered will need to be considered. It must be remembered, however, that codification in this field is by no means simple. International law develops slowly. States do not change overnight from methods and principles to which they have become accustomed. They, no less than individuals, are apt to be skeptical of new rules, the necessity for which may not be readily apparent. It is necessary in considering codification to keep ever in mind the realistic and practical approach. A program that is too ambitious in its inception may prove disappointing. On the other hand, a carefully planned program which would have for its purpose progressive codification on well-chosen subjects would present prospects of success."

Green H. Hackworth, Legal Adviser, Department of State, "The International Court of Justice and the Codification of International Law", address, Cincinnati, Ohio, Dec. 19, 1945, XIII *Bulletin*, Department of State, No. 339, Dec. 23, 1945, pp. 1000, 1002–1005.

As of January 1, 1944, certain jurists, chiefly American and Canadian, set forth certain "Postulates, Principles and Proposals", with comments, containing much well-accepted international law and proposing lines upon which future international law might be shaped. *The International Law of the Future: Postulates, Principles and Proposals* (Carnegie Endowment for International Peace, 1944) ; 38 Am. J. Int'l L. Supp. (1944) 41–139.

The Hague, 1930

The Conference for the Codification of International Law, held at The Hague March 13–April 20, 1930, under the auspices of the League of Nations, considered three subjects: (1) Nationality; (2) Territorial Waters; and (3) Responsibility of States for Damage Caused in Their Territory to the Person or Property of Foreigners. There were invited to the Conference, by invitation of the Council of the League, the members of the League, Brazil, Costa Rica, the Free City of Danzig, Egypt, Ecuador, United States of America, Iceland, Mexico, Monaco, San Marino, Turkey, and the Union of Soviet Socialist Republics. In addition to the Final Act of the Conference, the following documents were opened for signature on the final day of the Conference: Convention on Certain Questions Relating to the Conflict of Nationality Laws; Protocol Relating to Military Obligations in Certain Cases of Double Nationality; Protocol Relating to a Certain Case of Statelessness; Special Protocol Concerning Statelessness. The Conference in plenary session also received a "Report of the Second Commission (Territorial Sea)". The Conference adopted (without dissent) three recommendations: namely, on future codification; on inland waters; and on the protection of fisheries.

For the Bases of Discussion Drawn up for the Conference by the Preparatory Committee, in 3 vols., see I. Nationality (Doc. C.73.M.38.1929.V), Supplements (a), (b), and (c) ; II. Territorial Waters (Doc. C.74.M.39.-1929.V) with Supplements (a) and (b) ; and III. Responsibility of States for Damage Caused in their Territory to the Person or Property of Foreigners (Doc. C.75.M.69.1929.V), and Supplement (a). The volumes just cited include the replies made by the governments to the Schedule of Points.

The proceedings of the Conference are printed in Acts of the Conference for the Codification of International Law, in 4 vols., see I. Plenary Meetings (Doc. C.351.M.145.1930.V) ; II. Minutes of the First Committee—Nationality (Doc. C.351(a).M.145(a).1930.V) ; III. Minutes of the Second Committee—Territorial Waters (Doc. C.351(b).M.145(b).1930.V) ; and IV. Minutes of the Third Committee—Responsibility of States for Damage Caused in their Territory to the Person or Property of Foreigners (Doc. C.351(c).M.145(c).1930.V.)

For the Convention on Certain Questions Relating to the Conflict of Nationality Laws, see Doc. C.24.M.13.1931.V. For the Protocol Relating to Military Obligations in Certain Cases of Double Nationality, see Doc. C.25.M.14.1931.V. For the Protocol Relating to a Certain Case of Statelessness, see Doc. C.26.M.15.1931.V. For the Special Protocol Concerning Statelessness, see Doc. C.27.M.16.1931.V. The United States is not a party to the Convention on Nationality which came into force on July 1, 1937. The Protocol on Military Obligations entered into effect on May 25, 1937, as to the United States and other governments parties to it. 50 Stat. 1317; IV Treaties, etc. (Trenwith, 1938) 5261.

For the Report of the First Commission (Nationality), see Doc. C.229.M. 116. 1930.V. For the Report of the Second Commission (Territorial Sea), see Doc. C.230.M.117.1930.V. For the Report of the Third Commission (Responsibility of States), see Doc. C.231.M.117.1930.V.

For the Final Act, see Doc. C.228.M.115.1930.V.

See also MS. Department of State, file 504.418A2; 1930 For. Rel., vol. I, pp. 204–223, for correspondence of the Department of State on the subject of the Conference.

A Research in International Law was organized under the auspices of the faculty of the Harvard Law School in 1927 and 1928, initially for the purpose of preparing drafts of conventions on topics on the agenda of the Hague Codification Conference of 1930. The Research in International Law prepared drafts on the following subjects: (1) Nationality; (2) Responsibility of States for Injuries to Foreigners; (3) Territorial Waters; (4) Diplomatic Privileges and Immunities; (5) Legal Position and Functions of Consuls; (6) Competence of Courts in Regard to Foreign States; (7) Piracy; (8) Extradition; (9) Jurisdiction With Respect to Crime; (10) Law of Treaties; (11) Judicial Assistance; (12) Rights and Duties of Neutral States in Naval and Aerial War; and (13) Rights and Duties of States in Case of Aggression.

For copies of drafts on subjects (1) to (3), see 23 Am. J. Int'l L. Spec. Supp. (1929); subjects (4) to (7), see 26 *ibid.* Supp. (1932); subjects (8) to (10), see 29 *ibid.* Supp. (1935); subjects (11) to (13), see 33 *ibid.* Supp. (1939).

The First South American Congress on Private International Law was held at Montevideo in 1888–1889. Treaties were concluded on the following subjects: International Civil Law, International Commercial Law, International Penal Law, International Procedural Law, Literary and Artistic Property, Trade-Marks, Patents of Invention, Exercise of Liberal Professions, and an Additional Protocol. *Montevideo 1888–1889*

1939–1940

A second meeting on Private International Law was held at Montevideo in 1939. Treaties were signed on the following subjects: Political Asylum and Refuge, Intellectual Property, and Exercise of the Liberal Professions. At the 1939 meeting it was seen that there was need to hold a new Congress. The Second Congress took place at Montevideo in 1940, officially known as the Second South American Congress on Private International Law. This Congress drafted treaties on: International Civil Law, International Commercial Terrestrial Law, International Commercial Navigation, International Penal Law (including Extradition), International Procedural Law, and an Additional Protocol.

The revisions of 1939–1940 left the treaties on Trade-Marks and on Patents of Invention of the 1888–1889 Conference as they were. The Treaty of 1939 on Political Asylum and Refuge is an expanded version of articles 15–18, title II, of the Treaty on International Penal Law of the 1888–1889 Conference. The treaties on International Commercial Terrestrial Law and on International Commercial Navigation Law, signed March 19, 1940, constitute a division and amplification of the Treaty on

International Commercial Law concluded at the 1888–1889 Conference.
For the 1889 treaties, see *Actas y Tratados del Congreso Sud-Americano de
Derecho Internacional Privado, Montevideo 1888–1889* (compiled by Ernesto
Restelli, Buenos Aires, 1928). For the 1939 and 1940 agreements, see
*Segundo Congreso Sudamericano de Derecho Internacional Privado, Acta
Final* (Segunda Edición, Montevideo, 1940); *Segundo Congreso Sudameri-
cano de Derecho Internacional Privado, de Montevideo, Ministerio de Re-
laciones Exteriores y Culto de la República Argentina* (Buenos Aires, 1940);
and 37 Am. J. Int'l L. Supp. (1943) 99–152. The latter also contains an
English translation of the 1889 Treaty on Trade-Marks and of the 1889
Treaty on Patents of Invention. *Ibid.* 152–157.

". . . the Congresses of 1888–89 and 1939–40 adopted integrally and
without qualification, the principle of *territoriality*, in civil [Art. 56,
Tratado de Derecho Civil Internacional], criminal [Art. 1, *Tratado de
Derecho Penal Internacional*], and procedural [Art. 1, *Tratado de Derecho
Procesal Internacional*] matters.

"One of the many excellent features of these treaties is the demotion
of the foreign State to the position of a juristic person in private law, with
the corresponding responsibilities [Art. 3, *Tratado de Derecho Civil Internacional*], especially in regard to cases where such States employ vessels in
carrying on ordinary commercial transactions. [Arts. 34–42, Title X,
Tratado de Derecho de Navegación Commercial Internacional]." J. Irizarry
y Puente, "Treaties on Private International Law", 37 Am. J. Int'l L. Supp.
(1943) 95, 98–99.

Inter-American Neutrality Committee, 1939

In 1939 the First Meeting of Foreign Ministers of the American
Republics resolved that "With a view to studying and formulating
recommendations with respect to the problems of neutrality, in the
light of experience and changing circumstances, there shall be established, for the duration of the European war, an Inter-American
Neutrality Committee, composed of seven experts in international
law, who shall be designated by the Governing Board of the Pan
American Union before November 1, 1939." Recommendations of
the Committee were transmitted, through the Pan American Union,
to the Governments of the American Republics.

Res. V, "General Declaration of Neutrality of the American Republics",
*Report of the Delegate of the United States of America to the Meeting of
the Foreign Ministers of the American Republics, Held at Panamá, September 23–October 3, 1939*, pp. 54, 57. At its session held November 1, 1939,
the Governing Board of the Pan American Union proceeded to organize the
Inter-American Neutrality Committee. The Committee held its opening
session in Rio de Janeiro on January 15, 1940.

The work of the Inter-American Neutrality Committee has been summarized as follows:

"During the first half of 1940, the Committee formulated recommendations on the following subjects, which the Pan American Union
transmitted to the Governments, members of the Union:

"1. Internment.

"2. Vessels used as auxiliary transports of warships.

"3. Entry of submarines into the ports and territorial waters of
the American Republics.

"4. Security Zone.

"5. Inviolability of postal correspondence.

"6. Telecommunications.

"The foregoing recommendations furnished the basis of many laws, decrees and regulations issued by the American Governments on these particular subjects. In many instances, in the preamble to said laws and decrees, the Governments expressly refer to the recommendations of the Neutrality Committee.

"The Second Meeting of the Ministers of Foreign Affairs of the American Republics (Habana, 1940), requested the Committee, in Resolution I, to draft and submit to the Governments a preliminary project of convention dealing with 'the juridical effects of the Security Zone and the measures of international cooperation which the American States are ready to adopt to obtain respect for the said Zone'; and, furthermore, to prepare a project of inter-American convention 'which will cover completely all the principles and rules generally recognized in international law in matters of neutrality.'

"The first of these drafts, on the Security Zone, was completed by the Neutrality Committee early in 1941, and was submitted to the Governments by the Pan American Union in March of the same year. The observations and comments thereon made by the member Governments were transmitted to the Committee for its consideration.

"The draft convention on neutrality is partially completed. In the face of new world developments, the Committee found it necessary to postpone the completion of this project, in order to devote its efforts to the preparation of other projects of a more urgent character which were subsequently assigned to it by the American Governments.

"In July 1941 the Neutrality Committee formulated a Recommendation on the Treatment of the Crews of Merchant Ships Suspected of Sabotage and transmitted it to the Pan American Union. The Union forwarded this project to the member governments and the replies received were communicated to the Committee. In this recommendation the Committee suggested certain precautionary measures which the neutral States might adopt with respect to the treatment of members of the crews removed from merchant ships of the belligerents or of countries occupied by them which had taken refuge in the ports, harbors or territorial waters of these neutrals, when there was reason to believe that the crew members had committed or were about to commit acts of sabotage.

"Another of the projects formulated by the Committee during the period of neutrality in the Continent was that relative to the Extension of Territorial Waters. This project was based on a proposal presented to the Second Meeting of the Ministers of Foreign Affairs of the American Republics at Habana in 1940 by the Delegation of Uruguay and, in accordance with Resolution VIII of said Meeting, transmitted by the Pan American Union to the Inter-American Neutrality Committee and to the members of the Committee of Experts on the Codification of International Law.

"The Neutrality Committee's recommendation on the subject was forwarded to the Pan American Union in September 1941. . . ." Manuel S. Canyes, Chief of the Juridical Division, Pan American Union, "The Inter-American Juridical Committee", 1943 *Bulletin of the Pan American Union* (May) 268, 269–270.

The Minutes of the Inter-American Neutrality Committee do not appear to have been printed. A mimeographed copy, in Portuguese, *Atas da sessão ordinária, 1940–1942* (Rio de Janeiro, two vols.), is on deposit in the Library of Congress. Minutes, in Portuguese, of sessions of the Committee held from January 15 to February 2, 1940, together with minutes of the unofficial sessions held on May 15, 17, 20, and 21, 1940, are available (in mimeograph) in "Decrees and Regulations on Neutrality", Supp. No. 3, Law and Treaty Series No. 15 (Pan American Union).

For diplomatic correspondence of the United States concerning the Inter-American Neutrality Committee, see MS. Department of State, file 740.00111 A.R.; 1939 For. Rel., vol. V, pp. 45–47; 1940 For. Rel., vol. V, pp. 257–340; 1941 For. Rel., vol. VI, pp. 1–18.

In 1942, at the Third Meeting of the Ministers of Foreign Affairs of the American Republics, held at Rio de Janeiro, it was resolved that the profound alteration in the international situation in America demanded a substantial expansion of the scope of the Inter-American Neutrality Committee and that "the Inter-American Neutrality Committee at present existing will continue to function in its present form under the name of 'Inter-American Juridical Committee' ", with its seat in Rio de Janeiro. The resolution so providing also provided that the members (jurists) would be appointed by their respective governments and that they should have no other duties than those pertaining to the Committee. The Committee had as its object, *inter alia*, the development and coordination of the work of codifying international law, "without prejudice to the duties entrusted to other existing organizations".

"Inter-American Juridical Committee", 1942

Res. XXVI, *Report on the Third Meeting of the Ministers of Foreign Affairs of the American Republics, Rio de Janeiro, January 15–28, 1942*, submitted to the Governing Board of the Pan American Union by the Director General, pp. 53–54. The opening session of the Inter-American Juridical Committee was held at Rio de Janeiro on March 10, 1942.

"The first project which the Juridical Committee agreed to undertake, soon after the general lines of its work were laid down, was the formulation of a draft declaration entitled *Reaffirmation of fundamental principles of international law*. This draft was prepared on the basis of the project introduced by the Bolivian delegation at the Rio Meeting of Foreign Ministers and referred to the Committee by Resolution XXVIII.

.   .   .   .   .   .

"The Declaration, as formulated by the Juridical Committee, restates certain principles which are already incorporated into American conventional law or which are the object of resolutions and declarations approved at inter-American conferences and consultative meetings. In some instances, these principles were rephrased by the Committee so as to define them more precisely and clarify their application to present-day conditions.

.   .   .   .   .   .

"Following the drafting of the Declaration on Reaffirmation, the Committee proceeded to discuss at length its various plans for future work. With respect to problems arising out of the war the Committee found it difficult to formulate uniform rules on many subjects because of the conflicting positions taken by the different Governments. In view of this situation the Committee agreed to make preliminary inquiry of the Governments with respect to legislation and accompanying administrative regulations concerning such matters as the requisition of merchant vessels, the status of enemy aliens and of enemy alien property, the legal position of refugees and of stateless persons, the nationality of corporations, and the effect of war upon contracts.

"One of the problems arising out of the war on which the Committee believed that a uniform recommendation might be made, notwithstanding the different aspects it might present in a number of American States, was the legal position of refugees. On this subject an elaborate questionnaire was prepared for submission to the Governments . . .

"After completing these preliminary steps, the Committee proceeded to the study of post-war problems. The Resolution on Post-war Problems, adopted by the Rio Meeting of Ministers of Foreign Affairs, was the outcome of a number of projects which were presented to that conference by several delegations for the purpose of laying the foundation of the 'new order of peace' which must follow the present war.

. . . .

". . . the Committee . . . chose to begin its work with a Preliminary Recommendation, which sets forth certain ideas of a fundamental character bearing upon the establishment of international peace and the maintenance of law and order." Manuel S. Canyes, Chief of the Juridical Division, Pan American Union, "The Inter-American Juridical Committee", 1943 *Bulletin of the Pan American Union* (May) 268, 271–273. The Pan American Union published five volumes of the Minutes of the Inter-American Juridical Committee, in the original language (Portuguese), covering the period March 20, 1942–January 25, 1946.

Projects prepared by or in the Inter-American Juridical Committee from May 1943 to First Meeting of the Council of Jurists (May-June 1950):

Revised text, Reaffirmation of Fundamental Principles of International Law (Mar. 6, 1944) ; Draft Treaty for the Coordination of Inter-American Peace Agreements (Mar. 6, 1944) ; Draft of an Alternative Treaty Relating to Peaceful Procedures (Mar. 6, 1944) ; Report to Accompany the Draft Treaty for the Coordination of Inter-American Peace Agreements and Draft of an Alternative Treaty (1944) ; Recommendation for the Immediate Establishment of a Preliminary International Organization (June 6, 1944) ; Recommendation on a Reorganization of the Agencies Engaged in the Codification of International Law (Oct. 17, 1944) ; Report to Accompany the Recommendation on the Codification of Public International Law (Oct. 17, 1944) ; Dumbarton Oaks Proposals: Preliminary Comments and Recommendations (Dec. 8, 1944) ; Report on the International Juridical Status of Individuals as "War Criminals" (July 30, 1945) ; Draft of an Inter-American Peace System (Sept. 4, 1945) (unpublished) ; Report to Accompany the Draft of an Inter-American Peace System (Sept. 4, 1945) (unpublished) ; Draft Declaration of the International Rights and Duties of Man (Dec. 31, 1945) (unpublished) ; Report to Accompany the Draft Declaration of the International Rights and Duties of Man (Dec. 31, 1945) (unpublished) ; Opinion on the Guatemalan Project submitted to the Conference on Problems of War and Peace (Oct. 29, 1946) (unpublished) ; Carta Interamericana de Garantías Sociales—Proyecto que el Comité Jurídico Interamericano somete a la consideración de la IX Conferencia Internacional Americana de Bogotá (Oct. 21, 1947) (Spanish only) ; Exposición de Motivos de la Carta Interamericana de Garantías Sociales (Oct. 21, 1947) (Spanish only) ; Sistema Interamericano de Paz—Proyecto definitivo que el Comité Jurídico Interamericano presenta a la consideración de la IX Conferencia Internacional Americana de Bogotá (Nov. 18, 1947) (Spanish only) ; Informe anexo al Proyecto definitivo de "Sistema Interamericano de Paz" (Nov. 18, 1947) (Spanish only) ; Declaración de los Derechos y Deberes del Hombre—Proyecto definitivo que el Comité Jurídico

Interamericano presenta a la consideración de la IX Conferencia Internacional Americana de Bogotá (Dec. 8, 1947) (Spanish only) ; Informe anexo al Proyecto definitivo de Declaración de los Derechos y Deberes Internacionales del Hombre (Dec. 8, 1947) (Spanish only) ; Report on the Plan for the Development and Codification of Public and Private International Law (Sept. 6, 1949) ; Plan for the Development and Codification of Public and Private International Law—Draft Resolution (Sept. 6, 1949) ; Report to the Inter-American Council of Jurists Concerning Resolution XXXI of the Conference of Bogotá—Inter-American Court to Protect the Rights of Man (Sept. 26, 1949) ; Report and Draft Convention on Recognition of de Facto Governments (Sept. 27, 1949) ; Dictamen del Comité Jurídico Interamericano sobre Contenido de las Declaraciones, Recomendaciones y Otros Actos Análogos de las Conferencias y Reuniones de Consulta Interamericanas (May 15, 1950) (Spanish only) ; Dictamen del Comité Jurídico Interamericano Relativo a la Amplitud de las Facultades del Consejo de la Organización de los Estados Americanos (May 18, 1950) (Spanish only) ; Informe sobre el Derecho de Resistencia (May 20, 1950) (Spanish only) ; Informe sobre un Proyecto de Convenio que suprima el uso de pasaportes y establezca la cédula de identidad americana libre de visas e impuestos consulares (May 1950) (Spanish only).

By Resolution II of the Ninth Inter-American Conference, held at Bogotá in 1948, it was resolved that the Inter-American Juridical Committee of Rio de Janeiro, as then organized, should continue to perform its duties until such time as the Charter of the Organization of American States came into effect and the new procedures thereunder for constituting the Inter-American Juridical Committee were put into effect. *Ninth International Conference of American States,* Bogotá, 1948, Report of the Delegation of the United States of America, pp. 230–231.

Inter-American Council of Jurists

The Charter of the Organization of American States, signed at Bogotá in April 1948, contains provision for the establishment of the Inter-American Council of Jurists as an organ of the Council of the Organization of American States (article 57). By the terms of the Charter the purpose of the Inter-American Council of Jurists is "to serve as an advisory body on juridical matters; to promote the development of codification of public and private international law; and to study the possibility of attaining uniformity in the legislation of the various American countries, insofar as it may appear desirable" (article 67). The Inter-American Council of Jurists meets when convened by the Council of the Organization, at the place determined by the Council of Jurists at its previous meeting (article 72).

For the Charter of the OAS, see *Ninth International Conference of American States,* Bogotá, 1948, Report of the Delegation of the United States of America, pp. 166, 176, 178–179 ; U.S. TIAS 2361 ; 2 UST 2394 ; S. Exec. Rept. 15, 81st Cong., 2d sess. For the Statutes of the Inter-American Council of Jurists (With the amendments of 1957), see pamphlet of the Pan American Union, Washington, D.C., 1958, article 16 of which states that "The interval between meetings shall not exceed two years unless the Council of the Organization, for special reasons, finds a longer interval expedient."

The Inter-American Council of Jurists held its First Meeting at Rio de Janeiro in 1950. *Final Act of the First Meeting of the Inter-American Council of Jurists, Rio de Janeiro, Brazil, May 22–June 15, 1950* (Pan American Union, 1950). The Second Meeting of the Inter-American Council of Jurists was held at Buenos Aires in 1953. *Final Act of the Second Meeting of the Inter-American Council of Jurists, Buenos Aires, Argentina, 20 April–9 May 1953* (Pan American Union, 1953). The Third Meeting of the Council of Jurists was held at Mexico City in 1956. *Final Act of the Third Meeting of the Inter-American Council of Jurists, Mexico City, Mexico, January 17–February 4, 1956* (Pan American Union, 1956). The Fourth Meeting of the Council of Jurists was held at Santiago, Chile, in 1959. *Final Act of the Fourth Meeting of the Inter-American Council of Jurists, Santiago, Chile, August 24–September 9, 1959* (Pan American Union, 1959 [1960]) (CIJ–43).

The Charter of the Organization of American States further provides that "The Inter-American Juridical Committee of Rio de Janeiro shall be the permanent committee of the Inter-American Council of Jurists" (article 68). The Juridical Committee is, under the Charter, composed of jurists of the nine countries selected by the Inter-American Conference (article 69). The selection of the jurists is made by the Inter-American Council of Jurists from a panel submitted by each country chosen by the Conference. The members of the Juridical Committee represent all Member States of the Organization. The Council of the OAS is empowered to fill any vacancies that occur during the intervals between Inter-American Conferences and between meetings of the Inter-American Council of Jurists (*ibid.*). The Juridical Committee undertakes such studies and preparatory work as are assigned to it by the Inter-American Council of Jurists, the Inter-American Conference, the Meeting of Consultation of Ministers of Foreign Affairs, or the Council of the Organization. It may also undertake those studies and projects which, on its own initiative, it considers advisable (article 70). It is provided in the Charter of the OAS that the Inter-American Council of Jurists and the Juridical Committee should seek the cooperation of national committees for the codification of international law, of institutes of international and comparative law, and of other specialized agencies (article 71).

[marginal note: Inter-American Juridical Committee]

For the Statutes of the Inter-American Juridical Committee, referred to as the "Permanent Committee" of the Inter-American Council of Jurists, see the Statutes of the Inter-American Council of Jurists (With the amendments of 1957), pamphlet of the Pan American Union, Washington, D.C., 1958, arts. 26–47, 49, 50, 52–55, and 57.

Until 1955 the Inter-American Juridical Committee held its sessions on a continuing basis throughout the year. The Tenth Inter-American Conference, held at Caracas in March 1954, decided that, beginning in 1955, the Inter-American Juridical Committee "shall function on a permanent basis during three consecutive months each year, at a time that shall not coincide with any meeting of the Inter-American Council of Jurists, and without prejudice to the convocation of an extraordinary meeting whenever any important and urgent matter so requires." Res. LI, "Inter-American Juridical Committee", *Tenth Inter-American Conference,* Caracas, 1954, Report of the Delegation of the United States of America, pp. 120–121. The same resolution provided that for the better fulfillment of the aims of the Inter-American Juridical Committee "it is essential that the jurists selected to be members thereof devote themselves exclusively to the work of the Committee during the period of its meetings" (paragraph 3). It was also provided by that resolution that a quorum of five members should be required for meetings of the Juridical Committee, and that its opinions, resolutions, or decisions "shall be adopted by a minimum of five affirmative votes" (paragraph 4).

At the time of drafting of the Charter of the Organization of American States in 1948, there were—in addition to the Inter-American Juridical Committee—at least technically in existence the following inter-American juridical agencies whose work had in considerable measure come to a stand-still:

(a) International Conference of American Jurists;

(b) Committee of Experts for the Codification of International Law;

(c) Permanent Committee of Rio de Janeiro for the Codification of Public International Law;

(d) Permanent Committee of Montevideo for the Codification of Private International Law;

(e) Permanent Committee of Habana on Comparative Legislation and Uniformity of Legislation;

(f) Permanent Committee of Jurists for the Unification of the Civil and Commercial Laws of America.

The above-listed organizations ceased with the coming into existence of the Inter-American Council of Jurists and the Inter-American Juridical Committee, created pursuant to the Charter of the Organization of American States.

In 1950, at its First Meeting, the Inter-American Council of Jurists expressed "the opinion" that, "inasmuch as the Inter-American Council of Jurists and its Permanent Committee, the Juridical Committee of Rio de Janeiro, have been formally established, and the functions specifically assigned to them by Article 67 of the Charter of the Organization include each and all of the essential duties that formerly were entrusted to the aforesaid agencies [those listed *supra*]", they "have been replaced by and their duties entrusted to the Inter-American Council of Jurists and to its Permanent Committee, the Juridical Committee of Rio de Janeiro". *Final Act of the First Meeting of the Inter-American Council of Jurists, Rio de Janeiro, Brazil, May 22–June 15, 1950* (Pan American Union, 1950) 18–19.

The inter-American juridical agencies listed *supra* (a) to (f) had been established as follows under the following names and for the following described purposes:

In 1906 at the Third International Conference of American States held at Rio de Janeiro, there was drafted a Convention on International Law, pursuant to which an International Commission of Jurists was established, composed of one representative for each signatory State, charged with the preparation of a draft Code of Private International Law and one of Public International Law, regulating the relations between American States. Each signatory State was entitled to name one representative to the Commission. The Commission held its first meeting at Rio de Janeiro from June 26 to July 19, 1912. Committees were created to do preparatory work and to formulate projects for the consideration of the Commission at its second meeting, fixed for June 1914. However, World War I prevented the holding of the meeting. James Brown Scott, *The International Conferences of American States, 1889–1928* (1931) 144 and *ibid.* n.1. The United States ratified the Convention. III Redmond, Treaties, etc. (1923) 2885.

In 1923 at the Fifth International Conference of American States, a resolution was approved requesting each government to appoint delegates to constitute the "Congress of Jurists of Rio de Janeiro" and recommending that the committees appointed by the Congress of Jurists be reestablished. *Report of the Delegates of the United States of America to the Fifth International Conference of American States, Held at Santiago, Chile, March 25 to May 3, 1923*, p. 131.

The Sixth International Conference of American States, meeting at Habana in 1928, adopted a resolution which continued the International Commission of Jurists of Rio de Janeiro and which provided for the organization of three permanent committees: one in Rio de Janeiro for the work relating to public international law; another in Montevideo for the work relating to private international law; and another in Habana for the study of comparative legislation and uniformity of legislation. *Report of the Delegates of the United States of America to the Sixth International Conference of American States, Held at Habana, Cuba, January 16 to February 20, 1928*, appendix 73, p. 315.

At the Seventh International Conference of American States held at Montevideo in 1933, another resolution on "Methods of Codification of International Law" was approved. The Montevideo Resolution provided (1) for the maintenance of the Commission of Jurists; (2) for the creation by each government of a National Commission on Codification; and (3) for the creation of a Commission of Experts. The Commission of Experts—composed of seven members—was to organize in a preparatory character the work of codification. It was to list subjects considered susceptible of codification and to prepare questionnaires for submission to the National Commissions, which, in turn, should submit their views through the respective foreign offices to the Pan American Union. The Commission of Experts was to study the replies received from the National Commissions and to draft bases of discussion to be submitted to the International Commission of Jurists or Jurisconsults, as they were referred to in the resolution. Res. LXX, *Report of the Delegates of the United States of America to the Seventh International Conference of American States*, Montevideo, 1933, pp. 263–266.

At the Inter-American Conference for the Maintenance of Peace held at Buenos Aires in 1936, a resolution on the "Codification of International Law" was approved providing in effect (1) for the reestablishment of the Permanent Committees created at the Habana Conference "in order that they may undertake the preliminary studies for the codification of international law"; (2) that the National Committees on Codification of International Law provided for at the Montevideo Conference should undertake studies of the subjects to be codified and transmit the results to the Permanent Committees on Codification; (3) that the Permanent Committees should prepare draft conventions and resolutions as bases of discussion and the preparatory work for the International Commission of American Jurists; (4) that the studies of the Permanent Committees should be transmitted to the Committee of Experts, at Washington, "who will meet to revise and coordinate them", and (5) that upon completion of their work of general revision the Committee of Experts should transmit the preparatory studies with a detailed report to the Pan American Union for submission to the Governments of the American Republics and ultimately for consideration by the International Commission of American Jurists. Res. VI, *Report of the Delegation of the United States of America to the Inter-American Conference for the Maintenance of Peace*, Buenos Aires, 1936, pp. 211–212.

In 1938 at Lima, Peru, the Eighth International Conference of American States, by its resolution on "Methods for the Codification of International Law", provided that "The codification of international law shall be gradually and progressively accomplished through existing agencies, which are:

"(*a*) The national committees in each American country;
"(*b*) The three permanent committees, established in Rio de Janeiro, Montevideo and Habana, respectively;
"(*c*) The Committee of Experts, at Washington; and
"(*d*) The International Commission of American Jurists, which in the future shall be known as the International Conference of American Jurists."

Briefly, in maintaining in existence the then-existing codification agencies it was provided that the National Committees should elaborate preliminary drafts with explanatory summaries; that the three Permanent Committees of Rio de Janeiro, Montevideo, and Habana should prepare bases for conventions, declarations, or uniform laws, as appropriate; that the Committee of Experts, composed of nine members instead of seven, should make a technical examination of each subject treated by the three Committees just mentioned and prepare adequate drafts; and that the International Commission of American Jurists (to be known henceforth as the International Conference of American Jurists) should revise, coordinate, approve, modify, or reject the drafts thus prepared by the Committee of Experts; and that the conventions or other instruments thus prepared should be deposited with the Pan American Union which would transmit certified copies thereof to all the American Governments for appropriate action. Res. XVII, *Report of the Delegation of the United States of America to the Eighth International Conference of American States*, Lima, 1938, pp. 123–126.

For a "History of Codification of International Law in the Inter-American System", including, *inter alia*, pre-First World War efforts and a summary of accomplishments of the Fifth International Conference of American

States (Santiago, Chile, 1923), the Sixth International Conference of
American States (Habana, 1928), the Seventh International Conference of
American States (Montevideo, 1933), the Inter-American Conference for
the Maintenance of Peace (Buenos Aires, 1936), and the Eighth Inter-
national Conference of American States (Lima, 1938), see "Outline—The
Codification of International Law in the Inter-American System with
Special Reference to the Methods of Codification", U.N. Doc. A/AC.10/8,
May 6, 1947, and *ibid.*/Corr. 1, May 12, 1947. See also Final Acts of, and
Reports of the U.S. Delegation on, the respective Conferences.

The Inter-American Council of Jurists at its First Meeting, held
at Rio de Janeiro in 1950, adopted a resolution containing a plan for
the "Development and Codification of Public International Law and
Private International Law and the Attainment of Uniformity of
Legislation among the American States" (Resolution VII). The
first portion of the resolution dealt with work procedures. It was
provided that: in case of studies relating to the development of international law, the Permanent Committee should limit itself to writing
decisions or reports for consideration by governments and thereafter
prepare a new decision or report to be presented to the Council of
Jurists (article 4); in case of studies relating to the codification of
international law, the Permanent Committee should prepare, in addition to reports, draft conventions or treaties, or at least draft articles,
for consideration by governments, and thereafter prepare a second
report and draft document to be presented to the Council of Jurists
(article 5); in case of studies involving both codification and development of international law, the Permanent Committee should identify
such points together with sources (article 6); and in case of studies
relating to the attainment of uniformity of legislation, the Permanent
Committee was directed to proceed by preparing drafts of conventions
or treaties (or draft articles) for consideration by governments, submitting second drafts thereof to the Council of Jurists (article 7).

The second portion of Resolution VII listed topics to be studied
by the Juridical Committee, namely:

"I. Public International Law:

"(a) System of territorial waters and related questions.
"(b) Nationality and status of stateless persons.

"II. Private International Law:

"Possibility of revision, in so far as advisable, of the Bustamante Code, or the Code of Private International Law
adopted by the Sixth International Conference of American
States at Habana on February 20, 1928, in the light of the
Montevideo Treaties, approved by the South American
Congresses of Private International Law held in that city
in 1888–1889 and 1939–1940, and of the 'Restatement of

Res. VII,
1950

the Law of Conflicts of Laws' drawn up by the American Law Institute of the United States of America, in order to make these three codifications uniform.

"III. Uniformity of Legislation:

"(a) Aid and rescue;
"(b) Collision;
"(c) Rules concerning the immunity of State ships;
"(d) Uniform rules on the sale of personal property;
"(e) International commercial arbitration;
"(f) International cooperation in judicial procedures ('judicial assistance')."

Res. VII, *Final Act of the First Meeting of the Inter-American Council of Jurists, Rio de Janeiro, Brazil, May 22–June 15, 1950* (Pan American Union, 1950) 14–18. See also *infra* under "Consideration of topics" (item 26).

Consideration of topics:

1. *Territorial Waters and Related Questions*

The topic was assigned to the Inter-American Juridical Committee by Resolution VII of the First Meeting of the Council of Jurists (1950). Cited *supra*. The Juridical Committee considered the topic in 1952 and approved by a vote of 4 to 3 a "Draft Convention on Territorial Waters and Related Questions. CIJ–11. The Draft Convention was submitted to the Second Meeting of the Inter-American Council of Jurists at Buenos Aires in 1953, which decided, by Resolution XIX, to return the matter to the Juridical Committee for further study. *Final Act of the Second Meeting of the Inter-American Council of Jurists, Buenos Aires, Argentina, 20 April–9 May 1953* (Pan American Union, 1953) 52–54. By Resolution LXXXIV, entitled "Conservation of Natural Resources: The Continental Shelf and Marine Waters", it was decided in 1954 at the Caracas Conference that the Council of the Organization of American States should convoke a Specialized Conference for the purpose of studying as a whole the different aspects of the juridical and economic system governing the submarine shelf, oceanic waters, and their natural resources in the light of present-day scientific knowledge. *Tenth Inter-American Conference*, Caracas, 1954, Report of the Delegation of the United States of America, pp. 147–148. Thereafter, on October 6, 1954, and on September 2, 1955, the Juridical Committee approved resolutions providing for the suspension of study on the topic until it could learn the results of the Specialized Conference. A resolution in this sense was submitted to the Third Meeting of the Inter-American Council of Jurists. CIJ–25. The Council of Jurists at its Third Meeting, at

Mexico City, approved Resolution XIII containing the so-called "Principles of Mexico on the Juridical Régime of the Sea". *Final Act of the Third Meeting of the Inter-American Council of Jurists, Mexico City, Mexico, January 17–February 4, 1956* (Pan American Union, 1956) 36–38. The Council of Jurists by Resolution XIV, approved the same day (February 3, 1956), suggested that the Council of the Organization of American States transmit Resolution XIII, together with the minutes of the meetings, to the Specialized Conference called for by the Caracas Conference. *Ibid.* 39. The Inter-American Specialized Conference met at Ciudad Trujillo in March 1956 and adopted the "Resolution of Ciudad Trujillo" on the subject, submitting for consideration of the American States that the States were in agreement on certain aspects of the matter and that on certain others they were not in agreement. *Final Act, Inter-American Specialized Conference on "Conservation of Natural Resources: The Continental Shelf and Marine Waters", Ciudad Trujillo, March 15– 28, 1956* (Pan American Union, 1956) 13–14. "As the Council of Jurists has made the preparatory study on the juridical aspects of the matter entrusted to it in Resolution XIII and other documents, it appears that this matter no longer falls within the competence of the Committee." Report Submitted by the Chairman of the Inter-American Juridical Committee on the Status of Topics Entrusted to the Committee for Study, September 1956, CIJ–34, p. 7.

2. *Nationality and Status of Stateless Persons*

The topic was assigned to the Inter-American Juridical Committee by Resolution VII of the First Meeting of the Inter-American Council of Jurists (1950). *Final Act of the First Meeting of the Inter-American Council of Jurists, Rio de Janeiro, Brazil, May 22–June 15, 1950* (Pan American Union, 1950) 14, 17. A Report and Draft Convention on the Nationality and Status of Stateless Persons was prepared in 1952 by the Juridical Committee and submitted to the Second Meeting of the Council of Jurists. CIJ–12. By Resolution VII of that Meeting of the Council, the matter was returned to the Juridical Committee with instructions to make a methodical study of the subject, accompanied by the pertinent doctrinal and legislative antecedents. *Final Act of the Second Meeting of the Inter-American Council of Jurists, Buenos Aires, Argentina, 20 April–9 May 1953* (Pan American Union, 1953) 24. Because the Juridical Committee failed to receive a substantial amount of material on the subject from States members of the Organization of American States, as requested, the matter remained in abeyance, although in 1956 a rapporteur was appointed.   Report Submitted by the Chairman of the Inter-American Juridical Committee on the Status of Topics Entrusted to the Committee for Study, September 1956, CIJ–34, p. 2.

3. *Revision of the Bustamante Code*

The possibility of revising the Bustamante Code or the Code of Private International Law adopted by the Sixth International Conference of American States, held at Habana in 1928, in the light of treaties approved at conferences held at Montevideo in 1888–1889 and 1939–1940, and in the light of the Restatement of the Law of Conflict of Laws prepared by the American Law Institute, was assigned to the Inter-American Juridical Committee by Resolution VII of the Inter-American Council of Jurists in 1950.   The Juridical Committee prepared two reports prior to the Second Meeting of the Council of Jurists, namely : "Opinion on the Possibility of Revision of the Bustamante Code or the Code of Private International Law" (CIJ–13) ; and "Second Opinion on the Possibility of Revision of the Bustamante Code or the Code of Private International Law" (CIJ–13(A)). At Buenos Aires in 1953, at the Second Meeting of the Council of Jurists, the Council of Jurists decided (Resolution XII) that it would be advisable to entrust to the Juridical Committee the preparation of a comparative study of the provisions of the Bustamante Code, of the Montevideo Treaties, and of the Restatement of the Law of Conflict of Laws prepared in the United States by the American Law Institute; and that the Juridical Committee should engage in broad consultations for this purpose and transmit the comparative study to governments for comment within a period of 6 months, after which the Juridical Committee should prepare a report.   *Final Act of the Second Meeting of the Inter-American Council of Jurists, Buenos Aires, Argentina, 20 April–9 May 1953* (Pan American Union, 1953) 30–31.   A "Comparative Study of the Bustamante Code, the Montevideo Treaties, and the Restatement of the Law of Conflict of Laws" (CIJ–21) was prepared in the Juridical Committee by Dr. Caicedo Castilla, Colombian member of the Committee.   By a resolution of November 23, 1953, the Committee, without approving this Comparative Study, requested its distribution to governments for comment. This was done.   Observations were received from the Governments of the United States and Ecuador.   Report Submitted by the Chairman of the Inter-American Juridical Committee on the Status of Topics Entrusted to the Committee for Study, September 1956, CIJ–34, p. 4. At its 1958 session, the Juridical Committee approved a report on the "Possibility of Revising the Bustamante Code", for submission to the Inter-American Council of Jurists.   CIJ–40, pp. 3–4.

At the Fourth Meeting of the Inter-American Council of Jurists, that body by Resolution VIII resolved to continue the study of the possibility of the revision of the Bustamante Code, with the object of reaching uniformity in rules of private international law in the different American States. It recommended that the Pan American Union again transmit to the American Governments the "Comparative Study on the Bustamante Code, the Montevideo Treaties, and the Restatement of the Law of Conflict of Laws" prepared in the Juridical Committee, with the request that governments in turn transmit the study to persons and entities interested in its subject-matter. Further, it requested governments that made reservations to the Bustamante Code and nonratifying states to indicate in detail the nature of any conflict existing between the Code and their respective domestic legislation and to make suggestions as to the possible manner of resolving such conflict, such comments to be transmitted during the year 1960 to the Pan American Union. Finally, the Inter-American Juridical Committee was asked to prepare a general report on the subject for the Fifth Meeting of the Inter-American Council of Jurists. *Final Act, Fourth Meeting Inter-American Council of Jurists, August 24 to September 9, 1959* (Pan American Union, 1959), 26–27.

4. *Aid and Rescue*

This topic, which was among those referred to the Juridical Committee by Resolution VII of the First Meeting of the Council of Jurists, held at Rio de Janeiro in 1950, was assigned in August 1959 by the Inter-American Juridical Committee to Alvarez Aybar of the Dominican Republic as rapporteur.

5. *Collision*

This topic, assigned to the Juridical Committee by Resolution VII of the Council of Jurists at its First Meeting (1950), awaits study.

6. *Rules Concerning the Immunity of State Ships*

"This study is also included in Resolution VII of the First Meeting of the Inter-American Council of Jurists and background information was collected on the subject . . . [by the Juridical Committee]. Various phases of the matter were discussed during the 1956 period of meetings and a resolution on the subject was approved together with a questionnaire that was sent to the governments in order to obtain certain data that the Committee considered necessary for the study of this topic. Rapporteurs were appointed to prepare a study for consideration during the early part of the 1957 period of meetings." Report Submitted by the Chairman of the Inter-American Juridical Committee on the Status of Topics Entrusted to the Committee for Study.

September 1956, CIJ–34, p. 3. In 1957 the Juridical Committee adopted a Report on Rules Concerning the Immunity of State Ships. January 1958, CIJ–36. At its 1958 session the Juridical Committee included this subject among those recommended for inclusion in the agenda of the Inter-American Council of Jurists. CIJ–40, p. 4.

The Juridical Committee concluded, at its regular session in 1959, that there is no reason to create a regional régime on the subject different or separate from the Brussels Convention, which Convention represents the actual progressive doctrine on the subject. CIJ–45; CIJ–47, pp. 4–5. The Inter-American Council of Jurists meeting shortly thereafter at Santiago, Chile, adopted a resolution on "The Immunity of State-Owned Ships" wherein it recited that the Brussels Convention of April 10, 1926, and its additional Protocol of May 24, 1934, "contain the juridical principles universally accepted on the subject"; stated that the principles thereof had been recognized in the American hemisphere by, *inter alia*, Resolution XXXIII of the Eighth International Conference of American States of 1938 and by the Montevideo Treaty on International Commercial Navigation of 1940; affirmed that the juridical system of Brussels "has the commendable characteristics of universality and unification"; and decided to consider completed the work assigned by Resolution VII of 1950 on the subject. At the same time, the Council of Jurists recommended that the American States that had not ratified the Brussels Convention and additional Protocol, "the fundamental provisions of which have been incorporated in the *Tratado de Navegación Comercial Internacional* (Treaty on International Commercial Navigation) signed in Montevideo in 1940 (articles 34 to 40)", consider the possibility of ratifying or adhering to them. Res. IX, *Final Act, Fourth Meeting Inter-American Council of Jurists, August 24 to September 9, 1959* (Pan American Union, 1959) 28.

7. *Uniform Rules on the Sale of Personal Property*

This topic was among those assigned to the Juridical Committee by the First Meeting of the Council of Jurists in 1950. A Draft Uniform Law on the International Sale of Personal Property was prepared by the Juridical Committee in 1952. CIJ–14. The text was before the Council of Jurists at its Second Meeting in 1953. The Council of Jurists decided (Resolution XIII) to entrust to the Juridical Committee the preparation of a systematic study of the subject, taking into consideration a draft prepared by the Council of Jurists at its Second Meeting and the replies received to requests for opinions. *Final Act of the Second Meeting of the Inter-American Council of Jurists, Buenos Aires, Argentina, 20 April–9 May, 1953* (Pan American Union, 1953) 31 ff.; Report Submitted by the Chairman of the Inter-American Juridical Committee on the Status of Topics Entrusted to the Committee for Study, September 1956, CIJ–34, p. 5. Replies were slow in coming in.

During the regular session of the Inter-American Juridical Committee in 1959, the Committee discussed at length a project on the subject prepared by Dr. Hugo J. Gobbi of Argentina as rapporteur (CIJ–46), but considered it impossible to take action with respect to the project, other than to recommend to the Juridical Department of the Pan American Union that it transmit copies thereof to persons and entities interested in the subject, for the formulation of observations with respect to the preparation of a definitive project, and that the study be referred to governments for observations. CIJ–47, pp. 2–3. At the Fourth Meeting of the Inter-American Council of Jurists, held at Santiago, Chile, in 1959, that body included the subject on the list of topics recommended for study by the Inter-American Juridical Committee at its regular meeting in 1960. Res. XVII, *Final Act, Fourth Meeting Inter-American Council of Jurists, August 24 to September 9, 1959* (Pan American Union, 1959) 44.

8. *International Commercial Arbitration*

This topic was among those assigned to the Juridical Committee by the Inter-American Council of Jurists at its First Meeting in 1950. The Juridical Committee, on December 21, 1953, submitted an initial draft on the topic for consideration and comment by the respective American Republics. CIJ–20. On December 15, 1954, the Juridical Committee submitted a second draft Uniform Law on International Commercial Arbitration. CIJ–20(A). The latter draft was considered by the Council of Jurists at Mexico City in 1956, at its Third Meeting, with the result that a text entitled "Draft Uniform Law on Inter-American Commercial Arbitration" was approved. Res. VIII, *Final Act of the Third Meeting of the Inter-American Council of Jurists, Mexico City, Mexico, January 17–February 4, 1956* (Pan American Union, 1956) 23 ff. The Council of Jurists, treating the topic as one in which uniformity of legislation is desirable, recommended that "to the extent practicable, the American Republics adopt in their legislation, in accordance with their constitutional procedures, the draft Uniform Law on Inter-American Commercial Arbitration in such form as they consider desirable within their several jurisdictions", and requested the Secretary General of the Organization of American States to urge the respective American Republics to give publicity to the draft, in order that it "may be given appropriate consideration by the national legislative bodies". *Ibid.*

9. *International Cooperation in Judicial Procedures ("Judicial Assistance")*

This topic had its origin in Resolution VII of the First Meeting of the Inter-American Council of Jurists in 1950. The Inter-American Juridical Committee considered the topic in 1952, and its Report on Uniformity of Legislation on International Cooperation in Judicial Procedures (Judicial Assistance) was approved on September 23, 1952. CIJ–15. The report was submitted to the Inter-American Council of Jurists at its Second Meeting in 1953. By Resolution XIV the Council of Jurists recommended that the Council of the Organization request the Secretary General of the Organization to circulate copies of the 1952 report to agencies, etc., devoted to study of the subject and to print the comments received. *Final Act, op. cit.*, p. 43. By Resolution IX of the Third Meeting of the Council of Jurists, held at Mexico City, the Council decided that the Committee should continue study of the subject maintaining the same approach—that is, the preparation of "rules whose principles are capable of being adopted in the domestic legislation of the American Republics"—and that it give an account of its work at the Fourth Meeting of the Council of Jurists. *Final Act of the Third Meeting of the Inter-American Council of Jurists, Mexico City, Mexico, January 17–February 4, 1956* (Pan American Union, 1956) 29–30. See also "Observaciones al Informe sobre la Uniformidad de Legislación relativa de la Cooperación Internacional en Procedimientos Judiciales (Asistencia Judicial) (submitted to the Third Meeting of the Inter-American Council of Jurists)". CIJ–26. The Juridical Committee considered the topic at some length during 1956, and appointed a rapporteur to prepare a study, taking into account views expressed during the discussions and Resolution IX of the Council of Jurists approved at Mexico City. *Supra.* Report Submitted by the Chairman of the Inter-American Juridical Committee on the Status of Topics Entrusted to the Committee for Study, September 1956, CIJ–34, p. 4.

When the Inter-American Juridical Committee met in regular session in 1959, it resolved to ask the Pan American Union to circulate a resolution on the subject, with questions to be annexed, with a view to procuring the texts of laws and regulations of the respective states and information concerning practices and precedents, and recommending to Governments of the Americas the naming of national commissions to cooperate in the compilation of the materials and to formulate recommendations as to possible areas of agreement. The resolution further provided that on the basis of the materials obtained, the Pan American Union should prepare as soon as possible a technical study on the basis of which the Inter-American Juridical Committee would prepare a definitive project of uniform legislation to improve the administration of justice in this field. CIJ–44. At its 1960 meeting, the Committee approved a resolution requesting the Pan American Union to provide it with a collection of the laws, doctrines, and jurisprudence of the American Republics and to seek to obtain answers to the 1959 questionnaire. CIJ–60, p. 7. "Due reply" to the 1960 resolution had not been received by the 1961 meeting. CIJ–64, pp. 6–7.

10. *Recognition of de facto Governments*

By Resolution XXXVI approved at Bogotá in 1948, at the Ninth International Conference of American States, it was stated that whereas the Inter-American Juridical Committee of Rio de Janeiro as it then existed had not presented a report on the recognition of *de facto* governments, a topic submitted to the Conference for consideration, it was resolved to assign to the Inter-American Council of Jurists to be established under the Charter of Bogotá the preparation of a project and a report on the recognition of *de facto* governments. *Ninth International Conference of American States*, Bogotá, 1948, Report of the Delegation of the United States of America, p. 271.

The First Meeting of the Council of Jurists, held at Rio de Janeiro in 1950, considered a project and report on the subject of the Recognition of *de facto* Governments prepared by the Inter-American Juridical Committee, but because of divergent opinions on essential points, excluding the possibility of reaching agreement by an absolute majority, resolved to continue the consideration and study of the subject at the Second Meeting of the Council of Jurists. Report and Draft Convention on Recognition of de facto Governments (prepared by the Inter-American Juridical Committee and submitted to the First Meeting of the Inter-American Council of Jurists) CIJ–1; Res. IX, *Final Act of the First Meeting of the Inter-American Council of Jurists, Rio de Janeiro, Brazil, May 22–June 15, 1950* (Pan American Union, 1950) 23.

At the Second Meeting of the Council of Jurists, held at Buenos Aires, the Council of Jurists stated that an almost unanimous opinion had been expressed to the effect that it was "as yet premature to conclude a convention on the subject, and that neither is it opportune for an American inter-governmental organization to state at this time in declarative form the various principles which have been expounded by writers from time to time to govern the practice to be followed by States in this respect". Instead, it was decided to reaffirm adherence to the principles proclaimed in Resolution XXXV of the Ninth International Conference of American States. Res. III,

Final Act of the Second Meeting of the Inter-American Council of Jurists, Buenos Aires, Argentina, 20 April–9 May 1953 (Pan American Union, 1953) 10; *Ninth International Conference of American States*, Bogotá, 1948, Report of the Delegation of the United States of America, p. 271. See also "Recognition of de facto Governments" (documents submitted to the Second Meeting of the Inter-American Council of Jurists) CIJ–1(A).

11. *Right of Resistance*

By Resolution XXXVII approved in 1948 at the Ninth Inter-American Conference, held at Bogotá, it was resolved to forward to the Inter-American Juridical Committee for study a proposal of the Cuban delegation on the Right of Resistance, expressed in the following terms: "The right of resistance is recognized in case of manifest acts of oppression or tyranny", in order that the Committee may submit a report thereon to the Council of the Organization of American States. *Ninth International Conference of American States*, Bogotá, 1948, Report of the Delegation of the United States of America, pp. 271–272. The Inter-American Juridical Committee prepared a report on the subject, approved by the Inter-American Council of Jurists at its First Meeting in 1950, wherein it concluded that the so-called "right of resistance" is not yet recognized in the international juridical order, and that the latter does not have at its command adequate means to protect the exercise thereof. Res. XI, *Final Act of the First Meeting of the Inter-American Council of Jurists, Rio de Janeiro, Brazil, May 22–June 15, 1950* (Pan American Union, 1950) 24–25.

12. *Inter-American Court for the Protection of the Rights of Man*

Resolution XXXI of the Ninth Inter-American Conference contained provision that the Inter-American Juridical Committee should prepare a draft statute providing for the creation and functioning of an inter-American court to guarantee the rights of man, and that that project, after being submitted to governments for examination and comment, should be referred to the Tenth Inter-American Conference for study, if it were felt that the moment had arrived for a decision thereon. *Ninth International Conference of American States*, Bogotá, 1948, Report of the Delegation of the United States of America, p. 266. The Inter-American Juridical Committee duly presented a report on the subject in which it stated that "the lack of positive law on the subject is a serious obstacle to the preparation of such a Statute"; that it would be advisable first to prepare, with the approval of the States, a Convention thereon; and that the preparation of a Statute of such a nature "would necessarily imply a radical change in the constitutional systems in force". The report was considered by the Inter-American Council of Jurists at its First Meeting, held at Rio de Janeiro in 1950, with the result that the Council of Jurists approved the report, although it recommended to the Council of the Organization of American States that the same subject be placed on the agenda for the Second Meeting of the Council of Jurists. "Report to the Inter-American Council of Jurists Concerning Resolution XXXI of the Conference of Bogotá—Inter-American Court to Protect the Rights of Man", CIJ–2; Res. X, *Final Act of the First Meeting of the Inter-American Council of Jurists, Rio de Janeiro, Brazil, May 22–June 15, 1950* (Pan American Union, 1950) 23–24.

At the Tenth Inter-American Conference, held at Caracas in 1954, Resolution XXIX was adopted providing that the Council of the Organization of American States should continue its studies on the jurisdictional aspects of the protection of human rights, analyzing the possibility of the creation of an Inter-American Court for the Protection of Human Rights, in order that the matter be considered at the Eleventh Inter-American Conference. *Tenth Inter-American Conference*, Caracas, 1954, Report of the Delegation of the United States of America, p. 104. This resolution was referred by the Council of the OAS to its Committee on Juridical Political Matters for study.

The Fifth Meeting of Consultation of Ministers of Foreign Affairs, held at Santiago, Chile, in 1959, declared that 11 years after the adoption of the "American Declaration of the Rights and Duties of Man" (Res. XXX, Ninth Inter-American Conference, Bogotá, 1948)—progress having been made on the subject during the same period in both the United Nations and in the Council of Europe—the climate was favorable in the hemisphere to the conclusion of a convention in the matter. The Foreign Ministers resolved (I) that the Inter-American Council of Jurists prepare (for submission to the Eleventh Conference) a draft Convention on Human Rights and a draft convention or conventions on the creation of an Inter-American Court for the Protection of Human Rights and of other organizations appropriate for the protection and observance of those rights; (II) that the Council of the Organization of American States should organize an Inter-American Commission on Human Rights, which the Foreign Ministers thereby resolved to create, to have the specific functions that the Council should assign to it and to be charged with "furthering respect" for human rights. Res. VIII, *Final Act of the Fifth Meeting of Consultation of Ministers of Foreign Affairs, Held in Santiago,*

Chile, August 12–18, 1959, Doc. 89, Rev. 2, Oct. 12, 1959, pp. 10–11.
For the U.S. reservation, see *ibid.,* pp. 18–19.

The Inter-American Council of Jurists at its Fourth Meeting, held
at Santiago, Chile, in August–September 1959, prepared a draft Convention on Human Rights, including broad lists of "Civil and Political
Rights" and "Economic, Social and Cultural Rights", and containing
provision for the establishment of an Inter-American Commission for
the Protection of Human Rights and for the establishment of an Inter-
American Court of Human Rights. Res. XX, *Final Act, Fourth
Meeting Inter-American Council of Jurists, August 24 to September 9,
1959* (Pan American Union, 1959), pp. 47 ff. The draft is to be submitted to the Eleventh Inter-American Conference.

13. *Scope of the Powers of the Council of the Organization of American States*

The Council of the Organization of American States, by a resolution approved April 21, 1949, requested the Inter-American Council of
Jurists to prepare a technical study on the Scope of the Powers of the
Council of the Organization, as set forth in the applicable international instruments. Its Permanent Committee, the Inter-American
Juridical Committee, prepared and presented on May 18, 1950, a technical study, in preliminary form, submitted to the First Meeting of
the Inter-American Council of Jurists, and later studies prepared by
Dr. Alwyn V. Freeman, member of the Juridical Committee, and by
Dr. Charles G. Fenwick, Executive Secretary of the Council of Jurists,
were also submitted. The Inter-American Council of Jurists considered the documents submitted but was unable to complete study of
the problem because of divergent views on basic points. The Council
of Jurists resolved to continue the undertaking at its Second Meeting; to transmit to the Council of the Organization of American States
all the reports presented, minutes, etc., relating to the consideration
and study of the matter; and to charge the Juridical Committee with
continuing the technical study, obtaining the views of members of the
Council of Jurists "who may be so good as to send them" in the interval between the First and Second Meetings of the Council. Only
two such opinions were received, and the subject was not included on
the agenda of the Second Meeting of the Council of Jurists. "Amplitud de las Facultades del Consejo de la Organización de los Estados
Americanos (informe preparado por el Comité Jurídico Interamericano y sometido a la Primera Reunión del Consejo Interamericano de
Jurisconsultos)", CIJ–4; Res. XII, *Final Act of the First Meeting of
the Inter-American Council of Jurists, Rio de Janeiro, Brazil, May 22–
June 15, 1950* (Pan American Union, 1950) 25–26; Report Submitted
by the Chairman of the Inter-American Juridical Committee on the

Status of Topics Entrusted to the Committee for Study, September 1956, CIJ–34, p. 5.

14. *The Strengthening and Effective Exercise of Representative Democracy in America*

" Resolution V of April 8, 1950, approved by the Council of the Organization acting provisionally as Organ of Consultation, and Resolution VII of the Fourth Meeting of Consultation of Ministers of Foreign Affairs [1951] entrusted the preliminary studies on this matter to the Committee. The matter was fully discussed but it was impossible to obtain the majority vote required to reach an agreement that would express the opinion prevailing in the Committee." Report Submitted by the Chairman of the Inter-American Juridical Committee on the Status of Topics Entrusted to the Committee for Study, September 1956, CIJ–34, pp. 5–6.

At its regular session held in 1959, the Inter-American Juridical Committee considered that it would not be practical to make a study on this subject without having available a compilation of the laws in force in the American countries on this subject. Accordingly, the Committee concluded that its consideration of this subject should be postponed until it had at its disposal the compilation which the Pan American Union, in accordance with Resolution XXVII of the Tenth Inter-American Conference, was to prepare and which preparation the Committee deemed should not be delayed. *Informe del Comité Jurídico Interamericano sobre la Labor Desarrollada durante su Periodo de Sesiones de 1959, 4 de mayo–3 de agosto* (Pan American Union, 1959) 3–4 (CIJ–47).

At the Fifth Meeting of Consultation of Ministers of Foreign Affairs of the American Republics, held at Santiago, Chile, in 1959, the Foreign Ministers declared:

"1. The principle of the rule of law should be assured by the separation of powers, and by the control of the legality of governmental acts by competent organs of the state.

"2. The governments of the American republics should be the result of free elections.

"3. Perpetuation in power, or the exercise of power without a fixed term and with the manifest intent of perpetuation, is incompatible with the effective exercise of democracy.

"4. The governments of the American states should maintain a system of freedom for the individual and of social justice based on respect for fundamental human rights.

"5. The human rights incorporated into the legislation of the American states should be protected by effective judicial procedures.

"6. The systematic use of political proscription is contrary to American democratic order.

"7. Freedom of the press, radio, and television, and, in general, freedom of information and expression, are essential conditions for the existence of a democratic regime.

"8. The American states, in order to strengthen democratic institutions, should cooperate among themselves within the limits of their resources and the framework of their laws so as to strengthen and develop their economic structure, and achieve just and humane living conditions for their peoples . . ." Res. I, "Declaration of Santiago, Chile", *Final Act of the Fifth Meeting of Consultation of Ministers of Foreign Affairs, Held in Santiago, Chile, August 12–18, 1959*, Doc. 89, Rev. 2, Oct. 12, 1959, pp. 4, 5–6.

The Fifth Meeting of Consultation of Ministers of Foreign Affairs also entrusted to the Inter-American Council of Jurists "the study of the possible juridical relationship between respect for human rights and the effective exercise of representative democracy, and the right to set in motion the machinery of American international law in force." Res. III, *ibid.*, p. 7.

Further, the Fifth Meeting of Consultation of Ministers of Foreign Affairs cited article 5(d) of the "Principles" of the Charter of the Organization of American States stating that "The solidarity of the American States and the high aims which are sought through it require the political organization of those States on the basis of the effective exercise of representative democracy", and entrusted "to the Council of the Organization of American States the preparation, in cooperation with the technical bodies of the Organization and taking into consideration the views of the governments of the American states, of a draft convention on the effective exercise of representative democracy, and the establishment of the procedure and measures applicable thereto", the results of the work to be submitted to the Eleventh Inter-American Conference. Res. IX, *ibid.*, pp. 11–12.

The Inter-American Council of Jurists, meeting at Santiago, Chile, in August–September 1959, requested the Inter-American Juridical Committee to study the topic "Possible juridical relationship between respect for human rights and the effective exercise of representative democracy, and the right to put into motion the machinery of existing American international law in force", at the same time requesting the Council of the Organization of American States, if it deemed it advisable, to convoke a special session of the Juridical Committee in order that it might proceed with the preparation of the study. Res. XXI, *Final Act, Fourth Meeting Inter-American Council of Jurists, August 24 to September 9, 1959* (Pan American Union, 1959) 76. The Inter-American Juridical Committee, at its Special Session in October–November 1959, approved a study which, noting that the relationship between the respect for human rights and the effective exercise of democracy not only exists but is evident because a democratic régime must necessarily be based on certain essential rights and liberties, stated that the way to assure democratic systems of government in America is to recognize and protect the rights of the human being. The study stated that the only way to obtain the desired result was by means of a convention enunciating these rights and creating organs to guarantee such rights as well as punish violations of them. In support of this the study stated that there existed no organ in the Organization of American States authorized to impose sanctions in any form against any Member State whose political régime does not measure up to the standard of representative democracy, sanctions being authorized by the inter-American system only in those cases which, because touching on the peace and security of the continent, are covered by the Inter-American Treaty of Reciprocal Assistance. *Informe del Comité Jurídico Interamericano sobre la Labor Desarrollada durante su Periodo Extraordinario de Sesiones de 1959, 5 de octubre–5 de noviembre* (Pan American Union, 1959) 10–12 (CIJ–55).

15. *Regimen of Political Exiles, Asylees, and Refugees*

The Council of the Organization of American States, acting provisionally as organ of consultation, by Resolution V approved April 8, 1950, entrusted this subject to the Inter-American Juridical Committee. The Inter-American Juridical Committee prepared a draft convention on the "Regimen of Political Exiles, Asylees, and Refugees" and on "Diplomatic Asylum". "Regimen of Political Asylees, Exiles and Refugees (document prepared by the Inter-American Juridical Committee and submitted to the Second Meeting of the Inter-American Council of Jurists)". CIJ–10. The Second Meeting of the Council of Jurists considered these drafts and finalized two draft conventions on the basis thereof, namely, "Draft Convention on Regimen of Political Exiles, Asylees, and Refugees (Territorial Asylum)", and "Draft Convention on Diplomatic Asylum". The two conventions were forwarded to the Council of the Organization of American States. Res. XVII and XVIII, *Final Act of the Second Meeting of the Inter-American Council of Jurists, Buenos Aires, Argentina, 20 April–9 May 1953* (Pan American Union, 1953) 46, 49.

The two draft conventions served as working documents for the Tenth Conference, held in 1954 at Caracas, with the result that there were there concluded two conventions, the one on Diplomatic Asylum and the other on Territorial Asylum. The Convention on Diplomatic Asylum sets forth in a more comprehensive form than do the Habana

Convention of 1928 on Asylum and the Montevideo Convention of 1933 on "Political Asylum" the principles and procedures pertaining to diplomatic asylum. *Tenth Inter-American Conference*, Caracas, 1954, Report of the Delegation of the United States of America, p. 179. The Convention on Territorial Asylum contains a number of provisions which restate, in general, existing principles of international law. *Ibid.*, p. 175. Other provisions establish new obligations regarding control of activities of political refugees, such as restricting the right of assembly or association when it has as its purpose the use of force or violence against the government of the soliciting state and maintaining surveillance over, or interning at a reasonable distance from the border, certain categories of refugees. The United States did not sign either convention.

In 1959 at its Fourth Meeting, held at Santiago, Chile, the Inter-American Council of Jurists approved a Draft Protocol to the Conventions on Diplomatic Asylum, for submission by the Council of the Organization of American States, if considered appropriate, to the Eleventh Inter-American Conference. The Protocol as drafted was designed to supplement the 1928, 1933, and 1954 Conventions referred to above. By article II of the Protocol it is provided that "For the purposes of diplomatic asylum desertion may include any member of the regular armed forces." Certain other aspects of diplomatic asylum are dealt with in the Protocol, including safe conducts. Res. I, *Final Act, Fourth Meeting Inter-American Council of Jurists, August 24 to September 9, 1959* (Pan American Union, 1959) 10–11. The Fourth Meeting of the Inter-American Council of Jurists also entrusted to the Inter-American Juridical Committee the preparation of a draft article or articles to be incorporated into the draft Protocol, by means of which an attempt would be made "to avoid the requesting or the granting of asylum in a manner incompatible with the law in force in the Americas, without restricting the power of the State granting diplomatic asylum to determine the reasons for such asylum." Res. II, *ibid.*, p. 12. The Fourth Meeting of the Inter-American Council of Jurists also entrusted to the Inter-American Juridical Committee the preparation of a study and draft of a convention on "political offenses" for consideration by the Eleventh Conference. Res. III, *ibid.*, p. 13.

The Inter-American Juridical Committee, at its Special Session in October–November 1959, approved a report finding that (1) it was essential, for the survival of the institution of asylum, that the party granting asylum have the power to determine whether the one seeking asylum is a political offender or is being persecuted for political reasons; (2) the question of the desirability of creating a special procedure for recognizing and resolving differences between States caused by asylum should be answered in the negative; and (3) any serious attempt to improve the system of unilateral judgment in such cases was worthy of consideration, bearing in mind the lessons of past experience.

With regard to the latter, the Committee recommended the inclusion, in the proposed protocol to the conventions on asylum, the following provision, as a substitute for article 17 of the Caracas Convention:

"If there should be a difference of opinion over the judgment as to the propriety of the asylum, the territorial State may, on granting the safe-conduct and authorizing the asylee's departure, demand the detention of the asylee in the territory of the State which granted the asylum for a period of 60 days to enable the territorial State to present an extradition request.

"The State of asylum will be obliged to effect this detention and not permit the departure of the asylee for another country.

"The extradition request may be made even though no treaty on the subject exists between the two countries and will be resolved in conformity with the juridical norms which govern this subject in the State of asylum.

"If the extradition is not requested within the designated period, the obligation of the State of asylum to detain the asylee shall cease."

With regard to the matter of "political offenses", the Committee approved a report which set forth various views on the subject with the arguments supporting them, in the light of the question of whether or not it was desirable to include a definition of political offenses in conventions on diplomatic asylum and if, in such conventions, express mention of "terrorism" should be included. The report concluded:

"1. The conventional definition of political offenses would not improve the Conventions on diplomatic asylum now in force.

"2. Nevertheless, and on the supposition that the American governments deem a definition or characterization of political offenses in some international instrument desirable, the Committee believes that the following evaluations should be taken into consideration:

"1) Offenses against the organization and functioning of the State are political offenses.

"2) Offenses connected with the above are political offenses. The offense is connected when it is committed 1) to carry out or assist in the attempt to commit an offense coming within number 1); 2) to assist in escaping punishment for political offenses.

"3) Crimes of brutality and vandalism and, in general, all offenses which exceed the just limits of attack and defense are not political offenses.

"4) In conformity with the United Nations Convention, genocide is not a political offense." *Acta Final de la Reunion Extraordinaria del 5 de Octubre al 5 de Noviembre, Inclusive, de 1959, "Asilo Diplomatico"*, pp. 3 and 8 (mimeo., translation). The Report of the Inter-American Juridical Committee entitled *"New Articles on Diplomatic Asylum"* is contained in Doc. CIJ–49. *Report of the Inter-American Juridical Committee on the Work Carried Out During the Special Meeting held in 1959, October 5–November 5* (Pan American Union, 1960) 4–5, 12 (CIJ–55).

16. *Extradition*

The Tenth Inter-American Conference assigned to the Inter-American Juridical Committee the preparation of a draft convention on extradition to be submitted to the Third Meeting of the Inter-American Council of Jurists, which, in turn, should consult the American Republics regarding the draft. Res. CVII, *Tenth Inter-American Conference*, Caracas, 1954, Report of the.Delegation of the United States of America, pp. 166–167. A "Draft Convention on Extradition" was prepared by the Inter-American Juridical Committee and submitted to the Third Meeting of the Inter-American Council of Jurists held at Mexico City in 1956. CIJ–22. The Council of Jurists approved a draft Convention on Extradition at the Third ,Meeting, for transmittal to the Council of the Organization of American States pursuant to Resolution CVII of the Tenth Inter-American Conference. Res. VII, *Final Act of the Third Meeting of the Inter-American Council of Jurists, Mexico City, Mexico, January 17–February 4, 1956* (Pan American Union, 1956) 17–22. In conformity with Resolution CVII of the Tenth Conference, the Council of the OAS consulted the Member States regarding the draft, with the result that all comments were referred to the Juridical Committee, together with the draft prepared at Mexico City. Upon the basis of that draft and the comments received, the Juridical Committee in 1957 prepared a "Second Draft Convention on Extradition". March 1958, CIJ–37. In 1958 the Juridical Committee voted to recommend that this draft be considered at the next meeting of the Inter-American Council of Jurists. CIJ–40.

The Draft Convention was revised by the Inter-American Council of Jurists at its Fourth Meeting for submission to the Council of the Organization of American States, in order that it might, if it deemed it advisable, transmit the draft for consideration at the Eleventh Inter-American Conference. Res. IV, *Final Act, Fourth Meeting Inter-American Council of Jurists, August 24 to September 9, 1959* (Pan American Union, 1959) 15. See also Res. XIX, "Territorial Asylum", relating to the matter of political offenses, *ibid.*, p. 46.

However, because it had been unable at its Fourth Meeting to agree on what effect the Convention should have on existing extradition agreements between countries which might become parties to it, the Council of Jurists referred article 23 of the Draft Convention to the study of the Inter-American Juridical Committee for the drafting of alternative formulas for the consideration of the Eleventh Inter-American Conference. Res. V, *ibid.*, p. 23.

At its special session in October-November 1959, the Inter-American Juridical Committee drafted five formulas which ranged from one providing that the present convention would replace all existing bilateral and multilateral extradition conventions between the parties to one providing that the present convention would replace no existing conventions between the parties except if one of the existing conventions ceased to be in force the present convention would take effect. *Acta Final de la Reunion Extraordinaria del 5 de Octubre al 5 de Noviembre, Inclusive, de 1959*, "Definicion de Delitos Politicos", p. 8 (mimeo.); *Report of the Inter-American Juridical Committee on the Work Carried Out During the Special Meeting held in 1959, October 5–November 5* (Pan American Union, 1960) 13–14 (CIJ–55).

17. *Reservations to Multilateral Treaties*

This topic was assigned to the Inter-American Juridical Committee by resolution of the Council of the Organization of American States on May 17, 1950. Discussion of the topic took place at the meetings of the Juridical Committee in 1951 and 1952 without progress. In 1953 the topic was discussed at length by the Juridical Committee, and a report was on the point of being approved when the need of further studies on certain aspects of the matter became evident. In 1954 discussion of the topic was resumed by the Committee, with the result that on December 27, 1954, the Committee approved a "Report on the Juridical Effect of Reservations to Multilateral Treaties". CIJ–23. This report, together with dissenting votes and explanatory statements, was before the Third Meeting of the Council of Jurists at Mexico City in 1956. The Council of Jurists prepared a draft of proposed rules to govern reservations to multilateral treaties. Res. XV, *Final Act of the Third Meeting of the Inter-American Council of Jurists, Mexico City, Mexico, January 17–February 4, 1956* (Pan American Union, 1956) 40–42. The Council of Jurists, by the resolution just referred to, requested the Council of the OAS to forward its draft on the effects of reservations to multilateral treaties to the member governments in order that they might make any observations thereon considered advisable, and asked the Inter-American Juridical

Committee to consider such observations along with the Council of Jurists' draft prepared at Mexico City, in preparing a second draft of rules to be considered at the Fourth Meeting of the Inter-American Council of Jurists. *Ibid.* The subject was studied during the 1956 session of the Juridical Committee. See the Juridical Committee's "Study to Serve as the Basis for the Preparation of a Second Draft Text of Rules on Reservations to Multilateral Treaties", CIJ–33. At its 1958 session the Juridical Committee decided to transmit the study just referred to to the next meeting of the Inter-American Council of Jurists. CIJ–40, p. 2.

The Fourth Meeting of the Inter-American Council of Jurists, held at Santiago, Chile, in 1959, resolved to recommend to the Eleventh Inter-American Conference that it consider (for adoption) certain rules on reservations to multilateral treaties. Res. X, *Final Act, Fourth Meeting Inter-American Council of Jurists, August 24 to September 9, 1959* (Pan American Union, 1959) 29. At the same time the Council of Jurists agreed to submit a draft document prepared by the delegation of Paraguay on "Reservation of Theoretical Adherence" to the Inter-American Juridical Committee. Res. XI, *ibid.*, p. 43. The Juridical Committee concluded in its report in 1960 that it saw "no advantage" to adoption of "Theoretical Adherence". (CIJ–57, p. 5.)

18. *Contributions of the American Continent to the Development and Codification of the Principles of International Law That Govern the Responsibility of the State*

In 1954 the Tenth Inter-American Conference recommended to the Inter-American Council of Jurists and its permanent committee, the Inter-American Juridical Committee of Rio de Janeiro, the preparation of a study or report on the contribution which the American Continent has made to the development and to the codification of the principles of international law that govern the responsibility of the State. Res. CIV, *Tenth Inter-American Conference*, Caracas, 1954, Report of the Delegation of the United States of America, p. 165. At Mexico City, the Third Meeting of the Council of Jurists requested the Inter-American Juridical Committee to complete as soon as possible the study or report on this topic referred to it by the Tenth Conference and asked the Department of International Law of the Pan American Union to assist by making a preliminary study of the subject. Res. VI, *Final Act of the Third Meeting of the Inter-American Council of Jurists, Mexico City, Mexico, January 17–February 4, 1956* (Pan American Union, 1956) 16. The topic was discussed at length during the 1955, 1956, 1957, and 1958 sessions of the Juridical Committee, with the result that a draft was prepared at its 1958 session for submission to the Inter-American Council of Jurists at its next meeting. CIJ–40, pp. 4, 5–7.

The Fourth Meeting of the Inter-American Council of Jurists, held at Sàntiago, Chile, in 1959, had before it the Inter-American Juridical Committee document entitled "Contribution of the American Continent to the Principles of International Law that Govern the Responsibility of the State". CIJ–39. The Council of Jurists instructed the Juridical Committee that in continuing its task (a) the Department of Legal Affairs of the Pan American Union should supply additional background material to the Committee; (b) the Committee should prepare an objective and documented presentation that would demonstrate the contribution of the American Continent, utilizing all appropriate sources; and (c) it should indicate at the same time the differences that may exist on the subject. Res. XII, "Contributions of the American Continent to the Principles that Govern the Responsibility of the State", *Final Act, Fourth Meeting Inter-American Council of Jurists, August 24 to September 9, 1959* (Pan American Union, 1959) 32–33. For the majority opinion (and a dissenting opinion and a separate opinion) prepared by the Juridical Committee in 1961, for submission to the Fifth Meeting of the Council of Jurists, see CIJ–61.

19. *Possibility of Revising the American Treaty on Pacific Settlement*

The Tenth Inter-American Conference agreed that the Council of the Organization of American States should conduct an inquiry among the Member States to ascertain the suitability of, and the appropriate opportunity for, proceeding to revise the American Treaty on Pacific Settlement; and that, if the decision was in the affirmative, the Inter-American Council of Jurists and its permanent committee, the Inter-American Juridical Committee, should study the possibility of revising the Pact of Bogotá and formulate preliminary drafts of the various texts which may be expected to be accepted. Thus far, there has been little support for such revision. Res. XCIX, *Tenth Inter-American Conference*, Caracas, 1954, Report of the Delegation of the United States of America, pp. 161–162. For the American Treaty on Pacific Settlement ("Pact of Bogotá"), see *Ninth International Conference of American States*, Bogotá, 1948, Report of the Delegation of the United States of America, pp. 186 ff.

20. *Inter-American Court of Justice*

By Resolution C of the Tenth Inter-American Conference, held at Caracas in 1954, it was resolved that the Council of the Organization of American States should ascertain the position of Member States with respect to the establishment of an Inter-American Court of Justice and that "in the event that there is a majority which pronounces favorably upon it", the Inter-American Council of Jurists and its permanent committee, the Inter-American Juridical Committee, should prepare a preliminary draft of a statute for such court; and that the Council of the OAS, on the basis of the work thus done, should prepare a report and definitive draft of a statute and submit them to the Eleventh Inter-American Conference. The draft of such a statute was not prepared for the reason that a majority of states, members of the OAS, did not pronounce favorably upon the proposition. Res. C, *Tenth Inter-American Conference*, Caracas, 1954, Report of the Delegation of the United States of America, pp. 162–163.

21. *Prevention of Intervention by Totalitarian Powers in the Establishment of Governments*

The Tenth Inter-American Conference resolved to transmit to the Inter-American Juridical Committee the proposal of Uruguay on "Prevention of Intervention by Totalitarian Powers in the Establishment of Governments". Thus far, consideration of the topic has remained in abeyance, although in 1955 there was some discussion as to what the Committee might do on this topic. Res. CVIII, *Tenth Inter-American Conference*, Caracas, 1954, Report of the Delegation of the United States of America, p. 167.

22. *Elimination of Use of Passports*

By Resolution XII the Ninth Inter-American Conference entrusted to the Inter-American Council of Jurists and the Inter-American Economic and Social Council the preparation of a draft agreement to eliminate the use of passports and to establish an American identification certificate not requiring consular visas and fees. *Ninth International Conference of American States*, Bogotá, 1948, Report of the Delegation of the United States of America, pp. 237–238. In 1950 at its First Meeting, the Inter-American Council of Jurists resolved to transmit to the Inter-American Economic and Social Council, without expressing any opinion thereon, the matter of a draft agreement on the elimination of the use of passports and the establishment of an American identification certificate not requiring consular visas and fees, submitted by the Inter-American Juridical Committee (May 1950). Res. VIII, *Final Act of the First Meeting of the Inter-American Council of Jurists, Rio de Janeiro, Brazil, May 22–June 15, 1950* (Pan American Union, 1950) 22.

23. *Diplomatic Asylum and Military Personnel*

The Government of Colombia, through a note of June 12, 1958, addressed by the Ambassador of Colombia to the Organization of American States to the Council of that Organization, requested the technical services of the Inter-American Council of Jurists, under article 6 of the Statutes of the Inter-American Council of Jurists. Under article 6 requests from the governments for technical services may be submitted directly to the Inter-American Council of Jurists when it is in session, "or through the Council of the Organization in the interval between meetings of the Council of Jurists." Text of the *Statutes of the Inter-American Council of Jurists*, approved Apr. 18, 1951, and amended May 28, 1957, p. 2. Colombia called attention to the general and preeminently technical nature of the request for information on the institution of asylum, that is to say whether the granting of diplomatic asylum, in the light of the law on the subject of asylum, was or was not in accordance with the law in cases involving military personnel in active service. On June 30, 1958, the Council of the OAS resolved "To submit the above-mentioned request of the Government of Colombia for an opinion first to the Inter-American Juridical Committee, so that it may study it and report in due course to the Council of the Organization." Report on the Request of the Government of Colombia that a Technical Study on Asylum be made, presented by the General Committee (the resolution approved by the Council on June 30, 1958, is included), June 30, 1958, C–i–374, Rev. 2.

The Inter-American Juridical Committee at its 1958 session decided—in the light of article 6 of the Statutes—(a) to limit itself to a consideration of the matter raised by the Council's resolution of June 30, 1958; (b) to refer to the Council for such action, if any, as it might wish to take, a communication dated July 15, 1958, made by the Government of Colombia direct to the Committee; and (c) to advise the Colombian Government accordingly. Meanwhile, the cases giving rise to the original submission and the resolution of the Council of the OAS were disposed of by the Colombian Government. For the text of the July 15, 1958, communication, see C/INF–408, and addenda, including Add. 3, Aug. 21, 1958, and Add. 6, Oct. 27, 1958. For 1958 action of the Juridical Committee with respect to this subject, see *Report of the Inter-American Juridical Committee on the Work Accomplished during its 1958 Meeting, July 15–October 1* (Pan American Union, 1959) 7–11 (CIJ–40).

24. *Compilation of Treaty Principles*

At the First Meeting of the Inter-American Council of Jurists, held at Rio de Janeiro in 1950, the Council of Jurists recommended that the Inter-American Juridical Committee take into consideration, insofar as possible, the following directive with respect to the principles of international law embodied in public treaties or agreements:

"1. The systematic compilation of the principles already codified by the unanimous ratification of the signatory States of treaties or agreements signed at the International Conferences of American States;

"2. The systematic compilation of the principles that have been partially ratified; investigation of the reasons explaining the failure by some States to ratify; and as a result of this study a new enunciation of these principles so that they will be acceptable to all States;

"3. With respect to the principles contained in the treaties or agreements that have not been ratified by any State, to determine whether such principles are susceptible of codification and to study the most appropriate procedure for drafting them in codified form." Res. VII, pt. 7, *Final Act of the First Meeting of the Inter-American Council of Jurists, Rio de Janeiro, Brazil, May 22–June 15, 1950* (Pan American Union, 1950) 22.

Thus far, the Inter-American Juridical Committee has not prepared such systematic compilations of principles embodied in public treaties.

25. *Double Taxation*

In July 1957 the Inter-American Juridical Committee charged the Chairman of the Committee with the preparation of a preliminary study on "tax problems of international repercussions, particularly that of double taxation", in order that the Committee might decide whether to include in its agenda a topic covering the subject. A preliminary paper was submitted in the matter during the course of the 1958 session of the Juridical Committee. Preliminary Paper on "Double Taxation" submitted by Benedict M. English, U.S. member of the Inter-American Juridical Committee, Aug. 8, 1958.

26. *Revision of Resolution VII of the First Meeting of the Inter-American Council of Jurists*

This topic appears on the agenda of the Inter-American Juridical Committee by reason of consideration within the Juridical Committee, during its 1955 session, of the need for revision of Resolution VII of the First Meeting of the Council of Jurists (1950), having to do with the plan for codification and unification of law in the Americas. At that session the Inter-American Juridical Committee prepared a "Report on Resolution VII of the First Meeting of the Inter-American Council of Jurists" (CIJ–27), which was submitted to the Third Meeting of the Inter-American Council of Jurists in 1956. After considering the report, the Third Meeting of the Council of Jurists, by Resolution XII, requested the Juridical Committee to prepare preliminary draft amendments to Resolution VII. *Final Act of the Third Meeting of the Inter-American Council of Jurists, Mexico City, Mexico, January 17–February 4, 1956* (Pan American Union, 1956) 35.

The Juridical Committee approved a preliminary draft on the matter during its 1956 session, which was sent to governments by the Pan American Union in October of that year for observations. Report Submitted by the Chairman of the Inter-American Juridical Committee on the Status of Topics Entrusted to the Committee for Study, September 1956, CIJ–34, p. 2. During its 1957 session the Juridical Committee revised that draft in the light of further study. Second Draft of Amendments to Resolution VII of the First Meeting of Inter-American Council of Jurists, 1957, CIJ–35. At its 1958 session the Juridical Committee decided to recommend inclusion of this topic in the agenda for the 1959 meeting of the Inter-American Council of Jurists. *Report of the Inter-American Juridical Committee on the Work Accomplished during its 1958 Meeting, July 15–October 1* (Pan American Union, 1959) 4 (CIJ–40).

At its Fourth Meeting, held in 1959 at Santiago, Chile, the Inter-American Council of Jurists adopted Resolution XIV entitled "Amendments to Resolution VII of the First Meeting of the Inter-American Council of Jurists". By Resolution XIV the Inter-American Council of Jurists adopted a "plan in connection with its functions of promoting the development and codification of public and private international law and of studying the possibility of attaining uniformity in the legislation of the various American countries, insofar as it appears desirable." The plan was intended both to simplify and strengthen the procedures looking to this end.

By the plan adopted it was agreed that the Inter-American Council of Jurists should select the topics the study of which it wishes to undertake for the purpose of promoting the development and codification of international law or of determining the possibility of attaining uniformity of legislation, requesting, if it so desires, the Inter-American Juridical Committee to prepare reports and draft documents on the material that it deems advisable (article 1(1)). In the selection of topics the Inter-American Council of Jurists is to attend to requests and recommendations of Inter-American Conferences, Meetings of Consultation of Ministers of Foreign Affairs, and the Council of the Organization of American States, and the suggestions of the Inter-American Juridical Committee (article 1(2)(a)). The Council of Jurists in selecting topics and the Juridical Committee in recommending topics are to bear in mind considerations of urgency, necessity, usefulness, possibility of accomplishment, and opinions expressed by governments with respect to such considerations (article 1 (2) (b) and (3)).

It is provided that, when studying topics selected, the Inter-American Juridical Committee shall "investigate all the doctrinal and positive sources available to it, such as custom, legislation, treaties, jurisprudence, and theoretical works, endeavoring to obtain, in accordance with the requirements of each topic, the opinions of individuals and of public and private entities and organizations that are specialists in the study of the topic concerned or that, because of their functions and experience, have acquired practical knowledge of the topic in question." (Article 2(1).) It is to prepare a report as to each topic studied, containing therein a detailed account of the consultations carried out, and of the results achieved, together with the observations and recommendations which it deems advisable (article 2(2)). It is provided that "If the adoption of any specific rules of a juridical character, presented in the form of articles or otherwise, is recommended in the aforesaid report, the Committee shall indicate whether, in its opinion, its recommendations constitute rules of law or whether, on the contrary, they embody new precepts." Also, that "In any case . . . the recommendations that the Committee formulates should be reasoned, and citations of texts or sources that have been utilized should be included." (Article 2(3).) It was thought by members of the Inter-American Council of Jurists that by including these latter provisions the caliber of the work of the Inter-American Juridical Committee would be improved and made more valuable. Reports and drafts prepared by the Juridical Committee are to be transmitted, in preliminary form, through the General Secretariat of the Organization of American States, to governments for their information and in order that within such period as may be indicated by the Committee they may make observations thereon (article 2(4)). Any observations made by governments are to be transmitted, through the General Secretariat, to the Inter-American Juridical Committee, in order that they may be taken into consideration by the latter in preparing definitive reports or draft documents. Once the latter have been prepared, they are to be transmitted to governments, through the General Secretariat, for information (article 2(3)).

So far as the Inter-American Council of Jurists is concerned, it is to take into consideration, when studying the respective topics, the reports prepared by the Inter-American Juridical Committee, but it is not to give consideration to such reports or draft documents prepared by the Committee, unless they have been transmitted to governments at least 3 months prior to the date of the meeting of the

Council of Jurists (article 3). After studying the reports of the Committee, the Council of Jurists may approve them in whole or in part, amend them, postpone consideration of them, return them to the Juridical Committee for further study, or prepare its own report or draft (article 4).

When the Juridical Committee, on its own initiative, carries on studies, it is to follow procedures similar to those followed when studying an assigned topic (article 5).

Once a report or a draft document has been adopted by the Inter-American Council of Jurists, it is to be transmitted—through the General Secretariat of the Organization of American States—to the Council of the Organization, to the governments, and, when appropriate, to the Inter-American Conference, the Meeting of Consultation of Ministers of Foreign Affairs, or to a Specialized Conference. Res. XIV, *Final Act of the Fourth Meeting of the Inter-American Council of Jurists, Santiago, Chile, August 24–September 9, 1959* (Pan American Union, 1959 [1960]), pp. 37–40 (CIJ–43).

27. *Nonintervention*

At the Fifth Meeting of Consultation of Ministers of Foreign Affairs, held at Santiago, Chile, in 1959, it was agreed to transmit to the Inter-American Juridical Committee the draft declaration on nonintervention presented by the delegation of Mexico (Doc. 41) for study and report on its juridical aspect. Res. V, *Final Act of the Fifth Meeting of Consultation of Ministers of Foreign Affairs, Held in Santiago, Chile, August 12–18, 1959*, Doc. 89, Rev. 2, Oct. 12, 1959, pp. 8–9. The Inter-American Juridical Committee at its special session in October–November 1959, while noting that the Mexican draft declaration was not referred to it for consideration at the special session, also noted that the subject matter was included on the agenda for the Eleventh Inter-American Conference and, consequently, resolved to send the draft declaration to the General Secretariat of the Organization of American States for such use as it might deem appropriate with the understanding that it was being sent as a working document with respect to which the Committee expressed no opinion. *Acta Final de la Reunion Extraordinaria del 5 de Octubre al 5 de Noviembre, Inclusive, de 1959*, p. 10 (mimeo.); *Report of the Inter-American Juridical Committee on the Work Carried Out During the Special Meeting Held in 1959, October 5–November 5* (Pan American Union, 1960) 14–15 (CIJ–55).

By Resolution VII of the Fifth Meeting of Consultation of the Ministers of Foreign Affairs, held at Santiago, Chile, in 1959, it was agreed to recommend to the Council of the Organization of American

States that it have prepared (a) a draft instrument listing the greatest possible number of cases that constitute violations of the principle of nonintervention; and (b) a report on the possibility of establishing adequate procedures to insure, without constituting intervention in the internal or external affairs of states, strict observance of the principle of nonintervention. Such draft and report, it was agreed, should be submitted by the Council of the Organization of American States to the governments of Member States for information and for any observations they might wish to make and be included on the agenda of the Eleventh Inter-American Conference. *Final Act of the Fifth Meeting of Consultation of Ministers of Foreign Affairs, Held in Santiago, Chile, August 12–18, 1959*, Doc. 89, Rev. 2, Oct. 12, 1959, pp. 9–10. The Council of the Organization of American States referred the matter to the Inter-American Juridical Committee. That body, meeting in special session in October–November 1959, elaborated an instrument enumerating violations of the principle of nonintervention. *Acta Final de la Reunion Extraordinaria del 5 de Octubre al 5 de Noviembre, Inclusive, de 1959*, pp. 3–6 (mimeo.); *Report of the Inter-American Juridical Committee on the Work Carried Out During the Special Meeting Held in 1959, October 5–November 5* (Pan American Union, 1960) 5–8 (CIJ–55).

> For "A Systematic Classification of the Treaties, Conventions, Resolutions, Declarations, and Recommendations Adopted at Inter-American Conferences and Meetings of Consultation", including materials on codification of public and private international law and unification of law in the Americas, see *Manual of Inter-American Relations (Revised)* (Pan American Union, 1956), particularly, "I. Principles of Inter-American Solidarity, Fundamental Rights and Duties of States", *ibid.* 1–16; "III. Maintenance of Peace and Security; The Inter-American Peace System", *ibid.* 70–96; "IV. Cooperation for the Promotion of the Common Interests of the American Peoples . . . B. Juridical Interests", *ibid.* 109–143.

U.N.:
Charter,
1945

"The wide-spread interest of governments [at San Francisco in 1945] in securing some provision in the Charter devoted to the development of international law is evidenced by the fact that fifteen governments submitted comments on the subject, eight of them also offering proposed amendments, and that the Four Sponsoring Powers included the subject in one of their joint proposed amendments. [Documentation for Meetings of Committee IV/2, Development of International Law, UNCIO Doc. 225, IV/2/9, May 11, 1945.] Accordingly, the topic appeared on the agenda of the tenth meeting of Committee IV/2 for May 23, 1945. [UNCIO Doc. 522, IV/2/25, May 23, 1945.] It was speedily pointed out in debate, however, that Committee II/2 on 'Political and Security Functions,' was also dealing with this question and had already passed two motions on the matter. [Summary Report of Tenth Meeting of Committee II/2, May

21, 1945, UNCIO Doc. 507, II/2/22, May 23, 1945.] The questions put to Committee II/2 were: (1) 'Should the Assembly be empowered to initiate studies and make recommendations for the codification of international law?' and (2) 'Should the Assembly be empowered to initiate studies and make recommendations for promoting the revision of the rules and principles of international law?' For both the vote was in the affirmative. But on the following question, the vote of Committee II/2 was 26 to 1 in the negative: (3) 'Should the Assembly be authorized to enact rules of international law which should become binding upon members after such rules shall have been approved by the Security Council?' Confronted with this voting record of a fellow committee, Committee IV/2 declined to proceed with its agenda item. [Summary Report of Tenth Meeting of Committee IV/2, May 23, 1945, UNCIO Doc. 554, IV/2/28, May 25, 1945.] In its final report it submitted no recommendation on the subject [Report of the Rapporteur of Committee IV/2, UNCIO Doc. 933, IV/2/42/(2), June 12, 1945, p. 6], but the decisions of Committee II/2 are embodied in the clause dealing with international law in article 13 of the Charter."

Reiff, "Work of the United Nations 'Legal Committees'", XV *Bulletin*, Department of State, No. 366, July 7, 1946, pp. 3, 6–7.

Article 13 of the Charter of the United Nations reads: Article 13

"1. The General Assembly shall initiate studies and make recommendations for the purpose of:

"a. . . . encouraging the progressive development of international law and its codification".

U.S. TS 993; 59 Stat. 1031, 1039. On Aug. 2, 1946, the Acting U.S. Representative to the United Nations, Herschel V. Johnson, requested that the Secretary-General of the United Nations include in the provisional agenda for the second part of the first session of the General Assembly an item looking toward the carrying out of this provision of the Charter. U.N. press release, Aug. 8, 1946, XV *Bulletin*, Department of State, No. 373, Aug. 25, 1946, p. 355.

By Resolution 94(I) of December 11, 1946, the General Assembly established a 17-member committee to study the methods by which the General Assembly could implement its obligations under article 13, paragraph 1a, of the Charter.   International Law Commission

The Committee on the Progressive Development of International Law and its Codification, which met at Lake Success from March 12 to June 17, 1947, recommended (A/331) the establishment of an International Law Commission.

For the Report of the Committee, see Doc. A/AC.10/51, June 17, 1947. For the Report of the U.S. Representative (Philip C. Jessup) on the "U.N. Committee on the Progressive Development of International Law and Its Codification", see Doc. US/A/AC.10/4, June 19, 1947; XVII *Bulletin*,

Department of State, No. 420, July 20, 1947, pp. 121–127. For "Suggestions by the United States" made in the Committee, see Doc. A/AC.10/14, May 12, 1947; XVI *Bulletin*, Department of State, No. 412, May 25, 1947, pp. 1026, 1029.

Statute, 1947

Following consideration of this recommendation by the Sixth Committee at its 40th meeting, October 2, 1947, the General Assembly at its 123d plenary meeting, November 21, 1947, by Resolution 174(II) resolved to establish an International Law Commission to be constituted and to function according to the provisions of the annexed Statute.   (A/CN.4/4, Feb. 2, 1949.)

Under the provisions of the Statute of the International Law Commission, the Commission is charged with the promotion of the progressive development of international law and its codification.

Membership

The composition of this originally 15-member, now 25-member, Commission, elected by the General Assembly from a list of candidates nominated by governments of Member States, no two of whom can be nationals of the same State, is designed to reflect the main forms of civilization and the principal legal systems of the world. The members serve in a personal capacity rather than as representatives of States or governments, and although originally (in 1948) elected to serve a 3-year term of office, members beginning with those elected in 1957 now serve for 5 years (chapter I, articles 2–14). (General Assembly Resolution 985 (X), December 3, 1955.)

"Progressive development"; "codification"

In delineating the functions of the International Law Commission, the Statute clarifies the expression "progressive development of international law" as meaning the preparation of draft conventions on subjects which have not yet been regulated by international law or in regard to which the law has not yet been sufficiently developed in the practice of States, and correspondingly, the expression "codification of international law" is interpreted as the more precise formulation and systematization of rules of international law in fields where there already has been extensive State practice, precedent, and doctrine (chapter II, article 15).

Method of work

Upon receiving a General Assembly proposal for the progressive development of international law, the Commission proceeds to appoint one of its members the rapporteur, formulate a plan of work, and invite the governments to supply information relevant to items listed in the plan of work. It then considers the drafts proposed by the rapporteur. If satisfactory, the Commission requests the Secretary-General to issue it as a Commission document including any information submitted by governments. The Commission then invites governments to submit their comments on this document and after the rapporteur considers these comments, a final draft and explanatory report is submitted for consideration and adoption by the Commission. The Commission submits the draft as adopted with its recommendations through the Secretary-General to the General Assembly (chapter II, A, article 16).

The Commission also considers proposals and drafts of conventions submitted by members of the United Nations, the principal organs of the United Nations other than the General Assembly, specialized agencies, or official bodies established by intergovernmental agreement to encourage progressive development of international law and its codification, and, if the Commission finds it appropriate to proceed with the study of such proposals or drafts, it formulates a plan of work and invites members of the United Nations, organs, specialized agencies, and official bodies concerned with the question to submit comments. The Commission submits its report and recommendations to the General Assembly, and if the General Assembly invites the Commission to proceed with its work the procedure followed when the General Assembly refers proposals to the International Law Commission applies (chapter II, article 17).

To promote the codification of international law, the Statute directs the Commission to survey the whole field of international law with a view to selecting topics for codification and then recommend to the General Assembly those topics the codification of which it considers necessary or desirable. Priority, however, must be given to requests for codification made initially by the General Assembly (chapter II, article 18).

The Commission is to request governments through the Secretary-General to furnish any necessary texts of laws, decrees, judicial decisions, treaties, diplomatic correspondence and other documents relevant to the topic under study (chapter II, article 19). A draft in the form of articles is then submitted to the General Assembly together with a commentary containing precedents, relevant data including treaties, judicial decisions, doctrine, conclusions regarding the extent of agreement on each point in the practice and doctrine of States, and divergencies, disagreements, and arguments favoring one solution or another (chapter II, article 20). If satisfactory, the Commission requests the Secretary-General to issue it as a Commission document, which is then published along with any information supplied to the Commission by governments and opinions of scientific institutions and individual experts if the Commission so decides (chapter II, article 21). Comments which governments are invited to submit are considered in the Commission's preparation of the final draft and explanatory report which it submits to the General Assembly through the Secretary-General (chapter II, articles 21, 22).

The Commission may recommend in the case of codification that the General Assembly take no action upon the report already published, take note of or adopt the report by resolution, or recommend the draft to members to conclude a convention. The General Assembly may refer drafts back to the Commission for reconsideration or redrafting (chapter II, article 23).

The Statute of the International Law Commission has since been amended or clarified in the following respects: In 1950, the General

Assembly at its 320th meeting, December 12, decided in Resolution 485(V), in accordance with authority given it by article 13 of the Statute, to increase the special allowance for members of the International Law Commission to $35 per day; by Resolution 486(V) adopted at the same session, the term of office of the then present members was extended by 2 years, making a total of 5 years of service from the date of their election in 1948 (*Yearbook of the United Nations 1950*, pp. 847-850); in 1955 the meeting place of the International Law Commission was changed from New York to its European office in Geneva by amendment to article 12 of the Statute effected by Resolution 984(X) adopted at the 550th plenary session of the General Assembly, December 3, 1955; and in Resolution 986(X) adopted at the same session, article 10 was amended so that members elected beginning in 1956 would serve for a period of 5 years instead of 3. *Yearbook of the United Nations 1955*, p. 337.

Although the United States as one of a substantial minority proposed a further amendment to the Statute which would permit the General Assembly to fill casual vacancies thereby divesting the Commission of this function, the General Assembly at its 623d plenary session, December 18, 1956, concluded that the Statute should remain unchanged in this regard. *Yearbook of the United Nations 1956*, p. 383.

By Resolution 1103 (XI), adopted on December 18, 1956, the General Assembly changed the number of members of the International Law Commission from 15 to 21, and subsequently, by Resolution 1647 (XVI), adopted November 6, 1961, enlarged the membership again to a total of 25 elected members, thereby amending each time article 2, paragraph 1, and article 9, paragraph 1, of the Statute of the International Law Commission accordingly.

The Secretary-General was instructed to undertake necessary preparatory measures to initiate the work of the International Law Commission, particularly with regard to questions referred to it by the second session of the General Assembly, such as the Draft Declaration on the Rights and Duties of States, by Resolution 175(II) adopted during the 123d plenary meeting of the General Assembly, November 21, 1947.

In compliance with article 18, paragraph 1, of its Statute, which directs the Commission to "survey the whole field of international law with a view to selecting topics for codification", the Commission provisionally selected 14 topics from a list of 25 in the Secretary-General's memorandum (A/CN.4/1/Rev. 1). The topics the codification of which the Commission deemed necessary or desirable are: Recognition of States and Governments; Succession of States and Governments; Jurisdictional Immunities of States and Their Property; Jurisdiction with Regard to Crimes Committed Outside National Territory; Régime of the High Seas; Régime of Territorial Waters; Nationality Including Statelessness; Treatment of Aliens; Right of Asylum; Law of Treaties; Diplomatic Intercourse and Immunities; Consular Intercourse and Immunities; State Responsibility; and Arbitral Procedure. Report of I.L.C. to the General Assembly on Work of First Session, *Yearbook of the International Law Commission 1949*, pp. 279–281.

Topics (margin note)

Survey of Work by Sessions of the International Law Commission:

During the Commission's first session, April 12 to June 9, 1949, 14 topics were provisionally selected for codification, 3 of which were chosen for priority consideration; work on a Draft Code of Offences Against the Peace and Security of Mankind was initiated; preliminary study of the desirability and possibility of establishing an international judicial organ for the trial of persons charged with genocide or other crimes over which jurisdiction would be conferred upon that organ by international conventions was begun; initial consideration of the ways and means for making the evidence of customary international law more readily available was undertaken; and a Draft Declaration on the Rights and Duties of States was prepared. Report of I.L.C. to the General Assembly on Work of First Session, *Yearbook of the International Law Commission 1949*, pp. 277–290; U.N. Gen. Ass. Off. Rec. 4th Sess., Supp. No. 10, A/925.

The Commission at its second session, June 5 to July 29, 1950, drafted a report on the Ways and Means for Making the Evidence of Customary International Law More Readily Available based on a working paper on this subject submitted at its second session; adopted a formulation of the principles of international law which were recognized in the Charter of the Nürnberg Tribunal and in the judgment of that Tribunal on the basis of a report on this subject; discussed reports concerning the question of International Criminal Jurisdiction, concluding that the establishment of an international judicial organ for the trial of persons charged with genocide was both desirable and possible; considered a report on a Draft Code of Offences Against the Peace and Security of Mankind and referred a provisional draft of a code prepared by the Drafting Sub-Committee to the special rapporteur who was requested to submit a further report at the next session; considered reports on the three topics given priority for codification and requested work be continued on each. Report of I.L.C. to the General Assembly on Work of Second Session, II *Yearbook of the International Law Commission 1950*, pp. 364–385; U.N. Gen. Ass. Off. Rec. 5th Sess., Supp. No. 12, A/1316.

At its third session, May 16 to July 27, 1951, the Commission gave priority, in pursuance of General Assembly Resolution 478(V), November 16, 1950, to a study of the question of reservations to multilateral conventions in connection with its work on the codification of the Law of Treaties and included its views in its report to the General Assembly; considering the question of Defining Aggression, decided to include any act of aggression and any threat of aggression among the offences defined in the draft code of offences against the peace and security of mankind; adopted a draft Code of Offences Against the Peace and Security of Mankind; considered additional draft articles on the Law of Treaties, provisionally agreed on tentative texts, and requested submission of final drafts at its fourth session; decided to communicate drafts on the Régime of the High Seas to governments; decided to initiate work on the topics of Nationality Including Statelessness, and Régime of Territorial Waters. Report of I.L.C. to the General Assembly on Work of Third Session, II *Yearbook of the International Law Commission 1951*, pp. 123–144; U.N. Gen. Ass. Off. Rec. 6th Sess., Supp. No. 9, A/1858.

The Commission, during its fourth session, June 4 to August 8, 1952, considered a second preliminary draft on Arbitration Procedure and adopted a Draft on Arbitral Procedure; considered a report on Nationality Including Statelessness, which contained two working papers: a draft convention on Nationality of Married Persons and a paper on Statelessness covering three subtopics—Elimination of Statelessness, Reduction of Presently Existing Statelessness, and Reduction of Statelessness Arising in the Future, and requested preparation of further drafts for consideration at its next session; discussed the subject Régime of the Territorial Sea on the basis of a report on the same submitted at the fourth session, and, after expressing tentative views on this matter, requested a further report for its fifth session; deferred consideration on the subject Régime of the High Seas although it had before it reports on the topic along with draft articles on the Continental Shelf and related subjects; refrained from discussing a report on the Law of Treaties due to absence of its author and requested a further report at its next session. Report of I.L.C. to the General Assembly on Work of Fourth Session, II *Yearbook of the International Law Commission 1952*, pp. 57–70; U.N. Gen. Ass. Off. Rec. 7th Sess., Supp. No. 9, A/2163.

At its fifth session, June 1 to August 14, 1953, the Commission considered the Draft on Arbitral Procedure in the light of comments of governments, adopted substantial changes, and directed that a commentary prepared by the Secretariat be revised and supplemented in the light of certain decisions and be published; examined the provisional draft articles adopted at its third session and prepared final drafts on the following issues: Continental Shelf, Fishery Resources of the High Seas, and Contiguous Zones; discussed the two drafts on the Elimination of Future Statelessness and Reduction of Future Statelessness, adopted provisional drafts of both conventions, and asked the Secretary-General to issue them as Commission documents; requested further reports to be presented at its sixth session on the following subjects: Law of Treaties, Régime of the

High Seas, Nationality Including Statelessness, and a Draft Code of Offences Against the Peace and Security of Mankind. Report of I.L.C. to the General Assembly on Work of Fifth Session, II *Yearbook of the International Law Commission 1953*, pp. 200–269; U.N. Gen. Ass. Off. Rec. 8th Sess., Supp. No. 9, A/2456.

During its sixth session, June 3 to July 28, 1954, the Commission adopted draft conventions on the Elimination of Future Statelessness and on the Reduction of Future Statelessness as part I of its report on Nationality Including Statelessness. Part 2 of the report dealt with the elimination and the reduction of present statelessness. The Commission adopted draft articles on the reduction of present statelessness in the form of suggestions which governments may wish to take into account when attempting solution of this problem. Additionally, it made certain revisions in the previously adopted text of the Draft Code of Offences Against the Peace and Security of Mankind; and it considered the revised report on the Régime of the Territorial Sea and adopted a number of draft articles, with comments, for submission to governments; and decided to initiate work on the topic Diplomatic Intercourse and Immunities in pursuance of General Assembly Resolution 685(VII) of December 5, 1952, which requested the Commission to undertake the codification of this topic as soon as it considered it possible. Report of I.L.C. to the General Assembly on Work of Sixth Session, II *Yearbook of the International Law Commission 1954*, pp. 140–173; U.N. Gen. Ass. Off. Rec. 9th Sess., Supp. No. 9, A/2693.

The Commission at its seventh session, May 2 to July 8, 1955, considered anew questions regarding the High Seas in view of an additional report on this subject and adopted a provisional draft with commentaries to be submitted to governments for observations; amended several articles formerly drafted on the Régime of the Territorial Sea in the light of comments received from governments, and examined questions reserved for this session on breadth of the territorial sea, bays, groups of islands, and the delimitation of the territorial sea at the mouths of rivers, and adopted draft articles on the Régime of the Territorial Sea. Report of I.L.C. to the General Assembly on Work of Seventh Session, II *Yearbook of the International Law Commission 1955*, pp. 19–62; U.N. Gen. Ass. Off. Rec. 10th Sess. Supp. No. 9, A/2934.

During its eighth session, April 23 to July 4, 1956, the Commission drew up a final report on the Régime of the High Seas, and Territorial Sea, incorporating changes made in view of comments from governments, and adopted a final report on the Law of the Sea wherein it grouped together systematically all the rules it had adopted concerning the High Seas, the Territorial Sea, the Continental Shelf, the Contiguous Zone, and the Conservation of the Living Resources of the Sea; partially considered a report on the Law of Treaties; and requested work be continued on State Responsibility and Consular Intercourse and Immunities. Report of I.L.C. to the General Assembly on Work of Eighth Session, II *Yearbook of the International Law Commission 1956*, pp. 253–302; U.N. Gen. Ass. Off. Rec. 11th Sess., Supp. No. 9, A/3159.

The Commission during its ninth session, April 23 to June 28, 1957, adopted a provisional draft with commentaries concerning Diplomatic Intercourse and Immunities; discussed a second report on "International Responsibility" dealing with the particular topic of "Responsibility of the State for Injuries Caused in its Territory to the Person or Property of

Aliens—Part I: Acts and Omissions", and requested work to be continued thereon; concluded that the object to be attained in reviewing the draft on arbitral procedure should be a set of rules which might inspire States in the drawing up of provisions for inclusion in international treaties and special arbitration agreements, discussed certain of the key articles in the revised draft submitted by the special rapporteur in his report which took into consideration the comments of governments and the discussions in the Sixth Committee respecting the Commission's original (1953) draft, and adjourned the matter for final consideration and report at its tenth session after taking provisional decisions on certain points. Report of I.L.C. to the General Assembly on Work of Ninth Session, II *Yearbook of the International Law Commission 1957*, pp. 131–146; U.N. Gen. Ass. Off. Rec. 12th Sess., Supp. No. 9, A/3623.

The Commission at its tenth session, April 28 to July 4, 1958, adopted model Rules on Arbitral Procedure; examined the text of a provisional draft on Diplomatic Intercourse and Immunities in the light of observations of governments and of the conclusions drawn from them by the special rapporteur and recommended to the General Assembly that the draft articles on this subject should be recommended to Member States with a view to the conclusion of a convention. Report of I.L.C. to the General Assembly on Work of Tenth Session, II *Yearbook of the International Law Commission 1958*, pp. 78–139; U.N. Gen. Ass. Off. Rec. 13th Sess., Supp. No. 9, A/3859.

At its eleventh session, April 20 to June 26, 1959, the Commission began the codification of the Law of Treaties and completed 14 draft articles which as part of a planned code on the whole of the Law of Treaties cover part of the subjects of framing, conclusion, and entry into force of treaties, and part of the topic of signature and its legal effects; examined articles 1–17 of the draft on Consular Intercourse and Immunities. Report of I.L.C. to the General Assembly on Work of Eleventh Session, U.N. Gen. Ass. Off. Rec. 14th Sess., Supp. No. 9, A/4169; II *Yearbook of the International Law Commission 1959*, pp. 87–123.

At its twelfth session, April 25 to July 1, 1960, the Commission prepared draft articles on Consular Intercourse and Immunities, with commentary, and also draft articles on Special Missions, with commentary. Report of I.L.C. to the General Assembly on Work of Twelfth Session, U.N. Gen. Ass. Off. Rec. 15th Sess., Supp. No. 9, A/4425; II *Yearbook of the International Law Commission 1961*, pp. 88–174.

At its thirteenth session, May 1–July 7, 1961, the Commission produced a final text of draft articles on consular relations, recommending that the General Assembly convene an international conference and conclude one or more conventions on the subject. Report of I.L.C. to the General Assembly on Work of Thirteenth Session, U.N. Gen. Ass. Off. Rec. 16th Sess., Supp. No. 9, A/4843.

At its fourteenth session, April 24–June 29, 1962, the Commission adopted a provisional draft of articles on the conclusion, entry into force, and registration of treaties. Report of I.L.C. to the General Assembly on Work of Fourteenth Session, U.N. Gen. Ass. Off. Rec. 17th Sess., Supp. No. 9, A/5209.

Of the 14 topics provisionally selected for codification by the Commission, 3—Law of Treaties, Arbitral Procedure, and Régime of the High Seas—were chosen for priority consideration.

The scope of the International Law Commission's work on the Law of Treaties was broadened when in 1950 the General Assembly, at its 305th plenary session November 16, 1950, issued (Resolution 478(V)) a dual request: one to the Commission to consider the whole question of reservations to multilateral conventions both from the point of view of codification and from that of the progressive development of law; and, the other, to the International Court of Justice for an advisory opinion on questions concerning the effect of reservations to the Convention on Genocide. Submission of both reports was requested for the General Assembly's sixth session where they would be jointly considered. *Yearbook of the United Nations 1950*, pp. 873–879. Accordingly, the International Law Commission considered the question at its third session, taking into account two reports of the special rapporteur (A/CN.4/23 and A/CN.4/43), a "Report on Reservations to Multilateral Conventions" (A/CN.4/41), as well as memoranda presented by Mr. Amado (A/CN.4/L.9, Corr. 1) and by Mr. Scelle (A/CN.4/L.14), and submitted its report (A/1858) to the sixth session of the General Assembly where it was reviewed at the 264th to 278th meetings of the Sixth Committee from December 5, 1951, to January 5, 1952, and at the Assembly's 360th plenary meeting, January 12, 1952. Adopting the Sixth Committee's resolution as Resolution 598 (VI), which was addressed specifically to the Genocide Convention, the General Assembly recommended that organs of the United Nations, specialized agencies, and States should, in the course of preparing multilateral conventions, consider the insertion therein of provisions relating to the admissibility or nonadmissibility of reservations and to the effect to be attributed to them; and further recommended to all States that they be guided in regard to the Convention on the Prevention and Punishment of the Crime of Genocide by the advisory opinion of the International Court of Justice, *Reservations to the Convention on the Prevention and Punishment of the Crime of Genocide*, Advisory Opinion No. 12, May 28, 1951, I.C.J. Reports (1951) 15. The General Assembly requested the Secretary-General to conform his practice to the advisory opinion of the Court May 28, 1951, in relation to reservations to the Convention on the Prevention and Punishment of the Crime of Genocide and in respect to future conventions continue to act as depositary of documents containing reservations without passing on the legal effect of such documents; to communicate the text of such documents to all States concerned, leaving it to each State to draw legal consequences from such communication. *Yearbook of the United Nations 1951*, pp. 820–832. Although the General Assembly did not fully endorse either the League of Nations unanimity rule under which acceptance of a reservation by all contracting states is necessary, or the Pan

Law of
Treaties

American rule by which rejection of a reservation operates only to prevent the coming into force of the treaty as between the reserving and rejecting states, it refused to adopt the Commission's proposals which were strongly oriented in favor of the unanimity rule. U.S. participation in the U.N., report by the President to Congress for the year 1951, pp. 251–252. Although the Commission was in receipt of reports from both special rapporteurs on this subject at its ninth session (A/CN.4/107 and A/CN.4/108), the continuation of the work on Law of Treaties was requested for its tenth session. II *Yearbook of the International Law Commission 1957*, p. 144. The special rapporteur (Fitzmaurice) submitted his third report on the Law of Treaties to the tenth session of the ILC, March 18, 1958 (A.CN.4/115), where it was decided to continue discussion at the eleventh session. II *Yearbook of the International Law Commission 1958*, pp. 20–46, 106. Fourteen draft articles on the Law of Treaties adopted by the Commission at its eleventh session cover part of the subject of framing, conclusion, and entry into force of treaties, and part of the topic of signature, its function, incidents, and legal effects. Report of I.L.C. to the General Assembly on Work of Eleventh Session, II *Yearbook of the International Law Commission 1959*, pp. 87–123. The Commission at its fourteenth session, adopted provisional draft articles on the conclusion, entry into force, and registration of treaties, and submitted as its plan the drafting of another group of articles covering the validity and duration of treaties as well as a further draft of articles covering the application and effects of treaties. U.N. Gen. Ass. Off. Rec. 17th Sess., Supp. No. 9, A/5209, p. 3.

For U.N. and ILC documentation on the "Law of Treaties", see generally: Replies from Governments, Mar. 23, 1950, A/CN.4/19, II Yearbook of I.L.C. 1950, pp. 196–221; Report by Brierly, Special Rapporteur, on the Law of Treaties, Apr. 14, 1950, A/CN.4/23, II Yearbook of I.L.C. 1950, pp. 222–248; Report of I.L.C. Covering Work of Second Session, A/1316, II Yearbook of I.L.C. 1950, pp. 364, 380; Bibliography on the Law of Treaties, June 27, 1950, A/CN.4/31, printed as annex to document ST/LEG/SER.B/3, Dec. 1952; Memorandum on the Soviet Doctrine and Practice With Respect to the Law of Treaties, prepared by the Secretariat, Nov. 21, 1950, A/CN.4/37; Report by Brierly, Special Rapporteur, on Law of Treaties, replacing articles 6–10 as reported in A/CN.4/23, Apr. 10, 1951, A/CN.4/43, II Yearbook of I.L.C. 1951, pp. 70–73; Second Report on Law of Treaties, Redraft of articles suggested by Special Rapporteur in light of discussions and decisions of Commission, May 23, 1951, A/CN.4/L.4; Second Report on Law of Treaties, Text of articles tentatively adopted by the Commission at its 88th meeting, May 25, 1951, A/CN.4/L.5; Text of articles tentatively adopted by the Commission at its Third Session, July 19, 1951, A/CN.4/L.28, II Yearbook of I.L.C. 1951, pp. 73–74; Law of Treaties, Draft Report of I.L.C. Covering Work of Third Session, A/1858, II Yearbook of I.L.C. 1951, pp. 125–131; Third Report on Law of Treaties, by Brierly, Special Rap-

porteur, Apr. 10, 1952, A/CN.4/54, II Yearbook of I.L.C. 1952, pp. 50–56;
Report of I.L.C. Covering Work of Fourth Session, A/2163, II Yearbook of
I.L.C. 1952, pp. 57, 69.

Article prepared by Dr. Yuen-li Liang at request of Brierly, Special
Rapporteur, footnote 3 to Summary Record of 99th meeting, June 7, 1951,
A/CN.4/L.16; Draft Convention on Law of Treaties contained in first report
of Special Rapporteur (A/CN.4/23), footnote 11 to Summary Record of
98th meeting, June 7, 1951, A/CN.4/L.17; Articles tentatively adopted as of
June 11, 1952, A/CN.4/L.33; Law of Treaties, memorandum submitted by
Yepes, Aug. 13, 1953, A/CN.4/L.46; Report on Law of Treaties by Lauter-
pacht, Special Rapporteur, Mar. 24, 1953, A/CN.4/63; Second report on
Law of Treaties by Lauterpacht, Special Rapporteur, July 8, 1954,
A/CN.4/87; Working paper prepared by the Secretariat, May 10, 1955, reproduces texts of articles as amended by Lauterpacht's second report,
A/CN.4/L.55; Report on Law of Treaties by Fitzmaurice, Special Rap-
porteur, Mar. 14, 1956, A/CN.4/101; Second report by Fitzmaurice, Special
Rapporteur, Mar. 15, 1957, A/CN.4/107, II Yearbook of I.L.C. 1957, pp.
16–70; Third report of Fitzmaurice, Special Rapporteur, on Law of Treaties,
Mar. 18, 1958, A/CN.4/115, II Yearbook of I.L.C. 1958, pp. 20–46; Fourth
report by Fitzmaurice, Special Rapporteur, Mar. 17, 1959, A/CN.4/120, II
Yearbook of I.L.C. 1959, pp. 37–81.

Report by Brierly, Special Rapporteur, on Reservations to Multilateral
Conventions, Apr. 6, 1951, A/CN.4/41, II Yearbook of I.L.C. 1951, pp. 1–17;
Memorandum presented by Amado on Reservations to Multilateral Con-
ventions, May 31, 1951, A/CN.4/L.9, II Yearbook of I.L.C. 1951, pp. 17–23;
Reservations to Multilateral Conventions, memorandum presented by
Scelle, June 5, 1951, A/CN.4/L.14, II Yearbook of I.L.C. 1951, pp. 23–26;
Reservations to Multilateral Conventions, draft report by Brierly to
General Assembly, June 11, 1951, A/CN.4/L.18, II Yearbook of I.L.C. 1951,
pp. 26–27; Systematic Survey of Treaties for the Pacific Settlement of
International Disputes 1928–1948, 1949.V.3; Laws and Practices Concern-
ing the Conclusion of Treaties (ST/LEG/SER.B/3), Dec. 1952, 1952.V.4;
Signatures, Ratification, Acceptances, Accessions, etc., concerning the Multi-
lateral Conventions and Agreements in respect of which the Secretary-
General acts as Depositary, Nov. 15, 1949, 1949.V.9; Signatures, Ratifications, Acceptances, Accessions, etc., concerning the Multilateral Conventions and Agreements in respect of which the SYG acts as Depositary,
Corrigenda and addenda, Dec. 31, 1950, 1951.V.3; Status of Multilateral
Conventions, of which the Secretary-General Acts as Depositary, Oct. 10,
1952, 1952.V.2; see also *ibid.* in Sept. 30, 1959, 1959.V.6 (ST/LEG/3/Rev.1),
and suppls.: Supplement No. 4 to the Status of Multilateral Conventions,
of which the SYG acts as Depositary (ST/LEG/3), Mar. 1954, 1952.V.2
Suppl. 4; Supplement No. 5 to the Status of Multilateral Conventions, of
which the Secretary-General Acts as Depositary, Transmittal Sheet No. 5,
ST/LEG/3, Mar. 1954, 1952.V.2 Suppl. 5; Supplement No. 6 to the Status
of Multilateral Conventions, of which the Secretary-General Acts as Depositary, ST/LEG/3, June 1954, 1952.V.2 Suppl. 6; Supplement No. 7 to
the Status of Multilateral Conventions, of which the Secretary-General
Acts as Depositary, Transmittal Sheet No. 7, ST/LEG/3, Dec. 1954, 1952.V.2
Suppl. 7; Supplement No. 8 to the Status of Multilateral Conventions, of
which the Secretary-General Acts as Depositary, ST/LEG/3, Mar. 1955,

1952.V.2 Suppl. 8; Supplement No. 9 to the Status of Multilateral Conventions, of which the Secretary-General Acts as Depositary, ST/LEG/3, Mar. 31, 1955, 1952.V.2 Suppl. 9; Supplement No. 10 to the Status of Multilateral Conventions, of which the Secretary-General Acts as Depositary, ST/LEG/3, Aug. 1955, 1952.V.2 Suppl. 10; Supplement No. 11 to the Status of Multilateral Conventions, of which the Secretary-General Acts as Depositary, ST/LEG/3, Dec. 1955, 1952.V.2 Suppl. 11: Supplement No. 12 to the Status of Multilateral Conventions, of which the Secretary-General Acts as Depositary, ST/LEG/3, May 1956, 1952.V.2 Suppl. 12; Supplement Nos. 13–14 to the Status of Multilateral Conventions, of which the Secretary-General Acts as Depositary, ST/LEG/3, Oct. 1956, 1952.V.2 Suppl. 13–14; Supplement No. 15 to the Status of Multilateral Conventions, of which the Secretary-General Acts as Depositary, ST/LEG/3, Mar. 1957, 1952.V.2 Suppl. 15; Supplement Nos. 16–18 to the Status of Multilateral Conventions, of which the Secretary-General Acts as Depositary, ST/LEG/3, June 1957, 1952.V.2 Suppl. 16–18; Supplement No. 19 to the Status of Multilateral Conventions, of which the Secretary-General Acts as Depositary, ST/LEG/3, Dec. 1957, 1952.V.2 Suppl. 19; Supplement No. 20 to the Status of Multilateral Conventions, of which the Secretary-General Acts as Depositary, ST/LEG/3, Mar. 1958, 1952.V.2 Suppl. 20; Supplement No. 21 to the Status of Multilateral Conventions, of which the Secretary-General Acts as Depositary, ST/LEG/3, Apr. 1958, 1952.V.2 Suppl. 21; Supplement No. 22 to the Status of Multilateral Conventions, of which the Secretary-General Acts as Depositary, ST/LEG/3, June 1958, 1952.V.2 Suppl. 22; Supplement Nos. 23–24 to the Status of Multilateral Conventions, of which the SYG Acts as Depositary, ST/LEG/3, Mar. 1959, 1952.V.2 Suppl. 23–24. Reservations to Multilateral Conventions, Resolution adopted by Sixth Committee at its 277th meeting, Jan. 4, 1952, A/C.6/L.205.

Arbitral Procedure

The International Law Commission considered at its second session (1950) the first report (A/CN.4/18) on Arbitral Procedure, containing a preliminary draft code by Professor Scelle, special rapporteur, along with replies of governments (A/CN.4/19, pt. I, B) to a questionnaire circulated by it. *Yearbook of the United Nations 1950*, pp. 862–863. The second report (A/CN.4/46), considered at the fourth session, 1952, along with a Supplementary Note to the Second Report on Arbitral Procedure (A/CN.4/57), was followed by the adoption of a draft on Arbitral Procedure containing 32 articles covering such topics as the undertaking to arbitrate, constitution of the tribunal, the *compromis*, powers of the tribunal, the award, revision, and annulment of awards. *Yearbook of the United Nations 1952*, pp. 792–795. The Sixth Committee considered the draft submitted in 1953 by the ILC (A/2456), dealing with Arbitral Procedure, at its 382d to 389th meetings from November 9–18, 1953. The General Assembly adopted the Sixth Committee's draft resolution after consideration of its report (A/2589) at its 468th plenary meeting, on December 7, 1953, as Resolution 797 (VIII) wherein it decided to transmit to Member States the draft on Arbitral Procedure along with observations of the

Sixth Committee in order that governments might submit comments, and requested the Secretary-General to include this question in the provisional agenda of the General Assembly's tenth session. *Yearbook of the United Nations 1953*, pp. 670–676. In view of the fact that many of the delegations had been unable to take substantive positions on the draft convention, because of the comparatively short time between publication of the Commission's report and its consideration by the Assembly, the United States supported this Assembly decision. However, during debates in the Sixth (Legal) Committee, the United States noted that since the draft, which was designed to insure the continued validity and effectiveness of a freely undertaken obligation to arbitrate, introduced many innovations into traditional concepts of international arbitration, the General Assembly should have referred the draft convention to governments for use as a model for future bilateral or multilateral international arbitration agreements. U.S. participation in the U.N., report by the President to Congress for the year 1953, pp. 194–195. In the light of observations received from 14 governments, the Sixth Committee in its discussions at its 461st to 464th and 466th to 472d meetings (November 22–December 7, 1955) proposed that the draft convention be referred back to the International Law Commission for report at the thirteenth session of the General Assembly, 1958. The General Assembly in adopting the Committee's report (A/3083) at its 554th plenary meeting as Resolution 989(X), December 14, 1955, invited the International Law Commission to consider comments of governments and the discussions in the Sixth Committee and decided to place the question on the provisional agenda of the thirteenth session, along with the question regarding the desirability of convening an international conference of plenipotentiaries to conclude a convention on arbitral procedure. *Yearbook of the United Nations 1955*, pp. 339–340. The United States along with a substantial minority opposed the General Assembly's endorsement of the draft as it then stood and, indicating that its reconsideration by the International Law Commission was both premature and unpromising, proposed, instead, that the draft and comments be made available to governments for adaptation and use in future treaties and agreements and suggested an international conference under United Nations auspices if a sufficent number of States evidenced interest. U.S. participation in the U.N., report by the President to Congress for the year 1955, pp. 208–209. At its ninth session, in its report (A/3623), the International Law Commission considered the ultimate object to be attained in reviewing the draft and concluded that it should be simply to formulate a set of rules to guide States in the drawing up of provisions for·inclusion in international treaties and special arbitral agreements, and that upon completion of its final report the question would be resubmitted to the General Assembly in 1958. U.S. participation in the U.N., report by the President to Congress for the year 1957, p. 230; II *Yearbook of the International Law Commission 1957*, pp. 143–144. The Commission adopted a final text on Arbitral Procedure in the form of a model draft annexed at its tenth session (A/3859). II *Yearbook of the International Law Commission 1958*, pp. 83–86.

For U.N. and ILC documentation with respect to "Arbitral Procedure", see generally:

Report on Arbitration Procedure, Mar. 21, 1950, by Scelle, Special Rapporteur, A/CN.4/18, II Yearbook of I.L.C. 1950, pp. 114–151; Replies from Governments, Mar. 23, 1950, A/CN.4/19, II Yearbook of I.L.C. 1950, pp. 151–156; Bibliography on Arbitral Procedure, June 20, 1950, A/CN.4/29; Memorandum by the Secretariat, Nov. 21, 1950, A/CN.4/35, II Yearbook of I.L.C. 1950, pp. 157–180; Report of I.L.C. Covering Work of Second Session, A/1316, II Yearbook of I.L.C. 1950, pp. 364, 381–383; Memorandum on the Soviet Practice and Doctrine With Respect to Arbitral Procedure, by the Secretariat, Nov. 21, 1950, A/CN.4/36; Second report on Arbitration Procedure, Special Rapporteur, May 28, 1951, A/CN.4/46, II Yearbook of I.L.C. 1951, pp. 110–120; Supplementary note to second report on Arbitral Procedure, June 6, 1952, A/CN.4/57; Articles on Arbitral Procedure, decision of the Commission on July 3, 1952, July 4, 1952, A/CN.4/L.34; Draft on Arbitral Procedure, A/CN.4/L.35–36 and Corr. 1, July 25, Aug. 4, 1952, respectively; Arbitral Procedure: Comments by Governments on draft of Arbitral Procedure, May 1, 1953, A/CN.4/68; Arbitral Procedure: Commentary on draft of Arbitral Procedure, May 5, 1953, A/CN.4/L.40; Arbitral Procedure: Undertaking to arbitrate, constitution of tribunal, the *compromis*, powers of tribunal, award, revision, annulment of award, May 8, 1953, A/2163, A/CN.4/68/Add. 1; *ibid.*/Add. 2, Aug. 6, 1953; Consideration of the Chapter on Arbitral Procedure and text of draft convention on Arbitral Procedure in Report of the Commission Covering Work of Fifth Session, II Yearbook of I.L.C. 1953, pp. 201–212; Arbitral Procedure: Draft resolution adopted by Sixth Committee at its 388th meeting on Nov. 17, 1953, Nov. 18, 1953, A/C.6/L.321; Comments by Governments on draft of Arbitral Procedure prepared by I.L.C. at Fourth Session 1952 (A/2163, p. 2), A/2456, Annex 1, pp. 32–41; Supplementary Note by Scelle, Special Rapporteur, June 6, 1952, A/CN.4/57, II Yearbook of I.L.C. 1952, pp. 1–2; Draft on Arbitral Procedure, prepared by I.L.C. at Fourth Session, 1952, Sept. 16, 1952, A/CN.4/59; Commentary on the draft convention on Arbitral Procedure, adopted by I.L.C. at its Fifth Session, prepared by the Secretariat, Apr. 1955, A/CN.4/92, 1955.V.1; Arbitral Procedure, note by the Secretariat, Mar. 30, 1956, A/CN.4/L.64, II Yearbook of I.L.C. 1956, p. 232; Draft convention on Arbitral Procedure adopted by the Commission at its Fifth Session, report by Scelle, Special Rapporteur, with a model draft on Arbitral Procedure annexed, Apr. 24, 1957, A/CN.4/109, II Yearbook of I.L.C. 1957, pp. 1–15; Model draft on Arbitral Procedure by Scelle, Special Rapporteur, Mar. 6, 1958, A/CN.4/113, II Yearbook of I.L.C. 1958, pp. 1–15; Survey of views expressed in the Sixth Committee of the General Assembly and in written comments of Governments on the

draft Convention on Arbitral Procedure adopted by the I.L.C. at its Fifth
Session, A/2456; Working document prepared by Secretariat, Dec. 23, 1957,
A/CN.4/L.71; Model draft, I.L.C. Report (A/3859), II Yearbook of I.L.C.
1958, pp. 83–86.

Subsequent to the inclusion of the related topics, Régime of the
High Seas and the Régime of Territorial Waters, in its list of topics
provisionally selected for codification, the International Law Commission, during its second session, 1950, when it reviewed the first
report on the High Seas (A/CN.4/17) together with replies from
governments (A/CN.4/19, pt. 1, C), narrowed this first field of study   Law of the
to the following subjects: nationality of ships, collision, safety of   Sea
life at sea, the right of approach, slave trade, submarine telegraph
cables, resources of the sea, right of pursuit, contiguous zones, sedentary fisheries, and the continental shelf. *Yearbook of the United
Nations 1950*, p. 863. During its third session, 1951, the Commission
prepared draft articles on four of these eleven items, the provisions of which were related to jurisdiction over the seabed and subsoil of the continental shelf; resources of the sea (conservation of
marine life); sedentary fisheries; and contiguous zones for purposes of customs, fiscal, or sanitary regulations. Among other
items that the Commission adjudged insufficiently advanced to
warrant governmental comment at that time were: the question of
the nationality of ships, penal jurisdiction in matters of collision
on the high seas, rules relating to the safety of life at sea, and
submarine telegraph cables. U.S. participation in the U.N., report
by the President to Congress for the year 1951, pp. 254–255; *Yearbook of the United Nations 1951*, p. 845. The General Assembly,
in adopting the Sixth Committee's draft resolution (A/1196), in Resolution 374(IV) at its 270th plenary session, December 6, 1949, recommended that the ILC include the topic of the Régime of Territorial
Waters in its list of priorities because of its relationship with the topic
of Régime of High Seas. *Yearbook of the United Nations 1948–1949*,
p. 952. During this third session, the Commission initiated its study
of the topic Régime of Territorial Waters. On the basis of the Sixth
Committee's report after considering this dual subject at its 296th and
297th meetings on January 23–24, 1951, the General Assembly in Resolution 601(VI) merely noted the progress of the Commission on this
project. *Yearbook of the United Nations 1951*, pp. 845–846. The first
report (A/CN.4/53) containing a draft regulation on the Régime of
Territorial Sea, consisting of 23 articles together with comments, was
submitted at the fourth session of the ILC, 1952. The Commission,
in receipt of a third report (A/CN.4/51) on the Régime of the High
Seas, as well as comments from governments (A/CN.4/55 and Add. 1–

4) on its Draft Articles on the Continental Shelf and Related Subjects, deferred consideration on the report to its fifth session. *Yearbook of the United Nations 1952*, p. 796. The Commission at its fourth session decided to use the term "territorial sea" in lieu of "territorial waters" as the latter expression had sometimes been taken to include also inland waters. Report of I.L.C. to the General Assembly on Work of Fourth Session (A/2163), II *Yearbook of the International Law Commission 1952*, p. 68. On the basis of further reports by the rapporteur (A/CN.4/60 and A/CN.4/69), the Commission adopted draft articles at its fifth session on the following subjects: the Continental Shelf, Fisheries, and the Contiguous Zone. The Sixth Committee considered chapter III of the Commission's report (A/2456) containing these drafts at its 389th, 392d, and 393d meetings on November 18, 25, 1953. The General Assembly adopted the Sixth Committee's draft resolution contained in its report (A/2589) at its 468th plenary meeting on December 7, 1953, as Resolution 798(VIII) wherein it decided not to deal with any aspect of the Régime of the High Seas or of the Régime of Territorial Waters until all the problems involved had been studied by the International Law Commission and reported upon by it to the General Assembly. *Yearbook of the United Nations 1953*, pp. 676–679. The United States, opposing this decision as making possible the indefinite postponement of Assembly consideration of any of the important subjects relating to the Régime of the High Seas, favored instead early consideration of the draft articles on the Continental Shelf. U.S. participation in the U.N., report by the President to Congress for the year 1953, p. 195. The Commission, during its sixth session, 1954, considered the third report (A/CN.4/77) on the Régime of the Territorial Sea, together with a draft of certain articles which had been revised in the light of comments made by a Committee of Experts, meeting at The Hague from April 14–16, 1953 (A/CN.4/61, Add. 1, and Annex), and observations received from governments concerning the delimitation of the territorial sea between adjacent States (A/CN.4/71 and Add. 1, 2). The Commission adopted 27 provisional articles on the Territorial Sea with comments which were submitted to governments (A/2693). U.S. participation in the U.N., report by the President to Congress for the year 1954, p. 193; *Yearbook of the United Nations 1954*, p. 412. Since in the United States view these problems required early consideration in an international forum where the possibilities of arriving at some agreed solutions could be explored, the United States took the initiative, along with other interested governments, in proposing for the agenda of the ninth session of the General Assembly, 1954, two separate items: "Draft Articles on the Conti-

nental Shelf", and "Economic Development of Fisheries and Question of Fishery Conservation and Regulation". The United States, during the Sixth Committee's debates in 1954, urged the Assembly to begin at the tenth session its study of the problem of the high seas. Strong opposition in the Committee to the separate consideration of the Continental Shelf problem before the Assembly could review recommendations on all problems relating to the high seas and territorial sea was based on fear that any decision regarding the Continental Shelf might prejudice subsequent consideration of related problems. Following exhaustive debate by the Sixth Committee at its 430th to 435th meetings, from November 29 to December 3, the General Assembly at its 512th plenary meeting December 14, 1954, adopted the Sixth Committee's report (A/2849) as Resolution 899 (IX) in which it requested the Commission to devote the necessary time to the study of the Régimes of the High Seas and Territorial Waters and their related problems, in order to complete work on these topics and submit a final report at the eleventh session of the General Assembly. The Assembly thereby included the final report of the Commission in the provisional agenda for the eleventh session. U.S. participation in the U.N., report by the President to Congress for the year 1954, pp. 194, 195; *Yearbook of the United Nations 1954*, pp. 412–414. The United States proposal of the fisheries item was predicated upon the view that progress in solving fishery questions would facilitate progress in solving some of the other related problems, and that an understanding of technical and administrative aspects of international conservation and regulation of fisheries was essential to satisfactory solution of the fishery issues. The United States, therefore, joined in cosponsoring a resolution providing for the convening of a conference which, as amended, was adopted by the General Assembly at its 512th plenary meeting December 14, 1954, after discussion by its Sixth Committee at its 435th to 438th meetings, December 3–7, 1954 (A/2854) as Resolution 900(IX), wherein the Secretary-General was requested to convene an international technical conference at the headquarters (Rome) of the Food and Agriculture Organization April 18, 1955, to study and make technical recommendations. The General Assembly by this resolution on the problem of international conservation of living resources of the sea also decided to refer the report of this conference to the International Law Commission. U.S. participation in the U.N., report by the President to Congress for the year 1954, pp. 194–196; *Yearbook of the United Nations 1954*, pp. 423–426. At its seventh session, the Commission prepared two drafts (A/2934) regarding the international law of the sea. One contained provisional articles concerning the Régime of

the High Seas dealing with questions relating to the high seas other
than the continental shelf and contiguous zone, covering such topics
as navigation, fishing, submarine cables and pipe lines. In its discussion of fishing, the Commission considered the Report of the International Technical Conference on the Conservation of Living Resources of the Sea, held April 18 to May 10, 1955, in Rome (A/CONF.
10/6). The second included a new and more comprehensive draft
concerning the Régime of the Territorial Sea prepared in the light
of observations made by governments on the Commission's work during its sixth session, 1954. The Commission also decided upon additional articles not listed in the 1954 draft, including the breadth of
the territorial sea, bays, groups of islands, and the delimitation of
the territorial sea at the mouths of rivers. Report of I.L.C. to the
General Assembly on Work of Seventh Session, U.N. Gen. Ass. Off.
Rec. 10th Sess., Supp. No. 9, A/2934, p. 15. Amended drafts on the
régime of the territorial sea having been submitted to governments
for their comments, the Commission at its eighth session (1956) acted
upon and collected in a single and final report all the rules adopted
by it in respect of the high seas, the territorial sea, the continental
shelf, contiguous zone, fisheries, and the protection of the living
resources of the sea, for submission to the Assembly's eleventh session.
Report of I.L.C. to the General Assembly on Work of Eighth Session,
U.N. Gen. Ass. Off. Rec. 11th Sess., Supp. No. 9, A/3159, p. 3.

This report (A/3159) on the Law of the Sea consisted of 73 draft
articles, which set of articles was divided into two parts, the first
dealing with the Territorial Sea and the second with the High Seas.
The section on the Territorial Sea dealt with the juridical status of
the territorial sea; of the airspace over the territorial sea and of its bed
and subsoil; the limits of the territorial sea; and the right of innocent
passage. The section on the High Seas covered the general régime of
the high seas, including the subjects of navigation; fishing; submarine cables and pipe lines; contiguous zone; and the continental
shelf. The Commission recommended that the General Assembly
should summon an international conference to examine the law of the
sea, taking account not only of the legal but also of the technical,
biological, economic, and political aspects of the problem with a view
to concluding one or more international conventions or such other
appropriate instruments. *Yearbook of the United Nations 1956*, pp.
381–383. The United States, in cosponsoring a draft resolution to
convene an international conference, affirmed its adherence to the
3-mile limit, stating the view that international law does not require
States to recognize more than 3 miles as the outer limit of territorial
jurisdiction. The United States further contended that the prob-

lems that concerned coastal States, particularly those relating to fish stocks off their coasts, could be met by means other than through extensions of the territorial sea and announced its support of the Commission's proposals regarding conservation of the living resources of the high seas which accounts for the special interests of the coastal States. U.S. participation in the U.N., report by the President to Congress for the year 1956, p. 259. The draft as amended was approved by the Sixth Committee at its 485th–505th meetings on November 28 to December 20, 1956, and subsequently adopted by the General Assembly as Resolution 1105(XI) at its 658th plenary meeting, February 21, 1957, which called for the convocation of the international conference in early March 1958. U.S. participation in the U.N., report by the President to Congress for the year 1956, pp. 258–260; *Yearbook of the United Nations 1956*, pp. 382, 383. The U.N. Conference on the Law of the Sea concluded at Geneva in April 1958 a 9 weeks' session during which it adopted four international conventions: Territorial Sea and the Contiguous Zone, High Seas, Fishing and Conservation of the Living Resources of the High Seas, Continental Shelf; an Optional Protocol of Signature Concerning the Compulsory Settlement of Disputes; and nine resolutions.

The General Assembly at its thirteenth session, on December 10, 1958, adopted a resolution calling for a second international conference on the Law of the Sea for the purpose of considering further the questions of the breadth of the territorial sea and fishery limits, the conference to be convoked in March or April 1960 at Geneva. Res. 1307 (XIII). For results of Second U.N. Conference on the Law of the Sea, see *Summary Records of Plenary Meetings and of Meetings of the Committee of the Whole (Annexes and Final Act)*, Doc. A/CONF.19/8, and *post*, this work.

For U.N. and ILC documentation concerning the "Law of the Sea", see generally:

Report on the Law of the Sea by François, Special Rapporteur, Mar. 17, 1950, A/CN.4/17, II Yearbook of I.L.C. 1950, pp. 36–52; Replies from Governments concerning Régime of the High Seas, Mar. 23, 1950, A/CN.4/19, II Yearbook of I.L.C. 1950, pp. 52–65; Bibliography on the Régime of the High Seas, Apr. 25, 1950, prepared by the Secretariat, A/CN.4/26; Régime of High Seas (Memorandum presented by the Secretariat on questions under study by other organs of the United Nations or by Specialized Agencies— Safety of Life at Sea, Fisheries, Whaling, Pollution), June 23, 1950, A/CN.4/30, II Yearbook of I.L.C. 1950, pp. 65–66; Memorandum on the Régime of the High Seas (Presented by the Secretariat), July 14, 1950, A/CN.4/32, II Yearbook of I.L.C. 1950, pp. 67–113; Report of I.L.C. Covering Work of Second Session, A/1316, II Yearbook of I.L.C. 1950, pp. 364, 383–385; Memorandum on Soviet doctrine and practice with respect to the Régime of the High Seas, prepared by the Secretariat, Nov. 21, 1950, A/CN.4/38; Régime of the High Seas, Principles submitted as a basis of discussion by Yepes, July

11, 1950, A/CN.4/R.5, incorporated in A/CN.4/SR.64, footnote 4a, July 10, 1950; Régime of the High Seas, Principles proposed by Amado, A/CN.4/R.4, incorporated in A/CN.4/SR.64, footnote 1, July 10, 1950; Second report on Régime of the High Seas, by François, Apr. 10, 1951, A/CN.4/42, II Yearbook of I.L.C. 1951, pp. 75–103; Report of I.L.C. Covering Work of Third Session, U.N. Gen. Ass. Off. Rec. 6th Sess., Supp. No. 9, A/1858, II Yearbook of I.L.C. 1951, pp. 139–140; Draft Articles on Continental Shelf and Related Subjects Prepared by International Law Commission, July 30, 1951, A/CN.4/49, A/1858 and Annex, II Yearbook of I.L.C. 1951, pp. 141–144; Laws and Regulations on the Régime of the High Seas, Jan. 1951, vol. I, ST/LEG/SER.B/1 and Add. 1; Third Report by François, Special Rapporteur, on Régime of the High Seas, Feb. 28, 1952, A/CN.4/51; Report on the Territorial Sea by François, Special Rapporteur, Apr. 4, 1952, A/CN.4/53, II Yearbook of I.L.C. 1952, pp. 25–49; Report of I.L.C. Covering Work of Fourth Session, U.N. Gen. Ass. Off. Rec. 7th Sess., Supp. No. 9, A/2163, II Yearbook of I.L.C. 1952, pp. 57, 68–69; A/CN.4/L.45, July 30, 1953, ibid./Add. 1; Report of I.L.C. Covering Work of Fifth Session, U.N. Gen. Ass. Off. Rec. 8th Sess., Supp. No. 9, A/2456; Comments by Governments on Draft Articles on the Continental Shelf and Related Subjects prepared by the I.L.C. at its Third Session, 1951, printed in Summary Records and Reports of I.L.C. Covering Work of its Fifth Session, ibid., Annex II, pp. 42–72; Régime of the High Seas, Comments by Governments on Draft Articles on the Continental Shelf and Related Subjects, May 16, 1952, A/CN.4/55; ibid./Add. 1, June 18, 1952; ibid./Add.2, June 21, 1952; ibid./Add.3, July 8, 1952; ibid./Add.4, Aug. 4, 1952; ibid./Add.5, Sept. 5, 1952; ibid./Add.6, Oct. 23, 1952; Laws and Regulations on the Régime of the High Seas, Dec. 1951, vol. II, ST/LEG/SER.B/2; Fourth Report on the Régime of the High Seas, the Continental Shelf, and Related Subjects, by François, Special Rapporteur, Feb. 19, 1953, A/CN.4/60; Second Report on the Régime of the Territorial Sea, by François, Special Rapporteur, Feb. 19, 1953, A/CN.4/61, ibid./Add. 1, May 18, 1953; Fifth Report on the Régime of the High Seas, Penal jurisdiction in matters of collision, by François, Special Rapporteur, May 5, 1953, A/CN.4/69; Régime of the High Seas, Further Comments by Governments on Draft Articles on Continental Shelf and Related Subjects, May 7, 1953, A/CN.4/70; Régime of the Territorial Sea. Information and Observations Submitted by Governments Regarding the Question of Delimitation of Territorial Sea of Two Adjacent States, May 12, 1953, A/CN.4/71, ibid./Add. 1, May 13, 1953, ibid./Add. 2, Sept. 2, 1953; Régime of the High Seas, Draft resolution adopted by the Sixth Committee at its 393d meeting, Nov. 25, 1953, Nov. 27, 1953, A/C.6/L.326; Third Report on the Régime of the Territorial Sea, by François, Special Rapporteur, Feb. 4, 1954, A/CN.4/77; Sixth Report on Régime of the High Seas by François, Special Rapporteur, Mar. 22, 1954, A/CN.4/79; Régime of the High Seas, Draft Articles on the Continental Shelf, Fisheries, and the Contiguous Zone Adopted by the I.L.C. at its Fifth Session, Comments transmitted by the Government of Denmark, May 13, 1954, A/CN.4/86; Régime of the Territorial Sea, Comments by Governments on the Provisional Articles Concerning the Régime of the Territorial Sea adopted by I.L.C. at Sixth Session, Mar. 29, 1955, A/CN.4/90; ibid./Add.1, Apr. 19, 1955; ibid./Add.2, Apr. 22, 1955; ibid./Add.3, May 5, 1955; ibid./Add.4, May 17, 1955; ibid./Add.5, June 7, 1955; ibid./Add.6, Aug. 11, 1955; Régime of the Territorial Sea, Amendments Proposed by the Special Rapporteur, in the Light of the Comments by Governments, to the

Provisional Articles Adopted by the Commission at its Sixth Session, May 16, 1955, A/CN.4/93; Régime of the High Seas, proposal by Scelle, May 3, 1955, A/CN.4/L.51; Régime of the Territorial Sea, working paper prepared by the Secretariat, May 13, 1955, A/CN.4/L.54; Régime of the High Seas, proposal by Zourek, May 3, 1955, A/CN.4/L.52; Régime of the High Seas, Observations of the Government of Polish People's Republic, concerning freedom of navigation on the high seas, May 6, 1955, A/CN.4/L.53; Régime of High Seas, nationality of ships, proposal by Zourek, May 10, 1955, A/CN.4/L.56; Régime of the High Seas, Art. 21, proposal by Edmonds, May 11, 1955, A/CN.4/L.57; Régime of the High Seas, Observation of the Government of the Union of South Africa, concerning freedom of navigation on the High Seas, May 17, 1955, A/CN.4/L.58; Régime of the High Seas, Memorandum from the Legation of Ecuador to the I.L.C., July 6, 1955, A/CN.4/L.63; Régime of the High Seas and Régime of the Territorial Sea, Report by François, Special Rapporteur, Jan. 27, 1956, A/CN.4/97; *ibid.*/Add.1, May 1, 1956.; *ibid.*/Add.2, May 4, 1956; *ibid.*/Add.3, May 9, 1956, II Yearbook of I.L.C. 1956, pp. 1–37; Régime of the High Seas, Comments by Governments on the Provisional Articles Concerning the Régime of the High Seas and the Draft Articles on the Territorial Sea adopted by the I.L.C. at its Seventh Session, Mar. 12, 1956, A/CN.4/99; *ibid.*/Add.1, Apr. 5, 1956; *ibid.*/Add.2, Apr. 17, 1956; *ibid.*/Add.3, Apr. 24, 1956; *ibid.*/Add.4, Apr. 25, 1956; *ibid.*/Add.5, Apr. 30, 1956; *ibid.*/Add.6, May 7, 1956; *ibid.*/Add.7, May 22, 1956; *ibid.*/Add.8, June 25, 1956; *ibid.*/Add.9, July 3, 1956, II Yearbook of I.L.C. 1956, pp. 37–101; Régime of the High Seas, Comments by Inter-governmental Organizations on Articles Regarding Fishing Embodied in the Provisional Articles Concerning the Régime of the High Seas Adopted by the I.L.C. at its Seventh Session, Mar. 13, 1956, A/CN.4/100, II Yearbook of I.L.C. 1956, p. 102; Régime of the High Seas, The Rights of International Organizations to Sail Vessels Under Their Flags, Supplementary Report by François, Special Rapporteur, May 8, 1956, A/CN.4/103, II Yearbook of I.L.C. 1956, pp. 102–103; Laws Concerning the Nationality of Ships, ST/LEG/SER.B/5, Nov. 1955, 1956.V.I.; Laws and Regulations on the Régime of the Territorial Sea, ST/LEG/SER.B/6, Dec. 1956, 1957.V.2.

For preparatory documents for the 1958 United Nations Conference on the Law of the Sea, see: I *U.N. Conference on the Law of the Sea, Preparatory Documents*, pages v–vii of which contain a list of Docs. A/CONF.13/1 to 36.

For documents of the First Committee (Territorial Sea and Contiguous Zone), see: A/CONF.13/C.1/L.1–168/Add. 1; III *U.N. Conference on the Law of the Sea, First Committee (Territorial Sea and Contiguous Zone)*, pp. 212 ff. For documents of the Second Committee (High Seas: General Régime), see: A/CONF.13/C.2/L.1–153/Corr. 1; IV *U.N. Conference on the Law of the Sea, Second Committee (High Seas: General Régime)*, pp. 115 ff. For documents of the Third Committee (High Seas: Fishing: Conservation of Living Resources), see: A/CONF.13/C.3/L.1–93; V *U.N. Conference on the Law of the Sea, Third Committee (High Seas: Fishing: Conservation of Living Resources)*, pp. 134 ff. For documents of the Fourth Committee (Continental Shelf), see: A/CONF.13/C.4/L.1–67; VI *U.N. Conference on the Law of the Sea, Fourth Committee (Continental Shelf)*, pp. 125 ff. For documents of the Fifth Committee (Free Access to the Sea of Land-locked Countries), see: A/CONF.13/C.5/L.1–27; VII *U.N. Con-*

ference on the Law of the Sea, Fifth Committee (Question of Free Access to the Sea of Land-locked Countries), pp. 67 ff.

For Summary Records of the respective Committees and of the Plenary Sessions of the 1958 Conference, see: III *U.N. Conference on the Law of the Sea, First Committee (Territorial Sea and Contiguous Zone); IV U.N. Conference on the Law of the Sea, Second Committee (High Seas: General Régime); V U.N. Conference on the Law of the Sea, Third Committee (High Seas: Fishing: Conservation of Living Resources); VI U.N. Conference on the Law of the Sea, Fourth Committee (Continental Shelf); VII U.N. Conference on the Law of the Sea, Fifth Committee (Question of Free Access to the Sea of Land-locked Countries); and II U.N. Conference on the Law of the Sea, Plenary Meetings*.

For the Final Act of the 1958 Conference, see: A/CONF.13/L.58; II *U.N. Conference on the Law of the Sea, Plenary Meetings*, p. 146.

The Conventions, Resolutions, and Optional Protocol of Signature adopted by the 1958 Conference are printed in: II *U.N. Conference on the Law of the Sea, Plenary Meetings*, pp. 132 ff.; S. Exs. J. to N, Inclusive, 86th Cong., 1st sess., pp. 14 ff.; XXXVIII *Bulletin*, Department of State, No. 992, June 30, 1958, pp. 1111 ff. They include: (1) Convention on the Territorial Sea and the Contiguous Zone, A/CONF.13/L.52, Apr. 28, 1958; *ibid.*/Corr.1 and 2, June 11, 1958; (2) Convention on the High Seas, A/CONF.13/L.53 and Corr. 1, Apr. 29, 1958; *ibid.*/Corr.1, Apr. 30, 1958; *ibid.*/Corr.2, June 11, 1958; (3) Convention on Fishing and Conservation of the Living Resources of the High Seas, A/CONF.13/L.54, Apr. 28, 1958; (4) Convention on the Continental Shelf, A/CONF.13/L.55, Apr. 28, 1958; *ibid.*/Add.1, Apr. 29, 1958; Optional Protocol of Signature Concerning the Compulsory Settlement of Disputes, A/CONF.13/L.57, Apr. 30, 1958. The following resolutions were adopted by the Conference (A/CONF.13/L.56): Nuclear Tests on the High Seas, Apr. 27, 1958; Pollution of the High Seas by Radioactive Materials, Apr. 27, 1958; International Fishery Conservation Conventions, Apr. 25, 1958; Co-Operation in Conservation Measures, Apr. 25, 1958; Humane Killing of Marine Life, Apr. 25, 1958; Special Situations Relating to Coastal Fisheries, Apr. 26, 1958; Régime of Historic Waters, Apr. 27, 1958; Convening of a Second U.N. Conference on the Law of the Sea, Apr. 27, 1958; Tribute to the I.L.C., Apr. 27, 1958.

Nationality
Including
Statelessness

The study of "Nationality Including Statelessness" was initiated by the International Law Commission in 1951 at its third session, having been initially included as one of the 14 topics provisionally selected for codification. The development of the study of this broad topic eventually subsumed individual studies of such subjects as Status of Stateless Persons, the Problem of Statelessness, Nationality of Married Women, Elimination of Future Statelessness, and Reduction of Future Statelessness. Manley Hudson, as special rapporteur, submitted to the Commission's fourth session (1952) documents on The Problem of Statelessness (A/CN.4/56), Nationality of Married Women (E/CN.6/126 and E/CN.6/126/Rev.1 (E/CN.6/129/Rev. 1)), and A Study of Statelessness (E/1112 and Add.1), along with his own report (A/CN.4/50) which surveyed the subject of nationality in general. He included two working papers, the first of which was a draft of a convention on Nationality of Married Persons following closely the terms proposed by the Commission on the Status of Women and approved by the Economic and Social Council. The Commission decided that the question of nationality of married women could only be considered as an integral part of the whole subject of nationality including statelessness. The second working paper dealt with statelessness. The Commission directed that draft conventions on the Elimination of Statelessness and on the Reduction of Future Statelessness be prepared for its next session and elected Roberto Córdova to succeed Mr. Hudson as special rapporteur. *Yearbook of the United Nations 1952*, p. 795. His first report (A/CN.4/64) containing articles accompanied by detailed comment for two draft conventions—the Elimination of Future Statelessness and Reduction of Future Statelessness—was presented in 1953 to the Commission's fifth session, where also available for review were Mr. Hudson's report on Nationality Including Statelessness (A/CN.4/50), and a memorandum on national legislation concerning grounds for deprivation of nationality (A/CN.4/66) and the Secretary-General's reports on A Study of Statelessness (E/1112 and Add.1) and The Problem of Statelessness (A/CN.4/56 and Add.1). The Commission decided to invite governments to submit their comments on the two draft conventions provisionally adopted by it. U.S. participation in the U.N., report by the President to Congress for the year 1953, p. 194; *Yearbook of the United Nations 1953*, p. 680. During 1954 the question of statelessness was considered by the Economic and Social Council, a Conference of Plenipotentiaries called by the Council, the General Assembly, and the International Law Commission which, in the light of comments received on future statelessness, approved the texts of two draft conventions. The Commission, continuing its study of present statelessness, adopted a set of articles as suggestions that might be taken into account by governments when attempting a solution of the problem. A/2693; U.S. participation in the U.N., report by the President to Congress for the year 1954, p. 193; *Yearbook of the United Nations 1954*, p. 417. At its seventeenth session, 1954, the Economic and Social Council had before it a draft Protocol on The Status of Stateless Persons (A/CONF.2/1, p. 28) and a memorandum (E/2533) by the Secretary-General on action previously taken by the International Law Commission. The protocol was originally attached to the Convention on Refugees. The Convention alone was adopted at a Geneva Conference of Plenipotentiaries in July 1951 and came into force April 22, 1954.

The draft protocol and the problem of statelessness were discussed by the Council's Social Committee at three meetings on April 21–22,

1954, in pursuance of General Assembly Resolution 629 (VII), November 6, 1952. This Committee on April 26, 1954, adopted a resolution stating that the causes of statelessness were often different from those which justified recognition of the status of refugees, endorsed the principles underlying the work of the International Law Commission and requested it to continue to work for effective international instruments for the reduction and elimination of statelessness. This report (E/2580) was adopted by the Economic and Social Council at its 784th plenary meeting on April 26, 1954, as Resolution 526 A and B (XVII). *Yearbook of the United Nations 1954*, pp. 415–416. In accordance with this resolution, the conference, called by the Economic and Social Council, held September 13–23, 1954, approved a Convention Relating to the Status of Stateless Persons (E/CONF.17/5). After discussion of its report by the Sixth Committee at its 397th to 402d meetings, from October 4–13, 1954, the General Assembly at its 504th plenary meeting, December 4, 1954, adopted the report (A/2807) as Resolution 896 (IX) by which it gave approval to the convening of an international conference to conclude a convention on the reduction or elimination of future statelessness as soon as at least 20 States communicated to the Secretary-General their willingness to cooperate in such a conference. It requested the Secretary-General to communicate, together with the resolution, the revised draft conventions prepared by the International Law Commission (A/2693) to Member States and to each non-Member State which was or thereafter became a party to one or more of the specialized agencies of the United Nations or to the Statute of the International Court of Justice and invited governments of States to give early consideration to the merits of a multilateral convention on the elimination or reduction of future statelessness. *Yearbook of the United Nations 1954*, pp. 415–423. The General Assembly merely noted the Secretary-General's report to its eleventh session in 1956, that the required number of 20 States had not yet expressed a desire to take part in the conference. U.S. participation in the U.N., report by the President to Congress for the year 1956, p. 260.

For U.N. and ILC documentation concerning "Nationality Including Statelessness", see generally:

Letter from the Secretary-General to Chairman of I.L.C., on Nationality of Married Women, July 18, 1950, A/CN.4/33, II Yearbook of I.L.C. 1950, p. 363; Elimination of Statelessness, Note by Secretariat, May 31, 1951, A/CN.4/47; Report on Nationality, Including Statelessness, by Hudson, Special Rapporteur, Feb. 21, 1952, A/CN.4/50, II Yearbook of I.L.C. 1952, pp. 3–24; Report of I.L.C. Covering Work of Fourth Session, U.N. Gen. Ass. Off. Rec. 7th Sess., Supp. No. 9, A/2163, II Yearbook of I.L.C. 1952, pp. 57, 67–

68; The Problem of Statelessness, Consolidated Report by Secretary-General, May 26, 1952, E/2230 and Add.1, A/CN.4/56 and Add.1; Report on Elimination or Reduction of Statelessness by Córdova, Mar. 30, 1953, A/CN.4/64; Consideration of Chapter on Nationality, Including Statelessness in the Draft Report of the Commission Covering Work of Fifth Session, Aug. 8, 1953, A/CN.4/L.45/Add.2; Extracts from *The International Experiment of Upper Silesia* (1942) by Georges Kaeckenbeeck, prepared by Ivan S. Kerno, Expert of the I.L.C., Apr. 6, 1953, A/CN.4/65; National Legislation Concerning Grounds for Deprivation of Nationality, Memorandum prepared by Kerno, Apr. 6, 1953, A/CN.4/66; Analysis of Changes in Nationality Legislation of States since 1930 (keyed to Hague Convention on certain questions relating to conflict of nationality laws and Hague Protocol relating to a certain case of statelessness), Memorandum prepared by Kerno, Apr. 6, 1953, A/CN.4/67; Nationality Including Statelessness—Second Report on the Elimination or Reduction of Statelessness by Córdova, Special Rapporteur, Aug. 8, 1953, A/CN.4/75; Third Report on the Elimination or Reduction of Statelessness, by Córdova, Special Rapporteur, (including annexes), Mar. 11, 1954, A/CN.4/81; Comments by Governments on the Draft Convention on the Elimination of Future Statelessness and on the Draft Convention on the Reduction of Future Statelessness, Mar. 29, 1954, A/CN.4/82; *ibid.*/Add.1, Apr. 14, 1954; *ibid.*/Add.2, May 5, 1954; *ibid.*/Add.3, May 12, 1954; *ibid.*/Add.4, June 4, 1954; *ibid.*/Add.5, June 14, 1954; *ibid.*/Add.6, June 22, 1954; *ibid.*/Add.7, July 13, 1954; *ibid.*/Add.8, July 13, 1954; Report on Multiple Nationality, by Córdova, Special Rapporteur, Apr. 22, 1954, A/CN.4/83; Nationality Including Statelessness—Survey of the Problem of Multiple Nationality, prepared by the Secretariat, May 14, 1954, A/CN.4/84; Laws Concerning Nationality, U.N. Legislative Series, ST/LEG/SER.B/4, July 1954; *ibid.* Supp., ST/LEG/SER.B/9 (1959).

The Secretary-General's report to the General Assembly on October 24, 1946, proposing that the principles of the Nürnberg trials be made a permanent part of the body of international law, was followed by a United States proposal of a resolution that the General Assembly reaffirm the principles of international law recognized by the Nürnberg Charter and judgment and direct the Assembly Committee on the Codification of International Law to treat as a matter of primary importance the formulation of the principles of the Charter and judgment in the context of a general codification of offences against the peace and security of mankind or in an international criminal code. As adopted by the General Assembly at its first session, December 11, 1946, Resolution 95(I), in addition to affirming the principles of international law recognized by the Charter of the Nürnberg Tribunal and the judgment, directed the Committee to treat as a matter of primary importance plans for the formulation of these principles, in the context of a general codification of offences against the peace and security of mankind, or of an international criminal code. *Yearbook of the United Nations 1946–1947*, pp. 254–255; The U.S. and the U.N., report by the President to Congress for the year

Nürnberg Principles

1946, p. 20. This Committee's recommendation (A/332) was approved with modifications by the Sixth Committee. The latter Committee's report (A/505) proposing that the International Law Commission "formulate the principles of international law recognized in the Charter of the Nürnberg Tribunal and in the judgment of the Tribunal" and "prepare a draft code of offences against the peace and security of mankind, indicating clearly the place to be accorded" to these principles, was subsequently adopted by the General Assembly at its 123d plenary session, November 21, 1947, in Resolution 177(II). *Yearbook of the United Nations 1947–1948*, pp. 214–215; The U.S. and the U.N., report by the President to Congress for the year 1947, p. 79. The International Law Commission submitted the requested formulation of Nürnberg principles (A/1316) to the General Assembly following its second session in 1950. After the Sixth Committee's debates, during its 231st–239th meetings from November 2–14, 1950, the General Assembly at its 320th plenary meeting, December 12, 1950, neither approved nor disapproved the formulation as submitted, but requested (by Resolution 488(V)) the Commission to take account in its final work on the draft code of the observations of delegations at that session and the further observations which the General Assembly invited governments of Member States to furnish. *Yearbook of the United Nations 1950*, pp. 852–857; U.S. participation in the U.N., report by the President to Congress for the year 1950, p. 248. In preparing a draft Code of Offences Against the Peace and

**Draft Code
of Offences**

Security of Mankind, the Commission decided that a questionnaire be circulated to governments inquiring what offences, apart from those defined in the Charter and judgment of the Nürnberg Tribunal, should, in their view, be comprehended in the draft code. After considering at the second session the rapporteur's report (A/CN.4/25), and replies of governments to its questionnaire (A/CN.4/19, part II, A/CN.4/19/Add. 1 and 2), a drafting subcommittee, composed of Mr. Alfaro, Mr. Hudson, and Mr. Spiropoulos, prepared a provisional draft of a code (A/CN.4/R.6) which was referred by the Commission to the special rapporteur, Mr. Spiropoulos, with the request to continue work on the subject and to submit a further report to the Commission at its third session. *Yearbook of the United Nations 1950*, pp. 857, 861–862. The Commission at its third session considered a second report (A/CN.4/44) prepared by Mr. Spiropoulos. The report contained a revised draft code and a digest of the observations on the Commission's formulation of the Nürnberg principles made by delegations at the Assembly's fifth session. After considering observations from governments (A/CN.4/45 and Corr. 1 and Add. 1 and 2) on this formulation and inserting in article 2 of the draft code an enumeration of acts which it deemed offences against the peace and security of mankind, it adopted a draft code (A/1858) which was submitted to the General Assembly. The General Assembly at its 342d plenary session, November 13, 1951, held consideration of the draft code in abeyance until its seventh session (1952) because the draft code had not been submitted to governments. *Yearbook of the United Nations 1951*, pp. 841–843; U.S. participation in the U.N., report by the President to Congress for the year 1951, pp. 253–254. On the basis of the Sixth Committee's report resulting from its consideration at its 296th and 297th meetings, on January 23–24, 1952, the General Assembly in its Resolution 601(VI) merely noted the Commission's progress on this subject. The International Law Commission submitted in its 1954 report (A/2693) a revised version of a text for a draft Code of Offences Against the Peace and Security of Mankind. The earlier version was not discussed by the Assembly, which postponed consideration of the question in 1951 and for the 2 years, 1952 and 1953, omitted it from its agenda in view of the Commission's continuing study. This revised Draft Code consisted of four articles which defined offences against the peace and security of mankind as "crimes under international law, for which the responsible individuals shall be punished"; listed 13 specific acts considered offences; declared that a person committing any of these offences could not be absolved from responsibility because he acted as Head of State or as a responsible government official; and declared that a person charged with committing any of the offences could not be relieved of responsibility in international law because of the fact that he acted pursuant to an order of his government or of a superior—if, in the circumstances at the time, it was possible for him not to comply with the order. *Yearbook of the United Nations 1954*, p. 411. The Sixth Committee considered the report at its 396th and 420th to 425th meetings. Its report (A/2807) was adopted by the General Assembly at its 504th plenary meeting, December 4, 1954, as Resolution 897(IX) by which it postponed further consideration of the Draft Code until the Special Committee submitted its report on the definition of aggression. *Yearbook of the United Nations 1954*, pp. 408–412. The United States took the position that the project for a code of crimes under international law in today's world is impractical and inappropriate and that the project of the Draft Code should not be continued. U.S. participation in the U.N., report by the President to Congress for the year 1954, pp. 193–194. The majority of the Sixth Committee of the General Assembly in 1957 favored postponing further consideration of the Draft Code of Offences Against the Peace and Security of Mankind until the question of the definition of aggression was again considered by the General Assembly, which would not be earlier than its fourteenth session. The General Assembly at its 727th plenary meeting, December 11, 1957, adopted the Sixth Committee's recommendation as Resolution 1186(XII). U.S. participation in the U.N., report by the President to Congress for the year 1957, p. 233; *Yearbook of the United Nations 1957*, pp. 375–376.

> For U.N. and ILC documentation on the "Formulation of the Nürnberg Principles" and the Draft Code of Offences, see generally:
> Formulation of the Principles Recognized in the Charter of the Nürnberg Tribunal and in the Judgment of the Tribunal—The principles as stated by Sir Hartley Shawcross before the American Bar Association in 1946, May 9, 1949, A/CN.4/12, incorporated in A/CN.4/SR.17, par. 7; The Charter and Judgment of the Nürnberg Tribunal, Memorandum submitted by the Secretary-General, A/CN.4/5; Formulation of the Principles Recognized in the Nürnberg Tribunal and in the Judgment of the Tribunal—Draft proposed by the Sub-Committee on the Formulation of the Nürnberg Principles, May 11, 1949, A/CN.4/W.6, incorporated in A/CN.4/SR.25, footnote 9; Formulation of the Principles Recognized in the Charter of the Nürnberg Tribunal and in the Judgment of the Tribunal—Proposal by Scelle, A/CN.4/W.11, Add.2, incorporated in A/CN.4/SR.28, par. 88; Formulation of Principles recognized in the Charter of the Nürnberg Tribunal and in the Judgment of the Tribunal—Texts recommended by the Sub-Committee, incorporated in A/CN.4/SR.31, footnote 8; Draft Code of Offences Against the Peace and Security of Mankind, Replies from Governments, Feb. 28, 1950, A/CN.4/19; *ibid.*/Add.1, Mar. 28, 1950, *ibid.*/Add.2, Mar. 24, 1950, II Yearbook of I.L.C. 1950, pp. 249–253; Report by Spiropoulos, Special Rapporteur, on Formulation of Nürnberg Principles, Apr. 12, 1950, A/CN.4/22, II Yearbook of I.L.C. 1950, pp. 181–195; Draft Code of Offences Against the Peace and Security of Mankind, Apr. 26, 1950, Second Report by Spiropoulos, Special Rapporteur, A/CN.4/25, II Yearbook of I.L.C. 1950, pp. 253–278; Memorandum Concerning a Draft Code of Offences Against the Peace and Security of Mankind, Nov. 24, 1950, A/CN.4/39, prepared by Pella, II Yearbook of I.L.C. 1950, pp. 278–362; Report of I.L.C. Covering Work of Second Session, A/1316, II Yearbook of I.L.C. 1950, pp. 364, 379; Text of the Nürnberg Principles adopted by the I.L.C., June 24, 1950, A/CN.4/L.2, text also printed in the report, A/1316; Additional Crimes Proposed by Members of the I.L.C. for Inclusion in the Draft Code of Offences Against the Peace and Security of Mankind, July 3, 1950, A/CN.4/R.1, incorporated in A/CN.4/SR.60, footnote 15 and A/CN.4/SR.61, footnote 4; List of Crimes Proposed in the Replies from Governments for Inclusion in the Draft Code of Offences Against the Peace and Security of Mankind, July 3, 1950, A/CN.4/R.2, see A/CN.4/19 and Adds. 1, 2; Systematic List of the International Crimes Proposed by Mr. Pella in his Memorandum, July 3, 1950, A/CN.4/R.3, incorporated in A/CN.4/SR.61, footnote 16; Draft Code of Offences Against the Peace and Security of Mankind: Text proposed by the drafting committee, A/CN.4/R.6, incorporated in A/CN.4/SR.72, footnote 3; Second Report on a Draft Code of Offences Against the Peace and Security of Mankind, by Spiropoulos, Special Rapporteur, Apr. 12, 1951, A/CN.4/44, II Yearbook of I.L.C. 1951, pp. 43–69;

Draft Code of Offences Against the Peace and Security of Mankind, Re-
draft suggested by the Special Rapporteur in the light of the decisions of
and discussions in the Commission, June 7, 1951, A/CN.4/L.15; Draft Code
of Offences Against the Peace and Security of Mankind, July 16, 1951,
A/CN.4/L.26; Observations of Governments of Member States Relating
to the Formulation of Nürnberg Principles, Prepared by I.L.C., Apr.
19, 1951, A/CN.4/45, II Yearbook of I.L.C. 1951, pp. 104–105; Addendum to
the observations of Member States, A/CN.4/45/Add.1, June 7, 1951, *ibid.*,
pp. 105–108; A/CN.4/45/Add.2, June 14, 1951, *ibid.*, pp. 108–109; Report of
I.L.C. Covering Work of Third Session, U.N. Gen. Ass. Off. Rec. 6th Sess.,
Supp. No. 9, A/1858, II Yearbook of I.L.C. 1951, pp. 123, 133–137; Draft Code
of Offences Against the Peace and Security of Mankind, 'Note by the Secretariat, May 13, 1953, A/CN.4/72; Third Report Relating to the Draft Code
of Offences Against the Peace and Security of Mankind, by Spiropoulos,
Special Rapporteur, Apr. 30, 1954, A/CN.4/85. And see *Historical Survey
of the Question of International Criminal Jurisdiction*, Memorandum submitted by the Secretary-General of the United Nations, A/CN.4/7/Rev. 1,
1949.

Pursuant to Resolution 260B(III), adopted by the General Assem- International
bly in December 1948, the International Law Commission, at its first Criminal
Jurisdiction
session (1949), began a preliminary study of the desirability and
possibility of establishing an international judicial organ for the
trial of persons charged with genocide or other crimes over which
jurisdiction would be conferred upon that organ by international conventions. The Commission, asked to consider the possibility of establishing a criminal chamber of the International Court of Justice,
noted that, since a criminal chamber of the International Court of
Justice could be established only by amending the Statute of the Court,
it would not recommend that course of action but reported its conclusion that the establishment of an international judicial (criminal)
organ is desirable and possible. On the basis of the report (A/1639)
of the Sixth Committee which dealt with this issue at its 240–246th
meetings, from November 16–29, 1950, inclusive, the General Assembly
at its 320th plenary session, December 12, 1950, adopted Resolution 489
(V) which called for an intergovernmental Committee to meet at
Geneva, August 1, 1951, to prepare "one or more preliminary draft
conventions and proposals relating to the establishment and the statute
of an international criminal court". The question was again placed on
the agenda of the General Assembly's seventh session, 1952. U.S.
participation in the U.N., report by the President to Congress for the
year 1950, p. 249; U.S. participation in the U.N., report by the President to Congress for the year 1951, p. 255; *Yearbook of the United
Nations 1950*, pp. 857–861. From the meeting held at Geneva from
August 1–31, 1951, emerged a draft statute for an international criminal court presented in its report (A/2136). The Committee examined questions posed in the Secretary-General's memorandum (A/

AC.48/1), including annexed drafts for a statute, and adopted a resolution stating its opinion that along with the instrument establishing
the international criminal court a protocol should be drawn up conferring jurisdiction on that court in respect of genocide. *Yearbook
of the United Nations 1951*, pp. 852–854. By September 23, 11 governments had submitted their observations (invited by the General
Assembly) (A/2186 and A/2186/Add. 1). The Sixth Committee
considered the item at its 321–328th meetings, from November 7–17,
1952. The General Assembly's discussions at its seventh session
focused on the question whether the Assembly should proceed at that
time with the project of establishing a permanent criminal court.
The United States delegation stated that the United States "has
neither favored nor disfavored the creation of an international criminal court." U.S. participation in the U.N., report by the President
to Congress for the year 1952, p. 209. The draft resolution submitted
by the Sixth Committee (A/2275) was adopted by the General Assembly at its 400th plenary meeting, December 5, 1952, as Resolution
687(VII), whereby the General Assembly decided to appoint a committee composed of one representative from each of 17 Member States
and directed the Committee to explore the implications and consequences of establishing an international criminal court and of the
various methods by which this might be done; to study the relationship
between such a court and the United Nations and its organs; to re-
examine the draft statute; and to submit a report to be considered by
the General Assembly at its ninth session in 1954. U.S. participation
in the U.N., report by the President to Congress for the year 1952, p.
209; *Yearbook of the United Nations 1952*, pp. 803–807; *Yearbook of
the United Nations 1953*, pp. 683–686. The Special Committee on International Criminal Jurisdiction met from July 27 to August 20,
1953, and its report was considered at the Assembly's ninth session. In
the report, the Committee dealt with the general principles involved in
establishing an international criminal court (including alternative
methods for its establishment), the organization, jurisdiction, and
procedure of the court, as well as questions regarding a committing
chamber and prosecuting attorney, clemency and parole, and special
tribunals. A revised draft for an international criminal court was
annexed to the report. The Sixth Committee considered the
matter at its 426th to 430th meetings, November 23–29, 1954, and
its report (A/2827 and Corr. 1) was adopted by the General Assembly
at its 512th plenary meeting, December 14, 1954, as Resolution 898
(IX), whereby the General Assembly decided to postpone consideration of the subject until it reviewed the report of the Special Committee on the question of defining aggression and took up again the

Draft Code of Offences Against the Peace and Security of Mankind. U.S. participation in the U.N., report by the President to Congress for the year 1954, p. 196; *Yearbook of the United Nations 1954*, pp. 430–433. The Sixth Committee's resolution that the questions of international criminal jurisdiction be deferred until the question of defining aggression and the Draft Code of Offences were again before the General Assembly was adopted by the General Assembly at its 727th plenary meeting, December 11, 1957 (Res. 1187(XII)). U.S. participation in the U.N., report by the President to Congress for the year 1957, p. 233; *Yearbook of the United Nations 1957*, pp. 376–377.

> For U.N. and ILC documentation with respect to "International Criminal Jurisdiction", see generally:
>
> Memorandum, Historical Survey of the Question of Criminal Jurisdiction, A/CN.4/7/Rev.1, Sept. 1949, 1949.V.8; Report on Question of International Criminal Jurisdiction, by Alfaro, Special Rapporteur, Mar. 3, 1950, A/CN.4/15, II Yearbook of I.L.C. 1950, pp. 1–18; Report by Sandström, Special Rapporteur, Mar. 30, 1950, A/CN.4/20, II Yearbook of I.L.C. 1950, pp. 18–23; Report of I.L.C. Covering Work of Second Session, U.N. Gen. Ass. Off. Rec. 5th Sess., Supp. No. 12, A/1316, II Yearbook of I.L.C. 1950, pp. 364, 378–379; Bibliography on International Criminal Law and International Criminal Court, June 6, 1950, A/CN.4/28; Report of 1953 Committee on International Criminal Jurisdiction, July 27–Aug. 20, 1953, A/2645; Report by Sixth Committee, Dec. 3, 1954, A/2827 and Corr. 1, Dec. 4, 1954.

The drafting of a Declaration on the Rights and Duties of States on the basis of Panama's text of a draft (A/285), initially assigned to the Committee on the Progressive Development of International Law and its Codification by the General Assembly by Resolution 38(I), December 11, 1946, was, in 1947, transferred to the prospective International Law Commission by the General Assembly on the basis of its Sixth Committee's recommendation (A/508) by Resolution 178 (II) formulated at its 123d plenary meeting, November 21, 1947. *Yearbook of the United Nations 1947–1948*, pp. 215–216. During its first session, April–June 1949, the International Law Commission prepared a "Draft Declaration on Rights and Duties of States". Report of I.L.C. to the General Assembly on Work of First Session, 1949 (A/925), pp. 7–10. After consideration of the International Law Commission's draft (A/925), the Sixth Committee at its 159th meeting, October 12, 1949, and its 168th–173d, 175th–183d meetings, from October 18 to November 3, 1949, the General Assembly at its 270th plenary meeting, December 6, 1949, requested in Resolution 375(IV) the transmission of the draft to Member States for their comments and suggestions, in particular, whether the Assembly should take any further action on the draft declaration and, if so, the nature of such action. *Yearbook of the United Nations 1948–1949*, pp. 946–949; U.S.

Rights and Duties of States

participation in the U.N., report by the President to Congress for the year 1949, p. 176. Because by its fifth session (1950) only 11 replies had been received, the General Assembly deferred this item to its sixth session (1951). U.S. participation in the U.N., report by the President to Congress for the year 1950, p. 249. Still owing to an insufficient number of replies, the General Assembly at its 352d plenary meeting, December 7, 1951, decided (Resolution 596(VI)) on the basis of its Sixth Committee's report (A/1982) to postpone consideration of the draft declaration until the requisite number of States had made comments. *Yearbook of the United Nations 1951*, pp. 846–849; U.S. participation in the U.N., report by the President to Congress for the year 1951, pp. 255–256.

> For U.N. and ILC documentation with reference to the "Rights and Duties of States", see generally:
> Preparatory Study Concerning a Draft Declaration on the Rights and Duties of States, Memorandum by the Secretary-General, Dec. 15, 1948, A/CN.4/2, 1949.V.4; Preparatory Study Concerning a Draft Declaration on the Rights and Duties of States, including a detailed table of contents of appendices, Apr. 22, 1949, A/CN.4/2/Add.1; Draft Declaration on Rights and Duties of States (A/925) (Text:—G. A. Res. 375(IV), *Yearbook of the United Nations 1948–1949*, pp. 948–949); Draft Declaration on Rights and Duties of States (A/CN.4/2), summary of action taken by the Commission with regard to the Draft, A/CN.4/W.4 and Rev. 1–4; Draft Declaration on Rights and Duties of States, as proposed by the Sub-Committee on the draft Declaration, A/CN.4/W.5, incorporated in A/CN.4/SR.19, footnote 2; Draft Declaration on Rights and Duties of States, summary of action taken by the Commission after second reading of the Draft, A/CN.4/W.7; Draft Declaration on the Rights and Duties of States, summary of action taken by the Commission after third reading, A/CN.4/W.8, Yearbook of I.L.C. 1949, pp. 163–164, footnote 1; A/CN.4/SR.23–25, *ibid.*, pp. 163–183.

State Re-
sponsibility

At its 393d and 394th meetings on November 25 and 28, 1953, the General Assembly's Sixth Committee considered a draft resolution submitted by Cuba (A/C.6/L.311) providing that the General Assembly "request the International Law Commission as soon as it considers it possible, to undertake the codification of the principles of international law governing State responsibility and to include it among topics to which it accords priority." State Responsibility was one of the 14 topics of international law which the Commission at its first session in 1949 had provisionally selected for codification. On the Sixth Committee's recommendation (A/2589) the General Assembly adopted this proposal at its 468th plenary meeting on December 7, 1953, as Resolution 799 (VIII), wherein the International Law Commission was requested to undertake as soon as it considered it advisable the codification of the principles of international law governing State Responsibility. *Yearbook of the United Nations*

1953, pp. 679–680. A memorandum on the question (A/CN.4/80) was submitted by the Cuban member, F. V. Garcia-Amador, but in view of the Commission's heavy agenda, it was decided not to begin work on the subject for the time being. Report of I.L.C. to the General Assembly on Work of Sixth Session, U.N. Gen. Ass. Off. Rec. 9th Sess., Supp. No. 9, A/2693, p. 21. The special rapporteur, in accordance with the request made by the Commission at its eighth session, submitted at the ninth session, 1957, a second report (A/CN.4/106), International Responsibility, dealing with the particular topic of Responsibility of the State for Injuries Caused in Its Territory to the Person or Property of Aliens, Part I: Acts and Omissions. While study was being continued on this subject a third report on the same subject, consisting of Part II: The International Claim (A/CN.4/111), was submitted to the Commission at its tenth session, 1958, where it was decided to take up the subject again at its eleventh session. At its eleventh session the subject was placed on the provisional agenda for the twelfth session. Report of I.L.C. to the General Assembly on Work of Ninth Session, II *Yearbook of the International Law Commission 1957*, pp. 131, 143; Report of I.L.C. to the General Assembly on Work of Tenth Session, II *Yearbook of the International Law Commission 1958*, pp. 78, 106; Report of I.L.C. to the General Assembly on Work of Eleventh Session, II *Yearbook of the International Law Commission 1959*, pp. 87, 122; U.N. Gen. Ass. Off. Rec. 14th Sess., Supp. No. 9, A/4169, p. 36.

For documentation of the U.N. and the ILC with respect to "State Responsibility", see generally:

Request of the General Assembly for the Codification of the Principles of International Law Governing State Responsibility, Memorandum submitted by Garcia-Amador, Special Rapporteur, member of I.L.C., Mar. 10, 1954, A/CN.4/80; International Responsibility, Report by Garcia-Amador, Special Rapporteur, including annexes and bibliography, Jan. 20, 1956, A/CN.4/96, II Yearbook of I.L.C. 1956, pp. 173–231; Second Report on International Responsibility, Responsibility of the State for Injuries Caused in Its Territory to the Person or Property of Aliens, Part I: Acts and Omissions, by Garcia-Amador, Special Rapporteur, Feb. 15, 1957, A/CN.4/106, II Yearbook of I.L.C. 1957, pp. 104–130; Request for Codification of the Principles of International Law Governing State Responsibility, Draft Resolution Adopted by Sixth Committee at its 394th Meeting, Nov. 28, 1953, Nov. 30, 1953, A/C.6/L.327; Responsibility of the State for Injuries Caused in Its Territory to the Person or Property of Aliens, Part II: The International Claim, Third Report by Garcia-Amador, Special Rapporteur, Jan. 2, 1958, including annex, A/CN.4/111, II Yearbook of I.L.C. 1958, pp. 47–73; International Responsibility, Fourth Report by Garcia-Amador, Special Rapporteur, Feb. 26, 1959, A/CN.4/119, II Yearbook of the I.L.C. 1959, pp. 1–36; International Responsibility, Fifth Report by Garcia-Amador, Special Rapporteur, Feb. 9, 1960, A/CN.4/125; International Responsibility, Sixth Report by Garcia-Amador, Special Rapporteur, Jan. 26, 1961, A/CN.4/134.

Making
Evidence of
Customary
International
Law More
Readily
Available

In accordance with article 24 of the Statute of the International Law Commission, the Commission undertook to consider ways and means for making the evidence of customary international law more readily available. On the basis of a working paper (A/CN.4/16 and Add. 1) prepared by Mr. Hudson, special rapporteur, the International Law Commission at its second session (1950) concluded that, since customary and conventional international law need not be mutually exclusive, materials of conventional international law could be considered in connection with this question. The list prepared of types of evidence of customary international law included: texts of international instruments, decisions of international courts, decisions of national courts, national legislation, diplomatic correspondence, opinions of national legal advisers, and practice of international organizations. The Sixth Committee at its 230th and 231st meetings, October 30 and November 2, 1950, considered recommendations of the International Law Commission (A/1316) on ways and means for making the evidence of customary international law more readily available. Its report (A/1639) was adopted by the General Assembly at its 320th plenary meeting, December 12, 1950, as Resolution 487(V). *Yearbook of the United Nations 1950*, pp. 850–851. In accordance with this resolution, the Secretary-General presented a report (A/1934) on the recommendations contained in paragraphs 90, 91, and 93 of part II of the International Law Commission's report on its second session to the General Assembly, and after consideration at the Sixth Committee's 297th to 301st meetings, from January 24 to 28, 1952, the General Assembly at the 369th plenary meeting, February 1, 1952, adopted the Committee's recommendation (A/2089) that the Secretary-General submit an additional report. Res. 602 (VI), *Yearbook of the United Nations 1951*, pp. 849–851. In compliance with this request, the Secretary-General presented to the seventh session of the General Assembly (A/2170) detailed plans as to the form, contents, and budgetary implications in regard to the possible publication of a United Nations juridical yearbook, a consolidated index to the *League of Nations Treaty Series*, a list of treaty collections supplementary to those already existing, a volume containing a repertoire of the practice of the Security Council. After discussion of the report by the Sixth Committee at its 317th to 320th meetings from November 3 to 5, 1952, the General Assembly adopted the Sixth Committee's report (A/2258) at its 400th plenary meeting, December 5, 1952, as Resolution 686(VII) by which it authorized the publication of a list of treaty collections and a repertoire of the practice of the Security Council, and requested the Secretary-General to prepare and circulate to the governments of Member States a comparative study of the extent to which developments in the field of customary international law and selected legal activities of the United Nations can be usefully covered by an expansion of existing United Nations publications, by the launching of new special publications of limited scope and by a United Nations juridical yearbook; such study to cover form, contents, and budgetary implications. *Yearbook of the United Nations 1952*, pp. 797–800; U.S. participation in the U.N., report by the President to Congress for the year 1952, p. 210.

> For U.N. and ILC documentation on "Ways and Means for Making the Evidence of Customary International Law More Readily Available", see generally:
>
> Ways and Means for Making the Evidence of Customary International Law More Readily Available, Mar. 7, 1949, A/CN.4/6, A/CN.4/6/Corr. 1, 1949.V.6; Working Paper Based on Part III of the Preparatory Work Done by the Secretariat upon Ways and Means of Making the Evidence of Customary International Law More Readily Available (A/CN.4/6), A/CN.4/W.9; Working paper by Hudson, Special Rapporteur, on Article 24 of the Statute of the I.L.C., Mar. 3, 1950, A/CN.4/16, II Yearbook of I.L.C. 1950, pp. 24–32; Addendum to the working paper by Hudson, Special Rapporteur, A/CN.4/16/Add. 1, Mar. 15, 1950, II Yearbook of I.L.C. 1950, p. 33; Comments on Hudson's working paper, June 6, 1950, A/CN.4/27, II Yearbook of I.L.C. 1950, pp. 33–35; Report of I.L.C. Covering Work of Second Session, II Yearbook of I.L.C. 1950, pp. 364, 367–374, U.N. Gen. Ass. Off. Rec. 5th Sess., Supp. No. 12, A/1316; Ways and Means for Making the Evidence of Customary International Law More Readily Available, Resolution adopted by the General Assembly at its 369th meeting, Feb. 1, 1952 (adopted on report of Sixth Committee, A/2089), Feb. 2, 1952, A/L.71; Ways and Means for Making the Evidence of Customary International Law More Readily Available, Report by Sixth Committee, Nov. 17, 1952, A/2258; Report of Secretary-General prepared in pursuance of General Assembly Resolution 686(VII) concerning ways and means for making the evidence of customary international law more readily available, Oct. 10, 1955, A/C.6/348.

Codification of "Diplomatic Intercourse and Immunities" was endorsed in 1952 for work by the International Law Commission, following a request by Yugoslavia, by the General Assembly at its 400th plenary meeting, December 5, 1952, where, acting on the recommendation (A/2252) of its Sixth Committee by which the question was considered during its 313th to 317th meetings, October 29 to November 3, 1952, Resolution 685(VII) was passed requesting the International Law Commission to treat this as a priority topic.   At its first session in 1949, the International Law Commission had included this subject in its provisional list of 14 topics the codification of which was deemed desirable and feasible.   Report of I.L.C. to the General Assembly on Work of First Session, *Yearbook of the International Law Commission 1949*, p. 281, *Yearbook of the United Nations 1952*, pp. 800–803; U.S. participation in the U.N., report by the President to Congress

Diplomatic Intercourse and Immunities

for the year 1952, pp. 207–208.   At its sixth session, the International
Law Commission decided to initiate work on the subject and appointed
A. E. F. Sandström as special rapporteur.   The rapporteur's first report was submitted in 1955 at the seventh session (A/CN.4/91). The
International Law Commission found it necessary to postpone consideration of the subject until its ninth session (1957) when it adopted
a provisional draft with commentaries which it circulated to governments for their observations.   The draft dealt only with permanent
diplomatic missions and covered in section I, Diplomatic Intercourse
in General, such subtopics as establishment of diplomatic relations
and missions, functions of a diplomatic mission, appointment of the
head of the mission, appointment of nationals of the receiving State,
persons declared *persona non grata*, limitation of staff, commencement
of the functions of the head of the mission, agreement on the class to
which heads of their missions are to be assigned, mode of reception, and
equality of status; in section II, Diplomatic Privileges and Immunities, such subtopics as mission premises and archives subsuming such subjects as accommodation, inviolability of the mission
premises, exemption of mission premises from tax, inviolability of
archives; and facilitation of the work of the mission, freedom
of movement and communication subsuming such subjects as facilities,
free movement, freedom of communication; Personal Privileges and
Immunities subsuming such subjects as personal inviolability, inviolability of residence and property, immunity from jurisdiction,
waiver of immunity, exemption from taxation, exemption from
customs duties and inspection, persons entitled to privileges and
immunities, acquisition of nationality, diplomatic agents who are
nationals of the receiving State, duration of privileges and immunities, and duties of third States.   A third section is entitled,
"Conduct of the Mission and of its Members Toward the Receiving
State", while the fourth is entitled, "End of the Function of a
Diplomatic Agent" and includes subtopics: modes of termination,
facilitation of departure, protection of premises, archives and
interests.   Section V concludes the draft with an article on the
Settlement of Disputes.   While the draft articles do not cover missions
accredited to or staffs of international organizations, the Commission
directed that such forms of "*ad hoc* diplomacy" as roving envoys,
diplomatic conferences and special missions sent to a State for limited purposes be studied in order to bring out the rules of law governing them and requested the special rapporteur to make such a study
and submit his report to the next session.   The draft was prepared
on the provisional assumption that it would form the basis of a convention but the final decision as to the form of the draft would await

the Commission's receipt of comments from governments. U.S. participation in the U.N., report by the President to Congress for the year 1957, p. 230; Report of I.L.C. to the General Assembly on Work of Ninth Session, II *Yearbook of the International Law Commission 1957*, pp. 132–143, U.N. Gen. Ass. Off. Rec. 12th Sess., Supp. No. 9, A/3623. The Commission, at its tenth session, 1958, re-examined the text of its provisional draft in the light of the observations received from governments and of the conclusions drawn from them by the special rapporteur (A/CN.4/116 and Add. 1 and 2) and made a number of changes in the provisional draft. The draft adopted continued to treat only of permanent diplomatic missions. At its tenth session the Commission also decided to submit to the General Assembly that the draft should be recommended to Member States with a view to the conclusion of a convention on diplomatic intercourse and immunities. II *Yearbook of the International Law Commission 1958*, pp. 16, 89; Report of I.L.C. to the General Assembly on Work of Tenth Session, 28 April–4 July 1958, U.N. Gen. Ass. Off. Rec. 13th Sess., Supp. No. 9, A/3859, pp. 11 ff.

On December 7, 1959, the General Assembly, at its Fourteenth Session, decided that an international conference should be convoked to consider the question of diplomatic intercourse and immunities, which should embody the results of its work in an international convention, together with such ancillary instruments as might be necessary. The Secretary-General was requested to convoke the conference at Vienna not later than the spring of 1961. Res. 1450 (XIV). For results of the Conference held at Vienna in 1961, see *post* this Digest.

For U.N. and ILC documentation with respect to "Diplomatic Intercourse and Immunities", see generally:

Request of the General Assembly concerning the codification of the topic Diplomatic Intercourse and Immunities, note by the Secretariat, May 18, 1953, A/CN.4/73; Report on Diplomatic Intercourse and Immunities, by Sandström, Special Rapporteur, Apr. 21, 1955, A/CN.4/91, II Yearbook of I.L.C. 1955, pp. 9–17; Codification of International Law Relating to Diplomatic Intercourse and Immunities, Memorandum by the Secretariat, Feb. 21, 1956, A/CN.4/98, II Yearbook of I.L.C. 1956, pp. 129–172; Laws and Regulations Regarding Diplomatic and Consular Privileges and Immunities, ST/LEG/SER.B/7, 1958, 1958.V.3; Observations of Governments on the Draft Articles Concerning Diplomatic Intercourse and Immunities, Mar. 17, 1958, A/CN.4/114; *ibid.*/Add.1, Apr. 15, 1958; *ibid.*/Add.2, Apr. 28, 1958; *ibid.*/Add.3, Apr. 30, 1958; *ibid.*/Add.4, May 6, 1958; *ibid.*/Add.5, May 20, 1958; *ibid.*/Add.6, May 27, 1958; Diplomatic Intercourse and Immunities, summary of observations received from governments and conclusions of the special rapporteur, Sandström, May 2, 1958, A/CN.4/116; *ibid.*/Add.1, May 21, 1958; *ibid.*/Add.2, May 27, 1958, II Yearbook of I.L.C. 1958, pp. 16–19. Summary of opinions expressed in the Sixth Committee of the General

Assembly in 1957 relative to draft articles concerning diplomatic intercourse and immunities, adopted by the I.L.C. at its ninth session, working
paper prepared by Secretariat, Mar. 12, 1958, A/CN.4/L.72 and A/CN.4/L.75,
May 16, 1958.

Consular
Intercourse
and
Immunities

At the first session of the International Law Commission, held in
1949, the topic "Consular Intercourse and Immunities" was included
as the 12th of the 14 topics provisionally selected for codification.
Report of I.L.C. to the General Assembly on Work of First Session,
12 April–9 June 1949, U.N. Gen. Ass. Off. Rec. 4th Sess., Supp. No. 10,
A/925, p. 3.   At its seventh session, in 1955, the Commission appointed
Jaroslav Zourek as special rapporteur for this topic.   Report of I.L.C.
to the General Assembly on Work of Seventh Session, 2 May–8 July
1955, U.N. Gen. Ass. Off. Rec. 10th Sess., Supp. No. 9, A/2934, p. 23.
The eighth session of the Commission devoted two meetings to a brief
exchange of views on certain points submitted to it by the special
rapporteur and requested him to continue his work in the light of the
debate.   Report of I.L.C. to the General Assembly on Work of
Eighth Session, 23 April–4 July 1956, U.N. Gen. Ass. Off. Rec. 11th
Sess., Supp. No. 9, A/3159, p. 46.   At the ninth session of the Commission, the special rapporteur submitted a report April 15, 1957,
A/CN.4/108, II *Yearbook of the International Law Commission,
1957*, pp. 71–103, which was not considered at that session for lack of
time.   Toward the end of its tenth session the Commission, after
an exposé by the special rapporteur, and a general exchange of views
on the subject as a whole and on the first article of the draft submitted
at the previous session, deferred further consideration of the topic
until its next session.   Report of I.L.C. to the General Assembly on
Work of Tenth Session, 28 April–4 July 1958, U.N. Gen. Ass. Off.
Rec. 13th Sess., Supp. No. 9, A/3859, p. 28.   At its eleventh session
the Commission examined the first 17 of the draft articles.   Report of
I.L.C. to the General Assembly on Work of Eleventh Session, 20
April–26 June 1959, U.N. Gen. Ass. Off. Rec. 14th Sess., Supp. No. 9,
A/4169, p. 23; II *Yearbook of the International Law Commission
1959*, pp. 87, 109–111; Report of I.L.C. to the General Assembly on
Work of Twelfth Session, 25 April–1 July 1960, U.N. Gen. Ass. Off.
Rec. 15th Sess., Supp. No. 9, A/4425, pp. 2–35.   The Commission at its
thirteenth session produced a final text of draft articles on consular
relations, recommending that the General Assembly convene an international conference and conclude one or more conventions on the subject.   Report of I.L.C. to the General Assembly on Work of Thirteenth
Session, 1 May–7 July 1961, U.N. Gen. Ass. Off. Rec. 16th Sess., Supp.
No. 9, A/4843.   For results of the 1963 Vienna Conference, see *post*
this Digest.

Question of
Defining
Aggression

The question of defining aggression was inconclusively considered
by the General Assembly's Political Committee in 1950 and was

referred to the International Law Commission by the General Assembly at its fifth session (1950) in Resolution 378B(V) as a result of a proposal by the U.S.S.R. in connection with the agenda item, "Duties of States in the Event of an Outbreak of Hostilities." *Yearbook of the United Nations 1950*, p. 213. Undertaking its study at its third session, May 16–June 27, 1951, the International Law Commission in its report (A/1858) to the General Assembly stated that the majority of the Commission interpreted the resolution as a request to attempt to define aggression and report results. They further reported that to this end it had decided that the only practical course was to aim at a general and abstract definition, rather than a detailed enumerative definition of aggression. The Sixth Committee discussed the question of the possibility and desirability of defining aggression at its 278th–295th meetings from January 5 to 22, 1952. The United States along with certain other States advocated discontinuing the attempt to define aggression because any definition enumerating acts of aggression would be incomplete while a broad and abstract formula would be too vague to prove useful. These States preferred to leave to the United Nations organs, responsible for determining an aggressor, full discretion to consider all circumstances. The United States in support of this view referred to the decision at the San Francisco conference not to include a definition of aggression in the Charter of the United Nations, but to leave to the Organization itself the determination of specific acts of aggression. Other delegations, however, felt that a definition would prove a useful supplement to the United Nations system of collective security. The Sixth Committee's report (A/2087), which the General Assembly at its 368th plenary meeting, January 31, 1952, adopted as Resolution 599(VI), postponed the question and included it on the agenda of its next session (seventh) and instructed the Secretary-General to submit a thorough report. U.S. participation in the U.N., report by the President to Congress for the year 1951, pp. 252–253; *Yearbook of the United Nations 1951*, pp. 833–840. In compliance with this resolution, the Secretary-General submitted his report (A/2211) to the seventh session of the General Assembly. After discussing the question at its 329th–346th meetings, from November 19 to December 10, 1952, the Sixth Committee submitted a draft resolution (A/2322 and Corr. 1, Amendment A/L.136) to the General Assembly which, in turn, decided at its 408th plenary session, December 20, 1952, by Resolution 688 (VII), to establish a Special Committee of 15 members to submit at the ninth session draft definitions of aggression or draft statements of the notion of aggression; to study all the problems referred to on the assumption of a definition being adopted; requested the Secretary-General to communicate the Special Committee's report to Member States for their comments; and decided to place the question on the provisional agenda of its ninth session. *Yearbook of the United Nations 1952*, pp. 784–791. The Special Committee, after studying during its meeting from August 24 to September 21, 1953, the Secretary-General's report (A/AC.66/1) containing an analysis of views expressed at the seventh session of the General Assembly together with comments of governments on the draft Code of Offences Against the Peace and Security of Mankind as well as on the question of aggression, decided to transmit various draft definitions of aggression to Member States and to the General Assembly because it was unable to agree upon a definition of aggression. *Yearbook of the United Nations 1953*, pp. 681–683; U.S. participation in the U.N., report by the President to Congress for the year 1954, pp. 196–197. This report was considered at the Sixth Committee's 403d–420th, 424th, 433d, and 434th meetings, from October 14 to November 10, 1954, where it was recommended (A/2806) that the Special Committee meet again in 1956. The General Assembly at its 504th plenary meeting, December 4, 1954, adopted this recommendation in Resolution 895(IX) whereby another Special Committee of 19 designated States was established to meet in 1956 and required to submit a detailed report at the eleventh session along with a draft definition of aggression, and the question was placed on the provisional agenda of the General Assembly's eleventh session. *Yearbook of the United Nations 1954*, pp. 426–430. The 1956 Special Committee held 19 meetings from October 8 to November 9, 1956, and decided (A/3574), as had the 1953 Committee, not to adopt any definition of aggression but to transmit draft definitions along with the report to the General Assembly. The General Assembly at its 577th plenary meeting decided on the basis of a proposal by the Secretary-General (A/BUR/143) to the General Committee, and on that Committee's recommendation (A/3350), to postpone this item until its twelfth session. *Yearbook of the United Nations 1956*, p. 385. In reviewing the report of the 1956 Special Committee, the Sixth Committee in its 514th to 528th and 530th to 538th meetings, from October 7 to November 4 and November 6 to November 21, 1957, failed again to define aggression. The resolution which the Sixth Committee recommended for adoption invited members to comment on the report of the Special Committee and recommended that the Secretary-General place the question on the provisional agenda of the General Assembly, not earlier than the fourteenth session, or whenever a Committee whose membership would correspond to the membership of the General Committee of the previous Assembly session should advise him that it considered the time appropriate again to consider the question. The General Assembly at its 724th plenary meeting, November 29, 1957, adopted this recommendation as Resolution 1181(XII). U.S. participation in the U.N., report by the President to Congress for the year 1957, pp. 231–233, *Yearbook of the United Nations 1957*, pp. 371–375.

For U.N. and ILC documentation with respect to the "Question of Defining Aggression", see generally:

The Possibility and Desirability of Defining Aggression, Chapter II (Annex) of Second Report by Spiropoulos, Special Rapporteur, on Draft Code of Offences Against Peace and Security of Mankind, Apr. 12, 1951, A/CN.4/44, II Yearbook of I.L.C. 1951, pp. 60–69; Memorandum presented by Amado, May 29, 1951, A/CN.4/L.6, II Yearbook of I.L.C. 1951, pp. 28–32; Determination of Aggressor, draft submitted by Yepes, May 30, 1951, A/CN.4/L.7, II Yearbook of I.L.C. 1951, pp. 32–33; Memorandum on Question of Defining Aggression, by Alfaro, May 30, 1951, A/CN.4/L.8, II Yearbook of I.L.C. 1951, pp. 33–40; Definition of Aggression, proposal by Córdova, June 4, 1951, A/CN.4/L.10, II Yearbook of I.L.C. 1951, p. 40; Definition of Aggression, proposal by Hsu, June 4, 1951, A/CN.4/L.11, II Yearbook of I.L.C. 1951, p. 40; Proposition by Yepes, June 4, 1951, A/CN.4/L.12, II Yearbook of I.L.C. 1951, p. 40; Definition of Aggression, Text tentatively adopted by Commission at its 95th meeting, June 4, 1951, footnote 1 in Summary Record of 96th meeting, A/CN.4/L.13; Memorandum on Question of Definition of Aggression presented by Scelle, Special Rapporteur, June 20, 1951, A/CN.4/L.19, II Yearbook of I.L.C. 1951, pp. 41–42; Report of I.L.C. Covering Work of Third Session, U.N. Gen. Ass. Off. Rec. 6th Sess., Supp. No. 9, A/1858, II Yearbook of I.L.C. 1951, pp. 123, 131–133; Question of Defining Aggression, draft resolution as adopted by the Sixth Committee at its 294th meeting, Jan. 21, 1952, A/C.6/L.217; Question of Defining Aggression, Resolution as adopted by the General Assembly at its 368th meeting, Jan. 31, 1952 (adopted on report of Sixth Committee, A/2087), Res. 599(VI).

Concluding that punishment of the crime of genocide, a denial of the right of existence to entire human groups, is a matter of international concern, the General Assembly at its first session, by Resolution 96(I), December 11, 1946, affirmed that genocide is a crime under international law for the commission of which private individuals or public officials are punishable whether the crime is committed on religious, racial, political, or other grounds, and requested the Economic and Social Council to undertake the necessary studies with a view to drawing up a draft convention on the crime of genocide for submission at the Assembly's second session. *Yearbook of the United Nations 1946–1947*, pp. 255–256; The U.S. and the U.N., report by the President to Congress for the year 1946, p. 20. Accordingly, the Economic and Social Council at its fourth session, February 28 to March 29, 1947, instructed (Resolution 47(IV)) the Secretary-General to draw up a draft convention and, after consultation with the General Assembly Committee on the Development and Codification of International Law and, if feasible, the Commis-

Genocide

sion on Human Rights and, after reference to all member governments for comments, to submit a draft to the next session of the Economic and Social Council. The Secretary-General's draft of a convention (E/447) consisted of a preamble and 24 articles with provisions for establishing a Permanent International Criminal Court for the Punishment of Acts of Genocide, annexed thereto. In subsequent notes the Secretary-General reported the status of this matter. The draft was then submitted to the Assembly Committee on the Progressive Development of International Law and its Codification, June 13, 1947, where further action was delayed until comments from member governments had been received. The subject again came before the Economic and Social Council at its 86th plenary meeting, fifth session, July 23, 1947, when it was transferred to the Social Committee of the Council, August 2, 1947, for discussion at its 15th meeting. The Social Committee's resolution (E/522), approved by the Council at its 107th meeting, August 6, 1947, noted that the draft convention had not been considered by the Committee on the Development and Codification of International Law or by the Commission on Human Rights, and by Resolution 77(V), which set forth the text of the convention, the Secretary-General was requested to transmit the draft convention to the General Assembly together with any comments received. ECOSOC at its 107th plenary meeting, August 6, 1947, during its fifth session, held further action in abeyance pending consideration by the General Assembly Committee on the Development and Codification of International Law and comments of member governments. The General Assembly, at its second session, November 21, 1947, adopted at its 123d plenary meeting Resolution 180(II) by which the Economic and Social Council was requested to continue its study. The latter, accordingly, discussed the question during its sixth session at its 139th, 140th, and 160th plenary meetings on February 12, 13, and March 3, respectively, and at the 37th meeting of its Social Committee, February 21, 1948. See Annex to ECOSOC, official records, third year, sixth session for other documents (note by Secretary-General, E/622; Secretary-General's statement of financial implications, E/622/Add.1; U.S. draft resolution, E/662/Add.1; Venezuelan draft resolution, E/663). The Council at its 160th plenary meeting, March 3, 1948, on its Social Committee's recommendation, established by Resolution 117(VI) an *ad hoc* committee composed of seven members of the Economic and Social Council, including the United States, and instructed it to prepare the draft Convention on the Crime of Genocide and submit it to the next session of the Economic and Social Council, taking into consideration the draft convention prepared by the Secretary-General. The *ad hoc* committee's draft of a convention was subsequently considered by the Commission on Narcotic Drugs (E/799) and by the Commission on Human Rights (E/800). The Economic and Social Council at its 202d plenary meeting (seventh session), August 17, 1948, recalled the report of the *ad hoc* committee from the Human Rights Committee and then considered it in its plenary session at its 218th and 219th meetings, August 26, 1948. The Council decided (Resolution 153(VII)) to transmit to the third session of the General Assembly the draft convention as submitted by the *ad hoc* committee (E/794) together with the records of proceedings of the Council at its seventh session. *Yearbook of the United Nations 1947–1948*, pp. 595–599. The Sixth Committee of the General Assembly considered the draft at its 63d and 67th to 110th meetings, September 30, 1948, and October 5 to November 18, 1948, respectively, and in its drafting committee from November 16–22, 1948. As revised by its drafting committee (A/C.6/289), the draft was reexamined by the Sixth Committee at its 128th to 134th meetings, November 29 to December 2, 1948. Three draft Resolutions A, B, and C proposed by the Sixth Committee (A/760) were approved by the General Assembly at its 179th plenary meeting, December 9, 1948, as Resolution 260(III) A, B, and C. Part A to which the text of the Convention was annexed recorded the General Assembly's approval of the Convention on the Prevention and Punishment of the Crime of Genocide for signature and ratification or accession; Part B invited the International Law Commission to study the desirability and possibility of establishing an international judicial organ for the trial of persons charged with genocide and requested the Commission to pay attention to the possibility of establishing a criminal chamber of the International Court of Justice; Part C recommended that parties to the Convention which administer dependent territories should take such measures as are necessary and feasible to enable the provisions of the Convention to be extended to those territories as soon as possible. After consideration by the Sixth Committee at its 208th to 209th meetings, November 28, 1949, of article XI, which provides that the Convention shall be open to signature and ratification or to accession on behalf of any Member or non-Member State to which the General Assembly addresses an invitation, the General Assembly, adopting the Sixth Committee's report (A/1168) at its 266th plenary meeting, December 3, 1949, decided by Resolution 368(IV) to dispatch invitations to each non-Member State which was or thereafter became an active member of one or more of the specialized agencies of the United Nations, or which was or thereafter became a party to the Statute of the International Court of Justice. *Yearbook of the United Nations 1948–*

1949, pp. 953–962.   The Genocide Convention entered into force pursuant to its terms on January 12, 1951, 20 States having become parties without reservations.   *Yearbook of the United Nations 1951*, p. 193.

> For U.N. documentation on "Genocide", see generally:
> Draft Resolution Relating to the Crime of Genocide, proposed by delegations of Cuba, India, and Panama, A/BUR/50; Amendments to Draft Resolution Relating to the Crime of Genocide, A/C.6/83, A/C.6/94, A/C.6/95; Draft protocol for the prevention and punishment of the crime of genocide, A/C.6/86; Draft Report and Resolution Adopted by Sub-Committee 3 Relating to the Crime of Genocide, A/C.6/120; Note by the Secretary-General on the Crime of Genocide, E/330; Draft Convention Prepared by the Secretary-General on the Crime of Genocide, E/447; Draft Convention on the Crime of Genocide, E/476; Draft Convention on the Crime of Genocide, A/362, reprinted as Annex 32 in Annexes to Gen. Ass. Off. Rec. 2d Sess., A/510; Report of Social Committee, Text of Draft in Social Committee's report, E/690, *ibid.*/Add.1; Report of *Ad Hoc* Committee, E/794, *ibid.*/Corr.1 (same as 7th ECOSOC Off. Rec., Supp. No. 6, and Corr.); Report of *Ad Hoc* Committee with text of Convention attached as Annex, E/1049; Report of Committee on Human Rights, E/800 (ECOSOC Off. Rec. 3d year, 7th sess., Supp. No. 2); Text of Convention attached as annex to Res. 260A(III); Final text: U.N. Treaty Series, vol. 78, p. 277; E/Res./77(V), where text is the same as in E/522.

Chapter II

STATES, TERRITORIES, AND GOVERNMENTS[1]

STATES

General Nature

§ 14

"A state is an *institution*, that is to say, it is a system of relations which men establish among themselves as a means of securing certain objects, of which the most fundamental is a system of order within which their activities can be carried on. Modern states are territorial; their governments exercise control over persons and things within their frontiers,. and today the whole of the habitable world is divided between about seventy of these territorial states. A state should not be confused with the whole community of persons living on its territory; it is only one among a multitude of other institutions, such as churches and corporations, which a community establishes for securing different objects, though obviously it is one of tremendous importance; none the less it is not, except in the ideology of totalitarianism, an all-embracing institution, not something from which, or within which, all other institutions and associations have their being; many institutions, e.g. the Roman Catholic Church, and many associations, e.g. federations of employers and of workers, transcend the boundaries of any single state. Nor should a state be confused with a nation, although in modern times many states are organized on a national basis, and although also the terms are sometimes used interchangeably, as in the title 'United Nations', which is actually a league of states, and even in the term 'inter*national* law'; a single state, like the British Empire, may include many nations, or a single nation may be dispersed among many states, as the Poles were before 1919. Further, the term 'state' is relative, for there may be states within a state. . . . It is not, however, with all the institutions which in common parlance are called states that international law is concerned, but only with those whose governmental powers extend to the conduct of their external relations. Whether a state has such powers or not is a question of fact which must be answered by examining its system of government; the terminology which is used in the classification of composite states, or states which are 'composed of' other states, is an unsafe guide, both because different writers use the same

Definition

---

[1] In this connection, see prior U.S. digests of international law, particularly: I Moore, *International Law Digest* (1906), ch. II, pp. 12 ff.; I Hackworth, *Digest of International Law* (1940), ch. II, pp. 47 ff.

terms in different senses, and also because the possible variations of state organization and interstate relations, ranging as they do from mere alliance for temporary purposes to complete amalgamation or subordination, are so many that a permanently valid classification is impossible.   But it is usual today to distinguish a *federal state*, that is to say, a union of states in which the control of the external relations of all the member states has been permanently surrendered to a central government so that the only state which exists for international purposes is the state formed by the union, from a *confederation of states*, in which, though a central government exists and exercises certain powers, it does not control all the external relations of the member states, and therefore for international purposes there exists not one but a number of states.   Thus the United States since 1787, the German Republic from 1918 to 1933, and the Swiss Confederation since 1848, each form a single federal state, whereas the United States from 1778 to 1787, and the German Confederation from 1820 to 1866, were confederations of many states.   This distinction would be convenient if it were always observed, but unfortunately it is not; for example, the Swiss Republic is always styled a *confederation*.   But even so it would be difficult to classify all the states to which the classification is relevant definitely under one or other of the two heads; for example, the German Empire from 1870 to 1918 was in essence a federal state, but in form it retained some traces of a confederation of states, since Bavaria and some of the other member states were separately represented in foreign countries for certain limited and mainly honorary purposes.

"The states with whose relations international law is primarily concerned are those which are 'independent' in their external relations; it is also to some extent concerned with a few states which 'depend' on other states in the conduct of those relations in a greater or less degree. . . . The proper usage of the term 'independence' is to denote the status of a state which controls its own external relations without dictation from other states; it contrasts such a status with that of a state which either does not control its own external relations at all, and is therefore of no interest to international law, like the State of New York, or controls them only in part.   The exact significance of the term appears most clearly in such a phrase as 'declaration of independence', whereby one state throws off its control by, or its dependence on, another.

". . . 'independence' does not mean freedom from law, but merely freedom from control by other states.   Unfortunately, such a method of argument is very common; the associations of sovereignty have become attached in the popular mind to the notion of independence, and the word is often used as though it meant freedom from any restraint whatsoever, and appealed to as a justification for arbitrary and illegal conduct.   The temptation to mistake catchwords for arguments is strong in all political controversy; it is especially dangerous in the controversies of states."

Brierly, *The Law of Nations* (5th ed., 1955) 118–122.

The Convention on Rights and Duties of States signed at Montevideo in 1933 provides (article 1) :

"The state as a person of international law should possess the following qualifications: *a*) a permanent population; *b*) a defined territory; *c*) government; and *d*) capacity to enter into relations with the other states."

U.S. TS 881; IV Trenwith, Treaties, etc. (1938) 4807, 4808; 1933 For. Rel., vol. IV, p. 214.

In reply to a question of whether the Republic of Indonesia constituted a "state" in the international sense as of August 1947, the Office of the Legal Adviser stated in a memorandum:

"A state in the international sense is generally described as a recognized member of the family of nations, an international person. Authorities differ in respect to the qualifications for such statehood, but there is general agreement on certain basic requirements. As expressed by Hyde, the following qualifications are necessary: *Indonesia*

" 'First, there must be a people . . .
" 'Secondly, there must be a fixed territory which the inhabitants occupy . . .
" 'Thirdly, there must be an organized government exercizing control over, and endeavoring to maintain justice within, the territory.
" 'Fourthly, there must be a capacity to enter into relations with the outside world . . . . Independence is not essential . . . . The requisite personality, in the international sense, is seen when the entity claiming to be a State has in fact its own distinctive association with the members of the international society, as by treaties, which, howsoever concluded in its behalf, mark the existence of definite relationships between itself and other contracting parties . . .
" 'Fifthly, the inhabitants must have attained a degree of civilization, such as to enable them to observe . . . those principles of law which are deemed to govern the members of the international society in their relations with each other.'

"Some authorities disagree with the statement that independence is not required, holding any state not fully independent, to be an international person for some purposes only.
"The territory of the Republic of Indonesia for a number of years before the war was generally considered a colony of The Netherlands. Since the war, it has asserted its independence and has been negotiating with the Government of the Netherlands for recognition of independence.
"Negotiations resulted on November 15, 1946 in the initialling of a draft agreement by representatives of the Netherlands and

of the Republic of Indonesia. . . . This agreement [Linggadjati Agreement] offers the colonies a dominion-like status, as a federated entity, in which the Republic would be one of the states, other territories of the colonies to be constituted into at least two major states, and the entity to be known as the United States of Indonesia (USI). . . .

.   .   .   .

"In examining the Indonesian situation in the light of Professor Hyde's qualifications which, on the question of sovereignty, are more favorable to Indonesia than those of other authorities, we may conclude that the first, second and fifth qualifications are met. With reference to the third, the situation is questionable. The Netherlands, in the agreement, recognize the Government of the Republic of Indonesia as exercising *de facto* authority over Java, Madoera and Sumatra. It does not, however, recognize it as the legal authority for those areas, and does not admit that the authority of the Netherlands no longer exists. Indeed, if this were true, there would be no need for many provisions of the agreement. This situation is apparently accepted by the Republic.

"On the fourth qualification, it is believed Indonesia is even further from meeting the requirements. While it is true that certain Arab states have recognized the Republic diplomatically, this is by no means conclusive. Recognition of a state is not purely a legal act, but in part political. While recognition is a factor, it is not determinative and must be considered among other factors. Further, the recognition by a few small states is overshadowed by the failure of the major nations and the majority of the smaller nations to extend recognition. Looking at the agreement, it appears that even if all intended acts were accomplished, the Republic would not have 'its own distinctive association with the members of the international society.' The agreement contemplates it becoming one of three or more parts of the United States of Indonesia, a federated (rather than a confederated) entity. Significant also is the undertaking of the Netherlands (accepted by Indonesia) to promote the admission to the United Nations Organization of the United States of Indonesia, not the Republic of Indonesia. . . .

"It is the opinion of this Office, therefore, that the Republic of Indonesia is not a state in the sense of being an international person. This opinion does not preclude a later contrary decision in the event of substantial changes in the situation."

The Office of the Legal Adviser (Brown) to the Office of Southwest Pacific Affairs (Rusk), memorandum, "Opinion on International Character of the Republic of Indonesia", Aug. 15, 1947, MS. Department of State, file 856D.00/8–1547.

Israel

A Department of State memorandum on "Recognition of Successor States in Palestine", May 13, 1948, analyzing the legal status of Palestine just prior to the proclamation of any new state in that country, stated:

". . . A Class 'A' mandate for Palestine, under Article 22 of the Covenant of the League of Nations, was conferred on Great Britain by the Principal Allied and Associated Powers. The mandatory power was given general powers of administration over Palestine. The mandate could be altered by Great Britain with the consent of the Council of the League of Nations, or could be terminated by completion of the tutelage of Palestine by Great Britain and the grant of full independence to the people of Palestine as contemplated in Article 22 of the League Covenant.

"On April 2, 1947 Great Britain asked the General Assembly to consider the question of the future government of Palestine. This request could lead either to a recommendation by the Assembly to the mandatory on the manner in which Palestine's tutelage should be completed and full independence granted, or to an act of consent by the General Assembly to alteration of the mandate terms. It is possible to interpret the General Assembly's resolution of November 29, 1947 as constituting either of the two actions just mentioned. When Great Britain first asked the General Assembly to examine the Palestine problem, the request appears to have been made with a view to securing a General Assembly *recommendation*. Later, at the regular 1947 session of the Assembly, Great Britain announced that the mandate would be terminated and that Britain would not take the undivided responsibility for implementing any solution which was not agreed to by both Arabs and Jews, thus implying a changed British theory concerning the nature of the action sought from the General Assembly. On either theory, the mandatory power and Great Britain [the Assembly?] together were competent to make a legally effective political settlement for Palestine. By virtue of the Assembly's passage of the resolution and Great Britain's 'acceptance' of the plan, these authorities appear to have made a legal disposition for the future of Palestine.

"The Palestine plan contained in the General Assembly's resolution of November 29, 1947 provided for termination of the mandate, provisional arrangements for administration, and subsequent emergence of two independent states and an international territory (the City of Jerusalem); the partition of Palestine was to be accompanied by economic union. The working out of this Plan required the active functioning of the General Assembly's Palestine Commission. That body has now suspended its political operations, and the Plan cannot be carried forward without a resumption of activity by the Commission (including the designation of provisional councils of government).

"On May 15, 1948 the mandate for Palestine will end, pursuant to the provisions of the Plan; at that time Great Britain will withdraw its mandatory administration, even though other steps contemplated by the Plan are not being taken and even though Great Britain herself has failed to take some important measures called for by the General Assembly resolution of November 29,

1947. . . . According to the plan, the Palestine Commission was to be legally responsible for the administration of Palestine upon termination of the mandate, pending transfer of authority to the successor governmental agencies. If the Commission after May 14 is suspended, or is paralyzed and makes no effort to administer Palestine, the question must be asked whether any other authority can have legal capacity to carry on with the governing of Palestine.

"At this point we must consider the role of the remaining Principal Allied and Associated Powers. It was these Powers which allocated the Palestine mandate to Great Britain after World War I. Possibly they retained some residuary rights of disposition over Palestine after the mandate was granted. If such rights persisted, they might be asserted in the event that the mandate ended abruptly without provision for a future political settlement. Such might be the case if the General Assembly before May 15, 1948 repealed its resolution of November 29, 1947 and no other legally effective disposition of Palestine should be made by the Assembly and Great Britain. But in the absence of such repeal by the Assembly of its resolution, it seems particularly doubtful that the remaining Principal Allied and Associated Powers could assert any residuary rights.

"We are then faced with the situation where the only agencies claiming to have governing powers over Palestine are organizations within that country. The law of nations recognizes an inherent right of people lacking the agencies and institutions of social and political control to organize a state and operate a government.

"Article 22 of the League Covenant provided

" 'Certain communities formerly belonging to the Turkish Empire have reached a stage of development where their existence as independent nations can be provisionally recognized subject to the rendering of administrative advice and assistance by a Mandatory until such time as they are able to stand alone.'

Palestine was covered by this Article, later being made a Class 'A' mandate. Just what constituted the 'communities' referred to in Article 22 was not made clear. Quite evidently Palestine as a whole was not a *community*, as is shown by the fact that the mandatory in 1946 detached the Trans-Jordan from Palestine and gave it independence. The Palestine mandate instrument referred specifically to 'communities' and in a manner so as to make clear that the principal religious communities of Palestine—Jewish and Arab—were intended by the reference.

"There is, of course, in the background of the mandate and of the League Covenant, the Balfour Declaration of November 2, 1917 by the British Government, declaring in favor of the establishment in Palestine of a national home for the Jewish people. When the Council of the League of Nations gave its approval to the Palestine mandate so that the instrument could become effective, the Council in its approving resolution cited the agreement of the Principal Allied Powers that Great Britain 'should be responsible for putting into effect the declaration originally made on November 2, 1917, by the Government of His Britannic Majesty, and adopted by the said Powers . . .' It is therefore apparent that the disposition of Palestine by the competent Powers after World War I included a provision, having the nature of a trust, in favor of a Jewish national home in Palestine. This was to be, however, without prejudice to the civil and religious rights of existing communities in Palestine. One of the ways in which this trust might be carried out would be through the establishment of a Jewish state in Palestine.

"The existence of this trust together with the inherent right recognized in international law afford a legal basis for the formation of a state and government by the Jewish community in the areas of Palestine which that community occupies. Such action would also have the moral sanction of the partially implemented disposition of Palestine made by the mandatory and the United Nations General Assembly in the Partition Plan. Similarly, the Arab Community would be entitled to organize a State and government in the areas of Palestine which it occupies.

"It should be noted that the proclamation of a state and government by either community during the current special session of the General Assembly would be contrary to the provisions of paragraph 1(d) of the Security Council truce resolution of April 17, 1948. This resolution does not bind legally either community nor would it bind the states and governments proclaimed, since none of these are or would then be members of the United Nations.

.   .   .   .

"One may conclude, therefore: (1) the United States probably should not recognize the existence of any new state in Palestine during the special session, unless the Security Council should repeal its April 17 resolution; (2) the United States, after the special session, will be legally free to recognize the existence of Jewish and Arab states in the areas of Palestine occupied by them, respectively; (3) the United States should not recognize the existence of either an Arab or Jewish unitary state for all of Palestine in the absence of consent by the communities, since to do so would contravene obligations and rights arising out of the provisions of the League Covenant, the mandate instrument, the General Assembly resolution of November 29, 1947, and the principles of the law of nations regarding self-determination of peoples."

The Legal Adviser (Gross) to the Under Secretary of State (Lovett), memorandum, "Recognition of Successor States in Palestine", May 13, 1948, MS. Department of State, file FW 867N.01/5–1048.

In providing for the termination of British jurisdiction in Palestine, the Palestine Act, 1948, stated:

"1. (1.) On the fifteenth day of May, nineteen hundred and forty-eight, or such earlier date as His Majesty may by Order in

Council declare to be the date on which the mandate in respect
of Palestine accepted by His Majesty on behalf of the League of
Nations will be relinquished . . . , all jurisdiction of His Majesty
in Palestine shall determine, and His Majesty's Government in
the United Kingdom shall cease to be responsible for the government of Palestine."

11 & 12 Geo. 6, c. 27. See in this connection: The Palestine (Revocations)
Order in Council, 1948 (Stat. Instr., 1948, No. 1004). See also Palestine,
Termination of the Mandate, 15th May 1948, a statement prepared for pub-
lic information by the Colonial Office and Foreign Office (published by His
Majesty's Stationery Office), pp. 1–11.

Secretary of State for the Colonies, Mr. Creech Jones, stated in the House
of Commons on March 10, 1948, that—

> "There are protests that the Bill fails to make provision for the
> independence of Jewish and Arab States in Palestine as provided by
> the United Nations decision. I should point out that the future form
> of government to be established in Palestine is not a matter for His
> Majesty's Government but for the United Nations Assembly. On
> termination of our exercise of an international Mandate it was proper
> that the international authority should determine the new form of
> government which Palestine should enjoy. The Resolution of the
> Assembly provides that independent Arab and Jewish States shall be
> established by the United Nations Commission. There is nothing in
> this Bill which will prevent that. Indeed an act of the United Kingdom
> could not establish these independent States. Their recognition is a
> matter for international agreement, and cannot be done in a Bill
> designed to terminate the jurisdiction of His Majesty in Palestine."
> 448 H.C. Deb. (5th ser.) col. 1250 (Mar. 10, 1948).
>
> "It is also protested that the Bill makes no provision for the
> orderly transfer of His Majesty's jurisdiction to the United Nations
> Commission. It is assumed that acts for the orderly transfer of
> jurisdiction should be written into an Act of Parliament. What the
> Bill does is to leave the legal position straight, that is, to leave
> Palestine law in a form for the successor Government authority to take
> over. Moreover, the High Commissioner in Palestine has, by Order
> in Council, been given power to make such legal provision as will be
> appropriate in preparation for the withdrawal of His Majesty's
> Government, thus leaving a body of law in a suitable state for the
> Commission to administer.
>
> "With the concurrence of the Commission, these powers are being
> exercised, for example, to transfer to municipal authorities certain
> administrative functions now exercised by the central Government. I
> repeat that the Bill makes the way clear for the establishment of the
> successor authority in Palestine and for the United Nations to take
> up its task. It places no impediment in the way of the United Nations
> Commission assuming the tasks required of it by the Assembly's
> Resolution. It terminates His Majesty's jurisdiction and everything
> that can be done by legislation is done to leave the house in order
> for the incoming tenant." 448 H.C. Deb. (5th ser.) cols. 1250–1251
> (Mar. 10, 1948). See also 154 H.L. Deb. (5th ser.) col. 1199 (Apr. 7,
> 1948).

In answer to a question raised in the House of Commons as to the
international status of Palestine after the British withdrawal on May
14, 1948, the Attorney General, Sir Hartley Shawcross, explained:

"... Palestine clearly will not be an independent sovereign
State and for some time, at least, it will not have an independent
government, assuming, as we must assume, that it has a govern-

ment at all. If the United Nations is able, as we all hope it will, to exercise effective control, then Palestine will become an area entitled to legal recognition in international law as a legal entity under the control of the United Nations and held in trust with a view to its development, according to the wishes of the United Nations.

"If, most unfortunately, the United Nations Commission does not succeed in its task and if then the Jews and the Arabs, faced as they would then be, by the dread alternative, do not find some accommodation between themselves and do something which no Act of this Parliament can ever do, establish for themselves their own form of government and make their own arrangements in Palestine, the position in that unhappy country will be that it would no longer have any *de jure* government or be entitled to recognition in international law. Until things had developed and had settled down, and some new organisation had gained power, the ultimate legal status of Palestine in international law would have to be suspended and wait upon the development of circumstances and facts. . . ."

448 H.C. Deb. (5th ser.) cols. 1320–1321 (Mar. 10, 1948).

The Jewish National Council, announcing the new Jewish State of Israel, issued a proclamation May 14, 1948, 8 hours before the British mandate officially terminated, which stated:

". . . WE, the members of the National Council, representing the Jewish people in Palestine and the World Zionist Movement, are met together in solemn assembly today, the day of termination of the British Mandate for Palestine; and by virtue of the natural and historic right of the Jewish people and of the Resolution of the General Assembly of the United Nations.

"WE HEREBY PROCLAIM the establishment of the Jewish State in Palestine, to be called Medinath Yisrael (The State of Israel).

"WE HEREBY DECLARE that, as from the termination of the Mandate at midnight, the 14th–15th May, 1948, and pending the setting up of the duly elected bodies of the State in accordance with a Constitution, to be drawn up by the Constituent Assembly not later than the 1st October, 1948, the National Council shall act as the Provisional Government of the Jewish State, which shall be known as Israel."

State of Israel Government Yearbook 5711 (1950) 43–45.

In a letter to President Truman of May 14, 1948, Eliahu Epstein, Agent of the Provisional Government of Israel, wrote:

"I have the honor to notify you that the state of Israel has been proclaimed as an independent republic within frontiers approved by the General Assembly of the United Nations in its Resolution of November 29, 1947, and that a provisional government has been charged to assume the rights and duties of government for preserving law and order within the boundaries of Israel, for defending the state against external aggression, and for discharging the obligations of Israel to the other nations of the world in accordance with international law. The Act of Independence will become effective at one minute after six o'clock on the evening of 14 May 1948, Washington time."

In response to the Provisional Government of Israel's request for recognition, President Truman, in a statement released May 14, 1948, declared:

"The United States recognizes the provisional government as the de facto authority of the new State of Israel."

XVIII *Bulletin,* Department of State, No. 464, May 23, 1948, p. 673.

Philip Jessup, Deputy United States Representative in the Security Council, speaking before the Security Council December 2, 1948, in connection with Israel's application for membership in the United Nations, outlined the legal basis for supporting Israel's claim to the status of a "state" in international law. He argued:

"State" within meaning art. 4, U.N. Charter

"The Charter of the United Nations in article 4 specifies that membership in the United Nations is open to . . . 'peace-loving states which accept the obligations contained in the present Charter and, in the judgment of the Organization, are able and willing to carry out these obligations'. This formulation comprises the requirements laid down by the Charter for admission of new members to the United Nations. Reduced to their essence these requirements are as follows: The political entity in question must be a state; it must be a 'peace-loving' state; it must accept the obligations contained in the Charter; and it must be able and willing, in the judgment of the United Nations, to carry out these obligations. My Government considers that the state of Israel meets these Charter requirements.

"The first question which may be raised in analyzing this fourth article of the Charter and its application to the membership of the state of Israel is the question whether Israel is a 'state', as that term is used in article 4 of the Charter. It is common knowledge . . . that while there are traditional definitions of a state in international law, the term has been used in many different ways. We are all aware that under the traditional definition of a state in international law all of the great writers have pointed to four qualifications:

"First: There must be a people.
"Second: There must be a territory.
"Third: There must be a government.
"Fourth: There must be capacity to enter into relations with other states of the world.

"So far as the question of capacity to enter into relations with other states of the world is concerned, learned academic arguments can be and have been made to the effect that we already have among the Members of the United Nations some political entities which do not possess full sovereign freedom to form their own international policy which traditionally has been considered characteristic of a state. We know, however, that neither at San Francisco nor subsequently has the United Nations considered that complete freedom to frame and manage one's own foreign policy was an essential requisite of United Nations' membership. . . . in this respect I believe that there would be unanimity that Israel exercises complete independence of judgment and of will in forming and in executing its foreign policy. The reason I mention the qualifications of this aspect of the traditional definition of a state is to underline the point that the term 'state' as used and applied in article 4 of the Charter of the United Nations may not be wholly identical with the term 'state' as it is used and defined in classic textbooks of international law. When we look at the other classic attributes of a state we find insistence that it must also have a government. No one doubts that Israel has a government. . . . Although, pending their scheduled elections, they still modestly and appropriately call themselves the 'Government of Israel', they have a legislative body which makes laws; they have a judiciary which interprets and applies these laws; and they have an executive which carries out the laws and which has at its disposal a considerable force which is responsive to its will.

"According to the same classical definition, we are told that a state must have a people and a territory. Nobody questions the fact that the state of Israel has a people. It is an extremely homogeneous people: a people full of loyalty and of enthusiastic devotion to the state of Israel.

"The argument seems chiefly to arise in connection with territory. One does not find in the general classic treatment of this subject any insistence that the territory of a state must be exactly fixed by definite frontiers. We all know that historically many states have begun their existence with their frontiers unsettled. Let me take as one example my own country—the United States. . . .

"Although the formulas in the classic treatises vary somewhat one from the other, both reason and history demonstrate that the concept of territory does not necessarily include precise delimitation of the boundaries of that territory. The reason for the rule that one of the necessary attributes of a state is that it shall possess territory, is that one can not contemplate a state as a kind of disembodied spirit. Historically the concept is one of insisting that there must be some portion of the earth's surface which its people inhabit and over which its government exercises authority. No one can deny that the state of Israel responds to this requirement."

"Discussion of Israeli Application for Membership", Security Council, Paris, Dec. 2, 1948, XIX *Bulletin*, Department of State, No. 493, Dec. 12, 1948, pp. 723–724.

State
distinct from
government

"The government of a state must not be identified with the state itself, but between states intercourse is only possible if each has a government with which the others may enter into relations and whose acts they may regard as binding on the state itself. What form of government a state should adopt, and whether it should replace an existing government by a new one, are domestic matters with which other states are not concerned. But they are concerned to know whether the person or persons with whom they propose to enter into relations are in fact a government whose acts will be binding at international law upon the state which they profess to represent.

"The law regarding this question has been clearly stated in an award of Chief Justice Taft in an arbitration between Great Britain and Costa Rica in 1923. [Reported in A.J.I.L., 1924, p. 147.] Great Britain claimed that certain British companies had acquired certain rights against Costa Rica by contracts entered into with one Tinoco. It appeared that in 1917 Tinoco over- threw the existing government of Costa Rica and established a new constitution which lasted till 1919, when the old constitution was restored; and that in 1922 the restored government passed legislation nullifying all engagements entered into by Tinoco's government. The Chief Justice held that if Tinoco's government was the actual government of Costa Rica at the time when the rights were alleged to have been acquired, the restored govern- ment could not repudiate the obligations which his acts had im- posed on the state of Costa Rica. He further said that this question must be decided by evidence of the facts. It was im- material that by the law of Costa Rica Tinoco's government was unconstitutional. Even the objection put forward by Costa Rica that many states, including Great Britain herself, had never recognized Tinoco's government, was only relevant as suggesting, though it did not prove, that that government had not been the actual government of Costa Rica; but since Tinoco 'was in actual and peaceable control without resistance or conflict or contest by any one until a few months before the time when he retired', he held that his acts were binding upon Costa Rica. On the further question of the merits of the companies' claims, his decision on the whole favoured that state.

"This decision therefore shows that a state is bound interna- tionally by the acts of the person or persons who in actual fact constitute its government. This is sometimes expressed by saying that a new government 'succeeds' to the rights and obli- gations of its predecessor, but the expression is a loose one, be- cause international rights and obligations belong to states and not to governments, and a new government 'succeeds' to them only in the sense that it becomes the government of a state to which they are attached. It follows, therefore, that the identity of a state is not affected by changes in the form or the persons of its government, or even by a temporary anarchy, as in China or Mexico in recent years. But constitutional changes may make it difficult for other states to know who, if any one, is in a position to bind the state, and may thus give rise to the problem of deciding whether or not they will recognize a new government. The recognition of a new government is not to be confused with the recognition of a new state, but it raises problems in some respects similar. In both cases a premature recognition is an intervention in the domestic affairs of another state, and in both the question which other states have to decide is one of fact."

Brierly, *The Law of Nations* (5th ed., 1955) 136–138.

Sovereignty

§ 15

Source

"In general there are two prevailing concepts regarding the source of sovereign power: (1) that sovereign power originates in the people themselves who erect their governmental institutions, and (2) that sovereignty is vested in a monarch or other supreme person, and stems downward as a grant to the people.

"Sovereign People

"The language of the constitutions on this point shows a substantial preponderance of opinion favoring the concept that sovereignty rests in the people. In sixty-six nations, constituting about 71 percent of the total number of nations and comprehending about 80 percent of the world's total population, this concept appears in existing constitutional provisions. [See Table III for references to Articles in individual constitutions. III Peaslee, *Constitutions of Nations* (2nd ed. 1956) pp. 805–807.] These nations include Albania, Andorra, Argentina, Austria, Belgium, (notwithstanding the fact that the constitution provides for an hereditary King), Bolivia, Brazil, Bulgaria, Burma, Byelorussian SSR (the 'whole body of citizens'), Chile (the 'nation'), China (the 'whole body of citizens'), Colombia (the 'nation'), Costa Rica (the 'nation'), Cuba, Czechoslovakia, Dominican Republic, Ecuador, Egypt, El Salvador, Finland, France, Germany, Greece (the 'nation'), Guatemala, Haiti (the 'whole body of citizens'), Honduras, Hungary, Iceland, India, Indonesia, Iran (conferred on the monarch by the people), Iraq (as a trust confided to the King by the people), Ireland, Italy, Japan (although an empire), Jordan, Korea, Laos, Lebanon, Liberia, Libya (the 'nation'), Luxembourg (the 'nation'), Mexico, the Mongolian People's Republic ('urban and rural workers'), Nicaragua, Panama, Paraguay, Peru, Philippines, Poland, Portugal, (the 'nation'), Rumania, San Marino, Spain, Switzerland, Syria, Thailand, Turkey (the 'nation'), Ukrainian SSR ('workers in cities and villages'), Union of Soviet Socialist Republics ('working people of town and country'), United States of America, Uruguay (the 'nation'), Venezuela, Viet Nam and Yugoslavia.

"In still others the concept of sovereign power is that it rests more or less jointly in a sovereign and the people. Included in this group of nations are Afghanistan, Australia, Canada, Ceylon,

Denmark, Netherlands, New Zealand, Norway Pakistan, Sweden and the United Kingdom. If these nations are added to the 66, the list becomes 77 nations; the percentage of nations becomes 85 percent; and the percentage of the world's total population who consider the people to be a source of sovereign power becomes over 95 percent.

"*Sovereign Monarchs*

"The constitutions of most of the nations which recognize a monarchical head of their government declare or imply that the source of sovereign power lies in the monarch, or in the monarch and the people. This is the situation in Afghanistan, Australia, Bhutan, Cambodia, Canada, Ceylon, Denmark, Ethiopia, Liechtenstein, Monaco, Muscat and Oman, Nepal, Netherlands, New Zealand, Norway, Saudi Arabia, Sweden, Union of South Africa, United Kingdom, Vatican City and Yemen.

"In Australia, Canada, Ceylon, Denmark, New Zealand, the Netherlands, Norway, Pakistan, Sweden, the Union of South Africa and the United Kingdom, there are strong concepts that sovereign power rests in the people. However there are frequently official references to the Crown as the source of sovereign power. Historically the grants of civil and constitutional rights in those countries have stemmed from the monarch or parliament to the people. The inhabitants of the United Kingdom are currently described as 'British subjects.' In most of the members of the Commonwealth of Nations a Governor General sits as the symbol of the Crown and the link of the Commonwealth. Hence although most power is in fact exercised by the people in those nations, sovereign power is treated from the constitutional standpoint as having originated in a monarch, and not in the people."

I Peaslee, *Constitutions of Nations* (2d ed., 1956) 5–7.

As a concept

"Sovereignty as a principle of international law must be sharply distinguished from other related uses of the term: sovereignty in its internal aspects and political sovereignty. Sovereignty in its internal aspects is concerned with the identity of the bearer of supreme authority within a State. This may be an individual or a collective unit. In the United Kingdom, for instance, such sovereignty rests with the Queen in Parliament. At least in law, internal sovereignty may be completely eliminated by a system of intricate balances between different organs as, for instance, in a federal State such as the United States of America.

"Even in this type of State, sovereignty in the political sense remains a potent reality, for, at any time, the people can overthrow the legal system which has endeavoured to dispense with the concept of sovereignty. In international relations, the scope of political sovereignty is still less limited. Political sovereignty is the necessary concomitant of the lack of an effective international order and the constitutional weaknesses of the international superstructures which have so far been grafted on the law of

unorganised international society. Thus, the pleasant illusion
that interdependence has increasingly replaced independence in
inter-State relations is at the most a half-truth. It is more true
for some than for others. Moreover, what is to some extent true
within each of the two halves of a divided world is hardly a
correct assessment of the relations between the two halves of
world society.

"For this reason alone, doctrinal attempts at spiriting away
sovereignty must remain meaningless. Actually, such efforts appear to minimise unduly the fundamental character of the principle of legal sovereignty within the realm of international law.
The rules underlying this principle derive their importance from
the basic fact that 'almost all international relations are bound
up' with the independence of States. Thus, the principle of
sovereignty in general, and that of territorial sovereignty in
particular, remains of necessity the 'point of departure in settling
most questions that concern international relations.' [*Island of
Palmas* case (1928), 2 R.I.A.A., pp. 829, 839.] Beyond this, as
the World Court re-emphasised in the *Corfu Channel* (*Merits*)
case (1949), 'between independent States, respect for territorial
sovereignty is an essential foundation of international relations.'
[1949 I.C.J. Reports, p. 35.]"

I Schwarzenberger, *International Law* (3d ed., 1957) 114–115.

On growth of the concept of sovereignty, see George W. Keeton, "National
Sovereignty and the Growth of International Law", 50 Jurid. Rev. (Edinburgh, 1938) 380 ff.

"The dogma of sovereignty has repeatedly been attacked by a
great number of international lawyers during the past two or
three decades. [*See e.g.*, Kelsen, *Das Problem der Souveränität
und die Theorie des Völkerrechts* (1920); Lansing, *Notes on
World Sovereignty* (1921) 15 Am. J. Int. L. 13; Verdross, *Die
Einheit des rechtlichen Weltbildes* (1923); Politis, *Le problème
des limitations de la souveraineté* (1925) 6 *Recueil des Cours*
(Hague Academy of Int. Law) 5; Garner, *Limitations on National Sovereignty in International Relations* (1925) 19 Am. Pol.
Sci. Rev. 1; Brierly, *The Law of Nations* (2d ed. 1936) 34 *ff.*;
Keeton & Schwarzenberger, *Making International Law Work*
(1939) c. 4; Eagleton, *Organization of the Community of Nations*
(1942) 36 Am. J. Int. L. 229, 234.] Many students of the problem have proposed to consider sovereignty not as an *absolute* concept, but rather as a *relative* one. [The relative character of
sovereignty has been emphasized, moreover, in Garner, *Recent
Developments in International Law* (1925) 812. "The task of reconstructing and increasing the effectiveness of international law
raises the question of how far certain of its existing fundamental
bases need to be altered. It is now generally admitted that certain changes of this character are desirable. . . . *The theories of
absolute sovereignty* and equality of states which have heretofore
been recognized as basic principles *should be definitely eliminated*
so that law will conform more nearly to the facts." (Italics sup-

plied). *See also* Eagleton, *International Government* (1932) 29.
"Sovereignty is not a unit, which a state either has or does not
have; it is a relative term." *Cf.* 1 Oppenheim, *International Law*
(5th ed. by Lauterpacht, 1935) 117. *"The very notion of International Law* as a body of rules of conduct binding upon States
irrespective of their Municipal Law and legislation implies the
idea of their subjection to International Law and *makes it impossible to accept their claim to absolute sovereignty in the international sphere."* (Italics supplied). On absolute sovereignty,
see Sukiennicki, *La Souveraineté des Etats en Droit International
Moderne* (1927) 59. See *also*, Shotwell, *The Great Decision*
(1944) 202. "Absolute, unqualified and unchecked sovereignty is
a conception of anarchy."]"

Hans Aufricht, "On Relative Sovereignty", XXX Cornell L. Q. (1944)
137. At a later point, the same author points out that "The doctrine of
'relative' sovereignty can also be contrasted with a doctrine of 'absolute'
sovereignty which explicitly denies the validity of international law and
which, by implication, denies the coexistence of states." *Ibid.* 145.

Extreme views with respect to sovereignty are brought together by
Wagner, as follows:

"The concept of sovereignty, undermined by the monistic school
of international law with H. Kelsen at its head, is completely
discarded by modern legal scholars such as Prof. G. Scelle, *Traité
élémentaire de droit international public* (1944), P. C. Jessup,
A Modern Law of Nations (1949), M. Korowicz, *La souveraineté
des états et l'avenir du droit international* (1945), and many
others. See also the chapter on the *Eclipse of Sovereignty* in
L. Duguit, *Law in the Modern State* (1919), and the interesting
discussion at the 47th Annual Meeting of the American Society of
International Law; report by E. H. Finch in 47 Am. J. Int'l L.
467, 468–469 (1953). *Cf.* W. J. Wagner, *Les Libertés de l'Air*, 160
ff. (1948). For a criticism of the idea of sovereignty by a modern
political philosopher, see J. Maritain, *Man and the State*, 29–30,
40–41, 53 (1951); by an outstanding diplomat, see G. Kennan,
Speech reported in *Diplomacy and Logic*, 3 The Federalist News-
letter 2 (Jan. 1956): 'Actually, I think, no one could be more
sadly conscious than is the professional diplomatist of the primi-
tiveness, the anarchism, the intrinsic absurdity of the modern
concept of sovereignty.' "

Wagner, *The Federal States and Their Judiciary* (1959) 21 n. 4.

"Static co-existence of sovereign entities in a state of splendid
isolation would be incompatible with the dynamic character of
international society. In fact, international law assists in a
number of ways in making possible limitations of sovereignty.
Rules of international customary law, general principles of law
recognised by civilised nations and, above all, treaties impose
far-reaching limitations on the sovereignty of States. In a sys-

tem of interrelated legal principles, sovereignty is necessarily a relative concept."

I Schwarzenberger, *International Law* (3d ed., 1957) 121.

". . . It [sovereignty] stands for the power of modern States, the power of their governments to decide and to act without consulting others and without concern for anything but their own interests as they themselves conceive those interests. . . ."

Brierly, "The Sovereign State Today", 61 Jurid. Rev. (1949) 3, 5.

"At the present time [August 1956] we have the Suez incident, which presents the opportunity for the use and abuse of the word sovereignty, a word familiar to international lawyers as representing a conception which, if absolute, would involve the negation of international law. When sovereignty is not limited by treaty, it is well recognised by lawyers that it is at least limited by the maxim *sic utere tuo ut alienum non laedas.*"

Lord Justice Hudson, President of the International Law Association, Aug. 27, 1956, International Law Association, *Report of the Forty-Seventh Conference, 1956* (1957) 1, 3.

Later on the same day, during a discussion of "Co-existence", Dr. Vladimir Dedijer of Yugoslavia stated:

"9. The second objection to the impossibility of international law is deduced from the principle of State sovereignty.
"Sovereignty is conceived as a legal freedom, but legal freedom in society can only exist within the limits which condition the latter, and these lie in equal freedoms for all members of society. There is no freedom without equality in rights." *Ibid.* 50.

"The totalitarian state constitutes the extreme development of the ideas of political sovereignty and of cultural nationalism. It is an evolution of the theory of territorial sovereignty toward the complete exclusion of the historic, religious, economic, cultural, and humanitarian inhibitions which had, in practice and in law, held sovereignty in check."

Wright, "International Law and the Totalitarian States", 35 Am. Pol. Sci. Rev. (1941) 738, 739.

"1. *State Sovereignty.* At different stages of the development of class society the concept of sovereignty had different class meanings. The concept of sovereignty, which arose at the time of feudalism, during the struggle of the royal power (particularly the French kings) against the feudal lords, the Papacy, and the Holy Roman Empire, was the expression of the unlimited supremacy of the absolute monarch, the sovereign. At the time of the struggle of the bourgeoisie against absolutism and serfdom, the ideologists of the bourgeoisie put forth the theory of 'popular sovereignty,' as the expression of the supremacy and independence of the 'people,' identifying the class interests of the bourgeoisie with the interests of the people.

"The sovereignty of the contemporary bourgeois state is the expression of the rule of the bourgeois class within it. This sovereignty governs both the domestic and foreign policy of the state. Included in state sovereignty as it is understood at the present time is the supremacy of the state, the totality of supreme rights belonging to the state and embodied in its supreme organs within the state and abroad.

"International law stresses not only the complete autonomy of the sovereign state in its internal affairs, since this law denies interference in the internal affairs of the state, but also a second quality of sovereignty, the independence of the sovereign state. A state which is deprived of the possibility of independent entry into the international arena is not a sovereign state, even though it might preserve a certain autonomy in its internal affairs. From the standpoint of the theory of international law, sovereignty means the independence and autonomy of the state in domestic and foreign relations.

"The theory of the sovereignty of every state was the official class theory of the bourgeoisie until recent times. However, in the period after the imperialist war of 1914–1918, the bourgeois literature on international law brought forth a number of writers who limited and denied the meaning of sovereignty, referring to the 'interdependence' of states . . . .

"2. *The International Legal Capacity and Competence of Sovereign States.* Expressing the will of the ruling class, the state appears abroad, in its international legal relations with other states as a juridical person representing all its citizens. As such, the state enjoys legal capacity and competence. The international legal capacity of the state is the capacity to have rights and duties established by international law. International law especially stresses the importance of the so-called 'fundamental rights' of the state, including among these rights political independence, autonomy, territorial inviolability, equality, and the protection of the honor of the state. . . . The international legal competence of the state finds its expression in the process of the realization by the state of the rights belonging to it and the duties incumbent upon it, particularly in the competence of the state: 1) to carry on diplomatic relations, 2) to conclude treaties, 3) to wage war and make peace, and 4) to bear responsibility under international law in case of a violation of international law by the state.

"3. *Sovereignty in the Stage of Imperialism.* In spite of the proclamation of the equality of states, the international reality of the stage of imperialism is gradually producing facts contradicting this.

"The sovereignty of the bourgeois state can in reality only be a paper sovereignty which conceals a very important dependence of any given state. In his work entitled 'Imperialism, The Highest State of Capitalism,' V. I. Lenin repeatedly stresses the existence in contemporary international reality of various forms of dependent countries, formally independent from a political point of view, but in fact entangled in the snares of financial and diplomatic dependence. That is why it is necessary, in studying sovereign states as subjects of international law, to consider the real importance of each of these states in international life."

Contribution by Professor Krylov, contained in sec. 15, "The Sovereign State—Entity with Full Powers in International Law", published in *International Law* (1947) 112–114 (translation).

"In international relations the sovereignty of a state is one and indivisible. The concept of 'two existing German states' representing the indivisible sovereignty of the German people is unacceptable, both in legal and in political theory, and would be wholly unworkable in practice. Who, it may be asked, will represent a sovereign 'Germany' or 'the German people' in other capitals or in the United Nations? To whom will the other signatories of the treaty look for fulfillment of the obligations of 'Germany' under the Soviet proposal?"

Secretary of State Herter, statement, May 18, 1959, Foreign Ministers Conference, Geneva, XL *Bulletin*, Department of State, No. 1041, June 8, 1959, pp. 819, 820–821.

By article 5 of the Charter of the Organization of American States (signed at Bogotá in 1948)

"The American States reaffirm the following principles:

.   .   .   .

"*b*) International order consists essentially of respect for the personality, sovereignty and independence of States . . . ."

Art. 5, U.S. TIAS 2361; 2 UST 2394, 2418.

In the *Monetary Gold Case*, Italy submitted a claim in conformity with a collective offer in a three-power statement, asking the International Court of Justice to declare that the gold that might be due Albania be delivered to Italy, and that Italy's right be given priority over that of the United Kingdom. Acknowledging that Italy and the three powers, France, the United Kingdom, and the United States by separate and successive acts had accepted the Court's jurisdiction and conferred jurisdiction on the Court under article 36(1), the Court concluded that it could not "decide such a dispute without the consent of Albania." It added: "To adjudicate upon the international responsibility of Albania without her consent would run counter to a well-established principle of international law embodied in the Court's Statute, namely, that the Court can only exercise jurisdiction over a State with its consent."

The Case of the Monetary Gold Removed from Rome in 1943 (Preliminary Question) (Italy *v.* France, United Kingdom of Great Britain and Northern Ireland, the United States of America), Judgment, June 15, 1954, I.C.J. Reports (1954) 19, 32.

"If the freedom of the seas and related matters are of central concern in the Suez crisis to nations using the canal, the matter of sovereignty, with all that it implies, is of central concern to all the nations of the areas of Asia and Africa which share a common pride in independence and have deeply held aspirations for economic and social development to match their political freedom. We in America cannot properly question this pride and these aspirations, for their situation of today was ours only a few generations ago, when we won our own freedom to join the circle of independent states.

"One of the most delicate points in achieving even the present limited resolution of the Middle East crisis was to respect Egypt's sovereignty while at the same time satisfying the desire of other nations for the protection of their rights and for freedom of the seas. One of the questions involved in further development of the capacity of the United Nations to deal with international disputes is that of insuring that its function can be effectively carried out while at the same time the sovereignty of individual nations is respected.

"The events of recent troubled times illustrate again that sovereignty, like citizenship, involves obligations as well as rights. Freedom has been defined as the opportunity for self-discipline, and experience shows that this applies to the freedom of nations as well as to that of men. A rule of law cannot exist except among those who will respect it."

Under Secretary of State Herter, "The Rule of Law Among Nations", address before the American Bar Association, New York, N.Y., July 15, 1957, XXXVII *Bulletin*, Department of State, No. 945, Aug. 5, 1957, pp. 223, 227.

"But nothing that I have said is to be construed as indicating that I regard the status quo as sacrosanct. Change is indeed the law of life and of progress. But when change reflects the will of the people, then change can and should be brought about in peaceful ways.

"In this context the United States respects the right of every Arab nation of the Near East to live in freedom without domination from any source, far or near.

"In the same context, we believe that the charter of the United Nations places on all of us certain solemn obligations. Without respect for each other's sovereignty and the exercise of great care in the means by which new patterns of international life are achieved, the projection of the peaceful vision of the charter would become a mockery."

President Eisenhower, address before the third emergency special session of the U.N. General Assembly, Aug. 13, 1958, "Program for the Near East", XXXIX *Bulletin*, Department of State, No. 1001, Sept. 1, 1958, pp. 337, 338.

In the course of the same address, President Eisenhower stated:

"I doubt that a single free government in all the world would willingly forgo the right to ask for help if its sovereignty were imperiled." *Ibid.*

In determining whether Okinawa, during the occupation of Japan, *De facto* was a "foreign country" within the meaning of the Federal Tort *and de jure* Claims Act, the United States Court of Appeals for the 9th Circuit *sovereignty* in *Cobb* v. *United States* distinguished between *de facto* and *de jure* sovereignty, stating:

> "By evicting the Japanese and affirmatively withdrawing Okinawa from the sovereignty of Japan, the belligerent occupants acquired the exclusive power to control and govern the island. This power, although perhaps acquired in the name of the Allied Powers, is lodged exclusively in the United States. The United States Military Government now governs, and will continue indefinitely to govern, the island of Okinawa, free from interference by other powers. The will of the United States is in fact the 'supreme will' on Okinawa. The United States has therefore acquired, and still retains, what may be termed a 'de facto sovereignty.'
>
> "However, the traditional 'de jure sovereignty' has not passed to the United States. The conqueror does not acquire the full rights of sovereignty merely by occupying and governing the conquered territory without a formal act of annexation or at least an expression of intention to retain the conquered territory permanently. It does not necessarily follow, therefore, that Okinawa is not a 'foreign country' within the meaning of the Tort Claims Act. So long as the ultimate disposition of that island remains uncertain, it offers a persuasive illustration of the observation that 'the very concept of "sovereignty" is in a state of more or less solution these days.' "

191 F. 2d 604, 608 (9th Cir. 1951).

"The right of a state to function within a certain territory, un- *Definition—* impeded by any interference from the outside, is called territorial *territorial* sovereignty. In the award, the *Island of Palmas (or Miangas)*, *sovereignty* the arbitrator, Dr. Max Huber, construed the nature of territorial sovereignty as follows:

> " 'The development of the national organization of states during the last few centuries, and, as a corollary, the development of international law, have established this principle of the exclusive competence of the state in regard to its own territory in such a way as to make it the point of departure in settling most questions that concern international relations. The special cases of the composite state, of collective sovereignty, etc., do not fall to be considered here [*sic*], and do not, for that matter throw any doubt upon the principle which has just been enunciated. . . .
> " 'Territorial sovereignty is, in general, a situation recognized and delimited in space. . . .
> " 'Sovereignty in the relation between states signifies independence, independence in regard to a portion of the globe is the right to exercise therein, to the exclusion of any other

state, the functions of a state . . . .' [22 Am. J. Int. L. (1928) 868, 875.]

.   .   .   .

"The exclusive territorial jurisdiction of a state is, or may be, restricted with respect to certain matters. Such limitations of territorial sovereignty are usually based upon customary international or treaty law."

Hans Aufricht, "On Relative Sovereignty", XXX Cornell L.Q. (1944) 137, 149, 150.

"Imperialists, nationalists, and internationalists, though all professing allegiance to international law which assumes the sovereignty of territorial states, have tended to interpret that system somewhat differently. Imperialists have sought to interpret territorial sovereignty in an absolute sense. The government of the state is said to have an unlimited freedom, so far as international law is concerned, to deal with subject peoples and nationalities within its territory. It may profess certain moral principles, as did Queen Isabella in respect to the Indians, and it may even extend certain constitutional and legal rights to them, but these are matters of domestic law, outside the realm of international discussion or protest. In principle, each sovereign government should not only refrain from interference in the domestic affairs of others, but should co-operate with others to suppress revolts, as did the Holy Allies of the post-Napoleonic period.

"Nationalists have accepted the sovereignty of the territorial state in law, but have asserted a moral and political right of subject nations to secede, a moral duty of third states not to interfere, and a legal freedom of such states to recognize rebelling nations once they have been established *de facto*. The political right of revolution, the legal right of recognition, and the policy of recognizing *de facto* governments, suggested by the American Declaration of Independence and Monroe Doctrine, were increasingly recognized by all states during the nineteenth century, and marked a considerable change in the practice of international law from that of the age of imperialism. The subject nations were deemed to have 'natural rights' which were morally superior to the legal rights of states.

"The spirit of internationalism has effected new changes. Treaties began to be made protecting aborigines and minorities from exploitation and organizing international supervision to assure their observance. Such treaties, and the occasional use of plebiscites to determine the destiny of territories in question after wars, gradually came to manifest the principle that subject peoples had a right of self-determination, a doctrine closely associated with the democratic thesis that government can only be justified by the consent of the governed. Procedures for the realization of this right came to be incorporated in international law through such institutions as the mandates system, the

trusteeship system, and the regime of non-self-governing territories under the United Nations."

Wright, "Recognition and Self-Determination", *Proceedings of the American Society of International Law* (1954) 23, 26–27.

In June 1930, at a time when it appeared that forces of the Nica-
raguan Guardia might be driven into Honduras by the bandit leader
Ortez, the Solicitor of the Department of State commented:

> "The troops here in question would be warranted in crossing
> the frontier only for the purposes of seeking asylum in Honduran
> territory.   They would under no circumstances be justified in con-
> ducting military operations from that territory without permis-
> sion of the Honduran Government."

Respect for
territorial
sovereignty

The American Minister at Managua (Hanna) to the Secretary of State
(Stimson), telegram No. 68, June 10, 1930, MS. Department of State, file
817.00/6655; the Solicitor of the Department (Hackworth) to Assistant
Secretary of State White, memorandum, June 12, 1930, MS. Department of
State, file 817.00/6658.

On September 20, 1939, Ambassador Bullitt reported from Paris:

> "The general situation appears to be as follows: The French
> Government made, as you know, intense appeals to the Belgian
> Government to permit the French forces to cross Belgian territory
> to attack Germany as soon as Germany attacked Poland.   It was
> the conviction of the French Government and the General Staff
> that a French attack by way of Belgium could have drawn suffi-
> cient German troops away from Poland to have made it impos-
> sible for Germany to overrun Poland.   The Belgian Govern-
> ment refused.
> "Further urgent appeals to the Belgian Government have been
> made by the French Government for permission for French
> troops to cross Belgium in case of a German attack on the Neth-
> erlands.   The French Government has been informed that the
> Queen of the Netherlands also has appealed personally to the
> King of the Belgians in this sense.   The King of the Belgians has
> refused flatly to consider any such proposal.

> .   .   .   .

> "Since the French certainly will not violate Belgian neutrality
> the only opening for attack against Germany remains the Sieg-
> fried Line.   To break that line will require vastly more heavy
> guns, munitions, and airplanes than the French and British now
> have.   It is therefore the general opinion that no successful at-
> tack against Germany can be envisaged until the spring of 1942
> and that successful attack at that time will be dependent on air-
> planes, cannons, and munitions from the United States."

The American Ambassador at Paris (Bullitt) to the Secretary of State
(Hull), telegram No. 2075, Sept. 20, 1939, MS. Department of State, file
811.04418/555; 1939 For. Rel., vol. I, pp. 444–445.

On November 7, 1939, the American Ambassador in Brussels reported:

"The Belgian Government has protested officially at Berlin against the flight of German planes over Belgian territory several days ago. Yesterday seven German planes are reported to have been seen near Alost within 20 miles of Brussels."

On November 8, 1939, the American Ambassador further reported:

"I have just returned from a visit to Foreign Minister Spaak who stated that the situation was most tense and grave. He stated (one) that there were very large concentrations of German shock troops and mechanized and motor divisions along the Belgian and Dutch frontiers; and, (two) that they were the same troops as those which invaded Poland and that their disposition indicated the same plan and manner of attack as that which was employed in Poland and that it indicated a simultaneous attack on Belgium and Holland. He then told me that in spite of the protest of the Belgium Foreign Office (my telegram No. 168, November 7, 6 p.m.) there had been persistent flights of German airplanes over Belgian territory and under such conditions as would warrant no other conclusion than that they were deliberate. (The Foreign Minister was evidently referring to a statement made earlier in the day by a Belgian officer to the effect that a dozen of these planes had been engaged in photographic work.) Notwithstanding official German denials the identity of the planes was clearly established."

The American Ambassador in Belgium (Davies) to the Secretary of State (Hull), telegram No. 168, Nov. 7, 1939, MS. Department of State, file 740.0011 European War 1939/942; same to same, telegram No. 174, Nov. 8, 1939, *ibid.*/958; 1939 For. Rel. vol. I, p. 528.

In his radio address on May 27, 1941, President Franklin D. Roosevelt stated that the "United States is mustering its men and its resources only for purposes of defense—only to repel attack"; that no one could foretell just when "the acts of the dictators will ripen into attack on this hemisphere"; but that "it would be suicide to wait until they are in our front yard". He added that "we shall be on our guard against efforts to establish Nazi bases closer to our hemisphere". In the course of the address he adverted several times to the fact that "the Azores and the Cape Verde Islands, if occupied or controlled by Germany, would directly endanger the freedom of the Atlantic" and "would become bases for submarines, warships, and airplanes raiding the waters which lie immediately off our own coasts and attacking the shipping in the South Atlantic." He added: "We in the Americas will decide for ourselves whether and when and where our American interests are attacked or our security threatened. . . . We will not hesitate to use our armed forces to repel attack."

On May 30, 1941, the Portuguese Minister in the United States (João Antonio de Bianchi) addressed a note to the Department of State, adverting to the direct reference in President Roosevelt's address to Portuguese territories "unaccompanied by any express mention of respect for the complete and centuries old sovereignty of Portugal over those territories" and without "the slightest reference to the fundamental principle of respect for the sovereignty of others". The Portuguese Government, the note went on to say, deemed it imperative to request a clarification "otherwise it might be interpreted as conducting [conducing?] to the admission that in order to defend other countries or for its own defense, a great nation would be at liberty to commit a violation similar to those the threat of which is said to exist from third States." It was stated in the note that although the Portuguese Government had recently received, with satisfaction and gratitude, from the United States Government through the words of the Secretary of State, assurances of the respect for their sovereignty, it would appreciate assurances that in the thesis expounded by President Roosevelt nothing existed which was contrary to the former declarations "or which may be interpreted as derogatory of the sovereign rights of Portugal." For its own part, the note stated, the Portuguese Government "reassert their indefectible determination to defend to the limit of their forces, their neutrality and their sovereign rights against all and any attack to which they may be exposed".

In reply, Secretary of State Hull stated that "For its part, the Government of the United States can state categorically that it harbors no aggressive intentions against the sovereignty or territorial integrity of any other country"; that "Our policy today is based upon the inalienable right of self-defense"; that "The Government of the United States can not but view with increasing anxiety the constantly expanding acts of aggression on the part of a certain belligerent power, which now threaten the peace and safety of the countries of this hemisphere"; and that "In referring to the Islands in the Atlantic it was the intention of the President to point out the dangers to this hemisphere which would result if these Islands were to come under the control or occupation of forces pursuing a policy of world conquest and domination." It was added: "The strategic importance of these Islands, because of their geographical location, was stressed by the President solely in terms of their potential value from the point of view of attack against this hemisphere." To this, the Portuguese Minister replied, on June 13, 1941, that "the Portuguese Government . . . can not but regret that . . . the Government of the United States of America should not have gone beyond a generical and vague declaration which did not even refer individually to the very country in question, and failed to. assert whether or not they maintained the former declarations made by the Secretary of State." Following several calls at the Department concerning the subject, and an explanation by the Portuguese Minister that a reply to his second note (that of June 13th) was not intended, President Roosevelt addressed the following letter to the President of the Council of Ministers of Portugal (Antonio de Oliveira Salazar):

"I am writing this entirely personal and informal letter to you in the belief that it may be easier for me, in this manner, to put an end effectively to certain misunderstandings which have regrettably arisen during recent weeks between our two Governments.

"May I say first of all that, in the opinion of the Government of the United States, the continued exercise of unimpaired and sovereign jurisdiction by the Government of Portugal over the territory of Portugal itself, over the Azores and over all Portuguese colonies offers complete assurance of security to the Western Hemisphere insofar as the regions mentioned are concerned. It is, consequently, the consistent desire of the United States that there be no infringement of Portuguese sovereign control over those territories.

"This policy of the United States I made emphatically clear in the message which I addressed yesterday to the Congress of the United States concerning the steps which had been taken to assist the people of Iceland in the defense of the integrity and independence of their country. [See message of July 7, 1941, 87 *Cong. Rec.*, pt. 6, p. 5868.]

"I feel sure that there has never been any doubt in your own mind with regard to this question and that the questions which have been raised with regard thereto in the press have had their origin in false reports deliberately circulated by propaganda emanating from governments which have desired to impair the traditional relations between our two countries.

"For all of the reasons I have mentioned above, this Government views with the greatest gratification the steps which already have been taken and which are being taken by your Government to strengthen the defense of the Azores and other outlying portions of the colonial possessions of Portugal so as to render any surprise attack upon them by Germany, or by powers cooperating with Germany, less likely of success.

"I need merely add that in view of the vital importance to the United States that Portuguese sovereignty over the Azores and certain other outlying Portuguese possessions remain intact, this Government will stand prepared to assist the authorities of Portugal in the defense of those possessions against any threat of aggression on the part of Germany, or of the powers responsive to Germany, should your Government express to me its belief that such aggression is imminent or its desire that such steps be taken. Any such measures would, of course, be taken in full recognition of the sovereign rights of Portugal and with categorical assurances that any American forces sent to Portuguese possessions would be withdrawn immediately upon the termination of the present war.

"In the event that this contingency were to arise and the Government of Portugal considered it desirable, because of the close relations which happily exist between Portugal and Brazil, to ask that the Brazilian Government participate in these measures of defense, such a step would be most satisfactory to the Government of the United States. I feel certain that Brazil and the United States would cooperate effectively and whole-heartedly in assisting the Portuguese Government and people in the defense of the Azores.

"I have felt it desirable to clarify the situation completely in order to have the assurance that there may not be the slightest misunderstanding of these facts between you and myself.

"Frankly, I have felt particularly chagrined that any question should have arisen concerning my own attitude with regard to complete respect for the sovereignty of Portugal. I say that because, as you will remember, during the World War of 1914–1918, the Government of Portugal made available to its allies and subsequently to the United States the port of Horta as a fueling base and the port of Punta Delgada as a naval base. At that time, as Assistant Secretary of the Navy, I had the privilege of visiting those ports in the interest of the United States Navy and I was thus afforded the opportunity of seeing for myself how particularly close and friendly the relations between the Portuguese people and the members of the naval forces of the United States had become. There existed a complete spirit of cooperation between them and of course as soon as the international emergency had passed, all of the forces of the allied and associated powers were immediately withdrawn without the slightest detriment to the sovereign jurisdiction of the Portuguese Government. Because of this experience which I had, I should have a personal interest in seeing to it that the relations between our two Governments and between the peoples of our two countries were always conducted with a full reciprocal respect for the sovereign rights of each and that in any form of cooperation which might be undertaken between Portugal and the United States the best interests of the Portuguese people were completely safeguarded."

In his reply, July 29, 1941, the President of the Council of Ministers of Portugal stated that it was particularly gratifying to receive President Roosevelt's letter and "to have been apprised through a direct message from Your Excellency, of the sentiments of the United States and of their Government toward Portugal and of their precise position as regards Portuguese territories in the Atlantic in relation to the security of North America."

Radio address of President Roosevelt, May 27, 1941, IV *Bulletin*, Department of State, No. 101, May 31, 1941, pp. 647, 649–653; the Portuguese Legation to the Department of State, third person note of May 30, 1941, MS. Department of State, file FW 853B.014/36; the Secretary of State (Hull)

to the Portuguese Minister (Bianchi), note dated June 10, 1941, *ibid.;* the
Portuguese Minister (Bianchi) to Secretary Hull, note No. 95, June 13, 1941,
ibid./27; memorandum of conversation between Under Secretary of State
Welles and the Portuguese Minister (Bianchi), June 13, 1941, *ibid.;* memo-
randum of conversation between the Adviser on Political Relations (Dunn)
and the Portuguese Minister (Bianchi), June 17, 1941, *ibid.*/53; President
Roosevelt to the President of the Council of Ministers of Portugal
(Salazar), letter dated July 14, 1941, *ibid.*/41a; and the President of the
Council of Ministers of Portugal (Salazar) to President Roosevelt, July 29,
1941, *ibid.*/41⅜; *see also* 1941 For. Rel., vol. II, 844–855.

The Agreement Relating to the Defense of Greenland was signed
by Secretary of State Hull for the United States of America and
Henrik de Kauffmann, "Envoy Extraordinary and Minister Plenipotentiary of His Majesty the King of Denmark at Washington", at
Washington on April 9, 1941, the anniversary of the day on which
German troops invaded Denmark (April 9, 1940). By the Agreement
the United States was granted the right to locate and construct air-
plane landing fields and facilities for the defense of Greenland and for
the defense of the American Continent. The preamble to the Agreement recited that "Although the sovereignty of Denmark over Greenland is fully recognized, the present circumstances for the time being
prevent the Government in Denmark from exercising its powers in
respect of Greenland." The Agreement recited that Secretary of
State Hull and "Henrik de Kauffmann, Envoy Extraordinary and
Minister Plenipotentiary of His Majesty the King of Denmark at
Washington, acting on behalf of His Majesty the King of Denmark in
His capacity as sovereign of Greenland, whose authorities in Greenland have concurred herein" had agreed in the manner set forth. In
article I it was explicitly recited:

> "The Government of the United States of America reiterates its
> recognition of and respect for the sovereignty of the Kingdom of
> Denmark over Greenland. Recognizing that as a result of the
> present European war there is danger that Greenland may be
> converted into a point of aggression against nations of the Ameri-
> can Continent, the Government of the United States of America,
> having in mind its obligations under the Act of Habana signed
> on July 30, 1940, accepts the responsibility of assisting Greenland
> in the maintenance of its present status."

It was further provided, in article VI, that "The Kingdom of Denmark retains sovereignty over the defense areas mentioned in the preceding articles."

U.S. EAS 204; 55 Stat. 1245, 1246, 1248. Further, concerning the
negotiation and conclusion of the Agreement Relating to the Defense of
Greenland, see *post*, under "Self-Defense".

From the outset it was contemplated on the part of the United States "that any arrangements would be entered into with respect on our part for Danish sovereignty in Greenland". Subsequently, on April 4, 1941, Secretary of State Hull explained that whereas it had been at first the intention of the United States to work out an arrangement by which defense facilities in Greenland might be constructed as an undertaking of the Danish authorities in Greenland with financial and technical assistance of the United States, it had now been decided that defense facilities in Greenland should be constructed and protected by and be under the sole jurisdiction of the United States. At the same time he stated that an informal exchange of views had been had with the Danish Minister at Washington (Henrik de Kauffmann) regarding "the measures, consistent with the maintenance of free Danish sovereignty over Greenland", which might be taken to guard against Greenland being used by a non-American power as a point of aggression against the rest of the American Continent.

Following the conclusion of the Agreement Relating to the Defense of Greenland, King Christian of Denmark, while indicating appreciation for "the respect of Denmark's sovereignty over Greenland", protested against "these unjustified measures" and informed President Roosevelt that Minister de Kauffmann "by arbitrarily signing the agreement of the 9th of April 1941 on the defense of Greenland has exceeded his authority as accredited Minister and acted against the Danish constitution, for which reason he has no more my confidence", and that the agreement was "invalid". To this message, President Roosevelt replied: "I am greatly distressed that Your Majesty has found it necessary to characterize as unjustified the measures which the Government of the United States of America deems it essential to take no less in the interests of Your Majesty's sovereignty over Greenland than for the protection of the Western Hemisphere. I trust that I am not misinformed as to the true feeling of deep friendship and of common ideals which the people of Denmark have for the United States of America, or that they have any doubt that the Government of the United States will not live up to its undertakings with respect to Your Majesty's sovereignty over Greenland."

The Secretary of State (Hull) to the American Consul at Godthaab (Penfield), telegram No. 13, Feb. 17, 1941, MS. Department of State, file 859B.7962/3; same to same, telegram No. 31, Apr. 4, 1941, MS. Department of State, file 859B.01/348a; the American Chargé d'Affaires in Denmark (Perkins) to the Secretary of State (Hull), telegram No. 146, Apr. 26, 1941, MS. Department of State, file 859B.7962/93; and Secretary of State Hull to the Chargé in Denmark (Perkins), telegram No. 69, May 5, 1941, *ibid.;* 1941 For. Rel., vol. II, pp. 37–38, 42, 58–59, 62.

On October 22, 1941, Minister de Kauffmann, in a note of that date addressed to the Secretary of State, requested "the views of the Government of the United States with respect to his proposal that in order that he might more effectively discharge his responsibilities for the direct supervision of all Danish Government agencies in the United States, he attach the members of the Greenland Delegation in New York to the Danish Consulate General in that city". In reply, Secretary of State Hull stated that he thought it advisable that a clear statement of relations be made. Secretary Hull then stated:

". . . Reference is had particularly to the very broad obligations assumed by the Government of the United States towards the Kingdom of Denmark in the Agreement Relating to the Defense of Greenland signed on April 9, 1941, and related exchange of notes, and especially to the assurances included in that Agreement and made simultaneously in a statement by the President of the United States that the sovereignty of the Kingdom of Denmark over and its rights in and to the Colony of Greenland would continue to be recognized and scrupulously respected by the Government of the United States.

"From these obligations and assurances, which have been welcome no less in Denmark than in Greenland, it follows that the responsibilities of the United States with respect to Greenland run directly to Denmark, even though by reason of the occupation of the country by German forces, the Government of Denmark is unhappily not at present in a position freely to act in Greenland or elsewhere in the Western Hemisphere. The duly accredited and recognized representative in the United States of His Majesty the King of Denmark and the Royal Danish Government is the Minister of Denmark at Washington, who was appointed prior to the occupation of his country by German forces. In consequence, the Government of the United States feels that it must look to him as the spokesman for all Danish interests, including Greenland, and that it is obligated to consult with him whenever those interests are involved.

"Note has been taken of the fact that the Colony of Greenland did not have autonomous powers within the framework of the Danish constitutional system, but that its internal administration and external relationships were in all respects determined and directed by the Government of Denmark. It follows that were the United States to enter into relations with the Colony or the Colonial officials other than through the duly accredited and recognized representative of the Danish Government, it would, in effect, be contributing to a separation of Greenland from its historic and constitutional relationship with Denmark; and such action would therefore tend to be in violation of the obligations assumed by the United States to respect Danish sovereignty over Greenland and to assist Greenland in the maintenance of its status.

"The dependence of the Colony of Greenland upon the Government of Denmark appears to extend not merely to matters of political significance, but likewise to economic and financial matters. This plainly establishes the principle which must be applied to the control over Greenland assets and expenditures, most of which revolve around the sale of cryolite and the use of the funds thus obtained for the purchase of supplies, the administration of Greenland, and the discharge of Danish obligations to the owners of the cryolite mine and to the miners. The Minister of Denmark at Washington is recognized by the Secretary of State as having the responsibility for the control and expenditure of all Danish Government funds and Central Bank funds in the United States. Similarly the various licensing orders issued by the Secretary of the Treasury have been drawn with a view to fixing the responsibility for control and expenditure of Greenland funds upon the Minister of Denmark as the recognized representative in the United States of Danish interests, including Greenland.

"Note has also been taken of the fact that contracts for the disposal of cryolite have in the past been made under the direction of the Danish Government. It would thus appear that at present the Danish Minister in Washington exercises the functions of the Danish Crown and Government in that regard.

"The Secretary of State has accordingly determined that all matters regarding finance, supplies, and the sale of Greenland products in the United States will, as a matter of policy be taken up with the Danish Legation in Washington. The Danish Minister has proposed that he attach the members of the Greenland Delegation in New York to the Danish Consulate General in New York, to the end that he may more effectively discharge his responsibilities for the direct supervision of all Danish Government agencies in the United States. As indicated above, Mr. Hull agrees to this step for the purpose of better safeguarding the position and interests of the Kingdom of Denmark, including the Colony of Greenland. American consular officers in Greenland will, of course, continue to transact with the Danish authorities in Greenland such official business as is customarily transacted between a consular officer and the local officials within his consular district."

The Secretary of State (Hull) to the Danish Minister (de Kauffmann), third-person note, Oct. 25, 1941, MS. Department of State, file 859B.01B11/6; 1941 For. Rel., vol. II, pp. 68–69.

In his message to the Congress dated July 7, 1941, transmitting a message received from the Prime Minister of Iceland and the reply of the President of the United States, relating to the defense of Iceland by United States forces upon the invitation of the Icelandic Government, President Franklin D. Roosevelt stated:

"This Government will insure the adequate defense of Iceland with full recognition of the independence of Iceland as a sovereign state."

White House press release, July 7, 1941, V *Bulletin*, Department of State, No. 107, July 12, 1941, pp. 15, 16. See also Defense of Iceland Agreement, July 1, 1941, U.S. EAS 232; 55 Stat. 1547.

At the First Meeting of the Ministers of Foreign Affairs of the American Republics, held at Panamá in 1939, the Governments of the American Republics by Resolution IX (paragraphs 4 and 5) declared:

"4. That they consider the violation of the neutrality or the invasion of weaker nations as an unjustifiable measure in the conduct and success of war; and

"5. That they undertake to protest against any warlike act which does not conform to international law and the dictates of justice."

In May 1940 the Uruguayan Minister for Foreign Affairs, Alberto Guani, proposed that the following message be transmitted by the President of Panama, Augusto Boyd, to the German Chancellor, Adolf Hitler, invoking paragraphs 4 and 5 of Resolution IX adopted at the Panamá meeting of Foreign Ministers in 1939:

"The American Republics in accord with the principles of international law and in application of the resolutions adopted in their inter-American conferences, consider unjustifiable the ruthless violation by Germany of the neutrality and sovereignty of Belgium, Holland and Luxemburg.

"In paragraphs 4 and 5 of the Ninth Resolution of the Meeting of Foreign Ministers held at Panama in 1939 entitled 'Maintenance of International Activities in Accordance with Christian Morality', it was established that the violation of the neutrality or the invasion of weaker nations as a measure in the conduct and success of war warrants the American Republics in protesting against this infraction of international law and the requirements of justice.

"The American Republics therefore resolve to protest against the military attacks directed against Belgium, Holland and Luxemburg, at the same time making an appeal for the reestablishment of law and justice in the relations between countries."

Agreement by each of the 21 American Republics to the text of the joint declaration proposed by Uruguay was obtained May 18, 1940, and the text duly transmitted to the German Government.

Report of the Delegate of the United States of America to the Meeting of the Foreign Ministers of the American Republics, Held at Panamá, September 23–October 3, 1939, Res. IX, p. 60; II *Bulletin*, Department of State, No. 47, May 18, 1940, pp. 541–542; *ibid.*, No. 48, May 25, 1940, p. 568; 1940 For. Rel., vol. I, pp. 727–743.

In reporting on activities of German agents in Iran, in August 1941 prior to British-Soviet occupation of Iran, the American Minister at Tehran informed the Department of State:

". . . Thus there are German agents in all important public services and in all parts of Iran. Their organization centers in a Nazi club in Tehran known as the Brown House. This club formerly went in for military drilling and target practice but this has been stopped by the Iranian authorities. The organization is said to be disciplined and efficient with each man trained as to his duties either for sabotage or as an adjunct to invading German forces. . . ."

The American Minister in Iran (Dreyfus) to the Secretary of State (Hull), telegram No. 99, Aug. 21, 1941, MS. Department of State, file 740.0011 European War 1939/14278; 1941 For. Rel., vol. III, pp. 401, 402.

In the *Corfu Channel Case*, the United Kingdom sought to justify its minesweeping operation in that part of the Albanian territorial waters constituting the Corfu Strait subsequent to the mining of the destroyers *Volage* and *Saumarez* as justifiable on the ground, *inter alia*, that the operation was based on the doctrine of "self-protection or self-help". So far as the specific plea of self-protection or self-help was concerned, the International Court of Justice held:

". . . The Court cannot accept this defence either. Between independent States, respect for territorial sovereignty is an essential foundation of international relations. The Court recognizes that the Albanian Government's complete failure to carry out its duties after the explosions, and the dilatory nature of its diplomatic notes, are extenuating circumstances for the action of the United Kingdom Government. But to ensure respect for international law, of which it is the organ, the Court must declare that the action of the British Navy constituted a violation of Albanian sovereignty."

The Corfu Channel Case (United Kingdom *v.* Albania), Judgment (Merits), Apr. 9, 1949, I.C.J. Reports (1949) 4, 35.

The following note was sent by the American Embassy at Prague to the Czechoslovak Ministry of Foreign Affairs on June 19, 1951, in reply to a note from the Czechoslovak Government dated May 21, making various charges against the United States with reference to border violations, broadcasts, and other matters:

"The American Embassy presents its compliments to the Czechoslovak Ministry of Foreign Affairs, and with reference to the Ministry's note of May 21, 1951, concerning the question of border violations, certain broadcasts in Czech and Slovak languages, and related matters, has the honor, pursuant to instructions of the United States Government, to make the following reply:

"With respect to the charges of violations of the border between Czechoslovakia and the Federal Republic of Germany by United States military personnel, the Ministry's note states that on May 4, at 6 or 7 a.m., military personnel in two autos crossed the. Czechoslovak frontier between frontier markers 22 and 23, drove around frontier barriers on both sides of the frontier, studied frontier installations, used field glasses and photographed certain objects.

"The Embassy informs the Ministry that the United States Government does not condone any violation of the Czechoslovak frontier by members of its armed forces whether on the ground or in the air.

"An investigation of the incident referred to in the Ministry's note has been made. The results of this investigation indicate that the crossing of the Czechoslovak frontier by American military personnel at the place indicated did in fact take place and that it was unintentional and inadvertent. The American military personnel in question entered Czechoslovak territory to the maximum depth of 95 yards and remained there approximately 5 minutes.

"The report received by the Ministry is inaccurate in two respects: Members of the American patrol, which numbered six men, took no photographs; furthermore, they drove around one road barrier but not two, as they stopped before reaching the second barrier.

"The explanation of this unwitting crossing of the Czechoslovak frontier appears to be that all members of the patrol, including the leader, were unfamiliar with this segment of the frontier and were carrying out their first patrol in this area. Furthermore, there was no sign indicating the presence of the border which led the patrol leader to assume that the second barrier marked the international boundary. He, as well as members of his patrol, failed to see the unpainted border stones in line with the first barrier. No member of this patrol realized he had been in Czechoslovakia until so informed later by the investigating officer.

"Although the border crossing was unintentional, the investigating officer has recommended that disciplinary action be taken against the patrol leader on the grounds that his failure to make reconnaissance before passing the first barrier constituted a failure to exercise good judgment.

"The Embassy assures the Ministry that all possible steps are being taken by the appropriate United States authorities to prevent the recurrence of such an incident.

"As stated, the United States Government does not tolerate any violation of the Czechoslovak frontier by members of its armed forces and by the same token will not tolerate the violation of the United States Zone of Germany by Czechoslovak personnel. In this connection the United States Government calls the attention of the Czechoslovak Government to two recent violations in which armed members of the Czechoslovak armed forces crossed the border. On May 24 from approximately 0930 to 1000 hours six Czechoslovak soldiers were illegally within the United States Zone of Germany at the Regnitz River east of Hof in the American area. Furthermore one of these soldiers threatened a German national, Margarete Rausch, with a machine-pistol while within the United States Zone of Germany.

"At approximately 0930 May 24 two Czechoslovak soldiers dismounted from vehicles in Czechoslovakia, crossed the border and the Regnitz River and penetrated into the territory of the United States Zone of Germany to the depth of approximately 35 yards. The soldiers told Mrs. Rausch that she had been cutting grass in Czechoslovakia and must return with them. Despite her insistence that at no time had she been in Czechoslovakia, one of the soldiers pushed a machine-pistol into her back and forced her to return across a stream to a place, likewise in Germany, where she had been working. Four more Czechoslovak soldiers joined the group and laughed when she told them they were all standing in Germany. Her husband, Max Rausch, came up and also told the soldiers they were in Germany. During the course of this conversation a seventh Czechoslovak soldier, presumably the one in command, remained in Czechoslovak territory near one of the border markers and finally signalled to the six soldiers who thereupon left the United States Zone.

"The American military authorities were immediately notified of this violation of the United States Zone of Germany and on the same morning (May 24) undertook an investigation. The investigating officer and a sergeant while standing at the spot in Germany where the Czechoslovak soldiers first intercepted Mrs. Rausch noticed two Czechoslovak soldiers partially concealed in the brush on the Czechoslovak side of the border with their weapons aimed at them. As the American soldiers started towards the Rausch house, the Czechoslovak soldiers fired two shots, apparently not aimed at the American soldiers.

"From the circumstances in which this frontier violation occurred, particularly the fact that the Czechoslovak soldier who was apparently directing this operation took care to remain inside of Czechoslovakia, the Embassy is justified in drawing the conclusion that this was an intentional violation of the territory of the United States Zone of Germany.

"Between 11:00 and noon on June 6 a tractor dragging logs and carrying three unarmed civilians and a member of the uniformed Czechoslovak Security Police armed with a machine pistol, was observed crossing the border twice and penetrating the United States Zone each time to a depth of 10 or 15 yards near Wies. The improvised road used by the Czechoslovak personnel was clearly in the United States Zone. After the second unauthorized entry of the armed member of the Security Police, he was apprehended by a patrol of the United States constabulary. He was returned to Czechoslovak authorities at approximately 2330 on June 7.

"The United States Government considers these actions as entirely uncalled for and regards the first incident as particularly flagrant. The Ministry is requested to undertake a careful investigation to determine who was responsible for these border violations and to insure that the guilty person or persons be appropriately disciplined. The Embassy expects the Ministry to show the same diligence in informing it of the results of the investigation and in assuring it that measures to prevent recurrence have been taken, as was shown by United States authorities in connection with the incident which is the subject of the first part of this note."

XXV *Bulletin*, Department of State, No. 627, July 2, 1951, pp. 12–13.

In 1957 the Department of State instructed the American Embassy at Madrid that the conduct of public hearings by a congressional committee is an exercise of a sovereign function by the legislative branch of the Government of the United States which, if conducted— as apparently was then contemplated by a member of the U.S. House of Representatives then in Spain—within the boundaries of another country, would be in derogation of that country's sovereignty. The Embassy was further instructed that use of United States premises or facilities for such a purpose would be inconsistent with the rec- ognized role of a diplomatic mission and that it would be inap- propriate for U.S. executive branch personnel to participate in any such proceedings.

Acting Secretary of State Murphy to the American Embassy, Madrid, telegram, Sept. 18, 1957, MS. Department of State, file 033.1100 FA/9–1757.

Following a request on the part of the United States, the Mexican Ministry of National Defense gave approval in January 1958 for the survey of waterfowl in Mexico by the Fish and Wildlife Service of the United States Department of the Interior. It was required that a rep- resentative of the Ministry of National Defense accompany the group. In addition, the Mexican Ministry of Communications and Public Works stated that it desired to receive information, once the survey party concluded its labors, as to the number of flights made, time re- quired for flights, points of operation, and number of kilometers flown. As a matter of fact, oral approval for the waterfowl survey preceded by some weeks the receipt of the formal permission of the Mexican Government.

The American Embassy, Mexico City, to the Department of State, des- patch No. 871, Feb. 17, 1958, enclosing texts of Mexican Foreign Office note No. 500873, Jan. 15, 1958, and note No. 500938, Jan. 30, 1958, MS. Department of State, file 102.53/2–1758.

Consent was obtained from the Canadian Government by the United States Air Force for use of a firing range at Goose Bay, Lab- rador, which was used upon invitation of the Canadian Government.

Acting Secretary of State Herter to the American Embassy, Ottawa, instruction No. A–253, Mar. 14, 1958, MS. Department of State, file 711.5442/2–558.

Replying to reports published November 3, 1959, that Cuban exiles Establishment of govern- ment-in-exile were attempting to set up a government-in-exile in the United States, the Department of State said:

"Establishment of a foreign government within the territory of the United States without the consent of the United States would violate the sovereignty of the United States and run counter to international law. No such consent, implied or otherwise, has been given by the United States."

Assistant Legal Adviser Whiteman, memorandum, "Reported Plans to Form Cuban Government-in-exile in the United States", Nov. 3, 1959; *cf.* New York *Times*, Nov. 4, 1959, p. 1.

When an opinion was requested by the U.S. High Commissioner Enlistments by occupying power for Germany in November 1952, as to whether the recruiting by an occupying power (France) for the French Foreign Legion of nationals of occupied territory (Germany) was incompatible with principles of international law, the Office of the Legal Adviser of the Department of State advised:

"There appears to be no question but that, as between fully sovereign States, no State has a right to recruit troops in another State without its consent. (VII Hackworth, p. 405; II Oppenheim, p. 564; II Moore, p. 446; V Hague Conventions, Art. IV, Malloy, Vol. 2, p. 2298 . . .).

.   .   .   .

"The only other clause of the Occupation Statute [XX *Bulletin*, Department of State, No. 511, Apr. 17, 1949, pp. 499, 500–501] that might be involved is the one relating to 'foreign affairs, including international agreements made by or on behalf of Germany'. Prior to March 7, 1951, it might have been contended that the Occupying Powers, under this clause, had the power to consent to such recruiting. However, the 1951 amendment made it clear that this power would be exercised in such a way as to permit the Federal Republic to conduct its own foreign affairs 'to the full extent compatible with the requirements of security, other reserved powers, and obligations of the Occupying Powers relating to Germany'. [XXIV *op. cit.*, No. 611, Mar. 19, 1951, pp. 443, 447–448.] It has already been demonstrated that there are no other reserved powers involved. I can see no basis for saying such recruiting has any connection with security requirements or with obligations of the Occupying Powers relating to Germany. It would therefore appear that under this clause of the Occupation Statute as it now reads the Federal Republic is the proper party to give or withhold the requisite consent to such recruiting.

"Therefore, it is my opinion that there is no right reserved under the Occupation Statute that would affect the general rule of international law on this point, and that, without the consent

of the Federal Republic, the recruitment of German nationals·
in the Federal Republic by one of the Occupying Powers is incompatible with the established principles of international law."

Col. John M. Raymond, Assistant to the Legal Adviser for German Affairs,
memorandum dated Nov. 28, 1952, MS. Department of State, file FW 751.551/
11–2252. It was reported in the incoming telegram that Federal Chancellor
Adenauer had called to the attention of the Allied High Commission that
recruiting by an occupying power of nationals of the occupied country for
military assignments was incompatible with the principles of international
law. Telegram from Bonn to the Department of State, No. 2359, Nov. 22,
1952, *ibid.* On February 13, 1953, the Director of the Bureau of German
Affairs (Riddleberger) handed an aide memoire to Minister de Juniac
of the French Embassy on the subject. It appears from the aide memoire
that the French authorities had emphasized the absence of formal recruiting agents in the territory of the Federal Republic for obtaining enlistments
in the Foreign Legion. It was stated in the aide memoire that—

> "The misgiving of this Government is reinforced by the absence of
> any clear legal basis, so far as it can ascertain, for the recruitment of
> French forces from German nationals in Germany against the expressed opposition of the German authorities. Neither the Occupation Statute now in effect nor the Contractual Agreements awaiting
> ratification at Paris and Bonn contains, in the Department's opinion,
> a clause to justify Occupying Power recruitment of German nationals
> in, or removal of such recruits from, Federal Republic territory without
> the same consent from the Federal Republic Government that would be
> called for between fully sovereign states under generally applicable
> rules of international law.

> ".... Under the circumstances, this Government hopes that the Government of France may be disposed to modify the existing recruitment
> practice in Germany and may be in a position so to inform the German
> authorities in the near future. The United States authorities would
> be pleased to associate themselves with a reply of this nature."
> *Ibid.*/2–1853.

Restriction by unilateral act

In holding that the Federal Tort Claims Act of the United States,
inapplicable by its terms to "any claim arising in a foreign country",
did not authorize a suit against the United States for an allegedly
wrongful death of a flight engineer at a Newfoundland air base,
which the United States held under a long-term lease from Great
Britain, the Supreme Court of the United States (Mr. Justice Reed
delivering the opinion of the Court) stated :

"In brief, though Congress was ready to lay aside a great
portion of the sovereign's ancient and unquestioned immunity
from suit, it was unwilling to subject the United States to liabilities depending upon the laws of a foreign power. The legislative
will must be respected."

United States v. *Spelar, Administratrix*, 338 U.S. 217, 221 (1949). Federal Tort Claims Act, 62 Stat. 984, 985 ; 28 U.S.C. § 2680(k).

"When a State assumes a treaty obligation, those of its rights   Restriction
which are directly in conflict with this obligation are, to that   by agreement
extent, restricted or renounced. . . ."

Bin Cheng, *General Principles of Law as Applied by International Courts and Tribunals* (1953) 123.

Wilhelm Grewe, writing in his capacity as Chief of the German Delegation for the Replacement of the Occupation Statute, commented on the effect of the "Convention on Relations between the Three Powers and the Federal Republic of Germany and Related Conventions" (referred to as "Deutschlandvertrag") on the element of sovereignty inherent in the exercise of "supreme authority" by the Allied occupation powers as follows:

". . . Certainly, it is a moot point, whether sovereignty is conceivable which does not contain the full measure of state authority, but is subject to certain restrictions as those imposed in Art. 1, para. 1 and Art. 2, para. 1 of the Deutschlandvertrag for the benefit of the Three Powers. In the text of the Convention the word 'sovereignty' was deliberately avoided, in order not to add fuel to the flame of academic discussions. If the thesis that there can be no curtailed sovereignty is correct in its core, it would be equally right to maintain at least that 'supreme authority', restricted to certain functional fields, has ceased to be 'supreme authority'. This consideration alone would make it evident that the former occupation regime has ceased to exist in its juridical quintessence. For it was the very assumption of this 'Supreme Authority' which endowed the Allied occupation regime after 1945 with its special character of unlimited sovereignty.

"In the future we shall often hear of the words coined by Carl Schmitt: 'Sovereign is he who decides on the state of emergency' (Ausnahmezustand). We hope that then the following statement made by the same author in connection with the same topic will also occasionally be quoted: 'Not every extraordinary power, every emergency measure taken by the police, every emergency decree constitutes already a state of emergency.' In Schmitt's opinion the state of emergency is rather characterized by 'power, fundamentally unlimited, i.e. suspense of the entire hitherto existing order' (Politische Theologie. Vier Kapitel zur Lehre von der Souveränität (Political Theology. Four Chapters on the Doctrine of Sovereignty), 1922, p. 13). One must be very biased to read such sweeping powers into Article 5 of the Deutschlandvertrag—the 'emergency article' which has given rise to many arguments. If under item 3 of the Occupation Statute the Occupying Authorities had reserved the right, 'acting under instructions of their Governments, to resume, in whole or in part, the exercise of full authority, if they consider that to do so is essential to security or to preserve democratic government in Germany or in pursuance of the international obligations of their Governments,' it is significant that Art. 5 of the Deutschlandvertrag does not provide for such possibility of re-

suming 'supreme authority'. On the contrary, the powers of the
Three Western Allies, upon the proclamation of a state of
emergency, are restricted to the taking of such measures 'as are
necessary to maintain or restore order and to ensure the security
of the forces' (Art. 5, para 3)."

Wilhelm Grewe, "Von Der Kapitulation Zum Deutschlandvertrag" (From
the Capitulation to the General Agreement), *Aussenpolitik* (July 1952)
414–427 (translation).

"International relations in a relatively highly integrated world
society would be at a standstill if the sovereign States of the
world had no means of arriving at understandings regarding
matters within their exclusive domestic control. Apart from rules
of customary law, growing only imperceptibly over prolonged
periods, international conventions are the means by which such
adjustments are achieved. The fact that any arrangement of
this kind emphasises the relativity of State independence is made
more bearable for the jealous guardians of the rights of sovereign
States by the reciprocity of rights and obligations inherent in the
conception of a treaty. As the Permanent Court of International
Justice pointed out in its Advisory Opinion on the *Exchange of
Greek and Turkish Populations* (1928), the Convention of January 30, 1923, between the two countries created obligations for
both States on a footing of absolute equality and reciprocity: 'It
is therefore impossible to admit that a convention which creates
obligations of this kind, construed according to its natural meaning, infringes the sovereign rights of the High Contracting
Parties.' [Series B 10, p. 21.] Yet, as the Court observed in the
Anschluss case (1931), reciprocity in form and law does not necessarily mean reciprocity in fact [Series A/B 41, p. 52], a position
which is only too apparent to any student of the functions of the
principle of freedom of contract within the realm of municipal
law. In this respect, States are their own masters and can dispose
of their sovereign rights as they please. [*Ibid*. p. 48.] In doing
so, they exercise their rights as independent States, and by the
very treaty by which they limit their rights manifest the status
which entitles them to do so. Right from the start, in the
Wimbledon case (1923) [Series A 1, p. 25], the Permanent Court
of International Justice took this position and strongly affirmed
it in two subsequent Advisory Opinions: [Series B 10, p. 21;
Series B 14, p. 36] 'The Court declines to see in the conclusion of
any treaty by which a State undertakes to perform or refrain
from performing a particular act an abandonment of its sovereignty. No doubt any convention creating an obligation of this
kind places a restriction upon the exercise of the sovereign rights
of the State in the sense that it requires them to be exercised in a
certain way. But the right of entering into international engagements is an attribute of State sovereignty.' It cannot be
denied that at a certain point it becomes sheer formalism to argue
that a restriction on the exercise of sovereign rights accepted by
treaty cannot be considered as an infringement of sovereignty.

Then, a position may have been created in which—to use Judge
Hudson's apt description in his Separate Opinion in the case of the
Lighthouses in Crete and Samos (1937)—the theoretical sovereignty remaining in the State consenting to such limitation of its
independence is 'shorn of the last vestige of power,' and in which
'a ghost of a hollow sovereignty cannot be permitted to obscure
the realities of this situation.' [Series A/B 71, p. 127.]   Yet even
if such a 'realistic' interpretation of the law should lead to the
conclusion that, in a case of this kind, a State may have ceased
to be a sovereign State or to exercise sovereignty in a certain
territory, it still remains true that any independent State is entitled to sign away sovereign rights to this extent."

I Schwarzenberger, *International Law* (1949) 58–59.

". . . Sovereignty cannot be absolute.   A state, in fact, exercises sovereignty when it joins with other states in policies and
agrees to mutual limitations upon individual freedom of action
in order to accommodate for the good of its own people to the
facts of interdependence.   The United Nations Charter, which
cuts deeply into the older absolute ideas of independence and
sovereignty, bears witness to this fact. . . ."

William Sanders, "Multilateral Diplomacy", XXI *Bulletin*, Department
of State, No. 527, Aug. 8, 1949, pp. 163, 169.

"The difference between the United Nations and the Soviet
plans [for an international control system for atomic energy]
reflects a fundamental cleavage between the aims of the majority
and the minority.   Representatives of Canada, China, France,
the United Kingdom, and the United States reported as follows
to the General Assembly in 1949:

> " 'All the Sponsoring Powers other than the U.S.S.R. put
> world security first and are prepared to accept innovations
> in traditional concepts of international cooperation, national
> sovereignty and economic organization where these are nec-
> essary for security.   The Government of the U.S.S.R. puts
> its sovereignty first and is unwilling to accept measures which
> may impinge upon or interfere with its rigid exercise of un-
> impeded state sovereignty.'

"The willingness to accept some restrictions on sovereignty is
one of the great and hopeful attitudes in the world today.   The
Schuman proposal with respect to the European coal and steel
industries is the most recent example of this progressive spirit."

Philip C. Jessup, Ambassador at Large, address delivered at Hamilton
College, Clinton, N.Y., June 11, 1950, XXIII *Bulletin*, Department of State.
No. 574, July 3, 1950, pp. 26, 28.

"Passionately devoted to the realization of a European federation which will put an end to secular antagonisms, France
has put aside her legitimate resentment against the enemy of yesterday, demanding of it only that it bring to the cause of coop-

eration the admission of its responsibilities as well as the proof of its redemption through the repudiation of its old regime and the sincere attachment to the cause of democracy. Convinced of the need for supranational institutions, France has declared herself prepared to grant to those bodies, in conformity with her Constitution and under condition of reciprocity, part of her sovereignty. And she hopes to convince the still hesitant nations that they will not curtail their sovereignty but on the contrary strengthen it by associating it with others, by uniting their resources and labor to increase their forces, by developing and coordinating their industrial and agricultural economies, by widening their markets, by raising the standard of living of their workers, in a word, by making of the old divided Europe, slow of decision, torn with antagonisms, distrustful of herself, a new and harmonious organism animated by one soul and adapted to the needs and exigencies of the modern world."

President Auriol of France, address before the Congress of the United States, Apr. 2, 1951, XXIV *Bulletin*, Department of State, No. 614, Apr. 9, 1951, pp. 563, 565, 575.

An example of limitation of sovereignty by agreement is contained in the Joint Statement by Secretary of State Dulles and Korean President Rhee of August 7, 1953:

"The armistice contemplates that a political conference will be convened within 3 months, that is, prior to October 27, 1953. At that conference the U.S. delegation, in cooperation with the ROK delegation and other delegations from the UNC side, will seek to achieve the peaceful unification of historic Korea as a free and independent nation. We and our advisers have already had a full and satisfactory exchange of views which we hope and trust will establish a preparatory foundation for coordinated effort at the political conference.

"If, after the political conference has been in session for 90 days, it becomes clear to each of our Governments that all attempts to achieve these objectives have been fruitless and that the conference is being exploited by the Communist delegates mainly to infiltrate, propagandize, or otherwise embarrass the Republic of Korea, we shall then be prepared to make a concurrent withdrawal from the conference. We will then consult further regarding the attainment of a unified, free, and independent Korea which is the postwar goal the United States set itself during World War II, which has been accepted by the United Nations as its goal and which will continue to be an object of concern of U.S. foreign policy.

"We recognize that the Republic of Korea possesses the inherent right of sovereignty to deal with its problems, but it has agreed to take no unilateral action to unite Korea by military means for the agreed duration of the political conference."

Joint Statement by Secretary of State Dulles and President Rhee, issued at Seoul, Korea, Aug. 8, 1953 (Korean time), press release 424, Aug. 7, 1953, XXIX *Bulletin*, Department of State, No. 738, Aug. 17, 1953, p. 203.

"Once a State has limited its independence by treaty, the State is only free to exercise its sovereignty subject to its treaty obligations. Yet the right of independence is so fundamental in the system of international law that, corresponding to the general presumptions in favour of State sovereignty, there are complementary rules which have to be duly kept in mind in the interpretation of treaties limiting the sovereignty of States.

"In the first place, if there is a choice between two possible interpretations, that interpretation must be preferred by which the lesser obligations are imposed on a contracting State; for it must be presumed that a State will accept only the minimum of restriction of its freedom. The Permanent Court of International Justice expressly adopted this rule in the *Mosul* case (1925): 'If the wording of a treaty provision is not clear, in choosing between several admissible interpretations, the one which involves the minimum of obligations for the Parties should be adopted. This principle may be admitted to be sound.' [Series B 12, p. 25.] *(Limitations strictly construed)*

"Secondly, there is the equally important rule that limitations of independence have to be interpreted restrictively. In the cases of the *Wimbledon* (1923) and of the *Free Zones of Upper Savoy and the District of Gex* (1932) [Series A 24, p. 12; Series A/B 46, p. 167], the Permanent Court of International Justice had recourse to this principle. Thus, when the Court had to interpret the duties incumbent upon Germany under the Peace Treaty of Versailles respecting the Kiel Canal, it held 'that Germany has to submit to an important limitation of the exercise of the sovereign right which no one disputes that she possesses over the Kiel Canal. This fact constitutes a sufficient reason for the restrictive interpretation, in case of doubt, of the clause which produces such a limitation.' [Series A 1, p. 24.]

"Yet the Court took precaution against the obvious possibilities of the abuse of these rules of interpretation and carefully balanced them in such a way as to prevent them from reducing validly undertaken international obligations to meaninglessness and insignificance. In a number of decisions, the Court emphasised that this rule of interpretation was merely a subsidiary rule. The principle has to be applied with the greatest caution, and it cannot operate where the intention of the parties is unequivocal. It must not impair a teleological interpretation of treaties, *i.e.*, an interpretation which is not merely grammatical, but takes into account the underlying principles and the functions of the provisions under consideration. [Series A 9, p. 24; Series B 2, pp. 22–23; Series B 7, pp. 16–17; Series B 11, pp. 37–39; Series B 13, p. 22.] The line consistently taken by the Court is well summarised in its Judgment regarding the *Territorial Jurisdiction of the Oder Commission* (1929). The Court refused to 'accept the Polish Government's contention that, the text being doubtful, the solution should be adopted which imposes the least restriction on the freedom of States. This argument, though sound in itself, must be employed only with the greatest caution. To rely upon it, it is not sufficient that the purely grammatical analysis of a text should not lead to definite results; there are many other methods of interpretation, in particular, reference is properly had to principles underlying the matter to which the text refers; it will be only when, in spite of all pertinent considerations, the intention of the Parties still remains doubtful, that that interpretation should be adopted which is most favourable to the freedom of States.' [Series A, p. 26.]

"The Permanent Court of International Justice not only limited this rule of interpretation in the interest of the effectiveness of international treaties, but also had to make it compatible with another important rule, *i.e.*, that exceptions are not to be interpreted extensively. In so far as the reservation of exclusive domestic jurisdiction was raised under Article 15, paragraph 8, of the Covenant, it was merely an exception to the general rule that all disputes likely to lead to a rupture which were not submitted to arbitration, had to be submitted to the Council's jurisdiction. Within the system of the Covenant, therefore, the general position under international customary law was reversed. By their signature of the Peace Treaties, by their accession to the Covenant or by their admission to the League, the members of the League voluntarily submitted themselves to the League's *lex societatis* and, to that extent, limit their sovereign rights. In this way, they had put themselves into a position in which any plea under paragraph 8 had to be considered as 'an exception to the principles affirmed in the preceding paragraphs,' and which, therefore, 'did not lend itself to an extensive interpretation.' [Series B 4, p. 25.] The same arguments apply to any plea under paragraph 7 of Article 2 of the Charter of the United Nations."

I Schwarzenberger, *International Law* (1949) 59–60.

". . . From a political point of view, it may be said that the limitations on sovereignty may not be extended by interpretation or that such limitations must be interpreted restrictively. Speaking more legally, it may be said that international law does not authorize extending by generalization, or more particularly by analogy, the norms restricting the liberty of States. [D. Anzilotti, *Cours de droit international*, tr. Gidel, p. 116. In its political expression the idea figures in the Judgment rendered on August 17, 1923 by the Permanent Court of International Justice in the "Wimbledon" case, p. 24, in the Judgment of September 7, 1927, in the "Lotus" case, p. 18, and in the Judgment of June 7, 1932 on the Free Zones, p. 167. In its Judgment relating to the Oder Commission (September 10, 1929), the Court sharply limited the scope of the argument by stating (p. 26) that "This argument, though sound in itself, must be employed only with the greatest caution . . . it will be only when, in spite of all pertinent considerations, the intention of the Parties still remains doubtful, that that interpretation should be adopted which is most favorable to the freedom of States."]"

De Visscher, *Theory and Reality in Public International Law* (Princeton, 1957, translated from French by P. E. Corbett) 354–355.

"The principle of sovereignty is buttressed by strong presumptions in its favour. Thus, in the case of the *North Atlantic Coast Fisheries* (1910), the Permanent Court of Arbitration held: 'Considering that the right to regulate the liberties conferred by the Treaty of 1818 is an attribute of sovereignty, and as such must be held to reside in the territorial sovereign, unless the contrary be provided; and considering that one of the essential elements is that it is to be exercised within the territorial limits, and that, failing proof to the contrary, the territory is conterminous with the sovereignty, it follows that the burden of the assertion involved in the contention of the United States (*viz.*, that the right to regulate does not reside independently in Great Britain, the territorial sovereign) must fall on the United States.' [*World Court Reports* (1916) 141, 157.] In the *Lotus* case (1927), the World Court summed up this position in still more categorical language: 'Restrictions upon the independence of States cannot be presumed.' [Series A, No. 10, p. 18.] Similarly, in the *Asylum* case (1950), the International Court of Justice emphasised the derogation from territorial sovereignty which the grant of diplomatic asylum involved. Any such derogation 'cannot be recognised unless its legal basis is established in each particular case.' [1950 I.C.J. Reports, p. 275.] On the international judicial level, other presumptions, such as those in favour of the good faith and law-abidingness of the parties, tend to operate in the same direction, that is to say, towards the non-liability of disputants under international law in the absence of convincing evidence to the contrary."

I Schwarzenberger, *International Law* (3d. ed., 1957) 119–120.

"In fact, through the entire branch of international law relating to state territory and territorial sovereignty there runs as a constant theme the phenomenon of limitation of sovereignty in various spheres and directions. This is not confined to so-called state servitudes or to those instances in which the exercise of sovereignty—actual control and jurisdiction—is divorced from residuary sovereignty as in the case of so-called political leases or grants in perpetuity. It is sufficient to mention the less sweeping limitations resulting from express treaty stipulations, such as the air bases granted in 1941 by Great Britain to the United States, or from rules of general international law such as the prohibition of nuisance or the limitations upon the state's freedom of action in respect of the use of non-national rivers. . . . But it [sovereignty] is an established term of a clarity transcending that of 'control and jurisdiction'. In particular it implies not only rights but also international responsibility . . . ."

Lauterpacht, "Sovereignty Over Submarine Areas", XXVII Brit. Yb. Int'l L. (1950) 376, 391–392.

Diplomatic asylum

"In the case of extradition, the refugee is within the territory of the State of refuge. A decision with regard to extradition implies only the normal exercise of the territorial sovereignty. The refugee is outside the territory of the State where the offence was committed, and a decision to grant him asylum in no way derogates from the sovereignty of that State.

"In the case of diplomatic asylum, the refugee is within the territory of the State where the offence was committed. A decision to grant diplomatic asylum involves a derogation from the sovereignty of that State. It withdraws the offender from the jurisdiction of the territorial State and constitutes an intervention in matters which are exclusively within the competence of that State. Such a derogation from territorial sovereignty cannot be recognized unless its legal basis is established in each particular case."

Asylum Case (Colombia/Peru), Judgment, Nov. 20, 1950, I.C.J. Reports (1950) 266, 274–275.

Residual, ultimate, or titular sovereignty:

The German District Labor Court of Karlsruhe, in upholding its jurisdiction over a labor dispute involving the German Federal Railway Company's notice of dismissal to one of its workers employed in the operation of the railway station at Basle, a right granted to Germany by Switzerland, stated:

German railway establishment at Basle

". . . Although the State cannot part with its people or with its territory, it is, according to the predominant doctrine, at liberty to give up part of its sovereignty so long as it retains a certain residuum of it. The grant of the rights connected with the railway establishment at Basle constitutes such a partial cession of sovereignty, for the building and maintenance of railways within the State belong to the exercise of sovereignty. By having granted the right to these establishments, Switzerland has parted with her rights of sovereignty in regard to railways in respect of the areas placed at the disposal of Germany. It follows that as the result of this grant Switzerland has parted with her judicial supremacy in regard to the area in question. For the grant of such rights cannot be separated from the rights of sovereignty directly and necessarily connected with this right. A State which hands over rights of sovereignty connected with railways at the same time also hands over the rights of sovereignty in respect of judicial supremacy in so far as they are directly connected with the undertaking. Not every grant of the exercise of the rights of sovereignty on foreign territory has the same result. First, it is necessary that these rights should be permanently exercised; it is not sufficient if they are exercised on a single occasion. Secondly, it is necessary that these rights should be exercised within a self-contained area. If these requirements are present, there is in existence the judicial supremacy directly connected with the undertaking."

German Railway Station at Basle Case, [1927–1928] Ann. Dig. 136, 137–138 (No. 90).

By article III of the Agreement for the Lease to the United States of Lands in Cuba for Coaling and Naval Stations—the Guantanamo Naval Base—it was agreed that—

". . . the United States recognizes the continuance of the ultimate sovereignty of the Republic of Cuba over the above described areas of land and water".

I Malloy, Treaties, etc. (1910) 358, 359.

Guantanamo

Article III of the Convention for the Construction of a Ship Canal, signed November 18, 1903, by the United States of America and the Republic of Panama, reads:

"The Republic of Panama grants to the United States all the rights, power and authority within the zone mentioned and described in Article II of this agreement and within the limits of all auxiliary lands and waters mentioned and described in said Article II which the United States would possess and exercise if it were the sovereign of the territory within which said lands and waters are located to the entire exclusion of the exercise by the Republic of Panama of any such sovereign rights, power or authority."

Panama: Canal Zone

In his now-famous statement made April 18, 1906, before the Committee on Interoceanic Canals, William Howard Taft, then Secretary of War, quoted article III of the 1903 Convention and stated:

"It is peculiar in not conferring sovereignty directly upon the United States, but in giving to the United States the powers which it would have *if it were sovereign*. This gives rise to the obvious implication that a mere titular sovereignty is reserved in the Panamanian Government. Now, I agree that to the Anglo-Saxon mind a titular sovereignty is like what Governor Allen, of Ohio, once characterized as a 'barren ideality,' but to the Spanish or Latin mind poetic and sentimental, enjoying the intellectual refinements, and dwelling much on names and forms it is by no means unimportant. . . ."

Hearings before the Committee on Interoceanic Canals, Apr. 18, 1906, S. Doc. 401, 59th Cong., 2d sess., vol. III (Serial 5099), pp. 2515, 2526–2527.

In an earlier statement contained in a letter addressed to President Theodore Roosevelt, Taft had also stated:

". . . The truth is that while we have all the attributes of sovereignty necessary in the construction, maintenance, and protection of the canal, the very form in which these attributes are conferred in

the treaty seems to preserve the titular sovereignty over the Canal
Zone in the Republic of Panama, and as we have conceded to us
complete judicial and police power and control over the Zone and the
two ports at the end of the canal, I can see no reason for creating a
resentment on the part of the people of the Isthmus by quarreling over
that which is dear to them but which to us is of no real moment whatever." Secretary of War Taft to President Theodore Roosevelt, letter
dated Jan. 12, 1905, printed *ibid*. 2393, 2399.

Deputy Under Secretary Livingston Merchant, upon his departure
from Panama on November 24, 1959, issued a statement in which he
declared that "the policy of the United States Government with respect to the status of the Canal Zone remains as it had been stated
more than 50 years ago to the effect that the United States recognizes
that titular sovereignty over the Canal Zone remains in the Government of Panama".

Press release 817, Nov. 24, 1959, XLI *Bulletin*, Department of State, No.
1068, Dec. 14, 1959, p. 859.

Article 3 of the Treaty of Peace with Japan provides:

Ryukyu
Islands

"Japan will concur in any proposal of the United States to the
United Nations to place under its trusteeship system, with the
United States as the sole administering authority, Nansei Shoto
south of 29° north latitude (including the Ryukyu Islands and
the Daito Islands), Nanpo Shoto south of Sofu Gan (including
the Bonin Islands, Rosario Island and the Volcano Islands) and
Parece Vela and Marcus Island. Pending the making of such
a proposal and affirmative action thereon, the United States will
have the right to exercise all and any powers of administration,
legislation and jurisdiction over the territory and inhabitants of
these islands, including their territorial waters."

*Conference for the Conclusion and Signature of the Treaty of Peace
with Japan, San Francisco, California, September 4–8, 1951, Record of
Proceedings* (1951), Department of State publication 4392, p. 314; U.S.
TIAS 2490; 3 UST, pt. 3, p. 3169; 136 UNTS 46.

Commenting on article 3 with regard to the issue of sovereignty,
John Foster Dulles, who as special representative of the President
had conducted the negotiations with respect to the Treaty, said in a
speech at the Japanese Peace Treaty Conference:

"Several of the Allied Powers urged that the treaty should
require Japan to renounce its sovereignty over these islands in
favor of United States sovereignty. Others suggested that these
islands should be restored completely to Japan.

"In the face of this division of Allied opinion, the United
States felt that the best formula would be to permit Japan to
retain residual sovereignty, while making it possible for these
islands to be brought into the United Nations trusteeship system,
with the United States as administering authority."

Conference for the Conclusion and Signature of the Treaty of Peace with Japan, San Francisco, California, September 4–8, 1951, Record of Proceedings (1951), Department of State publication 4392, p. 78.

The United States District Court in Hawaii had occasion to examine the question of residual sovereignty with respect to Okinawa, an island in the Ryukyu Archipelago, in the case of *The United States* v. *Ushi Shiroma* (123 F. Supp. 145 (D.C. Hawaii 1954)). Charged with failure as an alien to notify the Attorney General in writing of his current address and furnish such additional information as required by law, thus violating 8 U.S.C. § 1306(b), Ushi Shiroma in defense asserted that being a native of Okinawa, and Okinawa being a possession of the United States since World War II, he was not an alien but a national of the United States. Since the defendant was not a citizen of the United States, he could only qualify as a "national" of the United States, according to the definition in the Immigration and Nationality Act of 1952, 8 U.S.C. § 1101(a)(22), if he owed permanent allegiance to the United States which, as a correlative of the concept of sovereignty, is owed, in the Court's determination, only to a "de jure sovereign".

Discussing this concept of residual sovereignty, the Court declared:

> "The adjective 'residual' means of the nature of something left as residue. Thus the concept of 'residual sovereignty' starts with the assumption that sovereignty is capable of division.
>
> "Under Article 3 of the Treaty of Peace, Japan which previously had full sovereignty over Okinawa transferred a part of that sovereignty, while retaining the residue. That portion of the sovereignty which gives the United States 'the right to exercise all and any powers of administration, legislation and jurisdiction' under Article 3 may be labeled 'de facto sovereignty.' The residue or 'residual sovereignty' retained by Japan is the traditional 'de jure sovereignty.'"

Accordingly, the Court concluded that "Japan, and not the United States, having 'de jure sovereignty' over Okinawa since the ratification of the Treaty of Peace, the defendant is not a national of the United States. . . ."

In reaching its decision, the Court attributed great weight to the construction given the terms of article 3 of this Treaty by John Foster Dulles (*supra*) and acquiesced in by the other signatory powers. In addition, the Court quoted from a letter dated May 14, 1952, from the Office of the Legal Adviser of the Department of State which stated in part:

> "1. A legal opinion is requested on the request of the Japanese Vice Minister for Foreign Affairs dated 10 December 1951, that the United States confirm that the 'Southern Islands' (the

Ryukyus and the Bonins) remain under the sovereignty of Japan and that their inhabitants remain Japanese nationals.

. . . .

"6. It is concluded that sovereignty over the Ryukyu and Bonin Islands remains in Japan, and that the inhabitants thereof are Japanese nationals."

123 F. Supp. 145, 149 (D.C. Hawaii 1954). For determination of Okinawa as a "foreign country" after World War II and prior to the Treaty of Peace with Japan within the meaning of the Federal Tort Claims Act and distinction between *"de facto"* and *"de jure"* sovereignty, see *Cobb* v. *United States*, 191 F. 2d 604 (9th Cir. 1951).

In reply to a letter inquiring about the status of the Ryukyu Islands, the Office of the Legal Adviser of the Department of State in a letter of July 31, 1959, wrote:

"You inquire firstly whether any steps have been taken or are likely to be made in the future to place the islands under the United Nations trusteeship system. The United States Government has not made any such proposal to the United Nations, and, as to the future, has repeatedly declared its intention to exercise its present powers and rights so long as conditions of threat and tension exist in the Far East, thereby enabling the United States to contribute effectively to the maintenance of security in that area. The statement contained in the joint communique of June 21, 1957, issued by President Eisenhower and Prime Minister Kishi at the conclusion of their talks in Washington continues to be the definitive statement of United States policy on this subject. It is quoted below for your information:

" 'The Prime Minister emphasized the strong desire of the Japanese people for the return of administrative control over the Ryukyu and Bonin Islands to Japan. The President reaffirmed the United States position that Japan possesses residual sovereignty over these islands. He pointed out, however, that so long as the conditions of threat and tension exist in the Far East, the United States will find it necessary to continue the present status.' ('Department of State Bulletin', July 8, 1957, page 52.)

"Your second inquiry relates to the phrase 'residual sovereignty'.

"This phrase expresses the idea that, far from being a cession of sovereignty, Article 3 of the Peace Treaty contains provision only for the broad exercise of the rights and powers of sovereignty by the United States. Thus, the United States has not annexed the islands or claimed sovereignty over them; sovereignty remains in Japan—even though in a latent or residual form. But the right to exercise the rights and powers usually associated with sovereignty has been given to the United States.

"A discussion of the situation where one state actually exercises sovereignty which is, in law, vested elsewhere may be found in I Oppenheim, *International Law* 455 (8th ed., Lauterpacht 1955). Analysis of the concept of residual sovereignty took place in at least two court decisions: *Cobb* v. *United States*, 191 F. 2d 604, 608 (9th Cir. 1951), and *United States* v. *Ushi Shiroma*, 123 F. Supp. 145 (D.C. Hawaii 1954). Reference might also be made to the remarks of the Honorable Leon H. Gavin in the United States House of Representatives entitled, 'The Precise Status of the Ryukyu Islands', 104 Cong. Rec. App. 283 (daily ed. Jan. 15, 1958). For an instructive illustration of the concept of residual sovereignty in practice, study should be made of the relinquishment by the United States on December 25, 1953 of its right under Article 3 of the Japanese Peace Treaty in favor of resumption by Japan of authority over the Amami Oshima group in the Ryukyu Islands. (4 UST 2912; TIAS 2895)."

The Office of the Legal Adviser (Maurer) to John Brimley, letter, July 31, 1959, MS. Department of State, file 794c.0221/7–1759.

"Undoubtedly, on occasions, states exercise jurisdictional rights over territory—rights of 'jurisdiction or control' or 'exclusive jurisdiction and control' [the author is referring to the language of certain proclamations, etc., with reference to the continental shelf]—although they do not possess or claim sovereignty. This is so in all cases in which the exercise of sovereignty is divorced from residuary sovereignty vested with and delegated by a higher authority (as in the case of the mandates of the League of Nations or trust territories under the Charter of the United Nations) or by another state (as in the case of leases, grants in perpetuity, and the like). . . ."

Lauterpacht, "Sovereignty Over Submarine Areas", XXVII Brit. Yb. Int'l L. (1950) 376, 389, n. 2.

It is not unusual for the status of a particular state's sovereignty to be far from clear. Thus, it may be unclear, indeterminable, or even in some instances considered to be in suspense, at least by certain persons. *[margin: Sovereignty unclear, indeterminable, in suspense, etc.:]*

In an address before the White House Correspondents Association, February 12, 1943, President Roosevelt remarked: "French sovereignty rests with the people of France. Its expression has been temporarily suspended by German occupation. Once the triumphant armies of the United Nations have expelled the common foe, Frenchmen will be represented by a government of their own popular choice." *[margin: Expression in suspense (France)]*

VIII *Bulletin*, Department of State, No. 190, Feb. 13, 1943, p. 145.

"Despite the substantive resemblance of the State Treaty [for the Re-establishment of an Independent and Democratic Austria] to a treaty of peace, in that its nine parts contain provisions normally associated with the restoration of peaceful amicable relations between hostile States, it appears that the Allied Powers did not regard it as a treaty of peace. The United Kingdom, *[margin: Austria]* for example, had already, by unilateral declaration on September 16, 1947, terminated the state of war between itself and Austria. The view appears to have prevailed that the international personality of Austria was suspended upon her annexation by Germany on March 18, 1938. And although there may be a measure of inconsistency between this view and the reference in the Preamble of Treaty to the statement in the Moscow Declaration of November 1, 1943, that the Allied Powers regarded the annexation of Austria as 'null and void,' the assumption of the loss by Austria in 1938 of her separate legal personality has been followed throughout the Treaty. Thus the first article contains the recognition by the Allied Powers that Austria is '*re-established* as a sovereign, independent and democratic State.' And in Article 28 . . . this assumption is pursued in connection with both the public debt of Austria and the private debts due to and from Austrian nationals."

Lauterpacht, "The Contemporary Practice of the United Kingdom in the Field of International Law—Survey and Comment, V", 7 Int'l & Comp. **L.Q.** (1958) 92, 94–95.

Professor Kunz writes:

". . . an independent and sovereign Austria is, under Articles 1 and 2, only re-established by this treaty. But Austria, even if not sovereign, has existed again since May, 1945. . . . this Austria since 1945, and the sovereign Austria re-established by the treaty, are identical in law with the Republic of Austria of 1918. That this is so, is clearly shown by Article 10, paragraph 2, which obliges Austria to maintain the Austrian law of April 3, 1919. It is clearly shown by Article 28, paragraphs 2 and 4, as to Austrian laws before March 13, 1938, and prewar contracts concluded by the Government of Austria or persons who were nationals of Austria on March 12, 1938.

"The treaty, therefore, recognizes Austria's extinction in fact between March 13, 1938, and May 8, 1945, and yet recognizes her identity and continuity. It is therefore a treaty proving Marek's proposed 'fourth rule' as to the identity of states: complete but illegal suppression of a state in time of peace, but continuance of a mere 'ideal legal notion' of the state in question; identity and continuity, provided this state is re-established in fact within a reasonable time." Kunz, "The State Treaty With Austria", 49 Am. J. Int'l L. (1955) 535, 541.

For further discussion regarding identity of Austria, see chapter on "State Succession", *post* this work. On the question regarding "suspension" of German sovereignty, see *infra* this chapter.

Formosa

". . . In 1895 under the Treaty of Shimonoseki China ceded Formosa to Japan. In the Cairo conference in November 1943 the United States, United Kingdom, and China declared it was their 'purpose' that Manchuria, Formosa, and the Pescadores 'shall be restored to the Republic of China.' Thereafter in August 1945 in the Potsdam conference the United States, United Kingdom, and China declared that 'the terms of the Cairo Declaration shall be carried out.' This Potsdam declaration was subsequently adhered to by the U.S.S.R. On September 2, 1945, the Japanese Government, in the instrument of surrender, accepted the provisions of the declaration. The Supreme Allied Commander for the Allied Powers then issued Directive No. 1, under which the Japanese Imperial Headquarters issued General Order No. 1 requiring Japanese commanders in Formosa to surrender to Generalissimo Chiang Kai-shek of the Republic of China. Since September 1945 the United States and the other Allied Powers have accepted the exercise of Chinese authority over the island. In article 2 of the Japanese Peace Treaty, which entered into force April 28, 1952, Japan renounced all 'right, title and claim' to Formosa. Neither this agreement nor any other agreement thereafter has purported to transfer the sovereignty of Formosa to China.

. . . .

". . . neither in that treaty nor in any other treaty has there been any definitive cession to China of Formosa. The situation is, then, one where the Allied Powers still have to come to some agreement or treaty with respect to the status of Formosa."

Ely Maurer, Assistant Legal Adviser for Far Eastern Affairs, "Legal Problems Regarding Formosa and the Offshore Islands", address, XXXIX *Bulletin*, Department of State, No. 1017, Dec. 22, 1958, pp. 1005–1006, 1009.

The Assistant Legal Adviser for Far Eastern Affairs of the Department of State, in a formal communication of June 2, 1959, addressed to an Assistant United States Attorney, wrote in part as follows:

". . . you are informed that the United States recognizes the Government of the Republic of China as the legal Government of China. The provisional capital of the Republic of China has been at Taipei, Taiwan (Formosa), since December 1949.

"In 1895, under terms of the Treaty of Shimonoseki, China was compelled to cede Formosa to Japan. In the Cairo Conference, the United States, United Kingdom and China declared it was their 'purpose' that Manchuria, Formosa and the Pescadores 'shall be restored to the Republic of China.' Thereafter in August 1945 in the Potsdam Conference the United States, United Kingdom and China declared 'that the terms of the Cairo Declaration shall be carried out.' This Potsdam Declaration was subsequently adhered to by the U.S.S.R. On September 2, 1945 the Japanese Government, in the instrument of surrender, accepted the provisions of the Declaration. The Supreme Allied Commander for the Allied Powers then issued Directive No. 1 under which the Japanese Imperial Headquarters issued General Order No. 1 requiring Japanese commanders in Formosa to surrender to Generalissimo Chiang Kai-shek of the Republic of China. Since September 1945 the United States and the other Allied Powers have accepted the exercise of Chinese authority over the island. In Article 2 of the Japanese Peace Treaty, which entered into force April 28, 1952, Japan renounced all 'right, title and claim' to Formosa."

The Assistant Legal Adviser for Far Eastern Affairs (Maurer) to Assistant United States Attorney Asman, letter, June 2, 1959, MS. Department of State, file 793.02/6–259.

The United States Court of Appeals for the District of Columbia Circuit in the case of *Rogers* v. *Cheng Fu Sheng and Lin Fu Mei* (1960) held that Formosa was a "country" within the meaning of the Immigration and Nationality Act of 1952 on the grounds that "Formosa is a well-defined geographical, social and political entity" with "a government . . . which has undisputed control of the island". Discussing the meaning of the word "country" the Court quoted the Supreme Court as having pointed out that " 'the word "country" . . . is ambiguous. It may be taken to mean foreign territory or a foreign government. In the sense of territory, it may embrace all the territory subject to a foreign sovereign power. When referring more particularly to a foreign government, it may describe a foreign State in the international sense . . . or it may mean a foreign government which has authority over a particular area or subject matter, although not an international person. . . .' *Burnet* v. *Chicago Portrait Co.*, 285 U.S. 1 (1932)."

> 280 F.2d 663, 664–665.
>
> Prime Minister Eden of Great Britain stated February 4, 1955, that "Formosa and the Pescadores are . . . in the view of Her Majesty's Government, territory the *de jure* sovereignty over which is uncertain or undetermined". Written Answers, 536 H.C. Deb. (5th ser.) col. 159 (Feb. 4, 1959).

Gaza Strip

Commenting on the status of the Gaza Strip in a debate before the House of Commons on the political situation in the Middle East in March 1957, the British Secretary of State for Foreign Affairs, Selwyn Lloyd, stated:

> ". . . The facts about the Gaza strip seem to me to be these. No country has legal sovereignty. By the Armistice Agreement of 1949 the Gaza strip was not demilitarised. Egypt was left in military occupation. Since then, until October, 1956, Egypt exercised *de facto* authority, but the provisions of the Armistice Agreement were, of course, dictated solely by military considerations, and other matters were excluded from its scope. During the recent hostilities, Israel captured the area." [566 H.C. Deb. (5th ser.) col. 1320 (Mar. 14, 1957).]

An editorial note discussed this comment as follows:

> ". . . It is doubtful whether the statement made here by the Foreign Secretary that 'No country has legal sovereignty' over the Gaza Strip should be regarded as an expression of opinion that the area is *terra nullius* and thus open to occupation in the normal way. Any such construction of the Foreign Secretary's words would involve the assumption that Her Majesty's Government had formed firm views upon such intricate issues as that of

the location of residual sovereignty over Mandated Territories, the extent of the succession of the United Nations to the legal position of the League of Nations under the Mandates System, the exact legal character of the role played by the United Nations in 1947 and 1948 in the establishment of the State of Israel, the interpretation and effect of General Assembly Resolution 181 (II) of November 29, 1947, and the possible legal consequences of the hostilities between Egypt and Israel; for, as will be seen, each of these questions must be considered before it is possible to reach a conclusion on the status of the Gaza Strip.

"The only certain starting point in any consideration of the present status of the Gaza strip is the fact that prior to the coming into force of the Treaty of Lausanne on August 6, 1924, the Strip was part of an area which was formally Turkish territory. It is true that Palestine had in fact already, on July 24, 1922, been placed under British Mandate, but, applying the doctrine that an enemy cannot be deprived of territory *pendente bello*, it is clear that Turkey did not validly lose her title to the area until she renounced it in terms in Article 16 of the Treaty of Lausanne. Thereafter, it is difficult to determine the devolution of sovereignty over the area. Turkey did not identify the parties in whose favour she renounced her title; though reference was made to the fact that the future of the area was being settled by the parties concerned. Who those parties might be was not indicated, but since the Mandate for Palestine had already entered into force, 'the parties concerned' must, presumably, have been the parties to the Mandate Agreement.

"In those circumstances, what was the fate of Turkish sovereignty over Palestine? Did it pass to the League of Nations? If so, did it, upon the dissolution of the League devolve upon the United Nations? And if it did, has the United Nations effectively conveyed or abandoned it? Some of the difficulties to which these questions give rise may now be considered.

"In the first place, although the question of the location of sovereignty during the operation of the Mandates system has for long been a matter of controversy, it has in large part been of an academic nature. On the practical side, it was clear that the Administering Authority was not the absolute sovereign and possessed only those powers which it was granted under the Mandate. As the International Court of Justice observed in its Advisory Opinion on the *Status of South-West Africa*, 'the terms of this Mandate, as well as the provisions of Article 22 of the Covenant and the principles embodied therein, show that the creation of this new international institution did not involve any cession of territory or transfer of, sovereignty' to the Mandatory power. [I.C.J. *Reports*, 1950, p. 79, at p. 83.] Equally, it was clear and was affirmed by practice that the Council of the League and the Mandatory Power, acting in concert, were capable at the least of establishing a good root of title for the future exercise of sovereignty over a former Mandated area by an independent State newly established therein. Certainly, the Administering Authority did not by itself possess sufficient authority unilaterally

to modify the status of the Mandated area. In these circumstances, while it may not be possible to speak of the possession of
sovereignty by the League, it is impossible to say that the League
enjoyed no rights whatsoever of a proprietory kind in territories
under Mandate.

"It is, therefore, necessary to determine the effect of the dissolution of the League upon the role which it might play in
validating the acquisition of absolute title to areas formerly comprised within a Mandated territory. On this question some help
is again to be derived from the Advisory Opinion of the International Court on the *Status of South-West Africa*. The Court
declared that the appropriate mode of procedure for modifying
the status of a Mandated area after the dissolution of the League
was by agreement between the Administering Authority and the
General Assembly of the United Nations. [*Ibid.*, at. pp. 92–93.]
It is true that this view was expressed by the Court in relation to
a Mandated territory other than Palestine and at a time after the
Palestine Mandate had terminated; but it is not, for these reasons,
any the less helpful as a guide to the general consequences of the
termination of the League.

"However, it is this view—that agreement between the General
Assembly and the Mandatory Power can alter the status of the
territory—which gives rise to the difficulty in the present case.
For it will be recalled that no agreement was reached between the
United Kingdom and the General Assembly upon the future of
Palestine. The United Kingdom declared its intention to re-
nounce the Mandate and thus, in effect, abandoned to the General
Assembly the complete disposition of the area. The General
Assembly, in its turn, only partially discharged its task. By
Resolution 181 (II) of November 29, 1947, the Assembly recommended 'the adoption and implementation, with regard to the
future government of Palestine, of the Plan of Partition with
Economic Union. . . .' This Resolution was never implemented
and its recommendations were overtaken by events. The evacuation of Palestine by the United Kingdom was completed on May
14, 1948, and on that day a Jewish State was proclaimed in
Palestine. The boundaries of this new State have not, however,
at any time coincided with those laid down for the State of Israel
in the Partition Plan. Also, in May, 1948, forces of neighbouring
Arab States moved into areas of Palestine adjacent to their own
frontiers. Among the areas thus entered and occupied by Egypt
was the Gaza Strip. Egypt retained control of the Strip under
the terms of the Egyptian-Israeli General Armistice Agreement
of February 24, 1949 [U.N. *Treaty Series*, vol. 42, p. 252],
but subject to the proviso in Article V (2) that 'The Armistice
Demarcation Line is not to be construed in any sense as a political
or territorial boundary, and is delineated without prejudice to
rights, claims and positions of either Party to the Armistice as
regards ultimate settlement of the Palestine question.'

"It is not possible within this Note to examine the implications
in relation to sovereignty over the Gaza Strip, of this series of
events. But, in the circumstances, there can be little doubt that

the observations of the Foreign Secretary are not to be regarded
as an exact opinion on the status of the Strip or as suggesting
that the status of the Strip is such as might enable an occupant,
also possessing the intention to annex it, to acquire title to the area.
It is probably that the Foreign Secretary was saying no more than
that the question of sovereignty over the Gaza Strip is 'uncertain
or undetermined'—the formula employed in 1955 to describe the
position in respect of sovereignty over Formosa and the
Pescadores."

E. Lauterpacht, "The Contemporary Practice of the United Kingdom in
the Field of International Law—Survey and Comment, IV", 6 Int'l & Comp.
L.Q. (1957) 506, 513–516.

In a written answer to inquiries concerning what state has sov- Tiran
ereignty over the islands of Tiran and Sanafir in the Gulf of Aqaba, Sanafir
Secretary of State for Foreign Affairs Selwyn Lloyd stated:

"In the view of Her Majesty's Government, the status of these
islands has not yet been finally determined. They were occupied
by Egypt in January, 1950. The Egyptian Government, when
informing Her Majesty's Government of the occupation, stated
that it had been carried out with the full agreement of the Saudi
Arabian Government in order to protect the interests of the two
countries. Egyptian forces were withdrawn from the islands
during the recent operations and on 6th November, 1956, it was
announced in Tel Aviv that Israel had annexed Tiran."

Written Answers, 565 H.C. Deb. (5th ser.) col. 168 (Feb. 27, 1957).

In answer to questions addressed to the Department of State bearing
upon the status of Andorra, the Department concluded:

"By the terms of a treaty of 1278, still in force, Andorra is a Joint
'fief' under the joint suzerainty of the President of the French suzerainty:
Republic and the Bishop of Urgel (Spain) who are 'co-princes' of Andorra
Andorra where they are represented by 'viguiers'. A nominal
tribute of 960 francs and 450 pesetas per annum is paid to France
and Spain respectively. Andorra is administered by a council of
twenty-four members elected to four-year terms by heads of families. The Public Services are supervised by the French 'Préfet'
of the Pyrenees Orientales at Perpignan. Andorra does not
maintain diplomatic relations with foreign countries."

Department of State, French-Iberian Affairs (West) to Steven Gladin,
letter, Aug. 17, 1956, MS. Department of State, file FW 012.150c/8–656.

". . . Andorra essentially is a feudal state under the personal protection
of the President of France and the Spanish Bishop of Seo de Urgel, who
must approve the acts of the Councilors.

"Andorra's history is vague. It is thought to have been established as
an independent state by Charlemagne as a reward to the local mountaineers
for help in repelling the Saracens who threatened France. When Charlemagne's empire broke up, Andorra became a bone of contention between
the various Counts of Foix in France and the Bishops of Seo de Urgel.

"In 1278, the quarreling feudal lords signed a charter providing for a joint suzerainty by the Count and the Bishop. When feudalism died in France, the hereditary rights of France were passed first to the kings and later the presidents of France." New York *Times*, May 11, 1959, p. 15.

Reporting on some of the legal and historical aspects of this "joint sovereignty", a despatch from the American Embassy at Paris stated:

". . . When the two Co-Princes agree, which is rarely the case, they can jointly exercise complete sovereignty since the *Paréage* treaty of 1278 does not guarantee self-government to the Andorrans. That interpretation is in any event given by the French, who do not use the term suzerainty to describe their relationship to Andorra. According to their view, the President of France . . . and the Bishop of Urgel could theoretically agree to partition Andorra, or one could sell or otherwise cede his rights to the other. As a matter of fact, only in 1933 when both the French and the Bishop were alarmed at anarchist disorders fomented by Spanish laborers brought in to build the FHASA hydro-electric works, they agreed to send in the French *garde mobile*, dissolve the Council of the Valleys and rule Andorra by decree. The *garde mobile* withdrew only after the Spanish Civil War, in 1939, when self-government had been gradually restored to Andorra. Theoretically, any decisions of the Council of the Valleys require the approval of both Co-Princes in order to be valid, and either of them can invalidate any decision of that body.

.   .   .   .

"It is the French position, which has been accepted up to now by the Ecclesiastical Co-Prince, that neither Spain nor France have rights of sovereignty over Andorra but rather the Bishop of Urgel in his ecclesiastical capacity and the President of France individually in his capacity as lineal descendant of the Comte de Foix. Because of this situation, and since the Bishop of Urgel does not maintain diplomatic relations with the outside world, the President of France represents Andorra in international relations. Consequently, the French authorities normally issue passports to Andorran citizens, who are admitted to France and treated there like Frenchmen. Andorrans in foreign countries are supposed to register with the French consulates for protection although they could also appeal for protection to the Bishop of Urgel. The Spanish government has occasionally attempted to intervene in Andorra and after the war tried to represent Andorra at some international conferences; but the French have always contested this right and the Spanish Government has never, as far as is known, persisted in raising the issue. More recently, the Bishop of Urgel has questioned the French monopoly of the foreign representation of Andorra.

"Not only the decisions of the Council of the Valleys require approval of the Co-Princes, but so do elections in Andorra and appointments to key executive and legislative positions. The latter are represented by two *batlles* or judges who are selected and confirmed one each by each of the Co-Princes, from a list established by the Andorrans. As will be seen, the role of the *batlles* is an important and contentious one. In 1903, when the Ecclesiastical Co-Prince also had his troubles with the Andorrans, both he and the French Co-Prince opposed an attempt to levy taxes on French imports. The Co-Princes instructed the *batlles* not to enforce the Andorrans' regulations and exhorted the population not to pay the taxes. The Council of the Valleys thereupon fired the *batlles* but the Co-Princes reinstated them. The affair petered out when the Pope raised the Bishop of Urgel to the rank of Cardinal and transferred him to another diocese, and the taxes were no longer raised."

The Counselor of the American Embassy at Paris (Joyce) to the Secretary of State (Dulles), despatch No. 881, Sept. 28, 1953, MS. Department of State, file 650c.51/9–2853.

When all privately owned radio stations in France were nationalized after World War II, Radio-Andorra remained outside the new R.T.F. (Radio-diffusion-Television Française) network. Following a Paris Court's ruling that the subsequent jamming of Radio-Andorra by the R.T.F. in 1948 and 1949 was illegal, private and official opponents set up a rival station called Andorradio. The Co-Princes, President Coty of France and the Bishop of Urgel, agreed in September 1958 to permit the Andorradio permanently to function on a wavelength assigned by the R.T.F.

The Andorran Council of the Valleys called an exceptional *Assemblea Magna*, attended by heads of families from every parish, which voted a unanimous protest against this "violation of Andorran rights". "It was reported that the protest reminded both co-princes that the council alone was empowered to grant concessions."

USIS, Paris, to USIA, Washington, despatch No. 42, Sept. 30, 1958. See also the Counselor of the American Embassy at Paris (Joyce) to the Secretary of State (Dulles), despatch No. 881, Sept. 28, 1953, MS. Department of State, file 650c.51/9–2853.

The Tribunal de Perpignan of France in deciding the case of *Massip* v. *Cruzel*, December 6, 1951, which involved a suit by an Andorran subject domiciled in Andorra, rejected the defendant's contention that the plaintiff should as a foreigner furnish security for costs. Addressing itself to the argument that an Andorran is a foreigner, the Court said in part:

" 'Andorra is not a foreign state; it is not even a sovereign state having the power to conclude diplomatic conventions.

" 'Andorra is a principality of which the co-prince is the Chief of the French State, President of the French Republic. It is in law, as in fact, under the protectorate of France.

" 'Judgments rendered by French courts in penal matters may be executed in Andorra without need to resort to the procedure of extradition.

" '. . . The superior court of Andorra, where only French judges sit and which sits at Perpignan, renders judgments of last resort . . . in the name of the President of the French Republic, who is at the same time co-prince of Andorra, and who causes to be carried out in this latter capacity the decisions made in his name in the former capacity.'

"Although the French Prefect of Pyrénées-Orientales, permanent French Delegate for Andorra, informed the court that Andorran nationals came to France with passports granted by Andorran officials and visas issued by French officials, permitting them to dispense with the identity cards required of aliens in France and letting them engage in France in any sort of employment or profession, the Delegate explained that 'passport' was an inaccurate term, since 'only nationals of a sovereign state can have the benefit of a national passport.' He pointed out that 'Andorrans enjoy in foreign countries French diplomatic and consular protection'; and that in France 'they cannot therefore be assimilated to aliens but ought to be considered as French *protégés.*'

"The court appeared to accept these views of the Delegate, and added that even if Andorra were considered a foreign country, the principle of legislative reciprocity freed Andorrans from the requirement of giving security for costs, since this was not required of foreigners bringing cases before Andorran courts."

Massip v. *Cruzel,* Sirey, *Jurisprudence* (1952) II.151; 47 Am. J. Int'l L. (1953) 331–332.

"It follows from the general principles concerning territorial sovereignty that in peacetime under customary international law only the organs of *one* state are authorized to perform state functions within a given territory. By mutual agreement, however, states have occasionally joined hands as to the exercise of territorial sovereignty.

Condominium–
coimperium

". . . With reference to specific situations the joint exercise of territorial sovereignty by two states has been called *condominium* or *coimperium.* Although the two terms are usually considered as interchangeable it has been proposed to differentiate between them by reserving the term *coimperium* to those situations where joint rights of administration are conferred, whereas the term *condominium* would cover rights of administration plus the right to dispose of a territory. In accordance with this distinction the legal status of the Sudan [could have been until its independence January 1, 1956] and [that of] the New Hebrides can be styled a *coimperium.*

"The several agreements between Great Britain and Egypt concerning the Sudan are [were] designed to regulate, above all, the administration of the Sudan; but the agreement does [did] not regulate the right of the contracting parties to cede the territory of the Sudan.

". . . the protocol respecting the New Hebrides concluded between Great Britain and France on August 6, 1914 contains elaborate provisions on the administration of the New Hebrides. Yet, it is silent on the question of who is ultimately authorized to cede the territory of the New Hebrides. . . ."

Hans Aufricht, "On Relative Sovereignty", XXX Cornell L.Q. (1944) 137, 153–154.

Sudan's attainment of complete independence, January 1, 1956, effectively terminated the joint administration of Great Britain and Egypt over Sudan, which administration had been in the process of liquidation since the entry into force of the Anglo-Egyptian Agreement Concerning Self-Government and Self-Determination for the Sudan, signed February 12, 1953, at Cairo (Cmd. 8767, appendix 8).

In this Agreement, the Governments of Great Britain and Egypt in affirming the right of the Sudanese people to self-determination, agreed that "to enable the Sudanese people to exercise self-determination in a free and neutral atmosphere, a transitional period providing full self-government for the Sudanese shall begin on the day specified in Article 9 below" (article I).

"The transitional period, being a preparation for the effective termination of the dual Administration, shall be considered as a liquidation of that Administration. During the transitional period the sovereignty of the Sudan shall be kept in reserve for the Sudanese until self-determination is achieved." (Article 2.) Documents concerning the Constitutional Development in the Sudan and the Agreement between the Government of the United Kingdom of Great Britain and Northern Ireland and the Egyptian Government concerning Self-Government and Self-Determination for the Sudan, Feb. 17, 1953, Cmd. 8767 (1953), p. 60. See also *The Sudan* (Background), Department of State publication 6572 (1958), pp. 9–10.

". . . In 1902, a French and a British Resident Commissioner were appointed, and regular government was introduced in 1906 when a Convention between Britain and France established the Anglo-French Condominium of the New Hebrides. This Convention was superseded by the Anglo-French Protocol of 1914, which was ratified in 1922, and proclaimed in the Territory in 1923.

"Three administrations were formed: a French National Administration, headed by a Resident Commissioner; a British National Administration also headed by a Resident Commissioner, and one Joint Condominium Administration. Thus, British subjects and ressortisants are protected by British law, French nationals and ressortisants by French law, and the indigenous population is a joint responsibility of the United Kingdom and France. The New Hebrideans have a special status and the two Powers may not consider them as under the jurisdiction of one of their Governments or grant to them British or French nationality. This status gives the New Hebrideans fiscal immunity in that they are not required to pay direct taxes either in services or in

New Hebrides

money and also immunity from military conscription. Under the Condominium Administration, special courts and joint services have been provided and laws and regulations have been enacted pertaining to the area of joint responsibility. . . ."

Information from Non-Self-Governing Territories: Summary and Analysis of Information Transmitted Under Article 73e of the Charter. Report of the Secretary-General, Pacific Territories, New Hebrides, U.N. Doc. A/4088/Add. 11, Apr. 14, 1959 (mimeo.), p. 4.

Independent States

New States

§ 16

STATES ATTAINING INDEPENDENCE SUBSEQUENT TO 1940

Name	Year	Name	Year
Algeria	1962	Lebanon	(5)
Burma	1948	Libya	1951
Burundi	1962	Malagasy	1960
Cambodia	(1)	Malaya	1957
Cameroon	1960	Mali	1960
Central African Republic	1960	Mauritania	1960
Ceylon	1948	Morocco	1956
Chad	1960	Niger	1960
Congo (Brazzaville)	1960	Nigeria	1960
Congo (Léopoldville)	1960	Pakistan	1947
Cyprus	1960	Philippines	1946
Dahomey	1960	Rwanda	1962
Federation of Mali	1960	Senegal	1960
Gabon	1960	Sierra Leone	1961
Ghana	1957	Somali Republic	(6)
Guinea	1958	Sudan	1956
Iceland	1944	Syria	(7)
India	1947	Tanganyika	1961
Indonesia	(2)	Togo	1960
Israel	1948	Trinidad and Tobago	1962
Ivory Coast	1960	Tunisia	1956
Jamaica	1962	Uganda	1962
Jordan	1946	United Arab Republic	1958
Korea	(3)	Upper Volta	1960
Laos	(4)	Viet-Nam	(8)
		Western Samoa	1962

[1] 1942 (independence declared).
   1949 (independence recognized).
[2] 1945 (self-proclaimed independence).
   1949 (transfer of sovereignty).
[3] 1945 (liberation).
   1948 (government formed).

[4] 1945 (independence proclaimed).
   1949 (independence recognized).
[5] 1941 (independence declared).
   1944 (powers transferred).

[6] (Union of Somalia and Somaliland, each of which had achieved independence in 1960).
[7] 1941 (independence declared).
   1944 (powers transferred).
   1958 (formed part of United Arab Republic).
   1961 (separated from United Arab Republic; became Syrian Arab Republic).
[8] 1942 (independence proclaimed).
   1949 (independence recognized).

A brief historical account of the attainment of independence of each of the above-named states is set forth under appropriate section-headings of this chapter.

Unified States

§ 17

Cambodia;
Laos; Viet-
Nam

After the defeat of France in 1940, when Japanese occupation forces largely supplanted French influence within Indochina, Emperor Bao Dai proclaimed the independence of Viet-Nam, March 11, 1942, and the following day King Sihanouk declared Cambodia's independence. The Prime Minister of Laos proclaimed the independence of all of Laos September 15, 1945. Following the capitulation of Japan, the Governments of Cambodia and Laos reaffirmed the independence of their countries from France, and in Tonkin a Vietnamese nationalist movement led by Communists established itself in Hanoi as the independent "Democratic Republic of Vietnam" (DRV) on September 2, 1945, claiming authority over Tonkin, Annam, and Cochin China.

France concluded in 1945 and 1946 provisional agreements with Cambodia (November 9, 13, 1945) and Laos (June 12, July 5, 1946), and created a separate Government of Cochin China in southern Viet-Nam. An accord with Ho Chi Minh, followed by a *modus vivendi* signed September 14, 1946, was concluded March 6, 1946, whereby France recognized "the Viet-Nam Republic as a free state having its government, its parliament, its army, and its finances forming part of the Indochinese Federation and of the French Union . . ."

> The American Ambassador at Paris (Caffery)· to the Secretary of State (Byrnes), despatch No. 6202, Sept. 20, 1946, encl. No. 2, MS. Department of State, file 851g.00/9–2046.

When failure to implement this agreement resulted in the outbreak of hostilities between France and the Viet-Minh (the Communist regime) in December 1946, an agreement was concluded between France and Bao Dai, former Emperor of Annam, under which Annam, Tonkin, and Cochin China were incorporated into the new State of Viet-Nam.

"Associated
States"

Although these proclamations of independence had failed to prevent the reimposition of French rule in 1945, the three States, Viet-Nam, Cambodia, and Laos, achieved the new status of "Associated States" within the newly formed French Union under which an Indochinese Federation replaced the prewar Indochinese Union.

A series of bilateral accords were signed between France and each of the three States in 1946 under which France recognized their independence and they in turn affirmed their association with France as independent states within the framework of the French Union. Subsequently, a *"modus vivendi"* was signed between France and each of the three States outlining provisional solutions in effecting the change in relations according the States a larger degree of autonomy.

Provisional French-Laotian Modus Vivendi, Aug. 27, 1946, and French-Laotian Military Convention forming an Addendum to the Provisional Modus Vivendi Established Between France and Laos, Oct. 3, 1946, the American Ambassador at Paris (Caffery) to the Secretary of State (Byrnes), despatch No. 6527, Oct. 25, 1946, MS. Department of State, file 751.51g/10–2546; Agreement Determining the Provisional Modus Vivendi Between France and Cambodia, Feb. 7, 1946, the American Embassy (T. C. Wasson), Paris, to the Secretary of State (Marshall), despatch No. 7665, Feb. 20, 1947, encl. No. 1, *ibid.*, 851g.00/2–2047; Agreement Recognizing the Independence of Viet-Nam, June 5, 1948, cited *infra.*

According to the Agreement signed June 5, 1948, between France and the newly constituted State of Viet-Nam, France recognized "the independence of Viet-Nam, whose responsibility it will be to realize freely its unity." Viet-Nam in turn proclaimed "its adherence to the French Union as a state associated with France" and declared "The independence of Viet-Nam has no other limitations than those imposed by its membership in the French Union".

Agreement Recognizing the Independence of Viet-Nam, signed at Bay of Along, June 5, 1948, the American Ambassador at Paris (Caffery), telegram No. 3062, June 9, 1948, MS. Department of State, file 851g.00/6–948. In compliance with the Bay of Along Agreement, further special arrangements of a cultural, diplomatic, military, economic, financial, and technical nature were concluded effecting a considerable transfer of authority. They are embodied in a series of accords signed by President Auriol on the part of the French Government and by Emperor Bao Dai for the Vietnamese Government on March 8, 1949, and ratified on December 30, 1949. French-Viet-Namese Agreements, Mar. 8, 1949, the American Consul General at Saïgon (Abbott) to the Secretary of State (Acheson), despatch No. 129, July 6, 1949, MS. Department of State, file 851g.01/7–649.

In reply to an inquiry to the French Ambassador at Washington (Bonnet) as to whether ratification by the French Assembly of the March 8, 1949 Agreement and the June 5, 1948 Declaration would constitute the legal establishment of Viet-Nam, the French Foreign Office answered, "The ratification of these agreements [the Agreement and the Declaration] by Parliament will not imply, however, the 'legal creation' of the states with which France has signed them. These states already exist. Ratification will merely confirm (*consacrer*) the essential points of the new regime of independence granted to these states."

The American Embassy (W. Wallner, First Secretary), Paris, to the Secretary of State (Acheson), despatch No. 1101, Dec. 9, 1949, MS. Department of State, file 851g.01/12–949.

President Auriol in his March 8, 1949, letter to Emperor Bao Dai, confirming and defining principles of the unity and independence of Viet-Nam, stated in part:

"The foreign policy of the French Union, within the framework of which Viet-Nam shall exercise its rights through its delegates to the High Council and through its diplomatic service defined below, shall be examined and coordinated under the direction and responsibility of the Government of the French Republic, by the High Council of the Union, on which the Government of Viet-Nam will be represented by delegates freely chosen by it.

"In order to carry out the above general directives, in matters of foreign policy, H.M. the Emperor of Viet-Nam will link his diplomatic activity to that of the French Union.

"The heads of foreign diplomatic missions in Viet-Nam shall be accredited to the President of the French Union and to H.M. the Emperor of Viet-Nam.

"The heads of Viet-Namese diplomatic missions whom the Government of Viet-Nam will appoint in concurrence with the Government of the French Republic to represent it in Foreign States will receive credentials issued by the President of the French Union and initialed by H.M. the Emperor of Viet-Nam.

"The countries in which Viet-Nam will be represented by a diplomatic mission shall be determined after agreement with the French Government.

. . . .

"Viet-Nam is empowered to negotiate and to sign agreements concerning its own interests, with the express proviso that, prior to any negotiation, it shall submit its plans to the Government of the Republic for study by the High Council, and that such negotiations shall be conducted in conjunction with the diplomatic missions of the Republic. A favorable opinion of the High Council shall be required before agreements so concluded can become final."

With regard to military matters, President Auriol's letter explained:

"Viet-Nam shall have its National Army charged with the maintenance of order, internal security, and the defense of the Empire. In the latter case it may be supported by the Forces of the French Union. The Viet-Namese Army shall likewise take part in the defense of the frontiers of the French Union against all external enemies."

Commenting on the relationship between Viet-Nam and France with respect to questions of internal sovereignty, the President outlined in part the extent of Vietnamese prerogatives:

"The Government of Viet-Nam shall fully exercise the duties and prerogatives deriving from its internal sovereignty. It shall conclude with the High Commissioner of France in Indochina

special or provisional agreements which, taking circumstances
into account, will determine the ways and means of transferring
to Viet-Nam powers previously wielded by the French Authorities."

The American Consul General at Saïgon (Abbott) to the Secretary of
State (Acheson), despatch No. 129, July 6, 1949, MS. Department of State,
file 851g.01/7–649, encl. (translation).

Referring to President Auriol's letter to Emperor Bao Dai and
particularly to the meaning of this analysis with respect to the legal
status of Viet-Nam, the Office of the Legal Adviser in a memorandum
of January 5, 1950, observed:

". . . it is evident . . . that the French Government and the
Viet-Nam authorities have intended to establish Viet-Nam as a
state. Certain provisions of the basic agreement of March 8
disclose that the powers of Viet-Nam will be limited in some
important respects. For example, the foreign policy of Viet-
Nam, it appears, is to be determined ultimately in the High
Council of the French Union. The Government of Viet-Nam
shall be represented in the High Council, but the agreement does
not state in what manner the Council shall reach its decisions.
Examination of the English and French texts of the March 8
agreement discloses that the Government of the French Republic
will play a very important and perhaps predominant role in the
operations of the High Council. Also, under the agreement, 'The
countries before which Viet-Nam will be represented by a diplomatic mission shall be determined after agreement with the
French Government.' The agreement further provides: 'Viet-
Nam is empowered to negotiate and sign agreements concerning
its special interests, on the express condition that, before any
negotiation, it submit its proposals to the Government of the
Republic for study in the High Council and that such negotiations be conducted in liaison with the diplomatic missions of the
Republic. The approval of the High Council will be necessary
for agreements so concluded to become definitive.'

"It may be asked whether these limitations on the authority
of the Viet-Nam Government would serve to disqualify Viet-
Nam from being considered as a state in the community of
nations. It is believed that they would not. There have in the
past been a number of political entities whose foreign relations
were under the control of another State, but which were not on
that account considered disqualified from being considered as
states. Egypt, Tunis, and Morocco are examples of such cases.
The foreign relations of Tunis and Morocco remain even today
under the control of France. This status of Morocco, for
example, has not prevented foreign countries, such as the
United States, from entering into and maintaining treaty relations
with Morocco. . . ."

Assistant Legal Adviser Meeker to the Director of the Office of Philippine
and Southeast Asian Affairs (Reed), memorandum, "Viet-Nam", Jan. 5,

1950, MS. Department of State, file 751g.02/1–550. For treaty provisions similar to those summarized above by President Auriol, see also Franco-Viet-Namese Judiciary Agreement, Dec. 30, 1949; General Convention Between the French Republic and the Kingdom of Laos, signed July 19, 1949, the American Ambassador at Paris to the Secretary of State (Acheson), encl. No. 1 to despatch No. 710, Aug. 2, 1949, MS. Department of State, file 851g.01/8–249, and the special agreements annexed thereto, Feb. 6, 1950, file 020.51g/4–1250; and Franco-Cambodian Treaty, signed Nov. 8, 1949, and the special agreements annexed thereto, June 15, 1950, file FW 751h.02/10–651, published in *La Liberté*, Phnom Penh, Nov. 23, 1949.   Under article 61 of the French Constitution of October 27, 1946, the position of each Associated State in the French Union depended upon a bilateral agreement defining its relation to France.   Accordingly, the status of Viet-Nam, Laos, and Cambodia as Associated States was formally established in respective bilateral agreements.   These agreements, recording the intention of France to grant a greater measure of autonomy to these States, followed a common pattern in their provisions for further delimiting the relations between each of the three States and France.   In general, the accords granted each State internal autonomy but retained for France effective control over foreign relations, military, judicial, administrative, and economic activities. While France explicitly recognized each State as an independent State, each, in turn, reaffirmed its membership in the French Union as an Associated State.   French-Viet-Namese Agreements, Mar. 8, 1949, the American Consul General at Saïgon (Abbott) to the Secretary of State (Acheson), despatch No. 129, July 6, 1949, MS. Department of State, file 851g.01/7–649; General Convention between the French Republic and the Kingdom of Laos, July 19, 1949, the American Ambassador at Paris to the Secretary of State (Acheson), encl. No. 1, despatch No. 710, Aug. 2, 1949, *ibid.*, file 851g.01/8–249 (translated); Franco-Cambodian Treaty, Nov. 8, 1949, published in *La Liberté*, Phnom Penh, Nov. 23, 1949.

The French Government announced July 3, 1953, its intent "to perfect the independence of the Associated States" by transferring to each State certain powers and controls exercised by the French Government under the terms of the 1949 Agreements.

Negotiations undertaken between France and Cambodia culminated in a working-level agreement signed May 9, 1953, which envisaged the transfer of France's residual powers in police and judicial matters to Cambodia, and according to a French-Cambodian military protocol, signed in October 1953, the King of Cambodia received military command over his entire kingdom, although France retained temporary operational command east of the Mekong River.

Laos, the only one of the three States to conclude a new treaty with France in 1953, achieved recognition by the terms of the Treaty signed October 22, 1953, as "a fully independent and sovereign State." "Consequently", it was agreed, "it shall replace the French Republic in all rights and obligations resulting from any international treaties or special agreements entered into by the French Republic on behalf of the Kingdom of Laos or French Indochina prior to the present agreement" (article 1).

The Kingdom of Laos, on the other hand, freely reaffirmed its adherence to the French Union which was defined as "an association of independent and sovereign peoples, free and equal in rights and duties, in which all the members pool their means of guaranteeing the defense of the whole Union." Laos at the same time reaffirmed its decision to sit on the High Council where "the coordination of such means and the general direction of the Union are ensured" (article 2).

> Treaty of Friendship and Association between the French Republic and the Kingdom of Laos; Lao Legation to the Department of State, note No. 67/LW, encl., MS. Department of State, treaty file.

In compliance with its declaration of July 3, 1953, to perfect the independence of the Associated States, France concluded a Treaty of Independence and Association with Viet-Nam, the text of which was adopted April 22, 1954, by the Franco-Viet-Nam Political Committee of the Conference. By the terms of this treaty France recognized Viet-Nam as a completely sovereign and independent State to whom France undertook to transfer whatever remaining services and functions were still exercised by her on Vietnamese territory. In a second treaty concluded at the same time, the President of the French Republic was recognized as the President of the French Union and the presiding officer of the High Council, in which the two equal States agreed to coordinate their policies in common interest.

> Franco-Viet-Namese Treaties of Independence and Association, the American Chargé d'Affaires at Saïgon (McClintock) to the Secretary of State (Dulles), despatch No. 502, May 4, 1954, encl., MS. Department of State, file 751g.00/5–454; the American Ambassador at Paris (Dillon) to the Secretary of State (Dulles), telegram, July 3, 1953, MS. Department of State, file 751.00/7–353. In answer to an inquiry, the Department of State was informed that a treaty of independence, initialed on June 4, 1954, was never signed and that according to the Ministry of Foreign Affairs the treaty is therefore not in force. Counselor of the American Embassy at Paris (Kidder) to the Secretary of State (Herter), despatch No. 480, Oct. 1, 1959, MS. Department of State, file 751g.00/10–159.

The Geneva Conference, convened in 1954 to restore peace in Indochina after 8 years of war between forces of the French Union and Communist forces, issued a final Declaration dated July 21, 1954, which states:

> ". . . the Conference expresses its conviction that the execution of the provisions set out in the present declaration and in the agreements on the cessation of hostilities will permit Cambodia, Laos and Viet-Nam henceforth to play their part, in full independence and sovereignty, in the peaceful community of nations.

"11. The Conference takes note of the declaration of the French Government (Doc. IC/49/Rev. 1; *Report on Indochina*, p. 29) to the effect that for the settlement of all the problems connected with the re-establishment and consolidation of peace in Cambodia, Laos and Viet-Nam, the French Government will proceed from the principle of respect for the independence and sovereignty, unity and territorial integrity of Cambodia, Laos and Viet-Nam.

"12. In their relations with Cambodia, Laos and Viet-Nam, each member of the Geneva Conference undertakes to respect the sovereignty, the independence, the unity and the territorial integrity of the abovementioned states, and to refrain from any interference in their internal affairs."

Geneva Conference Doc. IC/43/Rev. 2; reprinted in *Report on Indochina: Report of Senator Mike Mansfield on a Study Mission to Vietnam, Cambodia, Laos*, Oct. 15, 1954 (Senate Foreign Relations Committee print, 83d Cong., 2d sess.) 26–27; I *American Foreign Policy, 1950–1955: Basic Documents* (1957) 785–787; XXXI *Bulletin*, Department of State, No. 788, Aug. 2, 1954, p. 164.

Article I of the Agreement on the Cessation of Hostilities in Viet-Nam of July 20, 1954, established a "provisional military demarcation line" to the north of which the forces of the People's Army of Viet-Nam were to regroup and to the south of which the forces of the French Union were to regroup. Pending the reunification of the country, the party whose forces were regrouped in each of these zones was charged with the conduct of civil administration in its zone. Geneva Conference Doc. IC/42/Rev. 2, July 20, 1954; reprinted in *Report on Indonesia: Report of Senator Mike Mansfield on a Study Mission to Vietnam, Cambodia, Laos*, Oct. 15, 1954 (Senate Foreign Relations Committee print, 83d Cong., 2d sess.) 16; I *American Foreign Policy, 1950–1955: Basic Documents* (1957) 750.

France, Cambodia, Laos, and Viet-Nam liquidated the Indochinese Federation with the conclusion of 13 quadripartite accords signed December 29, 1954, in Paris. These agreements in effect abrogated the quadripartite economic agreements regulating common services drafted in pursuance of the Pau Conventions of 1950. (MS. Department of State, treaty file.)

The chairman of the French delegation, speaking at the plenary session of the Quadripartite Conference December 29, 1954, said, ". . . at the close of the work of this Conference which now makes the independence promised to your States a reality, I extend to you the sincere good wishes of France for their future."

The chairman of the Cambodian delegation, speaking on the same occasion, confirmed that

"Cambodia, Laos, and Viet-Nam will, then, try the experiment of a completely separate national life. But this separation, which is far from being isolation, must not prevent the maintenance of our bonds of friendship and solidarity. . . .

"Henceforth, as far as Cambodia is concerned, the Agreements

signed today supplementing the previous Agreements relating
to the transfer of jurisdiction in political, technical, military,
judicial, and police matters, will establish its full independence
and sovereignty. . . .

"Enjoying all the powers and prerogatives of an independent
and sovereign State, internally as well as abroad, in conformity
with the aspirations of the Khmer Nation and the Royal Program, Cambodia will strive to broaden the horizons of its national
life and to avoid confining itself in too small a community. Thus,
freed from the shackles of the system instituted by the Treaty of
1949 and the Conventions of 1950, it will aspire to establish economic and financial relations with all friendly nations, in the
evident interest of all."

Speaking for the Viet-Nam delegation, its chairman having remarked on the liquidation of the Indochinese Federation noted:

". . . agreements have just been signed between Cambodia,
Laos, and Viet-Nam which will make it possible to harmonize
and strengthen the bonds between our three countries. Agreements to be concluded shortly between France and Viet-Nam will
also make it possible to define on new bases the economic and
financial relations between our two countries. Thus, the quadripartite conventions and agencies have ceased to exist in order
to enable new treaties, better adapted to reality, to survive the
recent political changes."

The chairman of the Lao delegation, commenting on the change in
status, observed: "At this time when each State is acquiring the attributes of its sovereignty in economic and financial matters through
the liquidation of quadripartitism, we are happy to note that the ideas
of solidarity and cooperation subsist, the gage of an understanding
that is all the more fruitful because it is freely entered into."

> The American Embassy (Joyce, Counselor), Paris, to the Secretary of
> State (Dulles), despatch No. 1416, Jan. 12, 1955, encl. No. 14, MS. Depart-
> ment of State, file 651.51g9/1–1255 (translation).

Formerly a German protectorate, "the Cameroon" after Allied oc- **Cameroon**
cupation in 1916 was divided into an eastern and western region,
which regions were then mandated respectively to France and Britain
on July 20, 1922, by the League of Nations. On December 13, 1946,
each Mandate became a United Nations Trust Territory, under the
same administering powers.

The French made their region a Trust "State" by enacting the Statute of Cameroon of April 16, 1957 (Decree No. 57–501, J.O.R.F. of
April 18, 1957) which authorized the Cameroonian Government to
exercise control over those matters essentially Cameroonian.

In accordance with article 59 of this Statute which reserved to the
Cameroon Legislative Assembly the possibility of requesting an

amendment to the Statute by resolution, the Legislative Assembly in Resolution No. 1 of June 12, 1958, requested the Government of the French Republic to amend the Statute of Cameroon in order to:

> "Recognize for the State of Cameroun its option for independence at the end of Trusteeship.
> "Transfer to the State of Cameroun all powers relative to the management of internal affairs."

This resolution in addition invited the Cameroonian Government "to negotiate along these lines the new Statute of Cameroun which will be submitted to it and which should constitute the transitional period to independence".

> The American Consul General at Yaoundé (Foulon) to the Secretary of State (Dulles), despatch No. 101, June 26, 1958, MS. Department of State, file 751u.00/6–2658.

With respect to the ensuing negotiations which took place from June to October in 1958, the French Government in a statement made at the 953d meeting, 23d session, of the Trusteeship Council, February 10, 1959, commented:

> "During the negotiations, France agreed to recognize the option of the Cameroons for independence on the termination of the trusteeship. The Cameroonian Government and all the people wanted a date to be fixed forthwith in accordance with the wishes they had expressed. Moreover, the Administering Authority, having acknowledged the need to transfer all internal powers to the Cameroonian authorities, could no longer assume the responsibilities of the trusteeship for an indefinite period. It was in those circumstances that the Legislative Assembly was consulted on the subject of a time-table for the attainment of the objectives of the Trusteeship System in the Cameroons."

> United Nations Visiting Mission to Trust Territories in West Africa, 1958, Report on the Cameroons Under French Administration together with related documents, U.N. Trusteeship Council Off. Rec. 23d Sess., Supp. No. 3, pp. 59, 60 (T/1441) (1959).

A second resolution, October 24, 1958, stated in part that the Cameroonian Legislative Assembly—

> "Notes with satisfaction the negotiations carried on by the Prime Minister which have resulted, in conformity with the resolution of 12 June 1958, in the transfer to the State of the Cameroons of all powers relating to the conduct of internal affairs as from 1 January 1959; and the agreement of the French Government that the procedures for the termination of international trusteeship should be initiated;

"Solemnly proclaims the will of the Cameroonian people that the State of the Cameroons should attain national independence on 1 January 1960".

Ibid., p. 18.

The preambular provisions of Ordinance No. 58–1375 of December 30, 1958, establishing the Statute of the Cameroons, which came into effect on January 1, 1959, in first noting the two resolutions adopted by the Cameroonian Legislative Assembly (quoted above), stated that "The present Statute, which ensures the full internal autonomy of the State of the Cameroons, marks the last stage in the evolution of institutions before the termination of the trusteeship, which will take place in accordance with the conditions set forth in the Charter of the United Nations and the Trusteeship Agreement."

This Statute provided for the transfer of the exercise of all internal legislative, administrative, and jurisdictional powers to the Cameroonian Government and also accorded it new powers in respect of nationality, justice, maintenance of order, and secondary and higher education. It further provided that during this final stage, France, as the trusteeship Power, should retain responsibilities only in the spheres of defense, external relations, and currency. However, conventions annexed to the Statute provide that the Trust "State" should be associated in the exercise of such powers.

Ibid., Annex II, pp. 38–50.

The French Government in its Memorandum Concerning the Future of The Cameroons Under French Administration, submitted to the Secretary-General of the United Nations on November 12, 1958, took note of these developments of the Cameroonian Government toward the attainment of independence and declared:

". . . the Government of the French Republic considers that the time has come when, in full agreement with the Government and Assembly of the Cameroons, the peoples of that Territory should be summoned to pass through the final stage of the Trusteeship System and that provision should be made forthwith for the abrogation of the Trusteeship Agreement.

"9. The Government of the French Republic believes, after considering—together with the representatives of the peoples concerned—all the solutions relating to their future status, that Cameroonian public opinion favours the attainment of independence. It is of the opinion that the Cameroonians have acquired the necessary abilities and also that all the powers of legislation and internal administration have been exercised satisfactorily for nearly two years by the Legislative Assembly and the Cameroonian Government, and that the progress which the Cameroons has made augurs well for its adoption of the democratic course as laid down in the United Nations Charter.

. . . .

"11. In order to avoid any delay in the realization of the wishes of the Cameroonian people, the Government of the French Republic proposes that the Trusteeship Council should be requested by the General Assembly to adopt, having in mind the report of the Visiting Mission, all appropriate steps to enable the General Assembly, during its fourteenth session, to make a decision concerning the termination of the Trusteeship System simultaneously with the attainment of independence by the Cameroons on 1 January 1960."

Memorandum Concerning the Future of The Cameroons Under French Administration, submitted by the French Government to the Secretary-General of the United Nations, Nov. 12, 1958, U.N. Gen. Ass. Off. Rec. 13th Sess., 4th Comm., Agenda item 13, Annexes, pp. 3, 4.

In Resolution 1925(XXIII) of February 17, 1959, the Trusteeship Council, after recording that it "considers that the Territory of the Cameroons under French administration is ready for independence, in accordance with the declarations of the Administering Authority and the Legislative Assembly of the Cameroons under French administration, without the need for any further consultation with the people of the Territory;" recommended that "the General Assembly at its resumed session, after considering the report of the Council and any further views that may be expressed before it, take a decision to terminate the Trusteeship Agreement upon the attainment of full national independence with effect from 1 January 1960 in accordance with Article 76b of the Charter of the United Nations".

United Nations Visiting Mission to Trust Territories in West Africa, 1958, Report on the Cameroons Under French Administration together with related documents, U.N. Trusteeship Council Off. Rec. 23d Sess., Supp. No. 3, p. 63 (T/1441) (1959).

With the adoption of Resolution 1349(XIII) on March 13, 1959, the General Assembly in *"Taking into account* the declarations of the Administering Authority and the Government of the Cameroons under French administration that the Territory will become completely independent on 1 January 1960, and the assurances given by the representative of France that his Government will sponsor the application that will thereupon be made by the Government of the Cameroons to be admitted to membership of the United Nations", *"resolves,* in agreement with the Administering Authority, that, on 1 January 1960, when the Cameroons under French administration becomes independent, the Trusteeship Agreement approved by the

General Assembly on 13 December 1946 shall cease to be in force in accordance with Article 76b of the Charter of the United Nations"; and recommended that "upon the attainment of independence on 1 January 1960, the Cameroons under French administration shall be admitted to membership of the United Nations according to Article 4 of the Charter".

U.N. Gen. Ass. Off. Rec. 13th Sess., Feb. 20–Mar. 13, 1959, 794th meeting, Supp. No. 18A (A/4090/Add.1), p. 1.

The Department of State was officially informed that documents and an exchange of letters initialed at Matighon on December 25, 1959, by the Governments of France and the Cameroons provided for the government of relations between the two States for a period of 6 months and that the exchange of letters in particular provided for formal recognition by France of the Cameroons as an independent and sovereign State.

The American Minister at Paris (Lyon) to the Secretary of State (Herter), telegram, Dec. 29, 1959, MS. Department of State, file 751u.02/ 12–2959. Initially, it was reported that the official French view regarding formal recognition of Cameroon was that as a trusteeship territory acceding to independence in accordance with the terms of a United Nations resolution, specific recognition by States intending to establish relations with it was not required, and that unless the Cameroonian Government so requested, the Government of France would not inform the General Assembly of the termination of the trusteeship and Cameroonian independence. The Director of the Office of African Affairs of the French Foreign Office stated that France had no formal responsibility for Cameroonian independence. The American Ambassador at Paris (Houghton) to the Secretary of State (Herter), telegram, Dec. 22, 1959, MS. Department of State, file 751u.02/12–2259. Explaining the discrepancy between the French Government's original attitude and the communique, the Director of the Office for African Affairs informed the Department of State that since the Cameroon Government had requested formal French recognition, the French Government acceded to this request and included recognition in the documents initialed on December 25, 1959. The American Minister at Paris (Lyon) to the Secretary of State (Herter), telegram, Dec. 29, 1959, MS. Department of State, file 751u.02/12–2959.

Prime Minister and Chief of State Ahmadou Ahidjo issued the proclamation of independence for the Republic of Cameroon on January 1, 1960, in which he declared "Cameroun is free and independent".

The American Chargé d'Affaires at Yaoundé (More) to the Secretary of State (Herter), despatch No. 89, encl. 1, Feb. 26, 1960, MS. Department of State, file 770c.02/2–2660 (translation).

Following the plebiscites held in the Trust Territory of the Cameroons under United Kingdom administration on February 11, 1961, in which the inhabitants of the northern section voted to join the Federation of Nigeria and those of the southern section voted to join the Republic of Cameroon, the General Assembly in its Resolution 1608 (XV), April 25, 1961, endorsed the results of the plebiscites and decided that the Trusteeship Agreement of December 13, 1946, concerning the Cameroons under United Kingdom administration, terminated with the Northern Cameroons joining the Federation of Nigeria on June 1, 1961, and with the Southern Cameroons joining the Republic of Cameroon on October 1, 1961. On October 1, 1961, Southern Cameroons federated with the Republic of Cameroon, becoming the Federal Republic of the Cameroon.

Congo

The Congo, formerly a Belgian colony, attained independence on June 30, 1960, in accordance with Resolution No. 1 adopted unanimously February 19, 1960, by the Round Table Conference which held discussions in Belgium between the Belgian Government and the Congolese political leaders from January 20–February 20, 1960. The 16 resolutions adopted by that Conference were designed to serve as a basis of the political and judicial organization of independent Congo. Resolution No. 2 on the organization of the Congo State provided:

"1. As of June 30 next the Congo, within its present frontiers, shall become an independent State whose inhabitants shall, under conditions to be enacted by law, have the same nationality and shall be free to move about and establish themselves within the confines of the said State, and in which goods and merchandise may also circulate freely.

"2. As of June 30, 1960 the Congo State shall be made up of six provinces whose geographical boundaries are those of the provinces now in existence.

"3. The decision as to the number and geographical boundaries of the provinces which shall thereafter form the Congo State, rests with the Constituent Assembly."

. Under Resolution 4 establishing the competence of the first Government of the Congo, it was decided that "As of June 30, the Congolese Government shall replace the Belgian Government" and that "Both Governments, the Belgian and the Congolese, shall agree on the manner in which mutual representational facilities are to be provided for".

Belgian Congo, Monthly Information Bulletin No. 2, February 1960, pp. 4–6 ff.

The Congo Constitution of May 19, 1960, provides in title II relating to the organization of the State, "The Congo constitutes, within its actual boundaries, an indivisible and democratic State".

A Belgo-Congolese Treaty of Friendship concluded "in respect to the sovereignty of each of the two independent States" was signed by both parties on June 29, 1960, but has not been ratified by either the Belgian or Congolese Parliaments.

First Secretary of the American Embassy at Brussels (Cleveland) to the Secretary of State (Herter), despatch No. 31, July 14, 1960, MS. Department of State, file 655.70g42/7–1460.

The official act of independence signed at Léopoldville June 30, 1960, by the Congolese Prime Minister, Patrice Lumumba, the Prime Minister of Belgium, Gaston Eyskens, the Congolese Minister of Foreign Affairs, Justin Bomboko, and the Belgian Minister of Foreign Affairs, Pierre Wigny, declared—"The Congo accedes, on this day, in full accord and friendship with Belgium, to independence and to international sovereignty".

Second Secretary of the American Embassy at Brussels (McKinnon) to the Secretary of State (Herter), despatch No. 133, encl. 2, Aug. 10, 1960, MS. Department of State, file 770g.00/8–1060.

Following the collapse of law and order and the mutiny of Congolese troops within less than a week after Congo declared its independence, Premier Tshombe of Katanga Province proclaimed on July 11, 1960, that his Province was a country independent of the Republic of the Congo, and on July 14 the Katanga provincial assembly ratified Katanga's secession from the Republic of the Congo. While no State complied with Premier Tshombe's request cabled on July 15 to all members of the United Nations for recognition of his Province's secession from the Congo and his demand of July 18 that the United Nations recognize Katanga within 48 hours, Premier Tshombe advised on July 16 that leaders in Kivu and Kasai Provinces in the Republic of the Congo, as well as in the Belgian Trust Territory of Ruanda-Urundi, had sent messages seeking federation with "independent Katanga" upon severing connections with the central Congolese Government. On July 18 nine States, Liberia, Libya, the Sudan, Ghana, the United Arab Republic, Guinea, Morocco, Tunisia, and Ethiopia, declared Katanga an integral part of the Congo.

By resolution of July 14, 1960, the Security Council, in response to the Congo Government's request for military assistance, authorized the Secretary-General to provide such assistance "as may be necessary, until, through the efforts of the Congolese Government with the technical assistance of the United Nations, the national security forces may be able, in the opinion of the Government, to meet fully their tasks" (S/4387). In its resolution of July 22, the Security Council requested "all States to refrain from any action which might tend to impede the restoration of law and order and the exercise by the Government of Congo of its authority and also to refrain from any action which might undermine the territorial integrity and the political independence of the Republic of the Congo" and commended the Secretary-General for his prompt implementation of the resolution of

July 14, 1960, and for his report containing his interpretation of the mandate of the United Nations Force in the Congo organized pursuant to the resolution (S/4405). Asserting that Katanga was independent, Premier Tshombe prevented the entry of United Nations Forces into Katanga with armed resistance. The Secretary-General requested further instructions from the Security Council, which were set forth in its resolution of August 9, 1960, the first operative paragraph of which confirmed the authority given to the Secretary-General by the Security Council in its resolutions of July 14 and 22 and requested him to carry out the responsibility specified therein. The resolution in addition called upon the Government of Belgium to immediately withdraw its troops from the Province of Katanga; declared that the entry of the United Nations Force into the Province of Katanga was necessary for the full implementation of this resolution; and reaffirmed that the United Nations Force in the Congo would not be a party to or in any way intervene in or be used to influence the outcome of any internal conflict, constitutional or otherwise (S/4426). On August 12 Secretary-General Hammarskjold arrived in Katanga with an advance force of 300 Swedish troops to replace Belgian army units in the Province.

The Secretary-General in his second report on the implementation of Security Council Resolutions S/4387 of July 14, 1960, and S/4405 of July 22, 1960 (S/4417, August 6, 1960), recalled that in his first report, on the implementation of Security Council Resolution S/4387 of July 14, 1960 (S/4389, July 18, 1960), he stated as his interpretation that the resolution clearly applied to the whole of the territory of the Republic as it existed when the Security Council only a few days earlier recommended the Congo for admission as a member of the United Nations. He reiterated in this second report, "Thus, the United Nations Force, under the resolution and on the basis of the request of the Government of the Congo, was entitled to access to all parts of the territory in the fulfilment of its duties"; that "actions of the United Nations through the Secretary-General, in respects covered by the resolution, must in view of the legal circumstances which the Secretary-General has to take into account, be considered by him as actions referring to the Republic of the Congo as an entity"; and additionally, that "the United Nations Force could not be a party to or intervene in any internal conflict."

Adverting in his second report to the resistance in Katanga to the United Nations Force, the Secretary-General stated the problem in these terms:

". . . Will United Nations participation in control of security in the Katanga submit the Province to immediate control and authority of the Central Government against its wishes? They consider this seriously to jeopardize their possibility to work for other constitutional solutions than a strictly unitarian one, e.g. some kind of federal structure providing for a higher degree of provincial self-government than now foreseen. The spokesmen for this attitude reject the unitarian formula as incompatible with the interests of the whole Congo people and as imposed from outside.

"This is an internal political problem to which the United Nations as an organization obviously cannot be a party. Nor would the entry of the United Nations Force in Katanga mean any taking of sides in the conflict to which I have just referred. Nor should it be permitted to shift the weights between personalities or groups or schools of thought in a way which would prejudge the solution of the internal political problem. . . ."

See *Staff Memorandum on The Republic of the Congo*, Aug. 24, 1960, 86th Cong., 2d sess. (House of Representatives Committee on Foreign Affairs).

On August 4 the Katanga Assembly adopted a Constitution of the State of Katanga comprising 66 articles, the first of which states that "Katanga is a sovereign, independent and constitutional state adhering to the principles of association with other countries of former Belgian Congo and willing to negotiate with them for creation of a confederation of equal partners." The American Consul at Elisabethville (Canup) to the Secretary of State (Herter), telegram, Aug. 9, 1960, MS. Department of State, file 770g.00/8–960. In application of the new Constitution, Tshombe was proclaimed the first President of the Katanga Republic on August 8. On August 9 the self-proclaimed provisional president, Albert Kalonji, declared the independence of the mining state which he explained as consisting of the southernmost regions of the present Province of Kasai. The appellation "mining state" was subsequently abandoned in favor of "Autonomous state of South Kasai". The American Consul at Elisabethville (Canup) to the Secretary of State (Herter), telegrams, Aug. 11 and Sept. 14, 1960, MS. Department of State, files 770g.00/8–1160 and 770g.00/9–1460.

Following the September 1960 Government crises involving President Kasavubu's dismissal of Premier Lumumba, Lumumba's reciprocal ousting of Kasavubu, Colonel Mobutu's subsequent *coup d'etat*, and the establishment of "the College of High Commissioners" with Kasavubu's approval to administer the country until the end of the year, the General Assembly passed a resolution September 20, 1960, in which it, fully supporting the three resolutions of the Security Council, requested the Secretary-General "to continue to take vigorous action in accordance with the terms of the aforesaid resolutions and to assist the Central Government of the Congo in the restoration and maintenance of law and order throughout the territory of the Republic of the Congo and to safeguard its unity, territorial integrity, and political independence in the interest of international peace and security" (A/1474 (ES–IV)). On November 22 the General Assembly voted to seat the Kasavubu delegation to represent the Republic of the Congo. Following the arrest of Lumumba which ended with his assassination in February 1961, an expanded power struggle ensued. Gizenga, Deputy Premier in Lumumba's government, established control in Stanleyville; the Ileo government in Léopoldville on February 9, 1961, announced the formation of a new "Provisional" Government and the dissolution of the College of Commissioners, with six ministerial posts held open for representatives of Katanga, Kivu, and Orientale Provinces; and the Tshombe government reasserted its independence. In the light of these developments, the Secretary-General's mandate was strengthened by the Security Council resolution of February 21, 1961. This resolution, *inter alia*, urged that the United Nations take all appropriate measures to prevent the occurrence of civil war in the Congo, including arrangements for cease-fires, halting of all military operations, the prevention of clashes, and the use of force, if necessary, in the last resort. (S/4741, Feb. 21, 1961)

Tananarive Conference

The "*de jure* and *de facto* Authorities of the ex-Belgian Congo" adopted at their Conference at Tananarive on March 12, 1961, a resolution which, in taking account of their March 10 resolution recognizing existing States and permitting the creation of new States within the limits of the territory of the ex-Belgian Congo, decided that "In its entirety the territory of the ex-Belgian Congo will form a Confederation of States" (article 1); that "The existing States or those to be constituted are sovereign in relation to each other" (article 5); and providing that "The President of the Confederation and the Presidents of the member States form the Council of State" (article 3) which would "determine the general domestic and international policy of the Confederation" by the unanimous decisions of the members (article 6).

> The American Ambassador at Tananarive (Bartlett) to the Secretary of State (Rusk), despatch No. 172, Mar. 15, 1961, encls. 1 and 3, MS. Department of State, file 770g.00/3–1561.
>
> The final communique of the Tananarive Conference was signed by both Joseph Kasavubu as President of the Republic of the Congo and President of the proposed Congolese Confederation and Moise Tshombe as President of the State of Katanga.

Coquilhatville Conference

At the Coquilhatville Conference which opened April 24, 1961, representatives of the Léopoldville, Katanga, and South Kasai governments as well as from Orientale, Kivu, and North Kasai Provinces decided that the Congo would become a "Federal Republic" composed of States created from the existing Provinces, with a single diplomatic representation, a unified military force, and one currency.

For the resolution on the political structure of the Congo, see airgram No. G–356, June 22, 1961, from American Chargé d'Affaires at Léopoldville (Godley) to the Secretary of State (Rusk), MS. Department of State, file 770x.00/6–2261.

Following Tshombe's arrest in his attempt to quit the Conference, he was subsequently released on his pledge to participate in parliament. Although this pledge was later revoked along with a reassertion of Katanga's independence, parliament was convened on July 15, and the formation of the Adoula government which brought all political elements in the Congo together except Tshombe was announced. This parliament further reported its agreement on the necessity of maintaining a unified Congo including Katanga. Tshombe's reversion to a secessionist policy led to increased tension between Katanga and the United Nations with the latter's increased pressure to remove mercenaries. Major fighting which ensued was ended by a provisional cease-fire agreement of September 20, 1961 (S/4940/Add.7, Sept. 20, 1961), which was implemented by a Protocol of Agreement on October 13, 1961 (S/4940/Add.11, Oct. 23, 1961).

In response to the Central Government's request for effective assistance to help restore law and order in Katanga, the Security Council on November 24, 1961, passed a resolution (S/5002) which deplored the secessionist activities and armed action being carried on by the Provincial Administration of Katanga with the aid of external resources and foreign mercenaries, completely rejected the claim that Katanga is a "sovereign independent nation", authorized the Secretary-General to use the "requisite measure of force, if necessary" to deport mercenaries and political advisers as described in the February 21 resolution, and declared full support for the Congo Central Government. Following the outbreak of heavy fighting between the United Nations and Katanga on December 5, a provisional truce was effected on December 18, and on December 21 Adoula and Tshombe, meeting at Kitona, signed an agreement whereby Tshombe, "President of the Government of Katanga Province", *inter alia*, accepted the application of the fundamental law of May 19, 1960, recognized the indivisible unity of the Republic of the Congo, recognized the authority of the Central Government over all parts of the Republic, and agreed that Katangan gendarmerie be placed under the authority of the President of the Republic and agreed to enforce respect for the U.N. resolutions.

The American Ambassador at Léopoldville (Gullion) to the Secretary of State (Rusk), telegram, Dec. 21, 1961, MS. Department of State, file 770g.00/12–2161.

On August 20, 1962, Acting Secretary-General of the United Nations U Thant proffered a plan for the reconciliation of the differences between the Central Government and Katanga which included as a means of inducing Mr. Tshombe to abandon his secessionist ambitions, among eight steps proposed, United Nations assistance in the drafting of a constitution for a federal system of government in the Congo; a new law governing division of revenues and, pending its operation, an agreement whereby the Central Government and Katanga share on a 50-50 basis revenues from taxes on imports and exports and royalties from mining concessions; the integration and unification of the entire Congolese Army; and the reconstitution of the Central Government to provide representation for all political and provincial groups. Failing such agreement, the Acting Secretary-General suggested "economic pressure upon the Katangese authorities of a kind that will bring home to them the realities of their situation and the fact that Katanga is not a sovereign State and is not recognized by any Government in the world as such. . . ." The Acting Secretary-General, in acknowledging the acceptance by both parties of the Plan, stated that one of the immediate implications of the acceptances is that "All pretensions to the secession of Katanga from the Republic of the Congo must be regarded as abandoned."

> For the text of the Plan, see U.N. Doc. S/5053/Add.11, Aug. 20, 1962, pp. 15–18. For Statement by the Acting Secretary-General on Congo Proposals, see U.N. press release SG/1315, Sept. 5, 1962.

Following the outbreak of hostilities in Katanga on December 26, 1962, at the initiative of the Katangan gendarmerie, which culminated in the United Nations Forces' occupation of key populated areas and mining centers in Katanga, the Secretary-General of the United Nations, U Thant, issued a statement on December 31 which, in denying that force was used for political ends, declared:

> ". . . we support the Central Government as the only legitimate government of the Congo and we do not and will not, therefore, recognize any claim to secession or to independence of the province of Katanga, or deal with Mr. Tshombe or any other official of Katanga in any status other than that of provincial officials."

> U.N. press release SG/1402, CO/277, Dec. 31, 1962. See statement by the U.S. Government on the Congo, Department of State press release 2, Jan. 4, 1963, reaffirming its support for the Secretary-General's Reconciliation Plan and endorsing the statement of Dec. 31,,1962.

In a message of January 14, 1963, addressed to Secretary-General U Thant and the Governments of Belgium, the United States, the United Kingdom, and France, Tshombe announced the termination of Katanga's secession and his readiness to arrange modalities for the integral application of the U Thant Plan.

Jordan was included in the British Mandate for Palestine until the Jordan conclusion of the Treaty of Alliance Between His Majesty in Respect of the United Kingdom and His Highness the Amir of Transjordan which was signed on March 22 and which entered into force on June 17, 1946, upon the exchange of instruments of ratification at Amman. Under article 1 of this Treaty, the United Kingdom recognized Transjordan as a fully independent State and His Highness the Amir as the sovereign thereof.

6 UNTS 143, 144.

The United Kingdom of Libya proclaimed its independence on Libya December 24, 1951, pursuant to a United Nations General Assembly resolution (Res. 289A(IV)) of November 21, 1949, which recommended in part:

> "1. That Libya, comprising Cyrenaica, Tripolitania and the Fezzan, shall be constituted an independent and sovereign State;
> "2. That this independence shall become effective as soon as possible and in any case not later than 1 January 1952."

For General Assembly Res. 289 (IV), see U.N. Gen. Ass. Off. Rec. 4th Sess., Res. (A/1251), pp. 10–13.

See also II *American Foreign Policy, 1950–1955: Basic Documents* (1957) 2302–2303.

The United Nations undertook the disposal of the former Italian colonies, of which Libya was one, in accordance with annex XI, paragraph 3, of the Treaty of Peace with Italy, signed February 10, 1947 (61 Stat. 1245). Under article 23 of the Treaty of Peace, Italy renounced all right and title to the Italian territorial possessions in Africa and agreed that the final disposition of these possessions be determined jointly by the Governments of the Soviet Union, of the United Kingdom, of the United States of America, and of France within one year from the coming into force of the Treaty. The Four Powers provided in paragraph 3 of annex XI that should they be unable to agree upon the disposal of these territories within one year from the coming into force of the Treaty of Peace with Italy, the matter should be referred to the General Assembly of the United Nations for a recommendation agreeing therein to accept the recommendation of the General Assembly and to take appropriate measures for giving effect to it. (61 Stat. 1382, 1457–1458.) Pending final disposition, Libya was under the administration of the United Kingdom. See also U.S. TIAS 1648; 61 Stat. 1245; 49 UNTS 3.

Philippine independence was proclaimed July 4, 1946, by United Philippines States Presidential proclamation which reads as follows:

> "WHEREAS the United States of America by the Treaty of Peace with Spain of December 10, 1898, commonly known as the Treaty of Paris, and by the Treaty with Spain of November 7, 1900, did acquire sovereignty over the Philippines, and by the Convention of January 2, 1930, with Great Britain did delimit the boundary

between the Philippine Archipelago and the State of North
Borneo; and

"WHEREAS the United States of America has consistently and
faithfully during the past forty-eight years exercised jurisdiction
and control over the Philippines and its people; and

"WHEREAS it has been the repeated declaration of the legislative
and executive branches of the Government of the United States of
America that full independence would be granted the Philippines
as soon as the people of the Philippines were prepared to assume
this obligation; and

"WHEREAS the people of the Philippines have clearly demonstrated their capacity for self-government; and

"WHEREAS the Act of Congress approved March 24, 1934, known
as the Philippine Independence Act, directed that, on the 4th
Day of July immediately following a ten-year transitional period
leading to the independence of the Philippines, the President of
the United States of America should by proclamation withdraw
and surrender all rights of possession, supervision, jurisdiction,
control, or sovereignty of the United States of America in and
over the territory and people of the Philippines, except certain
reservations therein or thereafter authorized to be made, and,
on behalf of the United States of America, should recognize the
independence of the Philippines:

"Now, THEREFORE, I, Harry S. Truman, President of the United
States of America, acting under and by virtue of the authority
vested in me by the aforesaid act of Congress, do proclaim that,
in accord with and subject to the reservations provided for in the
applicable statutes of the United States,

"The United States of America hereby withdraws and surrenders all rights of possession, supervision, jurisdiction, control,
or sovereignty now existing and exercised by the United States of
America in and over the territory and people of the Philippines;
and,

"On behalf of the United States of America, I do hereby recognize the independence of the Philippines as a separate and self-
governing nation and acknowledge the authority and control over
the same of the government instituted by the people thereof,
under the constitution now in force."

XV *Bulletin*, Department of State, No. 367, July 14, 1946, p. 66; 60 Stat.
1352–1353. See United States-Philippine Treaty of General Relations, and
protocol, signed July 4, 1946, U.S. TIAS 1568; 61 Stat. 1174; 7 UNTS 3.

Rwanda
and
Burundi

The General Assembly originally envisaged the emergence of the
former Belgian Trust Territory of Ruanda-Urundi into a single independent State, setting July 1, 1962, as the date for the termination
of the Trusteeship Agreement (Res. 1743 (XVI), February 23, 1962).
In its Resolution 1746 (XVI), June 27, 1962, the General Assembly,
noting the unsuccessful efforts to maintain the unity of Ruanda-
Urundi and the desire of the Governments of Rwanda and Burundi to
attain independence as separate States on July 1, 1962, decided "in

agreement with the Administering Authority, to terminate the Trusteeship Agreement of 13 December 1946 in respect of Ruanda-Urundi on 1 July 1962, on which date Rwanda and Burundi shall emerge as two independent and sovereign States".

By law dated October 5, 1962, which was made retroactive to July 1, 1962, the Belgian Government gave full force and effect to its agreement to abrogate on July 1, 1962 the Trusteeship Agreement of December 13, 1946, for the Territory of Ruanda-Urundi.

See *Moniteur Belge*, No. 228, Oct. 5, 1962.

On August 25, 1959, the Legislative Assembly of Somalia approved a motion which requested the Administrator of Somalia to convey to the Administering Authority (Italy) the unanimous desire of the Somali people that the Italian Government submit to the United Nations a request to advance the attainment of complete and full independence by Somalia at the earliest possible date, in derogation of article 24 of the Trusteeship Agreement (approved by the General Assembly December 2, 1950) which in effect provided for the expiration of the trusteeship on December 2, 1960, at which time "the Territory shall become an independent sovereign State".

Somali
Republic:
(Somalia)

Following the announcement by the representative of the Government of Somalia to the Fourth Committee of the General Assembly on November 27, 1959, that this Government in agreement with the Administering Authority had decided to ask that proclamation of independence be issued on July 1, 1960, the Fourth Committee unanimously approved a resolution fixing July 1, 1960, as the date for the proclamation of Somalia independence. The General Assembly on December 5, 1959, decided that on July 1, 1960, when Somalia would become independent, the Trusteeship Agreement approved by the General Assembly on December 2, 1950, would cease to be in force, the fundamental objectives envisioned in the Agreement then having been attained. Res. 1418 (XIV).

Memorandum submitted by the United Nations Advisory Council for the Trust Territory of Somaliland under Italian Administration on the remaining arrangements for the orderly transfer of all the functions of government to a duly constituted independent government of the Territory, A/C.4/434, Nov. 16, 1959. Report of the Government of Italy on the administration of the Trust Territory of Somaliland under Italian administration for the year 1959 (1960) 9–10 (translation).

Italian law No. 643 of June 28, 1960, provided for the termination of the trusteeship administration of Somalia by Italy on July 1, 1960, whereupon Somalia automatically acquired full sovereign powers.

Official Gazette of the Republic of Italy, July 13, 1960, p. 2610.

Reporting in pursuance of General Assembly Resolution 1418 (XIV) of December 5, 1959, on the implementation of the recommendation for the transfer of powers to Somalia, made by the Trusteeship Council at its 24th session (A/AC.4/435), the Government of Italy at the 26th session of the Trusteeship Council affirmed the following: that Law No. 6 of January 8, 1960 (enacted January 25, 1960, see Annual Report 1959, paragraph 19), which, in conferring on the Somalian Legislative Assembly "full constitutional powers for the preparation and approval of the Constitution of Somalia", reaffirmed the principle of the exclusive competence of the Constituent Assembly in all constitutional matters; the adoption on March 22, 1960, of a motion specifying the members of which the Political Drafting Committee was to be composed; and that the drafting of a Constitution which as provisionally enacted on July 1, 1960, would be submitted to a popular referendum within 1 year of that date.

Report of the Administering Authority to the Trusteeship Council on the measures taken by the Government of Somalia in relation to General Assembly Resolution 1418 (XIV), T/1534, May 24, 1960.

(Somaliland)

Taking note of General Assembly Resolution 1418 (XIV) of December 5, 1959, by which the General Assembly recognized July 1, 1960, as the date on which Somalia would attain independence and on which the Trusteeship Agreement would cease to be in force, the British Somaliland Protectorate Legislative Council passed a resolution on April 6, 1960, in favor of independence and union with Somalia on July 1, 1960. Subsequently, representatives from British Somaliland and Italian-administered Somalia, at a conference for the unification of Somaliland and Somalia held in Mogadiscio from April 16 to 22, 1960, issued a joint communique on April 23, 1960, which declared in part:

"The territories of Somalia and the Somaliland Protectorate shall be united on July 1, 1960, according to the unanimous votes of the respective Parliaments. The new Somali Republic will be a unitary, democratic and parliamentary state.

"The Legislative Assembly of Somalia and the Legislative Council of the Somaliland Protectorate shall be merged into a National Assembly by July 1, and the National Assembly will elect a President of the Republic. A coalition government will be formed by the political parties now in power in the two territories.

"The capital will be Mogadishu where the National Assembly and the government will have their seats . . . ."

The American Ambassador at London (Whitney) to the Secretary of State (Herter), telegram, May 5, 1960, MS. Department of State, file 745w.00/5–560. *The Christian Science Monitor,* June 23, 1960. The American Consul at Mogadiscio (Post) to the Secretary of State (Herter), telegram, Apr. 23, 1960, MS. Department of State, file 677.00/4–2360.

A Constitution for the Somaliland Protectorate agreed upon during a London Conference by the Secretary of State for the Colonies, the Governor of the Protectorate, and the four Somali Ministers of the Protectorate Government went into effect on June 26, 1960, and remained in force until union between Somaliland and Somalia was effected on July 1, 1960, at which time the Somalia Constitution became the Constitution for the united Somali State. Since the Constitution was scheduled to expire within a few days following its institution, there was no provision for a Head of State as such and the executive authority was vested in the Council of Ministers.

The American Consul at Mogadiscio (Post) to the Secretary of State (Herter), despatch No. 182, May 23, 1960, MS. Department of State, file 777.00/5–2360. By the Somaliland Order in Council, 1960, effective immediately before June 26, 1960, the annexed Constitution had the force of law in Somaliland. (Stat. Instr., 1960, No. 1060.)

The Queen by a Royal Proclamation terminating Her Majesty's protection over the Somaliland Protectorate signed June 23, 1960, proclaimed and declared that "as from the beginning of the appointed day, Our protection over the territories known as the Somaliland Protectorate shall cease, and all treaties and agreements in force immediately before the appointed day between Us or Our Government of the United Kingdom of Great Britain and Northern Ireland and any of the Tribes of the said territories, all Our obligations existing immediately before that day towards the said territories and all functions, powers, rights, authority or jurisdiction exercisable by Us immediately before that day in or in relation to the said territories by treaty, grant, usage, sufferance or otherwise, shall lapse".

The Somaliland Protectorate Gazette, vol. XX, No. 30, June 25, 1960, p. 57 ; Stat. Instr., 1960, No. 1060.

The Somaliland Legislative Assembly having approved its Act of Union on June 27 and the Somalian Legislative Assembly having approved its Act of Union on July 1, the two independent countries united to form the Somali Republic on July 1 when the two Legislative Assemblies met jointly as the National Assembly of the Republic and the provisional Head of State officially proclaimed the union.

A final Act of Union passed unanimously by the Somalian National Assembly in January 1961, but made retroactively effective as of July 1, 1960, by reconciling some dissimilar provisions of the two separate

Acts, omitting other provisions, and declaring the Constitution supreme, is regarded as having regularized the legal status of the union of Somaliland and Somalia. Article 1 (1) of this Act of Union provides: "Somaliland and Somalia, being united, constitute under the Constitution, the SOMALI REPUBLIC, which shall be an independent, democratic and unitary republic."

> The American Ambassador at Mogadiscio (Lynch) to the Secretary of State (Rusk), despatch No. 148, encl. 1, Jan. 24, 1961, MS. Department of State, file 777.00/1–2461.

Syria and Lebanon

Syria and Lebanon were entrusted to France July 24, 1922, by the League of Nations as a Class A Mandate. By the Treaty of Versailles of 1919 they were defined as communities that had "reached a stage of development where their existence as independent nations can be provisionally recognized subject to the rendering of administrative advice and assistance by a Mandatory until such time as they are able to stand alone."

The populations of Syria and Lebanon were for the first time declared independent June 8, 1941, by General Catroux, leading the Free French associated with the Allied forces invading Syria.

By way of subsequent clarification, Captain Lyttleton of the British forces reiterated the British Government's disinterestedness in Syria and Lebanon and admitted that France should enjoy a "predominant" position in those countries. General de Gaulle replied with an expression of satisfaction that Britain had recognized in advance the continuing "preeminent and privileged" position of France in the area after the war. This exchange of letters culminated in an unpublished British-Free French agreement, signed July 25, 1941, providing that the French should be paramount in all matters relating to civil administration, including public services and security, and the exploitation of local resources.

General Catroux, in a letter dated September 12, 1941, named Sheikh Mohamed Tajeddin el Hassani as President of the Syrian Republic to organize the new Syrian state in its independence and sovereignty. The Sheikh accepted with appreciation and gratification the fact that France was granting "the absolute independence and sovereignty" which the Syrian people had long desired.

On September 27, 1941, when the new Government of Syria was inaugurated, General Catroux issued a proclamation stating:

> "(a) Syria to exercise at once all rights and prerogatives of an independent state, limited only by the exigencies of war and territorial security;
> "(b) Ally of Free France and Great Britain;

"(c) By assuming independent international life Syria assumes of course the rights and obligations heretofore subscribed to in its name;

"(d) Syrian Foreign Service permitted;

"(e) Free France to approach friendly powers regarding recognition;

"(f) Free France to modify status of certain regions in order to centralize and unify Syria;

"(g) Guarantees under public law of individuals and religious communities to be respected;

"(h) Free France to assist economic collaboration between Syria and the Lebanon;

"(i) Allies to defend Syria during the war;

"(j) Independence of Syria to be definitely consecrated later by Franco-Syrian Treaty."

> F. D. Kohler, Division of Near Eastern Affairs, memorandum, "Regarding the Recognition of Syrian and Lebanese Independence", May 7, 1942, MS. Department of State, file 890D.01/611. See also 1919 For. Rel., vol. XIII, pp. 99–100.

The British Embassy, cognizant of a change in status not comporting with full independence, commented, ". . . the United States Government will see that the creation and recognition of an independent Syrian Government involves a change in but not a termination of the Mandate *in toto*, nor does it involve a termination of French responsibilities. It puts Syria in a position analogous to that of Iraq before the last Anglo-Iraqi Treaty of Alliance and before Iraq became a member of the League. Iraq was at that time recognized as an independent Government but His Majesty's Government nevertheless retained mandatory responsibilities which were not terminated until Iraq's admission to the League."

> R. E. Barclay, British Embassy, to W. Murray, Near Eastern Division, aide memoire, Nov. 18, 1941, MS. Department of State, file 890D.01/566; 1941 For. Rel., vol. III, p. 802.

Following the Proclamation of Lebanese Independence read by General Catroux on November 26, 1941, General de Gaulle announced in a letter addressed to the Secretary General of the League of Nations, November 28, 1941, that, as Chief of the Free French, he had, since July 14, 1941, assumed the powers and responsibilities which France held in the Levant States under the Mandate of 1922. He stated that while the proclaimed independence and sovereignty of Syria and the Lebanon would, in practice, be limited only by the exigencies of the war, the proclamations "do not, however, affect the legal situation created by the Mandate", which "could only be modified with the assent of the Council of the League of Nations, with the consent of the Government of the United States, as signatory to the Franco-American Convention of April 4, 1924, and only after the conclusion between the French Government and the Syrian and Lebanese Governments of treaties duly ratified in conformity with the legislation of the French Republic." He added that "General Catroux will therefore continue to exercise, on behalf of the French National Committee, the powers of the French High Commissioner in Syria, but taking into account the new *de facto* situation".

In this connection a Department of State memorandum noted:

". . . General de Gaulle has officially stated that the legal situation is unchanged by the proclamations of independence (the temporary continuation of the mandate is also recognized by the British). In practice General Catroux and other local authorities in the Levant States appear to be conducting themselves as though the mandate were continuing in force almost unimpaired, to the displeasure and disillusionment of Syrian and Lebanese leaders. The *Bureau Diplomatique* of the Free French *Délégation Générale* still exists, and is the practical office through which the Consul General in Beirut must continue to function to secure effective action.

"It could not, therefore, be said that either the Syrian or the Lebanese Government is 'in possession of the machinery of the state "or" in a position to fulfill all the international obligations and responsibilities incumbent upon a sovereign state.' And since the respective Presidents were appointed by General Catroux and in turn appointed the members of the Government, and in the absence of any elections and nonexistence of any elective bodies, it could hardly be said that the present régimes 'are administering the government with the assent of the people.' In this connection, it may be pointed out that there are indications of increasing opposition to the governments of these states for allowing themselves to be used by the French authorities as a *façade* for an independence that is not real.

. . . .

"Formal recognition of Syrian and Lebanese 'independence' as it now exists would appear to imply acceptance of the present control of the Free French authorities. . . .

. . . .

". . . while the present status of Syria and the Lebanon falls far short of real independence, the Catroux proclamations are a recorded step toward that goal, of which the United States might well take some positive cognizance."

F. D. Kohler, Division of Near Eastern Affairs, memorandum, "Regarding the Recognition of Syrian and Lebanese Independence", May 7, 1942, MS. Department of State, file 890D.01/611.

With reference to the status of Syria and Lebanon in 1942, a Department of State memorandum stated:

"Syria and the Lebanon may be regarded as semi-independent states. Their independence has been proclaimed in principle by representatives of the Free French, recognized by the Government of the United States to be in *de facto* control of the areas. These proclamations are subject to eventual juridical confirmation by the negotiation of appropriate instruments legally terminating the French mandate. In the meantime, local governments have been set up, with which this government desires to enter into contact, recognizing them, in effect, for what they are— *ad interim* régimes preparing the way for the full independence which will follow, and which this Government is prepared formally to recognize. The present recognition is intended to be of a limited type. The citation of the precedents of Egypt and Morocco in the memorandum of May 11 was not intended to demonstrate that exactly similar circumstances existed in those states at the time when it was decided to name diplomatic agents there, authorized to deal with the local governments. Close similarity of the initial circumstances is regarded, in fact, as not particularly relevant. The precedents were cited to show more generally that the American Government has used 'Diplomatic Agents' (i.e. diplomatic representatives of grade and authority less than full minister or envoy extraordinary and minister plenipotentiary) to conduct its representation in semi-independent states.

"According to Moore, 'the title of "agent" is used in the case of the representative to a semi-sovereign state.' (Vol. IV, p. 441, par. 628)."

F. D. Kohler, Division of Near Eastern Affairs, memorandum, May 15, 1942, MS. Department of State, file FW 890D.01/604.

"Independence for areas such as Syria and the Lebanon would be in accord with the traditional policy of this Government to favor self determination . . . In the present instance, however, we are faced with the fact that neither Syria nor the Lebanon in actuality enjoys an independent status. The local Governments in Beïrut and Damascus have been appointed by the Fighting French, and exercise only a very limited degree of sovereign independence. It may be doubted that the exigencies of the military situation will permit their being granted full independence during the war. General de Gaulle has even expressed the view recently that Syria and the Lebanon may not be ready for full independence 'for many years'."

Under Secretary of State Welles to President Roosevelt, letter, Sept. 1, 1942, MS. Department of State, file 890D.01/641, endorsed by President Roosevelt: "S.W. [Sumner Welles] OK if C.H. [Cordell Hull] concurs".

In January 1943, General Catroux was authorized to reestablish a constitutional regime and elections were held in Syria in July and in Lebanon in August of that year, under his successor M. Helleu. The elections returned strongly Nationalist Syrian and Lebanese Chambers. Notwithstanding the French contention that the Constitution could not be legally modified without their consent, the Lebanese Government reformed the Constitution by repealing all articles concerning French rights under the mandate.

On December 22, a communique was issued stating that an agreement had been reached between General Catroux and representatives of the Syrian and Lebanese Governments "regarding the transfer to these Governments of powers exercised in their name by the French authorities". The "*Intérêts Communs*", with the right of enacting laws and regulations, were transferred January 1, 1944.

> Richard Miles to Theodore Achilles, letter, Feb. 19, 1945, MS. Department of State, file 890D.01/2–1945, encl. memorandum, "France, Syria, and the Lebanon", Dec. 4, 1944, Foreign Office Research Department, Whitehall, S.W. 1, RR V/40/iii.
>
> See *infra:* Syria's union with Egypt forming the United Arab Republic, February 22, 1958, and her subsequent withdrawal forming the Syrian Arab Republic, September 28, 1961.

Togo

Togo, formerly Togoland, which had been since 1894 successively a German colony, a French mandate under the League of Nations, and a French-administered United Nations trust territory, attained independence on April 27, 1960, as officially signified by Premier Olympio's proclamation: "I solemnly proclaim the independence of Togo, motherland. . . ."

> New York *Times*, Apr. 28, 1960, pp. 1, 9.

In compliance with the directives in General Assembly Resolution 1182 (XII) of December 5, 1957, outlining the procedure for the early attainment of the final objective of the Togoland Trusteeship, France as the Administering Authority passed a decree (Decree No. 58–187 of 22 February 1958 amending the Decree of 24 August 1956 setting forth the Statute of Togoland and the Convention of 25 February 1958 between France and Togoland, T/1409, September 26, 1958) which, in transforming the Autonomous Republic of Togoland into the Republic of Togoland, transferred all powers except those of defense, diplomacy, and currency to the Togoland Government. In September 1958 France and Togoland issued a joint communique which, in addition to confirming the transfer of powers and changes in the Statute, recognized that Togoland had opted for independence at the termination of the trusteeship, and stated that in consequence thereof "agreement had been reached on the essential modifications to be made to the present Statute of Togoland in order to achieve the final stage in the development of Togoland's institutions before independence", and declared that "It has further been agreed that the procedure for the 'termination of trusteeship', initiated in 1956 in the

United Nations General Assembly in accordance with Article 76 of the United Nations Charter, would be continued during the present session in New York with a view to terminating the Trusteeship Agreement in 1960".

T/1410/Rev.1, Oct. 10, 1958.

The Trusteeship Council in Resolution 1921 (S–VIII) of October 20, 1958, accepted the conclusion of the Commissioner's report that the general outcome of the elections faithfully reflects the wishes of the people; recognized that the new Chamber is truly entitled to speak for the people of Togoland; and took note of Togoland's choice of independence upon the expiration of the trusteeship (citing T/1410/Rev.1 which mentions the year 1960 in connection with the termination of the Trusteeship Agreement).

The Togoland Chamber of Deputies passed a resolution on October 27, 1958, which invited the Togoland Government "to draft and negotiate with the Government of the French Republic the amendments to the present Statute required for a transition from internal autonomy to complete independence"; proposed that "independence should be proclaimed in 1960"; and requested the United Nations General Assembly "to maintain trusteeship over Togoland until the proclamation of independence".

The Future of Togoland Under French Administration, note by the Secretary-General communicating to the members of the General Assembly letter No. 355 of November 3, 1958, from the representative of France, annex I, Resolution Concerning the New Statute of Togoland and the Proclamation of Independence, G.A. Doc. A/C.4/382, Nov. 3, 1958.

By Ordinance No. 58–1376 of December 30, 1958, the New Statute of the Republic of Togo was promulgated which in pursuance of the resolution adopted by the Togoland Chamber of Deputies on October 27, 1958, stipulated in article I: "Togo is a democratic State which, upon its request, shall be proclaimed an independent and sovereign Republic at the end of the international trusteeship system".

With regard to the relations between the Republic of Togo and France during the transitional period between internal autonomy and independence, the Statute provided that "At the request of the Togolese Republic, the French Republic shall have charge of its foreign affairs, currency, and defense"—the terms and conditions of which cooperation were to be set forth in an agreement (article 31). It was further provided that "As long as Togo remains under the international trusteeship system, France will discharge her responsibilities as Administering Authority under the terms of Chapter XII of the United Nations Charter and of the Trusteeship Agreement of December 13, 1946, by exercising the veto right" (article 32). The veto right could be exercised by the French Ministry of Overseas Territories with respect to Togolese laws and by the High Commissioner with respect to decisions of the Council of Ministers and the individual Ministers provided it was exercised "within a period of ten clear days either from passage of the law or from the publication of the decision" (article 33).

The American Chargé d'Affaires at Lomé (Dean) to the Secretary of State (Herter), despatch No. 267, encl. 1, June 24, 1960, MS. Department of State, file 770d.02/6–2460 (translation). *Journal Officiel de la République Française*, Dec. 31, 1958, p. 12115.

The General Assembly passed Resolution 1253 (XIII) on November 14, 1958, wherein it noted that "the Governments of France and of the Republic of Togoland have decided, by mutual agreement, that Togoland shall attain independence in 1960, in accordance with the wishes of the Chamber of Deputies of Togoland" and resolved accordingly, in agreement with France, "that on the day which will be agreed upon between the Government of France and the Government of Togoland, and on which the Republic of Togoland becomes independent in 1960, the Trusteeship Agreement approved by the General Assembly on 13 December 1946 shall cease to be in force, in accordance with Article 76b of the Charter of the United Nations".

Gen. Ass. Off. Rec. 13th Sess., Supp. No. 18 (A/4090).

The French representative informed the Trusteeship Council on July 13, 1959, that France as the Administering Power "has accepted the proposal of the Government of the Republic of Togoland that 27 April 1960 should be fixed as the date of Togoland's independence" and that in accordance with General Assembly Resolution 1253 (XIII) the Trusteeship Agreement of 13 December 1946 would therefore cease to be in force as from April 27, 1960.

Letter dated July 13, 1959, from the representative of France on the Trusteeship Council to the Secretary-General, A/4138, July 16, 1959. The Trusteeship Council in Resolution 1950 (XXIV), July 14, 1959, took note of April 27, 1960, as the date for the proclamation of Togoland's independence.

In Resolution 1416 (XIV) of December 18, 1959, the General Assembly noted that "the Governments of France and of Togoland have agreed that the date on which the Republic of Togoland shall become independent is to be 27 April 1960" and reiterated its decision that "on the date of the independence of Togoland, which has now been established as 27 April 1960, the Trusteeship Agreement for

Togoland under French administration, approved by the General Assembly on 13 December 1946, shall cease to be in force".

Gen. Ass. Off. Rec. 14th Sess., Supp. No. 16 (A/4354). (For the termination of the Trusteeship Agreement, see *post* this chapter, pp. 904–905.)

The first Japanese offer of surrender, August 10, 1945, as trans- Japan
mitted through the Chargé d'Affaires ad interim of Switzerland, stated in part:

"The Japanese Government are ready to accept the terms enumerated in the joint declaration which was issued at Potsdam on July 26th, 1945, by the heads of the Governments of the United States, Great Britain, and China, and later subscribed by the Soviet Government, with the understanding that the said declaration does not comprise any demand which prejudices the prerogatives of His Majesty as a Sovereign Ruler."

In reply to this offer of surrender, August 11, 1945, Secretary of State Byrnes, commenting on this qualification of surrender, stated:

"From the moment of surrender the authority of the Emperor and the Japanese Government to rule the state shall be subject to the Supreme Commander of the Allied powers who will take such steps as he deems proper to effectuate the surrender terms."

The Axis in Defeat, Department of State publication 2423, pp. 29, 30. For the Potsdam Declaration of July 26, 1945, see XIII *Bulletin*, Department of State, No. 318, July 29, 1945, pp. 137–138.

The instrument of surrender, signed September 2, 1945, recited on behalf of the Emperor of Japan and the Japanese Government:

"We . . . hereby accept the provisions set forth in the declaration issued by the heads of the Governments of the United States, China and Great Britain on 26 July 1945, at Potsdam, and subsequently adhered to by the Union of Soviet Socialist Republics, which four powers are hereafter referred to as the Allied Powers.

"The authority of the Emperor and the Japanese Government to rule the state shall be subject to the Supreme Commander for the Allied Powers who will take such steps as he deems proper to effectuate these terms of surrender."

A Decade of American Foreign Policy: Basic Documents, 1941–49 (1950) 625–626.

In a document prepared jointly by the Department of State, the War Department, and the Navy Department and approved by the President on September 6, 1945, which set forth the United States initial post-surrender policy for Japan, it was provided among other principles governing the objectives of this policy that ". . . Japan's sovereignty will be limited to the islands of Honshu, Hokkaido,

Kyushu, Shikoku and such minor outlying islands as may be determined, in accordance with the Cairo Declaration and other agreements to which the United States is or may be a party".

With respect to the relationship of the Allied Authority to the Japanese Government, it was specified that

> "The authority of the Emperor and the Japanese Government will be subject to the Supreme Commander, who will possess all powers necessary to effectuate the surrender terms and to carry out the policies established for the conduct of the occupation and the control of Japan.
>
> "In view of the present character of Japanese society and the desire of the United States to attain its objectives with a minimum commitment of its forces and resources, the Supreme Commander will exercise his authority through Japanese governmental machinery and agencies, including the Emperor, to the extent that this satisfactorily furthers United States objectives. The Japanese Government will be permitted, under his instructions, to exercise the normal powers of government in matters of domestic administration. This policy, however, will be subject to the right and duty of the Supreme Commander to require changes in governmental machinery or personnel or to act directly if the Emperor or other Japanese authority does not satisfactorily meet the requirements of the Supreme Commander in effectuating the surrender terms. This policy, moreover, does not commit the Supreme Commander to support the Emperor or any other Japanese governmental authority in opposition to evolutionary changes looking toward the attainment of United States objectives. The policy is to use the existing form of Government in Japan, not to support it. . . ."

> *Ibid.* 627–629.

With the purpose of clarifying the authority to be exercised by General MacArthur in his position as the Supreme Commander for the Allied Powers, a message prepared jointly by the Department of State, War Department, and the Navy Department and approved by the President September 6, 1945, and transmitted to General MacArthur by the Joint Chiefs of Staff, provided:

> "1. The authority of the Emperor and the Japanese Government to rule the State is subordinate to you as Supreme Commander for the Allied powers. You will exercise your authority as you deem proper to carry out your mission. Our relations with Japan do not rest on a contractual basis, but on an unconditional surrender. Since your authority is supreme, you will not entertain any question on the part of the Japanese as to its scope.
>
> "2. Control of Japan shall be exercised through the Japanese Government to the extent that such an arrangement produces satisfactory results. This does not prejudice your right to act directly if required. You may enforce the orders issued by you by

the employment of such measures as you deem necessary, including the use of force.

"3. The statement of intentions contained in the Potsdam Declaration will be given full effect. It will not be given effect, however, because we consider ourselves bound in a contractual relationship with Japan as a result of that document. It will be respected and given effect because the Potsdam Declaration forms a part of our policy stated in good faith with relation to Japan and with relation to peace and security in the Far East."

The Axis in Defeat, Department of State publication 2423, pp. 114–115.

The United States Supreme Court, deciding in *Cobb* v. *United States* a tort-claim action arising out of an accident which took place on the Island of Okinawa in 1948 and determining more specifically whether Okinawa was at the time a "foreign country" within the meaning of the Federal Tort Claims Act, stated with respect to Japan's sovereignty during the occupation period:

". . . In the event the United States' occupation of Okinawa were of a clearly provisional character designed simply to maintain order on the island until Okinawa could be returned to a responsible Japanese government, it could be said that Japan did not lose her 'sovereignty' over the island but had been merely deprived temporarily of the power to exercise some of the rights of sovereignty. This theory would be particularly applicable to the Japanese home islands because in those islands a native Japanese government has been permitted to exercise most of the normal powers of government in matters of domestic administration, subject to the supervision of the Supreme Commander. . . ."

191 F.2d 604, 607 (9th Cir. 1951).

Article 9 of the Constitution of Japan, promulgated November 3, 1946, in providing for the renunciation of war, reads:

"Aspiring sincerely to an international peace based on justice and order, the Japanese people forever renounce war as a sovereign right of the nation and the threat or use of force as means of settling international disputes.

"In order to accomplish the aim of the preceding paragraph, land, sea, and air forces, as well as other war potential, will never be maintained. The right of belligerency of the State will not be recognized."

Commenting on this provision as it appeared first in the draft Constitution, General MacArthur said:

"Foremost of its provisions is that which, abolishing war as a sovereign right of the nation, forever renounces the threat or use of force as a means of settling disputes with any other nation and forbids in future the authorization of any army, navy, air force or other war potential or assumption of rights of belligerency by the state. By this undertaking and commitment Japan surrenders rights inherent in her own sovereignty and renders her future security and very survival subject to the good faith and justice of the peace-loving peoples of the world. . . ."

Occupation of Japan—Policy and Progress, Department of State publication 2671, Far Eastern Series 17, p. 133. For art. 9 of the Constitution of Japan, see II Peaslee, *Constitutions of Nations* (2d ed., 1956) 511, 512.

Commenting on article 1 of the Treaty of Peace with Japan which reads in part: "(b) The Allied Powers recognize the full sovereignty of the Japanese people over Japan and its territorial waters", the delegate of the United States, John Foster Dulles, stated at the second plenary session of the Japanese Peace Conference in San Francisco, September 5, 1951, that "Chapter I ends the state of war, with consequent recognition of the full sovereignty of the Japanese people. Let us note that the sovereignty recognized is the 'sovereignty of the Japanese people' ".

Conference for the Conclusion and Signature of the Treaty of Peace with Japan, San Francisco, California, September 4–8, 1951, Record of Proceedings (1951), Department of State publication 4392, p. 77. For the text of the Treaty of Peace with Japan, see *ibid.* 313–326; U.S. TIAS 2490; 3 UST 3169.

Referring to the Japanese Peace Treaty, President Truman in addressing the Japanese Peace Conference at San Francisco, September 4, 1951, stated:

"The treaty reestablishes Japan as a sovereign, independent nation. . . .

.   .   .   .   .   .

"The Peace Treaty, therefore, recognizes that Japan, as a sovereign nation, must possess the right of self-defense and the right to join in defense arrangements with other countries under the United Nations Charter".

Conference for the Conclusion and Signature of the Treaty of Peace with Japan, San Francisco, California, September 4–8, 1951, Record of Proceedings (1951), Department of State publication 4392, pp. 33, 35; U.S. TIAS 2490; 3 UST 3169.

In the case of *Japanese Government* v. *Commercial Cas. Ins. Co. et al.,* which involved an action instituted by the Japanese Government, August 17, 1951—after cessation of hostilities but before the signing or ratification of the treaty of peace—for breach of a contract, approved by the Supreme Commander for the Allied Powers, a United States federal Court rejected the defendant's argument that the Court lacked jurisdiction because the plaintiff was at the time of the commencement of the action a nonresident alien enemy and was not a government recognized by the Government of the United States.

Taking judicial notice of the fact that the Department of State had recognized the Government of Japan, the Court, in addressing itself to the issue of the legal status of Japan at the time of the suit, stated:

". . . Japan was and has continued to be occupied, not for purposes of subjugation, annexation or destruction. The occupation has been, essentially, provisional and temporary; Japan has continued as a sovereign with its rights and powers of sovereignty limited only by the directives of the Supreme Commander."

101 F. Supp. 243, 245 (S.D.N.Y. 1951).

Preservation of the *status quo* of Outer Mongolia ("The Mongolian People's Republic") was one of the stated conditions on which the Soviet Union agreed at the Yalta Conference to enter the war against Japan. Agreement Regarding Entry of the Soviet Union Into the War Against Japan, released to the press by the Department of State on Feb. 11, 1946; printed as U.S. EAS 498; also in 59 Stat. 1823; 1945 For. Rel., The Conferences at Malta and Yalta, p. 984.

On August 14, 1945, an agreement was concluded in which the Chinese Government announced that after the defeat of Japan, if the desire of the people of Outer Mongolia for independence is confirmed by a plebiscite, the Chinese Government will recognize the independence of Outer Mongolia within her existing frontiers. 10 UNTS (1947) 300, 342.

The result of the plebiscite held October 20, 1945, confirmed that the people were in favor of independence.

"As announced on the radio by the chairman of the Presidium of the Minor Hural, Bumatsende, 'the freedom-loving Mongolian people, under the leadership of state authority, confirm before the world their independent national existence.'" "The Mongolian People's Republic" in *Sputnik Agitatora* (The Agitator's Companion) as transmitted from American Embassy, Moscow, to the Secretary of State (Byrnes), despatch No. 2517, Mar. 16, 1946, encl. 1, MS. Department of State, file 893.00 MONGOLIA/3–1646.

The Government of the Republic of China in a communique to London reported that "This government now recognizes the independence of Outer Mongolia and the Executive Yuan has duly directed the Ministry of the Interior officially to notify the Government of Outer Mongolia of this decision." The American Ambassador at London (Winant) to the Secretary of State (Byrnes), telegram No. 3924, Apr. 9, 1946, MS. Department of State, file 893.00 MONGOLIA/4–946.

"The Mongolian People's Republic" and the Union of Soviet Socialist Republics signed a Treaty February 27, 1946, which converted the Protocol of March 12, 1936, into a Treaty of Friendship and Mutual Assistance to remain in force for a period of 10 years. 48 UNTS 184.

In an exchange of notes accompanying the Treaty of Friendship, Alliance and Mutual Assistance of February 14, 1950, Communist China and the Union of Soviet Socialist Republics abrogated the August 14, 1945, Sino-Soviet Treaty of Friendship and Alliance and the Agreements on the Chinese Changchun Railway, Dairen and Port Arthur and "acknowledge[d] that the independent status (*nezavisimoe polozhenie*) of the Mongolian People's Republic has already been fully secured as a result of the referendum conducted in Outer Mongolia in 1945, which confirmed the aspiration for independence of that country, and as a result of its establishment of diplomatic relations with the Chinese People's Republic." Unofficial English translation from Russian texts appearing in the *Vedomosti* (Proceedings) of U.S.S.R. Supreme Soviet for Nov. 16, 1950, p. 4, printed in *Reported Agreements Between the USSR and Communist China* (1956) 38–39.

On February 25, 1953, the Government of the Republic of China charged the Union of Soviet Socialist Republics with violation of the Treaty of Friendship and Alliance of August 14, 1945, and, considering that the Treaty and other Related Documents had been nullified by the action of the Soviet Union and that China was of right freed and exonerated from the stipulation thereof, declared the Treaty of Friendship and Alliance between the Republic of China and the U.S.S.R. of August 14, 1945, and other Related Documents null and void. Statement of Dr. George K. C. Yeh, Minister of Foreign Affairs, Feb. 25, 1953, *Treaties between the Republic of China and Foreign States (1927–1957)* (Ministry of Foreign Affairs, 1958) 523–524.

In voting against the application of Outer Mongolia for membership in the United Nations in 1957, the United States Representative, Henry Cabot Lodge, stated in the Security Council on September 9: ". . . We do not think it [Outer Mongolia] is independent and we do not think it is a state." He also said: ". . . We do not think it has the attributes of sovereignty. We think it is a Soviet colony. . . ." United States Mission to the United Nations, press releases Nos. 2719 and 2721, Sept. 9, 1957.

"The Mongolian People's Republic" was admitted to membership in the United Nations by General Assembly Resolution 1630 (XVI), October 27, 1961, upon recommendation by the Security Council.

Nonunified States

§ 18

Korea

"In the Joint Declaration issued at Cairo on December 1, 1943, the three subscribing Powers—the United States, China, and Great Britain—expressed their determination 'that in due course Korea shall become free and independent'. This determination was reaffirmed in the Potsdam Declaration of July 26, 1945, with which the Soviet Union associated itself upon its declaration of war against Japan on August 8 of that year. On December 27, 1945, in Moscow the Foreign Ministers of the Soviet Union, the United States, and Great Britain concluded an agreement, later adhered to by the Government of China, designed to re-establish Korea as an independent state.

Cairo and Potsdam Declarations

"Although the annexation of Korea by Japan was effectively terminated with the occupation of that country by the armed forces of the Soviet Union and the United States in August and September 1945, the freedom and independence of Korea so solemnly pledged by the Four Powers has proven slow of realization. After nearly two years of painstaking but unavailing effort to give effect to those pledges through negotiations with the other occupying power, the United States Government, on September 17, 1947, laid the problem of Korean independence before the General Assembly of the United Nations. The will of an overwhelming majority of that body was expressed in two resolutions adopted by it on November 14, 1947, the purpose of which was to make it possible for the Korean people to attain their long-sought freedom and independence through the holding of free and democratic elections and the establishment, on the basis thereof, of a national government."

XIX *Bulletin*, Department of State, No. 477, Aug. 22, 1948, p. 242.

The U.N. Temporary Commission on Korea, provided for in the General Assembly resolution of November 14, 1947 (Resolution 112 (II)) and under whose observation the elections in Korea south of the 38th parallel were held May 10, 1948, reported that the results of the election were found to be "a valid expression of the free will of the electorate in those parts of Korea which were accessible to the Commission and in which the inhabitants constituted approximately two-thirds of the people of all Korea."

XXV *Bulletin*, Department of State, No. 650, Dec. 10, 1951, p. 927; also printed in *Korea: 1945–1948* (1948), Department of State publication 3305, p. 66. Resolution of the U.N. General Assembly relating to Korean independence, Res. 112(II), Nov. 14, 1947; *A Decade of American Foreign Policy: Basic Documents, 1941–49* (1950) 677–678.

The Constitution of the Republic of Korea, adopted by delegates to a National Assembly and proclaimed on July 2, 1948, noted that the people were at that time "engaged in reconstructing a democratic, independent country" (preamble). The fact of the formation of the new government, August 5, 1948, pursuant to the provisions of the Constitution was notified to the United Nations Commission on August 6, 1948, and on August 15, 1948, the Republic of Korea was proclaimed in south Korea.

II Peaslee, *Constitutions of Nations* (2d ed., 1956) 546, 549.

The General Assembly, acknowledging the report of the Temporary Commission, passed a resolution (195(III), December 12, 1948), in which it declared "that there has been established a lawful government (the Government of the Republic of Korea) having effective control and jurisdiction over that part of Korea where the Temporary Commission was able to observe and consult and in which the greater majority of the people of all Korea reside; that this government is based on elections which were a valid expression of the free will of the electorate of that part of Korea and which were observed by the

Temporary Commission; and that this is the only such government in Korea".

U.N. Gen. Ass. Off. Rec. 3d Sess., 1st pt., Doc. A/810.

In the agreement of August 24, 1948, between the United States and the Republic of Korea regarding the transfer of jurisdiction over security forces, it is stipulated that "the provisions of this article shall not interfere with the sovereign rights of the Government of Korea in the administration of the Korean Security Forces . . .".

Background Information on Korea, Report of the Committee on Foreign Affairs pursuant to H. Res. 206, July 11, 1950, H. Rept. 2495, 81st Cong., 2d sess. (1950), p. 16. See also the preamble to the agreement on aid between the United States and Korea, December 31, 1948, in which the belief of the United States was stated that such assistance was being furnished "on terms consonant with the independence and security of the Government of the Republic of Korea". Ibid., p. 22.

The United States Government in extending full recognition to the Government of the Republic of Korea January 1, 1949, stated:

"In conformity with the General Assembly resolution of December 12, the United States Government will endeavor to afford every assistance and facility to the new United Nations Commission on Korea established thereunder in its efforts to help the Korean people and their lawful Government to achieve the goal of a free and united Korea."

A Decade of American Foreign Policy: Basic Documents, 1941–49 (1950) 679.

The United States Ambassador at Large to the United Nations, in September 1949 referred to Korea as having been "restored to independence". Commenting further on Korea's status, he remarked, "Unfortunately, however, that nation has been cut in two, and the writ of the Korean Government, recognized by the United Nations, does not run in the northern half of the country which is subject to a totalitarian regime. . . . It is of the utmost importance, therefore, that the United Nations Commission which has been dispatched by the General Assembly to Korea be maintained there and that its authority be confirmed and enlarged, until the security of the new state is no longer threatened. . . ."

Philip C. Jessup (Ambassador at Large), address before the American Association for the United Nations, New York, N.Y., Sept. 18, 1949, XXI Bulletin, Department of State, No. 535, Oct. 3, 1949, pp. 492, 494.

Secretary of State Acheson in an address on January 12, 1950, speaking of United States efforts in Korea, said: ". . . we have taken

great steps which have ended our military occupation, and in cooperation with the United Nations, have established an independent and
sovereign country recognized by nearly all the rest of the world."

XXII *Bulletin,* Department of State, No. 551, Jan. 23, 1950, pp. 111, 117;
II *American Foreign Policy, 1950–1955: Basic Documents* (1957) 2320.

In explaining the special provision made for Korea in article 21
of the Treaty of Peace with Japan, the United States Delegate to
the Japanese Peace Conference, John Foster Dulles, addressing the
Conference at its second plenary session, September 5, 1951,
commented:

". . . The Republic of Korea will not sign the Treaty of Peace
only because Korea was never at war with Japan. It tragically
lost its independence long before this war began, and did not
regain independence of Japan until after Japan surrendered. . . .
"Nevertheless, Korea has a special claim on Allied consideration, the more so as it has not yet proved possible for the Allies
to achieve their goal of a Korea which is free and independent.
Korea is, unhappily, only half free and only half independent;
and even that fractional freedom and independence has been
cruelly mangled and menaced by armed aggression from the
North.
"Most of the Allied Powers have been seeking to make good
their promise of freedom and independence and, as members of
the United Nations, to suppress the aggression of which Korea
is the victim. By this treaty, the Allies will obtain for Korea
Japan's formal recognition of Korea's independence, and Japan's
consent to the vesting in the Republic of Korea, of the very considerable Japanese property in Korea. Korea will also be placed
on a parity with the Allied Powers as regards post-war trading,
maritime, fishing and other commercial arrangements. Thus the
treaty, in many ways, treats Korea like an Allied Power."

*Conference for the Conclusion and Signature of the Treaty of Peace with
Japan, San Francisco, California, September 4–8, 1951, Record of Proceedings* (1951), Department of State publication 4392, pp. 84–85; U.S. TIAS
2490.

During the course of the Korean armistice negotiations at Panmun-
jom, United States Delegate to the General Assembly Ernest A. Gross,
referring to this attempt to achieve an armistice, said, "We hope this
will lead to the establishment of a unified, independent, and democratic Korea, and to the economic recovery and rehabilitation of that
devastated land".

XXVI *Bulletin,* Department of State, No. 660, Feb. 18, 1952, p. 260. See
also text of a note transmitted by the United Kingdom Government to
the Chinese Communist authorities on April 9, 1958, on behalf of the
Governments of the countries which contributed forces to the United
Nations Command in Korea, in reply to the Chinese Communist statement

issued in Peiping on February 7, 1958. This note also reaffirms that the aim of these Governments in Korea "is to see the establishment of a unified, independent and democratic Korea . . . ." XXXVIII *Bulletin*, Department of State, No. 984, May 5, 1958, pp. 735–736.

General Assembly Resolution 1455(XIV), December 12, 1959, in reaffirming its Resolutions 112(II) of November 14, 1947, 195(III) of December 12, 1948, 293(IV) of October 21, 1949, 376(V) of October 7, 1950, 811(IX) of December 11, 1954, 910 A(X) of November 29, 1955, 1010(XI) of January 11, 1957, 1180(XII) of November 29, 1957, and 1264(XIII) of November 14, 1958, and in also reaffirming "that the objectives of the United Nations in Korea are to bring about, by peaceful means, the establishment of a unified, independent and democratic Korea under a representative form of government, and the full restoration of international peace and security in the area", called upon "the communist authorities concerned to accept these established United Nations objectives in order to achieve a settlement in Korea based on the fundamental principles for unification set forth by the nations participating on behalf of the United Nations in the Korean Political Conference held at Geneva in 1954, and reaffirmed by the General Assembly, and to agree at an early date on the holding of genuinely free elections in accordance with the principles endorsed by the Assembly".

Gen. Ass. Off. Rec. 14th Sess., Supp. No. 16 (A/4354) ; see in general *The Record on Korean Unification 1943–1960* (1960), Department of State publication 7084.

Secretary of State Dulles, in a message to the Korean people on the occasion of the 10th anniversary of the independence of the Republic of Korea, August 15, 1958, stated: "The re-creation of the independent nation of Korea has required valiant effort, and even so Korea still unhappily remains divided".

Press release 468, Aug. 14, 1958, XXXIX *Bulletin*, Department of State, No. 1001, Sept. 1, 1958, p. 346.

Establishment of "Democratic People's Republic of Korea"

"At almost the same time that the Republic of Korea assumed authority in the southern zone, another government was brought into being in the northern zone. The newly elected Supreme People's Council in north Korea on September 9, 1948, proclaimed the establishment of a 'Democratic People's Republic of Korea' claiming jurisdiction over the entire country.

"The procedures followed in establishing the government in the northern zone were not in accordance with those outlined in the November 14, 1947, resolutions of the General Assembly. The elections for the delegates to the Supreme People's Council, held on August 25, were not observed by the United Nations Temporary Commission on Korea. The election was essentially undemocratic in that the voter was presented with lists of candidates drawn up by the North Korean People's Committee for his approval or disapproval.

"Both the United Nations Commission and the United States Military Government tried to secure information on the 'secret election' which north Korean leaders assert was held in south Korea. Evidence was extremely difficult to obtain, however, and it is certain that only a very small number of persons even received ballots.

"The south Koreans who allegedly occupy 360 of the 572 seats in the Supreme People's Council apparently represent only small Communist dissident factions in the southern zone. Both Communist and non-Communist dissident elements in the southern zone, which opposed and boycotted the U.N.-observed election of May 10 and participated in the first North-South Conference of Political Leaders (April 19–28, 1948) were repudiated by the people of the southern zone in the May 10 election. Before the second North-South Conference of Political Leaders (June 29– July 5, 1948) the non-Communist elements of these dissident groups generally refused to join in further discussions with the political organizations of the northern zone, and since that time they have repeatedly denounced both the second North-South Conference of Political Leaders and the August election of delegates to the Supreme People's Council of the 'Democratic People's Republic of Korea'."

Korea: 1945–1948 (1948), Department of State publication 3305, p. 21.

At the Crimea (Yalta) Conference, February 4–11, 1945, it was agreed that article 12(a) of the Surrender Terms for Germany should be amended to read as follows: German Federal Republic

"The United Kingdom, the United States of America and the Union of Soviet Socialist Republics shall possess supreme authority with respect to Germany. In the exercise of such authority they will take such steps, including the complete disarmament, demilitarisation and dismemberment of Germany as they deem requisite for future peace and security." Yalta

On June 5, 1945, the representatives of the United States, Great Britain, the Soviet Union, and France, "acting by authority of their respective Governments and in the interests of the United Nations", declared:

"The Governments of the United States of America, the Union of Soviet Socialist Republics and the United Kingdom, and the Provisional Government of the French Republic, hereby assume supreme authority with respect to Germany, including all the powers possessed by the German Government, the High Command and any state, municipal, or local government or authority. The assumption, for the purposes stated above, of the said authority and powers does not effect the annexation of Germany. Allied assumption of "supreme authority"

"The Governments of the United States of America, the Union of Soviet Socialist Republics and the United Kingdom, and the Provisional Government of the French Republic, will hereafter determine the boundaries of Germany or any part thereof and the status of Germany or of any area at present being part of German territory."

A Four Power statement on June 5, 1945, constituted the four Zone Commanders, the Control Council for the exercise of supreme authority within Germany, and provided:

"1. In the period when Germany is carrying out the basic requirements of unconditional surrender, supreme authority in Germany will be exercised, on instructions from their Governments, by the Soviet, British, United States, and French Commanders-in-Chief, each in his own zone of occupation, and also jointly, in matters affecting Germany as a whole. The four Commanders-in-Chief will together constitute the Control Council. Each Commander-in-Chief will be assisted by a political adviser.

"2. The Control Council, whose decisions shall be unanimous, will ensure appropriate uniformity of action by the Commanders-in-Chief in their respective zones of occupation and will reach agreed decisions on the chief questions affecting Germany as a whole."

The Berlin (Potsdam) Conference of August 1, 1945, reaffirmed this policy by providing:

Potsdam

"In accordance with the Agreement on Control Machinery in Germany, supreme authority in Germany is exercised, on instructions from their respective Governments, by the Commanders-in-Chief of the armed forces of the United States of America, the United Kingdom, the Union of Soviet Socialist Republics, and the French Republic, each in his own zone of occupation, and also jointly, in matters affecting Germany as a whole, in their capacity as members of the Control Council."

A Decade of American Foreign Policy: Basic Documents, 1941–49 (1950) 29–30, 36, 506, 507, 512.

Legal status of occupied Germany

In reaching the conclusion that the removal of indigenous archives, records, and documents by an occupying power violates international law unless an overriding public interest is established, a memorandum of March 17, 1947, prepared in the Office of Military Government for Germany (U.S.), discussed the legal status of occupied Germany as follows:

". . . The first paragraph of the Declaration of 5 June 1945 Regarding the Defeat of Germany states: 'The German armed forces on land, at sea and in the air have been completely defeated and have surrendered unconditionally, and Germany, which bears responsibility for the war, is no longer capable of resisting the will of the victorious Powers. The unconditional surrender of Germany has thereby been effected, and Germany has become subject to such requirements as may now or hereafter be imposed upon her'. But the Declaration of 5 June 1945, above cited, contains the further statement that the assumption of complete governmental authority in Germany 'does not effect the annexation of Germany'; and, apart from special cessions of territory, it is clear that there is no present intention on the part of the victorious nations to retain political sovereignty over Germany. [On the basis of this reasoning, the Obergericht of the State of Zurich, held, in an opinion published in the 1946 Swiss Law Journal, page 88ff. that the international agreement on laws of civil procedure of 17 July 1905, to which Germany and Switzerland were signatories, is still effective. The court distinguished between two stages of conquest: military occupation and annexation. It held that during the period of military occupation the treaties concluded by the occupied State remain in force, and that such treaties cease to exist only after annexation. It concluded that the present occupation of Germany is not equivalent to annexation, because in addition to complete conquest, or *debellatio*, an expressed intention to annex the territory of the conquered nation is required to accomplish a legal annexation. Since the present powers in occupation of Germany have expressed no such intention, the court reasoned that the present status is only that of military occupation (even if the period of *debellatio* has been entered). The fact that the occupying powers have permitted the reestablishment of German governments, in the opinion of the court demonstrates that, apart from annexation, the occupying powers do not intend to retain absolute political sovereignty over Germany.] Germany has been defeated and subjugated, but is not to be annexed or obliterated. This is not to say that following unconditional surrender of the German armed forces, the victorious powers might not have partitioned Germany, or may not yet have the right as victors to destroy Germany as a sovereign State; but some legal effects undoubtedly flow from the present agreement that Germany as a whole is not to be annexed and is to regain its political sovereignty.

". . . The situation in Germany today under quadripartite occupation is comparable in some respects to the situation in Cuba under United States occupation after the war with Spain. In both cases the occupying powers exercised supreme and unqualified authority over the occupied country, and in both cases the intention not to annex was declared. The Treaty of Paris of 10 December 1898 (proclaimed 11 April 1899) terminating war between the United States and Spain, and ceding Cuba to the United States, provided that the United States, 'will, so long as such occupation shall last, assume and discharge the obligations that may under international law result from the fact of its occupation, for the protection of life and property'. In *Neely* v. *Henkel* (1901) 180 U.S. 109, 23 S. Ct. 302, 306, the Supreme Court of the United States expressed the obligations of the United States toward Cuba during the period of occupation in these words:

> " 'It is true that as between Spain and the United States—indeed, as between the United States and all foreign nations—Cuba, upon the cessation of hostilities with Spain and after the treaty of Paris, was to be treated as if it were conquered territory. But as between the United States and Cuba that island is territory held in trust for the inhabitants of Cuba, to whom it rightfully belongs, and to whose exclusive control it will be surrendered when a stable government shall have been established by their voluntary action.' "

Col. J. Raymond, G.S.C., Associate Director, Legal Division, Office of Military Government for Germany (U.S.) to Restitution Branch, Economics Division, "Right of Occupying Power to Remove Indigenous Archives, Records and Documents", memorandum, Mar. 17, 1947, VII *Selected Opinions* January 1, 1947–March 31, 1947, Office of Military Government for Germany (U.S.) Legal Division APO 742, pp. 115, 120–121.

Professor Josef L. Kunz finds that the uniqueness of the legal status of Germany lies in two facts, "both of them unchallengeable, but difficult to reconcile legally: that Germany was undoubtedly conquered, but that equally undoubtedly Germany was not annexed. The problem of the legal status of occupied Germany, and all further problems, such as the legal nature of the occupation authorities, or the character of the legal rules now binding on individuals in the occupied territory, depend entirely on the solution of a preliminary question; namely, whether Germany has or has not ceased to exist as a sovereign state, as a state in the sense of international law".

Endorsing the view that Germany has continued to exist as a state, Professor Kunz concludes:

> "The status of occupied Germany is neither subjugation nor simple belligerent occupation. It is correct that, in general, the law cannot be deduced from the facts. But there is the principle of effectivity, which is a norm of positive general international law, and this norm applies to the status of states. As an ultimate construction of the status of occupied Germany it could be said that even if the present status of Germany had been brought about illegally, yet this illegality would have been healed by the norm of effectivity. And this norm is not valid, as is sometimes asserted, only against the aggressor. Italy's conquest of Ethiopia was certainly illegal, but it was effective, and Italy's sovereignty was recognized *de jure* by Great Britain and by many other states.
>
> "It is not necessary, however, to resort to the norm of effectivity, for general international law allows the conqueror not only to annex the conquered state, but also to determine its fate in a different way. He can restore the conquered state to its former sovereign and evacuate the territory; he can cede the conquered

territory to a third state; he can partition it. He can take over
the conquered territory temporarily with the intention of later
restoring its sovereignty. Even if his intention is to continue
the conquered territory as a sovereign state, the latter may cease
to exist by subsequent events, such as dismemberment, even if this
occurs against the intention of the conquerors. Should a unified,
sovereign Germany emerge within foreseeable time, the question
whether it is the old state continued or a new state will probably
always remain controversial, not only because of strong political
and emotional influences, but also because of the vagueness of the
international norm concerning the so-called identity of a state
in international law.

"General international law does not give to any victor, but to
the conqueror, the right to take such measures with regard to the
conquered territory as he thinks fit. This is the legal basis of the
status of occupied Germany. The victors are not the German
government, nor do they hold a dual position, nor are they the
representatives of Germany. They act by virtue of a right given
to them by general international law; all their acts, legislative,
executive, or judicial, have the character of international law.
Philip C. Jessup said in the United Nations Security Council
debate on the Berlin blockade, 'We are here by the right of victory.' Serini holds the same view.

"It is this right of the conqueror, that is shown when writers
state that the fate of the conquered territory depends on the will
of the conqueror, when Lauterpacht notes that the conquered
territory, even if not annexed, 'remains in possession and under
the sway' of the conqueror. That is why the same author can
declare that the exercise of all rights and prerogatives is vested
in the Occupying Powers 'with full effect in International Law.'

"Especially within the Pan-American orbit, resolutions have
been adopted to the effect that 'victory gives no right.' But that
is not the general international law actually in force. True, great
progress has been made. The rights of the conqueror are no
longer legally unlimited. But within these limits, the conqueror
is entitled to determine the fate of the conquered state, by annexation or otherwise. . . .

.   .   .   .

"On the one hand, the theories identifying either the unconditional surrender or the Potsdam Declaration with subjugation
are legally untenable. Germany was conquered, but not subjugated. Conquest alone does not extinguish the vanquished state,
nor does it end the war automatically. On the other hand, the
theories construing the present situation as mere belligerent occupation under the Hague rules are equally untenable in law; conquest is, historically and legally, exactly the opposite of belligerent occupation. The theories invented *ad hoc* are untenable,
because they have no basis in general international law. Neither
does general international law, to quote some 'third way constructions,' know a 'suspension' of sovereignty, or know a sovereign state that has no government and is deprived of its total
capacity to act, in both external and internal matters.

"While the situation, even if originally illegal, could be construed as healed by the principle of effectivity that is a norm of positive general international law, it is not necessary to resort to this construction. The legal basis of the present occupation is conquest; the conqueror has a right to annex the conquered state, but can also take other measures. He can, particularly, intend to preserve the sovereignty of the conquered state. That was the declared intention of the conquerors of Germany. . . ."

Kunz, "The Status of Occupied Germany Under International Law: A Legal Dilemma", 3 *Western Political Quarterly* (1950) 538, 540, 562–564.

Professor Kunz presents and analyzes various legal theories regarding the status of occupied Germany which fall into one of two categories—that of either supporting or denying the continued existence of Germany as a state. These two contending views are briefly summarized as follows:

1. The *tertium non datur* argument under which Germany though conquered but not subjugated does not cease to exist as a state; not being annexed, her legal status is simply that of belligerent occupation under the Hague Rules.

2. Kelsen's *debellatio-condominium*-sovereignty thesis under which the abolition of the German Government in consequence of *debellatio*—complete defeat—extinguished the state and without annexation or subjugation, unconditional surrender terms vesting supreme authority in the victors placed the sovereignty of German territory under the joined sovereignty of the occupant powers thus establishing a *condominium*.

Other theories affirming the continued existence of Germany as a sovereign State are identified by such phrases as "occupation of intervention", "fiduciary occupation", and "put under tutelage".

See Kunz, "The Status of Occupied Germany Under International Law: A Legal Dilemma", 3 *Western Political Quarterly* (1950) 538–565. See also Kelsen, "The International Legal Status of Germany To Be Established Immediately Upon Termination of the War", 38 Am. J. Int'l L. (1944) 689; "The Legal Status of Germany According to the Declaration of Berlin", 39 Am. J. Int'l L. (1945) 518.

Establishment of German Federal Republic

In connection with the establishment of the German Federal Republic, the Governments of France, the United States, and the United Kingdom proclaimed an Occupation Statute April 8, 1949, defining the powers to be retained by the occupation authorities. The Statute recites in part:

Occupation Statute

". . . During the period in which it is necessary that the occupation continue, the Governments of France, the United States and the United Kingdom desire and intend that the German people shall enjoy self-government to the maximum possible degree consistent with such occupation. The Federal State and the participating Laender shall have, subject only to the limitations in this Instrument, full legislative, executive and judicial powers in accordance with the Basic Law and with their respective constitutions."

In addition to the list of powers reserved to the occupying powers, the Statute provides that ". . . The occupation authorities, however, reserve the right, acting under instructions of their Governments, to resume, in whole or in part, the exercise of full authority if they consider that to do so is essential to security or to preserve democratic government in Germany or in pursuance of the international obligations of their governments. . . ."

With the establishment of the Federal Republic of Germany September 21, 1949, and the entry into force of the Occupation Statute on the same date, all authority with respect to the control of Germany or over any governmental authority thereof, was transferred from the Commanders-in-Chief of the forces of occupation of the United Kingdom, France, and the United States to the Allied High Commission as provided in the Charter of the Allied High Commission for Germany, June 20, 1949.

A Decade of American Foreign Policy: Basic Documents, 1941–49 (1950) 586–587, 603, 609.

The Federal Republic of Germany acquired full authority as a sovereign State May 5, 1955, with the signing at Bonn of the Allied High Commissioner's Proclamation which brought into force the Convention on Relations Between the Three Powers and the Federal Republic of Germany and the related Conventions of May 26, 1952, as amended by the Protocol on the Termination of the Occupation Regime in the Federal Republic of Germany of October 23, 1954. (Impending ratification of the Treaty on the Establishment of the European Defence Community, upon which the entry into force of the Convention on Relations between the Three Powers and the Federal Republic of Germany was made contingent under article 11 of the Convention, delayed the attainment of sovereignty and failing ratification of the EDC, a separate act was requisite before the sovereign status of the Federal Republic could become legally effective.) *Bonn Conventions*

Articles 1 and 2 of the Convention on Relations between the Three Powers and the Federal Republic of Germany, as amended, which define this new status, read as follows:

"Article 1

"1. On the entry into force of the present Convention the United States of America, the United Kingdom of Great Britain and Northern Ireland and the French Republic . . . will terminate the Occupation regime in the Federal Republic, revoke the Occupation Statute and abolish the Allied High Commission and the Offices of the Land Commissioners in the Federal Republic.

"2. The Federal Republic shall have accordingly the full authority of a sovereign State over its internal and external affairs.

"*Article 2*

"In view of the international situation, which has so far prevented the reunification of Germany and the conclusion of a peace settlement, the Three Powers retain the rights and the responsibilities, heretofore exercised or held by them, relating to Berlin and to Germany as a whole, including the reunification of Germany and a peace settlement. . . ."

U.S. TIAS 3425 ; 6 UST 4121–4122.

Executive Order No. 10608, signed May 5, 1955, by the President of the United States, prescribed the division of authority and functions of the United States representatives in Germany. Where former Executive orders thereby revoked (Executive Orders Nos. 10062 of June 6, 1949, and 10144 of July 21, 1950) referred to the United States High Commissioner for Germany, the new Executive order abolished that position and referred instead to the Chief of the United States Diplomatic Mission to the Federal Republic of Germany.

Since the United States continued to have occupation powers and functions relating to Berlin and to Germany as a whole as distinguished from the relationship between the United States and the Federal Republic of Germany, the Executive order of May 5, 1955, defined the respective authority and functions of the Ambassador on the one hand and the United States Military Commander on the other.

XXXII *Bulletin,* Department of State, No. 829, May 16, 1955, p. 792. For the text of the Executive order, see *ibid.,* pp. 792–793 ; 20 *Fed. Reg.* 3093.

Continuity of State

In consideration of the question whether the Government of the Federal Republic may be regarded as the successor of the German Reich, the Office of the Legal Adviser prepared a memorandum in 1950 which, in discussing first the issue of Germany's continued existence as a State, reads in part as follows:

"Since limited sovereignty is no bar to the existence of a State, we may proceed to examine the case of Germany in the light of the usual requisites of statehood. These are generally accepted as:

"(1) a territory
"(2) a people
"(3) a government

all of which should be distinct from those of another State. There is no dispute that Germany had a territory which has not been annexed, and a people, whose nationality has not been affected. These continued after the unconditional surrender and assumption of supreme authority. While the Hitler government and the Doenitz government had disappeared, there was from the time of the conquest a military government of the Allies, distinct from the governments of their respective countries though unilaterally receiving instructions from those countries. The relationship was analogous to that of the governor of a protectorate and his home government. The governments of the United Kingdom, of France, of the United States and of the Soviet Union were neither individually nor collectively the government of Germany. There was a distinct government of Germany, even though it was not German in personnel or origin. Gradually a measure of German government was reestablished, supplanting *pro tanto* the military government, until the Federal Republic was finally established. But at all times there not only was a territory and a people that were German but also there was a government of these people in that territory—a government of Germany. The requisites for a State were present and never ceased to exist.

"The State of Germany, therefore, seems not to have been obliterated by the conquest, the unconditional surrender or the assumption of supreme authority, although a distinct new government was imposed which was Allied, not German, in character. As German government was more and more restored the subordinate character of the State has become less and less. True, supreme authority still rests with the Allies; but a large measure of sovereign power is now being exercised by the Federal Republic. It is by no means a sovereign State, but there appears to be no legal difficulty in saying that it is a 'dependent' or 'not-full-sovereign' State, as the writers say.

"Courts and writers generally agree that the State of Germany has not ceased to exist. This position has the support of all English, Swiss and German legal authorities that have come to the attention of the United States Delegation, as well as the weight of authority in the United States, only Professor Kelsen taking the opposite view. It is the view expressed by the Netherlands Government in a memorandum furnished the Three Powers in February 1950. It is believed to be legally sound.

". . . The Government of the Federal Republic may be considered as the Government of Germany.

". . . [A special problem] is raised because of the present administrative division of Germany. Had it not been for that, and had the Federal Republic included the eastern zone, it would seem clear that, since Germany still exists, the Government of the Federal Republic would be the legal successor of the Reich.

"The government of a State does not cease to be the government of that State merely because, through circumstances beyond its control, it temporarily loses control of a portion of its territory.

The common cases are rebellion, secession, separatist movements or invasion, where temporary control of a part of the country is lost. This is true even where a different government is in full control of the lost territory, provided the situation is considered temporary. The means by which the government of the State is deprived of control of the territory is immaterial.

"True we do not have a case of an *existing government* losing control of territory, but, if the analysis is correct that the State of Germany continues to exist, there is a case of a *State* temporarily being divided by forces which cannot be controlled. If, in those circumstances, one and only one government appears which claims to be the government of the State, there is no reason why it should not be so recognized if it is otherwise politically desirable to do so. That would be the condition were there no government in the eastern zone, but the government of the Federal Republic were prevented, let us say, by a hostile army from entering and governing that territory.

"The position of the Three Powers is that the government of the Federal Republic is the one and only legitimate government qualified to speak for the German people. The existence of the eastern German government is not recognized as legitimate. Therefore, the situation is as if it did not exist. The Basic Law of the Federal Republic provides (Article 23) for the future accession of the Laender of the eastern zone although 'for the time being' it applies only in the western zones. Article 146 recognizes that a Constitution for a united Germany may supersede it, but in the meantime the Basic Law has been adopted, as the preamble states, 'for a transitional period.' Lacking the possibility of establishing a democratic legal government capable of controlling all Germany, the greatest step that was possible was taken to that end. A government was established with the intent of ultimately controlling all of Germany and with the legal machinery for such a development, but confined of necessity 'for the time being' to the western zones. . . ."

The Office of the Legal Adviser (Raymond), memorandum, "Memorandum on the Successorship of the Government of the Federal Republic to the Reich", July 13, 1950, MS. Department of State, file 762.00/7–1350.

On the occasion of the deposit by the Federal Republic of Germany of its instrument of accession to the North Atlantic Treaty on May 6, 1955, Secretary of State Dulles said:

"This act reflects the recovery of sovereignty by a people, the German people, who have demonstrated that they can, if they will, be great in the best sense of that word. Also, it reflects the exercise of that sovereignty to perfect a fellowship with other sovereign nations and to create unity out of what has been diversity."

XXXII *Bulletin*, Department of State, No. 829, May 16, 1955, p. 793.

Referring to the legal concept of sovereignty as it relates to Germany, Deputy Under Secretary of State Murphy explained:

". . . This means that the German Federal Republic has regained a political identity of its own. Thus it is imperative that we judge it on its own record, not on the record of its predecessors. It is equally imperative that we accord the Federal Republic the status and credit that we accord any other sovereign nation. The Federal Republic is no longer a dependent of the free world; it now stands on its own feet. On May 5 of this year the United States, with Britain and France, renounced the privilege of an occupying power to intervene in the national affairs of the Federal Republic. We do have jurisdiction in two or three areas that were voluntarily agreed to by the Germans, but, aside from those, we have no authority over Germany. From here on out, the Federal Republic is on its own and the course of its internal and external policy will be determined by its elected government."

Address before the Indiana University Conference on Problems of American Foreign Policy at Bloomington, Ind., June 25, 1955, press release 387, June 24, 1955; XXXIII *Bulletin*, Department of State, No. 837, July 11, 1955, pp. 43, 44.

Referring to the feasibility of a "peace treaty" with Germany, Secretary of State Herter, in a statement made May 18, 1959, before the Foreign Ministers Conference in Geneva, said:

"It is the position of the United States that under international law the international entity known as Germany remains in existence, notwithstanding what has happened since 1945 as an incident of Four Power occupation. The Government of the United States does not consider, and will not admit, that Germany as an international entity is permanently divided into new and separate states, as was the case of Austria after World War I. ". . . It was the international entity known as Germany with which the United States was at war and with which it has outstanding problems. Accordingly, any 'final settlement,' so far as our Governments are concerned, must await the establishment of a government which can act for and bind Germany as a whole.

.   .   .   .

"The Bonn conventions entered into by the Western Powers and the German Federal Republic are in no way inconsistent with the position of the United States I have just set forth. The United States participated in the Bonn conventions because it considered that the people of West Germany should be permitted to assume as normal an international role as possible under the circumstances. It appears on the face of the Bonn conventions that they constitute merely an effort to achieve an interim solution to the problem resulting from the lack of a definitive peace treaty.

"Specifically, in the Bonn conventions it is made clear that these arrangements are of an interim nature pending a final peace settlement. While the Federal Republic is recognized as having the full authority of a sovereign over its own internal and external affairs, the three Western Powers retain all the rights and responsibilities exercised or held by them relating to Berlin and Germany as a whole, including reunification of Germany and a peace settlement.

. . . .

"In international relations the sovereignty of a state is one and indivisible. The concept of 'two existing German states' representing the indivisible sovereignty of the German people is unacceptable, both in legal and in political theory, and would be wholly unworkable in practice. . . ."

XL *Bulletin*, Department of State, No. 1041, June 8, 1959, pp. 819–820.

In answer to the argument as advanced in *Clark, Attorney General, As Successor to the Alien Property Custodian*, v. *Allen, et al.* that the Treaty of 1923 with Germany must be held to have failed to survive the war, since Germany, as a result of its defeat and the occupation by the Allies, has ceased to exist as an independent national or international community, Mr. Justice Douglas, speaking for the United States Supreme Court, said:

". . . We find no evidence that the political departments have considered the collapse and surrender of Germany as putting an end to such provisions of the treaty as survived the outbreak of the war or the obligation of either party in respect to them. The Allied Control Council has, indeed, assumed control of Germany's foreign affairs and treaty obligations—a policy and course of conduct by the political departments wholly consistent with the maintenance and enforcement, rather than the repudiation, of pre-existing treaties."

331 U.S. 503, 514 (1947).

The United States District Court, in vacating a certificate adjudging the plaintiff had lost and forfeited her United States nationality and citizenship by voting in an election in 1946 in the American Zone of military occupation in Germany, cited a Department of State publication, *Occupation of Germany—Policy and Progress*, quoting in part as follows:

"The Allied powers, having completely destroyed the Nazi State and assumed for the time sovereign authority in Germany, have been confronted with the necessity of formulating policies for the rebuilding of the entire German state structure. . . .

. . . .

"United States policy has recognized the fact that political reconstruction cannot consist in the reestablishment of preexisting institutions or forms. The dissolution of the Nazi regime has left a political void and even yet few constructive political ideas have emerged from the general chaos. . . ."

The Court interpreting these passages declared:

". . . it is made clear that the area in which the election was held was not a foreign state or territory within the meaning of Section 801(e). [Nationality Act of 1940, § 401(e), 8 U.S.C.A. § 801(e).]

"1. My conclusion is that the election of January 27, 1946, at which plaintiff voted, was held in territory then ruled and governed by the United States and was held by permission and under the direction and by the authority of the United States. And that when plaintiff voted, she was not voting in a political election in a foreign state, nor was she participating in an election or plebiscite to determine the sovereignty over foreign territory within the meaning of Section 801. . . ."

Brehm v. *Acheson*, 90 F. Supp. 662, 665 (S.D. Tex. 1950).

The "German Democratic Republic" was established October 7, 1949, by the provisional People's Chamber which body on the same day promulgated a Constitution forming the basis of the so-called East German state. Establishment of "German Democratic Republic"

Soviet Zone Constitution and Electoral Law, Office of the U.S. High Commissioner for Germany (1951), p. 1.

In response to the Soviet Government's announcement of March 25, 1954, that East Germany had become a sovereign state, the United States, British, and French High Commissioners issued a joint declaration April 8, 1954, which read:

"The Allied High Commission desires to clarify the attitude of the governments which it represents toward the statement issued on March 25 by the Soviet Government, purporting to describe a change in its relations with the Government of the so-called German Democratic Republic. [New York *Times*, Mar. 26, 1954.] This statement appears to have been intended to create the impression that sovereignty has been granted to the German Democratic Republic. It does not alter the actual situation in the Soviet Zone. The Soviet Government still retains effective control there.

"The three governments represented in the Allied High Commission will continue to regard the Soviet Union as the responsible power for the Soviet Zone of Germany. These governments do not recognize the sovereignty of the East German regime which is not based on free elections, and do not intend to deal with it as a government. They believe that this attitude will be shared by other states, who, like themselves, will continue to recognize the Government of the Federal Republic as the only freely elected and legally constituted government in Germany. The Allied High Commission also takes this occasion to express the resolve of its governments that the Soviet action shall not deter them from their determination to work for the reunification of Germany as a free and sovereign nation."

XXX *Bulletin,* Department of State, No. 773, Apr. 19, 1954, p. 588; II *American Foreign Policy, 1950–1955: Basic Documents* (1957) 1756–1757.

Adverting to the Soviet Union Government's announcement of March 25, 1954, regarding the establishment of the same relations with the so-called German Democratic Republic as with other sovereign states, the Government of the German Federal Republic declared in a statement of April 7, 1954:

"By this declaration the Soviet Government seeks to create the impression that the part of Germany occupied by it has become an independent state with status equal to that of other sovereign states.

"The Soviet declaration cannot, however, alter in any way the fact that there is, was, and will be only one German state, and that it is solely the governmental organs of the Federal Republic of Germany which today represents this German state which has never perished. Nor is this fact altered by the painful reality which is that German sovereignty cannot at present be exercised uniformly in all parts of Germany."

II *Bundestag Stenografiche Berichte* (1954) 794.

Interdependent Independent States

§ 19

Morocco

The Franco-Moroccan Joint Declaration of March 2, 1956, recognizing the independence of Morocco, terminated Morocco's status as a Protectorate of France instituted by the Treaty of Fez, March 30, 1912, and made fully operative the Declaration of La Celle-Saint-Cloud of November 6, 1955, under which the Government of the French Republic recognized the right of Morocco to regain its independence.

Moroccan independence which "implies in particular the right to a diplomacy and an army—as well as its determination to respect, and to see to it that others respect, the integrity of Moroccan territory, as guaranteed by international treaties" was established within the framework of "interdependence of the two countries" calling for "cooperation on a basis of liberty and equality, especially in matters of defense, foreign relations, economy and culture . . .".

Ambassade de France, Service de Presse et d'Information, *Moroccan Affairs,* No. 12, Mar. 1956, "Documentary Background on the Franco-

Moroccan Agreements of March 2, 1956", pp. 1, 2; *Documents on International Affairs 1956* (1959) 691–692; and for the French text, see *L'Année Politique 1956*, pp. 300–301. The International Court of Justice in the *Case Concerning Rights of Nationals of the United States of America in Morocco* observed with respect to the status of Morocco under the Treaty of Fez of 1912 that "It is not disputed by the French Government that Morocco, even under the Protectorate, has retained its personality as a State in international law", and that "Under this Treaty, Morocco remained a sovereign State but it made an arrangement of a contractual character whereby France undertook to exercise certain sovereign powers in the name and on behalf of Morocco, and, in principle, all of the international relations of Morocco." *Case Concerning Rights of Nationals of the United States of America in Morocco*, Aug. 27, 1952, I. C. J. Reports (1952) 176, 185, 188.

To further define the modalities of this "interdependence" in the field of external relations, France and Morocco signed a Diplomatic Agreement May 28, 1956, affirming thereby "in complete equality and respect of their independence" their determination to "maintain and to strengthen the solidarity which unites them".

Under the provisions of this Agreement it was "resolved to maintain between them relations of permanent friendship, of mutual aid and of assistance . . ." (article 1) and the two States agreed to consult to meet any threat to their common interests if the situation required it (article 2); to meet periodically or at the request of one of the parties to assure concerted action in the field of foreign policy (article 3); to undertake not to adopt a policy which, after examining together, they might recognize as being incompatible with the interests of one of them (article 4); and to undertake not to conclude international conventions which render ineffective the rights of the other party which it might have recognized by agreement (article 5). To these provisions were added the qualifications that "none of the present provisions must be interpreted as affecting the obligations which result either from the Charter of the United Nations or from agreements, treaties or conventions in force between one of the High Contracting Parties and third powers"; and "none of the present provisions must be interpreted, moreover, as entailing, for one of the High Contracting Parties, any limitation whatever on its ability to negotiate and to conclude treaties, conventions or other international acts" (article 6).

The First Secretary of the American Embassy at Paris (McBride) to the Secretary of State (Dulles), May 23, 1956, despatch No. 2248, encl. No. 2, MS. Department of State, file 651.71/5–2356. On February 15, 1960, Morocco announced the abrogation of the French-Moroccan Diplomatic Agreement of May 28, 1956, in a communique which reported the note delivered to the French Foreign Minister as stating that "Morocco considers that there is no longer cause for continuing to apply the diplomatic agreement signed

between Morocco and France on May 28, 1956.   This position is based on
the unfriendly attitude of the Government of France which, disregarding
repeated approaches by the Government of Morocco and the United Nations
resolution, proceeded to explode its first atomic bomb at Reggane, that is,
at a place which has incontestably been part of Moroccan territory".   The
American Ambassador at Rabat (Yost) to the Secretary of State (Herter),
telegram, Feb. 15, 1960, MS. Department of State, file 751.5611/2–1560.

Protectorate status of the Spanish zone in Morocco, established by
the Spanish-Moroccan Agreement of November 27, 1912, was terminated by the joint Hispano-Moroccan Declaration signed April 7,
1956, by which Spain "recognizes the independence of Morocco, . . .
and its full sovereignty, together with all the attributes of the same,
including its own diplomatic service and army . . .".   Under this
Agreement, the Spanish Government "undertakes to lend His Imperial Majesty the Sultan the aid and assistance which will be determined as necessary by common agreement, especially with regard to
foreign relations and to defense".

> The First Secretary of the American Embassy at Madrid (McClelland) to
> the Secretary of State (Dulles), Apr. 9, 1956, despatch No. 1128, MS. De-
> partment of State, file 771b.02/4–956; XXXIV *Bulletin*, Department of
> State, No. 878, Apr. 23, 1956, pp. 667–668.

In recognition of the status of Morocco as an independent State,
the participating powers in the international regime of Tangier, Belgium, Spain, the United States, France, Italy, Morocco, the Netherlands, Portugal, and the United Kingdom, formally abrogated the
international regime of Tangier October 29, 1956, and restored it to
the "entire and sole sovereignty" of the Sultan of Morocco.   (See
post, pp. 595 ff.)

The United States Government announced its decision October 6,
1956, "to relinquish . . . consular jurisdictions which were accorded
to the United States of America in a Treaty of Peace and Friendship
first concluded with Morocco in 1787 and renewed in 1836 and in the
Act of Algeciras signed in 1906; as well as to cease to exercise jurisdiction over subjects of Morocco or others who may be designated as
proteges under the Convention of Madrid signed in 1880. . . ."

> The First Secretary of the American Embassy at Rabat (Dixon) to the
> Secretary of State (Dulles), despatch No. 91, Nov. 30, 1956, MS. Depart-
> ment of State, file 611.7141/11–3056.

Tunisia   As a French Protectorate in 1955, Tunisia acquired internal autonomy under a General Convention between France and Tunisia
signed at Paris June 3, 1955.   Article 4 of this Convention stated:

> ". . . France recognizes and proclaims the self-government of
> Tunisia, which shall have no restrictions or limitations other than

those resulting from the provisions of the present Conventions and of the Conventions now in force, it being understood that, in the fields of defense and foreign affairs, the present state of things shall continue and matters be dealt with as they have been up until this day."

Under article 8 it was agreed that the French Government would consult His Highness the Bey in the course of international negotiations which concern exclusively Tunisian interests and to keep him informed of all other international negotiations of interest to Tunisia; that treaties requiring measures of application by Tunisia would be communicated for that purpose to His Highness the Bey by the French Government; and that the Tunisian State would take the necessary measures for rendering applicable the treaties concerning Tunisia and for assuring their execution.

> *Tunisia faces the future,* Special Issue Series, "World's Documents" (1956), p. 172.

Tunisia achieved full sovereignty and independence with the signing, March 20, 1956, of the Franco-Tunisian Protocol of Agreement, thereby ending the 75-year-old Protectorate established by treaty May 12, 1881, and modifying or abrogating those provisions of the Conventions of June 3, 1955, contradictory to Tunisia's new status.

While the negotiations resumed under the authority of this Agreement acknowledged "that Tunisia will have the exercise of its responsibilities in matters of foreign affairs, security and defense", France and Tunisia, "with due respect for their sovereignties", agreed "to define or to perfect the modalities of a freely effected interdependence between the two countries by organizing their cooperation in the domains in which they have common interests, particularly in matters of defense and foreign relations".

> Ambassade de France, Service de Presse et d'Information, *Tunisian Affairs,* No. 12, Mar. 1956, "The Independence of Tunisia Recognized by France: The Agreement of March 20, 1956", pp. 1, 2; *Documents on International Affairs 1956* (1959) 692–693; *American Foreign Policy: Current Documents, 1956* (1959) 724–725; and for the French text, see *L'Année Politique 1956,* 509–510.

Commenting on the term "interdependence", the Tunisian official press organ, *Al Amal,* reported March 20, 1956:

"Interdependence is a form of co-operation, and co-operation, provided it is free, spells nothing but good and mutual benefit. The race between States and the internationalism, both of which characterize our century, oblige all countries to be independent.

The co-operation between France and her main Allies—America and Great Britain—constitutes a form of free interdependence. . . ."

Le Monde Economique, "World's Documents" Series, "Tunisia Faces the Future", June 1956, p. 70.

Neutralized and Neutral States

§ 20

"The following variations of the word 'neutral' are commonly found in writings on international law. The definitions are intended primarily to identify each as in fact falling into separate categories:

"1. *Neutrality*—In time of war, the condition of a state which is not at war with the belligerents and does not participate in the hostilities.

"2. *Neutral Establishments*—Special protection for the term of war, arranged in special conventions for certain establishments, such as Red Cross, hospitals, etc.

"3. *Neutralization or Neutralized State*—A state whose independence and integrity are for all time guaranteed by an international convention of the powers, under the condition that such state binds itself never to take up arms against any other state except for defense against attack, and never to enter into such international obligations as could indirectly involve it in war.

"4. *Neutralization of Parts of States, Canals, Rivers, etc.*—Imposed neutralization upon an area by agreement of the powers with respect to a geographic area of mutual interest.

"5. *Autonomous or Self-Neutralization*—The unilateral declaration of a state that it will always remain neutral.

"It will be noted that the first concept of 'neutrality' set forth above is transitory, being a status any state may adopt or reject in time of war without affecting its international status after conclusion of the war.

.   .   .   .

"A *neutralized State* is one whose independence and political and territorial integrity are guaranteed *permanently* by a collective agreement of Great Powers subject to the condition that the particular State concerned will never take up arms against another State—except to defend itself—and will never enter into treaties of alliance, etc., which may compromise its impartiality or lead it into war.

.   .   .   .

"Neutralization differs fundamentally from neutrality, which is a voluntary policy assumed temporarily in regard to a state of War affecting other Powers, and terminable at any time by the State declaring its neutrality. Neutralization on the other hand is a permanent status conferred by agreement with the interested Powers, without whose consent it cannot be relinquished."

Attorney, Office of the Legal Adviser (Wehmeyer) to the Legal Adviser (Phleger), memorandum, "Nature of Austria's Neutrality and Legal Implications of United States Response to the Neutrality Declaration", Nov. 16, 1955, MS. Department of State, file 663.0021/11–1655.

While the term "permanent neutrality" refers loosely to either a "neutralized" state or to a "self-neutralized" state, the practice of states is nearly unanimous in the view that a unilateral declaration alone cannot create in international law a status of permanent neutrality. In the absence of a treaty creating permanent neutrality, any unilateral declaration to that effect has only the force of municipal law. It has been concluded, therefore, that "Iceland's unilateral declaration of permanent neutrality, 1918, had only the value of a unilateral formulation of policy; it had no international effect and did not render Iceland a permanently neutral state in international law."

Kunz, "Austria's Permanent Neutrality", 50 Am. J. Int'l L. (1956) 418.

The status of permanent neutrality does not impair the sovereignty of the state concerned. Subject to its obligations as a neutral, its attributes of sovereignty still obtain as it may participate in general and regional treaties, international organizations of a nonmilitary nature, and can conduct its own internal and foreign nonmilitary policies without limitation.

Chancellor Raab of Austria, commenting on the unimpaired freedom of the press and opinion on the occasion of submitting the Federal Constitutional Law of Austria's neutrality to the Austrian Parliament October 26, 1955, said:

". . . Freedom of thought and political freedom of the individual, in particular freedom of press and opinion, is not affected by the permanent neutrality of a state. Neither does it imply an obligation to observe ideological neutrality . . . ."

The Counselor of the American Embassy at Vienna (Davis) to the Secretary of State (Dulles), despatch No. 442, encl. 1, Nov. 4, 1955, MS. Department of State, file 663.0021/11–455.

A comprehensive study of the various legal concepts of neutrality and review of the works of leading authorities on this subject were undertaken in the Office of the Legal Adviser and set forth in a memorandum on the "Nature of Austria's Neutrality and Legal Implications of United States Response to the Neutrality Declaration" of November 16, 1955, from which the following is quoted:

" 'The obligations of a neutralised State are as follows:—

" '(a) to abstain from hostilities except in self-defense;
" '(b) to abstain from alliances involving the risk of hostilities, e.g. treaties of alliance, guarantee, or protectorate, but not from non-political conventions, e.g. postal or tariff Conventions;
" ' (c) to defend itself against attack, even when calling on the guarantors for assistance, unless it has no means of defense.

" 'This last obligation (c) is most important, and is virtually a condition of the collective recognition of neutralisation. Thus in 1938 when the League of Nations Council recognized Switzerland's full neutrality it took note of the fact that Switzerland was ready and in a position to defend itself.' [Starke, *An Introduction to International Law* (1950), pp. 89–91.]

" '. . . To be effective [neutralization] must be guaranteed by many world-powers, each of which must agree, not only to respect, but also to maintain, the permanently neutral condition . . . . As the French writers put it, they must *respecter et faire respecter* that neutral character. Therein lies the whole difference between neutrality and neutralization. Any state may declare itself neutral, or obtain through its impartial attitude toward belligerents the general recognition of its neutral character. But neutrality is a transient condition, and a merely neutral state can at any time cease to be neutral and engage in the war. The neutrality of a neutralized state, attained by international agreement, is permanent, and results in its entire exclusion from all hostilities whatsoever except in its own defense.' [Wicker, Cyrus, "The United States and Neutralization", *The Atlantic Monthly*, Sept. 1910, p. 310.]

" 'It should be noted, however, that the guarantees to *respect* neutrality or *to cause it to be respected* were not tantamount to a territorial guarantee, and that whenever it appeared desirable, the additional and specific territorial guarantee was explicitly and separately given. Thus *it is of the utmost importance to note that the idea of neutralization does not of itself connote a territorial guarantee.*

" 'As to the methodology of guarantee, treaty provisions have usually stipulated either a "joint-and-several" pledge or a "collective" one, the former placing upon all signatories individually the obligation to make good their word, while the latter has been so loosely interpreted as to provide for little more than an assurance of moral support to the country neutralized.

" 'Thus viewed, (1) the collective guarantee merely to respect the principle of neutrality is so weak as to be meaningless, as was proved by the instances of Luxembourg and the Congo during the World War. (2) A collective guarantee to cause neutrality to be respected is somewhat stronger, and would probably be workable if some Power other than a signatory should attempt the violation of the neutrality of the area in question, though in actual fact such a guarantee is not likely to be invoked against a signatory who violates it. (3) A joint-and-several guarantee to respect is of no more significance than the cumulative self-restraint of the guarantors, but (4) the joint-and-several guarantee to cause to be respected involves, in strict theory, effective sanctions.

" 'A guarantee of the latter (fourth) type leaves the individual guarantor no option but to act, irrespective of the action taken by other cosignatories . . . This type of guarantee is almost invariably associated with a stringent territorial guarantee which would in itself involve armed assistance to the attacked state. The only effective test of such a guarantee of neutrality would appear to occur in the absence of the territorial guarantee.' [Graham, "Neutralization As A Movement in International Law", 21 Am. J. Int'l. Law (1927), pp. 79, 89–91.]

"The three outstanding instances of neutralized states have been Switzerland, Belgium and Luxembourg. Accordingly, it is useful to note the precise language which was adopted to achieve the neutralization in each case.

"*Switzerland*

" '. . . the Powers who signed the Declaration of Vienna of the 20th March declare, by this present Act, their formal and authentic Acknowledgment of the perpetual Neutrality of Switzerland; and they Guarantee to that country the Integrity and Inviolability of its Territory . . .' (Act of Paris, November 20, 1815) (Parties to the Act were Austria, France, Great Britain, Prussia and Russia.) Switzerland
[Enumerating more specifically the powers and duties of the Federal Council, article 102(9) of the Constitution of Switzerland states: It insures the external security of Switzerland and the maintenance of its independence and neutrality. III Peaslee, *Constitutions of Nations*, (2nd ed. 1956), pp. 329, 350.]
[In commenting on the Statement of Fundamental Principles set forth on July 16, 1937 by Secretary of State Hull, the President of the Swiss Federal Council (President Motta) stated:

"By entering into the League of Nations and by signing the Kellogg Pact, Switzerland gave proof that it was prepared to do its part in international collaboration leading to a general realization of the principles referred to. Switzerland is able to continue this collaboration up to a point where its neutrality, which is recognized in international law and of which the value has been historically demonstrated, will not be weakened. It is conditional upon this consideration that Switzerland can adhere to the program put forward by Secretary Hull." The Chargé d'Affaires of the United States in Switzerland (Bigelow) to the Secretary of State (Hull), desp. No. 5063, July 29, 1937, encl.: Aide-Mémoire by the President of the Swiss Federal Council (Motta), MS. Dept. of State, file no. 711.00 Statement July 16, 1937/126; 1937 For. Rels. vol. 1, pp. 727, 729–730.]

"*Belgium*

Belgium

"The neutral status of Belgium was inserted in three separate treaties concluded at London on April 19, 1839.

"The first was signed by the representatives of Austria, France, Great Britain and Russia on the one part, and the Netherlands (Holland) on the other, which, after acknowledging the dissolution of the union of the Netherlands and Belgium, declares that 'Belgium . . . shall form an independent and perpetually neutral State. It shall be bound to observe such neutrality towards all other States.'

"The second treaty is that which separates Belgium from Holland and in that also the perpetual neutrality of the former country is recognized.

"The third treaty is that concluded between the same five Powers and Belgium, in which the following article appears:

" '. . . they (the Five Powers) declare that the articles herewith annexed and forming the tenor of the treaty concluded this day . . . are considered as having the same force as if they were textually inserted in the present act, and they are thus placed under the guarantee of their said Majesties (of the Five Powers).'

"In commenting on the neutralization of Belgium, one writer has observed:

" 'It should be observed that Holland, although one of the contracting parties to one of the above instruments, did not guarantee the neutrality of Belgium, but merely recognized that fact; therefore, although bound to respect it, she is not under any obligation to defend it in case it is violated.' [Ion, "Treaties of Neutrality", 13 Mich. L. Rev. (1915), pp. 368, 369.]

"*Luxembourg*

Luxembourg

" 'The Grand Duchy of Luxembourg within the limits determined by the Act annexed to the treaties of the 19th April 1839, under the guarantee of the Courts of Great Britain, Austria, France, Prussia, and Russia shall henceforth form a perpetually Neutral State. It shall be bound to observe the same neutrality towards all other States. The High Contracting Parties engage to respect the principle of Neutrality stipulated by the present Article.

" 'That principle is and remains placed under the sanction of the collective Guarantee of the Powers signing Parties to the present treaty, with the exception of Belgium, which is itself a Neutral State.' (Treaty signed at London on May 11, 1867)

. . . .

"*Self-Neutralized States*

. . . .

"There have been several instances of nations adopting a policy of self-neutralization although for various reasons only for a very brief period. Estonia started to follow a path of self-neutralization in 1918 and requested an international guarantee of her neutrality or of her independence and actually obtained in advance recognition of her eventual neutralization by Soviet

Russia and the Ukraine (League of Nations, Treaty Series, Vol. II, pp. 57, 124, 131, 136). In joining the League, however, Estonia made no request for special status as did Switzerland, apparently on the ground that membership in the League was in itself a guarantee of the territorial integrity of all nations and thus the policy of neutrality was no longer necessary.

"Apparently Latvia also toyed with the idea of self-neutralization during the days at the end of World War I but she too abandoned the idea as inconsistent with membership in the League.

"Under the provisions of the Central American Peace Treaty of December 20, 1907 (Malloy, Treaties of the United States, II, 2393), Honduras adopted a status of neutrality by unilateral act. Article 3 of the Treaty provided:

" 'Taking into account the central geographical position of Honduras and the facilities which owing to this circumstance have made its territory most often the theater of Central American conflicts, Honduras declares from now on its absolute neutrality in event of any conflict between the other republics, and the latter, in their turn, provided such neutrality be observed, bind themselves to respect it, and in no case to violate the Honduranean territory.'

"With regard to the Honduras case, it has been observed that

" '. . . this was merely a voluntary declaration of policy by Honduras, and in no way implied an imposed status. It was no bar to Honduras' entry into the World War. Finally, it was accompanied by a distinct and separate territorial guarantee, which was in no wise made contingent upon Honduranean neutrality. The omission of this provision in the revised treaties of 1923 is mute evidence of the greater force of the guarantees provided by membership in the League of Nations.' [Graham, "Neutralization As A Movement in International Law", 21 Am. J. Int'l. Law (1927), p. 84, ftn. 26.]

"The Honduras case is an illustration of a limited type of self-neutralization. The 'absolute neutrality' assumed by Honduras was limited to conflict between the other specified republics. Also it was accompanied by a distinct and separate territorial guarantee.

.   .   .   .

"A brief reference to the use of the word 'perpetual' in such neutrality declarations may be in order. One writer has said

" '. . . the meaning of the word "perpetual" ought not to be misunderstood and by giving it a false construction try to show its so-called absurdity. It is used in treaties recognizing or guaranteeing the permanent neutrality of States in order to distinguish it from temporary neutrality, namely from that of the states who chose to remain neutral during a war between other Powers . . . It is, however, beyond question that notwithstanding the word perpetual, a new treaty may alter such situation . . .' [Ion, "Treaties of Neutrality", 13 Mich. L. Rev. (1915), pp. 368, 372]."

Attorney, Office of the Legal Adviser (Wehmeyer) to the Legal Adviser (Phleger), memorandum, "Nature of Austria's Neutrality and Legal Implications of United States Response to the Neutrality Declaration", Nov. 16, 1955, MS. Department of State, file 663.0021/11–1655.

Tangier

"So far as I am aware, no formal proclamation of neutrality has been issued in any foreign country, but a formal proclamation is not necessary, and the real question is whether a policy of neutrality has been in fact pursued. We may begin by examining the action taken at Tangier. The international statute which governs Tangier provides that the Tangier zone shall always be neutral in time of war, and the control of Tangier is entrusted to a committee composed of the principal foreign consuls. On August 8, 1936, this committee decided by a majority vote (the Spanish consul dissenting) that warships of both parties should be excluded from the harbour. They further decided that insurgents not in uniform should be admitted to the zone from Spanish Morocco, and that passports bearing the visas of the insurgent government in Morocco should be recognized as valid. Clearly these decisions, to which Great Britain is a party, amount in substance to a declaration of neutrality in the Tangier zone and to a recognition of the insurgent government for the duration of the war."

H. A. Smith, "Some Problems of the Spanish Civil War", XVIII Brit. Yb. Int'l L. (1937) 17, 26. (For a change in the status of Tangier, see *post*, pp. 595 ff.)

Austria

At the Berlin Conference in 1954, Austria declared her intention to "do everything to keep herself free from foreign military influence" meaning that she would "not concede any military bases to foreign powers". Subsequently, the reference to permanent neutrality was incorporated in the Soviet-Austrian Agreement of April 15, 1955, signed by the Soviet and Austrian delegations. In part I of this Agreement Austria undertook to make a declaration in a form which will "obligate Austria internationally to practice in perpetuity a neutrality of the type maintained by Switzerland."

The Austrian Parliament enacted on October 26, 1955, a Constitutional Federal Statute on Austria's permanent neutrality. In its principal article I the Statute reads:

"1. For the purpose of the lasting maintenance of her independence externally, and for the purpose of the inviolability of her territory, Austria declares of her own free will her perpetual neutrality. Austria will maintain and defend this with all means at her disposal.

"2. For the securing of this purpose in all future times Austria will not join any military alliances and will not permit the establishment of any foreign military bases on her territory."

In response to the Austrian Government's note of November 14, 1955, requesting the Government of the United States to recognize "the perpetual neutrality of Austria", the United States, in a note of December 6, 1955, replied "that the Government of the United States has taken cognizance of this constitutional law and recognizes the perpetual neutrality of Austria as defined therein."

Department of State press release 680, Dec. 6, 1955. *Foreign Ministers Meeting: Berlin Discussions, January 25–February 18, 1954*, Department of State publication 5399, pp. 200, 201. For text of Soviet-Austrian Agreement, see XXXII *Bulletin*, Department of State, No. 834, June 20, 1955, pp. 1011–1013.

In reply to the Soviet Foreign Minister's proposal in Vienna at the time of the Soviet-Austrian Agreement of April 15, 1955, for a four-power undertaking to respect and observe Austria's intended declaration of neutrality, Secretary of State Dulles stated that "the United States would have no objection in principle to expressing an intention to respect Austria's neutrality . . . . Such respect is indeed enjoined upon us by the United Nations Charter. For example, article 2(4) of the charter requires all members to refrain in their international relations from the threat or use of force against the territorial integrity or political independence of any state. . . ."

XXXII *Bulletin*, Department of State, No. 834, June 20, 1955, pp. 1010–1011.

The implications of the United States response to Austria's neutrality notification were commented on in a State Department memorandum on this subject:

"While agreeing in principle to the concept of Austria's assuming a status of neutrality, United States officials have made it clear repeatedly in international meetings (at Vienna, San Francisco and Geneva) and in private discussions with other interested governments that the United States is limited constitutionally in terms of guarantees of political situations abroad and, accordingly, would not likely be in a position to participate in a guarantee of neutrality for Austria. Accordingly, the principal powers concerned in this matter are on notice of this constitutional limitation on the United States.

"What, then are the legal implications of the proposed response to the Austrian announcement of neutrality? It has been seen that even in the case of imposed neutralization, there is no implication, no guarantee of territorial integrity, unless such a guarantee is expressly and clearly stated. If imposed neutralization carries with it no automatic guarantee, *a fortiori* mere recognition of self-neutralization would assuredly not imply such ·a guarantee.

"One writer who has considered the implications of dealing with a self-neutralized state has expressed the view that the obligation imposed on states which agree to respect such neutrality is that of self-restraint, while states which guarantee the neutrality undertake the obligation to exercise constraint upon violators of the neutrality.

"Other authorities who have considered this problem have expressed the following viewpoints:

> " 'When any nation, for economic, moral, or political reasons, determines to assume the obligations and to demand the rights of a permanently neutral state, and when it has proclaimed that fact . . . the world must accept such a nation's act as binding, sanctioned by that ideal of law which has alone inspired all international life.' [Robinson, "Autonomous Neutralization", 11 Am. J. Int'l L. (1917) 607, 609.]

"Another says:

> " '*Recognition* [of neutrality] connotes that *the recognizing state will not violate the neutrality; guarantee* connotes that *the recognizing state will defend this neutrality* . . . . It is not necessary that the powers which recognize a permanent neutrality also guarantee this neutrality.' [Pradier-Fodéré, 8 *Traité de Droit International Public* (1906) 885 (translation).

"In its response to the note from the Austrian Government announcing its neutrality, the United States will state that it has 'taken due cognizance of that constitutional law and recognizes the perpetual neutrality of Austria as defined therein.' The literal definition of the word 'recognize' is commonly accepted in terms of 'to act or take note of'. Insofar as it relates to an official acknowledgement of an international status such as neutrality as declared by a sovereign government it thus requires the recognizing state to refrain from taking those actions with regard to the other state which might violate the accepted concepts of a neutral state in the international community. This, then, is the extent of the obligation assumed by the United States in recognizing the Austrian announcement of its neutrality."

Attorney, Office of the Legal Adviser (Wehmeyer) to the Legal Adviser (Phleger), memorandum, "Nature of Austria's Neutrality and Legal Implications of United States Response to the Neutrality Declaration", Nov. 16, 1955, MS. Department of State, file 663.0021/11–1655.

Chancellor Raab in a speech before the Austrian Parliament October 26, 1955, when the Federal Constitutional Law on Austria's neutrality was under discussion, clarified the views of the Austrian

Government on the nature of Austrian neutrality. In the course of that speech he stated that:

". . . The declaration of Austria's neutrality is, in the first place, an expression of the desire of political elements to base the foreign policy of the government on a status of permanent neutrality. A declaration to this effect would not have to be laid down in the form of a constitutional law; according to the procedure followed by other countries, it would be sufficient were the National Council in a resolution to instruct the government to pursue a policy of permanent neutrality. . . . These considerations also justify a deviation from the customary technique of legislation, according to which the motives and aims of the policy of neutrality are founded on the law itself, and form an integral part of the contents of this highly significant act of foreign policy.

"I have stressed that the Federal Constitutional Law offers a possibility to commit legislation of the Federal State and of the provinces, as well as the execution of the laws, to a neutral foreign policy. . . .

.   .   .   .

". . . the idea of neutrality can be compatible with the currently highly popular slogans of 'cooperation' and 'coexistence'. The organized mobilization of free countries for joint promotion and safeguarding of law and order is the great task to be performed in the future in the field of national policy; it corresponds to the idea of the United Nations. If Austria takes an active part in the realization of these principles, it will act in the spirit of its old tradition, and pursue a policy the aim of which is significant for all its citizens, since neutrality will help us in ever increasing manner to maintain our independence.

"It has been repeatedly emphasized that Austria endeavors admittance to the United Nations; I wish explicitly to repeat this statement today. We are convinced that our neutrality is fully compatible with membership in the United Nations; we even feel that the principle of neutrality will be of special value for our co-operation in international organizations.

"It is the first time since the establishment of the Republic in 1918, that, by means of the State Treaty, Austria has been offered the possibility of pursuing a truly active and constructive foreign policy. Our neutrality will form a new, promising, and permanent basis for this foreign policy. The fact that in the draft submitted today, neutrality is referred to as a permanent status, is of decisive importance. Our neutrality is not a temporary, revocable restriction of our sovereignty, assumed by us reluctantly under pressing conditions. It is the permanent basis for our foreign policy that warrants peace and prosperity for our country and our people for ever and ever."

The Counselor of the American Embassy at Vienna (Davis) to the Secretary of State (Dulles), despatch No. 442, encl. 1, Nov. 4, 1955, MS. Department of State, file 663.0021/11–455.

In response to Mr. Khrushchev's statement made during his press conference in Vienna on July 8, 1960, that the Soviet Union will not look idly on, if Austrian neutrality were violated, and that in such an event the Soviet Union would make a decision on the basis of the then existing situation and take such measures as it would consider appropriate, the Austrian Cabinet issued an official communique on July 12, 1960, announcing that "this interpretation delivered by Minister President Khrushchev is not in accord with Austria's neutrality policy". The Cabinet then summarized Austria's neutrality policy as follows:

> "Through the enactment of the Federal constitutional law of October 26, 1955 on Austria's neutrality, which is in accordance with Article I of the Moscow Memorandum of April 15, 1955, Austria assumed the rights and obligations of a perpetually neutral state.
>
> "Austria's obligations include not joining any military alliances for all time, not permitting the establishment of military bases of foreign states *on its territory* and maintaining and defending this neutrality with all means at its disposal.
>
> "Austria's rights, however, in carrying out its sovereignty, which remains unrestricted, include determining for itself and itself alone when and how its neutrality might be threatened or violated and in the event of a possible threat or violation to decide in what way the threat or violation should be countered."

> Counselor of the American Embassy at Vienna (Bennett) to the Secretary of State (Herter), despatch No. 44, encl. 1, July 14, 1960, MS. Department of State, file 763.13/7–1460.

Following repeated Soviet warnings that the Austrian Government's application for economic arrangement with the European Economic Community would be regarded as a violation of Austrian neutrality and the State Treaty prohibition against political or economic union with Germany, the Austrian Government in its note to the Soviet Union of October 2, 1961, stated:

> "Austria is interested in the best possible economic relations with all states regardless of their political regime. For this reason Austria cannot remain a non-participant in certain economic developments in Europe. The Austrian Parliament therefore on June 21 in a unanimous resolution emphasized Austria's special interest in European economic integration.
>
> "The Austrian Federal Government agreed to the declaration of the European Free Trade Area states on July 31, 1961. In this connection, it once again stated that Austria will strive for only such economic arrangements within the framework of European economic integration which would especially take into account its commercial policy interests and will enter into only such obligations as are compatible with its foreign political status."

The Political Counselor of the American Embassy at Vienna (Devine) to the Secretary of State (Rusk), airgram No. A–153, Oct. 4, 1961, MS. Department of State, file 375.800/10–461.

"In 1955 the Austrian Government was invited to send a delegation to Moscow for another series of discussions on the terms of a state treaty. By now, the Russians had changed their minds. Mr. Molotov no longer attempted to tie the departure of troops from Austria to a treaty with Germany. He was adamant, however, on a firm guarantee against another Anschluss, which, per se, had long since ceased to be an issue either in Austria or in Germany.

"There were, however, military implications in the Russian attitude: Russia would be satisfied only with a declaration of neutrality on Austria's part. This the Austrian delegation was quite prepared to render. Austrian neutrality was defined as follows:

> " 'The Austrian Government, having already declared at the Conference that it will not accede to any military pact nor permit military bases to be established on its territory, will render a declaration containing a definite international commitment to Permanent Neutrality as practised by Switzerland.'

. . . .

"To venture out into the open without having sought shelter with one of the blocs seemed fraught with grave consequences. Whatever the merit of this argument, it had the flaw of presupposing a choice which in fact did not exist. At the very best, we could choose between neutrality and the status quo. At no time could we choose between neutrality and alignment with a bloc. And in fact what did the status quo amount to? Was it not itself a form of passive neutralization—neutralization by occupation? Under the circumstances, what alternative was open to a nation which longed to be master once again of its own destiny?

. . . .

"How has neutrality affected Austria's international policies? In the Moscow talks the Austrian delegation had laid great stress on the preamble of the draft treaty, in which the Allies had declared that they would support an Austrian application for admission to the United Nations. The Soviets, on their part, had held up Switzerland as an example for Austria to follow—and Switzerland, of course, is not a member of the United Nations. Did this mean, we had asked the Russian delegates, that the Soviet Union would insist upon having the relevant paragraph changed? The answer was no.

"When Austria became a member of the United Nations on December 14, 1955, there once again were misgivings in certain quarters; and, indeed, the pitfalls were obvious. Austria, one argument went, might be wise to shun the spotlight of the international arena, where, despite much vain posturing and empty bombast, nations are called upon to stand up and be counted. Why not keep at a modest distance and wait until things had settled down?

"We gave the matter much thought, knowing full well that membership in the United Nations would determine Austria's international posture for a long time to come. We also knew, however, that in addition to incurring some irksome obligations we would derive international recognition from membership. Such recognition implied a measure of security which we could not have found elsewhere. This was perhaps the decisive consideration.

"There are several neutral countries in Europe, and the form their neutrality takes differs considerably. In contrast with Switzerland, Sweden does not have any constitutional commitment to neutrality and its status is not guaranteed by other powers. It simply is determined to follow in time of peace a policy that should logically result in a neutral position in time of war. Indeed, when Swedes describe their status they prefer the term non-alignment to neutrality.

"Swiss neutrality, on the other hand, is a firmly established concept of international law. The powers which have given it recognition have also undertaken a commitment to guarantee the inviolability of Swiss territory. However, the Swiss themselves have never invited outside intervention or any sort of unilateral action by a foreign power in defense of their neutrality. This was clearly stated by the Swiss Parliament during World War I: 'Switzerland reserves to itself the right to decide whether, and under what terms, the aid of foreign powers might be called upon.'

"Clearly, the principle of Austrian neutrality bears a strong constitutional resemblance to that of Switzerland, whereas Austrian practice—membership in the United Nations being a case in point—is not far removed from that of Sweden. One may suppose that Austria will develop its own variant somewhere between the Swedish and the Swiss. There are historical and geographical differences as well as similarities between Austria and these countries, and they will account for the differences in approach.

"The general subject of course lends itself to any number of interpretations. Not even Swiss authorities on international law agree wholly on the precise relationship between neutrality and United Nations membership. In the case of Austria, there was one interpretation according to which membership would be 'strictly speaking, incompatible with permanent neutrality;' another advanced more flexible views, arguing that the Charter recognizes neutrality by implication. The latter noted that Article 43, Paragraph 3, governing the participation of member states in sanctions, provides that agreements are to be negotiated between the Security Council and members but implies that in certain circumstances a state may exclude itself. Attention was also drawn to Article 48, Paragraph 1, stating that either all members or certain members may be called upon to act for the maintenance of international peace and security, as the Security

Council may determine. Here again the implication is that neutral states can be excluded from participating in sanctions. This, incidentally, is also the opinion given by Professor A. Verdross, a leading Austrian expert in international law. He pointed to the fact that at the time Austria was admitted to the United Nations, Austrian neutrality had already received almost universal recognition, and that in consequence members are practically obligated to respect this status in case sanctions are invoked.

"Actually, it is not accurate to speak of neutrality in peacetime, because what the term really means is non-participation in war. An attitude of indifference toward the ideological struggle has more properly been called neutralism (as opposed to neutrality). But this should not be taken to mean that neutrality does not impose any obligations whatever upon a country in peacetime. Such obligations can be summarized as follows:

"1. A neutral country cannot join a military alliance in time of peace because in so doing it would destroy its ability to remain neutral in time of war.

"2. Similarly, a neutral country must bar foreign military bases from its territory, since they would diminish its freedom of action—or, rather, non-action—in time of war.

"3. A neutral country must not accept any obligations—political, economic or other—which would tend to impair its neutrality in wartime.

"The Swiss concept is that a neutral state should attempt to gain a position of trust with both potential adversaries; its attitude to any international conflict must be determined by this basic rôle. How the foregoing rules are to be interpreted, however, rests with the neutral country, since all such matters are part of its sovereign right.

"In order to avoid such a situation, the Austrian Government has repeatedly stressed that neutrality, as far as Austria is concerned, is exclusively a matter of its own determination in accord with its own foreign and, of course, military policies."

Bruno Kreisky, State Secretary for Foreign Affairs, Federal Chancellery, Vienna, "Austria Draws the Balance", 37 *Foreign Affairs* (1959) 269, 272–276.

As the participating Governments in the International Conference on the Settlement of the Laotian Question, held at Geneva from May 16, 1961 to July 23, 1962, Burma, Cambodia, Canada, the "People's Republic of China", the "Democratic Republic of Viet-Nam", France, India, Poland, the Republic of Viet-Nam, Thailand, the Soviet Union, the United Kingdom, and the United States signed a Declaration on the Neutrality of Laos which, together with the statement of neutrality by the Royal Government of Laos of July 9, 1962, entered into force on the date of signature, July 23, 1962, as an international agreement. The Royal Government in its statement of neutrality of

July 9, 1962, which "shall be promulgated constitutionally and shall have the force of law", declared that:

"(1) It will resolutely apply the five principles of peaceful co-existence in foreign relations, and will develop friendly relations and establish diplomatic relations with all countries, the neighbouring countries first and foremost, on the basis of equality and of respect for the independence and sovereignty of Laos;

"(2) It is the will of the Laotian people to protect and ensure respect for the sovereignty, independence, neutrality, unity, and territorial integrity of Laos;

"(3) It will not resort to the use or threat of force in any way which might impair the peace of other countries, and will not interfere in the internal affairs of other countries;

"(4) It will not enter into any military alliance or into any agreement, whether military or otherwise, which is inconsistent with the neutrality of the Kingdom of Laos; it will not allow the establishment of any foreign military base on Laotian territory, nor allow any country to use Laotian territory for military purposes or for the purposes of interference in the internal affairs of other countries, nor recognise the protection of any alliance or military coalition, including SEATO [Southeast Asia Treaty Organization];

"(5) It will not allow any foreign interference in the internal affairs of the Kingdom of Laos in any form whatsoever;

"(6) Subject to the provisions of Article 5 of the Protocol, it will require the withdrawal from Laos of all foreign troops and military personnel, and will not allow any foreign troops or military personnel to be introduced into Laos;

"(7) It will accept direct and unconditional aid from all countries that wish to help the Kingdom of Laos build up an independent and autonomous national economy on the basis of respect for the sovereignty of Laos;

"(8) It will respect the treaties and agreements signed in conformity with the interests of the Laotian people and of the policy of peace and neutrality of the Kingdom, in particular the Geneva Agreements of 1962, and will abrogate all treaties and agreements which are contrary to those principles."

The signatories of the Declaration for their part declared that they "recognise and will respect and observe in every way the sovereignty, independence, neutrality, unity and territorial integrity of the Kingdom of Laos" and undertook in particular that—

"(a) they will not commit or participate in any way in any act which might directly or indirectly impair the sovereignty, independence, neutrality, unity or territorial integrity of the Kingdom of Laos;

"(b) they will not resort to the use or threat of force or any other measure which might impair the peace of the Kingdom of Laos;

"(c) they will refrain from all direct or indirect interference in the internal affairs of the Kingdom of Laos;

"(d) they will not attach conditions of a political nature to any assistance which they may offer or which the Kingdom of Laos may seek;

"(e) they will not bring the Kingdom of Laos in any way into any military alliance or any other agreement, whether military or otherwise, which is inconsistent with her neutrality, nor invite or encourage her to enter into any such alliance or to conclude any such agreement;

"(f) they will respect the wish of the Kingdom of Laos not to recognise the protection of any alliance or military coalition, including SEATO;

"(g) they will not introduce into the Kingdom of Laos foreign troops or military personnel in any form whatsoever, nor will they in any way facilitate or connive at the introduction of any foreign troops or military personnel;

"(h) they will not establish nor will they in any way facilitate or connive at the establishment in the Kingdom of Laos of any foreign military base, foreign strong point or other foreign military installation of any kind;

"(i) they will not use the territory of the Kingdom of Laos for interference in the internal affairs of other countries;

"(j) they will not use the territory of any country, including their own, for interference in the internal affairs of the Kingdom of Laos."

In addition, they appealed to "all other States to recognise, respect and observe in every way the sovereignty, independence and neutrality, and also the unity and territorial integrity," of Laos and refrain from any action inconsistent with the provisions of the Declaration, and undertook to consult jointly with the Royal Government of Laos and among themselves in the event of a violation or threat of violation of the sovereignty, independence, neutrality, unity, or territorial integrity of Laos. The Protocol to the Declaration of Neutrality contains obligations by all parties to withdraw all foreign military personnel from Laos and not to introduce such personnel into Laos except for French military instructors; provides for the Co-Chairmen of the Conference (United Kingdom and Soviet Union) to exercise supervision over the observance of the Protocol and the Declaration of Neutrality; and defines the terms of reference of the International Commission for Supervision and Control in Laos.

XLVII *Bulletin,* Department of State, No. 1207, Aug. 13, 1962, pp. 259–263.

Political
neutrality:

During the cold war, "neutrality" or "neutralism" has been variously invoked, primarily by newly independent countries, to describe their respective foreign policies thereby characterizing only a political position.

President Eisenhower at his press conference of June 6, 1956, commented on "neutralism" as follows:

United
States

"If you are waging peace, you can't be too particular sometimes about the special attitudes that different countries take. We were a young country once, and our whole policy for the first hundred years was, or more, 150, . . . neutral. We constantly asserted we were neutral in the wars of the world and wars in Europe and antagonisms.

"Now, today there are certain nations that say they are neutral. This doesn't necessarily mean what it is so often interpreted to mean, neutral as between right and wrong or decency or indecency.

"They are using the term 'neutral' with respect to attachment to military alliances. And may I point out that I cannot see that that is always to the disadvantage of such a country as ours.

"If a nation is truly a neutral, if it is attacked by anybody— and we are not going to attack them—public opinion of the world is outraged.

"If it has announced its military association with another great power, things could happen to it, difficulties along its borders and people would say: 'good enough for it.' They asked for it.

"So let us not translate this meaning of the word 'neutral' as between contending military forces, even though the conflict is latent, and neutral as between right and wrong."

The New York *Times*, June 7, 1956, p. 10.

The following statement supplementing the President's informal press conference remarks on the subject of neutrality was issued in the form of a White House press release of June 7, 1956, under the authorization of the President:

"Questions have been presented to the White House concerning the exact meaning of expressions in the President's press conference yesterday defending the rights of certain nations to a neutral position. He particularly referred to neutrality as a refusal to take sides in any military lineup of world powers.

"It is obvious that in some countries of the world there are certain ideological, geographical, or other reasons making military alliances impractical. Such nations may declare themselves to be neutral, hoping thus to secure the support of world opinion against attack from any quarter. Neutrality does not mean either disarmament or immunity from attack. We have had historical examples of this kind of neutrality for many decades.

"The President believes in the principle of collective security whereby the nations associate themselves together for each other's

protection.   This is the modern and enlightened way of obtaining
security.   The United Nations was designed to provide collective
security for all.   In view, however, of the veto power in the
Security Council it has proved necessary to organize for collective
defense under the provisions of article 51 of the charter.   The
United States has such collective defense arrangements with 42
other nations, and it believes that, under present conditions,
these treaties represent the best and most effective means of preserving world order within the framework of the United Nations
Charter.   Our mutual security program is primarily designed to
reinforce that world order.   The President does believe that there
are special conditions which justify political neutrality but that
no nation has the right to be indifferent to the fate of another or,
as he put it, to be 'neutral as between right and wrong or decency
or indecency.'

"The President does not believe that association for mutual
security with the United States will involve any country in added
danger but, on the contrary, will provide added security on the
basis of mutuality and scrupulous respect for the independence
of each.   As the President pointed out, the United States is not
going to attack anybody; but some great powers have shown an
aggressive disposition, and military association with such a power
could lead to difficulties."

White House press release, June 7, 1956, XXXIV *Bulletin*, Department
of State, No. 886, June 18, 1956, pp. 1004–1005.

In discussing the meaning of neutralism on the program "U.N. in
Action" televised October 9, 1960, U Thant of Burma explained that
in his country "neutralism means military nonalignment only".   He
continued, "Of course, as far as political ideologies are concerned,
Burma is not neutral.   Burma is dedicated to parliamentary democracy.   Burma is against totalitarianism in any shape or form.   The
Burmese leaders believe in human freedoms and the dignity of man".

Alex Quaison-Sackey of Ghana, appearing on the same program,
said, "Neutralism means in fact, friendship to all, not taking sides
where there are quarrels going on in two main groups of people, and
that, in fact, you should use your neutral position to bring the two
sides together".

New York *Times*, Oct. 10, 1960, p. 3.

At the time of Sudan's admission to the United Nations, November   Sudan—
12, 1956, her Minister of Foreign Affairs and head of the delegation   "strict" and
to the United Nations enunciated Sudan's policy of neutrality,   "positive"
declaring: neutrality

"We quite realize that our immediate problem is to direct all
our energies toward the development of our vast potentialities,

to raising the standard of living and providing the necessary services for the people. In so doing we would not like to take any course of action which would impair our sovereignty or give chance of foreign interference in our local politics; we have therefore decided to follow the policy of strict neutrality between the West and East. . . ."

> *The Sudan—Middle East Bridge to Africa* (Background), Department of State publication 6572 (1958), p. 18.

Foreign Minister Mahgoub of Sudan elucidated the Sudan Government's concept of positive neutrality in a statement before the House of Representatives May 21, 1958, in which he declared:

"Our conception of positive neutrality is that we judge every international problem on its own merit and pass our judgement which shall be based on substantial evidence. . . . Our objectives in foreign policy are always a reflection and extension of the principles which guide our internal policy. In the first place our foreign policy must seek to maintain the security of the country and preserve our freedom and sovereignty, and we therefore have spared no effort to work with all the peace-loving nations in the Middle East, Africa and Asia and elsewhere in order to establish conditions of peace and international understanding. . . . It is not our intention to get involved in the ideological conflicts which divide the world. We have a vast store of good will towards all nations and have no quarrel nor difference with any of them."

> Joint American Embassy-USIS message, Khartoum, to Secretary of State Dulles, telegram, June 30, 1958, MS. Department of State, file 645w.00/6–3058.

U.A.R.— "neutral liberative policy"; "positive" neutrality

Following the proclamation of Syrian-Egyptian union, forming the United Arab Republic, Foreign Minister Bitar declared in a statement to the Middle East News Agency: "The United Arab Republic will follow neutral liberative policy which is responsible for the new Republic's existence and which violently opposes Zionism, imperialism, and intervention in internal affairs and espouses peace, cooperation and co-existence."

> The American Ambassador at Damascus (Yost) to the Secretary of State (Dulles), telegram, Feb. 12, 1958, MS. Department of State, file 786.00/2–1258.

President Nasser of the United Arab Republic in a broadcast by Cairo Radio on the seventh anniversary of the overthrow of King Farouk declared that "his policy toward the United States, Britain, and the Soviet Union is friendship on the basis of mutual respect and that his world policy is 'positive neutrality' ".

The Christian Science Monitor, July 23, 1959, p. 2.

The Cambodian National Assembly formally proclaimed itself neutral by law which was promulgated November 6, 1957.   The Cambodian Neutrality Law reads: Cambodia— "neutrality"

"*Article I.*

"The Kingdom of Cambodia is a neutral country.
"It abstains from all military or ideological alliances with foreign countries.
"It will undertake no aggression against foreign countries.

"*Article II.*

"In case it should be subject to a foreign aggression, it reserves the right to:

"—defend itself by arms
"—appeal to the UN
"—appeal to a friendly power . . ."

Commenting on Cambodia's legal commitment to abstain from alliances, the American Ambassador stressed that it "is taken with the full knowledge that no international agreement prevents Cambodia from joining alliances".   As evidence of this an enclosed press release from the Cambodian Embassy at Bangkok was quoted as saying, "Cambodia's abstention from 'blocs' is due only to its policy of neutrality and that the Geneva accords do not prevent Cambodia from having a completely independent foreign policy."

The American Ambassador at Phnom Penh (Strom) to the Secretary of State (Dulles), despatch No. 159, Nov. 21, 1957, MS. Department of State, file 751h.00/11–2157.

The Premier of Cambodia, Prince Sihanouk, stated in a press interview at Cairo on November 21, 1959, during a state visit in the United Arab Republic that—

". . . Cambodia has adopted the Swiss type of neutrality. Some of our foreign friends are sometimes confused and think that we have joined a third bloc, a neutralist bloc.   This is impossible for us because it would mean deviation from the principle of neutrality.
"I believe that neutralist non-aligned countries can strengthen their relations by holding periodical roundtable conferences to be attended by their leaders to discuss questions of mutual interest and to try to bring the two blocs together so that tolerance and

friendship may prevail among them and in order to defend peace and the political beliefs of peoples."

The American Counselor for Political Affairs at Cairo (Ross) to the Secretary of State (Herter), despatch No. 366, encl. 5, Dec. 12, 1959, MS. Department of State, file 751h.11/12–1259.

India—
"no war
area"

Commenting on the Indian Government's concept of India's role in world affairs, Assistant Secretary of State Jernegan said, "It has been described variously as the idea of a 'no war area' or 'neutral group' or as the center of a 'neutral bloc'. In the arguments against United States aid to Pakistan which have been advanced in India during the past few months, we find that one of the central themes is the fear that such a move would destroy the 'neutrality' of the subcontinent and bring the cold war to India's borders." He quoted Prime Minister Nehru as saying in a speech to the Indian Council of States December 24, 1953, "We have declared that we should be parties to no war . . . . We, in our own way, worked for and looked forward to this area, if I may say so, as the 'no-war area' in Asia. . . ."

XXX *Bulletin*, Department of State, No. 769, Mar. 22, 1954, pp. 444, 446.

Following the fighting in Tibet which led to the Dalai Lama's escape into India in March 1959, Prime Minister Nehru, replying to a debate in the Rajya Sabha, said with reference to Bhupesh Gupta's intimation that India will now have to consider how far she can adhere to the policy of nonalignment:

". . . All that shows a strange misunderstanding of our ways of thinking in our policies. Non-alignment—although the word is itself a kind of negative word—nevertheless has a positive concept, and we do not propose to have a military alliance with any country come what may, and I want to be quite clear about it, because the moment we give up that idea of non-alignment, we lose every anchor that we hold on to and we simply drift. . . ."

Chanakya Sen, *Tibet Disappears* (1960) 196.

At the time of the invasion of Indian territory by the Chinese Communists in November 1962, the Indian Ambassador to the United States, B. K. Nehru, stated on the television program "Meet the Press"—

"Nonalignment consists basically in a nation making up its own mind on international issues, whether peace or war—in this sense almost all nations are nonaligned."

New York *Times*, Sept. 19, 1962, p. 3.

Referring to what the Asians themselves have styled "nonalignment" or "active neutrality", an official of the Department of State explained: "They do not choose to join alliances pursuant to article 51 of the United Nations Charter for enhancing their security or that of their neighbors. Yet, they do mean to protect and preserve their independence."

Kenneth T. Young, Jr., Director, Office of Southeast Asian Affairs, "The Challenge of Asia to United States Policy", address, Univ. of Southern California, Los Angeles, Calif., Aug. 13, 1956, XXXV *Bulletin*, Department of State, No. 896, Aug. 27, 1956, pp. 340, 351.

Marginal note: Asians—"nonalignment" or "active neutrality"

Premier Abdul Karim Kassim, referring to Iraq's withdrawal from the Baghdad Pact on March 24, 1959, said that Iraq's policy of positive neutrality precluded her from remaining a party to any "aggressive grouping" or pacts.

The New York *Times*, Mar. 25, 1959, p. 6.

Marginal note: Iraq—"positive" neutrality

Commenting on the nonalignment concept of "neutrality", President Tito of the Federal People's Republic of Yugoslavia and Prime Minister Nehru of India in a joint statement said, "The President and Prime Minister desire to proclaim that the policy of non-alignment adopted and pursued by their respective countries is not 'neutrality' or 'neutralism' and therefore passivity, as sometimes alleged, but is a positive, active and constructive policy seeking to lead to collective peace, on which alone collective security can really rest."

Joint Statement by President of Federal People's Republic of Yugoslavia and Prime Minister of India, December 23, 1954, *Report 1954–55, Ministry of External Affairs*, Government of India (1955) 53; the Counselor for Political Affairs of the American Embassy at New Delhi (Weil) to the Secretary of State (Dulles), despatch No. 1139, Apr. 20, 1955, encl., MS. Department of State, file 020.91/4–2055.

Marginal note: Yugoslavia—"nonalignment"

At the opening of the first session of Parliament under a republican form of government on July 4, 1960, Ghana's first President, Kwame Nkrumah, asserting in a major policy address that the operation of the Republican Constitution would not involve a change in Ghana's foreign policy, stated that this foreign policy would continue to be one of "positive neutralism and non-alignment". Describing this policy, he said:

". . . As I have explained many times before this does not imply that the Government of Ghana will be a mere silent spectator of world events.

Marginal note: Ghana—"positive neutralism and nonalignment"

"On the contrary, the Government will continue to take positive steps through the United Nations Organization to promote and maintain peace and security among all nations. We shall always adopt whatever positive policies will do most to safeguard our independence and world peace.

"To that end the Government solemnly re-affirm their faith in the Charter of the United Nations and undertake to be friends with all nations and enemy to none.

"The Government will continue to denounce the arms race, and the manufacture and testing of nuclear weapons anywhere in the world. In particular, it will, in concert with other Governments of Africa, find ways of persuading the French or any other Government to desist from such tests on African soil. Secondly the stand we have taken on foreign policy will steadily add impetus to the role that Ghana has to play in the projection of the African personality in the international community.

"At an early stage we intend to urge that the independent African states should agree to the formation of a free African non-nuclear bloc, independent of East or West, on the basis of refusal to allow their territories to be used as military bases and particularly the rejection of alliances dependent upon nuclear weapons.

"I will even be bold to offer the proposal that all uncommitted non-nuclear countries of the world particularly of Africa and Asia should summon themselves into a conference with a view to forming a non-nuclear third force—a war preventing force—between the two blocs of the so-called East and West."

Second Secretary of the American Embassy at Accra (Gebelt) to the Secretary of State (Herter), despatch No. 1, encl. 1, July 4, 1960, MS. Department of State, file 745j.21/7-460.

Types of States

SIMPLE STATES

§ 21

Distinction between simple and federal States

"In a unitary state, its constituent parts, called provinces or otherwise, are freely created by the central authorities according to the administrative necessities of the state. In a federation, on the other hand, its members, usually referred to as states, are distinct entities which cannot be changed at the will of the union. In the classical federal unions, such as Switzerland or the United States, the members of the federation had their own history before the union was created, and their consent was necessary to establish the federation. The theory of those federations is that it was not the union which created the states or provinces, but that the latter established the federation.

"In a unitary state, there is but one legal system, which may permit some degree of autonomy to its territorial divisions, the autonomy being revocable at will. In a federation, each member of the union has its own laws, free from interference on the part of the federation. In specified matters, however, the union has exclusive jurisdiction. The federal legal order stands above the state legal system. Logically, this dualism should extend to all the branches of government: besides the federal legislature, executive, and judiciary, there exist the states' analogous powers. The mutual relations of the federal and state authorities, the scope of their jurisdiction, are determined in general outlines by the 'federal pact' or constitution. The duality of state and federal institutions gives rise to various complicated problems, sometimes difficult and delicate, which do not exist at all in the unitary states."

Wagner, *The Federal States and Their Judiciary* (1959) 13.

". . . The constitutions known to history are either unitary or federal. In a unitary constitution there is concentration of authority or sovereignty in the central polity, which is supreme. In a federal constitution there is a division of sovereignty, hence the existence of a central polity and other polities side by side, each being sovereign in the field assigned to it."

Unitary and federal constitutions

Joshi, *The Constitution of India* (1954) 22.

"International Persons are as a rule single sovereign States. In such single States there is one central political authority as Government, which represents the State, within its borders as well as without, in its international intercourse with other International Persons. Such single States may be called *simple* International Persons. And a State may remain a simple International Person, although it may grant so much internal independence to outlying parts of its territory that these parts become in a sense States themselves. Great Britain was before the First World War a simple International Person, although the Dominion of Canada, Newfoundland, the Commonwealth of Australia, New Zealand, and the Union of South Africa were States, because Great Britain was alone sovereign and represented exclusively the British Empire in the international sphere."

I Lauterpacht, *Oppenheim's International Law* (8th ed., 1955) 170.

UNITARY OR SIMPLE STATES [1]

Afghanistan	Greece	Panama
Albania	Guatemala	Paraguay
Algeria	Guinea	Peru
Andorra	Haiti	Philippines
Belgium	Honduras	Poland
Bhutan	Hungary	Portugal
Bolivia	Iceland	Rumania
Bulgaria	Indonesia	Rwanda
Burundi	Iran	San Marino
Byelorussian S.S.R.	Iraq	Saudi Arabia
Cambodia	Ireland	Senegal
Central African Republic	Israel	Sierra Leone
Ceylon	Italy	Somali Republic
Chad	Ivory Coast	Spain
Chile	Jamaica	Sweden
China	Japan	Sudan
Republic of China	Jordan	Syria
"People's Republic of	Korea	Tanganyika
China"	Laos	Thailand
Colombia	Lebanon	Togo
Congo (Brazzaville)	Liberia	Trinidad and Tobago
Congo (Léopoldville)	Liechtenstein	Tunisia
Costa Rica	Luxembourg	Turkey
Cuba	Malagasy	Ukrainian S.S.R.
Czechoslovakia	Mali	United Kingdom of Great
Dahomey	Mauritania	Britain and Northern
Denmark	Monaco	Ireland
Dominican Republic	"Mongolian People's	Upper Volta
Ecuador	Republic"	Uruguay
Egypt	Morocco	"Vatican City"
El Salvador	Nepal	Viet-Nam
Ethiopia	Netherlands	Republic of Viet-Nam
Finland	New Zealand	"Democratic Republic
France	Nicaragua	of Viet-Nam"
Gabon	Niger	Yemen
Ghana	Norway	Western Samoa

[1] *Cf.* table II in III Peaslee, *Constitutions of Nations* (2d ed., 1956) 800–804.

Abrogation
of Personal
Union—
Iceland

The Danish-Icelandic law of November 30, 1918, effective December 1, 1918, is considered to have established a personal union between Denmark and Iceland by virtue of part I, article 1 of this "Act of Union" which reads:

"Denmark and Iceland shall be free and Sovereign States united under a common King, and by the agreement contained in this Law of Union; the names of both States shall be indicated in the King's title." See I Hackworth, *Digest of International Law* (1940) 58, 59.

Article 7 of this "Act of Union" specified that "Denmark shall attend on Iceland's behalf to its foreign affairs . . . ."

On April 15, 1937, the Althing passed a resolution which stated:

"The Althing resolves to instruct the Government to prepare immediately, in cooperation with the Foreign Affairs Committee, the procedure for handling foreign affairs, at home and abroad, which will prove most suitable when the Icelanders take advantage of the abrogation clause of the Act of Union, and take the whole handling of their own affairs into their own hands . . . ."

An officer of the Department of State, writing in 1944, stated:

"The occupation of Denmark by Germany on April 9, 1940 prevented the King from executing his constitutional powers, and made it impossible for Denmark to handle Iceland's foreign relations and to protect its fisheries. Accordingly, on April 10, 1940, the Icelandic Cabinet introduced into the Icelandic Althing the following two resolutions, both of which were passed by unanimous vote: [Utanrikismalataduneytid, Reykjavik. Translation prepared by the American Consulate at Reykjavik.]

"'1. Having regard to the fact that the situation which has been created makes it impossible for His Majesty the King of Iceland to execute the Royal Power given to him under the Constitutional Act, the Icelandic Parliament declares that the Cabinet of Iceland is, for the time being, intrusted with the conduct of the said power.

"'2. Having regard to the situation now created, Denmark is not in a position to execute the authority to take charge of the Foreign Affairs of Iceland, granted to it under the provisions of Article 7 of the Danish Icelandic Act of Union, nor can it carry out the fishery inspection within Icelandic territorial waters in accordance with Article 8 of the same Act. Therefore, the Icelandic Althing declares that Iceland will, for the time being, take entire charge of the said affairs.'"

On May 17, 1941, the Althing passed three resolutions which read as follows:

"1. The Althing resolves to declare that Iceland has acquired the right to abolish entirely the Act of Union with Denmark, since Iceland has had to take into its own hands the conduct of all of its affairs, and since Denmark is not in a position to attend to the matters on behalf of Iceland which were agreed to under the Danish-Icelandic Act of Union of 1918. On the part of Iceland there shall be no question of renewing the Act of Union with Denmark, although it is not thought expedient in the present circumstances to effect the formal abolition of the union, nor to establish the final constitution of the state, but these will not be postponed beyond the end of the war.

"2. The Althing has resolved to appoint a regent, for a period of one year, to wield Supreme Power in matters of state which were placed in the hands of the cabinet on April 10, 1940.

"3. The Althing decides to announce its will that a republic be established in Iceland as soon as the union with Denmark has been formally dissolved."

The resolution abrogating the 1918 Act of Union, unanimously adopted by the Althing February 25, 1944, reads:

"The Althing resolves to proclaim that the Act of Union between Iceland and Denmark is abrogated.

"This resolution shall be placed before the electorate of the country for acceptance or rejection by secret ballot. If the resolution is approved, it shall become effective when it has again been passed by the Althing following the plebiscite."

Results of the plebiscite held on May 20–23, 1944, endorsed the termination of the union with Denmark and approved the Constitution Bill which, unanimously passed by the Althing on March 8, 1944, established a republic in place of a kingdom. The Althing ratified the action of the people on these two proposals by unanimous vote on June 16, 1944, and the Republic of Iceland formally came into being on June 17, 1944.

The Department of State observed that although the ties with the Danish Crown had been severed and the form of the Government of Iceland changed, these acts did not imply that only then (June 17, 1944) Iceland had become a sovereign state. As evidence of the fact that Iceland had enjoyed the status of a sovereign state since December 1, 1918, the United States Treaty of Arbitration with Iceland signed May 15, 1930, and the Defense of Iceland Agreement were cited.

William C. Trimble, "The Icelandic Independence Movement", X *Bulletin*, Department of State, No. 260, June 17, 1944, pp. 559–564.

Paragraph 2 of the Defense of Iceland Agreement (July 1, 1941) provided:

"United States further promise to recognize the absolute independence and sovereignty of Iceland and to exercise their best efforts with those powers which will negotiate the peace treaty at the conclusion of the present war in order that such treaty shall likewise recognize the absolute independence and sovereignty of Iceland."

U.S. EAS 232; 55 Stat. 1547.

Indonesia   At present a simple state, the Republic of Indonesia has undergone various modifications, including federation, in its legal structure and status in international law since her self-proclaimed independence of August 17, 1945.

President Sukarno issued a decree July 6, 1959, invalidating the provisional Constitution of August 15, 1950, and making effective from the date of the decree the Constitution of 1945.

Jakarta, Indonesian Home Service (in Indonesian), July 5, 1959.

The 1945 Constitution, taking note in its preamble of "Independent Indonesia", describes in article 1 the State as "unitarian with a republican form of government" (*Constitution of the Indonesian Republic*, printed in Jogjakarta).

Unitary government

Invalidation of the 1950 Constitution did not alter the nature of Indonesia as a simple or unitary state, the status and development of which is described in the Presidential Resolution promulgating the 1950 Constitution as follows:

". . . this unitary State is actually identical with the State of Indonesia whose independence was proclaimed by the people on August 17, 1945, which was originally a unitary Republic and which subsequently became a federal Republic;

". . . in order to carry out the will of the people in regard to the unitary Republic, the component States, the Negara Indonesia Timur and Negara Sumatra Timur, had empowered the Government of the Republic of the United States of Indonesia to negotiate with the Government of the component State the Republic of Indonesia;

". . . now Agreement has been reached between the two parties in said negotiations with a view to carrying out the will of the people, the time has come for the transformation, in accordance with said Agreement, of the Provisional Constitution of the Republic of the United States of Indonesia into the Provisional Constitution of the State which shall be a Unitary Republic by the name of Republic of Indonesia".

Having taken into consideration "the Charter of Agreement between the Government of the Republic of the United States of Indonesia and the Government of the Republic of Indonesia of May 19, 1950", it was resolved to draw up "The Act on the transformation of the Provisional Constitution of the Republic of the United States of Indonesia into the Provisional Constitution of the Republic of Indonesia".

Article I of the Provisional Constitution identifies the independent and sovereign Republic of Indonesia as a "democratic, constitutional State of unitary structure" with sovereignty "vested in the people and . . . exercised by the Government together with the House of Representatives".

II Peaslee, *Constitutions of Nations* (2d ed., 1956) 371, 372.

Independence of the Republic of Indonesia was consummated by the Act of Transfer of Sovereignty and Recognition of December 27,

1949, which brought into force the Round Table Conference Agreements: The Charter of Transfer of Sovereignty, The Statute of the Netherlands Indonesian Union, The Agreement on Transitional Measures, including special agreements regarding matters requiring regulation in consequence of transfer of sovereignty. (Since the Covering Resolution with attached draft agreements and exchanges of letters was adopted by the Round Table Conference at The Hague in plenary session on November 2, 1949, and the documents affixed to this resolution were ratified as was formally established on December 27, 1949, the word "draft" appearing in the attached documents should be deleted. See 69 UNTS 202, n. 1.)

The Charter of Transfer of Sovereignty, November 2, 1949, provided that "The Kingdom of the Netherlands unconditionally and irrevocably transfers complete sovereignty over Indonesia to the Republic of the United States of Indonesia and thereby recognizes said Republic of the United States of Indonesia as an independent and sovereign State". The Republic of the United States of Indonesia agreed to accept "said sovereignty on the basis of the provisions of its Constitution which as a draft has been brought to the knowledge of the Kingdom of the Netherlands" (article 1).

Partners

The Netherlands Indonesian Union, as characterized in article I of the Draft Union Statute, attached to the Covering Resolution of the Round Table Conference Agreements, "effectuates the organized cooperation between the Kingdom of the Netherlands and the Republic of the United States of Indonesia on the basis of free will and equality in status with equal rights; . . . does not prejudice the status of each of the two partners as an independent and sovereign State." The purpose of the Union as stated in article 2 was to aim at cooperation of the partners for the promotion of their common interests primarily in the field of foreign relations and defense, and, as far as necessary, finance, and also in regard to subjects of an economic and a cultural nature. An attached Draft Agreement to Regulate Their Cooperation in the Field of Foreign Relations specified in part that "On the primary consideration of the principle that each of the partners conducts his own foreign relations and determines his own foreign policy, they shall aim at coordinating their foreign policy as much as possible and at consulting each other thereon" (article 2).

While the Union Statute provided that all decisions should be taken in agreement between the two partners, it also provided that H.M. the Queen of the Netherlands and her lawful successors should be the Head of the Union and as such should "effectuate the spirit of voluntary and lasting cooperation between the partners" (articles 4, 5, and 6).

69 UNTS 206, 208, 210, 224. "Indonesian Dispute Settled at Hague Conference", based on excerpts from U.N. Doc. S/1417, dated Nov. 10, 1949,

printed in XXI *Bulletin*, Department of State, No. 547, Dec. 26, 1949, pp. 958, 959.

An Indonesian law unilaterally abrogating the Round Table Conference Agreements, passed by Parliament on April 23, 1956, specifically stated that the Charter of Transfer of Sovereignty, the instrument of transfer and exchange of letters concerning the status quo of West Irian were annulled and that the decisions and executive regulations related to the Union Statute, the Netherlands-Indonesian Union, and the relations based on all Round Table Conference Agreements were no longer valid.

The American Ambassador at Djakarta (Cumming) to the Secretary of State (Dulles), telegram, Apr. 23, 1956, MS. Department of State, file 656.56d/4–2356.

Article 2 of the Charter of Transfer of Sovereignty provided that the "status quo of the residency of New Guinea shall be maintained with the stipulation that within a year from the date of the transfer of sovereignty to the Republic of the United States of Indonesia the question of the political status of New Guinea be determined through negotiations between the Republic of the United States of Indonesia and the Kingdom of the Netherlands". The Netherlands and Indonesia signed an Agreement August 15, 1962, wherein, pending the adoption by the General Assembly of a resolution authorizing the Secretary-General to carry out tasks entrusted to him in the Agreement, it was agreed that the Netherlands would transfer administration of West New Guinea (West Irian) to a United Nations Temporary Executive Authority under the jurisdiction of the Secretary-General, which upon completion of the first phase of its administration on May 1, 1963, will have discretion to transfer all or part of the administration to Indonesia. The United Nations administrative authority will cease and all the United Nations security forces will be withdrawn upon the transfer of full administrative control to Indonesia. Under the Agreement, Indonesia will arrange for an act of self-determination for the people of West New Guinea with United Nations participation before the end of 1969 on the question (a) whether the inhabitants wish to remain with Indonesia, or (b) whether they wish to sever ties with Indonesia. By its own terms, this Agreement entered into force with the adoption of General Assembly Resolution 1752 (XVII) on September 21, 1962. The actual transfer of administration to the United Nations took place October 1, 1962.

West New Guinea

Text of Agreement printed in New York *Times*, Aug. 16, 1962, p. 6. See also U.N. Doc. S/5169 (Sept. 21, 1962) ; New York *Times*, Oct. 1, 1962, p. 1.

"This declaration [of independence, August 17, 1945, two days after the collapse of Japan and a month before Allied occupation forces arrived to receive the surrender of occupying Japanese forces] precipitated hostilities and negotiations between the Netherlands and the Republic of Indonesia. In November 1946, the two disputants over Indonesian independence initialed the Linggadjati agreement and formally signed it in March 1947. This agreement recognized the *de facto* authority of the Republic in Java, Sumatra, and Madura; provided for establishment by January 1, 1949, of a sovereign, democratic, federal United States of Indonesia (USI) composed of the Republic and at least two other states to be formed in Borneo and the eastern islands, and for the linking of the USI to the Netherlands in a Netherlands–Indonesian Union. The United States welcomed the agreement and recognized the Republic's *de facto* authority.

"Efforts to implement the agreement, however, renewed the conflict. The Republic agreed to Netherlands proposals for an interim government for all Indonesia but balked at letting Dutch forces share in the policing of Republican territory. On July 21, [1947] the Netherlands began a 'police action' against Republican troops which brought under its control economically important areas of Java, Madura, and Sumatra and reduced the Republic to three noncontiguous areas: central Java, westernmost Java, and parts of Sumatra.

"Australia and India brought the conflict to the attention of the Security Council of the United Nations, and on August 1, [1947] the Council called upon both parties to cease-fire and to settle their dispute by peaceful means. On August 25, [1947] the Council offered its good offices which both parties accepted, though the Netherlands maintained that the dispute was a domestic matter and denied the Council's competence to deal with it.

"Though fighting continued, a conference between the Good Offices Committee (Belgium, Australia, and United States) and the disputants aboard the U.S.S. *Renville* produced the Renville agreement which both parties accepted on January 17, 1948.

"This new agreement provided for a truce, establishment of United States of Indonesia with the Republic a component, and transfer of Netherlands sovereignty to the USI after a 'stated interval.' Netherlands sovereignty would be recognized meanwhile, and a central interim government formed with the Republic and all other states granted fair representation. Plebiscites would determine final delineation of the states and elect a constitutional convention to frame a USI constitution. When formed, the USI would be joined in a Netherlands-Indonesian Union under the Kingdom of the Netherlands. The disputants agreed to assistance of the Good Offices Committee in arriving at a political agreement and also agreed to serve advance notice of intent to terminate the truce.

"It soon became evident that the Netherlands and the Republic put differing interpretations upon the terms of the Renville agreement. Both parties accused the other of violations. The Republic protested Dutch creation of new states by decree and formation of a provisional federal government in which the Republic had no part, contrary to the Renville agreement. The Republic also charged Dutch efforts to strangle it economically by a trade blockade. In turn, the Netherlands charged the Republic with incitement of guerrilla activity and sabotage in Dutch-held territory, also with refusal to accept Netherlands sovereignty in the interim period.

"In June 1948 and again in September, the United States and Australian delegations on the Good Offices Committee put forward a compromise plan as a basis for renewing the deadlocked negotiations. The Republic agreed to both plans, but the Netherlands refused to discuss the first and in agreeing to the second, insisted upon changes which rejected the substance of the United States-Australian proposal.

". . . The Netherlands instituted direct talks with the Republic, but these failed to produce a solution. The Netherlands launched military action on December 18, [1948] and the following day the Republican capital Jogjakarta, was bombed and attacked by Dutch paratroops. President Sukarno, Prime Minister Hatta, the Minister of Foreign Affairs, and other high-ranking officials of the Republic were captured and later interned in two separate groups, one on Bangka Island, the other on Sumatra. Dutch land forces quickly penetrated Republican territory, capturing the major cities. Coinciding with this abrupt termination of the truce, the Netherlands promulgated a decree of an interim government of Indonesia which had been previously framed by the Netherlands and leaders of the Federal (Dutch-occupied) areas of Indonesia.

.   .   .   .

"The Security Council, concerned over the increased gravity of the situation, converted its Good Offices Committee into the United Nations Commission for Indonesia (UNCFI) and passed a resolution on January 28, 1949, calling upon both parties to cease-fire, to release all political prisoners, and to restore the Republican Government at Jogjakarta, to be followed by staged withdrawals of Netherlands forces from areas occupied by them after December 18 [1948].

"At this juncture, the Netherlands announced to the UNCFI its decision to speed up the transfer of sovereignty to a federal Indonesian government. The Netherlands Government invited Republican leaders, Federalist leaders, Indonesian minority groups, and the members of the Commission to meet in a round-table conference at The Hague on March 12 [1949], to work out an agreement on the transfer of sovereignty and on a union statute. However, the Netherlands Government said it could not concur in restoration of the Republican Government. The Republican leaders, therefore, declared their inability to cooperate.

". . . the United Nations Commission for Indonesia obtained on May 7, [1949] agreement of both parties to the following four points: the restoration of the Republican Government to the residency of Jogjakarta, the issuance of a cease-fire order, the release of Republican prisoners by the Dutch, and the holding of a conference at The Hague leading to a definitive political settlement. Indonesian Federalist leaders, representing states of the Dutch-occupied areas, agreed to the Hague conference when they were assured of the restoration of the Republican Government and participation of the Republican leaders at The Hague." "United States Policy in Indonesia", XXI *Bulletin*, Department of State, No. 534, Sept. 26, 1949, pp. 447–449. See also, *A Decade of American Foreign Policy: Basic Documents, 1941–49* (1950) 789–804.

COMPOSITE STATES

Real Union

§ 22

Commensurate with the completion of Italian occupation of Albania, an Albanian provisional committee convoked an Assembly composed of delegates from all Albanian provinces and having vested

Albania, 1939

itself with full powers declared on April 12, 1939, the decadence of the preceding regime and offered the crown of Albania to the King of Italy. The Italian law of April 16, 1939, n. 580, declared that the King of Italy, having accepted the crown of Albania, assumed for himself and for his successors the title of King of Italy and Albania, Emperor of Ethiopia.

Concluding that these developments effected the legal relationship between Italy and Albania and altered the legal status of Albania while not modifying the already existing political "protectorate" relationship, Professor Sereni lists a series of international agreements between Italy and Albania and several domestic measures which provided for and confirmed these changes as follows:

". . . *International Agreements.* (a) An agreement of April 20, 1939, concerning the rights of the respective citizens, by which Italian citizens in Albania and Albanians in Italy enjoy all the civil and political rights which they enjoy in their respective national territories. (b) An economic, tariff, and currency convention of April 20, 1939, by which the kingdoms of Italy and Albania were linked together in an economic union, both countries forming only one territory for the purpose of the application of the tariff law. Italy was entrusted with authority to conclude tariffs and other economic and currency agreements for the Union. A supplementary convention was signed on May 28, 1939, to regulate some technical details. (c) A treaty of June 3, 1939, by which the management of the diplomatic and consular services of Italy and Albania was unified and concentrated in the Italian Ministry of Foreign Affairs. (d) A tacit agreement, resulting from a resolution of the Albanian Council of Ministers of May 26, 1939, and from the Italian law of July 13, 1939, n. 1115, which merged the armed forces of Albania with corresponding Italian forces.

". . . *Domestic Measures.* (a) An Italian law of April 16, 1939, n. 580, creating the office of General Lieutenant for Albania, residing in Tirana and representing the king in Albania. Besides being an organ of the Italian state, the Lieutenancy is also an Albanian organ, provided for in the Albanian constitution (Art. 12). (b) An Italian royal decree of April 18, 1939, creating the office of Under-secretary of State for Albanian Affairs within the Italian Ministry of Foreign Affairs. (c) A new Albanian constitution, granted by Victor Emmanuel, in his capacity of king of Albania, on June 3, 1939. (d) An Albanian decree of June 2, 1939, issued by the General Lieutenant, approving the by-laws of the Albanian Fascist party. (e) In order to complete the union between the two countries, several Albanians in Italy were appointed members of the Senate, of the Foreign Service, and of the Academy of Italy; some were appointed army officers and university professors. Italian officials were also appointed counselors in the Albanian ministries."

With respect to the effect of this union between Italy and Albania on the international status of Albania, Professor Sereni states:

". . . It is a well-established principle of international law that a constitutional change, however profound, does not affect the international status of a state. If the events of 1939 consisted only in a change of régime, this by itself would not have produced the extinction of the Albanian state. In order not to arouse the susceptibilities of the Albanian people, it seems to have been the desire of Albania and Italy that the former should continue to be considered an international subject. The present Albanian state is assumed to have a complete social, political, and economic organization; it has its own name, flag, official language, national bank, currency, and stamps. Subsequent to the events of April, 1939, Albania concluded the above-mentioned conventions with Italy, which presupposed mutual assumption of Albania's status as an international subject. In their preambles, the Italian-Albanian conventions of April 20, 1939, declared that they were aimed to establish coöperation between the two countries 'within the framework of the sovereignty of the respective states.' After the Italian invasion, international acts were also performed by Albania with regard to international subjects other than Italy. [On the contrary, in the case of Austria, annexed by Germany on March 13, 1939, the notification to the League of Nations that Austria's membership had ceased on March 13, 1939, was addressed by Germany.] On April 13, 1939, Albania notified the League of Nations of her withdrawal. Her capacity to perform such an international act did not give rise to any objection. According to some sources, the Albanian declaration of war against Great Britain, in June, 1940, came later and independent from that of Italy.

". . . The above-mentioned international and domestic acts were aimed to establish an international union between Italy and Albania. Though the crowns of Italy and Albania are separate, the Italian law of April 16, 1939, n. 580, and Art. 1 of the Albanian constitution, which make the crown of Albania hereditary in the dynasty of Victor Emmanuel of Savoy, imply a tacit understanding between Italy and Albania that the crown of Albania shall always and only be vested in the Head of the Italian State. Furthermore, the above-mentioned international and domestic acts create a unified organization for the satisfaction of the common interests of the two countries in the field of economics, tariffs, and currency affairs, of international relations, and of external defense. The Italian-Albanian union is therefore not a 'personal union,' similar to that which existed from 1714 to 1837 between Great Britain and Hanover, which were linked together during that period by the accidental and non-prearranged fact that they had the same individual as monarch. The new union should rather be considered a 'real union' such as those which existed between Sweden and Norway and between Denmark and Iceland, where the community of the head of the state was prearranged and presupposed a wide coöperation between the members of the Union for several common purposes. In the absence of any provision for termination or dissolution, the Italian-Albanian union is to be perpetual and permanent. The Union is devoid of all agencies, its international relations being carried on by Italy, who acts through her own organs for herself and as an agent for Albania. [See Sereni, "Agency in International Law", *American Journal of International Law*. Vol. 34 (1940), p. 640.] Because of the absence of its own organs, the Union must be considered not to possess an international personality separate from that of its two members.

". . . The most peculiar feature of the Italian-Albanian union, which also confirms its character as a real union, is the pre-arranged community of régime between the two members. Membership in the Union presupposes the acceptance by Albania of the political and constitutional doctrines and institutions of the senior partner. Art. 1 of the Albanian constitution defines Albania as a constitutional monarchy. However, the truth is that the king of Albania is vested with unusually extensive powers comprising most of the exceptional powers that in Italy are entrusted to the head of the government. In Albania, it is the king alone who imposes upon the state its political direction. He exerts his powers through the General Lieutenant. There exists a legislative assembly, whose rôle is to coöperate with the king in the exercise of the legislative function (Art. 5 of the constitution) but the actual importance of the parliament is negligible. Practically, the reorganization and most of the present activities of the Albanian state are carried on through decrees of the General Lieutenant. These decrees are executive acts, having the effect of laws, and are only subsequently converted into formal laws by the Albanian parliament. The king is assisted by a council of ministers, whose president is not entrusted with special powers. The ordinary affairs of the state are transacted through the ministries

.   .   .   .

". . . This brings us to the question of whether Albania may still be considered a subject of international law. If the technical formal conception of the international personality of the state which up to now has prevailed, is still to be accepted, no doubt can be entertained that Albania is still a subject of international law. It may be alleged that Albania has a political organization, a territory, a population, and the capacity to carry on international relations, even though she has delegated this power to Italy. However, if we cut through the veil of legal fictions so as to reach the root of the relationship between Italy and Albania, it appears that the Albanian state which existed prior to April 1939, now remains only an empty shell. Albania, in fact, is only an annex of Italy; it exists only in function and for the advantage of the latter. In harmony with the principle that the controlling state is responsible for the international wrongs of the controlled state, Italy may certainly be held liable for the international wrongs committed by Albania, even where the latter is to be considered a subject of international law. But relying upon the fiction of the separate existence of the two states, Italy may disclaim every responsibility for the pecuniary international obligations of Albania prior to the Italian intervention, on the ground that there has been no international extinction of Albania and no succession of Italy.   In every international union in which both Italy and Albania are members, Italy from now on will practically control two votes, hers and that of Albania.   In a war in which Italy is a party, it may be convenient for her to keep Albania neutral, in order that the Albanian oil fields may continue to produce much-needed oil for Italy without danger of Albania being bombed. These are only a few possible consequences of such an anomalous situation.   If the conclusion that Albania is still an international subject is to be accepted, the inference is irresistible that the traditional rules of international law are inadequate to meet the new situations arising from the activities of the totalitarian states. Multiplication of situations analogous to that of Albania, in consequence of the occupation or control by the Axis Powers of apparently independent states, should, then, bring about the establishment of new rules of international law to take cognizance of these questions and of their possible consequences."

Sereni, "The Legal Status of Albania", 35 Am. Pol. Sci. Rev. (1941) 311, 313–317.

With reference to the Italian invasion of Albania on April 12, 1939, the deposition of King Zog I by the puppet Constituent Assembly, the King of Italy's acceptance, April 16, 1939, of the crown offered by the appointed government of Albania, and the treaties concluded between Italy and her puppet regarding economic, monetary, and customs matters and providing the direction of Albania's foreign relations by Italy along with the closing of Albanian Foreign Office and diplomatic and consular agencies abroad, Professor Langer has reviewed the official position of the British and United States Governments as it bears on the legal status of Albania, as follows:

". . . Informing the House of Commons of these developments, Mr. Chamberlain stated that under the circumstances the British representative would cease to have the title Minister, but would continue as Consul General.   Asked by Mr. Henderson whether the granting of this constitution would in no way affect the decision of His Majesty's Government not to recognize the annexation of Albania by the Italian Government, the Prime Minister replied: 'We have reached no conclusion on that.'   [348 H.C. Deb. 875.]   Yet on October 31, 1939, he announced that 'it is proposed to appoint a Consulate General in Durazzo, and it will be necessary to apply in the usual way to the Italian Government for an exequatur.'   [352 H.C. Deb. 1755.]

"According to the Government's own views such an application implied de facto recognition.   The British Consul General obtained his exequatur and left on November 21, 1939, for Durazzo.

"Thereafter very few traces of the Albanian diplomatic situation are to be found until 1942, when both Great Britain and the United States were at war with Italy.   On November 18, 1942, the British Foreign Secretary, Mr. Eden, told the House that 'At the final peace settlement, in so far as the future of Albania is concerned,' the British Government will not be influenced by any changes brought about by Italy's aggression.' [385 H.C. Deb. 321.]

"On December 17, 1942, Mr. Eden told the House: 'His Majesty's Government . . . wish to see Albania freed from Italian yoke and restored to her independence.' [*ibid.*, 2114.]

"The United States Department of State issued on December 12, 1942, the following statement: [7 D.S. Bull. 998.]

> " 'Consistent with its well established policy not to recognize territorial conquest by force, the Government of the United States has never recognized- the annexation of Albania by the Italian crown.

> " 'The restoration of a free Albania is inherent in that statement of principles.' [i.e., the Atlantic Charter . . . .]

"On September 3, 1943, Italy surrendered to the Allies. Under the terms of the armistice the Italians had also to evacuate Albania. Germany, however, continued the war, and her armies replaced the Italian troops who had been in control of the country. The Germans were able to enlist the support of a certain number of natives who established themselves as a German puppet government. Yet the collaborationists met with ever increasing resistance from Albanian partisans. The situation in Albania prompted the United States Government to make on April 6, 1944—the anniversary of the Italian invasion of 1939—the following statement:

> " 'On April 6, 1939—Good Friday—the forces of Fascism struck at Albania in sudden and shameless aggression, and Mussolini proclaimed its incorporation into Fascism's so-called Empire. Although the fall of Mussolini and the lifting of the Fascist yoke brought not freedom, but Nazi occupation, the Albanian people have not, since that Good Friday five years ago, abandoned their struggle to throw out the invader and regain their freedom.

> " 'As is well known, the Government of the United States never recognized the Fascist annexation of Albania. Today it looks to the Albanian people to unite their efforts against the Nazi enemy, thus hastening the restoration to their country of the freedom they so ardently desire'. [10 D.S. Bull. 315.]

   .   .   .   .

". . . A few weeks later, on June 2, 1944, the United States Department of State reiterated its declaration of non-recognition of the Italian annexation of Albania by the following statement:

> " 'Five years ago today, on June 3, 1939, a Fascist constitution was imposed upon the Albanian people by the Mussolini regime of Italy. The Albanian people never accepted this constitution nor the series of puppet governments set up to administer it.

> " 'The United States, of course, never recognized the Fascist annexation of Albania which followed the unpro-

voked aggression of April 7, 1939, and considers that the right to freedom under institutions of their own choosing resides in the people of Albania.

" 'Albanian patriots have fought, and continue to fight to drive the Nazis from their country. This is a part of the common struggle to which these sturdy people can make a precious contribution if they can achieve unity in the efforts of their arms. Thus they can hasten the day of their liberation.' [10 D.S. Bull. 510.]

". . . On October 28, 1944, the Albanian Quisling government resigned. On November 15, 1944, the United States Department of State commented on the new situation as follows:

" 'There are two or three resistance groups now fighting in Albania, and the Germans have been driven out of a major part of the country. . . .

" 'This Government has not recognized any single one of the groups as an Albanian authority. However, we have repeatedly emphasized our traditional friendship for the Albanian people and our desire that their full independence shall be achieved'. [11 D.S. Bull. 591.]

"On November 21, 1944, the national capital, Tirana, and the seaport of Durazzo were liberated by the newly formed Albanian National Army, and a national government headed by Colonel General Enver Hoxha established control over the country. No recognition, however, was granted to this government by the Great Powers. . . .

.   .   .   .

"Toward the end of 1945 the situation in the Balkans was complicated by a flare-up of the old dispute between Greeks and Albanians over the so-called 'Northern Epirus,' that is, the regions around Sarande, Argyrokastro, and Korcha. These regions contain a more or less strong admixture of Greeks; after the First World War they were finally assigned to Albania; now a section of Greek public opinion demanded the reconsideration of that border settlement. According to unofficial reports, the Greek Government submitted a memorandum to the major Allied Powers expressing a 'very strong desire' for Allied military occupation of all of Albania, and emphasizing that Albania 'is in reality an enemy country' and the 'Allied attitude towards Albania is inexplicable'.

"The statement that 'Albania is in reality an enemy country' is certainly indefensible as far as the United States is concerned. For the latter never recognized the Italian annexation of Albania, and consequently from the American standpoint Albania could not be regarded as an enemy country on the ground that she was an integral part of Italy; nor did a state of war ever come into being between Albania herself and the United States. Regarding Great Britain the situation may appear more uncertain. The British Government doubtless granted de facto recognition to the Italian annexation, and so far never withdrew that recognition in any form, but only uttered pious wishes for the restoration of Albanian independence. In particular, no declaration after the pattern of the Moscow Declaration on Austria was ever issued regarding Albania.

". . . On November 10, 1945, . . . the United States Government announced its readiness to enter into diplomatic relations with the existing regime in Albania 'as the provisional Government of Albania.' [13 D.S. Bull. 766.]   The statement added:

.   .   .   .

" 'The Government of the United States also desires that the Albanian authorities shall confirm that the treaties and agreements which were in force between the United States and Albania on April 7, 1939, remain valid. The United States Government, on its part, confirms the continuing validity of these instruments.

" 'Upon receipt of the assurances requested, the Government of the United States shall be prepared to proceed with the exchange of diplomatic representatives'.

"This statement made it clear that the United States Government considered Albania a liberated and not an enemy country. . . ."

Langer, *Seizure of Territory* (1947) 247–253.

Federal State

§ 23

Nature

"A federal State is . . . a political contrivance intended to reconcile national unity and power with the maintenance of 'States' rights'. It is a union of a number or body of independent States whose territories are contiguous and whose citizens have certain affinities, either racial, ethnological or traditional, who have a common historical background or heritage, a community of economic interests, and feel a craving for spiritual and national unity, but at the same time are anxious to maintain the identity and independence of their States, which are not strong enough in modern times to face external industrial competition or military menace. It is an organic union. A federal State is a distinct fact. The federating States also remain distinct facts. . . ."

Joshi, *The Constitution of India* (1954) 24.

The Convention on Rights and Duties of States signed at Montevideo in 1933 provides (article 2):

"The federal state shall constitute a sole person in the eyes of international law."

U.S. TS 881; IV Trenwith, Treaties, etc. (1938) 4807, 4808; 1933 For. Rel., vol. IV, p. 215.

". . . A federal State is a perpetual union of several sovereign States which has organs of its own and is invested with power, not only over the member-States, but also over their citizens. The union is based, first, on an international treaty of the member-States, and, secondly, on a subsequently accepted constitution of the federal State. A federal State is said to be a real State side by side with its member-States, because its organs have a direct power over the citizens of those member-States. This power was established by American jurists of the eighteenth century as a characteristic distinction between a federal State and confederated States, and Kent as well as Story, the two later authorities on the Constitutional Law of the United States, adopted this distinction, which is indeed kept up until to-day by the majority of writers on politics. Now if a federal State is recognised as itself a State, side by side with its member-States, it is evident that sovereignty must be divided between the federal State on the one hand, and, on the other, the member-States. This division is made in this way, that the competence over one part of the objects for which a State is in existence is handed over to the federal State, whereas the competence over the other part remains with the member-States. Within its competence the federal State can make laws which bind the citizens of the member-States directly without any interference by these member-States. On the other hand, the member-States are totally independent as far as *their* competence reaches.

"For International Law this division of competence is only of interest in so far as it concerns competence in *international* matters. Since it is always the federal State which is competent to declare war, make peace, conclude treaties of alliance and other political treaties, and send and receive diplomatic envoys, whereas no member-State can of itself declare war against a foreign State, make peace, conclude alliances or other political treaties, the federal State, if recognised, is certainly itself an International Person, with all the rights and duties of a sovereign State in International Law. On the other hand, the international position of the member-States is not so clear. It is frequently maintained that they are deprived of any status whatsoever within the Family of Nations. But there is no justification for that view. Thus, the member-States of the Federal State of Germany, under the German Constitution as it existed before the First World War, retained their competence to send and receive diplomatic envoys, not only in intercourse with one another, but also with foreign States. The reigning monarchs of these member-States were still treated by the practice of States as heads of sovereign States, a fact without legal basis if these States had been no longer International Persons. Similarly, Article 32 of the Constitution of the German Federal Republic of 1949 provides that in so far as the member-States are competent to legislate they may, with the approval of the Federal Government, conclude treaties with foreign States. Thirdly, the member-States of Germany, as well as of Switzerland, retained the right to conclude treaties between themselves without the consent of the federal States as well as the right to conclude treaties with foreign States as regards matters of minor interest. Fourthly, in the judicial settlement of disputes which have arisen from time to time among them the municipal courts in question have had recourse to rules of International Law whenever applicable. In view of this it must be acknowledged that the member-States of a federal State can be International Persons in a degree. Full subjects of International Law—International Persons with all the rights and duties regularly connected with international personality—they certainly cannot be. Their position, if any, within this circle is overshadowed by their federal State; they are part sovereign States, and they are, consequently, International Persons for some purposes only.

"But it happens frequently that a federal State assumes *in every way* the external representation of its member-States, so that, so far as international relations are concerned, the member-States do not make an appearance at all. This is the case with the United States of America and all those other American federal States whose Constitution is formed according to the model of that of the United States. Here the member-States are sovereign too, but only with regard to *internal* affairs. All their external sovereignty being absorbed by the federal State, it is certainly a fact that they are not International Persons at all so long as this condition of things lasts."

I Lauterpacht, *Oppenheim's International Law* (8th ed., 1955) 175–178.

". . . The terms 'federal state' may be used interchangeably with 'federated state', which should refer particularly to unions the members of which were before its establishment separate entities. Federal States, absorbing the international personality of their members, which as a rule may act thereafter, on the international scene, only through the federal authorities, may be called, for convenience, 'constitutional law federations'.

"Federal states . . . are the most closely knit form of federations. They are federations in the strict meaning of the term. This term, however, has also a broader sense, and covers looser forms of associations of states. Whenever close relations between two or more countries lead to the establishment of steady economic, political, or military cooperation, the result of which is the birth of a new legal order standing above the legal orders of the countries involved, we deal with another type of federation. There may be a great variety of such connections between states; their common characteristic is that their members retain their international law personality to the full extent, while the federation itself often also becomes a subject of international law. Such federations may be called 'international law federations', and are established by international treaties. Of course, however, the form does not go to the essence of the problem. International agreements entered into by states which retain their international law personality may take a form of 'constitutions' (such as the

Charter of the United Nations). On the other hand, it is possible to imagine federations the members of which abandon their international law personality and vest their representation in international life in the union, and which have no regular constitution but are governed by some pact possessing the form and the characteristics of an international treaty.

"The most common type of international law federations are confederations of states (French *confédérations d'états*, German *Staatenbunde*); a still looser form may be described as associations of states. The League of Nations and the United Nations Organization offer most famous examples of loose international law federations; they are associations of states. According to Prof. Scelle, whenever the legal order of the federation calls into being some federal institutions, common agencies of the federated countries, we face an 'institutional federalism'; otherwise, we deal only with a 'normative federalism'. [G. Scelle, *Traité élémentaire de droit international public*, 191 (1944).] The institutions of a loose federation will have 'international' character, whereas the agencies of a federal state will be 'national'."

Wagner, *The Federal States and Their Judiciary* (1959) 19, 20.

Professor Wagner, in differentiating between essential features of federal states and those many characteristics which although "applicable also to looser forms of federation" or "found in unitary states . . . do not seem to go to the essence of the federal state phenomenon", writes of the essential features in part as follows:

"One of the fundamental principles of states the structure of which is purely federal is that the division of powers between the central government and the members of the federation cannot be determined by the central government itself, without the consent of at least a majority of those latter. . . .

   .   .   .   .

"A basic problem in federal states is that of the distribution of powers between the central and the regional governments. Each complete legal system should possess the three branches of government. Therefore, in federal states, we find besides the federal legislative, executive, and judiciary, those of the member states. If one of the three powers is lacking in the central government, the federation is a loose one, and does not answer to the description of a federal state. If one of the powers is denied to the member states, their federal autonomy is not full and the balance between the central and regional governments is impaired. . . .

"It is not only necessary that the member states possess their own sphere of action, but also that their scope of power include matters of a certain degree of importance. Otherwise, if they are permitted to take decisions only as to trivial problems, the federal foundation of the whole will be only illusory, although at the first glance the requirements of federalism may seem to be complied with.

.   .   .   .

"Another essential requirement of federalism is that all the member states should be equal. Of course, there is no question of factual equality. . . . But before the law, all the member states must be equal. The scope of power of each is equal, and each is given an equal opportunity to participate in the government of the union. Where one member has a privileged position, even if no legally recognized hegenomy [hegemony], there can be no phenomenon of federalism. . . .

.   .   .   .   .   .

"A corollary of the principle of equality is the above mentioned right of the member states to participate in the administration of the affairs of the federal state. This right must exist in every federation, but is particularly important in federal states, since because of the close ties between the union and its members, the fate of the latter is more dependent upon the developments in the whole union than in loose types of federation. The participation of all member states and their residents in the two chambers of the federal legislature is in all the federal states guaranteed in their constitutions; that in the federal executive and judiciary is usually not settled by any provision of law, but should be assured, as far as possible, in practice. . . .

"Another important feature of a federal state is the supremacy of the constitution. The same is true in most unitary states; however, in federal states, the principle of supremacy has an additional sense: that of the superiority of the federal legal system over that of the member states. . . .

"The underlying rationale of the principle of supremacy is the theory of the 'hierarchy of legal orders', according to which the law and institutions of human groups of any degree must be consistent with the legal orders of the more comprehensive, superior groups. . . ."

Ibid. 27, 33, 35, 36, 38, 39.

Federalism in the United States of America

"The question of the relation of the states to the federal government is the cardinal question of our constitutional system . . . . It cannot, indeed, be settled by the opinion of any one generation, because it is a question of growth, and every successive stage of our political and economic development gives it a new aspect, makes it a new question."

Woodrow Wilson, *Constitutional Government in the United States* (1911) 173.

A SHORT BIBLIOGRAPHY ON THE NATURE OF AMERICAN FEDERALISM

Anderson, William, *The Nation and the States; Rivals or Partners?* (Minneapolis, 1955) ; Anderson, William, *The Units of Government in the United States; An Enumeration and Analysis* (Chicago, 1945) ; "Annals of the American Academy of Political and Social Science", *Intergovernmental Relations in the United States,* vol. CCVII (Philadelphia, Jan. 1940) ; "Annals of the American Academy of Political and Social Science", *Federal vs. State Jurisdiction in American Life*, vol. CXXIX (Philadelphia, Jan. 1927) ; Beard, Charles A., with the collaboration of William Beard, *American Government and Politics* (New York, 1949) ; Beloff, Max, *The American Federal Government* (New York, 1959) ; Benson, G. C. S., *The New Centralization; A Study of Intergovernmental Relationships in the United States* (New York, 1941) ; Beveridge, Albert J., *The Life of John Marshall* (Boston and New York, 4 vols. in 2, 1929) ; Binkley, Wilfred E., *A Grammar of American Politics; The National Government* (New York, 1958) ; Binkley, Wilfred E., *The Powers of the President; Problems of American Democracy* (New York, 1937) ; Binkley, Wilfred E., *President and Congress* (New York, 1947) ; Bowie, Robert R., and Carl J. Friedrich, *Studies in Federalism* (Boston, 1954) ; Bryce, James B., *The American Commonwealth* (New York, 2 vols., 1910) ; Burdick, Charles K., *The Law of the American Constitution; Its Origin and Development* (New York and London, 1929) ; Burns, James M., and Jack M. Peltason, *Government by the People; The Dynamics of American National Government* (Englewood Cliffs, N.J., 1957) ; Carey, Jane Perry (Clark), *The Rise of a New Federalism; Federal-State Cooperation in the United States* (New York, 1938) ; Cooley, Thomas M., *A Treatise on Constitutional Limitations Which Rest Upon the Legislative Power of the States of the American Union* (Boston, 1927) ; Corwin, Edward S., *The President; Office and Powers 1787–1957; History and Analysis of Practice and Opinion* (New York, 1957) ; Corwin, Edward S., ed., *The Constitution of the United States of America; Analysis and Interpretation* (S. Doc. 170, 82d Cong., 2d sess., Washington, 1953) ; Corwin, Edward S., and Louis W. Koenig, *The Presidency Today* (New York, 1956) ; Council of State Governments, Committee on Federal Grants-in-Aid, *Federal Grants-in-Aid* (Chicago, 1949) ; Council of State Governments, Commission on Organization of the Executive Branch of the Government, *Federal-State Relations* (S. Doc. 81, 81st Cong., 1st sess., Washington, 1949) ; *The Federalist*, edited by Sherman F. Mittell (Washington, 1938) ; Ferguson, John H., and Dean E. McHenry, *The American System of Government* (New York, 1959) ; Fesler, James W., *Area and Administration* (University, Ala., 1949) ; Friedrich, Carl J., *Constitutional Government and Democracy; Theory and Practice in Europe and America* (Boston, 1950) ; Griffith, Ernest S., *The American System of Government* (New York, 1954) ; Hyman, Sidney, *The American President* (New York, 1954) ; Jensen, Merrill, *The Articles of Confederation; An Interpretation of the Social-Constitutional History of the American Revolution, 1774–1781* (Madison, Wis., 1948) ; Kallenbach, Joseph E., *Federal Co-operation With the States Under the Commerce Clause* (Ann Arbor, Mich., and London, 1942) ; Key, Valdimer O., Jr., *The Administration of Federal Grants to States* (Chicago, 1937) ; Laski, Harold J., *The American Presidency; An Interpretation* (New York and London, 1940) ; Livingston, William S., *Federalism and Constitutional Change* (Oxford, 1956) ; Looper, Charles E., *The Nature of the American Union; A Study in Federalism* (Washington, 1948) ; McBain, Howard L., *The Living Constitution; A Consideration of the Realities and Legends of Our Fundamental Law* (New York, 1928) ; McLaughlin, Andrew C., *A Constitutional History of the United States* (New York and London, 1935) ; Macmahon, Arthur W., ed., *Federalism, Mature and Emergent* (Garden City, N.Y., 1955) ; Maxwell, James A., *The Fiscal Impact of Federalism in the United States* (Cambridge, Mass., 1946) ; Ogg, Frederic A., and Harold

Zink, *Introduction to American Government* (New York, 1949) ; Patterson, Caleb P., *Presidential Government in the United States; The Unwritten Constitution* (Chapel Hill, N.C., 1947) ; Pound, Roscoe, C. H. McIlwain, and Roy F. Nichols, *Federalism as a Democratic Process* (New Brunswick, N.J., 1942) ; Rossiter, Clinton L., *The American Presidency* (New York, 1956) ; Schwartz, Bernard, *American Constitutional Law* (Cambridge, England, 1955) ; Story, Joseph, *Commentaries on the Constitution of the United States* (Boston, 2 vols., 1891) ; Studenski, Paul, and Paul R. Mort, *Centralized vs. Decentralized Government in Relation to Democracy* (New York, 1941) ; Swisher, Carl B., *American Constitutional Development* (Boston, 1954) ; Taft, William H., *Our Chief Magistrate and His Powers* (New York, 1938) ; Thursby, Vincent V., *Interstate Cooperation; A Study of the Interstate Compact* (Washington, 1953) ; Tompkins, Dorothy L. C., *Materials for the Study of Federal Government* (Chicago, 1948) ; U.S. House of Representatives, Committee on Government Operations, *Intergovernmental Relations in the United States, A Selected Bibliography* (prepared by W. Brook Graves) (Committee print, Washington, 1956) ; United States Code Annotated, Constitution of the United States, annotated ; Vile, *The Structure of American Federalism* (1961) ; Warren, Charles, *The Supreme Court in United States History* (Boston, 1937) ; Wheare, Kenneth C., *Federal Government* (London, 1953) ; White, Leonard D., *The States and the Nation* (Baton Rouge, La., 1953) ; Willoughby, Westel W., *The American Constitutional System; An Introduction to the Study of the American State* (New York, 1919) ; Willoughby, Westel W., *The Constitutional Law of the United States* (New York, 3 vols., 1929) ; Wilson, Woodrow, *Congressional Government; A Study in American Politics* (Boston, 1942) ; Wilson, Woodrow, *Constitutional Government in the United States* (New York, 1927) ; Wiltse, Charles M., *John C. Calhoun* (Indianapolis, 3 vols., 1944–51) ; Wright, Benjamin F., *The Growth of American Constitutional Law* (Boston and New York, 1942) ; Zink, Harold, *Government and Politics in the United States* (New York, 1946).

"Federalism in the United States embraces the following elements: (1) as in all federations, the union of several autonomous political entities, or 'States,' for common purposes; (2) the division of legislative powers between a 'National Government,' on the one hand, and constituent 'States,' on the other, which division is governed by the rule that the former is 'a government of enumerated powers' while the latter are governments of 'residual powers'; (3) the direct operation, for the most part, of each of these centers of government, within its assigned sphere, upon all persons and property within its territorial limits; (4) the provision of each center with the complete apparatus of law enforcement, both executive and judicial; (5) the supremacy of the 'National Government' within its assigned sphere over any conflicting assertion of 'state' power; (6) dual citizenship.

"The third and fourth of the above-listed salient features of the American Federal System are the ones which at the outset marked it off most sharply from all preceding systems, in which the member states generally agreed to obey the mandates of a common government for certain stipulated purposes, but retained to themselves the right of ordaining and enforcing the laws of the union. . . .

"The sheer fact of Federalism enters the purview of Constitutional Law, that is, becomes a judicial concept, in consequence of the conflicts which have at times arisen between the idea of State Autonomy ('State Sovereignty') and the principle of National Supremacy. Exaltation of the latter principle, as it is recognized in the Supremacy Clause (Article VI, paragraph 2) of the Constitution, was the very keystone of Chief Justice Marshall's constitutional jurisprudence. It was Marshall's position that the supremacy clause was intended to be applied literally, so that if an unforced reading of the terms in which legislative power was granted to Congress confirmed its right to enact a particular statute, the circumstance that the statute projected national power into a hitherto accustomed field of state power with unavoidable curtailment of the latter was a matter of indifference. State power, as Madison in his early nationalistic days phrased it, was 'no criterion of national power,' and hence no independent limitation thereof.

"Quite different was the outlook of the Court over which Marshall's successor, Taney, presided. That Court took as its point of departure the Tenth Amendment, which reads, 'The powers not delegated to the United States by this Constitution, nor prohibited by it to the States, are reserved to the States respectively, or to the people.' In construing this provision the Court under Taney sometimes talked as if it regarded all the reserved powers of the States as limiting national power; at other times it talked as if it regarded certain subjects as reserved exclusively to the States, slavery being, of course, the outstanding instance.

. . . .

"It is, therefore, the Taney Court, rather than the Marshall Court, which elaborated the concept of Dual Federalism. Marshall's federalism is more aptly termed national federalism; . . .

. . . . . .

"The last element of the concept of Federalism to demand attention is the doctrine that the National Government is a government of enumerated powers only, and consequently under the necessity at all times of justifying its measures juridically by pointing to some particular clause or clauses of the Constitution which, when read separately or in combination, may be thought to grant power adequate to such measures. In spite of such recent decisions as that in United States v. Darby [312 U.S. 100 (1941)], this time-honored doctrine still guides the authoritative interpreters of the Constitution in determining the validity of acts which are passed by Congress in presumed exercise of its powers of domestic legislation—the course of reasoning pursued by the Chief Justice in the Darby Case itself is proof that such is the fact. In the field of foreign relations, on the contrary, the doctrine of enumerated powers has always had a difficult row to hoe, and today may be unqualifiedly asserted to be defunct.

"As early as the old case of Penhallow v. Doane, which was decided by the Supreme Court in 1795, certain counsel thought it pertinent to urge the following conception of the War Power:

'A formal compact is not essential to the institution of a government. Every nation that governs itself, under what form soever, without any dependence on a foreign power, is a sovereign state. In every society there must be a sovereignty. 1 Dall. Rep. 46, 57. Vatt. B. 1. ch. 1. sec. 4. The powers of war form an inherent characteristic of national sovereignty; and, it is not denied, that Congress possessed those powers . . . .' [Dall. 54, 74.]

To be sure, only two of the Justices felt it necessary to comment on this argument, which one of them endorsed, while the other rejected it.

"Yet seventy-five years later Justice Bradley incorporated closely kindred doctrine into his concurring opinion in the Legal Tender Cases [12 Wall. 457, 555 (1871)]; and in the years following the Court itself frequently brought the same general outlook to questions affecting the National Government's powers in the field of foreign relations. Thus in the Chinese Exclusion Case, decided in 1889, Justice Field, in asserting the unlimited power of the National Government, and hence of Congress, to exclude aliens from American shores, remarked:

'While under our Constitution and form of government the great mass of local matters is controlled by local authorities, the United States, in their relation to foreign countries and their subjects or citizens, are one nation, invested with the powers which belong to independent nations, the exercise of which can be invoked for the maintenance of its absolute independence and security throughout its entire territory'. [130 U.S. 581, 604.]

And four years later the power of the National Government to deport alien residents at the option of Congress was based by Justice Gray on the same general reasoning. [Fong Yue Ting, 149 U.S. 698 (1893).]

"Finally, in 1936, Justice Sutherland, speaking for the Court in United States v. Curtiss-Wright Corporation, with World War I a still recent memory, took over bodily counsel's argument of 140 years earlier, and elevated it to the head of the column of authoritative constitutional doctrine. He said:

'A political society cannot endure without a supreme will somewhere. Sovereignty is never held in suspense. When, therefore, the external sovereignty of Great Britain in respect of the colonies ceased, it immediately passed to the Union. . . . It results that the investment of the Federal government with the powers of external sovereignty did not depend upon the affirmative grants of the Constitution. The powers to declare and wage war, to conclude peace, to make treaties, to maintain diplomatic relations with other sovereignties, if they had never been mentioned in the Constitution, would have vested in the Federal government as a necessary concomitant of nationality'. [299 U.S. 304, 316–318.]

"In short, the power of the National Government in the field of international relationship is not simply a complexus of particular enumerated powers; it is an inherent power, one which is attributable to the National Government on the ground solely of its belonging to the American People as a sovereign political entity at International Law.   In that field the principle of Federalism no longer holds, if it ever did."

Corwin, ed., *The Constitution of the United States of America, Analysis and Interpretation* (1953), S. Doc. 170, 82d Cong., 2d sess., pp. xi, xii, xiv, xv, xvi.

The Supremacy Clause (article VI, paragraph 2) of the Constitution of the United States reads: "This Constitution, and the Laws of the United States which shall be made in Pursuance thereof; and all Treaties made, or which shall be made, under the Authority of the United States shall be the supreme Law of the Land; and the Judges in every State shall be bound thereby, any Thing in the Constitution or Laws of any State to the Contrary notwithstanding."   For an annotation of United States Supreme Court cases dealing with the Supremacy Clause, see Corwin, *op. cit.*, pp. 721 ff.

STATES OF THE UNITED STATES

State	Date of Admission	State	Date of Admission
Alabama	December 14, 1819	Montana	November 8, 1889
Alaska	January 3, 1959	Nebraska	March 1, 1867
Arkansas	June 15, 1836	Nevada	October 31, 1864
Arizona	February 14, 1912	New Hampshire	June 21, 1788
California	September 9, 1850	New Jersey	December 18, 1787
Connecticut	January 9, 1788	New Mexico	January 6, 1912
Colorado	August 1, 1876	New York	July 26, 1788
Delaware	December 7, 1787	North Carolina	November 21, 1789
Florida	March 3, 1845	North Dakota	November 2, 1889
Georgia	January 2, 1788	Ohio [1]	March 1, 1803
Hawaii	August 21, 1959	Oklahoma	November 16, 1907
Idaho	July 3, 1890	Oregon	February 14, 1859
Illinois	December 3, 1818	Pennsylvania	December 12, 1787
Indiana	December 11, 1816	Rhode Island	May 29, 1790
Iowa	December 28, 1846	South Carolina	May 23, 1788
Kansas	January 29, 1861	South Dakota	November 2, 1889
Kentucky	June 1, 1792	Tennessee	June 1, 1796
Louisiana	April 30, 1812	Texas	December 29, 1845
Maine	March 15, 1820	Utah	January 4, 1896
Maryland	April 28, 1788	Vermont	March 4, 1791
Massachusetts	February 6, 1788	Virginia	June 25, 1788
Michigan	January 26, 1837	Washington	November 11, 1889
Minnesota	May 11, 1858	West Virginia	June 19, 1863
Mississippi	December 10, 1817	Wisconsin	May 29, 1848
Missouri	August 10, 1821	Wyoming	July 10, 1890

[1] By H.J. Res. 121 of the 83d Congress, agreed to August 7, 1953 (67 Stat. 407), Congress corrected an oversight of one and a half centuries and formally admitted the State of Ohio to the Union, setting March 1, 1803, as the effective date of admission.

Senate Manual, S. Doc. 2, 87th Cong., 1st sess., pp. 769–773.

Admission
of Alaska
and Hawaii

Alaska and Hawaii, admitted to the United States as the 49th and 50th States on January 3 and August 21, 1959, respectively, were established as Incorporated Territories of the United States by Act of Congress on August 24, 1912, and June 14, 1900, respectively. In the case of each State, the Memorandum by the Government of the United States of America Concerning the Cessation of Transmission of Information under Article 73(e) of the Charter of the United Nations submitted to the Secretary-General on June 2 and September 17, 1959, respectively, in compliance with G.A. Resolution 222(III) of November 3, 1948, which required that the United Nations be informed of any change in the constitutional position and status of any non-self-governing territory as a result of which the responsible government thinks it unnecessary to transmit information in respect of that territory under article 73(e) of the Charter, noted that the respective States had "attained a full measure of self-government—the same as that enjoyed by the people of all the other 48 States of the United States".

> U.N. General Assembly Docs. A/4115, June 11, 1959; A/4226, Sept. 24, 1959.

Alaska

A Constitutional Convention, authorized by the Territorial Legislature of Alaska on March 19, 1955, concluded a draft Constitution February 5, 1956, which was approved by the electorate of Alaska on April 24, 1956, and, in accordance with the terms of ratification of the Constitution, a copy was then transmitted to the President of the United States for submission to the Congress.

On May 28, 1958, the United States House of Representatives passed H.R. 7999 which the United States Senate passed on June 30, 1958. On July 7, 1958, President Eisenhower approved the bill, which became Public Law 85–508 (72 Stat. 339), "An Act to provide for the admission of the State of Alaska into the Union", specifying that the admission of the State into the Union be "on an equal footing with the other States . . . ."

Concurrently with the election held on August 26, 1958, for the nomination of candidates for the United States Senate and House of Representatives, three propositions were adopted: (1) that Alaska immediately be admitted into the Union as a State; (2) that the boundaries of the State of Alaska be as prescribed in the Act of Congress approved July 7, 1958, and all claims of the State to any areas of land or sea outside the boundaries so prescribed be relinquished to the United States; (3) that all provisions of the Act of Congress approved July 7, 1958, reserving rights or powers to the United States, as well as those prescribing the terms or conditions of the grants of lands or other property therein made to the State of Alaska, are consented to fully by the State and its people.

In the general election of November 25, 1958, the people of Alaska chose two United States Senators and one Representative to serve in the Congress of the United States, the members of the Senate and House of Representatives of the Legislature of Alaska, the Governor and the Secretary of State of Alaska, and on January 3, 1959, Proclamation No. 3269, 24 *Fed. Reg.* 81 (1959), was issued by President Eisenhower certifying that the "procedural requirements imposed by the Congress on the State of Alaska to entitle that State to admission into the Union have been complied with in all respects and that admission of the State of Alaska into the Union on an equal footing with the other States of the Union is now accomplished."

U.N. General Assembly Doc. A/4115, June 11, 1959, pp. 3–4.

In the case of Hawaii, the ratification of a State Constitution by Hawaii
popular vote on November 7, 1950, preceded by 9 years the passage of the statehood bill (S. 50) by the United States Senate on March 11 and by the House of Representatives on March 12, 1959.   President Eisenhower approved the bill on March 18, 1959, and it became Public Law 86–3 (73 Stat. 4), "An Act to provide for the admission of the State of Hawaii into the Union", specifying that admission be "on an equal footing with the other States . . .".

In a special election of June 27, 1959, the three propositions specified in Public Law 86–3 were adopted: (1) that Hawaii immediately be admitted into the Union as a State; (2) that the boundaries of the State of Hawaii be as prescribed in the Act of Congress approved March 18, 1959, and that all claims of the State to any areas of land or sea outside the boundaries prescribed be relinquished to the United States; (3) that all provisions of the Act of Congress approved March 18, 1959, reserving rights or powers to the United States, as well as those prescribing the terms or conditions of the grants of lands or other property therein made to the State of Hawaii are consented to fully by the State and its people.

In the general election of July 28, 1959, the people of Hawaii chose two United States Senators and one Representative to serve in the Congress of the United States, the members of the Senate and House of Representatives of the Legislature of Hawaii, and the Governor and Lieutenant-Governor of Hawaii.   On August 21, 1959, Proclamation No. 3309, 24 *Fed. Reg.* 6868, was issued by President Eisenhower certifying that the "procedural requirements imposed by the Congress on the State of Hawaii to entitle it to admission into the Union had been complied with in all respects and that admission of the State of

Hawaii into the Union on an equal footing with the other States of the Union had been accomplished".

U.N. General Assembly Doc. A/4226, Sept. 24, 1959, pp. 2–4. The General Assembly in a joint resolution (1469(XIV)) dated December 12, 1959, adopted the Memoranda by the Government of the United States of America Concerning the Cessation of Transmission of Information under Article 73(e) of the Charter with respect to both Alaska and Hawaii.

Common-
wealth of
Puerto Rico

In accordance with General Assembly Resolution 222(III) of November 3, 1948, which states that "having regard to the provisions of Chapter XI of the Charter, it is essential that the United Nations be informed of any change in the constitutional position and status of any non-self-governing territory as a result of which the responsible government concerned thinks it unnecessary to transmit information in respect of that territory under article 73(e) of the Charter", the United States transmitted to the Secretary-General of the United Nations on March 20, 1953, along with the Constitution of the Commonwealth of Puerto Rico, a Memorandum by the Government of the United States Concerning the Cessation of Transmission of Information under Article 73(e) of the Charter with Regard to the Commonwealth of Puerto Rico. U.N. Doc. A/AC.35/L. 121, Apr. 3, 1953.

This memorandum recited:

"5. Puerto Rico has been administered by the United States since 1898 when Spain ceded its sovereignty to the island under terms of the Treaty of Paris. Puerto Rico had a military government until 1900 when the United States Congress enacted the first organic law providing for a civil form of government. The establishment of the Commonwealth in July 1952 marks the culmination of a steady progression in the exercise of self-government initiated by the first organic law.

"6. The first organic law, known as the Foraker Act, provided for a Governor appointed by the President of the United States, with the advice and consent of the Senate of the United States, a legislative assembly in which the lower house was elected but the upper house was composed of the heads of executive departments of the government and five other persons, all appointed by the President with the advice and consent of the Senate; and a supreme court, the members of which were also appointed by the President with the advice and consent of the Senate, justices of the lower courts being appointed by the Governor with advice and consent of the upper house of the legislature. The act provided for Puerto Rico's representation before all departments of the Federal Government by a popularly elected Resident Commissioner. The Resident Commissioner has a seat in the House of Representatives of the Congress of the United States.

"7. In 1917, the scope of self-government was increased with enactment by the Congress of a second organic law known as the

Jones Act. Under it, the people of Puerto Rico elected both houses of their legislature, and the popularly elected upper house advised and consented to the Governor's appointment of justices of the lower courts. The President retained authority to appoint the Governor, the justices of the supreme court, the heads of the departments of justice and education, and the auditor, but all other heads of executive departments were appointed by the Governor. The people of Puerto Rico became citizens of the United States. The protection of a bill of rights patterned on the bill of rights of the United States Constitution was extended to Puerto Rico. Provision for representation before the various departments of the Federal Government remained. The legislature could repass a bill over the Governor's veto, but if the Governor did not then approve it, it did not become law unless it received the approval of the President.

"8. In 1946, the President appointed as Governor, with the advice and consent of the Senate, a Puerto Rican who had formerly been Resident Commissioner from Puerto Rico. This was the first time that a Puerto Rican had been appointed Governor.

"9. In 1947, the Congress authorized the people of Puerto Rico to elect their Governor, beginning with the general election in 1948, and provided a line of succession in the event of a vacancy in the position of Governor or of the Governor's temporary absence or disability. The elected Governor was authorized to appoint all the members of his cabinet, the heads of the executive departments, including the attorney general and commissioner of education. No change was made at that time in the provisions respecting appointment of the auditor and justices of the supreme court.

"10. In 1948, the candidates for Governor and Resident Commissioner from Puerto Rico, who were elected by very substantial majorities, ran on a platform calling for the adoption by the people of Puerto Rico of a constitution of their own drafting, within the framework of a continuing relationship with the United States to which the people of Puerto Rico would consent. In that election, the candidates who advocated statehood for Puerto Rico and independence for Puerto Rico were defeated. An overwhelming number of candidates for the legislature who ran on the same program as the successful candidates for Governor and Resident Commissioner were also elected. In accordance with the expressed wishes of the people of Puerto Rico, there was introduced in the Congress a bill to provide for the organization of a constitutional government by the people of Puerto Rico. It was enacted on July 3, 1950 as Public Law 600, 81st Cong. (64 Stat. 319).

"11. That law expressly recognized the principle of government by consent, and declaring that it was 'adopted in the nature of a compact', required that it be submitted to the voters of Puerto Rico in an island-wide referendum for acceptance or rejection. If the act were approved by a majority of participating voters, the Legislature of Puerto Rico was authorized to call a constitutional convention to formulate a constitution, which would become effective upon its adoption by the people if approved by the Congress after a finding by the President that it conformed with the applicable provisions of the act and of the Constitution of the United States. Those provisions of the Organic Act which related to matters of local government would thereupon be repealed, while the remaining provisions of the Organic Act, relating to such matters as Puerto Rico's economic relationship to the United States, the force and effect of applicable Federal laws, and continued representation in Washington, would thenceforth be known as the Puerto Rican Federal Relations Act. The Congress made only two stipulations with respect to the content of the constitution to be adopted; that it provide a republican form of government and that it include a bill of rights.

"12. Four political parties participated in the campaign preceding the referendum: two advocated approval of Public Law 600, 81st Congress, one opposed it, and one was divided in its position. On June 4, 1951, 506,185 persons, 65.08 percent of the 777,675 qualified voters of Puerto Rico, participated in the referendum, and 76.5 percent of those voting approved the act. On August 27, 1951, ninety-two delegates were elected to a constitutional convention, representing the Popular Democratic, the Statehood and the Socialist parties. The convention met in September 1951, and concluded its painstaking work in February 1952. An official English and an official Spanish version of the constitution were adopted, and the text was published in the four daily newspapers of Puerto Rico in both languages. Copies of the document were distributed throughout the Island.

"13. On March 3, 1952, the constitution was submitted for adoption or rejection. Of the 783,610 qualified voters, 456,471 participated in the referendum. Of these, 373,594 or 81.84 percent of those voting supported adoption of the constitution; only 82,877 or 18.16 percent of those voting disapproved it. All of the elections and referenda held in Puerto Rico in connection with the development of the constitution were on the basis of universal adult suffrage without property or literacy requirements. Puerto Rico has had universal adult suffrage since 1929. There have been no property requirements since 1906 and the last literacy requirements were removed in 1935.

"14. On April 22, 1952, the President transmitted the Constitution to the Congress with his recommendation for approval, and by Public Law 447, 82nd Cong. (66 Stat. 327), signed by the President on July 3, 1952, the Congress approved the Constitution subject to certain conditions which were to be submitted for approval to the Puerto Rican Constitutional Convention. Public Law 447, in its preambular provisions, recalled that the Act of July 3, 1950 'was adopted by the Congress as a compact with the people of Puerto Rico, to become operative upon its approval by the people of Puerto Rico'; that the people of Puerto Rico had overwhelmingly approved this Act and that the Constitution of Puerto Rico had been drafted by a Constitutional Convention; that the Constitution was adopted by the people of Puerto Rico in a referendum; that the President of the United States had declared that the Constitution conformed fully with the applicable provisions of the Act of July 3, 1950 and the Constitution of the United States, that it contained a Bill of Rights, and provided for a republican form of government; and that the Congress of the United States had considered the Constitution and found that it conformed with the stipulated requirements. The operative part of Public Law 447 recorded the approval by the Congress of the United States of the Constitution of the Commonwealth of Puerto Rico subject to certain conditions, among which was that the following new sentence be added to Article VII: 'Any amendment or revision of this Constitution shall be consistent with the resolution enacted by the Congress of the United States approving this Constitution, with the applicable provisions of the Constitution of the United States, with the Puerto Rican Federal Relations Act, and with Public Law 600, 81st Cong., adopted in the nature of a compact.' The Puerto Rican Constitutional Convention considered and approved these conditions. On July 25, 1952, the Governor of Puerto Rico proclaimed the establishment of the Commonwealth of Puerto Rico under its Constitution.

"15. The Constitution of the Commonwealth, as it became effective with the approval of the Congress, provides that 'Its political power emanates from the people and shall be exercised in accordance with their will, within the terms of the compact agreed upon between the people of Puerto Rico and the United States of America' (Art. I, Section 1). The Constitution of the Commonwealth is similar to that of a State of the Federal Union. It establishes a tri-partite form of government, with a popularly elected Governor, a popularly elected bi-cameral legislature and a judicial branch. The heads of all executive departments are appointed by the Governor, with the advice and consent of the Puerto Rican Senate; appointment of the Secretary of State also requires the consent of the House of Representatives. It should be noted that with the establishment of the Commonwealth neither the President nor the United States Senate participates in any way in the appointment of any official of the government of the Commonwealth.

"16. The Legislative Assembly, which is elected by free, universal and secret suffrage of the people of Puerto Rico, has full legislative authority in respect to local matters. The Commonwealth has the power to impose and collect taxes, and to contract debts. Acts of the Legislative Assembly become law upon approval of the Governor, or, in the event that an act is vetoed by the Governor, upon its reenactment by two-thirds of the total number of members of which each house is composed. The President may no longer prevent a bill repassed over the Governor's veto from becoming law by disapproving it. The protection of a bill of rights is extended to persons in Puerto Rico. All public officials must take an oath to support the Constitution of the United States and the Constitution and laws of the Commonwealth. Amendments to the Constitution may be proposed by the Legislative Assembly, and will be voted on at a referendum, becoming effective if ratified by a majority of the electors voting thereon. The Constitution does not restrict the substance of future amendments, except to provide that they shall be consistent with the act approving the Constitution, with the applicable provisions of the Federal Constitution, with the Puerto Rican Federal Relations Act, and with the act of Congress authorizing the drafting and adoption of a constitution.

"17. The judiciary of the Commonwealth is independent under the Constitution. The justices of the Supreme Court are no longer appointed by the President but are appointed by the Governor with the advice and consent of the Senate of Puerto Rico. Justices hold office during good behavior and may be removed, after impeachment, for causes specified in the Constitution. The number of justices may be increased only by law at the request of the court itself. No judge may make a direct or indirect financial contribution to any political organization or party, or hold any elective office therein, or participate in any political campaign or be a candidate for elective office unless he has resigned his judicial office at least six months prior to his nomination. Although judgments of the Supreme Court of Puerto Rico may be appealed to the United States Court of Appeals, decisions of the United States Supreme Court have established that the Supreme Court of Puerto Rico is the final authority on the meaning of a Puerto Rican law and that its decision interpreting such a law may not be reversed unless the interpretation is 'inescapably wrong' and the decision 'patently erroneous'; it is not sufficient to justify reversal that the Federal Court merely disagree with the Puerto Rican Supreme Court's interpretation. There continues to be a Federal District Court in Puerto Rico, but its jurisdiction does not differ from the jurisdiction of Federal District Courts functioning within the boundaries of States.

"18. Under the Constitution, there is full and effective participation of the population of Puerto Rico in the Government of Puerto Rico. Article II, section 1, provides that no discrimination shall be made on account of race, color, sex, birth, social origin or condition, or political or religious ideas and requires the laws to embody these principles. Puerto Rico is divided by the Constitution into senatorial and representative districts for purposes of electing members of the Legislative Assembly, and provision is also made for election of senators and representatives elected at large. By a special procedure established by Article III of the Constitution, minority parties are assured of representation which recognizes their island-wide voting strength. Elections will be held every four years.

"19. Article II, section 2, requires that the laws shall guarantee the expression of the will of the people by means of equal, direct, and secret universal suffrage and shall protect the citizen against any coercion in the exercise of the electoral franchise. Article VI, section 4, provides that every person over twenty-one years of age shall be entitled to vote if he fulfills the other conditions determined by law and prohibits depriving a person of the right to vote because he does not know how to read or write or does not own property.

"20. The people of Puerto Rico continue to be citizens of the United States as well as of Puerto Rico and the fundamental provisions of the Constitution of the United States continue to be applicable to Puerto Rico. Puerto Rico will continue to be represented in Washington by a Resident Commissioner whose functions are not altered by the establishment of the Commonwealth. Matters of foreign relations and national defence will continue to be conducted by the United States, as is the case with the States of the Union.

"21. At the request of the people of Puerto Rico and with the approval of the Government of the United States, Puerto Rico has voluntarily entered into the relationship with the United States which it has chosen to describe as a 'commonwealth' relationship. The term 'commonwealth' was adopted by Puerto Rico as the official English designation of the body politic created by the Constitution (the official Spanish title is 'estado libre asociado'), to define the status of that body as 'a state which is free of superior authority in the management of its own local affairs but which is linked to the United States of America and hence is a part of its political system in a manner compatible with its Federal structure', and which 'does not have an independent and separate existence' (Resolution No. 22 of the Constitutional Convention). By the various actions taken by the Congress and the people of Puerto Rico, Congress has agreed that Puerto Rico shall have, under that Constitution, freedom from control or interference by the Congress in respect of internal government and administration, subject only to compliance with applicable provisions of the Federal Constitution, the Puerto Rican Federal Relations Act and the acts of Congress authorizing and approving the Constitution, as may be interpreted by judicial decision. Those laws which directed or authorized interference with matters of local government by the Federal Government have been repealed.

"22. . . . . The people of Puerto Rico will participate effectively in their government through universal, secret and equal suffrage, in free and periodic elections in which differing political parties offer candidates, and which are assured freedom from undemocratic practices by the Constitution itself. These elections will be conducted in the future, as they have been in the past, without interference by the United States. The people of Puerto Rico have complete autonomy in internal economic matters and in cultural and social affairs under a Constitution adopted by them and approved by the Congress.

"23. Under the Puerto Rican Federal Relations Act, there will still be free trade with the United States, only United States coins and currency will be legal tender in Puerto Rico, and the statutory laws of the United States not locally inapplicable will, with some exceptions, have the same force and effect in Puerto Rico as in the United States. United States internal revenue laws do not apply in Puerto Rico, and the people of Puerto Rico will continue to be exempt from Federal income taxes on the income they derive from sources within Puerto Rico. The proceeds of United States excise taxes collected on articles produced in Puerto Rico and shipped to the United States and the proceeds of customs collected on foreign merchandise entering Puerto Rico are covered into the Treasury of Puerto Rico for appropriation and expenditure as the legislature of the Commonwealth may decide.

"24. The final declaration of the Constitutional Convention of Puerto Rico (Resolution No. 23), expresses the views of the people of Puerto Rico as to the status they have now achieved.

> " 'When this Constitution takes effect, the people of Puerto Rico shall thereupon be organized into a commonwealth established within the terms of the compact entered into by mutual consent, which is the basis of our union with the United States of America.
>
> .   .   .   .
>
> " 'Thus we attain the goal of complete self-government, the last vestiges of colonialism having disappeared in the principle of Compact, and we enter into an era of new developments in democratic civilization.' "

XXVIII *Bulletin*, Department of State, No. 721, Apr. 20, 1953, pp. 585–587.

On July 25, 1961, President Kennedy signed a "Memorandum for the Heads of the Executive Departments and Agencies" of the Government of the United States, in which, after referring to the series of legislative and electoral steps culminating in the establishment of the Commonwealth of Puerto Rico under its Constitution, it was stated:

> "The Commonwealth structure, and its relationship to the United States which is in the nature of a compact, provide for self-government in respect of internal affairs and administration, subject only to the applicable provisions of the Federal Constitution, the Puerto Rican Federal Relations Act, and the acts of Congress authorizing and approving the constitution.
>
> .   .   .   .
>
> "All departments, agencies, and officials of the executive branch of the Government should faithfully and carefully observe and respect this arrangement in relation to all matters affecting the Commonwealth of Puerto Rico. If any matters arise involving the fundamentals of this arrangement, they should be referred to the Office of the President."

26 *Fed. Reg.*, No. 143, July 27, 1961, p. 6695.

". . . Among other manifestations of the tie between the United States and Puerto Rico under the Commonwealth status, the

United States conducts the foreign relations of Puerto Rico, and maintains its defense. The currency is United States currency. Puerto Ricans are U.S. citizens. Puerto Ricans, however, are not subject to federal income taxes on income earned within Puerto Rico, and while Puerto Rico is within the U.S. customs system, all customs and duties collected in Puerto Rico go to the Commonwealth Treasury for local use. They do not become part of the federal treasury.

.   .   .   .

"Although Puerto Ricans do not vote in national elections for President and Vice President they participate in the activities of the national committees of the Republican and Democratic parties, and send voting delegations to the national nominating conventions. The U.S. Republican and Democratic parties have State Committees in Puerto Rico, but neither is organized as a local party. The Puerto Rican people elect a Resident Commissioner to the U.S. who enjoys the privilege of voice but not vote in the House of Representatives in the United States Congress. . . ."

"Status of Puerto Rico and Political Aspects", MS. Department of State, Background Paper, PGW2 D–5/3, Feb. 19, 1960.

"By the Act of July 3, 1950, an Act 'To provide for the organization of a constitutional government by the people of Puerto Rico', whereby it was recognized that 'the people of Puerto Rico may organize a government pursuant to a constitution of their own adoption', it was expressly provided that upon adoption of the Constitution by the people of Puerto Rico, the President of the United States was authorized to transmit such Constitution to the Congress of the United States 'if he finds that such constitution conforms with the applicable provisions of this Act and of the Constitution of the United States.' (Sec. 3, Act approved July 3, 1950, 64 Stat. 319.)

"By the Joint Resolution of the Congress of July 3, 1952, the Constitution of the Commonwealth of Puerto Rico, drafted by the Constitutional Convention of Puerto Rico and adopted by the people of Puerto Rico in a referendum of March 3, 1952, in accordance with the Act of July 3, 1950 (*supra*), was approved by the Congress of the United States. 66 Stat. 327. Interestingly, the Joint Resolution of July 3, 1952, approving the Constitution further provided that any amendment or revision of the Puerto Rican Constitution 'shall be consistent with . . . the Constitution of the United States'. *Ibid.*

"The Constitution of the Commonwealth of Puerto Rico, proclaimed by the Governor as effective on July 25, 1952, contains provision that the 'executive power' shall be vested in a 'Governor' (Art. IV, § 1.) However, in listing the powers of 'The Executive' (Art. IV, § 4) no reference is made to the conduct of foreign relations. *Laws of Puerto Rico, Annotated* (1954) 173, 193, 194–195. See also §§ 9 and 37, Federal Relations Act, *ibid.*, pp. 157, 164, 167.

"In view of the fact that the Constitution of the Commonwealth of Puerto Rico was required to 'conform with . . . the Constitution of the United States', was found so to conform by the President of the United States, and was approved by the Congress on the understanding that it did so conform, the conduct of its foreign relations must reside where the Federal Constitution places the conduct of the foreign relations of the United States, *i.e.*, in the national Government."

Assistant Legal Adviser Whiteman, "Who conducts the foreign relations of Puerto Rico?", memorandum, Mar. 13, 1962, MS. Department of State, file FW 611.11c/3–1262.

Asked for his views "on the responsibility for Puerto Rican foreign relations", A. Fernós-Isern, Resident Commissioner of Puerto Rico, stated that "they belong completely to the Federal Government". Office of Inter-American Regional Political Affairs (Cates), memorandum, Mar. 12, 1962, MS. Department of State, file 611.11c/3–1262.

Luis Muñoz Marín, the Governor of the Commonwealth of Puerto Rico, in a letter to the President of the United States, dated January 17, 1953, stated:

". . . The legislative power of the Commonwealth under the compact and the Constitution essentially parallels that of the state governments. The laws enacted by the Government of the Commonwealth pursuant to the compact cannot be repealed or modified by external authority, and their effect and validity are subject to adjudication by the courts. Our status and the terms of our association with the United States cannot be changed without our full consent."

XXVIII *Bulletin*, Department of State, No. 721, Apr. 20, 1953, pp. 588, 589.

The United States Ambassador to the United Nations, Henry Cabot Lodge, speaking on November 27, 1953, in the plenary session of the General Assembly concerning the cessation of the transmission of information under article 73(e) of the Charter, conveyed a message from President Eisenhower, as follows:

"I am authorized to say on behalf of the President [of the United States, Dwight D. Eisenhower] that if at any time the Legislative Assembly of Puerto Rico adopts a resolution in favor of more complete or even absolute independence, he will immediately thereafter recommend to Congress that such independence be granted. The President also wishes me to say that in this event he would welcome Puerto Rico's adherence to the Rio Pact and the United Nations Charter.

"The President's statement is an expression of the traditional interest which the United States has always had in encouraging and promoting political freedom for all people in all parts of the world whenever conditions are such that their freedom will not be jeopardized by internal or external pressures."

United States delegation to the General Assembly, U.S.–U.N. press release 1833, Nov. 27, 1953; XXIX *Bulletin*, Department of State, No. 755, Dec. 14, 1953, p. 841.

Following President Eisenhower's statement thus conveyed to the General Assembly in plenary session, November 27, 1953, the Legislative Assembly of Puerto Rico on January 11, 1954, by Concurrent Resolution, declared that "the people of Puerto Rico have chosen democratically and for themselves to be a free people voluntarily associated with the United States and have rejected, as the Legislative Assembly in their name now rejects, any proposal for separation whatsoever."

House Concurrent Resolution No. 21, Jan. 11, 1954, 4 *Diario De Sesiones*, No. 1, Jan. 11, 1954, p. 34.

Resolution 748 (VIII) of November 27, 1953, of the General Assembly recognized that:

"2. . . . the people of the Commonwealth of Puerto Rico, by expressing their will in a free and democratic way, have achieved a new constitutional status. . . .

. . . .

"4. . . . when choosing their constitutional and international status, the people of the Commonwealth of Puerto Rico have effectively exercised their right to self-determination;

"5. . . . in the framework of their Constitution and of the compact agreed upon with the United States of America, the people of the Commonwealth of Puerto Rico have been invested with attributes of political sovereignty which clearly identify the status of self-government attained by the Puerto Rican people as that of an autonomous political entity; . . ."

U.N. Gen. Ass. Off. Rec. 8th Sess., Supp. No. 17 (A/2630) pp. 25–26; XXIX *Bulletin*, Department of State, No. 755, Dec. 14, 1953, pp. 841, 842.

"Territorial status has always been interpreted to mean the status of an area which is subject to the plenary authority of Congress. Whatever political authority is exercised by the people of the area is delegated to them by Congress. The political powers now exercised by the people of Puerto Rico emanate from themselves. Therefore, since the proclamation of the commonwealth, two Governments operate and coexist in Puerto Rico similarly as in the states of the Union—namely, the Federal and the commonwealth Governments, each within its respective sphere. To hold that the status of Puerto Rico continues to be territorial is to ignore the true meaning of territorial status and to give the term a new meaning.

"Neither Governor Muñoz Marin nor anyone who has had any

significant part in the advent of the Commonwealth of Puerto Rico has ever claimed that commonwealth is independence, for it is not separation but rather it is freedom in association.

"It is unfortunate that because commonwealth status, as created for Puerto Rico, has no precedent in the United States political system, it is not always properly comprehended. . . ."

A. Fernós-Isern, Resident Commissioner, Commonwealth of Puerto Rico, letter to the New York *Times*, Mar. 10, 1960, New York *Times*, Mar. 14, 1960, p. 28.

In August 1960, during the Seventh Meeting of Consultation of Ministers of Foreign Affairs of the American Republics, held at San José, Costa Rica, the Governor of Puerto Rico, Luis Muñoz Marín, addressed the following communication to the Secretary of State of the United States, then in San José:

"If charges of United States colonialism against Puerto Rico are raised at Ministers' Conference by Cuban Delegation I should appreciate your making known following views of Commonwealth Government. 'The people of Puerto Rico have been staunch supporters of the right of the Cuban people to carry out whatever revolutionary changes they desire so long as due recognition was given to the necessity of keeping the Hemisphere absolutely free of communist influence. The people of Puerto Rico, as recognized by the United Nations Assembly Resolution of November 1953, effectively exercised their right to self-determination in establishing the Commonwealth as an autonomous political entity on a mutually agreed association with the United States. The people of Puerto Rico therefore energetically condemn the campaign conducted by the Cuban Government to picture Puerto Rico as a colony, as well as Cuban attempts to interfere with the local political situation which has led the Commonwealth Government to refuse acceptance of Cuban consular officials until assurances were given that Cuban Consulate shall cease being a center of intrigues and activities against the Commonwealth Government. Puerto Rico has achieved great economic and social reform based on the utmost respect for democratic institutions and individual rights and above all for the principle of free representative elections. Puerto Rico therefore fully supports OAS efforts on behalf of democratic elections and the protection of human rights as absolutely essential to the well-being and security of Hemisphere.' "

Governor Luis Muñoz Marín to Secretary of State Herter, telegram, Aug. 26, 1960, MS. Department of State, file 371.04/8–2660 CS/MDR.

The following message from the Governor of the Commonwealth of Puerto Rico, Luis Muñoz Marín, September 27, 1960, was distributed at his request at the fifteenth regular session of the General Assembly, to the President of the General Assembly and to all members of the United Nations, in connection with the Soviet's proposed inscription of the agenda item "Declaration on the granting of independence to colonial countries and peoples". A/4501, Sept. 23, 1960.

"In view of the charges of United States colonialism against Puerto Rico, raised at the General Assembly of the United Nations by the Soviet and Cuban delegations, I have the honor of bringing to your attention the following views of the Commonwealth Government:

"The people of Puerto Rico strongly adhere to the democratic way of life, based on the respect of minority rights, the protection and furtherance of individual freedoms, and the effective exercise of the right to vote in free, unhindered elections. There can be no genuine self-determination unless these conditions are met.

"Puerto Rico has truly and effectively met them and it has freely chosen its present relationship with the United States. The people of Puerto Rico are a self-governing people freely associated to the United States of America on the basis of mutual consent and respect. The policies regarding the cultural and economic development of Puerto Rico are in the hands of the people of Puerto Rico themselves for them to determine according to their best interests.

"The United Nations General Assembly, by Resolution of November 1953, has solemnly recognized that the people of Puerto Rico effectively exercised their right to self-determination in establishing the Commonwealth as an autonomous political entity on a mutually agreed association with the United States. In further regard to the principle of self-determination, the Commonwealth Legislative Assembly has approved this very year a law authorizing another vote on Puerto Rico's status whenever 10 per cent of the electors request it.

"More than 13,000 visitors and trainees from all over the world, including thousands from the new states in Africa and Asia now represented at the United Nations, have seen with their own eyes the social and economic achievements of the Commonwealth under free, democratic institutions. As an example of Puerto Rico's great forward strides as a Commonwealth, the rate of growth of the net Commonwealth income in 1959 was 9.4%, one of the highest in the entire world.

"The People of Puerto Rico fully support the United Nations as a symbol of a world order, ruled by law and the principle of self-determination, and hope that through the United Nations a militant campaign for peace is developed that would avoid the nuclear extinction of our civilization."

A/4519, Sept. 29, 1960. The General Assembly, on October 13, 1960, approved by acclamation the allocation of the agenda item "Declaration on the granting of independence to colonial countries and peoples" to plenary. XLIII *Bulletin*, Department of State, No. 1113, Oct. 24, 1960, p. 657; A/903, Oct. 13, 1960.

In a letter dated November 25, 1961, from the Permanent Representative of the United States to the United Nations (Stevenson) addressed to the President of the General Assembly during the Sixteenth Session of the General Assembly, regarding its agenda item 88, entitled "The situation with regard to the implementation of the Declaration on the granting of independence to colonial countries and peoples", it was declared:

> ". . . we hold no people against its will. We are prepared to take the necessary measures to consult any or all of the approximately 100,000 people whose destinies are still associated with ours any time they request it. The people of Puerto Rico are fully self-governing, as the General Assembly has found after careful examination, enjoy the status of American citizens, and are free to request a change of status at any time. The remaining territories for which the United States exercises sovereignty are in the process of becoming self-governing."

> Doc. A/4985, Nov. 25, 1961, p. 4. For the "Declaration on the granting of independence to colonial countries and peoples", see G.A. Res. 1514 (XV), Dec. 14, 1960.

The precise status of the Commonwealth of Puerto Rico within the American constitutional system has not yet been considered by the United States Supreme Court.

> One United States Circuit Court of Appeals reversing a lower court concluded in *Detres* v. *Lions Building Corporation* (234 F. 2d 596 (7th Cir. 1956)) that Puerto Rico's status is still that of a Territory within the meaning of the diversity section of the Federal code of civil procedure (28 U.S.C. § 1332) which authorizes suits in Federal Courts between citizens of different States and defines the word "States" to include "the Territories and the District of Columbia". To clarify this issue, Congress enacted H.R. 9038 as Public Law 808 (70 Stat. 658) on July 26, 1956, amending section 1332(b) of title 28 of the United States Code to read as follows: "(b) The word 'States', as used in this section, includes the Territories, the District of Columbia, and the Commonwealth of Puerto Rico." See also H. Rept. 2481, 84th Cong., 2d sess., p. 2.

> On the other hand, the United States Circuit Court of Appeals for the First Circuit, with appellate jurisdiction for Puerto Rico, remarked in the case of *Figueroa* v. *People of Puerto Rico* (232 F. 2d 615, 620 (1st Cir. 1956)) that "the constitution of the Commonwealth is not just another Organic Act of the Congress".

> The United States Court of Appeals for the First Circuit, in the case of *Mora* v. *Mejias* (206 F. 2d 377 (1st Cir. 1953)), affirmed a judgment of the United States District Court for the District of Puerto Rico denying an application for a temporary injunction against the Secretary of Agriculture and Commerce of Puerto Rico in connection with an administrative order fixing maximum prices for the sale of rice in Puerto Rico. The Court said:

> > "No doubt under the Organic Act of 1917, 39 Stat. 951, the insular government was subject to the due process clause of the Fifth Amendment. See *Balzac* v. *People of Porto Rico*, 1922, 258 U.S. 298, 312–313, 42 S. Ct. 343, 66 L. Ed. 627. Under the terms of the 'compact' offered to the people of Puerto Rico by Pub. L. 600, 64 Stat. 319, 48 U.S.C.A. §§ 731b–731d, and by the Joint Resolution of Congress approving the

Constitution adopted by the people of Puerto Rico pursuant thereto, 66 Stat. 327, 48 U.S.C.A. Section 731d note, the government of the newly created Commonwealth of Puerto Rico is subject to 'applicable provisions of the constitution of the United States'. That must mean that the people of Puerto Rico, who remain United States citizens, are entitled to invoke against the Commonwealth of Puerto Rico the protection of the fundamental guaranty of due process of law, as provided in the federal Constitution. For our present purposes it is unnecessary to determine whether it is the due process clause of the Fifth Amendment or that of the Fourteenth Amendment which is now applicable; the important point is that there cannot exist under the American flag any governmental authority untrammeled by the requirements of due process of law as guaranteed by the Constitution of the United States. It is true, the Constitution of the Commonwealth of Puerto Rico contains a due process clause, which will be authoritatively interpreted and applied by the Supreme Court of Puerto Rico as a matter of local law. But the overriding federal constitutional guaranty of due process of law may be vindicated in the federal courts, and ultimately of course by the Supreme Court of the United States. . . . *Ibid.* 382.

The Puerto Rican Labor Relations Board, in determining its own jurisdiction in a case involving a hotel business, concluded in part that section 2(6) of the Labor Management Relations Act, which empowers the National Labor Relations Board to exercise jurisdiction over commerce within any Territory, was not applicable to the Commonwealth of Puerto Rico. *Hilton Hotels International, Inc. dba Caribe Hilton Hotel, San Juan, P.R. and Local 24918, Union De Trabajadores De La Industria Gastronomica Y Ramas Anexas De Puerto Rico, AFL,* Case No. P–958, and P–959, Nov. 9, 1955, 37 LRRM (Labor Relations Reference Manual) (1956), pp. 1474, 1477.

By way of dictum, the Court in the case of *Consentino* v. *International Longshoreman's Association* (126 F. Supp. 420, 422 (D.C. Puerto Rico, San Juan Div. 1954)) said that Puerto Rico is no longer a Territory as that term is used in the Constitution and cases and if Congress proposes in the future to make a statute applicable to Puerto Rico it would have to make it so, other than by use of the term "Territory". See also, *Moreno Rios* v. *United States* (256 F.2d 68 (1st Cir. 1958)); *Dario Sanchez* v. *United States* (256 F.2d 73 (1st Cir. 1958)); *Marquez* v. *Aviles* (252 F.2d 715 (1st Cir. 1958)).

On July 10, 1962, Governor Muñoz Marín, in informing President Kennedy that the people of Puerto Rico would celebrate the 10th anniversary of the establishment of the Commonwealth on July 25, stated that ". . . The Commonwealth Convention itself recognized from the beginning that there was room for growth and that this growth could and should be not towards independence or federal statehood but within the genius of the creative Commonwealth idea itself" and that "The time has now come when the people, in [sic] the basis of their own experience, should consider how to perfect the Commonwealth concept within their permanent association with the Federal Union". It was his intention, he stated, to request the Commonwealth legislature to enact a law pursuant to which proposals "to perfect the Commonwealth within its association with the United States would be submitted to the people of Puerto Rico". In expressing pride and pleasure at Puerto Rico's remarkable achievements in the 10-year period, President Kennedy stated in his reply of July 24:

"I am aware, however, as you point out, that the Commonwealth relationship is not perfected and that it has not yet realized its full potential, and

I welcome your statement that the people of Puerto Rico are about to begin the consideration of this with the purpose of moving towards its maximum development. I am in full sympathy with this aspiration. I see no reason why the Commonwealth concept, if that is the desire of the people of Puerto Rico, should not be fully developed as a permanent institution in its association with the United States. I agree that this is a proper time to recognize the need for growth and, both as a matter of fairness to all concerned and of establishing an unequivocal record, to consult the people of Puerto Rico, as you propose to do, so that they may express any other preference, including independence, if that should be their wish."

White House press release, July 24, 1962.

U.S.S.R. and Union Republics

The Constitution (Fundamental Law) of the Union of Soviet Socialist Republics, as amended December 5, 1936, describes the state as a "federal state" (article 13) and in proclaiming the sovereignty of the Union Republics which "is limited only in the spheres defined in article 14 of the Constitution" declares that "each Union Republic exercises state authority independently" (article 15). In 1944, each of the then 16 component republics of the federation was declared independent in the conduct of its foreign affairs. III Peaslee, *Constitutions of Nations* (2d ed., 1956) 480, 486–487.

A British aide memoire of December 10, 1943, informed the United States Government that the Soviet Union had requested representation on the War Crimes Commission for seven of the Soviet Republics contending that these entities were no less sovereign than the British Dominions and that their war suffering gave them a moral right to representation.

Notter, *Postwar Foreign Policy Preparation 1939–1945* (1949), Department of State publication 3580, p. 318, n. 19.

Commissar Molotov's proposal, February 7, 1945, at the Yalta Conference, that "three or at least two" of the Soviet Union Republics be accorded membership in the international organization, thereby modifying the Soviet Union's original request for membership for 16 Republics, is reported to have been discussed as follows:

". . . Mr. Molotov said that there was one question raised at Dumbarton Oaks, mainly [namely?] that of participation of the Soviet Republics as initial members of the World Organization. He said the Soviet views were known as were those of the British and American Governments. He said the Soviet views were based on the constitutional changes which had occurred in February of last year and he did not think that this Conference should ignore this request.

. . . .

"The President [Roosevelt] then inquired whether Mr. Molotov meant members of the Assembly.

"Mr. Molotov replied 'yes,' that they should be included among other members of that body. The Dominions of the British Commonwealth have gradually and patiently achieved their place as entities in international affairs. He said he felt that it was only right that three, or at least two, of these Soviet Republics should find a worthy place among the members of the Assembly. Their sacrifices and contributions to the war earned them this place. He said in closing that he wished to repeat that he fully agreed with the President's proposals and withdrew any objections or amendments but would request that three, or at least two, of the Soviet Republics mentioned above be given a chance to become equal members of the World Organization."

1945 For. Rel., The Conferences at Malta and Yalta (1955), p. 712.

Prime Minister Churchill, according to his own account, replied to the Soviet proposal as follows:

". . . We had four self-governing Dominions, who during the last twenty-five years had played a notable part in the international organisation of peace which had broken down in 1939. All four had worked for peace and democratic progress. When the United Kingdom had declared war against Germany in 1939 all of them had sprung to arms, although they knew how weak we were. We had had no means of compelling them to do this. They had done it freely, of their own accord, on a matter about which it had only been possible to consult them very partially, and we could never agree to any system which excluded them from the position they had held and justified for a quarter of a century. For these reasons I could not but hear the proposals of the Soviet Government with a feeling of profound sympathy. . . . I recognised that a nation of a hundred and eighty millions might well look with a questioning eye at the constitutional arrangements of the British Commonwealth, which resulted in our having more than one voice in the Assembly . . . ."

Churchill, *The Second World War: Triumph and Tragedy* (1953) 358–359.

At the San Francisco Conference, on the morning of April 27, 1945, during a meeting of the heads of delegations to organize the Conference, Molotov, adverting to the decision reached at Yalta that the United States and the United Kingdom would support a proposal to admit the Ukrainian and Byelorussian Republics to original membership in the international organization, said:

". . . He wished to remind the delegates of the constitutional aspects of this subject. The Soviet Republics are sovereign states. The Constitution of the Soviet Union, as well as the constitutions of the individual Soviet Republics, insure to them the right even to leave the Soviet Union whenever they desire to do so. Decisions adopted by the Supreme Soviets of the Ukrainian and White Russian Republics, as well as by the Supreme Soviet of the Soviet

Union, granted to the Republics the right to make treaties, to participate in international acts, to take part in international conferences, and to establish diplomatic relations with foreign countries."

Secretary of State Stettinius, endorsing Mr. Molotov's proposal, stated:

". . . In reaching this agreement, President Roosevelt had felt, and the United States still felt, that the importance of the Ukrainian and White Russian Republics in the Soviet Union and the sufferings which they had undergone in the war, as well as their contribution to the war, fully justified their admission to the Organization. . . ."

The meeting voted unanimously to endorse the request of Mr. Molotov that the Ukrainian and White Russian Soviet Socialist Republics be admitted as original members of the Organization.

The United Nations Conference on International Organization, San Francisco, California, April 25 to June 26, 1945: Selected Documents (1946), Department of State publication 2490, pp. 16, 17.

"The Russian claim that their member-States be recognised as subjects of International Law and members of the Comity of Nations rests on the amendment of the Constitution of the U.S.S.R. by the decree of February 1, 1944. . . .

.   .   .   .

"The amendment of February 1, 1944, . . . established the principle that the member-republics are capable of cultivating of their own right relations with foreign States, entering into direct relations with them and exchanging diplomatic and consular officers. . . .

.   .   .   .

"The amendment of 1944 represents no attempt at altering the structure of the Union. It is a mere internal measure which neither affects the federal character of the Union nor purports to enlarge the basis of the constitution with a view to introducing elements of a confederation. As long as the Soviet Union remains a federal republic with central powers vested in the Federal Government no question of defining the relationship between the member-republics and the Federal Government according to the principles of International Law arises. This relationship rests on the federal constitution and notwithstanding the amendment remains substantially the same since the right of the member-republics to cultivate relations with foreign States receives a corollary in the principle of the supervision of such relations by the Federal Government.

"It appears that States whose relationships with the members of the Comity of Nations are governed by federal constitutions cannot aspire to be subjects of International Law of their own right. They must be described as quasi-sovereign States but since sovereignty, at present, can hardly be employed in the absolute sense of the term, it would appear that not their sovereignty but the law governing their international position should be taken as the criterion of classification of subjects of the Law of Nations.

". . . It is true that they are not 'sovereign States,' being members of a Federal State, and their relationship to the Federal Government is governed by the constitution of the U.S.S.R., not by International Law. It is also true that, becoming co-founders of the U.N.O., 'an organisation based on the principle of the sovereign equality of all its members,' the republics of Ukraine and Byelorussia were given the status of full subjects of International Law. If, therefore, we can consider the Soviet-Russian member-republics as subjects of International Law it is by virtue of the decision of the Comity of Nations admitting them on an equal footing into the U.N.O. and not because of the law of February 1, 1944. . . .

.   .   .   .

"It appears that in composite States the constitution is the decisive factor in proving whether the member-States are subjects of International Law. . . . Consequently the federation as such represents a separate political entity and is, therefore, the only subject of International Law. A confederation, on the other hand, being based on treaties, *viz.*, a relationship governed by International Law, does not represent one separate political entity, but a group of such entities. It would appear, therefore, that members of a confederation would enjoy the status of subjects of International Law to the exclusion of a sole representation of the whole by one body.

.   .   .   .

"As to the argument that admission into the U.N.O. constitutes automatic recognition of a member of that body as a subject of International Law, the force of this assumption is considerably weakened in the case of the Ukraine and Byelorussia by the manner in which those members were admitted. Notwithstanding their *de facto* position they remain constitutionally what they were: member-States of a federation. Their status must be distinguished from that of new States such as Israel, Yemen, Syria, Lebanon and others, whose admission into the U.N.O. has a declaratory not a constituent character. . . . Those states enjoy an inherent quality of independent sovereign States whereas the claim to the statehood of the Ukraine of today and Byelorussia (and for that purpose of all remaining republics of the U.S.S.R.) falls back on their position within the Soviet Union. . . ."

Edward Dolan, "The Member-Republics of the U.S.S.R. as Subjects of the Law of Nations", 4 Int'l & Comp. L. Q. (1955) 629–635.

Writing on the sovereignty of the Union of Soviet Socialist Republics and the allied Republics, Professor Krylov, in asserting that sovereignty belongs to the Union Republics and to the Soviet Union as a whole, cites articles 14, 15, 16, 19, 20, and 21 of the Constitution of the U.S.S.R. as defining the sovereign rights of the U.S.S.R. Explaining further the meaning of sovereignty inherent in the relationship between the Union and the Republics, he writes:

"The sovereignty of the USSR cannot be placed in conflict with the sovereignty of the Union Republics. One complements and mutually strengthens the other. The sovereignty of the Union would not be sufficiently strong if it did not maintain and strengthen the sovereignty of the Union Republics. On the other hand, the sovereignty of the Union Republics would not be secure if it did not rest on the military might and material resources of the whole Union.

"From the foregoing it is evident that the Soviet understanding of sovereignty is basically different from the bourgeois.

"The Stalin Constitution recognizes the Union Republics as sovereign (Article 15) ; each of them has its constitution (Article 16), its territory (Article 18), its citizens (Article 21) ; the Union Republics are assured the right of self-determination even to the point of unimpeded withdrawal from the USSR (Article 17). It is precisely this recognition of the freedom of nations to self-determination, even to the point of separation, on which rests that indestructible union of sovereign nations which form the USSR.

"Some bourgeois writers, referring to the right of Union Republics to leave the Union, have expressed doubts as to the nature of the USSR as a state: If any Union Republic can secede from the USSR, is the USSR a state? Such is the formal logical approach of bourgeois 'theorists.' However, in spite of the fact, or perhaps thanks to the fact that the USSR grants every Republic the right of withdrawal, the USSR is a monolithic unit.

"The sovereignty of the USSR is an expression of the political and economic independence of the USSR from the capitalist world and its full independence in both domestic as well as in foreign policy. Only in the socialist Soviet state is sovereignty indeed the sovereignty of the people. Article 3 of the Constitution of the USSR indicates that 'all power in the USSR belongs to the toilers of the city and the countryside, embodied in the Council of Deputies of the toilers.'

"Taking its stand in international life for the sovereignty of the Soviet people, the Soviet state proceeds from the premise of the sovereignty of all members of the international community and defends the equality of all states.

"15. *Soviet Union Republics are Entities in International Law.* On February 1, 1944, the 10th Session of the Supreme Soviet of the USSR approved, after an exposition by Comrade V. M. Molotov, a law granting the Union Republics full powers in the field of foreign relations and, in connection with this, converting the People's Commissariat of Foreign Affairs from an All-Union to a Union-Republic People's Commissariat. (As of March 15, 1946, the People's Commissariats of the USSR and of the Union Republics were changed to Ministries of Foreign Affairs.)

"For the purpose of broadening international contacts and strengthening the collaboration of the USSR with other states and in consideration of the growing need of Union Republics to establish direct relations with foreign states, the law established that Union Republics 'may enter into direct relations with foreign states and conclude agreements with them.' A new Article 18 of the Constitution of the USSR specified that every Union Republic has the right to exchange diplomatic and consular representatives with foreign states.

"The law of February 1, 1944 permitted the Supreme Soviet of every Union Republic to establish the representation of the Union Republic in international relations but reserved the right of the Union to establish general order in the mutual relations of the Union Republics with foreign states.

"Being 'an important new step in the practical settlement of the nationalities question' (Molotov), the law of February 1, 1944 left no doubt that the Soviet Union Republics were entities in international law. As is well known, from 1918 to 1922 the Soviet Ukraine, Byelorussia, Georgia, Armenia, and Azerbaijan were active as such entities. The Union Republics did not lose this attribute of theirs even when, with the formation of the Soviet Union, they entrusted the handling of foreign relations to the Union. The law of February 1, 1944 granted Union Republics the right to direct relations with foreign states in as much as the Union Republics had 'not a few specific economic and cultural needs which cannot be satisfied in full measure by All-Union representation abroad or by treaties and agreements of the Union' (Molotov).

"In compliance with the law of February 1, 1944, all Union Republics established, at regular sessions of their Supreme Soviets, their own Union-Republic People's Commissariats of Foreign Affairs (since 1946, Ministries) and accordingly amended the texts of their constitutions."

Contribution by Professor Krylov, contained in sec. 15, "The Sovereign State—Entity with Full Powers in International Law", published in *International Law* (1947) 121–123 (translation).

Citing articles 15–18 in the 1944 Constitution of the Union of Soviet Socialist Republics, the Soviet Union delegate to the International Telecommunications Conference held at Atlantic City in 1947 contended that the Baltic States, Lithuania, Latvia, and Estonia—which the Soviet Union considered as incorporated into the Soviet Union in 1940—were members of the International Telecommunication Union and should be included in the list of countries with the right to vote in the Conference. The Conference voted against including the names of the Baltic States in the list. Minutes of the Second Plenary Session, July 18 and 19, 1947, *Documents of the International Telecommunications Conference at Atlantic City (1947)*, Bern, Bureau of the International Telecommunication Union (1948), pp. 53, 58.

The following articles of the Constitution of the Union of Soviet Socialist Republics pertain to its federal structure:

"Article 14. The jurisdiction of the Union of Soviet Socialist Republics, as represented by its highest organs of state power and organs of state administration, embraces:

"(a) Representation of the USSR in international relations, conclusion, ratification, and denunciation of treaties of the USSR with other States, establishment of general procedure governing the relations of union republics with foreign states;

"(b) Questions of war and peace;

"(c) Admission of new republics into the USSR;

"(d) Control over the observance of the Constitution of the USSR and ensuring conformity of the constitutions of the union republics with the Constitution of the USSR;

"(e) Confirmation of alterations of boundaries between union republics;

"(f) Confirmation of the formation of new territories and regions and also of new autonomous republics and autonomous regions within union republics;

"(g) Organization of the defense of the USSR, direction of all the armed forces of the USSR, determination of directing principles governing the organization of the military formations of the union republics;

"(h) Foreign trade on the basis of state monopoly;

"(i) Safeguarding the security of the state;

"(j) Determination of the national economic plans of the USSR;

"(k) Approval of the consolidated state budget of the USSR and of the reports on its fulfillment; determination of the taxes and revenues which go to the union, the republican, and the local budgets;

"(l) Administration of the banks, industrial and agricultural institutions and enterprises and trading enterprises of all-union importance;

"(m) Administration of transport and communications;

"(n) Direction of the monetary and credit system;

"(o) Organization of state insurance;

"(p) Contracting and granting of loans;

"(q) Determination of the basic principles of land tenure and of the use of mineral wealth, forests and waters;

"(r) Determination of the basic principles in the spheres of education and public health;

"(s) Organization of a uniform system of national economic statistics;

"(t) Determination of the principles of labor legislation;

"(u) Legislation concerning the judicial system and judicial procedure; criminal and civil codes;

"(v) Legislation concerning union citizenship; legislation concerning rights of foreigners;

"(w) Determination of the basic principles of legislation concerning marriage and the family;

"(x) Issuing of all-union acts of amnesty.

"Article 15. The sovereignty of the Union Republics is limited only in the spheres defined in Article 14 of the Constitution of the USSR. Outside of these spheres each Union Republic exercises state authority independently. The USSR protects the sovereign rights of the Union Republics.

"Article 16. Each Union Republic has its own Constitution, which takes account of the specific features of the Republic and is drawn up in full conformity with the Constitution of the USSR.

.   .   .   .

"Article 19. The laws of the USSR have the same force within the territory of every Union Republic.

"Article 20. In the event of divergence between a law of a Union
Republic and a law of the Union, the Union law prevails.
"Article 21. Uniform Union citizenship is established for citizens
of the USSR.
"Every citizen of a Union Republic is a citizen of the USSR." III
Peaslee, *Constitutions of Nations* (2d ed., 1956) 486–488.

The Constitution of India, enacted November 26, 1949, adopted a
federal form of government declaring "India, that is Bharat, shall be   India
a union of States" (part I, 1 (1)). II Peaslee, *Constitutions of Nations* (2d ed., 1956) 223.

"The distribution of legislative powers is determined by the
three Lists in Schedule VII, i.e. the Union List, the State List and
the Concurrent List [defence of India, foreign affairs—all matters which bring the Union into relation with any foreign country, and entering into treaties and agreements with foreign countries and implementing of treaties, agreements and conventions
with foreign countries, are the matters pertaining to international
relations which are reserved entirely to the Central Government].
. . . Any residuary legislative power not enumerated in these
lists goes according to article 248 to the Centre. India has in
this respect followed the Canadian pattern and not the solution
adopted in the United States and in Australia where the residue
goes to the local States. As to executive power, which is co-
extensive with legislative power, every local State has to use it in
such a way as to ensure compliance with the laws made by Parliament and with any existent laws which apply in that State
(article 256). Moreover the Executive power of every State has
to be so exercised as not to impede or prejudice the exercise of the
Executive power of the Union (article 257). The Union may
give appropriate directions to States according to articles 256 and
257, without prejudice, however, to their constitutional autonomy.
Article 258 refers to the power of the Union to entrust functions
to local States in certain cases and article 258A, introduced by the
Constitution (Seventh Amendment) Act 1956, provides for the
reciprocal power of the States to entrust certain functions to the
Union."

Alexandrowicz-Alexander, *Constitutional Developments in India* (1957)
159–160.

It has been said that India is a "quasi-federal" state because of article
249 and the emergency provisions contained in articles 352–360 of the
Constitution.

The principal paragraph of article 249 reads:

"(1) Notwithstanding anything in the foregoing provisions of
this Chapter, if the Council of States has declared by resolution
supported by not less than two-thirds of the members present and
voting that it is necessary or expedient in the national interest
that Parliament should make laws with respect to any matter
enumerated in the State List specified in the resolution, it shall

be lawful for Parliament to make laws for the whole or any part of the territory of India with respect to that matter while the resolution remains in force."

With the issuance of a Proclamation of Emergency provided for in article 352(1) "if the President is satisfied that a grave emergency exists whereby the security of India or of any part of the territory thereof is threatened, whether by war or external aggression or internal disturbance", the division of powers between the States and Parliament merge into the hands of Parliament thus, in the view of some authorities, virtually transforming a federal form into a unitary arrangement to the extent of the incompetency.

II Peaslee, *Constitutions of Nations* (2d ed., 1956) 287, 317–320. (Classification of States into Parts A, B, and C listed in the First Schedule of the Constitution has disappeared with the enactment of the States Reorganization Act, 1956, Act No. 37 of 1956 [31st August, 1956] (*Acts of Parliament 1956* (Government of India, Ministry of Law, New Delhi, 1957) 659); and the Constitution (Seventh Amendment) Act, 1956 (*Gazette of India (Extraordinary)* Part II, Section I, S. No. 45, 1956), which embodies the corresponding Constitutional changes.)

". . . in the expression 'quasi-federation' the word 'quasi' hints at a deviation from the federal principle without indicating what kind of special position a particular quasi-federation occupies between a unitary State and a federation proper. It may be suggested that federations established from above for administrative convenience only be termed 'administrative federations'. They are in fact federations with practically undivided sovereignty in which the Centre yields to the Units a limited share in the administration of local affairs only, not infrequently on the basis of delegation of powers. Where however the member States were originally independent and came together for the purpose of creating, from below, a federal Centre to which they transferred part of their sovereignty, but where they retained for themselves effectively a self-contained system of government, be it a parliamentary system or a presidential (Governor's) regime, there is no need to pin them down to a definition which reduces them to a vague quasi-federal status. Sovereignty is in these cases divided, whatever the amount of power left to local States. Even if the federal Centre in course of time tended to emancipate itself from the original 'federal arrangement' by which it was brought into being, the existence of a federation proper may still be presumed if the responsibility of local Executives to local Legislatures or the position of locally elected Governors endowed with real power, mean what they were intended to mean constitutionally. Such local responsibility is sufficient proof of internal local independence.

"India is a case of *sui generis*. Though the federation was created from above, the local States enjoy the rights of real parliamentary government whatever the distribution of powers between them and the Centre. . . .

. . . .

". . . A local executive fully responsible to a local Legislature ensures a good deal of local internal sovereignty and sovereignty means statehood, limited as it may be by the distribution of powers. Local States pursue local policies, sometimes in accordance with the policy of the Centre, sometimes not. This distinguishes them precisely from the position which prevails in administrative federations in which local units must toe the line and always follow the policy of the Centre. India is undoubtedly a federation in which the attributes of statehood are shared between Centre and local States. Instead of defining her by the vague term of 'quasi-federation', it seems more accurate to exclude her from the category of administrative federations and to consider her a federation with vertically divided sovereignty. . . ."

Alexandrowicz-Alexander, *Constitutional Developments in India* (1957) 158–159, 168–169. See also Joshi, *The Constitution of India* (1954) 22–37.

"Mr. E. M. S. Namboodiripad, Kerala Chief Minister, told journalists here tonight that while in Moscow he would explore the possibilities of bartering some of his State's products such as coir and pepper for Russian capital goods. This was what he meant by his remarks that he would sound the Kremlin for diversion of part of the Soviet aid to India for Kerala's development, he said.

"Answering a question, Mr. Namboodiripad said that he was quite aware that foreign trade was a Central subject. But this, he maintained, did not debar him from exercising the right of a citizen to explore a wider market for the exportable products of his home State. . . ."

The Hindustan Times, Jan. 20, 1959.

The Constitution of the Islamic Republic of Pakistan, passed by the Constituent Assembly of Pakistan February 29, 1956, assented to Pakistan by the Governor-General March 2, 1956, and promulgated March 23, 1956, 8½ years after Pakistan became an independent dominion under the Indian Independence Act, 1947, avowed ". . . sovereignty over the entire Universe belongs to Allah Almighty alone, and the authority to be exercised by the people of Pakistan within the limits prescribed by Him is a sacred trust".

Describing Pakistan as a "Federal Republic" (article 1), the Constitution specified the relation between the Federation and the provinces, according "Parliament . . . exclusive power to make laws with respect to any matters enumerated in the Federal List", which included all matters pertaining to national problems such as defense of every part of Pakistan, foreign affairs including all matters which bring

Pakistan into relation with any foreign country, international organization—participation in international bodies and implementing of decisions made thereat—war and peace making and implementation of treaties, conventions, declarations and other agreements with foreign countries (article 106(1), Fifth Schedule) ; according "a Provincial Legislature . . . exclusive power to make laws for a Province or any part thereof with respect to any of the matters enumerated in the Provincial List" (article 106(3)) ; and according both legislatures, subject to the provisions mentioned, "power to make laws with respect to any of the matters enumerated in the Concurrent List" (article 106(2)).

Article 108 empowered Parliament "to make laws for the whole or any part of Pakistan for implementing any treaty, agreement or convention between Pakistan and any other country, or any decision taken at any international body, notwithstanding that it deals with a matter enumerated in the Provincial List or a matter not enumerated in any list in the Fifth Schedule", reading :

> "Provided that no law under this Article shall be enacted except after consultation with the Governor of the Province to which the law is to be applied."

Subject to these provisions, residual legislative powers over any matter not enumerated in any list in the Fifth Schedule was vested in the Provincial Legislature (article 109).

However, under a proclamation of emergency, which might be issued "if the President is satisfied that a grave emergency exists in which the security or economic life of Pakistan, or any part thereof, is threatened by war or external aggression, or by internal disturbance beyond the power of a Provincial Government to control", Parliament might make laws for a Province with respect to any matter not enumerated in the Federal or Concurrent Lists, and the national executive might direct a Province as to the manner in which the executive authority of the Province was to be exercised (article 191).

> *The Gazette of Pakistan*, Mar. 2, 1956, Registered No. S. 1033, the First Secretary of the American Embassy at Karachi (Soulen) to the Secretary of State (Dulles), despatch No. 690, encl. 1, Apr. 3, 1956, MS. Department of State, file 790d.03/4–356.

On October 7, 1958, President Mirza of Pakistan by proclamation announced :

> "(A) The Constitution of the 23d March, 1956 will be abrogated.
> "(B) The Central and Provincial Governments will be dismissed with immediate effect.
> "(C) The National Parliament and Provincial Assemblies will be dissolved.

"(D) All Political parties will be abolished.

"(E) Until alternative arrangements are made, Pakistan will come under martial law. . . ."

The American Ambassador at Karachi (Langley) to the Secretary of State (Dulles), telegram, Oct. 8, 1958, MS. Department of State, file 790d.00/10–858.

The Laws (Continuance in Force) Order, October 10, 1958, stated:

"Notwithstanding the abrogation of the Constitution of the 23rd March, 1956, hereinafter referred to as the late Constitution by the Proclamation and subject to any order of the President or Regulation made by the Chief Administrator of Martial Law the Republic to be known henceforward as Pakistan, shall be governed as nearly as may be in accordance with the late Constitution".

The Counselor of the American Embassy at Karachi (Mallory-Browne) to the Secretary of State (Dulles), despatch No. 356, Oct. 13, 1958, MS. Department of State, file 790d.00/10–1358.

Under the Constitution enacted March 1, 1962, "the Republic of Pakistan", retaining its federal structure, consists of two Provinces, East and West Pakistan, and "such other States and territories as are or may become included in Pakistan, whether by accession or otherwise" (article 1). *The Constitution of the Republic of Pakistan* (Government of Pakistan Press, Karachi, 1962).

FEDERAL STATES [1]

Argentina	Germany	Switzerland
Australia	India	Uganda
Austria	Libya	Union of South Africa
Brazil		Union of Soviet Socialist Republics
Burma	Mexico	United States of America
Cameroon	Nigeria	Venezuela
Canada	Pakistan	Yugoslavia

[1] *Cf.* table II in III Peaslee, *Constitutions of Nations* (2d ed., 1956) 800–804.

Federation

§ 24

The Arab Union, proclaimed February 14, 1958, by King Faisal of Iraq and King Hussein of Jordan, was formally established May 14, 1958, after ratification of the Constitution and prior to the formation of the Arab Union Government on May 19, 1958.

The First Secretary of the American Embassy at Baghdad (Thacher) to the Secretary of State (Dulles), despatch No. 1132, encl. 1, June 2, 1958, MS. Department of State, file 786.02/6–258. For Agreement of Arab Federation, see despatch No. 747, Feb. 26, 1958, MS. Department of State, file 786.00/2–2658.

While article 1 of the Arab Union Constitution recites "The Arab Union shall be formed of the Kingdom of Iraq and the Hashemite

The Arab Union

Kingdom of Jordan . . .", article 2 stipulates "With due regard for the provisions of this Constitution, each member-state of the Union will maintain its independent international status and its existing system of rule."

Among the enumerated affairs confined to the Government of the Union in article 62(a) were foreign affairs and diplomatic and consular representation; negotiation of treaties, pacts, and international agreements; protection of the States of the Union and preservation of their security; establishment and management of the armed forces under the name of "The Arab Army" (no Member State may maintain armed units other than the police and internal security forces). "All other affairs and powers will remain the authority of the member-states." (Article 62(b).)

Article 63 prescribes the supremacy of the Union laws in its provision that "All Union laws, regulations, orders, decrees, and other decisions issued by Union authorities in accordance with the rules of this Constitution will be implemented directly and will be binding on all authorities and individuals in the member-states."

> The Second Secretary of the American Embassy at Amman (Walstrom) to the Secretary of State (Dulles), despatch No. 269, encl. No. 1, Mar. 20, 1958, MS. Department of State, file 786.03/3–2058.

A memorandum addressed in part to the question of Arab Union representation in the United Nations stated:

> "Jordan and Iraq have, by uniting, formed a single State with a federal government having exclusive power over all aspects of foreign affairs. Despite the completeness of the merger, as expressed in the Constitution of the Arab Union, and despite the example of the United Arab Republic, various officials in both Jordan and Iraq have suggested that, although the Arab Union will have only one diplomatic mission in each national capital, nevertheless separate Jordanian and Iraqi memberships in international organizations will be maintained. Such a position would be inconsistent with the nature of the Union they have established. . . . the United States should take the position that the Arab Union, like the United Arab Republic in the case of Egypt and Syria, should be regarded as the direct successor of Jordan and Iraq and, thus, as succeeding to membership in those international organizations of which either Jordan or Iraq was formerly a member. . . ."

> The Legal Adviser (Becker) to Assistant Secretary of State Rountree, memorandum, "Legal Problems Relating to the Union of Iraq and Jordan", Apr. 10, 1958, MS. Department of State, file 786.00/4–1058.

The Ministry of Foreign Affairs of the Arab Union Government, informing the American Embassy at Baghdad of the formation of the Arab Union Government on May 19, 1958, explained that, until the Arab Union Government actually takes over from the Governments of Jordan and Iraq, all the powers within the jurisdiction of the Arab Union according to the provisions of article 74 of the Union Constitution, including the external affairs of the Kingdom of Iraq, will be exercised as they are at the present time, and during the transitory period the Foreign Minister of the Arab Union will take care of and supervise these affairs.

Career Minister Gallman, American Embassy, Baghdad, to Secretary of State Dulles, telegram, May 20, 1958, MS. Department of State, file 786.00/5–2058. As to art. 74, see *infra*.

A note from the Jordanian Ministry of Foreign Affairs to the American Embassy dated May 19, 1958, as transmitted by telegram from Amman, stated:

"Ministry Foreign Affairs wishes to point out to the Embassy on this occasion that until the Union Government announces dates on which it will take over its powers in accordance with Article 74 of the Union's Constitution, foreign relations pertaining to HKJ are to remain as they are at present and the procedure of communicating between the Embassy and Ministry will continue to be the same as at present."

The Counselor of the American Embassy at Amman (Wright) to the Secretary of State (Dulles), telegram, May 20, 1958, MS. Department of State, file 786.00/5–2058.

In connection with the telegrams referred to above, a memorandum on the status of the Arab Union from the Legal Adviser's Office of the Department of State quoted article 74 of the Union Constitution, "the Union Government will fix the dates and define the measures necessary to give effect to transfer of authority from the governments of the member states", and concluded, "It now appears from the messages coming from both Amman and Baghdad that no real authority has yet been transferred from Jordan and Iraq to the Arab Union. In fact, it appears that such transfers may be delayed for quite some time."

The Office of the Legal Adviser (Maktos, Reid, Meeker, and Hewitt) to the Legal Adviser (Becker), memorandum, "Status of the Arab Union", May 22, 1958, MS. Department of State, file FW 786.00/5–2058.

A note received by the American Embassies at Amman and Baghdad respectively, July 1, 1958, from the Ministry of Foreign Affairs of the Arab Union, informed the United States Government that the Arab Union, in accordance with article 74 of the Arab Union Constitution, has taken over all its powers relevant to Foreign Affairs as prescribed in paragraph (a) 1–2 of article 62 of the Constitution, as of July 1, 1958.

The American Embassy, Amman, to Secretary of State Dulles, airgram No. G–2, July 10, 1958, MS. Department of State, file 786c.00/7–1058; Career Minister Gallman, American Embassy, Baghdad, to Secretary of State Dulles, telegram, June 26, 1958, MS. Department of State, file 786.00/6–2658.

In reply to a request from the Office of Near Eastern Affairs for comment on the recent amendments to article 33 of the Constitution of Jordan, concerning its treatymaking powers, the Office of the Legal Adviser of the Department of State advised:

"Article 33 of the Jordanian constitution was recently amended by deleting certain phrases which, in the following quotation, are indicated by parenthesis and underscoring [*italics*]:

"'33. (i) The King (*declares war, concludes peace and*) signs treaties.

"'(ii) Treaties (*of peace, alliance, trade, navigation, and treaties involving territorial changes or adversely affecting sovereignty, or*) incurring financial commitments, or affecting the general or private rights of Jordanians shall not be brought in to [into] force unless approved by the National Assembly. In no circumstances shall a secret clause in a treaty be contradictory to its published clauses.'

"The effect of these amendments is to deprive the King of Jordan of the right to declare war and conclude peace. The amendments leave intact, however, the right of Jordan to conclude treaties; the deletions in Article 33(ii) simply restrict the kinds of treaties which need to be submitted to the National Assembly before they can come into force. Article 33 is, therefore, clearly in conflict with Article 62(2) of the constitution of the Arab Union:

"'a) The following are affairs confined to the Government of the Union:

.   .   .   .

"'2) Negotiation of treaties, pacts and international agreements.'

"Apart from the obvious inconsistency pointed out in the preceding paragraph, there is also a question as to whether one of the constituent states of a federal union can maintain diplomatic relations and conclude treaties which are applicable solely to that constituent state. There are certain examples in the 19th century (Bavaria under the German Empire) that would provide precedents for this practice, and it would seem difficult to sustain the contention that as a matter of law such a practice was impossible and illegal. The trend in modern practice is, however, toward a single voice in foreign affairs . . . ."

The Office of the Legal Adviser (Meeker and Ford) to the Office of Near Eastern Affairs (Waggoner), memorandum, "The Treaty-making Powers of Jordan and Diplomatic Representation in Amman", Apr. 28, 1958, MS. Department of State, file 786.00/4–2858.

Following the military coup of the Iraqi Government, July 14, 1958, the American Embassy at Amman received a note from the Ministry of Foreign Affairs of the Arab Union Government dated July 14, 1958, which, as transmitted, stated, "in accordance with paragraph 1, Article V of the Arab Union Constitution and due to the absence of King of Iraq, the Royal Diwan upon order of King Hussein announces His Majesty's assumption of the constitutional authority as President of the Union as from 14 July, 1958 . . ."

The Counselor of the American Embassy at Amman (Wright) to the Secretary of State (Dulles), telegram, July 15, 1958, MS. Department of State, file 786c.00/7–1558. The Iraqi Republic announced its withdrawal from the Arab Union on July 18, 1958. The American Ambassador at Baghdad (Gallman) to the Secretary of State (Dulles), telegram, July 18, 1958, MS. Department of State, file 786c.00/7–1858.

Following the *coup d'etat* in Baghdad and the overthrow of the monarchy in Iraq in July 1958, Prime Minister Macmillan stated in the House of Commons on July 17, 1958, in informing that body of the sending of British forces to Jordan in answer to a Jordanian request for immediate assistance against a *coup d'etat* reportedly being organized by the United Arab Republic against Jordan, that—

"A question has been raised about the precise position of the Arab Union of the Kingdom of Iraq and the Hashemite Kingdom of Jordan. Article 2 of the agreement of association makes it clear that each member State of the Union shall retain its international status and its existing state of Government. Therefore, I should make it clear that it is to the Kingdom of Jordan that we are sending our help in this time of need.

"The right hon. Gentleman the Leader of the Opposition very fairly warned me yesterday that I could not assume that the Opposition would support the dispatch of British troops to Jordan to suppress the revolt in Iraq. That is certainly not the purpose of the small force which we have sent."

591 H.C. Deb. (5th ser.) cols. 1510–1511 (July 17, 1958).

The Council of Ministers of Jordan adopted a resolution suspending the Arab Union Constitution and resuming its status under the Jordanian Constitution effective August 1, 1958. The resolution which gained Royal ratification declared in part:

"1. Since the Arab Union, which was made up of the Hashemite
Kingdom of Jordan and the Iraqi Kingdom, was based in its
entity, basis and organization on a partnership between the two
Kingdoms in responsibilities and duties; and since the oppressive
insurrection and overthrow which took place recently in Iraq
made the Iraqi province of the Arab Union incapable of fulfilling
its responsibilities and duties in accordance with the Constitution
of the Arab Union; and since the Union's constitution does not
enable Jordan alone to carry out the executive, legislative and
international activities established by the provisions of the said
constitution, especially foreign relations and diplomatic representation with all other states; now that the Union's constitution
has become suspended in applicable and/or executable form from
a practical or a realistic viewpoint, the Council of Ministers, with
the approval of H.M. the King, has decided to carry out the
constitutional prerogatives of the Hashemite Kingdom of Jordan
in accordance with provisions of the Jordanian Constitution, as
of August 1, 1958."

The American Embassy at Amman (Wright) to the Secretary of State
(Dulles), airgram No. G–8, Aug. 7, 1958, MS. Department of State, file
601.0085/8–758.

United Arab
Republic

"Proclamation of the United Arab Republic" issued February 1,
1958, announced the decision of Egypt and Syria to unite into one
State "the United Arab Republic", which officially came into being
on February 22, 1958, following confirmation in the plebiscite of February 21, 1958.

The Counselor for Political Affairs of the American Embassy at Cairo
(Ross) to the Secretary of State (Dulles), despatch No. 774, encl. 4, Feb. 7,
1958, MS. Department of State, file 786.00/2–758.

The United Arab Republic as a union of two wholly independent
sovereign States, whereby each State surrendered its sovereignty to
an entirely new entity, has been termed unprecedented.

The Office of the Legal Adviser (Reid to Raymond), memorandum,
"Legal Consequences of Union of Syria and Egypt", Feb. 5, 1958, MS.,
Department of State, file 786.00/2–558.

". . . There have been, it is true, analogous situations, particularly in
19th Century Europe. However, the usual examples of one state losing its
sovereignty to another are those in which one state has been annexed or
conquered by another state, whereby the former submerged its international
personality into that of the stronger state, rather than as [an] amalgamation of two sovereign states into a wholly new state.

"One example is the annexation of Texas to the United States in 1845.
Obviously no new state was formed. In this instance the U.S. assumed
the debts of Texas [Moore, v. I, p. 343 ff.], but all the latter's treaties
were considered by the U.S. to be no longer of any effect. [Moore, v. V,
p. 349. MacNair, *The Law of Treaties* (1938), p. 390 ff.] The Union of
Norway and Sweden, following the Napoleonic wars, would seem on its

face to present an example of a nature similar to that under consideration in this memorandum. However, on examination it is revealed that Norway was not independent before the formation of the Union, but rather had been a part of Denmark for some centuries.

"The unification of Italy in 1860 and the creation of Yugoslavia after the first world war both present instances in which a small sovereign nation [state] (Sardinia and Serbia, respectively) managed to bring together people who considered themselves to be of a common nationality, but who had been under the subjugation of alien powers. In this process the small sovereign nation [state] expanded and changed its name. In these cases the dominant power was said to have absorbed other sovereign nations [states], rather than amalgamating or merging with them. [Draft Convention on Law of Treaties, 29 A.J.I.L. Supp. 1073–4 (1935).]

"The unification of Germany, in 1871, presents the most involved and most nearly analogous case. In this complex instance formerly independent, or semi-independent, states became members of the German empire. In addition territories possessing German people were freed by war and joined the new Empire. However, the dominating force of the Empire, both before and after unification, was Prussia. The other states which joined the Empire were (with the possible exception of Bavaria) relatively small and insignificant. Moreover they retained a certain amount of autonomy in the exercise of foreign relations after the union." *Ibid.*

Instructing the United States Mission to the United Nations of the United States position regarding the credentials of the United Arab Republic delegation, specifically to the Law of the Sea Conference which convened at Geneva on February 24, 1958, and in general to United Nations organs and agencies, the Department of State asserted:

"According to the reports, the United Arab Republic will have one army, one postal system, one parliament, one flag, one diplomatic corps (foreign embassies to be maintained only in Cairo), one president, and one capital. For international purposes it will speak with one voice and through a central government. It must therefore be represented at the Conference on the Law of the Sea by only one delegation, which can only have one vote. . . .

"Only Members of the United Nations and of the specialized agencies have been invited to participate in the Conference on the Law of the Sea. The question may therefore be raised as to whether the UAR is a Member of the United Nations. The U.S. Delegation should take the position that it is a Member. The UAR is the product of a merger between Syria and Egypt, both of which were Charter Members of the United Nations. The UAR is their successor and as such succeeds automatically to the membership in the United Nations and the specialized agencies of which either Egypt or Syria was a member. . . ."

The Acting Secretary of State (Herter) to the United States Mission to the United Nations, Geneva, London, USRO Paris, instruction No. CA–7037, Feb. 14, 1958, "Syro-Egyptian Union", encl., MS. Department of State file 786.00/2–1458.

The Provisional Constitution of the United Arab Republic, proclaimed March 5, 1958, describes the United Arab Republic as a "democratic, independent, sovereign Republic" (article 1), and assigns to the President of the Union the position of Supreme Commander of the Armed Forces (article 55), and accords to him alone the power to conclude treaties some of which require ratification by the National Assembly before becoming effective (article 56), and to declare a state of emergency (article 57).

> The Counselor for Political Affairs of the American Embassy at Cairo (Ross) to the Secretary of State (Dulles), despatch No. 887, encl. 1, Mar. 8, 1958, MS. Department of State, file 786.03/3–858 (Provisional Constitution of the UAR).

On September 28, 1961, Syria withdrew from the United Arab Republic and by Decree No. 1 of September 29, 1961, formed the transitional Cabinet of the Syrian Arab Republic.

> First Secretary of the American Embassy at Damascus (Jones) to the Secretary of State (Rusk), despatch No. 102, Nov. 3, 1961, MS. Department of State, file 783.00/11–361.

Eritrea

The General Assembly under authority of article 23 of the Treaty of Peace with Italy of February 10, 1947 (annex XI) undertook the final disposition of the former Italian colonies—Libya, Italian Somaliland, and Eritrea—and passed a resolution (289 (IV)) on November 21, 1949, recommending a specific plan of disposition for each of the colonies. For Eritrea, under British administration since the collapse of Italian administration in 1941, the General Assembly recommended the establishment of a United Nations Commission of five Member States—Burma, Guatemala, Norway, Pakistan, and the Union of South Africa—"to ascertain more fully the wishes and the best means of promoting the welfare of the inhabitants of Eritrea, to examine the question of the disposal of Eritrea and to prepare a report for the General Assembly . . . ." (G.A. Res. 289A (IV), section C, November 21, 1949.) A subsequent General Assembly resolution (390A(V)), December 2, 1950, recommended, on the basis of the reports of the United Nations Commission for Eritrea and of the Interim Committee of the General Assembly on the Report of the U.N. Commission for Eritrea, that "Eritrea shall constitute an autonomous unit federated with Ethiopia under the sovereignty of the Ethiopian Crown". It was further recommended that the Eritrean Government shall possess legislative, executive, and judicial powers in the field of domestic affairs but that the jurisdiction of the Federal Government shall extend to such matters as defense, foreign affairs, currency and finance, foreign and interstate commerce, and external and interstate communications, including ports.

In a note from the British Ambassador to the Ethiopian Minister for Foreign Affairs of August 27, 1952, it was recited—

"2. It is laid down in paragraph 14 of the Resolution No. 390 (V) of the 2nd December, 1950, which provided for the federation of Eritrea with Ethiopia under the sovereignty of the Ethiopian Crown, that the transfer of power shall take place as soon as the Eritrean Constitution and the Federal Act shall enter into effect. Since the Eritrean Constitution has already been ratified by His Imperial Majesty, it follows that, if the Federal Act is ratified, as proposed in paragraph 1 above, on the 11th September, it, as well as the federation, will enter into effect on that day.

"3. In our recent discussion on this matter, it has been agreed that the words 'as soon as' in paragraph 14 of the United Nations Resolution should be interpreted as meaning to provide the minimum of time actually necessary to effect the transfer (effectuer matériellement), that is, three or four days, and in any case by the 15th September. I have therefore the honour to propose that the transfer of power to the Federal and Eritrean Governments shall have been completed by the 15th September."

With the acceptance of these proposals by the Ethiopian Government in a note dated August 29, 1952, the exchange of notes constituted an Agreement which entered into force on August 29, 1952.

190 UNTS 330–331.

After ratification of the Federal Act, which incorporated paragraphs 1–7, inclusive, of General Assembly Resolution 390A(V), by the Emperor of Ethiopia September 11, 1952, following its adoption by the Eritrean Assembly July 10, 1952, the approval of the Eritrean Constitution by the United Nations Commission August 6, 1952, and ratification of the same by the Emperor of Ethiopia August 11, 1952, the Federation of Eritrea with Ethiopia under the sovereignty of the Ethiopian Crown officially entered into full force and effect September 15, 1952, with the promulgation of the Termination of Powers Proclamation by the Administering Power.

Final Report of the United Nations Commissioner in Eritrea, U.N. Gen. Ass. Off. Rec. 7th Sess., Supp. No. 15 (A/2188) (1952), pp. 43, 46, 73. For the texts of G.A. Res. 390A(V), the Federal Act, and the Eritrean Constitution, see *ibid.*, pp. 74–75, 45–47, 76–89, respectively.

By Resolution 617(VII) of December 17, 1952, the General Assembly, having noted, *inter alia*, that "the conditions laid down in paragraph 13 of resolution 390A(V) of 2 December 1950 have been fulfilled, and that on 11 September 1952 the Federation of Eritrea with Ethiopia was proclaimed", welcomed "the establishment of the

Federation of Eritrea with Ethiopia under the sovereignty of the Ethiopian Crown".

On November 15, 1962, union with Ethiopia was effected as a result of the Eritrean Assembly's unanimous adoption by acclamation of a motion abolishing the Federation.

> The American Consulate, Asmara (Johnson), to the Secretary of State (Rusk), telegram, Nov. 15, 1962, MS. Department of State, file 675.75A/11–1562.

> For federation of autonomous states within the French Community (Mali Federation), see *post* this chapter under "French Community", pp. 568 ff.

Confederation

§ 25

Secretary of State Dulles, in answer to a question raised at a news conference January 27, 1959, concerning the possibility of confederation as a means of reuniting East and West Germany, discussed the term "confederation" as follows:

> ". . . the word 'confederation' covers a very wide variety of political relationships. It can be a relationship between two utterly dissimilar and unrelated areas which tends to perpetuate their division, perhaps only having a surface unity with respect to certain particular matters. Or you can have a confederation which is, in fact, of very considerable progress toward reunification. I said in a sense you can call the present Federal Republic of Germany a confederation. . . ."

> XL *Bulletin*, Department of State, No. 1025, Feb. 16, 1959, pp. 223, 230.

United Arab
States

A separate Union, the United Arab States, was formally established March 8, 1958, with the signing of its Charter by President Nasser on behalf of the United Arab Republic and Amir Muhammad al-Badr, Crown Prince of Yemen, on behalf of the Kingdom of Yemen.

While the Charter specifies that "Each State will preserve its national identity and its system of government" (article 2), it directs that "Member States shall pursue the unified policy drawn by the Union" (article 6), that "Diplomatic and consular representation of the Union abroad shall be assumed by a single mission in those cases specified by the Union" (article 7), and that "the Union shall have unified Armed Forces" (article 8).

Control of Union affairs is vested in the Supreme Council, composed of the Heads of the Member States, assisted by the Union

Council (articles 13 and 14). It is the function of the Supreme Council to "define the higher policy of the Union with regard to political, defence, economic and cultural matters." As stipulated, "it enacts the laws which are necessary to this effect", and "is the supreme authority to which the determination of the functions shall be referred" (article 17).

The Counselor for Political Affairs of the American Embassy at Cairo (Ross) to the Secretary of State (Dulles), despatch No. 896, encl. 1, Mar. 12, 1958, MS. Department of State, file 786.00/3–1258.

"Yemen and the UAR will apparently maintain separate armies, but under joint command, separate currencies, but closely tied together, separate representation in international organizations, and separate diplomatic missions 'in most cases'.

. . . .

"The proper title for this union would seem to be a confederated state, as the term is defined by Hackworth and Moore. ('A confederated state—or band of states—comprises an organization of states in which each retains its internal and, to a greater or lesser extent, its external sovereignty.' Hackworth, v. I, p. 60). .

"On the basis of the above facts, it would seem dubious that the FAS [UAS] possesses the requisites of a state or person at international law, insofar as these require that there be 'an organized government exercising control over, and endeavoring to maintain justice within, the territory.' (Hyde, v. I, p. 22.) Neither legislative nor judicial authority is mentioned in the agreement as it has been reported. In any case, since evidently each head of state has a veto power, it would appear that the 'Government' of the FAS [UAS] is incapable of exercising control over either of its components without their consent. Moreover, the factor that each state will retain its own diplomatic service would indicate that the FAS [UAS] is not holding itself out to the world as an international person.

"Consequently it would seem . . . that the degree of sovereignty retained, as contrasted with that relinquished, is such that there is no new state, but rather a new organization of two States effectuating what amounts to a close alliance, for cooperation. . . ."

The Office of the Legal Adviser (Maktos to Raymond), memorandum, "The Federation of Arab States (Union of the UAR and Yemen)", Mar. 7, 1958, MS. Department of State, file 786.00/3–758. See also Cotran, "Some Legal Aspects of the Formation of the United Arab Republic and the United Arab States", 8 Int'l and Comp. L.Q. (1959) 346, 350–351.

On December 26, 1961, the Government of the United Arab Republic announced its decision "to terminate the functions of the United Arab States" which bound "the United Arab Republic federally with the

Government of His Majesty Ahmed Ben Hamid Eldin, Imam of Yemen".

The American Ambassador at Cairo (Badeau) to the Secretary of State (Rusk), airgram No. A–193, Dec. 29, 1961, MS. Department of State, file 786.00/12–2961.

Ghana-
Guinea
Union

A Joint Declaration on the Ghana-Guinea Union announced at Conakry on May 1, 1959, following a provisional agreement of November 23, 1958, by Prime Minister Nkrumah of Ghana and President Touré of Guinea, proposed "that the Independent States of Africa and all territories achieving independence later should build up a fraternal and prosperous African Community" and specified their intent to "seal the Ghana-Guinea Union in practice and immediately to lay the foundations of the African Community which will owe no allegiance to any power and will be called the Union of Independent African States".

According to the basic principles of the Union of Independent African States to be followed by the Constitution when drafted, "each State or Federation which is a member of the Union shall preserve its only individuality and structure" and "the member-States or Federation will decide in common what portion of sovereignty shall be surrendered to the Union in the full interest of the African Community". It is further provided that the States or Federations shall have their own foreign representation although every member of the Union can entrust any other Member State with its representation in certain countries. While Heads of States which are members of the Union are to determine common policy on matters of defense, each State or Federation will have its own army. An economic council of the Union composed of an equal number of members designated by each Member State is responsible for determining the general economic policy, and a common Bank of Issue known as the Union Bank is designed to issue and back the respective currencies of the different States or Federations which are members of the Union. In addition to the flag, anthem, and motto of each Member State or Federation, and the citizenship of nationals within their respective States or Federations, the Union will have a flag, anthem, and motto of its own, and nationals will acquire Union citizenship. While the acts of States or Federations which are members of the Union are to be determined in relation to the essential objectives, which are independence, unity, and the African personality, as well as the interest of the peoples, it is required that they shall not act in obedience to any one group or bloc but "take account of external forces working for or against them."

> The Second Secretary of the American Embassy at Accra (Lang) to the Secretary of State (Herter), despatch No. 696, encl. 1, May 8, 1959, MS. Department of State, file 645j.70b/5–859.

> In the provisional Ghana-Guinea accord announced November 23, 1958, the Prime Ministers of Ghana and Guinea respectively agreed to link the two States in a "confederacy" intended to be the "nucleus of a Union of West African states". As a first step, it was agreed to adopt a union flag and to develop between the two Governments "the closest contacts in order to harmonize the policies of our two states especially in the fields of defence, and foreign and economic affairs." The American Ambassador at Accra (Flake) to the Secretary of State (Dulles), telegram, Nov. 23, 1958, MS. Department of State, file 779.00/11–2358.

The joint Ghana-Guinea Declaration does not envisage actual union of the two countries but exemplifies more the idea of confederation. The 1960 Ghana Constitution makes provision for Ghana to relinquish degrees of its sovereignty to the Union.

> Office of the Legal Adviser (Frank to Whiteman), "Ghana-Guinea Union", memorandum, Nov. 27, 1962, MS. Department of State, file 645j.70 B/11–2762.

Ghana, Guinea, and Mali formally established the Union of African States on July 1, 1961. The Charter of the Union, open to all African States which accept its objectives, designates the Union as the "nucleus of the United States of Africa" and specifies the following aims: to strengthen cooperation between the member States politically, diplomatically, economically, and culturally; to pool the resources of the member States in order to consolidate their independence and territorial integrity; to achieve joint collaboration for the liquidation of imperialism, colonialism, and neocolonialism in Africa; and to harmonize the domestic and foreign policy of members. The Union's activities are to comprise the working out of a common orientation for the States, strict observance of a concerted diplomacy, the organization of a system of joint defense, definition of a common set of directives relating to economic planning, and the rehabilitation and development of African culture. Administratively, the supreme executive organ is to be the conference, meeting quarterly, of heads of state of the Union.

> *Charter for the Union of African States and a Joint Communiqué Issued Later after a Summit Conference between the Leaders of the Union* (Ghana, Government Printing Department, 1961) ; *Ghana Today*, vol. 5, No. 11, July 19, 1961, pp. 8–9.

Dependent or Semi-independent States

Suzerainty

§ 26

". . . Suzerainty lacks juristic precision and in principle each case of suzerain-vassal relationship must be considered on its own merits. However, it is possible for international lawyers to detect certain characteristic features which are common to all cases. Suzerainty was originally an institution of feudal law and was used to describe the particular relationship between feudal lord and his vassal. The latter owed allegiance to the suzerain ruler, he had to pay him tribute, give him his military support and was entitled to his protection. Feudal institutions were characteristic of the period of interdynastic relationships, when the overlord ruler, and not his people, was endowed with legal as well as political sovereignty, and was capable of receiving allegiance from the subordinate ruler. With the disappearance of feudalism and dynastic policies, this type of suzerainty, which was determined by the constitutional law of the suzerain state, disappeared entirely.

"The institution of suzerainty then entered the field of modern international law and became a kind of international guardianship. The vassal state of the nineteenth and twentieth centuries is deprived of external sovereignty though it retains internal sovereignty, which the suzerain state is under a duty to respect. Deprived of external sovereignty, the vassal state has no position of its own in the family of nations. It is essential to remember that it remains a portion of the suzerain state which represents it entirely in relations with other nations. In principle all treaties concluded by the suzerain state are *ipso facto* binding on the vassal; the latter is automatically party to a war in which the suzerain is engaged, and the suzerain state is externally responsible for all actions of the vassal. These are some of the main common features of vassal states in modern international law. The Indian Princely States were, until the independence of India, vassals of the British Crown which exercised the rights of paramountcy in relation to them. As mentioned above, the Balkan states which were vassals of the Ottoman Empire gradually achieved independence in the nineteenth century. Some of them were first allowed to enter into certain non-political treaties with other nations, without participation of the suzerain. Bulgaria, while still a vassal state, fought a war against Serbia which had already ceased to be one. On the other hand, Egypt, while still a vassal of Turkey, was not considered a belligerent when Turkey entered World War I in 1914. Thus it happened not infrequently that suzerainty, though still continuing on the basis of an historical relationship, became a *nominal* title ripe for elimination or conversion into a title more favorable to the subordinate state. This is of great importance in the consideration of the Tibetan case.

"A number of vassal states, in their striving for independence, attained before complete liberation first a higher status of dependence, that of protectorate. Protectorates have this in common with the suzerain-vassal relationship: that they both created a kind of international guardianship. Protected states have, however, not only internal sovereignty, but are able in a number of cases to exercise some of the attributes of external sovereignty, though the latter is in principle vested in the protector state. Not infrequently the relationship between protector and protected was or is of a contractual nature, a feature not inherent in the suzerain-vassal set-up. The basic treaty between protector and protected is of an international character and of interest to third Powers. Thus a protected state has to some extent a position within the family of nations, and therefore enters directly the orbit of international law. In distinction to a vassal state, the protected state is not part of the protecting state; it is not automatically a party in a war in which the latter is engaged, and treaties concluded by the protecting state are not *ipso facto* binding on the protected state. These are differences of outstanding importance to international lawyers who analyze a particular relationship between superior and inferior state and may find that what is called suzerainty by name is in fact a protectorate in law or vice versa. Further, it may not be out of place to mention the existence of so-called quasi-protectorates in which the status of the protected state is higher than in a protectorate proper. . . ."

Alexandrowicz-Alexander, "The Legal Position of Tibet", 48 Am. J. Int'l L. (1954) 265–267. As to the Indian Princely States, see *post* this chapter.

Protectorates

§27

"Primarily, . . . international law deals with the relations of   Nature
independent states to one another. It is also to some extent concerned with certain other states, which, though partly controlled by another state, still maintain some relations with states other than that which controls them. This relation of dependency is sometimes described as a *protectorate*, sometimes as a *suzerainty*, but it is difficult to give precise juristic signification to either term; the degree of control on one side and of dependency on the other may vary indefinitely, and in any case it must be deduced from the events or treaties which created the relation, and not from the term used to describe it. This was laid down in 1923 by the Permanent Court in the following terms [Advisory Opinion No. 4, p. 27, the case of the *Nationality Decrees issued in Tunis and Morocco*]:

" 'The extent of the powers of a protecting state in the territory of a protected state depends, first, upon the treaties between the protecting state and the protected state establishing the protectorate, and, secondly, upon the conditions under which the protectorate has been recognised by third powers as against whom there is an intention to rely on the provisions of these treaties. In spite of common features possessed by protectorates under international law, they have individual legal characteristics resulting from the special conditions under which they were created, and the stage of their development.' "

Brierly, *The Law of Nations* (5th ed., 1955) 125–126.

"The theory of a Protectorate is that a weak state with certain attributes of sovereignty is under the protection of a strong state which likewise exercises certain sovereign rights with respect to the protected state. The protecting state usually conducts the foreign affairs of the protected state and may also exercise control over other matters, particularly the military and customs. The extent to which the protecting state dominates the affairs—internal and external—of the protected state depends in each case upon the agreement establishing the Protectorate and also upon the attitude of the protecting state. Accordingly, Protectorates vary greatly in their characteristics. In other words, there is no 'yes' and 'no' answer to the question as to whether the sovereignty is in the protecting or in the protected state because, as a matter of fact, the rights of sovereignty are divided as between the two."

The Legal Adviser of the Department of State (Hackworth), memorandum, "Effect of Non-Recognition of the So-Called Protectorate of Bohemia and Moravia or of German Sovereignty in That Area", Apr. 10, 1939, MS. Department of State, file 860F.01/209.

"The term 'protectorate' has been used broadly by writers on international law to apply to cases wherein a comparatively powerful state assumes the duty of protecting a weaker state with the essential feature that the conduct of the external affairs of the protectorate are placed in the hands of the protecting state. Even though the protectorate has given up its external sovereignty, it has not lost the whole of its independence, for in internal affairs it has freedom of action for the most part as long as such action does not involve it with a foreign Power. A typical example often cited of a protectorate was that assumed by Great Britain over the Ionian Islands from 1815–1864. The basis of this protectorate was three identical treaties which Britain made with Russia, Austria, and Prussia, respectively, whereby it was declared that the islands should form a single state, free and independent under the immediate and exclusive protection of the King of Great Britain. During this period the islands

were governed under a constitution adopted by a local legislature
and had their own commercial flag. Even in internal affairs the
protecting Power exercised considerable control. The protectorate ceased in 1864 when the islands were ceded to Greece with
the consent of the guaranteeing Powers. The state had actual
identity in international law and is an example of what writers
have classified as 'real protectorates.' This type of protectorate
has usually been exercised over a state which is well developed,
and the general intention is that the state will not be absorbed
by the protecting state.

". . . In 'protected states' society has advanced beyond the Protected
tribal stage, and there is an established government which can States
agree to accept the protection of the guaranteeing Power. 'Protected states' differ from 'real protectorates' in that there is an
absence of an expressed intention not to absorb the former.

"A third class of protectorates includes those known as 'Colonial Colonial
Protectorates.' These protectorates result from protection trea- Protectorates
ties negotiated by the Great Powers with tribal chiefs since the
middle of the last century, whereby the protecting state secured
a first claim in view of possible occupation and annexation of the
territory at some future time. It is difficult to distinguish between a 'protected state' and a 'colonial protectorate' aside from
the fact that in the case of the former organized government was
an established fact when the state accepted the protection of a
powerful state, while government in the colonial protectorate had
experienced little development beyond the tribal state at the time
of the protection agreement. . . .

". . . International law recognizes a distinction between a 'real
protectorate' and 'colonial protectorate' in that it deals with the
former and not the latter. The scope of international law does
not, however, provide a distinction between a 'colonial protectorate' and a 'protected state.' No other Power in the international community can lawfully prevent the protecting state from
annexing a protectorate of the colonial type if it wills to do so."

Robbins, "The Legal Status of Aden Colony and the Aden Protectorate",
33 Am. J. Int'l L. (1939) 700, 713–715.

". . . A protectorate, even one very closely resembling a colony,
is not part of the national territory of the protecting state but
remains legally a foreign country. The natives of the protectorate
are not British subjects, but subjects of the local ruler. They do
not owe allegiance but only a limited 'obedience' to the British
Crown; see King v. The Earl of Crewe, ex parte Sekgome, *Law
Reports, King's Bench Division*, 1910, vol. 2, pp. 619–20. The
right of the Crown to exercise legislative and administrative functions in such areas is based, aside from treaties with the local

rulers, upon the Foreign Jurisdiction Act of 1890 (53 & 54 Victoria c. 37, as amended). . . ."

Liebesny, "International Relations of Arabia: The Dependent Areas", *The Middle East Journal*, vol. 1 (1947), note 6, p. 152.

Arabian Peninsula [1]

". . . On the basis of their legal relationship to Great Britain, the dependent states and territories in the Arabian Peninsula may be divided into three general categories: (a) British colonial territory (Aden Colony); (b) British protectorate (Aden Protectorate); and (c) semi-independent states under British protection (the Persian Gulf states)."

Liebesny, "International Relations of Arabia: The Dependent Areas", *The Middle East Journal*, vol. 1 (1947) 150.

In a written answer to a question as to which of the independent rulers and States in the Persian Gulf Her Majesty's Government have treaty obligations in respect of their security, Secretary of State for Foreign Affairs Selwyn Lloyd stated:

"Her Majesty's Government have a Treaty obligation to protect Kuwait, Bahrain and Qatar. A similar obligation is implicit in the Perpetual Maritime Treaties of 1853 to which all the present Rulers of the seven Trucial States, Abu Dhabi, Dubai, Sharjah, Ras al-Khaimah, Ajman, Umm al-Qaiwain and Fujairah have adhered. There is in addition an explicit undertaking to the Ruler of Fujairah that his State is under British protection."

Written Answers, 574 H.C. Deb. (5th ser.) col. 107 (July 29, 1957).

Aden Colony

"In speaking of Aden we must bear in mind that we are dealing with two areas between which Great Britain makes a legal distinction: Aden Colony and Aden Protectorate. This distinction is one of British constitutional law, but it is also of interest to international law which is concerned with the conditions to which the term 'protectorate' is applied in the international community. . . ."

Robbins, "The Legal Status of Aden Colony and the Aden Protectorate", 33 Am. J. Int'l L. (1939) 700, 702.

"The fundamental law for the Crown Colony of Aden is the Order in Council of September 28, 1936, which follows the usual lines of basic legislation for British colonies [*Statutory Rules and Orders*, 1936, pp. 1–17]. Only the basic legislation is enacted by the Crown. Ordinary legislation is enacted locally in the form of 'Ordinances enacted by the Governor of the Colony of Aden.' In the exercise of his legislative and executive functions,

---

[1] States within the Arabian Peninsula are thus geographically grouped herein without prejudice to their legal classification.

the Governor is assisted by an Executive Council and Legislative Council . . . ."

Liebesny, "Administration and Legal Development in Arabia—Aden Colony and Protectorate", *The Middle East Journal*, vol. 9 (1955) 385–386.

The *Colonial Office List, 1960* describes Aden Colony as comprising:

"(a) The peninsula on which are situated the main town known as Crater, the wharf and shipyard area of Maala, the modern harbour suburb known as Tawahi, adjacent to which is an area leased to the Air Ministry for R.A.F. and military purposes and known collectively as Steamer Point.

"(b) The isthmus known as Khormaksar where a large R.A.F. station is situated.

"(c) The strip of mainland between the two peninsulas which encloses the modern harbour and contains the township of Sheikh Othman and the villages of Hiswa and Imad.

"(d) The Little Aden peninsula where a modern refinery has been constructed by the Anglo-Iranian Oil Company Limited and where the two fishing villages of Bureika and Fukum lie.

"The Island of Perim and the Kuria Muria Islands off the Dhufar Coast of Oman, also form part of the Colony."

Colonial Office List, 1960, p. 56.

"The region is divided into two parts: the Western Protectorate and the Eastern Protectorate. With the exception of the Sultan of Lahej, the chiefs in the Western Protectorate generally possess only limited control over their subjects; the states in the Eastern Protectorate are more fully organized. In contrast with the Colony, the native governmental institutions in the Protectorate were left intact, and the area is administered according to the principles of indirect rule. The Crown has reserved the right to make laws for the peace, good order, and government of the Protectorate. At the same time the Governor may enact certain rules and orders and may especially extend to the Protectorate legislation enacted for the Colony. Such legislation, however, applies only to persons who are not natives of the Protectorate. This point is of considerable practical importance. For example, the mining legislation for the Colony of Aden, which was extended to the Protectorate by the Governor in 1937, would apply to all foreign, including British, companies, but not to a native unless it had been made a part of the local legislation in the individual state in question. The situation with regard to the judicial organization is similar in that the Supreme Court and the inferior courts of the Colony have jurisdiction in all matters arising in the Protectorate in which any person who is not a native is concerned.

"The relations of the British with the various native states in the Aden Protectorate are based on treaties concluded with the sultans and sheikhs in the course of the nineteenth and the early twentieth centuries. . . . The important features of these agreements are the extension of British protection to the native state

Aden
Protectorate

in question, and the promise of the local ruler not to enter into relations with any foreign government without British consent, or to dispose of any part of his territory in favor of a power other than Great Britain. . . .

"The protectorates thus established restrict the sovereignty of the local rulers to a very considerable degree. As far as international relations (including those with their immediate neighbors) are concerned, they are wholly unable to pursue an independent course. In internal affairs there exists a somewhat larger degree of autonomy, but British over-all control extends, in most cases, to all fields of administration, as far as such exists at all in the individual states.

"Treaties of the above type were concluded with rulers in the Eastern as well as the Western Protectorate. The relationship between the British and the important sultans in the so-called Hadramaut in the Eastern Protectorate was modified, however, in the nineteen thirties. On August 13, 1937, an agreement was concluded between the British Government and the Sultan of Shihr and Mukalla in which the former agreed to provide a Resident Adviser for the sultanate. This was followed in February 1939 by a similar agreement with the Sultan of Seyun, who had not been previously in direct treaty relations with the British. [Seyun had an agreement with Mukalla, concluded in 1918, in which it was stated that the Hadramaut 'being an appanage of the British Empire,' should be one province. The Agreement was renewed in a revised form in 1939.] In these treaties the native rulers agreed to take the advice of the Resident Adviser in all matters except those concerning Moslem religion and custom. These treaties did not abrogate earlier agreements, such as the protectorate treaty with the Sultan of Mukalla of 1890, but were supplementary to them. . . . In 1939 . . . a State Council was set up in Mukalla. It is presided over by the Sultan and consists of the Resident Adviser, the State Secretary, and two nominated Arab members. The Council acts as the Sultan's cabinet.

.   .   .   .

". . . The British have . . . refrained from establishing by general ordinance the rights and duties of native authorities and native courts, and from giving the Governor the right to constitute and abolish them. Constitutionally speaking, . . . the internal sovereign rights left to the Protectorate rulers are not regarded as derived from British authority but as inherent in the ruling chief.

"In this connection it should also be mentioned that a decision of the High Court of Bombay in 1897 accorded the Sultan of Shihr and Mukalla immunity from jurisdiction, thereby putting him into the same category as the Indian and Malay rulers. [Chandu Lal Kushalji v. Awad bin Umar, Sultan of Shihr and Mukalla, *Indian Law Reports, Bombay Series*, 1897, p. 351.] The chiefs of the African protectorates, on the other hand, are not granted immunity and may be sued in British courts like any private individual. [Tshekedi Khama v. Ratshosa, *Law Re-*

ports, Appeal Cases, 1931, pp. 784–98.] . . . The granting of immunity from jurisdiction means that the respective rulers are regarded as sovereigns and, as a basic rule, cannot be sued in foreign courts. . . . " [While the treaties between the British Government and the native rulers in the Aden Protectorate continue in force, Western Protectorate rulers of the Amirate of Beihan, the 'Audhali Sultanate, the Fadhli Sultanate, the Amirate of Dhala, the Upper 'Aulaqi Shaikhdom and the Lower Yafa'i Sultanate established a Federation of Arab Amirates of the South with the conclusion of an additional Treaty of Friendship and Protection with Great Britain, February 11, 1959. See *post*, pp. 470 ff.]

Liebesny, "International Relations of Arabia: The Dependent Areas", *The Middle East Journal*, vol. 1 (1947) 152–156.

Toward the end of World War II, States in the Western Aden Protectorate followed the pattern inaugurated in the Eastern Aden Protectorate (see above) of entering into advisory treaties which gave the British authority to intervene in the internal administration of these protected states. The first of the series of these treaties concluded with the Western Aden Protectorate States was that with the Sharif of Baihan, signed on March 22, 1944. In reaffirming the treaties entered into by himself and his predecessors for himself and his successors, the Sharif declared that he would "at all times cooperate fully with and accept the advice of the Governor of Aden in all matters connected with the welfare and development of the territory of Beihan and its Dependencies".

For the text of the Treaty with Baihan, see Ingrams, *A Survey of Social and Economic Conditions in the Aden Protectorate* (1949) 178–179. See also, Liebesny, "Administration and Legal Development in Arabia—Aden Colony and Protectorate", *The Middle East Journal*, vol. 9 (1955) 385, 389–390. Similar advisory treaties have been concluded since 1944 with the following Aden Protectorate States: Habili Amirate of Baihan, Lower 'Aulaqi Sultanate, Fadhli Sultanate, Amiri Amirate of Dhala, Lower Yafa'i Sultanate, Wahidi Sultanate of Balhaf, Upper 'Aulaqi Shaikhdom, 'Audhali Sultanate, 'Abdali Sultanate of Lahej, Mahri Sultanate of Quishn and Socotra, and Shaikhdom of Shu'aib (Upper Yafa'i). Office of Near Eastern Affairs (Eilts) to Office of Legal Adviser (Willis), memorandum, "Aden Protectorate Advisory Treaties", June 6, 1961, MS. Department of State, file 641.46c7/6–661.

The Western Aden Protectorate consists of the following States: (1) Federation of Arab Amirates of the South, comprising: (a) 'Abdali Sultanate of Lahej, (b) Fadhli Sultanate, (c) Lower Yafa'i Sultanate, (d) 'Aqrabi Shaikhdom, (e) Upper 'Aulaqi Shaikhdom, (f) Habili Amirate of Baihan, (g) Dathina Confederacy, (h) Lower 'Aulaqi Sultanate, (i) 'Audhali Sultanate, and (j) Dhala Amirate; (2) Upper 'Aulaqi Sultanate; (3) 'Alawi Shaikhdom; (4) Haushabi Sultanate; and (5) the Upper Yafa'i Sultanate.

The Eastern Protectorate is comprised of five units specified as follows: Qu'aiti Sultanate of Shihr and Mukalla; Kathiri Sultanate; Mahri Sultanate of Quishn and Socotra (*i.e.*, Socotra Island); Wahidi Sultanate of Balhaf which now includes the two former separate treaty shaikhdoms of Haura and Irqa; Wahidi Sultanate of Bir 'Ali.

For the text of treaties between these Protectorates and Great Britain, see XI Aitchison, *Treaties, Engagements and Sanads* (1933) 1–178.

With reference to the protection "treaties" concluded between the British Government and the native chiefs of Aden hinterland, Professor Robbins observes:

> "These instruments are recognizable internationally as following the pattern of protectorates, but in international law they are not regarded as treaties, conventions, or agreements. If the British Crown should decide to override them, no international liability would be incurred, nor would any procedure under the constitutional law of the Empire lie against the Crown. [. . . the dictum of M. Max Huber, Arbitrator of the Palmas Island Case, this Journal, Vol. 22 (1928), 897–8: "As regards contracts between a state or a company such as the Dutch East India Company and native princes or chiefs of peoples not recognized as members of the community of nations, they are not, in the international law sense, treaties or conventions capable of creating rights and obligations such as may in international law arise out of treaties. But on the other hand, contracts of this nature are not wholly void of indirect effects on situations governed by international law; if they do not constitute titles in international law, they are nonetheless facts of which the law must in certain circumstances take account."] . . . But the common feature is that in all cases there has been a cession to the Crown of complete control of all external affairs, and the position has always been taken that for external purposes the states are part of the British Empire. Thus principles of international law have no direct bearing upon the native states any more than they would upon unincorporated territory under the sovereignty of the United States. . . ." Robbins, "The Legal Status of Aden Colony and the Aden Protectorate", 33 Am. J. Int'l L. (1939) 705, 706.

". . . the countries of the Aden Protectorate cannot be regarded as subjects of international law, and the treaties concluded by Great Britain with these states would fall into the same category as those concluded with Indian rajahs and African chiefs; that is, they are not regarded as internationally binding and can be disregarded or unilaterally altered by the imperial power. This interpretation, which is often at variance with the construction placed upon these treaties by the local governments, is based upon the doctrine that the [such] African and Oriental states cannot be regarded as states at all or at least not as states in the Western sense. Therefore they cannot be members of the 'Western family of nations' and subjects of international law."

Liebesny, "International Relations of Arabia: The Dependent Areas", *The Middle East Journal*, vol. 1 (1947) 166.

Professor Robbins has summarized the distinguishing features between the Aden Colony and Aden Protectorate as follows:

". . . (1) Although the same British officials make up the magistracy of both areas, the organic laws of Aden and the Aden

Protectorate are separate Orders in Council. (2) Other states are precluded from the Protectorate to the same degree as they are from the Colony, for any political or diplomatic relations with the former must be carried on via the Colonial Office through which the Crown exercises jurisdiction in the Protectorate. (3) The inhabitants of the Colony are distinct from those of the Protectorate. All persons born in the Colony are British subjects. Legislation passed by the Crown for British possessions extends to the Colony. The inhabitants of the Protectorate are not British subjects, but rather 'British protected persons.' In foreign countries, these 'protected persons' are entitled to British diplomatic protection, and in foreign countries with independent governments in which the Crown exercises extraterritorial jurisdiction, they are treated as entitled to the same exemption from local law as are British subjects. Legislation by the Imperial Parliament extends to British protectorates only when it is clearly apparent from the terms of the Act in question that such is intended. (4) Despite the degree of British jurisdiction internally, and complete control of external affairs by the protecting state, the Protectorate does not in law form an integral part of the Crown's domains because it has never been acquired by settlement, cession, conquest, or annexed by His Majesty."

Robbins, "The Legal Status of Aden Colony and the Aden Protectorate", 33 Am. J. Int'l L. (1939) 707, 712.

". . . For a long time the relationship of the Persian Gulf principalities to the United Kingdom was defined merely as 'a special treaty relationship with H.M. Government'. [See, for example, the British note to the U.S. Government, *Papers Relating to the Foreign Relations of the United States*, 1932, vol. 3, p. 14.] Only very recently have these principalities been put officially into the category, at least for some purposes, of British-protected states. Thus the British Protectorates, Protected States and Protected Persons Order in Council of 1949 declared that for the purposes of the British Nationality Act of 1948, Kuwait, Bahrein, Qatar, and the Trucial States were regarded as protected states. They were thus put into the same category as the Malay States, Brunei, Tonga, and the Maldive Islands. [Statutory Instruments 1949, vol. 1, part 1, p. 522. See also Second Schedule, p. 526.] There appears to be a tendency to apply this terminology generally to the Persian Gulf principalities, thus systematizing their status more than had heretofore been the case. [See, for example, Sir Rupert Hay, "The Persian Gulf States and Their Boundary Problems," *Geographical Journal*, vol. 120 (1954), p. 433; *The Statesman's Yearbook 1952*, p. 762, which in contrast to prior years characterizes the Persian Gulf principalities as British-protected states.]

"At the same time, there is still a considerable difference in status between these principalities and the states in the Aden hinterland, which are part of a protectorate. [Statutory Instruments 1949, vol. 1, part 1, p. 526, First Schedule.] Until India became independent, the British Persian Gulf establishment was subordinated administratively to the Government of India. The highest official in the Gulf, the Political Resident, had his seat at Bushire on the Iranian side of the Gulf, from where he moved to Bahrein during World War II. After the independence of India was declared in 1947, the Persian Gulf establishment was subordinated to the Foreign Office in London. As a result the personnel of the establishment was gradually changed over from members of the India Political Service to members of the Foreign Service.

.   .   .   .

". . . The Persian Gulf principalities have remained outside the Colonial Office organization. Their administration by the Foreign Office appears to emphasize their character as basically independent states under the protection of a foreign power. Unlike Aden, there is no colonial establishment into which the administration of the area can be dovetailed. Also, unlike the Aden Protectorate, the British officials in the Persian Gulf are not at the same time advisers to the local rulers. While there are rather elaborate advisory establishments in the various principalities outside the Trucial Coast, they are staffed by individuals, generally British, who are employed and paid by the local rulers and who have no official connection with the British Political Resident Persian Gulf and his subordinates. The function of the Residency is therefore limited to the conduct of foreign relations and the safeguarding of peace and over-all British interests. In addition, the British officials in the Gulf exercise judicial jurisdiction with regard to British subjects and, to a varying extent, with regard to foreigners."

Liebesny, "Administration and Legal Development in Arabia: The Persian Gulf Principalities", *The Middle East Journal*, vol. 10 (1956) 33–35.   For accession of Aden Colony to Federation of South Arabia, see *post*, p. 472.

Persian Gulf
States:
Bahrein

The present status of Bahrein is based on the Agreement of December 22, 1880, wherein the Ruler of Bahrein bound himself and his successors "to abstain from entering into negotiations or making treaties of any sort with any State or Government other than the British without the consent of the said British Government, and to refuse permission to any other Government than the British to establish diplomatic or consular agencies or coaling depots in our territory, unless with the consent of the British Government."

While the Agreement of 1880 exempts from its terms "the customary friendly correspondence with the local authorities of neighbouring States on business of minor importance", the Agreement of March 13, 1892, in reaffirming the Agreement of 1880 with respect to the conduct of foreign relations stipulates that the Ruler of Bahrein "will on no account enter into any agreement or correspondence with any Power other than the British Government" and that he "will on no account cede, sell, mortgage or otherwise give for occupation any part of my [his] territory save to the British Government".

XI Aitchison, *Treaties, Engagements and Sanads* (1933) 237, 238.

". . . As a result of these stipulations, . . . the foreign relations of Bahrein were brought under full British control. The treaties with Bahrein do not contain any clause expressly extending British protection to the country; nevertheless, Bahrein can be regarded as a British-protected state enjoying a large degree of internal autonomy.

. . . . . .

"The position of Bahrein as an independent sheikhdom under British protection has been challenged repeatedly by the Iranian Government, which claims sovereignty over the islands on historical grounds. Protests have been made to the British Government intermittently since 1829, and have been as often repudiated. The most extensive airing of the dispute took place between 1927 and 1930, when Iran protested against Article 6 of the Treaty of Jidda concluded in 1927 between Great Britain and Saudi Arabia. There Bahrein had been referred to as a state in special treaty relations with the British Government. In a lengthy exchange of notes both governments set forth their points of view. Iran claimed that Bahrein had been under its unchallenged sovereignty before the British intervened, and that Iranian sovereignty over the islands had been recognized by Lord Clarendon, the British Foreign Secretary, in 1869. This claim was denied in the British notes, which stated that the Sheikh of Bahrein had on various occasions during the first half of the nineteenth century professed only 'an unwilling allegiance' to the Ottoman Empire, Persia, and various Arab countries, and that often conflicting claims to sovereignty over Bahrein had been put forward in the course of time by a number of countries. Britain denied that Lord Clarendon had ever recognized the Iranian claim.

"Iran forwarded its original note of protest to the League of Nations under Article 10 of the Covenant; all subsequent notes were likewise sent to the Secretary-General of the League. However, the League took no action in the conflict and no settlement was ever reached. Iran again asserted its position when it protested to the U.S. Government in 1933 against the Sheikh's grant of an oil concession to an American company, stating that it regarded the concession as null and void since it was granted by authorities who had no right to do so. Iran also reserved the right to claim all profits from the concession, and possible damages. The U.S. Government apparently did not reply to this note. Likewise, when Bahrein was bombed by Italian planes in October 1940, Iran, which was then neutral, protested to Italy against this alleged violation of its territory. The Iranian claim was brought up again in 1946 when it seems to have found some support in the Russian press.

"The dispute regarding the sovereignty over Bahrein is one of those territorial disputes, not uncommon in Asia, in which one party bases its claims on historical arguments dating back several centuries; but it is doubtful whether the yardstick of Western international law and its definition of sovereignty and undisturbed possession can be applied at all to the situation prevailing in the Persian Gulf in the seventeenth, eighteenth, and early nineteenth centuries. It is likely that the relationship between the large Eastern empires and the small tribal sheikhdoms was one of suzerainty rather than sovereignty, and that allegiances shifted fairly rapidly. However, it should be noted that the Iranian claim has never been settled. . . ."

Liebesny, "International Relations of Arabia: The Dependent Areas", *The Middle East Journal*, vol. 1 (1947) 157–160.

In reply to a question concerning the attitude of His Majesty's Government towards any change in the existing status (as of December 1947) of Bahrein Island in the Persian Gulf, the Secretary of State for Foreign Affairs (Bevin) declared:

"His Highness the Sheikh of Bahrein is recognised as the ruler of an Independent State under the protection of His Majesty's Government and in special Treaty relations with them. His Majesty's Government see no reason for any change in this status."

445 H.C. Deb. (5th ser.) cols. 1681–1682 (Dec. 17, 1947); see also 456 H.C. Deb. (5th ser.) col. 500 (Sept. 20, 1948).

Kuwait

The legal position of Kuwait was formerly determined by the Agreement of January 23, 1899, entered into by the Sheikh of Kuwait who pledged "not to receive the Agent or Representative of any Power or Government at Koweit, or at any other place within the limits of his territory, without the previous sanction of the British Government;" and "not to cede, sell, lease, mortgage, or give for occupation or for any other purpose any portion of his territory to the Government or subjects of any other Power without the previous consent of Her Majesty's Government for these purposes. . . ."

XI Aitchison, *Treaties, Engagements and Sanads* (1933) 262.

In connection with the application of Kuwait for admission to the United Nations Educational, Scientific and Cultural Organization as a full Member State in accordance with paragraph 2 of article II of the Constitution of the Organization, the United Kingdom Foreign Office stated in a letter of May 23, 1960, to the Director-General of UNESCO that—

". . . Her Majesty's Government regard Kuwait as responsible for the conduct of her international relations".

Application from Kuwait for membership in the United Nations Educational, Scientific and Cultural Organization, Provisional Agenda for the Thirtieth Session of the Economic and Social Council, E/3363/Add.2, June 17, 1960, p. 4.

The gradual return of jurisdiction to the Ruler of Kuwait by Queen's Regulations was provided for by the Kuwait (Amendment) Order, 1960 (Stat. Instr., 1960, No. 207) effective February 25, 1960, which in amending the Kuwait Order, 1959 (Stat. Instr., 1959, No. 1036) made further provision for the exercise of jurisdiction within the territories of the Ruler of Kuwait by treaty, capitulation, grant, usage, sufferance, and other lawful means, thereby repealing the Kuwait Orders, 1953 to 1957 which had originally ordered the exercise of such jurisdiction (see: Stat. Instr. 1953/1211, 1954/1702, 1956/828, 2034, 1957/1526 (1953 I, p. 931; 1954 I, p. 1029; 1956 I, pp. 1113, 1115; 1957 I, p. 1227)). In pursuance thereof, the Secretary of State for Foreign Affairs issued two Queen's Regulations dated February 25 and May 10, 1960, officializing the first two stages of the transfer of British legal jurisdiction to Kuwait authorities. The final Queen's Regulation of April 1, 1961, completing the transfer of jurisdiction, provided that outstanding cases would continue to be heard by British Courts. The Kuwait (Repealing) Order, 1961, terminating British jurisdiction within Kuwait, provided that proceedings under the Kuwait Order, 1959, pending on July 1, 1961, in any of the British Courts established by that Order, shall be transferred to the Ruler's Court on that date.

The American Consul in Kuwait (Seelye) to the Secretary of State (Herter), despatch No. 379, June 28, 1960, MS. Department of State, file 786d.022/6-2860; 1961 Stat. Instr., No. 1001.

The United Kingdom and the State of Kuwait, in an exchange of notes on June 19, 1961, constituting an Agreement, referred to discussions between the two Governments concerning the "desirability of adapting the relationship of the United Kingdom of Great Britain and Northern Ireland and the State of Kuwait to take account of the fact that Your Highness' Government has the sole responsibility for the conduct of Kuwait's internal and external affairs" and recorded the following conclusions reached during the course of the discussions:

"(a) The Agreement of the 23rd of January, 1899 [printed in the Annex], shall be terminated as being inconsistent with the sovereignty and independence of Kuwait.

"(b) The relations between the two countries shall continue to be governed by a spirit of close friendship.

"(c) When appropriate the two Governments shall consult together on matters which concern them both.

"(d) Nothing in these conclusions shall affect the readiness of Her Majesty's Government to assist the Government of Kuwait if the latter request such assistance."

Exchange of Notes regarding Relations between the United Kingdom of Great Britain and Northern Ireland and the State of Kuwait, Cmnd. 1409.

Commenting in the House of Commons on the Kuwait Exchange of Notes on June 19, 1961, the Lord Privy Seal (Edward Heath) stated:

"For some time past the State of Kuwait has possessed entire responsibility for the conduct of its own international relations, and, with the full support of Her Majesty's Government, Kuwait has already joined a number of international organisations as an independent sovereign State.

"This development has rendered obsolete and inappropriate the terms of the Anglo-Kuwaiti Agreement of 23rd January, 1899, under which Kuwait undertook not to receive representatives of other Powers or to dispose of her territory, without the prior agreement of Her Majesty's Government.

"Her Majesty's Government and the Ruler of Kuwait have agreed that the necessary formal step should be taken to cancel this agreement.

"The exchange of Notes which has achieved this also states that relations between the two countries shall continue to be governed by a spirit of close friendship and that when appropriate the two Governments shall consult together on matters of common interest. The Notes conclude by reaffirming the readiness of Her Majesty's Government to assist Kuwait if the Government of Kuwait so request."

642 H.C. Deb. (5th ser.) col. 955 (June 19, 1961).

On June 25, 1961, 6 days after the exchange of notes on June 19, the Baghdad Government claimed Kuwait as an integral part of Iraq. Troop movements in Iraq were reported and Iraq radio broadcasts reiterated Qassim's claim to the territory of Kuwait. Upon request of the Kuwaiti Government, the United Kingdom dispatched troops to Kuwait in compliance with paragraph (d) of the exchange of notes of June 19 (*supra*). Following requests by Kuwait on July 1 and by Iraq on July 2 for inscription of issues involved on the Security Council agenda, the Security Council on July 2 adopted agenda item " 'Complaint by Kuwait in respect of the situation arising from the threat by Iraq to the territorial independence of Kuwait, which is likely to endanger the maintenance of international peace and security' (S/4845 and S/4844) 'Complaint by the Government of the Republic of Iraq in respect of the situation arising out of the armed threat by the United Kingdom to the independence and security of

Iraq, which is likely to endanger the maintenance of international peace and security' (S/4847)" (S/Agenda/957/Rev. 1, July 2, 1961).

During the discussion of this agenda item on July 2, the United Kingdom representative, Sir Patrick Dean, made the following statement:

> ". . . for some time past the State of Kuwait has possessed entire responsibility for the conduct of its own international relations and, with the full support of Her Majesty's Government, Kuwait has in the past joined a number of international organizations as an independent sovereign State. This development rendered obsolete and inappropriate the terms of the Anglo-Kuwaiti agreement of 23 January 1899. Her Majesty's Government and the Ruler of Kuwait therefore agreed that the necessary formal step should be taken to cancel this agreement.
>
> "Accordingly, on 19 June last, Notes were exchanged by the Ruler of Kuwait and the British Political Representative in the Persian Gulf, the effect of which was formally to establish and recognize a state of affairs which had in fact obtained for some time previously. This step was in accordance with the wishes of and aspirations of Kuwait. It was also a step fully in accordance with the long established policy of the United Kingdom. It was in accordance with the Charter of the United Nations and with the aims which have often found expression at this Council and in the General Assembly." (S/PV.957, July 2, 1961, p. 12.)

In reference to a cable dated July 1, 1961, from the State Secretary of Kuwait to the President of the Security Council which read, "I am instructed by His Highness the Ruler of Kuwait and in accordance with paragraph two of Article 35 of the United Nations Charter, I have the honour to request you, in your capacity as President of the Security Council, to call a meeting of the Council to consider urgently the following question: "Complaint by Kuwait in respect of the situation arising from threats by Iraq to the territorial independence of Kuwait which is likely to endanger the maintenance of international peace and security", the permanent representative of Iraq, Adnan Pachachi, in a letter dated July 2, 1961, to the President of the Security Council, stated:

> "I would like to state emphatically on behalf of my Government that this 'complaint' is not receivable by the Security Council since paragraph 2 of Article 35 of the Charter relates to the right of States, not Members of the United Nations, to bring questions to the attention of the Security Council.
>
> "Kuwait is not and has never been an independent State. It has always been considered, historically and legally, a part of the Basrah Province of Iraq. There can be no question of an international dispute arising between Iraq and Kuwait since the

latter is an integral part of the Iraqi Republic." (S/4844, July 1, 1961; S/4848, July 2, 1961.)

The permanent representative of Iraq further developed this argument during the discussions of the Security Council on this agenda item which he prefaced with the declaration that his participation in the discussions of the Security Council was only in the context of the dispute between the United Kingdom and Iraq. (S/PV.957, July 2, 1961, pp. 32–36. See also S/PV.959, July 6, 1961, pp. 62–70.)

While addressing the whole of the Iraq argument in detail, the representative of Kuwait (admitted by invitation of the Security Council, S/PV.958, July 5, 1961, pp. 17–21) stated in part:

> "The agreement of 19 June 1961 between the Government of the United Kingdom and that of Kuwait did not in fact give birth to the independence of Kuwait; it merely recognized the status quo as it had become, as a result of the long-range strategy and wise diplomacy of His Highness, the Ruler of Kuwait. Previous to the formal announcement of her independence, Kuwait had already taken long strides in the field of international diplomacy, proving that she was a sovereign State. Even before the abrogation of the Treaty of 1899 with Great Britain, Kuwait had achieved all of the traditional aspects by which a sovereign State is recognized and defined.
>
> "The Government of Iraq has not only witnessed but aided Kuwait in its development as an independent State. Iraqi delegates themselves have backed Kuwait's applications for membership in many international organizations. Beginning with 24 July 1959, Kuwait has successively been admitted to the following International Organizations: the International Union for Telecommunication, the World Mail Union, the International Civil Aviation Organization, the World Health Organization, UNESCO and the International Labour Organization. Certainly membership in these organizations constitutes international recognition of the independence of Kuwait." (S/PV.958, July 5, 1961, p. 48.)

The United States representative, Mr. Plimpton, stated:

> "The United States regards Kuwait as a sovereign independent State and supports the desire of the Kuwait Government and the Kuwait people to remain fully independent and fully free. In 1960 we concluded an international agreement directly with Kuwait. Kuwait is a member of UNESCO, ICAO and the various other international agencies mentioned by its representative. The United States supported its admission to these agencies and we will fully support its application for membership of the United Nations." (*Ibid.*, p. 51. Two draft resolutions, S/4855, July 6, 1961, and S/4856, July 7, 1961, failed of adoption.)

In the Treaty of November 3, 1916, between the British Govern- Qatar
ment and the Sheikh of Qatar, the latter undertook not to "have relations nor correspond with, nor receive the agent of, any other Power
without the consent of the High British Government;" nor ". . . without such consent, cede to any other Power or its subjects, land either
on lease, sale, transfer, gift, or in any other way whatsoever" (IV).

The British Government in turn agreed to protect the Sheikh and
the territory of Qatar from all aggression by sea, do their utmost to
exact reparation for all injuries that the Sheikh or his subjects may
suffer when proceeding to sea upon lawful occasions, and to grant
good offices when attacked by land (X, XI).

An Agreement concluded in 1934 extended fuller British protection over Qatar.

> XI Aitchison, *Treaties, Engagements and Sanads* (1933) 258, 259–260.
> Liebesny, "International Relations of Arabia : The Dependent Areas", *The
> Middle East Journal*, vol. 1 (1947) 148, 162.

The legal relationship of Trucial Oman was established with the Trucial Oman
conclusion of the Exclusive Agreement of March 6, 1892, between
the Chief of Abu Dhabi with the British Government and the five
Agreements subsequently signed by the other Trucial Sheikhs—the
Chiefs of Dubai, Ajman, Shargah, Ras-ul-Khima, and Umm-ul-
Gawain. (The first three dated the 7th and the last two the 8th of
March, 1892, are identical in form.)

In the Exclusive Agreement, the Chief of Abu Dhabi bound himself, his heirs and successors that he "will on no account enter into
any agreement or correspondence with any Power other than the
British Government"; "That without the assent of the British Government . . . [he] will not consent to the residence within my [his]
territory of the agent of any other Government"; and "will on no
account cede, sell, mortgage or otherwise give for occupation any part
of my [his] territory, save to the British Government".

> XI Aitchison, *Treaties, Engagements and Sanads* (1933) 256, 257.

The Sultanate of Muscat and Oman is an independent State in close Muscat and
relations with the British Government. However, the Sultanate is Oman
not as closely tied to the United Kingdom as the principalities of the
Persian Gulf: the Sultan has retained more attributes of external
and internal sovereignty than have the other rulers. Thus the United
Kingdom is responsible for the conduct of foreign relations of the
Persian Gulf principalities but is not responsible for the foreign relations of this Sultanate. The Sultanate is within the purview of the
British Political Resident Persian Gulf, but the United Kingdom is

represented in Muscat and Oman by a Consul General and not by a Political Agent as in the principalities. Again in contrast to the usage with regard to the Persian Gulf principalities, relations are regulated at present by a Treaty of Friendship, Commerce and Navigation concluded on December 20, 1951. Treaty Series No. 44 (1952), Cmd. 8633.

The difference in relationship between the United Kingdom and the Persian Gulf principalities on the one hand and the Sultanate of Muscat and Oman on the other is illustrated by the Arbitration Agreement concerning the Buraimi oasis which was concluded between Saudi Arabia and the United Kingdom on July 30, 1954. Treaty Series No. 65 (1954), Cmd. 9272. The preamble to that Agreement states:

> "The Government of the United Kingdom of Great Britain and Northern Ireland and the Government of the Kingdom of Saudi Arabia;
> "Considering that there is a dispute as to the location of the common frontier between Saudi Arabia and Abu Dhabi and as to the sovereignty in the Buraimi oasis; that Abu Dhabi is a State for the conduct of whose foreign relations the Government of the United Kingdom is responsible and that His Highness Sultan Said bin Taimur [of Muscat and Oman] has appointed the Government of the United Kingdom to conduct all negotiations and proceedings on his behalf for the settlement of the dispute in so far as it relates to territory in the Buraimi oasis claimed by him to belong to Muscat and Oman; . . ."

It thus appears that while the United Kingdom intervened on behalf of Abu Dhabi on the basis of its general responsibility for Abu Dhabi's foreign relations, in the case of Muscat and Oman a special authorization was required.

Like the Persian Gulf rulers, the Sultan of Muscat and Oman by an Agreement of March 20, 1891, did

> ". . . pledge and bind himself, his heirs and successors never to cede, to sell, to mortgage or otherwise give for occupation, save to the British Government, the dominions of Muscat and Oman or any of their dependencies." (XI Aitchison, *op. cit.* 317–318.)

Unlike the Persian Gulf rulers, however, the Sultan did not pledge himself not to enter into any agreement with a third power or accept the agent of a third power. Such a pledge was impossible in the case of Muscat and Oman because treaty relations already existed with the United States (1833), France (1841 and 1844), and the Netherlands (1877).

> "The status of Muscat as an independent sultanate was affirmed by the Hague Court of Arbitration in its decision in the

Muscat Dow Case in 1905. Britain itself has indicated that it does not put Muscat into the same category as the other Persian Gulf shaikhdoms by giving, for example, the Political Agent in Muscat the official title of consul."

Liebesny, "International Relations of Arabia: The Dependent Areas", *The Middle East Journal*, vol. 1, (1947) 148, 163.

In answer to a question posed in the House of Commons concerning what action His Majesty's Government was taking in response to a request of the Sultan of Muscat and Oman for assistance during the July 1957 disturbances from dissidents in Central Oman, the Secretary of State for Foreign Affairs, Selwyn Lloyd, distinguished between simply responding to a request for assistance and doing so in virtue of a treaty obligation. He said—

"May I make it clear that we are not doing this under a treaty obligation? We have no treaty obligation to deal with internal affairs in the territory of Muscat. We have certain duties in respect of external affairs, but not in respect of internal affairs. We are giving the full support which we think a staunch friend requires."

574 H.C. Deb. (5th ser.) col. 34 (July 22, 1957).

In a written answer to a question concerning the position of Oman as of June 1958, the Minister of State for Foreign Affairs, Commander Allan Noble, wrote that ". . . Oman is part of the Sultanate of Muscat and Oman, which is an independent sovereign state and Her Majesty's Government have accordingly no responsibility for the internal affairs of the territory which are the concern of the Sultan of Muscat and Oman."

Written Answers, 589 H.C. Deb. (5th ser.) col. 83 (June 18, 1958). See discussion regarding the status of Oman in the Security Council between the representatives of Iraq and the United Kingdom in connection with a proposal for inscription of an item charging the British with armed aggression against the Imamate of Oman. S/3865 and Add. 1; S/PV.783. At the 17th session of the General Assembly, a draft resolution recognizing Oman's right to self-determination and independence was rejected. A/PV.1191, Dec. 11, 1962.

Reporting on the outbreak of hostilities between the British troops and Omanis in Oman, the New York *Times* on August 3, 1959, quoted the Imam of Oman as saying that the Omanis recognize him not only as their religious leader but also as "president of an independent republic". He was reported to have stated that the late Imam Mohamed ben Abdullah al-Khalili had recommended him as his successor. After the former Imam's death in 1954, Oman's leaders "elected him for life" as sole ruler.

A British Foreign Office spokesman was quoted as saying with reference to the Imam of Oman that "He is not a rebel against the British, but against the Sultan of Muscat."

The New York *Times*, Aug. 3, 1959, p. 4.

Tonga

Under the Treaty of Friendship between the United Kingdom and Tonga, concluded August 26, 1958, the United Kingdom remains responsible for the protection of Tonga and for the conduct of its foreign affairs.

Article III of the Treaty provides as follows:

"(1) The external relations of the Kingdom of Tonga shall be conducted by and be the responsibility of the Government of the United Kingdom, except in so far as the conduct of such relations may be entrusted by the Government of the United Kingdom to the Government of Her Majesty The Queen of Tonga (hereinafter referred to as the Government of Tonga).

"(2) The Government of the United Kingdom shall consult with the Government of Tonga regarding the conduct of the external relations of the Kingdom of Tonga and in particular shall consult with the Government of Tonga before entering into any international agreement for or in relation to the Kingdom of Tonga.

"(3) Her Majesty The Queen of Tonga shall take such steps as may appear to the Government of the United Kingdom to be necessary to secure compliance with any international agreement entered into by the Government of the United Kingdom for or in relation to the Kingdom of Tonga and any other obligation imposed by international law in relation to the Kingdom of Tonga."

Article IV, after providing that "Her Britannic Majesty shall at all times to the utmost of Her power take whatever steps may appear to the Government of the United Kingdom to be necessary for the defence and security of the Kingdom of Tonga; . . .", outlines more specifically the cooperation between the two States to this end.

The Government of Tonga's legislative powers were circumscribed within the limits set out in article V under which the Government of Tonga is obligated to consult with and obtain the consent of the Government of the United Kingdom before any legislation is enacted in the Kingdom of Tonga "(a) relating to defence, banking, currency and exchange; or (b) whereby persons who are not Tongan subjects may be subjected to or made liable to any disabilities or restrictions to which Tongan subjects are not also subjected or made liable."

Article VII, regulating judicial matters, provides for reduced jurisdiction of Her Britannic Majesty's Courts over British subjects and foreigners. While all civil actions are to be heard by the Tongan Courts, jurisdiction over criminal proceedings involving non-Tongans for offenses which are punishable by death or by imprisonment for more than 2 years are retained by Her Britannic Majesty's Courts.

"Treaty of Friendship between Great Britain and Tonga 1958 and Associated Papers", published by Command, 'I he Fekau Tungi, Premier, Palemia; the American Embassy, London, to the Secretary of State (Dulles), despatch No. 535, Aug. 28, 1958, MS. Department of State, file 641.46n4/8–2858.

A Memorandum on Revised Treaty of Friendship stated with respect to the official status of Tonga:

"The draft Treaty assumes that Her Majesty, the Queen of Tonga, will wish the Kingdom of Tonga to continue as a Protected State within the British Commonwealth, and has been drafted with a view to giving the Government of Tonga the maximum independence of action and control over its own affairs as is consistent with its constitutional status and its present state of development. . . ."

Ibid.

The August 8, 1949, Treaty between Bhutan and India which was ^{Bhutan} intended "to regulate in a friendly manner and upon a solid and durable basis the state of affairs caused by the termination of the British Government's authority in India . . ." provided in its principal article relating to the legal status of Bhutan:

"Article 2. The Government of India undertakes to exercise no interference in the internal administration of Bhutan. On its part the Government of Bhutan agrees to be guided by the advice of the Government of India in regard to its external relations."

The Counselor of the American Embassy, New Delhi (Donovan), to the Secretary of State (Acheson), despatch No. 60, Jan. 9, 1950, encl., MS. Department of State, file 690a.91/1–950; I Peaslee, *Constitutions of Nations* (1956) 172.

A Treaty between India and Sikkim, signed December 5, 1950, by ^{Sikkim} the Political Officer in Sikkim on behalf of the President of India and His Highness the Maharaja of Sikkim, stipulated in article II:

"Sikkim shall continue to be a Protectorate of India and, subject to the provisions of this Treaty, shall enjoy autonomy in regard to its internal affairs."

Defense and external relations provided for in articles III and IV, respectively, were regulated as follows:

"Article III. (1) The Government of India will be responsible for the defence and territorial integrity of Sikkim. It shall have the right to take such measures as it considers necessary for the defence of Sikkim or the security of India, whether preparatory or otherwise, and whether within or outside Sikkim. In particular, the Government of India shall have the right to station troops anywhere within Sikkim.

"(2) The measures referred to in paragraph (1) will as far as possible be taken by the Government of India in consultation with the Government of Sikkim.

"(3) The Government of Sikkim shall not import any arms, ammunition, military stores or other warlike material of any description for any purpose whatsoever without the previous consent of the Government of India.

"Article IV. (1) The external relations of Sikkim, whether political, economic or financial, shall be conducted and regulated solely by the Government of India; and the Government of Sikkim shall have no dealings with any foreign power.

"(2) Subjects of Sikkim travelling to foreign countries shall be treated as Indian protected persons for the purpose of passports, and shall receive from Indian representatives abroad the same protection and facilities as Indian nationals."

While under article VIII it was provided that "Indian nationals within Sikkim shall be subject to the laws of Sikkim and subjects of Sikkim within India shall be subject to the laws of India", it was agreed that whenever any criminal proceedings are initiated in Sikkim against any Indian national or any person in the service of the Government of India or any foreigner, if the Indian Representative in Sikkim so demands, such person shall be handed over to him for trial before such court as may be established for the purpose by the Government of India either in Sikkim or outside.

> India-Sikkim Treaty, the American Embassy (Loy Henderson), New Delhi, to the Secretary of State (Acheson), despatch No. 1295, Dec. 7, 1950, encl. 1, MS. Department of State, file 791.022/12–750.

In answer to a parliamentary query, August 28, 1959, as to the truth of newspaper reports that the Chinese were trying to extend their influence in Bhutan, Sikkim, Ladakh, and the border areas of Nepal, Prime Minister Nehru declared:

> ". . . We have no information as to their validity or any responsible person having said this. But the fact remains that so far as Bhutan and Sikkim are concerned they are in treaty relations with us and we are responsible for their defense. I cannot imagine any foreign authority doing anything which is an infringement of their sovereignty. In any event, any such infringement would be an infringement of our undertakings with Sikkim and Bhutan, and we shall certainly resist every such intrusion."

> *Daily Report*, Middle East and West Europe, Foreign Broadcast Information Service, No. 169, 1959, Friday, Aug. 28, 1959, p. 02.

The Treaty of Peace and Friendship concluded between Nepal and India July 31, 1950, in providing for the cancellation of "all previous Treaties, Agreements, and engagements entered into on behalf of India between the British Government and the Government of Nepal", did not affect the independent status of Nepal but reconfirmed it in article I wherein the two Governments agreed "to acknowledge and respect the complete sovereignty, territorial integrity and independence of each other". 94 UNTS 3, 4, 8.

Commenting on Indian Prime Minister Nehru's statement of November 30, 1959, that "any aggression on Bhutan or Nepal will be considered by us as aggression on India", Prime Minister Koirala of Nepal said, "Nepal is a fully sovereign independent country. She decides her external and home policy according to her own judgment and in her own light without ever referring to any outside authority. The treaty of peace and friendship with India confirms this. I take Nehru's statement as an expression of friendship that, in case of aggression in Nepal, India would send help if such help is ever sought for. It could never be taken as suggesting that India would take unilateral action."

In a further statement, Prime Minister Koirala repeated:

"Nepal is an independent sovereign nation and there can never be any doubt with regard to this fact. No one need ever have any doubts about our sovereign independence. Our membership of the United Nations is a clear evidence of our sovereignty and independence".

The American Ambassador at Katmandu (Stebbins) to the Secretary of State (Herter), telegram, Dec. 10, 1959, MS. Department of State, file 690c.91/12–1059. Prime Minister Nehru made public on December 3, 1959, a 9-year-old secret agreement between India and Nepal for joint action by the two countries to meet any "foreign aggression" threatening the security of either. He reported that the letters embodying the understanding did not constitute any formal military alliance but were an exchange of assurances that neither country would "tolerate any threat to the security of the other by foreign aggression" and in the event of any such threat would "advise" for the purpose of devising "effective countermeasures". The Indian Prime Minister supported the Nepalese Prime Minister's interpretation of the agreement to mean that India would not take unilateral action to meet aggression on Nepal, but would make its help available if requested. The Baltimore *Sun*, Dec. 4, 1959, p. 1.

Autonomous Regions

§28

The "People's Republic of China" is described in its Constitution, adopted September 20, 1954, as a "people's democratic state led by the working class and based on the alliance of workers and peasants" (article 1) where "all power . . . belongs to the people" (article 2).

As provided in Constitution of Communist China

Although described as a "single multi-national state", "Regional autonomy applies in areas where people of national minorities live in compact communities" with the provision that "National autonomous areas are inalienable parts of the People's Republic of China" (article 3).

The National People's Congress as the "highest organ of state power" (article 21) is expressly empowered, along with other specific functions and powers, "to decide on questions of war and peace", and "exercise such other functions and powers which the National People's Congress considers necessary" (article 27), while the Standing Committee of the National People's Congress is authorized, *inter alia*, "to annul decisions and orders of the State Council which contravene the Constitution, laws or decrees", "to revise or annul inappropriate decisions issued by the government authorities of provinces, autonomous regions, and municipalities directly under the central authority", and "to decide on the ratification or abrogation of treaties concluded with foreign states" (article 31).

Administratively, the "People's Republic of China" is divided into provinces, autonomous regions and municipalities directly under the central authority, counties, municipalities, municipal districts, *hsiang*, nationality *hsiang*, and towns which establish people's congresses and people's councils (articles 53, 54) and which are ". . . organs of government authority in their respective localities" (article 55), while autonomous regions, autonomous *chou*, and autonomous counties establish organs of self-government (article 54) which generally ". . . exercise the functions and powers of local organs of the state . . ." (article 69) but are specifically authorized in addition to ". . . administer their own local finances within the limits of the authority prescribed by law", ". . . organize their local public security forces in accordance with the military system of the state", and ". . . draw up statutes governing the exercise of autonomy or separate regulations suited to the political, economic and cultural characteristics of the nationality or nationalities in a given area, which statutes and regulations are subject to endorsement by the Standing Committee of the National People's Congress" (article 70).

Constitution of the People's Republic of China (Foreign Language Press, Peking, 1954) 9, 10, 19, 20–25, 33–35, 40–41.

The following autonomous regions are reported to have been established and formulated in accordance with the stipulations prescribed in section 5, chapter 2, of the Constitution of the "People's Republic of China":

Sinkiang Uighur Autonomous Region, ratified by the Standing Committee of the National People's Congress September 13, 1955 (New China News Agency, Sept. 13, 1955, *Survey of China Mainland Press*, No. 1129) ; Ninghsia Hui Autonomous Region, established October 25, 1958 (New China News

Agency, Yinchuan, Oct. 25, 1958, *Survey of China Mainland Press*, No. 1884) ; Inner Mongolia Autonomous Region, Regulations which govern the organization of people's congresses and people's councils at all levels, adopted November 11, 1955, at the 27th session of the Standing Committee of the National People's Congress (*Current Background*, No. 370, Nov. 28, 1955, American Consulate General, Hong Kong) ; Kwangsi Chuang Autonomous Region, Regulations which govern the organization of people's congresses and people's councils at all levels, ratified July 9, 1958, by the Standing Committee of the National People's Congress at its 97th meeting (New China News Agency, July 9, 1958, *Survey of China Mainland Press*, No. 1816).

The preliminary report of the International Commission of Jurists   Tibet
of 1959 on *The Question of Tibet and the Rule of Law* traced the historical relations between Tibet, China, and Great Britain in an attempt to determine the status of Tibet in international law during the various stages of its legal relationship vis-a-vis China and Great Britain. Citing the Chinese invasion of Tibet in 1950 as an event leading to the signing of the Sino-Tibetan Agreement of May 23, 1951, the report summarized the Tibetan Government's appeal of November 11, 1950, to the United Nations (U.N. Gen. Ass. Doc. A/1549, Nov. 24, 1950) as follows:

". . . The Tibetan Government . . . affirming that the problem which has arisen 'was not of Tibet's own making but largely the outcome of China's ambition to bring weaker nations on her periphery within her active domination'. . . asserted that 'racially, culturally and geographically, they are far apart from the Chinese'.

" 'As a people devoted to the tenets of Buddhism,' the appeal declared, 'Tibetans had long eschewed the art of warfare, practised peace and tolerance and, for the defence of their country, relied on its geographical configuration and in [on] non-involvement in the affairs of other nations. There were times when Tibet sought but seldom received the protection of the Chinese Emperor. The Chinese, however, in their urge for expansion, have wholly misconstrued the significance of the ties of friendship and interdependence that existed, between China and Tibet as between neighbours. To them China was suzerain and Tibet a vassal state. It is this which aroused legitimate apprehension in the mind of Tibet regarding the designs of China on her independent status.

" 'China's conduct during their expedition in 1910 completed the rupture between the two countries. In 1911–12, when Tibet, under the thirteenth Dalai Lama, declared her complete independence, even as Nepal, simultaneously broke away from allegiance to China, the Chinese revolution in 1911 which dethroned the last Manchurian Emperor snapped the last of the sentimental and religious bonds that Tibet had with China. Tibet thereafter depended entirely on her isolation, her faith in the wisdom of

Lord Buddha and occasionally on the support of the British in India for her protection.'

"The delegate for El Salvador moved that the Tibetan appeal be put on the agenda of the General Assembly, but on 24th November [1950] the Steering Committee of the Assembly decided unanimously that consideration of the appeal should be postponed, after the Indian delegate had suggested this course, expressing the belief that a peaceful settlement would be reached, safeguarding Tibet's autonomy while maintaining its association with China. [U.N. General Assembly, 24th November, 1950, U.N. Doc. A/1543 [1549]]."

The Report of the International Commission of Jurists continued:

"As a result of these 'negotiations', which the Tibetans had no alternative but to carry on, an agreement was signed in Peking dated 23rd May 1951, which is popularly known as the Seventeen Point Agreement. Its main features were:

"(1) Chinese armies were to be allowed to enter Tibet for consolidating national defence;

"(2) Tibetan people were entitled to regional autonomy under the leadership of the Central People's Government;

"(3) The Central Government was not to alter the existing political system or the status and functions and powers of the Dalai Lama;

"(4) A policy of religious freedom was to be carried out and religious beliefs and customs were to be respected and Lamas and monasteries were to be protected;

"(5) Language and school system, agriculture and economy were to be gradually developed and no reforms were to be carried out by compulsion;

"(6) While the Chinese were to handle external relations Tibet would be free to have commercial and trading relations with neighbouring countries;

"(7) For the implementation of the agreement, the Chinese Government would set up a military and administrative committee, in which 'patriotic' local personnel would be absorbed.

"Assuming that the treaty is valid the position in international law would be that Tibet thereafter ceased to be an international person. If Tibet was a sovereign state before the conclusion of this treaty, as has been argued, the validity of this treaty must be considered in accordance with the customary rules of international law.

"The first point is that there is clear evidence from the Dalai Lama himself that this agreement was not voluntary. In any event, the inference from the circumstances in which it was signed, is obviously that Tibet signed at pistol-point. The Dalai Lama's statement at Mussoorie on June 20th states:

" 'The agreement which followed the invasion of Tibet was also thrust upon its people and Government by threat of arms. It was never accepted by them of their own free will.

Consent of the Government was secured under duress and at the point of bayonet. My representatives were compelled to sign the agreement under the threat of further military operations against Tibet by invading armies of China leading to the utter ravage and ruin of the country . . . While I and my Government did not voluntarily accept that agreement we were obliged to acquiesce in it and decided to abide by its terms and conditions in order to save my people and country from the damages of total destruction.'

"What is the effect of a treaty signed under duress? There appears to be no decided case on this question, although it has been much discussed by writers. Lauterpacht took the view in 1927 that 'there are few questions in international law in which there is such a measure of agreement as this, that duress, so far as states are concerned, does not invalidate a contract'. However, in 1947, he subscribed to the view that 'a treaty concluded as a result of intimidation or coercion exercised personally against the representatives is invalid'. Dealing with the question of resort to war as a means of enforcing claims, he takes the view that where a victorious State is bound by neither the Charter of the United Nations nor the General Treaty for the Renunciation of War (as is the case with the People's Republic of China), 'there is room for the traditional rule disregarding the vitiating effect of physical coercion exercised against a State.' It seems that physical coercion, or, according to the Harvard Draft Research on International Law, mental coercion, will invalidate a treaty only if directed against the signing representatives and not against the state itself. It is at least an arguable point that the reasons given by the Dalai Lama for the signing of the Seventeen-Point Agreement point to mental coercion exercised against him and his signing representatives.

"The Harvard Draft advocates that the state alleging duress should not be judge in its own cause and suggests that 'a State which claims that it has entered into a treaty in consequence of duress may seek from a competent international tribunal or authority a declaration that the treaty is void.' This is of course the solution to be advocated in a fully developed international community. However, it is by no means clear that there is any possibility of the question being taken before an international tribunal. There is also no precedent in international law and relations which is precisely in point. The basic question is whether Tibet is an internal part of China or whether Tibet has *locus standi* before an international tribunal or political authority.

"The very existence of Tibet as a State is involved. It would be absurd to expect China to take up Tibet's case under her exclusive right to conduct Tibet's foreign relations. In any event that right itself depends upon whether the Seventeen-Point Agreement is valid. The preliminary question of Tibet's statehood can be examined on this point by the United Nations and her case against the People's Republic of China can be considered by that body. The facts are there and the appropriate conclusions of law may be drawn. It is at least arguable that the

1951 agreement is invalid for duress, or can be made so if the
Dalai Lama repudiates it on that ground as he appears to have
done, with the result that for United Nations purposes, the Sino-
Tibetan events are between two states and not an internal affair
of China. . . .

"The question of duress does not, however, end with the signing
of the Seventeen-Point Agreement. The terms of the Seventeen-
Point Agreement, again assuming it is valid, have led to a controversy between China and Tibet as to what is the autonomy contemplated by Article 3. The Chinese interpreted it as regional
autonomy within the framework of the Chinese State for cultural,
educational and religious purposes. The Tibetans assert that
the position could at the utmost be that, whilst in matters of
foreign relations and defence China was the final arbiter, in matters other than this the Tibetan Government was supreme and
the Chinese Central Government was not entitled to legislate or
decide in matters concerning the internal administration of Tibet.
The question then arises how far the Dalai Lama acquiesced in
the Chinese version of regional autonomy, and how far he was a
free agent during the period of his apparent acquiescence. This
matter is also relevant to the question of treaty violation by the
Chinese People's Republic. The following brief account should
be studied together with Documents 19 and 20 [Text of Dalai
Lama's statement at Mussoorie and statement from news conference by Dalai Lama at Mussoorie, June 20, 1959, printed in report
of International Commission of Jurists, *The Question of Tibet
and the Rule of Law* (1959), pp. 196, 200].

"According to Point 15, for the implementation of this agreement, China was to set up a military and administrative committee and a military area Headquarters in Tibet. As the result
of this, General Chang-Ching-Wai arrived in Lhasa in September
1951 at the same time as the Dalai Lama. Although there is
nothing in this agreement to suggest that Tibet was to be carved
out, Tibet was in fact divided into three parts, one of which was
put under the control of the Chamdo Liberation Committee
headed by General Wang Chi Mei, a Chinese general, and the
third part was placed under the control of the Panchen Lama.

"In September 1954 the Dalai Lama and the Panchen Lama
were invited to go to Peking and they remained there until March
1955. They attended a meeting of the Chinese State Council on
the 9th of March in 1955, where the Dalai Lama and the Panchen
Lama had to submit to a number of decisions on Tibetan affairs.
One of such decisions was the establishment of a 'Preparatory
Committee for the Autonomous Region of Tibet'. The Committee consisted of 51 members, 15 from the Lhasa administration,
10 from the 'Panchen Lama's Bureau', 10 from the Chamdo 'People's Liberation Committee', 11 from Monasteries and 'Peoples
Organizations' and 5 representing the Chinese Government, the
Dalai Lama being named the Chairman. It was declared that the
members of the Committee are appointed 'with the approval of
the Chinese' State Council and the three regions of Tibet were
subordinate to it. It was stated that the chief task of the Pre-

paratory Committee was to prepare for regional autonomy in accordance with the provisions of the Chinese Constitution, the agreement of 1951 and the concrete circumstances of Tibet.

"The first meeting of the Preparatory Committee was held on April 22, 1956 and thereafter there were in the next three years twenty-seven meetings out of which the Dalai Lama was present at twenty-five and presided over the meetings. It is therefore said by the Chinese that the Dalai Lama had accepted the 1951 Seventeen-Point Agreement and that his participation in the meetings show that the Dalai Lama was in full agreement with the appointment and the work of the Preparatory Committee.

"In his Tezpur statement the Dalai Lama has said that 'in practice, even this body had little power and decisions in all important matters were taken by the Chinese authorities.'

"The statements of the Dalai Lama and other Tibetan leaders regarding the way in which Tibet was compelled to accept the Seventeen-Point Agreement and of the statement of the Dalai Lama regarding the Preparatory Committee, will have to be borne in mind when the legal status of Tibet is under consideration.

"Another point on which the validity of the 1951 agreement may be attacked is that Tibet may be able to repudiate her treaty obligations on the ground that China has violated hers. The classic doctrine on denunciation of treaties is that if one side violates its obligations under a treaty, the injured party 'may by its own unilateral act terminate a treaty as between itself and a State which it regards as having violated such treaty.' This view has been judicially approved in three American cases [Ware & Hylton (1796) 3 Dallas 199, 261; In re Thomas (1874) 23 Fed. Cas. 927; Charlton & Kelly (1913) 229 U.S. 447, 473] and in one case before the Judicial Committee of the Privy Council [The Blonde (1922) A.C. 313], the supreme court of appeal for overseas territories of the British Crown. It is essential, as emerges from all of these cases, that the treaty be actually repudiated, for, unless this is done, the treaty remains in force, i.e., it is voidable only. The Dalai Lama made a statement to the press at Mussoorie on June 20th, 1959, repudiating the Sino-Tibetan agreement, and there is a strong case for arguing that the agreement can no longer remain in force. The Dalai Lama was asked: 'Do you consider the 1951 Treaty between Tibet and the Chinese Government still in force?' He replied: 'The Sino-Tibetan agreement imposed by the Chinese in accordance with their own desires has been violated by the Chinese themselves, thus giving rise to a contradiction. Therefore we cannot abide by this agreement.'

"Tibet can argue that she never lost her sovereignty on the ground of duress or on the ground of China's violation of the 1951 agreement. Alternatively, it might be argued that Tibet lost her sovereignty but regained it when the Dalai Lama denounced the agreement, possibly on the ground of duress and for violation by China."

International Commission of Jurists, *The Question of Tibet and the Rule of Law* (1959) 94–99. See also a leading Indian jurist's account of the historical and legal relationship between Tibet and China: J. P. Mitter, "Sino-Tibetan Relations", the *Statesman*, Apr. 11 and 12, 1960.

As directed by the International Commission of Jurists, the Legal Inquiry Committee on Tibet investigated events in Tibet and submitted its findings together with a detailed review of the facts and evidence upon which those findings were based in its report to the Commission in 1960. The Committee accepted as a fact that representatives of Tibet signed the Seventeen-Point Agreement under duress and concluded that, in consideration of the violation of the Agreement, the Tibetan Government was justified in repudiating the Agreement. *Tibet and the Chinese People's Republic* (1960).

The "Seventeen-Point Agreement Between the Chinese Central People's Government and the Tibetan Government on the Administration of Tibet" of May 23, 1951, which recognized the autonomous status of Tibet, provides in part as follows:

"1. The Tibetan people shall unite and drive out imperialist aggressive forces from Tibet so that the Tibetan people shall return to the big family of the motherland—the People's Republic of China.

"2. The local government of Tibet shall actively assist the People's Liberation Army to enter Tibet and consolidate the national defences.

"3. In accordance with the policy towards nationalities laid down in the Common Programme of the Chinese People's Political Consultative Conference, the Tibetan people have the right of exercising regional autonomy under the unified leadership of the Central People's Government.

"4. The central authorities will not alter the existing political system in Tibet. The central authorities also will not alter the established status, functions and powers of the Dalai Lama. Officials of various ranks shall hold office as usual.

"5. The established status, functions and powers of the Panchen Ngoerhtehni shall be maintained.

.   .   .   .

"8. Tibetan troops shall be reorganised step by step into the People's Liberation Army and become a part of the national defence forces of the People's Republic of China.

.   .   .   .

"14. The Central People's Government shall have the centralised handling of all external affairs of the area of Tibet; and there will be peaceful co-existence with neighbouring countries and the establishment and development of fair commercial and trading relations with them on the basis of equality, mutual benefit and mutual respect for territory and sovereignty."

New China News Agency, May 28, 1951, published in *Documents on International Affairs 1951* (Folliot ed., 1954) 577–579.

The Dalai Lama of Tibet, on June 20, 1959, read a prepared state-ment of considerable historical significance at a press conference in Mussoorie, India, where he had sought and received asylum. In the course of his statement, with reference to the "reign of terror" in Tibet instituted by the Chinese Communist regime, he said:

"To understand and appreciate the significance and implication of the recent tragic happenings in Tibet, it is necessary to refer to the main events which have occurred in the country since 1950.

"It is recognized by every independent observer that Tibet had virtually been independent by enjoying and exercising all rights of sovereignty whether internal or external. This has also been implicitly admitted by the Communist Government of China for the very structure, terms and conditions of the so-called agree-ment of 1951 conclusively show that it was an agreement between two independent and sovereign States. It follows, therefore, that when the Chinese armies violated the territorial integrity of Tibet they were committing a flagrant act of aggression. The agree-ment which followed the invasion of Tibet was also thrust upon its people and Government by the threat of arms. It was never accepted by them of their own free will. The consent of the Gov-ernment was secured under duress and at the point of the bayonet.

"My representatives were compelled to sign the agreement un-der threat of further military operations against Tibet by the in-vading armies of China leading to utter ravage and ruin of the country. Even the Tibetan seal which was affixed to the agree-ment was not the seal of my representatives but a seal copied and fabricated by the Chinese authorities in Peking and kept in their possession ever since.

"While I and my Government did not voluntarily accept the agreement we were obliged to acquiesce in it and decided to abide by the terms and conditions in order to save my people and coun-try from the danger of total destruction. . . ."

Text printed in full as Document 19, International Commission of Jurists, *The Question of Tibet and the Rule of Law* (1959) 196, also in the New York *Times*, June 21, 1959, p. 24.

When asked for a statement on the situation in Tibet in the light of the Sino-Tibetan Agreement of May 23, 1951, Minister of State Younger replied by written answer for the House of Commons that "This agreement purports to guarantee Tibetan autonomy and safe-guard her religious freedom, but the arrangements for the entry of the Chinese army, the setting up of a Chinese military and adminis-trative headquarters in Tibet and the recognition by the Tibetan Government of a Chinese-sponsored candidate for the office of Panchen Lama, throw considerable doubt on the value of these guarantees".

Written Answers, 488 H.C. Deb. (5th ser.) cols. 61–62 (June 4, 1951).

While the 1946 Chinese Constitution does not include Tibet in its description of the territory of China, several of its articles refer to Tibet: Article 120 provides that the "self-government system of Tibet shall be safeguarded", and provision is made in article 26 for delegates from Tibet to the National Assembly, and in article 64 for members of the Legislative Yuan from Tibet. Article 91 specifies "The Control Yuan shall be composed of Members who shall be elected by Provincial and Municipal Councils, the local Councils of Mongolia and Tibet and Chinese citizens residing abroad. . . ."

> *China Yearbook 1958–1959* (1959) 698, 700–701, 706, 709, 714. The Constitution of the Republic of China adopted by the National Assembly on December 25, 1946, and promulgated by the National Government on January 1, 1947, became effective on December 25, 1947. Temporary Provisions Effective During the Period of National Crisis, adopted by the National Assembly on April 18, 1948, and promulgated by the National Government on May 10, 1948, and as subsequently revised and adopted on March 11, 1960, do not affect the articles cited above.

The Outline Regulations Governing the Organization of the Preparatory Committee for the Tibet Autonomous Region, adopted by the First National People's Congress of the "People's Republic of China" at its 47th session on September 26, 1956, were formulated in accordance with the Constitution of the "People's Republic of China" and the Resolution Concerning the Establishment of the Preparatory Committee for Tibet Autonomous Region, which was adopted by the State Council at its 7th plenary meeting (March 12, 1955) and which referred to the Agreement Between the Central People's Government and the Local Government of Tibet Concerning Methods for the Peaceful Liberation of Tibet.

Article 2 of the Regulations describes the Preparatory Committee for the Autonomous Region of Tibet as "an authoritative body for consultations and planning during the transitional period before the establishment of the Autonomous Region of Tibet and [which] functions under the direction of the State Council."

Article 4 charges this Committee with carrying out the following tasks:

> "A. To gradually strengthen the responsibilities of the Committee, accumulate work experience, and create various conditions in order to set up formally the united Autonomous Region of Tibet.
>
> "B. To carry out all concrete work in preparation for the establishment of the united Autonomous Region.
>
> "C. To assume the responsibility of consultation and unified planning for carrying out the construction in Tibet region and

other tasks that are feasible and necessary; to adopt resolutions and submit same to the State Council for approval and implementation.

"D. To unite with people of all circles so as to strengthen further the unity between the nationalities as well as the unity within Tibet.

"E. To organize and supervise studies and raise the patriotism and understanding of the policy of anti-imperialism among the cadres; to elevate the level of work and actively cultivate cadres.

"F. To protect in accordance with provisions of law the lives and properties of all the people in Tibet, both ecclesiastical and lay, and of all nationalities and social strata.

"G. To practise freedom of religious belief and protect the lamaseries and their income."

New China News Agency, Sept. 27, 1956, *Survey of China Mainland Press*, No. 1449.

In separate Agreements concluded by the "People's Republic of China" with India on April 29, 1954, and with Nepal on September 24, 1956, for the purpose of promoting trade and intercourse between these respective States and Tibet, Tibet was referred to as "Tibet Region of China". In the Sino-Nepalese Agreement it was provided in addition that "All treaties and documents which existed in the past between China and Nepal including those between the Tibet Region of China and Nepal are hereby abrogated".

"Agreement Between the People's Republic of China and the Republic of India on Trade and Intercourse Between Tibet Region of China and India", New China News Agency, Apr. 29, 1954, *Survey of China Mainland Press*, No. 798. China-Nepal Agreement, New China News Agency, Sept. 24, 1956, *Survey of China Mainland Press*, No. 1378.

In a letter of April 29, 1953, the Department of State outlined the official position of the United States Government with regard to the legal status of Tibet. The letter stated:

"Historically, the United States Government has recognized a continuing claim of the Government of the Republic of China to suzerainty over Tibet and has never maintained direct diplomatic relations with Tibet. The United States Government believes Tibet should not be compelled by duress to accept violation of its autonomy and that the Tibetan people should enjoy the rights of self-determination commensurate with the autonomy Tibet has maintained for many years. This has consistently been the position of the United States.

"In October 1950 Communist China dispatched troops into Tibet. On May 23, 1951 Chinese Communist leaders and Tibetan 'representatives' signed an agreement in Peiping under which the Chinese Communists assumed control of Tibet's foreign relations and security matters. The United States Government, which has never recognized the Chinese Communist regime, neither recognizes nor condones the so-called 'agreement' of May 1951 under which the Chinese Communists deprived the Tibetan people of the *de facto* political autonomy which they had long enjoyed."

Assistant Secretary of State Morton to Senator Wiley, letter, Apr. 29, 1953, MS. Department of State, file 611.93b/4–1753.

In answer to a question concerning the status of Tibet, a Department of State spokesman stated at a press conference of September 11, 1959:

". . . the historic position of the United States has been that Tibet is an autonomous country under Chinese suzerainty. However, the United States Government has consistently held that the autonomy of Tibet should not be impaired by force. The United States has never recognized the pretensions to sovereignty over Tibet put forward by the Chinese Communist regime."

Transcript of press and radio news conference, Sept. 11, 1959.

Under Secretary of State for Foreign Affairs Mayhew addressed the following memorandum August 5, 1943, to the Chinese Government in answer to their inquiry as to the British Government's attitude on the subject of Chinese suzerainty over Tibet:

"Since the Chinese Revolution of 1911, when Chinese forces were withdrawn from Tibet, Tibet has enjoyed *de facto* independence. She has ever since regarded herself as in practice completely autonomous and has opposed Chinese attempts to reassert control.

"Since 1911, repeated attempts have been made to bring about an accord between China and Tibet. It seemed likely that agreement could be found on the basis that Tibet should be autonomous under the nominal suzerainty of China, and this was the basis of the draft tripartite (Chinese-Tibetan-British) convention of 1914 which was initialled by the Chinese representative but was not ratified by the Chinese Government. The rock on which this convention and subsequent attempts to reach an understanding were wrecked was not the question of autonomy (which was expressly admitted by China) but was the question of the boundary between China and Tibet, since the Chinese Government claimed sovereignty over areas which the Tibetan Government claimed belonged exclusively to their autonomous jurisdiction.

"The boundary question, however, remained insuperable and, since the delay in reaching agreement was hampering the development of more normal relations between India and Tibet, eventually in 1921 the Secretary of State for Foreign Affairs (Lord Curzon) informed the then Chinese Minister (Dr. Wellington Koo) that the British Government did not feel justified in withholding any longer their recognition of the status of Tibet as an autonomous State under the suzerainty of China, and intended dealing on this basis with Tibet in the future.

"This is the principle which has since guided the attitude of the British Government towards Tibet. They have always been prepared to recognise Chinese suzerainty over Tibet but only on the understanding that Tibet is regarded as autonomous. Neither the British Government nor the Government of India have any territorial ambitions in Tibet but they are interested in the maintenance of friendly relations with, and the preservation of peaceful conditions in, an area which is coterminous with the North-East frontiers of India. They would welcome any amicable arrangements which the Chinese Government might be disposed to make with Tibet whereby the latter recognised Chinese suzerainty in return for an agreed frontier and an undertaking to recognise Tibetan autonomy and they would gladly offer any help desired by both parties to this end."

Written Answers, 470 H.C. Deb. (5th ser.) cols. 255–256 (Dec. 14, 1949). See also 480 H.C. Deb. (5th ser.) col. 602 (Nov. 6, 1950) ; Written Answers, 602 H.C. Deb. (5th ser.) col. 126 (Mar. 25, 1959).

In a written answer to a question concerning Tibet, the British Secretary of State for Foreign Affairs, Selwyn Lloyd, quoted the Dalai Lama as saying at Tezpur on April 18, 1959:

" 'In fact after the occupation of Tibet by the Chinese armies the Tibetan Government did not enjoy any measure of autonomy even in internal matters and the Chinese Government exercised full powers in Tibetan affairs.' "

He then added, ". . . Her Majesty's Government have maintained that Tibet should be regarded as autonomous, and we therefore deplore any action by the Chinese Government which has in any way deprived the Tibetans of autonomy."

Written Answers, 604 H.C. Deb. (5th ser.) col. 81 (Apr. 27, 1959).

Professor Charles Henry Alexandrowicz-Alexander of the University of Madras, in his historical analysis of the legal status of Tibet, concludes that Tibet evolved from the status of a *feudatory* in a suzerain-vassal relationship with China to that of an independent state. See 48 Am. J. Int'l L. (1954) 265. In answer to Professor Alexandrowicz-Alexander's conclusion, Tieh-Tseng Li, former Chinese Ambassador to Iran and Thailand, denies the status of suzerainty and, in asserting China's historical claim of sovereignty over Tibet, concludes that Tibet has an autonomous status constituting an integral part of China. See 50 Am. J. Int'l L. (1956) 394. See also Alexandrowicz-Alexander, "Comment on the 'Legal Position of Tibet' ", V *The Indian Yearbook of International Affairs 1956* (1956) 172. William W. Bishop, Jr., *International Law: Cases and Materials* (1954) 193, classifies Tibet as of doubtful or unusual legal status because of Chinese suzerainty and control and Tibet's limited foreign relations. Professor H. Lauterpacht, in I *Oppenheim's International Law* (8th ed., 1955) 258, classified Tibet as a "half-sovereign" state nominally regarded as being under the protection or suzerainty of China.

During a foreign affairs debate in the Indian Parliament on December 6, 1950—at a time when the fighting pursuant to the movement of Chinese armies into Tibet in 1950 had practically ceased and there were talks of negotiations between the Tibetan Government and China—Prime Minister Nehru answered in reply to a question concerning the advance of the Chinese forces into Tibet—

> ". . . The story of Tibet, so far as we are concerned, is very simple. . . . Ever since the People's Government of China talked about the liberation of Tibet, our Ambassador told them, on behalf of the Government of India, how the latter felt about it. We expressed our earnest hope that the matter would be settled peacefully by China and Tibet. We also made it clear that we had no territorial or political ambitions in regard to Tibet and that our relations were cultural and commercial. We said that we would naturally like to preserve these relations and continue to trade with Tibet because it did not come in the way of either China or Tibet. We further said that we were anxious that Tibet should maintain the autonomy it has had for at least the last forty years. We did not challenge or deny the suzerainty of China over Tibet. We pointed all this out in a friendly way to the Chinese Government. . . ."

In reply to a debate in Parliament, Mr. Nehru stated on December 7, 1950:

> "I have spoken of China and, more particularly, of Tibet. Prof. Ranga seems to have been displeased at my occasional reference to Chinese suzerainty over Tibet. Please note that I used the word suzerainty, not sovereignty. There is a slight difference, though not much. I was telling the House about a historical fact; I was not discussing the future. It is a historical fact and in the context of things it is perfectly true that we have repeatedly admitted Chinese suzerainty over Tibet just as we have laid stress on Tibet's autonomy. . . ."

In opening a foreign policy debate in Parliament on May 15, 1954, Prime Minister Nehru read the preamble to the Sino-Indian Agreement on Tibet of April 29, 1954, in which Tibet was referred to as the "Tibet Region of China" (*White Paper, Notes, Memoranda and Letters Exchanged and Agreements Signed Between the Governments of India and China, 1954–1959* (Ministry of External Affairs, Government of India, 1959), p. 98), and declared:

> "So far as Tibet is concerned, it is a recognition of the existing situation there. In fact, that situation had been recognized by us two or three years ago. Some criticism has been made that this

is a recognition of Chinese sovereignty over Tibet. Apart from that fact, I am not aware of any time during the last few hundred years when Chinese sovereignty, or if you like suzerainty, was challenged by any outside country and all during this period whether China was weak or strong and whatever the Government of China was, China always maintained this claim to the sovereignty over Tibet. It is true that occasionally when China was weak, this sovereignty was not exercised in any large measure. When China was strong, it was exercised. Always there was a large measure of autonomy of Tibet, so that there was no great change in the theoretical approach to the Tibetan problem from the Chinese side. It has been throughout the last 200 or 300 years the same. The only country that had more intimate relations with Tibet was India, that is to say, British India in those days. Even then, when it was British policy to have some measure of influence over Tibet, even then they never denied the fact of Chinese sovereignty over Tibet, although in practice it was hardly exercised and they laid stress on Tibetan autonomy. Recent events made some other changes, factual changes, because a strong Chinese State gave practical evidence of exercising that sovereignty. So that what we have done in this agreement is not to recognise any new thing, but merely to repeat what we have said previously, and what, in fact, inevitably follows from the circumstances, both historical and practical today. The real importance, I repeat, of this agreement is because of its wider implications in regard to non-aggression, recognition of each other's territorial integrity and sovereignty and non-interference with each other, external, internal or any other like interference. . . ."

In another speech in the Lok Sabha on March 30, 1959, following the outbreak of fighting in Tibet which led to the escape of the Dalai Lama into India, Prime Minister Nehru said with regard to Tibetan autonomy:

". . . the position of all previous Governments in India and elsewhere has been the recognition of some kind of suzerainty or sovereignty of China over Tibet and Tibetan autonomy. That was normally the basis of approach. The measure of the autonomy has varied, because the strength of China, or the weakness of China, the strength of Tibet, and the weakness of Tibet has varied in the course of the last hundreds of years. But, that is the position. Every Government in China has claimed that. Many Governments in Tibet have repudiated that. So, there it is. . . .

". . . When the Premier of the Chinese Government came here three or four years ago or two-and-a-half years ago, he discussed this question of situation in Tibet with me at his own instance. I did not raise it so far as I remember. He told me then that Tibet had always been, according to him and according to the

Chinese position, a part of the Chinese State; that is, they have always claimed it and they have had it, according to him; but yet, Tibet was not China. Tibet is not China; Tibet is not a province of China. Tibet is an autonomous region which has been a part of the Chinese State. That was, as far as I remember, his words. Therefore, we want to treat it as an autonomous region and give it full autonomy. That is how he explained the Chinese Government's attitude to Tibet. All I can say is that we had to recognise Chinese sovereignty over Tibet. But, I was glad to hear Mr. Chou En-lai laying such stress on Tibetan autonomy. . . ."

In the debate on Tibet in the Lok Sabha on May 8, 1959, Mr. Khadilkar, member of the Congress Party from Maharashtra, made the point that ". . . though we have given up our extraterritorial rights, we have never accepted Chinese sovereignty—that distinction is there—we have only maintained Chinese suzerainty. We shall accept it in the larger interests."

Federation of Dependent States

§29

Federation
of South
Arabia

"At the time Captain Haines became the first British Resident in Aden some of the more powerful families in this rugged interior had assumed the style of 'daulah' or 'government' and their leaders titles such as 'Sultan' and 'Amir'. This pretentious façade of sovereignty concealed a pitiful weakness for the writ of none of these so called 'rulers' ran further than the unarmed and, consequently, inferior classes of society: the traders and labourers in the towns and the tenants on 'daulah' lands."

These Sultans and Amirs signed protectorate treaties with the United Kingdom. After 1937, when responsibility for Aden passed from the Government of India to the Colonial Office, serious thought was given to the merit of a loose British control. Consequently, between 1944 and 1953 the Rulers of the nine more important States in the Western Aden Protectorate signed new treaties undertaking to accept British advice, which led to the establishment of the Federation of the Arab Amirates of the South.

"Federation in the Western Protectorate", *The Times British Colonies Review* (1st quarter 1959), No. 33, p. 9.

The Federation of Arab Amirates of the South, inaugurated February 11, 1959, with the signing of the Constitution, joined six of the eighteen States of the Western Aden Protectorate: the 'Audhali, Lower Yafa'i and Fadhli Sultanates, the Amirates of Baihan and

Dhala, and the Upper 'Aulaqi Shaikhdom. In accordance with the constitutional provision for the accession of any other States that wish to join and are acceptable to the founder members, the Lahej and Lower 'Aulaqi Sultanates, the Shaikhdom of 'Aqrabi and the State of Dathina acceded to the Federation within the course of its first year of existence.

Under the terms of the Constitution, the governments of the six founder States remain intact but transfer to the Federal Government exclusive jurisdiction over external affairs, defense and internal security, borrowing money for Federal use, agriculture, fisheries, aviation, postal and telegraph services, public relations, building and maintenance of trunk roads, education above the primary level, health, currency, banking, insurance, exchange control, civil service, Federal revenue, regulation of trade and commerce, establishment of a Federal seat of government, acquisition of property for Federal use and the administration thereof, and "incidental matters".

According to the Treaty of Friendship and Protection between the United Kingdom of Great Britain and Northern Ireland and the Federation of Arab Amirates of the South, also signed on February 11, 1959, the contracting parties—

"Considering that the Rulers of the Amirate of Beihan, the Audhali Sultanate, the Fadhli Sultanate; the Amirate of Dhala, the Upper Aulaqi Sheikhdom and the Lower Yafa' Sultanate each having a Treaty of Friendship and Peace with the United Kingdom of Great Britain and Northern Ireland (hereinafter referred to as 'the United Kingdom') have, with the agreement of the United Kingdom, formed their States into a Federation called the Federation of Arab Amirates of the South (hereinafter referred to as 'the Federation') for the mutual defence of those States and their development in all social, political and economic matters for the betterment of the country and its people;

"Considering that the Federation desires to develop ultimately into an economically and politically independent State in friendly relations with the United Kingdom and that the United Kingdom undertakes to assist the Federation to become ultimately an independent State;"

agreed with respect to the conduct of foreign affairs that—

"(1) The United Kingdom shall conduct and have full responsibility for the Federation's relations with other States and their Governments and international organizations and the Federation shall not enter into any treaty, agreement correspondence or other relations with any such State, Government or international organization without the knowledge and consent of the United Kingdom.

"(2) The Federation shall promptly inform the United Kingdom of any interference, or attempt to interfere, with the affairs of the Federation by any other State or Government.

"(3) The United Kingdom shall consult the Federation regarding the conduct by the United Kingdom of the relations referred to in paragraph (1) of this Article and shall not enter into any treaty or agreement providing for any change in the frontiers of the Federation or otherwise recognize any such change without the consent of the Federation." (Article II.)

In addition the Treaty provides, *inter alia*, for the extension of Her Britannic Majesty's favor and protection to the Federation, stating that the Annex, dealing with mutual assistance and cooperation with respect to defense and internal security, shall have effect as part of the Treaty; the giving of United Kingdom advice; and financial and technical assistance to the Federation. The Federation is obligated by its terms to receive such advisory staffs as the United Kingdom may desire to provide and pledges itself to accept any advice given by the United Kingdom. The Treaty also provides for the accession of new States and the applicability of the Treaty to such States upon accession and for the continuing validity of all Agreements previously entered into between the United Kingdom and the six member States.

The American Consul at Aden (Crawford) to the Secretary of State (Dulles), despatch No. 124, Feb. 19, 1959, encl. 3, MS. Department of State, file 746c.00/2–1959.

A Treaty dated January 17, 1963, between the United Kingdom and the Federation of South Arabia (formerly known as the Federation of the Arab Amirates of the South), while expressly declaring that nothing in the Treaty shall affect British sovereignty over Aden, provided for the accession of the Colony of Aden as a State of the Federation and for its secession therefrom if after 6 years the Federation had unfairly prejudiced the interests of Aden. Accession took place January 18, 1963, the date appointed by the Federation of South Arabia [Accession of Aden] Order-in-Council 1963, which, in giving the force of law to the Constitution of the Federation in Aden, provided that in relation to Aden the executive and legislative authority of the Governor will prevail over that of the Federation on matters concerning defense, external affairs, and internal security.

Stat. Instr., 1963, No. 82. See also Cmnd. 1814, Aug. 1962.

"Inevitably, the federal constitution [of the Federation of Arab Amirates of the South] reveals concessions to the highly developed individualism of the States and their Rulers. In the place of an individual head of State there is a plural executive known as the Supreme Council, a constitutional device to overcome the awkward problem implied by elevating one of the Rulers to a position of paramountcy. The Supreme Council is composed of ministers elected by and from a legislative body known as the Federal Council and combines the functions of a head of State with those of a Cabinet. The Federal Government is responsible for agriculture, education (excluding primary education), health, communications (aviation, main roads, postal and telecommunications) and internal security. It continues the practice of its component States of vesting its jurisdiction in foreign affairs in the British Government and shares with it responsibility for defence. Partly for reasons of economy and partly because the Rulers are reluctant to permit a seemingly rival authority within their States, the federation disposes of only a limited executive and no judicial machinery of its own. Thus the State administrations are responsible for implementing its policy and decisions and the State courts for disposing of cases under federal law; similarly the Rulers, as local federal agents, are responsible for security and for this purpose have at their disposal detachments of a federal gendarmerie called the National Guard."

"Federation in the Western Protectorate", *The Times British Colonies Review* (1st quarter 1959), No. 33, p. 9.

Under authority of the British Caribbean Federation Act, 1956 (4 & 5 Eliz. 2, c. 63), the British Parliament passed the West Indies (Federation) Order in Council, 1957 (Stat. Instr., 1957, No. 1364), July 31, 1957, which established the Federation known as the "West Indies" consisting of the "Colonies of Antigua, Barbados, Dominica, Grenada, Jamaica, Montserrat, Saint Christopher Nevis and Anguilla, Saint Lucia, Saint Vincent, and Trinidad and Tobago" and their dependencies. The West Indies Federation formally came into being January 3, 1958, when the Governor-General assumed office.
West Indies Federation

The Constitution of the West Indies (Stat. Instr., 1957, No. 1364, Annex, July 31, 1957), establishing the Federation as a whole as a colony of the United Kingdom, serves a two-fold purpose in defining the powers of the Governor-General in the affairs of the Federation consistent with its colonial status and in regulating the relationship and division of powers between the Federal and Territorial Governments.

While the Crown is empowered to make laws for those purposes enumerated in article 53(1), among which are matters of defense, and relations between the Federation and any country outside the Federation or any international organization, including the discharge of the obligations of the Federation under any agreement with such country or organization, and while the executive authority of the

Federation is vested in Her Majesty (article 55(1)), the Federal Legislature, composed of Her Majesty, an appointed Senate and an elected House, has the power to make laws for the "peace, order and good government of the Federation with respect to any matter that is included in the Exclusive Legislative List [among which is defence, the only matter also within the province of the United Kingdom] or the Concurrent Legislative List and with respect to any matter incidental to any matter so included or incidental to any power conferred by or under this Constitution on the Governor-General, the Federal Judicature or any department, officer or other authority of the Federal Government". The Legislature of any Territory is empowered to make laws for that Territory with respect to any matter included in the Concurrent Legislative List (article 43).

Article 45 (1) further specifies:

> "If any law of the Legislature of a Territory is inconsistent with any law of the Federal Legislature which the Federal Legislature was competent to enact, whether the Federal law was made before or after the Territorial law, then the Federal law shall, to the extent of the inconsistency, prevail over the Territorial law; and a law of the Federal Legislature with respect to any matter for the time being within the legislative competence of that Legislature may amend or repeal, or provide for the amendment or repeal of, any law of the Legislature of a Territory with respect to that matter."

Article 56(1) of the Constitution provides that "The executive authority of the Federation shall extend to . . . such external relations as may from time to time be entrusted to the Federation by Her Majesty's Government in the United Kingdom".

The Federal Government in a press release on September 12, 1959, announced that the United Kingdom Government formally delegated a measure of authority over external affairs to the Federation. The text of the announcement is as follows:

> "As a result of a request made some months ago by the Federal Government to the Secretary of State for a definition of the external relations to be entrusted to the Federation by Her Majesty's Government under Article 56(1) of the Constitution, the Secretary of State recently conveyed formally the agreement of Her Majesty's Government to the following measure of delegation to the executive authority of the Federation:—

> "(a) the negotiation and signature of agreements for financial and technical assistance with the Member Countries of the Commonwealth, and of agreements for technical assistance with the United States of America;

"(b) negotiation and signature of agreements for immigration quotas for West Indians entering Commonwealth or foreign countries;

"(c) Her Majesty's Government will be ready, after consultation with the Government of The West Indies in each instance and at their request, to seek for The West Indies the right to be represented in all appropriate international organizations whose Constitutions provide (whether by full membership, associate membership, or some other means) for the participation of territories which are not fully responsible for their own international relations.

"In addition Her Majesty's Government have undertaken to give sympathetic consideration to any requests by the Federal Government for authority to take action on individual questions of external relations not specifically delegated and in particular to requests for delegation of authority to hold discussions and sign agreements with neighboring countries or administrations on matters of purely local concern.

"The Federal Government has accepted responsibility for the entrustments conveyed and has expressed to the Secretary of State its appreciation of the undertaking by Her Majesty's Government to consider sympathetically any requests for additional delegation of authority in the field of external relations."

The American Consul General at Port-of-Spain in transmitting this press release noted with reference to this extension of authority over external affairs under the authority of article 56(1) that under the Constitution the executive authority is exercised on behalf of the Crown by the Governor-General, and that he in turn acts in accordance with the advice of the Council of State (Cabinet), except that on matters of foreign affairs (among other things) he may act contrary to that advice if he considers it necessary. Commenting further, he reported:

"Thus, if any matter affecting external affairs is assigned to the Federation under Article 56(1), the Governor-General may still constitutionally override the Cabinet, but in practical terms he can be expected to accept the advice of his ministers.

"The Constitution therefore has in it the mechanism for the gradual assumption of authority over foreign affairs by the Federal Government at the discretion of the UK Government. This power has been exercised in limited fashion, as, for example, in the signing of technical assistance agreements by the Federation and West Indian associate membership in UNESCO, and has been given formal sanction . . . .

". . . the Federal Government now takes over authority for its own external affairs in such matters as external aid programs, immigration agreements, Caribbean Commission, and membership in UN bodies in which representation can appropriately be sought."

The American Consul General at Port-of-Spain (Moline) to the Secretary of State (Herter), despatch No. 121, Sept. 18, 1959, MS. Department of State, file 741j.00/9–1859.

The Federation achieved full internal self-government on August 16, 1960 (Constitution of The West Indies (Amendment) Order in Council, 1960), with the principal result that the Federal Government became fully responsible for all matters within its competence, except defense and external affairs, and the Governor-General ceased to preside over the Council of State which became the Cabinet. The West Indies Constitutional Conference held at London from May 31 to June 16, 1961, designated May 31, 1962, as the date for The West Indies' independence. In response to The West Indies' expressed desire to become on independence a member of the Commonwealth, the Secretary of State in welcoming the proposal undertook that at the appropriate time Her Majesty's Government would consult the other Commonwealth Governments with a view to securing their concurrence.

Under the Federal Constitution proposed by the Conference, the Federation was to be accorded "ultimate authority over and responsibility for" external affairs and the right to enter into treaties with foreign countries, while the unit territories were to be empowered to "enter into negotiations" with foreign governments on matters within their individual legislative competence, provided the Federal Government, after being informed of the negotiations, approved the agreement.

Report of the West Indies Constitutional Conference, 1961, Cmnd. 1417.

On September 19, 1961, the people of Jamaica voted in a referendum to withdraw from the Federation. In the light of this decision, the Secretary of State for the Colonies, Reginald Maudling, having discussed the situation with the leaders of the Governments in the West Indies Federation, announced in the House of Commons on February 6, 1962, the Government's decision to arrange for the dissolution of the West Indies Federation. He stated:

"My talks revealed that we face this situation: Jamaica has declared its determination to withdraw from the Federation and this decision has been accepted by Her Majesty's Government. The Government of Trinidad and Tobago have decided not to participate in any federation of the Eastern Caribbean. Finally, the Premier of Barbados and the Chief Ministers of the Leeward and Windward Islands, while advocating a new federation between their territories, are agreed that the present one should be dissolved.

"In these circumstances, Her Majesty's Government have with regret reached the conclusion that they have no alternative but to arrange for the dissolution of the present Federation."

653 H.C. Deb. (5th ser.) col. 230 (Feb. 6, 1962).

Her Britannic Majesty, authorized by the West Indies Act, 1962, to provide for a colony's ceasing to be included in the Federation established by virtue of section one of the British Caribbean Federation Act, 1956, and to dissolve the Federation, dissolved the Federation, and with it, the Federal Government, the Federal Legislature, the Federal Supreme Court, and the other Federal authorities established by the Constitution annexed to the West Indies (Federation) Order in Council 1957, on May 29, 1962, by the West Indies (Dissolution and Interim Commissioner) Order in Council 1962. In addition, the Order in Council made provision for the appointment of an Interim Commissioner for the West Indies and designated his functions, including that of administering for the benefit of the Territories certain specified services.

The West Indies Act, 1962, 10 & 11 Eliz. 2, c. 19; The West Indies (Dissolution and Interim Commissioner) Order in Council 1962, Stat. Instr., 1962, No. 1084. Under section 6 of the West Indies Act, Her Majesty is empowered to establish new forms of government in place of the West Indies Federation.

Under the authority of the Jamaica Independence Act, 1962 (10 & 11 Eliz. 2, c. 40), which made provision for the attainment by Jamaica of "fully responsible status within the Commonwealth", Jamaica was constituted an independent State on August 6, 1962, by The Jamaica (Constitution) Order in Council 1962 (Stat. Instr., 1962, No. 1550). The Jamaican Independence Conference, February 1–9, 1962, originally concluded Jamaica's independence Constitution and set August 6 as the date of independence, specifying that Jamaican independence be celebrated on the first Monday in August thereafter.

Jamaica

The American Consul at Kingston (Cheslaw) to the Secretary of State (Rusk), despatch No. 214, Feb. 28, 1962, MS. Department of State, file 741f.03/2-2862.

In its note of August 24, 1962, the British Government informed the United States Government that—

"Section 4 of the Jamaica Independence Act, read with the Jamaica (Constitution) Order in Council 1962, the Turks and Caicos Islands (Constitution) Order in Council 1962, and the

Cayman Islands (Constitution) Order in Council 1962 . . . has the general effect, as from the 6th of August, 1962, when Jamaica attained her sovereign independence, of breaking the constitutional links between the Turks and Caicos Islands and the Cayman Islands on the one hand and Jamaica on the other. Whereas prior to that date the Turks and Caicos Islands and the Cayman Islands were both regarded as dependencies of Jamaica, since then, by virtue of these instruments, they are each established as as a direct dependency of the United Kingdom with the status of a British Colony."

The British Embassy to the Department of State, note No. 323, Aug. 24, 1962, MS. Department of State, file V–18-3.

Trinidad and Tobago

Trinidad and Tobago attained independence within the Commonwealth on August 31, 1962, as provided in the Trinidad and Tobago Independence Act, 1962. By virtue of section 5, subsection (1), of the West Indies Act, 1962, whereby Her Majesty was empowered to make provisions for the government of certain West Indian colonies and empower them to make laws for the peace, order, and good government of the colony, Trinidad and Tobago received its independence Constitution by Order in Council which came into operation immediately before August 31, 1962.

Trinidad and Tobago Independence Act, 1962, 10 & 11 Eliz. 2, c. 54; West Indies Act, 1962, 10 & 11 Eliz. 2, c. 19; The Trinidad and Tobago (Constitution) Order in Council 1962, Stat. Instr., 1962, No. 1875.

Sui Generis Status
British Commonwealth
§30

The independent portion of the Commonwealth is an association of 16 sovereign independent States—the United Kingdom of Great Britain and Northern Ireland, Canada, Australia, New Zealand, India, Pakistan, Ceylon, Ghana, the Federation of Malaya, Cyprus, Nigeria, Sierra Leone, Tanganyika, Jamaica, Trinidad and Tobago, and Uganda.

Terminology

The first formal legal description of the status and mutual relationship of the independent Commonwealth members as *"equal in status, in no way subordinate one to another in any aspect of their domestic or external affairs, though united by a common allegiance to the Crown, and freely associated as members of the British Commonwealth of Nations"* [Report of the Inter-Imperial Relations Committee of the Imperial Conference of 1926, *Imperial Conference,*

1926, Summary of Proceedings (1926), Cmd. 2768, pp. 14, 15] has undergone modification and clarification as a result of the postwar evolution of former colonies to complete independence and, in some cases, the institution of a republican form of government.

The Commonwealth Relations Office List, 1955 described the Commonwealth as "the equivalent of what was formerly known as 'the British Empire', *i.e.* as comprising not only the United Kingdom and the countries previously known as Dominions, but also the dependencies of those countries, whether Colonies, Protectorates, Protected States or Trust Territories", and stated:

> "Within the Commonwealth . . . there are certain countries possessing a special status, namely that of a sovereign, independent country, recognized as a separate international entity, but associated with other Commonwealth countries of the same status in a relationship differing from that existing between foreign States. These countries are usually called 'the Members of the Commonwealth' as distinct from other countries within the Commonwealth such as Colonies which, though they may be described as 'Commonwealth countries', cannot properly be regarded as 'Members' of the Commonwealth. . . ."

The Commonwealth Relations Office List, 1955 (1955) 7.

> "The word 'Dominion' which implied certain associations with the past was regarded with disfavour by the new Asian members of the Commonwealth; it has gradually come to be discarded and is no longer used in official communications. Dominions are now referred to as 'Members of the Commonwealth' or 'Commonwealth countries'.
>
> "Thus Dominion status or independent or Commonwealth status means today simply independence coupled with the membership of the Commonwealth; it is, in the words of Mr. P. Frazer, former Prime Minister of New Zealand—'independence plus'. It is only in this sense that today we can talk of Dominion status."

Weinberg, *An Outline of the Constitutional Law of The Federation of Rhodesia and Nyasaland* (1959) 130.

> "When the stage was reached at which, as now seems established, 'Commonwealth' stands for the whole collection of communities, self-governing and non-self-governing, the need for the expression 'Commonwealth and Empire' disappears. All are countries of the Commonwealth and the self-governing countries are Members of the Commonwealth. And it is not perhaps surprising that 'Commonwealth' should be extended so widely in scope in the years since 1945. For with the granting of independence to India and Pakistan in 1947 and to Ceylon in 1948, the overwhelming majority of the peoples of the 'Empire' were now citizens of Members of the Commonwealth. . . ."

Wheare, *The Constitutional Structure of the Commonwealth* (1960) 6.

"Every one of the Member nations enjoys unfettered control of its own affairs. Thus it determines its foreign, domestic, and fiscal policies, defines its citizenship and immigration regulations, negotiates and signs treaties with other nations, maintains its own diplomatic service and decides for itself the issues of peace and war. No longer does the entry of the United Kingdom into war automatically involve the rest of the Commonwealth as was the case in 1914. In 1939, Australia, New Zealand, Canada and South Africa each made its own declaration of war, the last only after a proposal of formal neutrality had been debated and defeated in a free vote of its own Parliament. Eire, then a Member of the Commonwealth, decided to remain neutral and continued to maintain diplomatic relations with Germany, Italy and Japan with which the rest of the Commonwealth was at war, and that decision was accepted by the other Members of the Commonwealth. Members are free to join international organisations or not, irrespective of the decision of any other Member, and all have complete freedom on international issues.

. . . .

"The Commonwealth is not a federation, for there is no central government, defence force or judiciary, and no rigid obligations or commitments. Nor is it comparable with a contractual alliance such as the United Nations. It is no easy task to convey at one and the same time the essential freedom and the friendly intimacy of the Commonwealth relationship; yet both are equally real. Speaking of this relationship, the late Mr. Peter Fraser, when Prime Minister of New Zealand, said: 'It is independence with something added, and not independence with something taken away'."

The Commonwealth Association in Brief, British Information Services (1958) 2–5. See also Sandys, *The Modern Commonwealth* (1962).

In an address to members of the South African Parliament February 3, 1960, Prime Minister of Great Britain Macmillan, adverting to the choice to be made between the East and the West by the uncommitted independent members of the Commonwealth, stated:

"It is the basic principle for our modern Commonwealth that we respect each other's sovereignty in matters of internal policy. At the same time, we must recognize that in this shrinking world in which we live today, the internal policies of one nation may have effects outside it.

"We may sometimes be tempted to say to each other, 'Mind your own business.' But in these days, I would myself expand the old saying so that it runs: 'Mind your own business, but mind how it affects my business, too.'

"Let me be very frank with you, my friends. What governments and parliaments in the United Kingdom have done since the war in according independence to India, Pakistan, Ceylon, Malaya and Ghana, and what they will do for Nigeria and the other countries now nearing independence—all this, though we take full and sole responsibility for it, we do in the belief that it is the only way to establish the future of the Commonwealth and of the free world on sound foundations."

Excerpts from the address printed in the New York *Times*, Feb. 4, 1960, p. 6.

With the passage of the Royal Titles Act March 26, 1953, which recites "it is expedient that the style and titles at present appertaining to the Crown should be altered so as to reflect more clearly the existing constitutional relations of the members of the Commonwealth to one another and their recognition of the Crown as the symbol of their free association and of the Sovereign as the Head of the Commonwealth", the Parliament of the United Kingdom gave its assent to the "adoption by Her Majesty, for use in relation to the United Kingdom and all other the territories for whose foreign relations Her Government in the United Kingdom is responsible, of such style and titles as Her Majesty may think fit . . . ." **Royal Style and Title**

Accordingly, Her Majesty, by Proclamation dated May 28, 1953, adopted the following style and title:

"Elizabeth II, by the Grace of God of the United Kingdom of Great Britain and Northern Ireland and of Her other Realms and Territories Queen, Head of the Commonwealth, Defender of the Faith".

1 & 2 Eliz. 2, c. 9; *London Gazette*, 11th supp., May 29, 1953, No. 39873, p. 3023.

". . . the criterion of whether a country is inside the Commonwealth or outside it is now whether it recognizes the Queen as the symbol of its association with the other countries in the Commonwealth, and, as such, the Head of the Commonwealth. . . .

. . . .

". . . In this symbolic sense, the Queen or the Monarchy is an essential institution and the only essential institution of the Commonwealth as a whole. A Country in the Commonwealth, then, displays this badge of its association, and by this mark you can tell that it is in the Commonwealth and not outside."

Wheare, "The Nature and Structure of the Commonwealth", 47 Am. Pol. Sci. Rev. (1953) 1016, 1017, 1019. See also Moodie, "The Crown and the Commonwealth", 11 *Parliamentary Affairs* (1958) 180.

In answer to a question concerning the requests in 1948 of the Governments of India, Pakistan, and Burma to the British Government to assist them with respect to their diplomatic affairs in foreign countries, Under-Secretary of State for Commonwealth Relations Gordon-Walker replied:

> ". . . A feature of the structure of the Commonwealth is that the United Kingdom post in any foreign country is freely at the disposal of any other Commonwealth country which is not separately represented. This arrangement applies equally to India and Pakistan as to all other members of the Commonwealth, and no specific requests have been necessary to enable them to benefit by it. We are gladly doing what we can to meet any requests from India and Pakistan for assistance in establishing their own posts in foreign countries.
>
> "As for Burma, I understand that we are now, at the request of the Burmese Government, protecting their interests in certain countries where they have no representatives of their own, and have assisted them to the best of our ability in establishing their own Missions."

> Written Answers, 452 H.C. Deb. (5th ser.) cols. 82–83 (June 17, 1948).

Consultation
re
admission

In answer to a question concerning the British Government's practice of consultation with other members of the Commonwealth in regard to any decisions to establish self-government in a colony, Secretary of State for Commonwealth Relations Gordon-Walker stated in the House of Commons:

> "Whilst the United Kingdom Government alone carry the responsibility for internal constitutional developments in Colonies dependent upon the United Kingdom, we recognise the interest of the Governments of other members of the Commonwealth, and it is our practice to keep them informed of major developments in that sphere. Were any question of admission to full and independent membership of the Commonwealth to arise, all existing members would, following past practice, be consulted.

> . . . .

> "We must make quite clear the distinction between the grant of responsible self-government within the Commonwealth, which is a matter for the United Kingdom Government and the territory concerned, and for them alone, and the question of becoming a full member of the Commonwealth, which is of course a matter for all members of the Commonwealth. All steps towards responsible self-government within the Commonwealth are a matter between us and the territory concerned, and we must make that distinction quite clear and abide by it."

> 488 H.C. Deb. (5th ser.) col. 1199 (June 7, 1951). See also 502 H.C. Deb. (5th ser.) cols. 779–780 (June 16, 1952).

In January 1956, question was raised by a Member of the House of Commons as to what consultations had taken place during the past

5 years with members of the Commonwealth in respect of the procedure to determine the recognition of new members, and in what manner the distinction was drawn between Dominion status and Commonwealth membership. The Under-Secretary of State for Commonwealth Relations, Commander Allan Noble, replied:

"None. The position, which I think is well understood, is that the admission of a new member to the Commonwealth is a matter for consultation between the existing members as and when the occasion arises. The term 'Commonwealth membership' of course covers what was once known as 'Dominion status.'"

Written Answers, 548 H.C. Deb. (5th ser.) col. 41 (Jan. 26, 1956).

"There is one distinction between independence and 'Dominion status' which is of vital importance. The grant to a dependent territory of fully responsible government or 'independence' is a matter concerning exclusively that territory and the United Kingdom. Burma was granted independence and chose to quit the Commonwealth. The admission of such territory to the membership of the Commonwealth is a matter of concern to all its members.

"The position with regard to the rules of admission to the membership of the Commonwealth is, however, not altogether clear. According to Halsbury, the admission of a colony to full and independent membership of the Commonwealth must be preceded by consultation with all existing Members, but although the right of other Members to be consulted is implicit in the conception of equality of status, it does not follow that, where a dependency has been advanced by United Kingdom action to the verge of independent status, its admission to full membership must be delayed until the concurrence of every other Member has been secured. The principle of unanimity may be invoked more convincingly where the applicant for full membership is a state outside the Commonwealth. While, in 1941, the decision with regard to the admission of Ireland to the membership of the Commonwealth rested entirely with the United Kingdom, the position has [sic] changed in 1947. The admission of the three Asian Dominions, India, Pakistan and Ceylon was preceded by full consultation with other members of the Commonwealth who also have given their consent to the continued membership of India as a Republic within the Commonwealth.

"Amery in his 'Thoughts on the Constitution' points to new constitutional problems which may arise with regard to the actual membership of the Commonwealth. 'General consent—he says— was obviously required for the acceptance of an Indian Republic as a full and equal member of a Commonwealth hitherto based on allegiance to a common Crown. But how far has the Commonwealth, like the United Nations, become a corporate body whose assent is required for the admission of any new member of whatever origin? There is nothing in the new constitutional structure of the Commonwealth to prevent a foreign nation, whether monarchy or republic, wishing to join it. In that case admission would, no doubt, have to be subject to the approval of the existing partners. But does that apply equally to a community of British subjects which has attained to complete self-government? In other words could the United Kingdom Government, by conceding complete autonomy to the Gold Coast, secure its automatic admission as a partner in the Commonwealth? In answer to a question on this point the Secretary of State for Commonwealth Relations on 7th June, 1951, made it clear that in view of the interest of other Commonwealth Governments in constitutional developments in the Colonial Empire, it was the "practice to inform them of major developments in that sphere", and that, "following past practice", all existing Members would be consulted on any question of admission to full and independent membership, "which is, of course, a matter for all Members of the Commonwealth". It may be presumed—suggests Amery—that, when the case arises, it will be decided, again in accordance with Commonwealth practice, by general agreement and not as the result of any formal vote.'

"Professor Fitzgerald also takes the view that although the United Kingdom may confer full self-governing status on a territory under its jurisdiction, it cannot confer on it the full membership of the Commonwealth without the consent of the other member nations. He finds support for this view in the statement made by Lord John Hope, then Under-Secretary for Commonwealth Relations, during the second reading of the Ghana Independence Bill in the House of Commons on December 12, 1956. He said that whether Ghana would be a full Member of the Commonwealth was a matter for all the Members, and at the request of the Gold Coast Government the United Kingdom Government were approaching other Members on the subject. They had every hope that Ghana would become a full Member on the same day that she became independent. He pointed out that when the Bill became law Ghana would be the first of the British dependent territories in tropical Africa to attain full self-government as a sovereign and independent nation."

Weinberg, *An Outline of the Constitutional Law of The Federation of Rhodesia and Nyasaland* (1959) 132–134.

With regard to the practice of consultation with the members of the British Commonwealth, Prime Minister Attlee, speaking in the House of Commons, said:

"On questions of major importance to all members of the Commonwealth, there is, of course, the fullest consultation, and every endeavour is made to arrive at an agreed view. On many other questions the Commonwealth countries are kept fully informed. There are naturally many day-to-day questions of foreign policy of minor importance and limited interest, on which it is neither necessary nor practicable to co-ordinate the views of all the Commonwealth countries. It would not be possible in this sense to

integrate the policy of the Commonwealth over the whole field
of foreign affairs, nor would it be in accordance with the nature
of the Commonwealth as it has developed in the course of time to
attempt to do so. . . ."

478 H.C. Deb. (5th ser.) col. 241 (July 25, 1950).

"Whether the Commonwealth, clearly a symbol, may also become an instrument of action, is questionable. The former Dominions have come far since they were, from the standpoint of
international law, 'mere colonial portions of the mother country'.
As they have moved into an era of statehood they have created no
instrumentalities to which all are subject. There is but one
organ in the Commonwealth as such—the Prime Ministers' Conference. . . .

    .   .   .   .

"While the Commonwealth may not mean exactly the same
thing to each of its members, all of them appear to have found
substantial reasons for continuing in their unique association. It
is an instrument only in the sense of an organ of consultation. The
people whom the Prime Ministers in conference collectively represent include about one fourth of the world's total population.
Traditionally, the Commonwealth has symbolized especially the
idea of individual freedom as associated with British methods of
government. . . ."

Wilson, "The Commonwealth as Symbol and as Instrument", 53 Am. J.
Int'l L. (1959) 392, 394, 395.

Consultation—Prime Ministers' Conference

With regard to the admission to the Commonwealth of Nigeria,
whose independence was scheduled for October 1, 1960, the Prime
Ministers of the Commonwealth declared in a final communique issued
May 13, 1960, at the conclusion of their meeting at London that—

". . . They extended to the Federation their good wishes for
its future and looked forward to welcoming an independent
Nigeria as a member of the Commonwealth on the completion of
the necessary constitutional processes".

In confirmation of their consultation with respect to the impending
constitutional change in the Government of Ghana and that contemplated by the Union of South Africa, the Prime Ministers stated:

"The Meeting was informed that, in pursuance of the recent
plebiscite, the Constituent Assembly in Ghana had resolved that
the necessary constitutional steps should be taken to introduce a
republican form of constitution in Ghana by 1st July, 1960. In
notifying this forthcoming constitutional change, the Prime Minister of Ghana assured the Meeting of his country's desire to continue her membership of the Commonwealth and her acceptance
of The Queen as the symbol of the free association of its independent member nations and as such the Head of the Commonwealth. The Heads of Delegations of the other member countries

of the Commonwealth assured the Prime Minister of Ghana that the present relations between their countries and Ghana would remain unaffected by this constitutional change and they declared that their Governments would accept and recognise Ghana's continued membership of the Commonwealth.

"The Meeting noted a statement by the South African Minister of External Affairs that the Union Government intended to hold a referendum on the subject of South Africa becoming a republic. The meeting affirmed the view that the choice between a monarchy and a republic was entirely the responsibility of the country concerned. In the event of South Africa deciding to become a republic and if the desire was subsequently expressed to remain a member of the Commonwealth, the Meeting suggested that the South African Government should then ask for the consent of the other Commonwealth Governments either at a Meeting of Commonwealth Prime Ministers, or, if this were not practicable, by correspondence."

The American Embassy at London (Galbraith, First Secretary) to the Secretary of State (Herter), despatch No. 3362, May 17, 1960, MS. Department of State, file 741.022/5–1760.

Prime Minister Macmillan, referring to the request of the representative of the Union of South Africa that the Prime Ministers' Conference, 1960, agree in advance of its becoming a republic to the continued membership of republican South Africa in the Commonwealth, explained to the House of Commons:

"The Prime Ministers felt unwilling at that time [at the Prime Ministers' Conference, 1960] to agree. They were influenced by two considerations. First, such a decision might have been construed as an attempt to influence the referendum and therefore as an interference in a matter which was clearly one for the people of South Africa alone. Secondly, the precedents showed that although it was not necessary to withhold approval until all the constitutional processes had been completed, it was not proper to give approval before the decision to make a constitutional change of this kind was beyond all doubt. South Africa was accordingly invited to delay the application for renewed membership until after the referendum. . . ."

637 H.C. Deb. (5th ser.) col. 441 (Mar. 22, 1961).

In discussing the continuing links which the new Republic of Cyprus might have with the Commonwealth after independence, Archbishop Makarios and Dr. Kutchuk requested that the United Kingdom Bill providing for the Independence of Cyprus should be prepared in a form which would make Cyprus's future association with the Commonwealth possible and that it should also provide for Cyprus in the meantime to continue to be treated under United Kingdom law in the same way as the independent countries of the Commonwealth. The British Secretary of State explained that "if the Government of the Republic of Cyprus should transmit an application to Her Majesty's Government for Membership of the Commonwealth, this would be a matter for decision not by the United Kingdom Government alone but by all the existing Member Governments of the Commonwealth".

Statement issued from the Commonwealth Relations Office on Jan. 20, 1960, British White Paper, *Cyprus*, Cmnd. 1093, p. 177.

In a communique issued on March 13, 1961, the Prime Ministers' Conference, 1961, announced that—

"At their meeting this morning the Commonwealth Prime Ministers accepted a request from the Republic of Cyprus for admission to Commonwealth membership. They invited the President of the Republic to join the Meeting."

British Information Services, *Commonwealth Prime Ministers Conference*, Annex II, T.10, Mar. 20, 1961.

In a communique issued March 16, 1961, the Commonwealth Prime Ministers, noting that Sierra Leone would attain independence on April 27, 1961, announced: "They looked forward to welcoming Sierra Leone as a member of the Commonwealth on the completion of the necessary constitutional processes".

Ibid.

In accordance with the Commonwealth Prime Ministers' suggestion at their conference in 1960 (*supra*), the Union of South Africa made application at the Prime Ministers' Conference, 1961, for continued membership in the Commonwealth as a republic. Following their historic consideration of this application, the Prime Ministers issued the following communique on March 15, 1961:

Withdrawal of application of Union of South Africa

"At their meetings this week the Commonwealth Prime Ministers have discussed questions affecting South Africa.
"On 13th March the Prime Minister of South Africa informed the Meeting that, following the plebiscite in October, 1960, the appropriate constitutional steps were now being taken to introduce a republican form of constitution in the Union, and that it was the desire of the Union Government that South Africa should remain within the Commonwealth as a republic.
"In connection with this application the meeting also discussed, with the consent of the Prime Minister of South Africa, the racial policy followed by the Union Government. The Prime Minister of South Africa informed the other Prime Ministers this evening that in the light of the views expressed on behalf of other member Governments and the indications of their future intentions regarding the racial policy of the Union Government, he had de-

cided to withdraw his application for South Africa's continuing membership of the Commonwealth as a republic."

Ibid.

With regard to the issues presented at the Commonwealth Prime Ministers' Conference by the Union of South Africa's application to remain a member of the Commonwealth, Prime Minister Macmillan stated in the House of Commons:

". . . If it had been possible to deal with the application as a purely constitutional matter, there need have been no difficulty. For the great decision of principle as to whether the Commonwealth should continue to rest on allegiance to the Crown or whether republican States might be members was in fact settled in 1949.

"In that year India became a republic but remained a member of the Commonwealth, accepting the Sovereign as head of the Commonwealth as a symbol of our unity. Since then Pakistan and Ghana have become republics within the Commonwealth, and Ceylon has been given an assurance that she will continue to be welcome as a republican member, although she is in fact still a monarchy.

"It was clear that the Commonwealth Prime Ministers as a whole did not feel themselves able to treat the continued membership of South Africa as a purely formal or procedural question. In view of the strong feelings on the racial policies pursued by the Government of South Africa, the discussion could not be narrowed to the constitutional point. Because of the wide implications of South Africa's racial policies for other members of the Commonwealth and their effect on world opinion, this matter could not be dealt with on the basis of constitutional change alone.

"Dr. Verwoerd himself recognised this. Although it is an established convention of these meetings that we do not discuss the domestic affairs of a member country without the consent of that country, the Prime Minister of South Africa agreed that on this occasion the racial policy of the Union Government should be discussed. In this I am sure he was right, for this question had become, as I say, more than a matter of domestic interest to South Africa. It had aroused widespread international interest and concern. It affected in various ways the relations between South Africa and other members of the Commonwealth. It was even threatening to damage the concept of the Commonwealth itself as a multi-racial association. In all those circumstances it was impossible to overlook the racial issue. In fact, as the House knows, it became the dominant issue, and the purely constitutional point was overshadowed.

"May I say in passing that I do not at all accept the view, which I have seen expressed in the last few days, that this means that the Commonwealth will in future turn itself into a body for passing judgment on the internal affairs of member countries.

I see no reason why the existing convention to which I have referred should not be maintained. After all, it was not broken on this occasion, for the Prime Minister of South Africa agreed that this discussion should be held. There were, as I have indicated, good reasons why it should have been held on this occasion—because of the grave external effects of the policy to which I have drawn attention."

637 H.C. Deb. (5th ser.) cols. 442–443 (Mar. 22, 1961).

The Secretary of State for Commonwealth Relations (Duncan Sandys), speaking in the House of Commons during its discussion of the withdrawal of the application of the Union of South Africa to remain in the Commonwealth over the issue of South Africa's policy of *apartheid*, stated:

". . . to us, the Commonwealth means something more than a number of separate bilateral links between Britain and each of the members of the Commonwealth. To us, the Commonwealth is, above all, a collective relationship in which we consult together, think together and, as far as possible, work together for the advancement of broad, common objectives.

"I agree with my right hon. Friend the Member for Thirsk and Malton that the Commonwealth of Nations, as its name implies, is an association of peoples and not only of Governments. For reasons which we all regret, South Africa will no longer be represented in this Commonwealth fellowship. We hope, however, that its absence will be no more than temporary . . . and that the time will come when, in changed circumstances, we shall be able to welcome back a representative of South Africa at our Commonwealth family table.

.   .   .   .

"The Commonwealth Prime Ministers have always wisely resisted the idea of establishing a code of conduct to which all members are required to conform. Our relations are governed not by a book of rules but by what has been described as a general concensus of opinion. But although there may be no precise definition of the principles for which the Commonwealth stands, there are certain things for which it clearly does not stand and which are incompatible with the whole spirit which inspires it. One of those things is the policy of *apartheid* as preached and practised in South Africa.

"We must, of course, recognise that racial discrimination still exists in many countries of the world. Incidentally, these are not confined, as one might imagine yb [*sic*] reading some newspapers, entirely to British Colonial Territories. But South Africa's policy is different, not only in degree but in kind. As the Leader of the Opposition said, there is a difference between precept and practice. Everywhere else outside South Africa Governments are trying, more or less successfully, progressively to eliminate racial discrimination between their citizens. In

South Africa, on the other hand, discrimination and segregation have been elevated into a principle, an objective of policy, something to be proud of, an inspiring ideal.

"Anyone who attended the Prime Ministers' Conference last week must have felt that on this subject Dr. Verwoerd was talking a totally different language from that of the rest of his colleagues. He is deliberately trying to swim against the whole current of world thought. He is trying to put history into reverse. It may be said that, however wrong and ill-conceived *apartheid* may be, it is South Africa's internal affair and does not affect her external relations with other members of the Commonwealth. It must, however, be recognised that *apartheid* has aroused deep emotions throughout the world, and has ceased to be a matter of purely domestic concern.

"But, quite apart from the wider considerations of humanity, it is clear that South Africa's racial policy and her attitude towards racial matters has become incompatible with the effective operation of the Commonwealth relationship. The Commonwealth is essentially an association of nations of different races and colours who have established a close and special relationship with one another. That close and special relationship can be maintained in one way only, and that is by continuous and intimate consultation between their Governments.

"Yet, while applying for continued membership, the South African Government—and this is something which bit very deep into all other members—still firmly refuses to receive diplomatic representatives from any non-European members of the Commonwealth. This makes a mockery of consultation; and, in any case, we cannot accept that because of the colour of their skins certain members of the Commonwealth are to be treated as lepers.

"By this refusal to have normal external relations with the African and Asian countries, even when they are members of the Commonwealth family, South Africa has herself carried the principle of *apartheid* into the international sphere.

.   .   .   .

"Dr. Verwoerd has said that the withdrawal of South Africa would be followed by the disintegration of the Commonwealth. I must say something about that. I have no wish to hurt anybody's feelings. Had Dr. Verwoerd not raised the issue himself, I should have preferred not to discuss whether we would be worse off or better off for the departure of South Africa. Whatever view we may take of the events of last week, I think that we must agree on one thing—that the withdrawal of South Africa will have the effect not of dividing but of uniting more closely the nations of the Commonwealth.

"It seems that the South African Government have not understood the changed character of our modern Commonwealth association. The rôle of the Commonwealth is not to build a *bloc* of racially homogeneous nations. It is rather, as the hon. Member for Cardiff, South-East (Mr. Callaghan) said, to build a bridge between peoples of all races and creeds. Its purpose is not to present a united front, but to provide a unifying influence in a deeply divided world. With the exception of South Africa, each of the members of the Commonwealth has its own circle of friends with whom it has some special affinity whether through geography, race, religion or alliance. These various circles of friends, when put together, embrace in one way or another the greater part of the globe. In fact, outside the Communist world there is scarcely any group of nations in which members of the Commonwealth do not play a leading rôle."

637 H.C. Deb. (5th ser.) cols. 526–531 (Mar. 22, 1961). See, in general, Wheare, *The Constitutional Structure of the Commonwealth* (1960).

India—a "sovereign democratic republic"

The Indian Independence Act, 1947 (10 & 11 Geo. 6, c. 30) which came into force August 15, 1947, partitioned India and set up two independent Dominions to be known respectively as India and Pakistan.

In further delineating the independent relationship between the newly formed Dominions and the United Kingdom Government, the act provided in some of its more pertinent provisions:

"6–(1) The Legislature of each of the new Dominions shall have full power to make laws for that Dominion, including laws having extra-territorial operation.

"(2) No law and no provision of any law made by the Legislature of either of the new Dominions shall be void or inoperative on the ground that it is repugnant to the law of England, or to the provisions of this or any existing or future Act of Parliament of the United Kingdom, or to any order, rule or regulation made under any such Act, and the powers of the Legislature of each Dominion include the power to repeal or amend any such Act, order, rule or regulation in so far as it is part of the law of the Dominion. . . .

"7–(1) As from the appointed day—

"(a) His Majesty's Government in the United Kingdom have no responsibility as respects the government of any of the territories which, immediately before that day, were included in British India;

"(b) the suzerainty of His Majesty over the Indian States lapses, and with it, all treaties and agreements in force at the date of the passing of this Act between His Majesty and the rulers of Indian States, all functions exercisable by His Majesty at that date with respect to Indian States, all obligations of His Majesty existing at that date towards Indian States or the rulers thereof, and all powers, rights, authority or jurisdiction exercisable by His Majesty at that date in or in relation to Indian States by treaty, grant, usage, sufferance or otherwise; . . .

.   .   .   .

"(2) The assent of the Parliament of the United Kingdom is hereby given to the omission from the Royal Style and Titles of the words 'Indiae Imperator' and the words 'Emperor of

India' and to the issue by His Majesty for that purpose of His Royal Proclamation under the Great Seal of the Realm. . . ."

10 & 11 Geo. 6, c. 30; II Mansergh, *Documents and Speeches on British Commonwealth Affairs 1931–1952* (1953) 669–685.

The Prime Minister, Clement Attlee, explaining the Indian Independence Bill in the House of Commons July 10, 1947, commented, ". . . In this Bill, we set up two independent Dominions, free and equal, of no less status than the United Kingdom or the Dominion of Canada, completely free in all respects from any control by this country, but united by a common allegiance to the Sovereign and by a community of ideas, receiving from their membership of the Commonwealth great advantages, but in no way suffering any restriction. . . ."

439 H.C. Deb. (5th ser.) cols. 2441, 2446 (July 10, 1947); II Mansergh, *Documents and Speeches on British Commonwealth Affairs 1931–1952* (1953) 685, 689.

With the enactment of the Constitution of India, operative January 26, 1950, in the preamble of which it is stated in part: "WE, THE PEOPLE OF INDIA, . . . resolved to constitute India into a SOVEREIGN DEMOCRATIC REPUBLIC . . ." (II Peaslee, *Constitutions of Nations* (2d ed., 1956) 218, 219, 223), India adopted a republican form of government but at the same time exercised her option to retain membership within the Commonwealth.

Representatives of the Governments of all the Commonwealth countries having discussed in London, in April 1949, the effects of India's decision upon the existing structure of the Commonwealth and the constitutional relations between its members issued the following Declaration April 27, 1949:

"The Governments of the United Kingdom, Canada, Australia, New Zealand, South Africa, India, Pakistan and Ceylon, whose countries are united as members of the British Commonwealth of Nations and owe a common allegiance to the Crown, which is also the symbol of their free association, have considered the impending constitutional changes in India.

"The Government of India have informed the other Governments of the Commonwealth of the intention of the Indian people that under the new constitution which is about to be adopted India shall become a sovereign independent republic. The Government of India have however declared and affirmed India's desire to continue her full membership of the Commonwealth of Nations and her acceptance of The King as the symbol of the free association of its independent member nations and as such the Head of the Commonwealth.

"The Governments of the other countries of the Commonwealth, the basis of whose membership of the Commonwealth is not hereby changed, accept and recognise India's continuing membership in accordance with the terms of this declaration.

"Accordingly the United Kingdom, Canada, Australia, New Zealand, South Africa, India, Pakistan and Ceylon hereby declare that they remain united as free and equal members of the Commonwealth of Nations, freely co-operating in the pursuit of peace, liberty and progress."

II Mansergh, *Documents and Speeches on British Commonwealth Affairs 1931–1952* (1953) 846–847.

Commenting on this Declaration of April 27, 1949, Prime Minister Nehru in a speech before the Indian Constituent Assembly May 16, 1949, said:

". . . you will notice that while in the first paragraph there is the question of allegiance to the Crown which exists at present, later, of course, this question does not arise, because India by becoming a Republic goes outside the Crown area completely. There is a reference, in connexion with the Commonwealth, to the King as the symbol of that association. Observe that the reference is to the King and not to the Crown. It is a small matter, but it has a certain significance. But the point is this, that in so far as the Republic of India is concerned, her Constitution and its working are concerned, she has nothing to do with any external authority, with any king, and none of her subjects owe any allegiance to the King or any other external authority. The Republic may however agree to associate itself with certain other countries that happen to be monarchies or whatever they choose to be. This declaration, therefore, states that this new Republic of India, completely sovereign and owing no allegiance to the King, as the other Commonwealth countries do owe, will, nevertheless, be a full member of this Commonwealth and it agrees that the King will be recognized as a symbol of this free partnership or rather association.

.   .   .   .

". . . one of the objects of this kind of Commonwealth association is now to create a status which is something between being completely foreign and being of one nationality. Obviously, the Commonwealth countries belong to different nations. They are different nationalities. Normally either you have a common nationality or you are foreign. There is no intermediate stage. Up till now in this Commonwealth or the British Commonwealth of Nations, there was a binding link which was allegiance to the King. With that link, therefore, in a sense there was common nationality in a broad way. That snaps, that ends when we become a Republic, and if we should desire to give a certain preference or a certain privilege to any one of these countries, we would normally be precluded from doing so, because of what is called the 'most favoured nation clause' every country would be as much foreign as any other country. Now, we want to take away that foreignness, keeping in our own hands what, if any, privileges or preferences we can give to another country. That is a matter entirely for two countries to decide by treaty or arrangement, so that we create a new state of affairs—or we try to create it—that the other countries, although in a sense foreign, are, nevertheless, not completely foreign."

Indian Constituent Assembly, *Constituent Assembly Debates*, vol. 8, pp. 2–10; II Mansergh, *Documents and Speeches on British Commonwealth Affairs 1931–1952* (1953) 847–849.

"This declaration [the Declaration of April 27, 1949] marks a radical change in the accepted concept of the Commonwealth—a concept which has been historically altered under the pressure of circumstances and changing situations in world politics to meet new needs and aspirations, but at the same time strengthening the unity of its purpose. The new formula has been evolved to accommodate India to fit into the pattern of the Commonwealth. India remains a Sovereign Democratic Republic. Her sovereignty is in no way affected. The agreement recognizes a symbolic link between the members of the Commonwealth—the King. The core of the agreement is that India, which has become a Republic, continues to recognize the King as the unifying symbol of Commonwealth association and that she enjoys complete independence as a Republic. This new concept of a functionless and merely symbolic Kingship accommodates India in the Commonwealth without in any way affecting the link between other Dominions and the Crown. The King is not the King of India and he is regarded as the symbolic head of the Commonwealth without any function to perform in relation to India. In effect his headship of the Commonwealth, so far as India is concerned, is only notional, but it is a constitutional concept evolved and accepted by all the members of the Commonwealth."

Joshi, *The Constitution of India* (1954) 18–20.

Princely States of India

The term "Indian State" was defined in subsection (1) of section 311 of the Government of India Act, 1935, as including "any territory, whether described as a State, an Estate, a Jagir or otherwise belonging to or under the suzerainty of a Ruler who is under the suzerainty of His Majesty and not being a part of British India". The Government of India White Paper on Indian States noted that "In political practice the term applied to a political community occupying a territory in India of defined boundaries and subject to a common Ruler who enjoyed or exercised, as belonging to him, any of the functions and attributes of internal sovereignty duly recognised by the Paramount Power".

White Paper on Indian States, Government of India (1948) 3.

The White Paper on Indian States classified the Indian States in the three following categories:

"(i) States, the Rulers of which were members of the Chamber of Princes in their own right. 108 in number.

"(ii) States, the Rulers of which were represented in the Chamber of Princes by 12 members of their Order elected by themselves. 127 in number.

"(iii) Estates, Jagirs and others. 327 in number.

"The first category included the Ruling Princes who enjoyed permanent dynastic salute of 11 guns or more, together with other Rulers of the States who exercised such full or practically full internal powers as, in the opinion of the Viceroy, qualified them for individual admission to the Chamber. As a result of fresh admissions, the membership of the Chamber was enlarged to 140 States."

Ibid. 5.

While 40 of these States had treaties with the Paramount Power, and a larger number had some form of engagements or sanads, *i.e.*, acknowledgment of concession or authority or privileges generally coupled with conditions proceeding from the Paramount Power, the paramountcy of the British Crown was not coextensive with the rights of the Crown derived from the treaties. As the Indian White Paper noted, paramountcy was based rather on the treaties, engagements, and sanads as supplemented by usage and sufferance and by decisions of the Government of India and the Secretary of State embodied in political practice, and the rights of the Paramount Power covered both external and internal matters.

The Indian White Paper described the relationship between the Paramount Power and the Indian States more extensively as follows:

"20. For external purposes State territory and the State subjects were in the same position as British territory and British subjects. The States had no international life and in consequence of the loss by them of their power of negotiation and legation, the paramount power had the exclusive authority of making peace or war or negotiating or communicating with foreign States. The rights and duties assumed by the Paramount Power in regard to external affairs carried with them consequential rights and duties. The Paramount Power was responsible for implementing its international commitments; the Princes were required to give effect to the international obligations entered into by the Paramount Power.

"21. The right of intervention in the internal affairs could be exercised for the benefit of the Ruler, of the State, of India as a whole or for giving effect to international commitments. The authority of the Paramount Power could thus be interposed *inter alia* for the prevention of dismemberment of a State, the suppres-

sion of a rebellion against the lawful sovereign, the prevention
of gross misrule, the economic growth of the whole of India, checking inhuman practices or offences against natural law or public
morality.

"22. The Paramount Power was responsible for the defence of
both British India and the Indian States and exercised full control
over all matters connected with defence, such as the establishment
of cantonments, the regulation of the strength of the armed forces
of the States, the procurement of supplies, free passage of troops,
supply of arms and ammunition, etc.

"23. Lastly the Paramount Power claimed certain important
rights as derived from the Royal Prerogative. These included
the exclusive right to settle precedence and to grant honours; to
regulate ceremonies; to recognise all successions and to settle
disputes as to succession; to impose or remit *nazarana* or succession duties; to take charge of the States of minors and to provide
for their education; and to impose the duty of loyalty to the
Crown.

"24. Paramountcy thus made serious incursions into the internal sovereignty of the States and it was natural that the Rulers
should seek codification of the political practice. The appointment of the Indian States Committee in 1927 to report upon the
relationship between the Paramount Power and the Indian States
was an outcome of these efforts. The Committee, however, found
it impossible to evolve a formula which would cover the exercise
of Paramountcy. It expressed the view that 'Paramountcy must
remain paramount; it must fulfill its obligations, defining or
adapting itself according to the shifting necessities of the time
and the progressive development of the States.' "

Ibid. 5–7.

Lapse of
paramountcy

In recognition of the fact that India's attainment of independence
and institution of a new constitutional order would render the
British Government unable to carry out the obligations of paramountcy, a Cabinet Mission issued a Memorandum in regard to
States Treaties and Paramountcy on May 12, 1946, which, in announcing that "His Majesty's Government will cease to exercise the
powers of paramountcy", explained that "This means that the rights
of the States which flow from their relationship to the Crown will no
longer exist and that all the rights surrendered by the States to the
paramount power will return to the States. Political arrangements
between the States on the one side and the British Crown and British
India on the other will thus be brought to an end." In assuring the
Princes of these states that there was no intention on the part of the
Crown to initiate any change in their relationship with the Crown
or the rights guaranteed by their treaties and engagements without
their consent, the memorandum stated "The void will have to be filled
either by the States entering into a federal relationship with the

successor Government or Governments in British India, or failing this, entering into particular political arrangements with it or them."

Ibid., app. III, pp. 44–45.

The Cabinet Mission Plan, announced May 16, 1946, explained that "Paramountcy can neither be retained by the British Crown nor transferred to the new Government" and in providing for the entry of the states into the proposed Union of India, recommended that the states retain all subjects and powers other than those ceded to the Union, which as specified were: Foreign Affairs, Defence and Communications.

Ibid., app. IV, p. 45.

The Indian Independence Act of 1947, providing for the lapse of paramountcy without mention of a transfer of rights, recites in section 7b:

> ". . . the suzerainty of His Majesty over the Indian States lapses, and with it, all treaties and agreements in force at the date of the passing of this Act between His Majesty and the rulers of Indian States, all functions exercisable by His Majesty at that date with respect to Indian States, all obligations of His Majesty existing at that date towards Indian States or the rulers thereof, and all powers, rights, authority or jurisdiction exercisable by His Majesty at that date in or in relation to Indian States by treaty, grant, usage, sufferance or otherwise; . . ."

10 & 11 Geo. 6, c. 30, July 18, 1947.

An exchange between Sardar Vallabhbhai Patel, Deputy Prime Minister and Minister for States in the Indian Government, and the ruler of the State of Kawardha affirmed the Indian Government's adherence to this arrangement. When the ruler of Kawardha requested Sardar Patel to protect the State as it had been protected by the British in the past, Sardar Patel replied that protection from internal disorders could not be extended to the State unless it had specifically acceded to the Dominion Government in internal affairs as well. To the ruler's pronouncement that he was prepared to accept the paramountcy of the Dominion Government, Sardar Patel explained that there could be no justification for doing so because in free India all were alike and no Indian could be paramount over another.

Menon, *The Integration of the Indian States* (1956) 169.

The declared intention of the British Government that the Princely States should be left free to join either with India or with Pakistan or to remain independent was officially expressed by Lord

Listowel, Secretary of State for India, who in referring to August 15, 1947, the effective date of Indian independence, stated in the House of Lords July 16, 1947:

> "From that moment the appointments and functions of the Crown Representatives and his officers will terminate and the States will be the masters of their own fate. They will then be entirely free to choose whether to associate with one or the other of the Dominion Governments or to stand alone and His Majesty's Government will not use the slightest pressure to influence their momentous and voluntary decision. But I think it can hardly be doubted that it would be in the best interests of their own people, and of India as a whole, that in the fulness of time all the States should find their appropriate place within one or other of the new Dominions."

150 H.L. Deb. (5th ser.) col. 812 (July 16, 1947).

Accession With the adoption of the policy of accession the Indian States Department, set up to deal with matters arising between the Central Government and the Indian States, drafted an Instrument of Accession which in final form provided for the accession of the Princely States to the Dominion of India in the matters of Defence, External Affairs and Communications as defined in List I of Schedule VII to the Government of India Act of 1935, reproduced in a Schedule annexed to the Instrument of Accession. It was expressly stipulated therein that nothing in the Instrument affected the continuance of the ruler's sovereignty in and over his state or, excepting for the three subjects to which he acceded, the exercise of any powers, authority, and rights now enjoyed by him as ruler of that state or the validity of any law in force in that state at that time.

White Paper on Indian States, *op. cit.* 52–54.

Only the fully empowered states, of which there were 140, could sign this Instrument of Accession.

V. P. Menon, Secretary of the States Department, recorded:

> "Besides these 140 States, there were *estates* and *talukas*, where the Crown exercised certain powers and jurisdiction, that were also counted as 'States'. These, numbering over 300, were situated in Kathiawar and Gujarat. Under the Attachment Scheme of 1943 some of these *estates* and *talukas* were tagged on to adjoining bigger States. But with the lapse of paramountcy, the Attachment Scheme came to an end. In any case, the rulers of these *estates* and *talukas* desired that they should be reverted to their former position and that the Government of India should administer their *estates* as was done by the Political Department before 1943. Another Instrument of Accession, suitable for their status and requirements, was prepared for these *estates* and *talukas*. This document, while preserving the form of accession,

vested all the residuary powers and jurisdiction in the Central Government. Subsequently an ordinance termed the 'Extra Provincial Jurisdiction Ordinance' was promulgated for the exercise of the powers and jurisdiction acquired by the Government of India in these areas.

"There were a number of intermediate rulers, higher in status than the *talukdars* and *estate-holders* of Kathiawar and Gujarat, who exercised wide but not quite full powers. These States, numbering over 70, were in Kathiawar, Central India and the Simla Hills. We devised still another Instrument of Accession for these States, the object of which was to ensure that the rulers did not exercise higher powers than they had prior to 15 August 1947. The rulers recognized that it was a fair condition that they could not expect to rise in status suddenly because of the lapse of paramountcy."

Menon, *op. cit.* 110–111.

Each acceding state signed a Standstill Agreement, conditional upon the accession of the state concerned, which provided in part that "Until new agreements . . . are made, all agreements and administrative arrangements as to matters of common concern now existing between the Crown and any Indian State shall, in so far as may be appropriate, continue as between the Dominion of India or, as the case may be, the part thereof, and the State". *(Standstill Agreement)*

White Paper on Indian States, *op. cit.*, app. IX, p. 54.

Mr. Menon, writing of the effect of this policy of accession, comments:

"By the policy of accession we had ensured the fundamental unity of the country. India had become one federation, with the provinces and the States as integral parts. The Standstill Agreement had provided the basis for retaining intact the many agreements and administrative arrangements which had been built up over nearly a century for ensuring that all-India interests were safeguarded and which, with the termination of paramountcy, had threatened to disappear and in the process throw the whole country into a state of confusion. . . ."

Menon, *op. cit.* 120–121.

Integration of the Indian States involved a two-fold operation: accession of the individual states to the Dominion of India or to the Dominion of Pakistan; and the merger of regional groups of states with provinces of India or the formation of these territories of states into unions. These unions or mergers came into being under the terms of a Covenant signed by the rulers of the states, estates, and *talukas* comprising the new union which recorded their agreement to unite and integrate their territories in one state with a common *(Integration of Indian States)* executive, legislature, and judiciary. As a common feature, these Covenants guaranteed to the rulers concerned their succession, Civil List, personal property, rights, privileges, dignities, and titles. In addition to the Covenants, the unions, once formed, signed a fresh Instrument of Accession (sometimes required under a mandatory provision in the Covenant as in the cases of Madhya Bharat, Patiala and East Punjab States, and the Travancore-Cochin Unions) whereby the Rajpramukh acceded to India in respect to all the subjects in both the federal and concurrent list for legislation by the Dominion Legislature, excepting entries relating to taxation and duties. (See app. XVIII of White Paper on Indian States, *op. cit.* 94). In the Covenant constituting the United State of Travancore and Cochin, however, a permissive provision was included empowering the Rajpramukh to execute an Instrument of Accession on entries relating to taxation and duties.

The effect of the accession to India upon the federal relationship between the states and the Central Government of India as established by the initial Instruments of Accession was explained by Secretary Menon in his answer to Sir Pratap Singh's challenge to the legality of the merger of Baroda with Bombay in a letter, part of which is quoted as follows:

"Your Highness seems to lay great emphasis on the terms of the Instrument of Accession signed by Your Highness in August 1947. The whole object of this Instrument was to establish a limited constitutional relationship between the Dominion of India and the State of Baroda on a federal basis. I wonder if Your Highness's contention is that this federal relationship continued even after the cession by Your Highness to the Government of India of full and exclusive jurisdiction and power in relation to the governance of your State. As Your Highness has yourself stated, under the terms of the Agreement of Merger, the Dominion Government became competent to exercise the ruler's powers, authority and jurisdiction in relation to the governance of the State in such manner as it thought fit. Quite obviously, with the execution of the Agreement, which transferred all powers pertaining or incidental to the governance of the State to the Government of India, the Instrument of Accession as well as the Standstill Agreement stood completely superseded. The Government of India having succeeded to Your Highness's powers and authority both sovereign and non-sovereign took such measures as they considered necessary to give effect to the merger. . . ."

Menon, *op. cit.* 427.

In holding the Maharaja of Jammu and Kashmir's proclamation entrusting his full and plenary powers of legislation to Yuvraj valid and constitutional under the Jammu and Kashmir Constitution Act,

1996, the High Court of Judicature of Jammu and Kashmir rejected the appellant's contention that the Maharaja of Jammu and Kashmir was not an absolute sovereign and therefore could not entrust his legislative powers to any other person. Noting further the appellant's reasoning that, before the partition of India, the Maharaja was under the paramountcy of the British Crown, that after he executed the Instrument of Accession in favor of the Dominion of India he surrendered part of his sovereignty to the Dominion of India; that he was therefore a limited subordinated sovereign; and that he consequently could not delegate his legislative authority, the Court discussed the constitutional relationship that existed between the Jammu and Kashmir State and the British Crown before the partition of India and how it was affected by the Indian Independence Act of 1947 and by the subsequent execution of the Instrument of Accession by His Highness on October 26, 1947, as follows:

". . . Previous to the partition there was no doubt that the Ruler of the Jammu and Kashmir State was under the suzerainty of the British Crown inasmuch as foreign relations were under the exclusive control of the Crown representative. But in so far as the internal sovereignty of the Ruler was concerned it was absolutely unlimited and there were no fetters on it. In this connection it would be relevant to reproduce Sections 4 and 5 of the Jammu and Kashmir Constitution Act, 1996 as they stood before the Act was amended in November 1951:

" '4. The territories for the time being vested in His Highness, are governed by and in the name of His Highness and all rights, authority and jurisdiction which appertain or are incidental to the Government of such territories are exercisable by His Highness, except in so far as may be otherwise provided by or under this Act, or as may be otherwise directed by His Highness.

" '5. Notwithstanding anything contained in this or any other Act, all powers, legislative, executive and judicial, in relation to the State and its Government are hereby declared to be and to have always been inherent in and possessed and retained by His Highness and nothing contained in this or any other Act shall affect or be deemed to have affected the right and prerogative of His Highness to make laws, and issue proclamations, orders and ordinances by virtue of his inherent authority'.

". . . These provisions make it crystal clear that the territories comprised in the State of Jammu and Kashmir were vested in His Highness and governed by and in his name and all rights, authority and jurisdiction appertaining or incidental to the government of these territories was exercisable by His Highness except in so far as was otherwise provided under the Act or as it might otherwise be directed by him. Despite the fact that under the Act a Legislative Assembly, i.e. Praja Sabha, had been set up with certain circumscribed powers, all legislative, executive and judicial powers of His Highness in relation to the State and its Government were declared to be or to have always been inherent in and possessed by His Highness. In view of these clear provisions it is futile to argue that His Highness' powers to do what he pleased in relation to the State could be seriously questioned. So far as the internal sovereignty of the State was concerned the powers of the Ruler were similar to those of the British parliament. In this connection the following extract from the judgment of the late Chief Justice of the Supreme Court of India in The Delhi Laws Act, (1912), AIR 1951 S C 332 at p. 337 (A) may be aptly quoted:

> " 'The important question underlying the three questions submitted for the Court's consideration is what is described as the delegation of legislative powers. "A legislative body which is sovereign like an autocratic ruler has power" to do anything. It may, like a ruler, by an individual decision, direct that a certain person may be put to death or a certain property may be taken over by the State. "A body of such character may have power to nominate someone who can exercise all its powers and make all its decisions". This is possible to be done because there is no authority or tribunal which can question the right or power of the authority to do so'.

There is no doubt whatsoever that the observations set out above fully apply to the powers of an Indian ruler like the Ruler of the State of Jammu and Kashmir.

"In this connection reference may also be made to a Full Bench judgment of Pepsu High Court,—Gurdwara Sahib v. Piyara Singh', A. I. R. 1953 Pepsu 1 (B) cited by the learned Acting Advocate General. It is stated therein that sovereignty of a State has two aspects, i.e. 'external' as independent of all control from without and 'internal' as paramount over all actions within. A State by ceding certain powers with regard to external affairs to another state does not cease to be sovereign if its powers with regard to internal matters remain unrestricted. It was held that the erstwhile Patiala State in the above sense was an independent and sovereign State, and its Ruler, so far as internal matters were concerned, exercised powers identical with those exercised by parliament in England. In short though in matters relating to external affairs and relations with states he was controlled by the British Government, and even in internal matters the paramount power had the right to interfere in certain contingencies, in internal matters his words had the weight and authority of law, and he exercised all the powers of a sovereign and discharged all his functions as such in matters judicial, executive and administrative. In his sovereign capacity he had the fullest control over his subjects and their property in his territories and could pass all kinds of orders. Therefore where in his capacity as the ruler of the Patiala State the Maharaja passed an executive order depriving a subject of his property and conferred the same on a Gurdwara Committee the Full Bench of the High Court held in the above case that the Civil Courts had no jurisdiction to question the legality of the order.

"... While the Maharaja of Kashmir was under the Paramountcy of the British Crown before the partition of India from 15–8–1947 under Section 7, Indian Independence Act (10 & 11 Geo. VI Ch. 30) passed by the British Parliament suzerainty of His Majesty over the Indian States lapsed and all functions exercisable by His Majesty at that date with respect to the State of Jammu and Kashmir, all obligations of His Majesty towards the Jammu and Kashmir State or the ruler thereof and all powers, rights, authority or jurisdiction exercisable by His Majesty at that date in relation to the State of Jammu and Kashmir by treaty or otherwise lapsed and the State became an independent and sovereign State in the full sense of the International Law. Thus whatever limits to the sovereignty of His Highness in relation to matters coming within the sphere of paramountcy existed before 15–8–1947, these ceased to exist and His Highness became an uncontrolled and absolute sovereign even in relation to such spheres from that. Now let us examine what was the effect of the execution of the Instrument of Accession by His Highness on 26–10–1947. This Instrument of Accession which was executed by the Ruler of the independent and sovereign State of Jammu and Kashmir was executed by him under Section 6, Government of India Act 1935, as adopted by the Indian (Provisional Constitution) Order, 1947. By executing this Instrument of Accession the Ruler on behalf of the State acceded to the Dominion of India with the object that certain authorities specified in Section 6 (1) (a) shall, by virtue of the Instrument of Accession, 'but subject always to the terms thereof,' and for the purposes only of the Dominion, exercise in relation to the State such functions as would be vested in them by or under the Act. It is clear that, even if the Instrument of Accession had not made any specific reservations therein, the instrument read with Section 6, Government of India Act would leave the residuary sovereignty of the State entirely unaffected. But the Instrument of Accession does not leave this important matter to be determined by implication alone. Clause 8 of the Instrument of Accession runs as follows:

" '8. Nothing in this Instrument affects the continuance of my sovereignty in and over the State, or, save as provided by or under this Instrument, the exercise of any powers, authority & rights now enjoyed by me as Ruler of this State or the validity of any law at present in force in this State.'

In view of this clear and express reservation we see that no change whatsoever was affected in the residuary sovereignty of the State or the power of its Ruler so far as the succession of the State to the Dominion of India was concerned. It may not be out of place to mention here that on 5–3–1948 His Highness issued a proclamation by which he appointed a Cabinet to carry on the administration of the State. Sheikh Mohd Abdullah was appointed the Prime Minister and all other Ministers were appointed on his advice. The proclamation laid down that the Cabinet would act on the principle of joint responsibility. In the words of the Late Mr. Gopalaswami Ayyangar thus

" 'He instituted a kind of responsible government with a Prime Minister and colleagues who would own collective responsibility for their acts and regard themselves as jointly responsible for all the acts of the Government.' (Vide Constituent Assembly debates dated 17–10–1949, Vol. X No. 10 at page 426).

This Proclamation did not in any way affect the sovereign powers vested in the Ruler. The only effect of his proclamation was that thenceforward His Highness exercised his executive and legislative powers in accordance with the advice given to him by his government, i.e. his Council of Ministers while he continued to exercise his judicial powers in accordance with the advice given to him by the Board of Judicial Advisers provided under Section 71, Jammu and Kashmir Constitution Act, 1996. The inherent powers of the Ruler remained unchanged."

Magher Singh v. *Principal Secretary, Jammu and Kashmir Government,* All India Rep. 1953 J. and K. 25, 27–28 (vol. 40, C.N. 17), Mar. 25, 1953.

For an account of the initial formation of these States following their integration with India into mergers, unions, or chief commissioner's provinces, see Poplai, Selected Documents on Asian Affairs, I *India, 1947–50* (1959) ; Menon, *The Integration of the Indian States* (1956). For an account of their reorganization in 1949, see First Schedule to Constitution of India, Nov. 26, 1949, II Peaslee, *Constitutions of Nations* (2d ed., 1956) 335–337. For an account of their reorganization in 1956, see The States Reorganization Bill, 1956, Bill No. 30–F of 1956, as passed by the Houses of Parliament (New Delhi, India (1956)).

Hyderabad   With the lapse of paramountcy, Hyderabad considered that its legal status was that of an independent state. The position of the Indian Government as reviewed in an official Indian document, White Paper on Hyderabad 1948, was that such a claim controverted the British Government's policy and intentions regarding the lapse of paramountcy as indicated in the memorandum of May 12, 1946, in regard to States Treaties and Paramountcy, which specifically stated that the void created by the lapse of paramountcy will have to be filled either by the states entering into federal relationship with the successor Government or Governments in British India or, failing this, entering into particular political arrangements with it or them. The Indian Government contended: "These particular arrangements which were to be the only alternative to federal relationship, could not but be in the nature of paramountcy or subordinate association of the States with the successor Governments. The Cabinet Mission's Statement dated 16th May, 1946, also while recognising the principle that paramountcy was not to be transferred to the new Government presupposed the willing cooperation of the States and the plan had as its integral part the accession of the States to the Dominion of India in respect of the three subjects of defence, foreign affairs and communications. Although the Cabinet Mission's plan was superseded by the British Government's Statement of 3rd June, 1947, it undoubtedly embodied their considered policy as regards the position of the States under the future polity of India" (p. 6).

As a special concession to Hyderabad, India entered into a 1-year Standstill Agreement with Hyderabad on November 29, 1947, without requiring accession to the State of India as a condition precedent. The Government of India regarded this arrangement as establishing a period of *status quo* on the lines on which Hyderabad's relationship was regulated with the Crown Representative minus paramountcy, and as an arrangement under which Hyderabad had no external status. Article 3 of the Standstill Agreement specified that "nothing herein contained shall include or introduce paramountcy functions or create any paramountcy relationship" (p. 45).

Following repeated rejections of India's overtures to the Government of Hyderabad to accede and suggestions for a referendum or plebiscite on the question of accession, Hyderabad proposed that instead of an Instrument of Accession an Instrument of Association be concluded providing for the application of the legislation of the Government of India to Hyderabad in respect of the three subjects of defense, foreign affairs, and communications. This principle of overriding legislation by the Government of India to Hyderabad was repudiated by subsequent negotiations (p. 9).

Viewing Hyderabad's claim to independence as a threat to India's security, the Indian White Paper on Hyderabad stated:

> ". . . An independent State completely landlocked within the heart of another is an unheard of proposition. To compare Hyderabad to Switzerland or Austria, on the ground that they are landlocked and have no access to the sea, is to turn one's back to elementary history and geography. Switzerland and Austria have common frontiers with more than one State and their polities and economy have accordingly developed on a different basis. If all Provinces of India were independent States and one of the three Provinces bordering Hyderabad questioned the right of this State to independence on the ground that it was landlocked, the analogy of Switzerland and Austria would hold good. As it is, however, the distinctive and decisive feature of Hyderabad's geographical set-up is that if it makes with a foreign State any defence, economic or other arrangements,

which are prejudicial to India's interests, it cannot implement such arrangements without violating India's sovereignty over her own territories. . . ."   (Pp. 9–10.)

Deterioration in the relations between Hyderabad and India and the ensuing charges of border raids and breaches of the Standstill Agreement exchanged by both sides culminated in a decision of the Nizam of Hyderabad to present his case against India to the United Nations.

The complaint addressed to the President of the Security Council August 21, 1948, requesting that its dispute with India involving Hyderabad's independence be placed on the Security Council agenda, charged: "Hyderabad has been exposed in recent months to violent intimidation, to threats of invasion, and to crippling economic blockade which has inflicted cruel hardship upon the people of Hyderabad and which is intended to coerce it into a renunciation of its independence. The frontiers have been forcibly violated and Hyderabad villages have been occupied by Indian troops. The action of India threatened the existence of Hyderabad, the peace of the Indian and entire Asiatic Continent, and the principles of the United Nations. . . ."

U.N. Security Council Off. Rec. 3d year, Supp. Sept. 1948 (S/986), p. 5.

In a cablegram dated September 12, 1948, the Government of Hyderabad asked that the complaint be put on the agenda at the earliest possible date, such as Wednesday, September 15, as a result of the "officially proclaimed intention of India as announced by its Prime Minister to invade Hyderabad". On the following day, a cablegram informed the Secretary-General that Hyderabad had been invaded.

U.N. Docs. S/998 and S/1000, ibid., pp. 6, 7.

"The matter was discussed in the Security Council on September 16 with representatives of India and Hyderabad present. Although some doubt was expressed by certain members as to whether Hyderabad was a 'state' within the meaning of that article of the Charter which permits a state to bring a complaint to the attention of the Security Council, the Council decided, with the United States Representative voting in favor, to place the matter on its agenda for discussion without prejudicing the merits of the case."   U.S. participation in the U.N., report by the President to Congress for the year 1948, p. 83. Although the Nizam ordered his delegation in Paris to withdraw the complaint from the agenda of the Security Council September 23, 1948, the situation was again discussed by the Council on September 27 and 28. While the Security Council is still seized with this question (Security Council Docs. S/4098, Sept. 22, 1958; S/4155, Feb. 3, 1959), it was last discussed May 25, 1949 (S/1380, Aug. 19, 1949). See ibid., p. 84.

The Nizam shortly after the invasion dismissed his government and pledged his full cooperation with the Indian authorities. The resulting military occupation of Hyderabad was carried out in accord with the stated policy of the Indian Government to administer the State in cooperation and in the name of the Nizam. This policy was more specifically implemented under a formula which without affecting the subordination of the Military Governor in the service matters to the General Officer Commanding-in-Chief, Southern Command, invested him not only with full executive authority but also with power to issue regulations having the force of law. This formula, embodied in a *firman* promulgated by the Nizam, provided the basis for the authority India exercised in Hyderabad until the new Constitution came into force.

Following the installation of the Military Governor's administration, the Nizam issued a proclamation which brought the Hyderabad State into line with the other states on accession and other matters. On November 23, 1949, he issued a *firman* accepting the Constitution framed by the Constituent Assembly of India as the Constitution of Hyderabad.

> Menon, *The Integration of the Indian States* (1956) 378–380, 387. See also Eagleton, "The Case of Hyderabad before the Security Council", 44 Am. J. Int'l L. (1950) 277.

State of Jammu and Kashmir

By August 15, 1947, the State of Jammu and Kashmir had failed to signify its accession to either of the Dominions (India or Pakistan), although the Jammu and Kashmir Government signed a Standstill Agreement with Pakistan on August 15, 1947. As a result of tribal invasions which began on October 22, 1947, the Jammu and Kashmir Government appealed to India for arms, ammunition, and reinforcement of troops, but was informed that since Kashmir had not at that time acceded to India, it would be improper to move Indian troops into what was at that moment an independent country. The Maharajah then signed an Instrument of Accession on October 26, 1947, which was accepted by the Government of India with the stipulation that, as soon as law and order had been restored in Kashmir and its soil cleared of the invader, the question of the State's accession should be settled by a reference to the people.

The Government of Pakistan responded by issuing a statement on October 30, 1947, characterizing the Kashmir accession as "based on fraud and violence" and stating that as such it "cannot be recognized". There followed charges and countercharges of aggression until on January 1, 1948, the Government of India brought a complaint before the Security Council (S/628).

The Security Council's Resolution S/654 of January 20, 1948, establishing a three-member commission to exercise functions of good offices and investigation on the spot was followed by Security Council Resolution S/726 of April 21, 1948, providing for restoration of peace and order and the holding of a plebiscite to determine the future status of the State of Jammu and Kashmir.

The Commission's three-part resolution (S/995) of August 13, 1948, proposed a cease-fire; a truce agreement specifying the withdrawal of Pakistani troops the presence of which it was noted constituted a material change in the situation since it was represented by the Government of Pakistan before the Security Council, enlisting the cooperation of Pakistan to secure the withdrawal of tribesmen and Pakistani nationals not normally resident therein who had entered the State for the purpose of fighting, conditioning the withdrawal of the bulk of Indian forces in stages on the notification of the withdrawal of tribesmen and Pakistani nationals and Pakistani forces; and a reaffirmation by the Governments of India and Pakistan that the future status of the State of Jammu and Kashmir be determined in accordance with the will of the people coupled with an agreement that to that end, upon the acceptance of the Truce Agreement both Governments consult with the Commission to determine fair and equitable conditions whereby such free expression will be assured.

While India accepted the resolution in whole on August 25, 1948, the reservations attached to Pakistan's acceptance on September 6, 1948, were considered by the Commission to have gone beyond its jurisdiction (S/1100). Both Governments accepted the Commission's proposals of December 11, 1948, which were embodied in the Commission's resolution of January 5, 1949 (S/1196). In calling for a free and impartial plebiscite, the resolution declared the cessation of hostilities in the State of Jammu and Kashmir as from January 1, 1949. Full agreement on a cease-fire line was reached July 27, 1949.

Subsequent truce negotiations and demilitarization proposals (recorded in the following Security Council documents and Commission reports: S/1430, Dec. 5, 1949, Adds. 1–3, Dec. 9, 12, 16, 1949; S/1453, Feb. 3, 1950; S/1461, Feb. 24, 1950; S/1791, Sept. 15, 1950; S/2182, May 31, 1951; S/2375 and Corr. 1, Oct. 15, 1951; S/2390, Nov. 9, 1951; S/2448, Dec. 18, 1951; S/2611, Apr. 22, 1952; S/2783, Sept. 16, 1952; S/2883, Dec. 23, 1952) resulted in no agreement on part II of the August 13, 1948, resolution, a condition precedent to the fulfillment of part III providing for the determination of the status of Jammu and Kashmir in accordance with the will of the people.

The differing conceptions of India and Pakistan of their relationship to Jammu and Kashmir as summarized by the United Nations

Commission for India and Pakistan are, in general outline, as follows:

"India considered itself to be in legal possession of the State of Jammu and Kashmir by virtue of the instrument of accession of October 1947, signed by the Maharaja of the State and accepted by the then Governor-General of India.

"India held, therefore, that the assistance which Pakistan rendered to tribesmen who made incursions into the State was a hostile act and that the entry into the territory of Pakistan troops was an invasion of Indian territory. As a consequence of accession, India's armies were in Kashmir as a matter of right and India controlled the defence, communications, and external affairs of the State whereas Pakistan had no *locus standi* in Kashmir. Also as a consequence of accession, India was responsible for the security of the State, and demilitarization must take into account the importance of leaving in the State sufficient Indian and State forces to safeguard its security. A plebiscite in the State would be for the purpose of confirming the accession which was, in all respects, already complete.

"India's stand regarding the northern areas and the *Azad* Kashmir forces also stemmed from the position that India was in Kashmir by right and responsible for the security of the State and that Pakistan could not aspire to an equal footing. In the case of the *Azad* Kashmir forces it also held that forces in revolt against the Government of the State must be disbanded and disarmed. India's refusal to discuss with Pakistan or allow it to know the details of withdrawal of the bulk of the Indian forces similarly followed from its insistence that Pakistan was in Kashmir illegally and had no rights there.

"Pakistan's position was based on the contention that the accession to India of the State of Jammu and Kashmir was illegal. The State had executed a standstill agreement with Pakistan on August 15, 1947, which debarred it from entering into negotiation or agreement with any other country. The Maharaja had no authority to execute an instrument of accession in October 1947 because his people had successfully revolted, overthrown his Government and compelled him to flee from the capital. The act of accession was brought about by violence and fraud and, as such, was invalid. The Maharaja's offer of accession had been accepted by the Governor-General on condition that as soon as law and order had been established the question of the accession of the State would be decided 'by a reference to the people'; as the Indian Constitution did not recognize conditional accession the accession had no legal validity.

"According to Pakistan an *Azad* movement was indigenous and spontaneous, the consequences of the Maharaja's misrule, and the tribal incursions were also spontaneous, resulting from reports of cruelties inflicted on the Muslims in Kashmir and the East Punjab. The entry of Pakistani troops was necessary to protect Pakistan territory from invasion by Indian forces, to stem the movement of refugees into Pakistan and to prevent India from taking possession of the entire State by force.

"Pakistan considered itself as having equal status with India and entitled, as a party to the dispute, to equal rights and consideration. Thus, it considered that the truce should establish a balance of forces between the two parties and that it should be informed of plans for the withdrawal of the bulk of the Indian forces before signing a truce agreement. It held that the disbanding and disarming of the *Azad* Kashmir forces should be balanced by a similar disposition of the State forces, or by a further reduction of the Indian forces after the bulk withdrawal. As regards the Northern Areas it denied India's right to assume there the defence of Kashmir as a result of the established relations between India and the State."

The India-Pakistan Question, Background Paper No. 72, Dec. 31, 1952, U.N. Doc. ST/DPI/SER.A/72, pp. 31–32, and annexes I–XII. Menon, *The Integration of the Indian States* (1956) 399, 404.

For the list of States which acceded to Pakistan and their instruments of accession, see *Instruments of Accession and Schedules of States Acceding to Pakistan*, Feb. 14, 1949 (Constituent Assembly of Pakistan (1949)).

The tribal area states of Dir, Swat, Chitral and Amb are recorded to have acceded to Pakistan on the dates of February 18, 1948, November 24, 1947, February 18, 1948, and December 31, 1947, respectively. The validity of these accessions is challenged by Afghanistan which claims that these States lie within "Pushtunistan", an area for which Afghanistan supports the right of self-determination. The Ministry of States and Frontier Regions of the Government of Pakistan issued on June 27, 1950, a "Notification" acknowledging and accepting the request of "the inhabitants of the areas situated within the external Frontiers of Pakistan which are not included in any of the Provinces or in the Chief Commissioner's Province of Baluchistan or in any of the acceding States or in the Capital of the Federation". It formally declared these territories a part of the Federation of Pakistan as constituted on August 15, 1947. These States had acceded to Pakistan only in the matters of defense, foreign affairs, and communications and while this "Notification" effected the formal incorporation of these States as of August 15, 1947, they are classified as the unadministered tribal tract to which Pakistani law does not apply and which are administered on the basis of agencies. The Afghan Government by Royal Decree on November 5, 1955, announced the convening of a Loe Jergah, a grand national assembly of tribal elders whose decisions are final and binding on the Government, to consider the Pushtunistan Question. The assembly, meeting from November 15–20, 1955, issued a final resolution, November 20, 1955, which, in protesting the "forced merger" of these areas with Pakistan, read in part:

"The Loe Jergah, representing the people and on behalf of the people of Afghanistan, hereby announces that it does not recognize in any way whatsoever the territories of Pushtunistan as part of Pakistan without the assent and against the wishes of the Pushtun Nation, and in this respect the Loe Jergah reiterates and confirms Resolution 72 of the National Assembly and the Senate passed on the 17th of October 1955."

The American Ambassador at Karachi (Warren) to the Secretary of State (Acheson), despatch No. 75, July 10, 1950, MS. Department of State, file 790d.022/7–1050; Resolution of Nov. 20, 1955, of *loe jirga*, *Bakhtar*, Nov. 22, 1955.

Pursuant to the enactment of the Constitution Bill providing for the Islamic Republic of Pakistan February 29, 1956, signed by the Governor-General March 2, 1956, which declared Pakistan a Federal Republic, part 1, article 1, clause 1, the Constituent Assembly of Pakistan adopted a resolution March 2, 1956, ratifying a Declaration "on the continued membership of Pakistan as a Republic in the Commonwealth of Nations, as set out in the official statement issued at the conclusion of the Conference of the Commonwealth Prime Ministers in London on the 5th February, 1955." *The Islamic Republic of Pakistan*

Identifying this Declaration in substance with that issued in 1949 in the case of India (*ante*) when she decided to remain in the Commonwealth after becoming a Republic, Mr. Mohamad Ali elaborated upon the implications of this Declaration. He explained, ". . . When we become a Republic . . . we will naturally cease to owe allegiance to the Crown but by virtue of this Declaration we shall continue, nevertheless, our full membership of the Commonwealth. In doing so we accept the Queen as the Indian Republic accepts her, not as our sovereign but as the symbol of the free association of independent nations which constitute the Commonwealth and as such the Head of the Commonwealth. This would not imply any derogation whatsoever from our fully sovereign and independent status. Our association with the Commonwealth, as that of its other members would be a completely free and voluntary association. Under the Declaration it would be an association on a basis of absolute equality as between the various members of the Commonwealth. They all aim at co-operating in complete freedom in the promotion of peace, liberty and progress. Such an association implies no restriction whatever on the members' domestic or foreign policy. Each member country continues to remain the master of its own policy and free to seek the co-operation of and develop its relation with every other country in the world. Our continuing membership of the Commonwealth would thus involve no diminution of our independence or sovereignty. It would not in any way prevent Pakistan from going forward to her natural destiny as sovereign independent Islamic Republic free in every way to shape her future course in full conformity with her own genius and her own ideals. The Commonwealth link is in no way a limiting or restrictive influence on our progress. On the other hand by providing for collaboration with other like-minded countries it would help in promoting our common weal and international peace."

> *The Constitution of the Islamic Republic of Pakistan* (1956) 5. Pakistan Constituent Assembly, *Debates* (1956), Friday, Mar. 2, 1956, vol. 1, No. 81, pp. 3734–3735.

In the debates in the Constituent Assembly of Pakistan preceding the ratification of the Declaration on continued membership in the Commonwealth of Nations as a Republic, Pir Ali Mohammad Rashdi distinguished a Republic from a Dominion as follows: "In a Republic the Head of the State is a person who is elected by the country itself and the sovereignty vests in the people. In the case of a Dominion the sovereignty vests in the British Crown. Just at the moment we have the Governor-General, who is appointed by Her Majesty the Queen. All our ambassadors go under the Royal Sign Manual, which is signed by Her Majesty the Queen. This is not going to happen now, even though we may be members of the Commonwealth. Now these appointments are going to be made by the President of the Republic, because by becoming a Republic, we become completely free. We are no longer a dominion and membership of Commonwealth under these conditions is vitally different from a country being a Dominion or occupying the status of a Dominion. . . ."

> *Ibid.*, p. 3744.
>
> On the present day force of the distinction between a monarchy and a republic, see H. J. T. Johnson, "Monarchy in Eclipse", I *Cambridge Journal* (1947–1948) 267–278, and K. C. Wheare, *Modern Constitutions* (1951) 41. On the powers of heads of state, see Sir Ivor Jennings, *The Commonwealth in Asia* (1951) 92.
>
> As stated *supra*, Pakistan attained independence on August 15, 1947, under the Indian Independence Act, 1947 (10 & 11 Geo. 6, c. 30) which in partitioning India set up the two independent Dominions of India and Pakistan.

Republic of Ireland

The Constitution of Ireland, effective December 29, 1937, changed the name of the Irish Free State to that of Eire or Ireland and, with regard to the type of state thereby constituted, provided in certain of its articles: "Ireland is a sovereign, independent, democratic state" (article 5); "All powers of government, legislative, executive and judicial, derive under God, from the people, whose right it is to designate the rulers of the State and, in final appeal, to decide all questions of national policy, according to the requirements of the common good. These powers of government are exercisable only by or on the authority of the organs of State established by this Constitution" (article 6(1), (2)).

Referring to the type of state Ireland thus represents, the Taoiseach, Mr. E. de Valera, in a speech in Dáil Éireann July 17, 1945, declared, "The State whose institutions correspond to these Articles is, it seems to me, demonstrably a republic. . . . We are a democracy with the ultimate sovereign power resting with the people—a representative democracy with the. various organs of State functioning under a written Constitution, with the executive authority controlled by Parliament, with an independent judiciary functioning under the Constitution and the law, and with a Head of State directly elected by the people for a definite term of office . . . ."

> II Mansergh, *Documents and Speeches on British Commonwealth Affairs 1931–1952* (1953) 795.

The new legal status of Ireland as a Republic raised in issue the validity of the status of Ireland as a member of the British Commonwealth whose relations with the King were governed by the Executive Authority (External Relations) Act, 1936. (See I Mansergh, *Documents and Speeches on British Commonwealth Affairs 1931–1952* (1953) 321–322.)

In answer to the argument that because of the External Relations Act of 1936 Ireland was still a monarchy, Mr. E. de Valera said, "This External Relations Act is a simple statute repealable by the legislature and not a fundamental law. As a law it is, in fact, null and void to any extent whatever in which it conflicts with our only fundamental law, the Constitution. It is a simple enabling Act to permit of the carrying out of the external policy of the State in the field of international relations as indicated and provided for in Article 29(4) of the Constitution and nothing more. This may be regarded as a unique arrangement. . . . The position, as I conceive it to be, is this: We are an independent republic, associated as a matter of our external policy with the States of the British Commonwealth. To mark this association, we avail ourselves of the procedure of the External Relations Act . . . by which the King recognized by the States of the British Commonwealth therein named acts for us, under advice, in certain specified matters in the field of our external relations."

He then quoted from a statement issued by the Dominions Office of the United Kingdom Government, December 24, 1937, which reads in part—

> " 'His Majesty's Government in the United Kingdom have considered the position created by the new Constitution which was

approved by the Parliament of the Irish Free State in June, 1937, and came into force on December 29.

" 'They are prepared to treat the new Constitution as not effecting a fundamental alteration in the position of the Irish Free State—in future to be described under the new Constitution as 'Eire' or 'Ireland'—as a member of the British Commonwealth of Nations.

" 'His Majesty's Government in the United Kingdom have ascertained that His Majesty's Government in Canada, the Commonwealth of Australia, New Zealand, and the Union of South Africa are also prepared so to treat the new Constitution.' [For full text of the statement see: I Mansergh, *Documents and Speeches on British Commonwealth Affairs 1931–1952* (1953), pp. 366–367.]"

II Mansergh, *Documents and Speeches on British Commonwealth Affairs 1931–1952* (1953) 795–796.

The Republic of Ireland Act, 1948, enacted December 21, 1948, repealed the Executive Authority (External Relations) Act, 1936, and in declaring the State the "Republic of Ireland" it further provided that "The President, on the authority and on the advice of the Government, may exercise the executive power or any executive function of the State in or in connexion with its external relations".

Ibid. 802.

In a speech, the Taoiseach, Mr. Costello, in the Dáil Éireann November 24, 1948, stated:

". . . This Bill will end, and end forever, in a simple, clear and unequivocal way this country's long and tragic association with the institution of the British Crown and will make it manifest beyond equivocation or subtlety that the national and international status of this country is that of an independent republic. . . .

. . . .

". . . Ireland does not now, and when the Executive Authority (External Relations) Act of 1936 is repealed, does not intend to regard their citizens as 'foreigners' or their countries as 'foreign' countries. Throughout, the position of the Irish Government is that while Ireland is not a member of the Commonwealth, it recognizes and confirms the existence of a specially close relationship arising not only from ties of friendship and kinship but from traditional and long-established economic, social and trade relations, based on common interest with the nations that form the Commonwealth of Nations. This exchange of rights and privileges, which it is our firm desire and intention to maintain and strengthen, in our view constitutes a special relationship which negatives the view that other countries could raise valid objections on the ground that Ireland should be treated as a 'foreign' country by Britain and the Commonwealth countries for the purpose of this exchange of rights and privileges."

II Mansergh, *Documents and Speeches on British Commonwealth Affairs
1931–1952* (1953) 802, 806.

By the terms of The Ireland Act, 1949 (12 & 13 Geo. 6, c. 41) the
United Kingdom in clause 1(1) "recognized and declared that the
part of Ireland heretofore known as Eire ceased, as from the eighteenth day of April, nineteen hundred and forty-nine, to be part of
His Majesty's dominions."

It was further declared in clause 2(1) that, "notwithstanding that
the Republic of Ireland is not part of His Majesty's dominions, the
Republic of Ireland is not a foreign country for the purposes of any
law in force in any part of the United Kingdom or in any colony,
protectorate or United Kingdom trust territory. . . ."

II Mansergh, *Documents and Speeches on British Commonwealth Affairs
1931–1952* (1953) 821–822.

Prime Minister Attlee, in a speech before the House of Commons,
May 11, 1949, said "Clause 2(1) declares that the Republic of Ireland
shall not be a foreign country. I admit at once that this is a novel
conception. I admit that hitherto there had been this straight division between countries which were foreign and countries which were
not foreign. I admit we are introducing a new category. Here is a
country which is outside allegiance, outside the British Commonwealth, but which is not to be held as foreign. . . ."

II Mansergh, *Documents and Speeches on British Commonwealth Affairs
1931–1952* (1953) 833.

" . . . The Act [Ireland Act, 1949] did not remove Eire (now called the
Republic of Ireland) from the Commonwealth. On the contrary the long
title stated that it was an Act to 'recognize and declare the *constitutional*
position as to the part of Ireland heretofore known as Eire, and to make
provision as to the name by which it may be known and the manner in
which the law is to apply to it; to declare and affirm the constitutional
position and the territorial integrity of Northern Ireland. . . .' In other
words, its purpose was to regulate the constitutional position of two portions of the Commonwealth. . . . Thus, though in accordance with British
traditions no attempt has been made to define in any formula the exact
relation between the Commonwealth and the Republic of Ireland, it is not
a foreign country like Burma (for instance) but may be loosely described
as associated with the Commonwealth." Jennings and Young, *Constitutional Laws of the Commonwealth* (1952) 5. See also Mansergh, *The
Commonwealth and The Nations* (1948), ch. VIII, pp. 193–224.

Malaya, a multiple dependency prior to The State Agreements, The
Federation of Malaya Agreement, 1948, and The Federation of
Malaya Order in Council, 1948 (I Stat. Instr., 1948, pp. 1231, 1249,
1276 (No. 108)) which established the Federation of Malaya comprising the Malay States and the two Settlements, attained its

*The Federa-
tion of
Malaya—
an elected
monarchy*

independence within the Commonwealth August 31, 1957. **The** Federation of Malaya Independence Order in Council 1957 (Stat. Instr., 1957, No. 1533) recited in part: ". . . by the Federation of Malaya Independence Act, 1957 (5 & 6 Eliz. 2, c. 60), the approval of Parliament was given to the conclusion between Her Majesty and the Rulers of the Malay States of such agreement as appears to Her Majesty to be expedient for the establishment of the Federation of Malaya as an independent sovereign country within the Commonwealth."

The Federal Constitution (Stat. Instr., 1957, No. 1533, Annex) established the independent Federation of Malaya comprising the Malay States and the two former Settlements which became States, and provided that the "Settlements shall cease to form part of Her Majesty's dominions and Her Majesty shall cease to exercise any sovereignty over them, and all power and jurisdiction of Her Majesty or of the Parliament of the United Kingdom in or in respect of the Settlements or the Malay States or the Federation as a whole shall come to an end."

> The Constitution provides for an elective monarchy as the "Supreme Head of the Federation, to be called the Yang di-Pertuan Agong", but Her Majesty the Queen is recognized as Head of the Commonwealth.
>
> Prior to the Federation of Malaya Agreement of 1948, the multiple dependency of Malaya included Singapore, a settled Colony; the Malayan Union comprising nine Malay protected States: Johore, Kedah, Kelantan, Negri Sembilan, Pahang, Perak, Perlis, Selangor, and Trengganu: two Settlements: Malacca and Penang. In 1946, Singapore was constituted a Colony and thereby separated from the Straits Settlements.

A Memorandum Setting Out Heads of Agreement for a Merger between the Federation of Malaya and Singapore of November 11, 1961, provides for a constitutional framework within which the two territories would merge in a new Federation of Malayasia to embrace the Federation of Malaya, Singapore, North Borneo, Sarawak, and Brunei. In accordance with a prior agreement of August 23, 1961, the Heads of Agreement vests responsibility for defense, external affairs, and security in the Federation of Malaya and specifies that Singapore retain local autonomy, especially on matters of education and labor.

Following the British-Malayan Agreement of November 24, 1961, on the proposed merger (Cmd. 33 of 1961), the two Governments announced August 1, 1962, their decision that the proposed Federation should be established by August 31, 1963, and their intention to conclude an agreement within 6 months which would provide for the transfer of sovereignty in North Borneo, Sarawak, and Singapore by August 31, 1963; the relationship between Singapore and the new Federation as agreed; defense arrangements as set out in the British-Malayan statement of November 22, 1961; and the constitutional arrangements, including safeguards for the special interests of North Borneo and Sarawak, to be drawn up after consultation with the legislatures of the two territories. The two Governments also announced they had informed the Sultan of Brunei of this Agreement and that they had made it clear that they would welcome the inclusion of the State of Brunei in the new Federation.

664 H.C. Deb. (5th ser.) cols. 584–586 (Aug. 1, 1962).

Under the Rhodesia and Nyasaland Federation Act, 1953 (1 & 2 Eliz. 2, c. 30), Her Majesty, by the terms of The Federation of Rhodesia and Nyasaland (Constitution) Order in Council, 1953 (Stat. Instr., 1953, p. 1804 (No. 1199)), ordered that "Southern Rhodesia, Northern Rhodesia and Nyasaland . . . shall be associated in a Federation in accordance with the Constitution" (p. 1808). The provisions of the Constitution came partially into being September 3, 1953, and in becoming fully operative on October 23, 1953, formally established the Federation as of the latter date. (Federation of Rhodesia and Nyasaland (Commencement) Order in Council, 1953, Stat. Instr., 1953, p. 2800.) *Federation of Rhodesia and Nyasaland*

Specifying Southern Rhodesia as "part of Her Majesty's dominions" and Northern Rhodesia and Nyasaland as "territories under Her Majesty's protection", the preamble to the Constitution of the Federation of Rhodesia and Nyasaland provides that "the Colony of Southern Rhodesia should continue to enjoy responsible government in accordance with its constitution". The preamble also states:

". . . Northern Rhodesia and Nyasaland should continue, under the special protection of Her Majesty, to enjoy separate Governments for so long as their respective peoples so desire, those Governments remaining responsible (subject to the ultimate authority of Her Majesty's Government in the United Kingdom) for, in particular, the control of land in those territories, and for the local and territorial political advancement of the peoples thereof;".

The federal system, fully explained in a separate White Paper entitled "The Federal Scheme" (Cmd. 8754), is described in the Report by the Conference on Federation (Cmd. 8753) as a "true Federation". Outlining its main features, this report states:

". . . Its object is to create a strong central authority, compatible with the state of political development of the three Territories and having the necessary power to co-ordinate the economic life of the area. This it does, while reserving to the

Governments and Legislatures of the individual Territories the political and financial powers which they must retain to enable them to discharge the important duties and responsibilities which remain within their control. . . .

Responsibilities reserved for the Federal Government exclusively cover the matters of defense, external affairs, transport and communications, immigration, customs and excise, currency, health, education (except the primary and secondary education of Africans), European agriculture in Southern and Northern Rhodesia, and certain important economic functions necessary to coordinate the economic life of the country.

The matter of external affairs as included on the Federal Legislative List or Exclusive List is qualified therein as follows:

"(a) such external relations as may from time to time be entrusted to the Federation by Her Majesty's Government in the United Kingdom; and

"(b) the implementation of treaties, conventions and agreements with, and other obligations towards, countries or organisations outside the Federation affecting the Federation as a whole or any one or more of the Territories, whether entered into—

"(i) either before or after the date of the coming into force of this Constitution, by Her Majesty, or by Her Majesty's Government in the United Kingdom on behalf of the Federation or any of the Territories; or

"(ii) after the said date, by the Federation with the authority of Her Majesty's Government in the United Kingdom; or

"(iii) before the said date, by any of the Territories with the said authority;

but not including relations between the United Kingdom and any of the Territories."

Item 1 of the Second Schedule to The Federation of Rhodesia and Nyasaland (Constitution) Order in Council, 1953, Stat. Instr., 1953 (No. 1199), pp. 1804, 1855.

In examining the legal status of the territories within the Federation and of the Federation as such, in order to determine whether the Federation had the constitutional authority to negotiate a Treaty of Friendship, Commerce and Navigation with the United States, the Office of the Legal Adviser in a memorandum dated December 10, 1953, analyzed the question as follows:

". . . Southern Rhodesia was a colony of Great Britain and Northern Rhodesia and Nyasaland were protectorates of that country. Their status as such has not been changed by the Act of Federation according to the reference on page 9 of the Report by the Conference on Federation found in British Command Paper 8753. It is traditional in international affairs that areas having these relationships to the superior power do not have the authority to independently conduct their external relations. It is also necessary to recall that the authority for the present advancement of the relationships between these territories by virtue of the scheme of Federation is accomplished only by virtue of authority granted by the British Government. Thus, it must be assumed that all powers not specifically granted to the Federation continue to rest within the authority of the Government of Great Britain. An examination of the draft Constitution and of the Command Papers relating to the Federal scheme which preceded the drawing up of the constitutional provisions reveal no grant of specific authority to negotiate treaties or, in general, to conduct external affairs without the consent of the United Kingdom.

"As a matter of fact, the language of the draft constitution clearly indicates the absence of such authority. Article 29 authorizes the Federal Legislature to make laws with respect to any matter included in the second schedule annexed to the Constitution. That schedule includes 'external affairs' but defines them as (1) such external relations as may be entrusted to the Federation by the Government of the United Kingdom, and (2) the implementation of treaties, conventions, and agreements, with certain other limitations. The 'implementation of agreements' is not the negotiation and signing thereof. As to other matters in this field, the authority must be entrusted to the Federation before it may act.

"The documents preceding the preparation of the draft constitution are in agreement with the interpretation that independent constitutional authority does not exist for the general conduct of international relations by the Federation. Nowhere is there an indication that this power was to be included in the grant of additional authority under the Federation scheme and there is no mention of this matter in any of the documents. In addition, much the same language as appears in the Constitution is also found in the preceding documents. The 'implementation' of treaties, conventions, and agreements, is referred to in Command Paper 8754, page 7, and the same appears in the list of exclusive federal legislative functions found on page 10 thereof. At page 22 of Cmd. 8754, it is stated that the Queen of England must sign any Federal bill appearing inconsistent with England's international agreements. The only possible exception to the conclusion of the lack of Federal authority regarding these matters might be in connection with the negotiation of tariff rates with the Union of South Africa, some mention of which is made in Command 8672, pages 22–23.

"No additional authority for such action rests in the Executive Branch of the Government, since under Article 36(2) the Executive authority extends only to execution and maintenance of the Constitution, and to all matters with respect to which the Federal legislature has the power to make laws."

Office of the Legal Adviser (Crowe) to the Office of African Affairs (Durnan), memorandum, "Authority of the Federation of Rhodesia and Nyasaland to Negotiate International Agreements", Dec. 10, 1953, MS. Department of State, file FW 611.45c4/9–2453.

The British Ambassador to the United States officially informed the United States Government in a note of January 6, 1954, that—

". . . On the 30th of October the Governor-General issued a notice declaring External Affairs (as defined in Item 1 of the Second Schedule to the Constitution Order-in-Council) an exclusive Federal responsibility. From this date the Federation accordingly takes the place as far as international matters are concerned of the three individual Territories [Southern Rhodesia, Northern Rhodesia, and Nyasaland].

.   .   .   .

"Under the Constitution, the new Federation will now in effect enjoy the same position in the field of external affairs as Southern Rhodesia has enjoyed in the past. The United Kingdom Government, while remaining generally responsible for the external relations of the Federation, will delegate to the Federation a limited measure of autonomy to conclude on its own behalf trade agreements and agreements of purely local concern with neighbouring territories. The Federal Government will also be responsible for the implementation of international obligations applying to the Federal area."

The British Ambassador at Washington (Makins) to the Secretary of State (Dulles), note No. 4, Jan. 6, 1954, MS. Department of State, file 645c.00/1–654.

The powers previously exercised by the self-governing colony of Southern Rhodesia in the sphere of external relations which had been delegated or accepted in practice by the United Kingdom were then applied to the Federation of Rhodesia and Nyasaland. These powers, subject to the United Kingdom's general responsibility for the Colony's external relations and the consequent need for prior consultation between the Governments of the two countries before Southern Rhodesia entered into any commitments, were based on the following broad principles:

(a) Authority to negotiate and conclude agreements with foreign countries relating solely to the treatment of goods;

(b) Acceptance of the practice of Southern Rhodesia of concluding agreements with neighboring territories on matters of local concern, including appropriate representational arrangements;

(c) Participation by Southern Rhodesia in the General Agreement on Tariffs and Trade and membership in certain international technical organizations which Southern Rhodesia was eligible to join under the terms of their constitutions.

The Governments of the United Kingdom and of The Federation of Rhodesia and Nyasaland issued a joint announcement of April 27, 1957, following discussions held in London from April 12 to April 17, 1957, which in part dealt with the subject of external affairs as follows:

> "The Federal Constitution provides that matters of External Affairs may, from time to time, be entrusted to the Federation. The Federal Prime Minister represented that the time had come for the Federation to assume more responsibility in this sphere, particularly in the field of relations with other countries, and the appointment of representatives of the Federation in such countries. The United Kingdom Government have agreed to entrust responsibility for external affairs to the Federal Government to the fullest extent possible consistent with the responsibility which Her Majesty's Government must continue to have in international law so long as the Federation is not a separate international entity."

The Federal Prime Minister reviewing this part of the announcement in an official statement of April 27, 1957, commented:

> "In regard to external affairs the position of the Federal Government before the London talks was that trade agreements with foreign governments relating to the treatment of goods, agreements of purely local concern with any neighbouring State, Colony or Territory in Africa (including arrangements with them for the exchange of foreign representatives) multi-lateral agreements involving membership of an international technical organisation which the Federation would be entitled to join, and in addition agreements with the Commonwealth could be entered into after consultation with the United Kingdom Government. It followed from this that the Federation could exchange non-diplomatic representatives with foreign countries and the Federal Government had the additional right, after consultation with the United Kingdom Government, to exchange representatives with Commonwealth countries. The Federation was not precluded from entering into direct correspondence on minor matters of purely mutual interest with other Commonwealth countries without prior consultation with the United Kingdom Government.
>
> "The agreement now reached with London carries the Federal Government a long way further. Indeed it carries it as far as it can possibly be carried, until the Federal Government becomes an independent international organisation.
>
> "What the Federal Government now has, can be summarized in the following way:—
>
> "(a) the right to conduct all relations and to exchange representatives with Commonwealth countries without consultation with the United Kingdom Government;

"(b) the right to conduct all negotiations and agreements with foreign countries, subject to the need to safeguard the United Kingdom Government's international responsibilities.

"(c) the right to appoint representatives to the diplomatic staffs of Her Majesty's Embassies;

"(d) the right to appoint its own Diplomatic Agents, who will have full diplomatic status and who will be in charge of Federal missions, in any foreign country prepared to accept them, and to receive such Agents from other countries;

"(e) the right, on its own authority, to acquire the membership of international organisations for which it is eligible.

"It will be seen that the entrustments now made are considerable and give the Federation the fullest practical independence in external affairs."

Press statement 148/57/CB, the American Consul General at Salisbury (Steere) to the Secretary of States (Dulles), despatch No. 400, Apr. 25, 1957, encl. 1 and annex, MS. Department of State, file 745c.00/4–2557.

"The Federal power with respect to external affairs is further subjected to certain severe limitations. It is provided, in effect, in article 34 of the Constitution that where a Federal law makes provision in relation to any Territory with respect to any matter relating to implementation of treaties, obligations, etc. which is not otherwise included in the Federal or Concurrent Legislative List, such provision has no effect in relation to that Territory unless and until the Governor of the Territory has declared, by notice in the official Gazette of the Territory, that it shall so have effect.

"The operation of the system is best explained by a practical example.

"Under section 10 of the Immunities and Privileges Act, 1956, the Governor-General may exempt certain persons, like consuls or consular employees of foreign countries and their families, from taxes, rates and other charges levied by the Federal or a Territorial Government or a local authority. These taxes include income tax and customs duties, but they also include Territorial taxes like, say, death duty, and municipal rates. Now, income tax and customs duties are matters within the Federal competence under items 11 and 12 of the Federal Legislative List, and therefore an exemption of a foreign consul from liability for these taxes is covered not only by the Federal power to implement a consular convention with a foreign country which provides for such exemption, but also by the Federal power to make laws with respect to income tax or customs duty.

"With regard to death duty, the position is different. This is a purely Territorial matter and the Federal Legislature has neither power to impose nor exempt any person from this kind of taxation. Therefore, in order to make section 10 of the Immunities and Privileges Act operative with regard to a Territorial death duty, the declaration of the Governor of a Territory mentioned in article 34 of the Constitution is necessary.

"It must be very clearly understood that the limitation of the law making power of the Federal Legislature under article 34 of the Constitution has absolutely nothing to do with the questions of sovereignty, dominion status and so forth. The limitation flows from the federal system of government and applies with equal force to Canada as to the Federation.

.   .   .   .

". . . On the one hand, under the Second Schedule the Federal Legislature has power to make laws with respect to external affairs which include such external relations as may from time to time be entrusted to the Federation by the British Government and implementation of international agreements towards other countries or organizations which affect the Federation as a whole or any of the Territories.

"On the other hand that power is, in respect of non-Federal matters, subject to the limitations imposed by article 34 of the Constitution.

"Certain specific entrustments of external affairs were made in 1953 and 1956; they were concerned chiefly with relations with the neighbouring territories in Africa and with trade matters. The entrustments were considerably extended in 1957, and, at the present time, include—

"(i) all relations with other members of the Commonwealth, including exchange of High Commissioners and making arrangements with them of any kind;

"(ii) negotiations and agreements with any foreign country, subject in each case to the need to safeguard the responsibility of Her Majesty in international law so long as the Federation is not a separate international entity;

"(iii) exchange of diplomatic agents or consular or trade officers to deal with matters within the competence of the Federation, and

"(iv) acquisition by the Federation in its own right of the membership of international organizations which the Federation is eligible to join."

   Weinberg, *An Outline of the Constitutional Law of The Federation of Rhodesia and Nyasaland* (1959) 67–70.

The Ghana Independence Act, 1957 (5 & 6 Eliz. 2, c. 6, Feb. 7, 1957), was enacted "to make provision for, and in connection with, the attainment by the Gold Coast of fully responsible status within the British Commonwealth of Nations." *Ghana— independent status*

The Colonial Office's White Paper entitled *The Proposed Constitution of Ghana* (Cmnd. 71), published February 8, 1957, recited, "Ghana is to be an independent State within the Commonwealth with the Queen as Sovereign and with a Cabinet and Parliamentary system

of government of the same general type as is found in the United
Kingdom and other independent Commonwealth countries". [Since,
according to colonial practice, an Order in Council contained the Gold
Coast Constitution, amendments thereto necessary or desirable on
account of independence, had to be enacted through an Order in
Council. Thus, *The Ghana (Constitution) Order in Council, 1957*
(Stat. Instr., 1957, No. 277, February 22, 1957) was made after the
Ghana Independence Act had received the Royal Assent but before
"the appointed day" of independence, March 6, 1957.]

The Duchess of Kent, speaking for Her Majesty the Queen, before
the National Assembly of Ghana on the occasion of Ghana's attaining
independence March 6, 1957, declared

> ". . . the Gold Coast, under the name of Ghana, takes her place
> as a free, sovereign and independent country within the Common-
> wealth of Nations, recognised at the same time by all other mem-
> ber countries as herself a member of the Commonwealth.
>
> "Less than a month ago I gave My Assent to the Ghana Inde-
> pendence Act enacted by My Parliament in the United Kingdom.
> In consequence of this Act My Government in the United King-
> dom has ceased from to-day to have any authority in Ghana.
> Henceforward, all powers previously exercised by My Govern-
> ment in the United Kingdom will be exercised by My Ministers
> in Ghana who will be responsible to the National Assembly of
> Ghana. . . ."
>
> Ghana National Assembly, *Parliamentary Debates*, vol. 5, No. 1, Mar. 6,
> 1957, col. 4.

With reference to Ghana's attainment of independence, Prime Minister Macmillan, speaking before the House of Commons, stated:

> "On the 6th March, 1957, the territory formerly known as the
> Gold Coast achieved independent sovereign status within the
> Commonwealth under the name of 'Ghana'. At the same time
> the new State of Ghana was recognised by other Member coun-
> tries of the Commonwealth as a Member of the Commonwealth.
> The correct description of the country is therefore, 'Ghana'. The
> description of its status is 'An independent sovereign state within,
> and a Member country of, the Commonwealth.' "
>
> The First Secretary of the American Embassy at London (McClanahan)
> to the Secretary of State (Herter), despatch No. 2529, Apr. 29, 1959, MS.
> Department of State, file 745J.03/4–2959.

When Ghana became a republic on July 1, 1960, following a plebiscite from April 19–27, 1960, in which the people approved the republican constitution and selected Dr. Nkrumah as President, Queen
Elizabeth II ceased to be Queen of Ghana but stood in relation to

Ghana as head of the Commonwealth of which Ghana remains a member.

> The American Ambassador at Accra (Flake) to the Secretary of State (Herter), telegram, July 2, 1960, MS. Department of State, file 745j.02/7–260.

"In May 1956, the peoples of Togoland under United Kingdom Administration elected to unite with this country [Ghana] on the attainment of Independence. This decision was approved by the United Nations General Assembly in December of the same year."

> Governor-General Charles Noble Arden-Clarke, speech before Gold Coast Legislative Assembly, *Legislative Assembly Debates*, vol. 4, No. 2, Mar. 5, 1957, cols. 37–38. G.A. Res. 1044(XI), Dec. 13, 1956. See also "Togoland", *post* this chapter, and under "Territory, Acquisition and Loss", *post* this work.

> The Ghana (Constitution) Order in Council, 1957 (Stat. Instr., 1957, No. 277) in clause 63(1) designates the regions in which the whole of Ghana shall be divided and specifies in part: "(d) the Northern Region, which shall comprise the whole of the Northern Territories and Northern Togoland; (e) the Trans-Volta/Togoland Region, which shall comprise that part of Ghana which on the first day of January, 1957, was comprised in the Trans-Volta/Togoland Region of the Gold Coast."

The Ghana-Guinea Union, declared May 1, 1959, is not considered to have altered Ghana's relationship to the Commonwealth. While the joint declaration does not envisage actual union of the two countries but exemplifies rather the idea of confederation, the Ghana Constitution of 1960 makes provision for Ghana's relinquishment of its sovereignty by degrees to the Union.

> Office of the Legal Adviser (Frank to Whiteman), "Ghana-Guinea Union", memorandum, Nov. 27, 1962, MS. Department of State, file 645j.70 B/11–2762. See also Ghana-Guinea-Mali Union (Union of African States), *ante*, p. 429.

Independent status for Ceylon was achieved in law when the following orders, The Ceylon (Constitution) Order in Council, 1946, three Amending Orders and The Ceylon Independence Order in Council, 1947, cited together as the Ceylon (Constitution and Independence) Orders in Council, 1946 and 1947, took effect February 4, 1948. (See The Ceylon Independence Order in Council, 1947, art. 1, sec. 2, published in I Peaslee, *Constitutions of Nations* (1950) 375, 376, and the Ceylon Independence (Commencement) Order in Council, 1947, *ibid.* 375). *Ceylon—independent status*

On November 11, 1947, an "External Affairs Agreement" was signed at Colombo, on behalf of the Government of the United Kingdom of Great Britain and Northern Ireland and on behalf of the Government of Ceylon, to take effect on the day "when the constitutional measures necessary for conferring on Ceylon fully responsible status within the British Commonwealth of Nations shall come into force". The Agreement recited that "Ceylon has reached the stage in constitutional development at which she is ready to assume the status of a fully responsible member of the British Commonwealth of Nations, in no way subordinate in any aspect of domestic or external affairs, freely associated and united by common allegiance to the Crown". It was also agreed, *inter alia,* that "In regard to external affairs generally, and in particular to the communication of information and consultation, the Government of the United Kingdom will, in relation to Ceylon observe the principles and practice now observed by the Members of the Commonwealth, and the Ceylon Government will for its part observe these same principles and practice."

> Cmd. 7257 (1947) ; 86 UNTS 26–29. See also Ceylon Independence Act, 1947, 11 & 12 Geo. 6, c. 7.

> "The phrase 'Dominion Status' is not used in any of the documents, though it has been employed by the Secretary of State for the Colonies in the House of Commons and in his demi-official correspondence. The phrase is apt to be misunderstood as implying something less than independence. . . . The phrase used throughout the Ceylon documents is 'fully responsible status' though in the Agreements it is elaborated to 'the status of a fully responsible member of the British Commonwealth of Nations, in no way subordinate in any aspect of domestic or external affairs, freely associated and united by common allegiance to the Crown.' " Jennings *The Constitution of Ceylon* (1949) 25.

Burma— secession

"The Burma White Paper of May 1945 stated that Britain would assist Burmese political development 'till she can sustain the responsibility of complete self-government within the British Commonwealth and consequently attain a status equal to that of the Dominions and of this country.'

"During the ensuing debate on this White Paper statement Mr. Amery, Secretary of State for Burma, used the term 'Commonwealth status' in reference to Burma, which he defined not as independence minus something, but as independence plus the rights and privileges and practical advantages accruing from association with a world-wide free partnership. Such, he said, was the status of Britain herself."

> John F. Cady (Division of Middle Eastern and Indian Affairs), "Four Principal Aspects of Burma's Constitutional Problem", office memorandum, June 10, 1946, MS. Department of State, file 845c.01/6–1046.

In view of the intention of the Government of the United Kingdom of Great Britain and Northern Ireland to invite Parliament to pass legislation providing that Burma shall become an independent State, the Government of the United Kingdom and the Provisional Government of Burma signed a Treaty at London October 17, 1947, in which it was agreed in part that "The Government of the United Kingdom recognise the Republic of the Union of Burma as a fully independent sovereign State." (Article 1.)

Br. Treaty Series No. 16 (1948), Cmd. 7360; II Mansergh, *Documents and Speeches on British Commonwealth Affairs 1931–1952* (1953) 775.

The decision of Burma to withdraw from the Commonwealth upon the attainment of independence was acknowledged by the United Kingdom Government with the enactment of the Burma Independence Act, December 10, 1947, which reads in part: "On the appointed day [January 4, 1948], Burma shall become an independent country, neither forming part of His Majesty's dominions nor entitled to His Majesty's protection" (article 1(1) and (2)).

11 & 12 Geo. 6, c. 3; II Mansergh, *Documents and Speeches on British Commonwealth Affairs 1931–1952* (1953) 779–784.

The Secretary of State for Burma, the Earl of Listowel, commenting on the Burma Independence Act before the House of Lords November 23, 1947, declared with respect to Burma's exercise of the right of secession, ". . . we have always maintained that the peoples of the Commonwealth must decide their own future. The choice could lie only with Burma, and it was freely made by the unanimous vote of a fully representative body. We here do not regard membership of the Commonwealth as something to be thrust by force upon a reluctant people, but as a priceless privilege granted only to those who deeply desire it and are conscious of its obligations as well as its advantages. The essence of the Commonwealth relationship is that it is a free association of nations with a common purpose, who belong together because they have decided of their own volition to give and to take their fair share in a world-wide partnership. . . ."

II Mansergh, *Documents and Speeches on British Commonwealth Affairs 1931–1952* (1953) 789.

The Constitution of the Union of Burma enacted September 24, 1947, provides in part: "1. Burma is a Sovereign Independent Republic to be known as 'the Union of Burma'."

I Peaslee, *Constitutions of Nations* (1956) 279.

While the conversion of Cyprus from a British colony to an independent State was legally initiated February 19, 1959, when the Governments of Greece, Turkey, and the United Kingdom signed a Memorandum of Agreement officially adopting the annexed documents relating to the new status and settlement of Cyprus (Cmnd. 679), the actual transfer of sovereignty became effective August 16, 1960, when the Constitution initialed on July 28, 1960, came into force as desig-

Cyprus

nated and specified by The Republic of Cyprus Order in Council, 1960 (Stat. Instr., 1960 (No. 1368)), pursuant to the Cyprus Act, July 29, 1960 (8 & 9 Eliz. 2, c. 52).

Also, signed on August 15, 1960, were three separate Treaties: the Treaty Concerning the Establishment of the Republic of Cyprus between the United Kingdom, Greece, Turkey, and the Republic of Cyprus; the Treaty of Guarantee between the United Kingdom, Greece, Turkey, and the Republic of Cyprus; and the Treaty of Alliance between Greece, Turkey, and the Republic of Cyprus, the latter two of which were accorded constitutional force by article 181, a basic article of the Constitution of the Republic of Cyprus, in accordance with article 21 of the Greek-Turkish Zurich accords of February 11, 1959 (Cmnd. 679).

The Treaty of Establishment describes the territory of Cyprus as comprising the Island of Cyprus together with the islands lying off its coast, with the exception of the two areas (Akrotiri Sovereign Base Area and the Dhekelia Sovereign Base Area) "which areas shall remain under the sovereignty of the United Kingdom" (article 1). With respect to these base areas, the Republic of Cyprus agreed by the terms of article 2 to cooperate fully with the United Kingdom to insure the security and effective operation of the military bases and the full enjoyment by the United Kingdom of the rights conferred by this Treaty as set forth in annex B. Article 3 of the Treaty records the undertaking of the Republic of Cyprus, Greece, Turkey, and the United Kingdom "to consult and co-operate in the common defence of Cyprus".

In the Treaty of Guarantee, the Republic of Cyprus of the one part, and Greece, Turkey, and the United Kingdom of Great Britain and Northern Ireland of the other part, "I Considering that the recognition and maintenance of the independence, territorial integrity and security of the Republic of Cyprus, as established and regulated by the Basic Articles of its Constitution are in their common interest," and "II Desiring to co-operate to ensure respect for the state of affairs created by that Constitution", agreed in article I that "The Republic of Cyprus undertakes to ensure the maintenance of its independence, territorial integrity and security, as well as respect for its Constitution" and that it undertakes ". . . not to participate, in whole or in part, in any political or economic union with any State whatsoever". Accordingly, the Republic of Cyprus declared "prohibited any activity likely to promote, directly or indirectly, either union with any other State or partition of the Island".

The Treaty of Guarantee provisions reflecting in substance the stipulation in article 22 of the Greek-Turkish Zurich accords of

February 11, 1959, that "It shall be recognised that the total or partial union of Cyprus with any other State, or a separatist independence for Cyprus (*i.e.*, the partition of Cyprus into two independent States), shall be excluded" received constitutional force in article 185 of the Constitution of the Republic of Cyprus which states:

> "1. The territory of the Republic is one and indivisible.
> "2. The integral or partial union of Cyprus with any other State or the separatist independence is excluded." (Cmnd. 1093.)

Article II of the Treaty of Guarantee states:

> "Greece, Turkey and the United Kingdom, taking note of the undertaking of the Republic of Cyprus set out in Article I of the present Treaty, recognise and guarantee the independence, territorial integrity and security of the Republic of Cyprus, and also the state of affairs established by the Basic Articles of its Constitution.
> "Greece, Turkey and the United Kingdom likewise undertake to prohibit, so far as concerns them, any activity aimed at promoting, directly or indirectly, either union of Cyprus with any other State or partition of the Island."

By article III, the Republic of Cyprus, Greece, and Turkey undertook "to respect the integrity of the areas retained under United Kingdom sovereignty at the time of the establishment of the Republic of Cyprus, and guarantee the use and enjoyment by the United Kingdom of the rights to be secured to it by the Republic of Cyprus in accordance with the Treaty concerning the Establishment of the Republic of Cyprus signed at Nicosia on to-day's date" (August 15, 1960).

Under the Treaty of Alliance, the Republic of Cyprus, Greece, and Turkey agreed to "undertake to co-operate for their common defence and to consult together on the problems raised by that defence" (article I) and "to undertake to resist any attack or aggression, direct or indirect, directed against the independence or the territorial integrity of the Republic of Cyprus" (article 2).

British White Paper, Cyprus (1960), Cmnd. 1093.

Article I of the Constitution describes the State of Cyprus as "an independent and sovereign Republic with a presidential régime, the President being Greek and the Vice-President being Turk elected by the Greek and Turkish Communities respectively . . .".

Article 2 defines these Communities thus:

> "(1) the Greek Community comprises all citizens of the Republic who are of Greek origin and whose mother tongue is Greek

or who share the Greek cultural traditions or who are members of the Greek-Orthodox Church;

"(2) the Turkish Community comprises all citizens of the Republic who are of Turkish origin and whose mother tongue is Turkish or who share the Turkish cultural traditions or who are Moslems".

Each of the Communities respectively elects from amongst its own members a Communal Chamber which has expressly reserved legislative powers. Article 61 of the Constitution provides that the legislative power of the Republic be exercised by the House of Representatives in all matters except those expressly reserved to the Communal Chambers which are outlined in article 87 as follows: all religious matters; all educational, cultural and teaching matters; matters of personal status; composition and instances of courts dealing with civil disputes relating to personal status and to religious matters; matters where the interests and institutions are of purely communal nature such as charitable and sporting foundations, bodies and associations created for the purpose of promoting the well-being of their respective Community; imposition of personal taxes and fees on members of their respective Community in order to provide for their respective needs and for the needs of bodies and institutions under their control as in article 88 provided; matters where subsidiary legislation in the form of regulations or by-laws within the framework of the laws relating to municipalities will be necessary to enable a Communal Chamber to promote the aims pursued by municipalities composed solely of members of its respective Community; matters relating to the exercise of the authority of control of producers' and consumers' cooperatives and credit establishments and of supervision in their functions of municipalities consisting solely of their respective Community, vested in them by this Constitution: provided that (i) any communal law, regulation, by-law or decision made or taken by a Communal Chamber under this subparagraph (h) shall not directly or indirectly be contrary to or inconsistent with any law by which producers' and consumers' cooperatives and credit establishments are governed or to which the municipalities are subject; (ii) nothing in paragraph (i) of this proviso contained shall be construed as enabling the House of Representatives to legislate on any matter relating to the exercise of the authority vested in a Communal Chamber under this subparagraph (h); and in such other matters as are expressly provided by this Constitution.

Ibid.

Nigeria, initially administered by Great Britain in two parts—the Protectorate of Northern Nigeria and the Colony and Protectorate of Southern Nigeria—until 1914 when Northern and Southern Nigeria were amalgamated to form a Colony and Protectorate of Nigeria, attained independence on October 1, 1960.

The October 1, 1954, Constitution recognized to a limited extent the autonomy of Regional Governments for their internal administration and affairs, accorded responsibilities to Nigerian Ministers for the formation and execution of policy, and, while retaining the system of regionalization, instituted Nigeria as a Federation.

Under the 1954 Constitution as subsequently modified, the following subjects became exclusively matters for the Federal Legislature: external affairs, aviation, banks, census, customs, defense, maritime shipping, mines and minerals, posts and telegraphs, trunk roads and railways. While the Federal law prevailed with regard to those matters on the Concurrent List, all subjects not included in the Federal or Concurrent Lists were decreed matters within the exclusive executive and legislative competence of the Regional Governments.

The Colonial Office List, 1960, pp. 126–128.

As a result of decisions taken at the 1957 Constitutional Conference, amendments to the Constitution were made in August 1957 by which internal self-government was granted to the Eastern and Western Regions. While the Northern Region delegates declared at that time that they did not propose to ask for self-government for the Northern Region before 1959, the Legislative Houses of the Northern Region in July and August of 1958 approved a White Paper containing proposals for the attainment of self-government, and, following consideration of it at the 1958 Constitutional Conference, self-government was extended to the Region on March 15, 1959.

At the 1958 Conference, the Secretary of State for the Colonies, in announcing the British Government's consideration that the originally proposed date of April 2, 1960, allowed too short a time for the completion of preparations for independence, suggested the date of October 1, 1960, proposing that, if the new Federal Parliament passed a resolution early in 1960 asking for independence, Her Majesty's Government would agree to that request and would introduce a Bill in Parliament to enable Nigeria to become a fully independent country on October 1, 1960.

Report by the Resumed Nigeria Constitutional Conference held at London in September and October, 1958, Cmnd. 569, pp. 3, 13, 37–38.

Accordingly, the Nigerian Federal House of Representatives on January 16, 1960, passed the following resolution:

"That this House authorizes the Government of the Federation of Nigeria to request Her Majesty's Government in the United Kingdom as soon as practicable to introduce legislation in the Parliament of the United Kingdom providing for the establishment of the Federation of Nigeria on October 1, 1960 as an independent sovereign State, and to request Her Majesty's Government in the United Kingdom at the appropriate time to support with the other member Governments of the Commonwealth Nigeria's desire to become a member of the Commonwealth."

The American Consul at Lagos (Dorros) to the Secretary of State (Herter), despatch No. 468, Jan. 25, 1960, MS. Department of State, file 745h.02/1–2560.

The Nigeria Independence Act, 1960 (8 & 9 Eliz. 2 c. 55) was passed on July 29, 1960, which as "An Act to make provision for, and in connection with, the attainment by Nigeria of fully responsible status within the Commonwealth" specified that "On the first day of October, nineteen hundred and sixty . . . the Colony and the Protectorate as respectively defined by the Nigeria (Constitution) Orders in Council, 1954 to 1960, shall together constitute part of Her Majesty's dominions under the name of Nigeria" (article 1 (1)).

At a constitutional conference held at London from May 10–19, 1960, the Secretary of State for the Colonies informed the Nigerian Ministers that the Commonwealth Prime Ministers had, on May 9, agreed that, when Nigeria became independent, she would become a full member of the Commonwealth.

The First Secretary of the American Embassy at London (Hadsel) to the Secretary of State (Herter), despatch No. 3390, May 20, 1960, MS. Department of State, file 745h.00/5–2060.

The Constitution of the Federation of Nigeria which came into operation on October 1, 1960, under the Nigeria (Constitution) Order in Council, 1960 (Stat. Instr., 1960 (No. 1652)) describes Nigeria as consisting of three Regions—Northern Nigeria, Western Nigeria, and Eastern Nigeria—and a Federal territory. Article 3 further defines Northern and Eastern Nigeria as comprising those parts of the former Protectorate of Nigeria that on the thirtieth day of September, 1960, were comprised in these respective Regions of Nigeria; Western Nigeria as comprising those parts of the former Colony and Protectorate of Nigeria that on the thirtieth day of September, 1960, were comprised in the Western Region of Nigeria; and the Federal territory as comprising those parts of the former Colony of Nigeria that on the thirtieth day of September, 1960, were comprised in the Federal Territory of Lagos.

At the end of World War I, part of the adjacent territory of the German Cameroons, occupied during that war by the Anglo-French forces, was placed by the League of Nations under British Mandate and has since been administered as part of Nigeria. In 1923 an Order in Council made provision for the territory of the Southern Cameroons to be administered as part of the Southern Provinces while the Northern sections were attached for administrative purposes to the adjacent provinces of the north.

The General Assembly on December 13, 1946, approved a Trusteeship Agreement whereby the territory of the Cameroons, continuing under British administration, was placed under the International Trusteeship System. (T/Agreement/4, June 9, 1947.)

Taking note at the 1958 Conference of the divergence of views expressed by the representatives of the political parties, some holding as the objective the attainment by the Southern Cameroons of the status of a Region equal in all respects with other Regions in an independent Nigeria while others held as the objective for both Northern and Southern sections of the British Cameroons the secession from the Federation of Nigeria, the British Secretary of State for the Colonies stated that he was prepared to accept in principle that the Southern Cameroons should become, at the appropriate time, a Region fully equal in status to the other Regions of Nigeria. Such a development would be considered as being in fulfillment of one of the basic objectives of the Trusteeship Agreement while it would in no way commit the Southern Cameroons to permanent association with Nigeria, which would be a question for the people to decide. It was accordingly agreed at the Conference that no immediate constitutional changes should be made but that it would be open to the Southern Cameroon Government, which would be formed after the elections to be held in January 1959, to request the United Kingdom to bring into effect certain agreed measures of constitutional advance.

As a result of a plebiscite held in the Northern Cameroons Trust Territory on November 7, 1959, the majority voted to defer a decision on the territory's future until a later date. As a result of the plebiscite held on February 11, 1961, at which the two questions asked were: "Do you wish to achieve independence by joining the independent Federation of Nigeria?" and "Do you wish to achieve independence by joining the independent Republic of the Cameroons?", the inhabitants of the northern section voted to join the Federation of Nigeria and those of the southern section voted to join the Republic of the Cameroons. The General Assembly in Resolution 1608 (XV), April 25, 1961, endorsed the results of the plebiscites, called for the immediate implementation of these decisions, and decided to terminate the Trusteeship Agreement of December 13, 1946, concerning the Cameroons under United Kingdom administration as follows:

"(a) With respect to the Northern Cameroons, on 1 June 1961, upon its joining the Federation of Nigeria as a separate province of the Northern Region of Nigeria; (b) With respect to the Southern Cameroons, on 1 October 1961, upon its joining the Republic of Cameroun."

> *The Colonial Office List, 1960*, pp. 126–129. Report by the Resumed Nigeria Constitutional Conference held at London in September and October 1958, Cmnd. 569, pp. 30–31. Report of the United Nations Commissioner for the Supervision of the Plebiscites in the southern and northern parts of the Trust Territory of the Cameroons under United Kingdom Administration, T/1556, Apr. 3, 1961. The questions asked at the plebiscite were outlined with respect to the northern section in Resolution 1473(XIV) of December 12, 1959, and with respect to the southern section in Resolution 1352(XIV) of October 16, 1959.

Sierra
Leone

The Sierra Leone Constitutional Conference, April 20 to May 4, 1960, having agreed on certain final measures of constitutional advance before independence, designated April 27, 1961, as the date for the attainment of full independence by Sierra Leone (par. 29). The House of Representatives of Sierra Leone then passed a resolution on November 22, 1960, which authorized the Government of Sierra Leone to request the British Government to introduce, as soon as practicable, legislation providing for "the establishment of Sierra Leone on April 27th, 1961 as an independent sovereign state" and to request the British Government "to support with the other Member Governments of the Commonwealth, Sierra Leone's desire to become a Member of the Commonwealth". In consideration of this resolution, the Prime Ministers' Conference, 1961, noted the said date of independence and expressed a welcome to Sierra Leone "as a member of the Commonwealth on the completion of the necessary constitutional processes". As a further instrument in the legislative process, the Sierra Leone Independence Act, 1961, in providing for the attainment by Sierra Leone of fully responsible status within the Commonwealth, stipulated that on April 27, 1961, "the Sierra Leone Colony and the Sierra Leone Protectorate . . . shall together constitute part of Her Majesty's dominions under the name of Sierra Leone" (par. 1). In pursuance of this Act, the Sierra Leone (Constitution) Order in Council, 1961, provided a new constitution with effect as from the date of independence.

> *Report of the Sierra Leone Constitutional Conference*, Cmnd. 1029; American Consul at Freetown (Reiner) to the Secretary of State (Herter), despatch No. 97, Nov. 17, 1960, MS. Department of State, file 745m.02/11–1760; *Commonwealth Prime Ministers Conference*, Communique issued Mar. 16, 1961, Annex II, British Information Services, T.10, Mar. 20, 1961;

Sierra Leone Independence Act, 1961, 9 & 10 Eliz. 2, c. 16; The Sierra Leone (Constitution) Order in Council, 1961, Stat. Instr., 1961, No. 741.

As provided for in the Uganda Independence Act, 1962, Uganda, formerly a protectorate of the United Kingdom, became independent, attaining a "fully responsible status within the Commonwealth", on October 9, 1962. Under the terms of the Uganda Independence Constitution, which by virtue of the Uganda (Independence) Order in Council 1962, came into effect immediately before October 9, 1962, Uganda is a federal state consisting of Federal States (the Kingdoms **Uganda** of Buganda, Ankole, Bunyoro, and Toro and the territory of Busoga); Districts (Acholi, Bugisu, Bukedi, Karamoja, Kigezi, Lango, Madi, Sebei, Teso and West Nile); and the territory of Mbale. With respect to the division of powers under its federal form of government, the Government of Uganda is empowered "to make laws for the peace, order and good government of Uganda (other than the Federal States) with respect to any matter" (section 74). The consequent authority of the Federal States to legislate for the peace, order and good government of their respective States is exclusive of the power of the central government only with regard to those matters specified in separate schedules to the Uganda Constitution (schedules 7 and 8). The legislative powers, reserved exclusively to the central government as specified in part II of schedule 7 relating to Buganda, and also applicable to the other Federal States by virtue of section 75 (2) and (3) of the Uganda Independence Constitution, expressly concern such matters as external affairs, extradition, passports, defense, internal security, penal and criminal procedure codes, certain courts, public service of Uganda, and finance.

10 & 11 Eliz. 2, c.57; Stat. Instr., 1962, No. 2175 East Africa. See also Cmnd. 1778, July, 1962.

Newfoundland's suspension of its constitution as a self-supporting Dominion and consent to the institution of government by commission in 1934 was conditional upon a pledge given by the Government of the United Kingdom that when the island again became self-support- **Newfound-** ing the former constitutional status would be restored. Upon be- **land, a** coming self-supporting, the majority of the people of Newfoundland **of Canada** signified by referendum their wish to enter into confederation with Canada. The Terms of Union (Cmd. 7605) signed by representatives of Canada and Newfoundland December 11, 1948, provided in clause 1, ". . . Newfoundland shall form part of Canada and shall be a province thereof to be called and known as the Province of Newfoundland." The Terms of Union, approved by the Parliament of Canada and the Commission of the Government of Newfoundland

(153 Br. & For. St. Paps. (1949), part 1, p. 131), and confirmed by the British North American Act, 1949 (Mar. 23, 1949, 12 & 13 Geo. 6, c. 22), took effect immediately before the expiration of March 31, 1949, as provided in the Terms of Union.

The British Embassy at Washington informed the Secretary of State of the United States, in a note of March 28, 1949, that "after the 31st March 1949, His Majesty's Government in the United Kingdom will no longer be responsible for Newfoundland which will thereafter be a Province of Canada."

> The British Minister at Washington (Hoyer Millar) to the Secretary of State (Acheson), note No. 149, Mar. 28, 1949, MS. Department of State, file 842.014/3–2849.

"Dependent Empire"— classification

"*Legally*, it [British Commonwealth] means the sum of His Majesty's dominions; but *politically* it includes a very great number of territories which are not His Majesty's dominions in law. . . . But when we speak of the Dependent Empire we are talking in terms not of legal status but of mode of government. By the Dependent Empire we must be supposed to mean those parts of the Commonwealth that have not attained self-government and independence from imperial control—the Commonwealth, therefore, excluding its independent nations (formerly known as the Dominions) and also perhaps Southern Rhodesia. The juridical and political classifications of the Commonwealth, legal status and mode of government, cut across one another. . . .

". . . The Dependent Empire . . . is composed of territories possessing either legislatures subordinate to the Crown (but not always to the Crown exclusively), or rulers in treaty relations with the Crown, and in some cases both; and a political unit of the Dependent Empire, or a *dependency*, may be defined in either of these ways. [The Dependent Empire might also be defined as the sum of the territories that are represented internationally by His Majesty's government in the United Kingdom (with a requisite qualification in respect of the condominiums). Note that 'the one institution which is common to all the political entities which form part of or are associated with the British Empire is the Crown' (Jennings and Young, p. 1).]

.   .   .   .

" 'Dependency' is the only word that covers all the kinds of political community within the Dependent Empire. Not all these communities are *colonies*. Indeed, the majority of the population governed from the Colonial Office do not live in colonies. They are the inhabitants of *protectorates* or *trust territories*. It is sometimes impossible to avoid using the words 'colony' and 'colonial' to cover other kinds of territory to which they do not strictly apply, and official documents sanction the practice. [E.g. Colonial Regulation 2; Colonial Development and Welfare Act, 1940 (3 & 4 Geo. VI, c. 40), section 1 (5); *Statement of Policy*

on Colonial Development and Welfare, Cmd. 6175 (1940), para.
3; *Report of the Commission on Higher Education in the Colonies*, Cmd. 6647 (1945), ch. i, para. 2(b).]

"1. *Colonies*

"Colonies are dependencies that have been annexed by the
Crown. They are thus part of the King's dominions, and their
inhabitants are British subjects. Legally there are two kinds of
colony, *settled* and *conquered* or *ceded*. . . .

". . . The mode of acquisition no longer determines the mode
of government [representative or 'Crown Colony' government].
It determines only the source from which the constitution derives
its authority; the constitution itself is determined by the political
conditions of the colony. Thus there may be identical constitutions in a settled and in a ceded colony; but the constitution will
probably be based in the first place on the British Settlements Act
[1887 and 1945 (50 & 51 Vict., c. 54)], and in the second case on
the Crown's prerogative.

"2. *Protectorates*

"In its essential character a British protectorate is a territory in
which the Crown has acquired control of foreign relations and
defence. Whatever other powers the Crown may have acquired
. . . are not essential to the protectorate status. For, legally,
a protectorate is a dependency that has not been annexed: it is
not part of the dominions of the Crown, and its inhabitants are
not British subjects. . . .

"Not being part of the King's dominions, protectorates are technically foreign countries. They are administered under the Foreign Jurisdiction Act [1890 and 1913 (53 & 54 Vict., c. 37 and 3
& 4 Geo. V, c. 16)], which empowers the Crown to exercise any
jurisdiction which it has, or may come to have, in a foreign
country, in as ample a manner as if the jurisdiction had been
gained by the conquest or cession of territory. . . .

"(a) *Colonial Protectorates*

"Colonial protectorates may be described as dependencies which
are colonies in everything but legal status. Their administration
is that of crown colony government; in many cases they are administered as one with a contiguous colony; the only difference
is that their administration derives probably from the Foreign
Jurisdiction Act instead of from the prerogative, the British
Settlements Act, ...

"In some cases with colonial protectorates (as in all cases with
protected states) protectorate status originated in an explicit
treaty between the native ruler and the British Crown. These
treaties, however, are not considered as treaties in international
law, inasmuch as the native rulers did not enjoy sovereignty in

international law; neither have the treaties any validity in the constitutional law of the Empire.

"(b) *Protected States*

"Protected states illustrate the original meaning of the word 'protectorate'—a country that has ceded control of its international relations to the British Crown. There is a division of sovereignty based upon treaty agreements between Britain and the protected state. Britain controls the foreign relations of the protected state, but as a rule leaves its domestic affairs in the hands of its own ruler. British authority is generally represented by a resident or adviser, who is responsible to the Secretary of State for the Colonies. [To complete the picture, reference may be made to the range of protected states or states under British influence which are the concern of the Foreign Office, from the sheikhdoms of the Persian Gulf to states which have recently been or still are in permanent treaty relations with Britain—Iraq, Egypt, and Transjordan [as of 1947]. There are also two independent states in permanent treaty relations with India (formerly with the Indian Empire)—Bhutan and Nepal.]

.   .   .   .

"3. *Mandated and Trust Territories*

"Mandated and trust territories are another kind of dependency that is not British territory but is governed under the Foreign Jurisdiction Act. The mandate system was set up under the Covenant of the League of Nations for disposing of the non-self-governing territories taken from the Central Powers after the First World War, and it has been superseded by the trusteeship system of the United Nations. Mandated or trust territories are distinguished from protectorates in that their administration is subject to a degree of international supervision, formerly exercised by the Permanent Mandates Commission and now by the General Assembly and the Trusteeship Council, and that local legislation is void for repugnancy to the terms of the mandate or trust agreement if the constitution so provides. But the powers of the Crown itself in respect of mandated or trust territories are subject not to constitutional limitations, but only to respect for international obligations."

Wight, *British Colonial Constitutions 1947* (1952) 1, 2, 5–9, 11.

"The principal difference between a Crown colony and a protectorate is that the former is and the latter is not a part of the British dominions. Consequently, persons born within a colony are British subjects by birth, those born within a protectorate, who are not British subjects or aliens by reason of their personal law, are British protected persons. A protectorate is a concept somewhere between a British possession and a foreign country, like British protected person is a status between a British subject and an alien.

"Colonies are either (i) settled or (ii) conquered or ceded. The mode of acquisition determines the legislative power and the system of the general law prevailing in a colony. 'The basis of distinction—says Halsbury—is the stage of civilisation in the territory; if there is no population or no civilized form of government recognized in international law, possession is obtained by settlement; where there is an organized society, acquisition depends on cession or conquest.'

"With regard to settled colonies the rule is that British settlers take with them the common law of England and the statute law as existing in England at the time of the settlement. But the rule is qualified by considerations of expedience, as, obviously, statutes passed for the highly organized society in the British Isles is not always suitable for small communities living often in primitive conditions originally at least prevailing in overseas territories. Thus, for example, it was held by the Supreme Court of Alberta (*Flewelling* v. *Johnston*, 19 D.L.R. 419) that 'where resort is to be had to the common law the application of its principles is not necessarily to result in the same decisions as have been or may be given by the English courts, but account must be taken of the different conditions prevailing in this country, not merely physical conditions, but the general conditions of our public affairs'. On these grounds it was held that the common law rule that the navigability or otherwise of a river (for the purpose of determining the boundary between riparian owners) must be tested by the ebb and flow of the tide was not in force in Alberta with regard to those rivers which were in fact navigable.

"The Crown has no prerogative power to legislate for settled colonies but the British Settlements Act, 1887, authorized legislation by Order in Council for any settled colony which did not, at the time of the passing of the Act, possess its own legislature.

"In a conquered or ceded colony the old laws continue in force until repealed or amended by Order in Council. For example, Roman Dutch law continues to apply in Southern Rhodesia, where it was introduced by the British South Africa Company at the time of its government of the territory, and in the Union of South Africa; French law applies in Quebec, Mauritius and Seychelles, etc.

"With respect to this class of colonies the Crown has prerogative power to legislate by Order in Council, though by conferring a representative legislature on the colony the Crown is held to immediately and irrevocably divest itself of that power, except in so far as is provided to the contrary in the instrument by which the legislature is granted.

"'A British protectorate—says Sir Henry Jenkyns—is a country which is not within the British dominions, but as regards its foreign relations is under the exclusive control of the King, so that its government cannot hold direct communication with any foreign power, nor a foreign power with that government. . . . The British Crown, either by treaty, by sufferance, or by force, assumes over a defined territory a protectorate in this sense . . .; whilst on the other hand, the Crown undertakes to protect the inhabitants of the territory from interference by any foreign power.' Thus, for example, in a recent case Northern Rhodesia was described by the Lord Chief Justice as a foreign territory which was to all intents and purposes wholly under the subjection of Her Majesty (*In re Mwenya*, The Times, 4th July, 1959). The basis of a protectorate is in some sort of agreement, not necessarily formal or express, with the native tribes or rulers whereby the latter assent or acquiesce to the Crown taking over the responsibility for their external affairs and a degree of internal administration. These agreements are not binding on the Crown whether in domestic or international law. Some of the protectorates are governed as colonies, for example the High Commission Territories of Bechuanaland and Swaziland; others have acquired a considerable degree of autonomy (British North Borneo). According to the measure of their internal autonomy the protectorates are often referred to as 'colonial protectorates' or 'protected states', but the distinction is fluid.

"The power of the Crown to legislate for the protectorates is now based on the Foreign Jurisdiction Acts, 1890 and 1913, and may be exercised in as ample a manner as if Her Majesty had acquired that jurisdiction by the cession or conquest of a territory. The effect of the Acts is that the jurisdiction of the Crown in a protected country is indistinguishable in legal effects from what might be acquired by conquest.

"It rests with the Government of the day whether a conquered territory is to be treated as a protectorate or annexed as a Crown colony. Thus, Southern Rhodesia was a protectorate until annexed as a part of British dominions by the Southern Rhodesia (Annexation) Order in Council, 1923."

Weinberg, *An Outline of the Constitutional Law of The Federation of Rhodesia and Nyasaland* (1959) 40–42.

Condominium:

". . . a condominium is a territory over which responsibility is shared by two administering powers (e.g., the New Hebrides)."

Leased Territories:

"The term 'leased territories' applies only to that part of the mainland of China which was in 1898 leased to Great Britain for 99 years and is administered by the Government of Hong Kong."

Douglas Williams, Colonial Attaché, British Embassy, Washington, Jan. 6, 1959.

Federation of Rhodesia and Nyasaland

". . . The status of the Federation of Rhodesia and Nyasaland, though in some respects similar to that of the Members of the Commonwealth, does not amount to full Membership, since the United Kingdom remains responsible for its external relations except in so far as they are entrusted by the United Kingdom Government to the Federation. Southern Rhodesia, a self-governing Colony, is one of the component Territories of the Federation. . . ." [See *ante*, pp. 513–520.]

The Commonwealth Relations Office List, 1955 (1955) 7.

Although the Singapore (Constitution) Order in Council, 1958 (II Singapore Stat. Instr., 1958, No. 1956) gave Singapore the title of "The State of Singapore" and conferred upon the State of Singapore internal self-government, it reserved to the Government of the United Kingdom responsibility for defense and external affairs.

Prime Minister Macmillan, referring to the new Constitution conferring full internal self-government upon Singapore, said in a speech before the House of Commons, "The United Kingdom Government will remain responsible only for the defence and external affairs of the island. In recognition of this advanced status Singapore will be known in future as the State of Singapore. A separate Singapore citizenship will also be created. The necessary local legislation has now been enacted. We shall ask Parliament to amend the British Nationality Act, 1948, so that Singapore citizens will be recognised under the Act as British subjects and Commonwealth citizens. . . ."

577 H.C. Deb. (5th ser.) cols. 34–35 (Nov. 5, 1957).

"The former colony of Singapore has, by virtue of the State of Singapore Act, 1958 [6 & 7 Eliz. 2, c. 59], and the Singapore (Constitution) Order in Council, 1958 [Stat. Instr. 1958, No. 1956], been given internal self-government. The Government of the United Kingdom retains responsibility for defence and external affairs. At the same time, the Constitution Order anticipates some delegation by the United Kingdom Government to the Government of Singapore of the power to conduct certain classes of foreign relations. Section 73 (1) and (2) provide[s] as follows:

"'(1) The Government of Singapore, acting with the assent of the Government of the United Kingdom, shall be responsible for the conduct of matters concerning the trade and cultural relations of Singapore with other countries.

"'(2) The scope of the responsibility which is vested in the Government of Singapore by the preceding subsection shall be defined in a communication made to that Government by the Government of the United Kingdom; and any such communication may also, from time to time, delegate responsibility for the conduct, with the assent of the Government of the United Kingdom, of other matters relating to external affairs.'

"The following section (74) of the Order contains elaborate provisions enabling the Government of the United Kingdom to require the Government of Singapore to take such steps as may be necessary for the discharge by the United Kingdom of her international obligations in respect of Singapore. In case of disagreement between the government of the United Kingdom and the Singapore Government as to whether a matter is one of external or internal affairs, the question will be referred to the Internal Security Council. This body is to consist of an equal number of representatives of the two Governments plus one member appointed by the Government of the Federation of Malaya.

"The State of Singapore is to have a separate citizenship, possession of which shall entitle the holder to the status of a British subject or Commonwealth citizen. [See State of Singapore Act, 1958, s. 1 and British Nationality Act, 1948, s. 1 (1) and (2).]

"The extent of the separation between the State of Singapore and the Government of the United Kingdom is also illustrated by the fact that provision is made in the Constitution Order for the possession by the United Kingdom Commission 'of immunity from suit and legal process, . . . inviolability of residence, official premises and official archives, and to the like privileges as are accorded to the envoy of a foreign sovereign Power accredited to Her Majesty.' "

Lauterpacht, "The Contemporary Practice of the United Kingdom in the Field of International Law—Survey and Comment, VII", 8 Int'l & Comp L.Q. (1959) 146–148.

For legal descriptions of Colonies, The Isle of Man, the Islands of Jersey, Guernsey, and Alderney, and Sark, see Jennings and Young, *Constitutional Laws of the Commonwealth* (1952) 2, 3, 6–8.

Political status and legal classification distinguished

While the mode of government in each of its phases constitutes the political status of the dependency, it may coexist at any stage with any one of the legal classifications of dependent territories listed above. Generally speaking, these modes of government fall into four main phases in the evolution from "crown colony" government to complete sovereignty and independence.

From the early period of autocratic official control where local opinion has only limited power of advice, a machinery of government by consultation was established with the division of the Governor's Advisory Council into Legislative and Executive Councils. Local representatives, the "unofficials", are admitted to the Legislative Council but the "officials" retain the majority and the heads of departments.

The second major advance or "representative" stage is when the "unofficials" on the Legislative Council, both nominated and elected members, are increased in number to become a majority over the "officials".

"Semi-responsible" government, the third stage, is marked by the establishment by a new constitution of an Executive Council, the principal instrument of policy, with a majority of its members drawn, if possible, from the majority party in the newly-elected Assembly and made responsible for departments of government.

The final phase is attained when ex-officio members disappear from the Legislature, the powers of the secretary of state and the United Kingdom Parliament cease to operate and the Governor, divested of his discretionary powers, becomes the constitutional, formal head of a new independent State.

Austin, *West Africa and the Commonwealth* (1957) 68–69.

For early constitutional arrangements for the various stages of political development, see Keith, *An Introduction to British Constitutional Law* (1931).

While the units comprising the dependent empire are at various stages in their advancement toward independence, they are legally classified by the Colonial Office as follows:

Colonies:

Bahama Islands, Basutoland, Bermuda, British Guiana, British Honduras, Central and Southern Line Islands, Cyprus [independent, August 16, 1960], Falkland Islands and dependencies, Fiji (and Pitcairn Islands group), Gibraltar, Gilbert and Ellice Islands Colony (including Phoenix and Northern Line Island groups), Hong Kong, Malta (Malta, Gozo, Comino and islets—Filfla and Cominotto), Mauritius, North Borneo including Island of Lauban, St. Helena and dependencies (Ascension, Tristan Da Cunha, Nightingale, Inaccessible, and Gough), Sarawak, Seychelles, Virgin Islands, ten colonies each consisting of one or more islands [formerly comprising West Indies Federation dissolved May 29, 1962]: Barbados; Jamaica (including the Cayman Islands and the Turks and Caicos Islands [which remained colonies when Jamaica became independent, August 6, 1962]); the Leeward Islands of Antigua, Montserrat, and St. Christopher, Nevis and Anguilla; Trinidad and Tobago; and the Windward Islands of Grenada, Dominica, St. Lucia and St. Vincent. It does not include British Guiana, British Honduras or the Virgin Islands (Leeward Islands).

Protectorates:

Bechuanaland, British Solomon Islands, Somaliland Protectorate [independent, June 26, 1960], Swaziland, Uganda [independent, October 9, 1962], Zanzibar.

Colony and Protectorate:

Aden (Kamaran Island under British occupation since 1915 forms neither a part of the Colony of Aden nor of the Aden Protectorate, but the Governor of Aden is also the Governor of Kamaran under the provisions of the Kamaran Order in Council, 1949), The Gambia,

Kenya Colony and Protectorate, Federation of Nigeria including the Federal territory of Lagos [independent, October 1, 1960], Sierra Leone (Colony includes Sierra Leone Peninsula, Tasso Island, Banana Island, York Island, and township of Bonthe on Sherbro Island) [independent, April 27, 1961], Federation of Rhodesia and Nyasaland comprises the Colony of Southern Rhodesia and the Protectorates of Northern Rhodesia and Nyasaland.

Western Pacific High Commission is an administrative unit of the following groups: The Gilbert and Ellice Islands Colony (including the Phoenix and Northern Line Islands groups), The British Solomon Islands Protectorate, The New Hebrides, The Central and Southern Line Islands (including Flint, Caroline, Vostock, Malden and Starbuck).

Trusteeship Territories:

Cameroons [trusteeship terminated when Northern Cameroons joined Nigeria, June 1, 1961; Southern Cameroons joined Republic of Cameroon, October 1, 1961]; Tanganyika [independent December 9, 1961].

Tanganyika

Following agreement between the United Kingdom and Tanganyikan Governments reached at a constitutional conference held at Dar-es-Salaam from March 27–29, 1961, that Tanganyika become a fully independent State on December 28, 1961, and that in the meanwhile full internal self-government be introduced in Tanganyika on May 1, 1961, the General Assembly on April 21, 1961, adopted Resolution 1609 (XV) whereby it resolved, "in agreement with the Administering Authority, that the Trusteeship Agreement for Tanganyika, approved by the General Assembly on 13 December 1946, should cease to be in force upon the accession of Tanganyika to independence on 28 December 1961". In the light of the Tanganyikan Prime Minister's suggestion that the date of December 28, 1961, could prove inconvenient, particularly for representatives and guests from abroad, the United Kingdom and Tanganyikan Governments agreed that the date of independence should be advanced to December 9, 1961. Accordingly, the General Assembly in resolution 1642 (XVI) on November 6, 1961, resolved that the Trusteeship Agreement be terminated on December 9, 1961.

> Report of the Trusteeship Council, *The Future of Tanganyika*, Apr. 17, 1961, A/C.4/489, Apr. 17, 1961; A/Res/1609 (XV), Apr. 25, 1961; letter dated July 12, 1961, to the Secretary-General from the Permanent Representative of the United Kingdom of Great Britain and Northern Ireland to the United Nations, A/4806, July 20, 1961. Tanganyika is a member of the Commonwealth by virtue of the Tanganyikan Independence Act, 1961 (10 Eliz. 2, c. 1).

The United Nations Trusteeship Council by Resolution 2102 (XXVII) of July 7, 1961, noting with satisfaction the results of the plebiscite held on May 9, 1961, on Western Samoa, then a Trust Territory administered by New Zealand, that the people of Western Samoa expressed their agreement with the Constitution for an independent Western Samoa adopted by the Constitutional Convention on October 28, 1960, and agreed that on January 1, 1962, Western Samoa should become an independent State on the basis of that Constitution, recommended that the General Assembly decide in agreement with the Administering Authority to terminate on January 1, 1962, the Trusteeship Agreement approved by the General Assembly on December 13, 1946. The General Assembly in resolution 1626 (XVI) on October 18, 1961, resolved that the Trusteeship Agreement be terminated on January 1, 1962.

T/RES/2102 (XXVII), July 24, 1961.

British Protected States:

State of Brunei, Maldive Islands, Kingdom of Tonga.

Leased Territories:

New Territories and islands around Hong Kong.

Condominium:

New Hebrides.

Additionally:

State of Singapore.

> *Colonial Office List, 1960* (1960). See also *Commonwealth Relations Office List, 1960* (1960) 233.

> Holding that Hong Kong—frequently referred to as a Crown Colony—is a "country" within the meaning of that part of the Immigration and Nationality Act of June 27, 1952 (8 U.S.C.A. § 1253) which provides for deportation to a "country from which such alien last entered the United States", the United States District Court for the District of Columbia based its opinion on the definition of the word "country" given by the United States Supreme Court in *Burnet* v. *Chicago Portrait Co.* (285 U.S. 1 (1932)) which it quoted as follows: "'The word "country," in the expression "foreign country," is ambiguous. It may be taken to mean foreign territory or a foreign government. In the sense of territory, it may embrace all the territory subject to a foreign sovereign power. When referring more particularly to a foreign government, it may describe a foreign State in the international sense, that is, one that has the status of an international person with the rights and responsibilities under international law of a member of the family of nations; or it may mean a foreign government which has authority over a particular area or subject-matter, although not an international person but only a component part, or a political subdivision, of the larger international unit. The term "foreign country" is not a tech-

nical or artificial one, and the sense in which it is used in a statute must be determined by reference to the purpose of the particular legislation.' " *Peter Ying, Wong Chai Liang* v. *Rogers,* 180 F. Supp. 618, 619–620 (D.D.C. 1960).

French Community

§31

The French Community officially came into being April 5, 1959, and as instituted by the French Constitution of the Fifth Republic, adopted by referendum September 28, 1958, and promulgated October 4, 1958, constituted a union of two distinct groups: the French Republic, comprising the mother country, the Overseas Departments and the Overseas Territories; and the autonomous Member States.

Composition—

"The overseas dependencies of the Republic form two very distinct categories: the overseas departments and the overseas territories. The first are part of the policy called 'assimilation' and have a status as near as possible to that of departments in the mother country. The second, on the contrary, enjoy a very large measure of autonomy, often approaching federalism. Legally, they are integrated in the Republic; actually, they are in many respects rather like Member States of the Community.

Overseas Departments

"(1) *The Overseas Departments.* The general rule is that their status is identical with that of the metropolitan departments, but special arrangements make some exceptions to this principle. Three very different groups of overseas departments should be pointed out.

"The departments of Réunion, Guiana, Guadeloupe, and Martinique are almost completely assimilated to the mother country. The twelve departments of Algeria are much less so. The doctrine called 'integration', adopted by the parties of the right after May 13, [1958,] is quite new: from 1830 to 1958 the same parties were violently opposed to any equality between European colonists and native Moslems; at the very time of the framing of the Algerian 'basic-law' of February 3, 1958, they made great efforts to prevent the establishment, or to limit the effects, of a 'single electoral body', in other words, of equality at the polls for all inhabitants of Algeria. The two departments of Oasis and of Saoura in the Sahara are in a very complex situation, since they are not only French departments but also part of the Common Organization of the Sahara Districts, created in 1957, which includes in addition parts of the Sahara belonging to Member States of the Community. These two departments are under the Ministry of the Sahara, despite the wish of the partisans of Algerian integration to regard them as part of Algeria, which is historically untrue. [*Cf.* Chatelain, *La nouvelle Constitution et le Régime politique de la France* (1959) 327 (translation), who in considering the Departments of Oasis and Saoura as added to the 12 districts comprising Algeria notes, ". . .

the establishment, by the decree of April 14, 1958, of three new Algerian departments had not yet actually been carried out". The French Foreign Ministry reported that the French Government does not recognize the claims put forward by certain political groups in Algeria that the two Saharan Departments of Saoura and Oasis are a part of Algeria. The Foreign Ministry further observed that the Algerian Departments and the Saharan Departments are administered separately, the former coming directly under the authority of President de Gaulle and the latter coming under the authority of Minister Delegate Soustelle. The Counselor of the American Embassy at Paris (Kidder) to the Secretary of State (Herter), despatch No. 2112, May 14, 1959, MS. Department of State, file 751.00/5–1459.]

"Article 73 of the 1958 Constitution, reproducing a corresponding article of the 1946 Constitution, permits legal exceptions to the general principle of assimilation with respect to 'the legislative system and administrative organization', which may be the subject of 'adjustment measures.' But these exceptions are limited in two ways: (1) they may apply only to the legislative system and administrative organization and not to political relations with the mother country; (2) they may relate only to 'adjustments,' and this, according to opinions of the Council of State in 1946 and 1947, does not permit violation of the general spirit and essential provisions of the Constitution regarding assimilation.

"(2) *The Overseas Territories.* Prior to the Constitution of 1958, the overseas territories were those former colonies which had not been assimilated and which therefore had a status quite different from that of the mother country. This status had evolved toward a progressive autonomy, the 1946 Constitution, and especially the 'basic-law' of June 23, 1956, having been important steps in this direction. The Constitution of 1958 [Article 76] gave them the right to choose, within four months from the date of promulgation, between retention of their status, becoming overseas departments, or becoming Member States of the Community, the choice to be made by a resolution of their territorial assembly. Under this provision, the territories of Black Africa and Madagascar chose entry into the Community . . . . No territory chose to become a department. The following overseas territories have retained their status as such: Saint Pierre and Miquelon, New Caledonia and its dependencies, Tahiti and the remainder of French Oceania [Polynesia], French Somaliland, and the Comoro Archipelago. [The status of French Polynesia was modified by the *ordonnance* of December 23, 1958. See the *Journal Officiel* of December 27, 1958.]

"The status of the overseas territories, on the whole, remains as it was determined by the law of June 23, 1956. A Territorial Assembly, elected by direct universal suffrage, with a single electoral body, has a power of decision in financial and fiscal matters (maintained despite Article 34 of the Constitution, which reserves matters for the law, that is, for the Parliament of the Republic

Overseas
Territories

. . . it is generally agreed that the wording is faulty), in the matter of the public domain and of the establishment of public services; and has advisory powers in other fields (consultation is compulsory with regard to regulations issued by the Government Council, optional with regard to the organization of public services, to economic and social questions, and to police regulations). The Assembly elects the members of the Government Council by a majority vote from lists of candidates in three ballotings, without splitting of votes or preferential votes. It may register a vote of no confidence in the Government Council, which in practice (but not by constitutional right) obliges the Council to resign. The Government Council is a true ministry and has wider powers of decision than does a parliamentary government; the head of the Council has the title of Vice President, but is actually a Prime Minister. Finally, the 'head of the territory' is the representative of the Republic, who exercises approximately the functions of a parliamentary head of state.

"But the competence of the autonomous territorial organs (Territorial Assembly and Government Council) applies only to the territorial services. A fundamental distinction is made by the law of June 23, 1956, between the territorial and the state public services. The list of the latter is rather long, and was extended by the law of 1956 to offset the autonomy granted in the manage‑ ment of the territorial services. The State services are: foreign relations; national defense; the judiciary, inspection of work, services assuring public safety and respect for the freedom of the citizens, exterior communications (air services, radio broadcasting), the treasury, credit, and foreign exchange; higher education; mixed-economy companies."

Duverger, *Droit Constitutionnel et Institutions Politiques* (1959) 699–702 (translation).

Article 74 of the 1958 Constitution in confirming the status of the Overseas Territories provides, however, for a special organization which takes into account their own interests within the general interests of the Republic. This organization, the article provides, shall be defined and modified by law after consultation with the Territorial Assembly concerned. Article 75 specifies that citizens of the Republic who do not have ordinary civil status, the only status referred to in article 34, may keep their personal status as long as they have not renounced it.

"This special organization is defined by French law, but the latter cannot come into being except after consultation with the territorial assembly concerned. That, then, is a guarantee of the maintenance of the autonomy of these territories. The latter remains limited, however, since modification of status requires merely consultation with and not the agreement of the territorial assembly. . . ."

Chatelain, *op. cit.* 326 (translation).

Adherence to the Community, which is based on the free determina- Member States tion of the members, required of the former Overseas Territories electing to become members the duty to opt twice. Although such was not stipulated by the Constitution, it was specified by the head of the government that rejection of the Constitution at the time of the referendum of September 28 would be considered a refusal to adhere to the Community. (Only Guinea rejected the draft constitution. See *infra.*) Then each Overseas Territory had to vote through its local assembly upon which status it intended to adopt of the three offered to it: Overseas Department, Overseas Territory, or Member State of the Community (article 76). States which opted for membership in the Community have the right to withdraw or to change their status according to article 86 which, as amended June 4, 1960, provides as follows:

"A change of status of a member State of the Community may be requested, either by the Republic, or by a resolution of the legislative assembly of the State concerned confirmed by a local referendum, the organization and supervision of which shall be ensured by the institutions of the Community. The procedures governing this change shall be determined by an agreement approved by the Parliament of the Republic and the legislative assembly concerned.

"Under the same conditions, a member State of the Community may become independent. It shall thereby cease to belong to the Community."

The following paragraphs were added in 1960:

"A member State of the Community may also, by means of agreements, become independent without thereby ceasing to belong to the Community.

"An independent State that is not a member of the Community may, by means of agreements, become a member of the Community without ceasing to be independent.

"The status of such States within the Community shall be determined by agreements concluded for that purpose, particularly the agreements referred to in the preceding paragraphs and, should the occasion arise, the agreements provided for in paragraph two of Article 85 [as amended]."

French Constitution, French Text and English Translation, Ambassade de France, Service de Presse et d'Information, New York (1958); Amendments of June 4, 1960, *Journal Officiel de la République Française*, June 8, 1960, p. 5103.

Those Overseas Territories which elected to become Member States in the Community specified their new official names as follows:

Madagascar:	Madagascan Republic [Department of State Mailing Notice of Feb. 2, 1960, announced the proper designation for the Malgache Republic to be "Malagasy Republic".]
Soudan:	Soudanese Republic
Senegal:	State of Senegal
Mauritania:	Mauritanian Islamic Republic
Gabon:	Gabon Republic
Chad:	Republic of Chad
Middle Congo:	Republic of Congo
Ubangi-Shari:	Central African Republic
Ivory Coast:	Republic of Ivory Coast
Dahomey:	Republic of Dahomey
Upper Volta:	Volta Republic
Niger:	Republic of Niger

Department of State mailing notice, "Proper Designations for the Member States of the (French) COMMUNITY", Apr. 8, 1959.

"While it recognized that the term 'French Somaliland' might be generally accepted American usage, the Foreign Ministry commented that the only correct term in French was *Côte Française des Somalis*. The Foreign Ministry opined that the correct translation of the French term would be 'French Coast of the Somalis'.

"After verification with the Secretariat General of the Community, the Foreign Ministry confirmed that Senegal officially assumed on January 24, 1959, the title of 'Republique du Senegal' (Republic of Senegal). The Foreign Ministry and the Secretariat General explained that the term 'Etat du Senegal' (State of Senegal) was adopted temporarily upon Senegal's entry into the Community in December, 1958. The term 'state' was replaced by that of 'republic' in the new Senegalese constitution which entered into effect on January 24, 1959." The Counselor of the American Embassy at Paris (Kidder) to the Secretary of State (Herter), despatch No. 2112, May 14, 1950, MS. Department of State, file 751.00/5–1459.

"French West Africa and French Equatorial Africa have been vacated as political designations. Formerly, they were federations consisting of overseas territories: French West Africa including Dahomey, Guinea, Ivory Coast, Mauritania, Niger, Senegal, French Sudan, and Upper Volta; French Equatorial Africa including Chad, Gabon, Middle Congo, and Ubangi-Shari (now Central African Republic). Togo (Republic of) and Cameroun (State of) are both locally-autonomous Trust Territories under French administration. They are not members of the Community." Department of State mailing notice, "Proper Designations for Member States of the (French) COMMUNITY", Apr. 8, 1959.

"The French Government does not consider the Franco-British Condominium of New Hebrides to be a part of the French Republic or of the Community. The Foreign Ministry observed that New Hebrides is a territory over which the French Republic exercises certain responsibilities, in this case jointly with Great Britain, but is not considered to be an integral part of French territory, as are the Departments of Metropolitan France, Algeria, Sahara, the Overseas Departments and the Overseas Territories. Moreover, since New Hebrides is neither a part of the French Republic nor an autonomous state of the Community, it is not considered to be a part of the Community. In this respect only, New Hebrides might be considered to be in the same general category as the Republic of Togo and the State of Cameroun, which belong neither to the French Republic nor the Community but over which the French Republic exercises certain responsibilities." The Counselor of the American Embassy at Paris (Kidder) to the Secretary of State (Herter), despatch No. 2112, May 14, 1959, MS. Department of State, file 751.00/5–1459.

The statute and institutions of the French Community as established and defined under title XII of the French Constitution of the Fifth Republic form a legal entity whose unique status cannot be circumscribed within the traditional international law classifications of federation or confederation.

Status of French Community—

Thus, an official compilation of comments of the French Government on the Constitution of October 4, 1958, explaining in part the genesis of the text of title XII, states:

"When the text of the draft was submitted to the Advisory Committee the latter immediately established an overseas group that was more or less equally divided between two trends: one federative and the other confederative.

"The members of the group prepared two texts corresponding to the two trends, federative and confederative. However, after lengthy and rather chaotic discussion before the Committee it became apparent, on the one hand, that the two theses were not reconcilable and, on the other, that those advocating a Federation did not desire a genuine federation any more than the advocates of Confederation desired a genuine confederation.

"It was at this point, at a memorable meeting, that a member of the Committee, the President of the Government of Madagascar, proposed abandoning discussions of principles, on which agreement was not being reached, and endeavoring to establish concretely the elements it was possible and desirable to pool. The Committee adopted this very wise proposal and it was by working in this spirit, with the will to succeed, that it drew up the almost complete definitive text of Title XII. Its contribution in this regard was therefore a capital one. The word 'Federation' was eliminated entirely from the draft and superseded by 'community,' on which general agreement was achieved.

"The institutions of the Community were established to meet a concrete situation: they are geared to this situation such as it is and is felt to be now, but they are also susceptible of adaptation to the evolution of the French system as a whole and of the world of which this system is a part. They can, tomorrow, become the institutions of a true federation of equal States, if such is to be our historic destiny; they can also become the institutions of a simple confederation.

"Title XII of the Constitution is therefore characterized by maximum flexibility, owing in particular, to the organic laws and special agreements for which it provides. Those who helped in its preparation drafted it with the idea that it should not be an obstacle to the evolution of events, whatever this evolution may be. Even if this were the sole merit of the text, it is essential, for very great flexibility is necessary in this sphere. Despite a certain daring, the constitution of 1946 had the defect of being a somewhat Cartesian and one-sided structure, which did not facilitate (far from it) the very rapid development during the post-war years. It contained a constitutional definition of the French Union and the High Council of the French Union, on which it was necessary, not without difficulty, to superimpose a diplomatic definition acceptable to the interested parties, but this came too late, as we know.

"However, this flexibility cannot lead to anarchistic development; the customary law that will come into being will respect the constitutional framework, of which the broad outlines may not be called in question; their general nature is to a large extent the guarantee of their effectiveness. The President of the Community, guardian of the Constitution, is normally responsible for ensuring that customary law is in harmony with the Constitution."

La Documentation Française, "Commentaires Sur La Constitution Du 4 Octobre 1958 accompagnés du texte intégral De La Constitution", No. 2.530, 11 Avril 1959, Secrétariat Général Du Gouvernement Direction de la Documentation, Notes et Études Documentaires (translation).

Title XII of the French Constitution is reprinted in English as follows:

"*Article 77*—In the Community instituted by the present Constitution, the States shall enjoy autonomy; they shall administer themselves and, democratically and freely, manage their own affairs.

"There shall be only one citizenship in the Community.

"All citizens shall be equal before the law, whatever their origin, their race and their religion. They shall have the same duties.

"*Article 78*—The Community shall have jurisdiction over foreign policy, defense, the monetary system, common economic and financial policy, as well as the policy on strategic raw materials.

"In addition, except by special agreement, control of justice, higher education, the general organization of external and common transport and of telecommunications shall be within its jurisdiction.

"Special agreements may establish other common jurisdictions or regulate the transfer of jurisdiction from the Community to one of its members.

"*Article 79*—The member States shall benefit from the provisions of Article 77 as soon as they have exercised the choice provided for in Article 76.

"Until the measures required for implementation of the present title go into force, matters within the common jurisdiction shall be regulated by the Republic.

"*Article 80*—The President of the Republic shall preside over and represent the Community.

"The Community shall have, as organs, an Executive Council, a Senate and a Court of Arbitration.

"*Article 81*—The member States of the Community shall participate in the election of the President according to the conditions stipulated in Article 6.

"The President of the Republic, in his capacity as President of the Community, shall be represented in each State of the Community.

"*Article 82*—The Executive Council of the Community shall be presided over by the President of the Community. It shall consist of the Premier of the Republic, the heads of Government of each of the member States of the Community, and of the ministers responsible for the common affairs of the Community.

"The Executive Council shall organize the cooperation of members of the Community at Government and administrative levels.

"The organization and procedure of the Executive Council shall be determined by an organic law.

"*Article 83*—The Senate of the Community shall be composed of delegates whom the Parliament of the Republic and the legislative assemblies of the other members of the Community shall choose from among their own membership. The number of delegates of each State shall be determined, taking into account its population and the responsibilities it assumes in the Community.

"The Senate of the Community shall hold two sessions a year, which shall be opened and closed by the President of the Community and may not last more than one month each.

"The Senate of the Community, upon referral by the President of the Community, shall deliberate on the common economic and financial policy before laws in these matters are voted upon by the Parliament of the Republic and, should circumstances so require, by the legislative assemblies of the other members of the Community.

"The Senate of the Community shall examine the acts and treaties or international agreements, which are specified in Articles 35 and 53, and which commit the Community.

"The Senate of the Community shall take enforceable decisions in the domains in which it has received delegation of power from the legislative assemblies of the members of the Community. These decisions shall be promulgated in the same form as the law in the territory of each of the States concerned.

"An organic law shall determine the composition of the Senate and its rules of procedure.

"*Article 84*—A Court of Arbitration of the Community shall rule on litigations occurring among members of the Community.

"Its composition and its competence shall be determined by an organic law.

"*Article 85*—By derogation from the procedure provided for in Article 89, the provisions of the present title that concern the functioning of the common institutions shall be amendable by identical laws passed by the Parliament of the Republic and by the Senate of the Community.

[Article 85 as amended on June 4, 1960, reads as follows: "The provisions of this Title may also be amended by agreements between all the States of the Community; the new provisions shall be put into force under the conditions stipulated in the Constitution of each State." *Journal Officiel de la République Française*, June 8, 1960, p. 5103.]

"*Article 86*—A change of status of a member State of the Community may be requested, either by the Republic, or by a resolution of the legislative assembly of the State concerned confirmed by a local referendum, the organization and supervision of which shall be ensured by the institutions of the Community. The modalities of this change shall be determined by an agreement approved by the Parliament of the Republic and the legislative assembly concerned.

"Under the same conditions, a member State of the Community may become independent. It shall thereby cease to belong to the Community.

[Paragraphs 3, 4, and 5 as added to article 86 of the Constitution on June 4, 1960, read as follows:

"A member State of the Community may also, by means of agreements, become independent without thereby ceasing to belong to the Community.

"An independent State that is not a member of the Community may, by means of agreements, become a member of the Community without ceasing to be independent.

"The status of such States within the Community shall be determined by agreements concluded for that purpose, particularly the agreements referred to in the preceding paragraphs and, should the occasion arise, the agreements provided for in paragraph two of Article 85 [as amended]." *Journal Officiel de la République Française*, June 8, 1960, p. 5103.]

"*Article 87*—The particular agreements made for the implementation of the present title shall be approved by the Parliament of the Republic and the legislative assembly concerned."

Ambassade de France, Service de Presse et d'Information, *French Affairs*, No. 66, Sept. 1958, pp. 25–27.

Constitutional analysts and French jurists writing in 1959 of the 1958 French Constitution have variously described the status of the French Community.

Professor Chatelain remarks at the outset of his analysis of the French Community: "The Community constitutes an association of states, but it is quite original, because it does not fit into any of the traditional frameworks of federalism."

Chatelain, *op. cit.* 331 (translation).

Professor Duverger refers to the Community as a "semi-federate, semi-confederate group that unites the Republic and the Overseas Territories". Commenting further on the idea of the Community, he adds:

"The term 'Community' has replaced that of 'French Union', which was used in the Constitution of 1946 and succeeded the term 'Empire', employed by Mr. Daladier after 1938 and recognized in the draft constitution of Marshal Pétain. The term 'Empire', in turn, had taken the place of the traditional designation 'colonies' of the Third Republic. These changes in words show the evolution in conditions: 'colonies' indicated a status of inequality, 'Empire' expressed a desire for assimilation in an atmosphere of nationalism, 'French Union' marked a step toward federalism, and 'Community' goes clearly beyond this stage. . . ."

. . . .

". . . The Republic and the other Member States are not placed on a footing of absolute equality; first, because the Republic alone has external sovereignty and ensures the international representation of the Community, and, second, because the Republic has a preponderant voice in the management of common affairs . . . . Subject to these two reservations, the Member States have internal sovereignty."

Duverger, *op. cit.* 692, 702.

Professor Friedrich in describing the Community as a "new conception" explains:

". . . We are here faced by a definite step in the direction of further federalizing the French Union, in the sense in which that process needs to be understood. The concept of a Community is crucial as expressing the fact that there is recognized the existence of two levels of community, the comprehensive one of the union as a whole, and that of the component units. Whenever the pattern of common values, interests, and beliefs displays a structuring in terms of two such levels, federalism is indicated. . . .

"The Community is based on the principle that its member states shall enjoy autonomy, shall administer themselves and manage their affairs democratically and freely. (art. 77) They are united in one common citizenship. The Community has a clearly defined set of functions assigned to it; it must be presumed that the residual functions are, as in the United States, left to the member states—an important feature of many federal systems.

Foreign policy, defense, currency, common economic and financial policy, as well as raw materials, are its exclusive preserve. In addition there are other functions—the supervision of courts, higher education, 'the general organization of external and common transport and of telecommunications'—which will be handled by the Community, unless excluded by specific agreement. Special agreements may extend as well as contract this list. (art. 78) It is evident that the scope of communal (federal) activities is wide . . . . Yet they leave much . . . in the hands of the member states, such as primary and secondary education, police, labor, and civil and criminal law.

. . . .

"The legislative Senate (art. 83) is more definitely conceived in the federal spirit than was the former Assembly, whose function was strictly advisory (art. 71). The French Parliament continued to legislate for all the territories, restricting the former Assembly to far less than effective participation. Under the new constitution, which provides for balanced representation of all member states, the Senate is to hold two sessions a year; it does not wield genuine legislative power, except in the fields which, by delegation from the assemblies of the members of the Community, are within its jurisdiction. Its decisions are called executing (exécutoires). The court of the Community has jurisdiction only over conflicts between the states (art. 84), not over any of the broad issues involved in a true federalism."

Friedrich, "The New French Constitution in Political and Historical Perspective", 72 Harv. L. Rev. (1959) 801, 831–833.

Comments in the Paris press, prior to the meetings of the Community Executive Council from July 7–8, 1959, characterized the Community as essentially a confederation. As transmitted from the American Embassy in Paris, these reports were summarized as follows:

"*Le Monde* July 2, attributed choice of Tananarive as site of first non-Metropole Executive Council meeting to Tsiranana's role in the development of Community concept which was described as halfway between French-dominated federal organization and Senghor's multi-nation confederation. However, the paper believed that after nine months of existence the Community had become almost indistinguishable from confederation of independent states.

"*Figaro* said Community now possessed its structure, that its activities were continuously increasing, and that its place in the world was achieved. In the paper's opinion even difficulties which had had to be overcome showed that in contributing to the common effort each state had freely defended its own concepts. In the forthcoming Executive Council meetings it would be up to de Gaulle to determine orientation of the institution which is not a fixed concept but is continuously perfectible. *Figaro* also believed that if, as expected, the question of diplomatic representation of Community states in neighboring countries arose during Tananarive conference, this interest on the part of the Community leaders would show that the institution was gradually taking on characteristics of confederation."

The Counselor of the American Embassy at Paris (Kidder) to the Secretary of State (Herter), airgram No. G-4, July 2, 1959, MS. Department of State, file 751w.00/7-259.

Effecting an extension of autonomy from that accorded the overseas territories by the "basic-law" of 1956, article 77 sets forth the fundamental principle governing the general areas of competence of the Member States by providing in addition to the stipulation that "States shall enjoy autonomy" that "they shall administer themselves and manage their own affairs democratically and freely". The exercise of powers within the Member States' fields of competence must comport, however, with the further stipulation in article 77 that "There shall be only one citizenship in the Community" and that "All citizens shall be equal before the law, whatever their origin, their race and their religion." *Areas of competence*

Certain affairs are reserved, however, to the Community's jurisdiction in article 78 which enumerates them as follows:

> "The Community's jurisdiction shall extend over foreign policy, defense, currency, common economic and financial policy, as well as over policy on strategic raw materials.
>
> "It shall include, in addition, except in the case of specific agreements, the supervision of the tribunals, higher education, the general organization of external transportation and transporation within the Community, as well as of telecommunications."

It is further provided in article 78 that "Special agreements may create other common jurisdictions or regulate any transfer of jurisdiction from the Community to one of its members."

French Constitution, op. cit.

Some interpretations of article 78 distinguish between the central authority's direct action over those affairs enumerated in the first paragraph and the limitation of the central authority to the exercise of control over those powers appearing in the second paragraph. With regard to this second category of powers, it has been asserted that it is merely incumbent on the central authority to supervise so that this multiplicity of actions will not imperil the common interests and the solidarity of the whole.

See Chatelain, *op. cit.* 331-332; Friedrich, *op. cit.* 832.

In connection with the third paragraph of article 78, which renders these fields of competence subject to change through agreements, Professor Duverger, noting that the 1958 Constitution introduced elements of confederation into an organization based rather on the idea of federation, comments further that the agreements may reduce as well as increase the autonomy of Member States.

Duverger, *op. cit.* 704.

Institutions
of the
French
Community—

The recognized looseness of structure, flexibility of functional provisions, and consequent uniqueness of the status of the French Community is best illustrated by an examination of constitutional provisions governing the participation of the organs of the Community in the exercise of powers. For this purpose Professor Duverger's analysis of the Community institutions is substantially reprinted (in translation) as follows:

President

"(A) *The President of the Community*

"The President of the Community is the President of the French Republic; he is therefore an organ common to the Republic and the Community. This is not just a simple superimposing of powers, a sort of personal union, like that of 'King of France and Navarre.' The two categories of powers are linked one to the other, as is made clear by the election procedure, which associates in one and the same act the voters of the Republic and those of the Community.

"The President is not the only organ common to the Republic and the Community. The Economic and Social Council, . . . has two representatives from each Member State of the Community, by agreements concluded with the States, and in this sense is a common organ, but with a very minor role.

"(a) *The Legal Definition of the Powers of the President of the Community*

"The Constitution itself is very vague on this subject. Article 80 says only:

" 'The President of the Republic shall preside over and represent the Community. The organs of the Community shall be an Executive Council, a Senate, and a Court of Arbitration.'

"Article 5 of the *ordonnance* of December 19, 1958 [*ordonnances* of December 19, 1958, embody basic regulations for the institutions of the Community] provides that the President of the Community shall have the general function of enforcing respect for the Constitution, for the organic laws of the Community, agreements of the Community, decisions of the Community Court of Arbitration, and the international treaties and agreements binding on the Community. This defines a field of action rather than precise powers, ends rather than means. But paragraph 2 of the same article, and other provisions of the *ordonnances* dealing with organic laws of the Community, are much more definite. They bestow upon the President of the Community a general power of decision and also prerogatives with regard to the special organs of the Community. The *ordonnances* of December 19 go much further than the classical presidential system; there is almost a confusion of powers to the advantage of the President.

"*1. The General Power of Decision in Common Affairs.* Article 5 of the *ordonnance* of December 19, 1958, relating to the Executive Council of the Community, provides: 'The President of the Community . . . shall formulate and make known the measures necessary for the conduct of common affairs; he shall see to their execution.' This text should be read in connection with Article 4: 'The Executive Council . . . shall take cognizance of questions of general policy of the Community within the fields of competence enumerated in Article 78 of the Constitution.' This comparison of texts gives rise to some doubt. Two things are certain: (1) the Executive Council should take cognizance of problems regarding which the President of the Community 'formulates and makes known' decisions, when these problems concern general policy (in this field the President cannot decide alone); (2) the formulation of the decision, on the other hand, is the duty of the President, in a personal capacity; it is not the task of the Executive Council. But which makes the basic decision itself, in the field of general policy: the President of the Community or the Executive Council? It seems indeed that the decision should be made *in* the Executive Council; but that does not mean that it should be made *by* the Council, acting by majority vote as a deliberating body. How, indeed, could a deliberating body make a decision without formulating it, that is, without expressing it in an exact manner? But only the President has the power of formulating decisions; which actually implies that he plays the principal role in making the decision itself.

"These are approximately the rules applied in practice: All decisions regarding the Community are made by the President. Those concerning general policy are in the following form: 'The President of the Community . . . at the close of the meeting of the Executive Council . . . formulates and makes known the following decision. . . .' Those that do not concern general policy say simply: 'The President of the Community . . . formulates and makes known the following decision.' If we remember that the common affairs include foreign policy, defense, currency, common economic and financial policy, etc., we see the importance of the prerogatives of the President of the Community. No distinction is made between the legislative and executive functions: the President legislates and 'sees to the execution' of his decisions, the execution itself being assured by the organs of the Member States. The system is indeed one of confusion of powers. The President of the Community may delegate all or part of his powers to one or more members of the Executive Council; but such delegation is at his discretion. Moreover, of course, the exercise of the powers of the President of the Community is not subject to countersignature, since the Prime Minister and the ministers are organs of the Republic. [Chatelain, *op. cit.*, pp. 334–335: "The second question is that of knowing whether the president of the Community, will be subject to the procedure of countersignature. According to a strict interpretation of the law, it appears that it is necessary to conclude that he is, since the president of the Community is at the same time president of the French Republic, all of whose acts must, in principle, be countersigned by the prime minister, except for certain cases indicated in Article 19 of the constitution. Now, this article does not refer to the exercise of the powers specified in title XII. Moreover, the abolition of the procedure of countersignature would in the end make the president an organ exempt from all political control. Contrarily, we may assert that to submit the decisions of the essential organ of the Community to countersignature by the prime minister of the French Republic tends to make the Community, that is, the union, subordinate to the French Republic, that is, one of the component elements, a formula that is obviously not very acceptable either in logic or from the political point of view."]

"This power of decision of the President of the Community extends to the institutions of all Member States, including the institutions of the Republic. In particular, matters reserved to the law by Article 34 of the Constitution concern only the Republic. Article 34 should here be combined with Article 78: not only is the Parliament of the Republic unable to legislate for the Community, but it must, like all the legislative assemblies of the Member States, comply with the decisions of the President of the Community. If Parliament passes a law contrary to a Presidential decision concerning the common policy, this law may be referred to the Constitutional Council for annulment, on the basis of Article 78. This means that the President of the Republic, as President of the Community, has the power of supreme decision in such fundamental matters as foreign policy, defense, common economic and financial policy, etc. . . .

"*2. Powers over the Special Organs of the Community.* In addition to the general power of decision we have just analyzed, the President possesses very important prerogatives with regard to the special organs of the Community, which place these organs very definitely under his authority in practice.

"He possesses, in the first place, the power of appointment: he appoints the ministers responsible for common affairs; he may require ministers in the governments of Member States to sit in special cases on the Executive Council; he appoints the Secretary General of the Executive Council and the members of the staffs of the Community services; he names the seven judges of the Court of Arbitration. In the second place, he possesses the power of convoking the Executive Council and the Senate, and of closing their sessions. Third, he has the power of initiating action: it is the President who decides on the agenda of the Executive Council; he has priority for placing items on the agenda of the Senate of the Community; moreover, most problems can be considered by the Senate only at the instance of the President; and, lastly, he brings cases before the Court of Arbitration in the name of the Community. . . . Obviously, they [these prerogatives] give the President very effective means of action and great authority over these organs.

"(*b*) *Practical Exercise of the Powers of the President of the Community*

"Actually, the Community is governed by its President, and by him alone: the Executive Council has hardly any power of decision of its own, the Court of Arbitration renders only jurisdictional decisions, and the Senate of the Community can take decisions only on questions of constitutional amendment or of powers delegated by the legislative assemblies of Member States. The only important executory decisions, which are binding on all Member States, including the Republic and its Parliament, are taken by the President. . . .

.   .   .   .

"(*B*) *The Special Organs of the Community*

"The Community has three special organs: the Executive Council, the Senate, and the Court of Arbitration. It must not be thought that this 'trilogy' corresponds to the traditional pattern: executive, legislative, and judicial powers. The Executive Council has no power of decision of its own, at least not legally; and the Senate is chiefly an advisory body. The real legislative power belongs to the President of the Community.

"(*a*) *The Executive Council of the Community*

Executive Council

"Neither the composition nor the powers of the Executive Council of the Community are clearly defined in the Constitution itself or in the *ordonnance* of December 19, 1958. The vague character of the provisions on this subject can be attributed either to lack of skill on the part of their authors in using the French language, or to their desire to leave as much room as possible for evolution. The absence of preparatory work prevents a choice between these two hypotheses.

"*1. The Composition of the Executive Council.* The Executive Council is composed of regular members, having a permanent status, and persons specially called to sit on the Council. The regular members are: (1) the President of the Community, the Presiding Officer; (2) the Prime Minister of the French Republic and the chiefs of government of the other Member States; (3) the ministers responsible for common affairs. These regular members sit personally on the Council, but, with the consent of the President of the Community, they may be replaced at a particular meeting by a member of the government to which they belong. In addition to the regular members, ministers in the governments of the Member States may be called by exception to sit on the Executive Council, to consider specific matters. The decision in making such exceptional appointments is taken by the President of the Community.

"The main discussion concerns the 'ministers charged by the President of the Community with handling common affairs.' For some this can mean only appropriate ministers of the Republic, since many functions of the Community are exercised by organs of the Republic, particularly by the ministers responsible. [See F. Luchaire, *Droit d'outre mer* (Thémis Collection, 1959).] This interpretation is open to dispute. The Constitution distinguishes rather clearly, in fact, between the fields of competence of the Republic and those of the Community; the confusion results from certain organic laws like the *ordonnance* of January 7, 1959, dealing with the general organization of defense. The very phrase 'charged, by the President of the Community, with handling common affairs' is quite clear. In reality, the President is legally free to designate any persons of standing he may wish as ministers of common affairs: he may appoint appropriate ministers of the Republic, appropriate ministers of the government of another Member State, or special ministers for the Community.

"This last solution would in many respects be more logical: it would correspond better to the nature of the Community and to the strong presidential character of its political régime. Behind this debate, the whole interpretation of the Community is at issue. If its ministers are of necessity those of the Republic, the Community is a piece of bluff, a sham, a camouflage; it conceals a colonial régime. If its ministers are different from those of the Republic, the Community has a more authentic character. . . .

"*2. The Functioning and Powers of the Executive Council.* The Executive Council meets in Paris, unless the President of the Community decides to convene it in some other city. It is convoked by the President of the Community. A meeting is compulsory at the time of each session of the Senate of the Community, but meetings may also be held 'whenever common policy needs so require,' the President being the sole judge in the matter. The work of the Executive Council may be prepared by meetings between the ministers for common affairs and the appropriate ministers of Member States, under the direction of the Executive Council and, if occasion arises, under the chairmanship of one of the members of the Council. These preparatory meetings may consider only the matters referred to them. The agenda for the meetings of the Executive Council is fixed by the President of the Community, and is secret, as are the minutes of the meetings.

"The powers of the Executive Council are ill-defined. According to Article 82 of the Constitution, the Council 'shall organize the cooperation of the members of the Community at the governmental and administrative level.' The *ordonnance* of December 19, 1958 further defines this general formula from two points of view: (1) the Council 'shall take cognizance of the questions' of general policy of the Community; (2) the Council 'shall deliberate' on the expenditures required for the organs and services of the Community and on their distribution among the Member States, as well as on the distribution of common policy expenditures. The first provision seems to indicate that the powers are advisory only, the decision resting with the President of the Community. The second is still less clear, but apparently does not indicate, either, any power of decision, which in this field belongs to the President. However, it seems quite normal that the Executive Council should endeavor to obtain for itself the power of decision, by trying to arrange that the President of the Community take his decisions in Council and that he comply with the views of the majority. This is contrary to the ultra-presidential régime set up by the texts, but the Council will probably endeavor to apply them in a different sense. A development in this direction has already been observed at the first meetings of the Council, on February 3 and March 3, 1959. . . . [See also Chatelain, *op. cit.*, pp. 336–337: "With respect to its powers, the Executive Council must be considered more as a coordinating body than as a federal government. Article 82 of the constitution provides simply that it 'shall organize the co-operation of the members of the Community at governmental and administrative levels.' The *ordonnance* of December 19 specifies that it is 'the supreme organ' in this field and adds, among other provisions, that 'it shall debate with regard to the expenses necessitated by the establishment and functioning of the organs and services of the Community and on the allocation of such expenses among the Member States and with regard to the allocation among these States of the expenses of the common policies.' These provisions must, however, be interpreted taking into consideration the powers of the president and of the Senate of the Community. The fact that the Council does not draw up its agenda itself, which is determined by the president (Article 2 of the *ordonnance* of December 19) and the fact, also, that it is not collectively responsible to a specific assembly, also seem to make it impossible to see in it a true government. It is rather, at least at the first stage of implementation of the constitution, a body that serves the president in an advisory capacity, while the president remains the essential organ."]

"(*b*) *The Senate of the Community*   Senate

"The Senate of the Community is a representative assembly of all the Member States. Its powers are weak but are susceptible of development.

"*1. The Composition of the Senate.* The Senate of the Community is composed of delegates chosen from their own membership by the Parliament of the Republic, on the one hand, and the legislative assemblies of the other Member States, on the other hand. Each of the two chambers of the Republic sends the same number of representatives to the Senate of the Community; the delegation of the Republic must include equitable representation of the various overseas departments and territories.   Article 83 of the Constitution provides that the number of delegates from each State 'shall take into account the population of that State and the responsibilities it assumes in the Community.'   At the meeting of the Executive Council of February 3 and 4, 1959, it was decided that the Senate of the Community shall be constituted on the basis of one seat per 300,000 inhabitants or a fraction thereof, with a minimum of three seats for each State.   It will thus be composed of 284 members, 186 for the French Republic (mother country, Algeria, overseas departments, overseas territories of the Republic) and 98 for the other States of the Community.

"The term of each member of the Senate ends at the same time as his term as a member of the assembly that designated him, but shall not exceed five years.   It is renewable.   The senators enjoy immunities in all States of the Community.   Their irresponsibility [sic] is the same as that of members of the Parliament of the Republic; their freedom from arrest and legal proceedings is a little different: when the Senate is in session, any legal proceeding against a senator shall be suspended if the Senate so requests; when it is not in session, no action may be instituted without the authorization of the executive committee of the Senate, except in cases of *flagrante delicto*, authorized prosecution, or final judgment.

"*2. The Functioning of the Senate.*   The Senate of the Community holds two sessions a year, the maximum duration of each being one month.   Regular sessions are convened and closed by the President of the Community.   Special sessions, not exceeding ten days, may be called by the President, after consultation with the Executive Council (this consultation is not necessary in case of a declaration of war).   The meetings are public, unless the President of the Community or one-tenth of the senators request a secret session.   The president [of the Senate] and the executive committee are elected by secret ballot for each session.   The Senate draws up its rules of procedure and its agenda; but the President of the Community may request priority for inclusion on the agenda or immediate discussion, which are then obligatory. Members of the Executive Council are admitted to the Senate and may have the floor when they request it, if they have been designated for that purpose by the Executive Council.

"*3. The Powers of the Senate.*   The powers of the Senate of the Community are advisory, but it has some powers of decision. It has also some prerogatives with regard to ministers of the Community.

"(*a*) *Advisory Powers.*   The Senate of the Community gives opinions, at the request of the President of the Community, in four cases: (1) on proposals concerning the common economic and financial policy; (2) on treaties or international agreements, involving the Community, which must be ratified by the Parliament of the Republic; (3) on declarations of war; (4) on any common matter, especially the general aims of Community policy concerning economic, social, and cultural development.   [Art. 83.]

In the first three cases, it seems that consultation of the Senate by the President of the Community is compulsory; consultation is optional in the last case. In all cases, it is a question merely of giving an opinion.

"The Senate may also, on its own initiative, draw up recommendations 'for harmonizing the legislation of the Member States.' Recommendations and opinions are transmitted by the President of the Community to the authorities concerned.

"(*b*) *Power of Decision.* The Senate of the Community has the power of decision, in the first place, with respect to amendment of Title XII of the Constitution, relating to the Community. This title is amended by passing identically worded laws in the Parliament of the Republic, on the one hand, and the Senate of the Community, on the other hand . . . . Article 21 of the *ordonnance* of December 19, 1958 provides that the organic laws of the Community shall be amended by the same procedure, which is contrary to the terms of Article 46 of the Constitution, which provides for a special procedure for organic laws.

"In the second place, the Senate takes 'executory decisions' in the fields in which it has been delegated authority by the legislative assemblies of the States members of the Community. This is a conditional power, depending on the good will of the assemblies of the States. The system opens up possibilities of evolution. These executory decisions, or the constitutional or organic laws amended by the foregoing procedure, are promulgated in identical terms in each of the Member States concerned, within a period of one month, or within eight days in cases declared urgent by the President of the Community.

"(*c*) *Power to Question Ministers.* The members of the Senate of the Community may put questions to ministers for common affairs. But this right is strictly limited. First, it may be exercised only within the limits of competence of the Community. Second, and especially, the questions and answers must be in writing; it was desired to prevent anything that might start a debate in parliamentary form. [Following the inauguration of the Senate of the Community, July 15, 1959, by President De Gaulle, the body reconvened on July 28, 1959 at which time its new President, Gaston Monnerville, set forth his views on the role the Senate should play in the life of the Community. He said it should be kept above political differences and not be a forum for airing rival philosophies. While he pointed out that the Senate could not intervene in the political life of member states and that it could not play the role of arbitrator among the different parties represented in it, he warned against succumbing to the temptation of underestimating the Senate's role by measuring it solely by constitutional and organic texts; and declared that although the body was without "political responsibility", it could act by recommendations. The First Secretary of the American Embassy at Paris (Witman II) to the Secretary of State (Herter), despatch No. 292, Aug. 18, 1959, MS. Department of State, file 751.2/8–1859.]

Court of
Arbitration

"(*d*) *The Community Court of Arbitration.* The Community Court of Arbitration has as its principal function the settlement of disputes between Member States. It is an original institution, resembling somewhat the French Council of State, with the difference that the Community Court tries cases between States and not individuals. Nevertheless, it is not an arbitral body, but a true court.

"*1. The Composition of the Court of Arbitration.* The Court of Arbitration is composed of seven judges appointed for six years by the President of the Community and chosen from among: (1) the members of the courts of justice or of the administrative courts with at least ten years' service; (2) professors in law schools with at least ten years' service; (3) persons of standing possessing legal qualifications by reason of at least twenty years' service. The judges are from different States of the Community. Their term of office is renewable.

"The judges are independent; their appointment may not be revoked. They may not be prosecuted, arrested, detained, or tried for criminal offenses without the authorization of the Court, which may in such cases assign competence to a specific class of courts. They may exercise no political, administrative, or professional function, other than as members of the courts of justice or the teaching profession; they may not be appointed to public office during their tenure or accept any honor; if they are government officials at the time of assuming office, they may benefit from no promotion by selection. They may not take a position publicly on questions concerning the competence of the Court, or give any opinion. When entering on their duties, they must take a professional oath, swearing to perform their duties properly and to keep secret the deliberations and the votes.

"The judges may resign at will. The Court pronounces their discharge officially in four cases: (1) acceptance of an office or of employment incompatible with their position as a member of the Court; (2) conviction involving loss of civil and criminal rights; (3) systematic abstention, without a valid excuse, from performing their duties; (4) permanent physical disability preventing them from performing their duties.

"*2. The Jurisdiction of the Court of Arbitration.* The Court of Arbitration has three jurisdictions; it tries disputes concerning the interpretation or application of the rules of law binding on the Member States of the Community; it tries disputes regarding the appointment of members of the Senate of the Community; it renders opinions to the President of the Community.

"(*a*) *Trial of Disputes Concerning the Rules of Law Binding on the Member States of the Community.* The competence of the Court extends to the interpretation or the application of all the rules of law binding on the Member States of the Community. Article 1 of the *ordonnance* of December 19, 1958 indicates three categories: the provisions of the Constitution, the organic laws, and the agreements or conventions between the States of the Community. But it specifies that this list is not restrictive: the rules of law, in particular, arising from executory decisions of the President or the Senate of the Community come within the jurisdiction of the Court. Moreover, the jurisdiction of the Court may be extended to all other classes of disputes, by agreements concluded between States of the Community: here we see the possibilities for evolution already pointed out with regard to the Senate.

"The Court has full jurisdiction in this field; that is, it may determine the interpretation of a rule of law, set aside decisions contrary to such rule of law, and grant compensation for damage caused by violation or misinterpretation of the rule.

"(*b*) *Settlement of Disputes with Regard to the Appointment of Members of the Senate of the Community.* The Court of Arbitration is sole judge of the regularity of appointments of delegates to the legislative assemblies of the States of the Community. But disputes in this connection may be referred to it only by the President of the Community. The latter may act on his own authority or at the request of the interested parties, but is never obliged to comply with such request.

"(*c*) *Opinions Requested by the President of the Community.* The President of the Community may ask the Court of Arbitration for its opinion on any question of interpretation of the Constitutional provisions concerning the Community, the organic laws applying them, or the agreements of the Community. The opinions in question are addressed to the President alone and are not published. In such cases, the Court is acting as an advisory body, not in a judicial capacity.

"*3. Procedure before the Court of Arbitration.* We shall examine here only the jurisdictional activity of the Court. Appeals concerning the regularity of appointment of a member of the Senate may be referred to it only by the President of the Community. Appeals concerning any other litigious matter are referred to it either by a Member State or in the name of the Community. In no case may direct recourse be had to the Court by an individual. A Member State, however, may bring before the Court a claim for compensation for damage caused to one of its nationals by another State of the Community; it thus exercises a kind of 'diplomatic protection', like that accorded to States before international courts. In such cases, the suit is admissible only after all the internal remedies of the State accused of having caused the damage are exhausted, unless, in an exceptional case, the Court decides otherwise.

"The procedure before the Court calls for full argument on both sides, in writing, but the pleas may be developed orally in Court by the attorneys of the States concerned. The hearings are public. The decisions of the Court are rendered by at least five judges, the Presiding Judge having the deciding vote in case of a tie. The decisions of the Court are final and are enforceable throughout the territory of the Community. They are not liable to appeal, except for correction of a material error or in case of third-party opposition."

Duverger, *op. cit.* 705–708, 711–719. See also Pickles, *The Fifth French Republic* (1960) ; and Dumon, *La communauté franco-afro-malgache—ses origines, ses institutions, son evolution Octobre 1958—Juin 1960* (1960).

Mali
Federation

Prime Ministers of Soudan, Senegal, and Dahomey, and the leaders of a special delegation from Upper Volta signed, December 30, 1958, the "Bamako Proclamation" by which these four States out of the seven formerly comprising French West Africa agreed to submit to their respective Constituent Assemblies a motion to create a Federal Constituent Assembly. The motion provided that the Constituent Assemblies of the respective States, having opted for the status of State Member of the Community in application of article 76 of the October 4, 1958, Constitution, would then decide "with the other states of West Africa members of the Community, which have adhered in principle to participation in a Primary Federation, or which might express the will to do so before the first session, to create a Federal Constituent Assembly composed in addition to the President of the Constituent Assembly of each State of 10 delegates for each State".

The American Consul General at Dakar (Dumont) to the Secretary of State (Dulles), despatch No. 161, encl. 1, Jan. 7, 1959, MS. Department of State, file 779.00/1–759.

Senegal and Soudan, having unanimously approved the Federal Constitution establishing the Mali Federation, January 18, 1959, constituted the only State Members of the Federation. Upper Volta approved the "Bamako Declaration" January 7, 1959, but withdrew from the Federation March 1, 1959, and Dahomey, although having ratified the "Bamako Declaration" January 9, 1959, failed to adhere to the Mali Federation by the terms of her own Constitution approved on February 14, 1959, and is not considered a member of the Federation.

The American Consul General at Dakar (Dumont) to the Secretary of State (Dulles), airgram No. G–120, Jan. 26, 1959, MS. Department of State, file 751t.03/1–2659; the American Consul General at Dakar (Dumont) to the Secretary of State (Dulles), despatch No. 238, Mar. 19, 1959, MS. Department of State, file 751t.00/3–1959.

Reflecting their dual status as autonomous States in the French Community and as member Republics of the Mali Federation, the Constitutions of Senegal and Soudan provided for the delegation of such responsibilities as foreign affairs, defense, money, and higher education to the Community and such others as justice, customs, interstate commerce, postal and telecommunication services, labor code, economic planning, and Federal security to the Mali Federation.

The American Consul General at Dakar (Dumont) to the Secretary of State (Dulles), Feb. 6, 1959, despatch No. 199, MS. Department of State, file 751t.03/2–659; the American Consul at Dakar (Graham) to the Secretary of State, Feb. 27, 1959, despatch No. 216, MS. Department of State, file 751t.03/2–2759.

The Secretary General of the Mali Federation, in examining the question of Mali Federation's representation in the Community Executive Council, drew a distinction between a "federation of states" and a "federal state". Defining Mali as " 'a federation of states' which does not substitute itself for its component states", he contended that "a representative of the Mali Federation should therefore be allowed to sit in the Executive Council alongside representatives of individual component states".

The American Minister at Paris (Lyon) to the Secretary of State (Dulles), airgram No. G–1162, Feb. 26, 1959, MS. Department of State, file 751t.00/2–2659.

The Community's refusal to grant a special seat in the Executive Council was explained on the ground that Mali, a federation whose component states retain their personality, could not be considered as a state itself. The Secretary General of the Community added: ". . . There is certainly not opposition to the Federation of Mali; the states have full right to group themselves . . . . Because of the structure of the Community, Mali cannot be represented within the Executive Council. The States have entered the Community in an isolated manner and Mali could have been represented within the Executive Council only if the states of which it is composed had decided to unite into a single state at the time of their choice."

The American Ambassador at Paris (Houghton) to the Secretary of State (Herter), airgram No. G–1458, May 12, 1959, MS. Department of State, file 751t.00/5–1259.

Referring to the new status "to this rank, that the Mali Federation . . . and . . . the States of which it is composed, are going to accede with the support, the approval and the assistance of France", General de Gaulle, as President of the French Republic and of the Community, said in an address on December 13, 1959, before the Federal Assembly of Mali—

". . . in a few days, France, Mali and the States of which it is composed will enter into negotiations in order to modify the status of their relations. That was provided for, implicitly and even explicitly, by the Constitution of the Community, which we all voted in favor of. It is nonetheless true that this is going to lead the Federal State of Mali and the States of Soudan and of Senegal, of which it is composed, to a new position as far as they are concerned. The position which they were already occupying last year was a new one, and it will be even more so in the immediate future. To put it another way, the State of Mali is going to assume what some call the position of independence, and which I prefer to call that of international sovereignty.

"I have said that I prefer the latter term, without, however, disputing the attractiveness and the significance which the word independence can and must have for any people, and especially for this people. Nevertheless, I prefer international sovereignty because it seems to me to correspond better with the necessities that have always existed, and especially with the necessities of today. Independence is a word which signifies a desire, an attitude, an intention; but the world being as it is—so small, so cramped, so interfering with itself—real independence, complete independence does not in reality belong to anyone.

General de Gaulle's Statement to the Mali Federation on the Evolution of the Community, Ambassade de France, Service de Presse et d'Information, *Community Affairs*, No. 9, Dec. 1959, pp. 1, 2.

Since the amendment on June 4, 1960, of articles 85 and 86 of title XII of the Constitution of October 4, 1958 (see above), thereby enabling Community States by means of agreements to become independent without ceasing to belong to the Community and permitting independent non-Community States, also by means of agreements, to adhere to the Community in the degree and to the extent they themselves consider desirable, the following former autonomous members of the French Community have attained independence and subsequently signed accords of cooperation defining their relations with the Republic of France: Central African Republic, Republic of Chad, Republic of Congo, Republic of Dahomey, the Gabon Republic, Republic of the Ivory Coast, the Malagasy Republic, Republic of Mali, Republic of Mauritania, Republic of Niger, Republic of Senegal, and Republic of Upper Volta (see *infra*). Of these 12 independent States, the following 5 have become equal and sovereign members of the French Community by concluding in compliance with the French Constitution a special agreement with France entitled in each case an Agreement of Participation: the Central African Republic, the Republic of Chad, the Republic of Congo, the Gabon Republic, and the Malagasy Republic (and formerly also the Mali Federation).

Independent Federation of Mali and its dissolution

The Federation of Mali proclaimed its independence on June 20, 1960, after the Transfer of Powers Agreement between France and Senegal and Soudan became effective with the signing of this document at Dakar by the French and Malian representatives on June 19, 1960. This Agreement providing for the transfer of jurisdiction over those powers vested in the French Community under article 78 of the

Constitution of October 4, 1958, to the Republic of Senegal and the Soudanese Republic—forming the Federation of Mali—was originally signed by the Governments of France, Senegal, and Soudan on April 4, 1960, along with a second Agreement regarding transitional measures.

> The Second Secretary of the American Embassy at Dakar (Harary) to the Secretary of State (Herter), despatch No. 94, Oct. 13, 1960, MS. Department of State, file 770t.00/10–1360.   Law No. 60–569, June 17, 1960, *Journal Officiel de la République Française*, June 18, 1960, p. 5471.

In compliance with the constitutional procedure required under article 87 of the French Constitution, the Agreement was ratified by the French National Assembly and by the Senate on June 13 and 16, respectively, and by the legislative assemblies of Soudan and Senegal on June 7 and 10, respectively.   Soudan and Senegal by the same legislative acts which ratified the Agreement (Soudan by Law No. 60–1 and Senegal by Law No. 60–033) reconveyed the powers to the Mali Federation in accordance with the procedure for Mali's accession to independence as determined by the Directing Committee of the Parti de la Federation Africain.

> The Second Secretary of the American Embassy at Dakar (Harary) to the Secretary of State (Herter), despatch No. 94, Oct. 13, 1960, MS. Department of State, file 770t.00/10–1360.   The American Consul General at Dakar (Dumont) to the Secretary of State (Herter), airgram No. G–156, Apr. 18, 1960, MS. Department of State, file 751t.02/4–1860.   The American Consul General at Dakar (Dumont) to the Secretary of State (Herter), telegram, June 11, 1960, MS. Department of State, file 751.2/6–1160.

Additional Agreements concluded between France and the Mali Federation (an Accord on the participation of the Mali Federation in the Community; Accords of cooperation between France and Mali on foreign policy, defense, policy regarding strategic raw materials and products, economic, monetary and finance policies, higher education, and sea and air transportation) and a Convention of Establishment were initialed on April 4 and signed on June 22, 1960.

The Accord on Participation provided for Mali's participation in the Community on a contractual and not on a constitutional basis and specified that Mali as a member of the Community would participate in the Community under the conditions set forth in this Agreement and in the Franco-Malian Accords of cooperation.   Under the terms of this Agreement, Mali recognized the President of the French Republic as being *ex officio* President of the Community, and agreed to take part in a periodic conference of Chiefs of State and of Government, under the chairmanship of the President of the Community, and also to serve on committees of Ministers and committees of experts. Mali was given the option of sending a delegation to a consultative interparliamentary Senate composed of delegates from the Parliaments of the member States.

The Agreements of cooperation, defining new relations between the French Republic and the Mali Federation with respect to matters formerly within the jurisdiction of the Community were based upon two principles: (1) Franco-Malian relations will be those of one sovereign State with another; (2) the French Republic and the Mali Federation along with other States form a Community within which France will give assistance to Mali and the two States will cooperate voluntarily and coordinate their policies with those of the other members of the Community.

> Ambassade de France, Service de Presse et d'Information, *Community Affairs*, No. 13, June, 1960, pp. 12–16.

> These Accords were signed June 22, 1960, and approved by the Republic of France by Law No. 60–682, July 18, 1960 (discussed and adopted by the National Assembly July 6 and by the Senate July 11, 1960), promulgated in *Journal Officiel de la République Française*, July 19, 1960; by the Federation of Mali by Law No. 60–73, June 20, 1960 (discussed and adopted by the Federal Assembly June 20, 1960), promulgated in *Journal Officiel de la Fédération du Mali*, July 9, 1960, and by Law No. 60–28, July 1, 1960, authorizing the Federal Government to ratify the particular Accords of cooperation and Conventions concluded between the Governments of the French Republic and the Government of the Mali Federation, initialed April 4 and signed June 22, 1960; the Convention and Accord concluded between the representatives of the Malagasy Republic and those of the Mali Federation, initialed April 2 and 4 and signed June 22 and 27, 1960 (discussed and adopted by the Federal Assembly July 1, 1960), promulgated in *Journal Officiel de la Fédération du Mali*, July 16, 1960. See also *Journal Officiel de la République Française*, July 20, 1960; *Journal Officiel de la Fédération du Mali*, July 16, 1960; and *Journal Officiel de la Communauté*, Aug. 15, 1960.

> The two multilateral Conventions signed June 22 and 27, 1960, were approved by the French Republic by Law No. 60–683, July 18, 1960 (discussed and adopted by the National Assembly July 6 and by the Senate July 11, 1960), promulgated in *Journal Officiel de la République Française*, July 19, 1960; by the Republic of Malagasy by Law No. 60–009, July 5, 1960 (discussed and adopted by the National Assembly June 27 and by the Senate June 28, 1960), promulgated in *Journal Officiel de la République Malgache*, July 9, 1960; by the Federation of Mali by Law No. 60–13, June 20, 1960 (discussed and adopted by the Federal Assembly June 20, 1960), promulgated in *Journal Officiel de la Fédération du Mali*, July 9, 1960, and by Law No. 60–28, July 1, 1960, authorizing the Federal Government to ratify the particular Accords of cooperation and Conventions concluded between the Governments of France and Mali, initialed April 4 and signed June 22, 1960; and the Convention and Accord concluded between representatives of Mali and Malagasy, initialed April 2 and 4 and signed June 22 and 27, 1960 (discussed and adopted by the Federal Assembly July 1, 1960), promul-

gated in *Journal Officiel de la Fédération du Mali*, July 16, 1960. See also *Journal Officiel de la République Malgache*, July 9, 1960; *Journal Officiel de la Communauté*, Aug. 15, 1960; *Journal Officiel de la République Française*, July 20, 1960.

The Mali Federation concluded with France and the Malagasy Republic two Agreements which were initialed April 2 and 4 and signed June 22 and 27, 1960. One multilateral Agreement guaranteed to the nationals of each State of the Community a certain number of rights in the territory of each of the other States. This Agreement was supplemented by a Convention of Establishment between France and Mali granting privileged treatment to the nationals of one of the parties in the territory of the other. The other multilateral Convention recorded the agreement of the contracting parties to refer the disputes which might arise between them to a conciliation procedure and, in case of the failure of conciliation, to an arbitration procedure, the Court of Arbitration being composed of an equal number of members from each State.

The French Ministry of Foreign Affairs informed the American Ambassador at Paris that, in virtue of the Accords signed April 4, 1960, between the Government of the Republic of France of one part, the Governments of the Republic of Senegal and the Soudan Republic, forming the Federation of Mali, of the other part, the Federation of Mali acceded to independence and that the Republic of France recognized it as an independent and sovereign State June 20, 1960.

The Counselor of the American Embassy at Paris (Kidder) to the Secretary of State (Herter), despatch No. 1968, June 23, 1960, MS. Department of State, file 770e.02/6–2360.

The Mali Federation has since been dissolved as a result of the secession of Senegal effected by law adopted in the Senegalese National Assembly on August 20, 1960, providing for the resumption of powers it had transferred to the Mali Federation and proclaiming its independence as a separate nation from Soudan. Commenting on the legality of this secession, the Senegalese Foreign Minister was reported to have said that Senegal had legally taken back powers it had transferred to Mali and that the transfer had been made by Senegalese law and reversed by the same procedure. On September 22, 1960, the Soudanese National Assembly adopted laws by which the Soudanese Republic took the name of the Republic of Mali and declared itself an "independent and sovereign State free of all obligations and political ties". As enacted by law, the powers and jurisdiction transferred by Soudan to the Mali Federation were withdrawn and made to revert to Soudan as the Republic of Mali, and the laws passed by the Mali Federation approving cooperation agreements with the French and Malagasy Republics were declared obsolete. On August 26, 1960, the Senegalese National Assembly unanimously adopted a new Constitution which reinvested in the Government of

Senegal

Republic of Mali

the Republic of Senegal powers with respect to defense, justice, foreign affairs, postal and telecommunications services, and customs.

> The American Chargé d'Affaires at Bamako (Dean) to the Secretary of State (Herter), telegram, Sept. 22, 1960, MS. Department of State, file 770e.02/9–2260; the Second Secretary of the American Embassy at Dakar (Graham) to the Secretary of State (Herter), despatch No. 55, Sept. 6, 1960, MS. Department of State, file 770e.03/9–660 (transmitting an unofficial translation of the Constitution). See Cohen, "Legal Problems Arising from the Dissolution of the Mali Federation", XXXVI Brit. Yb. Int'l L. (1960) 375. For Ghana-Guinea-Mali Union (Union of African States), see *ante*, p. 429.

Malagasy

The Republic of France and the Malagasy Republic signed two Agreements April 2, 1960, one providing for the transfer to the Malagasy Republic of powers which formerly belonged to the Community and the other defining transitional measures.

At the same time the parties initialed several Accords of cooperation which were signed June 27, 1960. These Accords, in reflecting the principles that relations would henceforth be those of sovereign State to sovereign State and that the French and Malagasy Republics along with other States form a Community within which France would give assistance to Malagasy and both States would cooperate voluntarily and coordinate their policies with those of the other members of the Community, defined the new relations between the States with respect to those powers formerly vested in the Community: foreign policy, defense, monetary, economic and financial questions, judicial questions, higher education, sea and air transportation, and telecommunications.

The Accord of cooperation with regard to foreign policy declared that the Malagasy Republic, an independent and sovereign State, has the right of legation and of receiving diplomatic representatives and affirmed that it will exercise this right in its relations with France. It was provided that both Governments will keep each other informed, consult with regard to foreign policy, and regularly consult with each other and the other States of the Community to compare views and seek, before taking any important decision, to coordinate their positions and their actions.

With respect to matters of defense, it was agreed that, as an independent and sovereign State, the Malagasy Republic will have national armed forces at its disposal and that the two States will give each other mutual aid and assistance in order to insure their defense. The Malagasy Republic is responsible for its own external and internal defense; it may ask for assistance from the French Republic. It will take part, along with France, in the defense of the Community. It was also agreed that, in order to enable France to assume her responsibilities in the common defense and on a worldwide scale to guarantee, in every emergency and effectively, the support that she has pledged to the Malagasy Republic, France will have free use of military bases and installations along with necessary facilities (see annex 3).

Another Accord also initialed April 2 and signed June 27, 1960, provided for the participation of the Malagasy Republic in the Community on a contractual rather than on a constitutional basis. In recognition of Malagasy as an independent and sovereign State and of the expressed desire on the part of the Malagasy Republic to cooperate with the French Republic within the Community, it was agreed that as a member of the Community Malagasy would participate therein under the conditions set forth in this Agreement and in the Franco-Malagasy Cooperation Agreements.

By the terms of the participation Accord, Malagasy agreed to recognize the President of the French Republic as being *ex officio* President of the Community, to take part in a periodic conference of the Chiefs of State and of Government under the chairmanship of the President of the Community, and also to serve on committees of Ministers and committees of experts. Under this Agreement Malagasy was given the option of sending a delegation to a consultative interparliamentary Senate composed of delegates from the Parliaments of the member States.

The Malagasy Republic in addition concluded two multilateral Conventions with France and Mali, initialed on April 2 and 4 and signed June 22 and 27. The first multilateral Agreement guaranteeing to the nationals of each State of the Community a certain number of rights in the territory of each of the other States was supplemented by a Franco-Malagasy Convention of Establishment, signed June 27, 1960, which granted privileged treatment to the nationals of one of the parties in the territory of the other. By the other Convention the parties agreed to refer the disputes which might arise between them to conciliation, and, in case of the failure of conciliation, to arbitration, the court of arbitration being composed of an equal number of members from each State. Both multilateral Conventions may be subscribed to by any State of the Community and by other States with the unanimous consent of the parties.

Ambassade de France, Service de Presse et d'Information, *Community Affairs*, No. 13, June 1960, pp. 7-11.

Accords signed or initialed April 2, 1960, were promulgated by Law No. 60–568, June 17, 1960, *Journal Officiel de la République Française*, June 18, 1960, p. 5471. The initialed Accords were signed June 27, 1960, and ap-

proved by the French Republic by Law No. 60–681, July 18, 1960 (discussed
and adopted by the National Assembly July 6 and by the Senate July 11,
1960), promulgated in *Journal Officiel de la République Française*, July 19,
1960; by the Malagasy Republic by Law No. 60–009, July 5, 1960 (discussed
and adopted by the National Assembly June 27 and by the Senate June 28,
1960), promulgated in *Journal Officiel de la République Malgache*, July 9,
1960. See also *Journal Officiel de la République Française*, July 20, 1960;
Journal Official de la République Malgache, July 9, 1960; and the *Journal
Officiel de la Communauté*, Aug. 15, 1960.

The two multilateral Conventions signed June 22 and 27, 1960, were
approved by the French Republic by Law No. 60–683, July 18, 1960
(discussed and adopted by the National Assembly July 6 and by the
Senate July 11, 1960), promulgated in *Journal Officiel de la République
Française*, July 19, 1960; by the Republic of Malagasy by Law No. 60–009,
July 5, 1960 (discussed and adopted by the National Assembly June 27
and by the Senate June 28, 1960), promulgated in *Journal Officiel de la
République Malgache*, July 9, 1960; by the Federation of Mali by Law No.
60–13, June 20, 1960 (discussed and adopted by the Federal Assembly
June 20, 1960), promulgated in *Journal Officiel de la Fédération du
Mali*, July 9, 1960, and by Law No. 60–28, July 1, 1960, authorizing the
Federal Government to ratify the particular Accords of cooperation and
Conventions concluded between the Governments of France and Mali
initialed April 4 and signed June 22, 1960; and the Convention and Accord
were concluded between representatives of Mali and Malagasy, initialed
April 2 and 4 and signed June 22 and 27, 1960 (discussed and adopted by the
Federal Assembly July 1, 1960), and promulgated in *Journal Officiel de la
Fédération du Mali*, July 16, 1960. See also *Journal Officiel de la Répub-
lique Malgache*, July 9, 1960; *Journal Officiel de la République Française*,
July 20, 1960; *Journal Officiel de la Communauté*, Aug. 15, 1960.

The French Foreign Office informed the American Ambassador in
a note of June 25, 1960, that "by virtue of the accords signed April
2, 1960 by the Government of France and Malagasy Republic and in
conformance with the joint declaration issued June 26, 1960, the
Malagasy Republic has acceded to independence and France has
recognized it as an independent and sovereign state".

The American Ambassador at Paris (Houghton) to the Secretary of
State (Herter), telegram, June 29, 1960, MS. Department of State, file
770f.02/6–2960.

A joint Franco-Malagasy declaration of June 26 announced that
in consequence of the completion of the constitutional formalities
required for the entrance into force of the Accords signed by both
parties on "April 20 [2], 1960", and "counting from the date of the
present declaration, the Republic of Malagasy accedes to independence
and assumes the rights and prerogatives attached thereto as well as the
responsibilities which flow therefrom".

Le Monde, June 28, 1960, p. 2 (translation).

The four States formerly comprising French Equatorial Africa, Chad, Gabon, Congo, and Central African Republic (Ubangi-Shari), having elected to become autonomous Republics within the French Community, signed two protocols January 17, 1959, which set up a new loose association.

As reported by the American Embassy at Paris, these protocols establish between the four partners a customs union with provision for the management of railways, ports, and public works of common interest. Postal and telecommunications services are entrusted to a "public establishment" to the extent to which they do not fall within the field of Community affairs. This association, having a permanent secretariat but not a common government or assembly as in the case of the Mali Federation, has been referred to as "coordination" rather than "federation".

> The American Ambassador at Paris (Houghton) to the Secretary of State (Dulles), airgram No. G–950, Jan. 20, 1959, MS. Department of State, file 751u.00/1–2059.

The Republic of Chad, the Central African Republic, the Republic of Congo, and the Gabon Republic, formerly autonomous States within the French Community which had earlier comprised French Equatorial Africa, respectively proclaimed their independence on August 11, 13, 15, and 17, 1960, by virtue of Agreements signed with France by Chad, the Central African Republic, and the Republic of Congo on July 12 and by the Gabon Republic on July 15, 1960, providing in identical terms that each State "accedes, in full accord and friendship with the French Republic, to international sovereignty and independence by the transfer of the powers of the Community".

At the same time the Agreements providing for the transfer of Community powers as instituted by article 78 of the French Constitution were signed, each of the States and France initialed on July 15 Accords defining transitional measures effective pending the conclusion of Accords of cooperation. An Accord on Participation was also concluded with each State declaring that the State concerned "is a member of the Community in which it participates according to the terms defined by the accords of cooperation".

While the Accords of cooperation were to be signed and then ratified by these States as "sovereign" States immediately following the proclamation of independence, the procedure varied among the four Republics. In Chad the Agreements were signed and then ratified by its National Assembly on the morning of independence; in the Central African Republic the signing took place during a special session of the Assembly on the day of independence, but the ratification had been completed previously; in Congo the Accords were both signed and ratified on the morning of independence; and in Gabon the Accords which had already been ratified were signed on the morning of independence.

Two multilateral Accords to which each of the States in the French Community had already adhered—the Convention on Conciliation and the Court of Arbitrage and the Accord on the fundamental rights of nationals of Community States—plus the Accords of cooperation in the field of foreign affairs constitute the only Accords which are identical for all four States. The preamble to the Accord on cooperation in foreign affairs states that the two countries, each one of the four separately and France, having common bonds in the Community and in the Charter of the United Nations, depend on the same ideals and principles. It was agreed that the new States and France would consult on foreign policy, either at Chiefs of State or Foreign Ministers' meetings.

Other Accords, similar in their provisions although identical for Chad, the Central African Republic, and Congo, were signed with each of the four States. These concern technical military assistance; public domain or the disposal of nonmilitary property; cultural cooperation; defense; strategic raw materials, which for Chad, the Central African Republic, and Congo were annexed to the defense Accords; economic, financial, and monetary cooperation; and nationalities and their rights. The defense Agreements differ substantially from those concluded separately with each of the three States and that concluded with Gabon in that, with regard to the three States, the relations are based on a partnership idea along the lines of a regional defense pact. A Defense Council for Equatorial Africa to coordinate the efforts of the three local armies and the Community forces in the area is set up under the command of the French General. Under the Agreement the three countries are responsible for their internal and external security, but French forces are given all facilities and bases they need.

Additionally, France signed an aid program Agreement with each of the three States which was not concluded with Gabon as well as a separate Agreement on higher education. Franco-Gabonese relations with respect to higher education were provided for in the cultural cooperation Accord concluded between the two parties. France signed singularly with Gabon two additional Accords relating to merchant shipping and civil aviation. Also, in an exchange of letters between France and Gabon, Gabon requested France and France promised to comply with the request to ask the European Economic Community to continue their membership as an associated state.

The American Chargé d'Affaires at Brazzaville (Lukens) to the Secretary of State (Herter), despatch No. 17, Aug. 31, 1960, MS. Department of State, file 651.70n/8–3160.

The Accords between France of the one part and Chad, the Central African Republic, and Congo, respectively, of the other part were signed July 12, 1960, and approved by the French Republic by Law No. 60–733, July 28, 1960 (discussed and adopted by the National Assembly July 20 and by the Senate July 22, 1960), promulgated in *Journal Officiel de la République Française*, July 28, 1960; by the Republic of Chad by Law No. 10–60, July 23, 1960 (discussed and adopted by its Legislative Assembly July 23, 1960) ; by the Central African Republic by Law adopted by its Legislative Assembly July 21, 1960; by the Republic of Congo by Law No. 60–43, July 28, 1960 (discussed and adopted by the National Assembly July 28, 1960), promulgated in *Journal Officiel de la République du Congo*, July 28, 1960. See also *Journal Officiel de la République Française*, July 30, 1960, and *Journal Officiel de la République du Congo*, July 28, 1960. The Accords between France and the Republic of Gabon were signed July 15, 1960, and approved by the French Republic by Law No. 60–734, July 28, 1960 (discussed and adopted by the National Assembly July 20 and by the Senate July 22, 1960), promulgated in *Journal Officiel de la République Française*, July 29, 1960; by the Republic of Gabon by Law discussed and adopted by its National Assembly July 24, 1960. See also *Journal Officiel de la Communauté*, Aug. 15, 1960, p. 114. The Accords of cooperation signed by France with the Central African Republic, Congo, and Chad were promulgated by France on November 22, 1960, by Law No. 60–1225, *Journal Officiel de la République Française*, Nov. 23, 1960, p. 10427. The Accords signed between France and Gabon were promulgated November 22, 1960, by Law No. 60–1226, *Journal Officiel de la République Française*, Nov. 23, 1960, p. 10428.

The *Conseil de l'Entente*, instituted "in order to harmonize their relations on the basis of friendship, of fraternity and solidarity" is comprised of the Prime Ministers of the four former French West African States of the Ivory Coast, Upper Volta, Niger, and Dahomey. At its first meeting, held at Abidjan on May 29–30, 1959, six special commissions were established: Finance, Justice, Agriculture, Civil Service, Telecommunications and Railroads, for the purpose of harmonizing their laws and assuring the uniformity of legislation which existed in French West Africa before the establishment of the French Community. In addition, the *Conseil de l'Entente* created a Solidarity Fund, effective as of July 1, 1959, and a customs union designed to promote the homogeneity of the four countries in the fields of internal and external trade. The organization of such customs union is based on the creation of commissions made up of equal membership from each State. These commissions, empowered to facilitate harmonization of the internal structures in each State, make lump sum redistributions of funds from customs taxes and duties collected.

Conseil de l'Entente: Dahomey; Niger; Upper Volta; Ivory Coast

The American Consul at Abidjan (Norland) to the Secretary of State (Herter), despatch No. 199, June 29, 1959, MS. Department of State, file

751t.00/6–2959. The American Consul General at Dakar (Dumont) to the
Secretary of State (Herter), despatch No. 326, June 4, 1959, MS. Department
of State, file 851t.00/6–459. Referring to the name of the Committee "Conseil de l'Entente", sometimes referred to as the Sahel-Benin Union, the American Consul General reported in this despatch that "The nearest rendition to
anything meaningful in English probably would be something like 'Consultative Committee', but even this suggests an organization of more restrictive conception than is implied in the powers exercised by the 'Conseil
de l'Entente'. The term 'Council of Understanding', used in earlier des-
patches, while literally correct, is awkward because of its unfamiliarity
with political terminology in current usage".

The Republics of Dahomey, Niger, Upper Volta, and the Ivory
Coast, formerly autonomous States within the French Community,
comprising the *Conseil de l'Entente*, respectively declared their independence on August 1, 3, 5, and 7, 1960, by virtue of Agreements signed
separately by each State with France on July 11, 1960, which stipulated in identical terms that each State "accedes, in full accord and
friendship with the French Republic, to international sovereignty and
independence by the transfer of the powers of the Community".

Although the Entente States elected not to become members of the
French Community, which fact is confirmed by the absence of any
Agreements on Participation, each State signed with France on April
24, 1961, separate Treaties of Cooperation and Agreements of Cooperation in respect of economic, monetary, and financial matters;
military assistance; justice; higher education; cultural affairs; post
and telecommunication matters; civil aviation; merchant marine; and
technical assistance personnel. Additionally, a multilateral Defense
Agreement described as a supplement to the Military Assistance
Agreement was concluded between France and each of the States
excepting Upper Volta. The Treaties of Cooperation, a device used
for the first time in French-African relations, are patterned after the
earlier agreements governing political and diplomatic cooperation
signed between France and the newly independent States which were
former autonomous members of the Community. Each treaty, in
affirmation of "complete equality and respect for their independence",
provides for regular consultation on foreign affairs with the stipulation that acceptance of the principle of consultation not limit the
African States' right to negotiate treaties or other international agreements and that differences growing out of the treaty will be dealt with
according to international law. These treaties also specify that the
French Ambassador automatically be dean of the diplomatic corps
and that the French Government represent the Entente members in
international organizations where they do not have their own representatives.

The Agreements providing for the transfer of powers, signed by the respective parties July 11, 1960, were approved by the French Republic by Law No. 60–735, July 28, 1960 (discussed and adopted by the National Assembly July 20 and in the Senate July 22, 1960), promulgated in *Journal Officiel de la République Française*, July 29, 1960; by the Republic of Dahomey by Law No. 60–30, July 28, 1960 (discussed and adopted in the Legislative Assembly July 27, 1960), promulgated in *Journal Officiel de la République du Dahomey*, July 30, 1960; by the Republic of Niger by Law discussed and adopted by the National Assembly July 27, 1960; by the Republic of Upper Volta by Law discussed and adopted by the National Assembly July 27, 1960; by the Republic of the Ivory Coast by Law No. 60–206, July 27, 1960 (discussed and adopted by the National Assembly July 27, 1960), promulgated in *Journal Officiel de la République de Côte d'Ivoire*, July 30, 1960. See also *Journal Officiel de la République Française*, July 30, 1960; *Journal Officiel de la Côte d'Ivoire*, July 30, 1960; *Journal Officiel de la République du Dahomey*, July 30, 1960; *Journal Officiel de la Communauté*, Aug. 15, 1960. Counselor of the American Embassy at Paris (Kidder) to the Secretary of State (Rusk), despatch No. 1738, June 21, 1961, MS. Department of State, file 651.70m4/6–2161, transmitting the official texts of the Treaties and Accords; the American Ambassador at Paris (Gavin) to the Secretary of State (Rusk), airgram No. A–56, July 12, 1961, *ibid./*7–1261.

Mauritania, formerly an autonomous State within the French Community, proclaimed her independence on November 28, 1960, following the exchange of ratifications on November 27 of an Agreement signed with France on October 19, 1960, which provided for the accession of the Islamic Republic of Mauritania in full accord and friendship with France to international sovereignty and independence by the transfer of powers of the French Community. Mauritania, negotiating the cooperation agreements with France after attaining international recognition as a sovereign State, signed with France on June 19, 1961, the following Agreements: a Treaty of Cooperation and Agreements of Cooperation relating to defense; technical military assistance; financial, economic, and monetary matters; justice; cultural matters; civil aviation; merchant marine; posts and telecommunications; and technical cooperation in the field of personnel. *Mauritania*

The American Embassy, Paris (Davenport), to the Secretary of State (Herter), telegram, Oct. 20, 1960, MS. Department of State, file 771.022/10–2060. Decree No. 60–1229, Nov. 23, 1960, publishing the Transfer of Competences Agreement in *Journal Officiel de la République Française*, Nov. 24, 1960, p. 10459. The Agreement of October 19 was ratified by the Mauritanian Assembly on November 9 and by the French Assembly on November 15, 1960. The American Ambassador at Dakar (Villard) to the Secretary of State (Herter), airgram No. G–107, Nov. 15, 1960, MS. Department of State, file 751t.00/11–1560. Agreements of June 19 were ratified by the Mauritanian National Assembly on June 30.

President de Gaulle, on September 16, 1959, proclaimed recourse to self-determination offering Algeria as a future legal status a choice *Algeria* between three arrangements: secession leading to independence; out-and-out identification with France as implied in the equality of rights; government of Algeria by Algerians in relationship with France in economy, teaching, defense, and foreign relations.

The New York *Times*, Sept. 17, 1959, p. 10.

Following a referendum on January 8, 1961, in which the French people recognized the right of the Algerians to choose their own political destiny in relation to the French Republic, the French Government and the Algerian nationalist provisional government announced on March 19, 1962, the following conclusions:

1. A cease-fire agreement which stipulated that military operations throughout Algerian territory end on March 19.

2. A common agreement defining the guarantees relative to the application of self-determination to take place within a period of not less than 3 months and not exceeding 6 months, and providing for the organization of the public powers in Algeria during the transition period.

3. Declarations which state, *inter alia*, that the Algerian state will exercise its full and complete sovereignty both internally and externally. Further, that they are binding on the Algerian state if the solution of independence and cooperation is adopted, and that they are to be submitted to the approval of the electors at the time of the self-determination vote.

Text of a "general declaration" as an agreed summary of the agreements reached at Evian-les-Bains, the New York *Times*, Mar. 19, 1962, p. 10. These agreements were approved by the French people in an April 8, 1962, referendum.

Following the vote of the Algerian people on July 1, 1962, for independence in cooperation with France, President de Gaulle declared on July 3, 1962, that "relations between France and Algeria being henceforth founded on conditions defined by the Governmental Declarations of March 1962", "France gives solemn recognition to the independence of Algeria".

The American Ambassador at Paris (Gavin) to the Secretary of State (Rusk), telegram, July 3, 1962, MS. Department of State, file 751S.00/7–362.

Republic of Guinea

The Republic of Guinea, formerly a territory of the French West African Federation, attained its independence as a result of voting in the referendum of September 28, 1958, to reject the Constitution of the Fifth Republic. Before Guinea issued its own independence proclamation on October 2, 1958, Premier de Gaulle formally notified Sekou Touré that by its vote Guinea had separated itself from the

French Community and that "sovereignty passes to it as of midnight Tuesday."

The New York *Times*, Oct. 1, 1958, p. 36.

The Constitution of the Republic of Guinea, approved on November 10, 1958, by the National Assembly of Guinea and promulgated by Prime Minister Sekou Touré on November 12, 1958, states in its preamble, "The people of Guinea by its overwhelming vote of September 28, 1958 have rejected [foreign] domination and by this act have acquired its national independence and constituted a free and sovereign state." While sovereignty is vested in the people "who exercise it in all matters by their Deputies in the National Assembly, elected by Universal Suffrage, equal, direct and secret, or by means of the Referendum" (article 3), it may be surrendered as provided in article 34 which states "The Republic can conclude with any African State agreements of association or of community, including the partial or total surrender of sovereignty in order to achieve African Unity."

The American Consul General at Dakar (Dumont) to the Secretary of State (Dulles), despatch No. 129, Nov. 25, 1958, encl. 1, MS. Department of State, file 770B.03/11–2558.

The Joint Declaration on the Ghana-Guinea Union, issued May 1, 1959, did not effect the surrender in any degree of Guinea's sovereignty but in envisaging the union of two States declared "Each State of the Federation which is a member of the Union shall preserve its own individuality and structure". As a provision relating to the future, the declaration states that "the member-States of Federation will decide in common what portion of sovereignty shall be surrendered to the Union in the full interest of the African Community". For Ghana-Guinea-Mali Union (Union of African States), see *ante*, p. 429.

Twelve African States—Cameroon, Central African Republic, Chad, Congo (Brazzaville), Dahomey, Gabon, Ivory Coast, Malagasy, Mauritania, Niger, Senegal, and Upper Volta—comprising the African and Malagasy Union (UAM), adopted a Charter at the Tananarive Conference in September 1961, which declares as its aim the coordination of the foreign policy of member States to strengthen their solidarity, assure their collective security, assist their development, and secure peace. Membership is open to all independent African States whose admission is contingent upon the unanimous approval of member States. The Charter provides that an administrative Secretary-General be chosen for a 2-year term by a conference of heads of State and government and that the general policy of the

UAM

Union be determined by the conference of heads of State and government meeting twice a year with special sessions called on the initiative of one State supported by the majority of the members of the Union. In addition, the Conference adopted five economic protocols, a defense pact, several conventions on juridical matters covering, *inter alia*, diplomatic representation, establishment, and judicial cooperation, and approved the creation of the *Union africaine et malgache des postes et télécommunications*.

The American Ambassador at Tananarive (Bartlett) to the Secretary of State (Rusk), despatch No. 44, Sept. 13, 1961, MS. Department of State, file 377/9–1361; XVI *International Organization* (1962) 434–437.

Seventeen States of the Monrovian group—Cameroon, Central African Republic, Chad, Congo (Brazzaville), Congo (Léopoldville), Dahomey, Ethiopia, Gabon, Ivory Coast, Liberia, Mauritania, Niger, Nigeria, Senegal, Sierra Leone, Togo, and Upper Volta—established the Inter-African and Malagasy Organization by signing the Charter of the Organization on December 21, 1962, which Charter thereby became provisionally applicable pending the duration of 30 days following the deposit of the instruments of ratification of three-fifths of the signatory States, whereupon it should come into force and effect. For the realization of its expressly stated objectives, the signatories "as independent, sovereign States in Africa and Malagasy under indigenous African rule" reaffirmed the following principles: sovereign African equality of African and Malagasy States; noninterference in the internal affairs of Member States; respect for the sovereignty and territorial integrity of each State and for its inalienable right to independent existence; peaceful and harmonious settlement of all disputes arising among the African and Malagasy States; unqualified condemnation of any subversive activity; constant promotion of all available means of cooperation in the fields of economics, health, nutrition, education, and culture; and dedication to the total emancipation of the remaining dependent territories of Africa. The Charter provides for the establishment of three institutions: an Assembly of Heads of States and Governments to meet at least once a year, a Council of Ministers to meet twice a year, and a General Secretariat. In addition, the Charter establishes The Association of African and Malagasy Economic Cooperation and Development. It was also agreed that there should be concluded separate treaties establishing a Scientific Training and Research Institute and a Permanent Conciliation Commission for the pacific settlement of disputes.

First Secretary of American Embassy at Lagos (Bennett) to the Secretary of State (Rusk), airgram No. A–394, Jan. 3, 1963, MS. Department of State, file 377/1–363.

International Entities

§32

In its advisory opinion on *Reparation for Injuries Suffered in the Service of the United Nations*, the International Court of Justice's determination that the United Nations Organization has the capacity to bring an international claim turned on the more basic question whether the Organization possessed international personality.

Addressing itself to this question, the Court stated:

"The subjects of law in any legal system are not necessarily identical in their nature or in the extent of their rights, and their nature depends upon the needs of the community. Throughout its history, the development of international law has been influenced by the requirements of international life, and the progressive increase in the collective activities of States has already given rise to instances of action upon the international plane by certain entities which are not States. This development culminated in the establishment in June 1945 of an international organization whose purposes and principles are specified in the Charter of the United Nations. But to achieve these ends the attribution of international personality is indispensable.

"The Charter has not been content to make the Organization created by it merely a centre 'for harmonizing the actions of nations in the attainment of these common ends' (Article I, para. 4). It has equipped that centre with organs, and has given it special tasks. It has defined the position of the Members in relation to the Organization by requiring them to give it every assistance in any action undertaken by it (Article 2, para. 5), and to accept and carry out the decisions of the Security Council; by authorizing the General Assembly to make recommendations to the Members; by giving the Organization legal capacity and privileges and immunities in the territory of each of its Members; and by providing for the conclusion of agreements between the Organization and its Members. Practice—in particular the conclusion of conventions to which the Organization is a party—has confirmed this character of the Organization, which occupies a position in certain respects in detachment from its Members, and which is under a duty to remind them, if need be, of certain obligations. It must be added that the Organization is a political body, charged with political tasks of an important character, and covering a wide field namely, the maintenance of international peace and security, the development of friendly relations among nations, and the achievement of international co-operation in the solution of problems of an economic, social, cultural or humanitarian character (Article 1); and in dealing with its Members it employs political means. The 'Convention on the Privileges and Immunities of the United Nations' of 1946 creates rights and duties between each of the signatories and the Organization (see, in particular, Section 35). It is difficult to see how such a convention could operate except upon the international plane and as between parties possessing international personality.

"In the opinion of the Court, the Organization was intended to exercise and enjoy, and is in fact exercising and enjoying, functions and rights which can only be explained on the basis of the possession of a large measure of international personality and the capacity to operate upon an international plane. It is at present the supreme type of international organization, and it could not carry out the intentions of its founders if it was devoid of international personality. It must be acknowledged that its Members, by entrusting certain functions to it, with the attendant duties and responsibilities, have clothed it with the competence required to enable those functions to be effectively discharged.

"Accordingly, the Court has come to the conclusion that the Organization is an international person. That is not the same thing as saying that it is a State, which it certainly is not, or that its legal personality and rights and duties are the same as those of a State. Still less is it the same thing as saying that it is 'a super-State', whatever that expression may mean. It does not even imply that all its rights and duties must be upon the international plane, any more than all the rights and duties of a State must be upon that plane. What it does mean is that it is a subject of international law and capable of possessing international rights and duties, and that it has capacity to maintain its rights by bringing international claims."

Reparation for Injuries Suffered in the Service of the United Nations, Advisory Opinion, Apr. 11, 1949, I.C.J. Reports (1949) 174, 178–179.

Sovereign Order of Malta

In upholding the international personality of the Sovereign Military Order of St. John of Jerusalem, of Rhodes and of Malta, commonly called "The Order of Malta", the Court of Cassation of Italy stated:

". . . the solution arrived at by the court below can be justified on other grounds. These grounds are based on the essential juridical character of the Sovereign Order of Jerusalem and Malta and on the position which is, in our judgment, held by it as an international person existing apart from the national sovereignty of the State. . . .

"In order to dispose of the argument of the appellants it is necessary to trace the historical development of the international personality of the Sovereign Order of Jerusalem and Malta. Sovereignty is a complex notion, which international law, from the external point of view, contemplates, so to speak, negatively, having only in view independence vis-à-vis other States. For this reason it is sufficient to require merely proof of the autonomy of the Order in its relation to the Italian State. Historically, the essential element of such autonomy can be found in the political nature of the mission which the Order has been destined to fulfil, namely, by the aid of its arms to resist the Saracen and Mohammedan menace and to establish its hospitallers in the Levant. . . ."

The Court at this point recited in some detail the history of the Order and continued:

> "With the recognition of the Church and of the Byzantine Empire, the Order established, after the conquest of territory of its own, its independence and sovereignty. . . . The Grand Master was recognised as Sovereign Head of Rhodes with all the attributes of such a position, which included, for instance, among other rights, the right to create and confer titles of Knight Commanders, the right to be accompanied on ceremonial occasions by three Knights of the Order . . . and finally, the right of active and passive legation together with the right of negotiating directly with other States and of making conventions and treaties. . . . Such attributes of sovereignty and independence have not ceased, in the case of the Order, at the present day—at least not from the formal point of view in its relations with the Italian State. . . . But it is impossible to deny to other international collective units a limited capacity of acting internationally within the ambit and the actual exercise of their own functions, with the resulting international juridical personality and capacity which is its necessary and natural corollary. In accordance with these doctrines, such personality was never denied to the Holy See even before the Lateran Treaty of February 11, 1929, and it is unanimously conceded to the League of Nations, although it is neither a State, nor a Super-State, nor a Confederation of States. It is equally conceded to certain international administrative unions (see judgment of the Court of Cassation of May 13, 1931, in the *International Institute of Agriculture* v. *Profili, Foro Italiano*, 1931, I, 1424) [*Annual Digest*, 1929–1930, Case No. 254] which aim at the protection and furtherance of collective economic interests.

> .   .   .   .

> "We must therefore conclude that, given the position which is, according to our legal system, enjoyed by the Order as an international person, there was no necessity, for the valid acquisition of this property, to obtain the permission of the government."

> *Nanni and Others* v. *Pace and The Sovereign Order of Malta*, Court of Cassation, Italy, Decision affirming an order for restitution of certain property to the Order, Mar. 13, 1935, [1935–1937] Ann. Dig. 2, 4–6 (No. 2).

Farran's historical account of the Order of Malta establishes that the Order "while in Rhodes and Malta, was an ordinary international person: a sovereign 'State' ". In answer to his query whether it was the Order itself or Malta which was an international person, he concludes that the Order is the sovereign international person.

Referring to the treaty of 1798 under which the Grand Master of the Order was forced to cede Malta to France, Mr. Farran argues: "If it was the Order which was an International person, then nothing could be more natural than that, after the loss of Malta, its international personality should continue undiminished. If, on the other hand, the Grand Master was only sovereign *qua* head of Malta, its loss should logically have reduced him to the level of other exiled monarchs, with the consequent loss of international personality. Possibly (as Cansacchi suggests is arguable) the answer may be that there was until the loss of Malta a personal union, the same individual being head of the Order and head of the Maltese State. The fact remains that the loss of Malta did not end the Grand Master's status *as head of the Order* as an international person, since many States—France, Austria, the Holy See, Parma, the Two Sicilies, Modena, Spain, Hungary, Rumania, San Marino, Argentina, Panama, Dominican Republic, Haiti and Paraguay—have from time to time since then had diplomatic relations with the Order. . . ."

> Farran, "The Sovereign Order of Malta in International Law", 3 Int'l & Comp. L. Q. (1954) 217, 222–223. For a listing of additional historical facts in support of the contention that the Order was sovereign apart from its occupation of Malta, see *ibid.* 223–227.

In connection with his analysis of the special relationship between the Sovereign Order and the Holy See, Mr. Farran records a summary of the Cardinals' report to the Pope as issued to the press in April 1953, which is quoted in part as follows:

> "(i) The Order is indeed sovereign and an international person fully entitled to exchange diplomatic agents, make treaties and so on. Yet its powers and prerogatives are not equivalent, in the ordinary sense of the term, to those of a State.
>
> "(ii) It is also a religious order seeking the sanctification of its members. In this capacity it is governed by canon law and hence, indirectly, by the Congregation of Religious."

> *Ibid.* 231.

In a more recent note on the Sovereign Order of Malta, Mr. Farran has written of the conflict of legal opinion concerning the status of this Order:

> ". . . One writer [Count Zeininger de Borja, "The Order of St. John and Its Affiliates," *Scientia* (Malta), Oct.–Dec. 1954, pp. 150–83], even though he is a member of the Order, has contended at length that it is really a religious order and should therefore be subordinated to the Sacred Congregation of Religious. My earlier article (part IV) [3 The International and Comparative Law Quarterly (1954), pp. 217–234] shows the grounds for rejecting this view, but the contention throws into relief the highly unusual conflict of laws in this matter: for essentially it would seem to be a conflict question between international law and canon law. While the Order as being in part a religious congregation is subject in certain matters to the latter, it is suggested that as an international person it owes in case of conflict a prime allegiance to the former."

To substantiate his view, Mr. Farran offers a comparison between the Order of Malta and the continued existence of the Teutonic Order:

> ". . . Like it the Teutonic Order began as a hospital order in the Crusaders' Jerusalem, like it it turned to military activities against

the unbeliever . . . like it it was once sovereign over considerable
territories (Prussia till 1525, Livonia till 1561), like it it has an 'inner
core' of celibate monk-knights, . . . like it it has reverted to hospital
work, like it it has an unrecognised Protestant 'branch,' the Bailiage
of Utrecht. . . . Why, then, it may be asked, has not the Teutonic
Order achieved international personality? Briefly it is because it lost
its lands before the modern system of international law really developed, because it was never truly cosmopolitan, being confined to those
of 'Teutonic' race . . . and because the Reformation—with its an-
tagonism to non-territorial sovereignty—dealt it a blow from which
it has never recovered. Fate was kinder to the Maltese Order, enough
of whose knights came from counter-Reformation lands to ensure it
a permanent, even if highly unusual, sovereignty. . . ." Farran, "The
Sovereign Order of Malta: A Supplementary Note", 4 Int'l & Comp.
L.Q. (1955) 308–309.

Taking note of the fact that in 1884 Italy recognized the Sovereign
Order of Malta's right of legation, that a number of countries including France, Austria, the Holy See, Spain, Hungary, Rumania,
San Marino, Argentina, Panama, the Dominican Republic, Haiti,
Paraguay, and apparently Ecuador had from time to time had diplomatic relations with the Order, and that in 1935 an Italian Court held
that the Sovereign Order of Malta was an international person, the
Office of the Legal Adviser in a letter of October 28, 1959, stated that
"the United States on its part does not recognize the Order as a state".

Assistant Legal Adviser Whiteman to the Chargé d'Affaires *ad interim*
of the American Embassy at Quito (Little), letter, Oct. 28, 1959, MS.
Department of State, file 747b.02/10–2059.

Italy and the Holy See concluded a Treaty and Concordat February   Vatican
11, 1929. The articles which pertain to the status of the Vatican
City and Holy See read in part as follows:

"2. Italy recognizes the sovereignty of the Holy See in the
international domain as an attribute inherent in its nature, in
accordance with its tradition and with the requirements of its
mission in the world.

"3. Italy recognizes that the Holy See has full ownership, exclusive and absolute power, and sovereign jurisdiction over the
Vatican, as it is at present constituted with all its dependencies
and endowments, creating thus the City of the Vatican for its
special ends and with the characteristics set forth in the present
Treaty. . . .

.   .   .   .

"4. The exclusive sovereignty and jurisdiction of the Holy See
which Italy recognizes over the City of the Vatican implies the
consequence that no interference on the part of the Italian government may be there manifested, and that there will be no other
authority than that of the Holy See."

III Peaslee, *Constitutions of Nations* (2d ed., 1956) 668, 669.

Commenting upon the international status of the Vatican City in the light of these provisions, Professor Sereni has stated:

"Vatican City is undoubtedly a state. It is endowed with its own administrative, legislative, and judicial organization, its own flag, army, and monetary system. It is also an international subject, which came into being in 1929, on territory formally belonging to the Italian state. [Vatican City is a new state, not the continuation of the Papal State which ended by *debellatio* by Italy in 1870.] Its particular characteristics result from its relationship with the Holy See. As stated in the preamble of the Lateran Treaty, Vatican City is a state created 'to secure absolute and visible independence to the Holy See and to guarantee its indisputable sovereignty in international relations.' While the normal aim of a state is the welfare of the state itself and of its citizens, Vatican City has not an autonomous purpose. It is only intended to support a religious entity, the Holy See. For this reason Vatican City, like the medieval state and unlike the modern state, is an example of patrimonial sovereignty. It is owned entirely by its sovereign, the Holy See. The preamble of the Lateran Treaty declares that the Holy See has 'complete ownership, exclusive and absolute power, and sovereign jurisdiction' over Vatican City. This formula is repeated in Article 3. The functional character of Vatican City is also evident in its autocratic constitution, whereby all power is concentrated in the Holy See, and in the composition of its population, composed only of persons connected with the Holy See (Article 9 of the Treaty). If we accept the opinion that the Catholic Church is an international person, we must reach the conclusion that the Catholic Church and Vatican City are two distinct international persons united by a relationship similar to that of 'real union.' The two subjects have the same head, the Holy See: and the Vatican City exists only for the realization of the aims of the Catholic Church."

Sereni, *The Italian Conception of International Law* (1943) 292–293.

"Most of the erroneous treatments of this [status of the Holy See] problem follow about this line: Until 1870 the Pope was the sovereign of the Papal State, a normal person in international law. Since the Lateran Treaty of February 11, 1929, the Pope is again the sovereign of the State of the City of the Vatican (*Stato della Città del Vaticano*). But between 1870 and 1929 there was no Papal State, hence no international personality. This line of reasoning, wholly untenable in the light of the practice of states, stems mostly from the pseudo-positivistic prejudice that only sovereign states *can* be persons in international law. But the Holy See was always a subject of general international law. Modern developments show, for instance, international organizations, which certainly are not states, as persons in international law.

"The Holy See [Not the Catholic Church as such; not the Pope. The relation between the concepts of the Holy See and of the Pope are analogous to the relation in British constitutional law between the concepts of the Crown and of the King.] is . . . a *permanent* subject of *general* customary international law *vis-à-vis* all states, Catholic or not. That does not mean that the Holy See has the same international status as a sovereign state. But the Holy See has, under general international law, the capacity to conclude agreements with states (concordats). The Holy See can also conclude normal international treaties, formerly on behalf of the Papal State, now on behalf of the State of the City of the Vatican, but also in its own capacity. [The Lateran Treaty of 1929 is a normal international treaty. Recently the Holy See signed and ratified the four new Geneva Conventions of 1949.] . . .

"The Holy See has the active and passive right of legation under general international law, not restricted to Catholic states. The Protocol of Vienna of March 19, 1815, puts Papal nuncios into the rank of ambassadors under general international law. The Vienna Protocol also provides that 'the present regulations shall not cause any innovation with regard to the representatives of the Pope,' to whom Catholic states grant the privilege of being the Dean of the Diplomatic Corps. These norms are binding on all the states, Catholic or not. Cardinals, on the other hand, are not diplomatic agents of the Holy See.

"Prior to 1870, there were two subjects of international law: The Papal State and the Holy See. The Pope constituted in his person a personal union of two different organs, the highest organs of two different subjects of international law. Even prior to 1870, the more important of these two subjects was the Holy See. It is clear that Catholic states granted the privilege of deanship to the Papal nuncios not because of the political importance of the Papal State, but because of the supreme spiritual sovereignty of the Holy See.

"Of these two persons in international law the one, the Papal State, undoubtedly came to an end, under the rules of general international law, by Italian conquest and subjugation in 1870. But the Holy See remained, as always, a subject of general international law also in the period between 1870 and 1929. That this is so, is fully proved by the practice of states.

"The Holy See continued to conclude concordats and continued, with the consent of a majority of states, to exercise the active and passive right of legation. The legal position of its diplomatic agents—as the continuance of the Vienna Protocol also during this period proves—remained based on general international law, not on the Italian Law of Guarantee, a municipal law, but enacted under an international duty incumbent upon Italy. Hence, the confiscation by Italy in 1917 of the Palazzo Venezia, house of the Austro-Hungarian Ambassador to the Vatican, constituted a violation of international law.

. . . .

"The Cardinal-Secretary of State of the Vatican exercises the functions of a Foreign Minister. In many other respects the status of the Holy See as a person in general international law was also clearly demonstrated in the period 1870–1929. Pope Leo XIII acted as a mediator in the Carolina Islands dispute between Germany and Spain. The same Pope acted in 1895 as arbiter in a border conflict between Haiti and Santo Domingo. In 1898 Orthodox Russia sent her project for the Hague Peace Conference to the Holy See and solicited its support. The exclusion of the Holy See from the Hague Peace Conferences was due to the request by Italy, just as Italy in the London Treaty of 1915 made it a condition of her joining Great Britain and France in the first World War that the Holy See would not be invited to the Peace Conference. Italy also opposed the Holy See as a Member of the League of Nations; but the German project for a League of Nations of 1919 provided expressly that the Holy See could become a member. During the first World War its own flag was conceded to the Holy See and the vessel flying this flag declared to be neutral and assimilated to a state vessel. After the first World War new states or governments applied for recognition by the Holy See; such recognition was, for instance, granted to Poland and Estonia.

"The Lateran Treaty had the object of liquidating once for all the 'Roman Question' and bringing about a reconciliation between the Holy See and Italy, but it in no way created or changed the international position of the Holy See. [It is, therefore, not correct, as Oppenheim-Lauterpacht (International Law, Vol. I (7th ed., 1948) p. 228) states, that 'the hitherto controversial international position of the Holy See was clarified as a result of the Treaty.'] The treaty concluded between the Holy See and Italy presupposes the international personality of the Holy See. Italian recognition, in Article 2, of the sovereignty of the Holy See, and, in Article 12, of the active and passive right of legation under the norms of general international law, is purely declaratory.

"The Lateran Treaty created, furthermore the state of the City of the Vatican as a *new* state, for which Italy makes a cession of territory. The treaty, correctly speaking, did not create this state, but laid down only the necessary presuppositions. This state of the City of the Vatican is a state, a subject of international law, different from the Holy See. It has become a member of the Universal Postal Union. But it is not a sovereign state. As all writers correctly state, 'its activities are totally different from those inherent in national States.' [Oppenheim-Lauterpacht, *op. cit.*, p. 230.] Its constitution is not autonomous, but derived from the Holy See. It is a vassal state of the Holy See.

"During the second World War the Protestant Occupying Powers of Italy—Great Britain and the United States—were bound under international law to observe the neutrality of the state of the City of the Vatican and to grant free correspondence between the Holy See and all states, including those with which the Occupying Powers were at war.   In Article 24 of the Lateran Treaty the Holy See makes a unilateral statement that it will remain aloof from the temporal competitions of states and from congresses convoked for such purposes, *except* that the contending parties by common consent may appeal to its mission of peace. The Holy See reserves in any event the right to exercise its moral spiritual influence.   In this sense the Popes appealed to all belligerents during the two World Wars.   In his Christmas address, 1951, the Pope declared that the Holy See cannot remain neutral between right and wrong, but, on the other hand, can never consider political conflicts on purely political lines, but always '*sub specie aeternitatis.*'

"The Holy See, certainly, is not eligible to be a Member of the United Nations because, under Article 4 of the Charter, admission is only open to 'States.'   The City of the Vatican would not be admitted because of its exiguity, just as the sovereign Principality of Liechtenstein was not admitted to the League of Nations. But the Holy See may participate in some activities of the United Nations, just as Papal delegates participated in the League of Nations meetings concerning calendar reform.   The Holy See can, of course, be chosen as a mediator or arbiter, and can be invited to international conferences.   Recently the Holy See was invited to and participated in the diplomatic conference held at Geneva in 1949.   It signed and ratified and is a contracting party to the four new Geneva Conventions of 1949.   At this conference, nearly all the states, including the Soviet States, were represented; none objected to the invitation and participation of the Holy See."

Kunz, "The Status of the Holy See in International Law", 46 Am. J. Int'l L. (1952) 308, 309–313.

". . . The view seems to be dominant today . . . that the Holy See does, in fact, enjoy international personality.   Furthermore, this personality of the Holy See is distinct from the personality of the State of Vatican City.   One is a non-territorial institution, and the other a state.   The papacy as a religious organ is a subject of international law and capable of international rights and duties.

.   .   .   .

". . . The fact that the Holy See is a non-territorial institution is no longer regarded as a reason for denying it international personality.   The papacy can act in its own name in the international community.   It can enter into legally binding conventions known as concordats.   In the world of diplomacy the Pope enjoys the rights of active and passive legation.   He can send and receive representatives who are public ministers in the sense of international law.   But this is not new or original.   This was the view of the very men who in 1870 stripped Pope Pius IX of his temporal domains by armed invasion.

"For a full understanding of the verdict reached after the many decades of controversy, it is important to grasp the precise juridical point at issue. The issue was not whether the Pope was still temporal ruler of the papal states. It did not turn upon whether a dispossessed prince retained his right of legation. The question was rather this: whether, *despite* the assumed loss of the temporal sovereignty, the Pope continued to enjoy international personality at least as head of the Catholic Church, as a 'spiritual sovereign.' Some papal writers did attempt to argue that the Pope remained at least a *de jure* temporal prince. They adduced various reasons to establish this, such as the injustice of the annexation or the refusal of the Pope to acquiesce in the status quo. These arguments, however, were hardly convincing from a juridical point of view. They served rather the purpose of demonstrating that the Roman question was not as dead as the Italian government would like to have it believed. The intense debate reflected in the post-1870 literature on the subject was not given over to the temporal sovereignty of the Pope, but to his spiritual sovereignty.

"It is necessary to stress this point because it is a common error to suppose that the Lateran Treaty of 1929 finally reestablished the papacy as a subject of international law. This misapprehension ignores the evolution of legal thinking during the preceding decades. By the time the situation was politically ripe for the Lateran accord, legal opinion was already prepared to concede the Pope's legal status. Had the Vatican State never come into being in 1929, international law would have increasingly recognized the non-territorial sovereignty of the papacy. Yet it must be conceded that the long years of the Roman question tended to confuse the two different issues: the political and the spiritual sovereignty. Theoretically distinct and separable, they were linked politically and emotionally in the rupture between the papacy and Italy. Many pro-papal writers were themselves responsible for this confusion of thought. They wrote as though only the temporal power was the issue. They played down the spiritual sovereignty on the grounds that it was a purely imaginary, extra-legal invention of the Italians, tailor-made to suit the political purpose of usurping the papal states. They refused to be misled from the chase by what they considered the will-o'-the-wisp of spiritual sovereignty. For this reason they tended to pour scorn upon any sovereignty not based on territory. The Marquis de Olivart, one of the ablest of these writers, exclaimed, 'As for those more or less fanciful distinctions of titular, or honorary, or such-like sovereignty, these are encountered only in books and cannot exist in the world of reality.' They would settle for nothing but the restoration of territorial sovereignty. For them, spiritual sovereignty was not enough.

"Even the language of official papal spokesmen was less than clear on this point. On many occasions the Vatican curia seems to say that there was no sovereignty that was not based on territory. Papal spokesmen rarely expatiated upon papal sovereignty without linking it with temporal power. What they meant to imply, of course, was that spiritual sovereignty was not in itself sufficient for the full independence that the Pope needed. They

did not wish to say that the Pope was not also a spiritual sovereign
in international law.   In the end, the satisfactory guarantees were
achieved by the creation of the Vatican State.   In the meantime,
however, minds had become confused over the real issue of the
legal debate."

Graham, *Vatican Diplomacy, A Study of Church and State on the International Plane* (1959) 186, 201–202.

Corpus Separatum

Jerusalem

§ 33

The United Nations General Assembly passed three resolutions
(Resolutions 181(II), November 29, 1947; 194(III), December 11,
1948; and 303(IV), December 9, 1949) providing for and relating
to full territorial internationalization of Jerusalem.

Resolution 303(IV) restated "its intention that Jerusalem should
be placed under a permanent international regime, which should envisage appropriate guarantees for the protection of the Holy Places,
both within and outside Jerusalem" and confirmed specifically that
"(1) the City of Jerusalem shall be established as a *corpus separatum*
under a special international regime and shall be administered by the
United Nations . . . ."

In accordance with the request of the General Assembly in Resolution 303(IV) of December 9, 1949, the Trusteeship Council approved
a Statute for the City of Jerusalem on April 4, 1950, which was submitted to the Governments of Israel and the Hashemite Kingdom of
Jordan with a request for their full cooperation.   In view of its conclusion that neither Government appeared prepared to collaborate
in the implementation of the Statute, the Trusteeship Council decided
in a resolution of June 14, 1950, to submit the Statute to the General
Assembly.

*Question of an International Regime for the Jerusalem Area and Pro-
tection of the Holy Places*, special report of the Trusteeship Council, Gen.
Ass. Off. Rec. 5th Sess., Supp. No. 9 (A/1286).   The Ad Hoc Political
Committee recommended to the plenary the adoption of a resolution which
would instruct four persons, to be appointed by the Trusteeship Council,
to study, in consultation with the other States, authorities and religious
bodies concerned, "the conditions of a settlement capable of ensuring the
effective protection, under the supervision of the United Nations, of the
Holy Places and of spiritual and religious interests in the Holy Land;" and
would invite them to report to the Assembly at its Sixth Session (A/1724,
Dec. 14, 1950).   The recommended resolution failed to receive the required
two-thirds majority vote at the General Assembly plenary session of

December 15, 1950, and, consequently, the Assembly took no action at that session. Gen. Ass. Off. Rec. 5th Sess., 326th Plenary Meeting, A/PV.326, p. 684.

Referring to these resolutions, the American Consul General at Jerusalem, in a despatch on the status of Jerusalem, stated:

". . . Both governments directly concerned, that of Israel and that of Jordan, rejected internationalization thus in fact nullifying the United Nations Resolutions. The majority of UN member nations, including the United States and the Soviet Union, have continued to respect the United Nations Resolutions despite the *de facto* occupancy of the city of Jerusalem part by Israel and part by Jordan. As a result, an anomalous situation exists today embodied, in the case of the United States, by a Consulate General whose district is the 'international city' and certain adjacent areas on the Jordanian side. Other nations which maintain similar establishments are the United Kingdom, Turkey, Italy, Spain, Greece and Belgium. Many other countries mark their respect for the internationalization resolutions by establishing embassies in Tel Aviv thus avoiding recognition of Jerusalem as the capital of Israel and, by implication, as Israel's *de jure* sovereign territory."

The American Consul General at Jerusalem (Franklin) to the Secretary of State (Dulles), despatch No. 67, Dec. 30, 1958, MS. Department of State, file 122.491/12–3058.

Upon learning of the Jordanian plans to construct offices in Jerusalem for the King, the Cabinet, and the Parliament, the Department of State likewise made its position regarding the status of Jerusalem a matter of record with the Jordanian Government by the deliverance on April 5, 1960, of the following aide memoire to the Prime Minister of Jordan:

"The Government of the United States of America has noted recent reports to the effect that the Government of Jordan plans to treat the City of Jerusalem as its second capital and to construct certain offices there for agencies of the Central Government.

"The Government of the United States of America has adhered and continues to adhere to a policy which respects the interest of the United Nations in the status of Jerusalem. The United States Government therefore cannot recognize or associate itself in any way with actions which confer upon Jerusalem the attributes of a seat of government of a sovereign state, and are thus inconsistent with this United Nations interest in the status of that city."

The American Ambassador at Amman (Mills) to the Secretary of State (Herter), despatch No. 376, encl. 1, Apr. 5, 1960, MS. Department of State. file 785.02/4–560.

In response to the proposed move of the Israel Foreign Ministry from Tel Aviv to Jerusalem, the American Embassy at Tel Aviv delivered to the Israel Government on July 9, 1952, an aide memoire which stated:

"The Government of the United States has noted with concern the decision and announcement of the Israel Government on May 4, 1952, to move the Foreign Office to Jerusalem.

"The Government of the United States has adhered and continues to adhere to the policy that there should be a special international regime for Jerusalem which will not only provide protection for the holy places but which will be acceptable to Israel and Jordan as well as the world community.

"Since the question of Jerusalem is still of international importance the U.S. Government believes that the United Nations should have an opportunity to reconsider the matter with a view to devising a status for Jerusalem which will satisfactorily preserve the interests of the world community and the states directly concerned. Consequently, the U.S. Government would not view favorably the transfer of the Foreign Office of Israel to Jerusalem.

"The Government of the United States also wishes to convey that in view of its attitude on the Jerusalem question, it has no present intention of transferring the Ambassador of the United States and his staff to Jerusalem."

Department of State press release 576, July 22, 1952.

The International Zone of Tangier was established by a Convention concluded between France, Spain, and Great Britain in 1923 by which the Contracting Parties recognized the "sovereign rights of His Majesty the Sultan" (article 25) and provided that the Zone be permanently neutralized and demilitarized (article 3). See I Hackworth, *Digest of International Law* (1940) 93.

"On June 14, 1940 Spanish military forces, by unilateral decision of the Spanish Government, occupied the International Zone of Tangier and notified the Statutory powers that this action had been taken as a result of Spain's desire to preserve the neutrality of the Zone during the war in which the other major interested powers—Great Britain, France, and Italy—were then engaged." Press release, July 2, 1945, XIII *Bulletin*, Department of State, No. 315, July 8, 1945, p. 48.

When asked during a House of Commons debate whether the British Government would open negotiations with the Spanish Government for restoration of the international status of Tangier, Secretary of State for Foreign Affairs Eden answered:

"His Majesty's Government in the United Kingdom have always made it clear that the *modus vivendi* reached between them and the Spanish Government early in 1941, the terms of which were summarised in a statement by the then Under Secretary of State for Foreign Affairs on the 26th February, 1941, was of a provisional nature pending the possibility of a final settlement, and that it was without prejudice to our own rights or to those of third parties under the relevant international instruments. They have always maintained their protest against the original unilateral action of the Spanish Government in the Tangier Zone. Under this *modus vivendi* British rights in that Zone have been and are fully safeguarded.

"His Majesty's Government are, however, keeping the situation at Tangier under constant review and it is their intention to put forward at the first suitable opportunity for the consideration of other interested parties, proposals for the future of the Zone. In view of the present international situation and of the position of some of those parties it is not, however, practicable to open the necessary negotiations now.

"Meanwhile, His Majesty's Government have informed the Spanish Government that they are bound to take a serious view of the use of the Zone by the German Consul-General and by German nationals for unneutral activities directed against British interests. They have requested the Spanish Government to put an end to these abuses and to ensure the maintenance of the strict neutrality of the Zone, which the Spanish Government declared in June, 1940, to be the exclusive object of the Spanish occupation." 392 H.C. Deb. (5th ser.) cols. 176–178 (Sept. 22, 1943).

For the first 4 months of this occupation, the organs of government created by the 1923 Convention—the Mixed Court, the International Administration, the Legislative Assembly, and the Committee of Control—continued their functions, but on November 4, 1940, the High Command of the Spanish Army of Occupation ended their activities and made the Tangier Zone part of the Spanish Zone of Morocco. Gutteridge, "The Dissolution of the International Regime in Tangier", XXXIII Brit. Yb. Int'l L. (1957) 296.

At the Berlin (Potsdam) Conference, held in July–August 1945, the Heads of Governments of the United States, of the United Kingdom, and of the Union of Soviet Socialist Republics agreed with respect to the International Zone of Tangier that ". . . this Zone, which includes the City of Tangier and the area adjacent to it, in view of its special strategic importance, shall remain international". Protocol of Proceedings, August 1, 1945, *A Decade of American Foreign Policy, 1941–49: Basic Documents* (1950) 34, 46; Department of State press release 238, Mar. 24, 1947.

The Anglo-French Agreement of August 31, 1945, annexed to the Final Act of the Conference Concerning the Re-establishment of the International Regime in Tangier concluded the same date between representatives of the Governments of the United States, the United Kingdom, France, and the Union of Soviet Socialist Republics, restored the international regime in Tangier October 11, 1945. The Agreement stipulated that the Tangier Zone be provisionally administered in accordance with the Convention of December 18, 1923 (and the Agreement of July 25, 1928, amending the same), as modified by the provisions of the Anglo-French Agreement until the entry into force of a Convention drawn up at a Conference to be convoked by France not later than 6 months from October 11, 1945 (articles 1 and 2).

In reestablishing the international regime, the Anglo-French Agreement officially terminated the Spanish Government's occupation of Tangier by directing the Spanish Government to "hand over to the Committee of Control the administration of the Zone and the archives of the administration . . ." (article 4), and provided for the participation of the Governments of the United States and the Union of Soviet Socialist Republics, who were not parties to the 1923 Convention, by inviting them ". . . to collaborate in the provisional régime of the Tangier Zone" (article 3). *A Decade of American Foreign Policy, 1941–49: Basic Documents* (1950) 894, 898; XIII *Bulletin,* Department of State, No. 330, Oct. 21, 1945, pp. 613–618.

"The Conference provided for in Article 2 of the 1945 Agreement was never held, and the provisional regime continued under the 1945 Agreement without any changes until 1952, when it was amended . . . by a Protocol, signed at Tangier on 10 November 1952, which was concluded for a period of five years and was to be renewed for further periods of the same duration, unless six months before its expiration any member of the Committee of Control requested its revision.

.   .   .   .

". . . the duration of the 1952 Protocol was less than five years. On 2 March 1956 negotiations between the French and Moroccan Governments resulted in a Declaration affirming that 'following on the progress realised by Morocco the Treaty of Fez of March 30, 1912, no longer corresponds to the necessities of modern life and can no longer govern Franco-Moroccan relations', and stating that 'in consequence the French Government solemnly confirm their recognition of the independence of Morocco and their will to respect and make others respect the integrity of Moroccan territory guaranteed by international treaties'. Annexed to the Declaration was a Protocol which stated, amongst its other provisions, that 'Legislative power is exercised by His Majesty the Sultan in full sovereignty'.

"Following the Franco-Moroccan Declaration and Protocol of 2 March 1956, other States, including the United Kingdom, recognized the complete independence of Morocco. One result of this recognition was to set on foot arrangements for bringing to an end the international regime in Tangier, the existence of which the Moroccan Government asserted, and the other Powers concerned tacitly accepted, was incompatible with the full independence of Morocco. A Protocol, recording arrangements between the Moroccan Government and the representatives on the Committee of Control, of the following countries: The U.S.A., Belgium, France, Great Britain, Italy, the Netherlands, Portugal and Spain was drawn up on 5 July 1956.

"The purpose of the Protocol was to provide for a transitional period which should precede the conclusion of negotiations for a settlement of the questions raised by the contemplated abrogation of the International Regime. . . ." Gutteridge, "The Dissolution of the International Regime in Tangier", XXXIII Brit. Yb. Int'l L. (1957) 296, 299.

On September 14, 1956, the Moroccan Government published a royal dahir (Rabat *Official Bulletin* No. 2290) affixing the Sultan's seal of approval on the Rabat Protocol of July 5, 1956, which after being submitted to the members of the Committee of Control for the International Zone of Tangier on June 1, 1956, was used by the Moroccan Government as the basis for installing a Governor in the Tangier Zone on June 10, 1956. Another royal dahir (Rabat *Official Bulletin* No. 2296) published on October 13, 1956, established the Tangier Zone as one of the 19 Provinces of the Moroccan State. As a result of these two dahirs the Governor of Tangier was brought under the direction of the Ministry of the Interior at Rabat. The American Consul General at Tangier (Cyr) to the Secretary of State (Dulles), Nov. 21, 1957, despatch No. 85, Department of State, file 771.00/11–2157.

At the invitation of His Majesty the Sultan of Morocco, an international Conference, held at Fedala and Tangier from October 8 to October 29, 1956, issued at its conclusion a final Declaration announcing the abolition of the international regime of the Tangier Zone. With the stated desire "to establish the principles of the independence of Morocco and the unity and integrity of its territory", the signatories declared the international regime abrogated and "in so far as they have participated therein, all acts, agreements, and conventions concerning the said régime"; and recognized in consequence "that His Sherifian Majesty has been reinstated in all His powers and capacities in this part of the Sherifian Empire, which shall henceforth be under His entire and sole sovereignty, and that this gives Him the unrestricted right to determine the future régime of Tangier".

As signatories of the Declaration, the Governments of Belgium, Spain, the United States, France, Italy, Morocco, the Netherlands, Portugal, and the United Kingdom also adopted on October 29, 1956, a Protocol, annexed to the Declaration, the provisions of which were designed to settle administrative and legal questions raised by the abrogation of the Special Statute of the Tangier Zone. XXXV *Bulletin*, Department of State, No. 909, Nov. 26, 1956, pp. 842–844.

The Royal Charter of Tangier, dated August 26, 1957, stated in its preface, "Our entire and complete sovereignty is today reestablished over the Province of Tangier. The special regime that existed in that Province has been abolished. We have thus accomplished—as we had always wished and wanted—the unification of our Kingdom, all parts of which will henceforth come under the same legislative, judicial, and executive authorities". The American Consul General at Tangier (Cyr) to the Secretary of State (Dulles), Sept. 6, 1957, despatch No. 36, encl. No. 2, MS. Department of State, file 771.00/9–657 (translation).

As has been noted, the International Regime of Tangier has been variously described as "a condominium of select States", "an international protectorate" and "un régime de souveraineté dispersée ou de souverainetés communes". Gutteridge, "The Dissolution of the International Regime in Tangier", XXXIII Brit. Yb. Int'l L. (1957) 296, 302.

MANDATED TERRITORIES
Establishment of League of Nations Mandates System
§ 34

"The Territory of South-West-Africa was one of the German overseas possessions in respect of which Germany, by Article 119 of the Treaty of Versailles, renounced all her rights and titles in favour of the Principal Allied and Associated Powers. When a decision was to be taken with regard to the future of these possessions as well as of other territories which, as a consequence of the war of 1914–1918, had ceased to be under the sovereignty of the States which formerly governed them, and which were inhabited by peoples not yet able to assume a full measure of self-government, two principles were considered to be of paramount importance: the principle of non-annexation and the principle that the well-being and development of such peoples form 'a sacred trust of civilization'.

"With a view to giving practical effect to these principles, an international régime, the Mandates System, was created by

Article 22 of the Covenant of the League of Nations. A 'tutelage' was to be established for these peoples, and this tutelage was to be entrusted to certain advanced nations and exercised by them 'as mandatories on behalf of the League'."

International Status of South-West Africa, Advisory Opinion, July 11, 1950, I.C.J. Reports (1950) 128, 131.

The basic treaty provisions relating to the League of Nations Mandates System are contained in article 22 of the Covenant of the League of Nations (Part I, Treaty of Peace between the Allied and Associated Powers and Germany, signed at Versailles, June 28, 1919, III Redmond, Treaties, etc. (1923) 3336, 3342–3343); in articles 118 and 119 of the Treaty of Versailles, *ibid.* 3329, 3390–3391; in article 16 of the Treaty of Peace with Turkey, signed at Lausanne, July 24, 1923 (28 LNTS 11, 22–23); and in the various Mandates, *i.e.*, Agreements concluded between the Council of the League of Nations and the respective States which acted as Mandatories ("Terms of League of Nations Mandates", republished by the United Nations, U.N. Doc. A/70, Oct. 1946).

Legal basis of Mandates System

Article 22 of the Covenant (cited *supra*) states:

Covenant, League of Nations, article 22

"To those colonies and territories which as a consequence of the late war have ceased to be under the sovereignty of the States which formerly governed them and which are inhabited by peoples not yet able to stand by themselves under the strenuous conditions of the modern world, there should be applied the principle that the well-being and development of such peoples form a sacred trust of civilisation and that securities for the performance of this trust should be embodied in this Covenant.

"The best method of giving practical effect to this principle is that the tutelage of such peoples should be entrusted to advanced nations who by reason of their resources, their experience or their geographical position can best undertake this responsibility, and who are willing to accept it, and that this tutelage should be exercised by them as Mandatories on behalf of the League.

"The character of the mandate must differ according to the stage of the development of the people, the geographical situation of the territory, its economic conditions and other similar circumstances.

"Certain communities formerly belonging to the Turkish Empire have reached a stage of development where their existence as independent nations can be provisionally recognised subject to the rendering of administrative advice and assistance by a Mandatory until such time as they are able to stand alone. The wishes of these communities must be a principal consideration in the selection of the Mandatory.

"Other peoples, especially those of Central Africa, are at such a stage that the Mandatory must be responsible for the administration of the territory under conditions which will guarantee freedom of conscience and religion, subject only to the maintenance of public order and morals, the prohibition of abuses such as the slave trade, the arms traffic and the liquor traffic, and the prevention of the establishment of fortifications or military and naval bases and of military training of the natives for other than police purposes and the defence of territory, and will also secure equal opportunities for the trade and commerce of other Members of the League.

"There are territories, such as South-West Africa and certain of the South Pacific Islands, which, owing to the sparseness of their population, or their small size, or their remoteness from the centres of civilisation, or their geographical contiguity to the territory of the Mandatory, and other circumstances, can be best administered under the laws of the Mandatory as integral portions of its territory, subject to the safeguards above mentioned in the interests of the indigenous population.

"In every case of mandate, the Mandatory shall render to the Council an annual report in reference to the territory committed to its charge.

"The degree of authority, control, or administration to be exercised by the Mandatory shall, if not previously agreed upon by the Members of the League, be explicitly defined in each case by the Council.

"A permanent Commission shall be constituted to receive and examine the annual reports of the Mandatories and to advise the Council on all matters relating to the observance of the mandates."

Articles 118 and 119 of the Treaty of Versailles (cited *supra*), whereby Germany renounced sovereignty to her oversea possessions, read:

"ARTICLE 118.

Renunciation of German Oversea Possessions: articles 118 and 119

"In territory outside her European frontiers as fixed by the present Treaty, Germany renounces all rights, titles and privileges whatever in or over territory which belonged to her or to her allies, and all rights, titles and privileges whatever their origin which she held as against the Allied and Associated Powers.

"Germany hereby undertakes to recognise and to conform to the measures which may be taken now or in the future by the Principal Allied and Associated Powers, in agreement where necessary with third Powers, in order to carry the above stipulation into effect.

"In particular Germany declares her acceptance of the following Articles relating to certain special subjects.

.   .   .   .

"ARTICLE 119.

"Germany renounces in favour of the Principal Allied and Associated Powers all her rights and titles over her oversea possessions."

The following exposition of the legal situation created by the provisions of the Treaty of Versailles was presented in 1950 to the International Court of Justice by Ivan Kerno, as representative of the Secretary-General of the United Nations:

"1. Articles 118 and 119 of the Treaty of Versailles represent a *complete renunciation on the part of Germany* of all her rights and titles to her oversea possessions. It is therefore unnecessary for us to consider the status of the Territory of South-West Africa prior to World War I. That it was under the sovereignty of Germany has not been questioned and is inferentially recognized in the opening paragraph of Article 22 of the Covenant. In the early years of the war, the Territory was occupied by troops from the Union of South Africa and it was administered as an occupied territory until the end of the hostilities. By Article 118 of the Versailles Treaty, Germany undertook to recognize and to conform to the measures which might be taken by the Principal Allied and Associated Powers, in agreement where necessary with third Powers, to carry into effect the renunciation by Germany of its rights, titles and privileges.

"2. *The renunciation by Germany was in favour of the Principal Allied and Associated Powers*, that is the United States of America, the British Empire, France, Italy and Japan. It will be noted that the renunciation was not in favour of the League of Nations, nor of the Union of South Africa.

"It will be recalled that while the United States never ratified the Treaty of Versailles, it reserved for itself in a separate treaty, which it concluded with Germany in Berlin in 1921, all the rights and advantages stipulated in the Treaty of Versailles for the Principal Allied and Associated Powers, including those in respect of the former German colonies. The Treaty of Berlin also stipulated that the United States should not be bound by the provisions of the Treaty of Versailles relating to the Covenant of the League of Nations or by any action taken by the League of Nations, unless the United States should expressly give its assent to such action.

"Notwithstanding this reservation in the Treaty of Berlin, there are no grounds for the view that so far as the United States is concerned, its failure to ratify the Treaty of Versailles has invalidated or weakened in any way the dispositions made in the creation and the operation of the Mandates System. The point is moreover made quite clear in the written statement submitted to the Court by the Government of the United States in the present case.

"3. The Covenant of the League of Nations was an integral part of the Treaty of Versailles. Articles 118 and 119 of the Treaty must therefore be read and understood in connexion with Article 22 of the Covenant."

International Status of South-West Africa, Pleadings, Oral Arguments, Documents, pp. 188–189 (I.C.J. 1950).

An account of the special position of the United States with respect to the Mandates System is set forth in the Written Statement of the

Special position of U.S.

United States to the International Court of Justice in the advisory proceeding, *International Status of South-West Africa*, as follows:

"The United States did not ratify the Treaty of Versailles. However, it acquiesced in the establishment of the mandate system, including the approval of mandate instruments. Article I of the separate treaty which the United States subsequently concluded with Germany reads:

" 'Germany undertakes to accord to the United States, and the United States shall have and enjoy, all the rights, privileges, indemnities, reparations or advantages specified in the aforesaid Joint Resolution of the Congress of the United States of July 2, 1921, including all the rights and advantages stipulated for the benefit of the United States in the Treaty of Versailles which the United States shall fully enjoy notwithstanding the fact that such Treaty has not been ratified by the United States.' Article I of the Treaty of Berlin, signed August 25, 1921, ratifications exchanged November 11, 1921.

"So far as the United States is concerned, therefore, its failure to ratify the Treaty of Versailles should not be considered to invalidate or weaken the dispositions made in the creation and operation of the mandate system."

International Status of South-West Africa, Pleadings, Oral Arguments, Documents, p. 93 (I.C.J. 1950).

"The United States never formally consented to the administration of the Territory of South West Africa under mandate to the Union of South Africa. The acquiescence of this Government to the situation may probably be presumed, since no objection apparently was made to the mandate, even at the time of the organization of the United Nations when arrangements were made for replacement of the Mandatory System by the United Nations Trusteeship System. Nevertheless, the United States did acquire definite treaty rights with respect to the Territory of South West Africa, which, it is believed, have not fallen into desuetude." Marcia M. Fleming, Office of the Legal Adviser, Department of State, "Note on the Legal Rights of the United States of America with respect to the Territory of South West Africa", memorandum, Jan. 13, 1956, MS. Department of State, file 745x.022/1–1356.

Article 16 of the Treaty of Lausanne (cited *supra*) provides:

Renunciation of Turkish Territories: article 16, Treaty of Lausanne

"Turkey hereby renounces all rights and title whatsoever over or respecting the territories situated outside the frontiers laid down in the present Treaty and the islands other than those over which her sovereignty is recognised by the said Treaty, the future of these territories and islands being settled or to be settled by the parties concerned.

"The provisions of the present Article do not prejudice any special arrangements arising from neighbourly relations which have been or may be concluded between Turkey and any limitrophe countries."

In its Advisory Opinion of July 11, 1950 (*International Status of South-West Africa*), the International Court of Justice observed that the Mandates System created by article 22 of the Covenant of the League of Nations was a "new international institution." (I.C.J. Reports (1950) 132.) See also, Separate Opinion of Judge Sir Arnold McNair, *ibid.* 150–155, *passim.* As pointed out by Judge Sir Hersch Lauterpacht, the basic idea of the League Mandates System was the same as that of the International Trusteeship System of the United Nations. I Lauterpacht, *Oppenheim's International Law* (8th ed., 1955) § 94c. See also, Brierly, *The Law of Nations* (5th ed., 1955) 161–167; and Kelsen, *The Law of the United Nations* (1951) 566. A new
international
institution

Paragraph 3 of the Resolution on Mandates adopted by the Assembly of the League of Nations on April 18, 1946, "notes that Chapters XI, XII and XIII of the Charter of the United Nations embody principles corresponding to those declared in Article 22 of the Covenant of the League . . ." League of Nations Off. J., Spec. Supp. No. 194, annex 24(c) (1946), p. 254.

Article 77 of chapter XII of the United Nations Charter specifically contemplated that the mandated territories would be placed under the International Trusteeship System. See *Report to the President on the Results of the San Francisco Conference* (1945) 126–127, 133–136, 216; Bunche, "Trusteeship and Non-Self-Governing Territories in the Charter of the United Nations", XIII *Bulletin*, Department of State, No. 340, Dec. 30, 1945, pp. 1037–39, 1043–44; and *Postwar Foreign Policy Preparation 1939–1945*, (1949), appendices 39, 55, 63, 64. In fact, all of the mandated territories, except for those which became independent, and for South-West Africa, were transferred to the Trusteeship System. See Armstrong and Cargo, "The Inauguration of the Trusteeship System of the United Nations," XVI *Bulletin*, Department of State, No. 403, Mar. 23, 1947, pp. 511, 514–15; "Review of the United Nations Charter," S. Doc. 164, 83d Cong., 2d sess. (1955), pp. 261–264; Sayre, "Legal Problems Arising from the United Nations Trusteeship System," 42 Am. J. Int'l L. (1948) 263–268; Aufricht, *Guide to League of Nations Publications* (1951) 154–155; and Sady, *The United Nations and Dependent Peoples* (The Brookings Institution, 1956), chapter I. Thus, an understanding of the Mandates System is essential to an understanding of the International Trusteeship System.

In the last study of the League of Nations on the subject, it is stated that "the mandates system was an innovation in the fields of international law and of colonial policy" but that, "underlying this institution, are ideas which had for a long time been taking shape in the minds of idealists, statesmen and experts in colonial matters and in international law and which had been disseminated by philan- Origin of
concept thropic and progressive circles in different countries." This study further observes that it was not "until the institution of the mandates system of the League of Nations" that the "moral principles" of "humanitarian sentiment" were "in the case of some territories at least, transformed into principles of international law." League of Nations, *The Mandates System, Origin—Principles—Application* (1945.VI.A.1) 7, 13. See also, Wright, *Mandates under the League of Nations* (1930), chapter I; Bentwich, *The Mandates System* (1930), chapter I; and Hall, *Mandates, Dependencies and Trusteeship* (1948) 91–112.

Of the statesmen who participated in the Paris Peace Conference of 1919, the principal exponents of the concept of the new international institution were President Wilson of the United States and General Smuts of the Union of South Africa.

In an address to a Joint Session of the United States Congress on January 8, 1918, President Wilson proposed "Fourteen Points" for a program of world peace. President Wilson's Fifth and Twelfth Points pertained specifically to the disposition of the territories which were placed under the Mandates System. His Fifth Point read:

President Wilson's Fourteen Points

Fifth Point

> "V. A free, open-minded, and absolutely impartial adjustment of all colonial claims, based upon a strict observance of the principle that in determining all such questions of sovereignty the interests of the populations concerned must have equal weight with the equitable claims of the government whose title is to be determined."

> 1918 For. Rel., vol. I, supp. I, The World War, pp. 12, 15.

A subsequent interpretation of the Fifth Point, approved by President Wilson, stated:

> "It would seem as if the principle involved in this proposition is that a colonial power acts not as owner of its colonies, but as trustee for the natives and for the interests of the society of nations, that the terms on which the colonial administration is conducted are a matter of international concern and may legitimately be the subject of international inquiry, and that the peace conference may, therefore, write a code of colonial conduct binding upon [all] colonial powers." *Ibid.*, pp. 407, 421.

Twelfth Point

President Wilson's Twelfth Point read:

> "XII. The Turkish portions of the present Ottoman Empire should be assured a secure sovereignty, but the other nationalities which are now under Turkish rule should be assured an undoubted security of life and an absolutely unmolested opportunity of autonomous development, and the Dardanelles should be permanently opened as a free passage to the ships and commerce of all nations under international guarantees."

> *Ibid.*, p. 16.

A subsequent interpretation of the Twelfth Point, approved by President Wilson, stated:

"Syria has already been alloted to France by agreement with Great Britain.

"Great Britain is clearly the best mandatory for Palestine, Mesopotamia and Arabia.

"A general code of guarantees binding upon all mandatories in Asia Minor should be written into the treaty of peace.

"This should contain provisions for minorities and the 'open door'. The trunk railroad lines should be internationalized." *Ibid.*, pp. 412, 421.

Both the German request to President Wilson, presented October 6, 1918, and the Turkish request to President Wilson, presented October 14, 1918, for an armistice and peace negotiations, accepted as a basis for the negotiations the President's program laid down in his message to Congress of January 8, 1918. *Ibid.*, pp. 337–338, 359–360.

In an address to the Congress on February 11, 1918, President Wilson stated : "Peoples are not to be handed about from one sovereignty to another by an international conference or an understanding between rivals and antagonists. National aspirations must be respected ; peoples may now be dominated and governed only by their own consent. 'Self-determination' is not a mere phrase. It is an imperative principle of action, which statesmen will henceforth ignore at their peril." *Ibid.*, p. 110. For similar views with respect to the right of self-determination, see the address of the British Prime Minister, Lloyd George, before the Trade Union Conference at London, January 5, 1918, *ibid.*, p. 4 and especially pp. 7, 9, and 10. Thus, "Arabia, Armenia, Mesopotamia, Syria and Palestine are, in our judgment, entitled to a recognition of their separate national conditions" and, with regard to the German colonies, the "principle of national self-determination is, therefore, as applicable in their cases as in those of the occupied European territories." *Ibid.*, p. 10.

At the Paris Peace Conference of 1919 which formulated the Covenant of the League of Nations, President Wilson's further explanation of his concept of the Mandates System was reported as follows:

". . . in order that the field of discussion should be defined as clearly as possible perhaps it would be better to begin with a clear statement of what was the mind of those who proposed a trusteeship by the League of Nations through the appointment of mandatories. The basis of this idea was the feeling which had sprung up all over the world against further annexation. Yet, if the Colonies were not to be returned to Germany (as all were agreed), some other basis must be found to develop them and to take care of the inhabitants of these backward territories. It was with this object that the idea of administration through mandatories acting on behalf of the League of Nations arose. . . .

"This he assumed to be the principle: it was not intended to exploit any people; it was not intended to exercise arbitrary sovereignty over any people.

.   .   .   .

"It was in the mind of many people that the mandatory power might be subject to constant irritation and constant interference by the League of Nations. In his opinion, that would not be so, as long as the mandatory performed his duties satisfactorily. In

Paris Peace Conference, 1919: President Wilson's views

so far as the administration by the mandatory power became a financial burden, it was clearly proper that the League of Nations should bear a proportion of the expense. The fundamental idea would be that the world was acting as trustee through a mandatory, and would be in charge of the whole administration until the day when the true wishes of the inhabitants could be ascertained. . . ."

1919 For. Rel., vol. III, Paris Peace Conference (1946), pp. 740–741. See also, pp. 719–728, 758–771, 785–798 for discussion of the Mandates System.

In the discussions pertaining to territories under Turkish sovereignty, President Wilson expressed the following views:

". . . One of the fundamental principles to which the United States of America adhered was the consent of the governed. This was ingrained in the United States of America thought. Hence, the only idea from the United States of America point of view was as to whether France would be agreeable to the Syrians. The same applied as to whether Great Britain would be agreeable to the inhabitants of Mesopotamia. It might not be his business, but if the question was made his business, owing to the fact that it was brought before the Conference, the only way to deal with it was to discover the desires of the population of these regions. He recalled that, in the Council of Ten, Resolutions had been adopted in regard to mandatories, and they contained a very carefully thought out graduation of different states of mandate according to the civilisation of the peoples concerned. One of the elements in those mandates was the desire of the people over whom the mandate was to be exercised. . . ."

1919 For. Rel., vol. V, Paris Peace Conference (1946), p. 9.

General Smuts' and others' views

In the final League of Nations study of the Mandates System, there appears the following account of the Paris Peace Conference of 1919:

"2. Genesis of the Mandates System

"On taking up the question of the fate of the German colonies and of the territories of the Ottoman Empire inhabited by non-Turkish populations, the Peace Conference, in 1919, found itself confronted with a peculiarly complex problem. A medley of factors of different kinds had to be taken into account: the actual situation resulting from the war, the claims of Allied countries and the agreements reached between them, the interests of the inhabitants of the territories in question, the trends of public opinion, the principles formulated by the Governments which were to serve as criteria for the general peace settlement and, finally, the differing degrees of civilisation which had been attained by the peoples inhabiting these territories and which rendered a uniform solution impossible.

"The German colonies had been occupied during the war by the forces of the Allied countries and some of the latter, with the support of their public opinion, had manifested an intention to annex one or other of the colonies in question (in particular those situated in the Pacific), adducing as a reason either the sacrifices made during the war, or motives of national security, or again humanitarian considerations. Certain official circles were, however, less inclined to favour an extension of the national colonial domain. There was, however, general agreement that the German colonies could not be allowed to revert to their former sovereignty. With regard to those territories of the former Ottoman Empire the fate of which had to be settled, they too had been occupied by the Allied armies. Subject to certain reservations and without any precise definition of frontiers, negotiations conducted in 1915 between British representatives and the Emir of Mecca had envisaged the independence of the Arab countries. On the other hand, a Franco-British agreement concluded in May 1916 had contemplated a special régime for Palestine and the Holy Places. Finally, in the Balfour Declaration of November 2nd, 1917, the British Government had undertaken to 'view with favour the establishment in Palestine of a national home for the Jewish People', without prejudice to the 'civil and religious rights of existing non-Jewish communities in Palestine'. This Declaration had been approved by the American, French and Italian Governments.

"The principle that the peace settlement should not be accompanied by any annexation and that it should be based on the right of nations to self-determination had been proclaimed towards the end of the war by the leaders of the Russian Revolution and also found expression in the declarations of Allied statesmen. The principle of 'non-annexation', however, envisaged only the negative aspect of the problem, while the principle of self-determination could scarcely be applied automatically to peoples which had not yet attained an adequate degree of political maturity, and still less to populations devoid of any real national consciousness. In respect of such peoples, therefore, these principles had to be adapted to meet different requirements.

.   .   .   .

"In the plan for a League of Nations published by General Smuts in December 1918, on the eve of the Conference of Peace, we find for the first time the broad outlines of an international mandates system. [General Smuts: *The League of Nations, a Practical Suggestion*. London, 1918.] The author described in twenty-one points, each accompanied by a brief commentary, the main characteristics of what, in his view, should be the future international organisation. The first nine points related to the fate of countries which had belonged to the European or Near-Eastern Empires which had collapsed. In respect of these territories, General Smuts proposed that the League should be regarded as 'the reversionary in the most general sense and as clothed with the right of ultimate disposal in accordance with the fundamental principles. Reversion to the League of Nations should be substituted for any policy of national annexation.' The government of each of these countries should be established in accordance with the principle of self-determination. Nevertheless, the conditions prevailing in these territories varied considerably from one country to another and for some of them—General Smuts continues—'it will probably be found that they are as yet deficient in the qualities of Statehood and that, whereas they are perhaps capable of internal autonomy, they will in one degree or another require the guiding hand of some external authority to steady their administration. . . . In all these cases the peoples concerned are perhaps sufficiently homogeneous and developed to govern themselves subject to some degree of external assistance and control.' The author, however, foresees that there may be other cases where, 'owing chiefly to the heterogeneous character of the population and their incapacity of administrative co-operation, autonomy in any real sense would be out of the question and the administration would have to be undertaken to a very large extent by some external authority. This would be the case, at any rate for some time to come, in Palestine . . .' 'No State should—affirms General Smuts—make use of the helpless or weak condition of any of these territories in order to exploit them for its own purposes.' The foregoing considerations are summarised by General Smuts in the following recommendation:

"(4) That any authority, control, or administration which may be necessary in respect of these territories and peoples, other than their own self-determined autonomy, shall be the exclusive function of and shall be vested in the League of Nations and *exercised by or on behalf of it.*

.   .   .   .

"At the time of the opening of the Peace Conference, a congress of allied associations in favour of a League of Nations which was held in Paris (January 25th–30th, 1919) adopted a resolution asking that the Council of the League of Nations should be entrusted with 'the moral guardianship of uncivilised races' and made responsible for the conclusion and execution of the international conventions 'necessary for the protection and progress of these nations'. A resolution to the same effect was adopted by an international socialist conference at Berne on February 6th, 1919.

"The foregoing constitutes a brief summary of the main facts, of the rights and interests involved, of the proposals put forward and of the trends of public opinion, which had to be reckoned with in working out the new status of the wide regions of Asia, Africa and Oceania which had formerly belonged to the Central Empires. The only system which appeared to take account of all the factors mentioned was the mandates system. This system seemed calculated to safeguard the interests both of the natives and of those countries which had asserted special claims and, in addition, the interests of the international community in general. It also enabled the highest ideals of colonial doctrine and of advanced public opinion in civilised countries to be put into practice.

"President Wilson, much struck with General Smuts' idea, embodied the international mandates system in his first two drafts of the Covenant of the League of Nations, which were worked out in Paris in January 1919, extending it to include the German colonies. The British Delegation, for its part, presented a 'Draft Convention on Mandates', accompanied by a number of annexed declarations. In this plan, the principles to be applied by the mandatory administration were defined and a distinction drawn between 'vested territories' and 'assisted States'. Furthermore, the British plan envisaged the creation of a Commission or of Commissions whose duty would be to assist the League of Nations in its supervision of the mandatory States, to study the reports on their administration of the mandates and to submit to the Council such recommendations as they might consider expedient. The negotiations in regard to these matters which were conducted towards the end of January 1919 culminated on January 30th in the adoption—not without some difficulty—by the Council of Ten of a resolution, the text of which would appear, like the original plan, to have been due to General Smuts. After undergoing some modifications—in particular, the addition of the last two paragraphs concerning the powers of the Council and the creation of a Mandates Commission—this resolution of January 30th was embodied in the text of the Covenant of the League of Nations, of which it then formed Article 19. This text was unanimously adopted by the Conference on February 13th, 1919. After having once more been slightly amended—more particularly by the addition of the words 'and who are willing to accept it' in the second paragraph (regarding the nations to whom the tutelage of the territories in question might be entrusted)—Article 19 of the Covenant of February 13th became Article 22 of the final text of the Covenant, as adopted on April 25th, 1919.

"As David Hunter Miller, a member of the American Delegation to the Peace Conference, observes: '. . . the world took a very long step forward when Article 22 of the Covenant came into force'. [David Hunter Miller: *The Drafting of the Covenant*, I, page 105.]"

League of Nations, *The Mandates System, Origin—Principles—Application* (1945.VI.A.1) 13–18. See also, statement by Ivan Kerno, representative of the Secretary-General of the United Nations, to the International Court of Justice on May 16, 1950, *International Status of South-West Africa*, Pleadings, Oral Arguments, Documents, pp. 189–190 (I.C.J. 1950).

"Apart from what the Covenant and the Mandate themselves said about the purpose and scope of the system, it is well for us to remember, if only to recall and bear in mind the atmosphere and ideas out of which the system of Mandates was born, certain declarations and statements made by the leaders of some of the Principal Allied and Associated Powers who had a determining voice in its formulation. I should like to refer to only a few of them which throw particular light on the objectives which the framers of the system had in view.

"In his Declaration of 1917 on the subject of German Colonies, Lord Belfour [Balfour] stated that they should be 'internationalised'—an important and significant term. Mr. Lloyd George, the then British Prime Minister, speaking of the system in 1918, stated that the general principle of national self-determination was as applicable in the case of the German Colonies as in those of occupied European territories. In another statement, he went further and declared that the objective of the system was self-government. . . .

Then there are the Fourteen Points of President Wilson. Point Five reads as follows:—

> " 'A free, open-minded and absolutely impartial adjustment of all Colonial claims, based upon a strict observance of the principle that, in determining all such questions of sovereignty, the interests of the populations concerned must have equal weight with the equitable claims of the Government whose title is to be determined.'

"Referring to the system of Mandates in an address delivered in 1919, President Wilson emphasised that the basis of the system was the feeling which had sprung up all over the world against further annexations. 'If the process of annexation went on', the President continued, 'the League of Nations would be discredited from the beginning'.

"Finally, here is what Field Marshal Smuts himself said in 1918 about the duties of the Mandatory :—

> 'The Mandatory state should look upon its position as a great trust and honour, not as an office of profit or a position of private advantage for it or its nationals. And in case of any flagrant and prolonged abuse of this trust the population concerned should be able to appeal for redress to the League, who should in a proper case assert its authority to the full, even to the extent of removing the mandate, and entrusting it to some other state, if necessary.'

"Referring to the principle underlying the system, the same statesman, who was one of the principal architects of it, stated :—

> 'Reversion to the League of Nations should be the substitute for any policy of national annexation.'

"I have ventured to take the Committee through the above references and citations in order to show what the governing instruments themselves conveyed by way of duties and obligations and the intentions and purposes of those principally responsible for framing them. 'Promote to the utmost the material and moral well-being and the social progress of the inhabitants of the territory' is what the Mandate says, among other things. Submit annual reports regarding such measures, was another injunction. The Mandate was to be regarded as a sacred trust and was made subject to 'safeguards'—words used by the Covenant 'in the interests of the indigenous population'. The intention and purpose was to internationalise instead of annex, to make the principle of self-determination applicable, to keep in view the goal of self-government and, in case of abuse of the trust and appeal for redress, to exercise international authority to the full, even to the extent of removing the mandate." Statement of Nawab Ali Yavar Jung, representative of India, in Committee IV of the United Nations General Assembly, on Nov. 24, 1960. (Verbatim text, issued by the Permanent Mission of India to the United Nations, pp. 3–5.)

The territories allocated to the Mandates System consisted of three formerly under Turkish sovereignty and seven former German oversea possessions.   Following is an account of the decisions as to their allocation:

"The 'A' mandates (art. 22, par. 4) were allocated at a meeting of the Supreme Council held at San Remo, Italy, on April 25, 1920 and attended by the representatives of the British Empire, France, Italy, Japan, and the United States (in the capacity of an observer).   This decision read in part (file 763.72119/9869, document I.C.P. 106):

" '(a) To accept the terms of the Mandates Article as given below with reference to Palestine, on the understanding that there was inserted in the *procès-verbal* an undertaking by the Mandatory Power that this would not involve the surrender of the rights hitherto enjoyed by the non-Jewish communities in Palestine; this undertaking not to refer to the question of the religious protectorate of France, which had been settled earlier in the previous afternoon by the undertaking given by the French Government that they recognized this protectorate as being at an end.

.   .   .   .

" '(c) [Translation] The mandatories chosen by the Principal Allied Powers are: France for Syria, and Great Britain for Mesopotamia and Palestine.'

.   .   .   .

"The colonies renounced by Germany in favor of the Principal Allied and Associated Powers under article 119 of the Treaty of Versailles were administered under 'B' and 'C' mandates as described in paragraphs 5 and 6 of article 22.   On May 7, 1919 the territories referred to were allocated to mandatories for administration under the terms of article 22 by a decision of the representatives of the United States, France, Great Britain, and Italy. The decision read (file 180.03401/149):

" '(1) Togoland and Cameroons. France and Great Britain shall make a joint recommendation to the League of Nations as to their future.

" 'German East Africa.   The mandate shall be held by Great Britain.

" 'German South West Africa.   The mandate shall be held by the Union of South Africa.

" 'The German Samoan Islands.   The mandate shall be held by New Zealand.

" 'The Other German Pacific Possessions South of the Equator excluding the German Samoan Islands and Nauru, the mandate shall be held by Australia.

" 'Nauru.   The mandate shall be given to the British Empire.

" 'German Islands North of the Equator.   The mandate shall be held by Japan.'

"Certain changes in this rough allocation were made.

"France and Great Britain by a declaration of July 10, 1919 arranged to delimit frontiers in the Cameroons and Togoland eastward and westward respectively for mandatory administration.

"Owing to their stability and proximity to the Belgian Congo, the native kingdoms of Ruanda and Urundi were detached from the former German East Africa, which under British mandate was named Tanganyika. The mandate of the two kingdoms was assigned to Belgium.

"The deposits at Nauru had been exploited by a German corporation, the Pacific Phosphate Company, which was taken over by the British, Australian, and New Zealand Governments under an agreement of July 2, 1919. In virtue of that agreement the British Empire's mandate was assigned to Australia for 5-year periods."

1919 For. Rel., vol. XIII, Paris Peace Conference (1947), pp. 94, 97–98. Also under title *The Treaty of Versailles and After: Annotations of the Text of the Treaty* (1947), pp. 94, 97–98 (prepared by Denys P. Myers, Division of International Organization Affairs, Department of State).

Confirmation of Mandates   The role of the Council of the League of Nations was described as follows by Ivan Kerno, representative of the Secretary-General of the United Nations, in his statement of May 16, 1950, to the International Court of Justice:

"4. Paragraph 8 of Article 22 prescribed that the degree of authority, control or administration to be exercised by the mandatory would, if not previously agreed upon by the Members of the League, be explicitly defined in each case by the Council, but no provision was made regarding the authority which would appoint the mandatory.

"Basing himself on the intentions of the authors of the Covenant, on the text of Articles 118 and 119 of the Treaty of Versailles, Mr. Hymans, Rapporteur of the Council of the League, concluded, and the Council agreed, that the right to appoint mandatory Powers should belong to the Principal Allied Powers and that 'the legal title held by a mandatory Power must therefore be a double one, one conferred by the Principal Powers and the other by the League of Nations'. [See League of Nations, *Responsibilities of the League arising out of Article 22 (Mandates).*—Report by the Council to the Assembly (20/48/161), page 2 (Folder 1), and Annex 4, Report presented by the Belgian representative, Mr. Hymans, and adopted by the Council of the League of Nations meeting at San Sebastian, 5 August, 1920, *id.*, page 14.]

.   .   .   .

"5. While agreeing that the mandatory Powers must, in accordance with the Treaty of Versailles, be selected by the Principal Allied and Associated Powers, the Council of the League held that it was in the last resort itself responsible for approving and, if necessary, for drawing up the terms of the mandates. It decided, however, that it was prepared to receive the proposals of any of its Members with regard to the terms of mandates provided these proposals were made within a reasonable time."

International Status of South-West Africa, Pleadings, Oral Arguments, Documents, pp. 190–191 (I.C.J. 1950).

In the Written Statement of the United States submitted to the International Court of Justice in the advisory proceeding, *International Status of South-West Africa*, there appears the following account:

"3. *Action by the League Council on mandates.*

"On August 5, 1920, the Council of the League of Nations, meeting at San Sebastian, heard and unanimously adopted a report submitted by the representative of Belgium, Mr. Hymans, entitled 'The Appeal of the Council to the Principal Allied and Associated Powers to Define the Mandates to be Conferred under Article 22 of the Covenant.' League of Nations Council P.V. 20/29/14 (8th sess., San Sebastian, July 31–August 5, 1920) 39–43, 63, 176–191; League of Nations Official Journal No. 6 (September, 1920), 313, 317, 334–351. Among the measures which the report found necessary to 'ensure the observance of Article 22 and to apply the Mandatory system' was the following:

" '(c) The Mandatory Powers chosen must be invested with the authority and the necessary powers for administering territories by means of an instrument which will legally bind them.' League of Nations Council P.V. 20/29/14 (8th sess., San Sebastion, July 31–August 5, 1920), 179.

Continuing to review steps taken, the report found as to the decision of the Principal Allied and Associated Powers of May 5, 1919 (as supplemented by a decision of August 7, 1919):

'This agreement has not been expressed in a form implying a legal obligation, although the territories in question are actually being administered by the Mandatory Powers to whom it was intended to entrust them.' *Ibid.*

The report then went on to explain the necessity for agreement by both the Principal Allied and Associated Powers and the Council in completing the legal investiture of the mandatory with the right to administer the mandate. [The report by Mr. Hymans read, in part:

"I.—*Allocation of the mandates and legal title of the mandatories*

"There is one point on which there seems to be no divergency of opinion, namely, that the right to allocate the mandates—that is to say, to appoint the mandatory Powers and to determine the territories over which they shall exercise authority—belongs to the Principal Allied and Associated Powers. Article 22 of the Covenant makes no provision regarding the authority which shall appoint the mandatories; but Article 119 of the Treaty of Versailles transfers the sovereignty over the former German overseas possessions to the Principal Allied and Associated Powers, and Article 118 expressly stipulates that measures shall be taken by the Principal Allied and Associated Powers, in agreement, where necessary, with third Powers, in order to carry into effect the full consequences of the provision by which Germany renounces her rights outside Europe. . . . The Allied Powers have adopted the same interpretation of Article 22 of the Covenant by inserting articles in the Treaty of Peace of Saint-Germain dated September 10, 1919, with Austria, and in the draft treaty with Turkey, which stipulate expressly that the right to appoint mandatory Powers shall belong to the Principal Allied Powers. There can be no question, moreover, as to the intentions of the authors of the Covenant with regard to this question.

"It is not enough, however, that the mandatory Powers should be appointed; it is important that they should also possess a *legal title*—a mere matter of form, perhaps, but one which should be settled, and the consideration of which will help towards a clear understanding of the conception of mandates.

"It must not be forgotten that, although the mandatory Power is appointed by the Principal Powers, it will govern as a mandatory and in the name of the League of Nations.

"It logically follows that the legal title held by the mandatory Power must be a double one: one conferred by the Principal Powers, and the other conferred by the League of Nations. The procedure should, in fact, be the following:—

"1. The Principal Allied and Associated Powers confer a mandate on one of their number or on a third Power.

"2. The Principal Powers officially notify the Council of the League of Nations that a certain Power has been appointed mandatory for such a certain defined territory.

"3. The Council of the League of Nations takes official cognizance of the appointment of the mandatory Power, and informs the latter that it [the Council] considers it as invested with the mandate, and at the same time notifies it of the terms of the mandate, after ascertaining whether they are in accordance with the provisions of the Covenant." *Id.*, at 181.

The report contained the following comment concerning the relationship of responsibility as between the League and the mandatory:

"III.—*The extent of the League's right of control.*

.   .   .   .

"The practical and positive question appears to me to be the following: What will be the responsibility of the mandatory Power before the League of Nations, or in other words, in what direction will the League's right of control be exercised: Is the Council to content itself with ascertaining that the mandatory Power has remained within the limits of the powers which were conferred upon it, or is it to ascertain also whether the mandatory

Power has made a good use of these powers, and whether its administration has conformed to the interests of the native population?

"It appears to me that the wider interpretation should be adopted. Paragraphs 1 and 2 of Article 22 have indicated the spirit which should inspire those who are entrusted with administering peoples not yet capable of governing themselves, and have determined that this tutelage should be exercised by the States in question as mandatories and in the name of the League. The annual report stipulated for in Article 7 should certainly include a statement as to the whole moral and material situation of the peoples under the mandate. It is clear, therefore, that the Council also should examine the question of the whole administration. In this matter the Council will obviously have to display extreme prudence, so that the exercise of its rights of control should not provoke any justifiable complaints, and thus increase the difficulties of the task undertaken by the mandatory Power." *Id.*, at 187.]

"After adopting Mr. Hymans' report, the League Council passed the following resolutions:

" 'I. The Council decides to request the Principal Powers to be so good as to (a) name the Powers to whom they have decided to allocate the Mandates provided for in Article 22; (b) to inform it as to the frontiers of the territories to come under these Mandates; (c) to communicate to it the terms and the conditions of the mandates that they propose should be adopted by the Council from [*sic*] following the prescriptions of Article 22.

" 'II. The Council will take cognizance of the mandatory Power appointed and will examine the draft mandates communicated to it, in order to ascertain that they conform to the prescriptions of Article 22 of the Covenant.

" 'III. The Council will notify to each Power appointed that it is invested with the mandate, and will, at the same time, communicate to it the terms and conditions.

" 'IV. The Council instructs the Secretary-General, following the recommendations set forth in this report, to prepare a draft scheme for the organization of the Commission of Control provided for by Article 22, para. 9.' *Id.* at 191.

"At a meeting of the Council of the League at Brussels, October 28, 1920, a further report by Mr. Hymans, entitled 'Mandates', was read and unanimously adopted. League of Nations Council P.V.20/29/16 (10th sess., 1920), 21–27, 59, 189–197; League of Nations *Official Journal* No. 8 (1920), 28, 30–33. Mr. Hymans' report noted that agreement had still not been reached on the terms of the mandates and stated unequivocally the power and duty of the Council to intervene:

" 'Beyond doubt, it is in every way desirable that the Principal Powers should be able to arrive at a complete understanding and to submit agreements to the League. Failing this very desirable agreement, however, the Covenant provides for the intervention of the Council with a view to determining the degree of authority, of control or of administration to be exercised by the mandatories.

" 'The Council, whose duty is to ensure the carrying out of the Covenant, will, without doubt, have to inform the Assembly as to the present position with regard to this matter. We sincerely hope, therefore, that before the end of the Assembly the Principal Powers will have succeeded in settling by common agreement the terms of the mandates which they wish to submit to the Council. The latter would certainly be disposed to reserve its report upon this question until the end of the Assembly meeting at Geneva, so as to allow the Powers adequate time for the purpose.'

"By letter of October 27, 1920, this view was communicated by the League Council to the Principal Allied Powers. The entire matter was also fully reported by the Council to the League Assembly. See II, *League of Nations Official Records*, Assembly (1st sess., 1920, Sixth Committee), 371 *et seq.*, Annex 17 *b*. On December 1, 1920, agreement still not having been reached, the letter of October 27 was followed up by the following telegram:

" 'In the name of the Council of League of Nations I have the honour to refer to letters which Council addressed to you on the subject of mandates on August 5th and October 27th, 1920 *Stop* In order to give to Principal Allied Powers the necessary time to complete their negotiations regarding terms and conditions of the mandates which they decide to propose should be adopted by the Council the Council had arranged not to present this report to the Assembly on this subject until the last days of the meeting *Stop* This Council has received no draft mandate up to the present and in view of the strong public feeling on the subject it ventures to urge the extreme importance of a quick settlement *Stop* Anxious as it is to see the mandates drafted by previous agreement between the Principal Allied Powers, the Council cannot indefinitely postpone the fulfillment of the duties which will fall to it if such agreement is not reached *Stop* It is to be anticipated that the Assembly will remind the Council of the clause in the Covenant which declares that the degree of authority control or administration to be exercised by the Mandatory shall if not previously agreed upon be determined by the Council *Stop* The Council therefore most earnestly begs that any draft mandates upon which agreement may have been reached by the Principal Allied Powers should be communicated to it at a sufficiently early date to enable the Council to give all necessary information to the Assembly before the end of the present meeting *Stop* HYMANS President of the Assembly.' League of Nations Council P.V. 20/29/17 (11th sess., 1920), 92."

Pleadings, Oral Arguments, Documents, pp. 89–92 (I.C.J. 1950).

Accordingly, the various Mandates were submitted by the Mandatory governments to the Council of the League of Nations, which reviewed and, with some revisions, approved their terms. Pertinent data for each mandated territory is given in the following table:

"DATA ON MANDATED TERRITORIES

Mandate	Mandatory	Terms defined by Council	Population (1931)	Area sq. mi.
'A' Mandates				
Palestine . .	United Kingdom	July 24, 1922	1, 035, 154	9, 010
Trans-Jordan.	United Kingdom	Sept. 16, 1922	305, 584	15, 444
Syria and Lebanon.	France	July 24, 1922	2, 656, 596	62, 163
'B' Mandates				
Cameroons .	France	July 18, 1922	2, 186, 015	165, 928
Cameroons .	United Kingdom	July 18, 1922	774, 585	34, 236
Ruanda-Urundi.	Belgium	July 20, 1922	3, 450, 000	20, 541
Tanganyika .	United Kingdom	July 20, 1922	5, 063, 660	374, 085
Togoland . .	France	July 18, 1922	725, 580	20, 077
Togoland . .	United Kingdom	July 18, 1922	293, 671	13, 240
'C' Mandates				
Islands, North Pacific.	Japan	Dec. 17, 1920	73, 027	830
Nauru . . .	British Empire (Australia acting)	Dec. 17, 1920	2, 692	8. 43
New Guinea and Islands.	Australia	Dec. 17, 1920	392, 816	93, 000
South-West Africa.	South Africa	Dec. 17, 1920	242, 290	322, 393
Western Samoa.	New Zealand	Dec. 17, 1920	46, 023	1, 133"

1919 For. Rel., vol. XIII, Paris Peace Conference, p. 101.

"The United States concluded treaties or conventions with mandatory states defining rights of its nationals in several of the mandated territories. These instruments stipulated that the United States should receive copies of the annual reports which mandatories by article 22, paragraph 7, were obligated to make to the League of Nations. The rights defined are equivalent to those possessed by members of the League of Nations.

"The conventions concluded with respect to 'A' mandated territories were signed after the negotiation of the Treaty of Lausanne of July 24, 1923 and state in the preamble that by that treaty concluded 'with the Allied Powers Turkey renounces all her rights and titles over' the area concerned.

"The convention and protocol defining the rights of the United States of America and of its nationals in Iraq was signed with the United Kingdom and Iraq, at London, January 9, 1930; in force February 24, 1931 (Treaty Series 835; 47 Stat. 1817; *Treaties, Conventions, etc.*, 1923–37, IV, 4335). The assent of the United States was required by article 6 to 'any change in the rights of the United States' as defined in the convention in case of the termination of the special relations existent between the United Kingdom and Iraq in accordance with the treaty of alliance of 1922 and the treaty of 1926, both of which were schedules to the convention. Article 7 of the convention provided for its ceasing to have effect upon the termination of those special relations, which, as between the United Kingdom and Iraq, occurred with the entry into force on October 3, 1932 of the superseding treaty of alliance of June 30, 1930. A treaty of commerce and navigation between the United States and Iraq signed at Baghdad, December 3, 1938 and in force June 19, 1940 (Treaty Series 960) supplants the provisions of the convention 'so far as commerce and navigation are concerned' as a consequence of negotiations stipulated by article 7 of the convention to be entered into 'on the termination of the said special relations' between the United Kingdom and Iraq.

"The mandate of France with respect to Syria and the Lebanon came into force on September 29, 1923. On April 4, 1924 the United States concluded with France a convention concerning rights in Syria and the Lebanon, in force July 13, 1924, (Treaty Series 695; 43 Stat. 1821; *Treaties, Conventions, etc.*, 1923–37, IV, 4169).

"The mandate of the United Kingdom with respect to Palestine came into force on September 29, 1923. On December 3, 1924 the United States concluded a convention defining the rights of nationals in Palestine with the United Kingdom; in force December 3, 1925 (Treaty Series 728; 44 Stat. 2184; *Treaties, Conventions, etc.*, 1923–37, IV, 4227).

"The conventions of the United States concerning 'B' mandates held by Belgium and France recognize the assignment of administration under the mandate to the respective mandatory and in

their preambles state that 'the benefits accruing under the aforesaid Article 119 of the Treaty of Versailles were confirmed to the
United States by the treaty between the United States and Germany, signed August 25, 1921'. These instruments are as follows:

"The convention defining the rights of nationals in the
Cameroons with France, signed at Paris, February 13, 1923; in
force June 3, 1924 (Treaty Series 690; 43 Stat. 1178; *Treaties,
Conventions, etc.*, 1923–37, IV, 4153).

"The convention defining the rights of nationals in Togoland
with France, signed at Paris, February 13, 1923; in force June 3,
1924; (Treaty Series 691; 43 Stat. 1790; *Treaties, Conventions,
etc.*, 1923–37, IV, 4160).

"The treaty concerning rights in the territory of Ruanda–
Urundi with Belgium, signed at Brussels, April 18, 1923, and
protocol signed at Brussels, January 21, 1924; in force November
18, 1924; (Treaty Series 704; 43 Stat. 1863; *Treaties, Conventions,
etc.*, 1923–37, IV, 3954).

"The other conventions concerning 'B' mandates were concluded in view of the facts that 'His Britannic Majesty has
accepted a mandate for the administration of part of the former
German colony' and that the two Governments were 'desirous of
reaching a definite understanding as to the rights of their respective Governments and of their nationals in the said territory'.
These instruments are:

"The convention defining the rights of nationals in the
Cameroons with His Britannic Majesty, signed at London,
February 10, 1925; in force April 8, 1926 (Treaty Series 743;
44 Stat. 2422; *Treaties, Conventions, etc.*, 1923–37, IV, 4235).

"The convention defining the rights of nationals in East Africa
(Tanganyika) with His Britannic Majesty, signed at London,
February 10, 1925; in force April 8, 1926 (Treaty Series 744;
44 Stat. 2427; *Treaties, Conventions, etc.*, 1923–37, IV, 4239).

"The convention defining the rights of nationals in Togoland
with His Britannic Majesty, signed at London, February 10,
1925; in force July 8, 1926 (Treaty Series 745; 44 Stat. 2433;
Treaties, Conventions, etc., 1923–37, IV, 4244).

"A single treaty was concluded by the United States with
respect to a 'C' mandate:

"Treaty with Japan regarding rights of the two Governments
and their respective nationals in former German islands in the
Pacific Ocean north of the Equator, and in particular the Island
of Yap, signed at Washington, February 11, 1922; in force July 13,
1922 (Treaty Series 664; 42 Stat. 2149; *Treaties, Conventions,
etc.*, 1910–23, III, 2723)."

1919 For. Rel., vol. XIII, Paris Peace Conference (1947), pp. 101–104.

Legal Nature of Mandates

§ 35

An
international
regime

In its Advisory Opinion of July 11th, 1950, *International Status of South-West Africa*, the International Court of Justice made the following observations regarding the general legal nature of the Mandates System:

> "It is now contended on behalf of the Union Government that this Mandate has lapsed, because the League has ceased to exist. This contention is based on a misconception of the legal situation created by Article 22 of the Covenant and by the Mandate itself. The League was not, as alleged by that Government, a 'mandator' in the sense in which this term is used in the national law of certain States. It had only assumed an international function of supervision and control. The 'Mandate' had only the name in common with the several notions of mandate in national law. The object of the Mandate regulated by international rules far exceeded that of contractual relations regulated by national law. The Mandate was created, in the interest of the inhabitants of the territory, and of humanity in general, as an international institution with an international object—a sacred trust of civilization. It is therefore not possible to draw any conclusion by analogy from the notions of mandate in national law or from any other legal conception of that law. The international rules regulating the Mandate constituted an international status for the Territory recognized by all the Members of the League of Nations, including the Union of South Africa."

> I.C.J. Reports (1950) 128, 132.

A detailed analysis appears in the Separate Opinion of Judge Sir Arnold McNair in this same proceeding, as follows:

> "2. *The objective character of Article 22 of the Covenant of the League of Nations*

> "From time to time it happens that a group of great Powers, or a large number of States both great and small, assume a power to create by a multipartite treaty some new international régime or status, which soon acquires a degree of acceptance and durability extending beyond the limits of the actual contracting parties, and giving it an objective existence. This power is used when some public interest is involved, and its exercise often occurs in the course of the peace settlement at the end of a great war. In 1920 the Council of the League had to deal with a dispute between Finland and Sweden, which, *inter alia*, involved an examination of the existing condition of a Convention dated March 30, 1856, between France and Great Britain on the one hand and Russia on the other, whereby Russia, in compliance with the desire of the other two States, declared 'that the Aaland Islands shall not be fortified, and that no military or naval base shall be maintained

or created there'.   (This Convention was attached to and became an integral part of the General Treaty of Peace of the same date, made between seven States, which brought the Crimean War to an end.)   Sweden claimed that this status of demilitarization was still in force in 1920 in spite of many intervening events, and that she, though not a party to the Convention or Peace Treaty of 1856, was entitled to the benefit of it; her claim was based on the allegation of an international servitude.   As the Permanent Court of International Justice had not then come into existence, the Council of the League set up a Commission of Jurists, Professor F. Larnaude (President), Professor A. Struycken and Professor Max Huber, and referred certain legal questions to them.   They received written statements and heard oral arguments on behalf of Finland and Sweden.   The Jurists rejected the argument based on an alleged servitude and reported that the provisions of the Convention and Treaty of 1856 for demilitarization were still in force.

> " 'These provisions [they said] were laid down in European interests.   They constituted a special international status, relating to military considerations, for the Aaland Islands.   It follows that until these provisions are duly replaced by others, every State interested [including Sweden which was not a party] has the right to insist upon compliance with them.   It also follows that any State in possession of the Islands must conform to the obligations binding upon it, arising out of the system of demilitarization established by these provisions.'

"The Report contains many expressions which illuminate this conclusion, e.g.,

> " 'The Powers have, on many occasions since 1815, and especially at the conclusion of peace treaties, tried to create true objective law, a real political status the effects of which are felt outside the immediate circle of contracting parties',

and again, 'the character of a settlement regulating European interests', 'European law', and 'the objective nature of the settlement'.

"It may seem a far cry from the Aaland Islands to South-West Africa, but reference to this case is demanded by the high standing of the members of the Commission and by the relevance of their reasoning to the present problems.   I may also refer to the statement by the Permanent Court in the SS. *Wimbledon* case (Series A. No. 1, p. 22) that as a result of Article 380 of the Treaty of Versailles of 1919 the Kiel Canal 'has become an international waterway intended to provide under treaty guarantee easier access to the Baltic for the benefit of all nations of the world'—which was referred to as 'its new régime'.

"The Mandates System seems to me to be an *a fortiori* case. The occasion was the end of a world war.   The parties to the treaties of peace incorporating the Covenant of the League and establishing the system numbered thirty.   The public interest extended far beyond Europe.   Article 22 proclaimed 'the principle that the well-being and development of such peoples form a sacred trust of civilization and that securities for the performance of this trust should be embodied in the Covenant'. A large part of the civilized world concurred in opening a new chapter in the life of between fifteen and twenty millions of people, and this article was the instrument adopted to give effect to their desire. In my opinion, the new régime established in pursuance of this 'principle' has more than a purely contractual basis, and the territories subjected to it are impressed with a special legal status, designed to last until modified in the manner indicated by Article 22. The dissolution of the League has produced certain difficulties, but, as I shall explain, they are mechanical difficulties, and the policy and principles of the new institution have survived the impact of the events of 1939 to 1946, and have indeed been reincarnated by the Charter under the name of the 'International Trusteeship System', with a new lease of life."

I.C.J. Reports (1950) 128, 153–155.

In addition, Judge McNair stated:

"What is the duty of an international tribunal when confronted with a new legal institution the object and terminology of which are reminiscent of the rules and institutions of private law? To what extent is it useful or necessary to examine what may at first sight appear to be relevant analogies in private law systems and draw help and inspiration from them? International law has recruited and continues to recruit many of its rules and institutions from private systems of law. Article 38 (1) (c) of the Statute of the Court bears witness that this process is still active, and it will be noted that this article authorizes the Court to 'apply . . . . (c) the general principles of law recognized by civilized nations'. The way in which international law borrows from this source is not by means of importing private law institutions 'lock, stock and barrel', ready-made and fully equipped with a set of rules. It would be difficult to reconcile such a process with the application of 'the general principles of law'. In my opinion, the true view of the duty of international tribunals in this matter is to regard any features or terminology which are reminiscent of the rules and institutions of private law as an indication of policy and principles rather than as directly importing these rules and institutions. I quote a sentence from a judgment by Chief Justice Innes in the decision of the Supreme Court of South Africa in *Rex* v. *Christian*, South African Law Reports [1924], Appellate Division, 101, 112:

"'Article 22 [of the Covenant] describes the administration of the territories and peoples with which it deals as a tutelage to be exercised by the governing Power as mandatory on behalf of the League. Those terms were probably employed, not in their strict legal sense, but as indicating the policy which the governing authority should pursue. The relationship between the League and the mandatory could not with any legal accuracy be described as that of principal and agent.'

"Let us then seek to discover the underlying policy and principles of Article 22 and of the Mandates. No technical significance can be attached to the words 'sacred trust of civilization', but they are an apt description of the policy of the authors of the Mandates System, and the words 'sacred trust' were not used here for the first time in relation to dependent peoples (see Duncan Hall, *Mandates, Dependencies and Trusteeships*, pp. 97–100). Any English lawyer who was instructed to prepare the legal instruments required to give effect to the policy of Article 22 would inevitably be reminded of, and influenced by, the trust of English and American law, though he would soon realize the need of much adaptation for the purposes of the new international institution. Professor Brierly's opinion, stated in the *British Year Book of International Law*, 1929, pages 217–219, that the governing principle of the Mandates System is to be found in the trust, and his quotation from an article by M. Lepaulle, are here very much in point, and it is worth noting that the historical basis of the legal enforcement of the English trust is that it was something which was binding upon the conscience of the trustee; that is why it was legally enforced. It also seems probable that the conception of the Mandates System owes something to the French *tutelle*.

"Nearly every legal system possesses some institution whereby the property (and sometimes the persons) of those who are not *sui juris*, such as a minor or a lunatic, can be entrusted to some responsible person as a trustee or *tuteur* or *curateur*. The Anglo-American trust serves this purpose, and another purpose even more closely akin to the Mandates System, namely, the vesting of property in trustees, and its management by them in order that the public or some class of the public may derive benefit or that some public purpose may be served. The trust has frequently been used to protect the weak and the dependent, in cases where there is 'great might on the one side and unmight on the other', and the English courts have for many centuries pursued a vigorous policy in the administration and enforcement of trusts.

"There are three general principles which are common to all these institutions:

"(*a*) that the control of the trustee, *tuteur* or *curateur* over the property is limited in one way or another; he is not in the position of the normal complete owner, who can do what he likes with his own, because he is precluded from administering the property for his own personal benefit;

"(*b*) that the trustee, *tuteur* or *curateur* is under some kind of legal obligation, based on confidence and conscience, to carry out the trust or mission confided to him for the benefit of some other person or for some public purpose;

"(*c*) that any attempt by one of these persons to absorb the property entrusted to him into his own patrimony would be illegal and would be prevented by the law.

"These are some of the general principles of private law which throw light upon this new institution, and I am convinced that in its future development the law governing the trust is a source from which much can be derived. The importance of the Mandates System is marked by the fact that, after the experience of a quarter of a century, the Charter of the United Nations made provision for an 'International Trusteeship System', which was described by a Resolution of the Assembly of the League of April 18th, 1946, as embodying 'principles corresponding to those declared in Article 22 of the Covenant of the League'."

I.C.J. Reports (1950) 128, 148–150.

"The territories or entities for which mandates have been conferred and accepted are not States, although they may be States in the making. They are populated areas which the Principal Allied Powers have, in consequence of their control thereof, and with the approval of the Council of the League of Nations, placed under the administration of designated mandatories on conditions set forth in the terms of the particular mandates, and in pursuance of the requirements of the Covenant. Those terms and conditions indicate the measure of authority of the mandatories, and emphasize the obligation of each to accept the coöperation and oversight of the League, and to make annual reports to the Council. The mandatory is not free to deal with the territory or people assigned to it as though either were its own; the relationship sharply differs from that existing, in an international sense, between the United States and its colonial possessions such as the Philippine Islands. A territory or entity under mandate is thus to be distinguished from the colonial possession which, in international contemplation, is a part of the State to which it belongs. The outstanding, and perhaps novel, feature of the mandatory system is the international obligation imposed upon and accepted by the mandatory to administer a territorial area not its own, and not constituting a State, under the supervision of an international agency."

I Hyde, *International Law Chiefly as Interpreted and Applied by the United States* (2d ed., 1945) 102–103.

Main characteristics

In the final League of Nations study on the Mandates System, there appears the following account of the main characteristics of this regime established by the provisions of article 22 of the Covenant of the League of Nations:

"Without going into controversial questions regarding the legal nature of the mandates, it may be said that the following main principles emerge from these provisions:

"The *aim* of the institution is to ensure the *well-being and development of the peoples* inhabiting the territories in question.

"The *method* of attaining this aim consists in entrusting the *tutelage* of these peoples to certain advanced nations. The acceptance by a nation of this mission carries with it certain obligations and responsibilities established by law. Like guardians in civil law, they must exercise their authority in the interests of their wards—that is to say, of the peoples which are regarded as minors—and must maintain an entirely disinterested attitude in their dealings with them. The territories with the administration of which they are entrusted must not be exploited by them for their own profit.

"Again, the phrase 'peoples not *yet* able to stand by themselves' is used. It follows from this and from the very conception of tutelage that this mission is not, in principle, intended to be prolonged indefinitely, but only until the peoples under tutelage are capable of managing their own affairs.

"The nations upon which such powers of guardianship are conferred exercise them 'as *Mandatories* on behalf of the League'. In other words, the administration of these territories is delegated to them. This involves *an obligation* on their part *to render account of their administration* to the League of Nations.

"This is made plain by paragraph 7, which prescribes that the Mandatory is to render to the Council an annual report on the administration of the territory committed to its charge. Finally, the last paragraph (No. 9) of the Article briefly describes *the machinery to be established for the internationl supervision of the mandatory administration.*

"Such are the main characteristics of the mandates system. But although the principle is uniform, it is applied in a variety of ways. It will be appreciated that the definition 'peoples not yet able to stand by themselves' covers a wide range of situations; the degree of civilisation attained by different peoples is extremely varied. Again, the geographical, economic, demographic, etc., conditions of the mandated territories differ very greatly. Accordingly, the Covenant (paragraphs 3 to 6 of Article 22) distinguishes between *three categories of mandates*, taking into account differences in the stage of development of the population, in the geographical situation of the territory, in the economic conditions prevailing and any other circumstances which may be relevant."

League of Nations, *The Mandates System, Origin—Principles—Application* (1945.VI.A.1) 23–24.

The same study on the Mandates System then states:

"2. The Mandate 'Charters'

"The various Mandates or 'charters' adopted by the Council comprise a collection of provisions defining the manner in which the principles laid down by the Covenant are to be applied. Under the terms of the latter, the degree of authority or control to be exercised by the Mandatory varies according to the character of the territory.

"Certain clauses, however, are common to all Mandates: the Mandatory has full power of administration and legislation subject to the terms of the Mandate [provision to this effect appears in all the mandates except that relating to Syria and Lebanon] ; he is under an obligation to make to the Council an annual report to the satisfaction of that body, giving full information as to the measures taken to carry out the provisions of the Mandate; he agrees that, if any dispute whatever should arise between him and another Member of the League of Nations relating to the interpretation or application of the Mandate, such dispute, if it cannot be settled by negotiation, shall be submitted to the Permanent Court of International Justice. [The Mandate for Tanganyika Territory, differing on this point from the other mandates, expressly provides that States Members of the League of Nations may likewise bring before the Court for decision any claims on behalf of their nationals for infractions of their rights under the Mandate.]‾ Any modification of the terms of the Mandate requires the consent of the Council of the League.

"The remaining clauses vary according to the category to which the Mandate in question belongs."

Ibid. 24–25.

As noted above, there are three distinct categories of Mandates under article 22 of the Covenant of the League of Nations classified as "A", "B", and "C" Mandates, according to the particular circumstances in each case.

"A"
Mandates

"In a first group—'A' Mandates (Syria and Lebanon, Palestine and Transjordan, and Iraq)—the nation is provisionally recognised as independent, but receives the advice and assistance of a Mandatory in its administration until such time as it is able to stand alone."

Ibid. 24.

"The *'A' Mandates* differ appreciably from those of the other two categories. In the countries to which they apply, the inhabitants had reached a more advanced stage of development and their independence could, in principle, be recognised by the Covenant itself, subject to the conditions which have been mentioned above. The mission of the Mandatories in these countries has therefore consisted mainly in developing their capacity to govern themselves, and in establishing their economic systems and social and other institutions on a more secure footing in order to fit them to take their position as independent nations.

"The 'A' Mandates, however, also differ from one another in some important respects, as their terms were drafted so as to take into account the special conditions of the various countries in question. In particular, the mandate for Iraq, which was terminated in 1932, was of a very special character in that, amongst other things, there was no actual charter conferring the mandate."

Ibid. 27.

". . . the conditions governing the Mandate for *Iraq* were never formulated in a special 'charter', but were embodied in treaties and subsidiary agreements concluded between the mandatory Power and the Government of Iraq [Treaty of Alliance of October 10th, 1922, Protocol of April 30th, 1923, Agreement concerning British Officials of March 25th, 1924, Military Agreement of March 25th, 1924, Judicial Agreement of March 25th, 1924, Financial Agreement of March 25th, 1924, and Treaty of January 13th, 1926. League of Nations document C.216.M.77.1926.VI.], and approved by the Council of the League of Nations as giving effect to the provisions of Article 22 of the Covenant. [Decisions of the Council of September 27th, 1924 (*Minutes of the Thirtieth Session of the Council*, pages 1345–1347) and of March 11th, 1926 (*Minutes of the Thirty-ninth Session of the Council*, page 502).]

"Under the first of these treaties, the British Government undertook, at the request of the King of Iraq, to provide the State of Iraq with such advice and assistance as might be required during the period of the treaty, without prejudice to her national sovereignty.

"For the period of the treaty, no official of other than Iraq nationality was to be appointed without the concurrence of the British Government.

"The King of Iraq undertook to frame an organic law to be put into force after presentation to the Constituent Assembly of Iraq. This law was to take account of the rights, wishes and interests of all populations inhabiting Iraq and to ensure freedom of conscience and the free exercise of all forms of worship, subject only to the maintenance of public order and morals. It was also to provide against discrimination of any kind between the inhabitants on the ground of race, religion or language, and to secure the right of each community to maintain its own schools for the education of its own members in its own language.

"The King of Iraq was to consult the British High Commissioner on what was conducive to a sound financial and fiscal policy.

"Iraq also had the right of representation in London and in such other capitals and places as might be agreed upon between her and the British Government. Where Iraq was not represented, the protection of Iraq nationals was to be entrusted to the British Government. Exequaturs were to be issued to representatives of foreign Powers in Iraq by the Iraqi Government, after the British Government had agreed to their appointment. The British Government undertook to provide such support and assistance to the armed forces of Iraq as might from time to time be agreed by the two parties.

"No territory in Iraq was to be ceded or leased or in any way placed under the control of any foreign Power.

"The treaty also contained clauses resembling fairly closely those in the Mandates for Syria and Lebanon and for Palestine concerning judicial matters, the activities of missionaries and non-discrimination between the nationals of States Members of the League of Nations in economic matters, etc.

"Lastly, the British Government undertook to use its good offices to secure the admission of Iraq to membership of the League of Nations as soon as possible."

Ibid. 31–32.

In its Advisory Opinion, *Interpretation of Article 3, paragraph 2, of the Treaty of Lausanne (Frontier between Turkey and Iraq)*, Nov. 21, 1925 (P.C.I.J., Series B, No. 12), the Permanent Court of International Justice, in response to a request of the Council of the League of Nations, expressed the opinion that "the 'decision to be taken' by the Council of the League of Nations in virtue of Article 3, paragraph 2, of the Treaty of Lausanne, will be binding on the Parties and will constitute a definitive determination of the frontier between Turkey and Iraq". *Ibid.*, at p. 33. In the League Council's proceedings in the matter of the Turkish-Iraq frontier, the "interested Parties", *i.e.*, the parties to the dispute, were Great Britain, as Mandatory for Iraq, and Turkey. *Ibid.*, pp. 15–18.

Palestine "The *Palestine* Mandate is of a very special character. While it follows the main lines laid down by the Covenant for 'A' Mandates, it also contains a number of provisions designed to apply the policy defined by the 'Balfour Declaration' of November 2nd, 1917. By this declaration, the British Government had announced its intention to encourage the establishment in Palestine of a national home for the Jewish people, it being clearly understood that nothing should be done which might prejudice the civil and religious rights of existing non-Jewish communities in Palestine, or the rights and political status enjoyed by Jews in any other country. The Mandate reproduces the Balfour Declaration almost in full in its preamble and states that 'recognition has thereby been given to the historical connection of the Jewish people with Palestine and to the grounds for reconstituting their national home in that country'.

"Accordingly, under the terms of the Mandate, the Mandatory is to be responsible for placing the country under such political, administrative and economic conditions as will secure the establishment of the Jewish national home, and the development of self-governing institutions, and also for safeguarding the civil and religious rights of all the inhabitants of Palestine, irrespective of race and religion. The Mandate also provides for the recognition as a public body of a Jewish agency which is to advise and co-operate with the administration of Palestine in such economic, social and other matters as may affect the establishment of the Jewish national home and the interests of the Jewish population in Palestine, and, subject always to the control of the Administration, to assist and take part in the development of the country. At first and in accordance with the terms of the Mandate, this rôle was entrusted to the Zionist Organisation; later, however, from 1929 onwards, that organisation was replaced by the 'Jewish Agency for Palestine', which includes representatives not only of the Zionist Organisation but also of other Jewish bodies in various countries. In consultation with the Mandatory, this agency takes steps to secure the co-operation of all Jews willing to assist in the establishment of the Jewish national home. While ensuring that the rights and position of other sections of the population are not prejudiced, the Administration, for its part, must facilitate Jewish immigration under suitable conditions and, in co-operation with the Jewish agency, encourage close settlement by Jews on the land, including State lands and waste lands not required for public purposes. A nationality law is to be enacted containing provisions framed so as to facilitate the acquisition of Palestinian citizenship by Jews who take up their permanent residence in Palestine.

"The Administration is to take all necessary measures to safeguard the interests of the community in connection with the development of the country, and, subject to any international obligations of the Mandatory, to provide for public ownership or control of any of the natural resources of the country, or of public works, services and utilities. The land system must be appropriate to the needs of the country, having regard to the desirability of promoting the close settlement and intensive cultivation of the land. The Administration may arrange with the Jewish agency, provided for by the Mandate, to construct or operate, upon fair and equitable terms, any public works, services and utilities, and to develop any of the natural resources of the country, in so far as these matters are not directly undertaken by the Administration. No profits, however, distributed by the Jewish agency are to exceed a reasonable rate of interest on the capital, and any further profits are to be utilised by it for the benefit of the country in a manner approved by the Administration.

"English, Arabic and Hebrew are the official languages of Palestine. Any statement or inscription in Arabic on stamps or money is to be repeated in Hebrew and *vice versa*. Holy days of the respective communities are legal days of rest for the members of such communities.

"All responsibility in connection with the Holy Places and religious buildings or sites in Palestine, including that of preserving existing rights and of securing free access to the Holy Places, religious buildings and sites and the free exercise of worship, while ensuring the requirements of public order and decorum, is assumed by the Mandatory. The latter has no authority to interfere with the fabric or management of purely Moslem sacred shrines, the immunities of which are guaranteed. The Mandate also provides for the appointment by the Mandatory of a special commission to study, define and determine the rights and claims in connection with the Holy Places and those relating to the different religious communities in Palestine. The method of nomination, the composition and the functions of this commission were to be submitted to the Council of the League for its approval. In the event of the termination of the mandate, it is for the Council to make all necessary arrangements for safeguarding in perpetuity, under guarantee of the League, the rights secured by the mandate in respect of the Holy Places."

League of Nations, *The Mandates System, op. cit.* 29–31.

"Of Palestine it may be said that, if the mandate system had not been evolved for other purposes, it would have had to be created for the government of the Holy Land. For Palestine, by its history, its geography, its population, and its destiny, is an international country, and its well-being and development form, without express declaration, a sacred trust of civilization. At one period in the inter-allied bargaining of the war years it seemed to be marked out for an international government, a form of administration which has scarcely ever prospered. It was saved that trial by the invention of statesmanship which happily combines the protecting authority of a single state with the supervision of an international body. It has been said of the introduction of the mandate system to the territories detached from Turkey that the conditions in those areas precluded immediate independence; principle precluded annexation; experience precluded internationalization. The application of the mandate to Palestine indicates the benefit which may be obtained through the administration of a country with complex national problems by one guardian Power subject to a trust to protect both national and international interests, and subject to the sympathetic scrutiny of a permanent international council which has as its function to assist and advise the Mandatory, while it is the function of the Mandatory itself to direct the local Government."

Bentwich, "The Mandate for Palestine", X Brit. Yb. Int'l L. (1929) 137, 143.   See also Bentwich, *The Mandates System* (1930), chapter II.

Transjordan

"In the Mandate for Palestine, *Transjordan* is dealt with separately. Under Article 25 of the Mandate, the Mandatory is entitled, with the consent of the Council of the League of Nations, to postpone or withhold application to this part of the territory of such provisions of the Mandate as he may consider inapplicable to the existing local conditions and to make such provision for its administration as he may consider suitable, subject to the clauses relating to freedom of conscience, non-discrimination between the inhabitants, the supervision of religious institutions, economic equality, etc. On September 16th, 1922, the Council, in accordance with this article, approved a proposal by the mandatory Power to the effect that the provisions of the Mandate respecting the Jewish national home and the Holy Places should not be applied to Transjordan. At the same time, the British Government expressly accepted full responsibility as Mandatory for Transjordan and undertook that such provision as might be made for the administration of that territory should conform to those provisions of the Mandate which had not been declared inapplicable. By a special Agreement concluded on February 20th, 1928, the British Government recognised the existence of an independent Government in Transjordan. It once more declared itself responsible to the Council for the application of the Mandate in that country. On September 1st, 1928, the Council took note of this declaration and recognised that the Agreement in question was in conformity with the principles of the Mandate."

League of Nations, *The Mandates System, op. cit.* 31. See also Bentwich, *op. cit.*, chapter II.

"2. Article 25 of the mandate permitted the mandatory to withhold application of such provisions of the mandate as were inapplicable to the existing local conditions in the territory of the mandate east of the River Jordan, which is inhabited by an Arab population not concerned with the establishment of a Jewish national home. The applicable parts of the Palestine mandate were recited in a decision of September 16, 1922, which provided for the separate administration of Trans-Jordan. The government of that territory was, subject to the mandate, formed by the Emir Abdullah, brother of King Feisal of Iraq, who had been at Amman since February 1921. That status was not altered by an agreement between the United Kingdom and the Emirate concluded on February 20, 1928 (League of Nations, *Official Journal*, 1928, p. 1574) which recognized the existence of an independent government in Trans-Jordan and defined and limited its powers. The ratifications were exchanged on October 31, 1929." 1919 For. Rel., vol. XIII, Paris Peace Conference (1947), p. 100. For a summary of the Agreement of February 20, 1928, between the United Kingdom and the Emir of Transjordan, see Bentwich, "The Mandate for Transjordan", X Brit. Yb. Int'l L. (1929) 212.

"The Mandate for *Syria and Lebanon* contains a special provision to the effect that the Mandatory is to frame for these countries an organic law taking into account the rights, interests and wishes of all their populations and that he is to facilitate the progressive development of the two countries as independent States. French and Arabic are the official languages of Syria and Lebanon. The Mandatory is to encourage public education, which is to be given through the medium of the native languages in use in the territories of Syria and Lebanon.

"In the Mandate for Syria and Lebanon, the Article establishing the principle of economic equality contains clauses similar to those included in the 'B' Mandates . . . with regard to concessions and monopolies."

League of Nations, *The Mandates System, op. cit.* 29.

"The 'A' mandate of Syria and Lebanon underwent an evolution bringing the two entities involved to the verge of independence. The mandate provided for an organic law, which was promulgated only on May 14, 1930 (League of Nations, *Official Journal*, 1930, p. 1099). This law embodied constitutions of the Lebanese Republic and the State of Syria, organic regulations of the Sanjak of Alexandretta, and organic statutes of the Governments of Latakia and the Jebel Druse. The Sanjak of Alexandretta, having been placed under a statute by decision of the Council on May 29, 1937 (*ibid.*, 1937, pp. 329, 580), was transferred to Turkey by an arrangement between France and Turkey of June 23, 1939, in force on July 13 (*ibid.*, 1939, p. 356). . . ."

1919 For. Rel., vol. XIII, The Paris Peace Conference (1947), p. 99. See also Myers, *Handbook of the League of Nations* (1935) 107–108.

The final League of Nations study of the Mandates System contains the following summary of the provisions of the Palestine Mandate and of the Mandate for Syria and Lebanon which are essentially similar:

External relations; international conventions

"The external relations of the territory are controlled by the mandatory Power. The latter is responsible for seeing that no part of the territory is ceded to or in any way placed under the control of a foreign Power. The privileges and immunities of foreigners, including the benefits of consular jurisdiction and protection as formerly enjoyed by capitulation or usage, are not applicable in the mandated territories. The judicial system which is to be established under the terms of the mandate must, however, assure to foreigners, as well as to natives, a complete guarantee of their rights.

"In the case both of Syria and Lebanon and of Palestine, the mandatory Power must adhere, on behalf of the territory, to any general international conventions already existing or which may be concluded subsequently with the approval of the League of Nations, respecting the slave traffic, the traffic in arms and ammunition, or the traffic in drugs, or relating to commercial equality, freedom of transit and navigation, aerial navigation, and postal, telegraphic and wireless communications, or literary, artistic or industrial property. So far as religious, social and other conditions permit, the Mandatory is to co-operate on behalf of the territory in the execution of measures adopted by the League of Nations for preventing disease, including diseases of plants and animals.

"The Mandatory is under an obligation to see that complete freedom of conscience and the free exercise of all forms of worship, subject only to the maintenance of public order and morals, are ensured to all. He must see that there is no discrimination of any kind between the inhabitants on the ground of race, religion or language; respect for the personal status of the various communities and for their religious interests is guaranteed; each

Civil rights

community is entitled to maintain its own schools for the education of its members in its own language, provided that it conforms to any educational requirements of a general nature which may be laid down. The supervision exercised by the Mandatory over religious institutions and missions is to be limited to that which is strictly necessary for the maintenance of public order and good government.

"The Mandatory is entitled to use the roads, railways and ports of the territory for the movement of his armed forces and the carriage of fuel and supplies. In Syria, the Mandatory is entitled to maintain his troops in the territory for its defence; and he may, as a temporary measure, organise such local militia as may be necessary for the defence of the territory and employ it for defence and also for the maintenance of order. Subsequently, this militia is to be under the local authorities, subject to the control of the Mandatory. In Palestine, the local Administration may, subject to the supervision of the Mandatory, organise on a voluntary basis the forces necessary for the preservation of peace and order and also for the defence of the country; except for such purposes, no military, naval, or air forces may be raised or maintained by the Administration. *Military forces*

"The Mandatory is to see that there is no discrimination against the nationals of any State Member of the League of Nations as compared with his own nationals or those of any other State in matters concerning taxation or commerce, the exercise of industries or professions, or navigation, or in the treatment of merchant vessels or civil aircraft. Similarly, there is to be no discrimination against goods originating in or destined for any of these States. Freedom of transit across the mandated territory is to be guaranteed under equitable conditions. Subject to these provisions, the Mandatory or the local Administration may take any steps calculated to promote the development of the natural resources of the territory and to safeguard the interests of the population. Special Customs agreements may be concluded between the territory and neighbouring countries. *Open door*

"The Mandatory must also enact a law concerning antiquities in accordance with certain principles defined in the mandate and ensuring equality of treatment in the matter of excavations and archæological research to the nationals of all States Members of the League of Nations.

"As regards the political regime of the territory, both the mandates in question lay down that the Mandatory is to encourage local autonomy, so far as circumstances permit. *Local autonomy*

"Lastly, both the mandates contain a special clause providing that, on the termination of the mandatory regime, it will be incumbent on the Council of the League of Nations to use its influence to ensure that financial obligations legitimately incurred by the Administration of the countries in question during the period of the mandate are henceforward duly honoured." *Financial obligations*

League of Nations, *The Mandates System, Origin—Principles—Application* (1945) 27–29.

"In the second group—'B' Mandates (the Cameroons, Togoland, Tanganyika, Ruanda-Urundi)—as it is impossible to grant autonomy, the Mandatory is 'responsible for the administration' under certain specified conditions. These conditions, which are briefly indicated in the Covenant, are designed to prevent certain abuses and to ensure that the Administration has the welfare of the natives constantly in mind. They aim also at securing respect for the rights and interests of other Members of the League of Nations. *"B" Mandates—main characteristics*

"The '*B*' *Mandates* go into more detail. They repeat most of the provisions of the 'C' Mandates, with certain variations; some clauses are expanded, while a number of important new provisions are added.

"As in territories under 'C' Mandate, the Mandatory must promote the material and moral well-being and the social progress of the inhabitants; the 'B' Mandates further lay down that he is responsible for the peace, order and good government of the territory. He must suppress all forms of slave trade, provide for the emancipation of slaves and for as speedy an elimination of domestic and other slavery as social conditions will allow. Forced labour is only authorised under the same conditions as in the case of 'C' Mandates; the Mandatory must protect the natives from measures of fraud and force by the careful supervision of labour contracts and the recruiting of labour. A strict control is to be exercised over the traffic in arms and ammunition and over the sale of spirituous liquors. (The provisions of the 'B' Mandates are thus less rigid in this respect than those of the 'C' Mandates, which 'prohibit' the supply of intoxicants to the natives.)

"With regard to the holding or transfer of land, the mandatory Power, when framing laws, must take into consideration native laws and customs and safeguard native rights and interests. The transfer of land from a native to a non-native and the creation of real rights over native land in favour of a non-native are to be subject to the previous consent of the public authorities. The Mandatory must also enact strict regulations against usury.

"The military clauses of the 'B' Mandates are almost identical with those of the 'C' Mandates. As an exception to the general principle, however, the French mandates for the Cameroons and Togoland provide that native troops raised in the territories may, in the event of general war, be utilised to repel an attack, or, for the defence of the territory outside the boundaries of the latter.

"The provisions relating to freedom of conscience and the free exercise of all forms of worship do not differ much from those in the 'C' Mandates. The 'B' Mandates, however, contain a special provision giving missionaries the right to acquire property in the territory, to erect religious buildings and to open schools. They also expressly recognise the right of the Mandatory in this connection to exercise such control as may be necessary for the maintenance of public order and good government.

"The Mandatory is authorised to constitute the territory under his mandate into a Customs, fiscal, or administrative union with the adjacent territories, provided that the measures adopted do not infringe the provisions of the mandate (that is to say, subject in particular to the principle of economic equality).

"The 'B' Mandates contain detailed provisions for the application of the principle of the 'open door' or of *economic equality*. The Mandatory must secure to all nationals of States Members of the League of Nations the same rights as are enjoyed in the territory by his own nationals, in respect of entry into and residence in the territory, the protection afforded to their property, the acquisition of property and the exercise of their profession or trade. The Mandatory has to ensure to the nationals of such countries, on the same footing as to his own nationals, freedom of transit and navigation, and complete economic, commercial and industrial equality except in the matter of essential public works and services. Concessions for the development of the natural resources of the territory must be granted without distinction on grounds of nationality. Concessions having the character of a general monopoly must not, however, be granted; but this provision does not affect the right of the Mandatory to create monopolies of a purely fiscal character in the interest of the territory, or to carry out the development of natural resources, either directly by the State or by a controlled agency, provided that no monopoly for the benefit of the Mandatory or his nationals results therefrom either directly or indirectly."

Ibid. 24–27.

"Finally, the territories in the third group—the 'C' Mandates (South West Africa and the Islands of the Pacific)—are 'administered under the laws of the Mandatory as integral portions of its territory' and subject to the same safeguards in the interests of the indigenous population as the territories under 'B' Mandate. | "C" Mandates— main characteristics

. . . .

"The '*C' Mandates*, which are all almost identical, are relatively simple. The Mandatory is authorised to apply his own legislation to the territory, subject to such local modifications as circumstances may require. He must promote to the utmost the material and moral well-being and the social progress of the inhabitants. In particular, he must see that the slave trade is prohibited; that no forced labour is permitted except for essential public works and services and then only for adequate remuneration. The traffic in arms and ammunition must be strictly controlled and the supply of intoxicating spirits and beverages to the natives prohibited.

"No military training may be given to the natives save for purposes of internal police and the local defence of the territory. No military or naval bases are to be established or fortifications erected.

"Freedom of conscience and the free exercise of all forms of worship are to be guaranteed. Missionaries, nationals of any State Member of the League of Nations, are to be free to prosecute their calling in the territory."

Ibid. 24–25. A detailed account of the application of international conventions in all three categories of Mandates appears in Hall, *Mandates, Dependencies and Trusteeship* (1948) 234–255.

The foregoing general description of the main characteristics of the Mandates System admittedly avoided discussion of questions regarding the legal nature of this new international regime. The principal legal characteristics distinctive of this System arise in connection with the following subjects: sovereignty, cession of territory, state | Principal legal characteristics succession, nationality, and belligerency.   In addition, as noted above, all the Mandate instruments contained provision for compulsory reference of disputes to the Permanent Court of International Justice, to which jurisdiction the International Court of Justice has now succeeded.

Locus of
sovereignty—
no transfer

"The terms of this Mandate, as well as the provisions of Article 22 of the Covenant and the principles embodied therein, show that the creation of this new international institution did not involve any . . . transfer of sovereignty to the Union of South Africa. . . ."

International Status of South-West Africa, Advisory Opinion, July 11, 1950, I.C.J. Reports (1950) 128, 132.

"Upon sovereignty a very few words will suffice.   The Mandates System (and the 'corresponding principles' of the International Trusteeship System) is a new institution—a new relationship between territory and its inhabitants on the one hand and the government which represents them internationally on the other—a new species of international government, which does not fit into the old conception of sovereignty and which is alien to it.   The doctrine of sovereignty has no application to this new system.   Sovereignty over a Mandated Territory is in abeyance; if and when the inhabitants of the Territory obtain recognition as an independent State, as has already happened in the case of some of the Mandates, sovereignty will revive and vest in the new State. What matters in considering this new institution is not where sovereignty lies, but what are the rights and duties of the Mandatory in regard to the area of territory being administered by it.   The answer to that question depends on the international agreements creating the system and the rules of law which they attract.   Its essence is that the Mandatory acquires only a limited title to the territory entrusted to it, and that the measure of its powers is what is necessary for the purpose of carrying out the Mandate.   'The Mandatory's rights, like the trustee's, have their foundation in his obligations; they are "tools given to him in order to achieve the work assigned to him"; he has "all the tools necessary for such end, but only those".'   (See Brierly, referred to above.)"

Separate Opinion of Sir Arnold McNair, ibid. 150.   The reference to Brierly in Judge McNair's Separate Opinion is to the note, "Trusts and Mandates", X Brit. Yb. Int'l L. (1929) 217–219.   A more recent statement of Professor Brierly's views may be found in his The Law of Nations (5th ed., 1955) 166–167.

". . . The Mandatory Power, as such, was not the sovereign of the territory.   It had no right of disposition, no jus dispondendi: it was merely a Mandatory on behalf of the League. . . ."

Separate Opinion of Judge Read, International Status of South-West Africa, Advisory Opinion, July 11, 1950, I.C.J. Reports (1950) 128, 168.

". . . In fact, no question of sovereignty is raised: the question does not arise with regard to South-West Africa. As to the Union of South-Africa, she cannot exercise a sovereignty which the Mandated Territory does not possess. She has not acquired any sovereignty over the Territory. She has only certain faculties, particularly in matters of administration, under the mission which has been entrusted to her."

Dissenting Opinion of Judge Alvarez, *ibid.* 180–181.

A review of the various theories of sovereignty advanced during the operation of the Mandates System was presented to the International Court of Justice in 1950 by Ivan Kerno, representative of the Secretary-General of the United Nations, in the advisory proceeding, *International Status of South-West Africa*, as follows:

"B. *Jurists' discussion on location of sovereignty*

"In the report which I mentioned a moment ago and which was adopted by the Council of the League on 5 August, 1920, the Rapporteur, Mr. Hymans, dealing with the question of the determination of the terms of the mandates, remarked:

" 'The degree of authority, control or administration is, so far as "B" or "C" Mandates are concerned, a question of only secondary importance. In the former case, as in the latter, the mandatory Power will enjoy in my judgment a full exercise of sovereignty, in so far as such exercise is consistent with the carrying out of the obligations imposed by paragraphs 5 and 6. In paragraph 6, which deals with "C" Mandates, the scope of these obligations is perhaps narrower than in paragraph 5, thus allowing the mandatory Power more nearly to assimilate the mandated territory to its own.' [League of Nations, Responsibilities of the League arising out of Article 22 (Mandates).—Report by the Council to the Assembly (20/48/161), Annex 4, page 15 (Folder 1).]

But a little further on and discussing the extent of the League's right of control, he stated:

" 'I shall not enter into a controversy—though this would certainly be very interesting—as to where the sovereignty actually resides. We are face to face with a new institution. Legal erudition will decide as to what extent it can apply to this institution the older juridical notions. . . .' [*Id.*, page 17.]

"Throughout the life of the League, this official position of refraining from an examination of the exact location of sovereignty was maintained by all its organs. This was true not only because the question was recognized as extremely difficult with chances of agreement small, but also because at no time did a solution appear indispensable in dealing with the practical problems involving the responsibility of the mandatory Power before the League of Nations.

"However, while League organs have observed this prudent attitude, eminent jurists of many nations eagerly accepted Mr. Hymans' challenge, and there is a wealth of legal literature on the subject. In spite of this abundance of legal theory, there exists no consensus, nor even a clearly discernible preponderance of opinion. In reviewing the literature on the subject, it may be observed that sovereignty has been variously attributed by jurists to the Principal Allied and Associated Powers [for example, see Fauchille, in second part of his Treatise, *Traité de Droit international public*, tome 1, 2me partie, 1925, p. 849; Potter, *Origin of the System of Mandates under the League of Nations*, "The American Political Science Review", Vol. 16, No. 4, November 1922, pp. 563–583], to the mandatories [for example, see Rolin, *Le Système des Mandats coloniaux*, "Revue de Droit international et de Législation comparée", troisième série, tome I (1920), pp. 329–363; Lindley, *The Acquisition and Government of Backward Territory* (1926), pp. 266–267; Diena, *Les Mandats internationaux*, "Académie de Droit international, Recueil des Cours", tome 5 (1924, IV), pp. 215–261] in their own right or on behalf of the League of Nations, to the mandated communities [for example, see Stoyanovsky, *La Théorie générale des Mandats internationaux* (1925) ; Pic, *Le Régime du Mandat d'après le Traité de Versailles, son application dans le Proche-Orient*, «Revue générale de Droit international public», vol. 30 (1923), pp. 321–371] or to the League of Nations [for example, see Lauterpacht, *Private Law Sources and Analogies of International Law* (1927), pp. 191–202; Schücking and Wehberg, *Die Satzung des Völkerbundes* (2nd ed., 1924), pp. 688–711; Redslob, *Théorie de la Société des Nations* (1927), pp. 175–216] either as such or as representing the international community. Nearly every possible combination of these four basic theories has been advanced, including theories of joint, divided and suspended sovereignty. [For example, see Hall, *International Law* (Higgins 8th ed., 1924), pp. 158–163; Corbett, *British Yearbook of International Law* (1924), p. 134.] Further, many jurists have expressed the opinion that there is no sovereignty with respect to mandated territory [Scelle, *Manuel de Droit international public* (1948), pp. 222–238; Hales, *Some Legal Aspects of the Mandates System: Sovereignty—Nationality—Termination and Transfer*, "Transactions of the Grotius Society", Vol. 23 (1938), pp. 85–126] or have argued that existing conceptions of sovereignty have little practical application to such a novel state of affairs as that presented by the Mandates System. [Oppenheim, *International Law*, Vol. I (McNair, 4th ed., 1928), pp. 201–215.]

"With the Court's permission, I should like to refer very briefly to some of the arguments which have been advanced with regard to these various theories of sovereignty.

"Those supporting the view that sovereignty is in a condominium of the Principal Powers point to the fact that Germany renounced its rights in favour of those Powers, and to the absence of an explicit transfer of sovereignty thereafter. Against this it has been stated that the function of the Principal Powers was limited to the designation of the mandatory and to participation in the setting up of the mandates. Upon the performance of this function, it was argued, their rights under Articles 118 and 119 of the Treaty of Versailles came to an end.

"Those supporting the view that sovereignty is in the mandatory Power emphasized the completeness of the powers of government possessed by the mandatory. They did recognize that such sovereignty would be subject to the limitations and servitudes set forth in the Covenant and in the Mandate. The arguments opposed to the view that sovereignty is in the mandatory have been numerous, and I will deal with some of these in more detail in a few minutes when I consider the work of the Permanent Mandates Commission. They are based in part on inferences from the words mandate, tutelage and trust; in part on the incongruity of a State at the same time possessing sovereignty and administering in the name of the League, and in part on the absence of the usual legal relations which accompany sovereignty.

"The theory that sovereignty resided in the mandated community was advanced with particular strength with regard to the 'A' Mandates, but was also argued with respect to 'B' and 'C' Mandates. It was sometimes stated that the exercise of sovereignty was in suspense. Those supporting this view attached particular significance to the term 'tutelage' as used in Article 22, and also to the principles of non-annexation strongly insisted upon at Versailles. Those opposing the view that sovereignty is in the inhabitants pointed to the absence in these territories of a community capable of possessing sovereignty and to the political immaturity of the peoples.

"The publicist supporting theories attributing sovereignty in full or in part to the League of Nations placed emphasis on the phrase 'on behalf of the League' appearing in Article 22, and also on the necessity for the consent of the Council for the modification of a mandate. Some writers found additional support for this theory in an analogy to the private law concept of mandate. Against the view that sovereignty was in the League, it was stated that the powers of supervision given to the League were not those of a sovereign. A few were of the opinion that the League was not capable of possessing sovereign powers, while others who recognized that the League might have sovereignty over a territory believed that it had not been given such powers in the case of the mandate.

"In view of these conflicting theories, it is not surprising that a number of international jurists have expressed the opinion that sovereignty is not a useful concept in describing the status of the mandates. It was suggested that a new relationship had been created under the Covenant and the mandates, and that the international status of the territory was to be determined from the terms of these instruments without attempting to force them into preconceived concepts of sovereignty."

International Status of South-West Africa, Pleadings, Oral Arguments, Documents, pp. 191–194 (I.C.J. 1950).

In this same Statement to the Court on behalf of the United Nations, Mr. Kerno recalled that in 1927 and in 1930 the Council of the League of Nations had adopted resolutions on the basis of reports of the Permanent Mandates Commission expressing the view that the legal relationship between the Mandatory and the mandated Territory is a new one in international law, and that sovereignty, in the traditional sense of the word, does not reside in the Mandatory Powers.

Ibid. 198.

The views set forth in various national court decisions were summarized in this same Statement to the International Court of Justice as follows:

"The question of the status of mandated territory has been involved in a number of national court decisions [for example Rex v. Christian, *South-African Law Reports*, 1924, Appellate Division, pp. 101–137; Ffrost v. Stevenson, 58 *C.L.R.* (1937), p. 528; Att.-Gen. v. Goralschwili, *L. R. Palestine*, 1920–1933, p. 353; Rex v. Ketter, 108 *L. J.* 345, 1 KB 787 (1940), (1939) 1 ALL E. R. 729; Talagoa v. Inspector of Police (1927), *N.Z.L.R.* 883; Delegate of the High Commissioner in Alexandretta, *Gazette des Tribunaux libano-syriens*, 3rd year, 1927, p. 1010, *Annual Digest* 1927–1928, Case No. 32; Antoine Bey Sabbagh v. Mohamed Pacha Ahmed, *Gazette des Tribunaux mixtes d'Égypte*, 18th Year, 1927–1928, p. 13; In re Caussègue and Cot, Sirey, 1930, Part 3, p. 7, *Annual Digest* 1929–1930, Case No. 15, p. 30; In re Karl and Toto Sané, *Dalloz*, 1931, Part 3, p. 36, *Sirey*, 1931, Part 3, p. 129, and other cases noted, *Annual Digest* 1931–1932, Case No. 22, pp. 48–49; *Re* Tamasese (1929), New Zealand, *L.R.* 209; Nelson v. Braisby (1934), *New Zealand Law Reports* 559], and the closely related question of the nationality status of the inhabitants has been the subject of considerable litigation. Perhaps the best known, and most interesting with relation to the present question, of the cases arising in the courts of the mandatory Powers is that of Rex v. Christian [*South-African Law Reports*, 1924, Appellate Division, pp. 101–137], decided by the Supreme Court of the Union of South Africa in 1923. Jacobus Christian, a leading figure in the Bondelzwarts Rebellion in 1922, was convicted by the Courts of South-West Africa on the charge of high treason. The case came to the Supreme Court of the Union by way of appeal on a question of law relating to the international status of the Mandate. Put in its simplest terms, the question was whether the Union of South Africa as mandatory possessed the sovereignty necessary to maintain a charge of treason. The conviction was affirmed by the unanimous decision of five judges. Three of the judges (Chief Justice Innes, Associate Justices Solomon and Katzé) expressed the opinion that the crime of high treason can be committed against a State which possesses internal sovereignty, even though its external powers may be limited. They held that the Union, as mandatory, possessed sufficient internal sovereignty, or *majestas*, to warrant a charge of treason. The two other judges (Associate Justices de Villiers and Wessels), in expressing the view that sovereignty over the Territory was in the Union, did not distinguish between internal and external sovereignty.

"In the four separate opinions written in this case, the position of the mandated Territory of South-West Africa under the Treaty of Versailles, the Covenant and the Mandate is examined at length.

"I shall not attempt to present these opinions in full, but should like to mention a few points of special interest. Chief Justice Innes, in considering Article 119 of the Treaty of Versailles, stated that, while the expression 'renounce in favour of' was used elsewhere in the Treaty to mean 'cede to', it did not have that meaning in Article 119. The *animus* essential to legal cession was not present on either side. This, he believed, was not only supported by Article 22, but also by a comparison of Articles 254 and 257 of the Treaty. Under the first of these Articles a State to whom territory was ceded was compelled to assume responsibility for a proportion of the German debt, whereas no such obligation was imposed on the mandatory under Article 257.

"This opinion of Chief Justice Innes, although recognizing that South Africa did not possess full sovereignty, expressed the view that it had full legislative and administrative power and was not itself subject to the sovereignty of another State. It was argued that neither the League nor the Principal Powers as such constituted a State, and therefore that they could not possess sovereignty. Justice de Villiers developed this point further by stating that while the exercise of sovereignty by the Union was limited by the terms of the Mandate, such limitation did not deprive the sovereign of *majestas* so long as there was no abdication of sovereignty in favour of another State.

"While the arguments in these opinions have been cited in support of the view that sovereignty is in the mandatory, the decision itself did not rest on a finding that the Union of South Africa possessed sovereignty so far as the international status of the Territory was concerned.

"The status of mandated territory has been the subject of Court decisions in a number of cases in the Australian Courts. It appears that some of the earlier Australian cases imply the existence of sovereignty in the mandatory. However, in Ffrost *v.* Stevenson [58 *C.L.R.* (1937), p. 528] now cited as the leading Australian case, the Court considered at length the nature of the mandates and did not accept the view that sovereignty had been acquired over the Territory of New Guinea. In this case the High Court of Australia was called upon to decide a question relating to the extent of legislative powers in mandated territories. Chief Justice Latham expressed doubt whether any light could be thrown on the question by considering the applicability to mandated territories of a conception itself so uncertain and so disputable as that of sovereignty. The grant of mandates, he thought, introduced a new principle into international law, and he concluded that a mandated territory is not a possession in the ordinary sense. Justice Evatt in his opinion in this same case expressed the view that every recognized authority on international law accepts the view that the mandated Territory of New Guinea is not part of the King's Dominions.

"There are, of course, a large number of cases arising in Palestine and the other 'A' Mandates. [*L.R. Palestine*, 1920–1923, p. 353.] I will only mention one of these. The High Court of Palestine in Attorney-General *v.* Goralschwili held that the British Crown had not acquired full sovereignty by accepting the Mandate for Palestine, and the subjects of this Territory had not become British nationals."

International Status of South-West Africa, Pleadings, Oral Arguments, Documents, pp. 194–196 (I.C.J. 1950).

No cession

"The terms of this Mandate, as well as the provisions of Article 22 of the Covenant and the principles embodied therein, show that the creation of this new international institution did not involve any cession of territory . . . to the Union of South Africa."

International Status of South-West Africa, Advisory Opinion, July 11, 1950, I.C.J. Reports (1950) 128, 132.

In his Separate Opinion in this proceeding, Judge Sir Arnold McNair observed that "the Mandatory acquires only a limited title to the territory entrusted to it . . ." *Ibid.* 150. Judge McNair had previously observed:

"First, the question is sometimes asked, Wherein does the mandate system differ from the old-fashioned annexation which was a frequent result of a war ending in a preponderant victory? From the point of view of the dispossessed owners, there is little difference, except that if and when they are admitted to the League they take part in the measure of supervision which the League exercises over the working of the system, and also become entitled to participate with other members of the League in the benefits of the 'open door' as to trade and commerce which the 'A' and 'B' mandatories undertake to secure. From the point of view, however, of the mandatory and of the inhabitants of the mandated area, there is a substantial difference from annexation, as the mandatory is precluded by the terms of the mandate from doing a number of things which an owner of territory can lawfully do. That Germany and Turkey have divested themselves of all rights of ownership in the mandated areas is clear. That the mandatories have not acquired all of those rights is equally clear; for (i) by the terms of the mandates they agree to exercise their mandates on behalf of the League, and the mandates, at any rate, contain no cession of the territory to the mandatory; (ii) the mandatory has no power without the consent of the Council of the League to annex, cede, or otherwise to dispose of the mandated territory; . . ."

I McNair, *Oppenheim's International Law* (4th ed., 1928) 203–204.

In his Separate Opinion in the advisory proceeding, *International Status of South-West Africa*, Judge McNair made the following additional observations on the subject of cession of territory:

"Some practical confirmation of these suggestions of the relevant principles can be obtained from judgments delivered by the Courts of two Mandatories—the Union of South Africa and the Commonwealth of Australia. (As the Reports of these decisions are not available everywhere, I must quote extracts from them.) In *Rex* v. *Christian*, . . . [So. Afr. L.R. [1924], Appellate Div., 101], before the Supreme Court of South Africa, the Honourable J. de Villiers, Judge of Appeal, said:

" 'It is true there is no cession of the territory to the Union Government as in the case of other possessions which formerly belonged to Germany. By Article 257 South-West Africa is said to be transferred to the Union Government in its capacity as mandatory. But, as I shall show, by that is meant that the Union Government is bound by the terms of the treaty, as well as in honour, scrupulously to carry out the terms of the Mandate. South-West Africa is transferred to the people of the Union not by way of absolute property, but in the same way as a trustee is in possession of the property of the *cestui que trust* or a guardian of the property of his ward. The former has the administration and control of the property, but the property has to be administered exclusively in the interests of the latter. The legal terms employed in Article 22—trust, tutelage, mandate—cannot be taken literally as expressing the definite conceptions for which they stand in law. They are to be understood as indicating rather the spirit in which the advanced nation who is honoured with a mandate should administer the territory entrusted to its care and discharge its duties to the inhabitants of the territory, more especially towards the indigenous populations. In how far the legal principles of these analogous municipal institutions should be applied in these international relations I shall not take upon myself to pronounce. But I may be permitted to say that in my opinion the use of the term shows that, in so far as those legal principles are reasonably applicable to these novel institutions, they should loyally be applied. No doubt most difficult questions will arise. In municipal law a principal can, e.g., revoke his authority at his own mere pleasure. Such is the rule. Could this be done in the case of South-West Africa where the Union Government, if there is a principal at all, must be considered as a joint principal together with all the other high contracting parties?' (P. 121.)"

International Status of South-West Africa, Advisory Opinion, July 11, 1950, I.C.J. Reports (1950) 128, 150–151.

Judge McNair's Separate Opinion continued:

"In *Ffrost* v. *Stevenson* (1937), 58 Commonwealth Law Reports 528, *Annual Digest and Reports of Public International Law Cases*, 1935–1937, Case No. 29, the High Court of Australia, on appeal from the Supreme Court of New South Wales, had to decide, on a matter of extradition, whether or not 'the Mandated Territory of New Guinea [also a C Mandate] is a place out of His Majesty's Dominions in which His Majesty has jurisdiction. . . .'. The High Court gave an affirmative answer. This decision involved a consideration of the nature of a Mandate and the powers of a Mandatory, and the following extracts from the judgments of Chief Justice Latham and Mr. Justice Evatt are of interest. The former said:

"'The grant of mandates introduced a new principle into international law. . . .' (P. 550.)
"'The position of a mandatory in relation to a mandated territory must be regarded as *sui generis*. The Treaty of Peace, read as a whole, avoids cession of territory to the mandatory, and, in the absence of definite evidence to the contrary, it must, I think, be taken that New Guinea has not become part of the dominions of the Crown.' (P. 552.)
"'The intention of this provision [Article 257 of the Treaty of Peace] must be taken to have been to provide for the transfer of the territory to the mandatory, but only in its capacity as a mandatory. The mandatory, as a kind of international trustee, receives the territory subject to the provisions of the mandate which limit the exercise of the governmental powers of the mandatory. Thus the article quoted, while recognizing that the territory is actually to be transferred to the mandatory, emphasizes the conditions and limitations upon governmental power which constitute the essence of the mandatory system. Thus the title under which the territory is to be held as a mandated territory is different from that under which a territory transferred by simple cession would have been held. The article shows that the intention was to achieve a transfer of a territory without making that territory in the ordinary sense a possession of the mandatory. A territory which is a "possession" can be ceded by a power to another power so that the latter power will have complete authority in relation to that territory. Such a cession by a mandatory power would be quite inconsistent with the whole conception of a mandate. A mandated territory is not a possession of a power in the ordinary sense.' (Pp. 552, 553.)

"Mr. Justice Evatt, after referring to a number of British decisions on the status of protectorates, said:

" 'It is quite fallacious to infer from the fact that, in pursuance of its international duties under the mandate, the Commonwealth of Australia exercises full and complete jurisdiction over the territory as though it possessed unlimited sovereignty therein, either that the territory (a) is a British possession, or (b) is within the King's dominions, or (c) has ever been assimilated or incorporated within the Commonwealth or its territories. . . .' (P. 581.)

" 'Therefore, it can be stated that, despite certain differences of opinion as to such questions as sovereignty in relation to the mandated territories, every recognized authority in international law accepts the view that the Mandated Territory of New Guinea is not part of the King's dominions. Over and over again this fact has been recognized by the leading jurists of Europe including many who have closely analyzed such matters in relation to the organization and administration of the League of Nations.'   (P. 582.)

"He then adopted Professor Brierly's view ["Trusts and Mandates", X Brit. Ybk. Int'l L. (1929) 217–219] . . ., as to the governing principle of the Mandates System.

"Reference should also be made to Mr. Justice Evatt's judgment in *Jolley* v. *Mainka* (1933), 49 Commonwealth Law Reports 242, at pages 264–292, *Annual Digest, 1933–1934*, Case No. 17, relating to the same Mandated Territory."

International Status of South-West Africa, Advisory Opinion, July 11, 1950, I.C.J. Reports (1950) 128, 151–153.

Article 257 of the Versailles Treaty, mentioned above, provided:

"In the case of the former German territories, including colonies, protectorates or dependencies, administered by a Mandatory under Article 22 of Part I (League of Nations) of the present Treaty, neither the territory nor the Mandatory Power shall be charged with any portion of the debt of the German Empire or States.

"All property and possessions belonging to the German Empire or to the German States situated in such territories shall be transferred with the territories to the Mandatory Power in its capacity as such and no payment shall be made nor any credit given to those Governments in consideration of this transfer.

"For the purposes of this Article the property and possessions of the German Empire and of the German States shall be deemed to include all the property of the Crown, the Empire or the States and the private property of the former German Emperor and other Royal personages."   III Redmond, Treaties, etc. (1923) 3331, 3442.

Article 254 of the same Treaty obligated the "Powers to which German territory is ceded" to assume a proportionate share of the debt of the German Empire. *Ibid.* 3441.   Article 256 provided in part:

"Powers to which German territory is ceded shall acquire all property and possessions situated therein belonging to the German Empire or to the German States, and the value of such acquisitions shall be fixed by the Reparation Commission, and paid by the State acquiring the territory to the Reparation Commission for the credit of the German Government on account of the sums due for reparation." *Ibid.* 3442.

A comparison of articles 254 and 256 with article 257 indicates that the latter provision did not contemplate "cession" of the former German territories to the Mandatory Powers. The question of "cession of territory" to the Mandatory Powers was not involved in the case of the former Turkish territories, which according to paragraph 4 of article 22 of the Covenant of the League of Nations, had "reached a stage of development where their existence as independent nations can be provisionally recognized," and which became the "A" Mandates.

"Integral portion" of territory

Paragraph 6 of article 22 of the Covenant of the League of Nations stated that certain territories such as South-West Africa and the Pacific Islands "can be best administered under the laws of the Mandatory as integral portions of its territory." Accordingly, all of the "C" Mandate instruments contained provisions conferring upon the Mandatory "full power of administration and legislation over the territory" "as an integral portion of" the Mandatory's territory. (Article 2, Mandate for German South-West Africa, U.N. Doc. A/70, Oct. 1946, "Terms of League of Nations Mandates"; article 2, Mandate for the German Possessions in the Pacific Ocean lying north of the Equator, *ibid.;* article 2, Mandate for the German possessions in the Pacific Ocean situated south of the Equator other than German Samoa and Nauru, *ibid.;* article 2, Mandate for Nauru, *ibid.*) The "B" Mandate instruments, with the exception of the British Mandate for East Africa (Tanganyika Territory) contained provisions authorizing the Mandatory to administer the area subject to the Mandate "as an integral part of his territory." (Article 9, British Mandate for the Cameroons, *ibid.;* article 9, French Mandate for the Cameroons, *ibid.;* article 9, French Mandate for Togoland, *ibid.;* article 9, British Mandate for Togoland, *ibid.;* article 10, Belgian Mandate for East Africa (Ruanda-Urundi), *ibid.*) In the early days of the League of Nations, the question arose as to whether, in view of these provisions, the Mandates were not, in fact, equivalent to "annexation" by the Mandatory Powers. In the Statement of Ivan Kerno as representative of the Secretary-General of the United Nations, to the International Court of Justice on May 17, 1950, the matter was summarized as follows:

". . . Field Marshal Smuts, in a letter to M. Rappard, Director of the Mandates Section of the League Secretariat, in 1922 referred to the fact that under Article 22 South-West Africa could be administered under the laws of the Union as an integral portion of its territory and stated the view that the 'C' Mandates are in effect not far removed from annexation. [Annex to the Minutes of the second session of the Permanent Mandates Commission, pp. 91–93.] Field Marshal Smuts further amplified this position in a statement before the South-African Parliament which was called to the attention of the ninth session of the Permanent Mandates Commission in 1926. In this statement, he said that the Mandate gives the Union 'such complete power of sovereignty not only administrative but legislative that we need not ask for anything more'. He continued: 'When the Covenant of the League of Nations and, subsequently, the Mandate gave to us the right to administer that country as an integral portion of the Union, everything was given to us. I remember at the Peace Conference one of the great Powers tried to modify the position, and, instead of saying "as an integral portion", an amendment was made to introduce the word "if", so that it should read—"as if an integral portion of the mandatory Power". But, after consideration, the "if" was struck out. We therefore have the power to govern South-West Africa actually as an integral portion of the Union.' [Permanent Mandates Commission, Minutes of ninth session, p. 33.]

"The members of the Permanent Mandates Commission were quick to state their opposition to this position. Mr. Van Rees remarked that the Mandates Commission had always interpreted paragraph 6 of Article 22 of the Covenant in the sense that the mandated territory should be administered 'as if it were an integral portion of the territory of the mandatory'. Sir Frederick Lugard at the same time stated that he did not think that the insertion or omission of the word 'if' made any real difference in practice. Mr. Orts did not believe that what had been said during the discussions preceding the adoption of the Covenant could be used as an argument, as no minutes had been kept of the Conference, and M. Rappard concurred in this view. M. Merlin stated 'that the "C" Mandate for South-West Africa laid upon the mandatory the same obligations as the "B" Mandates, except that concerning economic equality. Both "B" and "C" Mandates involved the obligation to present an annual report and recognized the right of the inhabitants to present petitions. These were the points which made it impossible to describe the mandates as an equivalent to annexation.' [*Ibid.*, p. 34.]

"Mr. Van Rees, at the eleventh session, after a review of a number of the decisions of the Council and of the Commission, concluded 'that on no occasion had the Commission or the Council, or the mandatory Powers themselves, ever agreed to recognize that mandated territories formed in reality an integral part of the territory belonging to those Powers'. [Minutes of the eleventh session, p. 88.]

"Somewhat similar discussions of the proper conception of the mandate ensued with regard to other territories. I might mention, for example, discussions which took place at the 10th session of the Commission in 1926 and at the 12th session in 1927 with regard to statements concerning the status of Western Samoa. At the former session, great satisfaction was expressed with regard to a statement by the Governor-General of New Zealand that 'Western Samoa is not an integral part of the British Empire, but a child of which we have assumed the guardianship'. [Minutes of the tenth session, p. 24.] On the other hand, at the latter session the following year, the Chairman of the Commission viewed with concern a statement made by the Administrator during the celebration of the King's birthday which referred to Western Samoa as 'part of the British Empire'. [Minutes of the twelfth session, p. 103.]

"The representative of New Zealand assured the Commission that the New Zealand Government was content to accept the view which, if he remembered rightly, was taken by the Commission, that a new sort of relationship, unknown in international law hitherto, had been created by the mandates."

International Status of South-West Africa, Pleadings, Oral Arguments, Documents, pp. 202–203 (I.C.J. 1950).

Cf., Chow Hung Ching etc. v. *The King*, reported in [1948] Ann. Dig. 147 (No. 47) (1948), 77 C.L.R. 449, [1949] A.L.R. 29, where the High Court of Australia construed article 2 of the Mandate for New Guinea. Philip, J., said ([1948] Ann. Dig. at 149) : "But in Article 2 of the New Guinea Mandate it was expressly declared that 'the Mandatory shall have full power of administration and legislation over the Territory subject to the present Mandate as an integral portion of the Commonwealth of Australia and may apply the laws of the Commonwealth of Australia to the territory, subject to such local modifications as circumstances may require.' In the face of that declaration it seems to me beyond doubt that, wherever the ultimate sovereignty of the Territory of New Guinea may reside, Australia may, as Mandatory Power, and subject to the terms of the Mandate, exercise powers of administration and legislation over New Guinea that are equivalent to and as full as those of a Sovereign State : in other words, Australia's powers of administration over New Guinea include exclusive jurisdiction over all persons and things within that Territory, except in so far as Australia concedes immunity from that exclusive jurisdiction." For a similar interpretation of article 2 of the Mandate for Western Samoa, see *Nelson* v. *Braisby* (*No. 2*), Supreme Court of New Zealand, [1933–34] Ann. Dig. 36 (No. 15). Thus, Myers, C.J.: ". . . that full power of administration and legislation involves plenary authority to make laws and to enforce them, which authority covers the whole sphere of government." *Ibid.* 39.

Territorial adjustments

Article VIII of the Treaty between His Britannic Majesty and His Majesty the King of Iraq, signed October 10, 1922, provided in part: "No territory in Iraq shall be ceded or in any way placed under the control of any foreign Power . . ." Article 4 of the Mandate for Syria and Lebanon provided: "The Mandatory shall be responsible for seeing that no part of the territory of Syria and the Lebanon is ceded or leased or in any way placed under the control of a foreign Power." A similar provision appeared in article 5 of the Mandate for Palestine. (The texts of these instruments may be found in U.N. Doc. A/70, Oct. 1946.)

Sanjak of Alexandretta

In 1939 the Sanjak of Alexandretta was transferred to Turkey by agreement between France, as Mandatory Power, and Turkey. 1919 For. Rel., vol. XIII, Paris Peace Conference (1947), p. 99. As to this, Lauterpacht commented: "It is difficult to admit that in concluding on June 23, 1939, the agreement with Turkey in which she ceded the Sanjak of Alexandretta, France remained within the limits of her powers as mandatory. See Reports of the Mandates Commission to the Council, Minutes of the 36th Session (1939), p. 278)." I Lauterpacht, *Oppenheim's International Law* (8th ed., 1955) 214, n. 2. See also Hall, *Mandates, Dependencies and Trusteeship* (1948) 11.

On December 16, 1925, the Council of the League of Nations took a decision, under article 3, paragraph 2, of the Treaty of Lausanne signed July 24, 1923 (28 LNTS 11), fixing the frontier between Turkey and Iraq. Myers, *Handbook of the League of Nations* (1935) 317–319. *Cf.*, Advisory Opinion, *Interpretation of Article 3, paragraph 2, of the Treaty of Lausanne (Frontier between Turkey and Iraq)*, Nov. 21, 1925 (P.C.I.J., Series B, No. 12); and Hudson, *The Permanent Court of International Justice 1920–1942* (1943) 517–518. {.margin: Iraq frontier}

On November 25, 1932, the Council of the League of Nations appointed a commission to fix the Iraqi-Syrian frontier, since France and the United Kingdom had found the previous treaty delimitation to be unsatisfactory. By agreement of October 31, 1931, France and the United Kingdom laid down the Syrian-Jebel Druse-Transjordan boundary, which was approved by the Council on January 30, 1932. Myers, *op. cit.* 110–111. {.margin: Syrian frontier}

The "B" and "C" Mandate instruments did not contain formal provisions similar to the "A" Mandate prohibiting the cession of territory. That the Mandatory, in the words of McNair had "no powers without the consent of the Council of the League to annex, cede, or otherwise to dispose of the mandated territory," was clear from the practice of the League of Nations. I McNair, *Oppenheim's International Law* (4th ed., 1928) 204. The practice of the League with regard to boundary adjustments for the "B" and "C" Mandates has been summarized as follows: {.margin: "B" and "C" Mandates: boundary adjustments}

> "*Boundary Adjustments.* The mandates which were formerly German colonies were established within the area of those colonies. The territories which were formerly Turkish had less well defined provincial boundaries. In general, the mandates embody specific geographical descriptions of the limits of the mandated territory. Even where the frontier was fully delimited, the territory's change of status rendered further agreements necessary between the mandatory and the state controlling the conterminous territory. In one case, the former German East Africa became two mandated territories, Tanganyika and Ruanda Urundi, entailing a further agreement between Belgium and Great Britain. All agreements respecting the boundaries of the

mandates are discussed in the annual reports of the mandatories and their texts are submitted to the Mandates Commission and then to the Council for its approval. In one case the Council asked for the submission of, and eventually approved, a protocol which had been registered and published in the *Treaty Series* several years before.

"The Council, finding that the boundary between Ruanda Urundi and Tanganyika as defined by the mandates approved July 20, 1922, did not conform to native interests, Belgium and Great Britain submitted modifications of the mandates, which were approved by the Council August 31, 1923.

"A Council recommendation to modify the frontier between French and British Cameroons so as to leave native holdings intact was found unnecessary to carry out.

"The Council accepted a draft British-German agreement of 1914 as the definitive line between Kenya and Tanganyika.

"South Africa and Portugal at the request of the Council allocated a strip of no-man's land along the northern boundary of Southwest Africa by an agreement of June 22, 1926."

Myers, *Handbook of the League of Nations* (1935), pp. 109–110. See also Hall, *Mandates, Dependencies and Trusteeship* (1948) 175–176.

State
Succession—
"A"
Mandates

Ottoman
State
property

The terms of the Treaty of Lausanne (28 LNTS 11) provided for the application of principles of state succession to the "A" Mandates. Thus, Norman Bentwich, in commenting on the case of *Heirs of the Prince Mohamed Selim* v. *The Government of Palestine* (reported in [1935–1937] Ann. Dig. 123 (No. 39)), states: ". . . The Article [60] of the Treaty [of Lausanne] transferred to the Government of Palestine only those properties which were passed from the Civil List to the Ottoman State by the Irades. But there was nothing in the discussions on the Treaty of Lausanne which could upset the natural interpretation of the words of the Article, that the imperial decrees had transferred properties of Sultan Abdul Hamid to the Ottoman State and that these properties were ceded to the allied *successor states*." (Italics supplied.)

Bentwich, "State Succession and Act of State in the Palestine Courts", XXIII Brit. Yb. Int'l L. (1946) 330, 333.

"In the *Ottoman Public Debt* case, which concerned the apportionment of the annuities of the Ottoman Public Debt among the various states whose territories, in whole or in part, had formerly belonged to Turkey, and which was decided on April 18, 1925 by Eugène Borel, of Switzerland, appointed Arbitrator by the Council of the League of Nations pursuant to the provisions of article 47 of the Treaty of Lausanne of July 24, 1923 [18 *American Journal of International Law*, Supp. (1924) 1, 17], a deposit had been made by the parties to the arbitration in order to guarantee the costs of the arbitration. Borel held that 'any court having jurisdiction on the fundamental question also has jurisdiction with respect to the costs'; that 'the costs of the arbitration, including the fees of the Arbiter' should be borne in equal shares by the parties to the arbitration (Bulgaria, Greece, Italy, Turkey, Syria and Lebanon under French mandate, and Iraq, Palestine, and Trans-Jordan under British mandate); that it was irrelevant to inquire as to the extent to which the respective parties had proved successful or unsuccessful in their pleadings; that such a test would be contrary not only to international practice but also to article 85 of the Hague convention of 1907 for the pacific settlement of international disputes; that such a procedure was especially inapplicable in a case such as the *Ottoman Public Debt* case where the arbitration was conducted in the interest of the parties to the dispute; and that it would be impossible to determine the proportional interests of the parties. [*Sentence arbitrale* (Geneva, 1925) 106 *et seq.*]"

III Whiteman, *Damages in International Law* (1943) 2029–2030.

The text of the award has been reprinted in I *Report of International Arbitral Awards* (United Nations, 1948) at 529.

Article 46 of the Treaty of Lausanne provided that the Ottoman Public Debt "shall be distributed . . . between Turkey" and, among others, "the States newly created in territories in Asia which are detached from the Ottoman Empire under the present Treaty." (28 LNTS 11, 37.) The Ottoman Debt Arbitration is also reported in the Annual Digest, with the following "Note":

"The arbitrator, after having adopted the principle that the costs have to be equally divided between the States parties to the arbitration, said: 'The difficulty arises here how one is to regard the Asiatic countries under the British and French mandates. Iraq is a Kingdom in regard to which Great Britain has undertaken responsibilities equivalent to those of a Mandatory Power. Under the British mandate, Palestine and Transjordan have each an entirely separate organisation. We are, therefore, in the presence of three States sufficiently separate to be considered as distinct Parties.

" 'France has received a single mandate from the Council of the League of Nations, but in the countries subject to that mandate, one can distinguish two distinct States: Syria and the Lebanon, each State possessing its own constitution and a nationality clearly different from the other.' "

[1925–1926] Ann. Dig. 42 (No. 29).

In its Judgment No. 5, *The Mavrommatis Palestine Concessions*, the Permanent Court of International Justice decided that certain concessions granted to a Greek national by Ottoman authorities for public works in Jerusalem were valid under Protocol XII of the

Ottoman
concessions

Treaty of Lausanne, a "Protocol relating to certain concessions granted in the Ottoman Empire", and were entitled to readaptation in conformity with new economic conditions. Article 9 of this Protocol provided in part: "In the territories detached from Turkey under the Treaty of Peace signed this day, the State which acquires the territory is fully subrogated as regards the rights and obligations of Turkey towards the nationals of the other Contracting Powers . . . who are beneficiaries under concessionary contracts entered into before the 29th October, 1914, with the Ottoman Government or any local Ottoman authority. . . ." (28 LNTS 203, 211.) Great Britain, the Mandatory for Palestine, was a party to Protocol XII as well as to the Treaty of Lausanne. In its Judgment No. 5, however, the Permanent Court of International Justice specifically stated that the Palestine Administration, not Great Britain as Mandatory, was subrogated to the obligations of Turkey with respect to these concessions. Thus, the Court observed: ". . . It is therefore in the exercise of this full power that the Palestine Administration must, under Article 11 [of the Mandate], respect the international obligations accepted by the Mandatory in regard to which that article makes an express reservation. In the opinion of the Court these international obligations there referred to are constituted solely by the Protocol of Lausanne. For no other instrument creating international obligations contracted by the Mandatory has been brought to the Court's knowledge, and it does not appear that any such exist. . . ."

At another point in its decision, the Court observed:

"The provision, therefore, contained in Article 9 of Protocol XII, to the effect that Palestine is subrogated as regards the rights and obligations of Turkey towards the nationals of contracting Powers other than Turkey, who are beneficiaries under the concessionary contracts entered into with the Ottoman authorities before October 29th, 1914, is applicable to M. Mavrommatis' concessions."

Still farther on, the Court stated:

"In order to determine M. Mavrommatis' position in relation to the Palestine Administration, which is subrogated as regards the rights and obligations of Turkey in respect of concessions granted by that country in Palestine, one matter of fact must be verified: had the contracts concluded between M. Mavrommatis and the Ottoman authorities begun to be put into operation at the date of the signature of Protocol XII? . . ."

The Mavrommatis Palestine Concessions, Judgment (Merits), P.C.I.J., Series A, No. 5, Mar. 26, 1925, pp. 23, 27, 32, 46.

In its Judgment of August 30, 1924 (Jurisdiction), the Permanent Court of International Justice had stated in the case of *The Mavrommatis Palestine Concessions:*

"The powers accorded under Article 11 [of the Mandate] must, as has been seen, be exercised 'subject to any international obligations accepted by the Mandatory.' This qualification was a necessary one, for the international obligations of the Mandatory are not, *ipso facto*, international obligations of Palestine. Since Article 11 of the Mandate gives the Palestine Administration a wide measure of autonomy, it was necessary to make absolutely certain that the powers granted could not be misused in a manner incompatible with certain international engagements of the Mandatory. The obligations resulting from these engagements are therefore obligations which the Administration of Palestine must respect; the Mandatory is internationally responsible for any breach of them since, under Article 12 of the Mandate, the external relations of Palestine are handled by it."

> Judgment No. 2 (Jurisdiction), P.C.I.J., Series A, No. 2, Aug. 30, 1924, p. 23.

In *Arab Bank Ld.* v. *Barclays Bank*, a proceeding in the English House of Lords ([1954] A.C. 495, also reported in [1954] Int'l L. Rep. 443), it was held that the appellant Arab Bank which had a credit balance in the respondents' Allenby Square Branch, Jerusalem, at the time of the termination of the British Mandate for Palestine, would have to look to the State of Israel for recovery. Thus, Lord Morton of Henryton stated: *(Credit balances)*

"My Lords, I do not attempt the task of formulating an exhaustive description of the rights which do and the rights which do not survive the outbreak of war; but I am quite satisfied that the right to be paid a credit balance on a current account is a right which survives. . . . It was therefore suspended, and not destroyed, by the outbreak of war, and immediately after the outbreak of war it was locally situate in the newly created State of Israel. Thus it became subject to the legislation of that State, was vested in the custodian, and was rightly paid to the custodian by the respondents. There was a difference of opinion in the court below as to whether the necessity for a demand survived the outbreak of war. I incline to the view that it did, but I do not regard a decision on this question as being necessary for the decision of this case.

"The question whether the appellants will or will not ultimately recover the large sum already paid by the respondents to the custodian is one which will be answered by Israeli legislation, or by the arrangements made between the State of Israel and the Arab countries when a treaty of peace is signed; but they cannot recover that sum from the respondents."

Lord Reid observed:

"Accordingly, I am of opinion that on May 15, 1948, there was a debt of £P582,931 due by the respondents to the appellants and that it was a debt situated in Jerusalem where alone it was payable. Further performance of the contract of current account was prevented by the outbreak of war so that no further banking services could be performed by the respondents for the appellants, but the debt fell within the class of accrued rights and was not abrogated. The respondents have paid the amount of the debt to the Custodian of Absentee Property in Israel, and if this was a debt situated in Israel after May 15 they were bound to make that payment and the appellants cannot recover anything in this action. To succeed, the appellants would have somehow to establish that any debt owing to them was not after May 15 situated in Israel, because it is only in that case that the respondents would have been wrong in making payment to the custodian in Israel."

And Lord Cohen stated:

"My Lords, it is common ground between the parties that: (I) Had the appellants demanded the balance standing to their credit with the Allenby Square branch of the respondents immediately before the outbreak of war the resultant debt would have been locally situate in Palestine. (II) The contract of current account made between the parties on February 14, 1939, was frustrated by the outbreak of war at least in the sense that the further performance by the respondents of their obligation to render banking services to the appellants was prohibited by the law of Israel as contrary to public policy. (III) If, notwithstanding frustration, the respondents remained bound to pay to the appellants at the Allenby Square branch the amount of the credit balance due to the appellants, that obligation was a chose in action locally situate in Israel and became vested in the Custodian of Absentee Property under the Absentee Property Regulation which was superseded by the Absentee Property Law, 1950.

. . . .

". . . It was of the essence of the original contract that the debt should be payable at the Allenby Square branch and that Palestine law should govern the obligations of the parties. So long as the appellants have to found their claim on the contract, it must, I think, be regarded as a right situate down to the outbreak of war in Palestine and thereafter in Israel."

[1954] A.C. 529, 534, 537, 541.

With respect to the financial obligations of the Administration of Palestine, a settlement was negotiated between Israel and the United Kingdom in 1950. 156 Br. & For. St. Paps. (1950, pt. I) 608. See O'Connell, *Law of State Succession* (1956) 178–179. The Palestine concessions "were, however, in a rather unusual situation since, consequent upon the decision in the *Mavrommatis Case*, and in exercise of the powers granted by the protocol to the Treaty of Lausanne, Great Britain, as Mandatory of Palestine, had regulated their exercise by municipal ordinance. [See, for example, Electricity Concession Ordinance, Drayton, *Law of Palestine*, vol. 1, p. 633; Electricity Concessions Jerusalem Ordinance, *ibid.*, p. 658; Dead Sea Concessions Ordinance, no. 3 of 1937; *Palestine Gazette Supplement*, no. 1 of August 1937, p. 195.] Such acts of legislation were undoubtedly continued in force after the setting up of the State of Israel by Act of the Knesseth maintaining the law of Palestine as it existed on 14 May 1948. [Transition (Temporary Provisions), no. 2 (Amendment Law), art. 11, Statute Book 14 of the 23rd day of Tamuz, 5709, p. 72.] At the present time these concessions are being 'readapted to the new economic circumstances' in accordance with the powers contained in the Palestine ordinances." O'Connell, *Law of State Succession* (1956) 129.

In several cases, the Supreme Court of Israel has had to consider the extent to which the law of Palestine under the Mandate continued to apply in the new State of Israel. Thus, in *Abmed Shauki el Kharbutli* v. *Minister of Defence*, that Court, sitting as the High Court of Justice, observed: ". . . It is perhaps surprising that after the establishment of the State of Israel we should still have to consider the question whether the Mandate was once part of the law in force in Palestine, or whether it was simply a 'document' containing a declaration of intentions without binding force. But bearing in mind that under the Law and Administration Ordinance all the laws which have been left from the period of the Mandate remain in force, it follows that whether any of these laws was valid is not an academic question but one of great practical importance.

"At this point we feel it necessary to hold without hesitation that the Mandate, as part of international law, was binding on the Power to which the Mandate was entrusted—the more so as by virtue of the Mandate that Power assumed authority over the country—and that every act done, or law promulgated, by the Mandatory Power in contravention of the terms of the Mandate was a violation both of international law and of the law of Palestine." [1949] Ann. Dig. 41, 42 (No. 19). See also Note in [1948] Annual Digest 42–43, commenting on the case of *Leon* v. *Gubernik* in the same Court, in which it is stated: "However, we must not ignore the argument . . . that Imperial statutes which were inconsistent with the Mandate are of no validity. During the Mandate the Courts rejected such arguments on the ground that the Mandate was only law in so far as its provisions had been incorporated into the Palestine Order in Council, 1922. The attitude of this Court is different. We are prepared to examine laws passed by the Mandatory in the light of the provisions of the Mandate." According to this same Note, decisions of the Mandatory's courts do not constitute binding precedents on the Courts of Israel, *Rosenbaum* v.

Law and judicial precedent

Rosenbaum, decided by the Supreme Court of Israel on April 3, 1949, but "continuity and stability in the law led the Court generally to follow the decisions of the former Supreme Court of Palestine . . . ." *Ibid*. 43 (*cf., Jerusalem-Jaffa District Governor* v. *Suleiman Murra*, [1926] A.C. 321, the "Urtas Springs" case, where, on appeal from the Supreme Court of Palestine, the British Privy Council held, at p. 327, that "it was the right and duty of the Court to consider whether the [Urtas Springs] Ordinance was in any way repugnant to those terms [of the Mandate]," but relied on the stipulation in the Order in Council of May 4, 1923, that no Ordinance should be promulgated which was repugnant to or inconsistent with the provisions of the Mandate. This case is also reported in [1925–1926] Ann. Dig. (No. 32)).

Criminal jurisdiction
    In the course of the Judgment in the case of Adolf Eichmann for crimes against the Jewish people, crimes against humanity, and war crimes, the District Court of Jerusalem stated:

> "36. Counsel contended that the protective principle cannot apply to this case because that principle is designed to protect only an existing State, its security and its interests, while the State of Israel had not existed at the time of the commission of the crime. He further submitted that the same contention was effective with respect to the principle of the 'passive personality' which stemmed from the protective principle, and of which some States have made use for the protection of their citizens abroad through their penal legislation. Counsel pointed out that in view of the absence of a sovereign Jewish State at the time of the catastrophe the victims of the Nazis were not, at the time they were murdered, citizens of the State of Israel.
>
> "In our view learned Counsel errs when he examines the protective principle in this retroactive law according to the time of the commission of the crimes, as is the case in an ordinary law. This law was enacted in 1950 with a view to its application during a specified period which had terminated five years before its enactment. The protected interest of the State recognised by the protective principle is in this case the interest existing at the time of the enactment of the law, and we have already dwelt on the importance of the moral and protective task which this law is designed to perform in the State of Israel.

> "38. All this is said in relation to the accused; but may a new State, at all, try crimes that were committed before it was established? The reply to this question was given in *Katz-Cohen* v. *Attorney-General*, C.A. 3/48 (Pesakim II, p. 225) wherein it was decided that the Israel Courts have full Jurisdiction to try offences committed before the establishment of the State, and that 'in spite of the changes in sovereignty there subsisted a continuity of law'. 'I cannot see', said President Smoira, 'why that com-

munity in the country against whom the crime was committed should not demand the punishment of the offender solely because that community is now governed by the Government of Israel instead of by the Mandatory Power'. This was said with respect to a crime committed in the country, but there is no reason to assume that the law would be different with respect to foreign offences. Had the Mandatory legislator enacted at the time an extraterritorial law for the punishment of war criminals (as, to give one example, the Australian legislator had done in the War Criminals Act, 1945, see Section 12) it is clear that the Israel Court would have been competent to try under such law offences which were committed abroad prior to the establishment of the State. The principle of continuity also applies to the power to legislate: the Israel legislator is empowered to amend or supplement the mandatory legislation retroactively, by enacting laws applicable to criminal acts which were committed prior to the establishment of the State.

"Indeed, this retroactive law is designed to supplement a gap in the laws of Mandatory Palestine, and the interests protected by this law had existed also during the period of the Jewish National Home. The Balfour Declaration and the Palestine Mandate given by the League of Nations to Great Britain constituted an international recognition of the Jewish people, (see *N. Feinberg*, 'The Recognition of the Jewish People in International Law', Jewish Yearbook of International Law 1948, p. 15, and authorities there cited), the historical link of the Jewish people with Eretz Israel and their right to reestablish their National Home in that country. The Jewish people has actually made use of that right, and the National Home has grown and developed until it reached a sovereign status. During the period preceding the establishment of the sovereign State the Jewish National Home may be seen as reflecting the rule 'nasciturus pro jam nato habetur' (see Feinberg ibid.). The Jewish 'Yishuv' in Palestine constituted during that period a 'State-on-the-way', as it were, which reached in due time a sovereign status. The want of sovereignty made it impossible for the Jewish 'Yishuv' in the country to enact a criminal law against the Nazi crimes at the time of the commission thereof, but these crimes were also directed against that 'Yishuv' who constituted an integral part of the Jewish people, and the enactment with retroactive application of the law in question by the State of Israel filled the need which had already existed previously."

The Attorney-General of the Government of Israel v. Adolf, the son of Karl Adolf Eichmann, District Court of Jerusalem, Criminal Case No. 40/61, Judgment delivered Dec. 11, 1961, unofficial English translation, the American Embassy, Tel Aviv, to the Department of State, despatch No. 444, Feb. 13, 1962, encl., MS. Department of State, file 662.0026/2–1362. The case was tried before Mr. Justice Moshe Landau, President, Judge Benjamin Halevi, and Judge Yitzhak Raveh. Affirmed, Supreme Court of Israel, May 29, 1962, same to same, despatch No. 659, June 5, 1962, encl., MS. Department of State, file 662.0026/6–562.

Rosenne, writing in 1950, stated:

". . . The short point in *Katz-Cohen* v. *Attorney-General* [*Pesakim* (*Israel Law Reports* (unofficial)), vol. ii (5709–1949), p. 216; [1949] Ann. Dig. 68 (No. 26)] was whether a crime (murder) committed in Tel Aviv before the termination of the Mandate and the establishment of the state of Israel could be tried in the courts of Israel and punishment inflicted. A few days after the establishment of the state of Israel the Law and Administration Ordinance, 5708–1948 [*Iton Rishmi* (*Official Gazette* of the Provisional Government of Israel) of 21 May 1948 Supplement No. 1, p. 1], was enacted, which provided, *inter alia*, that the law which existed in Palestine on 14 May 1948 (the date of the termination of the Mandate) [cf. the Palestine Act, 1948, s. 1] shall remain in force. It was argued on behalf of the accused that murder is a crime against the state, and that on a change of sovereignty the crime cannot be punished in the absence of clear and express provisions in the law of the new sovereign. The Israel Supreme Court rejected this argument. It said:

" 'Feelings of justice rise in revolt against a conclusion such as this which would imply a gap in the criminal law brought about by the transition from sovereign to sovereign . . . and only an express term of the law will compel me to accept it. . . . The root of the appellant's argument is the fundamental distinction between civil and criminal procedures. He repeatedly stressed that every criminal act is a blow to the community and the State. This is correct, and from it it emerges that not the individual, but the injured community demands the punishment of the offender. Why, then, in the present case should not the same community, against whom the offence was committed, not demand its punishment merely because the Government of Israel has now replaced the Mandatory Government?'

After citing passages from Oppenheim's *International Law* (vol. i, §§ 80 and 81) and Hyde's *International Law* (2nd ed., 1945, vol. i, §§ 120 and 122) the Court said:

" 'Neither of these books says anything to suggest that there is no right to punish for acts committed before the creation of the new sovereign. On the contrary, Hyde is strong authority for the reverse proposition. From him we learn the golden rule of continuity of law despite change of sovereignty. The exception, as he rightly points out, is in the case of laws which stand in contradiction to the Constitution and laws of the new sovereign. . . . Murder and manslaughter are offences against the person, and they, as well as most other criminal offences, are such that continuity of law and continuity of power to punish from sovereign to sovereign are axiomatic, and change of sovereignty does not affect this continuity, for the public welfare demands this result, as the change of sovereignty does not prevent it. . . . The Law and Administration Ordinance . . . establishes the continuity necessary for the power of punishment. . . . Under Section 11 . . . the law was not re-enacted as new law of the State of Israel . . . but *remained* in force, and this gives us continuity from the legal point of view. . . . There is no authority in international law against such continuity. On the contrary, there are ample authorities in favour of it on changes of sovereignty, even without specific enactment. . . .' [This precedent was followed in the later case of *Wahib Saleh Kalil* v. *Attorney-General, Piskei-Din* (*Israel Law Reports* (official)), vol. iv (5710–1950), p. 75. The facts here were identical, save that when the offence was committed the *locus in quo* was outside the area which was to have formed part of the Jewish State under the original United Nations Resolution 181 (II) recommending the partition of Palestine, although by the time of the trial the whole had come under Israel sovereignty. It may be mentioned that the Israel courts adopted towards an amnesty granted early in 1949 an attitude similar to that adopted by the Italian courts.]"

Rosenne, "The Effect of the Change of Sovereignty upon Municipal Law," XXVII Brit. Yb. Int'l L. (1950) 267, 284–285.

In the debate in the United Nations Security Council on October 30, Treaties 1953, on the complaint by Syria against Israel concerning work on the west bank of the River Jordan in the demilitarized zone, the representative of Israel, Mr. Eban, made the following statement:

"124. Secondly, with respect to water, the Government of Israel reserves its position on some of the legal assumptions in General Bennike's letter, especially the suggestion, which we really think remarkable, that Israel in its relations with Syria must be governed by the Franco-British agreement entitled 'Agreement of good neighbourly relations concluded between the British and French Governments on behalf of the territories of Palestine, on the one part, and on behalf of Syria and Great Lebanon, on the other part, signed at Jerusalem, February 2, 1926'.

"125. Israel does not inherit the international treaties signed by the United Kingdom as mandatory power, and I do not know if Syria inherits the treaties signed by France. That we should be bound in the context of Syria's attitude of belligerency and hostility to Israel to recognize a defunct treaty of good neighbourly relations between the United Kingdom and France is a thought of which the humorous possibilities are infinite. I really have not heard that Syria wishes to maintain such a treaty relationship with Israel, although if Syria will now announce its readiness to sign such a treaty we shall not, of course, fail to respond. Nevertheless, despite the absence, in our view, of any legal commitment, the Government of Israel is prepared to undertake that the supply of irrigation water to the Buteiha farm area—that is, towards the southern part of the map—will be maintained. That is the only irrigable area which has been invoked in the course of this discussion as being affected by any change in the level of the Jordan water. The Government of Israel is prepared to give a binding undertaking that the volume of Jordan water required by Arab land owners or cultivators for irrigation purposes in the demilitarized zone will remain available in the future. I have already pointed out that the hydro-electric project makes it entirely possible to ensure that at all seasons sufficient water should continue to be available to satisfy existing irrigation needs. In this I am responding, on my Government's behalf, to an implication contained in General Bennike's letter of 20 October, in paragraph 7(d). In that paragraph, the Chief of Staff asserts that prejudice to existing water interests would arise 'unless definite obligations are entered into to protect existing water rights.' That is a very valid point, and I am empowered to express my Government's readiness to enter into such 'obligations' and we are willing to embody them in a formal instrument which can, if necessary, be invoked internationally by the parties concerned. This applies both to the operating water mill, the solitary water mill involved in the north of the area, and to the Buteiha lands further to the south in the Jordan's course. I think the Security Council would like to have some picture of the dimensions of this problem."

U.N. Security Council Off. Rec., 633d Meeting, Oct. 30, 1953, S/PV.633, pp. 26–27.

Lebanon: Extradition Agreement

In an extradition case, the Supreme Court of Palestine, sitting as a High Court, held that the change of status of Lebanon from a Mandate to an independent Republic did not invalidate the Provisional Agreement for the Extradition of Offenders between Syria and Lebanon and Palestine, concluded between the High Commissioner of the French Republic for Syria and Lebanon and the High Commissioner for Palestine in 1921. The Court's judgment stated, in part: ". . . It cannot be doubted that the sovereignty, in so far as it affected treaty-making power, vested in the French Republic in the case of the Lebanon and in the Mandatory in the case of Palestine, and their duly accredited representatives could lawfully make the treaty. . . . That treaty, unless it is abrogated, binds the successor Government. It is, therefore, still effective between the Lebanese Republic and Palestine."

Shehadeh et al. v. *Commissioner of Prisons, Jerusalem,* Oct. 31, 1947, reported in [1947] Ann. Dig. 42, 43 (No. 16) ; 14 P.L.R. 461.

"B" and "C" Mandates: public property

In the case of the "B" and the "C" Mandates, which were the oversea possessions renounced by Germany under article 119 of the Treaty of Peace with Germany (III Redmond, Treaties, etc. (1923) 3331, 3391), the special provisions of article 257 of that Treaty (*ibid.* 3442) appear to preclude the application of the doctrine of state succession. Article 257, quoted *ante*, p. 645, while transferring the public property of the German State situated in the mandated territories "with the territories to the Mandatory Power in its capacity as such," stipulated that no payment or credit should be given in consideration of this transfer, and, in addition, that neither the mandated territory nor the Mandatory Power "shall be charged with any portion of the debt of the German Empire or States." (By contrast, as noted above, article 254 of the Treaty charged the Powers to which German territory was ceded with a proportionate share of the German public debt.) **Public debt**

The Written Statement of the Government of India before the International Court of Justice in 1950 read in part:

"(v) The administration of the territory was to be disinterested. The mandate, according to the terms of Article 22 of the Covenant, 'was a system of "tutelage" and tutelage implied a disinterested activity. Further, it was stated, in the reply of the Allied and Associated Powers to the observations of the German delegation on the condition of peace, that the Allied and Associated Powers are of opinion that the colonies should not bear any portion of the German debt nor remain under any obligation to refund to Germany the expenses incurred by the Imperial administration of the Protectorate—in fact, they consider that it would be unjust to burden the natives with a debt which appears to have been incurred in Germany's own interest and that it would be no less unjust to make this responsibility rest upon the mandatory Powers, which, in so far as they may be appointed trustees by the League of Nations, will derive no benefit from such trusteeship.' The mandatory was obliged to use all the revenue and profits from the property of the mandated territories for the benefit of the territories. It could not hold any of the property of the mandated territory in full dominium."

Written Statement of the Government of India, *International Status of South-West Africa*, Pleadings, Oral Arguments, Documents, p. 143 (I.C.J. 1950).

In *Verein für Schutzgebietsanleihen E. V. v. Conradie, N. O.*, October 28, 1936, the Supreme Court of South Africa held that the Mandated Territory of South-West Africa was not liable for loans raised for the benefit of the Protectorate of German South-West Africa, pursuant to enactments of the German Imperial Government. ([1935–1937] Ann. Dig. 128 (No. 40); So. Afr. L.R. (1937), App. Div. 113.) The report of this case states:

"His Lordship then turned to the argument for the appellant that the Peace Treaty in terms safeguarded and preserved the juristic *persona* of the Protectorate. Reliance was placed in this connection on Article 22, and it had been said that the effect of the Treaty and the Mandate taken together was to remove the

juristic *persona* of the territory from the care of the old tutor
and entrust it to the care of a new tutor, the Mandatory.   His
Lordship first pointed out that in Article 22 the term 'tutelage'
was applied to 'peoples', not to 'territories', and continued :

> " 'As already pointed out, the German Protectorate of
> South-West Africa, though in name a protectorate, was in
> fact a colony under the sovereignty of the German Reich.
> Before the grant of the Mandate there was no tutor and no
> ward.   There is therefore no similarity between the position
> in which the territory, known as the "Protectorate of German
> South-West Africa", formerly stood, as a colony, in relation
> to the Government of the German Reich, and the position
> in which the same territory now stands, as a Mandated Terri-
> tory, in relation to the Government of the Union as a Man-
> datory.   The allegation contained in the declaration as to the
> identity of the Juristic Persona of the Mandated Territory
> with the Juristic Persona of the former Protectorate can
> derive no support from this argument as to the identity of
> a ward remaining unaffected by change of tutor, as the
> premises on which the argument are based do not bear ex-
> amination.' "   *Ibid.*, pp. 135–136.

Cf., State Succession (Windhuk in South West Africa) Case, January 2,
1925, [1925–1926] Ann. Dig. 75 (No. 55), *Juristische Wochenschrift*, 1926,
p. 205, where the Civil Senate of the German Chamber Court held that the
German State was not liable for money deposited as bail with the Imperial
District Court in Windhuk, German South-West Africa, in 1914, and indicated that the British Empire, as the successor State, succeeded not only to
the rights but also to the duties of its predecessor.   Confirmed by the
Supreme Court of the Reich, April 27, 1926.   *Entscheidungen des Reichs-
gerichts in Zwilsachen,* vol. 113, p. 281.

"A unique exception to the universal principle adopted with
respect to local debts in the Peace Treaties is that afforded by the
case of the German colonies placed under mandate.   The Treaty
of Versailles enacted that 'neither the territory nor the Mandatory
is to be charged with any portion of the debt of the German
Empire or States'.   [Treaty of Versailles, *British Treaty Ser.*
1919 (Cmd. 153), art. 257 at p. 125.]   The Reparations Commission found itself in the position of having to decide whether this
exclusion was intended to embrace the bonded debts of the German colonies themselves.   [It was considered that art. 257 referred only to the debts of the German Empire and States, and
not to the debts of the colonies themselves : Mann in *Journal of
Comparative Legislation and International Law*, 3rd ser., vol.
XVI (1934), no. 4, pp. 281–8.]   These debts were owed by the
colonies as joint debts to the creditors and each other, and were
thus undoubtedly debts of fiscally autonomous regions.   [Feil-
chenfeld, *Public Debts and State Succession* (1931) 557.]   The
mandatory Powers refused to recognize a responsibility with respect to such debts because, it was contended, the colonial budgets
had shown deficits and the colonies had not benefited from for-

eign investments. Some controversy on the matter persisted between Great Britain and Germany until 1930 when the latter abandoned its claims. [Feilchenfeld, p. 562.]

"The question of the unbonded debts of the colonies was no less controversial. In 1922 the Reichsgericht held that the German Government was liable for rent payable by the administration of German East Africa in 1916–20, on the ground that, even though by general principles of law Great Britain would have been responsible for the private law liabilities of the ceded territories, the Treaty of Versailles had expressly excluded this principle. Germany was therefore held precluded from arguing that it had ceased to be liable for obligations of its lost colonies. [*Tanganyika Succession Case, Annual Digest*, 1919–22, Case no. 34.] The same court decided later, however, that as the debts of the colonies had not been debts of the German Empire they were not within the provisions of the Treaty, and Germany was not responsible for them. [R.G.Z. 137, 1 (415), see Mann, *loc. cit.* p. 285.] In a further case the same view was adopted with respect to deposits made during the war to a court in the colonies. [*S. Th.* v. *German Treasury, Annual Digest*, 1923–4, Case no. 29.]"

O'Connell, *Law of State Succession* (1956) 177.

The Statement of Ivan Kerno, representative of the Secretary-General of the United Nations, addressed to the International Court of Justice in the advisory proceeding, *International Status of South-West Africa*, summarized the views of the Council and of the Permanent Mandates Commission of the League of Nations as to the liability of a "C" Mandated territory for financial obligations assumed by the Mandatory, as follows: "C" Mandates:

"The status of the Territory was also discussed by the Commission during its consideration of the question of loans, advances and investments of public and private capital. [For discussion in the Permanent Mandates Commission, see: Minutes of third session, pp. 76–78, 90, 161, 191, 197–199, 311–312; Minutes of fourth session, pp. 140–141, 146; Minutes of fifth session, pp. 154–156, 161–162, 176–180; Minutes of sixth session, pp. 52–54, 117–119, 145, 151–153, 154–156, 156–158, 171–172; Minutes of seventh session, p. 6.] The Commission, at its third session, was impressed by the fact that the mandated territories might be placed under an economic disadvantage owing to the uncertainty in their status, particularly with regard to the possibility of revocation or transfer of the Mandate. [Minutes of third session, pp. 311–312.] I shall return to the discussion of revocability, which the Commission considered highly theoretical, in a latter part of this statement. It may be mentioned here that the Commission considered that a pronouncement by the Council of the League, tending to remove the lack of confidence arising from the uncertainty of status, would greatly promote the economic prospects of the Territory. The Commission subsequently, at its sixth session [Minutes of sixth session, pp. 171–172], recommended that the Council declare that obligations assumed by a mandatory Power in a mandated territory and rights of every kind regularly acquired under its administration should have under all circumstances the same validity as if the mandatory Power were sovereign. It further recommended that the Council should decide that: 'In the event of a cessation of a mandate or of its transfer—however improbable this may be— to a fresh mandatory Power, the Council, without whose approval no such change could take place, should not give such approval unless it has been assured in advance that the new government undertaking the administration of the Territory will accept responsibility for the fulfilment of the financial obligations regularly assumed by the former mandatory Power and will engage that all rights regularly acquired under the administration of the latter shall be respected.'

"The Council considered this recommendation during its 35th Session. M. Undén, in his report to the Council on 15 September, 1925, noted that the text as proposed by the Commission used the word 'sovereign'. This, he thought, raised certain complicated questions of international law which it did not seem necessary to take up at that time. The paragraph was, therefore, redrafted in order to eliminate reference to the word 'sovereign'. The resolution, as adopted, declared that the validity of financial obligations assumed by a mandatory Power on behalf of a mandated territory in conformity with the provisions of the Mandate and all rights regularly acquired under the mandatory régime were in no way impaired by the fact that the territory was administered under mandate. [League of Nations, *Official Journal*, 6th year, No. 10, pp. 1510–1511.]"

Pleadings, Oral Arguments, Documents, pp. 200–201 (I.C.J. 1950).

National status of inhabitants

It is clearly established that in no case did the native populations of the mandated territories acquire the nationality of the respective Mandatory Powers, as a consequence of the transfer of the territory to the Mandates System. Thus, in an early commentary on this nationality question, McNair stated: "Have the inhabitants of the mandated areas acquired any new nationality? If so, what is it? These questions can only be answered by an examination of the terms of the particular mandate and of the other relevant circumstances. It may be accepted that in no circumstances have the inhabitants *ipso facto* acquired the nationality of the mandatory. It does not necessarily follow that they have acquired any nationality at all; for, in our opinion, the creation of a new nationality could only be the act of a mandated area well advanced on the road to statehood." I McNair, *Oppenheim's International Law* (4th ed., 1928) 210–211.

"A" Mandates

As noted above, the "A" Mandates were former Turkish territories detached from Turkey by the Treaty of Lausanne signed July 24, 1923 (28 LNTS 11). Article 30 of that Treaty (*ibid.* 29) provided:

"Turkish subjects habitually resident in territory which in accordance with the provisions of the present Treaty is detached from Turkey will become *ipso facto*, in the conditions laid down by the local law, nationals of the State to which such territory is transferred." The terms of the "A" Mandate instruments, leave no doubt, however, that the inhabitants of the former Turkish territories which were placed under the Mandates System acquired a nationality separate and distinct from that of the Mandatory Power. Thus, article V of the Treaty Between His Britannic Majesty and His Majesty the King of Iraq, signed October 10, 1922, provided, in part: "Where His Majesty the King of Iraq is not represented, he agrees to entrust the protection of Iraq nationals to His Britannic Majesty." (Terms of League of Nations Mandates, U.N. Doc. A/70, Oct. 1946). Article 3 of the Mandate for Syria and the Lebanon provided, in part: "Nationals of Syria and the Lebanon living outside the limits of the territory shall be under the diplomatic and consular protection of the Mandatory." (*Ibid.*) In the case of Palestine, article 7 of that Mandate stated: "The Administration of Palestine shall be responsible for enacting a nationality law. There shall be included in this law provisions framed so as to facilitate the acquisition of Palestinian citizenship by Jews who take up their permanent residence in Palestine." Article 12 of the Mandate authorized the Mandatory "to afford diplomatic and consular protection to citizens of Palestine when outside its territorial limits." (*Ibid.*) McNair described the creation of separate nationality in the "A" Mandates, as follows: ". . . in Iraq, as the result of the Iraq Law of October 9, 1924; in Palestine, where by a British Order in Council of July 24, 1925, Palestinian 'citizenship' [which is equivalent to nationality; see Bentwich, Brit. Ybk. Int'l L. 1926, at p. 102. . . . some hold the view that, as a result of the constitutional relationship between Great Britain and the Government of Palestine, and because (according to this view) Palestine is not a 'foreign State' within the meaning of § 13 of the British Nationality and Status of Aliens Act, 1914, a British subject who acquires Palestinian citizenship by naturalisation does not thereby cease to be a British subject] has been created; [but as to Transjordan, see Bentwich, *op. cit.*, at p. 106] and in Syria and Lebanon, in which case the existence of a distinct nationality is recognized by Article 3 of the mandate, and has been established by decrees of the French High Comissioner. [For details in all three cases, see Bentwich, *op cit.*, at p. 106, and, as to Palestine, Stoyanovsky, *The Palestinian Mandate* (1928), and, as to Syria and Lebanon, Nicolas in *Revue de droit international privé*, etc. XXI (1926), pp.

481–503.]" I McNair, *Oppenheim's International Law* (4th ed., 1928) 211. See also, Bentwich, *The Mandates System* (1930) 36–37, 78–79. "What is most remarkable in the law as to nationality in the mandated territories detached from Turkey is that in place of the Ottoman subjection there are now five new nationality systems, each with its distinctive features as to acquisition, retention, and loss. There has been no such national particularism in the Middle East for nearly two thousand years." *Ibid.* 79.

National cases

"The question of the status of mandated territory has been involved in a number of national court decisions, and the closely related question of the nationality status of the inhabitants has been the subject of considerable litigation. [See summary of eleven cases by Hales in *Transactions of the Grotius Society*, 1937, Vol. 23, pp. 95–112. See also international arbitration between France and Mexico involving nationality status of inhabitants of mandated territory, Navera Case, *Annual Digest of Public International Law Cases*, 1927–1928, Case No. 30, pp. 52–53.]"

Statement of Ivan Kerno, representative of the Secretary-General of the United Nations, addressed to the International Court of Justice, in the advisory proceeding, *International Status of South-West Africa*, Pleadings, Oral Arguments, Documents, pp. 194 (I.C.J. 1950).

Palestinian citizenship

In various national decisions, it has been affirmed that there existed a distinct Palestinian citizenship status. A leading case in the courts of the Mandatory, *The King* v. *Ketter*, [1940] 1 K.B. 787, also reported [1938–1940] Ann. Dig. 46 (No. 21), held that article 30 of the Treaty of Lausanne, quoted *supra*, as to Turkish subjects in the detached territories, did not confer British nationality on persons resident in Palestine. The Court quoted the provision of the Palestinian Citizenship Order, 1925, "Turkish subjects habitually resident in the territory of Palestine upon the 1st day of August, 1925, shall become Palestinian citizens." The Court cited *Attorney-General* v. *Goralschwili*, reported [1925–1926] Ann. Dig. 47 (No. 33), where the High Court of Palestine, in an extradition case, had held that subjects of the mandated territory of Palestine had not become British subjects. The Palestine Supreme Court has held that Transjordanian nationality was separate and distinct from Palestinian citizenship. *Jawdat Badawi Sha' ban* v. *Commissioner etc.*, reported [1943–1945] Ann. Dig. 15 (No. 5); [1945] 12 P.L.R. 551.

In *Kletter* v. *Dulles*, 111 F. Supp. 593 (D.D.C. 1953), affirmed 268 F. 2d 582 (1959), certiorari denied 361 U.S. 936 (1960), it was held by the United States District Court for the District of Columbia that naturalization in Palestine in 1935 according to Palestinian law would constitute an act of expatriation under the United States nationality laws. "The contention . . . that Palestine, while under the League of Nations mandate, was not a foreign state, within the meaning of the [expatriation] statute is wholly without merit." *Ibid.* 598. In the *Palestinian Nationality Case*, [1951] Int'l L. Rep. 55 (No. 25); (1952) 19 E.A.C.A. 187, the Court of Restitution Appeals of Nuremberg, Federal Republic of Germany, ruled that a Palestinian national was entitled to claim the benefits of German currency legislation conferred on "nationals of the United Nations," on the ground that the "territory of Palestine, where the appellant acquired his nationality, was under the administration and control of the United Kingdom", and that "That part of Palestine which became the State of Israel took part in the war against Germany, by virtue of the fact that the United Kingdom was at war with Germany." For the situation in the State of Israel subsequent to the termination of the Palestine Mandate, see, *inter alia*, *Hussein* v. *Governor of Acre Prison*, Supreme Court of Israel, Nov. 6, 1952, noted in [1950] Int'l L. Rep. 112 (published in 1956) (No. 27), and *Naqara* v. *Minister of the Interior*, Supreme Court of Israel, Oct. 16, 1953, [1953] Int'l L. Rep. 49. According to these cases, under the Nationality Law of Israel, Palestinian citizens were eligible, under certain stated conditions, to acquire Israel nationality, but did not automatically become nationals of Israel as a consequence of the transfer of the territory of the former Palestine Mandate to the State of Israel.

With respect to the native populations of the former German colonies which became the "B" and "C" Mandates, article 127 of the Treaty of Versailles provided: "The native inhabitants of the former German oversea possessions shall be entitled to the diplomatic protection of the Governments exercising authority over those territories." III Redmond, Treaties, etc. (1923) 3331, 3392. (*Cf.*, article 122: "The Government exercising authority over such territories may make such provisions as it thinks fit with reference to the repatriation from them of German nationals and to the conditions upon which German subjects of European origin shall, or shall not, be allowed to reside, hold property, trade or exercise a profession in them." *Ibid.* 3391.)

"B" and "C" Mandates

On April 23, 1923, the Council of the League of Nations adopted the following resolution concerning the national status of the native populations of the "B" and "C" Mandates:

"The Council of the League of Nations,
"Having considered the report of the Permanent Mandates Commission on the national status of the inhabitants of territories under B and C mandates,

"In accordance with the principles laid down in Article 22 of the Covenant:

"Resolves as follows:

"(1) The status of the native inhabitants of a mandated territory is distinct from that of the nationals of the Mandatory Power and cannot be identified therewith by any process having general application.

"(2) The native inhabitants of a mandated territory are not invested with the nationality of the Mandatory Power by reason of the protection extended to them.

"(3) It is not inconsistent with (1) and (2) above that individual inhabitants of the mandated territory should voluntarily obtain naturalisation from the Mandatory Power in accordance with arrangements which it is open to such Power to make, with this object, under its own law.

- "(4) It is desirable that native inhabitants who receive the protection of the Mandatory Power should in each case be designated by some form of descriptive title which will specify their status under the mandate."

League of Nations Off. J. (1923), pt. 1, 3d Ass., p. 604.

In the words of Judge McNair: "On the other hand, the 'B' and 'C' mandated areas cannot be said yet to have minted a nationality of their own, and we must be content to say that the native inhabitants of those areas have a status which is distinct from their former German or Turkish nationality and from the nationality of their mandatory, but does not yet amount to full nationality itself."

I McNair, *Oppenheim's International Law* (4th ed., 1928) 211.

Japanese Mandated Islands

On December 16, 1946, John B. Howard, Office of the Legal Adviser, Department of State, expressed the opinion that Micronesian natives of the former Japanese mandated islands are not and have never been nationals of Japan, except as individual natives may have become naturalized pursuant to the laws of Japan; that, while such natives are "residents of the islands", they cannot be regarded as "citizens of the islands" because the islands do not constitute a sovereignty sufficiently advanced for citizenship or even nationality as one of its attributes.

John B. Howard, Attorney, Office of the Legal Adviser, to Hugh Borton, Division of Japanese Affairs, Department of State, memorandum, Dec. 16, 1946, MS. Department of State, file 411.00—War Damages/12–1646.

National cases: British Commonwealth

"In *Wong Man On* v. *The Commonwealth and Others* [(1952), 86 C.L.R. 125; [1952] Int'l L. Rep. 324 (No. 58)] . . .

.   .   .   .   .   .

". . . [the] plaintiff relied on the fact of British military administration at the time of his birth, or alternatively on the words 'as an integral part of the Territory of the Commonwealth', which

appear in the Mandate itself as well as in the preamble to the
Act.   The first proposition was readily dismissed. . . . The second proposition occasioned more difficulty.   In the High Court
in 1924 [*Mainka* v. *Custodian of Expropriated Property* (1924),
34 C.L.R. 297, at p. 300] Isaacs J. had said that the words   Australia
'integral part of the Territory of the Commonwealth' meant not
that the mandated territory was deemed to be physically part of
the territory of the mandatory, but that it was territory belonging
to the King in right of the mandatory.   The plaintiff in *Wong*'s
case relied on this statement to support his assertion that New
Guinea had been incorporated in the Commonwealth of Australia,
so that British nationality had extended to its inhabitants under
the rule in *Campbell* v. *Hall* [(1774) I Comp. 204].

"The original draft of the Covenant of the League provided
that 'C' class Mandates were to be administered as *if* integral
portions of the mandatory's territory.   On the suggestion of the
Japanese delegate the word 'if' was omitted.   It was concluded
by Latham C.J. in *Ffrost* v. *Stevenson* in 1937 [(1937), 58 C.L.R.
528, at p. 550] that the intention was to confer on the mandatory
the fullest powers of government.   That did not, however[,] imply, the Chief Justice went on, that the Commonwealth exercised
sovereignty over its mandated territory.   'The position of a
mandatory in relation to a mandated territory must be regarded
as *sui generis*.   The Treaty of Peace, read as a whole, avoids
cession of territory to the mandatory, and in the absence of
definite evidence to the contrary, it must, I think, be taken that
New Guinea has not become part of the dominions of the Crown.'
The title, he concluded, under which the territory was to be held
as a Mandated Territory was different from that under which a
territory transferred by simple cession would have been held.
Neither this case nor that of *Jolley* v. *Mainka* [(1933), 49 C.L.R.
242, at p. 280], in which Evatt J. gave utterance to similar views,
determined the national status of persons resident in New Guinea
at the date of the coming into force of the mandate; nevertheless,
the Court in *Wong*'s case drew from the discussions of Latham
C.J. and Evatt J. the conclusion that 'Territory the subject of a
"C" mandate does not become part of the dominions of the
mandatory in such a sense as to confer on the inhabitants the
nationality of the mandatory.' [The New Zealand courts adopted
a similar opinion on the question of the sovereignty over Samoa,
and although not quoted in *Wong*'s case may be taken as supporting the basis of decision: *Tagaloa* v. *Inspector of Police*,
(1927) N.Z.L.R. 883; *In re Tamasese*, (1929) N.Z.L.R. 209; *Nelson* v. *Braisby* (No. 2), (1934) N.Z.L.R. 559.]   The words of
Isaacs J. on which the plaintiff relied had, it was held, to be
interpreted in the light of the two subsequent cases.

"The decision confirms the generally accepted view on na-   South
tionality in 'C' class Mandates. . . .   In addition, despite its claims Africa
to sovereignty over South-West Africa and judicial confirmation
of those claims in the South African courts, the South African
Government made no claim that the inhabitants of the Mandated

Territory acquired British nationality *ipso facto*. Pursuant to an Agreement with the German Government in 1923, and with the consent of the Council of the League, the South African Government passed legislation in 1924 [Act 30 of 1924; see this *Year Book*, 6 (1925), pp. 188–91] which automatically naturalized adult Europeans resident in South-West Africa who had previously enjoyed German nationality unless they signed a declaration that they were desirous of not being naturalized. The Act did not affect persons who had left the territory before 1924 but after the coming into force of the Mandate. In an unreported case of 1947 [*Rimpelt* v. *Clarkson*, referred to with approval by Steyn J. in *Westphal and Westphal* v. *Conducting Officer*, (1948) 2 S.A.L.R. 18, at p. 21, reported in *Annual Digest*, 1947, Case No. 12], the Transvaal Provincial Division of the High Court held that, although South Africa in 1920 acquired sovereignty over South-West Africa, there was no cession of the territory to the Crown, and hence no extension of British nationality to Germans who were in it at the time but subsequently departed. Article 122 of the Treaty of Versailles, which provided for the repatriation of 'German nationals' from the mandated territories, tended, it was held, to repudiate the theory of automatic change of nationality. [In view of the South African decisions on the question of sovereignty over South-West Africa the case may be considered illogical, although satisfactory as to its conclusion. The accepted theory is that inhabitants of territory becoming subject to British sovereignty automatically acquire British nationality: *Campbell* v. *Hall*, 1 Cowp. 204, at p. 208; *Donegani* v. *Donegani*, (1935) 3 Knapp. 63, at p. 85; *Mostyn* v. *Fabrigas*, (1774) 1 Cowp. at p. 171; *Mayor of Lyons* v. *The East India Co.*, (1836) 1 Moo. I.A. 175. If South Africa acquired sovereignty over the territory this conclusion should follow, unless Article 122 constituted an alteration of the Common Law. South Africa, of course, was entitled to refrain from extending British nationality to the inhabitants in question (see *P.C.I.J.*, Series B, No. 4, p. 24), but had not legislated to alter the rule in *Campbell* v. *Hall*.]

"If the residents of 'C' Mandates did not acquire British nationality, did they lose their German nationality? On this point there seems to be a fundamental disagreement between judicial decision in South Africa and administrative action of Australia and New Zealand. In 1942 the Union Parliament enacted legislation [Act 35 of 1942] providing that every person who became a British national exclusively in virtue of the Act of 1924, which has already been mentioned, should henceforth be treated as an alien. In 1946 a Commission was appointed to make recommendations with respect to undesirable aliens. It recommended the deportation of certain persons who had been naturalized under the Act of 1924. It was held [*Minister of the Interior* v. *Bechler et Al.; Beier* v. *Minister of the Interior*, (1948) 3 S.A.L.R. 409 (App. D.)*; see also Ex parte Schwietering*, (1948) 3 S.A.L.R. 378] on appeal against a deportation order pursuant to this recommendation that residents of South-West Africa had not been deprived of their German nationality in virtue of Article 278

["Germany undertakes to recognize any new nationality which has been or may be acquired by her nationals under the laws of the Allied and Associated Powers and in accordance with the decisions of the competent authorities of these Powers pursuant to naturalization laws or under treaty stipulations, and to regard such persons as having, in consequence of the acquisition of such new nationality, in all respects severed their allegiance to their country of origin"] of the Treaty of Versailles because that Article had not been incorporated into German municipal law. The apellants [sic] had therefore reverted to the status of aliens after 1942. The decision seems to be confirmatory of the assumptions on which both the Union and Germany are alleged to have acted during the negotiations preceding the enactment of 1924. If Germany did not regard the inhabitants of the territory as its nationals in 1924, so it is argued, it is difficult to see why it was referred to at all. [Lewis in *Law Quarterly Review*, 39 (1923), p. 471; Emmett in *Journal of Comparative Legislation and International Law*, 9 (1927), p. 117; *Oppenheim's International Law*, vol. i (7th ed. by Lauterpacht, 1948), p. 201.] The Australian and New Zealand Governments, on the other hand, while proceeding on the assumption that the inhabitants of their mandated territories are not British subjects, have not regarded them as aliens. It has been accepted that persons born in the territories before the Mandates came into force were German nationals under the provisions of the German Nationality Law of 22 July 1913, but that under Section 25 of that Law they lost their nationality upon the dereliction of the territories by Germany. They and their descendants have been treated as lacking nationality but enjoying an administrative status analogous to that of inhabitants of British protectorates. [Whose status is discussed in *R.* v. *Earl Crowe, Ex parte Sekgome*, [1910] 2 K.B. 576, esp. *per* Kennedy J. at p. 620; *Sobhuza II* v. *Miller*, [1926] A.C. 518; Evatt J. in *Ffrost* v. *Stevenson* (1937), 38 C.L.R. 528, at p. 581.] They have been designated in relevant legislation as 'British protected persons' [Immigration Ordinance, 1932–1940, of the Territory of New Guinea accords local officers the power to exclude British nationals from the territory on the assumption that local residents are not British nationals], and their passports are specially endorsed for the territory in which they reside. The South African decision is open to the criticism that it examined the relevant provisions of the Treaty of Versailles but not the German legislation, and the assumptions underlying the Australian and New Zealand executive policy seem to be well founded."

O'Connell, "Nationality in 'C' Class Mandates", XXXI Brit. Yb. Int'l L. (1954) 458–461.

"The inclusion of all the League mandates in the League's sanctions against Italy in 1935–6 was a prelude to their role in the war. [*Minutes of First Session of Committee of Experts*, 27 November–12 December 1935: League of Nations, *Official Journal*, Special Supplement No. 147. See ibid., Special Supplement No. 150

Belligerency of Mandated territories

(1936), for the replies of governments.]   In September 1939 the British, French, Australian, New Zealand, and South African (and nine months later Belgian) mandates were involved in the belligerency of their respective mandatory Powers.   At its final Session in December 1939 the Mandates Commission, being engaged on the discussion of the annual reports for 1938, 'deliberately refrained', as it put it, 'from anticipating the events of 1939'.   Questions by some members of the Commission to accredited representatives revealed uneasiness as to the legal point involved in belligerency.   'Everyone knew', Lord Hailey pointed out, 'that the mandated territories had been treated as involved in a state of belligerency', and if there was any doubt as to the propriety of such an act from a legal point of view the matter should be discussed at once, and not in a year's time.   Professor Rappard expressed the view that mandates were 'not under the sovereignty of the belligerent Powers; the latter administered them in the name of the League of Nations, which was not at war'.   [*Permanent Mandates Commission, Minutes*, 37 (1939), pp. 120–2.]   But the League had never claimed sovereignty, nor would the mandatories have admitted any such claim.   They were charged by their trust with the defence of their mandates, which proved to be as much liable to attack as any portion of their own possessions. Their action was no doubt guided by the view that '. . . the mandatory is entitled, subject to the fundamental principles of the regime of mandates . . . , to extend to the mandated territory his relevant war legislation . . .'.   [Oppenheim, *International Law*, vol. ii (6th ed. by Lauterpacht, 1940), p. 192.]   An important decision of the Supreme Council in 1919, bearing on the question of automatic belligerency, had slipped out of the record and was not apparently known when these words were written nor when the relevant legislation was drafted.   It was brought to light again by the recent publication of the Paris Conference records by the United States State Department.   [*U.S. For. Rels.: Paris Peace Conf.* 1919, vol. ix, pp. 542–4 and 836.]   The Supreme Council decided on 9 December 1919 that the words 'defence of territory' in Article 22 and in the text of the 'B' mandates should be interpreted in the sense of permitting military training of the natives for use for defence purposes outside the territory in the case of general war.   [Article 22 has "defence of territory" in the English text, and "la défense du territoire" in the French.   The "B" mandates read "the defence of the territory", whilst the "C" mandates read "the local defence of the territory".   All the mandates permit the raising of native defence forces.   Except in the case of Palestine they do not restrict such forces to volunteers, as do the Charter (Art. 84) and the Trusteeship Agreements.]   The interpretation was in general terms and applied to all the 'B' mandates.   But it arose out of a discussion of the desire of France to have this right made clear.   In the text of the two French mandates, after the clause common to all the 'B' texts permitting the training of natives 'for the defence of the territory', a clause was inserted as follows: 'It is understood, however, that the troops thus raised may, in the event of general war, be utilised to repel an attack or for the defence of the territory outside that subject to the mandate.' The approval of the United States Government of an interpretation of Article 22 in this sense was indicated to the Supreme Council on 10 January 1920. [Under the Neutrality Act of 4 November 1939, the "B" and "C" mandates were regarded as belligerent countries, whereas the "A" mandates were not so regarded. See U.S. Dept. of Commerce, Bureau of Foreign and Domestic Commerce, *Comparative Law Series*, vol. iii, No. 5, May 1940, p. 284.] An 'understanding' of a clause in the Covenant valid for one League Member but not another would have been an anomaly even if this decision had not been on record. Since the words of Article 22 'for defence of territory' applied to the 'C' as well as to the 'B' mandates, the interpretation would seem to be valid also for the 'C' mandates. [Moreover, the mandatory was empowered to administer a "C" mandate as an "integral portion" of his own territory. The Trusteeship Agreements support the interpretation of the Supreme Council.]

"The Mandates Commission at its third session in 1923 had ruled that the use even of volunteer troops outside the territory would be a violation of the 'B' mandates other than the French. This interpretation would appear to be untenable. It was not accepted by the Governments, though in practice they deferred to the wishes of the Commission. [*P.M.C. Min.* 3 (1923), pp. 196–7; also *L.N. Documents*, C.519(1), 1923, vi, and C.317, 1926, vi.]

"In the case of several of the mandates (e.g. Palestine and Tanganyika) troops recruited from the native population on a voluntary basis took part in military operations outside their territories.

. . . .

". . . League mandates were thus involved in the belligerency of the mandatory, despite the vague flavour of neutralization that clung to a mandate. . . ."

Hall, "The Belligerency of the Mandated Territories During the Second World War", XXIV Brit. Yb. Int'l L. (1947) 389–392.

"Apart from its last meeting in December 1939, the Mandates Commission of the League of Nations did not function during the first four years of the second World War. But Great Britain and the other members of the British Commonwealth, as Mandatory Powers, continued to submit to the League annual reports on the territories under their administration. Palestine, Syria and Transjordan, in particular, the 'A' Mandates, were deeply involved in the war in the Middle East. Of the 'B' and 'C' Mandates, New Guinea and the Island of Nauru shared the fate of the islands in the Southern Pacific, which were overrun by Japan. [The other Pacific islands which had been under a Japanese mandate were also involved in warlike operations. The conditions of the mandate with regard to them had not been observed by Japan for years before the outbreak of the war, and the failure of the Council of the League to investigate the allegations that the islands were being turned into military and naval bases was forcefully brought home.]"

Bentwich, "The Mandated Territories During the Second World War, 1939–1942", XXI Brit. Yb. Int'l L. (1944) 164.

Territories under British Mandate

"War between His Majesty and Germany involved the territories under His Majesty's jurisdiction, including the mandated territories. In the procedure followed at the outbreak of the war no difference was made between colonies, protectorates, and mandated territories. Thus, the circular telegram sent by the Colonial Office on September 3, 1939, announcing the existence of a state of war with Germany, was addressed to all colonies, protectorates, protected states, and mandated territories. All these territories had received specimen legislation drawn up in advance in case of the emergency of war. The Emergency Powers (Defense) Act of 1939, passed on August 24 in the United Kingdom, empowered the government to make defense regulations in respect of the United Kingdom. It provided further that 'His Majesty may by Order in Council direct that the provisions of this Act . . . shall extend, with such exceptions, adaptations and modifications, if any, as may be specified in the Order' to overseas territories, including 'any territory in respect of which a mandate on behalf of the League of Nations has been accepted by His Majesty, and is being exercised by His Majesty's Government in the United Kingdom.' Next day, August 25, the Emergency Powers (Colonial Defense) Order in Council, 1939, was issued under the Act. It extended the provisions of the Act to overseas territories, including those under United Kingdom mandate. [". . . the Prize Law Act of 1939 was made applicable to the mandated territories administered by Great Britain, Australia, and New Zealand." Oppenheim, *International Law*, 6th ed., revised by Lauterpacht, 1944, Vol. II, p. 192.] Under this Order in Council the governors of the mandated territories and the High Commissioner for Palestine had the same power as the United Kingdom Government to make local defense regulations. (The regulations made in the United Kingdom did not, of course, apply in the overseas territories.) In addition to this power of legislation by defense regulation, the local legislatures in mandated territories, as in colonies, could legislate by ordinance. This method was used, for example, to deal with trading with the enemy.

"Trans-Jordan was an exception to this procedure. Since it was a territory under an independent sovereign, bound to the United Kingdom by treaty of alliance, and exercising its own jurisdiction, the Emergency Powers (Defense) Act was not applicable to it. Under the treaty of February, 1928 (following the general lines of the Iraq treaty), the mandatory transferred full powers of legislation and administration to the Emir of Trans-Jordan and the local legislature, retaining only the right to offer advice and assistance. The war legislation of Trans-

Jordan thus appears to have been made by the government of the territory under powers conferred by local statute."

Hall, *Mandates, Dependencies and Trusteeship* (1948) 262–263.

"At the outbreak of the War the Palestine Administration at once applied legislation on the lines of the British war measures, including the defence emergency powers, the prohibition of trading with the enemy, the control of the economic life of the country in all its aspects, and the appointment of a custodian of enemy property.   Power was given also to constitute the Supreme Court of Palestine as a prize court, and in fact several German prizes were dealt with by the Palestine tribunal.   The population of Palestine included a large number of enemy subjects, namely, nationals of Germany.   Many were members of the German religious sect known as the 'Temple', which had settled in Palestine in the latter part of the nineteenth century and had established flourishing suburbs in Jerusalem, Jaffa and Haifa as well as several prosperous agricultural villages.   In addition, a very large number of Jewish German, Austrian and Czech subjects, refugees from Nazi oppression, had immigrated into Palestine since 1933 and were not yet naturalized.   The ('Aryan') enemy subjects were either placed in an internment camp in Acre or gathered in the German agricultural colonies, where they were under supervision.   The latter were allowed to manage their own agricultural properties, and religious institutions belonging to enemy subjects were not touched.

"At the outbreak of war with Germany the High Commissioner of Palestine issued a proclamation that Great Britain was at war, but no proclamation was issued by him that Palestine was at war. Until Italy entered the struggle Palestine was regarded as a neutral by the United States, at least to the extent that American ships were allowed to sail to and from Palestine ports.   From the time, however, that Italy came into the war Palestine was brought within the sphere of military operations.   Air raids on the coastal towns of Tel-Aviv and Haifa followed immediately.   The collapse of France and the ensuing events in Syria brought close the prospect of invasion.   One outcome of these events was to stimulate the recruitment of volunteers, particularly amongst the Jews. Their total enrolment in the military, naval and air forces rose to over 20,000; in addition 7,000 men were enlisted in the defence force.   The number of Arabs volunteering was considerably smaller.   No attempt was made to introduce conscription.   In fact, the Government intervened by legislation in 1942 to check measures of certain Jewish bodies, in relation to volunteering for military service, which were regarded as amounting to coercion. The Government, however, introduced measures for the use of the man power in the defence of the country and in the development of its agricultural and industrial life in order to make it more self-supporting.   Palestine was linked in its economic realtions [relations] with all the surrounding countries of the Middle East; and the Middle East Supply Centre, which was set up in 1941 after the

"A"
Mandates:
Palestine

Conference of Delhi, exercised a large control over local production and foreign trade. Palestine became in the following years an important supply base of the Allied Forces in the Middle East and an important military arsenal. The Jewish units rendered signal service in the Middle East campaigns, and so did the Transjordan Frontier Force, which was a permanent part of the defence established in Transjordan and composed partly of Arabs, partly of Sudanese and other native peoples under British officers. In 1941 the Administration passed a Volunteer Defence Force Ordinance which provided for the enrolment of Palestinians as well as British subjects for the defence of the country. In 1942 it agreed to the formation of a special Palestinian regiment of combatant troops. Jews and Arabs were included in the regiment, but formed in separate companies."

Bentwich, "The Mandated Territories During the Second World War, 1939–1942", XXI Brit. Yb. Int'l L. (1944) 164–165.

"The territory of Palestine, where the appellant acquired his nationality, was under the administration and control of the United Kingdom. That part of Palestine which became the State of Israel took part in the war against Germany, by virtue of the fact that the United Kingdom was at war with Germany. It follows, without the slightest doubt, that the appellant is entitled to claim the benefits referred to above [as a national of the United Nations]."

Palestinean Nationality Case, The Court of Restitution Appeals of Nuremberg, Federal Republic of Germany, [1951] Int'l L. Rep. 55, 56 (No. 25). For a case involving "detention" of an alien enemy in Palestine, see *Nathan* v. *Inspector-General of Police*, reported in [1941–1942] Ann. Dig. 450 (No. 142), where, at 453, the Court said: "This Territory is in a peculiar position with regard to enemy aliens, owing to the provisions of the Order in Council and the Immigration Ordinance and Regulations. In my view, an enemy alien who is entitled to the protection of Government and who is not stated to be a prisoner of war can only be detained under regulation 17. [Regulation 17, Palestine Defense Regulations, 1939]." Case also reported in *The Law Reports of Palestine*, vol. 8, 1941, p. 363.

". . . Was Palestine in fact a neutral country? The action of the Director of Selective Service in listing it as such did not make it so. It was governed by Great Britain as the mandatory power, and Great Britain was at war long before the registration of the petitioner with his Selective Service Board. The industrial and political life of Palestine was geared to that of Great Britain, as its mandatory, in the war effort. [United Press Dispatch from Rome, to Detroit News, Sept. 8, 1940: "A high command communique said today Italian planes had bombed the railroad between Alexandria and Marsah Matruh, Egypt, oil plants at Haifa, Palestine, and a British ship convoy in the Red Sea."

New International Year Book for 1941: "Palestine during 1940 became one of the main bastions protecting British communications and interests in the Near East."

Associated Press Dispatch from Jerusalem, Detroit News, Jan. 28, 1943 : "In the meantime, Palestine is at war, at war on the side of the United Nations. * * * The streets and countryside are rigidly blacked out each night as thoroughly as London itself. Tel Aviv and Haifa were bombed earlier in the war."] There was no change in the relationship of Palestine to Great Britain between the date of petitioner's registration and December, 1943, when Palestine was deleted from the list of neutral countries. It follows therefore, that the petitioner's claim for exemption as a citizen of a neutral country was a nullity and without legal effect, since he was not in fact a citizen of such a country and the section could have no application in his case."

Petition of Ajlouny, 77 F. Supp. 327, 329–330 (E.D.S.D. Mich. 1948). *Cf. Jubran* v. *United States,* 255 F. 2d 81, 83 (5th Cir. 1958) which criticized the decision in the *Ajlouny* case on the ground that the determination of the neutral status of a foreign country is a political and not a judicial function.

"Syria and the Lebanon were from the outbreak of war important French bases. The French authorities, who had negotiated treaties as far back as 1936 for the creation of independent republics in place of the two mandated states, suspended any action calculated to give effect to the treaties. The administration was carried on by a small body of ministers who were, in fact, controlled by the French High Commissioner and the military authorities. France had a large army in the Levant states, estimated at some 200,000 men, which included native levies. The collapse of France produced a very grave situation in Syria. At first the High Commissioner for the Mandated Territories, M. Puaux, in consultation with the French High Command, declared that France would continue the fight and would not surrender to the Axis Powers. When, however, General Weygand was sent by the Vichy Government to Syria, a sudden change of policy was announced. The civil and military authorities accepted the terms of the armistice, by which the forces in Syria were to be demobilized under the control of a Disarmament Commission of the Axis. Some high officers of the French Army and a number of the military and air force units made their way across the frontier into Palestine and joined the British forces. But the mass were compelled to accept the surrender of the military commanders. There was reason to fear that the French bases might be used as bases of the Axis; the danger was greatest in Syria, and was a matter of equal concern to Great Britain and Turkey. The British Government lost no time in making clear the action which it would take in certain circumstances to guard against that danger. On July 1st, following the declaration of General Mittelhauser, Commander-in-Chief of the French forces in the Levant, that hostilities had ceased in Syria, it issued the following declaration :

Territories under French Mandate : Syria and Lebanon

" 'His Majesty's Government assume that this does not mean that if Germany or Italy sought to occupy Syria or the

Lebanon, and were to try to do so in the face of British command of the sea, no attempt would be made by the French forces to oppose them. In order, however, to set at rest doubts which may be felt in any quarter, His Majesty's Government declare that they could not allow Syria or the Lebanon to be occupied by any hostile Power, or to be used as a base for attacks upon those countries in the Middle East which they are pledged to defend, or to become the scene of such disorder as to constitute a danger to those countries. They therefore hold themselves free to take whatever measures they may in such circumstances consider necessary in their own interests. Any action which they may hereafter be obliged to take in fulfilment of this declaration will be entirely without prejudice to the future status of the territories now under French mandate.'

"An Italian Disarmament Commission and, subsequently, a mixed German-Italian Commission were sent to Syria. When in 1941 a rising broke out in Iraq, and the Axis Powers were preparing for general hostilities in the Middle East, the German authorities, without any effective French opposition, used the Syrian aerodromes as bases and began to tighten their hold on the communications and strategic positions in the country. It was apparent that they intended to take control of the country as a base. The British commanders in the Middle East then took action. In May the British air forces bombed the aerodromes at Palmyra, Rayak, Beyrouth and Damascus. That drew a protest from the French High Commissioner, and the British Consul-General and his staff were obliged to leave Beyrouth, while the French consular staff left Jerusalem. In June British troops, accompanied by a Free French contingent, entered Syria. The French forces resisted, and for a month there was stiff fighting.

"At the outset the British Government, together with General Catroux, representing General de Gaulle, issued a declaration that they would grant liberty and independence to Syria and the Lebanon, and negotiate a treaty with the governments of those countries to assure that object. The British Government added: 'Should you support and join the Allies, His Majesty's Government offer you all the advantages enjoyed by the free countries which are associated with them. The blockade would be lifted, and you may enter into immediate relations with the Sterling Block which will give you advantages for your exports and imports. You will be able to sell your products and buy freely in all the free countries.' By the beginning of July French resistance was broken, and there were pourparlers for an armistice. The German forces in Syria and the Italian members of the Armistice Commission and their consuls left the country, while the French warships were removed to Alexandretta, which was regarded as a neutral port. A purely military armistice was signed at Acre between the French and the British military forces. The Vichy Government declined to give its direct approval, but authorized General Dentz to act as he thought best.

"On the occupation of Beyrouth, General Catroux was named delegate-plenipotentiary and Commander-in-Chief of the Free French in the Levant, and assumed all the powers of the High Commissioner. He took over many of the former officials. The British Government associated itself with the administration by the appointment of a diplomatic minister who, in fact, shared the control. The General declared that he would bring into being as quickly as possible legislative assemblies, and would negotiate fresh treaties on the lines of the treaties of alliance concluded by the French Republic in 1936. His declaration ended: 'I will take steps to transmit to the League of Nations at the appropriate moment suggestions substituting the mandate régime by a new régime which will conform to the ends for which the mandate was devised.' The British Minister of State in Cairo sent a letter to General de Gaulle affirming Great Britain's approval of these arrangements; but more than a year passed before any steps could be taken to implement them fully. A proclamation issued in September 1941 declared the new status of independent republics with the prerogatives of independent sovereign states and the right to nominate diplomatic representatives in a country where Syria had a special interest involved, e.g., Iraq, and to raise military forces.

"However, the proclamation included a reservation that, during the war, policy must conform to the requirements of the Allies, and that the Allied commanders could dispose of the harbours, aerodromes, etc., in the countries concerned. Nothing was said about the relation of Syria to the other Arab states. In the meantime the economic linking up with other Middle Eastern countries under Allied control was effected. In a message sent at that time Mr. Churchill said: 'We have no ambitions in Syria, and we do not intend to replace or supplant the French or to substitute British for French interests. Our policy is that Syria shall be handed back to the Syrians, who will assume at the earliest possible moment their independent sovereign rights.' There was considerable political unrest in the country during 1942, because of the delay in introducing representative institutions. The government was, in fact, carried on during that year by a few ministers, nominated by the Free French administration, with the approval of the British representative. It was not until March 1943 that General Catroux proclaimed the intention to restore the constitution and to hold elections for representative chambers. The United States Government appointed a Consul-General in the Lebanon who, when presenting his credentials, emphasized that President Roosevelt wished by the appointment to manifest the sympathy of his Government with the aspirations of the Lebanese people for independence. The exercise of full powers was suspended by the limitations of war conditions, but the President looked forward to 'the time when the Lebanese people would undertake the rights and responsibilities of full independent statehood'."

Bentwich, "The Mandated Territories During the Second World War, 1939–1942", XXI Brit. Yb. Int'l L. (1944) 164, 165–167.

On November 29, 1941, the leader of the Free French, General Charles de Gaulle, addressed a communication to the American Ambassador to the Polish Government-in-Exile (Biddle), reading as follows:

"(1) Since the attempt to transform Syria and Lebanon into a German military base has led the Free French Forces, in cooperation with British troops, to take in hand the defense of these countries, I have the honor to inform you that, in my capacity as Leader of the Free French, on July 14, 1941 I assumed in the Levant States under French mandate the powers and responsibilities which France has under the Mandate Act of July 24, 1922, which entered into force September 29, 1923.

"(2) I have vested General Catroux, Delegate General and Plenipotentiary in the Levant, with the powers exercised by the French High Commissioner in the Levant States.

"(3) In conformity with the principles laid down by the Mandate Act and with the traditional policy of France, General Catroux, acting on behalf of the Leader of the Free French, on September 27, 1941 proclaimed, by virtue of and within the framework of the Mandate, the independence and sovereignty of the Syrian State, of which Sheik Taj-ed-Din has become the President.

"On the same bases, and taking into account the special relations between France and Lebanon, General Catroux, acting on behalf of General de Gaulle, Leader of the Free French and Chairman of the French National Committee formed in London on September 24, 1941, proclaimed, on November 26, the independence and sovereignty of Lebanon, with Mr. Naccache as President.

"(4) The independence and sovereignty of Syria and Lebanon will not, in fact, involve limitations other than those resulting from the exigencies of the war.

"(5) They do not, however, affect the juridical situation as it results from the Mandate Act. Indeed, this situation could be changed only with the agreement of the Council of the League of Nations, with the consent of the Government of the United States, a signatory of the Franco-American Convention of April 4, 1924, and only after the conclusion between the French Government and the Syrian and Lebanese Governments of treaties duly ratified in accordance with the laws of the French Republic.

"(6) General Catroux will continue, therefore, to exercise on behalf of the French National Committee, with due regard for the new *de facto* situation, the powers of the High Commissioner of France in Syria.

"(7) I should appreciate it very much if you would be good enough to inform the Government of the United States, which, together with the French Government, signed the Franco-American Convention of April 4, 1924.

"I have the honor to enclose the text of the proclamations of

General Catroux with respect to the independence and sovereignty of Syria and Lebanon."

1941 For. Rel., vol. III, pp. 809–810.

" 'B' and 'C' Mandates

"The reports (unpublished) on Togoland, the Cameroons and Tanganyika, which were under British mandate, for 1939–41, indicate the steadily increasing integration of the territories in the war effort.   A special difficulty arose from the presence of a considerable number of German planters, business houses and missionaries in these former German colonies.   While in the early stages of the war internment was restricted to those who were suspect, as the war spread and the position in Africa became more serious, it was found necessary to remove most of the German male inhabitants, and to take control through a custodian of enemy property of the estates and business owned by them.   It was found necessary also to introduce legislation for compulsory service, which, however, was made to apply only to British subjects and not to the natives.

"The Ordinances of the colony of Nigeria concerning special war measures, except the naval defence ordinance, were applied in the Cameroons.   For the defence of the territory a special force of police, replaced later by a force of the Nigerian regiment, was drafted. Sea-going and river craft belonging to German planters, as well as aircraft, were seized as prize at the outbreak of hostilities.   The German members of the Basel and Baptist missions were permitted to continue their activities on parole— probably having regard to the provisions of Article 7 of the Mandate relating to missionary activities.   When later many of them were interned, the American Baptist Missionary Society came to the aid of the missions.   The report on the Cameroons for 1940 is mainly confined to statistical tables, relating to financial, economic, and social questions.

The measures in the vast mandated territory of Tanganyika were more systematic.   There the German resident population was about equal to the British resident population, and serious problems of internal security had to be met.   Already at the crisis of September 1938, the necessity for preparing complete defence plans had been recognized.   The defence of the territory was secured by a force of the King's African Rifles and the Naval Volunteer Force and the enrolment of special constables from the British residents.   A Custodian of Enemy Property, and Information Office for the purpose of giving the native peoples news of the war, and a voluntary service register were instituted. In May 1939 a man-power commission was appointed.   On the declaration of war these departments came into immediate working, and volunteering for labour service was organized amongst the natives.   At first only a maximum of 10 per cent. of the adult males was accepted.   No attempt was necessary to encourage

"B" and "C" Mandates

recruiting. Many Africans enlisted in the Naval Volunteer Force, and were soon transformed into able seamen.

"A central internment camp was set up for Germans of military age, and some hundreds of German refugees in the country were interned for a time, until a commission on aliens could make a sifting. In the end five hundred Germans were marked for compulsory repatriation; about two hundred, found to be the victims of Nazi oppression, were released. The wives and husbands of the interned Germans were left on the farms, and provision was made for their maintenance, when necessary. The Custodian of Enemy Property took over plantations and businesses owned by the Germans, and carried on those which could be profitably worked.

"The one 'C' Mandate for which a full report is available, for 1940, is New Guinea. At the outbreak of war the Defence Act of the Australian Commonwealth was extended to the territory, and the organization of volunteers to assist the local defence was taken in hand. It was restricted, however, to British subjects. Under the National Security Act of the Commonwealth, which was extended to the territory, a number of enemy aliens were detained and removed to Australia for safe custody."

Bentwich, "The Mandated Territories During the Second World War, 1939–1942", XXI Brit. Yb. Int'l L. (1944) 164, 167–168. See also Hall, *Mandates, Dependencies and Trusteeship* (1948) 261–262.

"The 'C' mandates in the Pacific, unlike the 'B' mandates in Africa, were all deeply affected by the war. The special case of the Japanese mandated islands is referred to below.

"Probably no mandated territory was more profoundly affected than New Guinea. By the middle of 1942, the Japanese forces had overrun the mandated territory and a considerable part of the adjoining Australian territory of Papua. It took over two years of arduous warfare to eject them. The normal life of a large part of the estimated population of a million native people was completely disrupted. There resulted immense destruction of facilities and property and, more important still, profound changes in mental attitudes and social structure. The loyalty and cooperation of the native people was a very important contributing factor to Allied success. The chief political and military lesson of the war in this region was perhaps that the well-being and good-will of native peoples is essential to the defense of the South-West Pacific. The territory gained immensely in the matter of capital equipment and communications, which gave some access to its highlands and helped towards an ultimate mastery of the tropical environment. The war brought also an immense change in the attitudes of the Australian people to its near north. 'The New Guinea campaigns spread a new knowledge of, and an utterly new and vivid interest in, Australia's own island empire.' [K. H. Bailey, "Dependent Areas of the Pacific: An Australian View," *Foreign Affairs*, April, 1946, p. 512.]

"War opened up much of Papua and New Guinea, not only economically, but also from a political and a military point of view. During the war the territories were—

'administered as a unity by a military administration. They are, in fact, a physiographic, economic, social, and ethnological unity. Military transport, communications and supply methods have now unified them functionally. The political division is historical and arbitrary, and unrelated to these underlying real unities.' ["New Guinea Under War Conditions," by W. E. H. Stanner, *International Affairs*, October, 1944 (Royal Institute of International Affairs), p. 492.]

The war indeed brought an immense change in the political and strategical, as well as probably the economic, relationship of the whole island of New Guinea and its outlying islands with respect to Australia. It became for Australia a vital strategical base for defense of the continent: 'The facts of military geography strongly indicate that under foreseeable conditions of the future the Territory of New Guinea and Papua will be one of a series of increasingly critical strategic areas of vital importance to the military security of the British Commonwealth, and the United States.' [*Ibid.*, p. 494; on the United States bases, see *New York Times*, June 25, 1946, article by James Reston; and statement by the Australian Minister for External Affairs before Parliament, November 8, 1946, *Current Notes*, Department of External Affairs, Canberra, Vol. 17, No. 11.] During the war the latter [the United States] built a base on Manus Island at a cost estimated at over $150,000,000. The use of this base has been under discussion between the United States and Australia since the end of the war with a view to the latter taking over on December 1, 1947.

"The civil administrations in Papua and New Guinea were suspended on February 11, 1942, and the two territories were placed under the authority of the Commander in Chief of the Australian-New Guinea forces. A semimilitary administration covering both territories was set up under the name of the Australian-New Guinea Administrative Unit. This, although served in part by former administrative officials, was organized and run on military lines with the task of administering the two territories as a single unit. It followed the advance of the armies in the field and took over after them.

"The restoration of civil administration was provided for in the Papua-New Guinea Act of October 30, 1945, introduced in the Australian Parliament in July. By June, 1946, the whole of Papua and New Guinea were once more under civil control. [*The Mandated Territory of New Guinea.* Memorandum of information supplied by the Australian Delegation to Subcommittee I, Fourth Committee, United Nations General Assembly, December, 1946.] . . ."

Hall, *Mandates, Dependencies and Trusteeship* (1948) 267–269.

In 1948 the High Court of Australia sustained the jurisdiction of the Supreme Court of Papua-New Guinea over offenses committed within the Mandated Territory of New Guinea. Philips, J., of the New Guinea Court had rejected the contention of the appellants "that the Australian Courts were precluded from exercising jurisdiction over the accused in respect of offences committed in Manus Island because during war operations against Japan that island had, in agreement with the Government of Australia, been occupied by the forces of the United States of America and because no formal relinquishment of control in favour of the Australian Government had taken place," with the following observations:

"If this alternative submission, put by the accused in support of their plea to the jurisdiction, is sound, it would mean that the United States of America had the right, because its forces had allegedly recaptured Manus from a common enemy who was in temporary possession of that Island, to regard Manus as its own American territory 'by right of conquest'; that is to say, to take possession for itself of part of the Territory which had been entrusted to an ally and co-belligerent, Australia, as Mandatory, but from which Australia had, by the fortunes or misfortunes of war, been temporarily expelled. To put it more briefly, this contention of the accused amounts to this: that America had the right to regard the Manus operations as a privateering venture of her own, with Manus, part of the Mandated Territory of a comrade-in-arms, as the booty. This is a startling proposition and one that, to me, is distinctly novel. When Mr. Jones, for the Defence, suggests that the American forces at Manus were a 'force of occupation', I think he is confusing their case with that of the occupation, by a conquering force, of *enemy* country, that is, of country that had already been enemy country before the outbreak of hostilities.

.   .   .   .

"What was the Australian Government's attitude towards Manus after the Japanese invaded the Territory of New Guinea in late January, 1942? The Government left no doubt about its attitude. On 12th February 1942, National Security (Emergency Control) Regulations made under the National Security Act 1939–1940 were gazetted. Those Regulations provided that, in such parts of the Commonwealth of Australia and its Territories as might be proclaimed, specified military authorities might do or direct to be done whatever they thought necessary for the purpose of meeting any emergency, in the proclaimed areas, arising out of the war, or for the purpose of providing for the defence of the areas proclaimed. But regulation 7 of those Regulations expressly preserved (subject of course to the emergency orders of the military authorities) the civil and criminal jurisdiction of the existing civil Courts. On the same date, notification was given that the Territory of Papua and the Territory of New Guinea had been proclaimed as areas to which the Regulations applied. The rapid advance of the enemy made administrative changes necessary in New Guinea. Accordingly the National Security (External Territories) Regulations (S.R. 1942, No. 200) were made under the National Security Act and were gazetted on 27th April 1942. Those Regulations, as amended, provided for the suspension of various officers and administrative authorities of New Guinea and for the exercise (under what were called 'Temporary Administrative Provisions') of their powers and functions (except those of the Courts) by the Minister for External Territories in Australia, the General Officer Commanding New Guinea Force, and their delegates. The jurisdiction of the Supreme Court of the Territory was vested for the time being in the Supreme Court of the Australian Capital Territory. But the law of the Territory of New Guinea was never abrogated (save as affected by emergency military measures) and was enforced wherever practicable in the Territory throughout the war. Gradually, the ground lost to the enemy was regained and the way cleared for the civil administration of the Territory from a centre less remote than Canberra. On 3rd August 1945, the Governor-General assented to the Commonwealth Parliament's Papua-New Guinea Provisional Administration Act, 1945. Section 3 of that statute read as follows: 'This Act shall apply to and in relation to the Territory of Papua and such portions of the Territory of New Guinea as from time to time cease to be areas to which the National Security (Emergency Control) Regulations apply, and the whole of the area to and in relation to which this Act from time to time applies shall be called the Territory of New Guinea'. Even then some parts of New Guinea had been notified as areas to which the National Security (Emergency Control) Regulations had ceased to apply: but by a series of further proclamations, the remaining parts of the Territory had, by mid-June 1946, been declared areas to which those Regulations had ceased to apply. Finally, by an amending Act (No. 77 of 1946), section 3 of the Papua-New Guinea Provisional Administration Act was amended so that it declared that that Act 'shall apply to and in relation to the Territory of Papua and the Territory of New Guinea . . . .' Thus the whole of the Territory of New Guinea was again entirely under a Civil Administration—free from any concurrent military control. The words 'Territory of New Guinea' in the section, as amended, are not qualified in any way: they permit no inference to be drawn that the Commonwealth Parliament recognised or admitted that any part of that Territory was within the control of any other nation: in short, those words mean what they say, and mean that the Commonwealth Parliament had yet again asserted its claim to the administrative control of the whole Territory of New Guinea. There is nothing inconsistent between that claim and an agreement, tacit or express, on the part of Australia, that America should have time to evacuate its armed personnel and war material from Manus. Apart from the doctrine enunciated in *de Jager* v. *The Attorney-General of Natal* [[1907] A.C. 326], the legislation and regulations made in respect of the Territory of New Guinea by the Australian Government during the war show, very plainly, that the Government at no time abandoned, but at all times asserted, its claim to administrative control of the whole of that Territory. The declaration in section 3 of the Papua New Guinea Provisional Administration Act 1945–1946 is a declaration of the Australian Parliament's will, and it is conclusively binding on this Court."

Chow Hung Ching v. *The King*, [1948] Ann. Dig. 147, 148, 154–156 (No. 47); 77 C.L.R. 449; [1949] Argus L.R. 29. For cases involving enemy aliens in the Mandated Territory of South-West Africa, see *Westphal* v. *Conducting Officer of Southern Rhodesia*, [1948] Ann. Dig. 211 (No. 54); and *Minister of the Interior* v. *Bechler*, *ibid.* 237 (No. 67).

Japanese
Mandated
Islands

"Authority for military government in the Japanese Mandated Islands was derived from the laws of belligerent occupation. The President of the United States, in his capacity as Commander in Chief of the Army and Navy, appointed the Commander in Chief Pacific and Pacific Ocean Areas (Cin C Pac/Cin CPOA) the Military Governor of all islands and atolls and adjacent waters in the Mandated Islands occupied by the forces under his command. . . ."

I *United States Naval Administration of the Trust Territory of the Pacific Islands* (1957) 169.

Thus, Proclamation One for the Marshall Islands stated:

"*To the People of the Marshall Islands:*

"In prosecuting their war against the Japanese it has become necessary for the armed forces of the United States under my command to occupy this and other islands of the Marshall Islands.

"It is the policy of the United States Forces not to make war upon the civilian inhabitants of these islands but to permit them to continue their normal lives and occupations in a peaceable manner, so far as war necessities and their own behavior permit.

"In order to preserve law and order and provide for the safety and welfare both of my forces and of yourselves, it is necessary to establish Military Government in the islands occupied by United States Forces.

"Therefore, I, C. W. Nimitz, Admiral, United States Navy, Commander in Chief, United States Pacific Fleet and Pacific Ocean Areas and Military Governor of the Marshall Island Areas occupied by United States Forces, do hereby proclaim as follows:

I

"All powers of government and jurisdiction in the occupied territory and over the inhabitants therein, and final administrative responsibility, are vested in me as Admiral, United States Navy, Commanding the United States Forces of occupation, and Military Governor, and will be exercised through subordinate commanders by my direction.

II

"The exercise of the powers of the Emperor of Japan shall be suspended during the period of military occupation.

III

"All persons will obey promptly all orders given by me or under my authority; must not commit acts hostile to the United States Forces under my command or in any way helpful to the Japanese; must not commit acts of violence or any act which may disturb public safety in any way.

IV

"Your existing personal and property rights will be respected and your existing laws and customs remain in force and effect, except to the extent that it is necessary for me in the exercise of my powers and duties to change them.

V

"Until further notice, United States dollar currency, overprinted 'Hawaii' and United States coins will be legal tender in the occupied territory and all persons are warned against accepting or dealing in any other currency whatever, except as permitted under my orders.

VI

"So long as you remain peaceable and comply with the orders of the United States Forces of occupation, you will be subject to no greater interference than is made necessary by war conditions, and may go about your normal occupations without fear.

VII

"Further proclamations and orders will be issued by me or under my authority from time to time. They will state what is required of you and what you are forbidden to do and will be displayed at police stations and in your villages.

C. W. NIMITZ,
*Admiral, United States Navy, Commander in Chief,
United States Pacific Fleet and Pacific Ocean Areas,
Military Governor of the Marshall Islands.*"

Ibid., appendix 2, pp. 651–652. Executive Order No. 9875, July 18, 1947, terminated the United States Military Government in the former Japanese Mandated Islands concurrently with the entry into force of the Trusteeship Agreement designating the United States as Administering Authority for the "Territory of the Pacific Islands, consisting of the islands formerly held by Japan under mandate. . . ." 12 *Fed. Reg.* 4837. See further, "Trust Territory of the Pacific Islands", § 41, *infra*.

"The natives of the islands were not classified as enemy nationals. They were not Japanese subjects but because the mandate definition of nationality was not clear, the United States could assume that they were liberated peoples and therefore base all military government policies and activities on that assumption. . . ."

I *United States Naval Administration of the Trust Territory of the Pacific Islands* (1957) 164.

The following account is given of the ceremony investing native officials of Majuro Atoll, the Marshall Islands, with civil authority:

"On 29 February 1944, the No. 1 and No. 2 kings, their wives, the chief magistrate, the village scribe, the native medical practitioner and several elders, made a formal call on the Atoll and Island Commander. They were received by him and his staff, entertained at dinner and official presents were exchanged. As symbolic of the end of Japanese sovereignty [*sic*], their Japanese insignia of authority had been voluntarily surrendered. To evidence that the authority they now exercised came from the United States, the Atoll and Island Commander presented each official with a new badge of authority. These badges, designed on heavy three inch brass discs, with the American Eagle, were for evident reasons, considerably larger and more ornate than the cloth discs supplied by the Japanese. Large brass stars were issued for the village policemen. Typical is the badge of the No. 1 king which bears the inscription 'King, Majuro Atoll, U.S.A.'."

> *Ibid.* 332, 334.

"It is the view of the Department of State that the Island of Saipan on October 16, 1945 was an area under military occupation by forces of the United States following conquest from Japan, the power to which a mandate had been entrusted after World War I pursuant to Article 22 of the Covenant of the League of Nations."

> Ernest A. Gross, Legal Adviser, Department of State, to Tom C. Clark, Attorney General of the United States, letter, Dec. 16, 1947, MS. Department of State, file 411.11 Brunell, Beverly/12–147. See also *Brunell* v. *United States*, 77 F. Supp. 68 at p. 70 (S. D. N. Y., 1948).

Adjudication of disputes: PCIJ

All of the mandate instruments contained provisions for their interpretation by the Permanent Court of International Justice.

"A" Mandates

In the case of the "A" Mandates, these provisions were as follows: article XVII, Treaty between His Britannic Majesty and His Majesty the King of Iraq, signed October 10, 1922 ("Any difference that may arise between the High Contracting Parties as to the interpretation of the provisions of this Treaty shall be referred to the Permanent Court of International Justice provided for by Article 14 of the Covenant of the League of Nations. In such case, should there be any discrepancy between the English and Arabic texts of this Treaty, the English shall be taken as the authoritative version.") ; article 26, Mandate for Palestine ("The Mandatory agrees that, if any dispute whatever should arise between the Mandatory and another Member of the League of Nations relating to the interpretation or the application of the provisions of the mandate, such dispute, if it cannot be settled by negotiation, shall be submitted to the Permanent Court of International Justice provided for by Article 14 of the Covenant of the League of Nations.") ; article 20, Mandate for Syria and the Lebanon (identical with article 26, Mandate for Palestine). (These texts may be found in "Terms of League of Nations Mandates," U.N. Doc. A/70, Oct. 1946).

The "B" and "C" Mandates instruments all contained provisions identical to article 26, Mandate for Palestine. (Article 12, British Mandate for the Cameroons; article 12, French Mandate for the Cameroons; article 12, French Mandate for Togoland; article 12, British Mandate for Togoland; article 13, Belgian Mandate for East Africa (Ruanda-Urundi); article 13, British Mandate for East Africa (Tanganyika Territory); article 7, Mandate for German South-West Africa; article 7, Mandate for the German possessions in the Pacific Ocean lying north of the Equator; article 7, Mandate for German possessions in the Pacific Ocean situated south of the Equator other than German Samoa and Nauru; article 7, Mandate for German Samoa; article 7, Mandate for Nauru. "Terms of League of Nations Mandates", U.N. Doc. A/70, Oct. 1946).

In addition, article 13 of the Mandate instrument for Tanganyika provided: "States Members of the League of Nations may likewise bring any claims on behalf of their nationals for infractions of their rights under this mandate before the said Court for decision." *Ibid.*

The jurisdiction of the Permanent Court of International Justice was invoked only once under the Mandate instruments, *i.e.*, in Judgment No. 2, *The Mavrommatis Palestine Concessions* (P.C.I.J., Series A, No. 2), where the Court interpreted article 26 in the Mandate for Palestine, quoted *supra*. With respect to the Mavrommatis Jerusalem Concessions, the Court found that there existed a "dispute" within the meaning of article 26 ("a disagreement on a point of law or fact, a conflict of legal views or of interests between two persons," *ibid.* 11); that the dispute was between the Mandatory and another Member of the League of Nations, Greece, which had taken up the case of a Greek national (*ibid.* 12); that the dispute was one "which cannot be settled by negotiations" (*ibid.* 15); and that the dispute did relate "to the interpretation or the application of the provisions of the Mandate" in that "the question whether the Administration of Palestine can withhold from M. Mavrommatis the readaptation of his Jerusalem concessions, is a question concerning the interpretation of Article 11 of the Mandate, and consequently the provisions of Article 26 are applicable to it." (*Ibid.* 27.)

In reaching these conclusions, the majority opinion took account of the basis of the Court's jurisdiction, as follows:

> "For this reason the Court, bearing in mind the fact that its jurisdiction is limited, that it is invariably based on the consent of the respondent and only exists in so far as this consent has been given, cannot content itself with the provisional conclusion that the dispute falls or not within the terms of the Mandate. The Court, before giving judgment on the merits of the case, will satisfy itself that the suit before it, in the form in which it has

been submitted and on the basis of the facts hitherto established, falls to be decided by application of the clauses of the Mandate. For the Mandatory has only accepted the Court's jurisdiction for such disputes." (*Ibid.* 16.)

It should be noted that five of the Judges, Lord Finlay and Judges de Bustamante, Moore, Oda, and Pessôa, dissented on the ground that the conditions of article 26 of the Mandate had not been fulfilled. In their Dissenting Opinions, Judges de Bustamante and Oda specifically referred to article 13 of the British Mandate for East Africa, *supra*. Thus, Judge Oda stated:

> "Since the Mandate establishes a special legal relationship, it is natural that the League of Nations, which issued the Mandate, should have rights of supervision as regards the Mandatory. Under the Mandate, in addition to the direct supervision of the Council of the League of Nations (Articles 24 and 25) provision is made for indirect supervision by the Court; but the latter may only be exercised at the request of a Member of the League of Nations (Article 26). It is therefore to be supposed that an application by such a Member must be made exclusively with a view to the protection of general interests and that it is not admissible for a State simply to substitute itself for a private person in order to assert his private claims. That this is the case is clearly shown by a reference to Article 13 of the Mandate for East Africa, in which Members of the League of Nations are specially authorized to bring claims on behalf of their nationals. It is impossible to ascertain why this special provision was only inserted in the East African Mandate; but, as it appears that in all the drafts of 'B' Mandates the same provision was inserted, but deleted in the final documents, except in the case of the Mandate for East Africa, it is at all events clear that it was intended to establish a difference between 'B' and 'A' Mandates to which latter category the Palestine Mandate belongs. The logical conclusion is that an action in support of private interests is excluded under Article 26 of the Mandate now in question, and that, precisely from this standpoint, the Court has no jurisdiction in the case of the Mavrommatis concessions." *Ibid.* 86–87.

See also Hudson, *The Permanent Court of International Justice 1920–1942* (1943), pp. 441–442, 634–636. The Court's Judgments Nos. 5 and 10 dealt with the merits of the Mavrommatis claims (P.C.I.J. Series A, No. 5 and No. 11). See also *ante*, pp. 651–653.

Jurisdiction of ICJ

"According to Article 7 of the Mandate, disputes between the mandatory State and another Member of the League of Nations relating to the interpretation or the application of the provisions of the Mandate, if not settled by negotiation, should be submitted to the Permanent Court of International Justice. Having regard to Article 37 of the Statute of the International Court of Justice, and Article 80, paragraph 1, of the Charter, the Court is of opinion that this clause in the Mandate is still in force and that, therefore, the Union of South Africa is under an obligation to accept the compulsory jurisdiction of the Court according to those provisions."

International Status of South-West Africa, Advisory Opinion, July 11, 1950, I.C.J. Reports (1950) 128, 138.

"The *judicial supervision* has been expressly preserved by means of Article 37 of the Statute of the International Court of Justice adopted in 1945:

" 'Whenever a treaty or convention in force provides for reference of a matter to a tribunal to have been instituted by the League of Nations, or to the Permanent Court of International Justice, the matter shall, as between the parties to the present Statute, be referred to the International Court of Justice.'

"This article effected a succession by the International Court to the compulsory jurisdiction conferred upon the Permanent Court by Article 7 of the Mandate; for there can be no doubt that the Mandate, which embodies international obligations, belongs to the category of treaty or convention; in the judgment of the Permanent Court in the *Mavrommatis Palestine Concessions* (*Jurisdiction*) case, Series A, No. 2, p. 35, the Palestine Mandate was referred to as an 'international agreement'; and I have endeavoured to show that the agreement between the Mandatory and other Members of the League embodied in the Mandate is still 'in force'. The expression 'Member of the League of Nations' is descriptive, in my opinion, not conditional, and does not mean 'so long as the League exists and they are Members of it'; their interest in the performance of the obligations of the Mandate did not accrue to them merely from membership of the League, as an examination of the content of the Mandate makes clear. Moreover, the Statute of the International Court empowers it to call from the parties for 'any document' or 'any explanations' (Article 49) ; and to entrust any 'individual, body, bureau, commission or other organization that it may select, with the task of carrying out an enquiry . . . .' (Article 50). Article 94 of the Charter empowers the Security Council of the United Nations to 'make recommendations or decide upon measures to be taken to give effect to the judgment' of the Court, in the event of a party to a case failing to carry out a judgment of the Court. In addition, the General Assembly or the Security Council of the United Nations may request the Court to give an advisory opinion on any legal question (Article 96 of the Charter)."

Separate Opinion of Judge McNair, *ibid.* 158–159.

"These obligations have one point in common. Each Member of the League had a legal interest, *vis-à-vis* the Mandatory Power, in matters 'relating to the interpretation or the application of the provisions of the Mandate'; and had a legal right to assert its interest against the Union by invoking the compulsory jurisdiction of the Permanent Court (Article 7 of the Mandate Agreement). . . .

.   .   .   .

"First: the Mandate survived, together with all of the essential and substantive obligations of the Union.

"Second: the legal rights and interests of the Members of the League, in respect of the Mandate, survived with one important exception—in the case of Members that did not become parties to the Statute of this Court, their right to implead the Union before the Permanent Court lapsed."

Separate Opinion of Judge Read, *ibid.* 165, 169. See also Lauterpacht, *The Development of International Law by the International Court* (1958) 278–279, n. 33.

The United Nations Committee on South West Africa, in a Special Report, "A study of legal action to ensure the fulfilment of the obligations assumed by the Mandatory Power under the Mandate for South-West Africa," commented: "32. There would therefore appear to be little doubt that the right to invoke Article 7 of the Mandate is enjoyed at any rate by those former Members of the League which were Members at the date of dissolution of the League and which are now Members of the United Nations or are otherwise parties to the Statute of the Court. For the article to apply, there must be a dispute between the Mandatory and such former Members, which cannot be settled by negotiation and which relates to the interpretation of the Mandate." U.N. Gen. Ass. Off. Rec. 12th Sess., Supp. No. 12A (A/3625), p. 5.

On November 5, 1960, the Registry of the International Court of Justice issued the following statement:

"On November 4th, 1960 applications were filed in the Registry of the Court on behalf of the government of Ethiop[i]a and on behalf of the government of Liberia instituting separate proceedings before the Court against the Union of South Africa.

"In both applications, the subject of the dispute is stated to be the continued existence of the mandate for Southwest Africa and the duties and performance of the Union, as mandatory, thereunder. The applications refer to Article 80, paragraph 1, of the Charter of the United Nations, and found the jurisdiction of the Court on Article 7 of the mandate for German Southwest Africa made at Geneva on December 17th, 1920, and on article 37 of the Statute of the Court.

.   .   .   .

"The applications respectively state that a dispute exists and has existed for more than ten years between the applicants and the Union regarding the interpretation and application of the mandate."

Reported in the American Embassy, The Hague, to the Department of State, airgram No. 140, Nov. 8, 1960, MS. Department of State, file 360/11–860. See § 37, "South-West Africa", *post*, for substantive aspects of these proceedings. On December 15, 1960, the Government of the Union of South Africa notified the Registrar of the International Court of Justice of the appointment of its Agent in these cases. Orders of 13 January 1961, I.C.J. Reports (1961) 3, 4, 6, 7.

On December 18, 1960, the General Assembly of the United Nations adopted the following resolution:

> "1565 (XV). *Legal action to ensure the fulfilment of the obligations assumed by the Union of South Africa in respect of the Territory of South West Africa*
>
> "*The General Assembly*,
>
> "*Recalling* its resolution 1361 (XIV) of 17 November 1959, in which it drew the attention of Member States to the conclusions of the special report of the Committee on South West Africa concerning the legal action open to Member States to submit to the International Court of Justice any dispute with the Union of South Africa relating to the interpretation or application of the provisions of the Mandate for the Territory of South West Africa, if such dispute cannot be settled by negotiation,
>
> . . . .
>
> "2. *Concludes* that the dispute which has arisen between Ethiopia, Liberia and other Member States on the one hand, and the Union of South Africa on the other, relating to the interpretation and application of the Mandate has not been and cannot be settled by negotiation;
>
> "3. *Notes* that Ethiopia and Liberia, on 4 November 1960, filed concurrent applications in the International Court of Justice instituting contentious proceedings against the Union of South Africa;
>
> "4. *Commends* the Governments of Ethiopia and Liberia upon their initiative in submitting such dispute to the International Court of Justice for adjudication and declaration in a contentious proceeding in accordance with article 7 of the Mandate."

G.A. Res. 1565 (XV), Dec. 18, 1960, U.N. Doc. A/4684, pp. 31, 33. This resolution was adopted by a vote of 86 in favor, including the United States, with none opposed, and 6 abstentions.

"My Delegation believes that by far the greatest possibility of substantial progress in this matter rests with the International Court of Justice, which now has before it a case involving contentious proceedings brought by the Governments of Liberia and Ethiopia against the Union of South Africa. Considering the matter realistically, I think we must conclude that no important action can be taken by the United Nations, with a reasonable prospect of solving the problem of South West Africa, until we have the answers to the several questions now before the Court. . . ."

Statement by Senator Wayne Morse, United States Representative, in Committee IV of the United Nations General Assembly, Nov. 22, 1960 (U.S.-U.N. press release No. 3583/Rev. 1, Nov. 22, 1960).

Termination of Mandates

§ 36

"A"
Mandates:
Iraq

". . . After various negotiations the British Government on November 4, 1929 informed the League of Nations that it would recommend Iraq for admission to the League in 1932 (League of Nations, *Official Journal*, 1929, p. 1838). A fresh treaty of alliance, signed at Baghdad on June 30, 1930 and in force from October 3, 1932 for 25 years (132 League of Nations Treaty Series, p. 363), replaced the treaties of October 10, 1922 and January 13, 1926. A special report by the mandatory gave the Permanent Mandates Commission evidence that the progress of Iraq during the period 1920–31 satisfied the *de facto* conditions requisite for termination of the mandate. On May 19, 1932 the Council of the League adopted the conditions to be met for its termination (League of Nations, *Official Journal*, 1932, pp. 1212, 1347), which were ratified by Iraq in July (*ibid.*, pp. 1483, 1557). Admission to the League was unanimously voted by the Assembly on October 3, 1932, at which date the mandated status of Iraq terminated."

1919 For. Rel., vol. XIII, Paris Peace Conference (1947), p. 99. Also printed under title "The Treaty of Versailles and After: Annotations of the Text of the Treaty". See also League of Nations, *The Mandates System, Origin—Principles—Application* (1945.VI.A.1) 31–32.

Syria and
Lebanon

"The 'A' mandate of Syria and Lebanon underwent an evolution bringing the two entities involved to the verge of independence. . . . France signed treaties of friendship and alliance with Lebanon at Beirut on November 13, 1936 and with Syria at Damascus on December 22, 1936 (France, Ministère des affaires étrangères, *Rapport à la Société des Nations sur la situation de la Syrie et du Liban* (*année 1936*), pp. 201, 229). These treaties were to come into force, along with new organic statutes of the Jebel Druse and the Aluite (Latakia), upon the admission of Syria and Lebanon to the League of Nations. France delayed the ratification of the treaties while the Alexandretta matter was being settled and the arrangements for admission to the League were being completed. After the surrender of France in June 1940 the Free French National Committee, which was later succeeded by the French Committee of National Liberation, took over the administration of the territories from the Vichy French forces with the aid of British contingents. On June 8, 1941 the commander of the Free French forces in the Middle East, in the name of the committee, assumed the powers, responsibilities, and duties of the representative of France in the Levant and as such informed the people of Syria and the Lebanon that 'I come to put an end to the mandatory regime and proclaim you free and independent'. On September 7, 1944 the Department of State extended formal recognition to both. Lebanon and Syria signed the Declaration by United Nations, April 12, 1945 and are Members of the United Nations."

1919 For. Rel., vol. XIII, Paris Peace Conference (1947), pp. 99–100.

"Syria

[A. H. Hourani, *Syria and Lebanon; A Political Essay* (Issued under the auspices of the Royal Institute of International Affairs, London, New York, etc.: Oxford University Press, 1946) gives all the recent documents, against a luminous analysis of the background.]

"An Allied force, consisting of Free French and British Commonwealth troops, entered Syria and Lebanon on June 8, 1941, and took over the territory after a campaign lasting a month. In simultaneous Free French and British proclamations, issued that day, the peoples of Syria and Lebanon were declared 'from henceforth sovereign and independent peoples.' The French proclamation announced that their 'independent and sovereign status' would be guaranteed by a treaty defining the mutual relations between them and France. General Catroux proclaimed the independence of Syria as a sovereign state on September 28, and of Lebanon on November 26. British recognition was accorded to Syria on October 27, and to Lebanon on December 26, 1941. War conditions and the difficulties that stood in the way of negotiating a treaty between France and the new states slowed up the establishment of constitutional rule. The French view was that legally the mandate still held, that neither France nor the new states could end its obligations except by a legal process through the League of Nations or its successor, and that the Iraq precedent of a treaty, as worked out by the League and the Mandates Commission, was the proper method of termination of the mandate. The view of Syria and Lebanon was that the mandate had ceased to exist—at least *de facto*—with the declaration of independence made in 1941, and that a treaty of friendship and alliance with France was not necessary. In October, 1943, the Lebanese government and parliament eliminated all references to the mandatory power and the League of Nations from the constitution. Meanwhile, the new states began to receive unconditional recognition by an increasing number of powers: by the Arab states in the fall of 1943, by the U.S.S.R. in July, 1944, and by the United States of America in September, 1944. In February, 1945, Syria and Lebanon declared war against Germany and Japan. After signing the Declaration of the United Nations they were invited on March 29, 1945, by the United States and the other sponsor powers to the San Francisco Conference. On December 13, 1945, an agreement was signed between Britain and France providing for the evacuation of their troops from Syria and Lebanon.

"Thus, the Syrian mandate may be said to have been terminated without any formal action on the part of the League or its successor. The mandate was terminated by the declaration of the mandatory power, and of the new states themselves, of their independence, followed by a process of piecemeal unconditional recognition by other powers, culminating in formal admission to the United Nations. Article 78 of the Charter ended the status of tutelage for any member state: 'The trusteeship system shall not apply to territories which have become Members of the United

530309 O—63—45

Nations, relationship among which shall be based on respect for the principle of sovereign equality.' "

Hall, *Mandates, Dependencies and Trusteeship* (1948) 265–266. For statement of General de Gaulle of November 29, 1941, concerning the Mandate for Syria and Lebanon, see *ante*, pp. 680–681.

Palestine:
Transjordan

In article 1 of the Treaty of Alliance between the United Kingdom and Transjordan, signed at London on March 22, 1946, ratifications of which were exchanged at Amman, June 17, 1946, it was stated that "His Majesty The King recognises Trans-Jordan as a fully independent State and His Highness The Amir as the sovereign thereof." (146 Br. & For. St. Paps. (1946) 461, 462.) This followed upon a declaration of the British Foreign Minister in the General Assembly of the United Nations on January 17, 1946, of his Government's intention to establish Transjordan "as a sovereign independent state" and to recognize "its status as such." (U.N. Gen. Ass. Off. Rec. 1st Sess., 1st pt., Jan. 10–Feb. 14, 1946, p. 167, A/P.V.11.) In its Resolution 11(I), February 9, 1946, the General Assembly welcomed the declaration by the Mandatory "in respect of Transjordan, to establish its independence." (G.A. Res. 11(I), Feb. 9, 1946, U.N. Doc. A/64, p. 13.) (In a letter of April 23, 1946, from Secretary of State Byrnes to Senator Francis J. Myers, the history of this Mandate was reviewed and assurance given that the Treaty of March 22, 1946, did not "violate any treaties existing between Great Britain and the United States, including the Convention of December 3, 1924, or deprive the United States of any rights or interests which the United States may have with respect to Trans-Jordan." The letter reserved the position of the United States with respect to recognition of Transjordan as an independent state and made no comment as to its status as a Mandated Territory. XIV *Bulletin*, Department of State, No. 357, May 5, 1946, pp. 765–766.) According to one authority, the Treaty of March 22, 1946, "terminated the mandate." Thus, "Trans-Jordan might be regarded as one of the territories 'now held under mandate,' in the words of Article 77 of the [United Nations] Charter. But the mandate ended in independence before the trusteeship system was in effect." Hall, *op. cit.* 266. Nevertheless, the same authority observed: "The mandate charters were the basic law applying within the territories the principles of Article 22 of the Covenant. Each charter was in the nature of a treaty between the League and the mandatory which defined the terms upon which the mandatory had agreed with the Council of the League to advise or assist or govern the territory. Being treaties, the mandates could not be amended unilaterally, and each text specifically stated that it could not be modified without the consent of the Council of the League." *Ibid.* 149.

In fact, only the mandated status of Iraq was terminated with the consent of the Council of the League of Nations. The activities of the League were suspended by the Second World War; and the question of the future of the Mandates System, among a number of other questions, was considered by the League of Nations Assembly in 1946. The following resolution was adopted by that body on April 18, 1946:

Action, last League Assembly

"The Assembly,
"Recalling that Article 22 of the Covenant applies to certain territories placed under mandate the principle that the well-being and development of peoples not yet able to stand alone in the strenuous conditions of the modern world form a sacred trust of civilisation:

"1. Expresses its satisfaction with the manner in which the organs of the League have performed the functions entrusted to them with respect to the mandates system and in particular pays tribute to the work accomplished by the Permanent Mandates Commission;

"2. Recalls the rôle of the League in assisting Iraq to progress from its status under an 'A' Mandate to a condition of complete independence, welcomes the termination of the mandated status of Syria, the Lebanon and Transjordan, which have, since the last session of the Assembly, become independent members of the world community;

"3. Recognises that, on the termination of the League's existence, its functions with respect to the mandated territories will come to an end, but notes that Chapters XI, XII and XIII of the Charter of the United Nations embody principles corresponding to those declared in Article 22 of the Covenant of the League;

"4. Takes note of the expressed intentions of the Members of the League now administering territories under mandate to continue to administer them for the well-being and development of the peoples concerned in accordance with the obligations contained in the respective Mandates, until other arrangements have been agreed between the United Nations and the respective mandatory Powers."

League of Nations Off. J., 21st Ass. (1946), Spec. Supp. No. 194, p. 58.

At the time the above-quoted resolution was adopted by the Assembly of the League of Nations, Professor Bailey of Australia, rapporteur, commented to the Assembly:

"I draw the Assembly's attention now to pages 3 and 4 of the Committee's Report and to the resolutions which are relevant to that page. The Assembly comes now to three major activities of the League, which as activities of the League will, of course, from now on be brought to their termination. That does not mean, however, that the activities themselves as international activities will come to an end. It means rather that they will be continued in some other form.

. . . .

"Though the immediate process on which the Assembly is engaged is a process of technical dissolution, it is only part of an essentially constructive and continuing process in the work of international organisation. It is neither necessary nor appropriate for me to add more than a word to what is said in the body of the report, but the Assembly may desire to be reminded of the achievements of the League and, in particular, of the Permanent Mandates Commission as regards the international supervision of the administration of certain dependent territories; . . ."

On the same occasion Mahmoud Mohamed El Darwiche Bey of Egypt stated:

"The terms of Article 22 of the Covenant of the League of Nations, referred to in the preamble of the resolution under consideration, provide that the system of mandates was meant for peoples not yet able to stand alone in the strenuous conditions of the modern world. Palestine, after the last war, was considered to be a territory coming under this provision. The opinion of my Government is that Palestine has intellectually, economically, and politically reached a stage where it should no longer continue under mandate or trusteeship or whatever other arrangements may be considered. Palestine is not behind the countries the independence of which has lately been admitted, and to which reference is made in the resolution; she is not behind Iraq, Syria, the Lebanon or Transjordan. I therefore feel that I have to make all reservations in the Assembly, as I did in the Committee, with regard to the fourth paragraph of the resolution, whereby the Assembly

" 'Takes note of the expressed intentions of the Members of the League now administering territories under mandate to continue to administer them . . . in accordance with the obligations contained in the respective Mandates . . .'

"It is the view of my Government that mandates have terminated with the dissolution of the League of Nations, and that, in so far as Palestine is concerned, there should be no question of putting that country under trusteeship. I have not chosen the procedure of submitting a formal resolution whereby the Assembly expresses the wish that the independence of Palestine shall be declared; I chose in the Committee, and I intend here, simply to abstain from voting on this resolution."

Ibid., pp. 58–59.

Thus, the Assembly of the League of Nations appears to have given *ex post facto* recognition to the termination of the "A" Mandates, except for Palestine.

It is clear that the Palestine Mandate was considered by the Man- Palestine
datory Power and other States to have survived the dissolution of the
League of Nations. The circumstances of the termination of the
Palestine Mandate were described in a judgment of the highest court
of the Mandatory Power, the House of Lords, as follows:

"The facts were stated by Lord Morton of Henryton as follows:
The appellants sought to be paid by the respondents a sum of
£582,931 3s. 0d., being the equivalent in sterling of 582,931·146
Palestine pounds. The latter sum was standing to the credit of
the appellants on May 14, 1948, in their current account at the
respondents' branch at Allenby Square, Jerusalem. The British U.K.
mandate over Palestine ended at midnight on May 14–15, 1948. action
Immediately on the determination [*sic*] of the mandate, by a Declaration of Independence and a proclamation made thereunder,
the provisional Council of State and the provisional Government
of the State of Israel were constituted and, although there was no
formal declaration of war, war in fact broke out at once between
the State of Israel on the one hand and the Arabs in Palestine and
certain States which supported them on the other hand, including
the Hashemite Kingdom.

. . . .

"Prior to midnight on May 14–15, 1948, Palestine was mandated territory administered by a High Commissioner. The
adjoining territory of Transjordan had originally been a British
Protectorate, administered by a High Commissioner, but in the
year 1946 Transjordan was recognized as an independent State
under the rule of King Abdullah. Palestine and Transjordan
had the same currency and were treated as a single currency area
for the purposes of exchange control.
"In January, 1948, His Majesty's Government announced that
the mandate would end at midnight on May 14–15, and from the
time of that announcement until the end of the mandate, disturbances which had already begun rapidly increased.

. . . .

"On April 27, 1950, de jure recognition was accorded by His
Majesty's Government to Israel, but a reservation was made in
that no more than de facto recognition was accorded in respect
of Israeli sovereignty over that part of Jerusalem occupied by
Israel. In April, 1951, His Majesty's Government accorded de
jure recognition to the Hashemite Kingdom of Jordan which
included that part of Palestine occupied and controlled by the
Arabs, but His Majesty's Government made a similar reservation
in respect of that part of Jerusalem occupied and controlled by
the Arabs."

Arab Bank Ld. v. *Barclays Bank*, L.R. [1954] A.C. 495, 496–498.

"ACT OF PARLIAMENT to make provision with respect to the
termination of His Majesty's jurisdiction in Palestine, and for

purposes connected therewith.—[11 & 12 Geo. 6. c. 27.]—29th April, 1948

"Be it enacted by the King's Most Excellent Majesty, by and with the advice and consent of the Lords Spiritual and Temporal, and Commons, in this present Parliament assembled, and by the authority of the same, as follows:—

"1.—(1) On the fifteenth day of May, nineteen hundred and forty-eight, or such earlier date as His Majesty may by Order in Council declare to be the date on which the mandate in respect of Palestine accepted by His Majesty on behalf of the League of Nations will be relinquished (in this Act referred to as 'the appointed day'), all jurisdiction of His Majesty in Palestine shall determine, and His Majesty's Government in the United Kingdom shall cease to be responsible for the government of Palestine.

"(2) Nothing in this Act shall affect the jurisdiction of His Majesty, or any powers of the Admiralty, the Army Council or the Air Council, or of any other authority, in relation to any of His Majesty's forces which may be in Palestine on or after the appointed day."

150 Br. & For. St. Paps. (1948, pt. I) 278, 279.

By subsequent Orders in Council, the 15th day of May 1948 was confirmed as "the appointed day" for the relinquishment of the Palestine Mandate, when the "jurisdiction of His Majesty in Palestine will . . . determine . . ."

Order in Council making transitional provisions with regard to the termination of Jurisdiction in Palestine, London, 12th May, 1948. 150 Br. & For. St. Paps. (1948, pt. I) 299; Order in Council revoking certain provisions in Orders in Council relating to Palestine and the application of certain Acts thereto, London, 12th May, 1948. *Ibid.* 302. See also Order in Council making provisions for the government of Palestine pending the termination of the Mandate, London, 26th January, 1948. *Ibid.* 28; and Agreement between the United Kingdom and Israel for the settlement of financial matters outstanding as a result of the termination of the Mandate for Palestine, with Exchanges of Letters, London, 30th March, 1950. 156 Br. & For. St. Paps. (1950, pt. I) 608.

"B. *Termination of Mandates: Palestine*

"The General Assembly was heavily occupied during 1947 with the problems involved in the termination of the Palestine Mandate. In a formal communication to the Secretary-General of the United Nations, dated April 2, 1947, the United Kingdom, as Mandatory, announced its intention to ask the General Assembly, at its next regular session, to make recommendations, under Article 10 of the Charter, concerning the future government of Palestine. In this same communication, the United Kingdom requested the Secretary-General to summon a special session of the General Assembly for the purpose of constituting and instructing a special committee to prepare for the consideration of this question at

U.N.
action

the next regular session of the General Assembly. Accordingly, a Special Session was convened on April 28, 1947, which established a Special Committee on Palestine.

"After consideration of the report of this Special Committee and extensive debate in its *Ad Hoc* Committee on Palestine, the General Assembly adopted Resolution 181 (II), Future Government of Palestine, on November 29, 1947. This resolution called for the termination of the Mandate for Palestine not later than August 1, 1948, and the partition of the territory into independent Arab and Jewish States, together with a special international regime for the City of Jerusalem. This resolution was adopted by a two-thirds majority vote, 33 in favor, 13 against, with 10 abstentions (including the United Kingdom).

"The United Kingdom subsequently announced its intention to abandon the Mandate on May 15, 1948. At midnight May 14, 1948, the Provisional Government of Israel proclaimed the independence of the State of Israel. This State was later admitted, in May 1949, as a member of the United Nations.

"The General Assembly's debate and resolution on the Palestine question in 1947 provide an example of Assembly action, to terminate a mandate, by a two-thirds vote where that vote was considerably short of being unanimous and was not joined in by the mandatory power."

Written Statement of the United States of America, *Voting Procedure on Questions Relating to Reports and Petitions concerning the Territory of South-West Africa*, Pleadings, Oral Arguments, Documents, pp. 67–68 (I.C.J. 1955). A detailed account of the United Nations action with respect to the Palestine Mandate, together with the text of General Assembly Resolution 181 (II), appears in The U.S. and the U.N., report by the President to Congress for the year 1947, pp. 42–57, 164–187. See also U.S. participation in the U.N., report by the President to Congress for the year 1948, pp. 39–56. As noted in the report for 1947, the United States voted with the majority for Resolution 181 (II).

"You inquire whether a mandatory or trust power can relinquish its responsibility except '(a) by agreement with the other party or parties to the contract, and (b) when proper provision is made to carry on its responsibilities in order to avoid a complete breakdown which might otherwise occur'. U.S. views

"Whether or not a mandatory, or administering authority in the case of a trust territory, can unilaterally relinquish its mandate or trust, depends upon the terms of the particular treaty situation obtaining in a given case. Thus the mandate treaty for Iraq, contained provision in Article 18 that the treaty should remain in force for a specified period (25 years as amended) though termination was made subject to confirmation by the League of Nations (unless Iraq should be admitted to the League of Nations under Article 6). In the case of the Palestine Mandate there is no similar provision, Article 27 merely provides that 'The consent of the Council of the League of Nations is required for any modification of the terms of this mandate.'

"The question is not entirely new. The Permanent Mandates Commission, at its third session (July-August 1923) pointed out to the Council of the League of Nations that the opinion existed in some quarters that a mandate was revocable, and that this opinion, together with the possibility of the voluntary rendition or transfer of a mandate was regarded by some as a defect of title presenting an obstacle to the investment of private capital in a mandated territory. P.M.C. Minutes, 3, pp. 77, 198–199. The question, at least so far as it involved the manner of 'voluntary rendition' of a mandate was never resolved.

"Henry Goudy, a British professor writing in 1919, at the time of the institution of the mandates system, in analyzing the Roman law concept of *mandatum*, expressed the view that a mandate was 'even renounceable by the mandatory under certain circumstances'. He stated that the Roman mandate 'might be revoked . . . by the mandant at any time, but subject to liabilities incurred by part-execution, and it might correspondingly be renounced by the mandatory *re adhuc integra* or under circumstances involving no blame on his part'. Speaking of the projected mandates system, he said:

"'. . . How is the mandate to be terminated: If once partially executed, can it be revoked? Undoubtedly, on legal principle, failure by the Mandatory State to carry out its instructions will warrant revocation. But what kind of indemnification, if any, will then have to be given? Dissolution, moreover, of the League of Nations will doubtless put an end to the mandate, as will a change, say by conquest, in the Mandatory State'. 1 J.C.L. 175, 176, 180–181.

"While Barriedale Keith, another British professor and writer, speaks of the mandatory Power 'resigning the mandate', he apparently has in mind the modification or transfer of a mandate, and at least does not go into the matter of how a mandate may be resigned. 4 J.C.L. 71, 80–81 (1922).

"Quincy Wright after pointing out that 'The A mandates expressly provide that "on the termination of the mandate, the council of the League of Nations shall use its influence" to assure the fulfillment of financial obligations by the mandated territory and, in the case of Palestine, the security of holy places', states:

"'. . . Some writers have interpreted the article referred to in A mandates as authority for resignation by the mandatory with assurance of reimbursement of administrative expenses in such an event. The general principle of international law which forbids the unilateral termination of international agreements in the absence of breach of duty or express provision is, however, opposed to this interpretation. The mandate, while the constitution of the area, is also an international agreement between the League represented by the Council and the mandatory and can normally be terminated only by agreement of the two.' Mandates Under the League of Nations (1930) 519–520.

"James C. Hales, a British barrister, concluded, in a paper written in 1937 and apparently relying largely on Wright, that

" 'It is also probable that the consent of the Mandatory Power to the ending of the trust is essential, for the Mandate came into existence as the result of an agreement between the League and the Mandatory Power, which is very much in the nature of a Treaty. Consequently, the latter can only come to an end with the consent of all parties to it, subject to its unlikely end by revocation. . .' 'Some Legal Aspects of the Mandate System: Sovereignty—Nationality—Termination and Transfer', 23 Transactions of the Grotius Society, pp. 85, 117.

"Because of the confused legal situation, obtaining in part as a result of the extinction of the League of Nations, it is extremely doubtful whether the United States should permit itself to become involved in a discussion of the legal question raised."

Marjorie M. Whiteman, Assistant Legal Adviser, to Benjamin O. Gerig, Chief, Division of Dependent Areas, "Unilateral Right to Relinquish a Mandate or Trust Agreement", memorandum, Oct. 28, 1947, MS. Department of State, file 501–BB Palestine/9–2647.

In a memorandum of October 27, 1947, the Legal Adviser of the Department of State (Gross) stated: "It is not entirely clear . . . just what procedures would be necessary in order to effect a legal termination of the mandate and to put into application in a legal and orderly manner whatever measures may be decided upon for Palestine." FW *ibid.*/10–2747.

One authority has observed: "The Resolution [181(II)] was never fully implemented, and the declaration was never made. Israel came into existence by its own act. . . . The Mandate had been terminated by Great Britain, and with it the Government of Palestine, without any arrangement having been made for the disposal of the latter's assets and liabilities." O'Connell, *The Law of State Succession* (1956) 10–11.

Another authority has observed: "On 29 November 1947 the General Assembly adopted, in Resolution 181(II), a plan of Partition with Economic Union for the future Government of Palestine. Nevertheless, from the legal point of view, the termination of the Mandate was achieved by the unilateral action of the British Parliament in passing the Palestine Act, 1948." Rosenne, "The Effect of Change of Sovereignty upon Municipal Law", XXVII Brit. Yb. Int'l L. (1950), pp. 267, 268, n. 2. *Cf.:* "The international status of the Territory results from the international rules regulating the rights, powers and obligations relating to the administration of the Territory and the supervision of that administration, as embodied in Article 22 of the Covenant and in the Mandate. It is clear that the *Union has no competence to modify unilaterally the international status of the Territory* or any of these international rules. This is shown by Article 7 of the Mandate, which expressly provides that the consent of the Council of the League of Nations is required for any modification of the terms of the Mandate." (Italics supplied.) *International Status of South-West Africa*, Advisory Opinion, July 11, 1950, I.C.J. Reports (1950) 128, 141.

"When the General Assembly met for the first part of the first session in London from January 10 to February 14, 1946, it con-

"B" and "C" Mandates

sidered the problems relating to the establishment of the trusteeship system. Among the most important developments were the statements by the powers holding mandates concerning the disposition of these territories. On January 17, 1946 Foreign Minister Bevin announced for the United Kingdom that preliminary negotiations to place Tanganyika, the Cameroons, and Togoland under the trusteeship system had already commenced. Mr. Bevin further declared that steps would be taken to establish Trans-Jordan as an independent state, but that proposals concerning Palestine must await the report of the Anglo-American Committee of Inquiry. The Governments of Belgium, New Zealand, and Australia also announced their intention to transfer Ruanda-Urundi, Western Samoa, and New Guinea respectively to the trusteeship system. Australia, with the concurrence of the United Kingdom and New Zealand, announced a similar course of procedure regarding Nauru. The French Government announced that it was prepared to study the terms by which Togoland and the Cameroons might be placed under trusteeship. However, a note of opposition was sounded by the Government of the Union of South Africa whose representatives stated in the General Assembly on January 17, 1946 that South-West Africa occupied a special position with respect to the Union which differentiated that territory from any other 'C' mandate. Pending consultations with the people of South-West Africa regarding the form of their future government, the South African Government would reserve its position concerning the future of the mandate. In the meanwhile the Union would continue to administer the territory in accordance with the obligations and responsibilities of the mandate.

"The General Assembly in its London session concluded its consideration of trusteeship problems by the adoption of a resolution on February 9, 1946 welcoming the declarations made by the Mandatory Powers and expressing the expectation that the realization of the objectives of the Charter referring to the trusteeship system, the Trusteeship Council, and non-self-governing territories would make possible the attainment of the aspirations of non-self-governing peoples as a whole. The resolution also invited states administering mandated territories to undertake practical steps, together with the other states directly concerned, for the negotiation of trusteeship agreements. [*The United States and the United Nations.* Report of the United States Delegation to the First Part of the First Session of the General Assembly of the United Nations, London, England, Jan. 10–Feb. 14, 1946, p. 10. Submitted to the President of the United States by the Secretary of State in Washington, D.C., Mar. 1, 1946. Department of State publication 2484.]"

Armstrong and Cargo, "The Inauguration of the Trusteeship System of the United Nations," XVI *Bulletin*, Department of State, No. 403, Mar. 23, 1947, pp. 511, 513–514.

"A. *Termination of Mandates: Transfer to the United Nations Trusteeship System*

"As noted above, Article 18, paragraph 2, of the Charter requires a two-thirds vote of members of the General Assembly present and voting for decisions of the General Assembly on questions relating to the operation of the Trusteeship System.

"On February 9, 1946, the General Assembly adopted resolution 9 (I), inviting all States administering territories under Mandate to submit trusteeship agreements for approval and welcoming the declaration of the United Kingdom of its intention as mandatory to terminate the Mandate of Trans-Jordan and to establish the independence of that country. [Prior to that date, the following League Mandates had been terminated by the establishment of the independence of the countries involved: Iraq, Syria and Lebanon.]

"On December 13, 1946, the General Assembly adopted resolution 63 (I) approving the following eight trusteeship agreements placing League of Nations Mandates under the United Nations trusteeship system:

Territory	Administering Authority	VOTE Affirmative	Negative	Abstention
New Guinea ...	Australia	41	6	5
Ruanda-Urundi .	Belgium	41	6	5
Cameroons	France	41	5	6
Togoland	France	41	5	6
Western Samoa .	New Zealand	41	6	5
Tanganyika ...	United Kingdom ..	41	6	5
Cameroons	United Kingdom ..	41	6	5
Togoland	United Kingdom ..	41	6	5

"On November 1, 1947, the General Assembly, by a vote of 46 to 6, adopted resolution 140 (II), approving the Trusteeship Agreement for the former Mandate, Nauru, submitted by the Governments of Australia, New Zealand and the United Kingdom. [During this same year, 1947, arrangements were completed for the placing of the Marshall, Caroline and Mariana Islands (formerly mandated to Japan) under the United Nations trusteeship system, with the United States of America as administering authority. Since this territory, the Trust Territory of the Pacific Islands, was designated a strategic trust territory, this trusteeship agreement was approved, on behalf of the United Nations, by the Security Council of the Organization, in accordance with Article 83 of the Charter. The vote in the Security Council on April 2, 1947, approving the trusteeship agreement, was unanimous. As pointed out above, even in that body the "unanimity" rule does not prevail, since the majority required is a majority of seven members, including the concurring votes of the five permanent members.]

.   .   .   .

"It may be noted at the same time that these General Assembly decisions to approve trusteeship agreements had also the character of actions to modify and in fact terminate League of Nations Mandates. Under the League such action might have been taken by the League Council, where the unanimity rule was in force. In the General Assembly the actions were taken by less than unanimous vote and in accordance with the Charter provisions governing Assembly voting."

Written Statement of the United States of America, *Voting Procedure on Questions Relating to Reports and Relations concerning the Territory of South-West Africa*, Pleadings, Oral Arguments, Documents, pp. 66–67 (I.C.J. 1955). See also, The U.S. and the U.N., report by the President to Congress for the year 1946, pp. 67–71; report for the year 1947, pp. 137–138.

South-West Africa

§ 37

"What do we know of South West Africa? We know that the respected Chief Hosea Kutako was born in a time when the people of South West Africa were masters of their own destinies—the problem is not yet a hundred years old. We know that the territory was taken from Germany after World War I and that the Union of South Africa was designated the Mandatory Power. Parenthetically, one might note the present status of other former German colonies. Both Togos are self-governing: one as a part of Ghana; one as a sovereign state represented here. Cameroun is an independent state and the British Cameroons will exercise their right to determine their own future within three months. Tanganyika will soon be independent; Ruanda-Urundi is on the way. South West Africa seems to be the only one of the former German African colonies whose people are in doubt about the time when they too will have secured the fundamental rights which their African brothers enjoy.

"Five years ago in this Committee, the United States Representative said, 'In our view, the Committee's report would have been better if a representative of the Union Government had participated in the Committee's sessions and given it additional facts and explanations. My delegation regrets both the Union's failure to transmit reports and petitions on South West Africa and its failure to cooperate with the Committee.'

"This view has not changed, but we are all five years older and I would hope five years wiser.

"Four years ago, our representative said, 'We will also support resolution 443, recommending again the view of the International Court of Justice that the normal way of modifying the international status of the territory would be to place it under the International Trusteeship System'.

"This view stands. What did we say three years ago? It went like this: 'Most delegations are agreed that it is the welfare of the inhabitants of the Territory with which we are and should be primarily concerned. In this spirit the United Nations has repeatedly offered its considerable experience for solving the status of South West Africa. . . . My delegation believes that it would be an act of the highest statesmanship for the Union of South Africa to make it possible for this experience to be applied to the mandated territory of South West Africa.'

"In 1958 we appealed in most earnest terms, 'to the Government and people of the Union and also to the delegations represented in this Committee, that further efforts be made so that the hopes and aspirations of the peoples of that Territory will be developed and safeguarded to the end that they will be able to live out their lives in dignity and in harmony with their neighbors, and that their political and economic development will take place as President Wilson, Lord Robert Cecil, Field Marshall Smuts and others intended when the Mandate was first formulated.'

"Also in 1958, 'we strongly protest the subjection of any peoples no matter in what part of the world they may live.'

"In [An] examination of the record, Mr. Chairman, shows clearly that every possible opportunity has been given the Union to cooperate in friendship and trust with other members of the United Nations. In this, we have been disappointed. Alone among the Mandatory Powers, the Union refused to place its territory under the United Nations Trusteeship System. We cannot help but conclude that the racial policies of the Union, which are so universally condemned, are an important factor in this refusal."

Statement by Senator Wayne Morse, United States Representative, in Committee IV of the United Nations General Assembly, Nov. 22, 1960 (U.S.-U.N. press release No. 3583/Rev.1).

"After World War 1, the Principal Allied and Associated U.K. Powers, acting upon behalf of the League of Nations, transferred the administration of South West Africa to the Union Government. The mandate executed by the League Council, confirming and defining this transfer, used the formula normal for such purposes at that time, by conferring it on and through the Head of State of South Africa. They conferred it, in the words of Art. 1 of the operative paragraph of the Mandate, upon His Britannic Majesty 'for and on behalf of the Government of the Union of South Africa.' As South Africa at that time was a monarchy, and in the then prevailing constitutional position and circumstances, the mandate would not have been conferred upon the South African Government without mention of its Head of State, the Crown.

"Now the distinguished representative of India in this Committee is always quick to point out, and quite rightly so, that the Commonwealth is 'the Commonwealth' and not the 'British Commonwealth.' But at the time of the Treaty of Versailles it was still known as the 'British Empire' and was invariably referred to as 'British' that term covering its various component parts. The use of the word 'Britannic,' therefore, did not at that time have any local significance; it did not, in fact, relate to the United Kingdom, but was the usual means of identifying the Crown in relation to the Government of South Africa, or of other parts of the Empire. It certainly cannot be argued by anybody familiar with the situation as it then existed, that the term 'Britannic' referred in that context in any way to the Crown in relation to the United Kingdom Government. It most certainly did not. It is natural that as the Head of State exists in the person of a monarch, the idea should be current that the Crown has rights and duties in the international field which attach to the person of the Monarch. This is simply not so. The Crown can exercise no functions in an international sense, except upon the advice of the Ministers of one or another of the countries of the Commonwealth which acknowledge the Monarch as Head of State. Not only is the Crown incapable of so acting by itself, but it is also a perfectly clear and well established doctrine that the Crown has a quite separate relationship with each such country, and that Ministers in one country cannot be substituted and act for those of another. Indeed, were the contrary to be the case, the independence and sovereignty of members of the Commonwealth who recognise the Monarch as Head of State, would be meaningless. In short, the same individual acts as a separate Monarch of each of those countries of the Commonwealth that recognise him or her as Head of State.

"It is therefore clear that the conferment of the Mandate on the Crown 'for and on behalf of the Government of the Union of South Africa' by implication and constitutional practice excluded any other set of Ministers from assuming rights or duties under the Mandate. It is equally clear that at no time did the United Kingdom Government possess any rights or duties whatsoever in connection with it. Some delegates have spoken from time to time as though the United Kingdom Government, or His Britannic Majesty, conferred the Mandate on South Africa. This is a plain error of fact. At no time did the United Kingdom Government either possess the Mandate or have power to confer it; and at no time did His Britannic Majesty have any connection with the Mandate except as Head of State of the Government of the Union of South Africa, nor did he have any power to exercise it through ministers other than South African Ministers. As the Minister of State for Commonwealth Relations put it recently in the House of Commons:—

> 'The fact is that our legal position in relation to South West Africa in no way differs from that of any other member of the United Nations which was also a former member of the League of Nations.' "

Statement by Peter Smithers, M.P., United Kingdom Representative, in Committee IV of the United Nations General Assembly, Mar. 22, 1961 (Document, United Kingdom Mission to the United Nations).

In its Advisory Opinion on the *International Status of South-West Africa*, the International Court of Justice concluded:

"The Court is of opinion,
"*On the General Question:*
"unanimously,
"that South-West Africa is a territory under the international International
Mandate assumed by the Union of South Africa on December 17th, status
1920;
"*On Question (a):*
"by twelve votes to two,
"that the Union of South Africa continues to have the international obligations stated in Article 22 of the Covenant of the League of Nations and in the Mandate for South-West Africa as well as the obligation to transmit petitions from the inhabitants of that Territory, the supervisory functions to be exercised by the United Nations, to which the annual reports and the petitions are to be submitted, and the reference to the Permanent Court of International Justice to be replaced by a reference to the International Court of Justice, in accordance with Article 7 of the Mandate and Article 37 of the Statute of the Court;
"*On Question (b):*
"unanimously,
"that the provisions of Chapter XII of the Charter are applicable to the Territory of South-West Africa in the sense that they provide a means by which the Territory may be brought under the Trusteeship System;
"and by eight votes to six,
"that the provisions of Chapter XII of the Charter do not impose on the Union of South Africa a legal obligation to place the Territory under the Trusteeship System;
"*On Question (c):*
"unanimously,
"that the Union of South Africa acting alone has not the competence to modify the international status of the Territory of South-West Africa, and that the competence to determine and modify the international status of the Territory rests with the Union of South Africa acting with the consent of the United Nations."

International Status of South-West Africa, Advisory Opinion, July 11, 1950, I.C.J. Reports (1950) 128, 143–144.

In the course of its Advisory Opinion on the *International Status of South-West Africa*, the International Court of Justice stated:

". . . the Principal Allied and Associated Powers agreed that a Mandate for the Territory of South-West Africa should be conferred upon His Britannic Majesty to be exercised on his behalf by the Government of the Union of South Africa and proposed the terms of this Mandate. His Britannic Majesty, for and on behalf of the Government of the Union of South Africa, agreed to accept the Mandate and undertook to exercise it on behalf of the League of Nations in accordance with the proposed terms. On

December 17th, 1920, the Council of the League of Nations, confirming the Mandate, defined its terms.

"In accordance with these terms, the Union of South Africa (the 'Mandatory') was to have full power of administration and legislation over the Territory as an integral portion of the Union and could apply the laws of the Union to the Territory subject to such local modifications as circumstances might require. On the other hand, the Mandatory was to observe a number of obligations, and the Council of the League was to supervise the administration and see to it that these obligations were fulfilled.

"The terms of this Mandate, as well as the provisions of Article 22 of the Covenant and the principles embodied therein, show that the creation of this new international institution did not involve any cession of territory or transfer of sovereignty to the Union of South Africa. The Union Government was to exercise an international function of administration on behalf of the League, with the object of promoting the well-being and development of the inhabitants.

"It is now contended on behalf of the Union Government that this Mandate has lapsed, because the League has ceased to exist. This contention is based on a misconception of the legal situation created by Article 22 of the Covenant and by the Mandate itself. The League was not, as alleged by that Government, a 'mandator' in the sense in which this term is used in the national law of certain States. It had only assumed an international function of supervision and control. The 'Mandate' had only the name in common with the several notions of mandate in national law. The object of the Mandate regulated by international rules far exceeded that of contractual relations regulated by national law. The Mandate was created, in the interest of the inhabitants of the territory, and of humanity in general, as an international institution with an international object—a sacred trust of civilization. It is therefore not possible to draw any conclusion by analogy from the notions of mandate in national law or from any other legal conception of that law. The international rules regulating the Mandate constituted an international status for the Territory recognized by all the Members of the League of Nations, including the Union of South Africa.

"The essentially international character of the functions which had been entrusted to the Union of South Africa appears particularly from the fact that by Article 22 of the Covenant and Article 6 of the Mandate the exercise of these functions was subjected to the supervision of the Council of the League of Nations and to the obligation to present annual reports to it; it also appears from the fact that any Member of the League of Nations could, according to Article 7 of the Mandate, submit to the Permanent Court of International Justice any dispute with the Union Government relating to the interpretation or the application of the provisions of the Mandate.

"The authority which the Union Government exercises over the Territory is based on the Mandate. If the Mandate lapsed, as the Union Government contends, the latter's authority would equally have lapsed. To retain the rights derived from the Mandate and to deny the obligations thereunder could not be justified.

"These international obligations, assumed by the Union of South Africa, were of two kinds. One kind was directly related to the administration of the Territory, and corresponded to the sacred trust of civilization referred to in Article 22 of the Covenant. The other related to the machinery for implementation, and was closely linked to the supervision and control of the League. It corresponded to the 'securities for the performance of this trust' referred to in the same article.

"The first-mentioned group of obligations are defined in Article 22 of the Covenant and in Articles 2 to 5 of the Mandate. The Union undertook the general obligation to promote to the utmost the material and moral well-being and the social progress of the inhabitants. It assumed particular obligations relating to slave trade, forced labour, traffic in arms and ammunition, intoxicating spirits and beverages, military training and establishments, as well as obligations relating to freedom of conscience and free exercise of worship, including special obligations with regard to missionaries.

"These obligations represent the very essence of the sacred trust of civilization. Their *raison d'être* and original object remain. Since their fulfilment did not depend on the existence of the League of Nations, they could not be brought to an end merely because this supervisory organ ceased to exist. Nor could the right of the population to have the Territory administered in accordance with these rules depend thereon.

.   .   .   .

"This view results, moreover, from the Resolution of the League of Nations of April 18th, 1946 . . . .

"As will be seen from this resolution, the Assembly said that the League's functions with respect to mandated territories would come to an end; it did not say that the Mandates themselves came to an end. In confining itself to this statement, and in taking note, on the other hand, of the expressed intentions of the mandatory Powers to continue to administer the mandated territories in accordance with their respective Mandates, until other arrangements had been agreed upon between the United Nations and those Powers, the Assembly manifested its understanding that the Mandates were to continue in existence until 'other arrangements' were established.

"A similar view has on various occasions been expressed by the Union of South Africa. In declarations made to the League of Nations, as well as to the United Nations, the Union Government has acknowledged that its obligations under the Mandate continued after the disappearance of the League. In a declaration made on April 9th, 1946, in the Assembly of the League of Nations, the representative of the Union Government, after having declared his Government's intention to seek international recognition for the Territory of South-West Africa as an integral part of the Union, stated: 'In the meantime, the Union will continue to administer the Territory scrupulously in accordance with

the obligations of the Mandate for the advancement and promotion of the interests of the inhabitants as she has done during
the past six years when meetings of the Mandates Commission
could not be held.' After having said that the disappearance of
the Mandates Commission and of the League Council would
'necessarily preclude complete compliance with the letter of the
Mandate', he added: 'The Union Government will nevertheless
regard the dissolution of the League as in no way diminishing
its obligations under the Mandate, which it will continue to discharge with the full and proper appreciation of its responsibilities
until such time as other arrangements are agreed upon concerning
the future status of the Territory.'

"In a memorandum submitted on October 17th, 1946, by the
South-African Legation in Washington to the Secretary-General
of the United Nations, expression was given to a similar view.
Though the League had at that time disappeared, the Union
Government continued to refer to its responsibility under the
Mandate. It stated: 'This responsibility of the Union Government as Mandatory is necessarily inalienable.' On November 4th,
1946, the Prime Minister of the Union, in a statement to the
Fourth Committee of the United Nations General Assembly,
repeated the declaration which the representative of the Union
had made previously to the League of Nations.

"In a letter of July 23rd, 1947, to the Secretary-General of the
United Nations, the Legation of the Union referred to a resolution of the Union Parliament in which it was declared 'that the
Government should continue to render reports to the United
Nations Organization as it has done heretofore under the Mandate'. It was further stated in that letter: 'In the circumstances
the Union Government have no alternative but to maintain the
status quo and to continue to administer the Territory in the
spirit of the existing Mandate.'

"These declarations constitute recognition by the Union Government of the continuance of its obligations under the Mandate
and not a mere indication of the future conduct of that Government. Interpretations placed upon legal instruments by the
parties to them, though not conclusive as to their meaning, have
considerable probative value when they contain recognition by a
party of its own obligations under an instrument. In this case
the declarations of the Union of South Africa support the
conclusions already reached by the Court.

. . . . . .

"The international status of the Territory results from the international rules regulating the rights, powers and obligations relating to the administration of the Territory and the supervision of
that administration, as embodied in Article 22 of the Covenant and
in the Mandate. It is clear that the Union has no competence to
modify unilaterally the international status of the Territory or
any of these international rules. This is shown by Article 7 of the
Mandate, which expressly provides that the consent of the Coun-

cil of the League of Nations is required for any modification of the terms of the Mandate.

"The Court is further requested to say where competence to determine and modify the international status of the Territory rests.

"Before answering this question, the Court repeats that the normal way of modifying the international status of the Territory would be to place it under the Trusteeship System by means of a Trusteeship Agreement in accordance with the provisions of Chapter XII of the Charter.

"The competence to modify in other ways the international status of the Territory depended on the rules governing the amendment of Article 22 of the Covenant and the modification of the terms of the Mandate.

"Article 26 of the Covenant laid down the procedure for amending provisions of the Covenant, including Article 22. On the other hand, Article 7 of the Mandate stipulates that the consent of the Council of the League was required for any modification of terms of that Mandate. The rules thus laid down have become inapplicable following the dissolution of the League of Nations. But one cannot conclude therefrom that no proper procedure exists for modifying the international status of South-West Africa.

"Article 7 of the Mandate, in requiring the consent of the Council of the League of Nations for any modification of its terms, brought into operation for this purpose the same organ which was invested with powers of supervision in respect of the administration of the Mandates. In accordance with the reply given above to Question (a), those powers of supervision now belong to the General Assembly of the United Nations. On the other hand, Articles 79 and 85 of the Charter require that a Trusteeship Agreement be concluded by the mandatory Power and approved by the General Assembly before the International Trusteeship System may be substituted for the Mandates System. These articles also give the General Assembly authority to approve alterations or amendments of Trusteeship Agreements. By analogy, it can be inferred that the same procedure is applicable to any modification of the international status of a territory under Mandate which would not have for its purpose the placing of the territory under the Trusteeship System. This conclusion is strengthened by the action taken by the General Assembly and the attitude adopted by the Union of South Africa which is at present the only existing mandatory Power.

"On January 22nd, 1946, before the Fourth Committee of the General Assembly, the representative of the Union of South Africa explained the special relationship between the Union and the Territory under its Mandate. There would—he said—be no attempt to draw up an agreement until the freely expressed will of both the European and native populations had been ascertained. He continued: 'When that had been done, the decision of the Union would be submitted to the General Assembly for judgment.'

"On April 9th, 1946, before the Assembly of the League of Nations, the Union representative declared that 'it is the intention of the Union Government, at the forthcoming session of the United Nations General Assembly in New York, to formulate its case for according South-West Africa a status under which it would be internationally recognized as an integral part of the Union'.

"In accordance with these declarations, the Union Government, by letter of August 12th, 1946, from its Legation in Washington, requested that the question of the desirability of the territorial integration in, and the annexation to, the Union of South Africa of the mandated Territory of South-West Africa, be included in the Agenda of the General Assembly.   In a subsequent letter of October 9th, 1946, it was requested that the text of the item to be included in the Agenda be amended as follows: 'Statement by the Government of the Union of South Africa on the outcome of their consultations with the peoples of South-West Africa as to the future status of the mandated Territory, and implementation to be given to the wishes thus expressed.'

"On November 4th, 1946, before the Fourth Committee, the Prime Minister of the Union of South Africa stated that the Union clearly understood 'that its international responsibility precluded it from taking advantage of the war situation by effecting a change in the status of South-West Africa without proper consultation either of all the peoples of the Territory itself, or with the competent international organs'.

"By thus submitting the question of the future international status of the Territory to the 'judgment' of the General Assembly as the 'competent international organ', the Union Government recognized the competence of the General Assembly in the matter.

"The General Assembly, on the other hand, affirmed its competence by Resolution 65 (I) of December 14th, 1946.   It noted with satisfaction that the step taken by the Union showed the recognition of the interest and concern of the United Nations in the matter.   It expressed the desire 'that agreement between the United Nations and the Union of South Africa may hereafter be reached regarding the future status of the Mandated Territory of South-West Africa', and concluded: 'The General Assembly, therefore, is unable to accede to the incorporation of the Territory of South-West Africa in the Union of South Africa.'

"Following the adoption of this resolution, the Union Government decided not to proceed with the incorporation of the Territory, but to maintain the *status quo*.   The General Assembly took note of this decision in its Resolution 141 (II) of November 1st, 1947.

"On the basis of these considerations, the Court concludes that competence to determine and modify the international status of South-West Africa rests with the Union of South Africa acting with the consent of the United Nations."

International Status of South-West Africa, Advisory Opinion, July 11, 1950, I.C.J. Reports (1950) 128, 132–136, 141–143.

In the Written Statement of the United States of America sub- U.S. position
mitted to the International Court of Justice in the advisory proceeding, *International Status of South-West Africa*, the following views
were expressed:

"I. Obligations of the Mandate for South-West Africa

"The obligations of the Mandate for South-West Africa continue to bind the Union of South Africa at the present time. This
proposition seems fairly well established with respect to the substantive obligations laid down in the mandate instrument,
although some difficulties on the procedural side are obvious in
view of the dissolution of the League of Nations.

.   .   .   .

"1. *The Mandate has not expired according to its terms.*

"(*a*) The Mandate has not been terminated under the provisions of Article 7 of the Mandate.

"Article 7 of the Mandate provides: 'The consent of the Council
of the League of Nations is required for any modification of the
terms of the present Mandate.' The League of Nations Council
never gave its consent to a modification of the Mandate resulting
in its termination, nor has the United Nations done so.

"(*b*) Independence has not been granted by the mandatory.

"The question of possible ways of modifying the international
status of South-West Africa consistently with the terms of the
Mandate is discussed in Part IV below (pages 127 *et seq.*). Assuming, however, that one method of modification or termination
is by giving independence to the territory, it is clear that this
has not been done. The letter which the deputy permanent representative of the Union of South Africa to the United Nations, on
July 11, 1949, addressed to the Secretary-General, and the accompanying text of the South-West Africa Affairs Amendment Act
of 1949 make abundantly clear the continued status of the Territory as a dependent area of the Union of South Africa. U.N.
Doc. A/929 (July 13, 1949).

"(*c*) South-West Africa has not been incorporated in any
other country.

"It has been suggested that South Africa can incorporate
South-West Africa because this was the future planned for the
Territory at the Paris Peace Conference. See U.N *Official
Records*, General Assembly (3rd sess., 1st part, Fourth Committee, 1949), 294 (statement by representative of Union of South
Africa). But cf. *id.*, at 313–314 (statement by representative of
Uruguay). Termination of the Mandate by incorporation was
foreseen by President Wilson, but only on the basis that it should
not be annexation and that it be based on the wishes of the people
of South-West Africa after their development had reached the
stage which would 'qualify them to express a wish as to their
ultimate relations. . . . The fundamental idea would be that
the world was acting as trustee through a mandatory, and would

be in charge of the whole administration until the day when the true wishes of the inhabitants would be ascertained.' See III, *Foreign Relations of the United States* (Paris Peace Conference, 1919), 740. It seems clear that the guaranty of impartiality, in determining when unification might be proper, was to be found and was intentionally made to reside in the considered opinion of the world community.

"As will be brought out below (pages 102, 129–130), the Union of South Africa requested approval of incorporation by the General Assembly of the United Nations in 1946, and the General Assembly in Resolution 65 (I) of December 14, 1946, declined to accede to such incorporation. Unilateral action by the Union of South Africa to effect incorporation would be contrary to the Mandate, and appears not in fact to have been proclaimed by the Union Government. See U.N. *Official Records,* General Assembly (4th sess., Fourth Committee, 1949), 213–215, 239–240 (statements by representative of Union of South Africa).

"2. *The Mandate was not terminated by the Second World War.*

"(*a*) General principles of international law.

"It seems unnecessary to dwell at length on the question of the effect of the Second World War upon this mandate. It is generally accepted that treaties to which belligerents alone are parties are not necessarily abrogated by war. It is even clearer that a multipartite agreement of such general interest to the community of nations as a League of Nations Mandate could not be abrogated, *ipso facto,* by the outbreak of war. *The North Atlantic Fisheries Case,* Hague Court Reports (ed. Scott, 1916), 141, 159. *Accord: Clark* v. *Allen,* 331 U.S., 503 (1947); *Techt* v. *Hughes,* 229 N.Y., 222 (1920); see also, *Resolution of Institute of International Law on Effect of War on Treaties,* Christiania, 1912, Oxford University Press (ed. Scott, 1916), 173–174; V, Hackworth, *Digest of International Law,* sec. 513; II, Oppenheim, *International Law* (6th ed., 1944), sec. 99."

International Status of South-West Africa, Pleadings, Oral Arguments, Documents, pp. 86, 94–95 (I.C.J. 1950).

The Written Statement of the United States, *supra,* continued:

"3. *Dissolution of the League and establishment of the United Nations did not end the Mandate.*

"(*a*) Effect of a mandatory's withdrawal from the League.

"That the obligation of a mandatory under Article 22 and the mandate instrument are not dependent on continuance of the membership of such mandatory in the League of Nations has been demonstrated in the case of Japan. On March 27, 1935, Article 22 as part of the Covenant defining obligations of membership ceased to bind Japan; but Article 22, as incorporated by reference in the mandate for the former German possessions in the North Pacific Ocean, continued to have and receive binding legal effect. The League asserted and Japan recognized the continuing jurisdiction of the Permanent Mandates Commission, as an agent of the League Council, to receive and consider Japan's annual reports under paragraph 7 of Article 22 of the Covenant and Article 6 of the mandate instrument. These positions were taken notwithstanding any existing theoretical uncertainties as to the location of 'sovereignty', and notwithstanding the very practical difference that upon Japan's withdrawal the participation of Japan as a Member of the Council in reviewing reports and in designating the members of the Commission automatically terminated. See League of Nations *Official Journal*, Permanent Mandates Commission (28th sess., 1935) 125, 183–184.

"The case of Japan differs from the case of the Union of South Africa. In the latter the Union of South Africa has not withdrawn, but the Council of the League has been dissolved as the instrument for supervising the carrying out of the obligations of the mandate instruments and Article 22 of the Covenant; this dissolution was effected by the Union and the other remaining Members of the League. The Union remains a Member of the United Nations, which it, together with the other remaining Members of the League and other States has generally entrusted with functions formerly exercised by the League. It cannot be contended that the Union Government, in concert with the other governments referred to, has released the mandatory from the obligations of the Mandate."

Ibid. 96–97.

Further, the Written Statement of the United States said:

"II. APPLICABILITY OF THE PROVISIONS OF CHAPTER XII OF THE UNITED NATIONS CHARTER TO THE TERRITORY OF SOUTH-WEST AFRICA

"The General Assembly, in one of the particular inquiries which it has submitted to the Court, has asked: '(*b*) Are the provisions of Chapter XII of the Charter applicable and, if so, in what manner, to the Territory of South-West Africa?' This particular inquiry raises, first, the issue whether South-West Africa, as one of the mandated territories, comes within the general purview of Chapter XII. It is concluded that Chapter XII does provide for the placing of mandated territories under the international trusteeship system of the United Nations, but that the placing of mandated territories under trusteeship is not compulsory.

. . . .

"III. APPLICABILITY OF THE PROVISIONS OF CHAPTER XI OF THE UNITED NATIONS CHARTER TO SOUTH-WEST AFRICA

"A. *By reason of the continuing existence of the mandate, South-West Africa is a non-self-governing territory within the meaning of Chapter XI.*

"1. *Nature of the mandate.*

"Article 22 of the Covenant of the League referred to certain territories formerly under German sovereignty—including South-

West Africa—as territories 'inhabited by peoples not yet able to stand by themselves under the strenuous conditions of the modern world'. In pursuance of this provision, South-West Africa was placed under the tutelage of the Union of South Africa, within the mandate system. Indeed the Territory was made a class C Mandate (see the sixth paragraph of Article 22), since its stage of development toward self-government or independence was considered not far advanced. There is nothing to suggest that this status has altered so radically in thirty years that South-West Africa no longer requires tutelage. Indeed, the Union Government's proposal for incorporation of the Territory (discussed in I, B, above) clearly shows that in the mandatory's judgment South-West Africa is not yet able to stand by itself.

.   .   .   .

"IV. Competence to modify the international status of the Territory of South-West Africa

"In the question submitted to the Court by the General Assembly, the following particular inquiry is made:

" '(c) Has the Union of South Africa the competence to modify the international status of the Territory of South-West Africa, or, in the event of a negative reply, where does competence rest to determine and modify the international status of the territory?'

"In Part I of the present statement, the view is expressed that the mandate for South-West Africa continues in force at the present time. In Part III above, the view is expressed that, while the mandate continues, South-West Africa remains a non-self-governing territory within the meaning of Chapter XI of the Charter. In view of these conclusions, it is submitted that the question of competence to modify the international status of the Territory of South-West Africa is essentially a question of competence to modify the mandate.

"A. *The mandate for South-West Africa may be replaced by trusteeship.*

"The provisions of Chapter XII in the Charter make quite clear that mandated territories, including South-West Africa, can be placed under the international trusteeship system of the United Nations. This is probably the clearest way in which the mandate may be modified. In view of the discussion contained in Part II above, it is not believed necessary to present further discussion here on this point.

"B. *The Union of South Africa does not have competence unilaterally to modify the Mandate.*

"In part (c) of the General Assembly's question, it is asked specifically whether the Union of South Africa has 'the competence to modify the international status of the Territory of South-West Africa'. Presumably the question is whether the

Union may effect such modification unilaterally. It is the view of the Government of the United States that the Union is not competent to bring about modifications unilaterally.

. . . .

"C. *The Mandate for South-West Africa may be modified by agreement between the mandatory Power and the United Nations General Assembly.*

"As has been shown earlier in this statement, the Union of South Africa assumed authority and administration in the Territory of South-West Africa pursuant to the Treaty of Versailles, the allocation made by the Principal Allied and Associated Powers, and the mandate terms approved by the Council of the League of Nations. Thus the Union became a trustee, and exercised its powers in South-West Africa on behalf of the large portion of the international community which were parties to the Treaty of Versailles and Members of the League of Nations. It has been seen that under the mandate system modifications of the mandate required the assent of the international community, to be given through the Council of the League. In the view of the Government of the United States, the termination of the League of Nations did not end the interest of the international community in the mandate for South-West Africa and did not leave that community without means of asserting its interest.

. . . .

"D. *Modification of the mandate without the consent of the mandatory.*

"There remains the possibility that the appropriate organ representing the international community might, in certain circumstances, be competent to modify a mandate regardless of consent by the mandatory Power. Such circumstances might include (*a*) breach by the mandatory of mandate obligations, and (*b*) events making Article 22 of the League Covenant and the mandate itself no longer applicable to the situation of the mandated territory. Professor Wright, in his *Mandates under the League of Nations* (1930), 440–441, has stated:

> " 'Whether the League can appoint a new mandatory in case one of the present mandatories should cease to function has not been determined. Nor has it been decided whether the League can dismiss a mandatory though both powers may be implied from the Covenant assertion that the mandatories act "on behalf of the League", and members of the Permanent Mandates Commission have assumed that they exist. Furthermore, it would seem that the mandate of a given nation would automatically come to an end in case the mandatory ceased to meet the qualifications stated in the Covenant and that the League would be the competent authority to recognize such a fact. Australia, however, has declared that the League has no power to dismiss a mandatory, and in reply to the question of her representative the Council's *Rap-*

porteur said the decision with regard to the guarantee of loans in case of transfer of mandate carried no implication in regard to the way in which that might take place. Since the areas subject to mandate are defined in Article 22 of the Covenant, it would seem that the League, whose competence is defined by the Covenant, could not withdraw a territory from the status of mandated territory unless through recognition that the conditions there defined no longer exist in the territory.'

There appears to have been no settled law on these questions during the life of the League of Nations. Had a dispute arisen it could have been settled pursuant to paragraph 2 of Article 7 in the terms of the Mandate for South-West Africa. . . .

"Whether, since the termination of the League of Nations, any League power unilaterally to modify a mandate has survived in an organ of the United Nations such as the General Assembly is similarly unclear. The League Assembly Resolution of April 18, 1946, looked toward *agreed* arrangements between the mandatory Powers and the United Nations concerning the future of mandates. That resolution was adopted, of course, under circumstances in which the mandatory Powers without exception had declared their intentions to discharge the obligations of the mandates. An obviously different situation is created if a mandatory Power denounces or breaches its mandate. It may be questionable then whether the element of consent on the part of the mandatory is relevant to action by the appropriate international organ.

"In the event of need, an authoritative determination on the above points might be secured pursuant to Article 7 of the mandate instrument taken in conjunction with Article 37 of the Statute of the International Court of Justice. That Article provides:

> " 'Whenever a treaty or convention in force provides for reference of a matter to a tribunal to have been instituted by the League of Nations, or to the Permanent Court of International Justice, the matter shall, as between the parties to the present Statute, be referred to the International Court of Justice.'

"If no organ of the United Nations were competent, or able, to make new provision for a mandated territory where the mandatory was breaching its obligations or the situation had so changed that the purpose of the mandate was no longer being effectuated, there might be a residuum of authority in the remaining Principal Allied and Associated Powers which could then be employed to make a new disposition. See Wright, *op. cit. supra*, 320, 502. The necessary determination of facts and establishment of rights might have to be accomplished, in such circumstances, through a proceeding before an appropriate international tribunal."

Ibid. 111, 124, 127–128, 135, 137–139.

"The General Assembly,

"Having accepted, by resolution 449 A (V) of 13 December, 1950, the advisory opinion of the International Court of Justice of 11 July 1950 with respect to South-West Africa,

U.N. supervision: Voting procedures

. . . .

"Requests the International Court of Justice to give an advisory opinion on the following questions:

"(*a*) Is the following rule on the voting procedure to be followed by the General Assembly a correct interpretation of the advisory opinion of the International Court of Justice of 11 July 1950:

> " 'Decisions of the General Assembly on questions relating to reports and petitions concerning the Territory of South-West Africa shall be regarded as important questions within the meaning of Article 18, paragraph 2, of the Charter of the United Nations'?

"(*b*) If this interpretation of the advisory opinion of the Court is not correct, what voting procedure should be followed by the General Assembly in taking decisions on questions relating to reports and petitions concerning the Territory of South-West Africa?

. . . .

"THE COURT IS UNANIMOUSLY OF OPINION with regard to Question (*a*):

> " 'Is the following rule on the voting procedure to be followed by the General Assembly a correct interpretation of the advisory opinion of the International Court of Justice of 11 July 1950:

> " ' "Decisions of the General Assembly on questions relating to reports and petitions concerning the Territory of South-West Africa shall be regarded as important questions within the meaning of Article 18, paragraph 2, of the Charter of the United Nations"?'

that the said rule is a correct interpretation of the Advisory Opinion of July 11th, 1950."

Voting Procedure on Questions Relating to Reports and Petitions concerning the Territory of South-West Africa, Advisory Opinion, June 7, 1955, I.C.J. Reports (1955) 67–69, 78.

In the course of its Advisory Opinion of June 7, 1955, on *Voting Procedure on Questions Relating to Reports and Petitions concerning the Territory of South-West Africa,* the International Court of Justice stated:

"The Court, in the previous Opinion, was answering the question: 'Does the Union of South Africa continue to have international obligations under the Mandate for South-West Africa and, if so, what are those obligations?' It was dealing with two kinds of international obligations assumed by the Union of South Africa under the Mandate.

"The first kind of obligation was directly related to the administration of the Territory and corresponded to the sacred trust of civilization referred to in Article 22 of the Covenant. The Court found that these obligations did not lapse on the dissolution of the League of Nations.

"The second kind of obligations related to the supervision of the administration of the mandated Territory by the League. The Court, taking into account the Resolution of the Assembly of the League of Nations of April 18th, 1946, and the provisions of Articles 10 and 80 of the Charter, recognized that the General Assembly was legally qualified to exercise the supervisory functions which had previously been exercised by the Council of the League. It was necessary for the purpose of defining the international obligations of the Union to indicate the limits within which it was subject to the exercise of supervision by the General Assembly.

"In order to indicate those limits, it was necessary to deal with the problem presented by methods of supervision and the scope of their application. The General Assembly was competent, under the Charter, to devise methods of supervision and to regulate, within prescribed limitations, the scope of their application. These were matters in which the obligations could be subjected to precise and objective determination, and it was necessary to indicate this in a clear and unequivocal manner. This was done when it was said in the previous Opinion that: 'The degree of supervision to be exercised by the General Assembly should not therefore exceed that which applied under the Mandates System. . . .'

"On the other hand, in marking out those limits, the Court did not need to deal with the system of voting. In recognizing that the competence of the General Assembly to exercise its supervisory functions was based on the Charter, the Court also recognized implicitly that decisions relating to the exercise of such functions must be taken in accordance with the relevant provisions of the Charter, that is, the provisions of Article 18. If the Court had intended that the limits to the degree of supervision should be understood to include the maintenance of the system of voting followed by the Council of the League of Nations, it would have been contradicting itself and running counter to the provisions of the Charter. It follows that the statement that 'The degree of supervision to be exercised by the General Assembly should not therefore exceed that which applied under the Mandates System' cannot be interpreted as extending to the voting system of the General Assembly.

"Accordingly, the Court finds that the statement in the Opinion of July 11th, 1950, that 'The degree of supervision to be exercised by the General Assembly should not therefore exceed that which applied under the Mandates System', must be interpreted as relating to substantive matters, and as not including or relating to the system of voting followed by the Council of the League of Nations.

*

*   *

"In the course of the proceedings in the General Assembly and Committees of the United Nations, it was contended by representatives of the Union of South Africa that Rule F would not correspond to a correct interpretation of the previous Opinion. It was argued that the rule of unanimity governed the proceedings in the Council of the League of Nations, in which the mandatory Power was entitled to participate and vote; and that Rule F, by substituting a two-thirds majority rule, would lead to a degree of supervision exceeding that which applied under the Mandates System.

"These contentions were questioned by representatives of other Governments and also in the written statements submitted to the Court in the present proceedings.

"In view of the finding of the Court that the statement in the Opinion of 1950 that 'The degree of supervision to be exercised by the General Assembly should not therefore exceed that which applied under the Mandates System' does not include or relate to the system of voting, it is unnecessary to deal with the issues raised by these contentions or to examine the extent and scope of the operation of the rule of unanimity under the Covenant of the League of Nations.

*

*   *

"The Court will now consider whether Rule F is in accord with the statement in the Opinion of 1950, that the supervision to be exercised by the General Assembly 'should conform as far as possible to the procedure followed in this respect by the Council of the League of Nations'.

"While, as indicated above, the statement regarding the degree of supervision to be exercised by the General Assembly over the Mandate of South-West Africa, relates to substantive matters, the statement requiring conformity 'as far as possible' with the procedure followed in the matter of supervision by the Council of the League of Nations, relates to the way in which supervision is to be exercised, a matter which is procedural in character. Thus, both substance and procedure are dealt with in the passage in question and both relate to the exercise of supervision. The word 'procedure' there used must be understood as referring to those procedural steps whereby supervision is to be effected.

"The voting system of the General Assembly was not in contemplation when the Court, in its Opinion of 1950, stated that 'supervision should conform as far as possible to the procedure followed in this respect by the Council of the League of Nations'. . . . To transplant upon the General Assembly the unanimity rule of the Council of the League would not be simply the introduction of a procedure, but would amount to a disregard of one of the characteristics of the General Assembly. Consequently the question of conformity of the voting system of the General Assembly with that of the Council of the League of Nations presents insurmountable difficulties of a juridical nature. For these reasons, the voting system of the General Assembly must be considered as not being included in the procedure which, according to the previous Opinion of the Court, the General Assembly should follow in exercising its supervisory functions.

.   .   .   .

"When the Court stated in its previous Opinion that in exercising its supervisory functions the General Assembly should conform 'as far as possible to the procedure followed in this respect by the Council of the League of Nations', it was indicating that in the nature of things the General Assembly, operating under an instrument different from that which governed the Council of the League of Nations, would not be able to follow precisely the same procedures as were followed by the Council. Consequently, the expression 'as far as possible' was designed to allow for adjustments and modifications necessitated by legal or practical considerations."

Ibid. 73–77.

In his Separate Opinion on *Voting Procedure on Questions Relating to Reports and Petitions concerning the Territory of South-West Africa, supra,* Judge Lauterpacht commented:

". . . I am unable to accept the contention advanced by the Government of the Union of South Africa that there is an inconsistency between the proposed Rule F and the procedure followed by the Council of the League of Nations for the alleged reason that the latter was based on the rule of absolute unanimity, including the vote of the Mandatory State concerned. This has been the principal view put forward by the Government of South Africa in the matter. I have given reasons why it was desirable that the Court should examine it in all its aspects.

"Admittedly, the procedure of the Council of the League of Nations was governed by the principle of unanimity not only of the Members of the Council but of States who, though not ordinarily Members thereof, were invited to sit at its table in connection with a matter under its consideration—a rule which applied also to the representatives of the Mandatory State invited to take part in the proceedings of the Council. However, having regard both to principle and practice, as I interpret them, the ruling of the Court given in its Twelfth Advisory Opinion on the *Interpretation of the Treaty of Lausanne* must be held to apply also to the question with which the Court is now concerned. In that case, the Court held that the principle which was enshrined in Article 15 of the Covenant and which excluded the vote of the parties to the dispute from the requirement of unanimity as a condition of the validity of a recommendation made by the Council, was of general application in so far as it embodied the 'well-known rule that no one can be judge in his own suit' (Series B, No.

12, p. 32). That 'well-known rule', henceforth sanctioned by a pronouncement of the Permanent Court of International Justice, must be held to apply to the case in which an international organ, even when acting otherwise under the rule of unanimity, judges in a supervisory capacity the legal propriety of the conduct of a State administering an international mandate or trust. The supervisory organ may do so either directly by pronouncing a verdict upon the conformity of the action of the administering State with its international obligations or indirectly by calling upon it to adopt—or desist from—a certain line of action.

. . . .

". . . While the powers of the General Assembly in the matter are to be exercised primarily in pursuance of the Charter as interpreted by the Court in its Opinion rendered in 1950, and in particular of Articles 10 and 80, they are also to be exercised in pursuance of the continuing system of Mandates whose obligations were declared by the Court to be binding upon the Union of South-West Africa in respect of the territory which continues to be held under the international Mandate assumed by her in 1920. In view of this, there is room, as a matter of law, for the modification of the voting procedure of the General Assembly in respect of a jurisdiction whose source is of a dual character inasmuch as it emanates both from the Charter and the Mandate. In so far as considerations of international interest constitute a legitimate factor in the situation, they do so with much cogency in a situation which concerns the exercise of an international trust in respect of a territory which is endowed with an international status, which is the subject of an Opinion of this Court, and which has been the cause of international friction.

"The question which calls for an answer is whether in the present case there exists a treaty of a character as described above. The words of the Opinion of 1950 seem to suggest a negative answer inasmuch as the Opinion lays down that 'the competence of the General Assembly of the United Nations to exercise such supervision and to receive and examine reports is derived from the provisions of Article 10 of the Charter' (at p. 137). However, the passage must be read not in isolation but in the general context of the Opinion and in the light of the dual character of the source of the supervisory function of the General Assembly. The true meaning of the passage in question is that Article 10 of the Charter confers upon the General Assembly the competence to fulfil the functions as derived from the international instrument which establishes the international status of the territory in question, namely, the Mandate. It is the Mandate which is the original source of the powers of the General Assembly. The competence to apply the Mandate is derived from Article 10.

"It follows from what has been said above that there is no warrant for considering as a dogma, for which no proof is required and with regard to which any contrary evidence can be ignored, the rule that under no circumstances may the General Assembly act under a voting procedure other than that laid down in Article 18. This being so, what are the modifications of the voting procedure of the General Assembly which may properly be contemplated in this connection? It is clear that any application of the principle of absolute unanimity—which in any case would be ruled out by virtue of the answer given above to Question 1—is inadmissible under the legal principle here formulated for the reason that it offends against a fundamental tenet of the constitution of the United Nations, namely, the abandonment of the doctrine of unanimity. For the same reason there would seem to be no room for a system of qualified unanimity not including the vote of the administering State—a system which would be open to the additional objection that it would place South Africa in some ways in a better position than that obtaining under the procedure of the Council of the League. For the number of States required for unanimity in the General Assembly is about four times as large as in the Council of the League."

Ibid. 98–99, 112–113.

U.S.
views

"The Advisory Opinion of July 11, 1950 (International Status of South-West Africa), concluded that the General Assembly is legally qualified to exercise the supervisory functions previously exercised by the League of Nations with regard to the administration of the Territory of South-West Africa. The Court did not state that in exercising these functions the General Assembly must follow procedures identical with those of the League of Nations: the Court stated that such procedures 'should conform as far as possible to the procedure' of the League of Nations Council. The Court particularly noted that the supervisory functions of the General Assembly, though similar to those of the League's Council, are 'not identical'. Finally, the Court expressly stated that the same procedure followed by the General Assembly for the approval of a trusteeship agreement, should be followed by the General Assembly for the approval of any modification of the international status of a territory under Mandate. This procedure includes a two-thirds majority vote of the General Assembly, as expressly required by Article 18, paragraph 2, of the Charter of the United Nations.

"Mandatory powers were not invariably members of the League Council, where a rule of unanimous decision prevailed on many matters. Although invited to sit with the Council in the consideration of mandate questions, such a power could not have claimed a right of veto. There is even question whether a mandatory power occupying a Council seat could have exercised a power of veto so as to frustrate proper League supervision of the territory mandated to that power, by analogy to the principle that no one shall be a judge in his own cause. One of the fundamental features of the Charter of the United Nations is the adoption of the general principle of majority voting and the abandonment of the requirement of unanimity in voting. For most of the principal organs of the United Nations, including the Court itself, the requirement of a simple majority vote prevails.

Even in the Security Council, which has primary responsibility under the Charter for the maintenance of international peace and security, a system of qualified majority voting prevails rather than one of complete unanimity.

"The United Nations Conference on International Organization considered various proposals for voting requirements in the General Assembly and decided that a two-thirds majority vote should be the highest vote required, and that this special majority should be required only for 'important' questions. It is believed that when the Court concluded, in its Advisory Opinion of July 11, 1950 (International Status of South-West Africa), that the General Assembly is legally qualified to exercise supervisory functions with regard to the Territory of South-West Africa, the Court referred to the General Assembly as constituted by the Charter of the United Nations, including the express provisions governing voting procedures in that body.

. . . .

"VII. Conclusion

"When in 1950 the Court advised that supervision of the mandate for South-West Africa devolved upon the United Nations General Assembly, it followed that the function of supervision must be carried out by the Assembly in accordance with the Charter provisions governing that body. The Charter provided for Assembly voting by simple majority and by two-thirds majority; there was no provision for a requirement of Assembly unanimity in any case.

"Article 18 (2) of the Charter states that Assembly decisions on important questions shall be by a two-thirds majority; on all other questions, including the matter of adding to the category of important questions, decisions shall be by a simple majority. The Article specifies among the important questions: 'questions relating to the operation of the trusteeship system'. Assembly decisions 'on questions relating to reports and petitions concerning the Territory of South-West Africa' do not come within this class. Under the Charter such decisions could be taken by a simple majority. But, in framing the rule on voting procedure which is the subject of the current request for an advisory opinion, the Assembly has chosen—as Article 18(3) authorized—to determine that these questions shall be decided by a two-thirds majority.

"In the view of the United States, the General Assembly acted quite properly in choosing to determine that this additional category of questions shall require a two-thirds vote for decision. Such a choice, and the adoption of a rule based on it, accord with a correct interpretation of the Court's Advisory Opinion of July 11, 1950.

"It is submitted that question (a) should be answered in the affirmative and that, in consequence, question (b) does not call for any answer."

Written Statement of the United States of America, *Voting Procedure on Questions Relating to Reports and Petitions concerning the Territory of*

South-West Africa, Pleadings, Oral Arguments, Documents, pp. 55, 69 (I.C.J. 1955).

"The General Assembly,

"Having been requested by the Committee on South West Africa to decide whether or not the oral hearing of petitioners on matters relating to the Territory of South West Africa is admissible before that Committee (A/2913/Add.2),

"Having instructed the Committee, in General Assembly resolution 749 A (VIII) of 28 November, 1953, to examine petitions as far as possible in accordance with the procedure of the former Mandates System,

"Requests the International Court of Justice to give an advisory opinion on the following question:

> " 'Is it consistent with the advisory opinion of the International Court of Justice of 11 July 1950 for the Committee on South West Africa, established by General Assembly resolution 749 A (VIII) of 28 November 1953, to grant oral hearings to petitioners on matters relating to the Territory of South West Africa?'

.   .   .   .

"THE COURT IS OF OPINION,

"by eight votes to five,

"that the grant of oral hearings to petitioners by the Committee on South West Africa would be consistent with the Advisory Opinion of the Court of 11 July 1950."

Admissibility of Hearings of Petitioners by the Committee on South West Africa, Advisory Opinion, June 1, 1956, I.C.J. Reports (1956) 23, 24, 32.

In the course of its Advisory Opinion on *Admissibility of Hearings of Petitioners by the Committee on South West Africa, supra,* the International Court of Justice stated:

> "It has been contended that the Court, in its Opinion of 11 July 1950, intended to express the view that the Mandates System and the degree of supervision to be exercised by the General Assembly in respect of the Territory of South West Africa must be deemed to have been crystallized, so that, though the General Assembly replaced the Council of the League as the supervisory organ in respect of the Mandate, it could not, in the exercise of its supervisory functions, do anything which the Council had not actually done, even if it had authority to do it. The Court does not consider that its Opinion of 11 July 1950 supports this position.

> "There is nothing in the Charter of the United Nations, the Covenant of the League, or the Resolution of the Assembly of the League of April 18th, 1946, relied upon by the Court in its Opinion of 1950, that can be construed as in any way restricting the authority of the General Assembly to less than that which was conferred upon the Council by the Covenant and the Man-

Hearing of oral petitions *(margin note)*

date; nor does the Court find any justification for assuming that the taking over by the General Assembly of the supervisory authority formerly exercised by the Council of the League had the effect of crystallizing the Mandates System at the point which it had reached in 1946.

"The Court having determined that the General Assembly had replaced the Council of the League as the supervisory organ, it was proper for it to point out that the General Assembly could not enlarge its authority but must confine itself to the exercise of such authority as the Mandates System had conferred upon the supervisory organ. The Court was not called upon to determine whether the General Assembly could or could not exercise powers which the Council of the League had possessed but for the exercise of which no occasion had arisen.

"The Court held that the obligations of the Mandatory under the Mandate continued unimpaired, and that the supervisory functions in respect of the Mandate were exercisable by the United Nations, the General Assembly replacing in this respect the Council of the League. It followed that the General Assembly in carrying out its supervisory functions had the same authority as the Council. The scope of that authority could not be narrowed by the fact that the Assembly had replaced the Council as the supervisory organ.

.   .   .   .

"The Court notes that, under the compulsion of practical considerations arising out of the lack of co-operation by the Mandatory, the Com[m]ittee on South West Africa provided by Rule XXVI of its Rules of Procedure an alternative procedure for the receipt and treatment of petitions. This Rule became necessary because the Mandatory had refused to transmit to the General Assembly petitions by the inhabitants of the Territory, thus rendering inoperative provisions in the Rules concerning petitions and directly affecting the ability of the General Assembly to exercise an effective supervision. This Rule enabled the Committee on South West Africa to receive and deal with petitions notwithstanding that they had not been transmitted by the Mandatory and involved a departure in this respect from the procedure prescribed by the Council of the League.

"The particular question which has been submitted to the Court arose out of a situation in which the Mandatory has maintained its refusal to assist in giving effect to the Opinion of 11 July 1950, and to co-operate with the United Nations by the submission of reports, and by the transmission of petitions in conformity with the procedure of the Mandates System. This sort of situation was provided for by the statement in the Court's Opinion of 1950 that the degree of supervision to be exercised by the General Assembly 'should conform as far as possible to the procedure followed in this respect by the Council of the League of Nations'."

Ibid. 29–30, 31–32.

"IV. Conclusion

U.S. views

"The Court's Advisory Opinion of July 11, 1950, concluded that the General Assembly of the United Nations should act in the place of the Council of the League of Nations in exercising international supervision over the administration of the Territory of South West Africa and should conform as far as possible to the procedure followed in this respect by the Council of the League of Nations. The Council never authorized the Permanent Mandates Commission to grant oral hearings of petitioners. The Council and the Mandates Commission did, however, receive extensive information concerning the Territory from direct sources such as annual reports, written petitions, and hearings of accredited representatives. What action the Council would have taken, had that body and the Mandates Commission been denied such information, must necessarily be a matter of speculation. It does appear, however, that the Council considered itself competent to authorize the Mandates Commission to obtain information through such appropriate means as circumstances might require for the effective supervision of the Mandates System. Where the United Nations body charged with supervision of a mandate is denied access to direct sources of information concerning the mandated territory—through absence of annual reports, comments of the mandatory on written petitions, and appearance of a representative of the mandatory at meetings of the supervisory body—it would seem that the General Assembly (as the United Nations body responsible for supervision) could properly authorize resort to other sources in order to gain information on the mandate, including the oral hearing of petitioners from the territory."

Written Statement of the United States of America, *Admissibility of Hearings of Petitioners by the Committee on South West Africa*, Pleadings, Oral Arguments, Documents, p. 36 (I.C.J. 1956).

Ethiopia,
Liberia,
and
Mandate

"On November 4th, 1960 applications were filed in the Registry of the Court on behalf of the government of Ethiopia and on behalf of the government of Liberia instituting separate proceedings before the Court against the Union of South Africa.

"In both applications, the subject of the dispute is stated to be the continued existence of the mandate for Southwest Africa and the duties and performance of the Union, as mandatory, thereunder. The applications refer to article 80, paragraph 1, of the Charter of the United Nations, and found the jurisdiction of the Court on article 7 of the mandate for German Southwest Africa made at Geneva on December 17th, 1920, and on article 37 of the Statute of the Court.

"Both applications, after reciting the circumstances in which a mandate for the former German protectorate of Southwest Africa was conferred upon His Britannic Majesty to be exercised on his behalf by the government of the Union of South Africa, set forth the duties which, it is contended, thereupon devolved upon the mandatory. The applicants allege that the Union, acting through official bodies created by it to administer the territory, has violated, and continues to violate, article 2 of the mandate and article 22 of the Covenant of the League of Nations, by failing to promote to the utmost the material and moral well-being and social progress of the inhabitants; by distinguishing as to race, color, national and tribal origin in establishing the rights and duties of the peoples of the territory by the practice of apartheid; by legislation which is arbitrary, unreasonable, unjust and detrimental to human dignity; by the suppression of rights and liberties of the inhabitants essential to their orderly evolution towards self-government.

"The applicants further allege that the Union has violated, and continues to violate, article 6 of the mandate by its failure to render to the General Assembly of the United Nations annual reports with regard to the territory; and article 2 of the mandate and article 22 of the Covenant, by the exercise of powers of administration and legislation inconsistent with the international status of the territory and in violation of its duty to exercise an international function of administration on behalf of the United Nations; that the Union has violated, and continues to violate, the League of Nations rules by refusing to transmit petitions to the General Assembly of the United Nations, and article 2 of the mandate and article 22 of the Covenant by preventing residents of the territory from appearing before United Nations bodies. It is contended that the Union has thereby substantially modified the terms of the mandate without the consent of the United Nations.

"The applications respectively state that a dispute exists and has existed for more than ten years between the applicants and the Union regarding the interpretation and application of the mandate.

"The applications seek declarations by the Court in accordance with their allegations."

Statement issued by Registry of International Court of Justice, Nov. 5, 1960. Reported in American Embassy, The Hague, to the Department of State, airgram No. 140, Nov. 8, 1960, MS. Department of State, file 360/11–860.

TRUST TERRITORIES

Establishment of the International Trusteeship System

§ 38

Chapter XII, articles 75 through 80, of the United Nations Charter, signed at San Francisco, June 26, 1945, provides:

"*Article 75*

"The United Nations shall establish under its authority an international trusteeship system for the administration and supervision of such territories as may be placed thereunder by subsequent individual agreements. These territories are hereinafter referred to as trust territories.

U.N. Charter

"Article 76

"The basic objectives of the trusteeship system, in accordance with the Purposes of the United Nations laid down in Article 1 of the present Charter, shall be:

"a. to further international peace and security;

"b. to promote the political, economic, social, and educational advancement of the inhabitants of the trust territories, and their progressive development towards self-government or independence as may be appropriate to the particular circumstances of each territory and its peoples and the freely expressed wishes of the peoples concerned, and as may be provided by the terms of each trusteeship agreement;

"c. to encourage respect for human rights and for fundamental freedoms for all without distinction as to race, sex, language, or religion, and to encourage recognition of the interdependence of the peoples of the world; and

"d. to ensure equal treatment in social, economic, and commercial matters for all Members of the United Nations and their nationals, and also equal treatment for the latter in the administration of justice, without prejudice to the attainment of the foregoing objectives and subject to the provisions of Article 80.

"Article 77

"1. The trusteeship system shall apply to such territories in the following categories as may be placed thereunder by means of trusteeship agreements:

"a. territories now held under mandate;

"b. territories which may be detached from enemy states as a result of the Second World War; and

"c. territories voluntarily placed under the system by states responsible for their administration.

"2. It will be a matter for subsequent agreement as to which territories in the foregoing categories will be brought under the trusteeship system and upon what terms.

"Article 78

"The trusteeship system shall not apply to territories which have become Members of the United Nations, relationship among which shall be based on respect for the principle of sovereign equality.

"Article 79

"The terms of trusteeship for each territory to be placed under the trusteeship system, including any alteration or amendment, shall be agreed upon by the states directly concerned, including the mandatory power in the case of territories held under mandate by a Member of the United Nations, and shall be approved as provided for in Articles 83 and 85.

"Article 80

"1. Except as may be agreed upon in individual trusteeship agreements, made under Articles 77, 79, and 81, placing each territory under the trusteeship system, and until such agreements have been concluded, nothing in this Chapter shall be construed in or of itself to alter in any manner the rights whatsoever of any states or any peoples or the terms of existing international instruments to which Members of the United Nations may respectively be parties.

"2. Paragraph 1 of this Article shall not be interpreted as giving grounds for delay or postponement of the negotiation and conclusion of agreements for placing mandated and other territories under the trusteeship system as provided for in Article 77."

U.S. TS 993; 59 Stat. 1031, 1048–1049.

"Arrangements for International Trusteeship

"Additional Chapter Proposed by the United States

U.S. proposal

"(*Note:* This draft deals with principles and mechanism only and makes no assumption about the inclusion of any specific territory.)

"1. The Organization should establish under its authority a system of international trusteeship for the administration and supervision of such territories as may be placed thereunder by subsequent agreement.

"2. The basic objectives of the trusteeship system should be: (a) to further international peace and security; (b) to promote the political, economic, and social advancement of the trust territories and their inhabitants and their progressive development toward self-government; and (c) to provide for non-discriminatory treatment in trust territories with respect to the economic and other appropriate civil activities of the nationals of all member states.

"3. The trusteeship system should apply only to such territories in the following categories as may be placed thereunder by means of trusteeship arrangements: (a) territories now held under mandate; (b) territories which may be detached from enemy states as a result of this war; and (c) territories voluntarily placed under the system by states responsible for their administration. It would be a matter for subsequent agreement as to which territories would be brought under a trusteeship system and upon what terms.

"4. The trusteeship arrangement for each territory to be placed under trusteeship should be agreed upon by the states directly concerned and should be approved as provided for in paragraphs 7 and 8 below.

"5. The trusteeship arrangements in each case should include the terms under which the territory will be administered.

"6. There may be designated, in the trusteeship arrangement, a strategic area or areas which may include part or all of the territory to which the arrangement applies.

"7. All functions of the Organization relating to strategic areas, including the approval of the trusteeship arrangements and their alteration or amendment, should be exercised by the Security Council.

"8. The functions of the Organization with regard to trusteeship arrangements for all other areas should be exercised by the General Assembly.

"9. In order to assist the General Assembly to carry out those functions under the trusteeship system not reserved to the Security Council, there should be established a Trusteeship Council which would operate under its authority. The Trusteeship Council should consist of specially qualified representatives, designated (a) one each by the states administering trust territories; and (b) one each by an equal number of other states named for three-year periods by the General Assembly.

"10. The General Assembly, and under its authority, the Trusteeship Council, in carrying out their functions, should be empowered to consider reports submitted by the administering authorities, to accept petitions, to institute investigations, and to take other action within their competence as defined by the trusteeship arrangements.

"11. The administering authority in each trust territory within the competence of the General Assembly should make an annual report to the General Assembly upon the basis of a questionnaire formulated by the Trusteeship Council."

3 *Documents of the United Nations Conference on International Organization San Francisco, 1945* (1945) 607, Doc. 2 (English), G/26(c), May 5, 1945. Also printed in appendix 63, *Postwar Foreign Policy Preparation 1939–1945* (1949) 686–687.

"BACKGROUND OF UNITED STATES POLICY

San Francisco Conference

"In 1918, two principal views on this subject were advanced by President Wilson, namely, that colonies should be governed in the interest of the native peoples, and that the principle of equal economic opportunity for all nations should be generally recognized. The first view—native welfare—had emerged partly as a result of the Congo scandals toward the end of the nineteenth century. The second—equal economic opportunity—had been applied to the Congo Basin by the Berlin Convention of 1885 and the Brussels Convention of 1890, and it was proposed further to extend this principle.

"American policy with respect to non-self-governing peoples had also been reflected in the grant of independence to Cuba; in the Jones Act of 1916 foreshadowing the independence of the Philippines; and in the Jones Act of 1917 granting full American citizenship and a substantial measure of home rule to Puerto Rico.

"At the end of the war of 1914–1918, the United States Government took the position that none of the dependent territories which were detached from Germany and Turkey should be annexed by any of the Allied and Associated Powers.

"In order to avoid annexation and to give effect to the two fundamental principles of native welfare and equal economic opportunity, the mandates system was devised. This placed upon the League of Nations responsibility for supervision over the administration of the dependent territories taken from Germany and Turkey. In this way, the welfare of the dependent peoples involved in the mandates system, and the actions of the mandatory powers specifically entrusted with responsibilities of administration over them, became matters of continuing international concern.

"The United States, although not a member of the League or a party to the Treaty of Versailles, safeguarded its interests in the mandated territories, resulting from its membership in the Allied and Associated Powers, by a series of treaties with the mandatory powers which protected its national rights and its international position.

"Early in 1942 when the United States Government began to develop its policies with respect to a new international organization, the need for the establishment of some international mechanism to replace the mandates system of the League of Nations was clearly recognized.

"The projected new international machinery to deal with these territories came to be described as a trusteeship system, a description which differentiated it from the League of Nations mandates system. It was designed to be not only a substitute for, but also a definite improvement over, the old mandates system.

"The trusteeship question was also the subject of study by the other governments which later participated in the Dumbarton Oaks Conversations. It had been tentatively placed on the agenda of these Conversations, but discussion of this subject was temporarily postponed pending completion of studies of the many complex factors involved. It was understood by the governments represented at Dumbarton Oaks that the question would be taken up later and placed on the agenda of the prospective United Nations Conference.

"Subsequently, an Interdepartmental Committee on Dependent Area Aspects of International Organization was set up to examine further into the question and to draft proposals as to the kind of trusteeship system which this Government could support. This Interdepartmental Committee developed a program designed to reflect our historic attitude toward dependent peoples and to safeguard American security and economic interests in the future.

"Secretary Hull, in 1943, had submitted to the President, who endorsed them, certain proposals on dependent territories. They set forth that there should be opportunity to achieve independence for those peoples who aspire to independence, and that it is the duty and purpose of those United Nations which have responsibilities for the future of colonial areas to cooperate fully with the peoples of such areas in order that they may become qualified for independent national status. The Hull proposals called on these governments to fix, at the earliest practicable moment, the dates upon which colonial peoples under their authority would be accorded the status of full independence within a system of general security. They also urged that in order effectively to carry out these purposes and functions, the United Nations should establish an international trusteeship administration.

"Agreement Reached at Yalta

"President Roosevelt was deeply interested in this question and took with him to Yalta certain recommendations on dependent territory and trusteeship matters as to proposals which might be advanced at the Crimea Conference. The subject was considered at Yalta by President Roosevelt, Prime Minister Churchill, and Marshal Stalin, and the following policy was agreed upon:

"(a) That the five governments with permanent seats in the Security Council should consult each other prior to the United Nations Conference on providing machinery in the World Charter for dealing with territorial trusteeships which would apply only to (a) existing mandates of the League of Nations; (b) territory to be detached from the enemy as a result of this war; and (c) any other territory that may voluntarily be placed under trusteeship.

"(b) That no discussions of specific territories were to take place during the preliminary consultations on trusteeships or at the United Nations Conference itself. Only machinery and principles of trusteeship should be formulated at the Conference for inclusion in the Charter, and it was to be a matter for subsequent agreement as to which territories within the categories specified above would actually be placed under trusteeship.

"Upon the basis of this new decision of general policy, the Interdepartmental Committee, after President Roosevelt's return from Yalta, reviewed its previous work and developed new proposals, within the limits of the Yalta agreement, for a Chapter on Trusteeship to be included in the proposed Charter of the new organization.

"Approval of United States Policy by Presidents Roosevelt and Truman

"These revised proposals were approved by Secretary of State Stettinius and were transmitted formally by the Secretary of State to the Secretaries of War and Navy. They were submitted to President Roosevelt by the Secretary of State on April 10, together with recommendations that they constitute the basis of the position of this Government on the subject in the discussions at San Francisco. The President replied to the Secretary of State on April 10, saying that he approved in principle the draft proposal on international trusteeship.

"President Roosevelt died on April 12. On April 18 at a meeting held in the State Department at which were present the

Secretary of State, the Secretaries of War and Navy, the United States Delegation to the San Francisco Conference, and the Advisers to the United States Delegation, including advisers from the Departments of War, Navy, and Interior, a memorandum was prepared for President Truman and submitted to him by the three secretaries. The memorandum was approved in the following terms:

"It is not proposed at San Francisco to determine the placing of any particular territory under a trusteeship system. All that will be discussed there will be the possible machinery of such a system.

"The United States Government considers that it would be entirely practicable to devise a trusteeship system which would apply only to such territories in the following categories as may, by trusteeship arrangements, be placed thereunder, namely: (a) territories now held under mandate; (b) territories which may be detached from enemy states as a result of this war; and (c) territories voluntarily placed under the system by states responsible for their administration. It shall be a matter for subsequent agreement as to which of the specific territories within the foregoing categories shall be brought under the trusteeship system and upon what terms.

"This system would provide, by agreements, for (1) the maintenance of United States military and strategic rights, (2) such control as will be necessary to assure general peace and security in the Pacific Ocean area as well as elsewhere in the world, and (3) the advancement of the social, economic, and political welfare of the inhabitants of the dependent territories.

"GUIDING PRINCIPLES FOR THE UNITED STATES DELEGATION

"The policy toward dependent territories and trusteeship had now been carefully coordinated within our own Government. The United States Delegation had a set of guiding principles, the chief points of which were:

"(1) Recognition that the principles of the Atlantic Charter are applicable to all peoples of the world, including dependent peoples;

"(2) Recognition of the principle that the administration and development of dependent peoples is a proper concern of the world community and of the international organization;

"(3) That, subject to prior agreement of the states directly concerned,

"(a) territories now administered under the mandates system may be placed under the new trusteeship system if and when such agreement is reached;

"(b) territories which are detached from enemy states in this war may be placed and administered under the trusteeship system when such agreement is reached; and "(c) the trusteeship system should be available to dependent territories other than those in (a) and (b) above when the states controlling them voluntarily agree;

"(4) That the trusteeship system evolved as a part of the Charter should be so designed as fully to protect the security interests of an administering power;

"(5) That self-government or independence should be the ultimate goal for all peoples who are capable of exercising the responsibilities involved, and that administering states should be responsible for the political advancement of the peoples under their authority;

"(6) That all dependent territories should be administered in accordance with the principles that the interest of the inhabitants and their welfare and development are a primary concern;

"(7) That the welfare and development of dependent peoples and the maintenance of international peace and security are closely inter-related;

"(8) That the trust territories should be administered under the principle of equal treatment in social, economic, and commercial matters for all members of the international organization and their nationals;

"(9) That the proposed Trusteeship Chapter of the Charter in and of itself should not alter the existing rights of any states or any peoples, but that alterations of the terms of existing mandates or other territories could be made only by subsequent agreement of the states directly concerned subject to the approval of the Organization.

"On May 27, 1945 in a radio broadcast to the people of the United States and the world, Secretary of State Stettinius summarized the United States position as follows:

"'. . . We have stood with equal firmness for a trusteeship system that will foster progress toward higher standards of living and the realization of human rights and freedoms for dependent peoples, including the right to independence or another form of self-government, such as federation—whichever the people of the area may choose—when they are prepared and able to assume the responsibilities of national freedom as well as to enjoy its rights.

"'The United States has demonstrated this long standing policy in the Philippines. It looks forward to the time when many other now dependent peoples may achieve the same goal.

"'I regard the provisions which are being made in the Charter for the advancement of dependent peoples, and for the promotion of human rights and freedoms, as of the greatest importance.'

"AGREEMENT BY UNITED NATIONS REACHED AT SAN FRANCISCO

"As soon as the Conference convened in San Francisco, steps were taken to initiate the Five Power consultations on trusteeship which had been provided for in the Yalta agreement. The Five

Powers consisted of the four Sponsoring Powers and France. The preliminary consultations among these powers were held at San Francisco simultaneously with the Committee sessions of the Conference. In the course of these consultations the Five Powers also took into consideration proposals advanced by other delegations. These consultations resulted in the formulation of a Working Paper on Trusteeship which formed, in the absence of any Dumbarton Oaks provision on the subject, the basic document for the deliberations of the Conference Technical Committee on Trusteeship.

"After weeks of negotiation and discussion in the Technical Committee, the final draft was completed and approved by the Conference. The finished chapters represent the most comprehensive set of guiding principles for states administering dependent.territories ever agreed upon by an international body, together with the mechanism of a practical and workable system of international trusteeship . . . ."

Report to the President on the Results of the San Francisco Conference by the Chairman of the United States Delegation, the Secretary of State, June 26, 1945, pp. 126–132. In this connection, see vol. II, United States Naval Administration of the Trust Territory of the Pacific Islands (1957) 55–82, for views of the Secretaries of Navy and War with respect to proposals for international trusteeship. See also The Private Papers of Senator Vandenberg (1952) 169.

"During the Second World War the question of the mandates system came under consideration in connection with preparations for the formation of the United Nations. At Yalta in early 1945 the United States, Great Britain, and the Soviet Union decided that, prior to the forthcoming San Francisco Conference on the United Nations Charter, they would consult each other on creating machinery for dealing with what they called 'territorial trusteeship.'

"The intent at that time was that the proposed trusteeship system, at least in the beginning, should be primarily a means of handling the mandates held under the old League of Nations and such territories as would be detached from enemy states as a result of the Second World War. [In practice, only these 2 types of territories have actually been placed under trusteeship.] Provision for a third type—territories voluntarily placed under trusteeship—was made in the hope that in time the success of the system would induce countries with dependencies to take this step. [This interpretation of the agreement at Yalta is given in the United Nations and Non-Self-Governing Territories. International Conciliation (New York) No. 435. November 1947: 703.]

"At the San Francisco Conference it soon became clear that the agreement reached at Yalta provided too narrow a foundation on which to build the kind of international structure for dependencies desired by many of the participating nations. Some delegations proposed that the charter should provide not just for the territories that might be brought under trusteeship by one of the methods mentioned above but for all dependencies.

"It was finally agreed at San Francisco to devote separate chapters of the charter to trusteeships and to non-self-governing territories. Chapters XII and XIII of the charter create a system of international supervision for a particular category of non-self-governing territories, the trust territories. Chapter XI contains a 'Declaration' of principles for all other non-self-governing territories, but specifically provides for little or no international supervision.

"In working out the final wording of these chapters, controversy arose over whether 'independence' should be stipulated as a goal for all dependent peoples. It was finally decided to mention only 'self-government' as the objective for non-self-governing territories under chapter XI. For the trust territories, however, the objective was set forth as—

> 'progressive development towards self-government or independence as may be appropriate to the particular circumstances of each territory * * *.' [It appears to be a matter of dispute whether or not the objective of "self-government" under chapter XI includes the goal of "independence." See, for example, L. Larry Leonard, International Organization, New York, McGraw-Hill Book Co., 1951, p. 491; and Josef L. Kunz, Chapter XI of the United Nations Charter in Action, American Journal of International Law (Washington), vol. 48, January 1954: 105.
>
> At the San Francisco Conference those who opposed the use of the term "independence" in connection with non-self-governing territories gave various arguments, among which was the contention "that the use of 'self-government' alone did not exclude the possibility of independence. * * * In the discussion the delegate of the United Kingdom stated that his Government had never ruled out independence as a possible goal for dependent territories in appropriate cases but objected to putting it forward as a universal coequal alternative goal for all territories." Leland M. Goodrich and Edvard Hambro, Charter of the United Nations: Commentary and Documents. Boston, World Peace Foundation, 1949, p. 410.]"

"The United Nations and Dependent Territories," Staff Study No. 9, June 27, 1955, Review of the United Nations Charter, S. Doc. 164, 83d Cong., 2d sess., pp. 253, 262.

5-Power Consultations, San Francisco

"The Five-Power Consultations

"It proved impossible to convene the representatives of the five powers on the trusteeship question prior to the opening of the United Nations Conference. Immediately following the convening of the Conference at San Francisco, however, steps were taken to get under way consultations among the four sponsoring governments and France. In the course of these consultations the United States, the Soviet Union, the United Kingdom, China, and France submitted proposals for a system of trusteeship.

There was substantial divergence between the American and British proposals, but the Soviet, Chinese, and French papers adhered quite closely to the pattern of the American paper.

"Although not a member of the five-power group, Australia had also submitted to the Conference a trusteeship proposal which was very broad in some of its provisions and which at a late stage of the deliberations of the Conference Committee on Trusteeship contributed no little to the provisions of chapter XI of the Charter.

"Owing to the absence of any Dumbarton Oaks Proposals on the subject, the Conference Technical Committee on Trusteeship, through its chairman, Peter Fraser, Prime Minister of New Zealand, asked the American chairman of the five-power group to assume responsibility for presenting to the committee a working paper on trusteeship as a guide for its discussions. The working paper was to take account of the several proposals formally submitted to the Conference.

"On May 15 the chairman of the five-power group submitted to the Committee on Trusteeship the proposed working paper on a system of international trusteeship. This paper was made available as a basis for discussion only and without prejudice to the individual proposals previously submitted by the several national delegations. There were points in the working paper which were still at issue among the five powers, and it was necessary for the five-power consultations to continue throughout the Conference.

"These consultations were characterized by an intense seriousness of purpose, extensive give and take, and a sincere effort to reach the maximum possible measure of agreement. They were held under considerable pressure of time, in view of the fact that the Conference Committee on Trusteeship, composed of representatives of the 50 nations, was meeting simultaneously with the five-power consultations and from time to time had to be asked to await agreement on the part of the five powers in order to proceed with consideration of the working paper upon which the committee's deliberations were based.

"The Main Issues

"The discussions in the five-power consultation group and in the Conference Committee revolved about several vital issues. The working paper was divided into two parts. Part A covered the provisions finally appearing in chapter XI of the Charter, the Declaration Regarding Non-Self-Governing Territories, while Part B was devoted to the principles and procedures of the trusteeship system, ultimately chapters XII and XIII. The issue which received most public notice was that of political objectives, both in the trusteeship system and in the Declaration. Some delegations took the position that a forthright statement of independence as a goal toward which all dependent peoples might aspire should be included. Other delegations felt that it would be unwise to establish the goal of independence for all dependent peoples without exception, since there were some dependent territories which, because of their meager population and resources, could never become fully independent. The United States trusteeship proposal had set forth the objective of self-government which, in the American interpretation, included independence for those peoples who aspired to it and were capable of assuming the responsibilities involved.

"The issue as it affected the trusteeship system was finally resolved by providing alternative goals of self-government or independence in accordance with the particular circumstances of each territory and its peoples and their freely expressed wishes. In the Declaration a different formulation was adopted which did not specifically mention independence but which, by official Conference interpretation, recognized it as one of the possible alternatives.

"Another issue arose in connection with the provision in the American proposal for equal treatment in economic and commercial matters for all members of the United Nations and their nationals in trust territories. It was pointed out in the course of the debates that an unqualified provision of this nature would have the actual effect of altering the status of the 'C' mandates and of automatically imposing a limitation which does not now obtain on the present mandatory of any 'C' mandate which might be transferred to the trusteeship system. The principle of equal treatment was incorporated in chapter XII, however, with the proviso that its application would be subject to the provisions of article 80 of the Charter. This would have the effect of protecting the present position of 'C' mandatories except as this position might be altered in the terms of any trusteeship agreement by which a 'C' mandate would be placed under the trusteeship system.

"The proposal that certain areas might be designated as strategic areas under the trusteeship system was advanced by the American Delegation and was accepted by the Conference. In addition to the strategic-area provisions, a principle set forth in the British proposal was also incorporated. This would make it an obligation upon the administering authority in any trust territory, whether or not it might be a strategic area, to contribute to the maintenance of international peace and security and to use whatever volunteer forces, facilities, and assistance from the trust territory it might find necessary in discharging its obligations to the Security Council and for purposes of local defense and the maintenance of law and order.

"One important issue was related to the fact that there would inevitably be an interim period between the adoption of the Charter of the United Nations and the placing of eligible territories under the trusteeship system. Some delegations felt it important to provide strong reassurance that the Charter itself did not in any way affect the status of any territory or the rights of any states or peoples in that territory. In other words, until trusteeship agreements would be drawn up by means of which particular territories would be placed under the trusteeship system, no provision of the Charter could be interpreted as affecting the rights of anyone in that territory or the status of the territory itself. This provision came to be known at the Conference as the 'conservatory clause' and appears in the Charter as article 80.

"There was difference of opinion as to the composition of the Trusteeship Council and also as to its status in the Organization. The American position from the outset—this position was sustained in the Charter—was that the Trusteeship Council should be one of the principal organs of the Organization and that its membership should be selected on a basis which would insure a balance between those states having responsibility for the administration of trust territories and those having no such responsibility. Agreement was eventually reached on a formula which incorporated not only these points but also the position that all the permanent members of the Security Council should be included in the Trusteeship Council as permanent members, irrespective of whether or not they might have administering responsibility for trust territories.

"There were also some divergences of view, although the problem was less one of substance than of drafting, on the power of the Organization to receive petitions and to visit the trust territories for purposes of inspection. There was no apparent opposition to the principle involved, but it was felt by some delegations that great care should be taken not to imply that the administering authority might be irresponsible, nor to belittle the administering authority in the eyes of the people administered.

"Agreement on the Proposals

"The subjects dealt with in the three chapters devoted to non-self-governing peoples proved to be among the most difficult of all those considered by the Conference, and they were among the last on which agreement could be reached. In fact it was not until the final week of the Conference that agreement on some of the provisions of these chapters could be reached. In the subsequent London deliberations of both the Executive Committee of the Preparatory Commission and the Preparatory Commission itself, debates have developed around the correct interpretation of some of the provisions of these chapters.

"The United States Role

"Throughout the prolonged deliberations on trusteeship at San Francisco the role of the United States Delegation was one of constructive leadership in reconciling differences not only among the sponsoring powers and France but also among the other delegations which submitted proposals. The American position was a dual one of standing steadfastly for the basic principles set forth in the original American proposal submitted to the Conference while attempting at the same time to bring together the divergent viewpoints of other interested nations."

Bunche, "Trusteeship and Non-Self-Governing Territories in the Charter of the United Nations", XIII *Bulletin*, Department of State, No. 340, Dec. 30, 1945, pp. 1037, 1038–1040.

"It is evident from a reading of Chapter XII in the United Nations Charter, from a consideration of the history of its provisions, and from the circumstances and situation which the Charter's provisions were intended to meet, that Chapter XII is applicable to mandated territories and, among them, to South-West Africa. The mandate system, which was established following the First World War, was still in existence at the end of the Second World War, when the United Nations Charter was being framed. Under the Charter, a new international organization was to be created, and the League of Nations would go out of existence. Chapter XII of the Charter was designed for the purpose of setting up an international trusteeship system under the authority of the United Nations. This trusteeship system was by no means limited in its intended scope to the mandated territories, but it was clearly contemplated that existing mandates not yet ready for independence would be converted into trust territories under the United Nations international trusteeship system. Organs of the League of Nations had played an important role in the operation of the mandate system. Since the League was to terminate, obviously new machinery was required to take over the functions of the League organs. And, indeed, there were reasons for reexamining some substantive aspects of the concept of international trusteeship, so that revisions of the mandate system might be made in the course of converting mandated territories into trust territories.

Trusteeship and Mandates

"1. *The Charter provisions: Articles 77, 79, 80 (2).*

"That the provisions of Chapter XII are applicable to mandated territories, including South-West Africa, is made evident first of all in the language of the Charter itself. Article 77 of the Charter provides:

> " '1. The trusteeship system shall apply to such territories in the following categories as may be placed thereunder by means of trusteeship agreements:
>
> > " '(a) territories now held under mandate;
> > " '(b) territories which may be detached from enemy States as a result of the Second World War; and
> > " '(c) territories voluntarily placed under the system by States responsible for their administration.
>
> " '2. It will be a matter for subsequent agreement as to which territories in the foregoing categories will be brought under the trusteeship system and upon what terms.'

Sub-paragraph 1 (a) of this article refers directly to 'territories now held under mandate' as included within the general scope of the international trusteeship system to be set up pursuant to Chapter XII.

"Article 79 provides:

" 'The terms of trusteeship for each territory to be placed under the trusteeship system, including any alteration or amendment, shall be agreed upon by the States directly concerned, including the mandatory Power in the case of territories held under mandate by a Member of the United Nations, and shall be approved as provided for in Articles 83 and 85.'

Here again the language of the Charter makes quite clear that mandated territories are covered by the trusteeship chapter.

"Article 80 contains what has been referred to as the 'conservatory' clause:

" 'Except as may be agreed upon in individual trusteeship agreements, made under Articles 77, 79, and 81, placing each territory under the trusteeship system, and until such agreements have been concluded, nothing in this chapter shall be construed in or of itself to alter in any manner the rights whatsoever of any States or any peoples or the terms of existing international instruments to which Members of the United Nations may respectively be parties.

" '2. Paragraph 1 of this article shall not be interpreted as giving grounds for delay or postponement of the negotiation and conclusion of agreements for placing mandated and other territories under the trusteeship system as provided for in Article 77.'

Paragraph 2 of this article refers directly to mandated territories as being the subject of the negotiation and conclusion of agreements for placing them under the international trusteeship system of the United Nations.

"These provisions of the Charter leave no doubt that the provisions of Chapter XII are applicable to the Territory of South-West Africa as one of the mandated territories.

"2. *History of Chapter XII at the San Francisco Conference*

"Since the terms of the Charter are in themselves so clear, it is scarcely necessary to refer to the proceedings at the San Francisco Conference in order to gain a definite understanding of the scope of Chapter XII so far as its applicability to mandated territories is concerned. Accordingly, no extended discussion of the San Francisco Conference will be undertaken at this point and only a few illustrative instances will be cited.

"Throughout the proceedings of Committee II/4 at San Francisco, there was a complete understanding that the provisions which later became Chapter XII of the Charter would be applicable to mandates with a view to converting these into trust territories. This is indicated in the statements of a number of representatives on the Committee. See, e.g., U.N.C.I.O. Docs. 241 (May 11, 1945), 1; 260 (May 12, 1945), 2; 310 (May 15, 1945), 2; 448 (May 13, 1945), 2; 512 (May 23, 1945), 1; 552 (May 24, 1945), 3; 877 (June 9, 1945), 3.

"The report of the Rapporteur of Committee II/4 to Commission II at San Francisco contained the following statement:

" 'The Committee recommends that the trusteeship system shall be applicable to such territories in certain specified categories as may be placed thereunder by trusteeship agreements. The categories are (a) territories now held under mandate. . . .' U.N.C.I.O. Doc. 1115 (June 20, 1945), 4."

Written Statement of the United States of America, *International Status of South-West Africa*, Pleadings, Oral Arguments, Documents, pp. 111–113 (I.C.J. 1950).

At the San Francisco Conference a number of interpretative statements were made. Among them were the following:

Smuts
(Union of
South Africa)

"The scheme of trusteeships before us, Ladies and Gentlemen, is somewhat difficult and involved. The subject breaks new ground. There is nothing in the original Dumbarton Oaks draft to guide us. Practically all that the Committee had before it was a section in the old Covenant of the League of Nations, which dealt with the subject of mandates. The treatment which has been given to this subject by the Committee expands it far beyond the old mandate conception and makes the principle of trusteeship of very general application today. As most of you know, the old trusteeship, the old mandate system, was applied to the ex-German and ex-Turkish colonies which the Paris Peace Conference had to dispose of. The subject, therefore, was a very limited one. So far as there was a system of trusteeship, it was applied to only a small group of colonies, those that were taken from Germany and Turkey.

"This scheme diverts in scope very largely from that old Covenant scheme. The principle of trusteeship is now applied generally. It applies to all dependent peoples in all dependent territories. It covers all of them, and therefore an extension has been given to the principle of a very far-reaching and important character. That has added largely to the difficulties of the subject, because this wide application of the trusteeship principle to all sorts of territories—to colonies of half a dozen powers and not merely to ex-colonies of defeated powers—has complicated the subject very much and made its treatment very much more difficult.

"If you look at the report and at the annexed recommendations, you will see that the scheme is divided into two parts, *A* and *B*. *B* covers on a much more thorough ground than before the field covered by the old mandate commission. . . .

.   .   .   .

"*B* deals to some extent with the old field already covered in the Covenant of the League of Nations and the provision there is this: That with regard to certain types of dependent territories, old mandate territories, territories newly conquered and taken from existing powers, and also colonies where the governing power is prepared voluntarily to place them under trusteeship—

all these various types of territories will fall under the trusteeship system, which will impose stricter conditions than those prescribed in Section A. You will find all this set out in the recommendations and in the report. If these additions for the advancement of these dependent peoples, politically, socially, economically, are carried out, I have no doubt that the results will be very far-reaching indeed. A Trusteeship Council will be elected representing partly the powers who are trustees and partly other members of the United Nations in equal numbers. This Council will see that the obligations undertaken are carried out, and reports will have to be submitted annually by the responsible trustees in which they set out the work that has been done and the progress that has been made and keep the United Nations Organization fully informed of what is going on. The result will be that as both Sections A and B are applied to dependent peoples all over the world wherever you have territory inhabited by dependent peoples—peoples that are not advanced enough to look after themselves, peoples that are still backward in development in one way or another, and in one degree or another—they will all have the benefits of this new administration. They will also have the United Nations Organization seeing that they do get these benefits, that these principles which have been evolved for their government and their advancement are duly carried out."

Statement of Field Marshal Smuts (Union of South Africa), in Third Meeting of Commission II, June 20, 1945, 8 *Documents of the United Nations Conference on International Organization San Francisco, 1945* (1945) 125, 126–128, Doc. 1144 (English), II/16, June 21, 1945. The verbatim minutes of this meeting are reprinted in *United Nations Conference on International Organization: Selected Documents* (1946) 678–702.

"The work which we had to do was specially difficult and delicate. No doubt the Covenant of the League of Nations could offer to the long and patient studies of members of the Committee indications which were worthy of the greatest attention, and, in certain cases, both guiding lines and precedents. But between the work accomplished in 1919 under the high inspiration of President Wilson and that which the San Francisco Conference had to bring to a conclusion while remaining faithful to the memory of President Franklin Roosevelt, there was that difference—that in 1919 the mandate clauses of the Covenant, which was an integral part of the Treaty of Peace, referred to concrete cases of well-defined territories, taken from ex-enemy countries, whereas in 1945 the San Francisco Conference, which meets before any Treaty of Peace is drafted, had to delineate the general principle of the trusteeship system which had to be considered somewhat in abstracto, without any possibility of referring to specific territories.

Naggiar
(France)

"For that reason, the difficulty of our task was greater, as also in the case of other chapters of the Charter, but more particularly in this case, since such a system, however closely one may have wanted to define it, could not actually come to life independently of concrete cases of application. That difficulty was overcome, however, as the Commission can see in the excellent report which is before us now. The principles which were laid down, the conservatory measures which were prescribed, and the mechanism which was defined at its different stages are so well conceived and so well defined that the United Nations will find in our text for every specific case for which a special agreement will have to be prepared all the provisions necessary for a satisfactory working of the trusteeship system."

Statement of Mr. Naggiar (France), in the Third Meeting of Commission II, June 20, 1945, 8 UNCIO 131.

Al-Jamali
(Iraq)

"I wish, however, to show you a point of view that is slightly different from what you have heard so far and from what you have seen in the report. I am not one of those who believe that this draft is perfect. I do believe, however, that we have worked hard to make it as good as it is. There is still much to be desired. I am going to enumerate for you just a few points as examples of what could be done in the future.

"First of all, this chapter of the Charter does not guarantee the rights of those territories now under mandate in the new arrangements when they are put under trusteeship. Their rights are being preserved up to the time the new arrangements are made. But after the new arrangements are made, we don't know what happens. There is no specific guarantee that the rights of these territories now under mandate will be preserved. Some of you may know that paragraph 4 of Article 22 of the Covenant of the League of Nations has recognized that territories formerly belonging to the Ottoman Empire are provisionally recognized as independent. The recognition of this right is not specified in the Charter. That has been mentioned and referred to in the report. But there is no mention in the Charter that rights already acquired shall not be diminished.

"Second, under the same paragraph of Article 22 of the Covenant of the League of Nations, the wishes of the people are to be taken into account in the selection of the mandatory power. There is no such provision in the trusteeship system. Now I said in Committee, and I say again, there are peoples who are advanced enough so that their wishes could be taken into consideration in the choice of the mandate and the trustee power. The wishes of the people in the choice of the trustee power are of great significance to the success of trusteeship itself because it is our experience and our knowledge that some territories under the mandate have had hard times with the mandatory powers because their wishes were not taken into account in the choice of the mandatory powers. The same may hold true about trusteeship. Consideration of the wishes of the people should have been included in the Charter. That was not done.

"Third, there is no specific regulation in the Charter as to how to terminate a trusteeship. A territory under trusteeship has no specific way of applying for independence and being granted that independence. It is at the mercy of the trustee power. Had provision been made for that, the Charter would have been better.

"Fourth, I believe that the Charter should have given greater chance to the peoples of the territories under trusteeship to have their voice heard by the Trusteeship Council and by the Organization. The trustee power is always the channel which carries the voice of the people to the Organization. There is no direct access of the people to the Organization. That direct access and direct inspection by the Organization of the territories would have made the Charter much better.

"These are only samples of some of the points which could have been more perfect from my point of view. I do think, however, that we in this Conference are being guided by hope and confidence, by faith in the powers who are undertaking these obligations. It is our sincere hope that the right to independence will be recognized and will be granted without any complications, without problems, without bloodshed. Iraq is often referred to—and was referred to in the Committee—as a country with a happy experience with the mandatory power. That is true. The mandatory power helped the people of Iraq to realize their wishes and aspirations. We hope that all powers in all territories will take Iraq as a good example. We hope that principles of the chapter on Trusteeship will not be only ink on paper. We shall want acts and not words. We hope that fraternity, liberty, equality, will be active forces and not mere words. We hope that human brotherhood will be the motive in this trusteeship business, and we hope that racial discrimination, which is a purely Nazi philosophy, will be discarded forever, and that nations who are entrusted with dependent territories will feel that the peoples of these territories are their brothers and that there is no superiority of any sort, national, racial, or religious."

Statement of Mr. Al-Jamali (Iraq), *ibid*. 133–134.

"This important document on trusteeship achieves two main objects. Section B takes care of the intricate problem of providing for the administration and international supervision of territories taken from enemy states, and of such other territories as may be placed under the supervision of the United Nations. We look for fine results, both for the peoples concerned, and for the world from the machinery agreed to by the Committee.

Forde (Australia)

.   .   .   .

". . . As a nation which accepted a trustee's responsibilities in respect to neighboring islands after the last war, Australia welcomes the inclusion of this chapter on trusteeship in the United Nations Charter. We have had no reason to be ashamed of our own trusteeship record in the Pacific. It has been vindicated by the progress we were able truthfully and regularly to report to the Mandates Commission of the League of Nations. It was even more strikingly, and indeed touchingly, vindicated by the magnificent loyalty and affection which the native peoples of

those territories have shown to American and Australian service-
men fighting in those theaters of war.   The stories of their devotion and self-sacrifice in aiding our wounded and in speeding our
supplies are amongst the outstanding, if all too little known, epics
of this war and must never be forgotten by the democracies of
the world."

Statement of Mr. Forde (Australia), *ibid.* 134, 135–137.

"The Egyptian Delegation has taken very keen interest in the
deliberations of the Trusteeship Committee and has followed
with great attention every phase of its prolonged discussions.
Our main concern in this chapter, as in several other chapters of
the Charter, has been that it should be an instrument worthy of
the United Nations and of the great objects for which they are
gathered here in San Francisco.   On the other hand, my country,
Egypt, is very well informed about the conditions of certain
territories and peoples and of the relations between the latter
and the administering authorities.   We have followed with great
concern what has been happening in other territories.   The

Awad
(Egypt)

history of these peoples has not always been a very happy one,
and has not always been free from a certain amount of hardship
and a certain amount of suffering.   Hence, we have taken a very
keen interest in the deliberations of this Committee in order to
see to it that the lot of the peoples in the future should be much
happier and much better than it has been in the past.   We have
not done so by producing a new document to add to the other six
or seven that have been offered, but our attitude has been one, I
hope, of intelligent criticism.   Our earnest wish has been to
establish and make everyone familiar with the concept that the
dependent territories be considered as a sacred trust.

"We believe that humanity and the human communities at
the present stage of civilization should be able to understand that
the trustee territory can no longer be considered as an investment
or as a business affair.   We believe that it is the duty of the
administering authority to go to no end of sacrifice in order to
enable the people of those territories to achieve the greatest
measure of independence and happiness possible.   This is not only
good for the trust territories themselves, but it is a noble achievement for the trustee power itself, and the latter cannot possibly
feel fully happy until it has fulfilled this particular obligation.

.   .   .   .

"We have objected to making trusteeship subject to an agreement with the countries now administering dependent territories,
and especially mandated territories.   We equally objected to the
composition of the Trusteeship Council because we considered
that the Trusteeship Council is an organ of the Assembly, and
therefore the Assembly should have a far greater hand in nominating its members than is now provided by this chapter, which
enables the Assembly only to nominate a minority of the members of the Trusteeship Council.   Under these circumstances, Mr.
President, it has been only natural that the Delegation of Egypt

cannot consider this document as a fully ideal one, but rather as one which falls a little short of the ideal for which we have aimed and for which we have struggled. The mere fact that so much important material is lying in a shy place called Annex B, and not embodied right in the heart of the chapter, indicates that there is still great room for improvement. In this connection, I remember a word said by Commander Stassen in the Committee, that this document is a living document and like all living beings, I wish to comment, it must evolve, it must change, and it must grow into something greater and better. This is the reason why, even though the Egyptian Delegation does not look upon this document as in any way an ideal document, nevertheless it considers that it presents a great step forward, and in the right direction, and we hope that it opens for the peoples under trusteeship a brighter and happier future than what they have experienced in the past, and that it will help in bringing many of them to the goal of complete independence at the earliest possible moment."

Statement of Mr. Awad (Egypt), *ibid.* 147–149.

"Now may I just say this. I am deeply moved by the things that have been said about this chapter tonight and the other evening in the technical Committee as we concluded our work, and by some of the Delegates who have spoken to me between those sessions. I trust and hope that this is a great document that we are meeting to approve this evening, but I also say, let us not overestimate it. It does affect directly in some degree the futures of hundreds of millions of men and women and children in various parts of the world. But let's not forget that tonight it is only a document; it is only a series of words in a mimeographed piece of paper; that if it is to become a great document the peoples of the world, including particularly the peoples and the governments who are represented here tonight, must breathe into it the light that only sincere adherence and support to these principles can give it. This document can open the door to millions of people; it can mark out a path. But only the helping hand of the peoples of the world, particularly those in the more advanced and privileged nations, only the constant and continuous, alert, intelligent, humanitarian attention of the peoples of the world can make it live, can make it mean progress and the progressive development of the freedoms and the rights of these peoples. It is based upon the dignity of man, wherever he may be found, whatever his color, or race, or creed. It has within it so much of what was envisioned by that great humanitarian, Franklin Delano Roosevelt. It has in its background so much of what has been discussed in parliaments and in gatherings throughout the world, and what has been present in the hopes and the hearts of men.

Stassen (U.S.)

"But let us not think that when tonight we adopt this document, we have solved a problem. We will have indicated in a tremendously encouraging way the manner in which the nations of the world can meet and reach agreement through very frank consultations and deliberations, but it is only machinery. It is only principles on paper. The test will be, do we the peoples of the world give it the life that sincerity in our future action can give it, and in that way do we make it really mean something to those millions of men and women and children throughout the world who do not now have representatives seated at these distinguished council tables of the United Nations?"

Statement of Commander Stassen (United States), *ibid.* 151. In his opening remarks, Mr. Stassen made the following attributions:

"Distinguished President, Mr. Fraser, Honored Delegates, Ladies and Gentlemen, I respond briefly to the kind invitation of the President merely to say to this Commission that this document, this chapter, is the result of the work of many men. This entire Committee, under the distinguished chairmanship of Mr. Fraser, worked long hours and diligently in bringing to you this evening the document that has been so eloquently and ably described. Associated with the work of the Committee there were very extensive consultations and studies which played a very large part in the successful conclusion of the work. I would like this evening, as we conclude our discussion in this Commission, to acknowledge and pay tribute to those who participated particularly in those consultations.

"In the first instance, may I say to you that there was a very distinct and marked contribution made to this chapter by the Delegates of that great nation that played such a large part in rolling back the Nazi hordes at the peak of their onslaught—I speak of the Delegates of the Soviet Union. Participating in the five-power consultations which took place continually on the various suggestions and documents affecting this chapter, Mr. Novikov of that Delegation frankly and directly and earnestly made a very marked and cooperative contribution, attended every meeting of the Committee, and joined with us there in the formulation of its final work. At various special stages of the consultations Ambassador Gromyko and Mr. Sobolev of that Delegation made very distinct contributions.

"Likewise, the very able contribution of the Delegates of heroic China deserves special mention tonight. Dr. Wellington Koo, who many speak of as the very youthful figure at Geneva after the last war, and who has been with us through this Conference, and Mr. Liu of that Delegation, with their great knowledge of the Orient, played a very large part in the successful conclusion of these consultations and the drafting of this document.

"You have heard tonight and have observed the ability and the background and the deep understanding of the Delegates of the United Kingdom and of France. Lord Cranborne and Mr. Poynton, and Mr. Naggiar, Mr. Pleven, and Mr. Bouchinet-Serreules of those two Delegations made an extremely valuable contribution that was so evident to you as you heard their presentation tonight.

"And then may I say to you very frankly that the contribution made by my Delegation was really made by those who did the work. It fell to my lot simply to have the honor of standing up in the Committee and making the motions. The work was done by Mr. Gerig and Mr. Bunche of our Delegation. Great advice was given by Congressman Bloom and the able military advisers under Admirals Hepburn and Train and Generals Embick and Fairchild participating thoroughly throughout.

"Of course, in the deliberations of the Committee and in the special consultations, many of these governments whom you have heard speak tonight and others played their part and played it well. I speak of the Delegates of Australia under the leadership of Mr. Forde and Mr. Evatt, who had a distinct and constructive interest from the very opening of our discussions, and many of whose marks appear in the final document. In the Committee, the Delegate of Greece, Mr. Goulimis; of Mexico, Mr. de la Colina; of Belgium, Mr. De Schryver; and that eloquent and thoughtful Delegate of the Philippines, General Romulo; Mr. Smit of South Africa, who undoubtedly brought to us at least some part of the wisdom of the years of experience of the great Field Marshal who presides over us tonight; and Mr. van der Plas of the Netherlands. In the general discussions in the Committee, each played a part. The contribution of our friends of Egypt and Iraq and of Syria, Lebanon, and Saudi Arabia, with their background of intimate contact in a different way with this entire question of the assistance to peoples who have not yet attained self-government, and its relationship to those who have attained self-government, after having been in the other classification, was extremely valuable and had a marked effect upon the final document." *Ibid.* 150–151.

"It is something that nations that have mandated territories express a willingness to frame this new means of administrating that trust, of at least supervising the administration in the name of the world of that trust. It is something even more that great colonial nations or empires, like the United Kingdom, Belgium, France, and the Netherlands, were willing also to adopt Section A, which is truly interpreted as steps toward self-expression, self-determination, and self-government.

Fraser (N.Z.)

"To us of the British Commonwealth, it is very difficult to distinguish between self-government and independence, for to the self-governing sovereign states of the British Commonwealth, self-government is independence and independence is self-government. But we have also learned that there is something additional to independence and something that is more secure and lasting in our modern world, where phrases become out of date so rapidly and titles and names that signified something a few years ago become meaningless with such precipitation, and that is, that as well as being independent, we are interdependent, and that the future of the British Commonwealth depends upon our cooperation. I go further: The future of the world depends upon our recognition of interdependence and upon our cooperation, one nation with another. That is a greater thing, of building up, of consolidating. It is even a greater thing than a nation realizing its own genius and wanting to break away from others.

"However, there is the road to those who want self-government and self-determination and it's a splendid thing the nations were so united. We have built the road, or a considerable part of it. The point is, as Commander Stassen has put it in referring to the document—will the nations take it? Will we go forward on that road? That is the test of our sincerity. I believe we will.

"In the name of the Rapporteur, of the Secretary, of the staff, of all those who have helped to make our Committee work and our Commission work here tonight a great success, I want to thank the delegates for their support.

"All that has been said of the staff is correct. What has been said of myself, I take with great mental reservations. We have all done our best and I think the document is worthy of the Committee, and worthy of the Conference, and I hope that it will bring light, the light of renewed hope and life into many places of the earth that have been dark. Those of us of the mandatory powers have a great responsibility. We have to ask who is to be the authority to transfer the mandate? Who will represent the Allied and Associated Powers that met in Versailles in 1919? That must be thought of. The nations who are represented there must come to some conclusion about that matter. There is the question of the Japanese mandates, and all these questions to be settled.

"But whatever difficulties there are, the rule that we will be guided by—I know I speak for my own country, but I feel I speak also for every country in a similar position—is that we have accepted a mandate as a sacred trust, not as part of our sovereign territory. The mandate does not belong to my country or any other country. It is held in trust for the world. The work immediately ahead is how those mandates that were previously supervised by the Mandates Commission of the League of Nations can now be supervised by the Trusteeship Council with every mandatory authority pledging itself in the first instance as the test of sincerity demands, whatever may happen to the territory afterwards, to acknowledge the authority and the supervision of this Trusteeship Council that has been helped toward its formation this evening."

Statement of Mr. Fraser (New Zealand), *ibid.* 153–154.

Conclusion of Trusteeship Agreements

§ 39

U.N.
Charter

Trusteeship agreements for 10 of the 11 United Nations trust territories were negotiated with, and approved by, the General Assembly of the United Nations in accordance with the following provisions of the Charter of the United Nations:

"Article 79

"The terms of trusteeship for each territory to be placed under the trusteeship system, including any alteration or amendment, shall be agreed upon by the states directly concerned, including the mandatory power in the case of territories held under mandate by a Member of the United Nations, and shall be approved as provided for in Articles 83 and 85.

"Article 80

"1. Except as may be agreed upon in individual trusteeship agreements, made under Articles 77, 79, and 81, placing each territory under the trusteeship system, and until such agreements have been concluded, nothing in this Chapter shall be construed in or of itself to alter in any manner the rights whatsoever of any states or any peoples or the terms of existing international instruments to which Members of the United Nations may respectively be parties.

"2. Paragraph 1 of this Article shall not be interpreted as giving grounds for delay or postponement of the negotiation and conclusion of agreements for placing mandated and other territories under the trusteeship system as provided for in Article 77.

"*Article 81*

"The trusteeship agreement shall in each case include the terms under which the trust territory will be administered and designate the authority which will exercise the administration of the trust territory. Such authority, hereinafter called the administering authority, may be one or more states or the Organization itself.

. . . .

"*Article 84*

"It shall be the duty of the administering authority to ensure that the trust territory shall play its part in the maintenance of international peace and security. To this end the administering authority may make use of volunteer forces, facilities, and assistance from the trust territory in carrying out the obligations towards the Security Council undertaken in this regard by the administering authority, as well as for local defense and the maintenance of law and order within the trust territory.

"*Article 85*

"1. The functions of the United Nations with regard to trusteeship agreements for all areas not designated as strategic, including the approval of the terms of the trusteeship agreements and of their alteration or amendment, shall be exercised by the General Assembly.

"2. The Trusteeship Council, operating under the authority of the General Assembly, shall assist the General Assembly in carrying out these functions."

U.S. TS 993; 59 Stat. 1031, 1049–1050. See *infra*, §§ 40 and 41, with respect to negotiation of the one "strategic" trusteeship agreement, that for the Trust Territory of the Pacific Islands, which was concluded between the United States and the Security Council of the United Nations, and is printed as U.S. TIAS 1665; 61 Stat. 3301; 8 UNTS 189.

The following resolution was adopted at the first part of the First 1st U.N. Assembly Session of the General Assembly of the United Nations:

"1. NON-SELF-GOVERNING PEOPLES

"The United Nations, meeting in its first General Assembly, is keenly aware of the problems and political aspirations of the peoples who have not yet attained a full measure of self-government and who are not directly represented here.

"Chapters XI, XII and XIII of the Charter recognize the problems of the non-self-governing peoples as of vital concern to the peace and general welfare of the world community.

. . . .

"By Chapters XII and XIII, the Charter provides for the establishment of an international trusteeship system, the basic objectives of which are, among others, to promote the political, economic, social and educational advancement of the inhabitants of trust territories, and to promote their progressive development towards self-government or independence.

"The General Assembly regrets that the Trusteeship Council cannot be brought into being at this first part of the first session, not because of any lack of desire to do so but because, before the Trusteeship Council can be established, trusteeship agreements must be concluded.

"The General Assembly holds the view that any delay in putting into effect the system of international trusteeship prevents the implementation of the principles of the trusteeship system, as declared in the Charter, and deprives the populations of such territories as may be brought under the trusteeship system of the opportunity of enjoying the advantages arising from the implementation of these principles.

"With a view to expediting the conclusion of these agreements and the establishment of the Trusteeship Council, the Preparatory Commission recommended that the General Assembly should call on those Members of the United Nations which are now administering territories held under mandate to undertake practical steps, in concert with the other States directly concerned, for the implementation of Article 79 of the Charter.

"Without waiting for the recommendation of the Preparatory Commission to be considered by the General Assembly, the Members of the United Nations administering territories held under mandate took the initiative in making declarations in regard to these territories.

"*Therefore*

.   .   .   .

"*with respect to Chapters XII and XIII of the Charter, the General Assembly:*

"3. *Welcomes* the declarations, made by certain States administering territories now held under mandate, of an intention to negotiate trusteeship agreements in respect of some of those territories and, in respect of Transjordan, to establish its independence.

"4. *Invites* the States administering territories now held under mandate to undertake practical steps, in concert with the other States directly concerned, for the implementation of Article 79 of the Charter (which provides for the conclusion of agreements on the terms of trusteeship for each territory to be placed under the trusteeship system), in order to submit these agreements for approval, preferably not later than during the second part of the first session of the General Assembly.

"*In conclusion, the General Assembly:*

"5. *Expects* that the realization of the objectives of Chapters XI, XII and XIII will make possible the attainment of the political, economic, social and educational aspirations of non-self-governing peoples."

G.A. Res. 11 (I), Feb. 9, 1946, U.N. Doc. A/64, p. 13.

"CONSULTATIONS WITH THE MANDATORY POWERS

"In the intervals between the London and New York meetings of the General Assembly, trusteeship drafts were prepared by the Mandatory Powers and submitted to certain other interested powers for information. Early in 1946 the United States Government received copies of proposed trusteeship agreements for Tanganyika, Togoland, and the Cameroons from the United Kingdom; for Ruanda-Urundi from Belgium; and later for Togoland and the Cameroons from France; for Western Samoa from New Zealand; and for New Guinea from Australia. The United States Government communicated to each of these Mandatory Powers its comments on their proposed terms of trusteeship.

Negotiation of Trusteeship Agreements: Mandated Territories

"In the course of the summer of 1946 consultations concerning a number of provisions of the draft trusteeship agreements took place between experts of this Government and of the governments of the Mandatory Powers. In conversations with the United Kingdom Government the United States was represented by Benjamin Gerig, Chief of the Division of Dependent Area Affairs, and Edwin L. Smith of the Division of African Affairs; and in conversations with the Belgian Government the United States was represented by Henry S. Villard, Deputy Director of the Office of Near Eastern and African Affairs.

"In its comments on the draft trusteeship proposals and in its consultations with the Mandatory Powers with regard to them, the United States particularly sought the addition of provisions which would enlarge upon the rights of the inhabitants of trust territories and specify in greater detail the obligations of the administering authority under article 76 of the Charter to insure their political, economic, social, and educational advancement. Agreement was reached with the Mandatory Powers to add a significant number of such provisions to the original draft agreements. Two of the proposals put forward by the United States were designed especially to guarantee the fundamental freedoms of the inhabitants of the territories and to set forth the obligations of the administering authority to promote the educational advancement of the inhabitants. In the trusteeship agreement for Tanganyika they are stated in the following terms:

" 'Subject only to the requirements of public order, the Administering Authority shall guarantee to the inhabitants of Tanganyika freedom of speech, of the press, of assembly, and of petition.

" 'The Administering Authority shall, as may be appropriate to the circumstances of Tanganyika, continue and extend a general system of elementary education designed to abolish illiteracy and to facilitate the vocational and cultural advancement of the population, child and adult, and shall similarly provide such facilities as may prove desirable and practicable in the interests of the inhabitants for qualified students to receive secondary and higher education, including professional training.'

"Such provisions appear in one form or another in each of the eight trusteeship agreements approved by the Assembly.

"In many cases agreement was readily reached with the Mandatory Powers to include further provisions relating to the welfare of the inhabitants in the trusteeship drafts which they would present to the General Assembly. In some cases, however, the Mandatory Powers expressed the view that the inclusion of such clauses was unnecessary, either because the administering authority was already bound by international agreements to these ends, or because it was felt that the Charter obligations automatically assumed by any administering authority were sufficiently broad to cover such matters.

"Thus the process of alteration of the draft trusteeship proposals was begun well in advance of the General Assembly session in New York. Although this process was continued by the General Assembly itself, the extent of the alterations made in the draft trusteeship agreements at the Assembly stage was, except in the case of the New Guinea agreement, relatively small. That the pre-Assembly consultations between the Mandatory Powers and the United States were regarded as constructive and helpful is suggested in the comment made by Ivor Thomas, the British Representative on the Trusteeship Committee at the General Assembly in New York. As reported in the Summary Record of the 26th meeting of Committee 4 (Dec. 11, 1946), Mr. Thomas stated that 'when the texts had been circulated in January, the Government of the United States had been the only one to suggest any amendments. Those had been discussed fully, with the result that some were adopted as they stood, others adopted in modified form, others were withdrawn by mutual agreement and one left over to be raised before the General Assembly. Only two articles of the original draft remained unchanged.'

"Two outstanding questions remained, so far as the United States Delegation was concerned, when the draft trusteeship agreements were submitted to the General Assembly in New York. The first was the thorny procedural question regarding the problem of 'states directly concerned', arising from the provisions of article 79 of the Charter, and the second concerned the monopolies clauses of the draft agreements for the African mandates of the United Kingdom, France, and Belgium."

Armstrong and Cargo, "The Inauguration of the Trusteeship System of the United Nations," XVI *Bulletin*, Department of State, No. 403, Mar.

23, 1947, pp. 511, 514–515. For an account of the negotiations relative to the monopolies clauses, see *post*, p. 886.

"THE PROCEDURAL ISSUE: 'STATES DIRECTLY CONCERNED'

"The language of article 79 of the Charter led to the principal procedural issue involved in drawing up and approving the trusteeship agreements. Article 79 provides, in part, that 'The terms of trusteeship for each territory to be placed under the trusteeship system . . . shall be agreed upon by the states directly concerned, including the mandatory power in the case of territories held under mandate by a Member of the United Nations. . . .' The importance of the 'states directly concerned' in this procedural conception is readily apparent. Although this matter was clearly of less importance with respect to the operation of the trusteeship system than the terms of the trusteeship agreements themselves, it was an important hurdle which had to be surmounted if chapters XII and XIII of the Charter were to be given effect and the Trusteeship Council brought into operation.

"The San Francisco Conference established in articles 79, 83, and 85 of the Charter the procedure by which territories may be placed under the trusteeship system of the United Nations. Article 83 relates to strategic trusteeship agreements and was therefore not applicable to the eight draft agreements considered by the recent General Assembly. Article 85 provides in clear terms that the General Assembly shall approve trusteeship agreements which are non-strategic in character. The interpretation of this article presented no difficulties. It was article 79 which contained the crux of the procedural problem.

"No clear indication is offered either by the Charter itself or by the records of the San Francisco Conference, which drew up the Charter, as to the meaning of the phrase or the method by which the 'states directly concerned' mentioned in article 79 should be determined. . . .

"Speaking on behalf of the United States Delegation to the General Assembly, John Foster Dulles on November 7, 1946 placed the whole procedural problem relating to 'states directly concerned' before the Trusteeship Committee of the Assembly. After pointing out the numerous possible interpretations of the phrase 'states directly concerned' and the great difficulty of arriving at any agreed interpretation, Mr. Dulles put forward the following proposal:

> " 'In the light of these considerations the United States Delegation urges that the Assembly, and this Committee on its behalf, should not become involved in all these questions. We prefer a practical procedure which, in harmony with the letter and spirit of the Charter, will, as quickly as possible, permit the establishment of the trusteeship system and the giving to the inhabitants of the trust territories the benefit of that system. Concretely, we propose:

"States directly concerned"

" '1. That a small subcommittee of this Committee should be established to consider the draft trusteeship agreements before us and to negotiate on our behalf in relation to them;

" '2. That all states which are interested be given the opportunity promptly to submit to this subcommittee and to the mandatory power involved their suggestions regarding these proposed trusteeship agreements;

" '3. That after hearing such suggestions and after consultation with the subcommittee, the mandatory power concerned shall promptly advise the subcommittee as to the acceptability of those suggestions;

" '4. That the agreements reflecting any such modifications shall then be considered by this Committee and referred by it to the General Assembly with the recommendation of this Committee, in each case, as to approval or disapproval.

" 'Under this procedure every state which. is interested, whether or not technically a state "directly concerned", whether it be large or small, whether it be near or far, will have an equal opportunity to present its views. All would, however, without prejudice to any rights they may possess, now forego formal classification as being, or not being, states "directly concerned", and would forego formal signature of the preliminary agreement, accepting the verdict of a two-thirds vote of the Assembly.' [BULLETIN of Dec. 1, 1946, p. 993.]

"The Trusteeship Committee followed the suggestion put forward by the United States Delegation and selected a subcommittee which undertook the initial consideration of the eight draft trusteeship agreements. Moreover, the solution which was ultimately reached regarding the procedure to be followed with respect to 'states directly concerned' was along the lines suggested in the final paragraph of the proposal quoted above.

"In the subcommittee's consideration of the draft trusteeship agreements the question of 'states directly concerned' was raised owing to the fact that the preambles of the draft agreements stated that the provisions of article 79 had been complied with. Certain delegations, including principally the Soviet Delegation, contended that the Charter provisions had not been fulfilled, and called for an attempt to define the 'states directly concerned'. At the request of the Chairman of the subcommittee the Delegates from the Soviet Union and the United States undertook consultations in an attempt to find an agreed solution to the problem. Following the announcement that these consultations had been unsuccessful the subcommittee, on the initiative of the United States Delegation, approved the following proposal regarding 'states directly concerned':

" 'Approval of any terms of Trusteeship by this session of the General Assembly should be on the following understanding with respect to "states directly concerned":

"'All Members of the United Nations have had an opportunity to present their views with reference to the terms of Trusteeship now proposed to the General Assembly for approval. There has, however, been no specification by the General Assembly of "states directly concerned" in relation to the proposed Trust Territories. Accordingly, the General Assembly in approving the terms of Trusteeship does not prejudge the question of what states are or are not "directly concerned" within the meaning of Article 79. It recognizes that no state has waived or prejudiced its right hereafter to claim to be such a "state directly concerned" in relation to approval of subsequently proposed Trusteeship agreements and any alteration or amendment of those now approved, and that the procedure to be followed in the future with reference to such matters may be subject to later determination.' [General Assembly doc. A/258, Dec. 12, 1946, p. 13.]

This statement was approved by an overwhelming majority of the full Trusteeship Committee of the General Assembly and constitutes, therefore, the understanding on which the Assembly approved the eight trusteeship agreements."

Ibid., pp. 518–520.

"APPROVAL OF THE TRUSTEESHIP AGREEMENTS BY THE GENERAL ASSEMBLY

"After long weeks of discussion the subcommittee approved the eight draft agreements and referred them to the Fourth Committee where they were approved by a vote of 35 for, 8 against, with no abstentions.

Approval first trusteeship agreements

"At the sixty-third plenary meeting of the General Assembly on December 13, 1946 the Soviet Delegation moved a resolution calling on the Assembly to reject the draft trusteeship agreements as having been drafted contrary to the fundamental requirements of the Charter. The three principal grounds asserted were: (1) that the states directly concerned had never been specified; (2) that the agreements made the trust territories an integral part of the administering power; and (3) that the agreements did not provide for approval by the Security Council of military arrangements in the trust territories. This resolution was defeated by a vote of 34 against, 6 for, with 8 abstentions. The eight trusteeship agreements were then approved by the General Assembly by more than the required two-thirds vote. The United States Delegation voted in favor of all eight agreements. Opposing votes were cast by the Delegations of the Soviet Union, Byelorussia, Ukraine, Yugoslavia, and Liberia. The Polish Delegation also voted in the negative except in the case of the French agreements on which it abstained from voting.

"The territories thus placed under the trusteeship system, with their administering authorities, are as follows:

Trust territory	Administering authority
Cameroons (British)	United Kingdom
Cameroons (French)	France
New Guinea	Australia
Ruanda-Urundi	Belgium
Tanganyika	United Kingdom
Togoland (British)	United Kingdom
Togoland (French)	France
Western Samoa	New Zealand"

Ibid., p. 520.

See also The U.S. and the U.N., report by the President to Congress for the year 1946, pp. 67–71.   The texts of these eight agreements appear in 8 UNTS 71–187, having been registered by the United Nations Secretariat.

"By approving the eight trusteeship agreements the General Assembly made possible the establishment of the Trusteeship Council, the last major organ of the United Nations to be set up.   On December 14, 1946 the General Assembly elected Mexico and Iraq to the Trusteeship Council in order to balance the number of non-administering states with the number of administering states as required by the Charter.   The Soviet Delegation again stated the view that the trusteeship agreements were contrary to the Charter, and contended that they could not be used as a basis for the creation of the Trusteeship Council.   Accordingly, the Soviet Delegation did not participate in these elections.

"The 10 members of the Trusteeship Council are:

Administering states	Non-administering states
Australia	China
Belgium	Iraq
France	Mexico
New Zealand	United States
United Kingdom	Union of Soviet Socialist Republics

"The first meeting of the Trusteeship Council is scheduled for March 26, 1947.   Francis B. Sayre, former Assistant Secretary of State and former High Commissioner to the Philippines, has been appointed as the United States Representative on the Council."   Armstrong and Cargo, *op. cit.*, p. 521.   See also The U.S. and the U.N., report by the President to Congress for the year 1946, pp. 71–72.

Nauru

On November 1, 1947, the General Assembly approved a Trusteeship Agreement for the mandated island of Nauru in the Pacific. The Agreement was submitted on behalf of Australia, New Zealand, and the United Kingdom; Australia was designated to administer the territory on behalf of these three States.

The U.S. and the U.N., report by the President to Congress for the year 1947, p. 137.   The Agreement is printed in 10 UNTS 3.

Somaliland

In 1948 the disposition of the former Italian colonies was referred to the United Nations General Assembly in accordance with article 23 and annex XI of the Treaty of Peace with Italy, dated at Paris February 10, 1947, reading as follows:

"SECTION IV—ITALIAN COLONIES

"*Article 23*

"1. Italy renounces all right and title to the Italian territorial possessions in Africa, i. e. Libya, Eritrea and Italian Somaliland.

"2. Pending their final disposal, the said possessions shall continue under their present administration.

"3. The final disposal of these possessions shall be determined jointly by the Governments of the Soviet Union, of the United Kingdom, of the United States of America, and of France within one year from the coming into force of the present Treaty, in the manner laid down in the joint declaration of February 10, 1947, issued by the said Governments, which is reproduced in Annex XI.

. . . .

"ANNEX XI

"Joint Declaration by the Governments of the Soviet Union, of the United Kingdom, of the United States of America and of France concerning Italian Territorial Possessions in Africa

"(See Article 23)

"1. The Governments of the Union of Soviet Socialist Republics, of the United Kingdom of Great Britain and Northern Ireland, of the United States of America, and of France agree that they will, within one year from the coming into force of the Treaty of Peace with Italy bearing the date of February 10, 1947, jointly determine the final disposal of Italy's territorial possessions in Africa, to which, in accordance with Article 23 of the Treaty, Italy renounces all right and title.

"2. The final disposal of the territories concerned and the appropriate adjustment of their boundaries shall be made by the Four Powers in the light of the wishes and welfare of the inhabitants and the interests of peace and security, taking into consideration the views of other interested Governments.

"3. If with respect to any of these territories the Four Powers are unable to agree upon their disposal within one year from the coming into force of the Treaty of Peace with Italy, the matter shall be referred to the General Assembly of the United Nations for a recommendation, and the Four Powers agree to accept the recommendation and to take appropriate measures for giving effect to it.

"4. The Deputies of the Foreign Ministers shall continue the consideration of the question of the disposal of the former Italian Colonies with a view to submitting to the Council of Foreign Ministers their recommendations on this matter. They shall also send out commissions of investigation to any of the former Italian Colonies in order to supply the Deputies with the necessary data on this question and to ascertain the views of the local population."

U.S. TIAS 1648; 61 Stat. 1245, 1382, 1457; 49 UNTS 3, 139, 214.

On November 21, 1949, the General Assembly adopted Resolution 289(IV), which provided, with respect to the former Italian colony of Somaliland, in part:

"1. That Italian Somaliland shall be an independent sovereign State;

"2. That this independence shall become effective at the end of ten years from the date of the approval of a Trusteeship Agreement by the General Assembly;

"3. That, during the period mentioned in paragraph 2, Italian Somaliland shall be placed under the International Trusteeship System with Italy as the Administering Authority;"

U.N. Gen. Ass. Off. Rec. 4th Sess., Resolutions (1949), pp. 10, 11. U.S. participation in the U.N., report by the President to Congress for the year 1949, pp 51–57.

On December 2, 1950, by Resolution 442(V), the General Assembly approved a Trusteeship Agreement for Somaliland under Italian administration.

U.S. participation in the U.N., report by the President to Congress for the year 1950, pp. 214–216. The Agreement was printed in 118 UNTS 255.

By 1950 eleven territories had been placed under the International Trusteeship System. The following table sets forth pertinent data with respect to these territories.

"Territory	Area (square miles)	Population (thousands)	Administering state
Cameroons	34, 081	991	United Kingdom.
Do	166, 797	2, 703	France.
New Guinea	93, 000	1, 006	Australia.
Nauru	82	3	Australia (on behalf of the United Kingdom, New Zealand, and Australia).
Pacific Islands [1]	687	60	United States.
Ruanda-Urundi	20, 916	3, 719	Belgium.
Somaliland	194, 000	915	Italy.
Tanganyika	362, 688	7, 080	United Kingdom.
Togoland	13, 040	382	Do.
Do	21, 236	944	France.
Western Samoa	1, 133	73	New Zealand.
Total	907, 660	17, 876	

[1] This is the only strategic trust territory."

S. Doc. 164, 83d Cong., 2d sess., p. 263.

Kinds of Trust Territories: Strategic and Nonstrategic

§ 40

The United Nations Charter provides for the establishment of two types of trust territories, "strategic" and "nonstrategic". Provisions in the Charter for "strategic" trusteeships are:

"Article 82

"There may be designated, in any trusteeship agreement, a strategic area or areas which may include part or all of the trust territory to which the agreement applies, without prejudice to any special agreement or agreements made under Article 43.

"Article 83

"1. All functions of the United Nations relating to strategic areas, including the approval of the terms of the trusteeship agreements and of their alteration or amendment, shall be exercised by the Security Council.

"2. The basic objectives set forth in Article 76 shall be applicable to the people of each strategic area.

"3. The Security Council shall, subject to the provisions of the trusteeship agreements and without prejudice to security considerations, avail itself of the assistance of the Trusteeship Council to perform those functions of the United Nations under the trusteeship system relating to political, economic, social, and educational matters in the strategic areas."

U.S. TS 993 ; 59 Stat. 1031, 1050. For the text of article 76, see *ante*, p. 732.

"Strategic Areas

"The strategic areas provided for in article 82 of the Charter are trust territories and come under the trusteeship system. The strategic-area concept is designed to meet the special situation wherein a particular territory or a part of a territory is of vital importance to security, and must therefore be maintained and operated as a military or naval base or security zone. Any areas designated as strategic would normally be areas in which strategic considerations are clearly controlling.

"Because of the vital strategic importance of such areas and the security considerations involved, the administering authorities would exercise, within an agreed scope of international responsibility subject only to such international supervision as the trusteeship agreements with the approval of the Security Council might specify, a maximum degree of control over such areas. In other words the administering authority would have as much control over a strategic area as it would find necessary to preserve the essential function of the area. The administering authority would be bound, however, to protect and promote the well-being of the civilian inhabitants of the area in conformance with the basic objectives of the trusteeship system.

"The Security Council will not only approve the trusteeship agreements for strategic areas but will also exercise all functions of the Organization with regard to these areas. The Security Council, however, may avail itself of the assistance of the Trusteeship Council in handling political, economic, social, and educational matters in the strategic areas."

Bunche, "Trusteeship and Non-Self-Governing Territories in the Charter of the United Nations," XIII *Bulletin,* Department of State, No. 340, Dec. 30, 1945, pp. 1037, 1043.

In fact, only one "strategic" Trusteeship Agreement has been concluded, that for the Trust Territory of the Pacific Islands, which was approved on April 2, 1947, by the Security Council of the United Nations, and on July 18, 1947, by the President of the United States, pursuant to authority of a Joint Resolution of the United States Congress of that date. U.S. TIAS 1665; 61 Stat. 3301; 8 UNTS 189. See § 41, *infra,* for a detailed statement as to this "strategic" trust territory. The other 10 Trusteeship Agreements were of a "non-strategic" character and were negotiated with and approved by the General Assembly of the United Nations, under the following provisions of the United Nations Charter:

"*Article 85*

"1. The functions of the United Nations with regard to trusteeship agreements for all areas not designated as strategic, including the approval of the terms of the trusteeship agreements and of their alteration or amendment, shall be exercised by the General Assembly.

"2. The Trusteeship Council, operating under the authority of the General Assembly, shall assist the General Assembly in carrying out these functions."

U.S. TS 993; 59 Stat. 1031, 1050.

"The San Francisco Conference established in articles 79, 83, and 85 of the Charter the procedure by which territories may be placed under the trusteeship system of the United Nations. Article 83 relates to strategic trusteeship agreements and was therefore not applicable to the eight draft agreements considered by the recent General Assembly. Article 85 provides in clear terms that the General Assembly shall approve trusteeship agreements which are non-strategic in character. The interpretation of this article presented no difficulties. It was article 79 which contained the crux of the procedural problem."

Armstrong and Cargo, "The Inauguration of the Trusteeship System of the United Nations", XVI *Bulletin,* Department of State, No. 403, Mar. 23, 1947, pp. 511, 519. In the case of some of the "non-strategic" Trusteeship Agreements, the Administering Authority reserved the right to propose the designation of the whole or part of the particular Territory as a "strategic" area. See article 17, Tanganyika; article 17, Ruanda-Urundi;

article 17, Cameroons (British) ; article 11, Cameroons (French) ; article 17, Togoland (British) ; article 11, Togoland (French). 8 UNTS 102, 116, 130, 146, 162, 176.

"What the role of the Trusteeship Council should be in carrying out U.N. functions relating to strategic trusteeships was debated in the Security Council on June 18. The discussion centered on Charter interpretation, but there were overtones deriving from the fact that the only strategic trusteeship now in effect is that of the United States over the Pacific Islands formerly mandated to Japan.

Role of U.N. Trusteeship Council

"Article 83 of the Charter states: 'All functions of the United Nations relating to strategic areas . . . shall be exercised by the Security Council', but goes on to say that the Security Council 'shall, subject to the provisions of the trusteeship agreements and without prejudice to security considerations, avail itself of the assistance of the Trusteeship Council to perform those functions of the United Nations under the trusteeship system relating to political, economic, social, and educational matters in the strategic areas.'

"Whether the phrase 'shall . . . avail itself of the assistance of the Trusteeship Council' is mandatory or merely permissive is the main point in issue. The June 18 debate's point of departure was a report from the Council's Committee of Experts recommending that the Council authorize the Trusteeship Council to act on its behalf in functions relating to the welfare of inhabitants of strategic trust territories.

"Mr. Gromyko of the U.S.S.R. and Mr. Tarasenko of the Ukrain[e] attacked this proposal, contending that the Charter language, 'all functions . . . shall be exercised by the Security Council', meant just that. Mr. Gromyko maintained that, although the Security Council is free to ask the assistance of the Trusteeship Council on particular problems, 'a decision for a wholesale transfer of the Security Council's functions to the Trusteeship Council is as inadmissible as it is illegal.'

"The attitude of Belgium, China, France, the United Kingdom, and the United States, as stated by their representatives in the Committee of Experts, is that it is obligatory for the Security Council to avail itself of the assistance of the Trusteeship Council and that general principles of inter-Council collaboration need to be formally established.

"The June 18 meeting ended with a 9–0 vote (U.S.S.R., Ukraine abstaining) to approve President El Khouri's proposal that the President and the Belgian and Ukrainian Representatives meet with a Trusteeship Council committee to explore informally the possibility of a formula acceptable to both Councils."

XVIII *Bulletin*, Department of State, No. 469, June 27, 1948, pp. 830–831.

"Strategic Trusteeships

"Debates in the Trusteeship Council on June 25 and 28 regarding the relationship of the Trusteeship Council and the Security Council with respect to strategic trusteeships followed the same general lines as earlier debate in the Security Council. S. K. Tsarapkin, Soviet Representative, echoed what Mr. Gromyko had said in the Security Council, i.e. that all U.N. functions for strategic trusteeships were vested in the Security Council and were in no way the concern of the Trusteeship Council unless and until the Security Council asked its help or advice on particular problems.

"The representatives of Australia, China, Mexico, New Zealand, and the Philippines said that in their view the language of article 83 of the Charter obliged the Security Council to entrust to the Trusteeship Council U.N. functions having to do with political, economic, social, and educational matters in the strategic trust areas.

"The only strategic trusteeship now in effect is that under which the United States administers the Pacific islands formerly mandated to Japan, and the discussion, in which Ambassador Sayre of the United States took no part, often adverted to this particular arrangement. After William D. Forsyth of Australia had said that the Trusteeship Council could not act before the Security Council asked its help, as it was obliged to do, Luis Padilla Nervo of Mexico argued that in effect the Security Council had already done so with respect to the Pacific islands by ratifying the trust agreement, which applies articles 87 and 88 of the Charter, subject to the right of the United States to close any area for security reasons. These articles authorized the Trusteeship Council to inspect trust territories, to receive petitions from their inhabitants, and to obtain public-welfare data from administering authorities."

XIX *Bulletin*, Department of State, No. 470, July 4, 1948, pp. 15–16.

By resolution of March 7, 1949, the Security Council, referring to article 83, paragraph 3, of the Charter, requested the Trusteeship Council, "subject to the provisions of the Trusteeship Agreements or parts thereof in respect of strategic areas, and subject to the decisions of the Security Council made having regard to security considerations from time to time, to perform in accordance with its own procedures, on behalf of the Security Council, the functions specified in Articles 87 and 88 of the Charter relating to the political, economic, social and educational advancement of the inhabitants of such strategic areas". This resolution also requested the Trusteeship Council "to submit to the Security Council its reports and recommendations on political, social, economic and educational matters affecting strategic areas under trusteeship".

Report of the Security Council to the General Assembly covering the period from 16 July 1948–15 July 1949, U.N. Gen. Ass. Off. Rec. 4th Sess., Supp. No. 2 (U.N. Doc. A/945), pp. 91–92. Accordingly, the Trusteeship Council submits an annual report to the Security Council with respect to the Trust Territory of the Pacific Islands, the sole "strategic" trust territory.

Trust Territory of the Pacific Islands

§41

"Description of the Area

"The islands of the Trust Territory are located in the Western Pacific Ocean north of the Equator. Here some 96 island units lie scattered over an oceanic area larger than the continent of Australia or the continental United States of America. The 96 island units, variously small islands or atolls, have, however, a land area of only 687 square miles. Of the islands, only 64 are regularly inhabited.

"A division into three major island groups—the Marshalls, the Carolines, and the Marianas—can be made. Extending from latitude 1° to 20° north and from longitude 130° to 172° east, the Territory stretches some 2,700 miles in an east-west direction and 1,500 miles in a north-south direction. The southernmost atoll, Kapingamarangi, lies 1° above the Equator while the northernmost, Farallon de Pajaros in the Marianas, is situated at 20° north latitude. Tobi Island in the Western Carolines, 130° east longitude, and Mili Atoll in the Marshalls, at 172° east longitude, respectively delineate the western and eastern boundaries of the area. The approximate geographic center of the Trust Territory falls at Truk in the east-central Carolines.

"The islands of the Territory form part of Micronesia, a zone of the Pacific which also includes the Gilbert Islands, Ocean Island, Nauru Island, and Guam. Although the term 'Micronesia' tends to be used synonymously with 'Trust Territory of the Pacific Islands,' this usage is neither geographically nor culturally correct. The Trust Territory's two southernmost islands, Kapingamarangi and Nukuoro, culturally are Polynesian, whereas, as noted above, Guam and the neighboring islands of the Gilbert group together with Ocean Island and Nauru culturally and geographically fall in the Micronesia zone. The many different island groups of the Territory necessitate the use of a general term in referring to the inhabitants, and in this report the term 'Micronesian' is used to designate the people of the Territory."

Trust Territory of the Pacific Islands, 1960, 13th Annual Report to the United Nations (Department of State publication 7183, 1961), p. 1.

On November 6, 1946, President Truman made the following statement: | President Truman's offer

"The United States is prepared to place under trusteeship, with the United States as the administering authority, the Japanese Mandated Islands and any Japanese islands for which it assumes responsibilities as a result of the Second World War. Insofar as the Japanese Mandated Islands are concerned, this Government is transmitting for information to the other members of the Security Council (Australia, Brazil, China, Egypt, France, Mexico, the Netherlands, Poland, the Union of Soviet Socialist

Republics, and the United Kingdom) and to New Zealand and the Philippines a draft of a strategic area trusteeship agreement which sets forth the terms upon which this Government is prepared to place those islands under trusteeship. At an early date we plan to submit this draft agreement formally to the Security Council for its approval."

Draft Trusteeship Agreement for the Japanese Mandated Islands, With Article by Article Explanatory Comments (Department of State publication 2784, 1947), p. 1; U.S. Delegation Doc. US/S/119, Feb. 26, 1947, p. 1.

Sen. Austin in U.N.

By letter of February 17, 1947, Senator Warren R. Austin, the United States Representative on the Security Council, transmitted to Trygve Lie, the Secretary-General of the United Nations, the text of a draft trusteeship agreement for the former Japanese Mandated Islands, and requested "that this matter be placed on the agenda of the Security Council at an early date." *Draft Trusteeship Agreement for the Japanese Mandated Islands, op. cit.*, p. 2; U.N. Doc. S/281; U.N. Security Council Off. Rec. 2d year, Supp. No. 8, Annex 17, p. 69. Accordingly, on February 26, 1947, the Security Council, at its 113th meeting, began consideration of the United States offer to place this territory under the International Trusteeship System of the United Nations. At that time Senator Austin stated:

"The United States, like other nations adhering to the United Nations Declaration of 1 January 1942, subscribed to the Atlantic Charter principle that they 'seek no aggrandizement, territorial or otherwise.'

"It was for the purpose of making clear that the United States adheres unswervingly to this principle that on 6 November 1946, the President of the United States declared our intentions regarding Pacific islands whose control by Japan enabled her to attack the United States. . . .

"Final disposition of the islands belonging to Japan must, of course, await the peace settlement with Japan. The draft trusteeship agreement submitted to the Security Council for its approval relates only to the former Japanese mandated islands, which never belonged to Japan, but were a part of the League of Nations mandate system. The United States has consistently and strongly supported the position of the General Assembly that former mandated territories should be placed under the trusteeship system as soon as possible.

"The General Assembly, during the first part of its first session, called on those Members of the United Nations which are 'administering territories now held under mandate to undertake practical steps . . . for the implementation of Article 79 of the Charter'. Since the United States was, and is, occupying the territory formerly mandated to Japan, the United States desires to play its part in attaining the objectives of the General Assembly's resolution, so that trusteeship agreements for all former mandated territories should be concluded promptly and the trusteeship system organized as soon as possible.

"The Japanese mandated islands, the Marshalls, Marianas and Carolines, consist of some ninety-eight islands and island clusters with a total area of only 846 square miles, a total population of only about 48,000 native inhabitants and negligible indigenous economic resources.

"The tremendous strategic value of the mandated islands to Japan is evident, however, from the way these islands were used in carrying out its basic plan of aggression. Before Japan entered the war on 7 December 1941, she had established fortified positions, naval bases and air bases in these islands. As a whole, the islands formed a deep, well-defended barrier between the United States on the one hand and Guam, the Philippines, and its British and Dutch allies in the Far East on the other.

. . . .

"Tens of thousands of American lives, vast expenditure and years of bitter fighting were needed to drive the Japanese aggressors from these islands, which constitute an integrated strategic physical complex vital to the security of the United States. The American people are firmly resolved that this area shall never again be used as a springboard for aggression against the United States, or any other Member of the United Nations. U.S. terms: A "Strategic Area":

"Most of the strategically important areas of the world, including those of the Pacific, are at present under the exclusive sovereignty of various of the larger nations. The United States, however, is proposing trusteeship rather than annexation as the basis for its administration of these highly strategic islands.

"In undertaking to place under trusteeship a territory of such strategic importance to the United States as these islands, the United States is expressing its faith in the United Nations. Our purpose is to defend the security of these islands in a manner that will contribute to the building up of genuine, effective and enforceable collective security for all Members of the United Nations.

"The first of the four basic objectives of the trusteeship system set forth in Article 76 of the Charter is 'to further international peace and security.' Since the area of the former Japanese mandated islands is of paramount strategic importance, the United States proposes, in accordance with Article 82 of the Charter, that the trust territory 'be designated . . . a strategic area.'

"In preparing this draft trusteeship agreement, the Government of the United States gave long and careful study not only to the Charter as a whole, and to its specific provisions for strategic needs in special areas, but also to the draft agreements for non-strategic areas recently submitted to the General Assembly by five of the mandatory Powers. This draft trusteeship agreement is viewed by the Government of the United States as conforming, in substance and in form, with the Charter, and as promoting the interests both of the inhabitants of the islands and of the United

Nations. It contains the terms upon which the United States is prepared to administer the former Japanese mandated islands as a trust territory."

U.N. Security Council Off. Rec., 113th Meeting, Feb. 26, 1947, pp. 407, 408–410.

Basis of
U.S. authority

"The United States Government does not consider that there is any obstacle to the placing of these islands under trusteeship in accordance with the Charter as soon as the Security Council approves the draft agreement.

"As a result of the war, Japan has ceased to exercise, or to be entitled to exercise, any authority in these islands. These islands were entrusted to Japan under mandate from the League of Nations after the first world war. In utter disregard of the mandate, Japan, contrary to the law of nations, used the territories for aggressive warfare against the United States and other Members of the United Nations. Japan, by her criminal acts of aggression, forfeited the right and capacity to be the mandatory Power of the islands. The termination of Japan's status as the mandatory Power over the islands has been frequently affirmed: in the Cairo Declaration of 1943, subsequently reaffirmed in the Potsdam Declaration and in the instrument of surrender accepted by the Powers responsible for Japan's defeat.

"All authority in these islands is now exercised by the United States. The United States, in repelling Japanese aggression occupied, and is in possession of, the former Japanese mandated islands.

"All the Members which may have special interests in the islands have been sent copies of the draft agreement which the United States, as the responsible administering authority in the islands, has submitted to the Security Council. My Government is not aware that any other Member of the United Nations has asserted any claim for trusteeship of these islands.

"In the above circumstances, it is the view of my Government that the conclusion of a trusteeship agreement, pursuant to the Charter, for the former Japanese mandated islands clearly can take effect at this time, and does not depend upon, and need not await, the general peace settlement with Japan."

Statement of Senator Warren R. Austin, United States Representative, U.N. Security Council Off. Rec., 113th Meeting, Feb. 26, 1947, p. 413.

U.S. position
in Security
Council

During the course of the consideration of the United States draft text of a trusteeship agreement in the Security Council, Senator Austin made the following statement as to the position of the United States:

"At this point I think I ought to state my position here, in view of the fact that the United States delegation cannot admit the idea of exercising the veto in the Security Council in a case where it would appear to be acting in a dual capacity, sitting on both sides of the table. Here we are one of the parties to the agreement that we are proposing, and it does not seem ethical to us that we should exercise a veto on any question as a member of the Security Council, when we should be trading with you at arm's length, were it not for the necessity of dealing with the Security Council in this manner under the Charter.

"Therefore, I want you to know in advance that this question, upon which we are firmly decided, will have to be determined by you without our vote. On the question of whether this amendment should be accepted or not, if we voted, we would of course vote 'no', but we are not going to use our vote to exercise the veto. We state this in advance, so that you can clearly understand our position and also understand that your position in the matter cannot be safeguarded at all or balanced by the veto right of the United States. On such questions as this, it is perfectly clear—to us at least—that, when faced with the possibility of being obliged, in view of its responsibilities, to withdraw the tender of an agreement, the United States should certainly not also exercise its right of veto in the Security Council. I just want you to understand that. This is a precautionary statement. I have not made it as strongly as I might, for I have really very strong personal feelings about what we ought to do and what I ought to do as the representative of one of the permanent members of the Security Council."

U.N. Security Council Off. Rec., 124th Meeting, Apr. 2, 1947, pp. 665–666. The proposed United Kingdom amendment (which was rejected by the Security Council) would have deleted the last four words of article 8, paragraph 1, *i.e.*, "except the Administering Authority", set forth in full *post*, pp. 809–810. *Ibid.*, pp. 662, 666.

The Agreement for the Trust Territory of the Pacific Islands— formally referred to as the Trusteeship Agreement for the former Japanese Mandated Islands and which entered into force on July 18, 1947—under which the United States of America is designated as the administering authority of the trust territory, contains the following provisions in the Preamble and in article 1:

"PREAMBLE

"WHEREAS Article 75 of the Charter of the United Nations pro- Establishment vides for the establishment of an international trusteeship system for the administration and supervision of such territories as may be placed thereunder by subsequent agreements; and

"WHEREAS under Article 77 of the said Charter the trusteeship system may be applied to territories now held under mandate; and

"WHEREAS on 17 December 1920 the Council of the League of Nations confirmed a mandate for the former German islands north of the equator to Japan, to be administered in accordance with Article 22 of the Covenant of the League of Nations; and

"WHEREAS Japan, as a result of the Second World War, has ceased to exercise any authority in these islands;

"Now, THEREFORE, the Security Council of the United Nations, having satisfied itself that the relevant articles of the Charter have been complied with, hereby resolves to approve the following terms of trusteeship for the Pacific Islands formerly under mandate to Japan:

"ARTICLE 1

"The Territory of the Pacific Islands, consisting of the islands formerly held by Japan under mandate in accordance with Article 22 of the Covenant of the League of Nations, is hereby designated as a strategic area and placed under the trusteeship system established in the Charter of the United Nations. The Territory of the Pacific Islands is hereinafter referred to as the trust territory."

Trusteeship Agreement for the former Japanese Mandated Islands, U.S. TIAS 1665; 61 Stat. 3301; 8 UNTS 189, 190. See also S. Rept. 471, 80th Cong., 1st sess; H. Rept. 889, 80th Cong., 1st sess.; H. Doc. 378, 80th Cong., 1st sess.; and, *ante*, § 35, "Legal Nature of Mandates": Belligerency, pp. 671 ff.

Japanese consent

The Treaty of Peace with Japan, signed at San Francisco September 8, 1951, contains the following provision:

"Article 2

.   .   .   .

"(d) Japan renounces all right, title and claim in connection with the League of Nations Mandate System, and accepts the action of the United Nations Security Council of April 2, 1947, extending the trusteeship system to the Pacific Islands formerly under mandate to Japan."

U.S. TIAS 2490; 3 UST 3169, 3172; 136 UNTS 45, 48–50. By a Convention between the United States and Japan, signed February 11, 1922, the United States had consented (in article I) "to the administration by Japan, pursuant to the aforesaid Mandate, of all the former German Islands in the Pacific Ocean, lying north of the Equator." (U.S. TS 664; 42 Stat. 2149, 2150; III Redmond, Treaties, etc. (1923) 2723, 2725.)

"That the obligation of a mandatory under Article 22 and the mandate instrument are not dependent on continuance of the membership of such mandatory in the League of Nations has been demonstrated in the case of Japan. On March 27, 1935, Article 22 as part of the Covenant defining obligations of membership ceased to bind Japan; but Article 22, as incorporated by reference in the mandate for the former German possessions in the North Pacific Ocean, continued to have and receive binding legal effect. The League asserted and Japan recognized the continuing jurisdiction of the Permanent Mandates Commission, as an agent of the League Council, to receive and consider Japan's annual reports under paragraph 7 of Article 22 of the Covenant and Article 6 of the mandate instrument. These positions were taken notwithstanding any existing theoretical uncertainties as to the location of 'sovereignty', and notwithstanding the very practical difference that upon Japan's withdrawal the participation of Japan as a Member of the Council in reviewing reports and in designating the members of the Commission automatically terminated. See League of Nations *Official Journal*, Permanent Mandates Commission (28th sess., 1935), 125, 183–184."

Written Statement of the United States of America, *International Status of South-West Africa*, Pleadings, Oral Arguments, Documents, p. 30 (I.C.J. 1950). Information as to the administration of the Mandate by Japan may be found in the final League of Nations study, *The Mandates System, Origin—Principles—Application* (1945.VI.A.1), especially pp. 24, 58, 105–108, and Wright, *Mandates under the League of Nations* (1930). See also volumes I and II, *United States Naval Administration of the Trust Territory of the Pacific Islands;* and *United States Army in World War II: The War in the Pacific: The Approach to the Philippines* (1953) 457–461; *ibid., Seizure of the Gilberts and the Marshalls* (1955) 206–209; *ibid., Campaign in the Marianas* (1960) 53–55. On March 27, 1935, Japan ceased to be a member of the League of Nations.

The texts of the Preamble and of article 1 of the Trusteeship Agreement for the former Japanese Mandated Islands, set forth *ante*, pp. 773–774, are identical with the texts in the United States proposal. *Draft Trusteeship Agreement for the Japanese Mandated Islands, With Article by Article Explanatory Comments* (Department of State publication 2784, 1947), pp. 3, 4; U.S. Delegation Doc. US/S/119, pp. 1–2.

The United States comment on draft article 1 stated:

"The entire Territory of the Pacific Islands is designated as strategic under the provisions of Article 82 of the Charter in order to enable the United States to safeguard its own national security and at the same time to discharge its obligations for general security under the United Nations. The importance of these requirements was clearly shown in the last war.

"It should be noted, of course, that the geographical extent of the trust territory is based upon the mandate formerly held by Japan. The three archipelagos in the trust territory include 98 islands and island clusters, with a total land area of 846 square miles inhabited by 48,297 natives. This agreement applies only to the Japanese Mandated Islands and does not apply to any islands under Japanese sovereignty for which the United States may become responsible."

Draft Trusteeship Agreement for the Japanese Mandated Islands, op. cit., pp. 3–4; U.S. Delegation Doc. US/S/119, p. 1.

"First of all, I would like to remind the committee that the Trust Territory of the Pacific Islands is a strategic area and I would like to read to the committee, begging their indulgence, the wording of Article 83 of the Charter: 'All functions of the United Nations relating to strategic areas, including the approval of the terms of the trusteeship agreements and of their alteration or amendment, shall be exercised by the Security Council.' — Strategic area

"The only reply that I would make to the substance of what the Soviet delegate said about the Pacific Trust Territory is to suggest to the members that if they are interested in the facts that they examine for themselves the report of the Visiting Mission to the Pacific Trust Territory last year, which included among its membership as the distinguished chairman the representative of Bolivia, Ambassador Salamanca, and our distinguished colleague from India, Mr. Rasgotra, that they look first of all at that report and then they look at the report to the Security Council of the Trusteeship Council covering the facts as the Trusteeship Council saw them and including a number of recommendations. And the great bulk of that report was unanimous again and again; the only abstaining vote or the only adverse vote in voting on the paragraphs came from the Soviet Union.

. . . .

"He [the Soviet representative] implied that the United States had been opposed to and had objected to discussion of the conditions in the Pacific Trust Territory in the Security Council. That is not so. We have never objected to discussion of the matters of that territory in the Security Council and we do not today object. We are prepared to discuss those matters in the Security Council at any time."

Statements by Jonathan B. Bingham, Alternate United States Representative, in the Fourth Committee, United Nations General Assembly, U.S.-U.N. press release No. 3789, Oct. 9, 1961.

Nuclear tests

"The Trusteeship Agreement in its very first Article sets up the strategic area and the Security Council has accepted the United States' use of the area for test purposes from the very beginning—which is now six times.

"I would like to add here that it is not a question of the Security Council giving the United States this right. They did not give us this right, rather they recognized this right which was incorporated into the very first Article of the Trusteeship Agreement itself—and no one has tried to amend it since."

Statement by Mason Sears, United States Representative in the Trusteeship Council, June 26, 1958, U.S.-U.N. press release No. 2949. See also article 13, *post*, pp. 825 ff., as to nuclear tests.

U.S. designated administering authority

Article 2 of the Trusteeship Agreement for the Trust Territory of the Pacific Islands reads:

"Article 2

"The United States of America is designated as the administering authority of the trust territory."

U.S. TIAS 1665; 61 Stat. 3301; 8 UNTS 189, 190.

The United States comment on draft article 2 stated:

"Although the United States has not been the mandatory power responsible for these islands, the United States was primarily responsible for their liberation, is presently responsible for their administration, and considers them essential to the security of this country and to the maintenance of international peace and security. For these reasons this Government considers that the United States should be designated as the sole administering authority. Such a designation is in accord with action recently taken by the General Assembly with respect to the several trusteeship agreements, wherein in each case a single Member of the United Nations is designated as the administering authority."

Draft Trusteeship Agreement for the Japanese Mandated Islands, op. cit., p. 4; U.S. Delegation Doc. US/S/119, p. 2.

Article 3 of the Trusteeship Agreement for the Trust Territory of the Pacific Islands reads:

"The administering authority shall have full powers of administration, legislation, and jurisdiction over the territory subject to the provisions of this agreement, and may apply to the trust territory, subject to any modifications which the administering authority may consider desirable, such of the laws of the United States as it may deem appropriate to local conditions and requirements." Full U.S. authority

U.S. TIAS 1665; 61 Stat. 3301, 3302; 8 UNTS 189, 192.

The language of article 3 which the United States originally proposed included the phrase, "as an integral part of the United States," after the phrase "subject to the provisions of this agreement," with the following comment: "Integral part"

"This article is similar to the relevant provision of Article XXII of the Covenant of the League of Nations and of the terms of the original 'C' Mandates, as well as to corresponding articles in the trusteeship agreements recently approved by the General Assembly. The words 'as an integral part' of the United States are carried over from the original mandate to Japan, and appear in other trusteeship agreements approved by the General Assembly. The phrase does not, of course, imply sovereignty over the territory."

Draft Trusteeship Agreement for the Japanese Mandated Islands, op. cit., pp. 4–5; U.S. Delegation Doc. US/S/119, p. 2.

In the negotiation of the trusteeship agreement in the United Nations Security Council, the United States Representative, Senator Warren R. Austin, accepted the amendment proposed by the Representative of the Union of Soviet Socialist Republics to delete the words "as an integral part of the United States." In this connection the United States Representative made the following statement:

> ". . . In employing the phrase 'as an integral part of the United States,' in article 3, my Government used the language of the original mandate and also the language used in six of the agreements recently approved by the General Assembly. It does not mean the extension of United States sovereignty over the territory, but in fact it means precisely the opposite.
>
> "There has, however, been some misunderstanding on this point and, for the sake of clarity, the United States Government is prepared to accept the amendment suggested by the Soviet Union, and to delete that phrase. In agreeing to this modification, my Government feels that for record purposes it should affirm that its authority in the trust territory is not to be considered as in any way lessened thereby. My Government feels that it has a duty towards the peoples of the trust territory to govern them with no less consideration than it would govern any part of its sovereign territory. It feels that the laws, customs and institutions of the United States form a basis for the administration of the trust territory compatible with the spirit of the Charter. For administrative, legislative and jurisdictional convenience in carrying out its duty towards the peoples of the trust territory, the United States intends to treat the trust territory as if it were an integral part of the United States. . . ."

U.N. Security Council Off. Rec., 116th Meeting, Mar. 7, 1947, p. 473.

U.S. law applicable

The Trusteeship Agreement, having been approved by the President pursuant to authorization of the Congress (Joint Resolution of July 18, 1947; 61 Stat. 397, 3301; 48 U.S.C. § 1681 note), is part of the law of the United States.

In *Pauling* v. *McElroy*, 164 F. Supp. 390 (D.D.C. 1958); affirmed, 278 F.2d 252 (D.C. Cir. 1960); certiorari denied, 364 U.S. 835 (1960), Judge Keech of the United States District Court stated, at page 393:

> "The provisions of . . . the Trusteeship Agreement for the Trust Territory of the Pacific Islands . . . relied on by plaintiffs are not self-executing and do not vest any of the plaintiffs with individual legal rights which they may assert in this Court. . . ."

By the Act of June 30, 1954 (68 Stat. 330; 48 U.S.C. § 1681), Congress has authorized continuance of civil government of the Trust Territory until Congress shall further provide for its government. See discussion of article 12, *post*, for detailed statement as to this legislation, and of article 6, *post*, as to the Code of the Trust Territory, including a basic "Bill of Rights", promulgated by the High Commissioner of the Trust Territory. See discussion of article 14, *post*, as to the application of treaties of the United States. As to articles 6, 12, and 14, see *post*, pp. 790–791, 822–823, and 830–834.

The following United States laws apply by their own force to the Trust Territory:

1. *Coast Guard*

The Act of June 22, 1951, 65 Stat. 89, 14 U.S.C. § 81, extended the authority of the Coast Guard to establish, maintain, and operate aids to navigation to include the Trust Territory of the Pacific Islands.

2. *Coconut Oil—Exemption from Processing Tax*

The Act of August 16, 1954, 68A Stat. 536–537, 26 U.S.C. § 4513, provides that the additional domestic processing tax (26 U.S.C. § 4511(b)) shall not apply to coconut oil which is "wholly the production of . . . the Territory of the Pacific Islands" or "was produced wholly from materials the growth or production of . . . the Trust Territory. . . ." (See discussion of article 9, *post*, for text of Decision of September 8, 1948, "Waiver in respect of the Trust Territory of the Pacific Islands," Contracting Parties to the General Agreement on Tariffs and Trade.)

3. *Courts*

The Act of June 4, 1958, 72 Stat. 178, 179, 48 U.S.C. § 1424b, provides:

> "The Chief Judge of the Ninth Judicial Circuit of the United States may assign . . . a judge of the High Court of the Trust Territory of the Pacific Islands . . . to serve temporarily as a judge in the District Court of Guam whenever it is made to appear that such an assignment is necessary for the proper dispatch of the business of the court."

4. *Authority of Secretary of Interior*

The Act of August 23, 1958, 72 Stat. 837, 5 U.S.C. § 485 note, extends the authority vested in the Secretary of the Interior "to perform surveys, investigations, and research in geology, biology, minerals and water resources, and mapping" to "include Antarctica and the Trust Territory of the Pacific Islands."

5. *Narcotics Control*

The Narcotics Control Act of 1956, 70 Stat. 572, 18 U.S.C. § 1401, provides that for the purposes of that law the term "United States" shall include, *inter alia*, "the Trust Territory of the Pacific."

6. *Narcotics Tax*

The Act of August 16, 1954, 68A Stat. 557, 26 U.S.C. § 4731(h), amends the Internal Revenue Code so that with respect to the tax imposed on dealers in, and importers, manufacturers and producers of, narcotic drugs, "the word 'territory' shall include the Trust Territory of the Pacific Islands". Further, it provides, 68A Stat. 558, 26

U.S.C. § 4735(a), that in the Trust Territory "the collection of the special tax imposed by section 4721 [of Title 26], and the issuance of the order forms specified in section 4705 [of Title 26] shall be performed by the appropriate internal revenue officers" of the Government of the Trust Territory, "and all revenues collected thereunder in . . . the Trust Territory of the Pacific Islands shall accrue intact" to that government. It also provides that "The highest court of original jurisdiction of the Trust Territory of the Pacific Islands shall possess and exercise jurisdiction in all cases arising in such Territory under sections 4701 to 4707, inclusive, and sections 4721 to 4726, inclusive [Title 26]."

The House Report on H.R. 5257, the bill on which the Act of August 16, 1954, *supra*, was based, states:

> "The Committee on Ways and Means, to whom was referred the bill (H. R. 5257) to extend to the Trust Territory of the Pacific Islands certain provisions of the Internal Revenue Code relating to narcotics, having considered the same, report favorably thereon without amendment and recommend that the bill do pass.

> "PURPOSE

> "H. R. 5257 makes applicable to the Trust Territory of the Pacific Islands the sections of the Internal Revenue Code which are derived from the Harrison Antinarcotic Act, enacted in 1914. The legislation is required to provide for the orderly supply of narcotic drugs for medical purposes in the trust territory.

> "GENERAL STATEMENT

> "The need for this legislation has arisen from the transfer of the administrative responsibility for the government of the trust territory to the Department of the Interior, pursuant to Executive Order No. 10265 on June 29, 1951. Prior to that date, the trust territory was the administrative responsibility of the Department of the Navy and narcotic requirements were met through Navy supplies. Since the transfer of control to the Department of the Interior, it has become necessary to devise a system of procuring narcotics through civilian channels. The problem of procurement is complicated by the fact that of the two relevant Federal statutes one is applicable, while the other is not.

> "The Narcotic Drugs Import and Export Act (21 U. S. C., 1946 ed., sec. 171 et seq.) applies generally to the United States and 'any territory under its control or jurisdiction,' and it therefore is applicable to the trust territory, over which the United States has 'full powers of administration, legislation, and jurisdiction' pursuant to article 3 of the trusteeship agreement approved by the President on July 18, 1947, by authority of the act of July 18, 1947 (61 Stat. 397). The Narcotic Drugs Import and Export Act makes it unlawful to import into the United States or territory under its control or jurisdiction any narcotic drug,

except for such amounts of crude opium and coca leaves as the Commissioner of Narcotics finds to be necessary for medical or legitimate uses. This exception, however, is not of practical value to the trust territory, since it does not extend to manufactured drugs.

"On the other hand, the provisions of the Internal Revenue Code which are derived from the Harrison Antinarcotic Act (26 U. S. C., 1946 ed., secs. 2550–2565, 3220–3228) apply only to the continental United States, its Territories and possessions (26 U. S. C., 1946 ed., sec. 2563). They therefore do not apply to the trust territory, which is not a territory or possession of the United States. The Harrison Act established a system for the internal control of narcotics, requiring the registration with the appropriate collector of internal revenue of those who have a legitimate reason for dealing in narcotics, the purchase of narcotics only on approved order forms or by means of a certificate of exemption, and the payment of certain taxes incident to the purchase and handling of narcotic drugs.

"Because the Narcotic Drugs Import and Export Act applies, the trust territory cannot import from foreign sources the narcotic drugs which it requires. Since the Harrison Act provisions do not apply, there is no system for the internal control of narcotic drugs, and the usual method by which purchases are made in the continental United States cannot be employed in the trust territory. Trust territory doctors cannot register with a collector of internal revenue, secure official order forms, or pay the narcotic taxes, and as a consequence they cannot procure narcotic drugs through regular commercial channels. It is therefore of the greatest importance that section 2563 of the Internal Revenue Code, which sets forth the extent of territorial application of the Harrison Act provisions, be amended to include the Trust Territory of the Pacific Islands. This will be accomplished by your committee's bill.

"In addition, H. R. 5257 amends subsection (a) of section 2564 of the Internal Revenue Code to add the trust territory to those areas in which local administration and enforcement of the Harrison Act provisions are authorized. Such local administration and enforcement by the government of Puerto Rico has proved singularly successful. If local administration and enforcement are authorized for the trust territory, a system can be devised which will be somewhat simpler and far more expeditious than the Federal scheme, yet wholly adequate to meet the trust territory's requirements.

"CONCLUSION

"In view of the urgent need for providing a system of control of narcotics for medical purposes in the trust territory, your committee unanimously recommend prompt enactment of this bill."
"Extending Certain Narcotic Drug Provisions to Trust Territory of the Pacific Islands", H. Rept. 858, 83d Cong., 1st sess., pp. 1–3.

7. *Federal Aviation Act*

Section 1110 of the Federal Aviation Act of 1958, 72 Stat. 731, 800, 49 U.S.C. § 1510 provides: "Whenever the President determines that such action would be in the national interest, he may, to the extent, in the manner, and for such periods of time as he may consider necessary, extend the application of this Act to any areas of land or water outside of the United States and the overlying airspace thereof in which the Federal Government of the United States, under international treaty, agreement or other lawful arrangement has the necessary legal authority to take such action." By Executive Order No. 10854, Nov. 30, 1959, 24 *Fed. Reg.* 9565, the President extended the application of this Act "to those areas of land or water outside the United States and the overlying airspace thereof over or in which the Federal Government of the United States, under international treaty, agreement or other lawful arrangement, has appropriate jurisdiction or control: . . ." See article 8, *post*, pp. 809–810, as to air transit rights in the Trust Territory, and article 14, *post*, pp. 830–834, as to application of international treaties.

8. *Industrial Property*

Trademark law

The Act of July 5, 1946, 60 Stat. 427, 443, 15 U.S.C. § 1051, provides (section 45): "The United States includes and embraces all territory which is under its jurisdiction and control." This seems broad enough to include the Trust Territory, over which the United States has "full powers of administration, legislation and jurisdiction" by virtue of article 3 of the Trusteeship Agreement. U.S. TIAS 1665; 61 Stat. 3301, 3302; 8 UNTS 189, 192.

Patent law

The Patent Act, Act of July 19, 1952, 66 Stat. 792, 797, 35 U.S.C. § 100, defines the United States as "the United States of America, its territories and possessions". This language would not seem broad enough to include the Trust Territory.

"It is probable that the patent laws of the United States [35 U.S.C.] do not govern [the Trust Territory of the Pacific Islands]. The Code [T.T.C.] provides that in the absence of any other applicable section, those laws of the United States are in effect, which, by their own force, shall apply. [T.T.C., Section 20(b).] This is interpreted as meaning those acts in which Congress expressly or impliedly has included the Trust Territory. Examples of these would be the Narcotics Control Act [18 U.S.C., Section 1401] and parts of the Internal Revenue Code [26 U.S.C., Section 4731(h), Section 4735, and Section 4513].

"Moreover the Patent Act of the United States by its very terms applies by its own force only in the United States and its territories. [35 U.S.C., Section 100(c).] 'Territory' is so defined as to include Puerto Rico, Canal Zone, the Virgin Islands, and the insular possessions of the United States. [15 U.S.C., Section

77(b).] These insular possessions include Samoa and Swains Islands. [48 U.S.C.] Hence, the Trust Territory is not considered a territory or an insular possession of the United States. The inhabitants are considered citizens of the Trust Territory [T.T.C., Section 660] and not United States nationals. The Code defines 'citizens of the Trust Territory' to include citizens by birth [T.T.C., Section 660] and citizens by naturalization. [T.T.C., Section 668.] An immigration quota into the United States is imposed upon the Trust Territory, which is thus treated similarly, at least in our immigration laws, as a foreign country. [8 U.S.C.] For these reasons—admittedly not finally conclusive—it may be argued that the Patent Act of the United States by its own force does not apply to the Trust Territory.

"It would appear that no patent law is currently applicable in the Territory. The Office of the High Commissioner states that this absence of patent emphasis is due to the nature of the Territory's economy. [Letter dated 28 October 1959 from the Acting Deputy High Commissioner in response to a query.] This economy is based primarily upon subsistence agriculture and fishing. Supplemental cash income is provided through the making of copra, harvesting of trochus, government employment, the sale of handicraft, sale of farm produce, and through other miscellaneous activities. [11th Annual Report to the United Nations on the Administration of the Trust Territory of the Pacific Islands, July 1, 1957 to June 30, 1958, Department of State Publication 6798, page 49.] In view of the terms of the Trusteeship Agreement under which the United States has agreed among other things to promote the economic advancement of the inhabitants by encouraging the development of fisheries, agriculture, and industries [Trusteeship Agreement for the former Japanese Mandated Islands, which entered into force on July 18, 1947, Article 6, Section 2], the need for a patent system may arise.

"A patent system would require provisions for the granting of Letters Patent by the sovereign and the enforcement of the rights granted by the patentee. The High Commissioner, by Executive Order, may promulgate additional laws to the existing regulations. [T.T.C., Section 28.] Hence the Patent Act of the United States could be made applicable to the Trust Territory by the High Commissioner. Since a non-resident alien is always free to obtain a United States patent [35 U.S.C., Section 111], the effect of an Executive Order of the High Commissioner would be to extend the rights of a holder of a United States patent to the Trust Territory of the Pacific Islands. It is conceivable that should commerce and industry increase in the Trust Territory of the Pacific Islands, the High Commissioner will adopt the United States patent laws.

"Should the United States patent laws be applied to the Trust Territory, the question of enforcement of the patentee's rights would arise. Under the Patent Act, a patentee shall have remedy by civil action for infringement of his patent. [35 U.S.C., Section 281.] The Code of the Trust Territory provides that the

Trial Division of the High Court shall have original jurisdiction to try all causes, civil and criminal. [T.T.C., Section 123.] This Trial Division of the High Court consists of the Chief Justice and the Associate Justice appointed by the Secretary of the Interior. [T.T.C., Section 120.] Decisions of the Trial Division of the High Court are reviewable by the Appellate Division of the High Court, the court of last resort. [T.T.C., Section 124.] The Appellate Division consists of three temporary Judges appointed by the Secretary of the Interior. [T.T.C., Section 122.] Thus a judicial system now exists in the Trust Territory which could try patent causes."

Chovanes, "Patents, Trademarks and Copyrights in the Trust Territory of the Pacific Islands", 42 J. Pat. Off. Soc'y (Apr. 1960) 254, 257–259.

9. Merchant Marine Academy

By the Act of September 14, 1961, 75 Stat. 514, the Secretary of Commerce is authorized to permit, upon designation of the Secretary of the Interior, "not to exceed four persons at a time from the Trust Territory of the Pacific Islands to receive instruction in the United States Merchant Marine Cadet Corps and at the United States Merchant Marine Academy at Kings Point, New York," who "shall receive the same pay, allowances, and emoluments . . ." and "shall be subject to the same rules and regulations governing admission, attendance, discipline, resignation, discharge, dismissal, and graduation as cadets at the Merchant Marine Academy appointed from the United States; . . ."

Federal
Tort
Claims Act

". . . Despite the powers undertaken by the United States pursuant to the trust agreement, for purposes of the Federal Tort Claims Act, 28 U.S.C.A. § 2680(k), it cannot follow that Kwajalein became part of the United States. It remained a foreign country. In United States v. Spelar, 338 U.S. 217, 70 S.Ct. 10, 11, 94 L. Ed. 3, it was said that 'the coverage of the Federal Tort Claims Act was geared to the sovereignty of the United States.' And the reason for this, as Spelar points out, was because under the Act the *lex delicti* was applicable and consequently, if 'foreign countries' were to be included, it would lead 'to a good deal of difficulty.' Although the nature of this 'difficulty,' which was recognized in the legislative history of the Act, was not particularized we think it reasonable to infer that Congress foresaw that a United States court might find it difficult to ascertain and apply the local law in regions not under the sovereignty of the United States—especially in regions where the local law had not crystallized through established legislative or judicial definition or where its content was subject to change by administrative authority. In United States v. Spelar an American air base in Newfoundland was held to be a foreign country for purposes of the Federal Tort Claims Act.

"The question presented on this appeal as to what is a foreign territory under the Federal Tort Claims Act, is thus not a new one. Indeed the question was well discussed by Judge Ryan in 1948 in Brunell v. United States, D.C.S.D.N.Y., 77 F.Supp. 68. That case involved the status of Saipan, under the act in question. Judge Ryan made a careful review of the authorities and concluded that Saipan was a foreign country.

". . . Whatever administration is exercised by the United States Government is solely and wholly in the capacity of a trustee designated by the United Nations. Whether the United Nations may be responsible for the acts of its trustee is not before us. Nor, indeed, is the United States being sued as a trustee. On the contrary, it is sued in its status as a sovereign—i.e., a sovereign of its own territorial components, i.e., the forty-eight States of the Union and the territories concerning which the United States has the power to enact laws. It makes no laws as a sovereign for the Island of Kwajalein. From a letter attached to the affidavit of counsel for the plaintiffs which he received from the Director of the United States Department of the Interior, it appears

'that any law of negligence which may be in force on Kwajalein is contained in the local common law or the British common law as it existed before July 4, 1776.'

Certainly such is not the law of the United States, for there is no general common law within the federal jurisdiction. See Erie R. Co. v. Tompkins, 304 U.S. 64, 58 S.Ct. 817, 82 L.Ed. 1188."

Opinion of Judge Galston, *Callas* v. *United States*, 253 F.2d 838, 840 (2d Cir. 1958) ; certiorari denied, 357 U.S. 936 (1958). Judge Ryan, in the *Brunell* case mentioned above, quoted from a letter dated December 16, 1947, to Tom C. Clark, Attorney General of the United States, from Ernest A. Gross, Legal Adviser, Department of State. This letter stated, in part:

"In further answer to your inquiry and to that made by the United States Attorney, no treaty of cession has been signed ceding Saipan to the United States, and no Federal legislation has been enacted incorporating Saipan into the United States. A Trusteeship Agreement with respect to the former Japanese mandated islands, including Saipan, between the United States as administering authority and the Security Council of the United Nations, came into force on July 18, 1947. The United States does not have sovereignty over Saipan by virtue of this Agreement. The Agreement does not provide for a termination date.

"Accordingly, it is concluded that Saipan has not been and is not a part of the United States, nor a territory or possession of the United States. * * *" MS. Department of State, file 411.11 Brunell, Beverly/12–147.

Circuit Judge Hincks, concurring in the above-quoted decision, stated:

"I fully concur in Judge Galston's opinion but also place reliance on additional considerations. As was recognized in Cobb v. United States, 9 Cir., 191 F.2d 604, whether the Pacific Islands are a 'foreign country' within the meaning of the Federal Tort Claims Act is a question of considerable difficulty. But whether the problem is reached by the common-sense approach advocated by Judge Pope in his concurring opinion in the Cobb case (which strongly appeals to me) or by the more legalistic approach of the majority opinion, the result here is the same. For if Okinawa was properly classified as a 'foreign country' notwithstanding the unlimited power of the United States which had occupied and thereafter (until the date of the Cobb decision) maintained absolute control of the island by force of arms, *a fortiori* is Kwajalein a foreign country. For the comparable power which the United States had acquired over Kwajalein was voluntarily translated into a fiduciary responsibility to the United Nations which carried specified accountability to its Security Council through an express trust agreement, 61 Stat. 3301, approved by the Joint Resolution of Congress of July 18, 1947, c. 271, 61 Stat. 397, Historical Note to § 1435 of Title 48 U.S.C.A."

Callas v. *United States, op. cit.*, 841. *Cf.* dissenting opinion of Judge Lumbard, who expressed the view at pages 843–844 that "Kwajalein is not now a 'foreign country' as Congress used the term in the Federal Tort Claims Act . . ." for the following reasons:

"In the international law sense, Kwajalein and related islands hold a unique position. A coral atoll and site of a United States naval station, Kwajalein is part of the Marshall Islands, this island group being one of the six districts of the Trust Territory of the Pacific Islands. [See generally, Report of the Special Subcommittee on Territorial and Insular Affairs of the Committee on Interior and Insular Affairs, Trust Territory of the Pacific Islands, 83d Cong., 2d Sess. (1955).] The territory is controlled by the United States by virtue of a Trusteeship Agreement with the United Nations, allowing in practical effect the exercise of full sovereign power by the United States although a residual sovereignty remains in the territory, divisions thereof, or the United Nations. See 1 Oppenheim, International Law 236 (8th Ed. 1955) for the latter view. In common with all trust territories, termination of the trust requires the consent of the administering authority as well as the consent of the United Nations. Moreover, this territory is the only area designated as a strategic trust, a designation which results in the United States being responsible to the Security Council rather that [than] the General Assembly for administration of the trust, permits preferential treatment of the United States in economic and commercial matters, and allows this country unilaterally to declare all or any part of the islands a closed area within which the United States may determine the extent to which trustee functions shall be exercised and from which it may bar anyone, including the United Nations.

"The area is administered from a headquarters on Guam, a territory of the United States, and for the most part through the Department of the Interior. A system of courts has been established, applying local law and law which this country has introduced through codes, orders, and Congressional legislation. The local law apparently pertains primarily to property rights and criminal acts, and personal injury law, at least to the extent that United States citizens are involved, apparently would be based upon an incorporation of United States concepts in the absence of developed indigenous law. This is apparently what the Director of the Office of Territories of the Department of the Interior had in mind in his letter, referred to by Judge Galston, when he stated that the law of the trust territory included '* * * the common law of England and all statutes of Parliament in and thereof in force and effect on July 3, 1776, as interpreted by American courts.'

"The Charter of the United Nations and the Trusteeship Agreement impose binding legal obligations upon this country to promote self-government and other enumerated objectives. It is clear, however, that political development in the territory is elementary and that it will be a considerable time before the trust obligations are fulfilled and the trust terminated. Although the purpose of the trust is to prepare for independence, the furtherance of that purpose will require administration by the United States for an indefinite period in the future."

See discussion of article 9, *post*, pp. 814 ff., as to the Tariff Act, and discussion of article 11, *post*, pp. 819 ff., as to the Immigration and Nationality Act.

Cf., Pauling v. *McElroy*, 164 F. Supp. 390 (D.D.C. 1958); affirmed, 278 F.2d 252 (D.C.Cir. 1960); certiorari denied, 364 U.S. 835 (1960); wherein Judge Keech of the United States District Court said, at p. 393: "It is doubtful that this Court has jurisdiction under 28 U.S.C. § 1350 [alien's action for tort] of the claim asserted by the residents of the Marshall Islands who are plaintiffs in Civil Action No. 1566–58, and no other provision of law gives this Court jurisdiction of such claim".

"War damage claims

"23. A number of claims for compensation for war damage suffered by the inhabitants of the Trust Territory have concerned the Council since 1950 and have been the subject of recommendations both by the Council itself and by each Visiting Mission. At its twenty-sixth session, the Council expressed concern that no settlement had yet been reached concerning the war damage claims of Micronesians against the Government of Japan. It reiterated its previous recommendations concerning the need for a prompt and definitive decision and hoped that the Governments of the Administering Authority and of Japan would make every effort to reach a speedy decision.

. . . .

"28. At its twenty-seventh session, the Council adopted the following conclusion and recommendations:

"The Council, recalling its previous recommendations concerning the need for a prompt and definitive settlement of claims in respect of war damage suffered by the inhabitants of the Territory, notes with satisfaction the statement of the Administering Authority to the Visiting Mission that it recognizes its obligation to ensure that every effort is made to deal promptly and equitably with such claims and its assurance that the problem is receiving the highest priority. The Council endorses the views of the Visiting Mission that payment of compensation should be made without further delay and that, except in respect of cases of acute individual hardship in which claims can be clearly determined on the basis of evidence, the amount of compensation should be determined on a territory-wide basis and disbursed to the maximum benefit of the people as a whole." Report of the Trusteeship Council to the Security Council on the Trust Territory of the Pacific Islands covering the period from 1 July 1960 to 19 July 1961, U.N. Doc. S/4890, July 27, 1961, pp. 8–10.

Negotiations in the matter with Japan are continuing.

"Sec. 22. Common law applicable; exceptions. The rules of the common law, as expressed in the restatements of the law·approved by the American Law Institute, and to the extent not so expressed, | Common law applicable

as generally understood and applied in the United States, shall be the rules of decision in the courts of the Trust Territory in cases to which they apply, in the absence of written law applicable under Section 20 hereof or local customary law applicable under Section 21 hereof to the contrary and except as otherwise provided in Section 24 [Land Law not affected] hereof; Provided, That no person shall be subject to criminal prosecution except under the written law of the Trust Territory or recognized local customary law not inconsistent therewith. (As amended by Executive Order 76 dated May 11, 1959.)"

Code of the Trust Territory of the Pacific Islands, as amended, ch. 2, sec. 22.

U.S. obligations

Article 4 of the Trusteeship Agreement for the former Japanese Mandated Islands reads:

"The administering authority, in discharging the obligations of trusteeship in the trust territory, shall act in accordance with the Charter of the United Nations, and the provisions of this agreement, and shall, as specified in Article 83 (2) of the Charter, apply the objectives of the international trusteeship system, as set forth in Article 76 of the Charter, to the people of the trust territory."

U.S. TIAS 1665; 61 Stat. 3301, 3302; 8 UNTS 189, 192.

The text of article 4 is the same as that submitted to the United Nations Security Council by the United States Representative. The following comment accompanied the United States draft text:

"This article explicitly places the United States under obligation to apply the objectives of the international trusteeship system to the people of the trust territory. Since these objectives were designed primarily for the protection and benefit of the inhabitants this undertaking on the part of the United States is of fundamental importance. In articles 5, 6, 7 and 8 the draft agreement outlines the specific measures by which the United States proposes to implement these objectives." *Draft Trusteeship Agreement for the Japanese Mandated Islands, op. cit.,* p. 5; U.S. Delegation Doc. US/S/119, p. 2.

Article 5 of the Trusteeship Agreement for the former Japanese Mandated Islands provides:

Military measures

"In discharging its obligations under Article 76 (a) and Article 84, of the Charter, the administering authority shall ensure that the trust territory shall play its part, in accordance with the Charter of the United Nations, in the maintenance of international peace and security. To this end the administering authority shall be entitled:

"1. to establish naval, military and air bases and to erect fortifications in the trust territory;

"2. to station and employ armed forces in the territory; and

"3. to make use of volunteer forces, facilities and assistance from the trust territory in carrying out the obligations towards the

Security Council undertaken in this regard by the administering authority, as well as for the local defense and the maintenance of law and order within the trust territory."

U.S. TIAS 1665; 61 Stat. 3301, 3302; 8 UNTS 189, 192.

The text of article 5 is the same as that proposed by the United States. The comment which accompanied the United States draft text of article 5 stated:

"This article specifies the military measures which the United States may take in the trust territory to assist in the maintenance of international peace and security and to safeguard the security of the United States.

"Similar provisions are contained in the trusteeship agreements approved by the General Assembly.

"Since, according to Article 84 of the Charter, it is the duty of the administering authority to ensure that the trust territory shall play its part in the maintenance of international peace and security, this article has been designed to list some of the powers necessary to fulfill that obligation and any obligation assumed under Article 43 of the Charter."

Draft Trusteeship Agreement for the Japanese Mandated Islands, op. cit., pp. 5–6; U.S. Delegation Doc. US/S/119, p. 3. *Cf.* article 4, Mandate for the German Possessions in the Pacific Ocean Lying North of the Equator, U.N. Doc. A/70: "The military training of the natives, otherwise than for purposes of internal police and the local defense of the territory, shall be prohibited. Furthermore, no military or naval bases shall be established or fortifications erected in the territory."

In presenting the United States draft trusteeship agreement to the United Nations Security Council, Senator Warren R. Austin, the United States Representative, made the following statements pertaining to article 5:

"In conformity with the provisions of the Charter for strategic areas, the trust territory will contain bases. Many atolls in the territory have potential value as base sites or as anchorages. Few such sites, however, are being developed and maintained at present.

"The United States will administer this strategic trust territory in accordance with the provisions of the Charter. In particular, the United States will administer the territory in accordance with the obligations contained in article 2, paragraph 4, and according to which 'All members shall refrain in their international relations from the threat or use of force against the territorial integrity or political independence of any state, or in any other manner inconsistent with the purposes of the United Nations.'

"The United States, as administering authority, will insure that this trust territory shall play its part in the maintenance of international peace and security, in accordance with its obligation, under article 1 of the Charter—'. . . to take effective collective measures for the prevention and removal of threats to the peace and for the suppression of acts of aggression or other breaches of the peace. . . .' Its administration will also be in accordance with Article 84 of the Charter, relating to the part to be played by trust territories 'in carrying out the obligations towards the Security Council' of the administering authority.

"The United States, therefore, intends to include this trust territory as fully as those territories under its sovereignty in the special agreement or agreements it will conclude with the Security Council for the provision of the United Nations with armed forces, assistance and facilities, including rights of passage, necessary for the purpose of maintaining international peace and security as envisaged under Article 43 of the Charter.

"Pending conclusion of these permanent agreements under Article 43, the United States will undertake that these islands play their part in whatever action the United States may be called upon to take in accordance with the obligations imposed by article 106 relating to transitional security arrangements."

U.N. Security Council Off. Rec., 113th Meeting, Feb. 2, 1947, pp. 410–411. Article 5 was adopted unanimously in the Security Council without comment. U.N. Security Council Off. Rec., 124th Meeting, Apr. 2, 1947, p. 659.

Article 6 of the Trusteeship Agreement for the former Japanese Mandated Islands reads:

"In discharging its obligations under Article 76(b) of the Charter, the administering authority shall:

Political development

"1. foster the development of such political institutions as are suited to the trust territory and shall promote the development of the inhabitants of the trust territory toward self-government or independence, as may be appropriate to the particular circumstances of the trust territory and its peoples and the freely expressed wishes of the peoples concerned; and to this end shall give to the inhabitants of the trust territory a progressively increasing share in the administrative services in the territory; shall develop their participation in government; shall give due recognition to the customs of the inhabitants in providing a system of law for the territory; and shall take other appropriate measures toward these ends;

Economic advancement

"2. promote the economic advancement and self-sufficiency of the inhabitants, and to this end shall regulate the use of natural resources; encourage the development of fisheries, agriculture, and industries; protect the inhabitants against the loss of their lands and resources; and improve the means of transportation and communication;

Social advancement

"3. promote the social advancement of the inhabitants, and to this end shall protect the rights and fundamental freedoms of all elements of the population without discrimination; protect the health of the inhabitants; control the traffic in arms and ammunition, opium and other dangerous drugs, and alcohol and other spirituous beverages; and institute such other regulations as may be necessary to protect the inhabitants against social abuses; and

"4. promote the educational advancement of the inhabitants, **Educational** and to this end shall take steps toward the establishment of a **advancement** general system of elementary education; facilitate the vocational and cultural advancement of the population; and shall encourage qualified students to pursue higher education, including training on the professional level."

U.S. TIAS 1665; 61 Stat. 3301, 3302–3303; 8 UNTS 189, 192–194.

The text of article 6 is the same as that proposed by the United States except for the first paragraph. The text of article 6, paragraph 1, as proposed by the United States provided:

"1. foster the development of such political institutions as are suited to the trust territory and shall promote the development of the inhabitants of the trust territory toward self-government, and to this end shall give to the inhabitants of the trust territory a progressively increasing share in the administrative services in the territory; shall develop their participation in local government; shall give due recognition to the customs of the inhabitants in providing a system of law for the territory; and shall take other appropriate measures toward these ends".

Draft Trusteeship Agreement for the Japanese Mandated Islands, op. cit., p. 6; U.S. Delegation Doc. US/S/119, p. 3.

The comment accompanying the United States proposed text for article 6 stated:

"These provisions elaborate the general objectives of article 76 (b) of the Charter and constitute a considerable advance over the terms of the original mandate.

"This article refers to the development of the people of the territory as being directed specifically toward 'self-government' rather than 'Self-government or independence' incorporated in article 76 (b) of the Charter. This article is not a prior judgment of the ultimate status of the trust territory, but merely reflects its sparse, highly scattered population, its relatively underdeveloped, indigenous central government, and its lack of economic resources."

Draft Trusteeship Agreement for the Japanese Mandated Islands, op. cit., p. 7; U.S. Delegation Doc. US/S/119, p. 4.

The word "local" was deleted on motion of the United States Representative at the 124th meeting of the Security Council, at the suggestion of the Representative of India who observed that "in certain countries 'local government' means 'municipal government', and that surely would not be what the United States representative intended." U.N. Security Council Off. Rec., 124th Meeting, Apr. 2, 1947, pp. 660–661.

The United States proposal for article 6 was amended to include **"Independ-** the language, "or independence, as may be appropriate to the par- **ence"** ticular circumstances of the trust territory and its peoples and the freely expressed wishes of the peoples concerned". This additional language was included after extensive discussion in the Security Council, prompted by the proposal of the Representative of the U.S.S.R. to insert the words "or independence" after the words "towards self-government." In the 116th meeting of the Security Council, Senator Warren R. Austin, the United States Representative stated:

> "Now, we come to the second Soviet amendment, which consists in inserting the words *or independence* in article 6 after the words 'towards self-government'.

> "The United States is going to accept this principle, but it wants to place on record its views on this matter and to have the principle properly safeguarded by certain additional language. . . .

. . . .

> "Now, the proposed amendment would make this read as follows:

>> " '1. Foster the development of such political institutions as are suited to the trust territory and shall promote the development of the inhabitants of the trust territory toward self-government or independence . . .'

> "Instead of merely adding the words, 'or independence' the deviation which the United States would like to suggest is the addition of the following words: *or independence, as may be appropriate to the particular circumstances of the trust territory and its people.*

> "In accepting article 6 as modified in order to include the objective of independence of the trust territory, the United States feels that it must record its opposition, not to the principle of independence, to which no people could be more consecrated than the people of the United States, but to the idea that in this case independence could possibly be achieved in the foreseeable future. To be free and independent, a community of people must have acquired at least some of the attributes of a sovereign State. Until this community of persons becomes an integrated community, capable of undisputed and exclusive control over all persons and things within the trust territory, and can regulate its internal affairs independently and give a sufficient guarantee of stability, this area must continue to be maintained by an outside Power capable of providing for its needs and interests.

> "In the present instance, the trust territory covers a vast area, comprising numerous islands with a sparse, primitive population. The inhabitants are scattered and diverse. They have many different customs and languages. Communication between the islands is difficult. Because of their weakness, the inhabitants have been unable to provide for their own protection against unscrupulous individuals from outside the area. Except possibly for the larger islands, such as Saipan, the basic economy is but

little above subsistence level, and cannot be expected to support a society capable of exercising the minimum rights and duties of an independent state. Therefore, it appears that for such an area, independence can be but remote and entirely unforeseeable at the present time.

"Therefore, the United States makes a qualified acceptance of the language, but accepts the principle of the second Soviet amendment."

U.N. Security Council Off. Rec., 116th Meeting, Mar. 7, 1947, pp. 473–475.

At the 124th meeting of the Security Council, when the final text of article 6 was approved, the following discussion took place:

"The PRESIDENT: There is a proposal of the Union of Soviet Socialist Republics to add, after the words 'towards self-government' in article 6, the words *or independence*. The United States representative has indicated his willingness to accept this addition, but modified to read 'or independence *as may be appropriate to the particular circumstances of the Trust Territory and its peoples*'.

"I think I will put the United States modification to the vote first.

"Mr. GROMYKO (Union of Soviet Socialist Republics). (*translated from Russian*): I have no objections to the inclusion of an additional phrase in the text of article 6, after the words 'or independence' proposed by me. That additional phrase is in accordance with Article 76 of the Charter. It does not however fully express the sense of Article 76. I therefore wish to propose an amendment to this United States amendment, whereby the corresponding Article of the Charter, Article 76, will be most adequately reflected in this amended text of article 6 of the agreement. The members of the Council will shortly receive the Soviet amendment to the United States amendment. Inasmuch as this addition is entirely in agreement with the terms of Article 76 of the Charter, I wish to express the hope that Mr. Austin will agree to accept this amendment. I have already said that I have no objections to the text proposed by the representative of the United States.

"The PRESIDENT: May I ask the United States representative if this suggested addition by the Soviet Union representative is agreeable to him?

"Mr. AUSTIN (United States of America): I accept the suggested amendment.

"The PRESIDENT: Then I will ask the Council to vote on article 6 as originally amended by the Soviet Union, then further amended by the United States, and finally amended again by the representative of the Soviet Union."

U.N. Security Council Off. Rec., 124th Meeting, Apr. 2, 1947, p. 660. Article 6, as thus amended, was unanimously adopted. *Ibid.*, p. 662.

"257. At the twenty-seventh session, the Representative of the Administering Authority informed the Council that the Administering Authority considered that the essential elements of the resolution on the granting of independence to colonial countries and peoples were applicable to the Trust Territory. The Administering Authority had always insisted upon the view which was stated in operative paragraph 2 of this resolution that all peoples have the right to self-determination and that by virtue of that right they freely determine their political status and freely pursue their economic, social and cultural development. The Administering Authority was taking immediate and continuing steps to stimulate the political development of the Territory in the direction of increased self-government, with a view to giving to the people of the Territory free choice with respect to their political future. It thus considered that its policy with regard to the Trust Territory of the Pacific Islands was entirely consistent with the main policy recommendations for action contained in resolution 1514 (XV). Accordingly, the Administering Authority welcomed discussion in this Council of the political development of the Territory and encouraged this discussion in the context of the principles and criteria set forth in resolution 1514 (XV) and in the relevant Articles of the Charter of the United Nations.

"258. At its twenty-seventh session, the Council adopted the following conclusions and recommendation:

. . . .

"*The Council also notes the statement of the Administering Authority that 'the essential elements' of General Assembly resolution 1514 (XV) on the granting of independence to colonial countries and peoples are applicable to the Trust Territory of the Pacific Islands.*

"*The Council considers that it is necessary to establish realistic target dates reflecting a proper sense of urgency for the rapid and planned advance of the Territory in all aspects of its political life; and invites the Administering Authority to establish such targets in the light of the Charter of the United Nations, the Trusteeship Agreement and General Assembly resolution 1514 (XV).*"

Report of the Trusteeship Council to the Security Council (1961), *op. cit.*, pp. 72, 73.

"I would now, with your permission, like to say a word on the subject that was raised the other day by the representative of the Soviet Union and which then became a topic of discussion briefly in this Council, and that is the application to this Territory of General Assembly resolution 1514 (XV). I think it is generally understood that in adopting this resolution the Assembly intended that its principles should have universal application. The members of this Council should know that the United States Government considers that the essential elements of this resolution on the granting of independence to colonial countries and peoples are applicable to the Trust Territory. We have always insisted upon the view which is stated as follows in operative paragraph 2 of this resolution:

" '2. All peoples have the right to self-determination; by virtue of that right they freely determine their political status and freely pursue their economic, social and cultural development.'

"As will appear in more detail from the opening statement of our Special Representative, my Government is taking immediate and continuing steps to stimulate the political development of the Territory in the direction of increased self-government, with a view to giving to the people of the Territory free choice with respect to their political future. My Government thus considers that its policy with regard to the Trust Territory of the Pacific Islands is entirely consistent with the main policy recommendations for action contained in resolution 1514 (XV). Accordingly, we welcome discussion in this Council of the political development of the Territory and encourage this discussion in the context of the principles and criteria set forth in resolution 1514 and in the relevant Articles of the Charter of the United Nations."

Statement of the United States Representative, Jonathan Bingham, in the 1147th meeting of the Trusteeship Council, June 13, 1961, U.N. Doc. T/PV.1147, p. 7.

"The question posed by the representative of the Soviet Union is one of interpretation of language, particularly the language of paragraph 5 of the declaration on the granting of independence to colonial countries and peoples. I do not feel that the statement which I made on 13 June is in any way in conflict with that paragraph, nor was it intended to detract from that paragraph as a general statement of principle which my Government is prepared to accept in terms of its general application to the Territory. We do not make any distinction in this respect between the terms 'self-government' and 'independence'.

"As I pointed out on previous occasions, the term 'independence' is one which can take a number of forms. The basic question here is one of self-determination—a choice by the people themselves as to their political future. That is what I was referring to when I said that it was our policy to stimulate that development with a view to giving to the people of the Territory free choice regarding their political future. That free choice would, of course, make independence possible in any one of various forms.

"Concerning the further interpretation of paragraph 5, it is the view of my Government that this paragraph, in referring to immediate steps, means steps which must be taken in a certain direction—not steps which must be taken on any given date to complete the process referred to.

"I think this is all I can add to the statement which was made on 13 June."

Statement of the United States Representative, Mr. Bingham, in the 1149th meeting of the Trusteeship Council, June 15, 1961, U.N. Doc. T/PV.1149, pp. 43–45.

"In accordance with our belief in the principle of self-determination, and in accordance with Resolution 1514, I am glad to advise this Assembly that the United States is proceeding to consult with the appropriate elected councils in Guam, in American Samoa, and in the Virgin Islands, as to what steps might be taken in each territory, in the light of its own particular conditions, to determine the wishes of its people regarding their political future. (We are also doing the same in the Trust Territory of the Pacific Islands, but that territory is the concern of the Security Council.)"

Statement by Jonathan Bingham, Alternate United States Representative, in the United Nations General Assembly, U.S.-U.N. press release No. 3851, Nov. 22, 1961.

System of law

"*Sec. 20. Laws applicable in the Trust Territory.* The following are declared to be in full force and to have the effect of law in the Trust Territory of the Pacific Islands, hereinafter referred to in the laws and regulations as 'Trust Territory': (a) the Trusteeship Agreement; (b) such laws of the United States, as shall, by their own force, be in effect in the Trust Territory, including Executive Orders of the President; (c) these laws and regulations of the Government of the Trust Territory and amendments thereto; (d) District Orders promulgated by the District Administrators of the Trust Territory either with the approval of the High Commissioner or in accordance with Section 29; (e) the acts of legislative bodies convened under charter from the High Commissioner when these acts are approved by the High Commissioner or otherwise confirmed as law as may be provided by charter or the laws and regulations of the Trust Territory; and (f) duly enacted Municipal Ordinances. (As amended by Executive Order No. 55, dated March 27, 1956, and Executive Order No. 60, dated Oct. 10, 1956.)

" *Sec. 21. Local Customs.* The customs of the inhabitants of the Trust Territory not in conflict with the laws of the Trust Territory or the laws of the United States in effect in the Trust Territory shall be preserved. The recognized customary law of the various parts of the Trust Territory in matters in which it is applicable, as determined by the courts, shall have the full force and effect of law, so far as such customary law is not in conflict with the laws mentioned in Section 20.

"*Sec. 22. Common law applicable; exceptions.* The rules of the common law, as expressed in the restatements of the law approved by the American Law Institute, and to the extent not so expressed, as generally understood and applied in the United States, shall be the rules of decision in the courts of the Trust Territory in cases to which they apply, in the absence of written law applicable under Section 20 hereof or local customary law applicable under Section 21 hereof to the contrary and except as otherwise provided in Section 24 hereof; Provided, That no person shall be subject to criminal prosecution except under the written law of the Trust Territory or recognized local customary law not inconsistent therewith. (As amended by Executive Order 76 dated May 11, 1959.)

"*Sec. 23. Spanish, German, and Japanese laws repealed.* All laws, regulations, orders and ordinances heretofore enacted, issued, made or promulgated by Spanish, German or Japanese authority which are still in force in the Trust Territory or any part thereof, are hereby repealed, except as provided in Section 24 hereof: Provided, however, that nothing herein shall change the effect of local custom which may have been included within the scope of laws, regulations, orders, or ordinances enacted, issued, made or promulgated as aforesaid.

"*Sec. 24. Land Law not affected.* The law concerning ownership, use, inheritance, and transfer of land in effect in any part of the Trust Territory on December 1, 1941, shall remain in full force and effect except insofar as it has been or may hereafter be changed by express written enactment made under the authority of the Trust Territory of the Pacific Islands."

Code of the Trust Territory of the Pacific Islands, as amended. Promulgated by Executive Order No. 32, High Commissioner of the Trust Territory of the Pacific Islands, Dec. 22, 1952. See discussion of article 3, *ante*, as to United States laws applicable by their own force to the Trust Territory; article 12, *post*, as to legislation and Executive orders implementing the Trusteeship Agreement; and discussion of article 14, *post*, as to United States treaties applicable to the Trust Territory. For articles 3, 12, and 14, see pp. 777, 822, and 830 of this chapter.

Chapter 1 of the *Code of the Trust Territory of the Pacific Islands*, as amended, consists of a "Bill of Rights", reading as follows:

"*Sec. 1. Freedom of religion, conscience, speech, press, rights of assembly and petition.* No law shall be enacted in the Trust Territory respecting an establishment of religion or prohibiting the free exercise thereof, or abridging the freedom of conscience, or of speech, or of the press, or the right of the people to form associations and peaceably to assemble and to petition the government for a redress of grievances. No public money shall ever be appropriated, supplied, donated, or used, directly or indirectly, for the use, benefit, or support of any sect, church, denomination, sectarian institution or association, or system of religion, or for the use, benefit, or support of any priest, preacher, minister, or other religious teacher or dignitary as such. [Bill of Rights]

"*Sec. 2. Slavery and involuntary servitude.* Neither slavery nor involuntary servitude, except as a punishment for crime whereof the party shall have been duly convicted, shall exist in the Trust Territory.

"*Sec. 3. Protection against unreasonable search and seizure.* The rights of the people to be secure in their persons, houses, papers, and effects, against unreasonable searches and seizures, shall not be violated, and no warrants shall issue but upon probable cause, supported by oath or affirmation, and particularly describing the place to be searched and the persons or things to be seized.

"*Sec. 4. No deprivation of life, liberty, or property without due process.* No person shall be deprived of life, liberty, or property, without due process of law; nor shall private property be taken for public use, without just compensation; nor shall any person be subject for the same offense to be twice put in jeopardy of life or limb; nor shall any person be compelled in any criminal case to be a witness against himself. In all criminal prosecutions the accused shall enjoy the right to a speedy and public trial; to be informed of the nature and cause of accusation; to be confronted with the witnesses against him; to have compulsory process for obtaining witnesses in his favor, and to have the assistance of counsel for his defense. No crime under the laws of the Trust Territory shall be punishable by death.

"*Sec. 5. No ex post facto law.* No bill of attainder, ex post facto law, or law impairing the obligations of contracts, shall be enacted.

"*Sec. 6. Excessive bail, excessive fines, cruel and unusual punishments prohibited.* Excessive bail shall not be required, nor excessive fines imposed, nor cruel and unusual punishments inflicted.

"*Sec. 7. No discrimination on account of race, sex, language or religion.* No law shall be enacted in the Trust Territory which discriminates against any person on account of race, sex, language, or religion; nor shall the equal protection of the laws be denied.

"*Sec. 8. Freedom of migration and movement.* Subject only to the requirements of public order and security, the inhabitants of the Trust Territory shall be accorded freedom of migration and movement within the Trust Territory.

"*Sec. 9. Education.* Free elementary education shall be provided throughout the Trust Territory.

"*Sec. 10. No imprisonment for failure to discharge contractual obligation.* No person shall be imprisoned solely for failure to discharge a contractual obligation.

"*Sec. 11. Writ of habeas corpus.* The privilege of the writ of habeas corpus shall not be suspended, unless, when in cases of rebellion or invasion or imminent danger thereof, the public safety shall require it.

"*Sec. 12. Quartering of soldiers.* No soldier shall, in time of peace, be quartered in any house without the consent of the owner, nor in time of war but in a manner to be prescribed by law.

"*Sec. 13. Trade and property rights protected.* The High Commissioner may restrict or forbid the acquisition of interests in real property and in business enterprises by persons who are not citizens of the Trust Territory.

"*Sec. 14. Local customs recognized.* Due recognition shall be given to local customs in providing a system of law, and nothing in this Chapter shall be construed to limit or invalidate any part of the existing customary law, except as otherwise determined by the High Commissioner.

Ibid., ch. 1.

"255. At its twenty-sixth session, the Council noted the con- Organic
sistent progress reported by the Administering Authority in the legislation
achievement of intermediate targets and dates in the political and
other fields, and hoped that no effort would be spared to enact
organic legislation which would fully reflect the needs and
interests of the people of the Territory.

.   .   .   .

"258. At its twenty-seventh session, the Council adopted the
following conclusions and recommendation:

*"The Council notes the progress achieved in the various fields of
development and that work on the preparation of organic legislation is continuing. It notes further that the Administering
Authority has fixed a date, which it hopes to advance, for the
establishment of a Territorial Legislature. The Council requests
the Administering Authority to inform it, at its next session, of
any steps taken in that direction."*

Report of the Trusteeship Council to the Security Council on the Trust
Territory of the Pacific Islands covering the period from 1 July 1960 to
19 July 1961, U.N. Doc. S/4890, July 22, 1961, pp. 72, 73. For bills providing
organic legislation for the Trust Territory, see H.R. 5381, 83d Cong., 1st
sess.; H.R. 7427 and S. 2992, 82d Cong., 2d sess.; H.R. 9278, 87th Cong.,
1st sess. Provisions for appeal to the U.S. Court of Appeals, Ninth Circuit,
from the highest court, Trust Territory of the Pacific Islands, are found in
these bills.

General economy

"124. The economic system of the Territory rests on subsistence Economic
agriculture and fishing, with cash income being provided from advancement
the making of copra, the harvesting of trochus, the sale of handicrafts, fish and vegetables, and employment in Government and
in private business.

"125. At its twenty-sixth session, the Council expressed the
hope that the results of a proposed comprehensive survey of the
economic potentialities of the Territory would be submitted to the
Council as soon as possible and that in its preparation for this
survey, the Administering Authority would draw upon the best
experience available including, where appropriate, the specialized
agencies of the United Nations and other international bodies.
It also urged the Administering Authority to continue its policy
of introducing new crops into the Territory and of developing
its available resources with a view to achieving at least a measure
of economic self-sufficiency as soon as possible."

Report of the Trusteeship Council, *op. cit.*, p. 38. "133. As in previous
years, funds derived from local taxation and revenues during fiscal year
1960 fell far short of meeting the Territory's expenditures. Total expenditures during the year under review, including typhoon damage costs,
amounted to $8,224,897 compared with $8,169,303 in 1959, of which $1,407,148
and $1,825,083, respectively, were derived from local revenue collections.
It is estimated that during fiscal year 1961, expenditures will amount to
$7,875,000 with revenues totalling $1,350,000 leaving a deficit of approxi-

mately $6.5 million to be made up by the Administering Authority." *Ibid.,* p. 42.

U.N. recommendations

"132. At its twenty-seventh session, the Council adopted the following conclusions and recommendations:

"The Council, noting the views of the Visiting Mission concerning the economy of the Territory, considers that a concentrated effort to develop the Territory's economic potential is called for in the next few years. It endorses in general the recommendations of the Visiting Mission, in particular (1) that machinery for Territory-wide economic planning should be set up under the direction of an Economic Development Officer, with which representatives of the people would be closely associated; (2) that a long-term plan with well-defined priorities and stages for the entire Territory should be prepared; (3) that substantial contributions should be made by the Administering Authority for economic development, which might be paid into a separate development fund; (4) that funds for economic development should be made available on a long-term basis rather than annually and that the development budget should be separate from the current revenue and expenditure budget; (5) that greater facilities for savings and the mobilization of internal capital for development purposes should be provided, particularly through co-operatives; and (6) that more Micronesians should be given vocational and technical training in various fields including practical training abroad in such fields as tropical agriculture.

"The Council notes with satisfaction the assurance of the Special Representative that the detailed recommendations of the Visiting Mission concerning economic development will receive the careful attention of the Administering Authority and that action has already been taken on a number of recommendations of the Mission. It welcomes his statement (1) that the time has now come for an intensification of the Administering Authority's efforts in the economic field; (2) that the economic staff is being strengthened and that an Economic Development Officer will be appointed; (3) that the Administering Authority hopes to increase materially the resources which can be used for an economic development fund; and (4) that the Administering Authority will give careful attention to see what further funds can be made available for accelerating the much-needed economic progress of the Territory.

"The Council draws the Administering Authority's special attention to the Visiting Mission's observation that the Territory has an impressive potential for a tourist industry, that limited facilities for tourism already exist and that on the basis of these an experimental beginning might be made to find out where expansion could be brought about to the maximum advantage."

Ibid., pp. 40–41.

"THE REQUEST OF THE UNITED STATES FOR A WAIVER IN RE-
SPECT OF PREFERENTIAL TREATMENT FOR THE TRUST TERRI-
TORY OF THE PACIFIC ISLANDS

"Report adopted by the CONTRACTING PARTIES *on 8 September
1948*

"(GATT/CP.2/36)

"According to its terms of reference, the working party has considered the request of the United States for a waiver in respect of
preferential treatment for the Trust Territory of the Pacific
Islands on the basis of the information submitted by the United
States representative. After a detailed discussion in which the
members of the working party and a certain number of observers
expressed their views as regards the legal and economic implications of the request of the United States, the working party
reached the following conclusions:

"1. It is appropriate for the CONTRACTING PARTIES to consider
the request under Article XXV of the General Agreement on
Tariffs and Trade. There is no other provision of the General
Agreement under which that request could be examined.

"2. The working party examined whether the request of the
United States was based on the existence of 'exceptional circumstances'. It came to the conclusion that such exceptional circumstances existed as indicated in the following paragraphs.

"3. The islands of the Trust Territory were accorded preferential treatment by Japan so long as they remained under Japanese
mandate, and such preferential treatment would be eliminated
with the inauguration of the United States administration. If
the waiver requested were granted to the United States, the
islands would remain in a position similar to that existing before
the inauguration of the United States administration and would
enjoy the same privileges comparable to those enjoyed by other
Trust Territories which, in accordance with the exceptions provided for in Article I of the General Agreement, receive preferential treatment for their imports into the territories of the
respective administering authorities.

Exports:
preferential
treatment

"4. Also, unlike the situation prevailing under Japanese mandate, the Administering Authority would not enjoy any preference for their imports into the Trust Territory of the Pacific
Islands.

"5. Moreover, the working party considered that the exodus of
the 70,000 Japanese who were mainly employed in the sugar,
alcohol and dried bonito industries of the islands would probably
lead to the practical disappearance of those industries and that
the transformation undergone by the economy of the islands
would justify certain exceptional measures in order to enable the
administering authority to fulfil its obligations in accordance
with Article 6, paragraph 2, of the Trusteeship Agreement for the
former Japanese mandated islands.

"6. The working party was of the opinion that the production figures and export possibilities of the islands were so unimportant that, under the conditions expected to exist, the granting of the waiver would not be likely to cause substantial injury to the trade of the other contracting parties.

"The export values of the five main export commodities of the islands amounted to about 11 million dollars in 1936, but sugar exports, which accounted for more than half of those export values, are not likely to be continued and the phosphate exports are expected to terminate by 1951, on account of the depletion of resources. The copra exports ranged from ten to fifteen thousand tons during the 1930s, but it is unlikely that future production will exceed a yearly average of 10,000 tons. This estimated production would correspond to about 5 per cent of the total United States imports of copra.

"Most of the products are now admitted duty-free, and the system of sugar import quotas allocated by areas now in force in the United States would not allow an increase in the imports of sugar originating in the islands. While the reduction by 2 cents per pound in the tax on the processing of coconut oil from copra will improve the income derived by the islands from copra exports, it is not expected that it will bring about a substantial increase in the total volume of such exports, which have to compete with the more efficient production of the Philippines.

"It was, however, understood that if the underlying economic factors on which the decision of the CONTRACTING PARTIES would be based were modified so as to cause or threaten substantial injury to the trade of contracting parties, the decision to be taken at this session could be reconsidered by the CONTRACTING PARTIES. . . ."

Basic Instruments and Selected Documents, vol. II, General Agreement on Tariffs and Trade (1952), pp. 173, 174. This preferential treatment was agreed to, at the request of the United States, by the Contracting Parties to the General Agreement on Tariffs and Trade, by the Decision of September 8, 1948. See discussion *post*, pp. 815–816, for text of the Decision.

"166. The value of exports during the year under review totalled $1,891,300, an increase of some $650,000 over the previous year. Copra remained the most valuable commodity of export, 10,717 short tons being exported at a value of $1,587,767. This represented a production increase of some 1,300 short tons which is attributed to better transportation service and the higher price. Production of trochus for export increased by approximately 100,000 lbs. to 636,201 lbs. although its value decreased by some $26,000 to $148,366 owing to a drop in price. The value of vegetables exported mainly from Saipan and Rota, rose from $60,000 to $104,988 while the value of handicrafts exported rose significantly from $13,000 to $20,711."

Report of the Trusteeship Council to the Security Council on the Trust Territory of the Pacific Islands covering the period from 1 July 1960 to 19 July 1961, U.N. Doc. S/4890, p. 49.

Copra (*i.e.*, dried coconut meat from which coconut oil is processed), Copra the principal commercial product of the Trust Territory, is on the "free list" under the United States tariff law, and thus may be imported into the United States exempt from customs duty. Paragraph 1727, Tariff Act of 1930, 46 Stat. 590, 679; 19 U.S.C. § 1201, paragraph 1727. In addition, copra produced in the Trust Territory has been exempted from the additional United States domestic processing tax.

Act of August 16, 1954, 68A Stat. 536–537; 26 U.S.C. § 4513. See article 3, *ante*, p. 777 and article 9, *post*, p. 812.

". . . There is also a heavy duty on Micronesian handicrafts imported into the United States and this is a severe handicap on what might be a profitable market. A Micronesian economic fair held in Guam in 1960, in which Trust Territory handicrafts were displayed, has created a demand for them. During the same year handicrafts Handicrafts valued at some $20,000.00 were exported from the Territory." U.N. Doc. T/1560, May 26, 1961, p. 40. In the discussion of this problem in the Trusteeship Council, the Representative of New Zealand, Mr. Edmonds, stated: ". . . From history and from current data, it seems unlikely that the Trust Territory can hope to rise very much above the subsistence level unless its economy is also linked much more closely with that of a larger, wealthier country. Once this economy was Japan's; now it most logically should be that of the United States, a country which has always been most careful to respect the rights and opinions of the Micronesians and protect them from mere exploitation. While such matters have to be approached with due caution, they also call for the exercise of imagination and for long-range planning which should now be regarded as urgent. If special provision is required to ensure a market in the United States for certain Micronesian products, the necessary steps should be taken."

U.N. Trusteeship Council Off. Rec., 1152d Meeting, June 21, 1961, pp. 18–19.

"The islands of the Trust Territory are located in the Western Land Pacific Ocean north of the Equator. Here some 96 island units lie scattered over an oceanic area larger than the continent of Australia or the continental United States of America. The 96 island units, variously small islands or atolls, have, however, a land area of only 687 square miles. Of the islands, only 64 are regularly inhabited."

Trust Territory of the Pacific Islands 1960, 13th Annual Report to the United Nations (Department of State publication 7183, 1961), p. 1.

"A. (2) Population of the Trust Territory for years ending June 30, 1956, through June 30, 1960

Year	Population	Year	Population
1956	65, 039	1959	73, 052
1957	67, 199	1960	75, 836"
1958	70, 594		

Ibid., p. 179. Thus, there has been a steady increase in the population. In 1947, when the United States offered to place this territory under trusteeship, the native population was estimated at 48,297. *Draft Trusteeship Agreement for the Japanese Mandated Islands, op. cit.*, p. 4. *Cf.* League of Nations, *The Mandates System, Origin—Principles—Application* (1945. VI.A. 1), according to which the native population increased from 48,505 in 1920 to 50,868 in 1938 (p. 106). "The Mandates Commission has continuously concerned itself with the stagnation of the native population of this Territory—in some of the mandated Islands (particularly the Island of Yap) there has been an actual *decrease*. It has repeatedly drawn the attention of the Council and of the mandatory Power to this state of affairs." [See the Commission's reports on its fifth session (1924), fourteenth session (1928), nineteenth session (1930), twenty-first session (1931), twenty-fourth session (1933), twenty-eighth session (1935); thirtieth session (1936), thirty-third session (1937), and thirty-fifth session (1938).] *Ibid.*, p. 108.

"183. At its twenty-seventh session, the Council adopted the following conclusions and recommendations:

"*The Council, noting the observations of the Visiting Mission, recommends that full information concerning all public domain land, including plans for its future use, should be made available to the people. It also recommends that all private claims against public domain land should be settled with the utmost speed.*

"*The Council notes the intention of the Administering Authority to appoint a separate Land and Claims Administrator and hopes that he will be provided with the necessary trained staff so that the homestead programme can be accelerated. It hopes that in returning public land to the people under the homestead programme, the Administering Authority will keep in mind the growing needs of the Territory and the desirability of applying, as pointed out by the Visiting Mission, a consistent land policy better adapted to the changing economic needs of its people.*

"*The Council, recalling its resolution 2063 (XXVI) concerning land claims in Kwajelein and Majuro Atolls, notes that active negotiations are now being conducted looking to a mutually agreeable and satisfactory settlement of the problem and hopes that such a settlement will soon be reached. In this connexion, it endorses the suggestion of the Visiting Mission that, if a satisfactory solution is not arrived at in the very near future, the amount of compensation and the manner in which such compensation is to be paid should be determined by arbitration.*"

Report of the Trusteeship Council to the Security Council on the Trust Territory of the Pacific Islands covering the period from 1 July 1960 to 19 July 1961, U.N. Doc. S/4890, July 27, 1961, pp. 52–53.

These recommendations were based on the following findings of fact:

"174. Customary forms of land tenure, which vary from place to place, prevail throughout the Territory. A handbook on customary land tenure was published in 1959 which is designed to serve as a preliminary guide for use of administrative and judicial personnel.

"175. Land holdings by non-indigenous persons are small and date from previous administrations. Such alienation is now prohibited under the Trust Territory Code.

"176. Previous administrations claimed as public domain all land not then in actual use by the inhabitants and in addition acquired title to other lands. The title to this land now rests with the present administration [government of the Trust Territory]. In recent years there have been a number of private claims against public domain land, as a result of which land has been returned to the former indigenous owners. Since 1957 some 1,700 acres of public domain lands in Palau have been returned in this way. In each district there is a Land Advisory Board, the membership of which includes at least two Micronesians. The function of these boards is to advise the High Commissioner regarding the use and development of public lands, including its use for homesteading.

"177. Under the government's homesteading programme, public domain land has been made available for individual farms to Micronesians who do not have land and need it. Activity in this field is of major significance only in Palau, Ponape, Rota and Saipan districts, since these are the only districts where sizeable areas of public domain are to be found.

"178. The Visiting Mission felt that the Administration should endeavour to apply a consistent policy calculated to produce a pattern of land holdings better adapted to the economic needs of the people. These needs could be met either by the establishment of land-holding co-operatives or by the individualization of land tenure. The Mission noted that the latter formed the basis of the homesteading programme, but felt that experiments could be made with the former system. It also suggested that experiments might be made in the operation of plantations, using wage labour.

"179. With regard to land classified as public domain, the Mission noted that a number of private claims against such land remained unsettled. It felt that the necessary staff should be provided urgently to investigate these claims which should be settled expeditiously. The Mission also felt that a feeling it had observed among the people that the government had decided to keep for its own use all land designated as public domain, should be dispelled and, to this end, it recommended the circulation of a detailed statement describing such land, as defined by the Trust Territory Code. The Mission also felt it was essential that all public domain land should be brought under cultivation with the utmost speed. In this connexion, the Mission considered that the homestead programme, which was a good one, needed to be strengthened and speeded up in every possible way.

"180. In connexion with the Kwajelein land question, the Mission regretted that no negotiations had yet taken place between the parties concerned as called for by the Trusteeship Council's resolution, 2063 (XXVI), on the matter. The failure to settle this and similar claims concerning the peoples' most precious commodity was causing discontent and seemed to be generating undesirable political overtones. The Mission believed therefore that these claims should be settled without delay. It further recommended that, should these cases not be settled in the very near future, the amount of compensation and the manner of its being paid should be determined by arbitration.

"181. In connexion with the recent transfer of the people living on the islands of Roi and Namur to another island, which was brought to the attention of the Visiting Mission, the Mission expressed the view that transfer of populations from one island to another, not desirable in itself, was particularly inadvisable without written orders from the appropriate authorities.

"182. At the twenty-seventh session, the Special Representative informed the Council that active negotiations were now being conducted in connexion with the Kwejalein [Kwajalein] land claims."

Ibid., pp. 51–52.

Educational advancement

"The legal provisions governing education in the Territory are set forth in chapter 8 of the Code of the Trust Territory of the Pacific Islands. The following are its principal provisions:

"(1) It provides for the establishment of a free public school system in which elementary schools are supported, maintained, and operated from revenues derived from the local Micronesian community; within limits of available funds the Code also provides for the establishment of intermediate (junior high school), secondary, professional, technical, and adult education.

"(2) It establishes a Department of Education and sets up as its administrative officer the Director of Education on the High Commissioner's staff, whose duty it is to supervise education in the Trust Territory, formulate and recommend educational policy to the High Commissioner, establish educational procedures, and insure their practical application.

"(3) It authorizes the establishment of a Board of Education in each district and each local community. Most districts have a District Board of Education, and one district has local community boards of education.

"(4) It describes the duties and responsibilities of the educational personnel in each district—the district educational administrator, the district superintendent of schools, school principals, and teachers.

"(5) It sets forth the conditions under which nonpublic schools can be established and operated.

"(6) It requires compulsory school attendance of all children between 8 and 14 years of age. Attendance requirements, however, are regulated and carried out by local authorities. It is recognized that compulsory formal schooling will not be effective until local authorities become convinced that the school as an educational institution meets some very real needs of the people. [Executive Order No. 88, September 18, 1961, of the High Commissioner for the Trust Territory of the Pacific Islands amended Section 577, Trust Territory Code, lowering the age requirement for school attendance to 7 and 13 years of age.]

.   .   .   .

"There are no institutions of higher education beyond senior secondary or high school level within the Trust Territory nor any other specialized formal school other than the School of Nursing and School for Dental Hygienists. The Administration did provide a rather extensive program of higher education during the year outside the Trust Territory through its scholarship program. Fifty-six students were receiving advanced education under various Trust Territory scholarships outside the Territory, and transportation for some half dozen other students was subsidized by the Administration from the scholarship fund. Seventeen scholarship students were at the University of Hawaii or other institutions in Hawaii. Twelve were at the Territorial College on Guam. Ten were medical students at the Central Medical School in Suva, Fiji. Three were studying in universities in the Philippines and four additional students departed in June to enroll for the opening term at the College of Agriculture. Two special degree scholarship students attended colleges in mainland United States. These students formed the vanguard of those which the Trust Territory Government hopes some day will replace Americans in all fields of administrative activity. The bulk of the present scholarships are for 2 years. There is also a special degree scholarship program. Six of the 1959–60 scholarship students fell in this category, and one additional special degree grant for 1960–61 was made during the year. These degree scholarships are in the fields of education, law, agriculture, public administration, fisheries, and food technology.

"Although the Territory does not have institutions of higher learning as such, specialized training is given at the schools that are conducted at regular intervals for such employees as sanitarians, public defenders, and public prosecutors. Preservice and inservice teacher training programs are conducted in each district by the district educational staffs. In addition a few teachers have attended the Territorial College on Guam for special teachers' sessions during the summer months. . . ."

530309 O–63—52

Trust Territory of the Pacific Islands 1960, 13th Annual Report to the United Nations (Department of State publication 7183, 1961), pp. 120, 139–140.

By the Act of September 14, 1961, the Secretary of Commerce is authorized to permit, upon designation of the Secretary of the Interior, four persons at a time from the Trust Territory of the Pacific Islands to receive instruction in the United States Merchant Marine Cadet Corps and at the United States Merchant Marine Academy at Kings Point, New York. These persons "shall receive the same pay, allowances, and emoluments, to be paid from the same appropriations, and subject to such exceptions as shall be jointly agreed upon by the Secretary of Commerce and the Secretary of the Interior, shall be subject to the same rules and regulations governing admission, attendance, discipline, resignation, discharge, dismissal, and graduation as cadets at the Merchant Marine Academy appointed from the United States; . . ." 75 Stat. 514.

By Public Law 87–541 (S. 2775), the Congress of the United States amended section 2 of the Act of June 30, 1954, providing for continuance of civil government in the Trust Territory of the Pacific Islands, 68 Stat. 330, by increasing the authorization for appropriations from $7,500,000 to $17,500,000. In signing the bill into law, President Kennedy stated (*inter alia*):

"We have a great and challenging responsibility for the development of the peoples and resources of the Trust Territory, and, by the passage of this legislation, the Congress has taken the first step toward providing the means whereby a new and vital phase of development may be instituted. This administration has recognized the fundamental changes that are taking place in the outlook of the people in this area, and we intend to meet this challenge with accelerated economic and social programs commensurate with the responsibilities of our stewardship.

"The accelerated program that is contemplated will place great emphasis upon education for, in our opinion, education is the key to all further progress—political, economic, and social. It is our hope that, with this authorization, funds will be made available to meet the urgent need for the immediate initiation of programs leading to striking improvement of education at all levels in the Trust Territory, upgrading education to a level comparable to the level which has been taken for granted in the United States for decades. At the same time, we intend to move forward as rapidly as possible and with the cooperation and the full participation of the citizens of the Trust Territory in all other areas requiring development.

"The people of the Trust Territory, I am sure, will mark this day as the beginning of a new era of progress for the Trust Territory and its inhabitants."

76 Stat. 171; White House press release, July 20, 1962, XLVII *Bulletin,* Department of State, No. 1207, Aug. 13, 1962, p. 272.

Article 7 of the Trusteeship Agreement for the former Japanese Mandated Islands provides: **Civil rights**

> "In discharging its obligations under Article 76 (c), of the Charter, the administering authority shall guarantee to the inhabitants of the trust territory freedom of conscience, and, subject only to the requirements of public order and security, freedom of speech, of the press, and of assembly; freedom of worship, and of religious teaching; and freedom of migration and movement."

U.S. TIAS 1665; 61 Stat. 3301, 3303; 8 UNTS 189, 194.

This text is the same as that originally proposed by the United States with the exception that, at the proposal of the United States Representative, the phrase "freedom of conscience" was moved forward so as not to be "subject to the requirement of public order and security." U.N. Security Council Off. Rec., 124th Meeting, Apr. 2, 1947, p. 662. For the "Bill of Rights" of the Trust Territory of the Pacific Islands, see *ante*, pp. 797–798.

The comment which accompanied the United States proposal for article 7 stated:

> "There were no comparable guaranties of freedom of speech, of the press, of assembly, and of migration and movement in the original mandate. The present article adds 'freedom of migration and movement' to the other freedoms referred to in the agreements approved by the General Assembly. The provision that these freedoms are subject not only to the requirements of public order, as in other trusteeship agreements, but also to the requirements of security, is considered necessary in view of the fact that the trust territory is a strategic area.
>
> "The right of petition is provided for in article 13 of this agreement."

Draft Trusteeship Agreement for the Japanese Mandated Islands, op. cit., p. 7; U.S. Delegation Doc. US/S/119, p. 4.

Article 8 of the Trusteeship Agreement for the former Japanese Mandated Islands reads: **"Most favored nation"**

> "1. In discharging its obligations under Article 76 (d) of the Charter, as defined by Article 83 (2) of the Charter, the administering authority, subject to the requirements of security, and the obligation to promote the advancement of the inhabitants, shall accord to nationals of each Member of the United Nations and to companies and associations organized in conformity with the laws of such Member, treatment in the trust territory no less favourable than that accorded therein to nationals, companies and associations of any other United Nation except the administering authority.
>
> "2. The administering authority shall ensure equal treatment to the Members of the United Nations and their nationals in the administration of justice.
>
> "3. Nothing in this Article shall be so construed as to accord traffic rights to aircraft flying into and out of the trust territory.

Such rights shall be subject to agreement between the administering authority and the state whose nationality such aircraft possesses.

"4. The administering authority may negotiate and conclude commercial and other treaties and agreements with Members of the United Nations and other states, designed to attain for the inhabitants of the trust territory treatment by the Members of the United Nations and other states no less favourable than that granted by them to the nationals of other states. The Security Council may recommend, or invite other organs of the United Nations to consider and recommend, what rights the inhabitants of the trust territory should acquire in consideration of the rights obtained by Members of the United Nations in the trust territory."

U.S. TIAS 1665; 61 Stat. 3301, 3303–3304; 8 UNTS 189, 194–196.

This article is the same as that contained in the draft trusteeship agreement submitted by the United States. The comment accompanying the United States proposal stated:

"1. The intent of this paragraph is to ensure the greatest freedom of international participation in the economy of the trust territory consistent with the basic prerequisite of ensuring that its role as a strategic area is not interfered with. Accordingly, it provides for most-favored-nation rather than national treatment in the territory for all Members of the United Nations.

"The United States does not intend to take advantage for its own benefit of such meager and almost non-existent resources and opportunities as may exist in these scattered and barren islands.

"The Charter makes a specific exception to the application of economic principles affecting Members of the United Nations when the area concerned is a strategic one. This exception is contained in article 83 (2) of the Charter of the United Nations which provides that the basic objectives of article 76 'shall be applicable to the *people* of each strategic area' rather than to the territory as a whole or to people in other territories. Article 76 (d) also provides that the objectives contained therein shall not prejudice 'the attainment of the foregoing objectives', including that of international peace and security. Since security is the overriding consideration in a strategic area, economic treatment is required which will be compatible with this objective.

"2. This provision is in accordance with article 76 (d) of the Charter and ensures equal treatment for the nationals of all members of the United Nations in the administration of justice.

"3. The purpose of this provision is to state explicitly what has already been accepted in international practice, namely, that air traffic rights which concern the picking up and discharge of passengers, mail, and cargo are subject to specific bilateral agreements. Thus, irrespective of what form of economic treatment for non-territorial interests might be provided in any trusteeship agreement, air traffic rights would remain subject to bilateral agreements. Air transit rights, on the other hand, are covered by the Chicago Convention on International Civil Aviation, a multilateral agreement.

"4. The intent of this paragraph is to protect the interests of the inhabitants of the trust territory in the economic treatment and other rights which they may obtain outside the trust territory. Since this agreement applies to a strategic area, the rights of other members of the United Nations in the territory are of a most-favored-nation character. The paragraph, therefore, provides that the United States may negotiate and conclude appropriate international agreements which will attain for the inhabitants of the trust territory most-favored-nation treatment by Members of the United Nations. In addition, it provides that the Security Council or, at its invitation, other organs of the United Nations may recommend what other rights the inhabitants of the trust territory should acquire in consideration of the rights obtained by members of the United Nations in the trust territory."

Draft Trusteeship Agreement for the Japanese Mandated Islands, op. cit., pp. 8–9; U.S. Delegation Doc. US/S/119, pp. 5–6. See discussion of article 6, *ante,* pp. 790 ff., additionally, as to the economy of the Trust Territory.

In the proceedings in the Security Council, the Representative of the United Kingdom proposed the omission of the last four words, "except the Administering Authority," from article 8, paragraph 1. The amendment was rejected by 6 votes against (Australia, Belgium, Brazil, Colombia, France, Syria), to 3 votes for (Poland, United Kingdom, U.S.S.R.), with 2 abstentions (China, United States). In response to the question of the Representative of the United Kingdom whether the phrase "without prejudice to security considerations" in article 83, paragraph 3, of the Charter would not be a "sufficient safeguard," the United States Representative answered in the negative and stated that

". . . [this provision] is not adequate in this particular case. Here we are concerned with a trusteeship, the purpose of which is security. There is no visible evidence at the present time that this proposal has any other purpose than security. The provision of the United States draft referred to is designed to ensure to all other Members of the United Nations the benefit of what is implied by the words 'most favoured nation' in the Trust Territory. This is true, notwithstanding the fact that Article 83, paragraph 2, provides that: 'The basic objectives set forth in Article 76 shall be applicable to the people of each strategic area.' That does not mean to the people generally; it specifies the people of the strategic areas.

. . . .

"I wish to state, and to have it recorded, that the United States Government has no intention, through this clause or any other clause, of taking advantage, for its own benefit and to the detriment of the inhabitants, of the meagre and almost non-existent resources and commercial opportunities that exist in these scattered and barren islands. The nature of this proposed clause is dictated by the fact that these islands are proposed as a strategic trusteeship area and by the obligation which the Administering Authority will assume under the Charter 'to further international peace and security' and to ensure that the Territory itself shall play its part in the maintenance of international peace and security.

"My Government would not have proposed the most favoured nation treatment for this prospective Trust Territory had it not believed that such a suggestion was in full accordance with the Charter.

"The proposal made by my Government is for the designation of the former Japanese mandated islands as a strategic area. In such an area the security objective must be an overriding consideration. Such a provision in a strategic area is justified, in the view of my Government, by Article 76 d and Article 83, paragraph 2, of the Charter, which I have already read. Article 76 d, it will be recalled, provides for equal treatment for all Members of the United Nations and their nationals 'without prejudice to the attainment of the foregoing objectives', one of which is the furtherance of international peace and security. Article 83, paragraph 2, provides for the manner in which Article 76 shall be carried out in a strategic area by stating that the provisions of Article 76 shall be applicable to the people of the Territory rather than to the people outside.

"It should be recognized that these islands, in the light of experience, are an economic liability and are not an asset to the Administering Authority, and therefore they do not present an opportunity for important economic development. We might have a different problem, as the representative of Belgium has stated, if it were a different country and territory which we were contemplating.

"Finally, my Government believes that the provisions of article 8, paragraph 1 of the draft trusteeship agreement are peculiarly appropriate to this Territory, not only on account of the overriding security aspects but also because of the meagreness of its indigenous resources and the paucity of its population."

U.N. Security Council Off. Rec., 124th Meeting, Apr. 2, 1947, pp. 644, 662, 664–665, 666.

Federation with U.S. territories

Article 9 of the Trusteeship Agreement for the former Japanese Mandated Islands reads:

"The administering authority shall be entitled to constitute the trust territory into a customs, fiscal, or administrative union or federation with other territories under United States jurisdiction and to establish common services between such territories and the trust territory where such measures are not inconsistent with the basic objectives of the International Trusteeship System and with the terms of this agreement."

U.S. TIAS 1665; 61 Stat. 3301, 3304; 8 UNTS 189, 196.

This article is identical with the draft text proposed by the United States which was accompanied by the following comment:

> "This article should be read in connection with article 3 of the draft agreement which provides in part that the administering authority shall have full powers of administration over the territory as an integral part of the United States. Both articles 3 and 9, it should be noted, are made subject to the terms of this agreement. The substance of article 9 permits customs, fiscal, or administrative union or federation, with other territories under United States jurisdiction. It is practically identical with similar provisions in four of the agreements approved by the General Assembly. Provision for such union or federation is obviously desirable to ensure the efficient administration of such island areas as Saipan which will face many problems common to the nearby island of Guam. However, such a provision does not imply sovereignty over the trust territory." *Draft Trusteeship Agreement for the Japanese Mandated Islands, op. cit.,* pp. 9–10; U.S. Delegation Doc. US/S/119, p. 6.

On February 5, 1961, a plebiscite was conducted among the people Saipan of the Saipan District, in which, of a total of 2,847 registered voters, 1,557 opted for unification with Guam while 818 opted for annexation by the United States as a separate territory.

> Report of the Trusteeship Council to the Security Council on the Trust Territory of the Pacific Islands covering the period from 1 July 1960 to 19 July 1961, U.N. Doc. S/4890, July 27, 1961, p. 19.

"66. In commenting on the apparent reasons which led the people to demand the separation of Saipan from the rest of the Trust Territory, the Mission noted that both political parties wanted to join the United States either by integration with Guam or as a separate territory and thereby become entitled to United States citizenship and all the advantages flowing from it as they see them. It understood that the comparative prosperity resulting from military expenditures was, in part, responsible for the demand. The Mission felt that, in making this move, the people of Saipan had overlooked the fact that they could not join the United States until they had achieved a greater degree of self-government and economic self-sufficiency and until all the people of the Trust Territory were ready to choose, at the same time, either self-government or independence.

. . . .

"69. At the twenty-seventh session, the representative of the Administering Authority informed the Council that the people of Saipan had been advised that the Administering Authority supported the conclusion of the Visiting Mission that the United Nations would not approve a partial termination of the Trusteeship Agreement, such as would be involved in an integration of Saipan with Guam. The Special Representative added that he believed the leaders understood the position and were prepared to abide by the view expressed to them by the Visiting Mission. The Special Representative informed the Council that the Administering Authority would be glad to prepare and distribute a document explaining the objectives of trusteeship, as suggested by the Visiting Mission.

"70. At its twenty-seventh session, the Council adopted the following conclusions:

> "*The Council, bearing in mind that the district of Saipan is only a single part of a Trust Territory, the Trust Territory of the Pacific Islands, and the right of the people to determine their future at the appropriate time, endorses the action taken and the views expressed by the Visiting Mission in respect of the so-called referendum held in Saipan in February 1961 concerning the future of that particular district. It notes with satisfaction the statement of the Administering Authority that the people of Saipan have been informed that the Administering Authority supports the conclusion of the Visiting Mission.*
>
> "*The Council also endorses the view of the Visiting Mission that in order to assist the people of the Territory in clarifying their thoughts about the future of the Territory, it would be useful for the Administration to prepare a document, for use all over the Territory, explaining the objectives of trusteeship and pointing out that the people themselves would, at the appropriate time, have the opportunity of freely expressing their wishes concerning their future. It notes with satisfaction that the Administering Authority has agreed to prepare and distribute such a document.*"

> *Ibid.*, pp. 20, 21–22.

In his closing statement to the Trusteeship Council on June 23, 1961, M. Wilfred Goding, the High Commissioner of the Trust Territory of the Pacific Islands, stated that "the Saipan District will send delegates to the September meeting of the [Inter-District Advisory] Committee, rather than observers as in the past. We anticipate that the active participation of the Saipan representatives as delegates will be a major contribution to the work of the Committee." U.S.-U.N. press release No. 3736, June 23, 1961. On this same occasion, Jonathan B. Bingham, United States Representative on the Trusteeship Council stated: ". . . We have heard much of the plebiscite which was conducted on Saipan by the Saipanese. Without reference to the many aspects of this, I would like to make it quite clear that we in the United States are proud that the Saipanese people think so highly of our society and political system that they expressed the hope of sharing its benefits and responsibilities." U.S.-U.N. press release No. 3737, June 23, 1961.

U.S. customs: "foreign territory"

Although the United States is entitled, under article 9, *supra*, to constitute the Trust Territory into a customs union with the United States, the Trust Territory at present is regarded as "foreign territory" for the purposes of United States customs laws. *Cf.* S. 2992, 82d Cong., 2d sess., "The Organic Act of the Trust Territory of the

Pacific Islands," section 26(b) : "No customs duties shall be levied in the customs territory of the United States upon articles which are the growth, produce, or manufacture of the Trust Territory, except to the extent that the President may determine and proclaim is required by any international obligation of the United States." A comparable provision was contained in section 21(b), H.R. 5381, 83d Cong., 1st sess., which was also a bill providing organic legislation for the Trust Territory. See also H.R. 9278, 87th Cong., 1st sess., section 18(b). None of these bills became law.

At the request of the United States, the Contracting Parties to the General Agreement on Tariffs and Trade agreed to a waiver in respect of the Trust Territory to permit the United States to accord preferential treatment to products of the Trust Territory. *Basic Instruments and Selected Documents*, vol. II, General Agreement on Tariffs and Trade (1952), p. 9. Accordingly, the Internal Revenue Code has been amended by the Act of August 16, 1954, 68A Stat. 536, 26 U.S.C. § 4513(b), so as to exempt coconut oil produced in the Trust Territory from an additional tax on domestic processing. See discussion of article 3 and article 6, *ante*, pp. 777 ff. and 790 ff. The text of the GATT decision states:

GATT waiver: preferential treatment

"ARTICLE I

"Waiver in Respect of the Trust Territory of the Pacific Islands

"Decision of 8 September 1948

"The Contracting Parties, acting pursuant to Article XXV: 5(*a*) of the General Agreement on Tariffs and Trade,

"*Taking note* of the request of the Government of the United States with respect to the establishment of preferential treatment for imports into the United States from the Marshall, Caroline and Marianas Islands (other than Guam), which islands were formerly held by Japan under mandate and which, by agreement with the Security Council of the United Nations approved on 2 April 1947, have been placed under the trusteeship system of the United Nations with the United States as the Administering Authority;

"*Considering* that, while under Japanese mandate, the exports of such islands were entitled to preferential treatment in the market of the metropolitan territory of Japan, upon which such exports were substantially dependent, and that such preferential treatment has been terminated upon the establishment of the trusteeship under the administration of the United States;

"*Considering* further that while under Japanese mandate such islands applied a system of preferential treatment for imports from Japan, which system will, under United States administration, be replaced by a system of non-discriminatory treatment for the goods of all countries; and

"*Considering* further that the replacement of preferential entry for the exports of such islands into the market of Japan by preferential entry into the market of the United States is not, in view of the nature and small volume of the production and trade involved and of the underlying economic factors affecting such production and trade, likely to result in substantial injury to the trade of any of the contracting parties,

"*Decide:*

"1. Subject to paragraph 2 of this Decision, the provisions of Article I, paragraph 1, of the General Agreement on Tariffs and Trade shall be waived to the extent necessary to permit the Government of the United States

"(*a*) to accord duty-free treatment, except as otherwise provided for in paragraph (*b*), to all products of the Trust Territory of the Pacific Islands imported into the customs territory of the United States without obligation thereby to extend the same treatment to the like products of the other contracting parties, and

"(*b*) to accord, in respect of products of the Trust Territory of the Pacific Islands imported into the customs territory of the United States, the same rate of internal tax on the processing of coconut-oil (or, if such internal tax should be converted into the equivalent import duty, the same rate of equivalent duty) as may be applied consistently with the General Agreement on Tariffs and Trade, in respect of the like products of the Philippine Republic, without obligation to extend the same treatment to the like products of the other contracting parties.

"2. The margins of preference created upon the institution of the treatment provided for in paragraph 1 shall thereafter be bound against increase in the same manner as other preferences under the General Agreement on Tariffs and Trade and for this purpose the date of 10 April 1947, referred to in sub-paragraphs (*a*) and (*b*) of the final paragraph of Article I of the General Agreement, shall be replaced by the date on which such treatment is instituted; such date shall be notified to the CONTRACTING PARTIES by the Government of the United States.

"3. In the event that the underlying economic factors affecting the production and trade of the Trust Territory of the Pacific Islands should change so that the preferences authorized by this decision should result or threaten to result in substantial injury to the competitive trade of any contracting party, the CONTRACTING PARTIES, upon the request of any affected contracting party, shall review this decision in the light of all relevant circumstances."

Basic Instruments and Selected Documents, vol. II, General Agreement on Tariffs and Trade (1952), pp. 9–10.

See discussion of article 6, *ante,* pp. 801 ff., for text of report of GATT working party, adopted by the GATT Contracting Parties on September 8, 1948.

Article 10 of the Trusteeship Agreement for the former Japanese Mandated Islands reads:

> "The administering authority, acting under the provisions of Article 3 of this agreement, may accept membership in any regional advisory commission, regional authority, or technical organization, or other voluntary association of states, may co-operate with specialized international bodies, public or private, and may engage in other forms of international co-operation."

International organizations

U.S. TIAS 1665; 61 Stat. 3301, 3304; 8 UNTS 189, 196.

This article is the same as that proposed by the United States. The comment accompanying the United States proposal stated:

> "This article, which is permissive in character, seems particularly appropriate for the trust territory in that it offers the inhabitants an opportunity to benefit from association with other peoples who face similar problems. Such association would enable them to develop a regional economy, to take advantage of technical studies on common problems, and to participate effectively in furthering their own development. The advantages of regional organization have been demonstrated by the Caribbean Commission. Similar developments are also under way in the South Pacific." *Draft Trusteeship for the Japanese Mandated Islands, op. cit.,* p. 10; U.S. Delegation Doc. US/S/119, p. 6.

The South Pacific Commission was established by an Agreement signed at Canberra February 6, 1947, on behalf of Australia, France, the Netherlands, New Zealand, the United Kingdom, and the United States. U.S. TIAS 2317; 2 UST 1787. Its original scope comprised "all those non-self-governing territories in the Pacific Ocean which are administered by the participating Governments and which lie wholly or in part south of the Equator and east from and including Netherlands New Guinea." *Ibid.* 1789. By a subsequent Agreement signed November 7, 1951, the territorial scope of the Commission was extended to include Guam and the Trust Territory of the Pacific Islands. U.S. TIAS 2458; 3 UST 2851, 2852.

"International and Regional Relations

"International Relations

"The Administration of the Trust Territory of the Pacific Islands maintains a number of important contacts with international and regional organizations. Official negotiation with international organizations is through the State Department of the Administering Authority.

"The basic and most important convention applying to the Territory is the Trusteeship Agreement approved at Lake Success, N.Y., on April 2, 1947.

"A list of international agreements applying to the Territory in 1960 is given in appendix A.

"The Trust Territory is a part of the Western Pacific Region of the World Health Organization (WHO). The standards of the

World Health Organization, such as communicable disease reporting and quarantine regulations, are used by the Public Health Division of the Territory.

"Technical assistance also has been made available to the Trust Territory by the various specialized agencies of the United Nations. In the year under review, the most important of these were as follows:

"(a) The Territory Director of Public Health attended a World Health Organization (WHO) Seminar on Tuberculosis Control held in Sydney, Australia.

"(b) The Territory Director of Dental Services attended a World Health Organization-sponsored Dental Congress in Adelaide, South Australia.

"(c) A Palauan medical officer was awarded a WHO Public Administration fellowship for study in the Philippines and Japan.

"(d) A Marshallese education staff employee spent 6 months as a UNESCO fellow in the study of radio broadcasting in New Zealand, Western Samoa, and Fiji.

"(e) A Palauan deputy sheriff received a United Nations fellowship for the study of police and welfare methods in Hawaii.

"Additionally, other applicants were under consideration for U.N. scholarship awards during the year.

"The Territory Administration receives free literature and also purchases materials on a variety of subjects relating to education, public health, and community development through the facilities of UNESCO and WHO. This is distributed to interested groups within the Territory.

"REGIONAL RELATIONS

"During the year the Administering Authority continued its membership in the South Pacific Commission, an advisory and consultative body set up in 1947 by the Governments of Australia, France, the Netherlands, New Zealand, the United Kingdom, and the United States of America, all of which administer non-self-governing territories in the Pacific.

"The scope of the Commission's activities is wide, and the Territory received valuable assistance in a variety of ways.

"Two members of the staff of the Trust Territory of the Pacific Islands are members of the Research Council of the South Pacific Commission. The Contracts and Programs Officer and the Staff Anthropologist serve on the Research Council in the fields of economic development and social development, respectively.

"In October 1959 the Director of Education of the Trust Territory attended the South Pacific Commission Regional Seminar on Education held in Brisbane, Australia.

"The Executive Officer for Social Development visited the Territory in August 1959. Arrangements also were made during the year for the Women's Interest Officer to visit the Territory in the fall of 1960 to conduct a training course for representatives of women's organizations. The Health Education Officer of the South Pacific Commission conducted a 3 weeks' course on health education during June 1960 at Saipan.

"Two Territory students were enrolled in the South Pacific Commission-sponsored Literature Production Training Center in Honiara, British Solomons, during the year. Preliminary arrangements were made to enroll one candidate in the boatbuilding training school to be established under the Commission's auspices in Auki, Malaita, British Solomons, in the summer of 1960."

Trust Territory of the Pacific Islands 1960, 13th Annual Report to the United Nations (Department of State publication 7183, 1961), pp. 12–13.

Article 11 of the Trusteeship Agreement for the former Japanese Mandated Islands reads:

"1. The administering authority shall take the necessary steps to provide the status of citizenship of the trust territory for the inhabitants of the trust territory.
"2. The administering authority shall afford diplomatic and consular protection to inhabitants of the trust territory when outside the territorial limits of the trust territory or of the territory of the administering authority." Citizenship

U.S. TIAS 1665; 61 Stat. 3301, 3304; 8 UNTS 189, 196–198.

This is identical with the text proposed by the United States. The comment accompanying the United States text read:

"1. The status of citizenship will tend to create a common bond amongst peoples who otherwise might feel no unity and consequently would have difficulty in working toward the objectives of the trusteeship system as set forth in Article 76 of the Charter.
"2. Diplomatic and Consular protection of the inhabitants of the trust territory when outside the territorial limits of the trust territory or of the territory of the administering authority serves not only to provide a necessary service, but also to establish the rights of the inhabitants under international law." *Draft Trusteeship Agreement for the Japanese Mandated Islands, op. cit.*, p. 10; U.S. Delegation Doc. US/S/119, p. 7.

"*Sec. 660. Nationality.* For the purposes of these Regulations, all persons heretofore or hereafter born in the Trust Territory shall be deemed to be citizens of the Trust Territory, except

"(a) persons, born in the Trust Territory prior to the effective date of this Chapter, who at birth or otherwise have acquired another nationality;
"(b) persons, born in the Trust Territory on or after the effective date of this Chapter, who at birth shall acquire another nationality; and
"(c) persons, born in the Trust Territory whose principal, actual dwelling place in fact has not been in the Trust Territory

or Guam at any time between July 18, 1947, and the effective date of this Chapter.

"Provided, that a child born outside the Trust Territory of parents who are citizens of the Trust Territory shall be considered a citizen of the Trust Territory if he becomes a permanent resident of the Trust Territory while under the age of 21 years. (As amended by Executive Order No. 70, dated Oct. 1, 1957.)"

Code of the Trust Territory of the Pacific Islands, as amended, ch. 10, § 660.

"STATUS OF INHABITANTS

"The legal status of inhabitants of the Trust Territory, likewise, did not change during the year under review. Section 660 of the Code of the Trust Territory defines all persons born in the Territory as citizens of the Trust Territory, except those persons who at birth acquire another nationality and those persons born in the Territory whose principal actual dwelling place in fact has not been in the Trust Territory or Guam at any time between July 18, 1947, and December 29, 1952, the effective date of the Trust Territory Code. No special national status as yet has been conferred by the Administering Authority. An amendment to the Trust Territory Code providing for naturalization was promulgated in October 1957, and some 107 individuals have been granted Trust Territory citizenship since that date.

"All persons resident in the Trust Territory are subject to the same laws regardless of whether they are citizens, resident noncitizens, or visitors. The High Commissioner, by specific authority, may grant non-Micronesian immigrants permanent residence status. Such grants, when made, generally involve wives or other dependents of citizens. Through the naturalization amendment mentioned above, immigrants can now acquire a status equal in all respects to that of native-born citizens of the Trust Territory.

"Citizens of the Trust Territory of the Pacific Islands may acquire U.S. citizenship in the same manner as other immigrants to the United States. Resident noncitizens of the Trust Territory of the Pacific Islands desiring U.S. citizenship would be governed by U.S. laws applying to the country of their origin."

Trust Territory of the Pacific Islands 1960, op. cit., pp. 10–11.

Diplomatic, consular protection

Passports for citizens or inhabitants of the Trust Territory are issued by the High Commissioner upon application through the District Administrator or at Trust Territory Headquarters at Guam. Sec. 661, Code of the Trust Territory of the Pacific Islands; Emigration and Immigration Regulation No. 1, Revised March 10, 1960. In addition to the description of the bearer and his photograph, the passport includes the pertinent parts shown on the following page.

No.

PASSPORT

Trust Territory of the
Pacific Islands

-1-

I, the undersigned, _____

_____ of the
Trust Territory of the Pacific Islands, hereby request all
whom it may concern to permit safely and freely to pass,
and in case of need to give all lawful aid and protection to

a citizen or inhabitant of the Trust Territory of the Pacific Islands.

The bearer is accompanied by his

Wife _____

Minor children _____

_____ and seal of the

_____

of the Trust Territory
of the Pacific Islands

19____

-2-

The rightful holder of this passport is a citizen
or inhabitant of the TRUST TERRITORY OF THE PACIFIC
ISLANDS under United States Administration entitled,
under Article Eleven of the Trusteeship Agreement
between the UNITED STATES and the United Nations Security Council, which entered into force on July 18,
1947, to receive diplomatic and consular protection
of the UNITED STATES OF AMERICA.

This passport, unless limited to a shorter period,
is valid for five years from its date of issue and
may be renewed once to permit a total of ten years
validity from date of issue, and is revocable at any
time upon order of the High Commissioner of the Trust
Territory or by a United States diplomatic or consular officer upon authorization of the Department of
State.

-5-

NOTICE

This passport, properly vissed, is valid for travel in all countries unless otherwise restricted.

When presented to any Trust Territory immigration
authority at a point of entry, this Document will be
accepted as evidence of the rightful holder's right
to enter the Trust Territory.

Any person whose passport has been lost or destroyed must render a report to such effect to the
nearest American Consular officer or his duly authorized representative. If the passport has
been recovered, the same must be done.

-6-

Immigration quota

Pursuant to the Immigration and Nationality Act of 1952, 66 Stat. 166, 175, 8 U.S.C. §§ 1101, 1151, an annual immigration quota of 100 was assigned to "Pacific Islands (trust territory, United States administered)" by Presidential Proclamation No. 2980, July 2, 1952, 17 F.R. 6019, 66 Stat. c 36, 8 U.S.C. § 1151.

"In view of the sweeping provisions of the trusteeship agreement, it is possible that Congress had the authority to declare that the trust territory was to be considered as part of the United States for purposes of naturalization. However, it has not done so and it must be concluded that Kwajalein is not a part of the United States and that petitioner's absence [in Kwajalein] operated to break the continuity of his residence."

Application of Reyes, 140 F. Supp. 130, 131–132 (U.S. Dist. Ct., D. Hawaii, 1956). See also *Aradanas* v. *Hogan*, 155 F. Supp. 546, 547 (U.S. Dist. Ct., D. Hawaii, 1957) (". . . under the 1917 [Immigration] Act Kwajalein was not within the meaning of the word 'United States', as defined by that Act.")

Visas

For the fiscal year ending June 30, 1961, a total of 1,566 immigrant and nonimmigrant United States visas were issued to citizens of the Trust Territory.

Department of State press release No. 597, Aug. 26, 1961.

Implementing legislation

Article 12 of the Trusteeship Agreement for the former Japanese Mandated Islands reads:

"The administering authority shall enact such legislation as may be necessary to place the provisions of this agreement in effect in the trust territory."

U.S. TIAS 1665; 61 Stat. 3301, 3304; 8 UNTS 189, 198.

This is the same as the text proposed by the United States, which was accompanied by the following comment: "This article constitutes an international commitment upon the part of the United States to implement by legislation the provisions of the trusteeship agreement." *Draft Trusteeship Agreement for the Japanese Mandated Islands, op. cit.*, p. 11; U.S. Delegation Doc. US/S/119, p. 7.

Approval of Agreement

By Joint Resolution of July 18, 1947, the United States Congress authorized the President "to approve, on behalf of the United States, the trusteeship agreement between the United States of America and the Security Council of the United Nations for the former Japanese mandated islands (to be known as the Territory of the Pacific Islands) which was approved by the Security Council at the seat of the United Nations, Lake Success, Nassau County, New York, on April 2, 1947."

61 Stat. 397; 48 U.S.C. § 1681 note.

The Act of June 30, 1954, provided for the continuance of civil government for the Trust Territory of the Pacific Islands, as follows: Civil government

"That until Congress shall further provide for the government of the Trust Territory of the Pacific Islands, all executive, legislative, and judicial authority necessary for the civil administration of the Trust Territory shall continue to be vested in such person or persons and shall be exercised in such manner and through such agency or agencies as the President of the United States may direct or authorize." (Section 2 authorized "to be appropriated such sums, not in excess of $7,500,000 per year, as may be necessary to carry out the provisions of this Act.")

68 Stat. 330; 48 U.S.C. § 1681.

"STATUS OF TERRITORY

"The legal status of the Trust Territory of the Pacific Islands is established by:

"(a) The Trusteeship Agreement between the United States and the United Nations Security Council which entered into force on July 18, 1947.

"(b) Executive Order No. 10265 signed by the President of the United States on June 29, 1951, placing administrative responsibility for the Trust Territory of the Pacific Islands with the Secretary of the Interior.

"(c) Department of the Interior Order No. 2658, describing the nature and extent of authority exercised by the High Commissioner.

"(d) The Proclamations of the High Commissioner.

"(e) The Code of the Trust Territory of the Pacific Islands enacted on December 22, 1952, which provides the laws for its government.

"(f) Executive Order No. 10408 signed by the President of the United States on November 10, 1952, providing for the transfer of responsibility for the civil administration of the islands of Saipan and Tinian in the Northern Marianas to the Secretary of the Navy.

"(g) Executive Order No. 10470 signed by the President of the United States on July 17, 1953, providing for the transfer of responsibility for the civil administration of the remaining islands in the Northern Marianas, with the exception of Rota, to the Secretary of the Navy.

"There was no legislation initiated during the year under review which affected the legal status of the Territory."

Trust Territory of the Pacific Islands 1960, 13th Annual Report to the United Nations (Department of State publication 7183, 1961), p. 10.

See discussion of article 6, *ante*, pp. 790 ff., as to the system of law in the Trust Territory. See also *Pauling* v. *McElroy*, 164 F. Supp. 390 (D.D.C. 1958); affirmed, 278 F.2d 252 (D.C. Cir. 1960); certiorari denied, 364 U.S. 835

(1960). In the District Court opinion, Judge Keech stated at page 393:
"The provisions of . . . the Trusteeship Agreement for the Trust Territory of the Pacific Islands, . . . relied on by plaintiffs are not self-executing and do not vest any of the plaintiffs with individual legal rights which they may assert in this Court. . . ."

Security rights

Article 13 of the Trusteeship Agreement for the former Japanese Mandated Islands reads:

"The provisions of Articles 87 and 88 of the Charter shall be applicable to the trust territory, provided that the administering authority may determine the extent of their applicability to any areas which may from time to time be specified by it as closed for security reasons."

U.S. TIAS 1665; 61 Stat. 3301, 3304; 8 UNTS 189, 198.

Article 13, as approved, is the same as that proposed by the United States. The comment accompanying the United States text stated:

"The intent of this paragraph is to ensure that the functions of the Trusteeship Council in regard to non-strategic trust territories may be appropriately applied to the strategic trust territory covered by this agreement.

"The Charter itself provides for supervision over strategic areas in only the most general terms. Article 83 states merely that 'all functions of the United Nations relating to strategic areas . . . shall be exercised by the Security Council' and that 'the Security Council shall . . . avail itself of the assistance of the Trusteeship Council to perform those functions . . . relating to political, economic, social, and educational matters in strategic areas.' No indication is given as to what those 'functions' should be. Accordingly, Article 13 of the draft agreement provides that Articles 87 and 88 of the Charter—relating to reports, petitions, visits, and questionnaires concerning non-strategic areas—shall be applicable to the trust territory, even though it is designated as a strategic area, except that the administering authority may determine the extent of applicability in any areas which may, from time to time, be specified by the administering authority as closed for security reasons.

"This exception has been made in recognition of the fact that an administering authority of a strategic trust territory should have, in the discharge of its responsibilities for the maintenance of international peace and security, the authority necessary to safeguard the installations established for that purpose. It is permitted under article 83 (3) of the Charter which wisely provides that the functions of the Trusteeship Council in strategic areas shall be 'subject to the provisions of the trusteeship agreements *and without prejudice to security considerations.*'

"Article 13 of the draft agreement states only that the *extent* of applicability of Article[s] 87 and 88 of the Charter may, in 'closed' areas, be determined by the administering authority. Hence, even in such areas the Trusteeship Council can, and normally would, be authorized to request and consider reports submitted by the administering authority, to accept petitions and examine them in consultation with the administering authority, and otherwise to keep itself informed of the political, economic, social, and educational development of the inhabitants.

"Any agreement arising out of (*a*) the regulation of armaments, including the principle of inspection, or (*b*) the assignment of forces and facilities to the Security Council under Article 43 of the Charter, would apply to the strategic areas of the Japanese Mandated Islands in the same way as to any United States territory."

Draft Trusteeship Agreement for the Japanese Mandated Islands, op. cit., pp. 11–12; U.S. Delegation Doc. US/S/119, pp. 7–8.

In his statement submitting the United States draft trusteeship agreement to the Security Council, the United States Representative, Senator Austin, made the following observations in connection with the proposed right to close areas in the Trust Territory: **Atomic energy control**

"The United States draft agreement provides that the administering authority may, from time to time, specify certain areas as closed for security reasons. This provision will not, of course, prejudice the full application to the entire trust territory of all international control and inspection measures that may become part of a system of international control of atomic energy, other weapons of mass destruction and conventional armaments."

U.N. Security Council Off. Rec., 113th Meeting, Feb. 26, 1947, p. 411.

"Although this is a strategic area vital to that system of international peace and security to which articles 73 and 76 refer, the United States draft agreement goes beyond the requirements of the Charter in strategic areas. It provides that articles 87 and 88, relating to reports, petitions, visits and questionnaires in non-strategic trusteeship areas, shall be applicable to the whole of this trust territory, except that the administering authority may determine the extent of applicability in any areas which may, from time to time, be specified by the administering authority as closed for security reasons. This exception has been made in recognition of the fact that an administering authority of a strategic trust territory should have the necessary authority to safeguard the installations established in the discharge of its responsibilities for the maintenance of international peace and security. **Safeguard installations**

"It is true that the fulfillment of the basic objectives of the trusteeship system will depend in all trust territories—and this territory is no exception—upon the good faith of the administering authority as well as upon effective supervision by the United Nations.

"I can assure you, on behalf of the Government of the United States, that the United States will faithfully support the principle of effective supervision by the United Nations as fully in this trust territory as in any other trust territory, within the limits imposed by its obligation to administer this area in such a way as to preserve the security of the United States and to strengthen collective security under the United Nations."

Ibid., p. 412.

In addition, Senator Austin made the following statement, in response to a proposal of the Representative of the United Kingdom that article 13 be redrafted to insert a provision notifying the Security Council when areas are closed:

"Sir Alexander CADOGAN (United Kingdom) : I do not think I need say very much about the amendment which stands in the name of my delegation. The text has already been circulated.

"In the view of my Government, article 13 is one of the most important articles of the United States draft. My Government realizes that it would be impossible to provide for any prior notification to the Security Council of any areas which may be closed for security reasons, but it hopes that some provision will be inserted for notifying the Security Council when areas are closed, giving reasons if possible. With that object, we have submitted, for the appreciation of the United States delegation, this re-draft which you will find in the paper circulated.

"Mr. AUSTIN (United States of America) : Perhaps the United Kingdom representative would be entirely satisfied if the records showed that the United States contemplates that notification should be made to the Security Council whenever the proviso that is contained in article 13 comes into effect. Article 13 seems to the United States of such great importance that it could not accede to a suggested change, and the United States is very anxious to find out whether my statement, as representative of the United States, is satisfactory this [thus] avoiding a prolonged discussion. If that is the case, I will not go into a full discussion of the matter.

"You will notice that the act of specification is an act of notification, and it is the purpose of the United States to keep the Security Council notified. Of course, the main element of the provision is to bring into operation Articles 87 and 88, which call for inspection, examination and reports. Obviously the proviso is a necessary one in the interest of security; otherwise it would not be there."

U.N. Security Council Off. Rec., 124th Meeting, Apr. 2, 1947, p. 668. The Representative of the United Kingdom expressed his satisfaction at the declaration that the word "specified" in article 13 "implied an act of notification", and that the United States Government "contemplated keeping the Security Council notified". *Ibid.*, pp. 668–669.

Notification of closure

Nuclear tests: Eniwetok

By letter of December 2, 1947, addressed to the President of the Security Council, Senator Warren R. Austin, United States Representative, notified the Security Council that "effective December 1, 1947,

Eniwetok Atoll in the Trust Territory of the Pacific Islands, is, pursuant to the provisions of the Trusteeship Agreement, closed for security reasons, in order that the United States Government, acting through its Atomic Energy Commission, may conduct necessary experiments relating to nuclear fission." In addition, the Security Council was "further notified that periodic visits provided for in Article 87 (c) of the Charter of the United Nations are suspended in the closed area until further notice, as permitted by Article 13 of the Trusteeship Agreement. With this exception, the provisions of Article 87 of the Charter will continue to apply. With respect to Article 88 of the Charter, the United States Government will, of course, report to the United Nations on the political, economic, social, and educational advancement of the inhabitants of the Trust Territory."

> The U.S. Representative to the United Nations (Austin) to the President of the Security Council (Hood), Dec. 2, 1947, certified copy of communication attached to "Motion of Defendants to Dismiss the Complaint", in *Linus C. Pauling, et al.*, Plaintiffs, v. *Neil H. McElroy, et al.*, Defendants, Civil No. 866–58, and *Dwight Heine et al.*, Plaintiffs, v. *Neil H. McElroy et al.*, Defendants, Civil No. 1566–58. (See *Pauling et al., v. McElroy et al.*, and *Heine et al., v. McElroy et al.*, 164 F. Supp. 390 (D.D.C. 1958) ; affirmed, 278 F. 2d 252 (D.C. Cir. 1960) ; certiorari denied, 364 U.S. 835 (1960).)

By letter of April 2, 1953, addressed to the Secretary-General of the United Nations, the United States Permanent Representative to the Security Council, Ambassador Henry Cabot Lodge, notified the Security Council that "effective April 2, 1953, Bikini Atoll in the Trust Territory of the Pacific Islands, is closed for security reasons pursuant to the provisions of the Trusteeship Agreement in order that the United States Government, acting through its Atomic Energy Commission, may conduct necessary atomic experiments." This letter further notified the Security Council "that periodic visits provided for in Article 87 (c) of the Charter of the United Nations are suspended in the closed area until further notice, as permitted by Article 13 of the Trusteeship Agreement. With this exception, the provisions of Article 87 will continue to apply. With respect to Article 88 of the Charter, the United States Government will, of course, report to the United Nations on the political, economic, social and educational advancement of the inhabitants of the Trust Territory."

Bikini Atoll

> The U.S. Permanent Representative to the Security Council of the United Nations (Lodge) to the Secretary-General of the United Nations (Lie), Apr. 2, 1953, certified copy of communication attached to "Motion of Defendants to Dismiss the Complaint" in *Linus C. Pauling, et al.*, Plaintiffs, v. *Neil H. McElroy et al.*, Defendants, *op. cit.*

U.S. position

"All I can do in commenting on this second major portion of his [the Representative of India's] address is to repeat categorically what I said to the Council a few days ago. At that time I stated that the Trusteeship Agreement was predicated on the fact that the Security Council of the United Nations knowingly approved the Pacific Islands as a strategic area in which the first great post-war nuclear tests had been held only a few months previously. Accordingly—from the very outset—it was clear that the right of the United States to close stategic areas for security reasons anticipated closing them for nuclear tests. . . ."

Statement of Mason Sears, United States Representative, in the Trusteeship Council, June 26, 1958, U.S.-U.N. press release No. 2949.

In *Pauling et al.*, v. *McElroy* certain residents of the Marshall Islands brought action, *inter alia*, to enjoin the Secretary of Defense and the Atomic Energy Commission from detonating nuclear weapons in the Marshall Islands. In dismissing the complaints, Judge Keech of the United States District Court stated:

"5. The nuclear weapons tests sought to be enjoined by plaintiffs are authorized by the Atomic Energy Act of 1954. The Atomic Energy Act of 1954 is not unconstitutional in any of the respects claimed by plaintiffs. The Act does not unconstitutionally delegate legislative power to the defendants, nor does it vest in the defendants vague and indefinite power in violation of the due process clause of the Fifth Amendment. The Act is a valid exercise of the authority of Congress to promote and protect the national defense and safety under the constitutional war power. Congress by its repeated appropriations of funds and authorizations of the weapons testing activities of the Atomic Energy Commission and the Department of Defense, made with full awareness of the present state of scientific knowledge as to the nature and extent of radioactive fallout resulting from such nuclear explosions and of the varying scientific views as to the claimed deleterious effects of such radioactive fallout upon human beings, has ratified and confirmed defendants' administrative construction that by the Atomic Energy Act of 1954 the Congress intended to authorize such tests as have been and are to be conducted.

"6. The Atomic Energy Act of 1954 does not conflict with the so-called human rights provisions of the Charter of the United Nations, the Trusteeship Agreement for the Trust Territory of the Pacific Islands, or the international principle of freedom of the seas. In any event, even if there were any such conflict, the Atomic Energy Act of 1954, being a part of the supreme law of the land under the Constitution and later enacted, would be paramount to any such conflicting provisions."

164 F. Supp. 390, 393 (D.D.C. 1958) ; affirmed, 278 F.2d 252 (D.C. Cir. 1960) ; certiorari denied, 364 U.S. 835 (1960).

"Displacement of population resulting from nuclear experiments U.N. position

"13. The situation of the Bikini and Eniweitok people, displaced in 1946 and 1947, respectively, because of nuclear experiments, who are now living on Kili and Ujdelong, and of the Rongelap and Utirik people, who were temporarily displaced in 1954 because of radioactive fall-out from thermonuclear experiments, has periodically occupied the attention of the Council.

"14. The 1961 Visiting Mission, which discussed the problems of Rongelap with the people themselves and with officials, observed that the people of Rongelap had not recovered from the shock of their experiences and that they were seized by fear and anxiety and felt that the Administering Authority should take active steps to rehabilitate the community. It considered that it might help to restore the confidence of the people if responsible officials were to live among them for a period, and it stressed the necessity of providing competent and qualified health personnel. It also believed that field trips to the island should be increased and that special attention should be given to the requirements of education, agricultural rehabilitation and community development. The Mission noted the statement made to it by the Administering Authority that it had no plans to resume nuclear tests in the Territory and expressed the hope that no nuclear or thermonuclear tests would be carried out in the future.

"15. On the question of claims for damages suffered by the people of Rongelap as a result of the 1954 fall-out, the Visiting Mission was informed that a civil suit brought by the people had been dismissed by the Chief Justice of the Trust Territory for want of jurisdiction. The Mission felt that the people should be assured of access to appropriate legal or other means for seeking satisfaction of their claims. It hoped that the Administering Authority would look into this question urgently and find the most fair and equitable means of solving it.

"16. At its twenty-seventh session, the Special Representative informed the Council that the medical team which had examined the people of Rongelap in 1959, 1960 and 1961, had found no existing physical illness attributable to exposure to radioactive fall-out. The Administering Authority would nonetheless continue regular physical examinations, making every effort to minimize their psychological impact on the Rongelap people. He also informed the Council that, in connexion with the claims for damages by the Rongelapese, legislation to overcome the legal difficulties was being prepared.

"17. At its twenty-seventh session, the Council adopted the following conclusions and recommendations:

"The Council, noting the observation by the Visiting Mission that the people of Rongelap have not recovered from the shock of their experiences and are seized by fear and anxiety, considers it urgent and essential that the Administering Authority should make further efforts to rehabilitate the community and, to that end, it commends to the Administering Authority the suggestions made by the Visiting Mission.

"The Council notes the statement of the Administering Authority that a team of experts conducted medical surveys in March 1951, March 1960 and March 1961 and that regular physical examinations will continue in the future, every effort being made to minimize their psychological impact on the people. The Council has also had before it the published report of the 1960 survey and notes that the findings of the team of experts as to the possible physical effects of the fall-out, both at present and in the future, are inconclusive. The Council recognizes the need for continued surveys, particularly in the light of the opinion of the team of experts that the next five years will be the critical period for the possible adverse developments, and expresses the hope that activities connected with such surveys will be conducted in such a manner as to avoid causing constant anxiety and apprehension in the minds of the people.

"The Council, noting the views of the Visiting Mission that the people of Rongelap should be assured of appropriate legal or other means of seeking satisfaction of their claims for compensation, which have been dismissed by the High Court of the Territory for lack of jurisdiction, recommends that the Administering Authority should take speedy action to solve the matter in a fair and equitable manner. In this connexion it notes the statement of the Administering Authority that the necessary legislation is already under preparation. The Council recommends that improved facilities of medical attention and care and other necessary assistance should be provided to the Rongelapese by the Administering Authority especially as recommended in paragraph 201 of the Visiting Mission's report.

"The Council notes the statement of the Administering Authority that it has no plans to resume nuclear or thermonuclear tests in the Territory and earnestly hopes that no nuclear or thermonuclear tests will be carried out in the future."

Report of the Trusteeship Council to the Security Council on the Trust Territory of the Pacific Islands covering the period from 1 July 1960 to 19 July 1961, S/4890, July 27, 1961, pp. 5, 6, 7.

Article 14 of the Trusteeship Agreement reads:

International conventions

"The administering authority undertakes to apply in the trust territory the provisions of any international conventions and recommendations which may be appropriate to the particular circumstances of the trust territory and which would be conducive to the achievement of the basic objectives of Article 6 of this agreement."

U.S. TIAS 1665; 61 Stat. 3301, 3304; 8 UNTS 189, 198.

U.S. treaties applicable

On May 21, 1961, Ambassador Graham A. Martin was authorized to address the following communication to the Director-General of the International Labor Office:

"I have the honor to inform you that the United States Government considers Convention No. 53 [Officers' Competency Certificates] applicable to the Trust Territory of the Pacific Islands by virtue of the understanding contained in the United States instrument of ratification of that Convention registered in 1938. That understanding reads in part:

'. . . the provisions of this Convention shall apply to all territory over which the United States exercises jurisdiction except the Government of the Commonwealth of the Philippine Islands and the Panama Canal Zone, with respect to which this Government reserves its decision.'

The inclusion of the above-quoted understanding in the United States instrument of ratification is regarded by my Government as fully meeting the requirements of Article 7, paragraph 1, of Convention No. 53 and Article 35, paragraph 2, of the Constitution of the International Labor Organization as in force when the United States ratification was registered in 1938. No part of that understanding has been cancelled by any subsequent declaration as provided for in Article 7, paragraph 3, of Convention No. 53.

"When the Trust Territory of the Pacific Islands came under the jurisdiction of the United States in 1947, the treaties and agreements applicable generally to territories under the jurisdiction of the United States were considered by this Government to become applicable to the Trust Territory without necessity of a declaration to that effect in any given case.

Generally

"In view of the foregoing, I have the honor to request that the International Labor Office rely upon the understanding contained in the United States instrument of ratification of ILO Convention No. 53 to consider the Convention as having been declared applicable to the Trust Territory of the Pacific Islands."

ILO

The Secretary of State (Rusk) to the American Consulate General, Geneva, instruction No. A-211, May 26, 1961, MS. Department of State, file 398.06-ILO/5-2661. By airgram, August 12, 1961, from Geneva, the Department was informed that this communication had been transmitted to the Director-General of the International Labor Office on June 6, 1961. The Consul General at Geneva (Martin) to the Secretary of State (Rusk), airgram No. A-27, Aug. 1, 1961, *ibid.*/8-161.

"PART I. AIR NAVIGATION

"CHAPTER I

"GENERAL PRINCIPLES AND APPLICATION OF THE CONVENTION

"*Article 1*

"The contracting States recognize that every State has complete and exclusive sovereignty over the airspace above its territory.

"*Article 2*

"For the purposes of this Convention the territory of a State shall be deemed to be the land areas and territorial waters adjacent thereto under the sovereignty, suzerainty, protection or mandate of such State.

Civil aviation

"*Article 3*

"(a) This Convention shall be applicable only to civil aircraft, and shall not be applicable to state aircraft.

"(b) Aircraft used in military, customs and police services shall be deemed to be state aircraft.

"(c) No state aircraft of a contracting State shall fly over the territory of another State or land thereon without authorization by special agreement or otherwise, and in accordance with the terms thereof.

"(d) The contracting States undertake, when issuing regulations for their state aircraft, that they will have due regard for the safety of navigation of civil aircraft.

"*Article 4*

"Each contracting State agrees not to use civil aviation for any purpose inconsistent with the aims of this Convention."

Convention on International Civil Aviation, signed at Chicago, Dec. 7, 1944, U.S. TIAS 1591; 61 Stat. 1180–1181; 15 UNTS 295, 296–298. See articles 3 and 8 of the Agreement for the Trust Territory of the Pacific Islands, *ante*, pp. 777, 782, 809, and comment thereon, as to air transit rights in the Trust Territory of the Pacific Islands.

"United States Treaties and Other International Agreements, Concluded Since Administration of the Trust Territory of the Pacific Islands Was Entrusted to the United States, Which Have Application to the Trust Territory—June 30, 1960

"BILATERAL

"*China:* Mutual defense treaty. Signed at Washington December 2, 1954.

"*Costa Rica:* Agreement relating to the exchange of third party messages between radio amateurs. Exchange of notes at Washington August 13 and October 19, 1956.

"*Cuba:* Agreement relating to the exchange of third party messages between radio amateurs. Exchange of notes at Habana September 17, 1951, and February 27, 1952.

"*Ecuador:* Agreement relating to the exchange of third party messages between radio amateurs. Exchange of notes at Quito March 16 and 17, 1950.

"*Ireland:* Consular convention and supplementary protocol. Signed at Dublin May 1, 1950, and March 3, 1952, respectively.

"*Japan:* Security treaty. Signed at San Francisco September 8, 1951.

"*Japan:* Air transport services agreement. Signed at Tokyo, August 11, 1952. Amended September 15, 1953.

"*Korea:* Mutual defense treaty. Signed at Washington October 1, 1953.

"*Liberia:* Agreement relating to the exchange of third party messages between radio amateurs. Exchange of notes at Monrovia November 9, 1950, and January 8, 9, and 10, 1951.

"*Nicaragua:* Agreement relating to the exchange of third party messages between radio amateurs. Exchange of notes at Managua October 8 and 16, 1956.

"*Panama:* Agreement relating to the exchange of third party messages between radio amateurs. Exchange of notes at Panamá July 19 and August 1, 1956.

"*Philippines:* Mutual defense treaty. Signed at Washington August 30, 1951.

"*Union of South Africa:* Treaty of extradition. Signed at Washington December 18, 1947.

"*United Kingdom:* Consular convention and protocol. Signed at Washington June 6, 1951.

"MULTILATERAL

"International telecommunication convention, final protocol, and radio regulations. Signed at Atlantic City October 2, 1947. (Convention and protocol superseded and replaced by convention signed at Buenos Aires December 22, 1952, as between contracting parties to the latter.)

"Protocol of provisional application of the General Agreement on Tariffs and Trade. Concluded at Geneva October 30, 1947.

"Agreement for the establishment of the Indo-Pacific Fisheries Council. Signed at Baguio February 26, 1948. (Revised at Tokyo September 30–October 14, 1955.)

"Convention on international recognition of rights in aircraft. Opened for signature at Geneva June 19, 1948.

"Protocol bringing under international control drugs outside the scope of the convention of July 13, 1931, for limiting the manufacture and regulating the distribution of narcotic drugs, as amended by the protocol signed at Lake Success on December 11, 1946. Opened for signature at Paris November 19, 1948.

"Telegraph regulations (Paris revision, 1949) annexed to the international telecommunication convention (Atlantic City, 1947), and final protocol. Signed at Paris August 5, 1949.

"Convention for the amelioration of the condition of the wounded and sick in armed forces in the field. Dated at Geneva August 12, 1949.

"Convention for the amelioration of the condition of wounded, sick and shipwrecked members of armed forces at sea. Dated at Geneva August 12, 1949.

"Convention relative to the treatment of prisoners of war. Dated at Geneva August 12, 1949.

"Convention relative to the protection of civilian persons in time of war. Dated at Geneva August 12, 1949.

"Convention on road traffic. Opened for signature at Geneva September 19, 1949.

"International sanitary regulations (WHO regulations No. 2), as amended. Dated at Geneva May 25, 1951.

"Security treaty between Australia, New Zealand, and the United States of America. Signed at San Francisco September 1, 1951.

"Treaty of peace with Japan. Signed at San Francisco September 8, 1951.

"Agreement extending the territorial scope of the South Pacific Commission to Guam and the Trust Territory of the Pacific Islands. Signed at Nouméa November 7, 1951.

"Agreement for the preparation and adoption of the new international frequency list for the various services in the bands between 14 kc/s and 27,500 kc/s with a view to bringing into force the Atlantic City table of frequency allocations. Signed at Geneva December 3, 1951.

"Universal Postal Union convention, final protocol, regulations, airmail provisions and final protocol to airmail provisions. Signed at Brussels July 11, 1952.

"International telecommunication convention, six annexes, and final protocol. Signed at Buenos Aires December 22, 1952.

"Convention of the Postal Union of the Americas and Spain, final protocol, and regulations of execution. Signed at Bogotá November 9, 1955.

"Agreement relative to parcel post, final protocol, and regulations of execution of the Postal Union of the Americas and Spain. Signed at Bogotá November 9, 1955.

"Agreement relative to money orders and final protocol of the Postal Union of the Americas and Spain. Signed at Bogotá November 9, 1955.

"International wheat agreement. Open for signature at Washington through May 18, 1956."

Trust Territory of the Pacific Islands 1960, Appendix A, 13th Annual Report to the United Nations (Department of State publication 7183, 1961), pp. 159–161.

Alteration, amendment, termination

Article 15 of the Trusteeship Agreement reads:

"The terms of the present agreement shall not be altered, amended or terminated without the consent of the administering authority."

U.S. TIAS 1665; 61 Stat. 3301, 3305; 8 UNTS 189, 198.

The wording of article 15 is the original text proposed by the United States. Accompanying the United States draft was the following comment:

"Under this provision, the United States as administering authority of the trust territory would occupy the same position with respect to amendment of this agreement as the administering authorities of other trust territories with respect to the agreements for those territories." *Draft Trusteeship Agreement for the Japanese Mandated Islands, op. cit.*, p. 12; U.S. Delegation Doc. US/S/119, p. 8.

Prior to the adoption of article 15, by a vote of 8 in favor (Australia, Belgium, Brazil, China, Colombia, France, United Kingdom, United States of America) with 3 abstentions (Poland, Syria, U.S.S.R.), there had been extended debate over proposals by Poland and the U.S.S.R. to amend the United States draft text of article 15. U.N. Security Council Off. Rec., 124th Meeting, Apr. 2, 1947, p. 680.

The U.S.S.R. had proposed an amendment of article 15 which the United States Representative, Senator Austin, declared to be unacceptable for the following reasons:

"Now, let us consider the third amendment which consists in reformulating article 15 as follows: *The term[s] of the present agreement may be altered and amended, or the term of its validity discontinued by the decision of the Security Council.* [Quotation of the interpretation of the amendments presented by the USSR representative at the hundred and thirteenth meeting, official translation of which will be found in *Official Records of the Security Council*, Second Year, No. 20.]
"The language of the article referred to is as follows:

" 'The terms of the present agreement shall not be altered, amended or terminated without the consent of the administering authority.'

"The United States stands on that proposition. There are several reasons why it does so. Primarily, it should be noted that this proposed amendment is in conflict with the Charter. Article 79 of the Charter reads as follows:

" 'The terms of trusteeship for each territory to be placed under the trusteeship system, including any alteration or amendment, shall be agreed upon by the States directly concerned, including the mandatory Power in the case of territories held under mandate by a Member of the United Nations, and shall be approved as provided for in Articles 83 and 85.'

"Now let us look at Article 83. You will notice that the idea of approval contained in Article 79 is expressed once more in Article 83, paragraph 1, which states that:

" 'All functions of the United Nations relating to strategic areas, including the approval of the terms of the trusteeship agreements and of their alteration or amendment, shall be exercised by the Security Council.'

"In other words, obviously it is not the Security Council which originates the amendment; certainly it cannot authorize the termination; the most it can do, under the Charter, is approve or disapprove. Moreover, the Charter is the guide and the law regarding the powers of the Security Council; we cannot sit here and change them by an agreement between the United States and the Security Council. We cannot grant to the Security Council powers that the Charter does not grant. The only way in which the Security Council could be granted the power to alter, amend and terminate this contract would be by amending the Charter; no less authority than that would be necessary. For that reason we are opposed to it.

"But let us consider the other side of the question in the spirit of the Charter, which provides that all interested parties have a chance to be heard. According to Article 79, the terms of trusteeship, including any alteration or amendment, 'shall be agreed upon by the States directly concerned, including the mandatory Power . . .' and approved by the Security Council.

"The United States wishes to record its view that the draft trusteeship agreement is in the nature of a bilateral contract between the United States, on the one hand, and the Security Council on the other. The agreement confines itself to provisions for the powers, duties, and responsibilities of the administering authority. Note the difference: it is the Charter that defines the duties, the powers, and the responsibilities of the Security Council, which is one party to this agreement; but it is this agreement which is necessary in order to define the powers that the United States may have if it becomes the trustee under the agreement. That is what we are dealing with: what power shall the mandatary [sic] have; what power shall the trustee exercise?

"Thus article 15 of the draft agreement defines the action which would be required of the administering authority with respect to changes in the agreement, and does not attempt to define the responsibilities of the Security Council in this respect. The latter are already defined; they are in the Charter; and no amendment or termination can take place without the approval of the Security Council. There is no need to repeat them here, though there would not be any harm in doing so. If you want to make a change just for the sake of making a change, the United States would see no harm at all in saying that alterations in the terms of trusteeship can only be undertaken by agreement between the United States and the Security Council. But we could not accept the amendment proposed here. Its meaning is apparent from the literal interpretation of the wording.

"The responsibilities of the Security Council, with regard to the approval of the original trusteeship agreement and to future changes in this agreement, are clearly set forth in Article 83, paragraph 1, of the Charter. The United States fully subscribes to the principles of this Article, and does not wish in any way to evade their application to the draft trusteeship agreement. It is the view of the United States that an amendment to article 15 of the agreement as drafted, such as that suggested by the Soviet delegation, is inconsistent with the bilateral conception of these agreements as laid down in the Charter, and therefore cannot be accepted."

U.N. Security Council Off. Rec., 116th Meeting, Mar. 7, 1947, pp. 475–476.

Senator Austin indicated a willingness to accept an alternative text for article 15 as follows: "The terms of the present agreement shall not be altered, amended or terminated, except by agreement of the administering authority and the Security Council." *Ibid.*, pp. 476–477. The Soviet Representative, Mr. Gromyko, considered this second text "worse than the first, for it still further restricts the rights and powers of the Security Council with regard to the revision of the conditions of agreements or the cancellation of a trusteeship agreement concerning strategic areas." U.N. Security Council Off. Rec., 124th Meeting, Apr. 2, 1947, p. 669. Senator Austin repeated the United States position as follows:

"This is an occasion when I shall not be able to vote, because if I did, I should have to vote against the amendment; that would constitute a veto, and, as I have stated, I am not going to exercise a veto here.

"As the United States is a party to the agreement, all I can do is to state, with all due deference, that an amendment in the nature of the one proposed by the representative of the Soviet Union would probably be unacceptable to the United States as a party to the agreement. It would clearly be in violation of the Charter. As a matter of principle, therefore, it ought not to be accepted since the whole theory of the Trusteeship System is based on the fact that there must be, in any case, at least two parties to any trusteeship agreement. It would be an astonishing interpretation of the Charter to assume that the function of determining the terms of the agreement should be given exclusively to that party which, under the Charter, has only the function of approval. An amendment leaving the terms of an agreement and the power of termination to the Security Council alone is in violation of the spirit of the Charter and of the theory of agreement.

"I think it is correct to say that the amendment which the United States indicated it might accept is worse than the original proposal; but it is worse for the United States, not for the Security Council.

"It therefore rests with the Security Council to say whether all our work has gone for naught, whether we should now abandon the idea of agreement and change the whole theory and policy of the United Nations Charter by this amendment, which would put the trusteeship under the exclusive control of the Security Council and the Trustee in a position of not knowing from one day to the next where he stood.

"I ask you merely to consider the position in which any Power accepting the great obligations and responsibilities assigned to it under this agreement would find itself, if its trusteeship term could be ended at any moment unless it saw fit to exercise a veto. I have already indicated our attitude on the subject. We do not wish to be put in the position of being obliged to veto an amendment which otherwise would give control to one party to the agreement.

"Our position is that we shall have to refrain from voting on this issue, and the whole matter may result in the withdrawal of the principal party, the United States, from executing the trust."

Ibid., p. 670. The Soviet amendment was rejected by 8 votes (Australia, Belgium, Brazil, China, Colombia, Poland, Syria, U.K.) to 1 (U.S.S.R.) with 2 abstentions (France, U.S.). *Ibid.*, p. 679.

A Polish proposal that article 15 should read: "The terms of the present agreement shall not be altered, amended or terminated, except as provided by the Charter" was also rejected. Senator Austin having declared that the second United States text "was only a tender of compromise, and it is not pending now," the original United States text of article 15 was adopted by 8 votes with 3 abstentions (Poland, Syria, U.S.S.R.).

Ibid., pp. 679–680.

"First of all, I would like to remind the committee that the Trust Territory of the Pacific Islands is a strategic area and I would like to read to the committee, begging their indulgence, the wording of Article 83 of the Charter: 'All functions of the United Nations relating to strategic areas, including the approval of the terms of the trusteeship agreements and of their alteration or amendment, shall be exercised by the Security Council.'"

Statement by Jonathan B. Bingham, Alternate United States Representative, in the Fourth Committee, United Nations General Assembly, U.S.-U.N. press release No. 3789, Oct. 9, 1961.

"ARTICLE 16

"The present agreement shall come into force when approved by the Security Council of the United Nations and by the Government of the United States after due constitutional process. [Approved by the Security Council of the United Nations, Apr. 2, 1947; and by the Government of the United States of America, July 18, 1947.]

Entry
into
force

Certified corrected true copy
For the Security Council Affairs Department

[signature]

D. Protitch
Director in charge of Security Council Affairs Department"

U.S. TIAS 1665; 61 Stat. 3301, 3305; 8 UNTS 189, 198.

The Trusteeship Agreement for the former Japanese Mandated Islands was registered *ex officio* as No. 123 in the United Nations Treaty Series by the Secretariat of the United Nations on October 1, 1947. The first footnote appended to the text of this Agreement by the Secretariat stated:

"Came into force on 18 July 1947, in accordance with Article 16, having been approved by the Security Council on 2 April 1947 and by the Government of the United States of America on 18 July 1947. (See United Nations documents S/P.V.124 and S/448.)" 8 UNTS 189, 190.

The text of article 16 of the Trusteeship Agreement is the same as that proposed by the United States, with the accompanying comment:

"This article merely defines the steps necessary for the agreement to come into force under the Charter of the United Nations and the Constitution of the United States. Article 83 of the Charter provides that the terms of trusteeship agreements relating to strategic areas must be approved by the Security Council."

Draft Trusteeship Agreement for the Japanese Mandated Islands, op. cit., p. 13; U.S. Delegation Doc. US/S/119, p. 8.

By Joint Resolution of July 18, 1947, the United States Congress authorized the President "to approve on behalf of the United States, the trusteeship agreement between the United States of America and the Security Council of the United Nations for the former Japanese mandated islands (to be known as the Territory of the Pacific Islands) which was approved by the Security Council" on April 2, 1947. The agreement was approved by the President on July 18, 1947, and on that same date, there was issued Executive Order No. 9875, terminating the military government in the former Japanese mandated islands", and providing "an interim administration for the Trust Territory of the Pacific Islands", "pending the enactment of appropriate legislation by the Congress of the United States providing for the future government thereof."

For the Joint Resolution of July 18, 1947, see 61 Stat. 397; 48 U.S.C. § 1435 note. For Executive Order No. 9875, July 18, 1947, see 12 *Fed. Reg.* 4837. See *ante*, under articles 3, 6, and 12 as to legislation, pp. 777 ff., 790 ff., and 822 ff.

Legal Nature of International Trusteeship System

§ 42

"The Mandates System seems to me to be an *a fortiori* case. The occasion was the end of a world war. The parties to the treaties of peace incorporating the Covenant of the League and establishing the system numbered thirty. The public interest extended far beyond Europe. Article 22 proclaimed 'the principle that the well-being and development of such peoples form a sacred trust of civilization and that securities for the performance of this trust should be embodied in the Covenant'. A large part of the civilized world concurred in opening a new chapter in the life of between fifteen and twenty millions of people, and this article was the instrument adopted to give effect to their desire. In my

An
international
regime

opinion, the new régime established in pursuance of this 'principle' has more than a purely contractual basis, and the territories subjected to it are impressed with a special legal status, designed to last until modified in the manner indicated by Article 22. The dissolution of the League has produced certain difficulties, but, as I shall explain, they are mechanical difficulties, and the policy and principles of the new institution have survived the impact of the events of 1939 to 1946, and have indeed been reincarnated by the Charter under the name of the 'International Trusteeship System', with a new lease of life."

Separate Opinion of Judge McNair, *International Status of South-West Africa*, Advisory Opinion, July 11, 1950, I.C.J. Reports (1950) 128, 154–155.

". . . It [the Court] further regarded a trusteeship agreement as being of a contractual nature. But no further conclusions—for instance, as to whether a trusteeship agreement is, or should be, exclusively an interstate treaty—are to be extracted from its Opinion. The keynote of its attitude, which is to be deduced from its remarks concerning the mandates system, is that the constitution of a trust territory involves the giving to that territory of a status *in rem*. [Advisory Opinion on the *International Status of South-West Africa*.]

"Status
in rem"

 . . . .

"1. The draftsmen of the Charter envisaged trusteeship agreements as inter-state agreements to which the United Nations would not—save possibly in the case where that organization itself became an administering authority—be a contracting party. There is some evidence that it was also the intention of the draftsmen that the negotiation and conclusion of trusteeship agreements with respect to mandated and ex-enemy territories should be the legal duty of Members of the United Nations concerned. It was probably assumed that the administering authority designated therein would always be a party to a trusteeship agreement. Whilst little consideration was given to conveyancing details, it would appear that the treaty-character envisaged for the agreements, taken together with the circumstance of its obligatory application to mandated and ex-enemy territories, involved that there would, with respect to these categories of territories at least, be other parties also.

"2. The intentions of the draftsmen were not, however, translated into law. The text of the Charter is, in relation to the trusteeship system, highly ambiguous. Authoritative interpretation has made it clear that the application of the trusteeship system is in no case obligatory, but that capacity to place a territory under that system is to be decided exclusively by the law of the Charter, without necessary regard to the rules of general international law respecting transfer of territorial title. This last circumstance is primarily a consequence of the fact that the status of a trust territory, as that of a mandated territory, is a status *in rem*, a new international legal conception to which the classical rules relating to territorial sovereignty do not apply.

"3. The implementation of the intentions of the draftsmen of the Charter and of the. sense of the text that trusteeship agreements should be inter-state treaties to which the appropriate organ of the United Nations should be a confirming, rather than a contracting, party has proved impossible in practice. Experience has demonstrated that the conception of such agreements is gradually altering and they have come—first unconsciously and then consciously—to be drawn up in effect as agreements of a contractual sort between the United Nations and the several administering authorities exclusively.

"4. As actually achieved in the form of treaties between the United Nations and the several administering authorities, the trusteeship agreements are legal acts distinct from the Charter. They possess, however, a dispositive (or conveyancing) as well as a contractual character. In their 'dispositive' aspect they are not independent of the Charter. Together with the relevant provisions of the Charter they constitute a quasi-statutory basis for the trusteeship system as in fact applied to specific territories. They have, as has the régime which they inaugurate and govern, an objective character. This is perhaps their most important aspect."

Parry, "The Legal Nature of Trusteeship Agreements", XXVII Brit. Yb. Int'l L. (1950) 164, 170, 184–185.

"Nearly every legal system possesses some institution whereby the property (and sometimes the persons) of those who are not *sui juris*, such as a minor or a lunatic, can be entrusted to some responsible person as a trustee or *tuteur* or *curateur*. The Anglo-American trust serves this purpose, and another purpose even more closely akin to the Mandates System, namely, the vesting of property in trustees, and its management by them in order that the public or some class of the public may derive benefit or that some public purpose may be served. The trust has frequently been used to protect the weak and the dependent, in cases where there is 'great might on the one side and unmight on the other', and the English courts have for many centuries pursued a vigorous policy in the administration and enforcement of trusts.

"There are three general principles which are common to all these institutions:

"(*a*) that the control of the trustee, *tuteur* or *curateur* over the property is limited in one way or another; he is not in the position of the normal complete owner, who can do what he likes with his own, because he is precluded from administering the property for his own personal benefit;

"(*b*) that the trustee, *tuteur* or *curateur* is under some kind of legal obligation, based on confidence and conscience, to carry out the trust or mission confided to him for the benefit of some other person or for some public purpose;

"(*c*) that any attempt by one of these persons to absorb the property entrusted to him into his own patrimony would be illegal and would be prevented by the law.

Anglo-American "Trust"

"These are some of the general principles of private law which throw light upon this new institution, and I am convinced that in its future development the law governing the trust is a source from which much can be derived. The importance of the Mandates System is marked by the fact that, after the experience of a quarter of a century, the Charter of the United Nations made provision for an 'International Trusteeship System', which was described by a Resolution of the Assembly of the League of April 18th, 1946, as embodying 'principles corresponding to those declared in Article 22 of the Covenant of the League'."

Separate Opinion of Judge McNair, *International Status of South-West Africa*, Advisory Opinion, July 11, 1950, I.C.J. Reports (1950) 128, 149–150.

"This Court is not unaware of the historical evolution of the old colonial systems and the new conception of colonial affairs as expressed in the Covenant of the League of Nations and now in the Charter of the United Nations. Nor is it unaware that by virtue of Article 1 of the Annex to the Trusteeship Agreement, which was brought into operation so far as Italy is concerned by Law No. 1301 of November 4, 1951, sovereignty over the territory of Somaliland is vested in its population, although under Article 2 of the Agreement, the Administration of the territory, for the period specified in the Agreement, has been entrusted to Italy. Moreover, we know—and it was mentioned in the report by Ambrosini to Parliament on the draft Bill for the ratification and bringing into operation of the Trusteeship Agreement—that the régime of Trusteeship Administration is connected, like that under the former Mandate system, with the Anglo-Saxon legal institution of trusteeship, which consists in entrusting the full administration of property to a person for the benefit of a third person."

Società A.B.C. v. *Fontana and Della Rocca*, Italy, Court of Cassation (United Chambers), Aug. 10, 1954, reported in [1955] Int'l L. Rep. 76, 77 (1958).

"Under Anglo-American law a trust is a device whereby property is held or duties undertaken by one for the benefit of another. The practice of establishing trusts originated in the practice of granting the legal estate in land to a person 'to the use' of a monastery in order to evade the statute of mortmain which sought to prevent alienations to the dead hand of the church with consequent loss of customary feudal perquisites on transfer. Generally speaking, in a trust the legal ownership of the property is held by the trustee while the beneficial or equitable ownership is in the beneficiary (*cestui que trust*).

.   .   .   .   .   .

"While it is probably desirable to take the position that generally (cases can be envisioned of the dissolution of the United Nations, of the organization itself acting as administering authority, etc.) the administering authority may not unilaterally relinquish the trust, and while it is true that normally a trustee cannot unilaterally relinquish his trust under the law of trusts as known to Anglo-American law, the extent to which the trusteeship agreements constitute trusts in the sense of Anglo-American law with all of their technicalities has not been passed upon, and it would seem to be unwise at this time to select a few desired characteristics of 'trusts' and argue that they are plainly applicable in the realm of trustee-ship agreements, when other common characteristics of 'trusts'—as for instance the holding of title—may be objectionable if carried over to the international field."

Marjorie M. Whiteman, Assistant Legal Adviser, to Benjamin Gerig, Chief, Division of Dependent Areas, "Unilateral Right to Relinquish a Mandate or Trust Agreement", memorandum, Oct. 28, 1947, MS. Department of State, file FW 501–BB Palestine/9–2647.

"It is true that, while Members of the League of Nations regarded the Mandates System as the best method for discharging the sacred trust of civilization provided for in Article 22 of the Covenant, the Members of the United Nations considered the International Trusteeship System to be the best method for discharging a similar mission. It is equally true that the Charter has contemplated and regulated only a single system, the International Trusteeship System. It did not contemplate or regulate a co-existing Mandates System. It may thus be concluded that it was expected that the mandatory States would follow the normal course indicated by the Charter, namely, conclude Trusteeship Agreements. . . ."

Similarity to Mandates System

International Status of South-West Africa, Advisory Opinion, July 11, 1950, I.C.J. Reports (1950) 128, 140.

"The obligation incumbent upon a mandatory State to accept international supervision and to submit reports is an important part of the Mandates System. When the authors of the Covenant created this system, they considered that the effective performance of the sacred trust of civilization by the mandatory Powers required that the administration of mandated territories should be subject to international supervision. The authors of the Charter had in mind the same necessity when they organized an International Trusteeship System. The necessity for supervision continues to exist despite the disappearance of the supervisory organ under the Mandates System. It cannot be admitted that the obligation to submit to supervision has disappeared merely because the supervisory organ has ceased to exist, when the United Nations has another international organ performing similar, though not identical, supervisory functions.

"These general considerations are confirmed by Article 80, paragraph 1, of the Charter. . . . It purports to safeguard, not only the rights of States, but also the rights of the peoples of mandated territories until Trusteeship Agreements are concluded. The purpose must have been to provide a real protection for those rights; but no such rights of the peoples could be effectively safeguarded without international supervision and a duty to render reports to a supervisory organ.

"The Assembly of the League of Nations, in its Resolution of April 18th, 1946, gave expression to a corresponding view. It recognized . . . that the League's functions with regard to the mandated territories would come to an end, but noted that Chapters XI, XII and XIII of the Charter of the United Nations embody principles corresponding to those declared in Article 22 of the Covenant. It further took note of the intentions of the mandatory States to continue to administer the territories in accordance with the obligations contained in the Mandates until other arrangements should be agreed upon between the United Nations and the mandatory Powers. This resolution presupposes that the supervisory functions exercised by the League would be taken over by the United Nations."

Ibid. 136–137.

"The trusteeship system provided for in this Charter marks a positive advance from the mandates system in several important respects. The new system preserves intact the principle of international responsibility for certain types of dependent territories while making an entirely realistic allowance for security requirements. It faces frankly the fact, as the mandates system failed to do, that such territories in the future must be administered in a manner that will further international peace and security.

Comparison between trusteeships and mandates

"The new system is also more elastic than the old. It avoids the rigid and artificial classification of territories into A, B, and C categories, typical of the mandates system, and permits each individual territory under the system to be dealt with according to the needs and circumstances peculiar to it. It thus recognizes the very great diversity with respect to population, resources, geographical location and stage of advancement of the peoples, characteristic of the territories which are eligible for the system.

"The Trusteeship Council established under the new system should prove to be a more important and effective organ than the Permanent Mandates Commission in that its membership will be composed of states, represented by official, specially qualified persons, and it will be listed as one of the principal organs of the United Nations.

"In the proposed trusteeship system more emphasis is placed on the positive promotion of the welfare of the inhabitants of the trust territories than in the mandates system, whose function was primarily negative and policing. Even in this latter respect, however, the new system, unlike the old, makes specific and formal provision for the power to accept petitions and the authority to make periodic visits to trust territories coming under the competence of the General Assembly.

"SUMMARY

"In brief, this chapter represents an agreement among the United Nations to set up an international trusteeship system which would make it possible for nations to continue to subscribe to the principle adopted at the end of the last war that neither the dependent territories detached from enemy states, nor the inhabitants thereof, should be objects of barter among victorious nations, or subject to exploitation by them, but should be administered in the interest of the native populations and in a manner which will provide equal economic opportunity for all nations.

"All these objectives can be achieved while, at the same time, the security interests of the administering power, and of all the other United Nations, in any territories now under mandate which may be placed under the trusteeship system, or any that may be detached from the enemy and which may be placed under the system, will be fully safeguarded. There is a broad freedom of action, however, for the future policy of the United States vis-à-vis any such territories."

Charter of the United Nations, Report to the President on the Results of the San Francisco Conference by the Chairman of the United States Delegation, The Secretary of State, June 26, 1945 (Department of State publication 2349, 1945), pp. 135–136.

"The trusteeship system of the United Nations is historically, though not legally, the successor of the mandates system of the League. When those writing the Charter of the United Nations in San Francisco toward the close of the Second World War wrestled with this exceedingly complex problem of rule over dependent peoples, they naturally turned to the mandates system and the League's experience with the concept of international accountability.

.   .   .   .

"The international trusteeship system set out in Chapters XII and XIII of the Charter goes considerably beyond the mandates system of the League. The trusteeship system is not limited to specified territories formerly belonging to the enemy but is open to any territory placed under the system by means of a trusteeship agreement. [Article 77 of the Charter was written in terms sufficiently broad to make possible the placing under trusteeship of almost any kind of territory, since clause (c) specifies "territories voluntarily placed under the system by states responsible for their administration." Unofficial suggestions have been made from time to time that such diverse territories as Trieste, the Ruhr, Palestine, and Antarctica should be placed under trusteeship. Recent petitions officially brought before the Trusteeship Council have included requests to extend international control, for instance, to the polar regions through an Arctic and an Antarctic Trusteeship. See UN docs. T/Pet/General 15 (4 Oct. 1947); T/Pet/General 16 (4 Oct. 1947); T/Pet/General 18 (9 Oct. 1947). Whatever may be the practical considerations involved, there would appear to be no legal barriers to the placing of these, or similar territories, under trusteeship.] It contains no arbitrary and fixed classification of territories, such as 'A,' 'B,' and 'C' mandates, but lends itself to far greater flexibility in administration. It provides for several possible forms of administering authority—one or more states or the United Nations itself. ["*Charter of the United Nations*, Article 81. Administration by more than one state may be politically expedient but can raise issues of great difficulty. The problem of the Ewe people of Africa occupying British and French Togoland illustrates the unhappy complexities and enormous difficulties which arise when a single people find themselves divided by political frontiers and administered under differing cultural and colonial systems. In the case of Togoland it is two administering states operating in adjoining but separate trust territories. Nevertheless, since the basic principles and objectives of British colonial policy differ widely from those of French colonial policy and since the two cultures also differ radically, the underlying problem is much the same.

"In the petition presented to the United Nations by the 'All-Ewe Conference on behalf of the Ewe people of Togoland' dated August 9, 1947 (UN doc. T/Pet. 6/5, 26 August 1947) it is stated (p. 4):

> " 'The permanent Anglo-French frontier cuts indiscriminately through local states, villages and farms, thus separating sections of the people from their chiefs, relations and farms. In fact, one has the impression that Togoland was Germany's personal property—a territory taken from her by Britain and France in the Great War of 1914, and was shared as a booty pure and simple, with little or no consideration for the people who live in it. Eweland has since remained three territories, namely, Gold Coast Eweland, British Mandated Togoland and French Mandated Togoland under two fundamentally different administrations, namely, British and French administrations.
>
> " '8. British policy which we may call the policy of adaptation, aims at educating colonial peoples for self-government, and for that reason, takes due account of indigenous culture and makes provisions for its development. On the other hand, French colonial policy, which we may call the policy of assimilation leads in an entirely different direction. The policy of assimilation aims at converting colonial peoples to full citizenship of France, and, for that reason, aims at imbuing the educated community with the best that French culture can give, rather than developing indigenous culture.
>
> " '9. It is inimical to the true development of the people of Eweland who are united by the closest ties of kinship, language and culture to be divided between these two totally different administrations.
>
> " '10. The division of Eweland between these two totally different administrations has therefore been felt by the Ewe people as unjust, and has led to a widespread dissatisfaction among both the literate and the illiterate.'

"The problem remains as yet unsolved. At its session in November 1947 the Trusteeship Council examined the Ewe petition; and in the hearing which followed the representatives of the United

Kingdom and of France proposed an arrangement to eliminate customs barriers, to develop a common educational program and to take such other steps as can be worked out to ameliorate the present difficulties. The Trusteeship Council approved the plan as an initial proposal and intimated its intention to send a visiting Mission to Togoland at the next dry season—probably in January 1949—to give further study to the problem. UN doc. T/109, 18 December 1947, pp. 4–5.

"The only trust territory thus far to be placed under multi-state administration is Nauru. In this case the three administering powers, the United Kingdom, Australia and New Zealand, possess the same basic culture, language, and colonial policy. In order to overcome difficulties and possible inefficiencies in administration, however, even in this case the actual administration of the territory has been delegated by the three powers to Australia alone."] In contrast to the mandates system, which demilitarized the mandated territories, the trusteeship system provides that each trust territory 'shall play its part in the maintenance of international peace and security' [*Charter of the United Nations*, Article 84] and that all or part of a trust territory may be designated as a strategic area. [Same, Article 82.]

"Moreover, the Trusteeship Council is made a principal organ of the United Nations. [Same, Article 7.] Whereas the Permanent Mandates Commission was a subsidiary body of the League Council, experts appointed by the League 'to receive and examine the annual reports of the Mandatories and to advise the Council on all matters relating to the observance of the mandates' [*Covenant of the League of Nations*, Article 22], the Trusteeship Council, on the other hand, speaks authoritatively for the governments concerned. It is the governments themselves, acting through their chosen representatives sitting in the Trusteeship Council, which have in their hands the translation of the progressive Charter objectives into a concrete program of achievement.

"One of the vital powers of the Trusteeship Council, which was never accorded to the Permanent Mandates Commission, is that of making periodic visits to trust territories. [*Charter of the United Nations*, Article 87(c).] Such visits can be of far-reaching effect. To the inhabitants of the trust territories a visiting mission gives concrete reality to the United Nations and its living concern in their welfare. To the administering authorities such visits are bound to quicken the sense of their responsibility and accountability to the United Nations. To the Trusteeship Council and especially to the members of the visiting missions, such first-hand contacts give tremendous vitality to their work, and bring home, as nothing else could, the realities and the possibilities of the Council's tasks.

"The international trusteeship system affects not only the lives of some fifteen million people who live in the ten trust territories now under international control but also the peace and prosperity of the rest of mankind. It at once protects the inhabitants of trust territories and fosters their advancement towards self-government or independence. In a world characterized by discriminatory practices in trade and investment, the trusteeship system provides, with certain qualifications, equal treatment in the trust territories for all Members of the United Nations and their nationals. It offers, moreover, a yardstick by which political, economic, and social advancement may be measured in the sixty-one non-self-governing territories, inhabited by 175 million people, which are outside the trusteeship system."

Francis B. Sayre, United States Representative in the Trusteeship Council and President of the Council, "Legal Problems Arising from the United Nations Trusteeship System", 42 Am. J. Int'l L. (1948) 263, 265–268.

"Chapters XII and XIII are devoted to the international trusteeship system. These chapters are in response to the continued recognition of the principle established at the end of World War I that dependent territories detached from enemy states should be administered as an international responsibility in accordance with principles internationally agreed upon and should be subject to international supervision.

"At the end of the last war the mandates system was established as a means of disposing of territories detached from the enemy states, Germany and Turkey. The operation of the mandates system was subject to criticism from many quarters, but the principle of international responsibilty upon which it was established and operated was sound, and the essential soundness of that principle has been reaffirmed in the Charter of the new Organization.

"The new trusteeship system which is to replace the mandates system has certain definite advantages over the latter. The new system preserves the principle of international responsibility for the trust territories which will be created, while making entirely realistic provisions for security needs.

"The trusteeship system has an elasticity which the mandates system lacked. It avoids the rigid and artificial classification of territories into 'A', 'B', and 'C' categories as in the mandates system. Each trust territory under the new system will be administered according to an agreement which has been tailored to the individual circumstances and needs of that territory. This is in recognition of the very great diversity characteristic of the dependent territories with respect to population, resources, geographical location, and stage of advancement of the people.

"The new system also makes possible the transfer of colonies to the trusteeship system by the voluntary action of the metropolitan state. No such possibility existed in the mandates system.

"The Trusteeship Council, functioning under the authority of the General Assembly, is designed to be a more important and effective organ than the Permanent Mandates Commission of the League. It is designated as a principal organ of the United Nations Organization. Its membership will be composed of official representatives of states, and it should prove better equipped than was the Mandates Commission to deal with the political problems which constitute so large a portion of the problems of the trust territories.

"The prestige and authority of the Trusteeship Council should certainly be greater than that enjoyed by the Mandates Commission, and its recommendations should carry correspondingly more weight. Moreover, article 81 of the Charter provides that the Organization itself may be designated as the administering authority in trusteeship agreements. In that event the Trusteeship Council, acting on behalf of the General Assembly, would shoulder direct responsibility of administration.

"In the trusteeship system more emphasis is placed on the positive promotion of the welfare of the inhabitants of the trust territories than under the mandates system. The new system introduces periodic visits by representatives of the Organization to the trust territories, which was not possible under the old. The power to accept and examine petitions, oral as well as written, which was practiced by the mandates system with respect to written petitions but which was not included in the Covenant of the League of Nations, is formalized in the Charter.

"The trusteeship system also provides that equal economic and commercial opportunities must be extended to the nationals of all members of the United Nations unless this prejudices the economic and social advancement of the inhabitants of the trust territories. No such qualification was made in the mandates system.

"Finally, the General Assembly of the United Nations is given important functions which were not attributed to the Assembly of the League of Nations in connection with the mandates. In addition, under article 87(d) new functions relating to the trusteeship system may be given to both the General Assembly and the Trusteeship Council."

Ralph J. Bunche, Acting Chief of the Division of Dependent Area Affairs, Office of Special Political Affairs, Department of State, "Trusteeship and Non-Self-Governing Territories in the Charter of the United Nations", XIII *Bulletin*, Department of State, No. 340, Dec. 30, 1945, pp. 1037, 1040–1041. See also Rappard, "The Mandates and the International Trusteeship Systems", 61 Pol. Sci. Q. (1946) 408.

The International Court of Justice had occasion to consider the provisions of chapter XII of the United Nations Charter in the advisory proceeding, *International Status of South-West Africa* (1950), and, by eight votes to six, concluded that this chapter did not impose a legal obligation upon a Mandatory Power to negotiate and conclude a Trusteeship Agreement for this Mandated Territory. In reaching this conclusion the majority opinion stated: **Voluntary character**

"Territories held under Mandate were not by the Charter automatically placed under the new International Trusteeship System. This system should, according to Articles 75 and 77, apply to territories which are placed thereunder by means of Trusteeship Agreements. South-West Africa, being a territory held under Mandate (Article 77a), may be placed under the Trusteeship System in accordance with the provisions of Chapter XII. In this sense, that chapter is applicable to the Territory.

"Question (*b*) further asks in what manner Chapter XII is applicable to the Territory. It appears from a number of documents submitted to the Court in accordance with the General Assembly's Resolution of December 6th, 1949, as well as from the written and the oral observations of several Governments, that the General Assembly, in asking about the manner of application of Chapter XII, was referring to the question whether the Charter imposes upon the Union of South Africa an obligation to place the Territory under the Trusteeship System by means of a Trusteeship Agreement.

"Articles 75 and 77 show, in the opinion of the Court, that this question must be answered in the negative. The language used in both articles is permissive ('as may be placed thereunder'). Both refer to subsequent agreements by which the territories in question may be placed under the Trusteeship System. An 'agreement' implies consent of the parties concerned, including the mandatory Power in the case of territories held under Mandate (Article 79). The parties must be free to accept or reject the terms of a contemplated agreement. No party can impose its terms on the other party. Article 77, paragraph 2, moreover, presupposes agreement not only with regard to its particular terms, but also as to which territories will be brought under the Trusteeship System.

"It has been contended that the word 'voluntarily', used in Article 77 with respect to category (*c*) only, shows that the placing of other territories under Trusteeship is compulsory. This word alone cannot, however, over-ride the principle derived from Articles 75, 77 and 79 considered as a whole. An obligation for a mandatory State to place the Territory under Trusteeship would have been expressed in a direct manner. The word 'voluntarily' incorporated in category (*c*) can be explained as having been used out of an abundance of caution and as an added assurance of freedom of initiative to States having territories falling within that category.

"It has also been contended that paragraph 2 of Article 80 imposes on mandatory States a duty to negotiate and conclude Trusteeship Agreements. The Court finds no justification for this contention. The paragraph merely states that the first paragraph of the article shall not be interpreted as giving grounds for delay or postponement of the negotiation and conclusion of agreements for placing mandated and other territories under the Trusteeship System as provided for in Article 77. There is nothing to suggest that the provision was intended as an exception to the principle derived from Articles 75, 77 and 79. The provision is entirely negative in character and cannot be said to create an obligation to negotiate and conclude an agreement. Had the parties to the Charter intended to create an obligation of this kind for a mandatory State, such intention would necessarily have been expressed in positive terms.

"It has further been maintained that Article 80, paragraph 2, creates an obligation for mandatory States to enter into negotiations with a view to concluding a Trusteeship Agreement. But an obligation to negotiate without any obligation to conclude an agreement can hardly be derived from this provision, which expressly refers to delay or postponement of 'the negotiation and conclusion' of agreements. It is not limited to negotiations only. Moreover, it refers to the negotiation and conclusion of agreements for placing 'mandated and other territories under the Trusteeship System as provided for in Article 77'. In other words, it refers not merely to territories held under Mandate, but also to the territories mentioned in Article 77 (*b*) and (*c*). It is, however, evident that there can be no obligation to enter into negotiations with a view to concluding Trusteeship Agreements for those territories.

"It is contended that the Trusteeship System created by the Charter would have no more than a theoretical existence if the mandatory Powers were not under an obligation to enter into negotiations with a view to concluding Trusteeship Agreements. This contention is not convincing, since an obligation merely to negotiate does not of itself assure the conclusion of Trusteeship Agreements. Nor was the Trusteeship System created only for mandated territories."

I.C.J. Reports (1950) 138–140, 144.

The Court continued with regard to chapter XII of the United Nations Charter:

"The Court is further requested to say where competence to determine and modify the international status of the Territory rests.

"Before answering this question, the Court repeats that the normal way of modifying the international status of the Territory would be to place it under the Trusteeship System by means of a Trusteeship Agreement in accordance with the provisions of Chapter XII of the Charter." *Ibid*. 141.

"1. *Provisions of the Charter.*

"Article 77 provides in paragraph 1 that: 'The trusteeship system shall apply to such territories in the following categories as may be placed thereunder by means of trusteeship agreements.' Paragraph 2 of the same article provides: 'It will be a matter U.S. views for subsequent agreement as to which territories in the foregoing categories will be brought under the trusteeship system and upon what terms.' These provisions indicate that a mandatory Power is not obligated to place a mandated territory under the international trusteeship system, and that it is not required to submit a trusteeship agreement for the approval of the appropriate United Nations organ. In defining the categories of territories which may be placed under trusteeship, Article 77 reads as follows:

" '(*a*) territories now held under mandate;

" '(*b*) territories which may be detached from enemy States as a result of the Second World War; and

" '(*c*) territories voluntarily placed under the system by States responsible for their administration.'

It will be noted that the word 'voluntarily' is used in Article 77 only with respect to category (c) and is not used with respect to categories (a) and (b). From this it might be argued that the placing of territories under trusteeship is compulsory with respect to territories in categories (a) and (b), and is optional only with respect to territories in category (c). However, this interpretation based on the appearance of the word 'voluntarily' in (c) alone is not sustained by a consideration of the provisions of Article 77 as a whole. The provisions of paragraph 2 of Article 77 are not limited in their operation to territories in category (c) but apply with respect to territories in all three categories. Likewise the word 'may' in Article 77 (1) applies to all three.

"Quite apart from the question whether the Charter makes the conversion of mandates into trust territories compulsory and requires the mandatory Powers at least to submit draft trusteeship agreements for the consideration of the United Nations, the Charter establishes that the agreement of the mandatory Power is necessary to any terms of trusteeship which may be proposed for a mandated territory. Thus, Article 79 provides:

> " 'The terms of trusteeship for each territory to be placed under the trusteeship system, including any alteration or amendment, shall be agreed upon by the States directly concerned, including the mandatory Power in the case of territories held under mandate by a Member of the United Nations, and shall be approved as provided for in Articles 83 and 85.'

"2. *History of the Charter provisions.*

"If the provisions of Chapter XII left any doubt as to the non-compulsory character of the placing of mandated territories under trusteeship, those doubts are dispelled by an examination of the history of Chapter XII at San Francisco. At the fourth meeting of Committee II/4, the United States representative 'pointed out that this Government did not seek to change the relations existing between a mandatory and a mandated territory without the former's consent, and it supported the principle of voluntary submission of territories to the system'. See U.N.C.I.O. Doc. 310 (May 15, 1945), 2.

"At the eighth meeting of Committee II/4, the representative of Egypt proposed an amendment to the proposal which later became Article 77. This amendment would have resulted in Article 77 reading as follows:

> " 'The trusteeship system shall apply to:
>
> " '(a) all territories now held under mandate;
> " '(b) territories which may be detached from enemy States as a result of the Second World War;
> " '(c) territories voluntarily placed under the system by States responsible for their administration.' See U.N.C.I.O. Doc. 512 (May 23, 1945), 1.

Objection was taken to the proposed amendment on the ground that it would have the effect of creating a compulsory system. The amendment was defeated. See *id.*, at 2.

"At the ninth meeting of Committee II/4, the United States proposed inclusion in the provision, which later became Article 79, of the phrase 'including the mandatory Power in the case of territories held under mandate by one of the United Nations. . . .'. This amendment, making clear that the agreement of the mandatory Power was requisite to placing a mandated territory under trusteeship, was adopted unanimously by the Committee. See U.N.C.I.O. Doc. 552 (May 24, 1945), 2.

"Subsequently, the representative of Egypt proposed in Committee II/4 that provisions embodying the following principles be included in the chapter on trusteeship:

" 'That in all trust territories, within its competence, the General Assembly shall have the power to terminate the status of trusteeship, and declare the territory to be fit for full independence, either at the instance of the administering authority, or on the recommendation of any Member of the Assembly.

" 'That whenever there is any violation of the terms of the trusteeship arrangements by the administering authority, or when the administering Power has ceased to be a Member of the United Nations, or has been suspended from membership, the Organization shall take the necessary steps for the transfer of the territory under trusteeship to another administering authority. . . .'

Against this proposal, it was urged 'that a provision for the termination or transfer of a trusteeship without the consent of the trustee Power would be contrary to the voluntary basis upon which the trusteeship proposals had been built'. See U.N.C.I.O. Doc. 1018 (June 16, 1945), 5. The representative of Egypt subsequently withdrew his proposal.

"The report of the Rapporteur of Committee II/4 to Commission II and the report of the Rapporteur of Commission II to the plenary session of the San Francisco Conference did not consider specifically the question whether the placing of mandated territories under the trusteeship system was to be compulsory or optional. These reports, which in part paraphrased the language of the provisions which were to become Chapter XII, contained no statements to indicate that the conversion of mandates to trust territories was to be compulsory. See U.N.C.I.O. Docs. 1115 (June 20, 1945), 4; 1210 (June 27, 1945)."

Written Statement of the United States of America, *International Status of South-West Africa*, Pleadings, Oral Arguments, Documents, pp. 120–122 (I.C.J. 1950).

"Controversy has twice arisen in the General Assembly as to whether or not the Charter provisions create a legal obligation on the part of mandatory states to place former mandated territories under trusteeship. During the debates over South West Africa, in both 1946 and 1947, a very vocal bloc of powers insisted with vigor that the Charter was based upon the assumption that all mandated territories should be placed under trusteeship and that all mandatory states are legally bound to do so. [In support of this contention they argued that Article 77(1) lists mandated territories as one category to which the trusteeship system "shall apply," and that Article 80(2) states that Article 80(1) "shall not be interpreted as giving grounds for delay or postponement of the negotiation and conclusion of agreements for placing mandated and other territories under the trusteeship system. . . ." It was further argued that if there were no binding obligation to place the mandated territories under trusteeship, and if they were consequently not placed under trusteeship, the Trusteeship Council, a principal organ of the United Nations, could not have been brought into being—a contingency which could not have been contemplated by the drafters of the Charter. See UN docs. A/250, Dec. 11, 1946; A/250/Add. 1/Rev. 1, Dec. 12, 1946; A/250/Add. 2/ Dec. 12, 1946; A/P.V./104, Nov. 1, 1947; A/P.V./105, Nov. 1, 1947.] An opposing group of powers, including the United States, maintained that whatever the moral obligations might be, there was clearly no binding legal obligation on the part of the Union of South Africa to place South West Africa under trusteeship.

"From a strictly legal point of view, the Charter provisions seem to leave little room for doubt. There is no Charter provision explicitly requiring a mandatory state to take such action; and Article 77 seems to point in quite the opposite direction. Article 77 states: 'The trusteeship system shall apply to such territories . . . as may be placed thereunder by means of trusteeship agreements'; and, again: 'It will be a matter for subsequent agreement as to which territories . . . will be brought under the trusteeship system and upon what terms.' These are not the words of a binding legal obligation. [In stating the position of the United States during the debate in the General Assembly on November 1, 1947, the author said: "The United States Government played an active role, both at the Crimea Conference and at the San Francisco Conference, in the formulation of the basic principles of the trusteeship system. It was always of the view that nothing in the Charter could or should compel the placing of any territory under the trusteeship system. At San Francisco, the United States Delegation was particularly concerned as members of the Assembly will remember, over the disposition of the former Japanese Mandated Islands, and was constitutionally unable in advance to commit the Congress of the United States to the conclusion of a trusteeship agreement for those islands. The United States Delegation therefore necessarily took the position that the conclusion of trusteeship agreements was to be a voluntary, and not a compulsory, process. To this end, it gave the most careful consideration to the wording of Article 77 of the Charter. The question is now an academic one in so far as the former Japanese Mandated Islands are concerned, but it would not be fair for the United States to alter its interpretation of Article 77 merely because its own interests are no longer involved." See UN doc. A/P.V./104, pp. 57–61.]

"In questions of international concern such as this, involving vital interests and fundamental issues of policy among sovereign states, the answer must be sought in the actual decisions reached by the powers involved, sometimes crystallizing into established practice, quite as often as in carefully considered determinations of judicial tribunals. In the South West African case the conflict of opinion was decided by vote in the Assembly in both 1946 and 1947. In both years resolutions were proposed reciting that the Union of South Africa was legally bound under the Charter to place South West Africa under trusteeship, and these were in each case voted down. [The Resolution recommended to the General Assembly by the Fourth Committee in 1947 recited that "it is the clear intention of Chapter XII of the Charter of the United Nations that all territories previously held under mandate, until granted self-government or independence, shall be brought under the International Trusteeship System." UN doc. A/422, October 27, 1947. The General Assembly amended the Resolution as proposed by striking out this particular provision.] In both Assemblies, on the other hand, resolutions were passed recommending that the mandated territory of South West Africa be placed under the international trusteeship system and *inviting* the Union Government to propose for the consideration of the General Assembly a trusteeship agreement for the territory. [As phrased in the General Assembly resolution passed on November 1, 1947, the General Assembly "firmly maintains its recommendation that South West Africa be placed under the Trusteeship System," and "urges the Government of the Union of South Africa to propose for the consideration of the General Assembly a Trusteeship agreement for the territory of South West Africa and expresses the hope that the Union Government may find it possible to do so in time to enable the General Assembly to consider the agreement at its third session." For 1946 resolution see UN doc. A/64/Add.1, Res. 65(1), January 31, 1947; for 1947 resolution see UN doc. A/429, October 29, 1947, and UN doc. T/52, Res. 141 (11), November 7, 1947.]"

Francis B. Sayre, United States Representative in the Trusteeship Council and President of the Council, "Legal Problems Arising from the United Nations Trusteeship System", 42 Am. J. Int'l L. (1948) 263, 272–273. See also Parry, "The Legal Nature of Trusteeship Agreements", XXVII Brit. Yb. Int'l L. (1950) 164–165.

"The trusteeship agreement will:

"(1) determine whether the area concerned will be wholly or partly strategic or non-strategic;

"(2) designate the administering authority, which can be one or more states, or the Organization itself;

"(3) define the extent of authority to be exercised by the administering authority;

Substantive content

"(4) indicate the extent of supervision to be exercised by the Organization;

"(5) state the objectives of the administration, which must be consistent with the basic objectives of the trusteeship system as defined in article 76;

"(6) incorporate whatever provisions for termination, alteration, or amendment may prove practicable; and

"(7) set forth whatever other provisions the states signatory may see fit to include.

"It is fully recognized that the effective operation of the trusteeship system will depend in large measure on the nature of the trusteeship agreements by means of which territories will be placed under the system.

"When accord has been reached among the states directly concerned on the terms of the trusteeship agreement for a territory, that agreement will be submitted to the Organization for approval. If the territory is a non-strategic area, the agreement will be submitted to the General Assembly for approval. The Security Council will approve those agreements or aspects of agreements relating to territories or parts of territories designated as strategic. The General Assembly and the Security Council, in exercising their power to approve and therefore their right to reject the agreements, may, of course, recommend revision of the agreements as a prior condition of approval. Such revisions must be agreeable to the states directly concerned."

Ralph J. Bunche, Acting Chief of the Division of Dependent Area Affairs, Office of Special Political Affairs, Department of State, "Trusteeship and Non-Self-Governing Territories in the Charter of the United Nations", XIII *Bulletin*, Department of State, No. 340, Dec. 30, 1945, pp. 1037, 1042.

Parties: "states directly concerned"

"It was envisaged in Article 79 of the Charter that trusteeship agreements would be concluded in two steps—agreement by the 'states directly concerned' and approval by the General Assembly or, in the case of strategic areas, by the Security Council. [See *Some Points of Procedure with Regard to Consideration of Trusteeship Agreements by the General Assembly*, UN doc. A/87, September 25, 1946.] It was thought that the agreement would take the form of a formal instrument, probably a treaty, entered into by the 'states directly concerned' and thereafter jointly submitted to the appropriate United Nations organ.

"The phrase 'states directly concerned' made its first appearance in the working paper which the United States Delegation submitted at the San Francisco Conference. [*Documents of the United Nations Conference on International Organization, San Francisco, 1945*, Vol. X, p. 646.] It was generally considered that it would be a matter for subsequent determination as to which states were directly concerned in any particular territory.

"The conception was based upon the fact that no territory could be placed under the trusteeship system without the consent of the states which were directly concerned—through sovereignty, administration, or other rights in such territory. In the case of the mandated territories, as has already been pointed out, it has always been a matter of dispute as to where sovereignty resided— in the Principal Allied and Associated Powers, in the League of Nations, in the mandatory power, or in the people of the territory. With respect to territories detached from enemy states, the signatories of the peace treaties would presumably be directly concerned. With respect to other territories, the states directly concerned would be those responsible for their administration. In any event, the 'states directly concerned' would themselves make this determination, after which the General Assembly or the Security Council, as the case might be, would be entitled to pass upon the determination.

"At the London meeting of the General Assembly in 1946 efforts were made to define the phrase 'states directly concerned' but no agreement was reached. [*The United States and the United Nations: Report of the United States Delegation to the First Part of the First Session of the General Assembly of the United Nations*, Department of State Publication 2484, 1946.] Later in the year, at the New York meeting of the General Assembly, the United States representative, Mr. John Foster Dulles, declared that, owing to the obvious difficulty of defining this phrase and to the danger that controversy over the matter might lead to delay in establishing the trusteeship system, it would be preferable to assume, for practical purposes, that the mandatory power was the state directly concerned. He added that the United States, which might well claim to be a state directly concerned in all mandated territories, would be willing to waive its claims with respect to the eight trusteeship agreements under consideration by the Assembly if all other Members would do the same. [*U.S. Position on Establishment of Trusteeship System;* Statement by Member of the U.S. Delegation, *The Department of State Bulletin*, December 1, 1946, pp. 991–992.]

"After prolonged controversy, the General Assembly, on December 13, 1946, approved the eight trusteeship agreements by overwhelming majorities, without attempting to determine which were the states directly concerned. [For a summary of the General Assembly's debates on the "states directly concerned" and other trusteeship topics, see Elizabeth H. Armstrong and William I. Cargo, *The Inauguration of the Trusteeship System of the United Nations, The Department of State Bulletin*, March 23, 1947, pp. 511–521.] It was contended by certain delegations, however, that the conclusion of these trusteeship agreements was contrary to Article 79 of the Charter and that, hence, the Trusteeship Council was being illegally organized. At the time of the election of members of the Trusteeship Council, the President of the General Assembly, in response to a challenge by the Byelorussian Delegate, declared that the General Assembly had adopted the trusteeship agreements by an overwhelming majority and that elections to the Trusteeship Council would therefore be perfectly regular. [See Official Records of the Second

Part of the First Session, the General Assembly (63d Plenary Meeting, Dec. 14, 1946), p. 1321.]

"The question of the interpretation of Article 79 of the Charter arose a second time when the Security Council was considering the United States trusteeship agreement for the former Japanese Mandated Islands. Here again the problem was settled without a determination of what states were the ones 'directly concerned.' In proposing the agreement to the Security Council the United States representatives stated that 'The United States believes it has fulfilled the requirements of Article 79 of the Charter, first by transmitting copies of a draft trusteeship agreement for the former Japanese Mandated Islands to all Members of the United Nations, which, in the view of the Government of the United States, may have special interests in these islands, and now by formally submitting the draft agreement to the Security Council for its approval.' [*Draft Trusteeship Agreement for the Japanese Mandated Islands*, Department of State Publication No. 2784, p. 19.]

"During subsequent discussions of the proposed agreement by the Security Council, however, two decisions were made which bear upon the interpretation of Article 79. First, after receipt of requests from the Indian and New Zealand governments that they be given an opportunity to present their views on the agreement, the Security Council decided to give a hearing to those two governments, as well as to any members of the Far Eastern Commission which might apply. As a result of this decision representatives of Canada, India, the Netherlands, New Zealand, and the Republic of the Philippines were present at subsequent discussions on the trusteeship agreement.

"The second decision bearing upon the question came during consideration of Article 15 [reading, "The terms of the present agreement shall not be altered, amended or terminated without the consent of the administering authority"] of the trusteeship agreement. It was pointed out by one member of the Security Council that no consideration had been given to 'states directly concerned' as stipulated in Article 79, and that some attempt should be made to define this phrase and to determine who those states might be. A proposal to adjourn the meeting in order to study this matter and prepare a full discussion on the point was defeated. [For a full discussion of this proposal see S/P.V./124, April 2, 1947.]

"At the recent session of the General Assembly, when the report of the Trusteeship Council was under consideration in the Fourth Committee, a delegate protested that since the trusteeship agreements were themselves invalid the Trusteeship Council had therefore been brought illegally into existence. [In the Fourth Committee of the Second General Assembly, the author, as President of the Trusteeship Council, in reply to the charge of illegality, referred to the previous actions of the General Assembly and the Security Council as justifying the legality of the Council, and concluded with the statement that "quite apart from the fact that there is no possible legal justification for questioning its validity, the time is now past when any justifiable attack can be made upon the Council's constitutional existence." United States Mission to the United Nations. Press Release No. 238, September 29, 1947. See also UN doc. A/C.4/SR. 34, September 29, 1947, pp. 1–2.] The Chairman of the Committee ruled that any further remarks challenging the legality of the Trusteeship Council would be ruled out of order as irrelevant. [Same, p. 1.]

"The approval of the draft trusteeship agreement for Nauru was objected to somewhat later in the session by the Soviet Delegation on the same ground, the claim being made that, *inter alia*, Article 79 of the Charter had been violated. [UN Doc. A/C.4/SC.1/SR. 30, October 6, 1947, pp. 1–4.] This objection was voted down and the trusteeship agreement for Nauru was approved."

Francis B. Sayre, United States Representative in the Trusteeship Council and President of the Council, "Legal Problems Arising from the United Nations Trusteeship System", 42 Am. J. Int'l L. (1948) 263, 283–285. See also Armstrong and Cargo, "The Inauguration of the Trusteeship System of the United Nations", XVI *Bulletin*, Department of State, No. 403, Mar. 23, 1947, pp. 511, 514–515. For further discussion of article 15, see § 41, "Trust Territory of the Pacific Islands", *ante*, pp. 834–838.

"(b) The identity of the parties to trusteeship agreements

"Nevertheless, it has been rightly pointed out that Article 77 is concerned only with, as it were, the geographical range of the new system [cf. Kelsen, *The Law of the United Nations* (1950), p. 574]—a conclusion confirmed by the fact that the next article, Article 78, is concerned with the limitation of that range. For it is provided there that the system 'shall not apply' to territories which have become Members of the United Nations. It is only in Article 79 that the question of trusteeship agreements proper is reached. It is stipulated there that 'the terms of trusteeship for each territory to be placed under the trusteeship system, including any alteration or amendment, shall be agreed upon by the states directly concerned, including the mandatory power in the case of territories held under mandate by a Member of the United Nations, and shall be approved as provided for in Articles 83 and 85'. This language is perhaps unfortunate. For in the first place it leaves open the question as to who are the parties to the treaties it envisages as requisite for the application of the trusteeship system to any particular territory. In the second place it gives some ground—as do also Articles 79 (2) and 82—for the drawing of a distinction between a trusteeship agreement and agreement upon 'terms of trusteeship'. It might thus be thought that, although the 'states directly concerned' were required to agree upon the terms—the general conditions as it were—of trusteeship with respect to a territory, these states need not necessarily be parties to the trusteeship agreement for that territory. The reference to Articles 83 and 85, which speak of 'approval of *the terms* of the trusteeship agreements' by the

Security Council or the General Assembly as the case may be, does not entirely exclude the possible distinction. [The substitution in the equally authentic French text of the phrase "Les termes du régime de tutelle, pour chacun des térritoires . . . feront l'objet *d'un accord* entre les états intéressés . . ." for the English "The terms of trusteeship shall be agreed upon . . .", as also the use in the French version of Art. 77 (2) of the expression "un accord ultérieur déterminera . . .", seem, however, to dispose of any such suggestion. Cf. also the French text of Art. 81, which speaks of "les *conditions* dans lesquelles le territoire sera administré" as opposed to the English "terms". . . .]

"As for the Organization itself, when not an administering authority, it is not possible to maintain with any confidence that the United Nations is, in the Charter, envisaged as a party to the trusteeship agreements. If that had been intended, it could scarcely have been stated more obscurely. That it was not so intended is sufficiently obvious both from the *travaux préparatoires* and the general scheme of the trusteeship system which, according to Article 75, the United Nations 'shall establish *under its authority* for the administration *and supervision*' of territories within its scope. The question thus remains open as to who the parties are. Some imperfect assistance is provided by Article 81, where it is laid down that 'the trusteeship agreement shall in each case include the terms under which the trust territory will be administered and designate the authority which will exercise the administration of the trust territory' and that 'such authority, hereinafter called the administering authority, may be one or more states or the Organization itself'. But even here (leaving aside in any event the prima-facie exceptional case where the Organization is the administering authority) there is no necessary implication that the administering authority must be a party to the trusteeship agreement. The fact that Article 84, which relates to the integration of trust territories into the general security system of the Charter, in laying a duty on the administering authority to ensure this, does so not by providing that 'the trusteeship agreement shall in each case enable . . .' but that 'to this end the administering authority *may* make use of volunteer forces . . .' perhaps implies that such authority will not so be a party. [See *British Year Book*, 26 (1949), pp. 108, 122–8.]

"*(c) Who can place a territory under the trusteeship system?*

"One possible approach to an answer to this question is to ask what authority has capacity to place a territory under the trusteeship system. The further question, which, incidentally, may throw light also on the problem as to whether or not the trusteeship system is exclusively voluntary in its application, must be answered in the first instance by reference to the Charter. This document gives only partial indications as to what the answer may be. As already mentioned, it provides in Article 77(1) (c) that the trusteeship system 'shall' apply to 'territories voluntarily placed [thereunder] by states responsible for their administration'. The plural form of that provision clearly follows from the fact that Article 77 is dealing with 'categories' of territories. The inference is that a single state responsible for the administration of a territory possesses exclusive capacity to place the latter under the system. [Cf. Kelsen, op. cit., p. 583, n. 8 for the suggestion, anent the phrase "the states directly concerned", that "A plural cannot be interpreted to mean the singular".] It may be objected that mere responsibility for administration does not give sufficient title to dispose of a territory in general international law. [Cf. Kelsen, op. cit., p. 573.] There may nevertheless be several explanations for the phraseology employed. Thus the draftsmen may have been merely guilty of loose language, in which case what they have provided will only apply to the normal circumstance—where a state is responsible for the administration of a territory because it has sovereignty over it. Or, alternatively, they may have intended that the Charter should override general international law and to mean what they have in fact said, namely, that administrative responsibility should give sufficient title to place a territory under the trusteeship system. The consequences of such a prima-facie departure from general international law amount to no more than the restriction of the administration's freedom of action by the observance of a 'trust' in favour of the inhabitants. Such an intention on the part of the draftsmen would be by no means unreasonable.

"In the second place the Charter indicates in Article 79 that the 'states directly concerned', whose 'agree[ment] upon the terms of trusteeship' for any territory is required, shall 'include the mandatory power in the case of territories held under mandate by members of the United Nations'. The acceptance of this as an indication of the identity of the parties to trusteeship agreements may depend, of course, upon acceptance of the thesis that 'agree-[ment] upon the terms of trusteeship' means the same thing as the conclusion of a trusteeship agreement. It may not do so, however. But if it be conceded only that a mandatory Power is a necessary party to 'agreement upon the terms of trusteeship', it may be asked who has capacity to place a mandated territory under the trusteeship system. The question is still relevant if the alternative thesis is accepted. For the Charter makes a distinction between mandatory Powers which are Members of the United Nations and others. The use of the word 'including' also implies that, even when the mandatory Power is such a 'Member' there should be other parties. Moreover, even if capacity in terms of the Charter be established, there remains the question of the compatibility of the solution with general international law.

"(d) The opinion of the International Court of Justice

"It is unprofitable to speculate concerning these questions on the basis of [the] bare text of the Charter. For it is evident that that text is not clear. Mere logic can only produce from it wholly untenable conclusions—such as that the only trusteeship agreement in fact achieved which conforms to the text is that for Nauru, by reason of the fortuitous circumstance that the original mandate for the territory was conferred upon 'His Britannic Majesty' and that the constitutional complexities of the Commonwealth cause the arrangements for its administration to present a wholly illusory appearance of an interstate treaty. Moreover, the text has been authoritatively interpreted by the International Court of Justice in its Advisory Opinion on the Status of South-West Africa. [*I.C.J. Reports*, 1950, p. 128.]

"The Court was directly presented with one aspect of the first problem adverted to above: the question as to whether the trusteeship system applies to any territories obligatorily. For it was asked this question in reference to a specific territory in respect of which a mandate had been given to a state which became a Member of the United Nations. By eight votes to six it returned the answer 'that the provisions of Chapter XII of the Charter do not impose on the Union of South Africa a legal obligation to place the territory under the Trusteeship System'. [Ibid., p. 144.] . . .

"The court's opinion does not relate directly to the territories within Article 77(1)(*b*)—territories to be detached from enemy states as a result of the Second World War. But the majority did express, as it were *obiter*, the view that Article 80(2) 'refers not merely to territories held under Mandate, but also to the territories mentioned in Article 77 (*b*) and (*c*)'. [*I.C.J. Reports*, 1950, pp. 128, 140.] If this is so it may well be asked, what possible reason there could be for providing: (1) in Article 77(1)(*c*), that a state might bring its own territory within the system voluntarily; and (2) in Article 80(1) that the rights of such states therein should not justify delay in doing this. The Court did indeed express the opinion, and that unanimously, that 'the provisions of Chapter XII of the Charter are applicable to the Territory of South West Africa in the sense that they provide a means by which the Territory may be brought under the Trusteeship System', and that 'the Union of South Africa acting alone has not the competence to modify the international status of the Territory of South-West Africa, and that the competence to modify the international status of the Territory rests with the Union of South Africa acting with the consent of the United Nations'. [Ibid., p. 144.] These points were made separately and the first of them was arrived at without discussion. [Cf. ibid., pp. 139, 140, 141.] In other words, the question of capacity to place a mandated territory under the trusteeship system was answered, in the context of the question as to how and in what manner Chapter XII of the Charter applied to South-West Africa, exclusively in terms of the law of the Charter, and not in terms of general international law. In the context of the different question as to whether the Union of South Africa had competence to modify the status of the territory and, if not, where such competence lay, the same answer was given on the same basis. In fact, the answer was somewhat more extensive. For, the Court said: 'Articles 79 and 85 of the Charter require that a Trusteeship Agreement be concluded by the Mandatory Power and approved by the General Assembly before the International Trusteeship System may be substituted for the Mandates System. . . . By analogy, it can be inferred that the same procedure is applicable to any modification of the status of a Territory under Mandate which would not have for its purpose the placing of the territory under the Trusteeship System.' [Ibid., pp. 141–2.] But the incompetence of the mandatory, acting alone, to modify the status of the territory was expressed to result 'from the international rules regulating the rights, powers and obligations relating to the administration of the Territory and the supervision of that administration, as embodied in Article 22 of the Covenant and in the Mandate'. [*I.C.J. Reports*, 1950, p. 141.] In other words, the reasons why the mandatory could not dispose of the territory unilaterally was that it had only a limited interest and that the provisions of the mandate constituted a status. The Court, both in this context and elsewhere, regarded the mandates system as still alive. [Contrast Kelsen, op. cit., pp. 594 ff.] It held Article 80(2) of the Charter itself to presuppose 'that the rights of States and peoples shall not lapse automatically on the dissolution of the League of Nations'. [*I.C.J. Reports*, 1950, pp. 128, 134.] However, it based its conclusion that the United Nations could supply the defective capacity of the mandatory exclusively on considerations relating to the real status of the territory. It held that notwithstanding the fact that the consent of the League Council was requisite to the modification of the mandate and that Article 22 of the Covenant could only be amended in accordance with the general procedure for the amendment of that instrument, the inapplicability of these methods of modification following the dissolution of the League did not permit one to 'conclude therefrom that no proper procedure exists for modifying the international status of South-West Africa'. However, despite the fact that all judges agreed with the conclusion, some of them did not accept the next step in the reasoning. For, the majority went on: 'Article 7 of the Mandate, in requiring the consent of the Council of the League of Nations to any modification of its terms brought into operation for this purpose the same organ which was invested with powers of supervision in respect of the administration of the Mandates. In accordance [with the earlier conclusion of the majority that the Union of South Africa had the obligation inter alia to make reports and present petitions to the Trusteeship Council in substitution for the appropriate League organs] those powers of supervision now belong to the General Assembly.' Accordingly by analogy it could be concluded that the General Assembly could supply the deficient capacity of the mandatory Power to modify the status of the territory. [Ibid., pp. 141–2.] Judges McNair and Read did not agree that South Africa had the obligation in question.

"For the rest, the language used by the Court indicates that it conceived of a trusteeship agreement as an instrument to which the mandatory, in the case of a mandated territory, would be a party. [See in particular the Separate Opinion of Judge Read, *I.C.J. Reports*, 1950, pp. 125, 168.] . . ."

Parry, "The Legal Nature of Trusteeship Agreements", XXVII Brit. Yb. Int'l L. (1950) 164, 165–170.

"The trusteeship agreements for Tanganyika, the Cameroons and Togoland under British Administration, the Cameroons and Togoland under French Administration, Ruanda-Urundi, and New Guinea each mention only one state by name—the single administering authority. It is also a common characteristic of this group of agreements that they are neither signed nor ratified, nor subjected to any similar process by any state. Whilst some of them speak of the administering authority being 'hereby designated', others merely refer to the state concerned as acting in the capacity of administering authority. . . .

.   .   .   .

"The agreement for Nauru is one the nature of which is often misunderstood. Its provision designating the three Governments of Australia, New Zealand, and the United Kingdom 'as the joint authority which will exercise the administration' [Art. 2] has thus been interpreted as making it 'unique' and as indicating that it 'was submitted as an agreement between these three Governments'. [Goodrich and Hambro, *The Charter of the United Nations, Commentary and Documents* (2nd ed. 1949) 440.] It has likewise been claimed that, because it is an agreement between these three Governments, the agreement in question is the only trusteeship agreement in existence which conforms to the Charter by constituting an agreement 'between the states directly concerned'. [Kelsen, *The Law of the United Nations* (1950) 602.] It is submitted, however, that these interpretations are open to question and that the agreement is not a treaty or quasi-treaty between the three Governments concerned. For the preamble recites the conferment of the mandate for Nauru 'upon His Britannic Majesty' and *His Majesty's* desire to place the territory under the trusteeship system. The three Governments are indeed 'designated as the joint [administering] authority' but 'in pursuance of an agreement made by the Governments of Australia, New Zealand and the United Kingdom [*scil*. distinct from the trusteeship agreement]' the first named will act on behalf of all of them and '*except and until otherwise agreed*' between them, will *continue* to exercise full governmental powers in the territory. [Art. 4.] It is thus difficult to regard the instrument, which merely perpetuates the pre-existing arrangement, as a treaty between 'states directly concerned' since Article 79 of the Charter requires, in addition to agreement between such states, approval by the United Nations of 'any alteration or amendment' of trusteeship terms. There has moreover to be taken into account the doctrine of the Commonwealth—which is not necessarily of significance in general international law—that inter-

Commonwealth relations are of a constitutional rather than an international nature."

Parry, "The Legal Nature of Trusteeship Agreements", XXVII Brit. Yb. Int'l L. (1950) 164, 179, 180–181.

". . . The preambles, wherein the requisite 'approval' of the organ of the United Nations concerned is declared, are likewise diverse, though all of them recite such approval all recite also the 'desire' or 'willingness' or 'undertaking'—significantly never the 'agreement'—of the mandatory to place the territory under the trusteeship system. Two only indicate a date of entry into force—the agreements for (French) Togoland and (French) Cameroons by reference to the approval of the General Assembly. None contains any indication as to how it may be terminated: a majority only stipulate that they shall not be altered or amended save in accordance with the relevant provisions of the Charter. [I.e. Art. 79; some of these agreements, perhaps curiously, pro- **Entry into** vide that nothing therein is to affect the right of the administer- **force** ing authority to *propose* their amendment for the purpose of the designation of all or part of the territory concerned as a strategic area "or for any other purpose not inconsistent with the basic objectives of the Trusteeship system". Cf. the agreement for Somaliland under Italian Administration, *infra*.]

"As already mentioned a statement of the approval of the competent organ of the United Nations is contained in the preamble to each agreement in the category under review. The General Assembly has also declared, by Resolution 63 (1) that it approves them 'separately (*séparément*)'. [*United Nations, Official Records of the Second Part of the First Session of the General Assembly, Resolutions*, p. 122.] The meaning of this word in this context is not wholly clear, and it is thus not apparent whether the definitive approval is to be found in the resolution referred to and is merely recited in the preamble to each agreement, or whether the statement in each agreement is the operative one and the resolution supererogatory. If the General Assembly can only act by resolution [see *British Year Book*, 26 (1949), pp. 108, 114], it must be the resolution which is in each case the operative instrument. [Compare the case of the agreement for Nauru, which is referred to in the resolution of approval (Resolution 140 (11)) as "the proposed agreement": *United Nations Official Record of the Second Session of the General Assembly, Resolutions*, p. 47.] On this basis the 'differentiation between the stage of negotiation' (between states) and the 'stage of approval' (by the United Nations) would seem correct with respect to this category of agreements and it would not seem possible to argue that the United Nations, or any organ thereof, is a contracting party to any of them. But, as the wording of Resolution 63 (1) perhaps shows, there is room for another view: that the process of approval is an integral part of the process of contracting such an agreement. If, therefore, the latter does not constitute an inter-state treaty, it may nevertheless constitute a treaty between the United Nations and an administering authority. The United Nations Secretariat seems to have taken this view in proceeding to the registration *ex officio* of the various agreements in pursuance of the regulations made under Article 102 of the Charter. Since none of the agreements authorized its *ex officio* registration, the basis of the latter must have been an opinion that they were instruments to which the United Nations is a party. [See Schachter in *British Year Book*, 25 (1948), pp. 91, 129–30.]

. . . .

U.N. a party

"The agreement for the 'Territory of Somaliland under Italian Administration', in its preamble, recites not only the approval of the General Assembly but also the fact of its negotiation and approval by the Trusteeship Council. The states members of the Advisory Council are not expressed to be parties to it though provision is made for the constitution and seat of that body. [Art. 2.] It is provided that the agreement shall not be altered or amended except in accordance with Articles 79 and 85 of the Charter, but that nothing therein shall affect the right of the Administering Authority or the Trusteeship Council to propose its alteration or amendment in the interests of the territory or for reasons not inconsistent with the basic objectives of the trusteeship system. [Art. 21.] It is not to enter into force until approved by the General Assembly and ratified by Italy, though provision for the temporary administration of the territory by Italy pending its entry into force is made. [Art. 23.] It is to cease to have effect ten years after the date of its approval by the General Assembly, the territory then becoming an independent state and its duly constituted independent government assuming all functions of the administering authority in accordance with a plan for 'orderly transfer' of such functions submitted by the latter to the Trusteeship Council not less than eighteen months before the expiry of the agreement. [Arts. 24, 25.]"

Parry, "The Legal Nature of Trusteeship Agreements", XXVII Brit. Yb. Int'l L. (1950) 164, 179–180, 181, 182.

Substantive content: "Sovereignty"

"Upon sovereignty a very few words will suffice. The Mandates System (and the 'corresponding principles' of the International Trusteeship System) is a new institution—a new relationship between territory and its inhabitants on the one hand and the government which represents them internationally on the other—a new species of international government, which does not fit into the old conception of sovereignty and which is alien to it. The doctrine of sovereignty has no application to this new system. Sovereignty over a Mandated Territory is in abeyance; if and when the inhabitants of the Territory obtain recognition as an independent State, as has already happened in the case of some of the Mandates, sovereignty will revive and vest in the new State. What matters in considering this new institution is not where sovereignty lies, but what are the rights and duties of the Mandatory in regard to the area of territory being administered by it. The answer to that question depends on the international agreements creating the system and the rules of law which they attract. Its essence is that the Mandatory acquires only a limited title to the territory entrusted to it, and that the measure of its powers is what is necessary for the purpose of carrying out the Mandate. 'The Mandatory's rights, like the trustee's, have their foundation in his obligations; they are "tools given to him in order to achieve the work assigned to him"; he has "all the tools necessary for such end, but only those".' "

Separate Opinion of Judge McNair, *International Status of South-West Africa*, Advisory Opinion, July 11, 1950, I.C.J. Reports (1950) 128, 150.

In discussing the matter of "where does sovereignty rest" with respect to trusteeships, Francis B. Sayre had the following to say:

"One of the most perplexing legal questions arising out of the mandates system was that of the location of sovereignty of the territories under mandate. It has been the subject of extended treatment by writers on international law. [See Quincy Wright, *Mandates Under the League of Nations* (1930), pp. 319 ff.]

. . . .

"Thus far, of the three groups referred to in Article 77(1) of the Charter, only former mandated territories have been placed under the trusteeship system. The question of sovereignty over these territories remains fluid.

"In spite of the unsolved question of exactly where sovereignty over mandated territories and over trust territories rests, there is general agreement with respect to certain aspects of the question. In the first place, there seems to be general concurrence with respect to the present trust territories, as there was with respect to mandated territories, that wherever sovereignty does rest it is not with the administering power. This view has been reënforced by statements of the United States, the United Kingdom and Australia as administering authorities of trust territories. Each of these has stated on separate occasions that it does not regard its administration of the trust territory as implying any claim of sovereignty. ["In an explanatory comment on the Draft Trusteeship Agreement for the former Japanese Mandated Islands, the United States Government, in discussing the phrase 'integral part' which appeared in the original draft of Article 3 of the proposed trusteeship agreement, declared that this did not 'imply sovereignty over the territory.' See Department of State Publication 2784, p. 5.

"In the discussions in the General Assembly preceding the approval of the first trusteeship agreements, the Delegate for the United Kingdom declared that the 'retention of the words "as an integral part" in the Trusteeship Agreement for Togoland and the Cameroons under British administration did not involve administration as an integral part of the United Kingdom itself and did not imply British sovereignty in these rights.' Report of the Fourth Committee on Trusteeship Agreements, UN doc. A/258, December 12, 1946, p. 6.

"The Australian representative in the Trusteeship Subcommittee of Committee 4 at the Second Part of the First Session of the General Assembly stated that sovereignty over New Guinea was not claimed by Australia. UN doc. A/C.4/ Sub. 1/19, November 21, 1946, p. 5. The Belgian representative stated to the same body that in using the phrase 'as an integral part' it was not the intention of the mandatory powers to imply a decision on the 'incidence of sovereignty.' The French representative supported these remarks. UN doc. A/C.4/Sub. 1/30, November 23, 1946, p. 3."]

"In the second place, little now is heard of the theory that sovereignty over the mandated territories resided in the League of Nations in view of the fact that the League of Nations has disappeared without any direct transfer of its mandates responsibilities or sovereignty to others and certainly without any suggestion that the League was transferring title to the mandated territories to the United Nations.

"Finally, it seems to be clear that the question of sovereignty over those trust territories which were formerly mandates is of lessening practical significance. The question of exactly where sovereignty over a trust territory rests is being reduced to one of sterility. Irrespective of where sovereignty may rest, a practical method has now been worked out and approved by the General Assembly for the placing of former mandated territories under trusteeship; and trusteeship may be lawfully terminated under the Charter by the grant of self-government or independence for the trust territory and its inhabitants. This is not to suggest that legal difficulties concerning title to mandated and trust territories do not still remain. But as long as the trusteeship system remains in operation they do not present insuperable or even baffling obstacles to progress."

Francis B. Sayre, United States Representative in the Trusteeship Council and President of the Council, "Legal Problems Arising from the United Nations Trusteeship System", 42 Am. J. Int'l L. (1948) 263, 268, 271–272.

"It is believed that to introduce the concept of sovereignty into any discussion of the nature either of mandates or of trust territories is, from the point of view of international law, merely confusing. Municipal law, as in *Rex* v. *Christian* [1923–1924 Annual Digest, Case No. 12, p. 27], may make it necessary to do so; international law does not. The notion that we must look for sovereignty in a mandated or a trust territory implies that sovereignty is an indestructible substance which we shall surely find in any area if only we look closely enough. But government under mandate or trust is surely an alternative to, not a species of, government under sovereignty; and, just as English law has two different regimes for the holding of property, namely private ownership and trusts, so now international law has acquired two regimes for government, that is to say, sovereignty and the mandate or the trust. Like the rights of a trustee in our law, so the rights of an international trustee state have their foundation in its obligations under the Charter and under the trust agreement; they are tools given it in order to achieve the work assigned to it, and the measure of its powers, the test by which its possession of any particular power must be determined, is that the law has provided it with all the tools that are necessary for its task, but with those only. [This view was originally suggested by Brierly in an article, "Trusts and Mandates", in Brit. Yb. Int'l L., 1929, p. 217, which was referred to with approval by Evatt, J., in the Australian case of *Ffrost* v. *Stevenson*, [1937] C.L.R. 528, 1935–1937 Ann. Dig., Case No. 29, p. 98.]"

Brierly, *The Law of Nations* (5th ed., 1955) 166–167.

". . . In the judgments to which I have been referring, the principles discussed were those which, in terms, related to the powers and jurisdiction of *Sovereign* States within their own Territory. It could, conceivably, be argued that those principles are not applicable in the case of a territory held under *Mandate* (as Australia had held the Territory of New Guinea) or under *Trusteeship* (as Australia is about to hold that Territory). Let us examine that argument. After the First World War, Germany renounced all her rights over her former Colony of New Guinea in favour of the Principal Allied and Associated Powers. Those Powers then conferred a Mandate on His Britannic Majesty, exercisable on his behalf by the Government of the Commonwealth of Australia, to administer the Territory of New Guinea in accordance with the terms of the Mandate. His Britannic Majesty accepted the Mandate and the Australian Government agreed to exercise it on his behalf. There is considerable difference of opinion about where, in the case of a Mandated Territory, the ultimate sovereignty resides. But in Article 2 of the New Guinea Mandate it was expressly declared that 'the Mandatory shall have full power of administration and legislation over the Territory subject to the present Mandate as an integral portion of the Commonwealth of Australia and may apply the laws of the Commonwealth of Australia to the territory, subject to such local modifications as circumstances may require'. In the face of that declaration it seems to me beyond doubt that, wherever the ultimate sovereignty of the Territory of New Guinea may reside, Australia may, as Mandatory Power, and subject to the terms of the Mandate, exercise powers of administration and legislation over New Guinea that are equivalent to and as full as those of a Sovereign State: in other words, Australia's powers of administration over New Guinea include exclusive jurisdiction over all persons and things within that Territory, except in so far as Australia concedes immunity from that exclusive jurisdiction. In the past Australia has certainly exercised, and at the date of the offences alleged in the present indictment certainly claimed to exercise, such powers

"Jurisdiction"

of administration and exclusive jurisdiction over the Territory of New Guinea. Will this position be altered when the Mandated Territory of New Guinea comes under the Trusteeship System? At San Francisco on 26th June 1945, Australia subscribed to the Charter of the United Nations. Australia has since subscribed to a Trusteeship Agreement for the Mandated Territory of New Guinea, in which Australia undertook to place that Territory under the Trusteeship System on the terms set forth in the Trusteeship Agreement. A Bill providing for a Permanent Administration of the Territories of Papua and New Guinea, and for Parliamentary approval of Australia's participation in the Trusteeship Agreement already mentioned, has recently been read for the first time in the Australian Parliament. Article 4 of the Trusteeship Agreement provides that Australia, as 'Administering Authority' of the Territory of New Guinea, 'will be responsible for the peace, order, good government and defence of the Territory and for this purpose will have the same powers of legislation, administration and jurisdiction in and over the Territory as if it were an integral part of Australia, and will be entitled to apply to the Territory, subject to such modifications as it deems desirable, such laws of the Commonwealth of Australia as it deems appropriate to the needs and conditions of the Territory'. That Article would give Australia powers of legislation, administration and jurisdiction over the Territory of New Guinea, Trust Territory, that are no less ample than those conferred on Australia as Mandatory Power administering the Mandated Territory of New Guinea—powers that may be exercised as fully, within their range, as those exercised by Sovereign States on the same subjects. It follows, in my opinion, that Australia, whether holding the Territory of New Guinea under Mandate or under Trusteeship, has exclusive jurisdiction over that Territory, subject to such immunities from that jurisdiction as Australia herself has conceded or may concede."

Phillips, J., in *Chow Hung Ching* v. *The King*, New Guinea, Supreme Court of Papau-New Guinea, Aug. 5, 1948, reported in [1948] Ann. Dig. 147, 149–150.

"The problem in our case is new and different. We must see whether the rules enacted by an organ of the Trusteeship Administration of Somaliland must be regarded as foreign in relation to the Italian legal system.

.   .   .   .

"From these preliminary remarks it is clearly wrong to say that acts performed by the State which has the power of administration over a Trust Territory can be regarded as foreign in relation to its own legal system, even though they concern another subject of international law.

"If we may refer to private law—from which, as we have said, the conception of trust is derived—the acts which are performed by the trustee, although they concern the beneficiary, are always within the sphere of will and action of the trustee. We should come to a similar conclusion in respect of the administration of a territory which was a colonial territory. The limits of the Italian legal system have become wider and more comprehensive. In addition to exercising sovereignty over its own territory, the Italian State, by virtue of Article 1 of the Annex to the Agreement exercises it also—although in the name of the population of Somaliland and under the conditions set forth in the Agreement— over Somaliland. The Trusteeship Administration which has been entrusted to Italy comes within the limits and the scope of the Italian legal system. It constitutes not a mere right but a power, and at the same time an obligation, of the administering State, which must be fulfilled by all the organs of the State itself within the limits of their respective competences.

.   .   .   .

"The idea, already examined, of the absolute separation between the Italian legal system and the Trusteeship Administration of Somaliland is repeated in this ground of appeal. The Court, however, is constrained by a number of considerations to reject the complaint. In the first place, the competencies of the Administration of Somaliland are not foreign to the Italian legal system. Article 2 of the Agreement confers on the administration authority all powers of legislation, administration and jurisdiction. The Trusteeship Administrator is designated by the President of the Italian Republic. According to paragraph 7 of Article 87 of the Constitution, this fact alone provides sufficient grounds for inferring that the Trusteeship Administrator constitutes an organ of the Italian State. It is irrelevant that Italy and Somaliland are two separate sovereign entities in their respective spheres and that therefore there cannot be interference by one in the legal system of the other. As a statement of fact, it is correct, but, on the one hand, the sovereignty of the Somali people is limited and confined within the limits of the power of the Trusteeship Administration of Italy, and, on the other hand, the Administrator derives his powers from the Italian State: therefore, he is in a position to designate Italian organs for the performing of functions which, as we have already said, belong to the sphere of the Italian legal system.

"It is not in point to say that the powers of the Administrator are limited to the territory of Somaliland. It is true that those powers are adherent to the territory of Somaliland, but the Administrator did not [in making his Decree of 1950] overstep the limits of his powers, seeing that the Decree concerns the exercise of jurisdiction with respect to that territory. It is of no importance whatsoever whether or not the seat of the organ which exercises judicial power is outside the territory concerned. This ground of appeal, therefore, must be rejected."

Società A.B.C. v. *Fontana and Della Rocca*, Italy, Court of Cassation (United Chambers), Aug. 10, 1954, reported in [1955] Int'l L. Rep. 76, 77–79 (1958).

"With the exception of the draft trusteeship agreements for Tanganyika and New Guinea, all the draft agreements submitted to the General Assembly for approval contained a provision empowering the administering authority to administer the trust territory as an 'integral part' of its territory. The New Guinea draft used the expression 'as if it were an integral part'. The Tanganyika draft had no such provision. It was pointed out by the states submitting the draft trusteeship agreements that the phrase 'integral part' was contained in the mandate agreements and that its continuance in the trusteeship agreements would have no new significance. They further stated that the phrase carried no implication of sovereignty and that it was proposed solely for administrative convenience. Nevertheless, certain delegations regarded the use of the expression 'integral part' as contrary to the spirit of the trusteeship system and felt that it revealed 'annexationist tendencies'. The Soviet Union and India proposed the deletion of the phrase from each of the trusteeship agreements in which it was used. The Trusteeship Subcommittee recommended to New Zealand, whose draft for Western Samoa was considered first, that the phrase be deleted. Similar recommendations were made by Committee 4 with regard to the other trusteeship drafts which used the phrase. The New Zealand Government accepted the recommendation, but the other Mandatory Powers found themselves unable to agree to delete the phrase from their drafts and made to the Fourth Committee formal statements of the reasons underlying their refusal. Thus, in the eight agreements finally approved by the General Assembly the phrase 'integral part' appears in all of the agreements except those for Tanganyika and Western Samoa.

"The Soviet Delegation carried its opposition to the phrase 'integral part' to the floor of the General Assembly. Before the final vote of the General Assembly approving the terms of trusteeship, the Soviet Delegation proposed a resolution advocating rejection of the trusteeship drafts partly on the grounds that they still contained the phrase 'integral part'. This resolution was rejected by a vote of 34 to 6 with 11 abstentions.

"The discussion in the General Assembly and its committees on the 'integral part' issue served the useful purpose of clarifying the meaning to be given to this phrase. In addition to general statements made by various representatives of the Mandatory Powers that they did not understand this phrase to connote sovereignty over the trust territories, the following declarations regarding the phrase were made by France, Belgium, and the United Kingdom and inserted in the report of the rapporteur on trusteeship agreements:

" 'With regard to the proposed deletion of the words "as an integral part" of the French and Belgian territory, as indicated by the modifications submitted to the Belgian agreement for Ruanda-Urundi and the French agreements for the Cameroons and Togoland by the Delegations of the Soviet Union and India, the Delegates for Belgium and France stated that it was the interpretation of their Governments that the words "as an integral part" were necessary as a matter of administrative convenience and were not considered as granting to the Governments of Belgium and France the power to diminish the political individuality of the Trust Territories.

" 'The Delegate for the United Kingdom informed the Sub-Committee that the retention of the words "as an integral part" in the Trusteeship agreement for Togoland and Cameroons under British administration did not involve administration as an integral part of the United Kingdom itself and did not imply British sovereignty in these areas.' [General Assembly Doc. A/258, December 12, 1946, p. 6.]"

Armstrong and Cargo, Division of Dependent Area Affairs, Office of Special Political Affairs, Department of State, "The Inauguration of the Trusteeship System of the United Nations", XVI *Bulletin*, Department of State, No. 403, Mar. 23, 1947, pp. 511, 517.

"Under the mandates provision of the Covenant of the League of Nations 'C' mandates were to be administered under the laws of the Mandatory 'as integral portions of its territory.' [*Covenant of the League of Nations*, Article 22, par. 6.] No such language was contained in the Covenant with respect to 'A' or 'B' mandates. All of the draft trusteeship agreements submitted to the General Assembly in 1946, except that for Tanganyika, contained a provision empowering the administering authority to administer the trust territory 'as an integral part' of its territory or (in the case of the New Guinea draft) 'as if it were an integral part.' These trusteeship agreements, however, included former 'B' mandates as well as 'C' mandates. Objection was raised to the phrase on the ground that it prepared the way for eventual annexation and violated the spirit of trusteeship. [UN docs. A/C.4/Sub. 1/30, November 23, 1946, pp. 1–2; A/C.4/Sub. 1/81, December 3, 1946, pp. 12–13.] The mandatory powers replied that this phraseology went back to the mandates system, that it carried no implication of sovereignty, and that it was proposed solely for administrative convenience. [UN doc. A/C.4/Sub. 1/81, December 3, 1946, pp. 8–12; A/258, December 12, 1946, p. 6.] Except for New Zealand [UN doc. A/C.4/Sub. 1/71, November 29, 1946, p. 2], the mandatory powers refused to accept proposals for the deletion of the phrase 'as an integral part.' In the plenary session of the General Assembly, the Soviet delegation proposed a resolution rejecting the trusteeship agreements on the ground *inter alia* that they still contained the phrase 'as an integral part.' [See *Official Records of the Second Part of the First Session of the General Assembly* (62nd Plenary Meeting, December 13, 1946), pp. 1276–1283.] The resolution was rejected by a vote of 34 to 6, with 11 abstentions, and the agreements were then approved by overwhelming majorities.

"In view of the debates which took place during the First Session of the Assembly and of the way the clause has been interpreted in practice in the actual administration of the trust territories it would seem as if the phrase in question confers upon the administering powers no substantive rights or powers which they would not possess in its absence. To all intents and purposes the phrase seems to carry little meaning and could easily be dispensed with.

"The United States draft trusteeship agreement for the former Japanese Mandated Islands, as submitted to the Security Council, similarly contained a provision that the territory was to be administered 'as an integral part' of the United States. [UN doc. S/281, February 17, 1947.] In accepting an amendment to delete this phrase, the United States representative said: 'In agreeing to this modification, my Government feels that it should affirm for the record that its authority in the trust territory is not to be considered in any way lessened thereby.' [Security Council Official Record 23, March 7, 1947, p. 473.]"

Francis B. Sayre, United States Representative in the Trusteeship Council and President of the Council, "Legal Problems Arising from the United Nations Trusteeship System", 42 Am. J. Int'l L. (1948) 263, 285–286.

Resolution 649 (VII) of the Seventh Session of the General Assembly made the following recommendations with respect to "Administrative unions affecting Trust Territories":

Administrative
unions

"*The General Assembly*,

"*Recalling* that the Trusteeship Agreements for the Trust Territories concerned authorize the Administering Authorities to establish customs, fiscal or administrative unions or federations,

"*Recalling* its resolution 224 (III) of 18 November 1948, recommending that the Trusteeship Council should investigate the question of administrative unions in all its aspects, and resolution 326 (IV) of 15 November 1949, recommending that the Trusteeship Council should complete the investigation,

"*Recalling*, further, that in resolution 326 (IV) it noted that the Trusteeship Agreements do not authorize any form of political association which would involve annexation of the Trust Territories in any sense, or would have the effect of extinguishing their status as Trust Territories, and affirmed the view that measures of customs, fiscal or administrative union must not in any way hamper the free evolution of each Trust Territory toward self-government or independence,

"*Recalling* its resolution 563 (VI) of 18 January 1952, requesting the Trusteeship Council to submit to it, at its seventh session, a special report containing a complete analysis of each of the administrative unions to which a Trust Territory is a party, and of the status of the Cameroons and Togoland under French administration arising out of their membership in the French Union,

"*Recalling* the studies [see *Official Records of the Trusteeship Council, Fifth Session, Annex*, agenda item 10, p. 255 and

Official Records of the General Assembly, Fifth Session, Supplement No. 4, annex] on administrative unions undertaken by the Trusteeship Council in 1949 and 1950, and in particular the important analysis of administrative unions contained in resolution 293 (VII) adopted by the Council on 17 July 1950,

"*Recalling* the regular annual reports adopted by the Trusteeship Council in 1951 and 1952 on each of the Trust Territories participating in an administrative union,

"1. *Takes note* of the special report [see *Official Records of the General Assembly, Seventh Session, Supplement No. 12*] submitted by the Trusteeship Council in compliance with General Assembly resolution 563 (VI), and the observations [see document A/2217] made thereon by the General Assembly Committee on Administrative Unions;

"2. *Calls* to the attention of the Administering Authorities the observations and conclusions contained in the special report of the Trusteeship Council and the observations of the General Assembly Committee on Administrative Unions;

"3. *Requests* the Administering Authorities to continue to transmit promptly to the Trusteeship Council information as complete as possible concerning the operation of the administrative unions affecting Trust Territories under their administration, indicating the benefits and advantages derived by the inhabitants of the Trust Territories from administrative unions;

"4. *Expresses the hope* that the Administering Authorities concerned will take into account the freely expressed wishes of the inhabitants before establishing or extending the scope of administrative unions;

"5. *Expresses the hope* that the Administering Authorities concerned will consult with the Trusteeship Council concerning any change in or extension of existing administrative unions, or concerning any proposal to establish new administrative unions;

"6. *Requests* the Trusteeship Council to continue its regular examination of each administrative union affecting a Trust Territory, and to study these administrative unions, not only with regard to the four safeguards enumerated in Trusteeship Council resolution 293 (VII), but also with regard to the interests of the inhabitants of the Territory and the terms of the Charter and the Trusteeship Agreements, as well as any other matters which the Council may deem appropriate.

*409th plenary meeting,
20 December 1952.*"

U.N. Gen. Ass. Off. Rec. 7th Sess., Supp. No. 20 (A/2361), pp. 35-36.

"*Administrative Unions*

"Administrative unions had existed under the League of Nations, but they did not raise any question of white settler domination. Soon after the trusteeship system of the United Nations was set in motion, however, Tanganyika, Kenya, and Uganda were joined for the administration of common services through the East African Territorial Organization, and New Guinea was joined with Papua in an administrative and legislative union. [Three other trust territories are involved in some form of administrative union: the political integration of British Togoland with the Gold Coast; the political integration of the British Cameroons with Nigeria; and the loose association of Ruanda Urundi with the Belgian Congo. Two others, the Cameroons and Togoland under French administration were assigned a status, not clearly defined, under the French constitution of 1946 as Associated Territories in the French Union. In 1956, French Togoland was declared to be an autonomous republic within the French Union.] Many Member states expressed concern over these unions, particularly over the former, which was established without prior consultation with the inhabitants of Tanganyika or the Trusteeship Council. The question has also been the subject of lively debate in both the Trusteeship Council and the General Assembly.

"In 1949, the General Assembly on the basis of a United States proposal, adopted a resolution setting forth the following principles in connection with administrative unions: that the Trusteeship Council be notified before new unions are established or old ones extended; that the unified administration be supervised as the Council deems necessary if separate data on the trust territory are not available; that a separate judicial organization and a separate legislative body be established for each territory; and that the freely expressed wishes of the people be taken into account before establishing or broadening an administrative union. [Res. 326(V), Nov. 15, 1949.] The resolution called on the Council to complete the study of administrative unions requested by the Assembly at its third session, paying particular attention to these principles, and to submit a report thereon including references to any safeguards that should be instituted.

"The Trusteeship Council had set up a Committee on Administrative Unions at its fourth session in 1949, and in 1950, it established a Standing Committee on Administrative Unions and spelled out four safeguards that the committee later looked for in its examination of administrative unions: (1) the existence of clear, precise, and separate data on the trust territories; (2) access of visiting missions to information on the unions; (3) maintenance of separate boundaries, status, and identity of the trust territories; and (4) public expenditures in a trust territory not to be less than revenues in the same year. [U.N. General Assembly, Seventh Session, *Official Records*, Supplement No. 12, "Special Report of the Trusteeship Council on Administrative Unions Affecting Trust Territories and on the Status of the Cameroons and Togoland under French Administration Arising Out of Their Membership in the French Union," p. 3.]

"Despite some initial reservations, the administering authorities concerned have co-operated in subjecting their administrative unions to scrutiny by the United Nations, but they opposed some of the principles set forth in the resolution of the General Assembly, which they regard as an intrusion on their legal authority. They emphasize the advantages to the trust territories from administrative integration with neighboring territories. They also point out that the 'balkanization' of Africa could have serious consequences, as the creation of small, independent states, lacking economic viability, would hardly benefit the people concerned or contribute to the well-being of the world. Many Members, however, have contended in the past, and a few still do, that some administrative unions, such as those involving Togoland and Cameroons under British administration, are incompatible with Article 76(b) of the Charter because the integration is so complete that it denies the people of the trust territory any real choice of their political future. They expressed dissatisfaction with the Standing Committee because it had based its work on the four 'safeguards' drawn up by the Council rather than the more exacting principles laid down by the Assembly. Also, the Standing Committee had limited itself to brief comments on the unions affecting only four territories, and no mention was made of those affecting the two Togolands, presumably because they were being considered in conjunction with the unification question.

"Over the objections of the administering authorities, the Assembly, in 1952, adopted another resolution, which created its own Committee on Administrative Unions, consisting of two administering and two nonadministering Members. The resolution called for a special report from the Council analyzing each administrative union from the standpoint of the principles laid down by the Assembly and asked its committee to review this report and present its observations thereon to the seventh session of the Assembly. [While Sady cites "Res. 649(VII), Dec. 20, 1952", the reference appears to be to Res. 563(VI) 18 Jan. 1952.] This was done, and the Assembly then adopted another resolution reiterating some of the principles contained in previous resolutions of the Assembly and the Council. [649(VII) 20 Dec. 1952.] Unlike the resolution of the Assembly in 1949, no mention was made in the resolution of 1952 of the desirability of separate legislative and judicial bodies for trust territories that form parts of administrative unions. The Soviet bloc was defeated, as it had been previously, in its effort to require the establishment of separate legislative and executive organs in all trust territories affected by administrative unions. The vote was 21 to 5 with 24 abstentions—the abstentions being indicative of the misgivings of many Members. [Another proposal by Iraq and Brazil to ask the International Court to give an advisory opinion on the compatibility of the administrative unions with the Charter and the relevant trusteeship agreements was withdrawn for lack of support. India had favored such a proposal in the Committee on Administrative Unions of the Assembly, but it may have been persuaded not to complicate further the question of the integration of British Togoland with the Gold Coast or of the integration of British Cameroons with Nigeria. Some opposition may have been induced by the confidence of administering authorities, such as Belgium, that the Court would only confirm the legality of the union of Ruanda Urundi with the

Congo. Another theory is that the proposal called for the Trusteeship Council to formulate the questions to be put to the Court, and the Soviet bloc, in particular, would prefer the Assembly itself to formulate the questions.]

"The concern of the General Assembly with administrative unions, although embarrassing to the Trusteeship Council at first, helped the Council produce several concrete results. The administering authorities have made a determined effort to provide separate financial and other data on the trust territories involved in administrative unions, even at the cost of reorganizing accounting and statistical reporting methods. Although the Council has not attempted to dissolve the unions that existed at the time the United Nations was established, it has scrutinized critically proposals for creating new unions or for extending existing ones. This was particularly evident in the case of New Guinea, in which the Council reviewed in detail the Australian legislation calling for joint administration of the territory with Papua [Papua and New Guinea Act, 1949], and in so doing, may have helped to ensure that the identity of the trust territory was maintained, and the interests of the inhabitants were not subordinated to those of European settlers. Finally, the Members of the United Nations have a better appreciation of the value, in some cases, of administrative unions to the inhabitants of trust territories.

"The doctrinaire opposition in the Assembly to administrative unions may also, however, discourage the creation of unions that would benefit the peoples concerned. For example, the United States has authority under the trusteeship agreement for the Trust Territory of the Pacific Islands to constitute the territory into an administrative union or federation with Guam, an island possession of the United States that is located in the heart of the Trust Territory. Guamanians have cultural and kinship ties with the people of other Mariana islands that are under trusteeship. Guam serves as headquarters for the Trust Territory and is the transportation, commercial, and cultural center for the whole territory. It is reasonable to assume that if any of the inhabitants of this trust territory ever attain full self-government, it will only be through some form of political association with Guam. However, the specter of international criticism that is raised at the suggestion of any such association has discouraged serious study of its possibilities."

Sady, *The United Nations and Dependent Peoples* (The Brookings Institution, 1956) 167–170. As to Saipan, see *supra*, § 41, "Trust Territory of the Pacific Islands", under discussion of article 9 (pp. 813–814).

"Independence"; "self-government"

"Article 76 of the Charter explicitly sets forth four basic objectives of the trusteeship system. These constitute a daring venture. Nothing so progressive and far-reaching within the realm of government over dependent peoples was ever before attempted.

"The second of these objectives—the promotion of political, economic, social, and educational advancement of the inhabitants and their progressive development towards self-government or independence—embodies the central conception of the mandates system, but goes beyond it. The Covenant (Article 22) confined the mandates objective to the 'well-being and development' of the inhabitants. To this the framers of the Charter at San Francisco boldly added 'progressive development towards self-government or independence.' The ideal of human freedom was written into a binding international agreement.

"The wording of this additional objective marks a compromise. Some delegations at San Francisco, particularly non-administering states, conceived the solution of problems of non-self-governing peoples in terms of rapid or even immediate attainment of full independence. In their minds the problem of dependent peoples can be at once solved by the grant of independence. Another group, composed largely of those states having long experience in governing and working with dependent peoples, felt equally strongly that the real problems go far deeper than mere political status, that genuine solutions can come only through slow processes of education and training in the complex tasks of government and administration. In their eyes the grant of independence to peoples who lack the trained administrators or popular education necessary for orderly processes of government or who perhaps lack the economic or financial resources necessary for independent statehood, is but to create and multiply international problems rather than to solve them. [See in this connection the interesting and able speech delivered by the United Kingdom's representative in the discussion on this subject in the Fourth Committee at the Second Session of the General Assembly. As there suggested, the ultimate welfare of dependent peoples can in some cases be best promoted by immediate independence, in others by self-government in a larger grouping of territories and in still others by remaining under the wing of a colonial power and drawing upon it for educational facilities, technicians, and defense. It is a naive misunderstanding to suppose that "sovereign status is a sovereign remedy for all ills." UN doc. A/C.4/SR. 36, October 4, 1947, pp. 2–5.]

"Between these two groups conflict raged, the former demanding that the objective of the trusteeship system should be the speedy grant of outright independence, the latter, including the United States, that the objective should be the gradual and orderly evolution toward whatever form of independence or self-government the inhabitants of a particular territory were capable and desirous of attaining. [See Ralph J. Bunche, "Trusteeship and Non-Self-Governing Territories in the Charter of the United Nations," *Department of State Bulletin*, December 30, 1945, p. 1039; and *The United States and Non-Self-Governing Territories* (Dept. of State Publ. 2812, Apr. 5, 1947), p. 11.] Agreement was finally found by a formula phrased in the alternative—'progressive development towards self-government or independence, as may be appropriate to the particular circumstances of each territory and its peoples and the freely expressed wishes of the people concerned.' [It is interesting that while each of the ten trusteeship agreements specifies in some detail the means for promoting political advancement, none specifically amplifies the words "self-government or independence." Efforts were made during the debates of the General Assembly to obtain such amplification but were rejected by the mandatory powers. A similar effort was made in the Security Council in the discussion of the trusteeship agreement for the Pacific Islands to modify the United States proposal which mentioned only "self-government." The United States representative, upon the request of the Soviet representative, agreed to the addition of the clause which follows in Article 76(b) of the Charter, but declared that "the United States feels that it must record its opposition not to the principle of independence, to which no people could be more consecrated than the people of the United States, but to the thought that it could possibly be achieved within any foreseeable future in this case." See UN doc. S/P.V./116, March 7, 1947, p. 47.]

"The view of the United States was set forth in the discussion in the Fourth Committee during the Second Session of the General Assembly:

" ' "Self-government" may take the form of independence; it may take the form of local autonomy within a larger association of some kind; it may take the form of assimilation to a sovereign state, provided that the people of the territory concerned have attained a degree of political autonomy and reached a stage of political development which will enable them to make a free and considered choice.

" 'Thus, it becomes evident that Chapter XI of the Charter provides for the steady progress of the peoples of non-self-governing territories toward a variety of goals encompassed in the phrase "self-government". It is equally evident, however, that immediate independence for all non-self-governing territories would not necessarily benefit those territories; in fact, it might retard their development, injure their peoples, and create confusion and chaos in many parts of the world.

" 'Indeed, it must be admitted that non-self-governing territories are not, in every case, in greater need of attention than some of the peoples of sovereign, self-governing nations. In fact, there are non-self-governing peoples who enjoy greater powers of self-government and greater protection for their individual rights than are enjoyed by some peoples within independent states.' [Statement by Mr. Sayre, representing the United States in the Fourth Committee, U.S. Mission Press Release No. 244, October 2, 1947, pp. 1–2.]"

Francis B. Sayre, United States Representative in the Trusteeship Council and President of the Council, "Legal Problems Arising from the United Nations Trusteeship System", 42 Am. J. Int'l L. (1948) 263, 279–281.

"The fourth of the basic objectives of the trusteeship system set forth in Article 76 is 'to ensure equal treatment in social, economic and commercial matters for all Members of the United Nations and their nationals.' This embodies a deep-rooted American ideal—the elimination of discriminatory practices in economic and commercial relations, expressed at various times as the 'Open Door' policy. It is here made an international obligation making for peace, binding in all non-strategic trust territories. *"Equal treatment"*

"The contentious issue of what constitutes 'equal treatment' was perhaps one of the most difficult problems at the San Francisco Conference. [See *The Question of Equal Treatment in Economic and Commercial Matters in Trust Territories (Article 76 d); Memorandum Prepared by the Secretariat*, UN doc. A/C.4/38, November 3, 1946.] It will be recalled that equal treatment was prescribed in the Covenant of the League for the 'A' and 'B' mandates, but not for the 'C' mandates. The United States Delegation at San Francisco introduced a proposal requiring non-discriminatory treatment in all trust territories. [*Documents of the United Nations Conference on International Organization, San Francisco*, 1945, Vol. X, p. 644.] The mandatory powers which administered 'C' mandates contended, however, that any provision in the Charter which would require equal treatment in 'C' mandates placed under trusteeship would have the effect of altering the terms of the mandate. Partly as a result of this contention, Article 80(1) was inserted in the Charter providing that, except as might be agreed upon in individual trusteeship agreements and until such agreements had been concluded, nothing in Chapter XII should be construed 'to alter in any way the rights whatsoever of any states or any peoples or the terms of existing international instruments to which Members of the United Nations might respectively be parties.'

"Article 76(d), as finally adopted, represented a compromise between these opposing points of view. Equal treatment was applied to all non-strategic trust territories but 'without prejudice to the attainment of the foregoing objectives'—that is, peace and security, the advancement of the inhabitants, and human rights. The effect of Article 76(d) is to strengthen the requirement of equal treatment with respect to the former 'C' mandates, where no such requirement previously existed, but to weaken it with respect to the former 'A' and 'B' mandates, where it was unqualified.

"Exactly how 'equal treatment' is to be defined is a problem still unsolved.

"The question also remains open whether in strategic trust territories the Charter requires equality of commercial treatment for all Members of the United Nations. Article 83, paragraph 2, of the Charter provides that 'the basic objectives set forth in Article 76 shall be applicable to the people of each strategic area.' It has been argued that these words, confining the applicability to *the people* of each strategic area, make the basic objectives set forth in paragraph (d) of Article 76 inapplicable to the 'Members of the United Nations and their nationals.' As yet no determination of the matter has been made either by vote in the General Assembly or by judicial decision.

"The position of the United States, the administering authority of the only existing strategic trust territory, was set forth before the Security Council, meeting on April 2, 1947 to consider the draft trusteeship agreement for the Trust Territory of the Pacific Islands. Ambassador Austin, the American representative in the Security Council, in discussing the Charter provision contained in Article 76(d), said: 'Now I wish to state as a matter of record that the United States Government has no intention, through this clause or any other clause, of taking advantage, for its own benefit and to the detriment of the welfare of the inhabitants, of the meager and almost non-existent resources and commercial opportunities that exist in the scattered and barren islands.' [UN doc. S/P.V./124, April 2, 1947, pp. 103–105. A similar statement was made at the time the draft trusteeship agreement was placed before the Security Council. See *Draft Trusteeship Agreement for the Japanese Mandated Islands*, State Department Publication 2784 (1947), p. 8.]"

Francis B. Sayre, United States Representative in the Trusteeship Council and President of the Council, "Legal Problems Arising from the United Nations Trusteeship System", 42 Am. J. Int'l L. (1948) 262, 281–283.

"Concessions"

"The problem of mineral concessions in Somaliland lasting beyond the period of trusteeship involves various issues: (1) Whether the Administering Authority can legally grant mineral concessions to extend beyond the ten years of trusteeship; (2) whether the independent state òf Somaliland would be bound by a concession after the ten-year period; and (3) what practical guarantees could be given to foreign investors interested in developing concessions.

"1. General Assembly resolution 289(IV) provides 'that Italian Somaliland shall be an independent sovereign state' and 'that this independence shall become effective at the end of ten years from the date of the approval of a trusteeship agreement by the General Assembly.' During the period of trusteeship, Italy is to serve as the Administering Authority. The powers and duties of the Administering Authority are laid down in the trusteeship agreement approved by the General Assembly on December 2, 1950. Under the Treaty of Peace with Italy, Italy gave up sovereignty over Italian Somaliland. For the present, however, Italy serves as Administering Authority, and must be thought to possess the usual powers of government in Somaliland in accordance with the terms of trusteeship. See, *e.g.*, Article 2, Somaliland Trusteeship Agreement. Article 14 of the trusteeship agreement provides, in part, as follows:

" 'In order to promote the economic and social advancement of the indigenous population, the Administering Authority shall, in framing laws relating to the holding or alienation of land or other natural resources, take into consideration the laws and customs of the indigenous population and respect their rights and safeguard their interests, both present and future.

" 'The Administering Authority shall not, without the consent in each case of a two-thirds majority of the members of the Territorial Council (provided for in article 4 of the annex to this Agreement), permit the acquisition by non-indigenous persons or by companies or associations controlled by such persons of any rights over land in the Territory save on lease for a period to be determined by law. In cases involving the alienation to non-indigenous persons or to companies or associations controlled by such persons of areas of agricultural lands in excess of one thousand acres, the Administering Authority shall also request in advance the advice of the Advisory Council. The Administering Authority shall include in its annual report to the Trusteeship Council a detailed account of such alienations.

" 'The Administering Authority shall prohibit the acquisition by non-indigenous persons or by companies or associations controlled by such persons of any rights over any other natural resources in the Territory, save on lease or grant of concession for a period to be determined by law.'

"The above-quoted provision shows that the trusteeship agreement contemplates the possibility of concessions being granted by the Administering Authority. Various requirements of principle and of detail are laid down in the article. None of these prevents the granting of a concession beyond the ten-year period of trusteeship. Accordingly, it would seem that the grant of a concession beyond the trusteeship period would be within the power of the Administering Authority provided the requirements of Article 14 are complied with. In certain cases these requirements involve consent or advice from the Territorial Council or the Advisory Council. It appears that both the Advisory Council and the Territorial Council have been consulted by the Administering Authority concerning the possibility of concessions running beyond the ten-year period of trusteeship. Both councils apparently agree that the Administering Authority has the power to grant such concessions.

"If the Italian administration granted concessions in Somaliland for a period exceeding the period of trusteeship, there is reason to believe that a considerable body of opinion in the Trusteeship Council and presumably the General Assembly would support such action, provided that Members of the United Nations were satisfied that the terms of such concessions adequately protected the interests of the territory and that the action was taken with the approval of the Territorial Council of Somaliland.

"2. Although the Administering Authority may be regarded as having the power to grant concessions intended to last beyond the trusteeship period, that would not determine the question of the right or ability of the independent state of Somaliland to terminate concessions when Somaliland has achieved independence. The attitude of the future government of Somaliland after independence cannot now be forecast; there are too many variables. Should a future Somaliland Government desire to terminate a concession, it might assert that any concession for the development of mineral resources in Somaliland was impliedly subject to a reserved right of nationalization. In the event of nationalization, fair compensation would be required. If, on the other hand, no such implied reservation of the right to nationalize should be asserted by the government in Somaliland, that government would still have the ability to terminate a mineral concession, even though to do so would constitute a breach of obligation. . . .

"For the above reasons it would seem impossible to assure that a concession received now from Italy could be enforced in the future against the will of the government in Somaliland. Private investors desiring concessions would, in the last analysis, have to depend for the security of their concession not so much on their bare legal rights as on the existence of a satisfactory working relationship with the government in Somaliland in regard to the concession in question. If the concession to begin with is a fair bargain, when judged in terms of Article 14 of the trusteeship agreement, and if the concessionaire maintains good relations locally in Somaliland, there would seem to be a good prospect for the concession being allowed to run its allotted term without prior cancellation. Some modifications in its terms might, of course, be necessary from time to time. Another important factor would be the attitude of the Advisory Council and the Trusteeship Council toward concessions in general and toward a particular concession. It would seem that both the Advisory Council and the Trusteeship Council are now aware of some of the problems standing in the way of economic development of Somaliland and probably see the necessity for the granting of certain concessions beyond the trusteeship period. If, in addition, the terms of individual concessions then receive approval from the Advisory Council or the Trusteeship Council, this would be an important added element of strength for the position of the concessionaire. But the concessionaires should understand that even with the fulfillment of all these conditions a post-trusteeship government in Somaliland could not be prevented from cancelling a concession.

"3. In the report of the Trusteeship Council and in the remarks of the Advisory Council on concessions there are references to 'adequate guarantees to external private investors' and 'guarantees which could be given to capitals from whom the investment is necessary to assure the economic development of the country.'

"The pertinent parts of the Trusteeship Council documents on this subject adopted on July 10, 1951, for inclusion in the report of the Council to the General Assembly are quoted below:

"PART I

"(TC document T/L/170)

"(1 June 1951)

" 'The Administering Authority, stressing the need for the investment of large sums of capital for the development of the Territory, expresses the view that under the circumstances private capital will be reluctant to provide the necessary sums. As alternatives it suggests that aid be provided by international organizations or that a guarantee for a period exceeding that of the Trusteeship administration be given to Italian or foreign capital.'

"PART II

"(TC document T/L/184)

"(27 June 1951)

" '9. The Council, noting with approval that the Administering Authority is desirous of encouraging further private and public investment in the Territory, noting that further capital investment is required for the development of local industries and other purposes, and noting that certain difficulties have been experienced in attracting capital, urges the Administering Authority to take all appropriate steps to encourage both public and private investment, and recommends in addition that in conjunction with the United Nations Mission for Technical Assistance which is about to visit Somaliland, the Administering Authority study all aspects of this question and in particular the methods which might be adopted to extend adequate guarantees to external private investors, and that, in consultation with the International Bank for Reconstruction and Development, the Administering Authority consider the measures which might be taken to augment the available resources for public investment in the Territory.'

"It is not clear what types of guarantees are intended by the reference in the above quotation. There are, however, no grounds upon which to conclude that approval, in principle, of such concessions by United Nations bodies would constitute a guarantee of the concessions beyond the trusteeship period. Furthermore, it is doubtful that the United Nations would agree to undertake such a guarantee itself or in any way limit the independence of any future Somali state. However, the normal presumption would be that any concession which was granted by the Italian administration with the approval of the Territorial Council and reviewed by the Trusteeship Council and the General Assembly would be fully honored by a future Somali administration."

"Concessions in Somaliland under Italian Trusteeship", memorandum (undated) attached to letter from Leo O. Cyr, Acting Director, Office of

African Affairs, to L. V. Stanford, Sinclair Petroleum Company, Aug. 24, 1951, MS. Department of State, file 357 AJ/8–2451.

"Monopolies"

"The initial trusteeship drafts put forward by France, the United Kingdom, and Belgium for the 'B' mandates in Africa authorized the administering authority to establish private monopolies under conditions of proper public control when this was in the interests of the economic advancement of the inhabitants of the trust territory. Under the provisions of the mandates it was possible for the Mandatory Powers to organize essential public works and services and to create monopolies of a purely fiscal character. There was no general authority, however, to create private monopolies. The United States Government did not challenge the premise that, in certain special circumstances, a private monopoly could be in the interests of the economic advancement of the inhabitants of the territory. However, the United States took the position that a definitive step such as the granting of a private monopoly, involving considerations both as to its possible effect on the inhabitants of the territory and on the equal-treatment provisions of the Charter, should be open to consideration by the Trusteeship Council or an appropriate United Nations agency at a stage where the recommendations of such a body might be effective. At the General Assembly in New York, the United States Delegation proposed a specific amendment to the trusteeship agreements in question which incorporated this idea.

"Although this United States proposal was defeated in the Trusteeship Subcommittee, the detailed discussion of the question resulted in significant alterations in the original monopoly clauses proposed by the Mandatory Powers and in interpretative declarations by these powers. The Delegations of the United Kingdom and Belgium included in the trusteeship agreements a provision to insure that any private monopoly contracts would be granted without discrimination on grounds of nationality against members of the United Nations or their nationals. The French Delegation stated that under French law private monopolies were not permitted at all in the trust territories which it would administer. Moreover, the United Kingdom and Belgian Delegations made the following declarations which form a part of the rapporteur's report to the General Assembly on the trusteeship agreements:

"'(a) The Governments of Belgium and the United Kingdom have no intention of using the grant of private monopolies in Trust Territories as a normal instrument of policy;

"'(b) Such private monopolies would be granted only when this was essential in order to enable a particular type of desirable economic development to be undertaken in the interest of the inhabitants;

"'(c) In those special cases where such private monopolies were granted they would be granted for limited periods, and

would be promptly reported to the Trusteeship Council.'
[General Assembly doc. A/258, Dec. 12, 1946, p. 6.]"

Armstrong and Cargo, Division of Dependent Area Affairs, Office of Special Political Affairs, Department of State, "The Inauguration of the Trusteeship System of the United Nations", XVI *Bulletin*, Department of State, No. 403, Mar. 23, 1947, pp. 511, 516–517.

"*9. Are administering authorities free to erect military and naval bases in non-strategic trust territories?*

"It was a basic conception underlying the League Mandates system that mandated territories should be kept free of all military and naval activities. Article 22 of the League Covenant laid it down in absolute terms that in 'B' and in 'C' mandates the Mandatory state must prevent 'the establishment of fortifications or military and naval bases and of military training of the natives for other than police purposes and the defence of territory.' Military and naval bases

"In writing the San Francisco Charter, however, an attempt was made to integrate trusteeship territories into the general program of the United Nations for the security of all peoples. Those framing the United Nations Charter at San Francisco felt strongly the lesson of the Second World War. They were determined that never again should Pacific Islands or other non-self-governing territories be permitted to serve as bases for aggression by militaristic nations. In so far as they possessed potential value as military or naval bases, they must be utilized for the common defense of the United Nations fighting for human rights and never for the aggressive designs of any single state acting in its own interests. [See *The Question of Fortifications and Volunteer Forces in Trust Territories (Article 84): Memorandum Prepared by the Secretariat*, UN doc. A/C.4/40, November 3, 1946.]

"Under the trusteeship system the attempt is being made to change such territories from possible international liabilities into assets. Not only are such territories removed from the area of international rivalry, but by means of the Charter provisions an effort is made to turn them into islands of security. Article 84 of the Charter makes it the positive duty of the administering authority 'to ensure that the trust territory shall play its part in the maintenance of international peace and security. To this end the administering authority may make use of volunteer forces, facilities, and assistance from the trust territory in carrying out the obligations towards the Security Council undertaken in this regard by the administering authority. . . .'

"All eight of the draft trusteeship agreements submitted to the General Assembly in 1946 contained similar clauses entitling the administering authority to establish bases and to station and employ armed forces in the trust territory. Strong opposition to these clauses was expressed on the ground that such powers would go beyond the limits of Article 84 which defines the forces which the administering authority may make use of as volunteer forces, facilities, and assistance. It was asserted that if the administering authority found it necessary to establish bases and employ forces in a trust territory, that territory would become a strategic area and would fall within the jurisdiction of the Security Council under Articles 82 and 83. [It was further maintained that any military measures taken in this connection would have to be set forth in special agreements negotiated on the initiative of the Security Council under Article 43. *Official Records of the Second Part of the First Session of the General Assembly*, 1946 (62nd Plenary, Dec. 13, 1946), pp. 1279–1280.]

"To this assertion the mandatory powers, supported by the United States, objected that, unlike the mandates system, the trusteeship system made it the duty of the administering authority to ensure that the trust territory shall play its part in the maintenance of international peace and security; and that in order to fulfill this positive duty it was often vitally necessary under modern conditions of warfare to erect military and naval bases. After long arguments the Soviet Delegation proposed in the Assembly a resolution for the rejection of the proposed trusteeship agreements on these and other grounds. The question was finally settled by the Assembly's voting down the Soviet resolution and with a large majority approving the trusteeship agreements containing the military bases clause. [Same, pp. 1282–1283, 1286.]

"In 1947 the same question arose with regard to the Nauru agreement and was settled in the same way. Australia, New Zealand, and the United Kingdom declined, as in the previous year, to accept the Soviet argument that establishment of bases in trust territories requires approval by the Security Council; but they accepted an amendment to Article 7 of the agreement which makes specific reference to Article 84 of the Charter. [UN doc. A/420, October 27, 1947.] The Nauru agreement, containing a clause permitting the establishment of military bases, was similarly approved by the Assembly. [A/P.V./104, November 1, 1947, p. 31.]"

Francis B. Sayre, United States Representative in the Trusteeship Council and President of the Council, "Legal Problems Arising from the United Nations Trusteeship System", 42 Am. J. Int'l L. (1948) 263, 287–288.

Responsibilities of Administering Authorities

§ 43

International responsibility

"A territory having been placed under trusteeship thenceforth becomes an international responsibility. The Organization will have become the trustee on behalf of the international community of the United Nations and of the inhabitants of the territory. The administering authority is the agent of the trustee and is responsible to the Organization for the conduct of its administration of the territory.

"The administering authority for non-strategic areas is required to submit annual reports to the General Assembly on the political, economic, social, and educational advancement of the inhabitants of the territory. These reports will be based upon a questionnaire to be formulated by the Trusteeship Council. The General Assembly and the Trusteeship Council may discuss these reports and may make recommendations concerning the administration of the territory. The General Assembly and the Trusteeship Council may also sponsor official visits to the trust territory for purposes of inspecting on the spot the nature of the administration and the progress being made by the inhabitants. Petitions from any source, either from within or from outside the trust territory, and either written or oral, concerning conditions in the territory may be accepted and examined by the same organs.

"The administration of the trust territories will thus be exposed to the strong influence of international appraisal and opinion."

Ralph J. Bunche, Acting Chief of the Division of Dependent Area Affairs, Office of Special Political Affairs, Department of State, "Trusteeship and Non-Self-Governing Territories in the Charter of the United Nations", XIII *Bulletin*, Department of State, No. 340, Dec. 30, 1945, pp. 1037, 1042.

"*4. What are the respective functions of the Trusteeship Council and of the administering powers with regard to the direction of policies controlling trust territories?*

"In the government and administration of a non-strategic trust territory two control agencies are primarily concerned—the administering power and the Trusteeship Council. Exactly what are the respective powers and functions of each relative to the other?

"The Charter itself and the various trusteeship agreements leave the question practically unanswered. The precise answer must be gradually evolved from current situations and from the give and take of day to day experience. [Implementation of resolutions]

"So far as practical detailed administration is concerned, it is readily apparent and universally agreed that this must fall within the scope of the administering power. The Trusteeship Council is by its structure and nature essentially a deliberative rather than an administrative body. It does not sit in continuous session. It lacks experience in carrying heavy police or financial responsibilities.

"On the other hand, when it comes to the question of overall policy which gives the direction to current administration, it is the Trusteeship Council which carries the ultimate responsibility. If, for instance, the administering power should in its administration depart from or violate the basic objectives of the trusteeship system as set forth in Article 76, it would unquestionably be the duty of the Trusteeship Council to make the fact clear and to bring all of its resources into play to secure a reversal of such policy. The administering power does not possess unlimited sovereign rights over the trust territory. The power of supervision over trust territories is given by the Charter to the Assembly and the Trusteeship Council.

"At the same time, it is to be remembered that the Trusteeship Council has no power to compel. It has no force at its command. In the exercise of its supervisory functions it secures compliance with its recommendations only through the force of persuasion and of public opinion.

"But these can be utilized as forces of great power. Instances are not lacking of the effectiveness of the Council's recommendations. When the Council sent a visiting mission in the summer of 1947 to the trust territory of Western Samoa in response to a petition for self-government, the mission, at the end of six weeks' intensive study on the spot, made concrete recommendations. [*Report of Western Samoa Mission.* UN doc. T/46, September 24, 1947, and T/46 Add. 1, September 25, 1947 (Annexes).] These include the taking of immediate steps to give Samoans a substantially greater measure of self-government than at present enjoyed, the setting up of a Government of Western Samoa, the institution of a legislative Assembly containing an absolute majority of Samoans, and other far-reaching reforms. The interesting fact is that following the mission's investigations the New Zealand Government laid before the Parliament in Wellington a new plan for the administration of Western Samoa; and this new plan embodies substantially every one of the mission's recommendations. [UN doc. T/62, November 21, 1947. The New Zealand bill embodying this new plan has now become law.]

"The Trusteeship Council has no power to oust the administering power, even should there be a flagrant case of maladministration. [The question of whether a Mandatory Power could be removed was a much-debated point under the Mandates system, particularly in connection with the withdrawal of Japan from the League of Nations and Japan's apparent violation of the military clauses of the mandate. See also Quincy Wright, *Mandates Under the League of Nations*, pp. 520–521.] The Charter is framed upon the basic principle that non-self-governing areas are placed under trusteeship only by the voluntary act of the administering power. The former mandatory powers were thus in a position themselves to determine the nature and character of the trusteeship agreement which each was willing to propose to the United Nations and to undertake to administer. This gives to the administering powers a practical independence in the exercise of their administration which can be curtailed only through persuasion, tactful influence and the force of opinion. These latter, however, can be of very great effect.

"In a hundred different ways the constant interplay between purely administrative functions and supervisory ones is shaping an evolving policy. For instance, in 1947, when the Trusteeship Council was considering more than a score of petitions from German and Italian residents of Tanganyika, each for the right to remain in or reënter the trust territory, the Trusteeship Council concerned itself, not with the individual situation of each petitioner but with the policy laid down and being followed by the administering authority with regard to the deportation and exclusion from Tanganyika of former German Nazis or Nazi sympathizers. The representatives of the United Kingdom, appearing before the Trusteeship Council and being questioned by the Council, stated the policy being followed and gave various assurances as to the carrying out of the policy. [See UN doc. T/43 (11 June 1947), *Resolutions adopted by the Trusteeship Council during its first Session*. For example: "The Trusteeship Council noted the United Kingdom assurance that no German is to be repatriated solely on account of his nationality. Those who are to be repatriated on grounds of enemy activities or sympathies are: persons associated with enemy espionage, sabotage or similar activities; persons who participated in anti-Allied or pro-Nazi activities, such as propaganda or the organization of local German nationalistic associations; and persons whose activities served to maintain German commercial or national interests or influence, whether or not such persons worked directly against Allied interests. All these twenty-four persons had mortgaged their properties in Tanganyika to a company which was, like the USAGARA Company, primarily a Nazi organization" (p. 5).] The Trusteeship Council in its resolution expressed its general approval of the policy. This general approval was reaffirmed in the Second Session during its discussion of an additional group of petitions bearing on the same subject. [See UN doc. T/P.V./ 32, December 1, 1947, and T/P.V./41, December 11, 1947.] While the Council refused to undertake to make detailed decisions with respect to the administration of the policy, it did of course consider charges made by individuals of the failure to carry out the declared policy in specific cases.

"It is clear that no precise fixed line of demarcation can be drawn between the respective functions of the Trusteeship Council on the one hand and the administering powers on the other. The lack of any such precise line could lead to endless irritation, frustration, and possible shipwreck. The fact is it has not. With tact and understanding on both sides, the work of the Trusteeship Council thus far has been notable for its harmony and resulting achievement. As long as this continues, there will be real progress. If it should ever disappear, the Trusteeship Council will be able only to mark time."

Francis B. Sayre, United States Representative in the Trusteeship Council and President of the Council, "Legal Problems Arising from the United Nations Trusteeship System", 42 Am. J. Int'l L. (1948) 263, 277–279.

On January 18, 1952, the General Assembly of the United Nations adopted the following resolution:

"*The General Assembly*,

"*Recalling* its resolutions 436 (V) and 433 (V) of 2 December 1950 concerning information on the implementation of Trusteeship Council and General Assembly resolutions relating to Trust Territories,

"*Having considered* the Secretary-General's memorandum [documents A/1903 and Adds. 1 and 2] regarding information on the implementation of Trusteeship Council and General Assembly resolutions relating to Trust Territories,

"1. *Takes note* of the Secretary-General's memorandum regarding information on the implementation of Trusteeship Council and General Assembly resolutions relating to Trust Territories;

"2. *Observes* that in certain cases effect has not yet been given to all Trusteeship Council and General Assembly recommendations and resolutions applicable to Trust Territories;

"3. *Observes* that the action thus far taken by the Trusteeship Council does not give effect to the wishes of the General Assembly as expressed in resolution 433 (V), paragraph 1(*d*);

"4. *Expresses the hope* that the Administering Authorities which have not yet given effect to all such recommendations and resolutions will implement them as speedily as possible and inform the Trusteeship Council of the steps which have been taken or which it is supposed to take in that respect;

"5. *Requests* the Trusteeship Council, in order to enable the General Assembly to have clearly at its disposal all the knowledge necessary for the fulfilment of its duties with regard to the International Trusteeship System, to include in each case in the appropriate section of its report to the General Assembly such conclusions as it may deem necessary regarding the action taken by the Administering Authority and regarding the measures which, in its opinion, should be adopted in view of those conclusions."

Res. 560 (VI), Jan. 18, 1952, U.N. Gen. Ass. Off. Rec. 6th Sess., Supp. No. 20/2119, p. 58. A detailed analysis of the measures taken by the administering authorities to implement resolutions of the Trusteeship Council and General Assembly may be found in the Secretary-General's memorandum, "Information on the Implementation of Trusteeship Council and General Assembly Resolutions Relating to Trust Territories", U.N. Doc. A/1903, Oct. 9, 1951 (Tanganyika, Ruanda-Urundi); U.N. Doc. A/1903/Add.1, Oct. 9, 1951 (Cameroons (British), Cameroons (French), Togoland (British)); U.N. Doc. A/1903/Add.2, Oct. 25, 1952 (Western Samoa, Nauru, New Guinea, Pacific Islands).

"*(c) The objective character of the agreements*

"In addition to clauses, such as quasi-'most-favoured-nation' clauses and the common-form jurisdictional clause . . ., which operate as between the administering authority and other states individually, the trusteeship agreements so far elaborated contain stipulations operating between the administering authorities and the United Nations as such. The standard undertaking to make 'to the General Assembly of the United Nations an annual report on the basis of a questionnaire drawn up by the Trusteeship Council in accordance with Article 88 of the United Nations Charter' [e.g. the agreement for (British) Togoland, 8 UNTS 152, Art. 16] is of this character. But when it is sought to multiply examples of obligations specifically undertaken towards the United Nations, it is not easy to find them. The undertaking to

Objective
character
of agreements

apply, in the trust territory concerned, 'the provisions of any international conventions and recommendations already existing or hereafter drawn up by the United Nations or by the specialized agencies . . . which may be appropriate or which would conduce to the achievement of the basic objectives of the International Trusteeship System' [cf. ibid., Art. 7] is of ambiguous quality. For presumably it refers to such conventions as those governing the drug traffic, which are inter-state agreements. The clause thus appears to amount to an agreement to agree—with other states. And, for different reasons, it is equally difficult to construe the primary undertaking to administer the territory 'in such a manner as to achieve the basic objectives of the International Trusteeship System laid down in Article 76 of the United Nations Charter . . . to collaborate fully with the General Assembly . . . and the Trusteeship Council in the discharge of all their functions as defined in Article 87. . . .' [Cf. ibid., Art. 3.] For, given that the territory is brought under trusteeship, this obligation follows directly from the Charter.

"Many of the provisions of the trusteeship agreements purport to confer rights on the administering authority rather than obligations. Of this nature are the provisions investing the administering authority with the legislative, administrative, and judicial power, with the authority to bring the trust territory into a customs, fiscal, or administrative union with territory under its own sovereignty, and with the power to provide for the defence of the territory. [Cf. ibid., Art. 5.] Such 'rights' of the administering authority are not, however, the correlatives of obligations of the United Nations, nor do they fall into the same category as rights which other states derive from the trusteeship agreements. They are to be taken together with the class of obligations of the administering authority—into which class the general obligation to administer the territory for the achievement of the basic objectives of the trusteeship system perhaps also comes—of which the beneficiary is not the United Nations or any other state but the population of the trust territory. Examples of obligations of this class are those of the administering authority to promote the development of free political institutions [cf. ibid., Art. 6] and to frame land laws with due regard to local custom. [Cf. ibid., Art. 8.] These rights and obligations together constitute the objective régime of the trust territory, and it is the creation of an objective status which is the principal legal effect of a trusteeship agreement.

"Their real nature, the quasi-constitutional or statutory character of the trusteeship agreements, is apparent in every one of them, though, in the case of those first drafted, it was to some extent obscured by a use of the language of mutual promises. In the agreement for Somaliland under Italian Administration it is, however, underlined by the annexure to that agreement, as 'an integral part' [118 UNTS 256, Art. 23] thereof, of a 'Declaration of Constitutional Principles'. Even in the body of that agreement its function as a partial written constitution is clear. For it is, for instance, provided that the administering authority

shall be represented by an administrator, who shall have his seat
in a particular place. [Art. 2.] The annexed Declaration stipulates that the administrator 'shall appoint a Territorial Council,
composed of inhabitants of the Territory and representatives of
its people'. [Art. 4.]"

Parry, "The Legal Nature of Trusteeship Agreements", XXVII Brit.
Yb. Int'l L. (1950) 164, 182–184.

Obligation
to apply
local law

" 'Tanganyika is not a Christian country . . . . The common
law of England might refuse to recognize as a "marriage" a poly-
gamous union between spouses of a different religion, whether
quasi-Christian or non-Christian. . . . But in my opinion the
law of Tanganyika could not from the date of the Mandate refuse
such recognition; and such a marriage would be recognized before,
no less than after, the enactment of section 2 of the Ordinance.
It follows that a divorce in due accordance with the incidents of
such a marriage would be similarly recognized. . . .'

"Sir Barclay Nihill, in his concurring judgment, supported the
arguments of Briggs J. A. He stated, *inter alia*, that: 'I have had
the advantage of reading the judgment delivered by my brother,
the learned Justice of Appeal, and I am in entire agreement with
the view he has expressed on the nature of the obligations imposed
on the mandatory power in Tanganyika by the Trusteeship Agreement of 1946. The regulation of the marriage state between
members of the same religious community is so intertwined with
the practice of religion that I am fully persuaded that the obligations imposed upon the administering authority under Article 13
of the Trusteeship Agreement must be taken to include recognition of the customary religious law of the community in respect
of marriage so far as the same is not inconsistent with the requirements of public order and morality. I am also fully persuaded that the same principle was recognized under the old
mandatory system which preceded the Trusteeship Agreement of
1946, in fact I consider that the right view to take of the Ordinance of 1923 (Cap. 112) is that it was nothing more than declaratory of the obligation resting on the then mandatory power to
recognize the personal law of non-Christian Asiatic communities
so far as this law was not inconsistent with the principles of good
order and natural justice. I agree, therefore, with the conclusion
reached by my learned brother that from the inception of British
rule in Tanganyika it has been recognized quite apart from statute
that the marriage and divorce of persons belonging to a recognized religious community were matters proper to be governed
by the religious and personal law of the community concerned
subject only to the proviso that the customs of any such community were not repugnant to good order and natural justice. . . .'

"Sir Herbert Cox C.J., in his concurring judgment, also referred to obligations of an Administering Authority under a Mandate or Trusteeship Agreement. On this point he said: 'The first
Order in Council establishing the Government of this territory

was the Tanganyika Order in Council, 1920, dated 22nd June, 1920, and which will be found at page 12 of Volume V of the current Laws of Tanganyika. In the recital to that Order it is stated:—

" ' "Whereas by the Treaty of Peace between the Allied and Associated Powers and Germany, signed at Versailles on the twenty-eighth day of June, 1919, Germany renounced in favour of the Principal Allied and Associated Powers all her rights and titles over her oversea possessions;

" ' "And whereas the said Treaty having been duly ratified as therein provided came into force on the tenth day of January, 1920;

" ' "And whereas it has been agreed between the Principal Allied and Associated Powers that the territories of Africa situate within the limits of this Order (being part of the territories formerly known as German East Africa) shall be administered by His Majesty the King, subject to and in accordance with the provisions of the said Treaty;

" ' "And whereas accordingly by treaty, capitulation, grant, usage, sufferance and other lawful means His Majesty has power and jurisdiction within the said territories (hereinafter called the Tanganyika Territory);

" ' "Now, therefore, His Majesty, by virtue and in exercise of the powers on this behalf by the Foreign Jurisdiction Act, 1890, or otherwise, in His Majesty vested, is pleased, by and with the advice of His Privy Council, to order, and it is hereby ordered, as follows: . . . " '

" 'The Tanganyika Order in Council, 1920, follows the general pattern of Orders in Council (under the Foreign Jurisdiction Act, 1890) but in its enactment a most important provision referred to in the recital had to be kept in mind, namely, that the territory was being administered by His Majesty the King, subject to and in accordance with the provisions of the Treaty of Peace signed at Versailles on June 28, 1919. It must also be borne in mind that Tanganyika was then being administered in accordance with Article 22 of the Covenant of the League of Nations under a Mandate conferred on the King of England, that the Mandate has been superseded by the present Trusteeship Agreement by means of which territories originally held under Mandate from the League of Nations can be placed under the international trusteeship of the General Assembly of the United Nations in accordance with Articles 75 and 77 of the United Nations Charter. The text of the present Trusteeship Agreement follows the pattern of the old Mandate and will be found at p. 1 of Vol. V of the current Laws of Tanganyika and one of the principal objects of the Mandate is the government of the territory in the interest of the inhabitants of the territory . . . .' "

Maleksultan v. *Jeraj*, East Africa, Court of Appeal of Nairobi, Jan. 22, 1955, [1955] Int'l L. Rep. 81, 85–86 (1958) ; 22 E.A.C.A. (1955) 142, 150 ff.

Alteration of Trusteeship Agreements

§ 44

Article 83 of the Charter of the United Nations contains the following provision in paragraph 1:

> "1. All functions of the United Nations relating to strategic areas, including the approval of the terms of the trusteeship agreements and of their alteration or amendment, shall be exercised by the Security Council."

Article 85 of the Charter reads:

> "1. The functions of the United Nations with regard to trusteeship agreements for all areas not designated as strategic, including the approval of the terms of the trusteeship agreements and of their alteration or amendment, shall be exercised by the General Assembly.
>
> "2. The Trusteeship Council, operating under the authority of the General Assembly, shall assist the General Assembly in carrying out these functions."

U.S. TS 993; 59 Stat. 1031, 1050.

The Advisory Opinion of the International Court of Justice, given July 11, 1950, on the *International Status of South-West Africa*, contains the following statements concerning modification, alteration, or amendment of Mandates and Trusteeships:

> "Article 7 of the Mandate, in requiring the consent of the Council of the League of Nations for any modification of its terms, brought into operation for this purpose the same organ which was invested with powers of supervision in respect of the administration of the Mandates. In accordance with the reply given above to Question (*a*), those powers of supervision now belong to the General Assembly of the United Nations. On the other hand, Articles 79 and 85 of the Charter require that a Trusteeship Agreement be concluded by the mandatory Power and approved by the General Assembly before the International Trusteeship System may be substituted for the Mandates System. These articles also give the General Assembly authority to approve alterations or amendments of Trusteeship Agreements. By analogy, it can be inferred that the same procedure is applicable to any modification of the international status of a territory under Mandate which would not have for its purpose the placing of the territory under the Trusteeship System. This conclusion is strengthened by the action taken by the General Assembly and the attitude adopted by the Union of South Africa which is at present the only existing mandatory Power."

I.C.J. Reports (1950) 128, 141–142.

". . . But the fact remains that the people of Saipan have, in a most impressive manner, demonstrated their desire to be part of the United States. Incidentally, I should like to make one comment on the position of the Administering Authority and the United Nations in connexion with the Saipan question. There is, of course, and this I must say sometimes gets obscured in the discussion of this question, no reason whatever in law why the Administering Authority should not come to the United Nations seeking an amendment to the Trusteeship Agreement to provide for the separate achievement of self-government by the people of Saipan, or any other district in the Trust Territory, in a form which is in accordance with their wishes. But the fact is that the United Nations which values the principle of the integrity of the Trust Territory and where there is also a feeling that the people of Saipan have something to offer to the rest of Micronesia if they remain in close association with it, is unlikely to agree to such a request. And more important still, since no one can predict with certainty what attitude the United Nations is going to adopt in any particular case, is the fact that the Administering Authority has declared that it has no intention whatever of taking any such initiative. In my delegation's view they are wise, and in my delegation's view again it is important that the people of the Trust Territory should fully understand this position. The fact is that they are part of a Trust Territory, that the Trust Territory is administered in an international context and that this context must form part of the thinking of the people of the Trust Territory, as it is of the Administering Authority, about their political future."

Statement of G. K. Caston, Representative of the United Kingdom, in the 1154th meeting of the Trusteeship Council, June 22, 1961. U.N. Doc. T/P.V.1154, June 22, 1961, p. 31. See *ante*, "Trust Territory of the Pacific Islands", § 41, pp. 813–814, 834–838, for discussion of article 9 of the Trusteeship Agreement as to Saipan plebiscite, and for discussion of article 15 as to amendment or alteration of the Trusteeship Agreement for the Former Japanese Mandated Islands (Trust Territory of the Pacific Islands), which was concluded pursuant to article 83, quoted above, as the only agreement for a strategic trust territory.

Termination of Trusteeship Agreements

§ 45

"There is no specific provision in the Charter for termination of trusteeship over any territory, except for the provision in article 78 that trusteeship cannot apply to territories which have become members of the United Nations and the provision for alteration and amendment in article 79. Specific provision for termination, however, even to the extent of stating an exact date, can be written into any trusteeship agreement. Moreover, the statement of political objectives in article 76 provides that the 'freely expressed wishes of the peoples' of the trust territories shall be taken into account."

Ralph J. Bunche, Acting Chief of the Division of Dependent Area Affairs, Office of Special Political Affairs, Department of State, "Trusteeship and Non-Self-Governing Territories in the Charter of the United Nations", XIII *Bulletin*, Department of State, No. 340, Dec. 30, 1945, pp. 1037, 1042–1043.

"The Charter of the United Nations, like the League Covenant, makes no specific provision for the termination of a trusteeship agreement. It is fair to assume, however, that an agreement may be terminated under Article 79, which states that the terms of trusteeship, 'including any alteration or amendment,' shall be agreed upon by the states directly concerned and approved by either the General Assembly or the Security Council. None of the nine agreements approved by the General Assembly contains any special provision with regard to termination other than that the agreement may not be altered or amended except in accordance with Article 79 and, in some instances, Articles 83 and 85. The United States trusteeship agreement for the former Japanese Mandated Islands contains, however, a specific provision in Article 15 that 'the terms of the present agreement shall not be altered, amended, or terminated without the consent of the administering authority.'

"As the trusteeship system matures one of its major problems will be the development of procedures for the termination of trusteeships, of standards for determining when a people under trusteeship is prepared for self-government or independence, and of guarantees which should be required as a condition precedent to independence. [It should be noted that the termination of a trusteeship or mandate does not necessarily require independence. The Charter itself refers to "self-government or independence." The General Assembly, in dealing with the question of South West Africa, has already considered proposals to terminate a mandate in a direction other than independence.]"

Francis B. Sayre, United States Representative in the Trusteeship Council and President of the Council, "Legal Problems Arising from the United Nations Trusteeship System", 42 Am. J. Int'l L. (1948) 263, 289–290.

For further discussion of article 15, see § 41, "Trust Territory of the Pacific Islands", *ante*, p. 834.

"You inquire whether a mandatory or trust power can relinquish its responsibility except '(a) by agreement with the other party or parties to the contract, and (b) when proper provision is made to carry on its responsibilities in order to avoid a complete breakdown which might otherwise occur'.

"Whether or not a mandatory, or administering authority in the case of a trust territory, can unilaterally relinquish its mandate or trust, depends upon the terms of the particular treaty situation obtaining in a given case. . . .

.   .   .   .

"While it is probably desirable to take the position that generally (cases can be envisioned of the dissolution of the United Nations, of the organization itself acting as administering authority, etc.) the administering authority may not unilaterally relinquish the trust, and while it is true that normally a trustee cannot unilaterally relinquish his trust under the law of trusts as known to Anglo-American law, the extent to which the trusteeship agreements constitute trusts in the sense of Anglo-American law with all of their technicalities has not been passed upon, and it would seem to be unwise at this time to select a few desired characteristics of 'trusts' and argue that they are plainly applicable in the realm of trustee-ship agreements, when other common characteristics of 'trusts'—as for instance the holding of title—may be objectionable if carried over to the international field."

Marjorie M. Whiteman, Assistant Legal Adviser, to Benjamin Gerig, Chief, Division of Dependent Areas, "Unilateral Right to Relinquish a Mandate or Trust Agreement", memorandum, Oct. 28, 1947, MS. Department of State, file FW 501–BB Palestine/9–2647.

In the following instances the Trusteeship Agreements for non-strategic areas have been terminated pursuant to resolutions of the General Assembly.

"1044 (XI). THE FUTURE OF TOGOLAND UNDER BRITISH
ADMINISTRATION

"*The General Assembly,*

"*Recalling* that, by resolution 944(X) of 15 December 1955, it recommended, in pursuance of Article 76 b of the Charter of the United Nations, that a plebiscite be organized and conducted in the Trust Territory of Togoland under British administration by the Administering Authority in consultation with and under the supervision of a United Nations Plebiscite Commissioner, in order to ascertain the wishes of its inhabitants in regard to the union of their Territory with an independent Gold Coast or otherwise,   Togoland (British)

"*Having received* the report of the United Nations Plebiscite Commissioner [*Official Records of the General Assembly, Eleventh Session, Annexes*, agenda item 39, documents A/3173 and Add. 1] on the organization, conduct and results of the plebiscite, and having noted in particular the conclusion contained in the report that the plebiscite was held in an atmosphere of freedom, impartiality and fairness,

"*Having also received* the report of the United Kingdom Plebiscite Administrator [*Official Records of the Trusteeship Council, Eighteenth Session, Annexes*, agenda item 12, documents T/1269 and Add. 1],

"*Noting* that the majority of the inhabitants of the Trust Territory participating in the plebiscite have expressed themselves in favour of the union of the Territory with an independent Gold Coast,

"*Noting also* the recommendation of the Trusteeship Council in its resolution 1496 (XVIII) of 31 July 1956 that appropriate steps be taken, in consultation with the Administering Authority, for the termination of the Trusteeship Agreement for the Territory to become effective upon the attainment of independence by the Gold Coast,

"*Having been informed* by the Administering Authority that it is the intention of the Government of the United Kingdom of Great Britain and Northern Ireland that the Gold Coast shall become independent on 6 March 1957,

"1. *Expresses its approval* of the union of the Territory of Togoland under British administration with an independent Gold Coast and accordingly invites the Administering Authority to take such steps as are necessary to this end;

"2. *Resolves*, with the agreement of the Administering Authority, that, on the date on which the Gold Coast becomes independent and the union with it of the Territory of Togoland under British administration takes place, the Trusteeship Agreement approved by the General Assembly in resolution 63(I) of 13 December 1946 shall cease to be in force, the objectives of trusteeship having been attained;

"3. *Requests* the Government of the United Kingdom of Great Britain and Northern Ireland to notify the Secretary-General as soon as the union of the Territory of Togoland under British administration with an independent Gold Coast has been effected;

"4. *Requests* the Secretary-General to communicate to all Member States and to the Trusteeship Council at its nineteenth session the notification by the Government of the United Kingdom of Great Britain and Northern Ireland, referred to in paragraph 3 above.

> *619th plenary meeting,*
> *13 December 1956.*"

U.N. Gen. Ass. Off. Rec. 11th Sess., Supp. No. 17 (A/3572), p. 24.

"On December 13, 1956, the General Assembly overwhelmingly recommended (64 (U.S.) to 0, with 9 abstentions) the termination of the trusteeship for the Trust Territory of Togoland under British administration, and its union with a free and independent Gold Coast (Ghana) to become effective during March 1957. This action followed long and serious consideration of the question of the future of Togoland and the freely expressed choice by the majority of the inhabitants of this territory in a U.N.-supervised plebiscite on May 9, 1956. The U.N. Plebiscite Commissioner supervised the conduct of this plebiscite and reported that it had been held in an atmosphere of freedom, impartiality, and fairness, and that of 160,587 voters, 58 percent (93,095) favored union with the Gold Coast while 42 percent (67,492) voted in favor of separation and continued trusteeship. A large majority of those opposing this action consisted of members of a tribe of Ewe-speaking people from Southern Togoland. This tribe also inhabits territory westward and southward into the

Gold Coast and eastward into Togoland under French administration. Many favored independence for both British and French Togoland while others favored a federal form of government in Ghana (formerly the Gold Coast) rather than the unitary form now envisaged.

"During the discussions on the future of British Togoland in the General Assembly, petitioners representing these various groups spoke both for and against the union of the territory with an independent Ghana. However, final U.N. action was based on the free choice of a majority of the people as to their political future after their attainment of the prerequisites necessary to govern themselves as an independent nation. The United States strongly supported this action but stressed the necessity and importance for all groups of the population to work together after the termination of the trusteeship agreement, and to prove themselves to be 'responsible, progressive, and politically mature' and consequently able to 'play a major role as a strong, free, and democratic state which can be an example for the entire free world'; thus as a result of the request of the United Kingdom to the United Nations to consider the political future of British Togoland, a territory was removed for the first time from the Trusteeship System and is pursuing its future course, as a result of its own choice, united with the larger independent nation."

U.S. participation in the U.N., report by the President to Congress for the year 1956, p. 233.

"1349 (XIII). THE FUTURE OF THE TRUST TERRITORY OF THE CAMEROONS UNDER FRENCH ADMINISTRATION

"*The General Assembly,*
"*Recalling* its resolution 1282 (XIII) of 5 December 1958 requesting the Trusteeship Council to examine, as early as possible during the twenty-third session, the reports of the United Nations Visiting Mission to the Trust Territories in West Africa, 1958, on the Cameroons under French administration and the Cameroons under United Kingdom administration, and to transmit them, with its observations and recommendations, to the General Assembly not later than 20 February 1959, to enable the Assembly, in consultation with the Administering Authorities, to take the necessary measures in connexion with the full attainment of the objectives of the Trusteeship System,

Cameroons (French)

"*Having examined* the special report of the Trusteeship Council [*Official Records of the General Assembly, Thirteenth Session, Annexes*, agenda item 13, document A/4094], as well as the report of the Visiting Mission on the Cameroons under French administration [*Official Records of the Trusteeship Council, Twenty-third Session, Supplement No. 3* (T/1441), documents T/1427 and T/1434] and the observations of the Administering Authority on it [*Official Records of the General Assembly, Thirteenth Session, Annexes*, agenda item 13, document A/4094, annex III],

"*Taking into account* the statements made in the Fourth Committee by the representatives of the Administering Authority and by the Prime Minister of the Cameroons under French administration [see *Official Records of the General Assembly, Thirteenth Session, Fourth Committee*, 845th, 846th, 849th, 860th and 871st meetings],

"*Noting with satisfaction* the adoption by the Legislative Assembly of the Cameroons under French administration of the amnesty law of 14 February 1959 and the assurances given by the Prime Minister of the Cameroons that this law is being put into effect on the widest possible basis and with the least possible delay,

"*Noting* the statements of the representatives of the Cameroons Government that it welcomes the return of all Cameroonians who in recent years have left the country and invites them to re-enter normal life without fear of reprisal,

"*Having been assured* by the representatives of the Administering Authority and the Government of the Cameroons that there exist in the Territory freedom of the Press, of assembly and of political association, and other fundamental freedoms,

"*Having been informed* by the Prime Minister of the Cameroons under French administration that his Government has issued a decree fixing 12 April 1959 as the date for elections to be held to fill the four seats in the Legislative Assembly allocated to the Sanaga-Maritime area, as well as two vacant seats in the Mbouda subdivision,

"*Noting with satisfaction* the statement of the Prime Minister of the Cameroons under French administration that there will be general elections after independence since such elections will then be necessary and useful in order to settle various constitutional and other questions,

"*Noting* the resolution adopted by the Legislative Assembly of the Cameroons on 24 October 1958, the conclusions of the Visiting Mission and the declarations of the Administering Authority and the representatives of the Cameroons Government concerning the desire and readiness of the people of the Cameroons for independence,

"*Taking into account* the declarations of the Administering Authority and the Government of the Cameroons under French administration that the Territory will become completely independent on 1 January 1960, and the assurances given by the representative of France that his Government will sponsor the application that will thereupon be made by the Government of the Cameroons to be admitted to membership of the United Nations,

"*Having heard* the views of the petitioners,

"1. *Resolves*, in agreement with the Administering Authority, that, on 1 January 1960, when the Cameroons under French administration becomes independent, the Trusteeship Agreement approved by the General Assembly on 13 December 1946 shall cease to be in force in accordance with Article 76 b of the Charter of the United Nations;

"2. *Expresses its confidence* that, at the earliest possible date after the attainment of independence on 1 January 1960, elections will be held for the formation of a new assembly which should take decisions regarding the establishment, in their final form, of the institutions of the free and independent Cameroons;

"3. *Recommends* that, upon the attainment of independence on 1 January 1960, the Cameroons under French administration shall be admitted to membership of the United Nations according to Article 4 of the Charter.

794th plenary meeting,
13 March 1959."

U.N. Gen. Ass. Off. Rec. 13th Sess., Supp. No. 18A (A/4090/Add.1), p. 1. The vote in the Assembly on Res. 1349 (XIII) was 56 in favor (including the United States) to none against, with 23 abstentions. Doc. A/PV.794, Mar. 13, 1959, p. 642.

"On the West Coast of Africa near Nigeria is the former Trust Territory of the Cameroun under French administration. It has a population of more than 3 million persons, of whom approximately 13,000 are Europeans.

"In recent years the 3 million inhabitants of the territory have enjoyed a progressively greater measure of self-government and achieved complete internal autonomy a year before independence. The Cameroun achieved independence on January 1, 1960. The United States appointed a delegation to the country's independence ceremonies headed by Ambassador Henry Cabot Lodge. . . .

"The future of French Cameroun was extensively debated by a resumed session of the 13th General Assembly which was held in February and March 1959. A resumed session had been felt necessary because of the presence in the territory of a U.N. Visiting Mission at the time the regular session of the 13th General Assembly was being held in the fall of 1958. The resumed session decided that 'on January 1, 1960, when Cameroun under French administration becomes independent, the Trusteeship Agreement approved by the General Assembly on 13 December 1946 shall cease to be in force in accordance with article 76(b) of the United Nations Charter.' The Assembly expressed its confidence that elections for the formation of a new legislative assembly would be held at the earliest possible time after the attainment of independence. Finally, the General Assembly also recommended that upon the attainment of independence on January 1, 1960, the Cameroun would be admitted to membership in the United Nations according to article 4 of the Charter.

"Speaking at the resumed session, Ambassador Lodge paid tribute to 'the democratically and freely elected' Government of the Cameroun. Its negotiation of independence, he said, 'entitles it to take its place among the great African nationalist movements of this era. It is in all truth an exhilarating experience to assist a people to attain their freedom and independence.'

"No resolution was required or adopted by the 14th regular session in view of the definitive decisions taken by the resumed session. An attempt by a number of member states to have the Assembly express its concern over a renewal of public disturbance in the territory, in terms derogatory of the Government of Cameroun, was defeated in the course of the session. During the debate Congressman Zablocki, U.S. Delegate to the 4th Committee, stated: 'In less than fifty-three days . . . Cameroun under French Administration will become fully independent. We hope this happy occasion will be the signal for full national reconciliation. However, it is difficult in the extreme to bring together a government, the custodian of civil order, and an external opposition determined to use force to achieve its objectives.' The U.S. Delegate was referring in this statement to attempts made since 1955 by dissident elements which have carried on sporadic guerrilla operations against a democratically elected government and spurned the government's invitation to accept an amnesty."

U.S. participation in the U.N., report by the President to Congress for the year 1959, pp. 186–187.

"1416 (XIV). DATE OF THE INDEPENDENCE OF THE TRUST TERRITORY
OF TOGOLAND UNDER FRENCH ADMINISTRATION

"*The General Assembly,*

Togoland
(French)

"*Recalling* its resolution 1253 (XIII) of 14 November 1958, by which it was decided, in agreement with the Administering Authority, that on the day which would be agreed upon between the Government of France and the Government of Togoland and on which the Republic of Togoland is to become independent in 1960, the Trusteeship Agreement approved by the General Assembly on 13 December 1946 shall cease to be in force, in accordance with Article 76 b of the Charter of the United Nations,

"*Having considered* the communication of 13 July 1959 sent to the Secretary-General by the representative of France to the Trusteeship Council [*Official Records of the General Assembly, Fourteenth Session, Annexes*, agenda item 13, document A/4138], Trusteeship Council resolution 1950 (XXIV) of 14 July 1959, and the statements made at the 933rd and 935th meetings of the Fourth Committee on 30 October and 2 November 1959 by the representative of France and by the representative of Togoland, duly accredited as a member of the delegation of France,

"1. *Notes* that the Governments of France and of Togoland have agreed that the date on which the Republic of Togoland shall become independent is to be 27 April 1960;

"2. *Expresses its satisfaction* with the terms and spirit in which this agreement has been concluded;

"3. *Reiterates its decision* that, on the date of the independence of Togoland, which has now been established as 27 April 1960, the Trusteeship Agreement for Togoland under French administration, approved by the General Assembly on 13 December 1946, shall cease to be in force;

"4. *Recommends* that, upon the attainment of independence on 27 April 1960, Togoland shall be admitted to membership in the United Nations in accordance with Article 4 of the Charter of the United Nations.

846th plenary meeting,
5 December 1959."

U.N. Gen. Ass. Off. Rec. 14th Sess., Supp. No. 16 (A/4354), p. 32. Res. 1416 (XIV) was adopted unanimously. Doc. A/PV.846, Dec. 5, 1959, p. 632.

"The French-administered Trust Territory of Togo will become independent on April 27, 1960. The territory, which lies between Ghana and the French West African territory of Dahomey, is approximately the size of West Virginia and has slightly more than one million inhabitants.

"The General Assembly at its 13th session in 1958 decided that the Trusteeship Agreement with France would be terminated on the date agreed upon by the Governments of France and Togo that Togo would receive its independence. That date subse-quently was established as April 27, 1960, and the General Assembly accordingly resolved at its 14th session that on that date the Trusteeship Agreement for Togo approved by the General Assembly on December 13, 1946, would cease to be in force. The Assembly also recommended that Togo should be admitted to membership in the United Nations upon its attainment of independence.

"For the second consecutive year the General Assembly adopted a resolution calling upon the Secretary-General and the Specialized Agencies to 'give urgent and sympathetic considera-tion' to requests from Togo for technical assistance. In this con-nection, Minister of State Paulin Freitas of the Government of Togo, speaking as a member of the French Delegation, paid tribute to the quality of assistance already received from the United Nations. Two technical experts, one in the field of public finance and the other in the field of money and credit, have al-ready visited Togo, and an expert in the field of public adminis-tration is expected shortly.

"The Minister also reported continued political advancement. Nationwide elections for local councils were held on August 9, 1959. Prime Minister Olympio's Committee for Togolese Unity (CUT) won all seats on the councils. Minister Paulin Freitas said that despite this electoral sweep political activity on the eve of independence has never been more intense. 'Our Republic has experienced these last days a flowering of political parties,' he said. U.S. spokesmen during Trusteeship Council and General Assembly debates on Togo during the year lauded the efforts of the people of the territory and its leaders as well as those of the Administering Authority and welcomed the forthcoming inde-pendence of the country."

U.S. participation in the U.N., report by the President to Congress for the year 1959, pp. 189–190.

"1418 (XIV). DATE OF THE INDEPENDENCE OF THE TRUST TERRITORY
OF SOMALILAND UNDER ITALIAN ADMINISTRATION

Somaliland
(Italian)

"*The General Assembly*,

"*Recalling* the terms of article 24 of the Trusteeship Agreement with respect to the Trust Territory of Somaliland under Italian administration (hereinafter referred to as Somalia) which provides that the Agreement shall cease to be in force ten years after the date of the approval of the Trusteeship Agreement by the General Assembly, at the conclusion of which the Territory shall become an independent sovereign State,

"*Recalling* its resolution 442(V) of 2 December 1950, by which it approved the Trusteeship Agreement,

"*Having considered* the information submitted by the Administering Authority [*Official Records of the General Assembly, Fourteenth Session, Annexes*, agenda item 13, document A/4262] to the effect that the Government of Somalia has conveyed the wish expressed by the Legislative Assembly that the Trusteeship Agreement be terminated as soon as possible so that the Trust Territory may achieve independence at a date earlier than 2 December 1960, as well as the statement of the representative of the Italian Government that the Administering Authority is prepared to support this wish,

"*Having heard* the statements made by the Chairman of the United Nations Advisory Council for Somalia,

"*Having heard* the views of the petitioners,

"*Noting* the wish expressed by the Government of Somalia that, as soon as possible after the date of attainment of its independence, Somalia should be admitted to membership in the United Nations, and noting further that the Government of Italy has expressed its readiness to sponsor the application that will be made by the Government of Somalia to be admitted to membership in the United Nations,

"1. *Takes note* of the statements made by the representative of Italy and the representative of the Government of Somalia that the preparations for independence will be completed by 1 July 1960 and that independence will be proclaimed on that date;

"2. *Congratulates* the Government of Italy, as Administering Authority, and the Government and the people of Somalia on taking steps in order to attain the basic objectives of the International Trusteeship System in advance of 2 December 1960;

"3. *Expresses its appreciation* for the aid and advice provided by the United Nations Advisory Council for Somalia to the Administering Authority and also to the Government and the people of Somalia in their progress towards independence;

"4. *Expresses its confidence* that the recommendations and observations of the Trusteeship Council, which have been accepted by the Administering Authority and by the Government of Somalia, concerning the broadening of the composition of the

Political Committee and the Constituent Assembly, a popular confirmation of the constitution now under preparation through a referendum, and a modification of the existing electoral law will be implemented before the date on which the Trusteeship Agreement is terminated, and that the Administering Authority will furnish a report on the implementation of these recommendations to the Trusteeship Council at its twenty-sixth session;

"5. *Resolves accordingly*, in agreement with the Administering Authority, that on 1 July 1960, when Somalia shall become independent, the Trusteeship Agreement approved by the General Assembly on 2 December 1950 shall cease to be in force, the basic objectives of trusteeship having been attained;

"6. *Recommends* that, upon the attainment of independence, Somalia shall be admitted to membership in the United Nations in accordance with Article 4 of the Charter of the United Nations.

846th plenary meeting,
5 December 1959."

U.N. Gen. Ass. Off. Rec. 14th Sess., Supp. No. 16 (A/4354), p. 33. Res. 1418 (XIV) was adopted unanimously. Doc. A/PV.846, Dec. 5, 1959, p. 633.

"The Trust Territory of Somaliland, under Italian administration, will become an independent nation on July 1, 1960. Somalia was unique among the trust territories in that its independence date had been specifically set for December 2, 1960, by the Trusteeship Agreement. After careful consideration of all the factors involved, the General Assembly, at its 14th session, acceded to the wish of the Somali Legislative Assembly, endorsed by the Government of Somalia and to which the Administering Authority agreed, for earlier independence. On December 5, in a resolution cosponsored by the United States with seven other countries, the General Assembly resolved 'that Somalia shall become independent on 1 July 1960, and that on that date the Trusteeship Agreement approved by the General Assembly on 2 December 1950 shall cease to be in force.'

"The trust territory, which covers an area of approximately 194,000 square miles along the eastern coast of the Horn of Africa, is still in the process of transferring governmental functions to a duly constituted government. It is expected that prior to independence the following measures will be adopted: (1) the Legislative Assembly will transform itself into a Constituent Assembly to draft and adopt a constitution; (2) the people of the territory will be called upon to ratify the constitution by some form of referendum; (3) the constitution will have to be promulgated, probably by the new Head of State as his first official act; (4) an electoral law will be drafted and an electoral register compiled; and (5) all governmental functions still carried on by the Italian administration will be absorbed by the Somali administration."

U.S. participation in the U.N., report by the President to Congress for the year 1959, p. 181.

"1608 (XV). THE FUTURE OF THE TRUST TERRITORY OF THE CAMEROONS UNDER UNITED KINGDOM ADMINISTRATION

Cameroons
(U.K.)

"*The General Assembly,*

"*Recalling* its resolution 1350 (XIII) of 13 March 1959 concerning the future of the Trust Territory of the Cameroons under United Kingdom administration in which the General Assembly recommended, *inter alia*, that the Administering Authority take steps, in consultation with the United Nations Plebiscite Commissioner for the Cameroons under United Kingdom Administration, to organize, under the supervision of the United Nations, separate plebiscites in the northern and southern parts of the Cameroons under United Kingdom administration, in order to ascertain the wishes of the inhabitants of the Territory concerning their future, and that the plebiscite in the Northern Cameroons be held about the middle of November 1959 on the basis of the two questions set out in paragraph 2 of the said resolution,

"*Recalling* its resolution 1352 (XIV) of 16 October 1959 whereby it decided, *inter alia*, that a plebiscite in the Southern Cameroons would be held between 30 September 1960 and March 1961, on the basis of the two questions set forth in paragraph 2 of the said resolution,

"*Recalling further* its resolution 1473 (XIV) of 12 December 1959 in which the General Assembly, having considered the results of the plebiscite in the northern part of the Cameroons under United Kingdom administration, recommended the organization by the Administering Authority, in consultation with the United Nations Plebiscite Commissioner, of a further plebiscite to be held in the Northern Cameroons under United Nations supervision between 30 September 1960 and March 1961, on the basis of the two questions defined in paragraph 3 of the said resolution,

"*Having examined* the report of the United Nations Plebiscite Commissioner concerning the two plebiscites held in the Northern and the Southern Cameroons in February 1961 [*Official Records of the General Assembly, Fifteenth Session*, agenda item 13, addendum, document A/4727] and the report of the Trusteeship Council thereon [*ibid.*, agenda item 13, document A/4726],

"*Having heard* the petitioners,

"1. *Expresses its high appreciation* of the work of the United Nations Plebiscite Commissioner for the Cameroons under United Kingdom Administration and his staff;

"2. *Endorses* the results of the plebiscites that:

"(*a*) The people of the Northern Cameroons have, by a substantial majority, decided to achieve independence by joining the independent Federation of Nigeria;

"(*b*) The people of the Southern Cameroons have similarly decided to achieve independence by joining the independent Republic of Cameroun;

"3. *Considers that*, the people of the two parts of the Trust Territory having freely and secretly expressed their wishes with regard to their respective futures in accordance with General

Assembly resolutions 1352 (XIV) and 1473 (XIV), the decisions made by them through democratic processes under the supervision of the United Nations should be immediately implemented;

"4. *Decides* that, the plebiscites having been taken separately with differing results, the Trusteeship Agreement of 13 December 1946 concerning the Cameroons under United Kingdom administration shall be terminated, in accordance with Article 76 b of the Charter of the United Nations and in agreement with the Administering Authority, in the following manner:

"(*a*) With respect to the Northern Cameroons, on 1 June 1961, upon its joining the Federation of Nigeria as a separate province of the Northern Region of Nigeria;

"(*b*) With respect to the Southern Cameroons, on 1 October 1961, upon its joining the Republic of Cameroun;

"5. *Invites* the Administering Authority, the Government of the Southern Cameroons and the Republic of Cameroun to initiate urgent discussions with a view to finalizing, before 1 October 1961, the arrangements by which the agreed and declared policies of the parties concerned will be implemented.

*994th plenary meeting,
21 April 1961.*"

U.N. Gen. Ass. Off. Rec. 15th Sess., Supp. No. 16A (A/4684/Add.1), pp. 10–11. Res. 1608 (XV) was adopted by a vote of 64 in favor (including the United States), to 23 against, with 10 abstentions. Doc. A/PV.994, Apr. 21, 1961, p. 77.

"1626 (XVI). THE FUTURE OF WESTERN SAMOA

"The General Assembly,

"Recalling its resolution 1569 (XV) of 18 December 1960 concerning the future of the Trust Territory of Western Samoa under New Zealand administration,

"Taking note of Trusteeship Council resolution 2102 (XXVII) of 7 July 1961,

"Having examined the report of the United Nations Plebiscite Commissioner concerning the plebiscite held in Western Samoa on 9 May 1961,

"Having heard the statements of the representative of the Administering Authority and of the Prime Minister of Western Samoa,

"1. *Expresses* its high appreciation of the work of the United Nations Plebiscite Commissioner for Western Samoa and his staff, and of the co-operation he received from the Administering Authority and from the Government and people of Western Samoa;

"2. *Endorses* the results of the plebiscite, namely that:

"(a) The people of Western Samoa have, by an overwhelming majority, expressed their agreement with the Constitution for an independent State of Western Samoa adopted by the Constitutional Convention on 28 October 1960;

Western Samoa

"(b) The people of Western Samoa have agreed by an overwhelming majority that on 1 January 1962 Western Samoa should become an independent State on the basis of that Constitution;

"3. *Resolves*, in agreement with the Administering Authority, that the Trusteeship Agreement for Western Samoa approved by the General Assembly on 13 December 1946 shall cease to be in force upon the accession of Western Samoa to independence on 1 January 1962;

"4. *Expresses the hope* that Western Samoa, on the attainment of independence, will be admitted to membership of the United Nations, should it so desire.

1039th plenary meeting,
18 October 1961."

G.A. Res. 1626 (XVI).   The resolution was adopted unanimously.
A/PV.1039, Oct. 18, 1961, p. 3.

"1642 (XVI). THE FUTURE OF TANGANYIKA

"*The General Assembly,*

"*Recalling* its resolution 1609 (XV) of 21 April 1961 concerning the future of the Trust Territory of Tanganyika,

"*Noting* that the Government of the United Kingdom of Great Britain and Northern Ireland and the Government of Tanganyika have since then agreed that Tanganyika should become independent on 9 December 1961,

"*Noting further* that the Trusteeship Council at its twenty-seventh session took note with satisfaction of the advancement of the date of independence for Tanganyika from 28 December 1961 to 9 December 1961 and drew the attention of the General Assembly to this date for appropriate action at its current session,

"1. *Resolves*, in agreement with the Administering Authority, that the Trusteeship Agreement for Tanganyika, approved by the General Assembly on 13 December 1946, shall cease to be in force upon the accession of Tanganyika to independence on 9 December 1961;

"2. *Recommends* that, upon the attainment of its independence on 9 December 1961, Tanganyika shall be admitted to membership in the United Nations in accordance with Article 4 of the Charter of the United Nations.

1047th plenary meeting,
6 November 1961."

G.A. Res. 1642 (XVI).   This resolution was adopted unanimously.
A/PV.1047, p. 7, Nov. 6, 1961.

The Trusteeship Agreement for Ruanda-Urundi was terminated as of July 1, 1962, by G.A. Res. 1746 (XVI), adopted June 27, 1962, by a vote of 93 (including the U.S.) to 0, with 10 abstentions (including the U.S.S.R.). By this resolution the General Assembly also decided that on July 1, 1962,

"Rwanda and Burundi shall emerge as two independent and sovereign States". U.N. Gen. Ass. Off. Rec. 16th Sess., A/PV.1118.

Ghana (formerly Togoland under British administration) was admitted to membership in the United Nations by Resolution 1118 (XI), adopted by the General Assembly of the United Nations March 8, 1957. U.N. Gen. Ass. Off. Rec. 11th Sess., Supp. No. 17 (A/3572), pp. 60–61. By Resolutions 1476 (XV), 1477 (XV), and 1479 (XV), adopted September 20, 1960, the General Assembly admitted the Republic of Cameroon (formerly Cameroons under French Administration), the Togolese Republic (formerly Togoland under French Administration), and the Republic of Somalia (formerly Somaliland under Italian Administration) to membership in the United Nations. U.N. Gen. Ass. Off. Rec. 15th Sess., Supp. No. 16 (A/4684), p. 64. By Resolution 1667 (XVI), adopted December 14, 1962, the General Assembly admitted Tanganyika to membership in the United Nations. A/PV.1078, p. 6.

GOVERNMENTS

Distinction Between State and Government

§46

". . . International law distinguishes between a government and the state it governs. This distinction makes it clear that the extinction of the Nazi Government and the temporary absence of any German Government did not necessarily mean that Germany as a state ceased to exist. States have frequently survived protracted periods of non-government, civil war, anarchy and hostile occupation. It has been noted that the American declaration of a state of war on December 11, 1941, and the Proclamation of the termination of that state of war in 1951 both referred to 'the Government of Germany.' This may have been intended to assist in a propaganda denominating the Nazis and not Germany as the enemy. In the President's Proclamation the term 'Germany' as distinguished from the Government of Germany does occur in the paragraph of the preamble which asserts that it is 'desirable to bring the existing state of war with Germany to a close and to remove Germany from its present enemy status, thus eliminating certain disabilities affecting German nationals.' This seems to imply that under American municipal law Germany, and not merely the German Government, was in a state of war with the United States."

Germany

Wright, "The Status of Germany and the Peace Proclamation", 46 Am. J. Int'l L. (1952) 299, 307.

The Declaration of June 5, 1945, regarding the defeat of Germany and the assumption of supreme authority with respect to Germany by the Governments of the United Kingdom, the United States of

America, and the Union of Soviet Socialist Republics, and the Provisional Government of the French Republic provides:

"The German Armed Forces on land, at sea and in the air have been completely defeated and have surrendered unconditionally and Germany, which bears responsibility for the war, is no longer capable of resisting the will of the victorious Powers. The unconditional surrender of Germany has thereby been effected, and Germany has become subject to such requirements as may now or hereafter be imposed upon her.

"There is no central Government or authority in Germany capable of accepting responsibility for the maintenance of order, the administration of the country and compliance with the requirements of the victorious Powers.

"It is in these circumstances necessary, without prejudice to any subsequent decisions that may be taken respecting Germany, to make provision for the cessation of any further hostilities on the part of the German armed forces, for the maintenance of order in Germany and for the administration of the country, and to announce the immediate requirements with which Germany must comply.

"The Representatives of the Supreme Commands of the United States of America, the Union of Soviet Socialist Republics, the United Kingdom and the French Republic, hereinafter called the 'Allied Representatives,' acting by authority of their respective Governments and in the interests of the United Nations, accordingly make the following Declaration:—

"The Governments of the United States of America, the Union of Soviet Socialist Republics and the United Kingdom, and the Provisional Government of the French Republic, hereby assume supreme authority with respect to Germany, including all the powers possessed by the German Government, the High Command and any state, municipal, or local government or authority. The assumption, for the purposes stated above, of the said authority and powers does not effect the annexation of Germany.

"The Governments of the United States of America, the Union of Soviet Socialist Republics and the United Kingdom, and the Provisional Government of the French Republic, will hereafter determine the boundaries of Germany or any part thereof and the status of Germany or of any area at present being part of German territory."

A Decade of American Foreign Policy: Basic Documents, 1941–49 (1950), pp. 506–507.

". . . The effect of the Allied Declaration of 5 June 1945 has been considered by the English courts in the case of *Rex* v. *Bottrill, ex parte Kuechenmeister.* [Proceedings in the King's Bench are reported in All E.R., [1946] i. 635; for the decision of the Court of Appeal see L.R. [1947] K.B. 41.] Kuechenmeister, a German national, had permanently resided in the United Kingdom since 1931, during which year he had married an Englishwoman. During the war he was interned as an enemy alien and it was now proposed to deport him. He applied to the court for a writ of habeas corpus. Counsel for the applicant accepted the proposition that the court will not issue habeas corpus on the application of an enemy alien; but he argued that Kuechenmeister was no longer an enemy alien because the effect of the Allied Declaration of 5 June was to destroy the existence of Germany as a sovereign state, from which conclusion it also followed that there could no longer be a state of war between Great Britain and Germany, and, further, that there was no longer a status of German nationality in international law. In answer to this argument the Attorney-General, opposing the application, put before the court a certificate signed by Mr. Ernest Bevin, Secretary of State for Foreign Affairs, in the following terms:

" '(1) That under paragraph 5 of the Preamble to the Declaration dated June 5, 1945, of the unconditional surrender of Germany, the Governments of the United Kingdom, the United States of America, the Union of Soviet Socialist Republics, and France assumed supreme authority with respect to Germany, including all the powers possessed by the German Government, the High Command, and any State, municipal, or local government or authority. The assumption for the purposes stated above does not effect the annexation of Germany.

" '(2) That in consequence of this declaration, Germany still exists as a State and German nationality as a nationality, but that the Allied Control Commission are the agency through which the Government of Germany is carried on.

" '(3) No treaty of peace or declaration by the Allied Powers having been made terminating the state of war with Germany, His Majesty is still in a state of war with Germany, although, as provided in the declaration of surrender, all active hostilities have ceased.'

The Court of Appeal upheld a decision of the Divisional Court refusing the application. It was held that the certificate of the Secretary of State was conclusive on the Court for the facts alleged in it, and in any case the action of the Executive taken in the interests of the safety of the state must be above challenge by habeas corpus. 'In our municipal law,' said Lord Justice Scott in the Court of Appeal, 'whether or not it differed in that respect from international law, a state of war could continue with a State in spite of the fact that that State no longer had any independent central government.' The actual decision of the Court rests, of course, on doctrines of English constitutional law; for the international lawyer the interest of the case lies in the propositions enunciated in the certificate of the Secretary of State. Although the certificate is conclusive of such matters in English law, it is not of itself conclusive in international law, and it will be convenient to consider the several propositions *seriatim*, together with certain other aspects of the operation of the Berlin Declaration not touched on in this case.

.   .   .   .

"The. Berlin Declaration states that the Allies have assumed 'supreme authority' over Germany, but that this does not effect the annexation of Germany. It has been argued that this is an assumption of sovereignty over Germany and that consequently Germany, lacking the prerequisite of an independent government, can no longer be said to exist as a state in the sense of international law. On the other hand, it is evident from *Rex* v. *Bottrill* [cited *supra*] that the British Government, at any rate, relies on the continued existence of Germany as a state. Which of these two contradictory views of the effect of the Berlin Declaration is correct?

"The view that the German state has ceased to exist rests very largely on the—it is submitted mistaken—assumption that the Allies have in fact vested themselves with full sovereignty over Germany in the ordinary sense of that term. The Berlin Declaration is obviously a carefully drafted document and it is significant that, far from declaring that the occupying Powers have assumed the sovereignty over Germany, it studiously avoids any reference to sovereignty. It speaks only of an assumption of 'supreme authority' (*l'autorité suprême: oberste Regierungsgewalt*), which is not necessarily the same thing. For the 'supreme authority' assumed by the occupying Powers is not without qualification: it is assumed for certain stated purposes; it is 'without prejudice to any subsequent decisions that may be taken respecting Germany'; it is a provisional régime to provide for 'the period when Germany is carrying out the basic requirements of unconditional surrender'; furthermore, it is specifically stated that 'the assumption, for the purposes stated above, of the said authority and powers does not effect the annexation of Germany'. Admittedly, sovereignty is not a term with a very precise legal connotation; nevertheless, it is quite clear that the powers assumed by the Allies fall something short of what is generally understood by sovereignty, and the content and legal effect of those powers must be established by an analysis of the Berlin Declaration, and not by an analysis of the general concept of sovereignty.

"If, indeed, the correct view is that the German state has ceased to exist, it would seem to follow that there has been a state succession, and that certain of the rights and duties of the former German state have passed by succession to the Allied states; for example, it would then be arguable that parts of the German debts are now chargeable on the public funds of the Allied states. It cannot be supposed that such a result was within the intention of the Allied Powers in making the Berlin Declaration. On the contrary, the expressed intention is that the assumption of supreme authority over Germany is not to effect the annexation of Germany, and this qualification of the rights assumed is an essential part of the instrument which must, if possible, be interpreted in such a way as to give undoubted effect to the qualification. If the qualification that Germany is not annexed is to be given any substantial content it can only be interpreted to mean that the Allied régime stops short of creating any sort of identity between the German state and the Allied states. In so far as there is any succession, it must be a succession of governments and not of states; or to put it another way, it means that in so far as the Control Authority is acting as 'the agency through which the Government of Germany is carried on', its acts are in law attributable not to the Allied states but to the state of Germany, which is accordingly deliberately maintained in being as a legal person.

"Thus to draw a distinction between government and state and to assume plenary powers of government unaccompanied by annexation of the state is admittedly unprecedented, and the question remains how far such a result is possible in law. There is, indeed, nothing novel in the idea that the persons who control one legal entity may also control a distinct legal entity. If the controlling shareholders of company X are also the controlling shareholders of company Y, the common lawyer finds no difficulty in still regarding company X and company Y as distinct legal persons; and there is no logical difficulty in applying the same reasoning to the artificial legal persons we call states. However, this does not dispose of the substantial objection that a state must nevertheless have an *independent* government if it is to qualify as a state in the sense of international as opposed to municipal law. It may very well be that Germany still exists as a legal person properly called a state but that, having no independent government, that legal personality is reduced to the sphere of constitutional law and has no validity in international law; just as Virginia is unquestionably a legal entity properly called a state in American constitutional law but, nevertheless, has no separate legal personality in international law. The criterion of statehood in international law must be the enjoyment of a sufficient degree of independent government, and the rule is fundamental to the international system: a state obviously could not be permitted to multiply itself by the creation of subsidiary states on the analogy of the subsidiary companies of company law and to claim for those subsidiary states legal personality in international law, including for example the right of separate representation on international assemblies. But in considering the relevance of this rule to the present status of Germany, the decisive factor is the purely temporary nature of the régime set up in the Berlin Declaration. For this is a question not of the emergence of a new state but of the continued existence of an old state with a long history of independence. The presumption is therefore of her continued existence as a state, and a merely provisional arrangement for carrying on her government through an agency set up by the four occupying Powers does not upset that presumption. It is of course true that the Allies have not yet finally committed themselves on the future of Germany, but their present intention is clearly that after a period of control and re-education in democratic responsibilities, Germany may be granted a new government which it is hoped will prove itself fitted eventually to resume the powers of the government of the German state."

Jennings, "Government by Commission", XXIII Brit. Yb. Int'l L. (1946) 112, 113–114, 119–123.

Adverting to that part of the Declaration of Berlin of June 5, 1945, which states "there is no central government or authority in Germany capable of accepting the responsibility for the maintenance of order, the administration of the country, and compliance with the requirements of the victorious powers", Professor Kelsen argued that ". . . The existence of an independent government is an essential element of a state in the eyes of international law. By abolishing the last Government of Germany the victorious powers have destroyed the existence of Germany as a sovereign state." Kelsen, "The Legal Status of Germany According to the Declaration of Berlin", 39 Am. J. Int'l L. (1945) 518, 519.

Secretary of State Herter, in discussing at Geneva May 18, 1959, the reason why the United States cannot negotiate or enter into a peace treaty of the nature proposed by the Soviet Union whereby "Germany" would be represented by the German Federal Republic and the so-called German Democratic Republic pending establishment of an all-German government, said:

". . . The German Federal Republic and the so-called German Democratic Republic do not, either separately or in combination, constitute an all-German government authorized to act for and bind the international entity known as Germany. That can be done only by an all-German government, freely chosen by the German people.

"True, the Soviet Union in its proposal pays lip service to the principle that any peace settlement, to be worthy of the name, must be with the whole of Germany, by the patent device of referring to 'Germany' as the contracting party to the treaty. But the 'Germany' of the Soviet proposal is a nonentity, and the only real parties are the Federal Republic of Germany and the so-called German Democratic Republic."

XL *Bulletin*, Department of State, No. 1041, June 8, 1959, p. 820.

Occupying power

"The recognition of the governments in London after the invasion of their countries in Europe is clearly in accord with the old and well established principle of international law that belligerent occupation does not affect the sovereignty of the occupied state. The occupying Power is not successor to the lawful sovereign in the occupied territory but is a government based on force exercised as a war measure. To refuse such recognition would also be contrary to the spirit of the Covenant of the League of Nations and to the principles of the Briand-Kellogg Pact that war is outlawed as an instrument of national policy and that neither military violence nor conquest is lawful title for acquiring territory."

Oppenheimer, "Governments and Authorities in Exile", 36 Am. J. Int'l L. (1942) 568, 571–572.

Classification

De Jure Governments

§ 47

". . . a *de jure* government means a government with uncontested legality, fully and permanently accepted as a partner in international relations."

von Schuschnigg, *International Law: An Introduction to the Law of Peace* (1959) 160.

"The terms '*de jure*' and '*de facto*' recognition had already come into Anglo-American terminology by the time of the revolt in Spanish America. A British Foreign Office instruction for the British plenipotentiary at the Congress of Verona, dated August 8, 1822, distinguished between three stages of recognition: '1st. The Recognition *de facto* which now substantially subsists. 2nd. The more formal Recognition of Diplomatic Agents. 3rd. The Recognition *de jure*, which professes to decide upon the Title, and thereby to create a certain Impediment to the assertion of the Rights of the former Occupant.' [H. A. Smith, *Great Britain and the Law of Nations* (1932) vol. I, p. 125.] At about the same time, President Monroe in his message to Congress declared that the policy of the United States in regard to Europe was 'to consider the Government *de facto* as the legitimate Government for us'. [Sir John Fischer Williams, "Recognition", 15 Grotius Transactions, 1929, p. 60.] In 1829, in an instruction to the American diplomatic representative in Colombia, Secretary Van Buren said: 'So far as we are concerned, that which is the Government *de facto* is equally *de jure*.' [Wharton, *Digest*, vol. I, p. 530.]

"By themselves, the terms '*de jure*' and '*de facto*' can, no doubt, with equal propriety, be used with reference to constitutional law as well as international law. In the constitutional law sense, a '*de jure* government' is synonymous with 'legitimate' or 'constitutional' government; while a '*de facto* government' is equivalent to an 'actual' or 'usurping' government. In the days of hereditary rulers, the constitutional legality of a government carried with it a certain measure of legality in international law. A ruler, deprived of actual control of his country, would nevertheless remain the *de jure* sovereign, while persons carrying on the actual administration would be regarded as 'usurpers', both constitutionally and internationally. [Grotius, *De Jure Belli ac Pacis, Libri Tres*, Bk. 1, Ch. IV, ss. 15–9.] With the decay of the doctrine of dynastic legitimacy in constitutional law, constitutional legality is no longer made the test of the international title to govern. There can be no *a priori* claim; the title to rule is to be determined by the fact of actual governing. Hence the constitutional law test of legality should have no significance

whatever in the consideration of international recognition.
[Noël-Henry, *Les Gouvernements de Fait Devant le Juge* (1927)
s. 2; de Visscher, *Les Gouvernements Etrangers en Justice*, 3
R.I., 1922, p. 149, at p. 156; Rougier, *Les Guerres Civiles et le
Droit des Gens* (1903) 496, n. 1. However, in Bernard's widely
quoted definition, constitutional legality still seems to be the
distinguishing feature of a *de jure* government: "A *de jure* government is one which, in the opinion of the person using the
phrase, ought to possess the powers of sovereignty, though at
the time it may be deprived of them. A *de facto* government is
one which is really in possession of them, although the possession may be wrongful or precarious" (*Neutrality of Great Britain
during the American Civil War*, 1870, p. 108, quoted in *Luther
v. Sagor* [1921] 3 K.B. 532, 543). See also Ralston (*Law and
Procedure of International Tribunals*, 1926, ss. 549–50, 556), who
seems to regard a *de facto* government as one without constitutional basis.] Since the terms '*de jure*' and '*de facto*' have reference to constitutional law only, it has been suggested that the
distinction should be disregarded in the question of international
recognition. [Noël-Henry, *op. cit.*, s. 222.]

"The alternative to abolishing the terms altogether in all references to the question of recognition is to use it in the international law sense. International law, in order to prevent a legal
vacuum, recognises the necessity of treating a government already
established as representing the State, although its authority may
be at times partially and temporarily undermined by insurgent
activities. This is not because the established government is
constitutionally legitimate (although, incidentally, it would be),
but rather because the insurgent authorities have not succeeded
in establishing themselves in its place. As long as this situation
persists, the established government is internationally the *de jure*
government; the insurgents remain, at most, a *de facto* government over a specified portion of the territory. [Baty, *Canons of
International Law* (1930) 207.]

"In principle, therefore, when we speak of '*de jure*' or '*de facto*'
with reference to a State or government, it is only legitimate
to use it in this sense. . . .

.   .   .   .

"Unlike the distinction between *de jure* and *de facto* recognition, which is mainly political, the distinction between *de jure*
and *de facto* governments is essentially legal. By '*de jure* government' we mean a government *de jure* in the international law
sense, that is, a government exercising unrivalled control over
the whole of the territory of a State, though, subsequent to the
establishment of such control, its authority may at times have
been challenged. [It is true, as Austin argues, that a *de jure*
government without *de facto* control is not a government (Austin,
Lectures on Jurisprudence, 1869, vol. I, p. 336), but a government

once having secured *de facto* control continues to be the government until definitely deprived of that control.] Such a challenge may come either from a belligerent community in a civil war or a foreign military occupant in an international war. As long as the war lasts the government which has hitherto been governing continues to be regarded internationally as the *de jure* government of the State, to whatever extent it may have lost actual control. The *de facto* government, although wielding actual power in the territory under its control, may not, according to the traditional view, be regarded as the sovereign of the territory. [See Oppenheim, vol. 2, s. 169; Baty, *op. cit.*, pp. 229–30, 469 *et seq.;* Baty, "Can Anarchy be a State?", 28 A.J.I.L., 1934, p. 446; Garner, *International Law and the World War*, 1920, vol. 2, p. 77; *Resolutions of the London Conference of International Law of 1943*, 38 A.J.I.L., 1944, pp. 291–2; Finch, Foreword to Lemkin, *Axis Rule in Occupied Europe* (1944) vii; Briggs, "De Facto and De Jure Recognition: The Arantzazu Mendi", 33 A.J.I.L., 1939, p. 698. As to practice of States, see the instruction of the United States Department [of State] to the American Ambassador in France, which, referring to the French occupation of the Ruhr, said: "Sovereignty over foreign territory is not transferred by such occupation . . ." (Hackworth, vol. I, p. 146). The United States declared the continued maintenance of the local laws when she was in occupation of the Philippines (*ibid.*, pp. 144–5, 156). A Belgian court held that the Belgian law of treason was applicable to a Belgian subject for acts committed in the territory under enemy occupation (*Kauhlen Case* (1920), *Annual Digest*, 1919–22, Case No. 323). The Legal Adviser of the State Department, however, stated on May 7, 1936, that a military occupant "to all intents and purposes, is the sovereign during the period of occupation" (Hackworth, vol. I, p. 156). See similar view of an Italian court in *Del Vecchio* v. *Connio* (1920), *Annual Digest*, 1919–1922, Case No. 320.] This is true even if the *de jure* government has been completely ousted, or, indeed, has disappeared. [Hall (*A Treatise on International Law*, p. 582) is of opinion that in the event of the conquest of one State by a State which is at the same time at war with another, the conquest cannot be considered complete if by any reasonable chance the other war might extend to the conquered territory. Baty thinks this will not apply to cases where the war is prolonged for many years (Baty, *op. cit.*, p. 482). Hall's view seems to have been acted upon during the late war (Oppenheimer, *Governments and Authorities in Exile*, 36 A.J.I.L., 1942, p. 568; Brown, *Sovereignty in Exile*, 35 A.J.I.L., 1941, p. 666).]"

Chen, *The International Law of Recognition* (1951, edited by Green) 270–272, 290–291.

De Facto Governments

§ 48

De facto government

"In determining whether or not a particular government is or was possessed of *de facto* character so as to have capacity to bind succeeding governments by its acts and obligations, a number of tests or *criteria* have been relied upon by courts and international commissions, with varying emphasis and results. The chief tests which have been applied, or at least mentioned by tribunals and commissions as having been considered in this connection are:

"1. Actual possession of supreme power by the government in the district or state over which its jurisdiction extends;

"2. The acceptance or acknowledgment of its authority by the mass of the people, as evidenced by their general acquiescence in and rendering habitual obedience to its authority; and

"3. The recognition of the government as *de facto*, or *de jure*, by foreign Governments."

Houghton, "The Responsibility of the State for the Acts and Obligations of General De Facto Governments—Importance of Recognition", 6 Ind. L. J. (1931) 422, 423.

Revolutionary forces

"Although international law does not stigmatize revolutions as unlawful, it does not ignore altogether the distinctions between the revolutionary forces and the established government. So long as the revolution has not been fully successful and so long as the lawful government, however adversely affected by the fortunes of the civil war, remains within national territory and asserts its authority, it is presumed to represent the State as a whole. . . ."

Lauterpacht, "Recognition of Governments: I", 45 Colum. L. Rev. (1945) 815, 821–822.

De facto authorities

In February 1958 the Department of State instructed the American Embassy at Djakarta, Indonesia, that American firms should protest requirement of payment of taxes to the dissident government which had been established by rebel forces in Sumatra, if request was made, but that if the dissident government was in *de facto* control of the area and in position to enforce such demand, the firms should pay under protest, making a record thereof, and obtain receipts of payment. The Department of State was of the view that under international practice payments made to *de facto* authorities of Sumatra who were in a position to compel obedience to their demands were considered due and proper payments, completely relieving the American firms making such payments from any further obligations to the central Government.

The Department of State to the American Embassy, Djakarta, telegram, Feb. 18, 1958, MS. Department of State, file 856f.2553/2–1858.

Governments-in-Exile

§ 49

"The term 'exiled' or 'refugee' government—although well-known today—is not very appropriate since it does not express clearly that such government is the only *de jure* sovereign power of the country, the territory of which is under belligerent occupation, but no better term has yet been coined. 'Authority' is used in English war legislation as referring to the Free French."

Oppenheimer, "Governments and Authorities in Exile", 36 Am. J. Int'l L. (1942) 568.

"Moreover, the effectiveness which we usually associate with the exercise of territorial jurisdiction may be wholly lacking in the case of a government in exile; its potential effectiveness depends upon the hazard of war. We may say of the governments of The Netherlands and of Norway, for example, when they were functioning in England during World War II, that their territorial supremacy was only momentarily in abeyance. There were fewer governmental authorities indeed who were prepared to say the same of the Emperor Hailie Selassie [of Ethiopia] in the winter of 1939. How do we know today whether the sovereignty of the Baltic states of Estonia, Latvia, and Lithuania is actually represented by their recognized diplomatic missions in Washington, or whether it has been permanently extinguished . . . ?"

Jessup, *Transnational Law* (1956) 62. See also Marek, *Identity and Continuity of States in Public International Law* (1954), 86–101.

"With respect to the governments-in-exile, two kinds of recognition have to be distinguished: one is the continuing recognition of the government existing in the country immediately preceding the occupation, and of their successors; and the other, recognition *ab origine* of a newly created governmental authority on Allied soil [e.g., the Czechoslovak Government]. While the international obligations of a government-in-exile of the first type cannot be legally repudiated by their states, the obligations of the governments of the second type have to be explicitly or by implication assumed by the states which they purport to represent.

"It is generally accepted that control over the territory of the country (or at least a substantial part of it) is a prerequisite to recognition. However, in the event of enemy occupation of its territory, this requirement is suspended, and recognition of the exiled government may be continued. Furthermore, recognition may be extended to newly created governments without territory and without continuity. The effects of recognition of governments-in-exile vary somewhat from the effects of recognition under normal circumstances. The absence of dominion over their own territories and their presence on foreign soil are dominating factors which condition this divergence. This is exemplified by various statutes enacted in Great Britain in order to enable the governments-in-exile to exercise governmental functions. [Diplomatic Privileges (Extension) Act, 1941, 4 & 5 Geo. VI, c. 7; The Allied Powers (Maritime Courts) Act, 1941, 4 & 5 Geo. VI: The Allied Forces Act, 1940, 3 & 4 Geo. VI, c. 51.] Without such enabling acts the governments-in-exile could perform no function on foreign territory outside of those activities pertaining to matters commonly embraced by the term 'external affairs'."

Lourie and Meyer, "Governments-in-Exile and the Effect of Their Expropriatory Decrees", 11 U. Chi. L. Rev. (1943) 26–27.

The United States Court of Appeals for the Second Circuit in the case of *State of the Netherlands* v. *Federal Reserve Bank of New York* (1953) declaring effective legislation passed by the Netherlands Government-in-exile concerning property within the occupied territory of the Netherlands discussed the authority of the absent sovereign and the limited administrative authority of the occupant as follows:

"The nineteenth century American view that military conquest completely displaced the sovereignty of the prior possessor, see, e.g., United States v. Rice, 4 Wheat. 246, 17 U.S. 246, 254, 4 L.Ed. 562; Fleming v. Page, 9 How. 603, 50 U.S. 603, 612, 13 L.Ed. 276, was substantially modified by the Regulations respecting the Laws and Customs of War on Land, ratified by the United States as an annex to the Fourth Hague Convention of 1907, 36 Stat. 2277, 2295. Since the adoption of these Regulations it is generally agreed that the occupant does not succeed to sovereignty over the occupied territory, but has only limited administrative authority. 6 Hackworth, Digest of International Law 385–6; Oppenheimer, Governments and Authorities in Exile, 36 Am. J. Int'l L. 568, 571. Article 43 of the Regulations specifies that authority as follows: 'The authority of the legitimate power having in fact passed into the hands of the occupant', the latter shall take all the measures in his power to restore, and ensure, as far as possible, public order and safety, while respecting, unless absolutely prevented, the laws in force in the country.' The word 'safety' in this article is not a literal translation of 'la vie publique,' the expression used in the original French version, and a somewhat broader concept may have been intended. Schwenk, Legislative Power of the Military Occupant under Article 43, Hague Regulations, 54 Yale L. J. 393; the author of this article suggests that 'civil life' would more accurately reflect the intent of the draftsmen. Id. at 393, n. 1. Be that as it may, the occupant's legitimate legislative authority is limited to necessary administrative measures, see Aboitiz & Co. v. Price, D. C. Utah, 99 F. Supp. 602, and is circumscribed by various other provisions in the Regulations, of which the prohibition against confiscation of private property is the most directly relevant here. See Comment, The Law of Belligerent Occupation in the American Courts, 50 Mich. L. Rev. 1066, 1071; Note, 65 Harv. L. Rev. 527.

"While it is clear that the preoccupation laws outside the legitimate scope of the occupant's control remain in force, Hague Regulations, Art. 43; Schwenk, supra at 406, the effectiveness of the absent sovereign's new legislation is not quite as certain. The Hague Regulations do not explicitly deal with this problem. Several foreign courts have, however, considered the issue; and, so far as we have been able to find, only those of Greece have refused to give effect to enactments of the legitimate sovereign applying to the occupied territory. See Occupation of Cavalla, Greece: Court of Thrace (1930), Annual Digest 1929–30, No. 292. All the others recognize the validity of such legislation, e.g., Agrocide v. Arsocid, Holland: Court of Appeal, The Hague (1946), Annual Digest 1947, No. 142; Public Prosecutor v. Reidar Haaland, Norway: Supreme Court, Appellate Division (1945), Annual Digest 1943–45, No. 154; Re Hoogeveen et al., Belgium: Court of Cassation (1944), Annual Digest 1943–45, No. 148; Stasiuk and Jagnycz v. Klewec, Poland: Supreme Court, Third Division (1927), Annual Digest 1927–28, No. 380; De Nimal v. De Nimal, Belgium: Court of Appeal of Brussels (1919), Annual Digest 1919–22, No. 311. Pitted against the array of precedent cited, the Cavalla case does not seem to us to merit the reliance the district court placed upon it.

"In support of its decision, the court below also pointed to a dictum in the De Nimal case to the effect that hostile measures aimed at combating the occupant and hampering his rule would not apply to occupied territory. Such a limitation appears quite reasonable, indeed essential; but rather than suggesting the ineffectiveness of the Netherlands decree, it supports our contrary conclusion. Obviously, absentee legislation intended to interfere with the occupant's *legitimate* rule should not be given effect. Otherwise the authority vested in the occupying power by Article 43 of the Hague Regulations would become nugatory. Mere hostility to the occupant should not, however, invalidate the absent sovereign's enactments. To have such an effect the hostile legislation must be directed against those aspects of governmental control which international law vests in the occupant. In short, the legitimate sovereign should be entitled to legislate over occupied territory insofar as such enactments do not conflict with the legitimate rule of the occupying power. This view is suggested by at least one prominent commentator on international law, who writes: 'Principle seems to demand that, assuming the new law to fall within the category of that large portion of national law which persists during the occupation and which the enemy occupant cannot lawfully change or annul, it ought to operate in occupied territory.' McNair, Municipal Effects of Belligerent Occupation, 57 L. Q. Rev. 33, 73; see also McNair, Legal Effects of War 382–3 (3d Ed. 1948). Somewhat similar is the position taken by Feilchenfeld in The International Economic Law of Belligerent Occupation 135 (1942), except that he would recognize absentee legislation in those fields not actually preempted by the occupant rather than those within his legal authority: 'Nevertheless, one would go too far in assuming, as has been done by various authorities, that an absent sovereign is absolutely precluded from legislating for occupied areas. The sovereignty of the absent sovereign over the region remains in existence and, from a more practical point of view, the occupant may and should have no objection to timely alterations of existing laws by the old sovereign in those fields which the occupant has not seen fit to subject to his own legislative power.'

"It has been pointed out, moreover, that refusal to recognize any new legislation by the displaced sovereign, while limiting the occupant's rule to the authority granted in Article 43 of the Hague Regulations, may well result in a hiatus of legislative control in fields inadequately covered by pre-existing enactments. Stein, Application of the Law of the Absent Sovereign in Territory under Belligerent Occupation: The Schio Massacre, 46 Mich. L. Rev. 341, 362. This author offers the rather utopian suggestion that the occupant's recognition of legislation by the absent sovereign in this no man's land would provide one possible solution. Stein also notes the 'modern tendencies in the British and American doctrine which require the occupant to give the widest possible application in occupied territory, within the limits of his legitimate military interests, to "absent" sovereign's "new" laws.' Id. at 370. Thus it is apparent that the commentators do not view international law as precluding all recognition of absentee decrees; and our own interpretation reconciles the Hague restrictions on the occupant with the need for continuous legislation in all fields of government control.

". . . In view of the vagueness of Article 43, it may occasionally be difficult in a particular case to determine where the occupant's authority ends and that of the absent sovereign begins. But that determination is greatly simplified here by Article 46 of the Hague Regulations, prohibiting confiscation of private property by the occupant. Decree A–1 was aimed directly at preventing or at least discouraging such illegal seizure; hence, while unquestionably a 'hostile' measure, it merely implemented a restriction upon the occupant, rather than interfered with his legitimate rule. See Stein, United States: Recovery of Property Confiscated by Enemy Occupant, 1 Am. J. Comp. L. 261, 266. . . ."

201 F.2d 455, 461–463 (2d Cir. 1953).

When offering the Diplomatic Privileges (Extension) Bill for a second reading in the House of Commons on February 20, 1941, the Under-Secretary of State for Foreign Affairs, Mr. Butler, stated that "the object of the Bill is to confer certain immunities and privileges upon members of foreign Governments and envoys accredited to Allied Powers". He further explained:

". . . We have in London at the present time a miniature Europe. We wish, consequently, to adjust the law of our country in order to meet the international character of our capital. I feel confident that the House will wish to honour these Allied Governments by giving to them the independent and dignified status to which their position and Sovereign powers entitle them. . . ."

369 H.C. Deb. (5th ser.) cols. 329, 330 (Feb. 20, 1941).

With the invasion of Nazi armed forces in World War II, eight European Governments (Belgium, Czechoslovakia, Greece, Luxembourg, The Netherlands, Norway, Poland, and Yugoslavia) and the Free French "authority" under General de Gaulle at the invitation of the British Government established governments or authorities in exile in the United Kingdom. With particular reference to their functions in exercising sovereignty and in representing their respective States, Oppenheimer wrote in 1942 of some of the legal aspects of these activities as follows:

"With the exception of Belgium, Czechoslovakia and Poland, the sovereignties continue to function in London without undergoing any material changes in their governments. The local authorities established in the territories under belligerent occupation and exercising administrative activities under the control of the occupying Power do not enjoy sovereignty. Under the circumstances the recognition of the governments in England of Greece, Luxembourg, The Netherlands, Norway and Yugoslavia does not call for any comment.

.   .   .   .

"On March 6, 1941, the British Parliament accorded diplomatic immunity and privileges to the members of sovereign allied governments established in the United Kingdom and their official staff as well as to envoys accredited to them. This statute does not, however, include the 'Heads of States' as it is generally admitted that they enjoy extraterritoriality. This is recognized by the British courts. By passing this Act, Parliament expressly conferred upon the governments-in-exile 'the independent and dignified status to which their position and sovereign power[s] entitles [sic] them.' [Statement by the Under Secretary of State for Foreign Affairs when introducing the Bill (369 Parl. Deb., H.C., 1940–1941, p[c]. 329).] . . . The exiled governments are receiving and sending envoys from and to the countries with which they maintain relations. The Act expressly extends the privileges to such envoys who, as in [the] case of the Czechoslovakian provisional government, are termed 'diplomatic representatives.' This distinction has, however, no legal significance. General de Gaulle and the members of his committee as a foreign non-sovereign authority enjoy also the diplomatic privileges which according to law, custom and usage are accorded to governments. The Free French authority maintains 'delegates' abroad, e.g., in the United States of America, and the representatives of foreign Powers are accredited to *Chef des Français Président du Comité National*.

"The governments-in-exile are displaying a rather intensive political activity. They have concluded treaties among themselves and with third countries. Each of them has signed a military agreement with the British Government. In addition the Czechoslovakian and Polish Governments concluded on November 11, 1940, an agreement of 'Confederation of States,' in execution of which a joint declaration was signed in London on January 25, 1942, defining the principles of the projected confederation. Furthermore, Greece and Yugoslavia on January 15, 1942, entered at London into a pact for a Balkan Union. Moreover, Czechoslovakia and Poland executed on July 18 and September 28, 1941, and July 30, and August 15, 1941, respectively, treaties with Russia pledging aid to the latter country and making arrangements for Czech and Polish army units on Russian soil.

"The American Government entered into treaty relations with the exiled government[s] not only by extending 'Lease-Lend' privileges to them but also by signing far-reaching declarations and agreements. The joint undertaking not to make a separate armistice or peace with the enemies was executed at Washington on January 1, 1942, by all the United Nations. Of still greater significance are the 'Mutual Aid Agreements' by which the signatory Powers pledge not only their mutual resources to a common victory but also their collaboration in economic policies to make possible a lasting peace. Substantially identical agreements were signed by the United States with Great Britain, the Union of Soviet Socialist Republics as well as China, and with the exiled governments of Belgium, Czechoslovakia, Greece, The Netherlands, Norway and Poland. It may be added that most of the governments-in-exile have declared war on Japan.

"All exiled governments, including the Fighting French, have formed, together with Great Britain, the Dominions and Russia, the 'Inter-Allied Council.' One of its most significant actions so far has been to adhere to the 'Atlantic Charter' at its meeting held in London on September 24, 1941.

.   .   .   .

Belgian
Government-
in-Exile

". . . Belgium is in the very exceptional position of being able to rely on the authority of its Supreme Court for the proposition that decrees issued without parliament by the executive power are valid if, as a result of hostile invasion, the legislative bodies cannot function. The constitutional legality of the royal decrees issued by the King and his government during the occupation of his country by Germany from 1914 to 1918 were upheld by the Belgian *Cour de Cassation*. [See the judgments of the Cour de Cassation of Feb. 11 and June 4, 1919, Feb. 18 and April 27, 1920, published in *Pasicrisie Belge*, 1919, Pt. I, pp. 9–16, 97–110, and 1920, Pt. I, pp. 62 and 124–125.] The Belgian Supreme Court of Justice based the decisions on the broad principles that: (1) belligerent occupation does not suspend or destroy the sovereignty of the occupied state (see Art. 43 of the Hague Convention of 1907 respecting the Laws and Customs of War on Land); (2) no nation can live without a sovereign government; (3) the legislative power is indispensable for the existence of a government. The tribunal concluded therefrom that since the Chamber of Deputies and the Senate were paralyzed, the legislative power is vested in the King alone. True, there is this difference between the conditions which prevailed during the first World War and today, that now also the King is in the occupied territory and the government alone functions abroad. But the constitution provides for the contingency that the King cannot govern. In this case the ministers have to convene the legislative bodies, which jointly are competent to devise means for replacing the King for the duration of such a contingency. Yet as long as the Chamber and the Senate cannot meet and have not adopted a joint resolution, the Belgian Cabinet can exercise the rights and prerogatives of the King. It is of interest to note in this respect that, similar to the action of the Norwegian Storting at its meeting at Hamar and afterwards at Elverum on April 9, 1940, the Belgian Parliament gave the King on September 7, 1939, extraordinary powers to take care of any emergency. Hence the Belgian Government keeps clearly within the framework of its constitution as interpreted by the *Cour de Cassation* at Brussels, if the Council of Ministers (*Ministres réunis en Conseil*) exercises legislative powers in England in the name of the Belgian people. In the preamble to the recent Belgian decrees any reference to the powers of the King is dropped and only the impossibility of convening the legislative bodies is emphasized. But it is not believed that the fact that the King is no longer mentioned in the Belgian decrees in London is intended to have any legal significance.

". . . The Queen of The Netherlands and her government followed a different course. The invasion of the kingdom in Europe was so sudden and overwhelming that no time was left to consider or to fulfill constitutional technicalities. In view of such extreme emergency, a temporary deviation from the wording of the constitution is justifiable if this is necessary to conserve the sovereignty and independence of the country. It is significant that the King's Bench Division of the High Court of Justice in England, in the Amand Case, held unanimously with regard to the Netherlands constitution, that there was 'in Netherland law an inherent power in the Netherlands governing bodies, or such of them as survive to make and execute acts of state legislation, which have the force of law during a time of emergency.' The Royal decrees (*Koninklijk Besluit*) are issued by the Queen in London upon the presentation of the competent Minister and published in *Staatsblad van het Koninkrijk Nederlanden* in England, but no article of the constitution as source of the powers of the Queen is mentioned.

Netherlands Government-in-Exile

". . . The temporary removal of the seat of the exiled government should, in the absence of express provisions in the constitution, not limit the exercise of the rights of sovereignty. It is not conceivable that sovereignties recognized by the English Crown should be prevented from doing in London what they could do if they were in their own countries. This issue was decided in October, 1927, by the Court of Appeal of Rome. In *Re* Sarsini and others, the tribunal considered the validity of acts of the Government of Montenegro, which took refuge on Italian soil as a result of the belligerent occupation of its territory in 1921 by Yugoslav troops. It held that

> 'a state may exist outside its natural boundaries and still pre-serve the character of a person in public international law in its relations with other states and particularly in its rela-tions with the state whose hospitality it enjoys. The Gov-ernment of such a state, however, must be enjoying full and formal recognition.'

Such recognition was denied by the Italian Crown to the Gov-ernment of Montenegro. But the English sovereign recognizes the 'Netherlands Queen and her government as *exclusively* com-petent to perform the *legislative* and administrative and other functions appertaining to the Sovereign and Government of the Netherlands.' Therefore, Mr. Justice Wrottesley rightly con-cluded that 'so far as His Majesty's Government is concerned, there is no flaw in the title of the Queen to do here what apper-tains to the Sovereign and Government of the Netherlands. . . .'

Norwegian Government-in-Exile

"With respect to the Norwegian Government in London, the King's Bench Division of the High Court of Justice declared that, according to a letter by the Foreign Office dated May 18, 1940, it is recognized as 'the *de jure* government of the entire Kingdom of Norway and that no other government is recognized either *de jure* or *de facto* of Norway or any part thereof.' Although no de-cisions concerning the other governments-in-exile are known, it can be safely assumed that the recognition accorded to them by the British Government and their powers are comparable to those vested in the Netherland and Norwegian sovereignties."

Oppenheimer, "Governments and Authorities in Exile", 36 Am. J. Int'l L. (1942) 568, 569, 576–577, 579–583.

In considering the international status of the Free French, M. Cas-sin, a French jurist, writing in 1941, observed:

Free French

". . . The problem would not exist if the German occupied zone included all of France, or if the President of the Republic and the Government had quit France in June 1940, either to establish themselves in some part of the Empire or to take up residence in Britain as the Governments of other invaded nations have done. In that case the *de jure* status of the French Government in exile, reinforced by a *de facto* position, would have been strong and clear.

"Actually, the present position of the Free French seems to resemble that of the Czechs. They too, from London, continue the fight for the deliverance of their country. In both cases a pseudo-government in the homeland gives the appearance of being a regularly constituted and sovereign power. In reality, neither is free; both are controlled by Berlin. The Czech situation is simpler because Hitler formally proclaimed that the sovereign Czecho-Slovak state had disappeared. Great Britain, the United States, France and the Soviet Union refused to acknowledge the legality of this act and continued to recognize the old diplomatic representatives of the Czech-Slovak Republic. The course of events in France was different. Nazi Germany did not claim to have annihilated the French State. The Vichy government occupied a *de facto* position in France which was not at first challenged seriously. And the principal foreign Powers did not dispute its claim to represent France in international relationships. According to the *Res Gentium*, the recognition of one government by others depends less on the domestic legitimacy of that government than on its ability to enforce its authority.

French at Vichy

"The rallying of important sections of the Empire to General de Gaulle greatly modified the original situation. His position now reminds one more of that of Mr. Venizelos during the First World War. King Constantine wished to keep Greece neutral; Venizelos insisted that Greece honor her alliance with Serbia and fight with the Allies. A patriotic uprising in Salonika, Crete and the Islands in 1916 gave him support; and he formed a Provisional Government which, after some months, received diplomatic recognition from France and Britain—though these two Powers still retained their representatives at the court of King Constantine. The abdication of the King late in 1917 brought Venizelos to power. Actually, the moral position of Free Frenchmen is even better than that of Mr. Venizelos twenty-five years ago. The latter merely resisted his sovereign who wished to remain neutral. Free France stands in opposition to a government which is subject to enemy orders—an enemy which is in occupation of a great part of the homeland and uses it as a base of operations against France's ally, Britain.

"On January 5, 1941, the British Government gave recognition to the Council of Defense of the French Empire, established at Brazzaville on October 27, and declared its readiness to deal with the Council in all matters touching those overseas possessions of France which had put themselves under General de Gaulle's orders. This recognition of General de Gaulle and the Council of Defense as territorial authorities prepared the way for the British Government to negotiate with them in respect to both the political and economic interests of the colonies. . . .

"The recognition accorded on January 5, 1941, was still short of recognition of a Free French government. . . ."

Cassin, "Vichy or Free France?", 20 *Foreign Affairs* (1941) 102, 109–111.

". . . The legal status of the 'Fighting French' is not dependent on the legality of the Petain régime. Whether the Vichy Government is both illegal and illegitimate, whether it usurped its power by a *coup d'état* and whether it enjoys sovereignty—all this seems rather immaterial for the determination of the status of the French supporting de Gaulle. Today the

'Free French' fight in alliance with the forces of the United Nations, and the National Committee is a non-sovereign authority which . . . enjoys in England most of the rights and the privileges to which the exiled governments are entitled. Although not recognized *de jure*, de Gaulle and his National Committee together with the Council of Defense of the French Empire constitute *de facto* a governmental institution."

Oppenheimer, "Governments and Authorities in Exile", 36 Am. J. Int'l L. (1942) 568, 576.

Tibet—
Dalai Lama's
exile in
India, 1959

In response to the claim reportedly made by the Dalai Lama that he is running the real Government of Tibet from his self-imposed exile in India and with reference to his statement at his news conference at Mussoorie, India, June 20, 1959, that "wherever I am, I am accompanied by my government, which the Tibetan people recognize as the government of Tibet", an official spokesman of the Indian Ministry of External Affairs issued the following statement, June 30, 1959, regarding the status within India of the Dalai Lama:

"So far as the Dalai Lama is concerned, the Prime Minister had made it clear on more than one occasion that while the Government of India are glad to give asylum to the Dalai Lama and show him respect due to his high position, they have no reason to believe that he will do anything which is contrary to international usage and embarrassing to the host country.

"The Government of India want to make it clear that they do not recognize any separate Government of Tibet, and there is therefore no question of a Tibetan Government under the Dalai Lama functioning in India."

The Christian Science Monitor, June 30, 1959, p. 2.

Insurgent and Revolutionary Governments

§ 50

Destruction
of life and
property

A note from Secretary of State Stimson to the Consul at Nogales (Damm) of April 25, 1929, at the time of an armed uprising against the legitimate Government of Mexico, distinguished between the destruction to American private property and noncombatant life as a result of bombardment by the recognized Mexican Government in an attempt to suppress the rebellion and that caused by the rebels whose belligerency was unrecognized by the United States Government as follows:

". . . Department does not perceive a legal basis upon which to found representations against bombardment of Empalme by forces of the recognized Mexican Government as part of its military campaign, thus far highly successful, to crush out a rebellion against the authority of that Government. Nor is this Government in a position to substitute its judgment for that of the regularly constituted Mexican authorities as to the wisdom, propriety, or effectiveness of legitimate military measures and operations undertaken by the regular Mexican forces to crush such rebellion, except to ask that due notice be given of military operations, particularly the bombardment of unoccupied or unfortified places, which might threaten either American property or American life, in order that Americans may take such precautionary measures against loss as may be possible under the circumstances. It is of course assumed that Federal forces will not wantonly destroy private property nor non-combatant life.

"The situation with reference to the rebel forces is entirely different. While the United States has recognized the existence of a condition of hostilities in certain areas in Mexico, this does not imply recognition of a legal state of war, the parties to which have been treated as belligerents. The belligerency of the rebels has not been recognized nor has this Government recognized in this conflict even a semi-belligerency in the form of a recognition that the military operations in Mexico are between two rival warring factions. This Government has recognized only that there is an armed uprising against the regularly constituted Government of Mexico which has adopted measures of suppression which seem now about to be successful. The rebels, therefore, have no international legal status and it would seem that nationally they stand as illegal groups of armed men attempting to overthrow their own Government, and therefore probably having the status of traitors. They are from the standpoint of legal principle, both international and national, in no better position than ordinary outlaws and bandits. Representations of the strongest character may therefore be made to them against injuries by them to American life and American property.

"It is of the utmost importance that you keep these legal distinctions in mind as otherwise this Government may find itself in a position where it is not properly fulfilling its international obligations."

1929 For. Rel., vol. III, pp. 402–403.

As to whether there is an obligation on the part of an alien with respect to payment of taxes to insurgent authorities in *de facto* control of a territory, and whether there is a legal right on the part of the *de jure* government to require a second payment of such taxes, it is well-settled that— *Payment of taxes*

Taxes are properly payable by an alien to insurgents in *de facto* control of an area and accordingly in a position to compel payment of taxes. However, protests should be made and receipts obtained, if possible.

A *de jure* government does not have the right to exact a second payment of taxes exacted by insurgents in *de facto* control of the same area.

However, if the insurgents are not in *de facto* control of an area, the *de jure* government may have grounds, under the authorities, not to recognize the validity of the first payment.

A memorandum dated December 18, 1957, prepared in the Office of the Legal Adviser of the Department of State, stated:

"A. *American authorities*

"The practice of the United States has been uniform. The United States has instructed American representatives to protest the requirement by insurgent forces that American citizens pay taxes. However, when such payments are, nevertheless, required, the United States has consistently taken the position that the legitimate or constitutional government may not subsequently collect those taxes a second time. The United States has also constantly instructed the United States representatives to protest against any discriminatory measures applied against American citizens.

"The following is set forth to illustrate what steps were taken by the Department of State, and in what sequence, in a typical case:

"Replying to the report of a consul that rebel forces in Sonora, Mexico, were exacting forced loans and payments from American citizens in his district under the guise of one kind of tax or another, the Department of State, on March 29, 1929, after stating that international law recognizes the right of *de facto* authorities actually in control of areas either by revolt or by occupation to compel obedience to their demands, instructed him to—

'protest orally to the appropriate persons now exercising *de facto* authority in your district, first, against the payment of all taxes to insurrectionary authorities by American citizens on the ground that such payment is not in accordance with local law, thus giving basis for the protest of the taxpayers themselves; second, and particularly, and on the additional ground of unfair discrimination, you will orally protest against all arbitrary or confiscatory exactions levied against American property or upon American citizens, when the levy in whatever form, whether as war or other taxes, or as "forced loans" or other similar measures or contributions, is not equally applied according to a fixed percentage amongst all the inhabitants, whether natives or foreigners, but is applied arbitrarily upon that part only of the community which includes Americans.'

"In an instruction of the same date to the Ambassador in Mexico, the Department, after quoting the above instructions to the consul, said that—

'you will bring the foregoing regarding . . . taxes to the attention of the Mexican Government and will state that the Government of the United States will regard payments of taxes of all kinds, made to *de facto* authorities in control of certain disturbed areas in Mexico under the circumstances set out in the telegrams, as constituting a due and proper payment of such taxes in the amounts paid and as completely relieving American citizens so paying such taxes from any and all further obligation in regard to such payment.'

"In reply to a report from a Consul that Mexican Federal officers were taking steps to enforce re-payment to the Federal Government of taxes already paid to the rebel leaders, the Department on May 3, 1929 stated that it was instructing the Ambassador in Mexico to protest to the Mexican Government. On May 8, 1929 the Department instructed the Ambassador as follows:

" 'International law and custom governing this question is so clearly recognized that it is difficult to understand the seeming insistence of local Mexican authorities in running contrary thereto. In taking the position that taxes and customs paid to *de facto* authorities in control of an area (whether they be rebel authorities or authorities of a foreign country) must be considered as if they were paid to the regular authorities of a country, this Government is not invoking a principle that has not been recognized by itself. In the celebrated Castine case which arose out of the occupation by British troops of the port of Castine in Maine, the Supreme Court of the United States itself held that goods imported into Castine during its occupation by British troops were not subject to payment of customs duties under the laws of the United States after the British withdrew, and the United States resumed the exercise of its sovereignty which, during British occupation, had been suspended. (See *United States* v. *Rice*, 4 Wheaton, p. 24.)

" 'Mr. Fish, Secretary of State, commenting upon the demand by the Mexican authorities for duty on goods imported into Mazatlán while that port was in the occupation of insurgents, stated as to the practice of the United States that "since the close of the Civil War in this country suits have been brought against importers for duties on merchandise paid to insurgent authorities. Those suits, however, have been discontinued, that proceeding probably having been influenced by the judgment of the Supreme Court adverted to," that is, the judgment of the Supreme Court in the Castine case noted above. (I Moore's *Digest*, p. 41 *et seq.*, particularly p. 49.)

" 'This Government confidently expects that the Mexican authorities will recognize this principle. It is no fault of Americans in Mexico that the regular constituted Mexican Government may not have been able at certain times and in given areas to enforce its own power and collect its own taxes, nor to protect Americans from the imposition of taxes and other duties by rebels, and therefore Americans, who were in no wise responsible for the conditions in such areas, must not now be punished for the forced payment by them of taxes to rebels because of this inability of the regular Mexican authorities to protect them against such payment.' (I Hackworth, *Digest of International Law*, pp. 140–142.)

"Numerous other cases, all to exactly the same effect, principally cases involving Mexico, are set forth at pages 137–140 of Volume I of Hackworth's *Digest of International Law*.

"B. *British authorities*

"With respect to British practice, the following appears typical:

"In 1865 an insurgent group was in possession of a customhouse in Peru. The *de jure* Peruvian Government issued a decree declaring that all duties collected by the insurgents would be considered as not paid and that the Government would require such duties to be paid again to its own offices as soon as its authority was re-established in the port.

"Law Officer Phillimore, of the British Foreign Office, recommended that an instruction to the British Chargé at Lima should contain the following:

" 'That according to the universal usage of nations dues paid by foreigners who take no part whatever in a civil war which breaks out in the country where they are peaceably resident and carrying on trade under the faith of Treaties and general international law, to a *de facto* Government which demands and has the power of compelling this payment, must be considered to be paid to the Government of the country.

" 'At the same time Her Majesty's Chargé d'Affaires should be instructed not to offer any encouragement to British subjects to pay these dues to the Insurrectionary Government, nor to give any pledge or promise to them that they will be protected from the repayment of such dues, but to warn them of the necessity of being very careful not to do any act which may be fairly treated as voluntarily aiding and abetting the Insurrectionary Government.' (II McNair, *International Law Opinions*, 1956, p. 398.)

"There appears to have been made often in practice distinctions between non-voluntary payments and voluntary payments and between payments made to a *de facto* government and to those made to a mere insurgent force which never became organic enough to form a government.

"The following authorities establishing this distinction are set forth in McNair's *International Law Opinions:*

" 'There is some evidence for the view (i) that a second payment can only be resisted or, if made, recovered, if the previous payment made to the *de facto* Government was made under compulsion, and (ii) that a regular Government cannot be called upon to admit as valid such payments as have been made to a mere insurgent force which never became organic enough to form a government.

" 'On 1 June 1874 [Spain], Baggallay, Holker and Deane reported that "the principle that payment to a *de facto* Government is a discharge of an obligation to the Government of a country could not with propriety be applied . . . [to] cases in which the taxes and contributions levied by the Carlists have been paid voluntarily or without protest, or under circumstances from which it may fairly be inferred that they were aiding the Carlist movement"—an Opinion which was reaffirmed by James, Herschell and Deane on 15 April 1885. [Peru]

" 'On 13 July 1875 [Mexico, presumably the "insurgent force" did not amount to a government], Baggallay, Holker and Deane reported:

> " ' "That the payment of the customs dues to an insurgent force, such as that which appears to have enforced payment in the present case, cannot, we think, be brought within the principle of payment to a *de facto* Government, which the regular or succeeding Government would be bound to admit as good payment. And we are of opinion that Her Majesty's Government cannot properly claim, as a matter of right, the repayment of customs dues levied by a foreign Government in cases where those dues, having been taken by an insurgent force in the first instance, have been subsequently levied a second time by the regular Government."

" 'On 24 August 1885 [Colombia], Webster, Gorst and Deane reported "that Her Majesty's Government are entitled to object to the exaction of such second payment by British Subjects of import duties, and of an additional duty in case of refusal, in respect of the importation of goods into territory which was not under the *de facto* sovereignty of the Colombian Government at the time of such importation."

" 'In the case of insurgency in Chile, Webster and Clarke on 9 April 1891 [Chile] declined to assent to the general view that export duties if paid to insurgents could later be refused when demanded by the parent Government and said that it depended on circumstances.' [*Ibid.* pp. 398, 399.]"

Office of the Legal Adviser (Whiteman and Neidle), memorandum, "Payment of Taxes to De Facto Insurgents and Possibility of Second Payment to De Jure Government", Dec. 18, 1957, MS. Department of State, file 856d.11/12–1857.

In the case of insurgency where the status of belligerency has not been recognized either by the legitimate government or by third powers thus according the insurgent authorities the status of *de facto* belligerent government, the United States has maintained that a legitimate government may not close to neutral commerce a port held

Closure of insurgent-held ports

by its insurgent enemies by mere proclamation. In such instances the legitimate government must maintain an effective blockading of the port as an assertion of its authority in that area. Cases supporting this position appear in I Hackworth, *Digest of International Law* (1940) 359, VII *ibid.* (1943) 125, 166; and 3 Hyde *International Law* 2187 (2d rev. ed., 1945). While most of the cases cited involved situations in which the United States Government did not actually recognize the effectiveness of the blockade and the consequent legality of the port closure, two cases in which the United States recognized the closure of insurgent-held ports combined with an effective blockade (the Brazilian revolution in São Paulo of 1932 and the Dominican Republic revolution in Puerto Plato in 1914) were reviewed as follows by the Office of the Legal Adviser in a memorandum of May 20, 1958:

Brazilian
Case

"During the revolution in Sao Paulo in 1932 the Brazilian Government closed all ports of that state to foreign and domestic shipping. Two American vessels which were then in the port of Santos, were allowed to depart under a ruling of the Brazilian Foreign Office that vessels anchored there at the time of publication of the decree closing the port might leave freely. The Department of State instructed the Embassy in Rio de Janeiro:

" 'If Santos is in the control of insurgents the Brazilian Government would have no right to close this port by decree as reported . . . unless this decree is enforced by an effective blockade.' (The Secretary of State (Stimson) to the Chargé in Brazil (Thurston), Telegram No. 49, July 16, 1932, MS. Dept. of State, File No. 832.00/260; 1932 *Foreign Relations* (vol. 5) 400). [Quoted from Hackworth, VII *op. cit.*, p. 168.]

"References in communications from Rio de Janeiro and Sao Paulo indicate that the port of Santos was effectively blocked and that no ships entered therein from July 13 until the armistice on October 3, 1932. The following excerpts support this contention:

" 'All ports Sao Paulo are declared temporarily closed to domestic and foreign shipping by a decree issued last evening.
" 'The cruiser *Rio Grande do Sul* was despatched last night to Santos which is in the hands of Sao Paulo forces.' (The Chargé in Brazil (Thurston) to the Secretary of State, Telegram No. 53, July 12, 1932, MS. Dept. of State, File No. 832.00 Revolutions/242, 1932 *Foreign Relations* (vol. 5) 391).
" 'Warships are patrolling off Santos which is decreed closed to commerce. . . . The Consul at Santos reports that no ships have entered since July 13, that all business is paralyzed and that shipments of coffee are suspended until further notice.' (The Chargé in Brazil (Thurston) to the Secretary of State, telegram No. 67, July 18, 1932, MS. Dept. of State,

File No. 832.00 Revolutions/242, 1932 *Foreign Relations* (vol. 5) 401).

" 'The Army and Navy, while said to display little enthusiasm continue actively to support the Government. Sao Paulo is blocked by sea and virtually surrounded by land. . . . With respect to the blockade I am advised by the Naval Attache that there is no doubt as to the ability of the Government to make it effective.' (The Chargé in Brazil (Thurston) to the Secretary of State, Telegram No. 79, August 3, 1932, MS. Dept. of State, File No. 832.00 Revolutions/242, 1932 *Foreign Relations* (vol. 5) 409).

"The issue of the legality of the port closure decree and the effectiveness of the blockade was presented by the following resolution of the American Chamber of Commerce of Sao Paulo, as reported in a telegram from the Consul General at Sao Paulo (Cameron) to the Secretary of State, September 24, 1932, MS. Dept. of State, File No. 832.00 Revolutions/381, 1932 *Foreign Relations* (vol. 5) 417):

" 'Whereas American and all other business interests domiciled in the State of Sao Paulo have suffered and are suffering tremendous losses in consequence of the closing of the port of Santos by decree of the Brazilian Provisional Government and whereas it appears that this act was not in accordance with accepted tenets of international law, and whereas we know of no action being taken to relieve the situation, it is resolved by the American Chamber of Commerce of Sao Paulo *respectfully to ask the Government of the United States to lodge a protest with the Brazilian Provisional Government against this closing and to take such steps as will guarantee the American interests their full rights.*' (Underlining [*italics*] supplied.)

"The Sao Paulo Chamber of Commerce requested that a copy of this resolution be forwarded to the United States Chamber of Commerce in Washington.

"In reply to these requests the Department of State instructed the Consul General at Sao Paulo in the following manner (September 27, 1932, MS. Dept. of State, File No. 832.00 Revolutions/ 389, 1932 *Foreign Relations* 419):

" '. . . If, as the Department understands, the Brazilian Government is maintaining an actual, effective blockade of the port of Santos, this Government cannot protest as requested by the American Chamber of Commerce.

" 'The Department feels that it cannot properly forward the resolution.'

"That the blockade continued to be effective until an armistice was arranged on October 3, 1932, is confirmed by the following correspondence:

" 'The blockade of Santos, regarding which Consul General Cameron telegraphed the Department a resolution of the American Chamber of Commerce of September 23rd, appears to be effective and is a measure of war which the Federal Government considers that it is justified in taking.' (The Ambassador in Brazil (Morgan) to the Secretary of State, despatch No. 3954, September 28, 1932, file No. 832.00 Revolutions/409, 1932 *Foreign Relations* 419).

" 'Great eagerness here for opening port of Santos; receipt of Rio de Janeiro mail retained since July 9 and various supplies such as wheat, fruit, gasoline and steel. Cable companies now open commercial intercourse.' (The Consul General at Sao Paulo (Cameron) to the Secretary of State, October 4, 1932, MS. Dept. of State, File No. 832.00 Revolutions/404, 1932 *Foreign Relations* 424).

" 'The Port of Santos is open to such steamers as are willing to accept the risk of passing through the channel which has been cleared of mines, and telegraphic and postal communication has been re-established with that City and with Sao Paulo. No foreign mails are detained in Rio de Janeiro.

" '. . . The influence of the American Naval Mission upon the Brazilian Navy is also evident in the loyalty of the officer corps, in spite of considerable sympathy with Sao Paulo, to take an active part in favor of that State. Had it done so the Port of Santos would have remained open, communication would have been established with the outer world and Sao Paulo would have been able to obtain the military supplies, the want of which caused her surrender.' (The Ambassador in Brazil (Morgan) to the Secretary of State, despatch No. 3958, October 7, 1932, MS. Dept. of State, File No. 832.00 Revolutions/415, 1932 *Foreign Relations* (vol. 5) 425).

"The excerpt from despatch No. 3954 of September 28, 1932, from Rio de Janeiro can be taken as a definitive statement that the blockade of Santos was effective at the time that the Department of State refused to act upon the resolution of the American Chamber of Commerce in Sao Paulo.

"It is submitted that this Brazilian case is a clear one of the United States respecting an effective blockade of closed, insurgent-held ports.

. . . .

Dominican Republic Case

"B. The Dominican Republic case is described as follows in VII Hackworth 127 (1940):

" 'The Department of State, being informed by the Dominican Government in 1914 that, because of a state of rebellion in the cities of Puerto Plata and Monte Christi, those ports had been closed to commerce and blockaded, replied:

" ' ". . . as this Government has been informed that the blockade at Puerto Plata is maintained effectively, the blockade of that port is recognized by this Government. As this Government is not in receipt of advices that the blockade of Monte Christi is effective, it will be impossible for it to recognize it until such a time as it is informed that this blockade is made effective." ' (The Acting Secretary of State (Lansing) to the Dominican Chargé d'Affaires (Cernuda), May 16, 1914, MS. Dept. of State, File No. 839.00/1225, 1914 *Foreign Relations* 231). (Underlining [*italics*] added).

"Further investigation of this case indicates that the United States Naval Forces in Dominican waters considered the blockade of Puerto Plata to be maintained effectively by a gunboat of the legitimate government. This factual determination was reflected in the American reply to the legitimate government's announcement of port closure, *supra.* The Department of State instructed the American Legation in Santo Domingo as follows, 'Commander U.S.S. *Washington* reports blockade Puerto Plata effective. This Government has today recognized blockade that port.' (The Secretary of State (Bryan) to the American Legation in Santo Domingo, May 16, 1914, MS. Dept. of State, File No. 839.00/1229A).

"Some six weeks after the United States had recognized the blockade, however, the Solicitor of the Department of State (Cone Johnson) indicated in a letter to a Mr. Stabler that the blockade of Puerto Plata may not have been truly effective. This communication reads as follows:

" 'Whether we shall continue to recognize the blockade at Puerto Plata must be decided by someone else. It appears that ours is the only government which has recognized the blockade and that our ships are the only ones which do not enter the port. I do not consider this in reality a blockade, and I know of no reason why we should continue to recognize it, unless there be something in the general situation in Santo Domingo to dictate that course and of which I am not advised.' (The Solicitor (Cone Johnson) to Mr. Stabler, July 30, 1914 . . .).

"This statement may have been made, because, although the blockade may have been initially effective, other powers were successful in obtaining safe passage for their merchant vessels through the presence of elements of their navies in the vicinity.

"For example, the Germans were trying to obtain shipment of a cargo on a Hamburg-American Line vessel from Puerto Plata. On June 11th, the American Commander at Puerto Plata received a copy of a letter from the Commander of the German cruiser *Strassburg* to the legitimate government indicating that the closure of the port had prevented German ships from picking up a cargo for several months at Puerto Plata. He stated that a German steamer would call for the cargo, that the vessel would do nothing to harm the operation of the blockade, and that German naval officers would be on board during her presence in port. On June 13 the German steamer *Mecklenburg* entered Puerto Plata, accompanied by boats from the *Strassburg.* The loading of the *Mecklenburg* was accomplished at gunpoint. A few shots were exchanged with forces of the legitimate government on shore. Apparently the blockading gunboats withdrew when the Germans moved in. (See the telegram from the U.S.S. *South Carolina* to the Secretary of the Navy, June 13, 1914, as forwarded to the Secretary of State by the Secretary of the Navy on June 18, 1914, MS. Dept. of State, File No. 839.00/1329).

"Similarly, the United States recognition of the blockade of Puerto Plata may have been partially motivated by Dominican willingness to permit fruit steamers to enter Sosua, a branch port some 10 miles away from Puerto Plata and outside the military zone. A note requesting free passage for such a steamer to Sosua was addressed to the Dominican Charge d'Affaires on the same day (May 16, 1914) as the United States recognition of the blockade. (See the note from the Acting Secretary of State (Lansing) to the Dominican Chargé d'Affaires (Cernuda), May 16, 1914, MS. Dept. of State, File No. 839.00/1222. Subsequent difficulties encountered in effecting the passage of this vessel to Sosua and the later resumption of service by the fruit steamers to the plantation appear in File No. 839.00/1222 to /1317).

"In summary the Dominican case appears to be one where the United States recognized initially an effective blockade of closed, insurgent-held ports, wavered as to the continuation of such recognition when it appeared that other countries' ships were being permitted to enter the port, but, as far as the record goes, never withdrew its recognition. The subsequent political intervention by the United States ended the revolution."

Office of the Legal Adviser (Fraley to Maurer), memorandum, "Respect of Effective Blockade of Closed, Insurgent-held Ports", May 20, 1958, MS. Department of State, file 611.0022/5–2058.

Chinese Case, 1949

The United States position requiring the legitimate government to maintain an effective blockade of the port as an assertion of its authority in that area was reiterated in the exchange of notes between the United States and the Government of the Republic of China in June 1949.

On June 20, 1949, the Chinese Ministry of Foreign Affairs announced the closure of certain Chinese ports in a note to the American Embassy at Canton, reading as follows:

"The Ministry of Foreign Affairs presents its compliments to the American Embassy and has the honor to state that the Government of China has now decided that the following regions from the north bank of the mouth of the Min River, longitude 119 degrees, 40 minutes east and latitude 26 degrees 15 minutes north to the mouth of the Liao River, longitude 122 degrees 20 minutes east and latitude 40 degrees 30 minutes north, which lie along the coast and within the territorial water of China shall be temporarily closed, and entry therein of foreign vessels shall be strictly forbidden. Instructions have already been issued by the Government of China that beginning from midnight of June 25 of this year prompt actions shall be taken to prevent violations of this decision by foreign vessels. All foreign vessels shall themselves be responsible for any danger resulting from their violation of this decision.

"The Ministry of Foreign Affairs also wishes to call the Embassy's attention to the fact that during the period of rebellion [and] suppression the Government of China decided on June 18 of this year to close all ports originally declared open but no longer under the actual control of the Government of China. Included in this category are Yungchia (Wenchow), Ningpo, Shanghai, Tientsen and Chinghuangtao (Chinwang Tao), where no commercial shipping by sea shall be permitted.

"The Ministry of Foreign Affairs requests the Embassy to give due consideration to this matter and to transmit the contents of this note to the American Government and promptly notify the American shipping companies concerned to act accordingly."

Department of State press release 483, June 23, 1949.

The United States reply contained in a note from the American Embassy at Canton on June 28, 1949, stated in part:

"As requested therein, the Ministry's note was transmitted to Washington. The Embassy is now instructed to state in reply that, despite the friendliest feelings toward the Chinese Government, the United States Government cannot admit the legality of any action on the part of the Chinese Government in declaring such ports and the territorial waters adjacent thereto closed to foreign vessels unless the Chinese Government declares and maintains an effective blockade of them. In taking this position, the United States Government has been guided by numerous precedents in international law with which the Chinese Government is doubtless familiar and has noted that the ports referred to are not under the actual control of the Chinese Government."

The American Embassy, Canton, to the Ministry of Foreign Affairs, China, note No. 265, June 28, 1949, MS. Department of State, file 893.801/6-2849.

The British Government, in a note to the Chinese Ministry of Foreign Affairs on June 30, 1949, stated, *inter alia:*

"The above declaration appears to His Majesty's Government to be a proclamation of blockade. In the opinion of His Majesty's Government, in cases where hostilities are in progress between the lawful government of a country and insurgent forces, the proclamation of a blockade by the lawful government amounts to the assertion of belligerent rights, which should be recognized by outside countries, with the further consequence that such rights are thus automatically conferred upon the insurgent party . . . .

"In the opinion of His Majesty's Government, moreover, a mere decree of a lawful Government purporting to close ports occupied by insurgents without the maintenance of a real and effective blockade, cannot be regarded as valid, inasmuch as it constitutes an attempt to secure rights of war without regard to conditions which International Law attaches to their exercise and such a decree cannot be recognized as resulting in a blockade in the sense of International Law".

The United Kingdom representative in Canton subsequently notified the Chinese Ministry of Foreign Affairs on July 2, 1949, that:

"His Britannic Majesty's Government in the United Kingdom cannot accept any disclaimer by the Chinese Government of responsibility on account of damages to British interests and property ashore or afloat arising out of the action of units of the Chinese Government's armed forces in application of decision announced by that Government. Moreover, His Britannic Majesty's Government must at same time hold the Chinese Government responsible for any untoward consequences of the exercise by the ships of the British Royal Navy or Mercantile Marine or by any other British craft or persons of their inherent right of self-defence or protection against hostile action."

The Minister-Counselor of the American Embassy at Canton (Clark) to the Secretary of State (Acheson), despatch No. 30, encls. 1 and 2, July 13, 1949, MS. Department of State, file 893.801/7–1349.

In reply to the United States note of June 28, 1949, the Chinese Ministry of Foreign Affairs stated, *inter alia*, that

". . . the Chinese Government deems it within the sovereign right of a state to declare open or closed any part of its territories, whenever conditions necessitate. In fact, the Chinese Government has exercised in the past on more than one occasion the right to close some of its ports, and no question of legality has been raised by any government, including that of the United States. Port Dairen, for instance, was declared closed at a time when it was not under the actual control of the Chinese Government. The closure order under reference is, in effect, of a similar nature and is, therefore, enforceable independently of a declaration of blockade, which has never been, and is not, under the contemplation of the Chinese Government."

The Minister-Counselor of the American Embassy at Canton (Clark) to the Secretary of State (Acheson), telegram No. 673, July 1, 1949, MS. Department of State, file 893.801/7–149.

In a legal analysis of the United States position with respect to the closure of Communist-held ports, a memorandum from the Office of the Legal Adviser stated:

"The action taken by the American Embassy at Canton on June 28, 1949, is in accord with the historic position of the United States with reference to the closure of ports in control of insurgents. Great Britain and the United States appear to have supported it for nearly 75 years, and certain writers have referred to it as the rule of international law. According to this theory the *de facto* control of ports by insurrectionists suspends the ordinary competence of the *de jure* authorities to close the ports by law or decree, but leaves them competent to close by effective blockade and 'by effective blockade only. It is not at all clear, however, whether the exercise of the blockade right is contingent upon recognition of the insurgent's belligerency or whether it has the effect of recognition. . . . [The British appear to hold in this case] that one of the conditions requisite to a blockade is recognition of the belligerent status of the other party. It is quite possible, however, that the American and British practice permits closure by belligerent blockade without recognition of belligerency. See Dickenson, 'Closure of Ports in Control of Insurgents', XXIV, Am. Journal, 69, 71.

"The present British suggestion is supported by some authority. Wheaton, Dana's 8th Ed. 34, note 15. This would hold that insurgency suspends the ordinary competence of the *de jure* authorities, but does not warrant blockade, or, in other words, that there is no way of closing insurgent-controlled ports without recognizing belligerency. Westloks [Westlake], on the other hand, holds that insurgency does not suspend the normal control of ports by the sovereign by municipal law or decree, but that other states may decline to recognize the closure and so by implication recognize the insurgent's belligerency. Still another theory holds that the status of insurgency and belligerency may be carefully distinguished, but that the closure of insurgent-held ports may be permitted only by methods practically analogous to blockade of belligerent-held ports. Wilson, 'Insurgency and International Law', I Am. J. (1907) 46, 58.

"While the practice has not been uniform, and there is little evidence of an international consensus, opinion has tended to support the position maintained officially by the Governments of Great Britain and the United States. . . ."

Office of the Legal Adviser (Snow) to the Office of Far Eastern Affairs (Merchant), memorandum, "The Closure of Communist-held Ports", Aug. 31, 1949, MS. Department of State, file 711.93112/8–3149.

Following the Central Chinese Government's announcement June 20, 1949, of its intention to blockade ports in Communists' hands, the British steamship *Anchises* was bombed while in the Whangpoo River. Describing this as an unwarranted attack from the air on a defenseless British merchant ship, the Under-Secretary of State for Foreign Affairs, Mr. Mayhew, stated before the House of Commons, "No more formal notification of this intention has, so far as I am aware, been given. The representative of His Majesty's Ambassador at

Canton has lodged an immediate protest and reserved the right of His Majesty's Government to demand full compensation. . . ."

466 H.C. Deb. (5th ser.) cols. 34–35 (June 21, 1949).

The efforts of the Chinese Nationalist Government to close Communist-held ports of China were challenged by ships of Isbrandtsen Company, Inc., an American flag line. In September of 1949 the *Flying Independent* and the *Flying Clipper* were intercepted by Chinese naval craft while outbound from Shanghai, and the *Flying Trader* was intercepted inbound for Shanghai. In November 1949, the *Flying Cloud* in leaving Shanghai was challenged by a shot across the bow and after getting underway without permission from the Chinese naval craft was damaged by the naval craft's open fire, and the *Sir John Franklin* while proceeding to the port of Shanghai was damaged by a barrage of fire from Chinese naval vessels. The *Flying Arrow*, when on the high seas approaching the Yangtze in January 1950, was attacked and disabled. The *Flying Clipper* subsequently in February 1950 experienced close misses during a strafing and bombing attack.

On November 30, 1949, Secretary of State Acheson released to the press the following statement of the Department's position regarding the port closure order of the Chinese Nationalist Government:

"Without becoming involved in technicalities I would like to state very simply what the Department's position has been and is regarding the port closure order of the Chinese Nationalist Government. From the outset this government refused to accept the port closure as constituting a legal blockade. That decision stands. Immediately upon the receipt of the Chinese Government's port closure order, steps were taken to inform American shipping companies, and later amendments to it were brought to their notice. It was also stated that any American ship which went into one of the closed ports would do so on its own responsibility. Moreover, to any reader of the newspapers it has been apparent since last June that by reason of the Nationalist naval and air activity in the port of Shanghai and its approaches, the area was in effect an area of hostilities and, in consequence, hazardous. To my knowledge no American ship entered or attempted to enter Shanghai from late June, when the port was stated to be closed, until late September, when arrangements had been made and publicly announced for the entrance of the *General Gordon*. As was stated at that time, the owners of the *General Gordon* secured through their local agents the assurance of the Shanghai authorities that the ship would not be molested during its call. It was similarly announced that the Department of State had secured from the Nationalist Government in Canton assurances that its entrance and departure from

Shanghai would not be interfered with in any fashion. All this was a matter of public knowledge.

"At about this time one American shipping line determined to start sending its ships into Shanghai. This line requested the Navy Department to provide a Naval escort which was refused, on the grounds that it was not this Government's policy to convoy American shipping through the so-called 'blockade'. That remains our policy.

"That same line has continued to send ships into Shanghai, notwithstanding the fact that the first two were detained for a considerable period by Nationalist patrol vessels after leaving Shanghai. More recently, two vessels of this line have been involved in incidents in which they have been shelled by Nationalist vessels. That is a serious matter. Fortunately, no one was hurt. Nevertheless, the endangering of American lives is, as I said, a serious matter. We immediately protested to the Nationalist Government and requested an explanation.

"I should like to commend the prudence, wisdom and perceptiveness displayed by the American shipping lines in the Pacific which during this troubled period have omitted Shanghai from their port of call. There has been only one exception among them, which I have already referred to above."

Department of State press release 930, Nov. 30, 1949.

In an announcement of December 12, 1949, the Chinese Nationalist Government, reiterating the closure order of June 20, further informed the United States Government that it had decided that any American registered vessel remaining in the closed territorial waters and ports, or their vicinities, would be allowed one week of grace to leave such waters and ports, and that the military authorities would afford safe-conduct to such vessels so as to avoid unnecessary risks, save where the vessels were attempting to enter such areas.

Department of State press release 990, Dec. 19, 1949.

On December 17, 1949, the Department published a "General Warning Regarding American Shipping In and Out of Port of Shanghai". The announcement read as follows:

"On November 28, 1949 the *Sir John Franklin*, an American flag ship, while proceeding to the port of Shanghai was subjected to a barrage of fire from two Chinese naval vessels in the lower estuary of the Yangtze, damaging the vessel and seriously endangering life aboard it. Although the vessel was permitted to leave Shanghai unmolested, the Chinese National Government stated that the fact that the vessel was so permitted to leave should not be regarded as a precedent.

"The Department of State must point out that the port of Shanghai and its approaches constitute a zone of danger and the conditions in it are such as to render this area extremely hazardous to shipping. In view of this situation, it is obvious that American lives and property should not be exposed to such risks and all masters of American flag ships are warned accordingly."

Department of State press release 986, Dec. 17, 1949.

On December 29, 1949, the Department was informed by the Chinese Government that the approaches to the Yangtze River and Shanghai had been mined within Chinese territorial waters and that no channel had been left open. The Department released the information to the press, with the statement that "United States shipping companies and masters who contemplate movements of vessels into the area are warned accordingly".

Department of State press release 1016, Dec. 29, 1949.

Indonesia,
1958

At the time of the Central Sumatran revolution in February of 1958, the Indonesian Embassy informed the Department of State, February 24, 1958, that "by a decree of February 17, 1958, of the Chief of Staff of the Indonesian Navy, the ports of Menado, Bitung, Kema and Padang will be closed until further notice to all vessels of both Indonesian and foreign ownership".

In a note of May 1, 1958, the Department replied that:

"While fully reserving the rights of the United States, the Department of State considers there is no occasion to comment on the contents of His Excellency's note, since it appears that no American ships call at the ports mentioned."

MS. Department of State, file 956D.734/2–2458. It appears that the view of the Department of State was still that it could not admit the legality of a decree of closure of insurgent-held ports by the legitimate government, unless the legitimate government declares and maintains an effective blockade of them. Office of the Legal Adviser (Maurer, Pender, Fraley), memorandum, "Legal Aspects of the Indonesian Government's Right to Block Certain Ports Held by Insurgents", Mar. 1, 1958, MS. Department of State, file FW 9560.734/2–2458.

Military Governments

§ 51

Nature:

Under the United States Department of the Army Field Manual on the Law of Land Warfare, military government is defined as "the form of administration by which an occupying power exercises governmental authority over occupied territory." In addition it is stated that "The necessity for such government arises from the failure or inability of the legitimate government to exercise its functions on account of the military occupation, or the undesirability of allowing it to do so." (Paragraph 362.)

In further providing rules for the administration of occupied territory, the Department of the Army Field Manual specifies:

"The authority of the legitimate power having in fact passed into the hands of the occupant, the latter shall take all the measures in his power to restore, and ensure, as far as possible, public order and safety, while respecting, unless absolutely prevented, the laws in force in the country. (HR, art. 43). [Paragraph 363.]

.   .   .   .

"a. *Paramount Authority of Occupant.* The functions of the hostile government—whether of a general, provincial, or local character—continue only to the extent they are sanctioned by the occupant.

"b. *Functions of Local Government.* The occupant may, while retaining its paramount authority, permit the government of the country to perform some or all of its normal functions. It may, for example, call upon the local authorities to administer designated rear areas, subject to the guidance and direction of the occupying power. Such action is consistent with the status of occupation, so long as there exists the firm possession and the purpose to maintain paramount authority. [Paragraph 367.]

"It is immaterial whether the government over an enemy's territory consists in a military or civil or mixed administration. Its character is the same and the source of its authority the same. It is a government imposed by force, and the legality of its acts is determined by the law of war." [Paragraph 368.]

U.S. Department of the Army Field Manual (FM 27–10) on the Law of Land Warfare (1956) 141–142.

The United States Department of the Army Field Manual on the Law of Land Warfare further provides with respect to military occupation:

"Being an incident of war, military occupation confers upon the invading force the means of exercising control for the period of occupation. It does not transfer the sovereignty to the occupant, but simply the authority or power to exercise some of the rights of sovereignty. The exercise of these rights results from the established power of the occupant and from the necessity of maintaining law and order, indispensable both to the inhabitants and to the occupying force.

"It is therefore unlawful for a belligerent occupant to annex occupied territory or to create a new State therein while hostilities are still in progress." [Paragraph 358.]

Provisional— no transfer of sovereignty

Distinguishing military occupation from subjugation or conquest, the Department of the Army Field Manual states:

"Belligerent occupation in a foreign war, being based upon the possession of enemy territory, necessarily implies that the sovereignty of the occupied territory is not vested in the occupying power. Occupation is essentially provisional.

"On the other hand, subjugation or conquest implies a transfer of sovereignty, which generally takes the form of annexation and is normally effected by a treaty of peace. When sovereignty passes, belligerent occupation, as such, of course ceases, although the territory may and usually does, for a period at least, continue to be governed through military agencies." [Paragraph 353.]

U.S. Department of the Army Field Manual (FM 27–10) on the Law of Land Warfare (1956) 138, 140.

"The most important principle of law incident to belligerent occupation—one that was not established until the last century—is that occupation does not displace or transfer sovereignty. The occupant is entitled to exercise military authority over the territory occupied, but he does not acquire sovereignty unless and until it is ceded to him by a treaty of peace (which is the commonest method), or is simply abandoned in his favour without cession, or is acquired by him by virtue of subjugation, that is, extermination of the local sovereign and annexation of his territory, as happened in the case of the South African Republic and the Orange Free State at the end of the South African War. For the same reason, occupation operates no change of nationality upon the inhabitants and no transfer of allegiance, though the occupant acquires a right against inhabitants who remain that they should obey his lawful regulations for the administration of the territory and the safety of his forces. The occupant's right and duty of administering the occupied territory are governed by international law. It is definitely a military administration and he has no right to make even temporary changes in the law and the administration of the country except in so far as it may be necessary for the maintenance of order, the safety of his forces and the realization of the legitimate purpose of his occupation. . . ."

M'Nair, "Municipal Effects of Belligerent Occupation" 57 L.Q. Rev. (1941) 33, 34–35.

A Federal District Court, discussing the relationship between Japanese occupation authorities and Manila and the surrounding territory, stated by way of *dictum* that—

". . . The relation was something more than invasion, and much less than sovereignty. [Since the close of the 19th Century, occupation alone does not transfer sovereignty. To do so requires cession by treaty of peace, abandonment in favor of the occupant, or extermination of the local sovereign and annexation of his realm. McNair, Legal Effects of War, 2d ed. pp. 319–320. Oppenheim, International Law, 6th Ed. Vol. II, pp. 337–338.] The Japanese Imperial Army took possession and set up an administration of the territory. It appears as a fact from the evidence before me and from the history of which I may take judicial knowledge, that the Japanese Government, through its officers, exercised effective governmental control over Manila and neighboring territory, from early in January 1942 until early in February 1945. But, the war was not over, and the United States government had not recognized that government. I conclude therefore, that the Japanese Imperial government was provisionally in effective control, exercising administration over, and therefore, in the international law sense, in belligerent military occupation of Manila and surrounding territory at the times important here."

Adverting to the defendant's reference to the Japanese military government of the Philippines as a "*de facto*" government, the Court stated:

". . . This is an ambiguous term. The situations in reference to which it has been used run the whole gamut from a government virtually the sovereign, although not yet *de jure*, down to belligerent invasion. Sometimes the term refers to recognition *de facto* and not *de jure* by the political departments of the recognizing power, e.g. the British Foreign Office, or our own State Department. . . . "Belligerent occupation" status

"Hence, in this opinion we use the term 'belligerent occupation' which is clearer and more accurate.

"McNair says this distinction between *de facto* and *de jure* 'should not be allowed to obscure the state of belligerent occupation and to attach to that status the rights and duties appertaining to conquest recognized as a *de facto* situation. Belligerent occupation creates a well established status which has been equipped by International Law with rights and duties in the interests of order and the welfare of the inhabitants of the occupied territory.'

"The relation of belligerent occupation is fully recognized by international law, and by a body of municipal law which has evolved through judicial decision in many countries, including our own.

"An enemy conqueror is not a very likely person in whom to repose the trust of administering the occupied territory. He is on the ground, however, and has the power to enforce his commands. And dangerous as it may be to recognize any authority in him, it is better to encourage some proper government than none at all. Without some kind of order, the whole social and economic life of the community would be paralyzed. So, international law has recognized the right of the occupant to make regulations for the protection of his military interests and the exercise of police powers. However, such law also imposes upon the occupant the duty to maintain public order and to provide for the preservation of the rights of the inhabitants."

Aboitiz & Co. v. *Price*, 99 F. Supp. 602, 608–610 (D. Utah, Cent. Div., 1951).

The United States District Court, denying an application for extradition for a United States army sergeant from the United States to Italy on charges of homicide and robbery committed in a portion of Italy then under occupation by German armies, and at a time subsequent to the Italian declaration of war against Germany but prior to the effective date of the Treaty of Peace between the United States and Italy, said with respect to the position of the Italian Government:

> "It may be true that the Italian government had not lost to Germany and the United States its sovereignty over the boundaries which it occupied prior to the war, yet while any of the enemy armies were within such boundaries, with or without the consent or permission of Italy's government, such presence may justly be considered as committing an act of hostility and certain of its rights were given up, ceded, severed or abandoned by that sovereign for the time. The Schooner Exchange v. McFaddon, 7 Cranch 116, 139–140, 3 L. Ed. 287; United States v. Rice, 4 Wheat. 246, 4 L. Ed. 562; Coleman v. Tennessee, 97 U.S. 509, 515, 517, 24 L. Ed. 1118."

In re Lo Dolce, 106 F. Supp. 455, 458–459 (W.D.N.Y. 1952).

The Legal Adviser of the Department of State, in a memorandum of April 17, 1945, to General Julius Holmes, Assistant Secretary of State, stated with respect to the position of the Allied Governments following unconditional surrender that—

> ". . . the Allied Governments would have all the rights of a military occupant, plus such additional rights as may be provided for in the terms of surrender. This presupposes that there will be a signed instrument. I do not consider that the Allied Governments would have the rights and obligations 'of a successor Government' under the terms of surrender. Such a situation would ordinarily result only from annexation or transfer of sovereignty.
>
> "Military occupation has the effect of suspending the exercise by the local government of customary sovereign rights, except to the extent that their exercise is permitted by the military occupant. His orders and decrees are supreme during the period of occupation."

Legal Adviser Hackworth to Assistant Secretary of State Holmes, memorandum, Apr. 17, 1945, MS. Department of State, file 740.00119 EW/4–1745.

General
powers

Judge McNair, stating the British view with regard to the effects of acts of government of the enemy occupant, wrote:

> ". . . Whether the territory under occupation is British or belongs to a co-belligerent with Great Britain or Great Britain is neutral, the principle is that, the occupant being under a duty to maintain order and to provide for the preservation of the rights of the inhabitants and having a right recognized by international law to impose such regulations and make such changes as may be necessary to secure the safety of his forces and the realiza-

tion of the legitimate purpose of his occupation, his acts, whether legislative, executive, or judicial, so long as he does not overstep these limits will be recognized by the British Government and by British courts of law—during and after the war if Great Britain is neutral, after it if Great Britain is belligerent. . . ."

As British authority for this proposition, W. E. Hall, in his reference to the right of *postliminium*, is quoted as saying:

" 'Thus judicial acts done under . . . [the control of the occupant], when they are not of a political complexion, administrative acts so done, to the extent that they take effect during the continuance of his control, and the various acts done during the same time by private persons under the sanction of municipal law, remain good. Were it otherwise, the whole social life of a community would be paralysed by an invasion [that is, occupation] ; and as between the state and individuals the evil would be scarcely less,—it would be hard for example that payment of taxes made under duress should be ignored, and it would be contrary to the general interest that sentences passed upon criminals should be annulled by the disappearance of the intrusive government.' "

M'Nair, "Municipal Effects of Belligerent Occupation", 57 L. Q. Rev. (1941) 33, 48–49.

With reference to the limitations imposed on the powers of a belligerent occupant, the Philippine Supreme Court in the case of *Peralta* v. *Director of Prisons*, (42 *Official Gazette* (1946) 198; 75 Phil. 285 at 298, 300) stated the law as follows:

"All law, by whomsoever administered, in an occupied district is martial law . . . . The words 'martial law' are doubtless suggestive of the power of the occupant to shape the law as he sees fit . . . . The only restrictions or limitations imposed upon the power of the belligerent occupant to alter the laws or promulgate new ones . . . so far as it is necessary for military purposes, that is, for his control of the territory and the safety and protection of his army, are those imposed by the Hague Regulations, the usages established by civilized nations, the laws of humanity and the requirements of public conscience.
[Applying these principles, the Philippine Courts have made the following holdings: that according to the Hague Regulations, a belligerent occupant gains the use to real property only during his occupation, but cannot authorize its alienation thereafter, *Banaag* v. *Encarnacion*, (P.I. 1949) 5 Decision L.J. 414; that in accordance with Rule 56 of the Hague Convention, public property of the legitimate sovereign devoted to religious, charitable, cultural, and educational purposes must be treated by the belligerent occupant in the same manner as private property, *ibid;* that present holders of goods and securities which were stolen or confiscated by the Japanese authorities in violation of the Hague Convention are not regarded as having title thereto, which, instead, is still deemed to be in the original owners, *Saavedra* v.

Pecson, (P.I. 1946), G.R. No. L–260 quoted in 30 J. Comp. Leg. & Int. L., part 3, 17 at 25 (1949) ; *Enriquez* v. *Manuel,* (P.I. 1946) 43 O.G. 104; that confiscation by the Japanese of a bank account in violation of the Hague Convention was void, *Milne* v. *Philippine National Bank,* Civil Case No. 71,200, Court of First Instance of Manilla, Feb. 4, 1946, cited in 30 J. Comp. Leg. & Int. L., part 3, 17 at 25 (1949).]"

Shanker, "The Law of Belligerent Occupation in the American Courts", 50 Mich. L. Rev. (1952) 1066, 1075, 1076, n. 58.

"Recent decisions by the federal courts in this country have clearly established that not only is public international law the test to be applied in determining the effect to be given the acts of state of a military occupying government within the occupied territory [*Aboitiz & Co.* v. *Price,* 99 F. Supp. 602 (D. Utah, Cent. Div., 1951)] but also the measure of the effect to be given the acts of the absent sovereign purporting to operate within the occupied territory.   The case of *State of the Netherlands* v. *Federal Reserve Bank of New York* [201 F. 2d 455 (2d Cir. 1953), 53 Col. L. Rev. 561] involved the applicability to the Netherlands during the German occupation of a royal decree of the Netherlands Government-in-Exile.   This decree purported to vest protective title in the Netherlands Government to all securities belonging to persons domiciled in the Netherlands for the purpose of conserving the rights of the former owners.   Counsel for the Kingdom of the Netherlands were able to convince the United States Court of Appeals for the Second Circuit that the view of international law adopted by the district court [*State of the Netherlands* v. *Federal Reserve Bank of New York,* 99 F. Supp. 655 (S.D.N.Y. 1951)]—that no such enactment of an absent sovereign with respect to property in the occupied territory could be recognized—was incorrect and that the more persuasive international law precedents and authorities sustained the rule that the absent sovereign should be entitled to legislate with respect to the occupied territory in so far as such legislation did not conflict or interfere with the legitimate rule of the occupying power; it followed that the decree, far from interfering with the legitimate rule of the occupying power, merely implemented Article 46 of the Hague Regulations prohibiting confiscation of private property by the occupying power.   [36 Stat. 2307 (1910).]"

Dean, "The Role of International Law in a Metropolitan Practice", 103 U. Pa. L. Rev. (1955) 886, 891–892.

Rhineland   Referring to the Inter-Allied Rhineland High Commission, established as the highest authority in the occupied Rhineland territory under the Rhineland Agreement of June 28, 1919, Ernst Fraenkel of the Foreign Economic Administration wrote in 1944 with respect to its nature as a military government:

". . . the powers of the High Commission cannot be separated into legislative, judicial, and executive. There is no profit in examining, for example, whether its right to approve German statutes was a legislative power, whether its right to cancel court decisions was judicial power, or whether both were attributes of executive power. Occupation represents not a constitutional government, characterized by a balance of powers, but rather a sort of emergency government in which all forms of power are concentrated in one centralized body. As Ireton, American analyst of the Rhineland occupation, has expressed it . . . :

" 'The High Commission . . . is the antithesis of the legal doctrine enunciated by Montesquieu and so readily accepted by the framers of our Constitution: the triune distinction of power, the separation of governmental authority into executive, legislative and judicial departments, each distinct and independent of the others, yet all so correlated as to make one consistent, harmonious and logical system of government. The Commission itself exercises executive, legislative and judicial authority, and not infrequently issues its administrative mandates, enacts important and far-reaching ordinances, and reviews, as would an appellate court, the action of a German civil or criminal court at one and the same sitting.' "

Fraenkel, *Military Occupation and the Rule of Law* (1944) 84–85.

In its determination that the United States Military Government for Germany has power to enter into proper export-import contracts, the Office of Military Government for Germany (U.S.), in a legal opinion addressed to this question, considered first the general nature and powers of Military Government in occupied enemy territory. The opinion cited the Supreme Court of the United States in *Dooley* v. *United States* (182 U.S. 222, 230, 21 Sup. Ct. 762, 765) where Halleck on *International Law* (vol. 2, para. 444) was quoted with approval as follows:

Regulation of foreign transactions

" 'The right of one belligerent to occupy and govern the territory of the enemy while in its military possession is one of the incidents of war, and flows directly from the right to conquer. We, therefore, do not look to the Constitution or political institutions of the conqueror for authority to establish a government for the territory of the enemy in his possession, during its military occupation, nor for the rules by which the powers of such government are regulated and limited. Such authority and such rules are derived directly from the laws of war, as established by the usage of the world and confirmed by the writings of publicists and decisions of courts,—in fine, from the law of nations. . . . The municipal laws of a conquered territory or the laws which regulate private rights, continue in force during military occupation, except so far as they are suspended or changed by the acts of the conqueror. . . . He, nevertheless, has all the powers of a de facto government, and can at his pleasure either change the existing laws or make new ones. . . .' "

The opinion continued:

"That the broad powers above outlined include the general power to enter into contracts seems obvious. In *New Orleans* v. *Steamship Co.*, 20 Wall. 387, the Supreme Court held that 'a contract for the use of a part of the water front of the city was within the scope of the Military occupant's authority . . .' Likewise, the power of Military Government to regulate commerce between the occupied territory and foreign countries is well established. 22 Op. Atty. Gen. 561; *Rutledge* v. *Fogg*, 3 Coldw. Tenn. 559, Magoon's Reports 302.

"3. The executive has very broad powers under the Constitution in the field of International relations. *United States* v. *Curtiss-Wright Export Corporation et al*, 299 U.S. 304, 57 S. Ct. 216. We know of no Congressional enactment which purports to limit the powers of the executive in the exercise of the powers of Military Government in occupied territory in any respect material to the present inquiry or of any directive or policy paper issued from Washington which deprives United States Military Government in Germany of the power to execute contracts in order to implement appropriate programs connected with the occupation. J.C.S. 1067/6 does not in express terms refer to the Zone Commander's power to contract. It does, however, charge him with the execution of many policies, including an export-import program, for the effectuation of which the power to enter into proper contracts appears desirable and appropriate, if not absolutely essential. . . ."

Charles Fahy, Legal Adviser of the Military Governor and Director of the legal division, Office of Military Government, legal opinion "Power to Enter into Contracts under Interim Export-Import Plan", Jan. 22, 1946, II *Selected Opinions* January 1, 1946–February 28, 1946, Office of Military Government for Germany (U.S.), Legal Division, APO 742, pp. 15–16.

Issuance of currency In a decision upholding the power of the Japanese military authorities under international law to order the liquidation of the China Banking Corporation and to appoint and authorize another bank as liquidator on the ground that such liquidation was a mere sequestration of its assets which required the liquidation and not confiscation of the properties of the bank, the Supreme Court of the Philippines affirmed in addition the validity of the payment of the debt with Japanese war notes. On this latter point, the Court said:

"The power of the Military Governments established in occupied enemy territory to issue military currency in the exercise of their governmental power has never been seriously questioned. Such power is based, not only on the occupant's general power to maintain law and order recognized in Art. 43 of the Hague Regulations . . . but on military necessity as shown by the history of the use of money or currency in wars."

Haw Pia v. *China Banking Corporation*, P.D. 1948A, 263, 282. See also *Hongkong & Shanghai Banking Corporation* v. *Luis Perez Samanillo, Inc., and Register of Deeds of Manila*, P.D. 1948B, 678. In its determination of a related issue, the Supreme Court of the Philippines held in the case of *Hilado* v. *De La Costa* that ". . . the character of the war notes as legal tender or currency impressed by the Japanese military authorities during the enemy occupation did not and could not transcend beyond the enemy occupation or after the territory of the Philippines has been liberated from the enemy occupant. In other words, while the Japanese military occupant had authority to make the war notes legal tender or acceptable as such during the enemy occupation, it had no power to make it so or the obligation created therewith payable with the same amount of Philippine currency or legal tender after the liberation." P.D. 1949B, 67, 73.

The case of *Dooply* v. *Chan Taik* involved a suit brought during the Japanese occupation of Burma to redeem certain property from an equitable mortgage created in 1941, plaintiff depositing Japanese military notes in court in full payment March 8, 1945. On the basis of this deposit the City Court of Rangoon on April 23, 1945, made a final decree for redemption. After reoccupation of Rangoon by forces of the lawful government, the High Court allowed an appeal by defendant and held that payment into court in Japanese military notes did not suffice. Plaintiffs appealed, but the Supreme Court of the Union of Burma affirmed the judgment of the High Court, saying in part:

"[appellants' counsel] claims that the enemy in occupation of Burma between the years 1942 and 1945 could have imposed on the inhabitants of the country, so long as the occupation lasted, the obligation to recognize the Japanese Military notes at their face value for use as media of exchange and that the appellants, so long as the occupation lasted, could have claimed as against the defendant that these notes which they were depositing in Court were worth their face value. This ingenious contention, however, does not help the appellants to surmount the difficulty inherent in such Japanese Military notes not being lawful money. They were no better than tokens which were given and had value as media of exchange so long as the occupation lasted. A Full Bench of the High Court of Judicature in *Ko Maung Tin* v. *U Gon Man* held that Japanese Military notes were documents with a value in exchange for goods, and had thus a purchasing value. Four of the five Judges held that Japanese Military notes never formed part of the currency system in Burma and was [were] not 'money'. . . . Nothing has been said before us on behalf of the appellants to justify our dissenting from the view held by the Full Bench of the High Court of Judicature. With the reoccupation of Burma by the lawful government Japanese Military notes became worthless and were not recognized by the lawful government as having any value after the re-occupation. If, then, Japanese Military notes were not 'money' the deposit into the City Court of Rangoon of these notes on the 8th March 1945 cannot, in itself, have the effect of discharging the obligation under the mortgage.

"True it is that if following the deposit into Court such deposit had been accepted by the defendant, such acceptance may . . . by reason of section 4 of the Japanese Currency (Evaluation) Act, 1947, have the effect of releasing the plaintiffs from their liability. . . . But we see no justification for extending the rule to cover a deposit into Court. . . .

"It is not relevant to the enquiry that so long as military occupation lasted, the military commander could have by exercise of irresistible force compelled acceptance of military notes at their face value. To contend . . . that the City Court of Rangoon on the 8th March 1945 could not have, without laying itself open to such pains and penalties as were held out by the military ordinance relating to military notes, refused the deposit of such notes in Court is to beg the question. Inherent in the contention is the proposition, which we have rejected, namely, that the military commander could have validly imposed a parallel currency system and equated such currency to the lawful currency of Burma." Supreme Court of the Union of Burma, June 29, 1950, 45 Am. J. Int'l L. (1951) 381.

In the case of *Laurel* v. *Misa*, decided on January 30, 1948, the Supreme Court of the Philippines held with respect to the governmental powers of the Japanese occupying authorities that:

Legislation

"Considering that, although the military occupant is enjoined to respect or continue in force, unless absolutely prevented by the circumstances, those laws that enforce public order and regulate the social and commercial life of the country, he has, nevertheless, all the powers of a *de facto* government and may, at his pleasure, either change the existing laws or make new ones when the exigencies of the military service demand such action, that is, when it is necessary for the occupier to do so for the control of the country and the protection of his army, subject to the restrictions or limitations imposed by the Hague Regulations, the usages established by civilized nations, the laws of humanity and the requirements of public conscience (*Peralta vs. Director of Prisons* . . . ; 1940 U.S. Rules of Land Warfare, 76, 77); and that, consequently, all acts of the military occupant dictated within these limitations are obligatory upon the inhabitants of the territory, who are bound to obey them, and the laws of the legitimate government which have not been adopted, as well and [as] those which, though continued in force, are in conflict with such laws and orders of the occupier, shall be considered as suspended or not in force and binding upon said inhabitants".

44 *Official Gazette*, Republic of the Philippines, No. 4, Apr. 1948, pp. 1176, 1181.

The Supreme Court of the Republic of the Philippines in the case of *Vicente Hilado*, April 30, 1949, discussing at one point the right of the Japanese military occupant to issue war notes as currency in order that they may be used in making payments of all kinds, due to military necessity, said—

". . . But such an order, being of political character, fell through as of course upon the cessation of the Japanese Military occupation; because it is a well-established rule in international law that 'the law made by the occupant within his admitted power, whether morally justifiable or not, will bind any member of the occupied population as against any other member of it, and will bind as between them all and their national government, so far as it produces an effect during the occupation. When the occupation comes to an end and the authority of the national govern-

ment is restored, either by the progress of operations during the
war or by the conclusion of a peace, no redress can be had for
what has been actually carried out but nothing further can
follow from the occupant's legislation. . . .' (Westlake, *International Law*, seventh edition, p. 518 . . .)".

P.D. 1949B, 67, 74.

". . . as long as an occupant merely enjoys a *de facto* position
in the invaded territory, he cannot collect debts (as distinct from
taxes) owed to the legitimate government, nor can he reduce such
debts, waive them entirely, or influence their status in any way
or by any method, inasmuch as he has no legal title to them.
The debts constitute agreements, contracts, or obligations between the debtors and the legitimate sovereign and the occupant
does not enter at all into the picture. Only if and when he
acquires *de jure* rights or title to the territory, such as through a
peace treaty or through *debellatio* followed by lawful annexation,
does the occupant acquire the legal right to take the former sovereign's place and henceforth to collect the debts owed to the
latter. In other words, during the period of belligerent occupation, that is, prior to a change in legal title to the territory, the
occupant cannot undertake the replacement of the sovereign by
collecting debts owed to that sovereign. . . ." Collection
of debts

von Glahn, *The Occupation of Enemy Territory* (1957) 157.

"The foregoing point of view has not been accepted by all jurists and
the wording of Article 53 of the Hague Regulations of 1907 has perpetuated
the older view that the occupant may collect debts owed to the legitimate
sovereign. The expression *valeurs exigibles* in the original text of the
regulations has been translated into English as 'realizable securities' (in
German, *eintreibbare Forderungen*) and has led to a confusion of the terms
'debts' and 'securities'. As a result, several publicists have maintained
that the occupant is entitled to collect all debts and monetary demands
owed to or collectible by the legitimate sovereign, provided they matured
or fell due *during the period of belligerent occupation*. This view represents only a minority opinion among international law experts and the
prevailing rule is that the occupant cannot collect such debts and at the
same time act in accordance with the prevailing rules of international law.
It should be pointed out, moreover, that still another group of writers has
held that bearer instruments belonging to the legitimate sovereign may be
seized as legitimate war booty and would thus become the legal property
of the occupying power." *Ibid.* 157–158.

In answer to the question "Do the US Courts for Germany derive
their jurisdiction completely from the authority of the US High
Commissioner or does a connection to the authority for Military Government Courts still exist ?", the Office of General Counsel in the Office
of the United States High Commissioner for Germany stated: Establish-
ment of
judiciary

"The true basis of the jurisdiction of the United States Courts
for Germany is to be found in the laws of war and the powers

and duties of an occupying power under international law. Among these powers and duties are the responsibility to establish and maintain law and order. Manifestly certain types of offenses cannot be entrusted to the local courts where the overriding interests of the military occupant are involved. On the occupation of Germany, additional factors dictated the need for Military Government courts. These included the announced national policy to eliminate the existing political regime and the desire to provide a system of tribunals in which persons who might be exposed to discrimination in the suspect local courts could be accorded a fair trial. The change to High Commission form of government does not alter the legal basis upon which occupation courts continue to function. They still partake of the nature of military commissions and the change in designation from Military Government courts to United States Courts for Germany is merely one of nomenclature."

XVI *Selected Opinions* August 16, 1949–December 31, 1949, Office of Military Government for Germany (U.S.), Legal Division, (August 16 to October 15) and Office of the United States High Commissioner for Germany, Office of General Counsel, (October 16 to December 31), pp. 77–78.

Jurisdiction of sovereign's courts

The Italian Court of Cassation, holding in *Marzola* v. *Società Teavibra* (August 3, 1949) that it retained jurisdiction in respect of appeals from decisions of the courts of the Free Territory of Trieste pronounced prior to the conclusion of the Treaty of Peace of February 10, 1947, and during the time of the Anglo-American occupation of Italy, based its finding of continuity of sovereignty on the laws of military occupation. In this regard the Court of Cassation said:

"The jurisdiction of the Italian courts to hear this case follows from two separate considerations. In the first place, the judgment of the Court of Appeal of Trieste is dated June 25–July 22, 1946. This means that it was pronounced before the Treaty of Peace of February 10, 1947, came into force (September 16, 1947). At that time the territory over which the Court of Appeal of Trieste exercised jurisdiction was still subject to Allied military occupation. It follows that the Court was undoubtedly an organ of the Italian judicial authorities, having regard to the rule that military occupation does not change the legal status of the occupied territory. The belligerent occupant is not permitted to take measures which must lead to the disintegration of the administration of law in the occupied State or which changes it, unless it has ceased to function regularly. Still less does military occupation affect the sovereignty of the State in regard to the occupied territory, although in effect military occupation diminishes this sovereignty or restricts its exercise to such an extent, at times, as to render it potential only. If this is true according to the generally recognized principles of international law in respect of belligerent occupation in general, it applies all the more in the case of Italy, following the Armistices of September 3 and 29, 1943. In virtue of these Armistices, allied occupation was transformed from belligerent occupation into occupation on the basis of an armistice. Thus jurisdiction of the Italian judicial authorities to hear this case is not affected by the fact that the final phase of the proceedings which culminated in the judgment of the Court of Appeal of Trieste under review here took place during Allied military occupation.

"In the second place, General Order No. 6 of the Allied Military Government, issued in Trieste on July 12, 1945, does not lead to any different conclusion. Article 2 of this Order provided: 'No appeal is permitted against the decisions of any judicial authority in the occupied territory to any judicial authority of whatever jurisdiction which operates outside the occupied territory.' It is true that, by prohibiting appeals to the Court of Cassation, General Order No. 6 weakened the jurisdictional links of the Italian State with the occupied territory. Nevertheless, it could not sever the ties based upon sovereignty; for until September 16, 1947, the Allied Military Government was nothing more than an organ of the Anglo-American forces of occupation. Its powers, rights and functions were governed by the Hague Convention of 1907. Consequently, the prohibition to appeal contained in General Order No. 6 could not abrogate the principle of Italian municipal law which is embodied in Article 15 of the Introductory Provisions to the Civil Code. This states that legislation, *i.e.*, in the present case the legislation regulating civil procedure, cannot be abrogated or modified except in the forms prescribed by the Constitution. Thus, leaving aside the question whether General Order No. 6 was lawful, the prohibition to appeal to the Court of Cassation laid down by the Order remains inoperative in the present case whether regard is paid to the parties to the dispute, who are both Italian nationals resident in Italy, or to the object of the dispute (land in the commune of S. Giorgio di Nogaro, Pretura of Palmanova, Court of Udine). The dispute was always, and is still, localised within territory over which Italy has never ceased to exercise sovereignty, whether before or after the conclusion of the Treaty of Peace. . . ."

[1949] Ann. Dig. 64–65 (No. 24).

"Military government is that form of government which is established and maintained by a belligerent over occupied territory of the enemy. When our troops invade enemy territory, the old government is gone and the responsibility for the maintenance of law and order rests with the occupant. As the military occupation suspends the operation of the enemy's civil government, it becomes necessary for the occupying Power to exercise the functions of the civil administration and to maintain public order. This is a command responsibility, and the authority is vested in the commanding general of the theater of operations. He is the military governor of the occupied territory, and it is

[right margin] Responsibility

to be noted that he is the sole military governor. His authority is limited only by the laws and customs of war and by his orders from higher authority."

> Wickersham, "The Government of Occupied Territory", *Proceedings of the American Society of International Law* (1943) 27–28.

Venezia Giulia

Adverting to reports concerning the removal by the order of Yugoslav authorities from the area of Zone B of Venezia Giulia of "various important industrial and other properties without the permission of the lawful owners, without appropriate compensation and without due process of law", the United States Government in a note to the Federal People's Republic of Yugoslavia referred to the responsibilities incumbent upon the Allied Military Government and the Yugoslav Military Government as authorities in charge of the administration of Zones A and B, respectively, in Venezia Giulia. In this connection, the note stated:

> "The Government of Yugoslavia will be aware of the well established principle of international law prohibiting the confiscation of private property by the occupying power administering military government in occupied territory, and the obligation to respect and protect the legitimate rights and interest of the population. It has been the firm policy of the United States Government, in the execution of its obligations in connection with the administration of Allied Military Government in Venezia Giulia, to respect those rights; and this Government expects that the Yugoslav Government will also observe these principles in the administration of military government in the areas of Italian territory under its administration.
>
> "As a party to the Duino Agreement under which Venezia Giulia is administered by Allied Military Government and Yugoslav Military Government, in Zone A and Zone B respectively, the United States Government requests that the Yugoslav Government take prompt measures to effect the immediate restoration to the rightful owners of all property which has been unlawfully seized and removed from the areas of Venezia Giulia under its military jurisdiction which will, upon the coming into force of the Treaty of Peace with Italy, constitute a part of the Free Territory of Trieste.
>
> "The Yugoslav Government is aware that the Security Council of the United Nations has agreed to accept responsibility for the assurance of the integrity and independence of the Free Territory of Trieste upon the coming into force of the Treaty of Peace with Italy. In the meantime, the proper administration of the area is the responsibility of the Military Government authorities who must exercise due care to prevent injury to the economy of the future Free Territory and who will be held accountable for all unlawful actions committed under their administration."

Acting Secretary of State Acheson to Ambassador Kosanovic of the Yugoslav Embassy at Washington, note, Mar. 27, 1947, MS. Department of State, file 740.00119 EW/3-2747.

The Yugoslav Government in its note, Pov. Br. 56 of January 13, 1947, addressed to the United States Government, initially protested against the removal from Julian March of "machines, industrial plants and transportation equipment" and their transportation "to Italy or those parts of Zone A which according to Draft Peace Treaties would not be allotted to Yugoslavia". The Yugoslav Government "consider that both the toleration of removal and active participation in it by Allied Military Authorities are on contradiction with clauses of Devin [Duino] Agreement". Ambassador Kosanovic of the Yugoslav Embassy at Washington to Secretary of State Byrnes, note Pov. Br. 56, Jan. 13, 1947, MS. Department of State, file 740.00119 Control (Italy)/1-1347.

In reply, the United States Government in a note of February 13, 1947, stated: "The Department has noted that the Yugoslav Government has protested against the removal of certain plant and industrial equipment by its owners from one part of Zone A to another part of Zone A of Venezia Giulia. The Yugoslav Government has also protested the removal to locations in Italy outside of Venezia Giulia of certain transportation equipment. In view of the fact that both actions are clearly permissible under the terms of the Duino Agreement, and that that Agreement remains at the present time in full force and effect, the United States Government cannot accept the protest of the Yugoslav Government against these legitimate activities, nor can it agree to the request of the Yugoslav Government that further removals be suspended and equipment already removed be returned." Secretary of State Marshall to Ambassador Kosanovic of the Yugoslav Embassy at Washington, note, Feb. 13, 1947, MS. Department of State, file 740.00119 Control (Italy)/1-1347.

The United States Government later informed the Yugoslav Government that "this Government considers that the transfer of property from one part of Venezia Giulia to another locality within that area is permissible under the terms of the Duino Agreement. This Government is not cognizant of any preparations for the transfer of facilities of the shipyards Sceglio Olivi in Pola away from that city. However, if indeed such action is, or has been, undertaken, it is presumed that it is in accordance with the desire of the owners and in conformity with correct legal procedures and, on the assumption that the equipment is not moved outside the present boundaries of Venezia Giulia, is in accordance also with the terms of the Duino Agreement." Secretary of State Marshall to Ambassador Kosanovic of the Yugoslav Embassy at Washington, note, Mar. 24, 1947, MS. Department of State, file 740.00119 Control (Italy)/1-1347.

The British Foreign Office, in response to the receipt of "further evidence that the Yugoslav Authorities, in that part of Zone 'B' of Venezia Giulia which is to be included in the Free Territory of Trieste, have, against the wishes of the owners of the property, removed important industrial plant from factories and ship yards belonging to Italian companies", delivered a note dated March 24, 1947, to the Yugoslav Ambassador in London which stated in part:

> "3. I do not doubt that the Yugoslav Government being bound by the terms of Annex I of the Duino Agreement of October, 1945, have refrained from moving this property outside the area of Venezia

Giulia. Nevertheless His Majesty's Government are of the opinion that such removals are improper, their nature being entirely different from the removals of industrial property undertaken from Pola. In the latter instance removals were carried out at the express wish and on the initiative of the owners of the firms concerned and without any assistance whatever from the Allied Military Authorities. On the other hand in the instances described in this note, the removals have been effected against the wishes of the owners and at the orders of the Yugoslav authorities, on the unfounded pretext that the companies concerned were of a Fascist character.

"4. I must ask Your Excellency to remind the Government of Yugoslavia that it is an established principle of International Law that the power administering the government of occupied territory is prohibited from confiscating private property and must undertake to respect the legitimate rights of the population. I most earnestly trust therefore that the necessary orders will be given for the restoration to its owners of all confiscated property in that part of Venezia Giulia which is under Yugoslav Military Administration.

"5. The confiscations of property to which I have referred have done a grave injury to the economy of the future Free Territory. The Yugoslav Government will no doubt be aware that the Security Council of the United Nations has now accepted responsibility for the integrity and independence of the Free Territory of Trieste. In the meantime it is the responsibility of the military government authorities in the area to see that no damage is done to the economy of the future Free Territory and thus to ensure that it will be as nearly self supporting as possible and able to enter into trading relations with neighbouring countries for the benefit of all concerned. Should the military government authorities fail in this task they will have to account to the Security Council for any actions they have committed which will injure the standing of the Free Territory and which are contrary to International Law." Note, Mar. 24, 1947, encl., MS. Department of State, file 740.00119 Control (Italy)/3–2747.

The Yugoslav Government in a subsequent note of May 14, 1947, to the United States Government reiterated its protest and request for immediate suspension of further removals and displacements of industrial plants and transport equipment at Pola and other parts of Zone A of Julian March and for the return of equipment already taken. Referring to that part of the United States note of March 27, 1947, which affirmed that the obligation to respect and protect the legitimate rights and interests of the population is a well established principle of international law, the Yugoslav Government's note commented:

"The Yugoslav Government is confident that the United States Government will agree with its opinion that it is one of the most essential among the legitimate rights of the population of an occupied territory, that it shall not be deprived of the economic basis of its existence. As a matter of fact this opinion precisely has been expressed in the following statement of the United States Note: . . . 'the proper administration of the area is the responsibility of the Military Government Authorities, who must exercise due care to prevent injury to the economy of the future free territory'. There is no rule of international law giving the Free Territory of Trieste a privileged position as to the responsibilities of the occupation authorities and therefore, if it is within the responsibility of the occupation authorities to see that no damage is done to its economy, it is, at least to the same degree, the responsibility of those authorities to see that no damage is done to the economy of the area which is to become part of allied Yugoslavia. The more so, as this latter responsibility has been, in addition, confirmed by the Devin [Duino] Agreement, the Annex I of which explicitly states that in order to 'insure minimum interference with the normal life of Venezia Giulia as a whole . . .' 'No plant or industrial facility will be moved out of Venezia Giulia'. It is obvious that the purpose and meaning of this provision is to prevent injury to the economy of the areas concerned, which is precisely what the United States Note of the 27th of March, 1947, considers to be the duty of the occupation authorities even in the absence of a special agreement as contained in the United States Note of February 13, 1947[.] [This note] which endeavours to justify the economic devastation of the area greatly interfering with the normal life of the Julian March . . . by the assertion that under the terms of Devin [Duino] Agreement removals inside zone A are permissible, cannot be accepted. Such an interpretation would completely frustrate the purpose of the provision.

"The obligation provided for by Annex I of the Devin [Duino] Agreement implies as a matter of course the responsibility of the occupation authorities to prevent, even against the will of the owners, the removal of private property. This is only natural, since the damage done to the economy of the area is in no way less extensive if the removal of the machinery is effected by the owners themselves. In accepting such an obligation, the United States Government has recognized that the responsibility relating to the preservation of the economic integrity of the area is independent of the assent of private owners, and, accordingly, that the interest of the population as a whole to preserve the economic basis of its existence is more important than the interest of a few private owners in the unrestricted disposal with their property." Ambassador Kosanovic of the Yugoslav Embassy at Washington to Secretary of State Marshall, note P. No. 767, May 14, 1947, MS. Department of State, file 740.00119 Control (Italy)/5–1447.

Insofar as sovereign powers of a military government are regulated by international law as codified in the Regulations Respecting the Laws and Customs of War on Land, annexed to the Fourth Hague Convention of 1907, and specifically in section III thereof, entitled "Military Authority Over the Territory of the Hostile State", they apply only to that type of military occupation called "belligerent" occupation meaning "where one belligerent has overrun a part of the territory of the opposing enemy belligerent, where the fighting is still in progress and no armistice agreement has been concluded".

Sovereign powers of military government:

"Belligerent" occupation

> Stein, "Application of the Law of the Absent Sovereign in Territory Under Belligerent Occupation: The Schio Massacre", 46 Mich. L. Rev. (1948) 341, 347.

The three contending views as to the application of these rules of international law in the case of an "armistice" occupation, or that occupation "continuing after or affected by virtue of an armistice agreement", are set forth briefly as follows:

"Armistice" occupation

1. Under the Anglo-American doctrine, the provisions of section III of the Regulations Respecting the Laws and Customs of War on Land apply not only to a "belligerent" occupation but also to "armistice" occupation unless otherwise specified in the armistice agreement.

Adverting to article 43 of section III of the Regulations Respecting the Laws and Customs of War on Land which states:

> "The authority of the legitimate power having in fact passed into the hands of the occupant, the latter shall take all the meas-

ures in his power to restore, and ensure, as far as possible, public order and safety, while respecting, unless absolutely prevented, the laws in force in the country",

Oppenheim, expressing the British view, commented that—

". . . through military occupation the authority over the territory and the inhabitants only *de facto*, and not by right, and only temporarily, and not permanently, passes into the hands of the occupant.

". . . since the occupant is *de facto* in authority, he has a right of administration over the territory, with the consequence that all administrative acts which he carries out in accordance with the laws of war and the existing local law must be recognized by the legitimate government after the occupation . . . ."

Oppenheim, "The Legal Relations between an Occupying Power and the Inhabitants," 33 L.Q. Rev. (1917) 363–364.

The British *Army Manual of Military Law* provides:

"The situation in occupied territory remains the same [that is, during an armistice] as during hostilities." (Amendment No. 12, paragraph 286)

British *Army Manual of Military Law, Amendments* (1929).

In a basic order issued in connection with the armistice occupation of the Rhineland after World War I, Marshal Foch, Supreme Commander of the Allied and Associated Powers, referred to the Hague Convention as the basis of the supervision to be exercised over the German administrative structure and asserted in conformance with the Hague Convention that the existing German laws and regulations would be respected unless they contravened the rights and security of the occupying powers.

Fraenkel, *Military Occupation and the Rule of Law* (1944) 8.

The other two views are:

2. In the German view, "armistice" occupation is considered an occupation *sui generis* and called "*occupatio mixta*" and is further distinguished as either a "genuine" armistice occupation of territory occupied by virtue of the armistice, and a "non-genuine" armistice occupation where a belligerent occupation established before the armistice is continued after the armistice. According to the German doctrine, the rules of section III of the Regulations Respecting the Laws and Customs of War on Land apply in the case of a "non-genuine" occupation but not in the case of a "genuine" occupation.

3. Related to this issue is a body of judicial precedents which developed in Belgium as a result of the German belligerent occupa-

tion during World War I which in connection with the "postliminy" aspect of the exercise of authority holds that article 43 of the Hague Regulations does not suspend the legal authority of the "absent" sovereign nor does it bestow any legal status upon the occupant and its acts.

While in the case of *Cambier* v. *Lebrun et al.*, December 4, 1919, the Belgium Court of Cassation dismissed an application to quash a judgment given in the exercise of jurisdiction of a court set up by the authority of the German occupying Power, holding that decisions given by courts established under the order of the German Governor-General in Belgium bind the parties, the Court added that ". . . these tribunals are not a creation of Belgian law" and that "the decrees of the occupying Power, whatever they may be, do not emanate from the exercise of national sovereignty. They have not the validity of Belgian laws, but are merely commands of the enemy military authority, and are not incorporated in the legislation or the institutions of the country. Accordingly, the judgment attacked is not to be regarded as an act emanating from a court established by the Belgian legislature".

> *Cambier* v. *Lebrun et al.*, Dec. 4, 1919, [1919–1922] Ann. Dig. 459 (No. 325).

An editorial note to this case citing other Belgian cases relating to this issue concluded that these decisions illustrate an important development in the case-law of the Court of Cassation and commented:

> ". . . While maintaining the legality of these arbitral tribunals and the obligatory character of their decisions, they refuse to assimilate the measures taken by the occupying Power to those emanating from the exercise of the national sovereignty. The Court of Appeal of Liège had already at an earlier date declared that 'orders of the occupying Power do not constitute part of the national system of law, which alone can be taken into consideration and whose sanctions alone can be examined by Belgian courts—courts the status of which has not been affected by the occupation' (7 May, 1919, *Belgique Judiciaire*, 1919, col. 1099). See also a decision of the same Court (19 February, 1919, *Pasicrisie belge*, 1919, vol. II, p. 45) declaring 'that it was not for the administrative officials nor for the judicial authorities to secure the execution of ordinances of the occupying Power, which are essentially different from the national legislation and can in no way be assimilated to it.' "

The note reports, however, a decision of the Court of Cassation of May 20, 1916, which admitted that by reason of the ratification of the Hague Convention by the Belgian Law of May 25, 1910, orders of the occupying Power made in pursuance of Article 43 of the annexed

Regulations derived from that law the same obligatory force as Belgian laws (*Pasicrisie belge*, 1915–1916, vol. I, p. 375; *Belgique Judiciaire*, 1919, cols. 148 *et seq.*).

> *Ibid.* 460.

> For an extensive discussion of these doctrines and their implementation in practice, see Stein, "Application of the Law of the Absent Sovereign in Territory Under Belligerent Occupation: The Schio Massacre", 46 Mich. L. Rev. (1948) 341.

The question of the application of article 43 of the Hague Rules on Military Authority Over the Territory of the Hostile State to the exercise of authority by the occupying Power during an "armistice" occupation arose obliquely in the decision of the Allied Military Court in Italy which, while confirming the right of the Allied Military Government to refuse implementation of a decree enacted by the legitimate government functioning outside of occupied territory, nevertheless deferred to the decree as a matter of policy.

Schio Massacre

The case arose out of the massacre of fifty-four prisoners of the Schio jail by seven partisans in June of 1945 in an area of Italy then under the rule of the Allied Military Government. The Allied Military Court acquitted two of the accused for lack of evidence, sentenced two to life imprisonment along with the imposition of other penalties, and sentenced the remaining three to death in application of the Italian Penal Code.

On review, judgment of the Court as to the life sentences and the acquittals was confirmed by the Chief Legal Adviser to the Chief Civil Affairs Officer of the Allied Military Government for Italy. The Chief Civil Affairs Officer commuted to sentences of life imprisonment the three death sentences. The decision as released to the press by the Allied Commission Public Relations Office in Rome on December 20, 1945, reads in part as follows:

> "2. The three death sentences were brought before me as Chief Civil Affairs Officer of Occupied Territory under Allied Military Government, Italy, for confirmation in pursuance to the established procedure. On review of the record of the trial, I am fully satisfied that the accused have received a full and fair trial, and that the sentences imposed were well founded.
>
> "3. The massacre committed at Schio was of such a nature as to put those responsible beyond consideration of clemency.
>
> "4. However, I felt bound to take into consideration the following facts:
>
> "(a) The fifty-four men and women murdered in the Schio jail were Italian men and women.
>
> "(b) The convicted murderers were Italian men.

"(c) The law which they outraged and under which they were charged and sentenced by the Allied Military Court was Italian law.

"(d) The crime they committed was a crime against Italian sovereignty.

"(e) The accused were not sentenced to death for violation of any order of the Military Governor.

"5. Italy in 1889 was among the first nations of the world to abolish the death penalty. The abolition of the death penalty is not exclusively an Italian legal concept. In Switzerland, and even in the United States in certain states where the law is purely of Anglo-Saxon origin, the death penalty cannot be imposed. The banishment of capital punishment became a firmly established principle in Italian pre-fascist legislation. It remained so until the advent of fascism. The Penal Code of 1930 enacted during fascist rule re-introduced the death penalty as a typical innovation serving the new regime, thus breaking the tradition of pre-fascist Italy. The first Bonomi Government passed the Decree of 10 August 1944 once again abolishing capital punishment as a general form of punishment under the Penal Code.

"6. At that time Allied military operations in Italy were in full progress, most of Northern Italy was in enemy hands, and this Decree was therefore not implemented by Allied Military Government in Northern Italy. As a result, the three accused in the present case were correctly charged and sentenced to death under the original and unamended text of the Penal Code. However, had the accused been charged with the same offence in territory restored to the Italian Government, they could not have been so sentenced, even in an AMG court. Similarly, the death sentence in this case could not have been confirmed by me had the northern regions been restored to Italian Government administration by this date.

"7. In deference to the pre-fascist concepts of punishment under Italian law, which the present Italian Government has reaffirmed, because I consider that military authorities governing under the law of occupation in a civilized state are but custodians of its fundamental legal institutions, and because I do not conceive it to be Allied policy toward Italy to override Italian basic concepts of justice with respect to a civil crime committed by Italians against Italians, regardless of how such a crime would be dealt with in Allied countries, the death sentences against FRANCESCHINI Renzo, FOCHESATO Antonio and BORTOLOSO Valentino are modified to sentences of imprisonment for life. Because of the nature of the crime, it is my intention to request of the Italian Government that no future general or individual amnesty be applied to these prisoners."

Press release, Dec. 20, 1945, by the Public Relations Branch, Allied Commission, Rome, as set forth in Stein, "Application of the Law of the Absent Sovereign in Territory Under Belligerent Occupation: The Schio Massacre", 46 Mich. L. Rev. (1948) 341, 342–343.

In discussing whether, in the light of international law, the Allied Military Government acted within its powers in refusing to implement the decree of the absent sovereign in occupied territory, Eric Stein noted in reviewing the practice of the Allied Military Government in Italy that—

"While the rest of liberated southern Italy was made subject to Allied Military Government, the four provinces of the Puglie Region were left to the exclusive jurisdiction of the new Italian Government. In these provinces the King with the new government exercised legislative power in accordance with Italian law. The laws thus enacted were published in the Italian Official Gazette. At that time, Allied authorities took the position that this new legislation could not have any effect and would not be given any force in that part of Italy which was occupied by Allied troops and administered by Allied Military Government. No announcement to this effect or any other formal act of Allied Military Government was made or deemed necessary.

"When in June, 1944 a politically more representative Italian government was established in Rome, the Allied Military Government laid down the following policy: (a) While the new legislation of the Italian Government did not become automatically effective in the Allied Military Government territory it would be extended to occupied areas to the rear of the zone of operation upon the order of a responsible Allied Military Government officer; only those laws or parts thereof inconsistent with Allied Military Government legislation or policy would be excluded from this 'implementation' procedure. (b) The 'implementation' was to take place by means of Allied Military Government orders, to be published from time to time on the last page of the Italian Gazette."

In support of his contention that the Hague Regulations applied to the Allied "armistice" occupation in Italy, the author, after noting that while hostilities with Italy had ended with the signing of the armistice agreements on September 3 and 29, 1943, fighting was still in progress in Italy, states:

"At the time of the signing of the documents of surrender, Sicily with adjacent islands and portions of southern Italy were being administered by the Allied Military Government under the regime of belligerent occupation governed by Section III of the Regulations. In view of the continuing hostilities, it was obviously the intention of the parties to the documents that the powers held by the Allied occupant under this regime should continue after the signing of the documents. In fact, the documents of surrender conferred upon the Allied occupant additional new power in areas occupied before the signing and to be occupied thereafter. Moreover, for reasons of military necessity, the documents granted the Allied Commander in Chief important powers, even in *unoccupied* Italian territory, such as the right of transit, and use of Italian facilities.

"The applicability of Section III is further supported by the already mentioned clause [Article 20] in the 'Long Terms' [Armistice Agreement of September 29, 1943] granting to the Allied occupant the 'rights of an occupying power,' for Section III is the only generally accepted source of international law defining such rights with a degree of certainty."

Citing article 43 of section III of the Hague Regulations as relevant in its provision that the occupant respect, "unless absolutely prevented, the laws in force in the country", the same author concludes that since the Italian decree was enacted after the signing of the documents of surrender it could not be considered as a law in force at the time of the establishment of the Allied Military Government, and that, therefore, the Allied Military Government was within its rights as an occupying Power in refusing implementation of the law of the absent sovereign.

> Stein, "Application of the Law of the Absent Sovereign in Territory Under Belligerent Occupation: The Schio Massacre", 46 Mich. L. Rev. (1948) 341, 344–345, 348–349.

In a legal opinion of March 17, 1947, concerning the right of an occupying power to remove indigenous archives, records, and documents, the Office of Military Government for Germany (U.S.) affirmed the observation of the Hague Convention rules during the period of hostilities but denied their application to a subjugated nation. Concluding that "the period of hostilities having ended, the provisions of Section III of the Regulations Respecting the Laws and Customs of War on Land annexed to the 1907 Hague Convention IV, do not literally apply to the present occupation of Germany", the opinion stated in addition:

"Subjugation"

> "But many of the provisions of Section III are merely expressive of principles bearing upon the relationships between victor and vanquished nations which have more general applicability, deriving their authority from the unwritten laws and customs of war and relations between civilized international communities. Thus in considering these very regulations, the International Military Tribunal held that 'by 1939 these rules laid down in the Convention were recognized by all civilized nations, and were regarded as being declaratory of the laws and customs of war . . .' And the source of the regulations was stated by the signatories to Convention IV in these words: 'The inhabitants and the belligerents remain under the protection and the rule of the principles of the law of nations, as they result from the *usages established among civilized peoples*, from the *laws of humanity*, and from the *dictates of the public conscience*' (underscoring [*italics*] supplied)."

Declaring the articles relevant to this issue, articles 46, 47, and 56 of the Regulations annexed to Convention IV, "expressive of general principles of international law", the opinion concluded that a removal of archives from Germany by one of the occupying powers would be a *prima facie* violation of international law, placing the burden upon the removing power to establish by clear and convincing reasons that an overriding public interest exists in each case.

Colonel Raymond, Associate Director, legal opinion "Right of Occupying Power to Remove Indigenous Archives, Records and Documents", Mar. 17, 1947, VII *Selected Opinions* January 1, 1947–March 31, 1947, Office of Military Government for Germany (U.S.), Legal Division, APO 742, pp. 115, 122–123. See also Colonel Raymond, Associate Director, legal opinion "Works of Art as External Assets of Germany", May 9, 1947, VIII *Selected Opinions* April 1, 1947–June 30, 1947, Office of Military Government for Germany (U.S.), Legal Division, APO 742, p. 73. For legal opinion affirming application of rules of Hague Convention during period of hostilities, see Colonel Raymond, Associate Director, legal opinion "Payment for Requisitions Prior to Occupation", Oct. 22, 1947, X *Selected Opinions* October 1, 1947–December 31, 1947, Office of Military Government for Germany (U.S.), Legal Division, APO 742, p. 25.

In determining the legal basis of requisitioning by the Allied occupying Powers in Germany, the Office of the Legal Adviser in a memorandum of January 25, 1960, affirmed the supreme powers of the Allies in making the following analysis of the legal basis of Allied rights in Germany after World War II:

". . . This basis is traced and perhaps best explained in the decision of *U.S.* v. *Altstoetter* (the Justice case) tried at Nuernberg, Germany, in 1947. The Opinion of the Court, found in III *Trials of War Criminals* before the Nuernberg Military Tribunals 954, 959–963, contains the following material:

"'The unconditional surrender of Germany took place on 8 May 1945. The surrender was preceded by the complete disintegration of the central government and was followed by the complete occupation of all of Germany. There were no opposing German forces in the field; the officials who during the war had exercised the powers of the Reich Government were either dead, in prison, or in hiding. On 5 June 1945 the Allied Powers announced that they "hereby assume supreme authority with respect to Germany, including all the powers possessed by the German Government, the High Command, and any state, municipal or local government or authority," and declared that "there is no central government or authority in Germany capable of accepting responsibility for the maintenance of order, the administration of the country, and compliance with the requirements of the victorious powers." The Four Powers further declared that they "will hereafter determine the boundaries of Germany or any part thereof and the status of Germany or of any area at present being a part of German territory."

.   .   .   .

" 'It is this fact of the complete disintegration of the government in Germany, followed by unconditional surrender and by occupation of the territory, which explains and justifies the assumption and exercise of supreme governmental power by the Allies. The same fact distinguishes the present occupation of Germany from the type of occupation which occurs when, in the course of actual warfare, an invading army enters and occupies the territory of another state, whose government is still in existence and is in receipt of international recognition, and whose armies, with those of its allies, are still in the field. In the latter case the occupying power is subject to the limitations imposed upon it by the Hague Convention and by the laws and customs of war. In the former case (the occupation of Germany) the Allied Powers were not subject to those limitations. By reason of the complete breakdown of government, industry, agriculture, and supply, they were under an imperative humanitarian duty of far wider scope to reorganize government and industry and to foster local democratic governmental agencies throughout the territory.

" 'In support of the distinction made, we quote from two recent and scholarly articles in "The American Journal of International Law."

" ' "On the other hand, a distinction is clearly warranted between measures taken by the Allies prior to destruction of the German Government and those taken thereafter. Only the former need be tested by the Hague Regulations, which are inapplicable to the situation now prevailing in Germany. Disappearance of the German State as a belligerent entity, necessarily implied in the Declaration of Berlin of 5 June 1945, signifies that a true state of war—and hence *belligerent* occupation—no longer exists within the meaning of international law." ' [Freeman, "War Crimes by Enemy Nationals Administering Justice in Occupied Territory," 41 Am. J. Int'l. L. (1947), p. 605.]

" ' "Through the subjugation of Germany the outcome of the war has been decided in the most definite manner possible. One of the prerogatives of the Allies resulting from the subjugation is the right to occupy German territory at their discretion. This occupation is, both legally and factually, fundamentally different from the belligerent occupation contemplated in the Hague Regulations, as can be seen from the following observations.

" ' "The provisions of the Hague Regulations restricting the rights of an occupant refer to a belligerent who, favored by the changing fortunes of war, actually exercises military authority over enemy territory and thereby

prevents the legitimate sovereign—who remains the legitimate sovereign—from exercising his full authority. The Regulations draw important legal conclusions from the fact that the legitimate sovereign may at any moment himself be favored by the changing fortunes of war, reconquer the territory, and put an end to the occupation. 'The occupation applies only to territory where such authority (i.e., the military authority of the hostile state) is established and can be exercised' (*Art. 42, 2*). In other words, the Hague Regulations think of an occupation which is a phase of an as yet undecided war. Until 7 May 1945, the Allies were belligerent occupants in the then occupied parts of Germany, and their rights and duties were circumscribed by the respective provisions of the Hague Regulations. As a result of the subjugation of Germany, the legal character of the occupation of German territory was drastically changed."'
[Fried, "Transfer of Civilian Manpower from Occupied Territory", 40 Am. J. Int'l. L. (1946), pp. 326–327.]

" 'The view expressed by the two authorities cited appears to have the support of the International Military Tribunal judgment in the case against Goering, *et al.* In that case the defendants contended that Germany was not bound by the rules of land warfare in occupied territory because Germany had completely subjugated those countries and incorporated them into the German Reich. The Tribunal refers to the "doctrine of subjugation, dependent as it is upon military conquest," and holds that it is unnecessary to decide whether the doctrine has any application where the subjugation is the result of the crime of aggressive war. The reason given is significant. The Tribunal said:

" ' "The doctrine was never considered to be applicable so long as there was an army in the field attempting to restore the occupied countries to their true owners, and in this case, therefore, the doctrine could not apply to any territories occupied after 1 September 1939." '
[Trial of the Major War Criminals, judgment, volume I, page 254.]

" 'The clear implication from the foregoing is that the Rules of Land Warfare apply to the conduct of a belligerent in occupied territory so long as there is an army in the field attempting to restore the country to its true owner, but that those rules do not apply when belligerency is ended, there is no longer an army in the field, and, as in the case of Germany, subjugation has occurred by virtue of military conquest.

" 'The views which we have expressed are supported by modern scholars of high standing in the field of international law. While they differ somewhat in theory as to the present legal status of Germany and concerning the situs of residual sovereignty, they appear to be in accord in recognizing that the powers and rights of the Allied Governments under existing conditions in Germany are not limited by the provisions of the Hague Regulations concerning land warfare. For reference see—

" ' "The Legal Status of Germany According to the Declaration of Berlin," by Hans Kelsen, Professor of International Law, University of California, American Journal of International Law, 1945.

" ' "Germany's Present Status," by F. A. Mann, Doctor of Law (Berlin) (London), paper read on 5 March 1947 before the Grotius Society in London, published in Sueddeutsche Juristen-Zeitung (Lawyers' Journal of Southern Germany), volume 2, No. 9, September 1947.

" ' "The Influence of the Legal Position of Germany upon the War Crimes Trial," Dr. Hermann Mosler, Assistant Professor of the University of Bonn, published in Sueddeutsche Juristen-Zeitung, volume 2, No. 7, July 1947.

" 'Article published in Neue Justiz (New Justice), by Dr. Alfons Steininger, Berlin, volume I, No. 7, July 1947, pages 146–150.

" 'In an article by George A. Zinn, Minister of Justice of Hessen, entitled "Germany as the Problem of the Law of States," the author points out that if it be assumed that the present occupation of Germany constitutes "belligerent occupation" in the traditional sense, then all legal and constitutional changes brought about since 7 May 1945 would cease to be valid once the Allied troops were withdrawn and all Nazi laws would again and automatically become the law of Germany, a consummation devoutly to be avoided.

" 'Both of the authorities first cited directly assert that the situation at the time of the unconditional surrender resulted in the transfer of sovereignty to the Allies. In this they are supported by the weighty opinion of Lord Wright, eminent jurist of the British House of Lords and head of the United Nations War Crimes Commission. For our purposes, however, it is unnecessary to determine the present situs of "residual sovereignty." It is sufficient to hold that, by virtue of the situation at the time of unconditional surrender, the Allied Powers were provisionally in the exercise of supreme authority, valid and effective until such time as, by treaty or otherwise, Germany shall be permitted to exercise the full powers of sovereignty.'

"This thesis is also expounded by Charles Fahy, now Judge of the United States Court of Appeals for the District of Columbia, in an article in 47 Michigan Law Review 11 entitled 'Legal Problems of German Occupation'. Judge Fahy states:

" 'A state has been subjugated by force and was without government of its own. The legal vacuum, if it may be so termed, was filled by the formal assumption of authority by the United States, the United Kingdom, the U.S.S.R. and

France. . . . Whatever ancient or modern theories or precedents may be advanced to describe the situation, the simple fact is that sovereign power in Germany was assumed and exercised by right of conquest accompanied by unconditional surrender of the armed forces and collapse of civil authority. This assumption of supreme authority cannot successfully be challenged under the law. It was a development of a war initiated and prosecuted by Germany in violation of international law. The allies defeated the aggressor and validly imposed terms which placed supreme authority as above noted. The question may arise whether this constituted an assumption of sovereignty. It is clear that it was the exercise of full sovereign power. It may well be that in theory sovereignty in an ultimate sense resides in the people of Germany but was suspended in exercise by them pending accomplishment of the purposes of the war and the occupation, and until a final settlement.

" ' . . . The interest of persons in responsible positions in the possible application of the Hague Convention was a manifestation of concern that the United States should proceed in accord with law notwithstanding the unlimited power residing in the victors. Undoubtedly these provisions of the convention were not legally applicable. The regulations contained in the convention were designed to govern the conduct of the military in its relations with the civilian population of an occupied territory during hostilities. They were designed to leave untouched so far as possible the sovereign authority of the enemy in the occupied territory. They are rules for the conduct of war in the area of impact of armed forces upon the territory and inhabitants of an enemy country still contesting. They do not govern or limit the right of the victor to impose terms and conditions when victory has been achieved, certainly where the victor in the eyes of the law has not forfeited its position by aggression in violation of international law. The imposition upon Germany of unconditional surrender, accompanied by such actual surrender and abandonment of governmental authority, created conditions making these provisions of the Hague Convention inapplicable. This is not to say that the regulations of the convention are of no effect. The acceptance of them by so large a part of the world caused them to be used as guides with persuasive but not obligatory effect in appropriate circumstances.' "

Other authorities are to the same effect.

"*U.S. v von Weizsaecker* XIV Trials of War Crimes 690.

"Rockwell, 'Postwar Problems in Occupied Germany', 36 ABAJ 359, 431, and opinion referred to on 'Right of Occupying Power to Remove Indigenous Archives,' VII Selected Opinions of Legal Division, OMGUS, 115, 119–120.

"Kelsen, 'The Legal Status of Germany According to the Declaration of Berlin', 39 AJIL 518.

"Kunz, 'The Status of Occupied Germany under International Law: A Legal Dilemma,' III The Western Political Quarterly, No. 4, page 538, particularly at page 564.

The same point is recognized by then Professor Wilhelm Grewe, present German Ambassador to the United States, in an article entitled, 'From the Capitulation to the General Agreement' in issue No. 7 of 'Aussenpolitik' for 1952. The following is from an English translation of that article by the U.S. Liaison/Interpreters Section of the Allied General Secretariat at Bonn. Ambassador Grewe states:

" 'Capitulation was followed, on 5 June 1945, by the Berlin Declarations by which the Allies assumed supreme governmental power in Germany, established the Control Council, and divided the country into zones of occupation. The Potsdam Agreement of 2 August 1945 reiterated and re-confirmed the most important principles of this control regime and added a number of additional basic agreements concluded between the United States, Great Britain and the Soviet Union (France did not participate in the Potsdam Conference).

" 'The status, under the aspect of international law, of the occupation regime thus established, has been very extensively discussed, written and argued about. There appears to be no need to deal with these arguments in this paper. It must, however, be stressed that the legal basis for the occupation regime was *not* the Capitulation Instrument of 8 May 1945. Doctrines according to which the capitulation constituted, from the standpoint of international law, some sort of self-extinction of the German State, are completely erroneous. *Military capitulation* as such does not affect the existence, under international law, of a state. Its only effect is what the term implies, i.e. capitulation of the armed forces, cessation of hostilities, discontinuance of military resistance. If such capitulation is "unconditional", this means only that the defeated is no longer able to obtain assurances with regard to its soldiers who become prisoners of war or, in addition, assurances with regard to future peace terms. To this extent, the defeated falls prey to the discretion of the victor; however, this discretion is not limitless. Unconditional capitulation does not release the victor from the obligation to observe the general rules of international law vis-à-vis the vanquished; the assumption that the vanquished state by the act of capitulation has lost its status as a state or as a subject of international law is wrong. In this respect, many erroneous ideas circulated after 1945, must be corrected.

" 'Therefore, the constitutive document in respect of the Allied occupation regime in Germany is not the capitulation instrument, but the Berlin Declaration of the Allies of 5 June 1945. After the disappearance or elimination of the last remnants of German governmental power, the Allies, in this Declaration, arrogated to themselves "Supreme Authority" in Germany. By this unilateral act which was exclusively based on the fact that there was no longer any effective German government in existence, the Allies went considerably beyond the powers to which an occupation power is normally entitled under general rules of international law (in particular, of the Hague Convention on Land Warfare).'

"The British Military Court of Criminal Appeal, *Grahame* v. *the Director of Prosecutions* published in Lauterpacht, Annual Digest and Reports of Public International Law Cases (1947) 228, held that the occupying powers in Germany were not 'restricted by the limitations placed by the Hague Convention on a belligerent occupant'."

The Deputy Legal Adviser (Raymond) to Assistant Chief, Council of Claims Section, the Department of Justice (Kendall Barnes), memorandum, "Court of Claims Cases Arising out of Requisitions in Germany, September 21, 1949–May 5, 1955," Jan. 25, 1960, MS. Department of State, file FW 200.6241/2–1160.

"The provisions of the Hague Regulations restricting the rights of an occupant refer to a belligerent who, favored by the changing fortunes of war, actually exercises military authority over enemy territory and thereby prevents the legitimate sovereign—who remains the legitimate sovereign—from exercising his full authority. The Regulations draw important legal conclusions from the fact that the legitimate sovereign may at any moment himself be favored by the changing fortunes of war, reconquer the territory, and put an end to the occupation. 'The occupation applies only to territory where such authority [i.e., the military authority of the hostile state] is established and can be exercised' (Art. 42, 2). In other words, the Hague Regulations think of an occupation which is a phase of an as yet undecided war. Until May 7, 1945, the Allies were belligerent occupants in the then occupied parts of Germany, and their rights and duties were circumscribed by the respective provisions of the Hague Regulations. As a result of the subjugation of Germany the legal character of the occupation of German territory was drastically changed. The occupants do no longer act *in lieu* of 'the legitimate sovereign.' They themselves exercise sovereignty. There is no legitimate German sovereign who is merely waiting, merely prevented from exercising his power. Whatever powers German authorities have during the post-surrender period, they must be construed as deriving from and delegated by the Allies. As a consequence of the doctrine that during belligerent occupation the sovereignty of the absent legitimate Government is merely suspended, the occupant must 'respect, unless absolutely prevented, the laws in force in the country.' But under the post-surrender occupation the abrogation instead of the preservation of National Socialist law is one of the principal aims of the Allies.

"The difference between the two types of occupation would be most apparent in case of withdrawal of the occupation forces. Had, for example, the German occupation forces voluntarily withdrawn from the Netherlands during the war, the German occupation regime would automatically have come to an end. But if the present occupation of Germany were not 'effective' or if the Allies would withdraw their occupation forces, their prerogatives over Germany would not be affected. During the post-surrender period, neither the extent nor the duration of the rights of the Allies is conditional upon establishing or maintaining an occupation,—whereas this is the first and foremost prerequisite for the exercise of the limited prerogatives of the belligerent occupant. The occupation of Germany is, in legal contemplation, only an incidental aspect of the post-surrender situation. Under belligerent occupation, the occupant's limited powers derive from the physical fact of military occupation; under the post-surrender occupation, the right to occupy derives from the occupant's unlimited powers. It is the essence of the provisions of the Hague Regulations concerning enemy civilians that the belligerent occupant does not possess sovereignty over them; whereas it is the essence of the legal situation prevailing during the post-surrender period that the Allies possess sovereignty over Germany."

Fried, "Transfer of Civilian Manpower From Occupied Territory", 40 Am. J. Int'l L. (1946) 303, 327–328.

"In Germany the governmental system had been so perverted by the Nazis that there remained nothing sound on which to build. Accordingly, the four powers have erected a temporary scaffolding of military government within which the work of rebuilding from the ground goes on. At the top is the Allied Control Commission, which exercises supreme authority and is for the present the national government of Germany. I take it that probably in the end we shall have a treaty of peace in Germany, just as we are about to have a treaty of peace with Italy. I take it that this will be done, however, with a view not to sanctioning what is past or to give legal effect to that which we have done by virtue of our effective power on the morrow of the unconditional surrender, but rather to fasten upon Germany continuing obligations to carry out those essential policies which up to that time we shall have been administering by our own hands. *{Position of Occupying Powers as actual government: Control Commissions}*

"The occupation of Japan follows a pattern of its own. As in Italy, the sound course was to carry forward the existing government and call upon it to adopt the essentials of liberalism. In Japan we share with no other power the primary responsibility for the conduct of the occupation.

"The control commission is a devise [device?] which has sprung from the occupations of this war. . . . The Allied Control Commission for Italy was the prototype. It was copied from an obverse point of view by the Soviet Government in its occupation of Hungary, Rumania, and Bulgaria. The great quadripartite Commission in Berlin has drawn upon this experience; but whereas it was possible for the British and Americans to operate a tightly combined agency in Italy, the four powers who had their hands on Germany could essay no more than the creation of four separate administrations, pinned together somewhat insecurely at the center, with much prayer and determination and very little cement. A control commission is composed of subcommissions— Fiscal, Industry and Commerce, Legal, Education, Transportation, and so on—like the ministries of a national government, the function of the whole being to carry out the policy of the occupation and supervise the operations of the indigenous administration or directly to govern the country, as the case may be."

Fairman, "Military Occupation and the Development of International Law", *Proceedings of the American Society of International Law* (1947) 131, 136–137.

Germany   Noting the dual position of the occupying Powers in Germany, as military victors of World War II maintaining armies of occupation and as powers constituting the government of Germany, Professor Rheinstein finds in international law, as a predicate for the distinction between the scope of the rights and duties inherent in the two positions, the applicability or nonapplicability of the Hague Rules. With regard to the rights and duties of the occupying Powers, he writes:

"Although hostilities have come to an end, the Hague Rules, which, by common consent but constitute a restatement of general international law, still fit the present situation in so far as they are concerned with the rights and duties of the army of occupation and the status of the occupation personnel."

After referring to that section of the Hague Rules which define an occupant's powers and duties in a situation of active warfare, Professor Rheinstein states—"But there are still applicable those rules articulated in the Hague Convention which limit the rights of the occupation, qua occupant, to the necessities of occupation, especially those obliging the occupant to respect private property. . . ."

With regard to their rights and duties as the Government of Germany, he observes:

". . . In this capacity the occupants have, subject to the far reaching limitations to be discussed below, all the powers which any government may legitimately exercise within its own territory and over its own nationals, including those abroad. These powers include those of legislation, of executive, judicial, and fiscal action, of economic regulation, and of administrative and governmental organization. However extensive, though, these governmental powers may be, they are not unlimited.

"The claim of unlimited governmental power is the mark of distinction of totalitarian government—that very form of government against which the war was waged, at least by the Western Allies. The very idea of the absence of any limitation upon governmental powers is contradictory to the political and legal foundations of democracy, particularly as understood in the United States, whose political and legal system is based upon the idea that no government is permitted to encroach upon the 'inalienable rights' of 'life, liberty and the pursuit of happiness.'

"These inalienable rights are now being recognized as guaranteed not only by national but also by international law, especially as the latter has been defined in Nuremberg. When by international law the individual is subject to duties, for the violation of which he is to be held personally responsible, he is, of necessity also entitled to rights. The general scope of these rights is clear; it comprises all those basic human interests the violation of which has been declared to constitute crimes against humanity. . . .

.   .   .   .

". . . Having assumed supreme authority with respect to Germany, a country having no government able to speak for herself and her people, the occupants are finding themselves in a fiduciary position. Fiduciary duties are well recognized already in international law even for a belligerent occupant. The existence of far-reaching fiduciary duties is recognized to be incumbent upon countries exercising powers not only over the inhabitants of trusteeship territories, but over all dependent peoples. The German people is at present a dependent people and as such is entitled to the observance of fiduciary duties by its guardian powers.

". . . The fiduciary position of the occupants implies, among others, a duty to preserve the capital assets of the German economy, to restore the productive capacity of the country, to provide for an efficient and clean administrative machinery, to preserve Germany's cultural identity, to reintegrate the German people into the economic and cultural world community, and to prevent disease and starvation. In the present food situation of Germany the incorporation by the occupants . . . of food into Germany is not simply an act of charity or generosity but the fulfillment of a duty of international law, which is part of the general duty of an occupant, even a belligerent one, to restore and maintain law and order in the occupied territory. The fulfillment of this duty has repeatedly been claimed of Germany by Allied Powers, when Germany found herself in the position of occupant. During the first World War the Allies declared Germany's responsibility for the proper feeding of the population of occupied Belgium and, being physically unable to fulfill this duty out of her own depleted resources, Germany, during that war consented to the establishment of an international Relief Organization for Belgium and, during the present war to the importation of food into occupied Greece and the British Channel Islands."

Rheinstein, "The Legal Status of Occupied Germany", 47 Mich. L. Rev. (1948–1949) 23, 27–31.

The Superior Restitution Court of Rastatt (Franco-German Cassation Jurisdiction) in the French Zone of Germany, in an action for restitution of a rotary press which had been transferred from claimants under the Nazi regime in what later became the French Zone, but which was at the time of the action found in the British Zone, reasoned in the course of its decision that the Allied Zone commanders legislated in two distinct capacities as exercising the supreme powers of German government and as exercising rights of military occupants (even *cessante bello*) ; that the exercise of the latter was subject to international law and article 43 of the Hague Convention; and that since restitution laws were not necessary for the security of the occupation troops or for the maintenance of public order, and had no military aspect, they had been enacted in the exercise of German legislative powers and regulated private law relations within the general framework of German law. The Court, therefore, regarding principles of private international law applicable by analogy, held that by virtue of ordinary rules of conflict of laws, Ordinance No. 120 concerning restitution in the French Zone, rather than Law No. 59 governing restitution in the British Zone, was applicable. The Court expressed the opinion that the French Zone restitution courts were competent to apply Law No. 59 in appropriate cases, subject to the requirements of *ordre public.*

> *Druckerei Und Verlagsgesellschaft M.B.H.* v. *Schmidts*, 43 *Revue Critique de Droit International Privé* (1954) 145; 49 Am. J. Int'l L. (1955) 96.

The Act of Military Surrender signed at Rheims on May 7, 1945, and at Berlin, on May 8, 1945, was unconditional and had the effect of placing Germany and the German people completely at the disposition of the victorious Allies. The Declaration on the Defeat of Germany of June 5, 1945, noting that there was "no central Government or authority in Germany capable of accepting responsibility for the maintenance of order, the administration of the country and compliance with the requirements of the victorious Powers", announced that the four occupying Powers thereby assumed "supreme authority with respect to Germany, including all the powers possessed by the German Government, the High Command and any state, municipal, or local government or authority . . . ."

Assumption of "supreme authority"

> For Acts of Military Surrender, see *The Axis in Defeat*, Department of State publication 2423, pp. 23, 24. XII *Bulletin*, Department of State, No. 311, June 10, 1945, p. 1051.

"When the Allies accomplished the conquest of Germany, the existing government disintegrated and disappeared. At this point the Allies could have annexed Germany; it follows that they could take any lesser step they wished. The Allies assumed supreme authority by the declaration of June 5, 1945, but expressly disclaimed annexation.

"The declaration of June 5, 1945, by the Allied Powers states: *Right to maintain occupation courts*

> " 'The German Armed Forces . . . have been completely defeated and have surrendered unconditionally and Germany . . . is no longer capable of resisting the will of the victorious powers . . . and Germany has become subject to such requirements as may now or hereafter be imposed upon her.
>
> " 'There is no central government or authority in Germany capable of accepting responsibility for the maintenance of order, the administration of the country and compliance with the requirements of the victorious powers.
>
> " 'It is in these circumstances necessary . . . to make provisions for . . . the administration of the country. . . .
>
> " 'The Governments of the United States of America, the Union of Soviet Socialist Republics, and the United Kingdom, and the Provisional Government of the French Republic, hereby assume supreme authority with respect to Germany, including all the powers possessed by the German Government, the High Command and any state, municipal, or local government or authority. . . .
>
> " 'The assumption . . . of the said authority and powers does not effect the annexation of Germany.'

"This declaration forms the basis of Allied authority. It has never been withdrawn or officially questioned by the German Government which succeeded the Government that carried on the war.

"The Supreme authority thus rightfully assumed has been and still is retained. An affirmative act by the Allies would be required to give it up. The authority derives not from the continued existence of a state of war but from the fact of conquest and assumption of supreme authority.

"One aspect of this power has received the attention of the courts. In *Madsen* v. *Kinsella*, decided on September 8, 1950, the court in discussing the right of the United States to maintain occupation courts said:

> " 'It may happen, as was the case with Germany, that unconditional surrender to a conquering army completely wipes out local sovereignty, leaving the territory of the conquered nation, pending a treaty of peace, without any body of enforceable law save that which may be imposed by the conqueror. The power, as well as the duty, then devolves upon the conquering nation, through the commander in chief of its occupying army, to provide a government to take the place

of that which has been overthrown. One of the essential functions of this substitute government is to enact or adopt and administer a body or code of criminal laws. Historically and according to the law of war this is accomplished through decrees of the military commander in chief, establishing the law, framing the system of courts, prescribing rules of procedure, and appointing the judges.

. . . .

" '. . . The situation in Germany is unusual in that the occupation has lasted more than 5 years; there is still no treaty of peace; and the occupying force still exercises all governmental functions which have not been restored to the German people by the occupation statute of September 21, 1949; yet despite this prolongation, the status remains that of a temporary occupation of conquered territory, and the relationships of all persons within its boundaries are fixed and determined by the law of war.

" 'The chain of authority whereby the military government courts were established and their jurisdiction delineated is clear. The Allied Powers, having conquered Germany, announced on June 5, 1945, their assumption of supreme authority with that country (93 F. Supp. 319, at 323 (Dist. Ct., W. Va.)).'

"The point was emphasized as recently as April 2, 1951, in a decision on the same case on appeal. The court said:

" 'The authority for military government is the fact of occupation. . . . There must be a full possession, a firm holding, a government de facto.

" 'Military government, thus founded, is an exercise of sovereignty, and as such dominates the country which is its theater in all branches of administration. Whether administered by officers of the army of the belligerent, or by civilians left in office or appointed by him for the purpose, it is the government of and for all the inhabitants, native or foreign, wholly superseding the local law and civil authority except insofar as the same may be permitted by him to subsist. . . .

" 'The status of military government continues from the inception of the actual occupation till the invader is expelled by force of arms, or himself abandons his conquest, or till, under a treaty of peace, the country is restored to its original allegiance or becomes incorporated with the domain of the prevailing belligerent (188 F. (2d) 272, at 274 (C.C.A. 4th)).'

"While the point being discussed in that case was the right to maintain courts, it is equally applicable to any other right exercised under our supreme authority. It would apply to the right to maintain occupation troops, to control the administration of Germany, the right to see that all foreign rights and claims are fully protected, and that no German asserts claims against the United States or its nationals in derogation of their rights.

"The position of the United States in Germany, together with the laws already in force in Germany, assure the rights of the United States. On September 20, 1945, the Allied Control Council for Germany enacted Proclamation No. 2, section VI of which provides:

> " 'The German authorities will carry out, for the benefit of the United Nations, such measures of restitution, reinstatements, restoration, reparation, reconstruction, relief, and rehabilitation as the Allied representatives may desire.'

"This is still the law in Germany and will remain so long as the United States desires."

"Terminating the State of War Between the United States and the Government of Germany", H. Rept. 706, 82d Cong., 1st sess., July 18, 1951, pp. 8–10.

The validity of the requisitioning powers of the Allies in the exercise of their supreme authority in Germany was described in a legal memorandum on Court of Claims Cases Arising out of Requisitions in Germany, September 21, 1949–May 5, 1955, prepared by the Deputy Legal Adviser of the Department of State. Part II of this memorandum, dated January 25, 1960, discusses this question as follows:

Power to requisition

"On June 5, 1945, at the same time that the Allied Powers announced the assumption of supreme authority, they also announced that each of the four powers was assigned a zone of occupation, and that supreme authority would be exercised by the respective Commanders-in-Chief, 'each in his own zone of occupation, and also jointly, in matters affecting Germany as a whole;' and for this latter purpose 'the four Commanders-in-Chief will together constitute the Control Council.' [The Axis in Defeat, Department of State Publication No. 2423, pp. 64, 68.]

"The Declaration of June 5, 1945 on the assumption of supreme authority contained the following in Article 13(b):

> " 'The Allied Representatives will impose on Germany additional political, administrative, economic, financial, military and other requirements arising from the complete defeat of Germany. The Allied Representatives, or persons or agencies duly designated to act on their authority, will issue proclamations, orders, ordinances and instructions for the purpose of laying down such additional requirements, and of giving effect to the other provisions of this Declaration. All German authorities and the German people shall carry out unconditionally the requirements of the Allied Representatives, and shall fully comply with all such proclamations, orders, ordinances and instructions.' [*Ibid.*, p. 69.]

"On September 20, 1945 the four Allied Governments signed an agreement regarding these additional requirements. Among the various requirements enumerated the German authorities were required to place at the disposal of the Allied Representatives the whole of the German communications systems (par. 10), and the whole of the German inland transport system (par. 29), as well as being required to supply free of cost such German currency as the Allied Representatives might require (par. 20). This agreement was incorporated in Proclamation No. 2 of the Control Council and published in the first volume of the Official Gazette. [*Ibid.*, p. 71.]

"Thus, the basis was laid for requisitioning tank cars and other means of transportation. The Army can undoubtedly document the mechanics whereby the requisitioning power was exercised.

"When the Soviet Union ceased to cooperate further in the administration of Germany, the other three Allied Occupying Powers agreed to a common administration for their three zones. They agreed to handle this administration of the three Western Zones through an Allied Commission consisting of the United States, British and French High Commissioners. [Charter of the Allied High Commission for Germany—See *A Decade of American Foreign Policy, 1941–1949*, Senate Document No. 123, 81st Congress, 1st Session, page 603.] They proclaimed an Occupation Statute which set forth the relationship between the Allied Governments and the Germans. However, it should be noted that paragraph 2(e) reserved to the three Allies powers in the fields of 'protection, prestige, and security of Allied forces, dependents, employees, and representatives, their immunities and *satisfaction of occupation costs and their other requirements.*' (Underscoring [*italics*] supplied). [*Ibid.*, p. 586.]

"While there were certain modifications from time to time of the Occupation Statute, paragraph 2(e) was never modified. This provision was finally ended when the Occupation Statute was revoked on May 5, 1955. [*American Foreign Policy 1950–1955*, Department of State Publication 6446, p. 1734.]

"Thus, it appears that at all times from June 5, 1945 to May 5, 1955 the three Western Allies retained full power to requisition transportation and transportation facilities for their needs, and to order the Government of the Federal Republic of Germany (which was established September 21, 1949) to pay for the same in German currency as part of the cost of the occupation."

The Deputy Legal Adviser (Raymond) to the Assistant Chief, Court of Claims Section, the Department of Justice (Kendall Barnes), memorandum, "Court of Claims Cases Arising out of Requisitions in Germany, September 21, 1949–May 5, 1955", Jan. 25, 1960, MS. Department of State, file FW 200.6241/2–1160.

Section III of the Agreement between the Governments of the United Kingdom, United States of America, and Union of Soviet Socialist Republics, and the Provisional Government of the French

Republic on Certain Additional Requirements To Be Imposed on Germany, dated September 20, 1945, provided in part:

> "5. The Allied Representatives will regulate all matters affecting Germany's relations with other countries. No foreign obligations, undertakings or commitments of any kind will be assumed or entered into by or on behalf of German authorities or nationals without the sanction of the Allied Representatives.
>
> "6. The Allied Representatives will give directions concerning the abrogation, bringing into force, revival or application of any treaty, convention or other international agreement, or any part or provision thereof, to which Germany is or has been a party."

XIII *Bulletin*, Department of State, No. 328, Oct. 7, 1945, pp. 515–516.

The Office of Military Government for Germany (U.S.), in a legal opinion of March 11, 1947, which affirmed the authority of the U.S. Zone Commander to conclude bilateral air agreements on a governmental level with foreign governments on the basis of Control Council Proclamation No. 2 in section III (*supra*), distinguished between the governmental authority of the Allied Control Council to "regulate all matters affecting Germany's relations with other countries" which affect Germany as a whole and the governmental authority of the respective Zone Commanders to regulate such matters which relate to the administration of areas of Germany under their respective jurisdictions. In reaching this conclusion, the opinion stated in part:

> "3. . . . the United States Zone Commander is the representative of the United States in the exercise of supreme authority in the United States Zone of occupation and, together with the representatives of France, Great Britain, and the Soviet Union, in the exercise of supreme authority in matters affecting Germany as a whole (Statement by the Governments of the United Kingdom, the United States of America, the Union of Soviet Socialist Republics, and the Provisional Government of the French Republic on Control Machinery in Germany, 5 June 1945). The authority of the United States Zone Commander is coextensive with the requirements of these functions; it does not go beyond them in any way unless there is a specific extension of his powers by the War Department in a particular case.
>
> "4. In his capacity as a member of the Control Council, the United States Zone Commander, undoubtedly may, together with the other members of that body, enter into international agreements necessary to the fulfillment of basic occupation policies. . . . Individual Zone Commanders may not . . . enter into an agreement with a foreign nation which affects Germany as a whole. But each Zone Commander undoubtedly may enter into such agreements which affect only his own Zone of Occupation.
>
> "5. In making the latter type of agreement, the United States

Zone Commander does not represent either the Allied Control Authority, which is supreme in matters affecting Germany as a whole, or his own Government in its sovereign capacity. He speaks merely as the representative of the United States in command of the United States Zone of Occupation, and his agreement is without legal validity and effect insofar as it purports to extend to matters which bear no reasonable relation to his functions as such representative."

Colonel Raymond, Associate Director, legal opinion "Bilateral Air Agreements", Mar. 11, 1947, VII *Selected Opinions* January 1, 1947–March 31, 1947, Office of Military Government for Germany (U.S.), Legal Division, APO 742, pp. 109, 110. See also Heath, Chief, Legal Advice Branch, legal opinion "Authority of Military Government to Enter Into Travel Control Agreement with Austria", July 2, 1948, XII *Selected Opinions* April 1, 1948–August 15, 1948, Office of Military Government for Germany (U.S.), Legal Division, APO 742, p. 90.

Power to legislate

Affirming the authority of Military Government to amend the laws and regulations relating to the payment of Civil Service pensions on the condition that it had been determined that this was not a matter upon which quadripartite action should be taken, the Office of Military Government for Germany (U.S.) based its conclusion as recorded in a legal opinion of August 17, 1946, on article 2 of SHAEF Proclamation No. 1 (MGR 23–200), continued in effect under Proclamation No. 1, U.S. Zone, July 14, 1945, which provided in part as follows:

"Supreme legislative, judicial and executive authority and powers within the occupied territory are vested in me as Supreme Commander of the Allied Forces and as Military Governor, and the Military Government is established to exercise these powers under my direction. All persons in the occupied territory will obey immediately and without question all the enactments and orders of the Military Government";

and also on MGR 1–200 which stated:

"The rights, powers and status of the Military Government in Germany are based on the unconditional surrender and total defeat of Germany. The Control Council for Germany possesses paramount authority throughout Germany on matters affecting Germany as a whole. Subject to the exercise by the Control Council of authority on matters within its jurisdiction, the Theater Commander, by virtue of his position, is clothed with supreme legislative, executive and judicial authority with[in] the U.S. Zone."

Alvin Rockwell, Acting Director, legal opinion "Payment of Civil Service Pensions", Aug. 17, 1946, V *Selected Opinions* August 1, 1946–October 15, 1946, Office of Military Government for Germany (U.S.), Legal Division, APO 742, p. 25.

The first directive issued in October 1945 by the Office of Military Government (U.S.) with regard to the relationship of Military Government to the German authorities stated that such relationship "is based upon the establishment of an autonomous state government in the three states of the United States Zone subject to a centralized Military Government control applied at the local state government level."

A subsequent directive of September 30, 1946, declaring that "the U.S. policy requires that the German people be permitted increasingly to govern themselves", and noting that "self-government is the object of U.S. Military Government policy", set forth specific restrictions "considered as superior to the authority of any German governmental agency, and to both statutory and constitutional law". Several of the restrictions listed are recorded here as follows:

> "a. All international agreements regarding Germany which have been or may be concluded;
> "b. All present and future quadripartite policy decisions, laws and regulations;
> "c. All basic policy decisions of the U.S.-British Bipartite Board affecting the fields of central agencies;
> "d. The rights of an occupying power under international law to maintain an occupying force within the zone, to preserve peace and order, to reassume at any time full occupation powers in the event the purposes of the occupation are jeopardized; . . ."

Pollock, Meisel, Bretton, *Germany Under Occupation* (rev. ed., 1949) 143, 146–147.

In a note to Soviet Ambassador Panyushkin, dated July 6, 1948, **Responsibility** in protest against the "actions of the Soviet Government in imposing restrictive measures on transport which amount now to a blockade against the sectors in Berlin occupied by the United States, United Kingdom and France", Secretary of State Marshall declared with **Berlin Blockade** respect to the responsibility of the occupying Powers that—

> "This Government now shares with the Governments of France and the United Kingdom the responsibility initially undertaken at Soviet request on July 7, 1945, for the physical well-being of 2,400,000 persons in the western sectors of Berlin. Restrictions recently imposed by the Soviet authorities in Berlin have operated to prevent this Government and the Governments of the United Kingdom and of France from fulfilling that responsibility in an adequate manner.
> "The responsibility which this Government bears for the physical well-being and the safety of the German population in its sector of Berlin is outstandingly humanitarian in character. This population includes hundreds of thousands of women and children, whose health and safety are dependent on the continued use of adequate facilities for moving food, medical supplies and

other items indispensable to the maintenance of human life in the western sectors of Berlin. The most elemental of these human rights which both our Governments are solemnly pledged to protect are thus placed in jeopardy by these restrictions. It is intolerable that any one of the occupying authorities should attempt to impose a blockade upon the people of Berlin."

XIX *Bulletin*, Department of State, No. 472, July 18, 1948, pp. 85–86.

In a statement before the Security Council during its discussion of the Berlin blockade, Deputy United States Representative in the Security Council Philip Jessup reiterated this element of responsibility when he said:

"The Soviet Union may pretend it cannot understand why it can be charged with threat or use of force against the United States, France, and the United Kingdom when a primary consequence of its action falls directly and intentionally upon the civilian population of Berlin for whose well-being the three Western occupying powers are responsible. That an effort should be made to deprive two and one-half million men, women, and children of medicines, food, clothing, and fuel, to subject them to cold and starvation and disease, may seem to some a small matter. But to us, the welfare of people committed to our charge is a matter of serious concern. We cannot be callous to the suffering of millions of people in any country, much less when we have responsibility for them as an occupying power."

XIX *Bulletin*, Department of State, No. 485, Oct. 17, 1948, p. 484.

The Acting President of the Allied Control Commission in Italy, Harold Macmillan, in announcing in Rome on February 24, 1945, further relinquishment of control by the Allied Control Commission to the Italian Government, remarked with regard to the relationship between these two governing authorities:

Italy

"Under the conventions of international law the landings at Salerno and the occupation of southern Italy were followed by proclamations setting up Allied Military Government. But even in those early days the concept of an independent Italian Government was kept in being; and from that moment all our minds were directed to the purpose of rebuilding, through such a Government, Italy as a free and democratic nation.

.   .   .   .

". . . from the earliest moment an Italian Government has been nurtured by the Allied authorities. From Brindisi it was moved early in 1944 to Salerno and there began, although subjected to great physical difficulties of communication and location, to grow in strength and stature. As soon as possible after the capture of Rome, arrangements were made for the members of the Government at Salerno to enter into close discussion with the heads of the parties in Rome. Thus Signor Bonomi's first administration rapidly emerged.

.   .   .   .   .   .

"This steady development of the Italian Government to its own authority is taking some further steps. The Chief Commissioner and I have today called upon the Prime Minister, Bonomi, and the Foreign Secretary, De Gasperi, to inform them of certain changes which are being made immediately. They are intended to carry out to the full the changed relationship between the Allied Commission and the Italian Government, which will in future be one of consultation and advice. Although the requirements of the Italian campaign and overriding military needs must be protected, the rights of the Allied governments will be held in reserve in the matter of day-to-day administration.

"What are the conditions of a sovereign state? I would say that they consist, first, in control of the external relations of that state; and secondly, in the control of the legislative functions and internal administration. Judged by this criterion, under the decisions which we have today communicated, the position of the Italian Government will be from a practical point of view incomparably reinforced. We have informed the Italian Government that it should conduct its relations with other governments no longer indirectly through the Allied Commission but directly. They have absolutely free right to appoint and receive ambassadors to and from all Allied and neutral countries. They will deal directly with their ambassadors in foreign countries and with their own secret channels of communication by diplomatic pouch. It is true that we have asked to be informed of any important negotiations in which the Italian Government may be engaged with foreign governments. That is a natural request, given the present situation, and one more likely to be beneficial to those negotiations than harmful. Externally, therefore, the Italian Government will resume once more those normal relations which every sovereign government has with the governments of all countries with which it is at peace. Internally, since there is no legislature, decrees and laws are passed by the Government. Up to now they have been submitted for the approval of the Commission. This requirement is abolished. Therefore the Italian Government regains full control over its legislative authority. As regards administration it has up to now been the practice that all appointments of the Italian Government must be approved by the Commission. This requirement also is abolished; and all appointments, from members of the Government down to the minor functionaries, will be the sole responsibility of the Italian Government itself. . . ."

"Allied Commission for Italy: Transcript of Remarks by the Acting President", Feb. 24, 1945, XII *Bulletin*, Department of State, No. 301, Apr. 1, 1945, pp. 539–541.

In contrast to the situation in Germany where the Allied Military Government actually supplanted the German Government in directly administering the area, the Allies in Italy tentatively accepted the Italian Government with the intention of building upon it and cooperating with it.

The directive of November 10, 1943, for the Allied Control Commission for Italy, which was established in Rome on July 15, 1944, at the time the Italian Government returned to the capital, distinguished between the Allied Military Government and the Allied Control Commission by delegating to the former "functions in territory in the forward areas behind the Allied lines where administration of Allied forces is necessary," and to the latter "functions in that territory more remote from the front line which it has been possible to restore to Italian administration". The directive further stipulated that "The Supreme Allied Commander will, however, continue to exercise supreme authority in all of liberated Italy through the Allied Control Commission of which he is president *ex officio*. The relationship of the Control Commission to the Italian Government and to Italian administration in liberated areas is one of supervision and guidance rather than one of direct administration as in the case of Allied Military Government."

XI Bulletin, Department of State, No. 267, Aug. 6, 1944, pp. 137–138.

Austria

The Agreement on Control Machinery in Austria concluded between the Governments of the United Kingdom, the United States of America, the Union of Soviet Socialist Republics, and the Government of the French Republic on June 28, 1946, provided for the exercise of governmental authority by the Four Powers as follows:

Article 1:

"The authority of the Austrian Government shall extend fully throughout Austria, subject only to the following reservations:
"(*a*) The Austrian Government and all subordinate Austrian authorities shall carry out such directions as they may receive from the Allied Commission;
"(*b*) In regard to the matters specified in Article 5 below neither the Austrian Government nor any subordinate Austrian authority shall take action without the prior written consent of the Allied Commission".

Article 2, part (*c*):

"The Allied Commission shall act only through the Austrian Government or other appropriate Austrian authorities except:
"(*i*) to maintain law and order if the Austrian authorities are unable to do so;

"(*ii*) if the Austrian Government or other appropriate Austrian authorities do not carry out directions received from the Allied Commission;

"(*iii*) where, in the case of any of the subjects detailed in Article 5 below, the Allied Commission acts directly".

Article 5:

"The following are the matters in regard to which the Allied Commission may act directly as provided in Article 2(*c*)(*iii*) above:

"(*i*) Demilitarization and disarmament (military, economic, industrial, technical and scientific).

"(*ii*) The protection and security of the Allied forces in Austria, and the fulfilment of their military needs in accordance with the Agreement to be negotiated under Article 8(*a*).

"(*iii*) The protection, care and restitution of property belonging to the Governments of any of the United Nations or their nationals.

"(*iv*) The disposal of German property in accordance with the existing agreements between the Allies.

"(*v*) The care and evacuation of, and exercise of judicial authority over prisoners of war and displaced persons.

"(*vi*) The control of travel into and out of Austria until Austrian travel controls can be established.

"(*vii*) (*a*) The tracing, arrest and handing-over of any person wanted by one of the Four Powers or by the International Court for War Crimes and Crimes against Humanity.

"(*b*) The tracing, arrest and handing-over of any person wanted by other United Nations for the crimes specified in the preceding paragraph and included in the lists of the United Nations Commission for War Crimes.

"The Austrian Government will remain competent to try any other person accused of such crimes and coming within its jurisdiction, subject to the Allied Council's right of control over prosecution and punishment for such crimes".

Article 6:

"(*a*) All legislative measures, as defined by the Allied Council, and international agreements which the Austrian Government wishes to make except agreements with one of the 4 Powers, shall, before they take effect or are published in the State Gazette be submitted by the Austrian Government to the Allied Council. In the case of constitutional laws, the written approval of the Allied Council is required, before any such law may be published and put into effect. In the case of all other legislative measures and international agreements it may be assumed that the Allied Council has given its approval if within thirty-one days of the time of receipt by the Allied Commission it has not informed the Austrian Government that it objects to a legislative measure or an international agreement. Such legislative measure or international agreement may then be published and put into effect. The Austrian Government will inform the Allied Council of all international agreements entered into with one or more of the 4 Powers.

"(b) The Allied Council may at any time inform the Austrian Government or the appropriate Austrian authority of its disapproval of any of the Legislative measures or administrative actions of the Government or of such authority, and may direct that the action in question shall be cancelled or amended."

For text of the Agreement, see XV *Bulletin*, Department of State, No. 369, July 28, 1946, pp. 175–178.

Responsibility   Acting Secretary of State James Webb, in a statement dated October 6, 1950, endorsing the action of the Austrian Government and police in suppressing Communist-inspired disturbances, adverted to that part of the Agreement on Control Machinery, signed by the four occupying Powers on June 28, 1946, which provided that the Allied Commission shall assist the Austrian Government to re-create a sound and democratic national life based on respect for law and order and affirmed:

". . . This agreement charges the Allied Commission with responsibility for maintaining law and order if the Austrian authorities are unable to do so and authorizes the High Commissioners to act independently to maintain law and order in their respective zones in the absence of action by the Allied Commission. Needless to say, this Government will take all proper action to fulfill its international commitments with respect to the maintenance of law and order in the areas of its responsibility in Austria."

XXIII *Bulletin*, Department of State, No. 589, Oct. 16, 1950, p. 616.

In its note of protest against Soviet interference with the Austrian Government, delivered by the American Ambassador at Moscow to the Acting Minister of Foreign Affairs of the U.S.S.R. on November 10, 1950, the United States Government, recalling "the discussions which took place in the Allied Council in Austria on October 13, 1950, during which the Soviet representative maintained the untenable point of view that mob violence in the Soviet zone of Austria is not properly the concern of the Allied Council and that actions taken by a local Soviet commander may not be discussed by the Council", declared:

". . . This assertion cannot, of course, be accepted by the Government of the United States since the control agreement for Austria of June 28, 1946, makes it clear that the Allied Council may and should concern itself with any matter relating to the maintenance of law and order and with any derogation of authority guaranteed by agreement to the Austrian Government".

Reiterating the responsibility of the Allied Commission in this matter, the note continued:

"As stated above, the Allied Council, by its terms of reference, clearly is called upon to concern itself with the maintenance of law and order in Austria. Thus, article 3D of the control agreement requires the Allied Commission to assist the Austrian Government to assume full control of the affairs of state in Austria. Suppression and obstruction of police is patently inconsistent with this objective, and it is clearly the responsibility of the Allied Commission to assist the Austrian Government to recreate the respect for law and order. The support of elements of the population acting against the authority of the Austrian Government and its police and forcing the surrender of a government building to a rioting mob are contrary to this principle and call for action by the Allied Commission.

"The Allied Commission did not consider that any of the three conditions set out in article 2C of the control agreement under which they were empowered to act directly rather than through the Austrian Government was relevant in this case. The Allied Commission, therefore, took no action. Paragraph 2D of the control agreement which authorized in certain circumstances independent action by the High Commissioners in the absence of action by the Allied Commission is equally inapplicable in this case. The Soviet commander had no justification to maintain law and order at Wiener Neustadt since Austrian authorities had already done so.

"Article 1 of the control agreement states unequivocally that the authority of the Austrian Government shall extend fully throughout Austria with two exceptions, execution of directions from the Allied Commission and questions defined in article 5. In these recent events, the Allied Commission had issued no directives and certainly no situation existed in which article 5 would apply. Any move to immobilize the police and to establish internal boundaries of their authority is in conflict with the duties of the signatories of the control agreement.

"The Government of the United States protests most emphatically against the perversion by the Soviet representative in the Allied Council in Austria of the clear language and intent of the control agreement of June 28, 1946, in attempting to justify unilateral controls over the Austrian police which would restrict or eliminate the authority of the Austrian Government in a part of its territory. The United States, therefore, calls upon the Soviet Government to issue appropriate instructions to the Soviet authorities in Austria to desist from interfering in the police functions of the Austrian Government."

XXIII *Bulletin*, Department of State, No. 594, Nov. 20, 1950, p. 819.

In its note of protest, November 10, 1950, the United States Government recounted the incidents which gave rise to this issue, asserting that the Soviet representative in the Allied Council "at no time denied that they had occurred". The incidents were briefly recapitulated as follows:

"In the course of demonstrations in the Soviet zone of Austria on October 4 and 5, 1950, the Soviet commander in the city of Wiener Neustadt obstructed efforts of the Austrian police to restore general order and ordered the police to return the federal post office to the control of the lawless mob, which had been ejected by the police, after it had illegally occupied the building. Further, this Soviet commander ordered the withdrawal of the police sent to Wiener Neustadt by the recognized Austrian authorities to maintain order and to protect life and property from the rioters. In taking these measures, the Soviet commander threatened that the Soviet armed forces would act against the Austrian police should they fail to comply with his orders.

"The law enforcement activities of the Austrian Government have been further hampered by the Soviet officer who commanded the president of the Vienna police immediately to recall to the Soviet sector any police forces employed outside that sector, not to execute the orders for dismissal and transfer of Austrian police officials without the consent of the Soviet element of the Interallied Command, and to forbid the employment of police forces of the Soviet sector of Vienna in any other sector." XXIII *Bulletin*, Department of State, No. 594, Nov. 20, 1950, p. 819.

Proclamation No. 1, which established Allied Military Government in Zone A of Venezia Giulia as Occupied Territory following Allied occupation of this area west of the Morgan Line on June 12, 1945, stated in its preamble:

Venezia Giulia

"In order to hasten the rehabilitation of areas which the Allied Forces have freed from German occupation and to ensure the proper administration thereof, to provide for the safety and welfare of yourselves and of the Allied Forces, and to preserve law and order, a Military Government must be established in this territory. This Military Government will have full control over the administration of this territory and will have power if necessary to try in its own courts and punish any persons who commit offences against any of the special laws and provisions promulgated by the Military Government or against the laws and usages of war or the law of the territory."

The Proclamation thereby vested "All powers of government and jurisdiction in those parts of the territory of Venezia Giulia occupied by Allied troops and over its inhabitants, and final administrative responsibility" in the Supreme Allied Commander, Mediterranean Theatre of Operations, as Military Commander and Military Governor, and declared the establishment of Allied Military Government "to exercise these powers" under his direction.

For text, see Allied Military Government, 13 Corps, Venezia Giulia, *The Allied Military Government Gazette*, No. 1, Sept. 15, 1946, pp. 3–6; XVI *Bulletin*, Department of State, No. 417, June 29, 1947, pp. 1265–1268. "Proclamation no. 1 establishing Allied Military Government bears no date. Since this proclamation was mentioned in the Duino agreement signed on June 20, 1945, it would appear that it was issued between June 12 and June 20". *Ibid.*, p. 1261, n. 19.

It was commented at the time that this Military Government in Zone A in Venezia Giulia is ". . . unique in several ways—only 'stakeholder' military government in the world—and probably the only one in history—carrying on the functions of government without any idea as to who the future sovereign might be, and without the program afforded by the example of parallel indigenous government which has solved so many problems in other places".

> *Allied Military Government Supplement, Blue Devil, Section II, Friday, July 19, 1946, Allied Military Government in Zone A*, p. 1.

> Upon the coming into force of the Treaty of Peace with Italy, September 15, 1947, Venezia Giulia constituted a part of the Free Territory of Trieste. "Venezia Giulia, according to the Yugoslavs, included the former provinces of Istria, Gorizia, Trieste, and part of Carniola. As employed by the Allied Powers the term Venezia Giulia denotes the 1939 Italian provinces of Gorizia, Trieste, Fiume (Carnaro) and Pola (Istria). The Yugoslav equivalent for Venezia Giulia is Julijska Krajina and the English term as employed by the Yugoslav Government is Julian March. The German term used by the Austrians prior to 1914 was Küstenland and referred to an administrative district composing Trieste, Gorizia, Gradisca, and Istria. The two terms—Venezia Giulia and Küstenland—are not quite identical." XVI *Bulletin*, Department of State, No. 417, June 29, 1947, p. 1258.

A directive from the President of the United States to the Supreme **Japan** Commander for the Allied Powers regarding the surrender of Japan stated in part:

> "From the moment of surrender, the authority of the Emperor and Japanese Government to rule the state will be subject to you and you will take such steps as you deem proper to effectuate the surrender terms.
> "You will exercise supreme command over all land, sea and air forces which may be allocated for enforcement in Japan of the surrender terms by the Allied Powers concerned."

> President Truman to Supreme Commander for the Allied Powers, Aug. 13, 1945, MS. Department of State, file FW 740.00119 Control (Japan)/8–1445.

Part II of the document entitled "U.S. Initial Post-Surrender Policy For Japan" outlined the relationship of Allied authority to the Japanese Government as follows:

> "The authority of the Emperor and the Japanese Government will be subject to the Supreme Commander, who will possess all powers necessary to effectuate the surrender terms and to carry out the policies established for the conduct of the occupation and the control of Japan.

"In view of the present character of Japanese society and the desire of the United States to attain its objectives with a minimum commitment of its forces and resources, the Supreme Commander will exercise his authority through Japanese governmental machinery and agencies, including the Emperor, to the extent that this satisfactorily furthers United States objectives. The Japanese Government will be permitted, under his instructions, to exercise the normal powers of government in matters of domestic administration. This policy, however, will be subject to the right and duty of the Supreme Commander to require changes in governmental machinery or personnel or to act directly if the Emperor or other Japanese authority does not satisfactorily meet the requirements of the Supreme Commander in effectuating the surrender terms. This policy, moreover, does not commit the Supreme Commander to support the Emperor or any other Japanese governmental authority in opposition to evolutionary changes looking toward the attainment of United States objectives. The policy is to use the existing form of Government in Japan, not to support it. Changes in the form of Government initiated by the Japanese people or government in the direction of modifying its feudal and authoritarian tendencies are to be permitted and favored. In the event that the effectuation of such changes involves the use of force by the Japanese people or government against persons opposed thereto, the Supreme Commander should intervene only where necessary to ensure the security of his forces and the attainment of all other objectives of the occupation."

XIII *Bulletin*, Department of State, No. 326, Sept. 23, 1945, pp. 423, 424. See also *The Far Eastern Commission, 1945 to 1952* (Department of State publication 5138, 1953).